3e

Physics Galaxy

Volume IIIB

Magnetism, EMI & Alternating Current

Ashish Arora
Mentor & Founder
PHYSICSGALAXY.COM

World's largest encyclopedia of online video courses on High School Students preparing for
JEE Main * JEE Advanced * NEET * NSEP/INPhO/IPhO

GKP

First Edition : December, 2000

Second Edition : May, 2016

Revised Edition : March, 2023

Title : Physics Galaxy : Vol. IIIB - Magnetism, EMI & Alternating Current, 3rd edition

Language : English

Author's Name : Ashish Arora

Typeset & Published by :

Career Launcher Infrastructure (P) Ltd.

A-45, Mohan Cooperative Industrial Area, Near Mohan Estate Metro Station, New Delhi - 110044

Marketed by :

G.K. Publications (A Unit of CL Educate)

14/4, Mathura Road, Faridabad, Haryana, 121003

ISBN : **978-93-95101-01-1**

Printer's Details : Printed in India, New Delhi.

For product information :

Visit ***www.gkpublications.com*** or email to ***gkp@gkpublications.com***

Dedicated

to

My Parents, Son, Daughter

and

My beloved wife

In his teaching career since 1992 Ashish Arora personally mentored more than 10000 IITians and students who reached global heights in various career and profession chosen. It is his helping attitude toward students with which all his students remember him in life for his contribution in their success and keep connections with him live. Below is the list of some of the successful students in International Olympiad personally taught by him.

NAVNEET LOIWAL	*International GOLD Medal in IPhO-2000 at LONDON*, Also secured **AIR-4** in **IIT JEE 2000** PROUD FOR INDIA : Navneet Loiwal was the first Indian Student who won first International GOLD Medal for our country in International Physics Olympiad.
DUNGRA RAM CHOUDHARY	**AIR-1** in **IIT JEE 2002**
HARSHIT CHOPRA	*National Gold Medal in INPhO-2002* and got **AIR-2** in **IIT JEE-2002**
KUNTAL LOYA	A Girl Student got position **AIR-8** in **IIT JEE 2002**
LUV KUMAR	*National Gold Medal in INPhO-2003* and got **AIR-3** in **IIT JEE-2003**
RAJHANS SAMDANI	*National Gold Medal in INPhO-2003* and got **AIR-5** in **IIT JEE-2003**
SHANTANU BHARDWAJ	*International SILVER Medal in IPhO-2002 at INDONESIA*
SHALEEN HARLALKA	*International GOLD Medal in IPhO-2003 at CHINA* and got **AIR-46** in **IIT JEE-2003**
TARUN GUPTA	*National GOLD Medal in INPhO-2005*
APEKSHA KHANDELWAL	*National GOLD Medal in INPhO-2005*
ABHINAV SINHA	*Hon'ble Mension Award in APhO-2006* **at** *KAZAKHSTAN*
RAMAN SHARMA	*International GOLD Medal in IPhO-2007* **at** *IRAN* and got **AIR-20** in **IIT JEE-2007**
PRATYUSH PANDEY	*International SILVER Medal in IPhO-2007* **at** *IRAN* and got **AIR-85 in IIT JEE-2007**
GARVIT JUNIWAL	*International GOLD Medal in IPhO-2008* **at** *VIETNAM* and got **AIR-10** in **IIT JEE-2008**
ANKIT PARASHAR	*National GOLD Medal in INPhO-2008*
HEMANT NOVAL	*National GOLD Medal in INPhO-2008* and got **AIR-25** in **IIT JEE-2008**
ABHISHEK MITRUKA	*National GOLD Medal in INPhO-2009*
SARTHAK KALANI	*National GOLD Medal in INPhO-2009*
ASTHA AGARWAL	*International SILVER Medal in IJSO-2009* **at** *AZERBAIJAN*
RAHUL GURNANI	*International SILVER Medal in IJSO-2009* **at** *AZERBAIJAN*
AYUSH SINGHAL	*International SILVER Medal in IJSO-2009* **at** *AZERBAIJAN*
MEHUL KUMAR	*International SILVER Medal in IPhO-2010* **at** *CROATIA* and got **AIR-19** in **IIT JEE-2010**
ABHIROOP BHATNAGAR	*National GOLD Medal in INPhO-2010*
AYUSH SHARMA	*International Double GOLD Medal in IJSO-2010* at *NIGERIA*
AASTHA AGRAWAL	*Hon'ble Mension Award in APhO-2011* at *ISRAEL* and got **AIR-93** in **IIT JEE 2011**
ABHISHEK BANSAL	*National GOLD Medal in INPhO-2011*
SAMYAK DAGA	*National GOLD Medal in INPhO-2011*
SHREY GOYAL	*National GOLD Medal in INPhO-2012* and secured **AIR-24** in **IIT JEE 2012**
RAHUL GURNANI	*National GOLD Medal in INPhO-2012*
JASPREET SINGH JHEETA	*National GOLD Medal in INPhO-2012*
DIVYANSHU MUND	*National GOLD Medal in INPhO-2012*
SHESHANSH AGARWAL	*International SILVER Medal in IAO-2012 at KOREA*
SWATI GUPTA	*International SILVER Medal in IJSO-2012 at IRAN*
PRATYUSH RAJPUT	*International SILVER Medal in IJSO-2012 at IRAN*
SHESHANSH AGARWAL	*International BRONZE Medal in IOAA-2013 at GREECE*
SHESHANSH AGARWAL	*International GOLD Medal in IOAA-2014 at ROMANIA*
SHESHANSH AGARWAL	*International SILVER Medal in IPhO-2015 at INDIA* and secured **AIR-58** in **JEE(Advanced)-2015**
VIDUSHI VARSHNEY	*International SILVER Medal in IJSO-2015 at SOUTH KOREA*
AMAN BANSAL	**AIR-1 in JEE Advanced 2016**
KUNAL GOYAL	**AIR-3 in JEE Advanced 2016**
GOURAV DIDWANIA	**AIR-9 in JEE Advanced 2016**
DIVYANSH GARG	*International SILVER Medal in IPhO-2016 at SWITZERLAND*
NALIN KHANDELWAL	**AIR-1 in NEET 2019**
MRIDUL AGARWAL	**AIR-1 in JEE Advanced 2021**

ABOUT THE AUTHOR

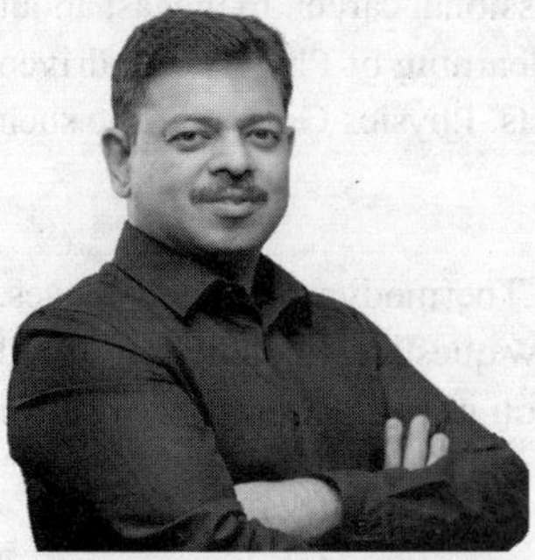

The complexities of Physics have given nightmares to many, but the homegrown genius of Jaipur- Ashish Arora has helped millions of students to live their dreams by decoding it.

Newton Law of Gravitation and Faraday's Magnetic induction force apply perfectly well with this unassuming genius. A Pied Piper of students, his webportal https://www.physicsgalaxy.com, The world's largest encyclopedia of video lectures on high school Physics possesses strong gravitational pull and magnetic attraction for students who want to make it big in life.

Ashish Arora, gifted with rare ability to train masterminds, has mentored over 10,000 IITians and Medicos in his past over three decades of teaching sojourn including lots of students made it to Top 100 in IIT-JEE/JEE(Advance) including multiple times AIR-1 and many in Top-10. Apart from that, he has also groomed hundreds of students for cracking International Physics Olympiad. No wonder his student Navneet Loiwal brought laurel to the country by becoming the first Indian to win a Gold medal at the 2000 - International Physics Olympiad in London (UK).

His special ability to simplify the toughest of the Physics theorems and applications rates him as one among the best Physics teachers in the world. With this, Arora simply defies the logic that perfection comes with age. Even at 18 when he started teaching Physics while pursuing engineering, he was as engaging as he is now. Experience, besides graying his hair, has just widened his horizon.

Now after encountering all tribes of students - some brilliant and some not-so-intelligent - this celebrated teacher has embarked upon a noble mission to make the entire galaxy of Physics inform of his webportal PHYSICSGALAXY.COM to serve and help global students in the subject. Today students from 183 countries are connected with this webportal. On any topic of physics students can post their queries in INTERACT tab of the webportal on which many global experts with Ashish Arora reply to several queries posted online by students.

Dedicated to global students of middle and high school level, his website *www.physicsgalaxy.com* also has teaching sessions dubbed in American accent and subtitles in 87 languages. For students in India preparing for JEE & NEET, his online courses will be available soon on PHYSICSGALAXY.COM.

Subscribe to

Physics Galaxy Mobile App — GET IT ON Google Play — Download on the App Store

PG Telegram
https://t.me/physicsgalaxyworld
High Quality Academic Resources for JEE(Main+Adv) & NEET

YouTube Channel
World's Largest Youtube Channel of 9000+ Video Lectures on High School Physics

Courses on Mobile App

- Complete JEE & NEET Concept Videos on Physics
- Complete Pre-Foundation Physics for Class 6-7-8
- Complete Foundation Physics for Class 9-10
- Complete NCERT Class 11 & 12 Physics Solutions
- Complete JEE Main 2002-2020 Video Solutions (Online & Offline)
- 700+ Advance Illustration Videos for JEE Advanced
- Tips & Tricks Guidance Videos for Competitive Exams
- Revision Checklist Videos for JEE Main & NEET
- Exam Memory Maps Videos for JEE Main & NEET

and much more...

FOREWORD

It has been pleasure for me to follow the progress Er. Ashish Arora has made in teaching and professional career. In the last about three decades he has actively contributed in developing several new techniques for teaching & learning of Physics and driven important contribution to Science domain through nurturing young students and budding scientists. Physics Galaxy is one such example of numerous efforts he has undertaken.

The third edition of Physics Galaxy provides a good coverage of various topics of Mechanics, Thermodynamics and Waves, Optics & Modern Physics and Electricity & Magnetism through dedicated volumes and many new questions included. It would be an important resource for students appearing in competitive examination for seeking admission in engineering and medical streams.

The structure of book is logical and the presentation is innovative. Importantly the book covers some of the concepts on the basis of realistic experiments and examples. The book has been written in an informal style to help students learn faster and more interactively with better diagrams and visual appeal of the content. Each chapter has variety of theoretical and numerical problems to test the knowledge acquired by students. The book also includes solution to all practice exercises with several new illustrations and problems for deeper learning.

I am sure the book will widen the horizons of knowledge in Physics and will be found very useful by the students for developing in-depth understanding of the subject.

Date : August 28, 2024

Prof. Sandeep Sancheti
Ph. D. (U.K.), B.Tech. FIETE, FIE (I), SMIEEE

Vice-Chancellor (Provost) Marwadi University, Rajkot
Member Executive Council, Association of Commonwealth Universities, London
Former President, AIU, New Delhi
Former Vice-Chancellor, SRMIST, Chennai
Former President, Manipal University, Jaipur
Former-Director NIT Surathkal, NIT New Delhi, NIT Trichy,
NIT Calicut, SPA Delhi; Former-Mentor Director NIT Goa,
NIT Sikkim, NIT Puducherry
Former-Member JEE Apex Board (JAB), MHRD, GoI
Former-Chairman, Central Counselling Board (CCB), AIEEE, MHRD, GoI
Former-Chairman, Direct Admission of Students Abroad (DASA), MHRD, GoI

PREFACE

For a science student, Physics is the most important subject, unlike to other subjects it requires logical reasoning and high imagination of brain. Without improving the level of physics it is very difficult to achieve a goal in the present age of competitions. To score better, one does not require hard working at least in physics. It just requires a simple understanding and approach to think a physical situation. Actually physics is the surrounding of our everyday life. All the six parts of general physics-Mechanics, Heat, Sound, Light, Electromagnetism and Modern Physics are the constituents of our surroundings. If you wish to make the concepts of physics strong, you should try to understand core concepts of physics in practical approach rather than theoretical. Whenever you try to solve a physics problem, first create a hypothetical approach rather than theoretical. Whenever you try to solve a physics problem, first create a hypothetical world in your imagination about the problem and try to think psychologically, what the next step should be, the best answer would be given by your brain psychology. For making physics strong in all respects and you should try to merge and understand all the concepts with the brain psychologically.

The book PHYSICS GALAXY is designed in a totally different and friendly approach to develop the physics concepts psychologically. The book is presented in five volumes, which covers almost all the core branches of general physics. This part of book, volume 3B covers Magnetic Effects of Current, Electromagnetic Induction and Alternating Current. These are most critical topics of Physics for building strong applications of whole section of electromagnetism. The things you will learn in this book will help in building your overall strength in the branch electricity and magnetism. In this book every chapter is explained in a simple, interactive and experimental way. The book is divided in the two major chapters, first chapters is covering all the applications of magnetic effects of current and force on moving charges or current carrying conductors due to magnetic field. This chapter also includes the calculation and analysis of magnetic effects produced by different current configurations. Second chapter covers the applications on electromagnetic induction and its several applications including time varying magnetic field and concept of self and mutual induction. The chapter at the end covers the major application of induction in form of alternating current and alternating current circuits.

The best way of understanding physics is the experiments and this methodology I am using in my lectures and I found that it helps students a lot in concept visualization. In this book I have tried to translate the things as I used in lectures. After every important section there are several solved examples included with simple and interactive explanations. It might help a student in a way that the student does not require to consult any thing with the teacher. Everything is self explanatory and in simple language.

One important factor in preparation of physics I wish to highlight that most of the student after reading the theory of a concept start working out the numerical problems. This is not the efficient way of developing concepts in brain. To get the maximum benefit of the book students should read carefully the whole chapter at least three or four times with all the illustrative examples and with more stress on some illustrative examples included in the chapter. Practice exercises included after every theory section in each chapter is for the purpose of in-depth understanding of the applications of concepts covered. Illustrative examples are explaining some theoretical concept in the form of an example. After a thorough reading of the chapter students can start thinking on discussion questions and start working on numerical problems.

Exercises given at the end of each chapter are for circulation of all the concepts in mind. There are two sections, first is the discussion questions, which are theoretical and help in understanding the concepts at root level. Second section is of conceptual MCQs which helps in enhancing the theoretical thinking of students and building logical skills in the chapter. Third section of numerical MCQs helps in the developing scientific and analytical application of concepts. Fourth section of advance MCQs with one or more options correct type questions is for developing advance and comprehensive thoughts. Last section is the Unsolved Numerical Problems which includes some simple problems and some tough problems which require the building fundamentals of physics from basics to advance level problems which are useful in preparation of NSEP, INPhO or IPhO.

In this third edition of the book I have included many new questions and solutions in different exercises at practice, conceptual, numerical and advance MCQs to support students who are dependent on their self study and not getting access to teachers for their preparation.

This book has taken a shape just because of motivational inspiration by my mother in 1997 when I just thought to write something for my students. She always motivated and was on my side whenever I thought to develop some new learning methodology for my students.

I don't have words for my best friend my wife Anuja for always being together with me to complete this book in the unique style and format.

I would like to pay my gratitude to Sh. Dayashankar Prajapati in assisting me to complete the task in Design Labs of PHYSICSGALAXY.COM and presenting the book in totally new format of third edition.

At last but the most important person, my father who has devoted his valuable time in finally presenting the book in such a format and a simple language, thanks is a very small word for his dedication in building the base structure of this book.

In this third edition I have tried my best to make this book error free but owing to the nature of work, inadvertently, there is possibility of errors left untouched. I shall be grateful to the readers, if they point out me regarding errors and oblige me by giving their valuable and constructive suggestions via emails for further improvement of the book.

Date : August 28, 2024 ***Ashish Arora***

PHYSICSGALAXY.COM
B-80, Model Town, Malviya Nagar, Jaipur-302017
e-mails: ashisharora@physicsgalaxy.com
ashash12345@gmail.com

CONTENTS

ANSWERS & SOLUTIONS

Magnetic Effects of Current & Magnetism 4

FEW WORDS FOR STUDENTS

First time playing with magnets is always a fun for every child. With age everyone gets aware that magnets have two poles, designated as north and south poles. All of you might have seen a compass used by travellers for the purpose of navigation. In ancient times compass was the only tool available for determining the directions. The needle of such a compass is a small, thin magnet. Magnets and magnetic effects are very important in different industrial applications as well as these are very important in understanding many natural and lab phenomenon related to magnetism. Even many birds use the magnetic field of Earth for navigation along with directions from the location of Sun and stars during long distance migrations. This whole chapter is covering effects and phenomenon of magnetism to strengthen understanding of this topic to a decent level.

CHAPTER CONTENTS

COVER APPLICATION

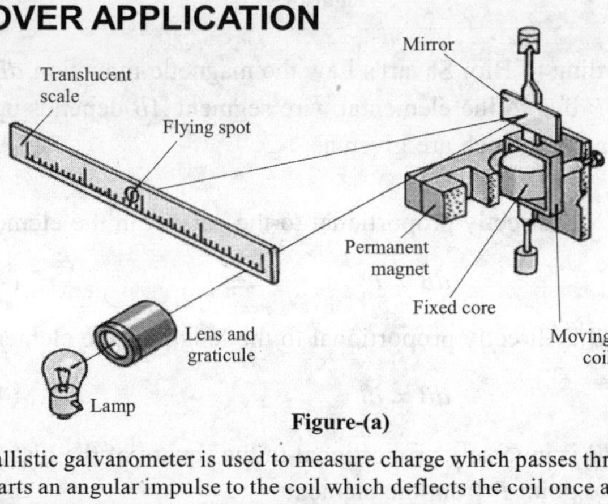

Figure-(a)

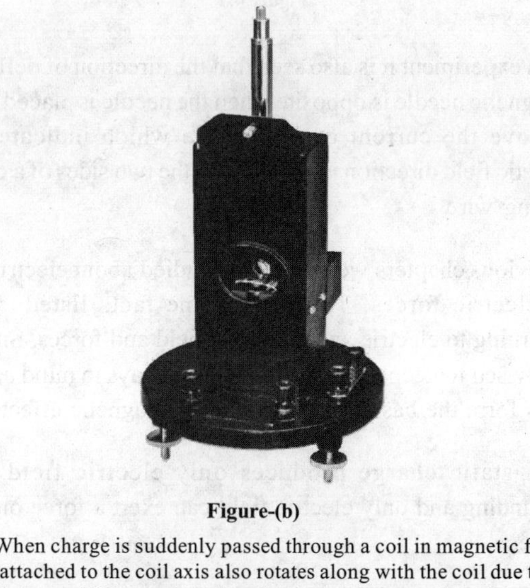

Figure-(b)

A ballistic galvanometer is used to measure charge which passes through the device. When charge is suddenly passed through a coil in magnetic field, it imparts an angular impulse to the coil which deflects the coil once and a small mirror attached to the coil axis also rotates along with the coil due to this. Torsional springs restores the position of coil back to normal but the deflection of a light beam falling on the mirror is measured on a scale and amount of charge can be calculated. Figure-(a) shows the setup of ballistic galvanometer experiment and figure-(b) shows the industrial or lab ballistic galvanometer at the center of which there is a small glass window through which a narrow light beam falls on the mirror and on the path of reflected beam a scale is placed.

'Magnetic forces of attraction and repulsion between magnetic poles are similar to the interaction between charges but magnetic poles and charges are not the same thing. However the way electric charges produce electric field in their surrounding is similar to that magnetic poles also have an associated magnetic field in their surrounding. Magnetic lines of forces are also similar to electric lines of forces used to trace the pattern of electric field in surrounding of charges. Tangent to a magnetic line of force in space gives the direction of magnetic field strength vector at that point and density of magnetic field lines in a region is a measures of the magnitude of magnetic field in that region. Similar to charges as we approach closer to a magnetic pole, density of magnetic lines increase.

It is also observed that in a region variation of electric field gives rise to induction of magnetic field and vice versa. A danish scientist Oersted observes magnetic field in the surrounding of current carrying conductor. Figure-4.1 shows the setup of Oersted's Experiment in which when a current is switched on, deflection in magnetic needle is observed which verified the presence of magnetic field in surrounding of current carrying wires. This is called '*Magnetic Effects of Electric Current*'.

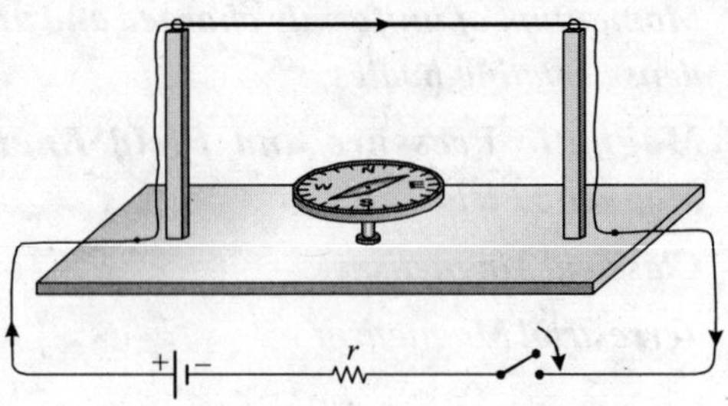

Figure 4.1

In this experiment it is also seen that the direction of deflection in magnetic needle is opposite when the needle is placed below or above the current carrying wire which indicates that magnetic field direction is opposite on the two sides of a current carrying wire.

In previous chapters we've already studied about electric field and electric forces. There are some facts listed below concerning to electric and magnetic field and forces. Students are advised to keep these below points always in mind as these points form the basis of understanding magnetic effects.

(1) A static charge produces only electric field in its surrounding and only electric field can exert a force on static charges.

(2) A moving charge produces both electric and magnetic fields in its surrounding and both electric and magnetic fields can exert force on moving charges.

(3) A current carrying wire produces only magnetic field in its surroundings and only magnetic field can exert a force on current carrying wires.

4.1 Biot Savart's Law

Biot Savart's Law is a basic law concerning electricity and magnetism which describes the magnetic field generated by a current carrying wire in its surrounding. The equation of Biot Savart's Law gives the strength of magnetic field at a specific point in surrounding of a current carrying wire. The magnetic field which is associated with electric field at any point for which we were discussing before this article is often referred as '*Magnetic Induction*' instead of magnetic field in technical terms. This is denoted by '$\vec{B}$' and also referred as magnetic flux density like electric field intensity '$\vec{E}$' in region of electric field.

This law analyzes that the magnetic induction produced due to an elemental length of a current carrying wire depends upon four factors. Consider a wire XY carrying a current I. To find the magnetic induction at a point P in its neighbourhood, we consider an elemental segment AB on this wire of length dl as shown.

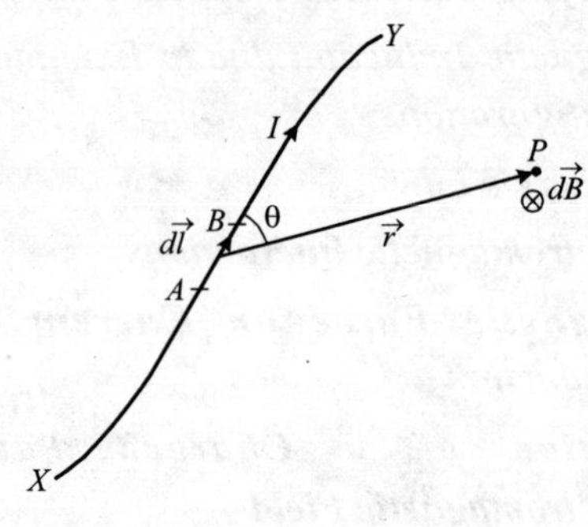

Figure 4.2

According to Biot Savart's Law the magnetic induction dB at point P due to the elemental wire segment AB depends upon four factors which are given as

(i) dB is directly proportional to the current in the element.

$$dB \propto I \quad \dots (4.1)$$

(ii) dB is directly proportional to the length of the element

$$dB \propto dl \quad \dots (4.2)$$

(iii) dB is inversely proportional to the square of the distance r of the point P from the element

$$dB \propto \frac{1}{r^2} \quad \dots (4.3)$$

(iv) dB is directly proportional to the sine of the angle θ between the direction of the current flow and the line joining the element to the point P

$$dB \propto \sin\theta \quad \text{... (4.4)}$$

Combining above factors, we have

$$dB \propto \frac{Idl\sin\theta}{r^2}$$

$$\Rightarrow \quad dB = K\frac{Idl\sin\theta}{r^2} \quad \text{... (4.5)}$$

Where K is a proportionality constant and its value depends upon the nature of the medium surrounding the current carrying wire. If the current carrying wire is placed in vacuum, then in SI Units its value is given as

$$K = \frac{\mu_0}{4\pi} = 10^{-7}\ \text{T-m/A}$$

Here μ_0 is called permeability of vacuum or free space. It is a physical quantity for a given medium which is a measure of a medium's ability on the extent to which it allows external magnetic field to polarize the material inside the volume of the body. Therefore Biot Savert's Law is written as

$$dB = \frac{\mu_0}{4\pi}\frac{Idl\sin\theta}{r^2} \quad \text{... (4.6)}$$

This constant μ_0 is similar in nature to the constant ϵ_0 we discussed in the topic of electrostatics. For a given medium its magnetic permeability is defined as

$$\mu = \mu_0\mu_r$$

Where μ_r is called '*Relative Permeability of Medium*' which is casually also referred as diamagnetic constant of the medium. Unlike to the case of electrostatics where dielectric constant of any medium is always greater than unity, in case of magnetism, depending upon the types of mediums value of μ_r can be greater or smaller than unity. In the topic of magnetic properties of material in next chapter we will discuss about the magnetic permeability in detail. As of now students can consider that if the current carrying wire is placed in a material medium then equation-(4.6) can be rewritten as

$$dB = \frac{\mu}{4\pi}\frac{Idl\sin\theta}{r^2} = \frac{\mu_0\mu_r}{4\pi}\frac{Idl\sin\theta}{r^2} \quad \text{... (4.7)}$$

Above equation-(4.7) gives the magnitude of magnetic induction produced due to a small current element. The direction of this magnetic induction is given by right hand thumb rule stated as "*Grasp the conductor in the palm of right hand so that the thumb points in the direction of the flow of current, then the direction in which the fingers curl, gives the direction of magnetic filed lines*". This is shown in figure-4.3.

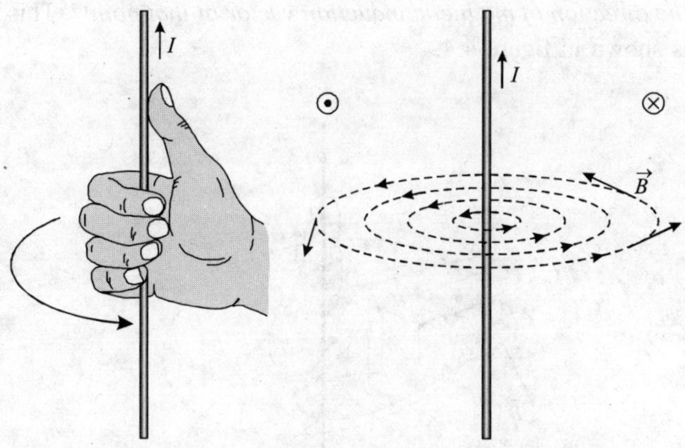

Figure 4.3

In the figure-4.2 using above rule we can see that direction of vector $\overrightarrow{dB}$ is into the plane of paper which is represented by $\otimes$ similarly on the points located on the left side of wire direction of $\overrightarrow{dB}$ is in outward direction from the plane of paper and it is represented by $\odot$. We can accommodate this direction in equation-(4.6) which can be rewritten as

$$\overrightarrow{dB} = \left(\frac{\mu_0}{4\pi}\right)\frac{I\vec{dl}\times\vec{r}}{r^3} \quad \text{... (4.8)}$$

In above equation you can see that the direction of cross product of the vector of elemental length and position vector of point P with respect to the element is giving the same direction as stated by right hand thumb rule.

At point P in figure-4.2 magnetic induction due to whole wire XY can be obtained by integrating the above expression for the entire length of the wire within proper limits according to the shape of the wire and it is given as

$$\vec{B} = \int\overrightarrow{dB} = \int\left(\frac{\mu_0}{4\pi}\right)\frac{I\vec{dl}\times\vec{r}}{r^3} \quad \text{... (4.9)}$$

In above equations many times the term '*Idl*' which is the product of current and length of element is also referred as a separate physical quantity called '*Current Element*' which is measured in units of '*Ampere-meter*' or '*A-m*'. In later articles of the chapter we will discuss its physical significance.

4.1.1 Magnetic Induction Direction by Right Hand Palm Rule

In previous article we studied that the direction of magnetic induction in surrounding of a current carrying wire can be obtained by right hand thumb rule. Same can also be obtained by '*Right Hand Palm Rule*' stated as "*Stretch your palm of right hand keeping fingers straight and put the thumb along the direction of current and point your fingers toward the point of application. The area vector of your palm face gives you the direction of magnetic induction vector at that point*". This is shown in figure-4.4.

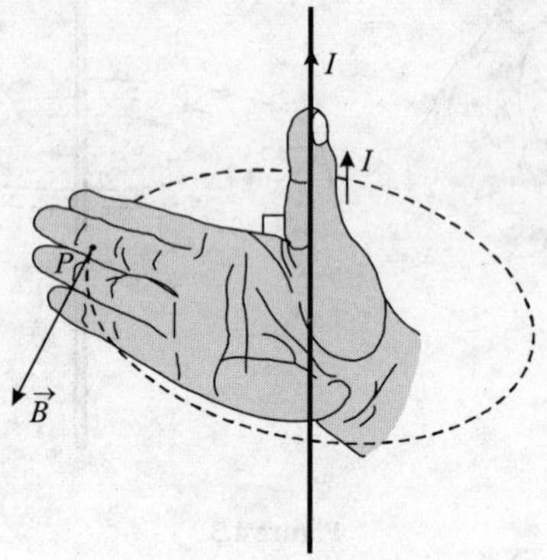

Figure 4.4

4.1.2 Magnetic Induction due to Moving Charges

As already discussed that moving charges produce magnetic field in their surrounding. Biot Savert's law is also defined for moving charges like current carrying wires we studied in article-4.1. To analyze the magnetic induction in surrounding of a moving charge we consider a charge q moving at velocity v as shown in figure-4.5. In this situation we will determine the magnetic induction at a point P located at a position vector r from the instantaneous position of charge as shown in figure.

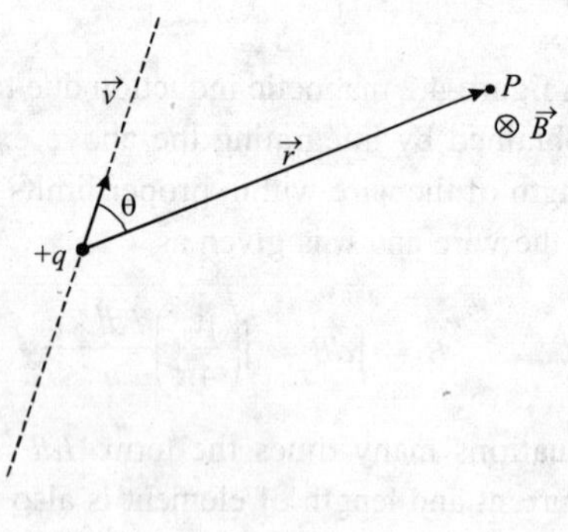

Figure 4.5

The magnetic induction B due to moving charges in surrounding depends upon four factors which are given as

(i) B is directly proportional to the charge

$$B \propto q \qquad \text{... (4.10)}$$

(ii) B is directly proportional to the speed of charge

$$B \propto v \qquad \text{... (4.11)}$$

(iii) B is inversely proportional to the square of the distance r of the point P from the element

$$B \propto \frac{1}{r^2} \qquad \text{... (4.12)}$$

(iv) B is directly proportional to the sine of the angle θ between the direction of the motion of positive charge and the line joining the charge to the point P

$$B \propto \sin\theta \qquad \text{... (4.13)}$$

Combining above factors we have

$$B \propto \frac{qv\sin\theta}{r^2}$$

$$\Rightarrow \qquad B = K\frac{qv\sin\theta}{r^2} \qquad \text{... (4.14)}$$

For free space we can use $K = \dfrac{\mu_0}{4\pi}$ so we have

$$B = \frac{\mu_0}{4\pi}\frac{qv\sin\theta}{r^2} \qquad \text{... (4.15)}$$

Vectorially above result can be rewritten including the direction of direction vector of magnetic induction is given as

$$\vec{B} = \frac{\mu_0}{4\pi}\frac{q(\vec{v}\times\vec{r})}{r^3} \qquad \text{... (4.16)}$$

In above expression of magnetic induction at point P due to the moving charge the cross product of velocity and position vector is written in such a way that the direction of magnetic field obtained by right hand thumb rule is same as that given by this cross product. In figure-4.5 direction of magnetic induction at point P is into the plane of paper (inward) as shown in this figure.

4.1.3 Units used for magnetic induction

In SI units magnetic induction is measured in '*Tesla*' denoted as '*T*' and magnetic flux in space through any area is measured in units of '*weber*' and denoted as '*Wb*'. As magnetic induction is also referred as magnetic flux density or flux passing through a unit normal area in a region like electric field was defined. The units tesla(T) and weber(Wb) are related as

$$1\ \text{T} = 1\ \text{Wb/m}^2 \qquad \text{... (4.17)}$$

4.2 Magnetic Induction due to different Current Carrying Conductors Configurations

Equation of Biot Savarts Law gives the magnetic induction due to a current element in its surrounding. For different shapes of current carrying conductors this needs to be integrated differently to obtain the net magnetic induction due to the conductors in their surrounding at specific points. Next we are going to discuss some standard configurations of the current carrying conductors.

4.2.1 Magnetic Induction due to a Long Straight Current Carrying Conductor

Figure-4.6 shows a long straight wire carrying a current I. To determine the magnetic induction due to the wire at point P situated at a normal distance r from the wire we consider an element of length dl in the wire at a distance y from the point O as shown. By right hand palm rule we can see that the direction of magnetic field at point P is into the plane of paper (inward).

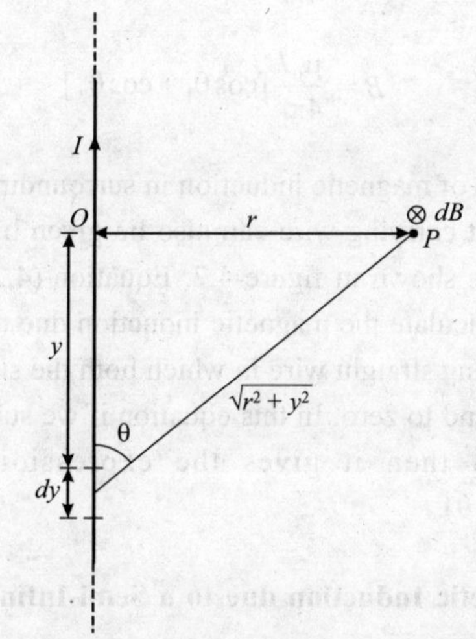

Figure 4.6

The magnetic induction dB at point P is into the plane of paper and given by Biot Savart's Law using equation-(4.6) as

$$dB = \frac{\mu_0}{4\pi} \times \frac{Idy\sin\theta}{(r^2+y^2)}$$

In above equation we can substitute $\sin\theta = \frac{r}{\sqrt{r^2+y^2}}$ gives

$$dB = \frac{\mu_0}{4\pi} \times \frac{Idyr}{(r^2+y^2)^{3/2}} \quad \text{... (4.18)}$$

As due to all the elements in the wire the magnetic induction is in inward direction at point P, the net magnetic induction at point P is given by integrating above equation-(4.18) for the whole length of wire within limits of y from $-\infty$ to $+\infty$ as

$$B = \int dB = \int_{y=-\infty}^{y=+\infty} \frac{\mu_0}{4\pi} \times \frac{I\,dy\,r}{(r^2+y^2)^{3/2}}$$

$$\Rightarrow \quad B = \frac{\mu_0 Ir}{4\pi} \int_{-\infty}^{+\infty} \frac{dy}{(r^2+y^2)^{3/2}}$$

To integrate the above expression we substitute

$$y = r\tan\theta$$

$$dy = r\sec^2\theta\, d\theta$$

With the above substitution limits of integration also changes as

$$\text{at } y = -\infty \rightarrow \theta = -\frac{\pi}{2}$$

and

$$\text{at } y = +\infty \rightarrow \theta = +\frac{\pi}{2}$$

$$\Rightarrow \quad B = \frac{\mu_0 Ir}{4\pi} \int_{-\frac{\pi}{2}}^{+\frac{\pi}{2}} \frac{r\sec^2\theta d\theta}{(r^2+r^2\tan^2\theta)^{3/2}}$$

$$\Rightarrow \quad B = \frac{\mu_0 Ir}{4\pi} \int_{-\pi/2}^{+\pi/2} \frac{r\sec^2\theta d\theta}{r^3\sec^3\theta}$$

$$\Rightarrow \quad B = \frac{\mu_0 I}{4\pi r} \int_{-\pi/2}^{+\pi/2} \cos\theta d\theta$$

$$\Rightarrow \quad B = \frac{\mu_0 I}{4\pi r} [\sin\theta]_{-\pi/2}^{+\pi/2}$$

$$\Rightarrow \quad B = \frac{\mu_0 I}{4\pi r} [1-(-1)]$$

$$\Rightarrow \quad B = \frac{\mu_0 I}{2\pi r} \quad \text{... (4.19)}$$

As already discussed that the direction of magnetic induction due to a long straight wire in its surrounding is along the tangent to the concentric magnetic lines as shown in figure-4.7. This is given by either of right hand thumb rule or right hand palm rule.

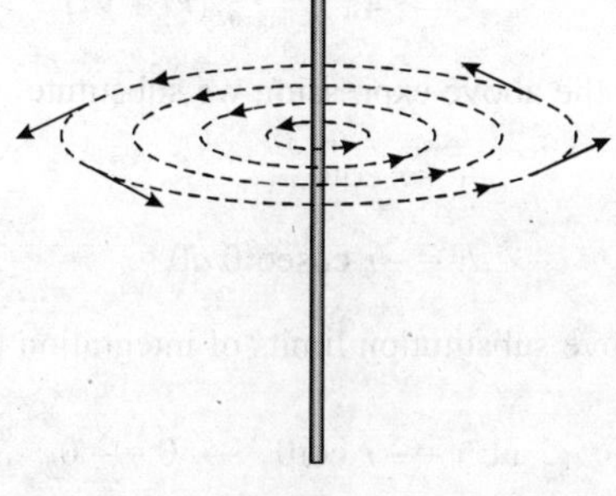

Figure 4.7

4.2.2 Magnetic Induction due to a Finite Length Current Carrying Wire

Figure-4.8 shows a wire AB of length L carrying a current I. In the surrounding of wire consider a point P as shown which is located at a perpendicular distance r from the wire such that the point is subtending angles θ_1 and θ_2 at the end points of the wire as shown in figure.

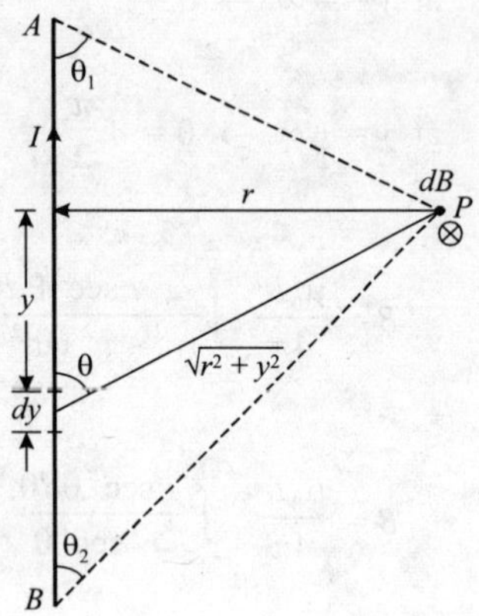

Figure 4.8

To calculate the magnetic induction at point P we consider an element of length dl at a distance y from the point O as shown in figure-4.8. By using Biot Savart's law the magnetic induction dB at point P due to this current element is given as

$$dB = \frac{\mu_0}{4\pi} \cdot \frac{Idl \sin\theta}{(r^2 + y^2)}$$

As due to all the elements in the wire the magnetic induction is in inward direction at point P, the net magnetic induction at point P due to wire AB is given by integrating above equation-(4.18) for the whole length of wire AB within limits of y from $-r\cot\theta_2$ to $+r\cot\theta_1$ as

$$B = \int dB = \int_{y=-r\cot\theta_2}^{y=+r\cot\theta_1} \frac{\mu_0}{4\pi} \times \frac{Idyr}{(r^2 + y^2)^{3/2}}$$

$$\Rightarrow \quad B = \frac{\mu_0 Ir}{4\pi} \int_{-r\cot\theta_2}^{+r\cot\theta_1} \frac{dy}{(r^2 + y^2)^{3/2}}$$

To integrate the above expression we substitute

$$y = r\cot\theta$$

$$dy = -r\,\text{cosec}^2\theta\, d\theta$$

With the above substitution limits of integration also changes as

$$\text{at } y = -r\cot\theta_2 \rightarrow \theta = -\theta_2$$

and $$\text{at } y = +r\cot\theta_1 \rightarrow \theta = +\theta_1$$

$$\Rightarrow \quad B = -\frac{\mu_0 Ir}{4\pi} \int_{-\theta_2}^{+\theta_1} \frac{r\csc^2\theta d\theta}{(r^2 + r^2\cot^2\theta)^{3/2}}$$

$$\Rightarrow \quad B = -\frac{\mu_0 Ir}{4\pi} \int_{-\theta_2}^{+\theta_1} \frac{r\csc^2\theta d\theta}{r^3 csc^3\theta}$$

$$\Rightarrow \quad B = -\frac{\mu_0 I}{4\pi r} \int_{-\theta_2}^{+\theta_1} \sin\theta d\theta$$

$$\Rightarrow \quad B = \frac{\mu_0 I}{4\pi r} [\cos\theta]_{-\theta_2}^{+\theta_1}$$

$$\Rightarrow \quad B = \frac{\mu_0 I}{4\pi r} [\cos\theta_1 - (-\cos\theta_2)]$$

$$\Rightarrow \quad B = \frac{\mu_0 I}{4\pi r} [\cos\theta_1 + \cos\theta_2] \quad \dots (4.20)$$

The direction of magnetic induction in surrounding of a finite length current carrying wire can also be given by right hand thumb rule as shown in figure-4.7. Equation-(4.20) can also be used to calculate the magnetic induction due to an infinite current carrying straight wire in which both the side angles θ_1 and θ_2 will tend to zero. In this equation if we substitute both angles zero then it gives the expression given in equation-(4.19).

4.2.3 Magnetic Induction due to a Semi-Infinite Straight Wire

Figure-4.9 shows a very long wire AB carrying a current I and P is a point at a perpendicular distance r from the end A of the wire. Using right hand thumb rule here we can state that the magnetic induction at point P is in outward direction.

The magnitude of the magnetic Induction at P can be calculated by using equation-(4.20). If we look at figure-4.9(b), we can see that at point A point P is making an angle 90° with the length of wire and at point B which is located far away distance, the angle between the line PB and wire can be considered as 0°. Thus magnetic induction at point P due to this semi infinite wire is given as

$$B = \frac{\mu_0 I}{4\pi r} [\cos(90°) + \cos(0°)]$$

$$\Rightarrow \quad B = \frac{\mu_0 I}{4\pi r} [0 + 1]$$

$$\Rightarrow \quad B = \frac{\mu_0 I}{4\pi r} \quad \dots (4.21)$$

(a)

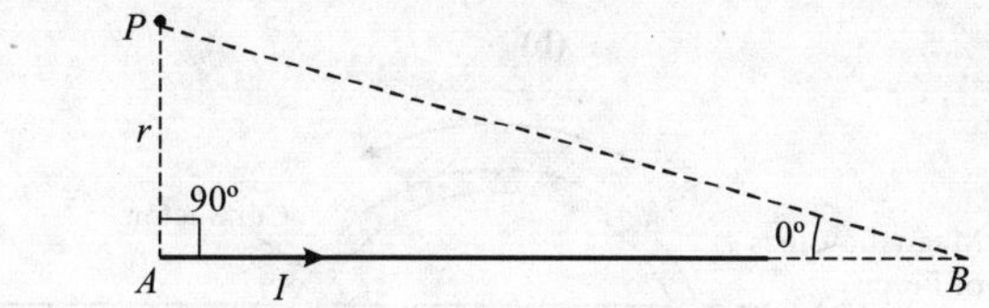

(b)

Figure 4.9

The magnetic induction given in above expression given in equation-(4.21) is half of that obtained due to an infinitely long wire as given in equation-(4.19) which can be directly stated as both the halves of an infinite wires are identical with respect to point P in figure-4.9 on the two sides of it and if one half is removed then due to the remaining half the magnetic induction is also reduced to half.

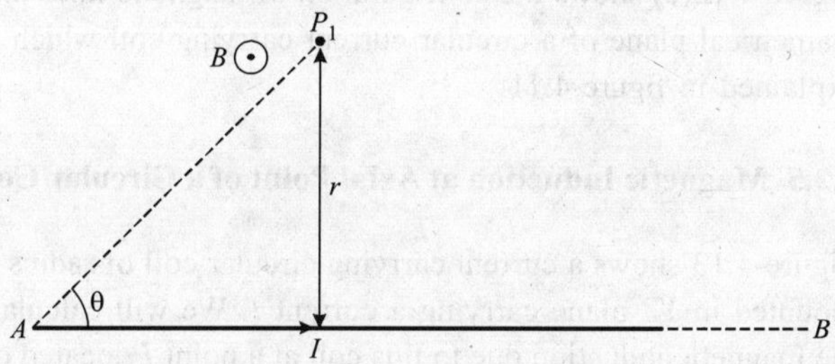

(a)

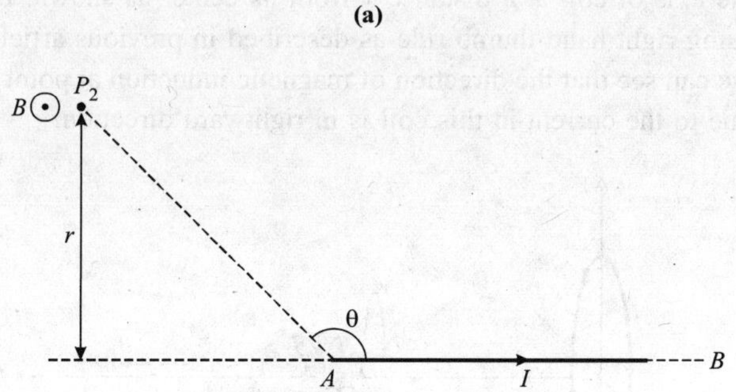

(b)

Figure 4.10

Figure-4.10(a) and (b) shows another semi infinite wire but in this case we will calculate the magnetic induction at points P_1 and P_2 which are located at same distance from end point A of wire at same perpendicular distance r from the line of wire. Again using equation-(4.20) we can calculate the magnetic induction at these points which is given as

$$B = \frac{\mu_0 I}{4\pi r}[\cos\theta + \cos(0^\circ)]$$

$$\Rightarrow \qquad B = \frac{\mu_0 I}{4\pi r}[1 + \cos\theta] \qquad \ldots (4.22)$$

In both of above cases the direction of magnetic induction is given by right hand thumb rule as shown in these figures.

4.2.4 Magnetic Induction at the Center of a Circular Coil

Figure-4.11(a) shows a circular coil of radius R carrying a current I. If we consider an element of length dl along its circumference as shown then due to this element by right hand thumb rule or palm rule we can see that the direction of magnetic induction dB at the center of coil is in outward direction as shown in figure-4.11(b). By Biot Savart's Law the magnetic induction at the center of this coil due to this current element is given as

$$dB = \frac{\mu_0}{4\pi}\frac{Idl\sin(90^\circ)}{R^2}$$

$$\Rightarrow \qquad dB = \frac{\mu_0 Idl}{4\pi R^2} \qquad \ldots (4.23)$$

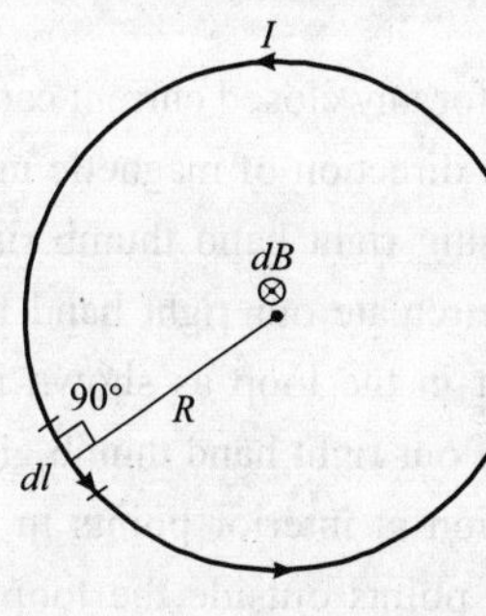

(a)

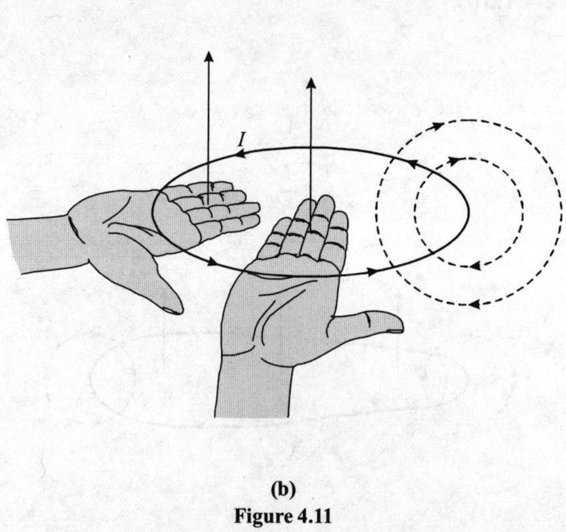

(b)

Figure 4.11

As shown in figure-4.11(b) the direction of magnetic induction due to all the elements of the coil are in same outward direction at every interior point of the coil and the magnetic lines are making closed loops from outside of the coil as shown. Thus net magnetic induction at center of coil can be given by integrating equation-(4.20) for the whole length of the coil which is given as

$$B = \int dB = \frac{\mu_0 I}{4\pi R^2} \int_0^{2\pi R} dl$$

$$\Rightarrow \quad B = \frac{\mu_0 I}{4\pi R^2} [2\pi R - 0]$$

$$\Rightarrow \quad B = \frac{\mu_0 I}{2R} \quad \dots (4.24)$$

If there are N turns of wire in the coil then total length of wire will be $2\pi RN$ so for N turns in coil, the magnetic induction at the center of coil is given as

$$B = \frac{\mu_0 IN}{2R} \quad \dots (4.25)$$

Like a circular coil for any closed current carrying coil of any shape in a plane the direction of magnetic induction can also be calculated by using right hand thumb rule in a different way. For this we circulate our right hand fingers along the direction of current in the loop as shown in figure-4.12(a) then the direction of our right hand thumb gives the direction of magnetic induction at interior points in the plane of the loop and at all the points outside the loop in its plane the direction of magnetic induction is opposite as shown in figure-4.12(b).

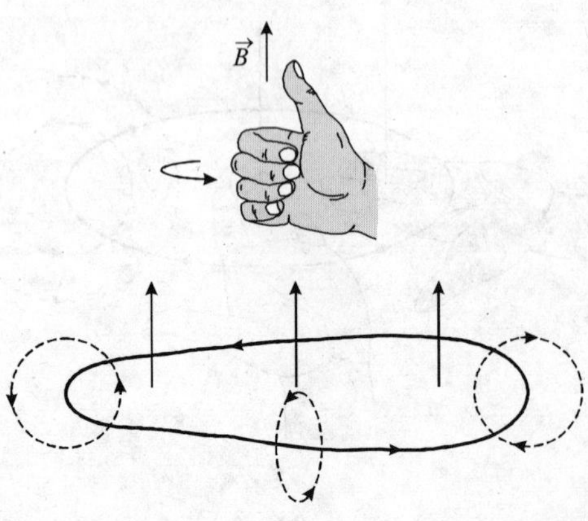

(a)

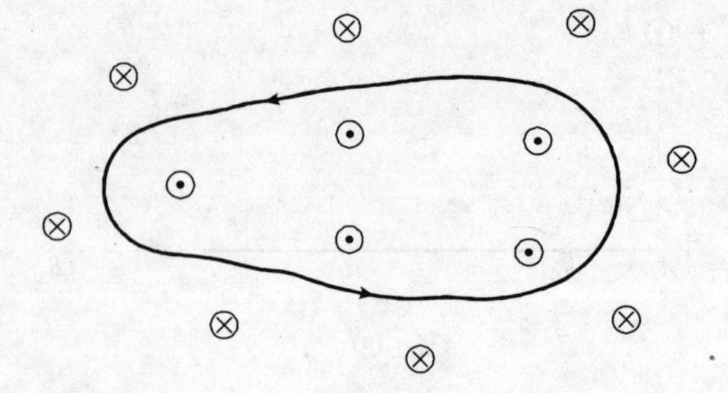

(b)

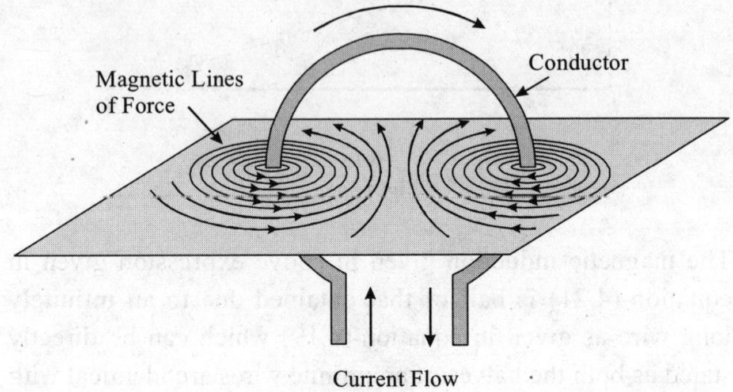

(c)

Figure 4.12

Figure-4.12(c) shows the configuration of magnetic lines in a diametrical plane of a circular current carrying coil which is explained in figure-4.11.

4.2.5 Magnetic Induction at Axial Point of a Circular Coil

Figure-4.13 shows a current carrying circular coil of radius R mounted in YZ plane carrying a current I. We will calculate the magnetic induction due to this coil at a point P located on the axis of coil at a distance x from its center as shown. By using right hand thumb rule as described in previous article, we can see that the direction of magnetic induction at point P due to the current in this coil is in rightward direction.

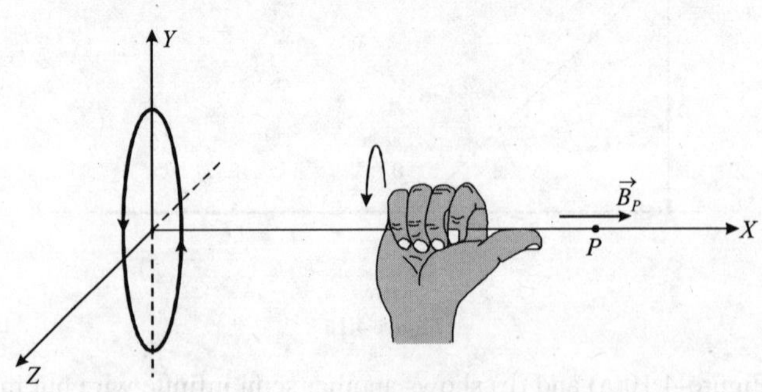

Figure 4.13

To calculate the magnitude of magnetic induction at P due to the coil we consider a small element of length dl at the top of the coil as shown in figure-4.14. Due to the current flowing in this element if we find the magnetic induction dB at point P then its direction can be given by right hand thumb rule as shown in figure. To understand the direction of dB at point P students can imagine their right hand palm placed in the figure with thumb along the direction of current in dl and fingers pointing toward the point P then you can feel that the direction of dB is perpendicular to the palm of your right hand.

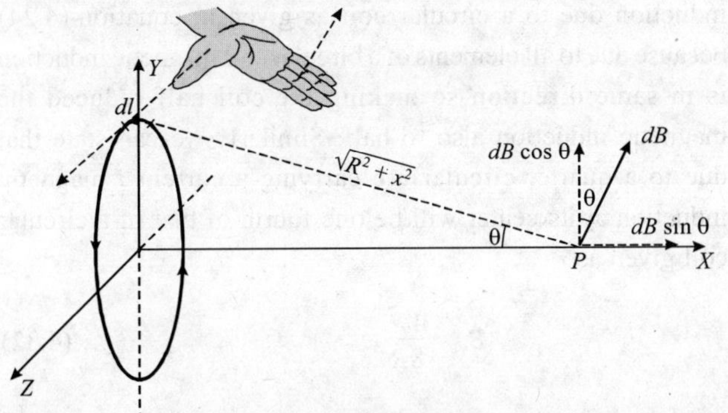

Figure 4.14

If we resolve the magnetic induction dB in mutually perpendicular directions along the axis and perpendicular to the axis as shown in figure then the component dB cosθ which is normal to axis gets cancelled out due to the element on coil which is diametrically opposite to the element considered and the other component dB sinθ which is along the axis will all get added up as due to all the elements on the coil these components are in same direction and the resultant magnetic induction at point P is in the direction as stated in figure-4.13.

The magnetic induction at point P due to the element considered can be given by Biot Savart's law as

$$dB = \frac{\mu_0}{4\pi}\frac{Idl\sin(90°)}{(R^2+x^2)}$$

$$\Rightarrow \quad dB = \frac{\mu_0}{4\pi}\frac{Idl}{(R^2+x^2)} \quad \ldots (4.26)$$

The magnetic induction at P due to the coil is given by integrating the above expression for the whole length of the circumference of the coil. Thus it is given as

$$B = \int dB\sin\theta$$

$$\Rightarrow \quad B = \int_0^{2\pi R}\frac{\mu_0}{4\pi}\cdot\frac{Idl}{(R^2+x^2)}\cdot\frac{R}{\sqrt{R^2+x^2}}$$

$$\Rightarrow \quad B = \frac{\mu_0 IR}{4\pi(R^2+x^2)^{3/2}}\int_0^{2\pi R} dl$$

$$\Rightarrow \quad B = \frac{\mu_0 IR}{4\pi(R^2+x^2)^{3/2}}[2\pi R - 0]$$

$$\Rightarrow \quad B = \frac{\mu_0 IR^2}{2(R^2+x^2)^{3/2}} \quad \ldots (4.27)$$

Above expression given in equation-(4.27) will be used as a standard result for many advance cases of determining magnetic induction. This result can be modified if coil has N turns and it can be given as

$$B = \frac{\mu_0 NIR^2}{2(R^2+x^2)^{3/2}} \quad \ldots (4.28)$$

4.2.6 Helmholtz Coils

A setup of two identical circular coaxial coils separated by a distance equal to their radius when carries current in same direction then in the region between the two coils near their common axis magnetic induction is found to be uniform. Such a system of two coils is called '*Helmholtz Coils*'. Figure-4.15(a) shows the setup of Helmholtz coils and the variation graph of magnetic field with distance of the two coils on their common axis.

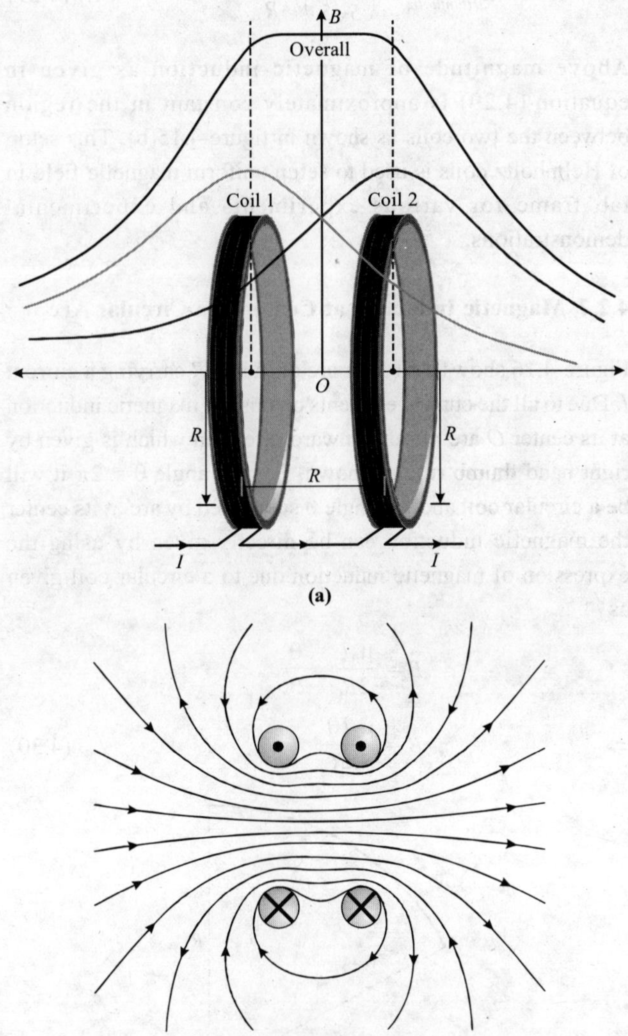

Figure 4.15

In above graphs it is observed that the drop in magnetic

induction due to one coil on either side from $\pm R/2$ position (mid point) is equal to the increase in magnetic induction due to other coil because of which the overall magnetic induction between the two coils remains almost uniform. The magnitude of this magnetic induction can be calculated by using equation-(4.28) at $x = R/2$ due to both the coils.

$$B_{Helmholtz} = 2\, B_{x=R/2}$$

$$\Rightarrow \quad B_{Helmholtz} = 2\left(\frac{\mu_0 NIR^2}{2\left(R^2+x^2\right)^{3/2}}\right)_{x=R/2}$$

$$\Rightarrow \quad B_{Helmholtz} = \frac{\mu_0 NIR^2}{(R^2+(R/2)^2)^{3/2}}$$

$$\Rightarrow \quad B_{Helmholtz} = \left(\frac{8}{5\sqrt{5}}\right)\frac{\mu_0 NI}{R} \qquad \ldots (4.29)$$

Above magnitude of magnetic induction as given in equation-(4.29) is approximately constant in the region between the two coils as shown in figure-4.15(b). This setup of Helmholtz coils is used to setup uniform magnetic field in lab frame for various experiments and experimental demonstrations.

4.2.7 Magnetic Induction at Center of a Circular Arc

Figure-4.16 shows a circular arc of radius R carrying a current I. Due to all the current elements on this arc magnetic induction at its center O are in same inward direction which is given by right hand thumb rule as shown. For the angle $\theta = 2\pi$ it will be a circular coil and for angle θ subtended by arc at its center the magnetic induction can be directly given by using the expression of magnetic induction due to a circular coil given as

$$B = \frac{\mu_0 I}{2R} \times \frac{\theta}{2\pi}$$

$$\Rightarrow \quad B = \frac{\mu_0 I\theta}{4\pi R} \qquad \ldots (4.30)$$

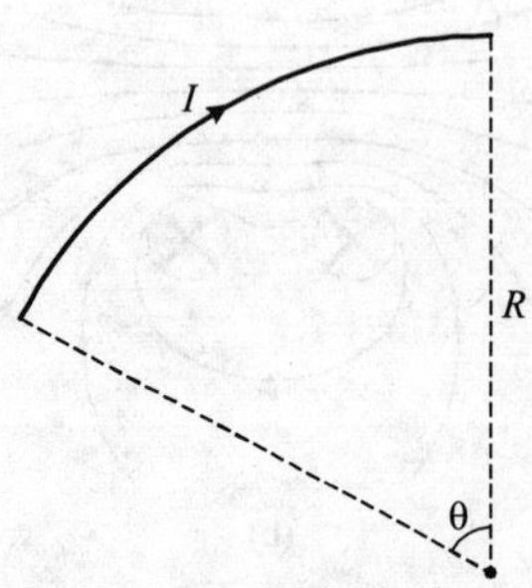

Figure 4.16

Using above expression given in equation-(4.30) we can calculate the magnetic induction due to a semicircular current carrying wire which is given by substituting $\theta = 2\pi$ as

$$B = \frac{\mu_0 I}{4R} \qquad \ldots (4.31)$$

Above expression in equation-(4.31) is half of the magnetic induction due to a circular coil as given in equation-(4.24) because due to all elements of a circular coil magnetic induction is in same direction so making the coil half reduced the magnetic induction also to half. Similarly we can state that due to a quarter circular arc carrying a current i magnetic induction at its center will be one fourth of that of a circular coil given as

$$B = \frac{\mu_0 I}{8R} \qquad \ldots (4.32)$$

Illustrative Example 4.1

A current $i = 1$ A circulates in a round thin wire loop of radius $r = 100$ mm. Find the magnetic induction

(a) At the centre of the loop

(b) At a point lying on the axis of the loop at a distance $x = 100$ mm from its centre.

Solution

(a) At the center of a circular loop magnetic induction is given as

$$B = \frac{\mu_0 i}{2r}$$

$$\Rightarrow \quad B = \frac{4\pi\times10^{-7}\times1.0}{2\times0.1}$$

$$\Rightarrow \quad B = 6.28 \times 10^{-6}\ \text{Wb/m}^2 \approx 6.3\ \mu\text{T}$$

(b) As studied at a point on the axis of the loop magnetic induction is given as

$$B = \frac{\mu_0}{4\pi}\times\frac{ir^2}{(x^2+r^2)^{3/2}}$$

$$\Rightarrow \quad B = \frac{4\pi\times10^{-7}\times1.0\times(0.1)^2}{2\times(0.02)^{3/2}}$$

$$\Rightarrow \quad B = 2.22 \times 10^{-6}\ \text{T}$$

$$\Rightarrow \quad B = 2.22\ \mu\text{T}$$

 # Illustrative Example 4.2

Find the magnetic induction at the point O due to the loop current i in the two cases given below. The shape of the loops are illustrated as

(a) In figure-4.17(a), the radii a and b, as well as the angle ϕ are known.

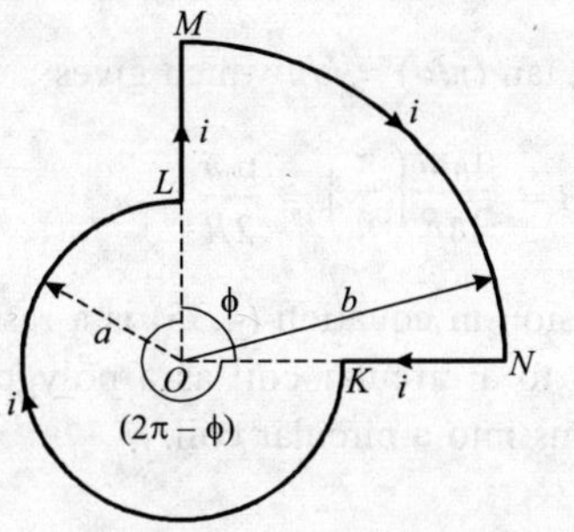

(a)
Figure 4.17

(b) In figure-4.17(b), the radius a and the side b are known.

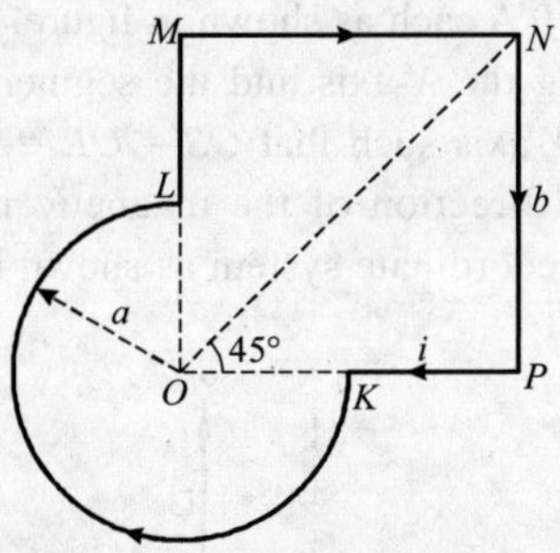

(b)
Figure 4.17

Solution

(a) Magnetic field at O due to segment KL which is a circular arc is given as

$$B_1 = \frac{\mu_0 i}{4\pi a} \times (2\pi - \phi)$$

Magnetic field at O due to part LM and KN is zero because the point O is located on the line of current

Magnetic field at O due to arc MN which subtend an angle ϕ is given by

$$B_2 = \frac{\mu_0 i}{4\pi b} \times \phi$$

Total magnetic induction at O is given as

$$B = B_1 + B_2 = \frac{\mu_0 i}{4\pi} \times \left[\frac{2\pi - \phi}{a} + \frac{\phi}{b}\right]$$

(b) Field at O due to arc KL is given as

$$B_1 = \frac{\mu_0 i}{4\pi a} \times \frac{3\pi}{2}$$

Field at O due to parts LM and PK is zero because the point O is located on the line of current.

Field at O due to part MN is given as

$$B_2 = \frac{\mu_0 i}{4\pi b} \times \sin 45° = \frac{\mu_0 i}{4\pi b} \times \frac{1}{\sqrt{2}}$$

Field at O due to part NP is given as

$$B_3 = \frac{\mu_0 i}{4\pi b} \times \sin 45° = \frac{\mu_0 i}{4\pi b} \times \frac{1}{\sqrt{2}}$$

Total magnetic induction at O is given as

$$B = B_1 + B_2 + B_3$$

$$\Rightarrow \quad B = \frac{\mu_0 i}{4\pi}\left[\frac{3\pi}{2a} + \frac{1}{\sqrt{2}b} + \frac{1}{\sqrt{2}b}\right]$$

$$\Rightarrow \quad B = \frac{\mu_0 i}{4\pi}\left[\frac{3\pi}{2a} + \frac{\sqrt{2}}{b}\right]$$

 # Illustrative Example 4.3

Figure-4.18 shows a current carrying wire bent at an angle α. Find magnetic induction at a point P located on the angle bisector at a distance x from the point O at the bend.

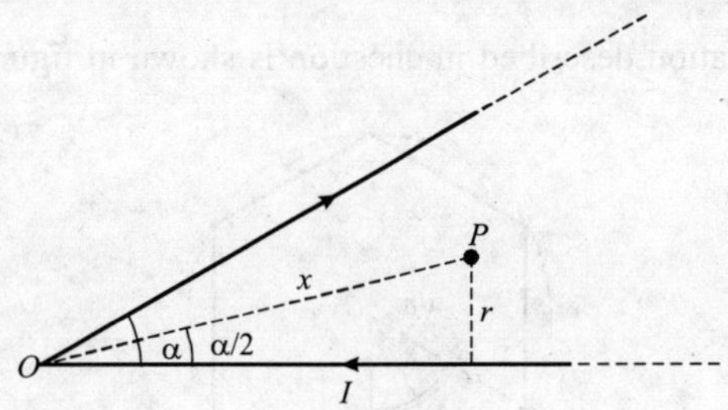

Figure 4.18

Solution

As shown in figure-4.19 below the angle subtended by point P at point O is $\alpha/2$ and at the other point at infinity is 0° so we can use the expression of magnetic induction due to a finite wire by considering these angles to find the magnetic induction at point P due to the two wires which is given as

$$B_P = 2B_{\text{one wire at } P}$$

$$\Rightarrow \quad B_P = \left[\frac{\mu_0 I}{4\pi x \sin \alpha/2}[\cos \alpha/2 + \cos 0]\right]$$

$$\Rightarrow \quad B_P = \frac{\mu_0 I}{4\pi x \sin\alpha/2}[1 + \cos\alpha/2]$$

$$\Rightarrow \quad B_P = \frac{\mu_0 I}{2\pi x \sin\alpha/2}[2\cos 2\,\alpha/2]$$

$$\Rightarrow \quad B_P = \frac{\mu_0 I}{4\pi x \sin\alpha/2 \cos\alpha/4} \times 2\cos^2\alpha/4$$

$$\Rightarrow \quad B_P = \frac{\mu_0 I}{2\pi x}\cot\frac{\alpha}{4}$$

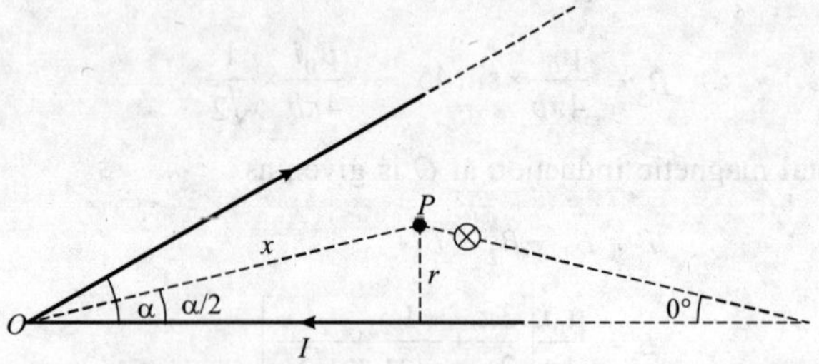

Figure 4.19

Illustrative Example 4.4

A current i flows along a thin wire shaped as a regular polygon with n sides which can be inscribed into a circle of radius R. Find the magnetic induction at the centre of the polygon. Analyses the obtained expression at $n \to \infty$.

Solution

The situation described in question is shown in figure-4.20.

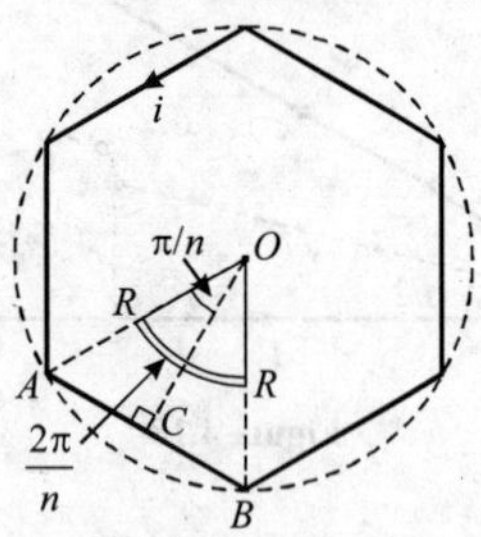

Figure 4.20

In figure, OC is the perpendicular distance of one segment of polygon from the centre. Here $\angle AOB = (2\pi/n)$ as there are n elements like AB thus distance OC is given as

$$OC = R\cos(\pi/n)$$

The magnetic induction at O due to a straight current carrying element AB is given as

$$B_1 = \frac{\mu_0 i}{4\pi} \times \frac{1}{R\cos(\pi/n)}\left[\sin\left(\frac{\pi}{n}\right) + \sin\left(\frac{\pi}{n}\right)\right]$$

$$\Rightarrow \quad B_1 = \frac{\mu_0 i}{4\pi} \times \frac{1}{R\cos(\pi/n)} \times 2\sin\left(\frac{\pi}{n}\right) \quad \ldots (4.33)$$

As there are n sides in the polygon, the total magnetic induction due to polygon is given as

$$B = \frac{\mu_0 n i}{2\pi R}\tan\left(\frac{\pi}{n}\right) \quad \ldots (4.34)$$

When $n \to \infty$, $\tan(\pi/n) \approx \pi/n$ which gives

$$B = \frac{\mu_0 n i}{2\pi R}\left(\frac{\pi}{n}\right) = \frac{\mu_0 i}{2R} \quad \ldots (4.35)$$

Above expression in equation-(4.35) is a result of magnetic induction due to a circular coil as a polygon with infinite sides transforms into a circular coil.

Illustrative Example 4.5

A pair of stationary and infinitely long bent wires are placed in the X-Y plane as shown in figure-4.21. The wires carry currents of $i = 10$ A each as shown in figure. The segments L and M are along the X-axis and the segments P and Q are parallel to the Y-axis such that $OS = OR = 0.2$ m. Find the magnitude and direction of the magnetic induction at the origin O of the coordinate system as shown in figure.

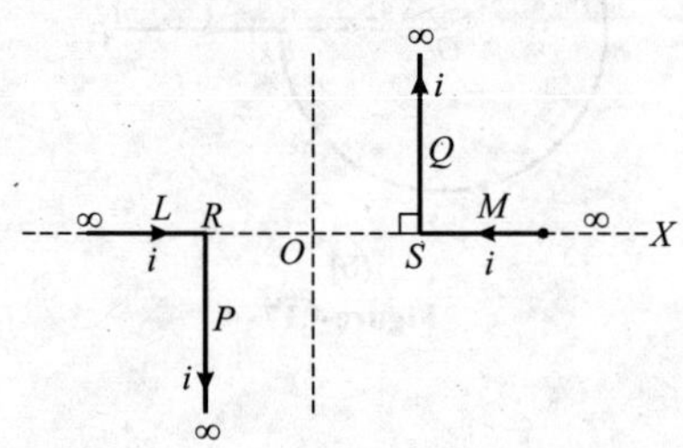

Figure 4.21

Solution

We consider the magnetic induction $\vec{B}$ at O due to each segment separately. Magnetic induction at O due segment L and M is zero because current point O is located on the line of these currents.

Magnetic induction at O due to segments P and Q are in same direction which can be seen by using right hand thumb rule in outward direction and equal in magnitude due to symmetry which is say B_1 can be calculated by using the result of magnetic induction due to a semi infinite wire given as

$$B_1 = \left(\frac{\mu_0}{4\pi}\frac{i}{r}\right)$$

$$\Rightarrow \quad B_1 = \left(\frac{4\pi\times10^{-4}}{4\pi}\times\frac{10}{10.02}\right)\text{Wb/m}^2$$

$$\Rightarrow \quad B_1 = 0.5\times10^{-4}\ \text{Wb/m}^2$$

As magnetic induction due to segments P and Q are equal, net magnetic induction at O is given as

$$B_O = 2B_1$$

$$\Rightarrow \quad B_O = 10^{-4}\ \text{Wb/m}^2$$

As discussed that the direction of B_O is perpendicular to X-Y plane and directed outward from the plane of paper.

Illustrative Example 4.6

Figure-4.22 shows two long wires A and B, each carrying a current I, separated by a distance l and oriented in a plane perpendicular to the plane of paper. The directions of currents are shown in figure. Find the magnetic induction at a point P located at a distance l from both wires as shown in figure-4.22.

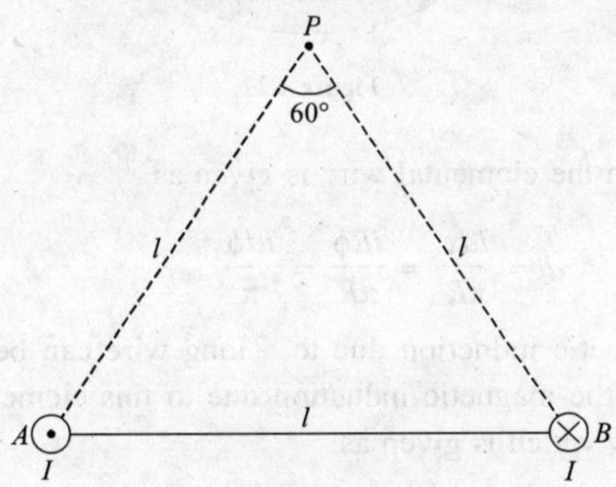

Figure 4.22

Solution

Magnetic induction at point P due to both wires is given as

$$B = \frac{\mu_0 I}{2\pi l}$$

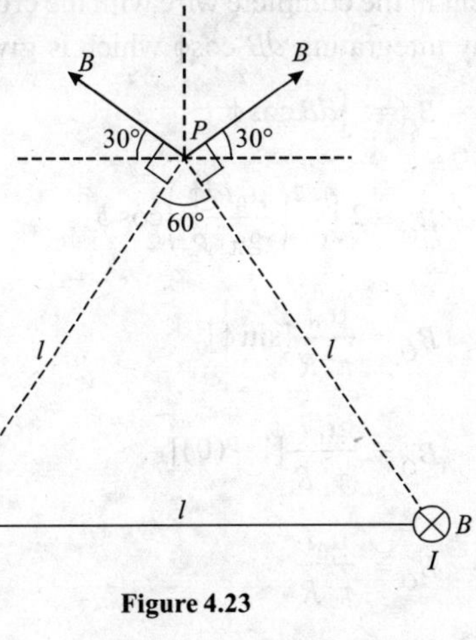

Figure 4.23

The directions of magnetic induction due to individual wires is perpendicular to the line joining the wire to point P. From above figure at point P net magnetic induction is given as

$$B_P = 2B\sin 30° = 2\times\frac{\mu_0 I}{2\pi l}\times\frac{1}{2}$$

$$\Rightarrow \quad B_P = \frac{\mu_0 I}{2\pi l}$$

Illustrative Example 4.7

In figure-4.24 a current carrying wire configuration is shown with current I. Find the vector of magnetic induction at origin of co-ordinate system O.

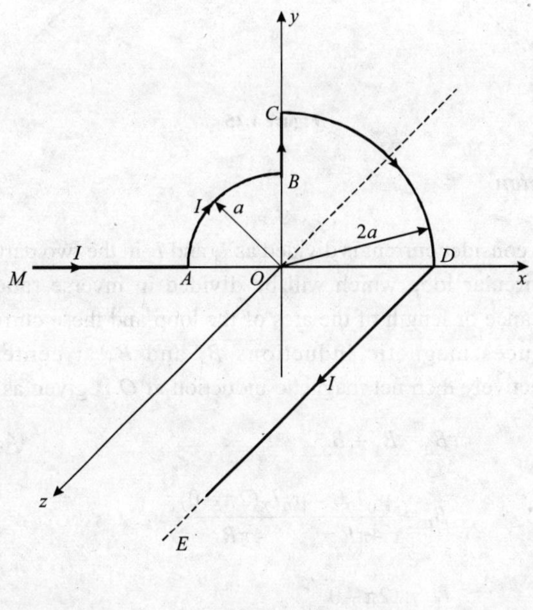

Figure 4.24

Solution

The magnetic induction at origin can calculated by vector sum of magnetic inductions due to separate segments of this wire configuration which is given as

$$\vec{B}_O = \vec{B}_{AB} + \vec{B}_{CD} + \vec{B}_{DE}$$

In above vector sum we have not considered the wire segments MA and BC as origin lies along the line of currents so

$$\vec{B}_O = \frac{\mu_0 I}{8a}(-\hat{k}) + \frac{\mu_0 I}{16a}(-\hat{k}) + \frac{\mu_0 I}{8\pi a}(-\hat{j})$$

$$\Rightarrow \quad \vec{B}_O = -\frac{\mu_0 I}{8a}\left[\frac{3}{2}\hat{k} + \frac{1}{\pi}\hat{j}\right]$$

Illustrative Example 4.8

Figure shows a circular wire loop in which a current I enters at point A and leaves from point B through straight wires. Find magnetic induction at centre O.

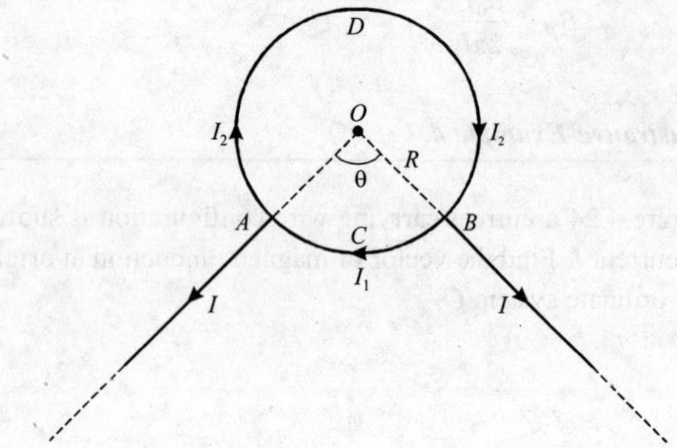

Figure 4.25

Solution

If we consider current is divided as I_1 and I_2 in the two parts of the circular loop which will be divided in inverse ratio of resistance or length of the arcs of the loop and these currents produces magnetic inductions B_1 and B_2 at center O respectively then net magnetic induction at O is given as

$$B_0 = B_1 - B_2 \qquad \ldots (4.36)$$

$$\Rightarrow \qquad B_0 = \frac{\mu_0 I_0 \theta}{4\pi R} - \frac{\mu_0 I_2 (2\pi - \theta)}{4\pi R}$$

$$\Rightarrow \qquad \frac{I_1}{I_2} = \frac{2\pi - \theta}{\theta}$$

$$\Rightarrow \qquad I_1 = I\left(\frac{2\pi - \theta}{\theta}\right)$$

$$\Rightarrow \qquad I_2 = I\left(\frac{\theta}{2\pi}\right)$$

Substituting above current values in equation-(4.36) we have

$$B_0 = B_1 - B_2 = 0$$

Illustrative Example 4.9

A current i flows in a long straight wire with cross-section having the form of a thin half-ring of radius R as shown in figure-4.26. Find the induction of magnetic field at the point O.

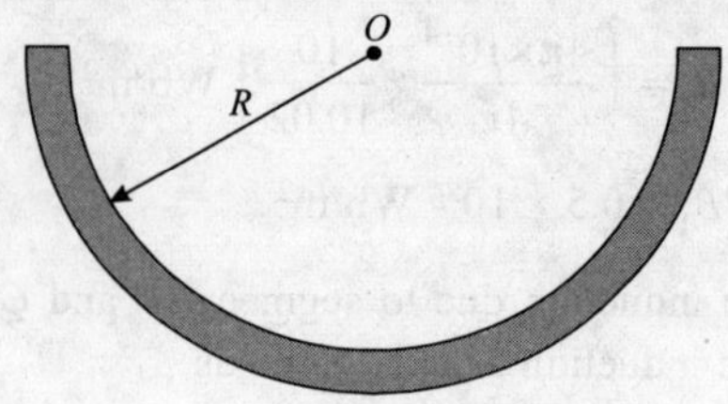

Figure 4.26

Solution

Consider elemental wire of width dx in the cross section as shown in figure-4.27

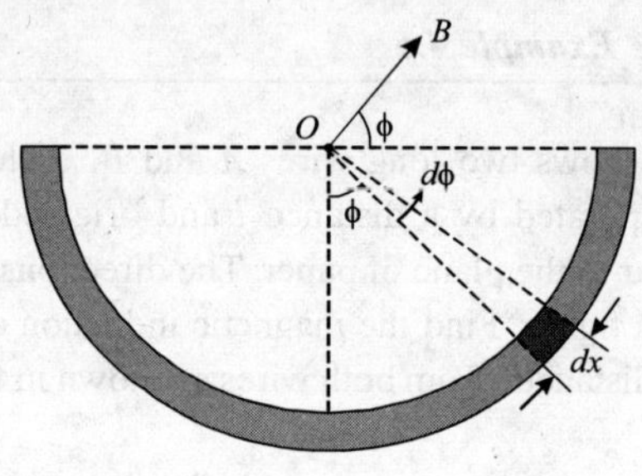

Figure 4.27

Current in the elemental wire is given as

$$di = \frac{idx}{\pi R} = \frac{iR\phi}{\pi R} = \frac{id\phi}{\pi}$$

The magnetic induction due to a long wire can be used to calculate the magnetic induction due to this elemental wire at point O which is given as

$$B = \frac{\mu_0 di}{2\pi R} = \frac{\mu_0 i d\phi}{2\pi^2 R}$$

All the components $dB \sin\phi$ will be cancelled out due to the corresponding elemental wires on the other half of the cross section as these are in opposite directions and the components $dB \cos\phi$ due to all the elemental wires are in same directions so will be added up. Thus net magnetic induction due to the total current in the complete wire with the cross section shown is given by integrating $dB \cos\phi$ which is given as

$$B_0 = \int dB \cos\phi$$

$$\Rightarrow \qquad B_0 = 2\int_0^{\pi/2} \left(\frac{\mu_0 i d\phi}{2\pi^2 R}\right) \cos\phi$$

$$\Rightarrow \qquad B_0 = \frac{\mu_0 i}{\pi^2 R} [\sin\phi]_0^{\pi/2}$$

$$\Rightarrow \qquad B_0 = \frac{\mu_0 i}{\pi^2 R} [1 - (0)]$$

$$\Rightarrow \qquad B_0 = \frac{\mu_0 i}{\pi^2 R}$$

Practice Exercise 4.1

(i) Find the magnetic induction at the centre of a rectangular wire frame whose diagonal length is equal to $d = 16$ cm and the angle between the diagonals is equal to $\phi = 30°$, the current flowing in the frame equals $i = 5.0$ A.

[0.1 mT]

(ii) Find the magnetic induction at the point O due to a current i flowing in a current carrying wire which has the shape as shown in figures-4.28 (a, b, c). The radius of the curved part of the wire is R and the linear parts are assumed to be very long.

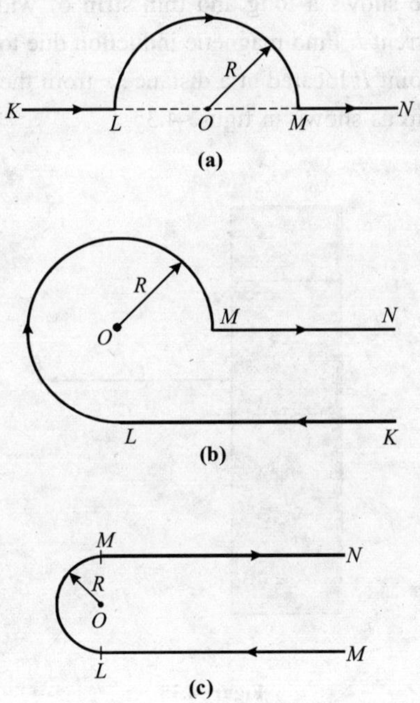

Figure 4.28

[(a) $\frac{\mu_0 i}{4R}$; (b) $\frac{\mu_0 i}{4\pi R}\left[1+\frac{3\pi}{2}\right]$; (c) $\frac{\mu_0 i}{4\pi R}(2+\pi)$]

(iii) Find the magnetic induction at the point O if the wire carrying a current I has a shape as shown in figure-4.29 (a, b, c). The radius of the curved part of the wire is R and consider the linear parts of the wire are very long.

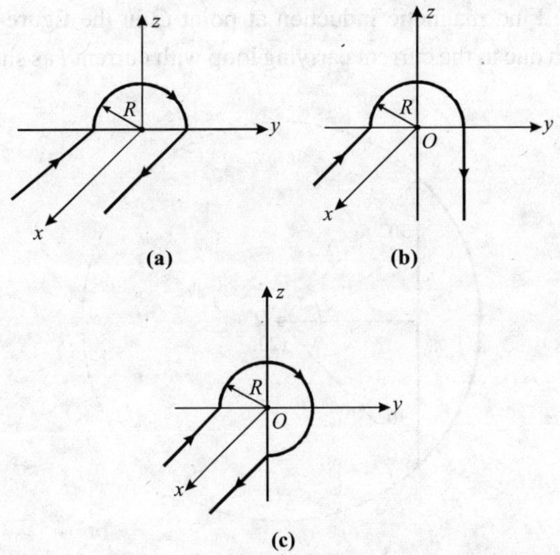

Figure 4.29

[$\frac{\mu_0}{4\pi}\frac{I}{R}\sqrt{\pi^2+4}$, $\frac{\mu_0}{4\pi}\frac{I}{R}\sqrt{1+(\pi+1)^2}$, $\frac{\mu_0}{4\pi}\frac{I}{2\pi}\sqrt{9\pi^2+8}$]

(iv) In the figure-4.30 shown two circular arcs are joined to make a closed loop carrying current I. Find the magnetic induction at the common centre O.

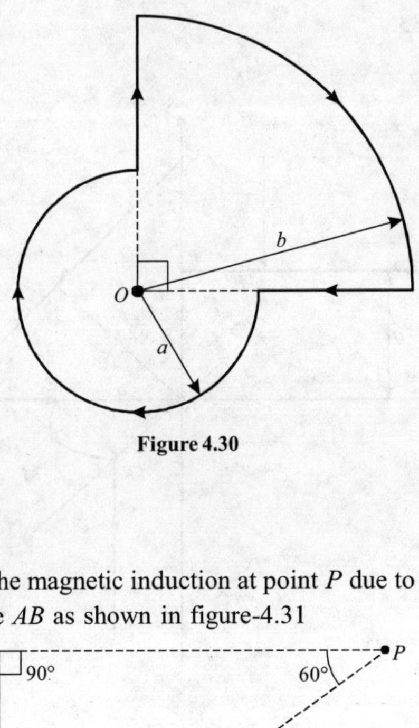

Figure 4.30

[$\frac{\mu_0 I}{8}\left(\frac{3}{a}+\frac{1}{b}\right)$]

(v) Find the magnetic induction at point P due to a current carrying wire AB as shown in figure-4.31

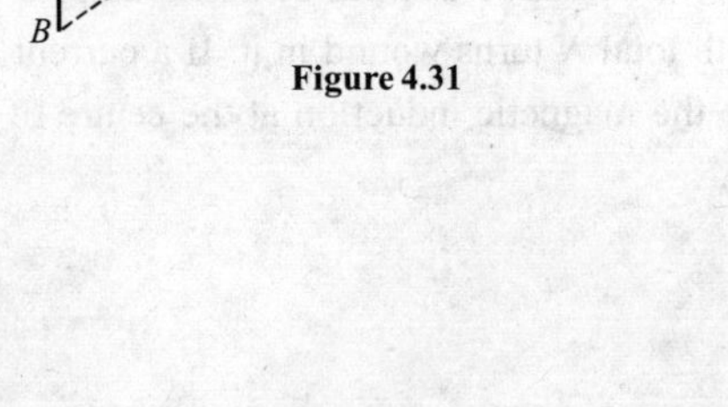

Figure 4.31

[$\frac{\sqrt{3}\mu_0 I}{8\pi l}$]

(vi) Find magnetic induction at point O in the figure-4.32 shown due to the current carrying loop with current I as shown.

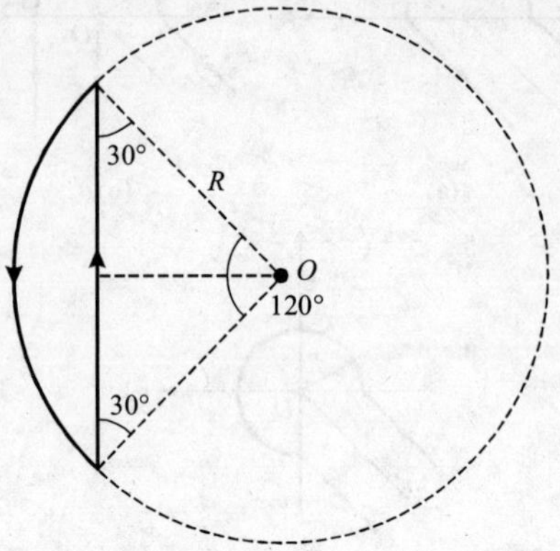

Figure 4.32

$[\frac{\mu_0 I}{2R}\left[\frac{\sqrt{3}}{\pi}-\frac{1}{3}\right]]$

(vii) Find the magnetic induction vector at origin O due to the current carrying wire configuration as shown in figure-4.33.

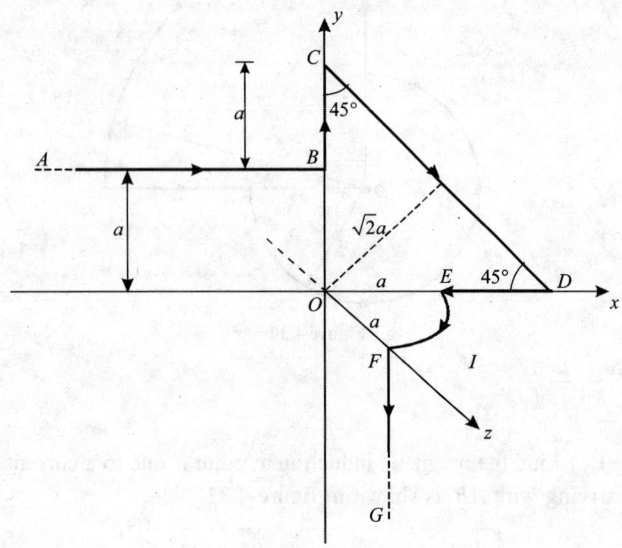

Figure 4.33

$[\frac{\mu_0 I}{4\pi a}\left[\hat{i}-\frac{\pi}{2}\hat{j}-2\hat{k}\right]]$

(viii) Figure-4.34 shows a spiral of inner radius a and outer radius b with total N turns wound in it. If a current i flows in it, calculate the magnetic induction at the centre of spiral.

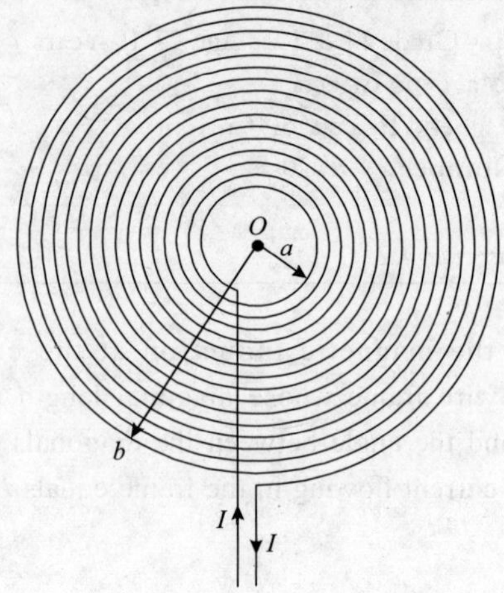

Figure 4.34

$[\frac{\mu_0 IN}{2(b-a)}\ln\left(\frac{b}{a}\right)]$

(ix) Figure shows a long and thin strip of width b which carries a current I. Find magnetic induction due to the current in strip at point P located at a distance r from the strip in the plane of strip as shown in figure-4.35.

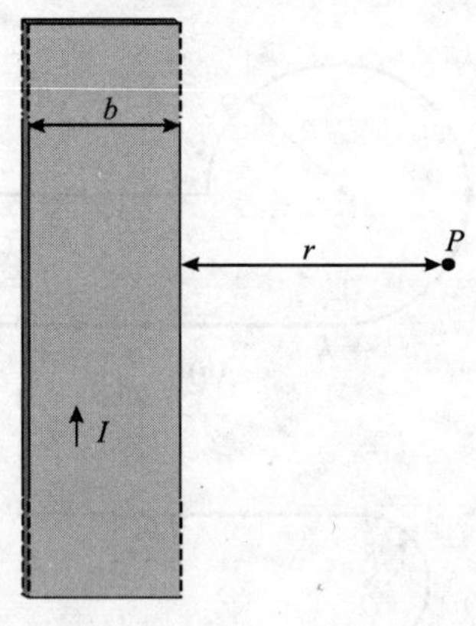

Figure 4.35

$[\frac{\mu_0 I}{2\pi b}\ln\left(\frac{r+b}{r}\right)]$

(x) Two long parallel wires carrying currents 2.5 A and 4 A in the same direction directed into the plane of the paper are held at points P and Q as shown in figure-4.36 such that they are perpendicular to the plane of paper. The points P and Q are located at a distance of 5 m and 2 m respectively from a collinear point R as shown.

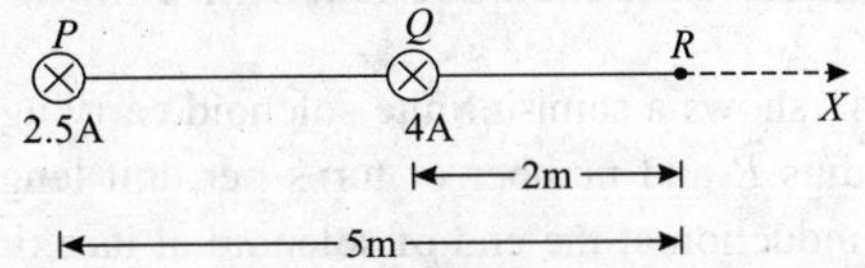

Figure 4.36

Find all the positions at which a third long parallel wire carrying a current of magnitude 2.5A may be placed so that the magnetic induction at R is zero.

[± 1 m from point R along x-axis]

4.3 Magnetic Induction due to Extended Current Configurations

In previous articles we've studied the magnetic induction due to current carrying long and finite straight wires, circular coil and arcs. In this section we will study the magnetic induction due to some current configurations in which the results obtained in previous articles will be used as building blocks. Such current configurations are called extended current configurations.

4.3.1 Magnetic Induction Inside a Long Solenoid

Figure-4.37 shows a long tightly wound solenoid with core radius R which carries a current I. The number of turns per unit length of solenoid are n. We consider tightly wound solenoid because in this case we can consider each turn of wire wound on solenoid core as a circular coil otherwise if it takes a helical shape then we cannot use the expression of magnetic induction due to a circular coil.

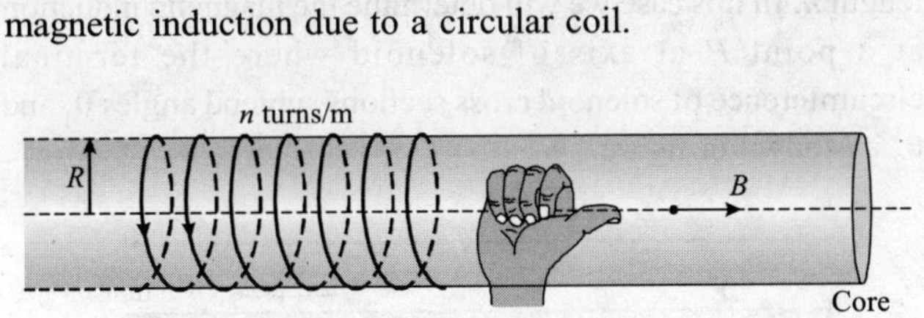

Figure 4.37

To determine the magnetic induction at the axial point of the solenoid we consider an elemental ring of width dx on the solenoid core at a distance x from an axial point O as shown in figure-4.38. Number of turns in this elemental ring will be ndx and due to this elemental ring, magnetic induction at point O is given by using equation-(4.28) as

$$dB = \frac{\mu_0 (ndx) IR^2}{2(R^2 + x^2)^{3/2}} \qquad \dots (4.37)$$

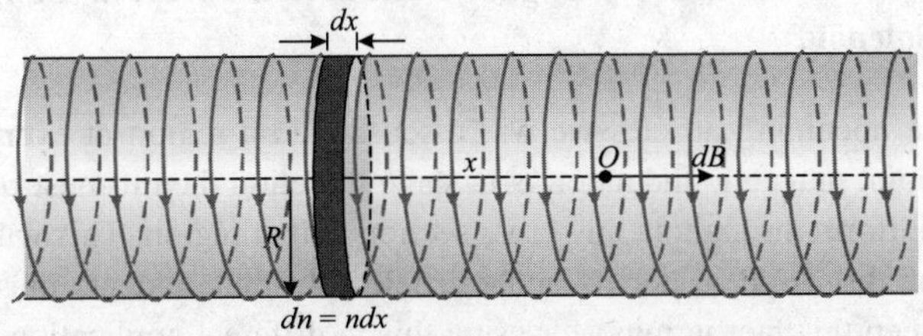

Figure 4.38

Net magnetic induction at point O due to whole solenoid can be calculated by integrating above expression within limits from $-\infty$ to $+\infty$ which is given as

$$B = \int dB = \int_{-\infty}^{+\infty} \frac{\mu_0 (ndx) IR^2}{2\left(R^2 + x^2\right)^{3/2}}$$

$$\Rightarrow \quad B = \frac{\mu_0 n I R^2}{2} \int_{-\infty}^{+\infty} \frac{dx}{(R^2 + x^2)^{3/2}}$$

To integrate the above expression we substitute

$$x = R \tan\theta$$

$$dx = R \sec^2\theta \, d\theta$$

With the above substitution limits of integration also changes as

$$\text{at } x = -\infty \rightarrow \theta = -\frac{\pi}{2}$$

and $$\text{at } x = +\infty \rightarrow \theta = +\frac{\pi}{2}$$

$$\Rightarrow \quad B = \frac{\mu_0 n I R^2}{2} \int_{-\frac{\pi}{2}}^{+\frac{\pi}{2}} \frac{R \sec^2\theta d\theta}{(R^2 + R^2 \tan^2\theta)^{3/2}}$$

$$\Rightarrow \quad B = \frac{\mu_0 n I R^2}{2} \int_{-\pi/2}^{+\pi/2} \frac{R \sec^2\theta d\theta}{R^3 \sec^3\theta}$$

$$\Rightarrow \quad B = \frac{\mu_0 n I}{2} \int_{-\pi/2}^{+\pi/2} \cos\theta d\theta$$

$$\Rightarrow \quad B = \frac{\mu_0 n I}{2} [\sin\theta]_{-\pi/2}^{+\pi/2}$$

$$\Rightarrow \quad B = \frac{1}{2} \mu_0 n I [1 - (-1)]$$

$$\Rightarrow \quad B = \mu_0 n I \qquad \dots (4.38)$$

Above expression given in equation-(4.38) is valid only for the case when the solenoid is very long and tightly wound on its core. If there is a gap between turns of solenoid then these turns cannot be considered as circular coils using which above result is derived.

4.3.2 Direction of Magnetic Induction Inside a Long Solenoid

In upcoming articles we will discuss if in a region at every point magnetic induction is in same direction then it must be uniform throughout any cross section in that region. This will be discussed in details under article-4.4.9 but students must keep this fact in mind for using this in different applications. As at every point on the axis of a long solenoid magnetic induction is given by equation-(4.38) which is a constant thus we can conclude that throughout the volume of solenoid at every cross section magnetic induction will remain uniform as shown in figure-4.39. It is also observed that for closed pack or tightly wound solenoid outside magnetic induction is zero as all magnetic lines form closed loop from negative infinity to positive infinity along the length of solenoid and at every exterior point of solenoid magnetic induction due to different parts on diametrically opposite sides of solenoid cancelled out.

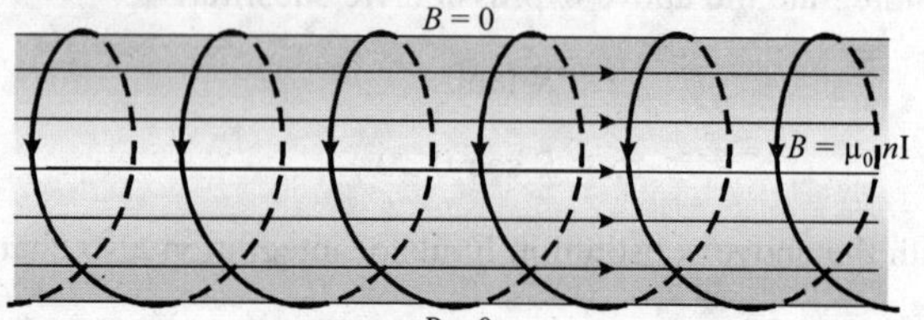

Figure 4.39

Figure-4.40 shows a loosely wound solenoid on a core. As the wires in turns are not closely packed magnetic induction due to each wire turn will be in form of concentric circles close to the wire and at some distance inside and outside the resulting magnetic induction is shown by the magnetic lines in this figure. As wire turns are not closely packed outside magnetic field exist in opposite direction. If turns are very close or almost touching each other the magnetic induction between the wire turns will be zero as due to the two close turns the magnetic field cancels because these are in opposite direction (See point A in figure).

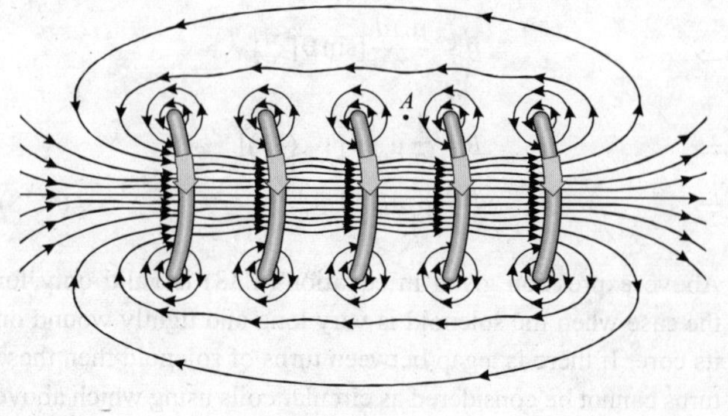

Figure 4.40

4.3.3 Magnetic Induction due to a Semi-Infinite Solenoid

Figure-4.41 shows a semi-infinite solenoid carrying a current I, core radius R and number of turns per unit length n. The magnetic induction at the end of solenoid at its axial point O can be directly given as half of that due to the long solenoid at any of its axial point. This is because if we consider another semi-infinite solenoid adjoining to this one to complete the infinite solenoid then at point O the magnetic induction due to two halves of the long solenoid will be equal which is given by equation-(4.38). Thus the magnetic induction at the point O on the axis at terminal cross section of this semi-infinite solenoid is given as

$$B = \frac{1}{2}\mu_0 nI \quad \dots (4.39)$$

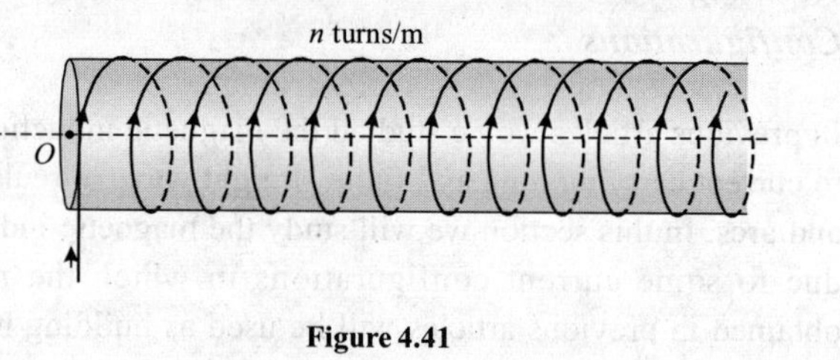

Figure 4.41

Students can also derive the above expression given in equation-(4.39) by integrating the result due to an elemental circular coil as considered in article-4.3.1 within limits from 0 to infinity for the magnetic induction at point O due to this semi-infinite solenoid.

4.3.4 Magnetic Induction due to a finite length Solenoid

Figure-4.42 shows a finite length tightly wound solenoid of core radius R and current I with number of turns per unit length n. In this case we will determine the magnetic induction at a point P at axis of solenoid where the terminal circumference of solenoid cross sections subtend angles θ_1 and θ_2 as shown in figure.

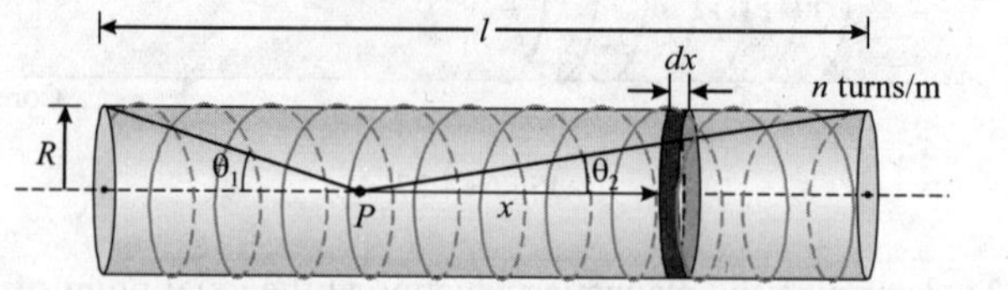

Figure 4.42

To find the magnetic induction at point P we consider an elemental coil of width dx at a distance x from P. Number of turns in this elemental coil are ndx. Magnetic induction due to the elemental coil dB at point P is given by using equation-(4.28) as

$$dB = \frac{\mu_0 (ndx) IR^2}{2(R^2 + x^2)^{3/2}} \quad \text{... (4.40)}$$

Net magnetic induction at point P due to whole solenoid can be calculated by integrating above expression within limits from $-R\cot\theta_1$ to $+R\cot\theta_2$ which is given as

$$B = \int dB = \int_{-R\cot\theta_1}^{+R\cot\theta_2} \frac{\mu_0 (ndx) IR^2}{2(R^2 + x^2)^{3/2}}$$

$$\Rightarrow \quad B = \frac{\mu_0 nIR^2}{2} \int_{-R\cot\theta_1}^{+R\cot\theta_2} \frac{dx}{(R^2 + x^2)^{3/2}}$$

To integrate the above expression we substitute

$$x = R\cot\theta$$

$$dx = -R\csc^2\theta \, d\theta$$

With the above substitution, limits of integration also changes as

$$\text{at } x = -R\cot\theta_1 \rightarrow \theta = -\theta_1$$

$$\text{and} \quad \text{at } x = +R\cot\theta_2 \rightarrow \theta = +\theta_2$$

$$\Rightarrow \quad B = \frac{\mu_0 nIR^2}{2} \int_{-\theta_1}^{+\theta_2} \frac{R\csc^2\theta d\theta}{(R^2 + R^2\cot^2\theta)^{3/2}}$$

$$\Rightarrow \quad B = \frac{\mu_0 nIR^2}{2} \int_{-\theta_1}^{+\theta_2} \frac{R\csc^2\theta d\theta}{R^3\csc^3\theta}$$

$$\Rightarrow \quad B = -\frac{\mu_0 nI}{2} \int_{-\theta_1}^{+\theta_2} \sin\theta d\theta$$

$$\Rightarrow \quad B = \frac{\mu_0 nI}{2} [\cos\theta]_{-\theta_1}^{+\theta_2}$$

$$\Rightarrow \quad B = \frac{1}{2}\mu_0 nI[\cos\theta_2 - (-\cos\theta_1)]$$

$$\Rightarrow \quad B = \frac{1}{2}\mu_0 nI[\cos\theta_1 + \cos\theta_2] \quad \text{... (4.41)}$$

Using above expression we can also calculate the magnetic induction due to the semi-infinite solenoid by substituting angles $\theta_1 = 90°$ and $\theta_2 = 0°$ which also verifies the expression obtained qualitatively as equation-(4.39) in article-4.3.3.

4.3.5 Magnetic Induction due to a Large Toroid

Figure-4.43 shows a large toroid with its radius R to be very large compared to its cross sectional radius r ($R >> r$). Due to large radius turns can be tightly wound on the toroidal core (also called as tore) of toroid. If there are total N turns of wire wound on the toroid then number of turns per unit length can be given as

$$n = \frac{N}{2\pi R} \quad \text{... (4.42)}$$

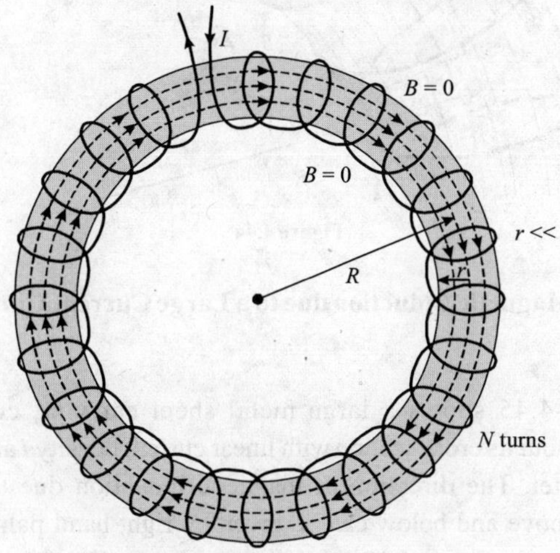

Figure 4.43

This toroid can also be imagined by considering a long solenoid is bent in circular shape so that its both far ends are joined together to close the loop for inside magnetic lines. In case of tightly wound turns with $R >> r$ the magnetic induction inside the cross sectional region of toroid can be given by equation-(4.38) as

$$B = \mu_0 \left(\frac{N}{2\pi R}\right) I$$

$$\Rightarrow \quad B = \frac{\mu_0 NI}{2\pi R} \quad \text{... (4.43)}$$

If the cross sectional radius of toroid is not very small compared to the average radius of the toroid then number of turns per unit length at inside and outside periphery of the toroid will be different due to which the magnetic induction inside the toroid cross section will also be different near to inside and outside edge as shown in figure-4.44 which approximately shows the magnetic lines density inside. As near to inner edge (at point 1 shown in figure-4.44) turns are closer so magnetic induction will be higher and at outer edge (at point 2 shown in figure-4.44) turns separation is large so magnetic induction will be lesser. In this case at outside points of toroid also magnetic induction will be non zero because of the same reason as discussed in article-4.3.2.

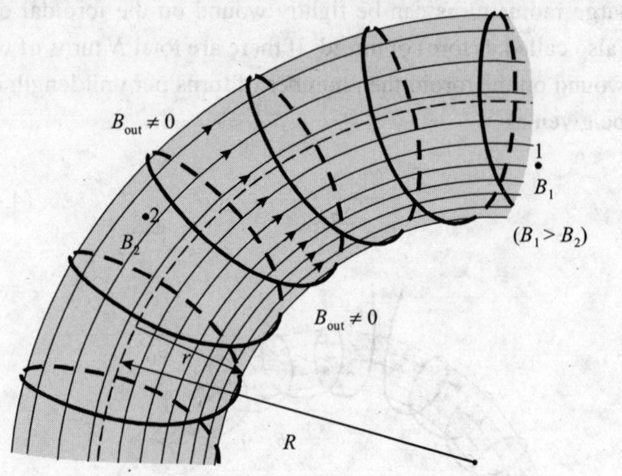

Figure 4.44

4.3.6 Magnetic Induction due to a Large Current Carrying Sheet

Figure-4.45 shows a large metal sheet carrying current throughout its cross section with linear current density i ampere per meter. The direction of magnetic induction due to this sheet above and below can be given by right hand palm rule as shown in figure-4.45(a). We can see that the direction of magnetic induction above and below the sheet are opposite and as the sheet is considered to be very large the direction of magnetic induction is considered uniform in the region. Figure-4.45(b) shows the cross sectional view of the sheet and the direction of magnetic induction due to the current in sheet.

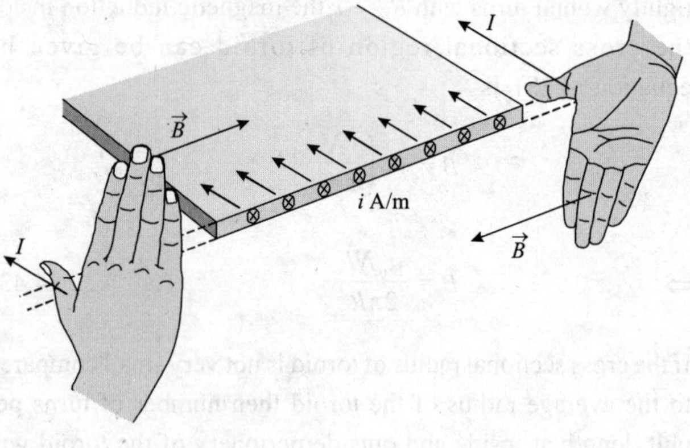

(a)

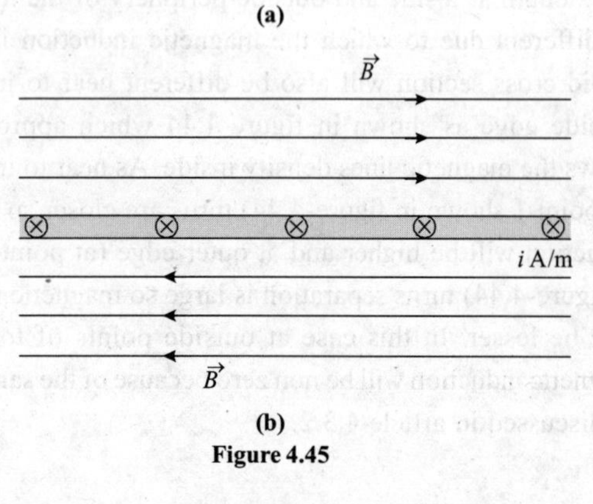

(b)

Figure 4.45

To determine the magnitude of magnetic induction at a point P located a distance r above the sheet we consider an elemental wire in the sheet of width dx at a distance x from the sheet as shown in figure-4.46. This figure shows the cross section of the sheet which carries a linear current density i A/m. The current in the elemental wire is given as

$$di = idx$$

Magnetic induction dB due to the elemental wire on sheet at point P can be calculated by equation-(4.19) as discussed in article-4.2.1 which is given as

$$dB = \frac{\mu_0 di}{2\pi\sqrt{x^2 + r^2}}$$

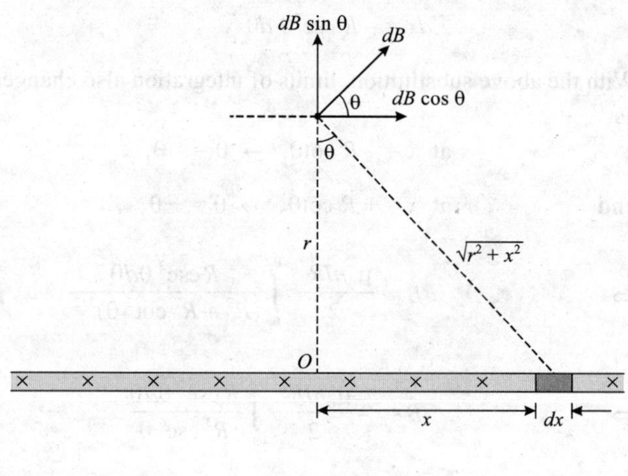

Figure 4.46

The direction of dB is shown in above figure which students can verify by placing their right hand thumb along the elemental wire pointing inward and fingers toward the point P so that right hand palm gives the direction of dB.

In figure-4.46 we can see that the component of dB normal to the sheet $dB \sin\theta$ will get cancelled out by the opposite direction component at P due to another elemental wire on sheet on the other side of point O at the same distance x. Other component of magnetic induction along the surface of sheet $dB \cos\theta$ will be added up due to all the elemental wires on the sheet thus net magnetic induction at point P due to whole sheet will be given by integrating $dB \cos\theta$ for the whole length of sheet from $-\infty$ to $+\infty$ given as

$$B = \int dB \cos\theta$$

$$\Rightarrow \quad B = \int_{-\infty}^{+\infty} \frac{\mu_0 (idx)}{2\pi\sqrt{x^2 + r^2}} \cdot \frac{r}{\sqrt{x^2 + r^2}}$$

$$\Rightarrow \quad B = \frac{\mu_0 ir}{2\pi}\int_{-\infty}^{+\infty}\frac{dx}{(x^2+r^2)}$$

$$\Rightarrow \quad B = \frac{\mu_0 ir}{2\pi}\left[\frac{1}{r}\tan^{-1}\left(\frac{x}{r}\right)\right]_{-\infty}^{+\infty}$$

$$\Rightarrow \quad B = \frac{\mu_0 i}{2\pi}\left[\left(\frac{\pi}{2}\right)-\left(-\frac{\pi}{2}\right)\right]$$

$$\Rightarrow \quad B = \frac{1}{2}\mu_0 i \qquad \ldots (4.44)$$

4.3.7 Magnetic Induction due to a Revolving Charge Particle

Figure-4.47(a) shows a point charge q is revolving in a circle of radius R with velocity v. If the charge is revolving at slow speed then the magnetic induction at its center due to motion of charge can be calculated by equation-(4.15) as discussed in article-4.1.2 which is given as

$$B = \frac{\mu_0 qv}{4\pi R^2} \qquad \ldots (4.45)$$

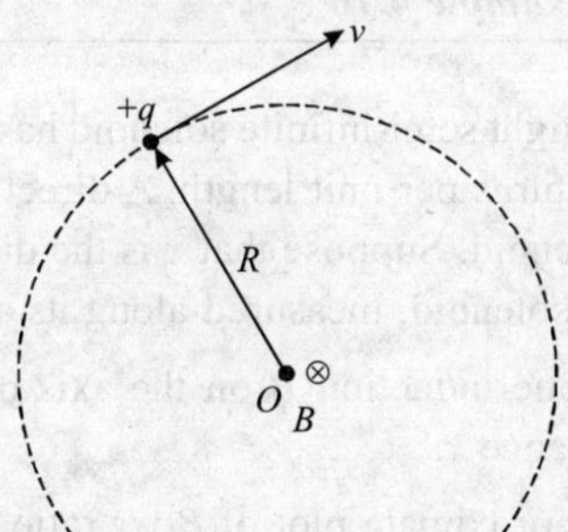

(a)

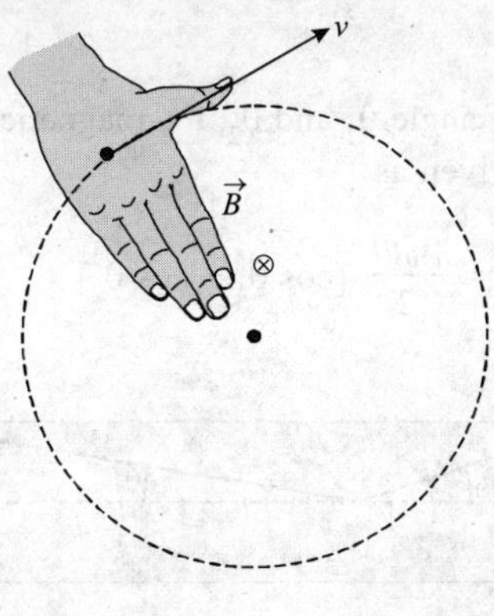

(b)

Figure 4.47

The direction of above magnetic induction is given by right hand thumb rule as shown in figure-4.47(b). If the charge is revolving at high speed then it can be considered as a continuously flowing current in coil. For a charge revolving at an angular speed ω then its equivalent current in the circular path is given as

Current = Charge × Frequency of revolution

$$\Rightarrow \quad I = q \times \frac{\omega}{2\pi} = \frac{q\omega}{2\pi} \qquad \ldots (4.46)$$

Thus magnetic induction at the center of this circle can be calculated by using equation-(4.24), given as

$$B = \frac{\mu_0 I}{2R}$$

$$\Rightarrow \quad B = \frac{\mu_0}{2R}\left(\frac{q\omega}{2\pi}\right)$$

$$\Rightarrow \quad B = \frac{\mu_0 q\omega}{4\pi R}$$

$$\Rightarrow \quad B = \frac{\mu_0 qv}{4\pi R^2} \quad \left[\text{As } \omega = \frac{v}{R}\right] \qquad \ldots (4.47)$$

Above equation-(4.47) is same as equation-(4.45). In case of magnetic induction at center of circle both of these results can be considered same but in case of a point on the axis of circle in first case due to revolution of charge particle the instantaneous direction of magnetic induction is shown in figure-4.48 which changes with the location of the particle on circular path in YZ plane as shown and its magnitude is given as

$$B = \frac{\mu_0 qv}{4\pi(R^2+x^2)} \qquad \ldots (4.48)$$

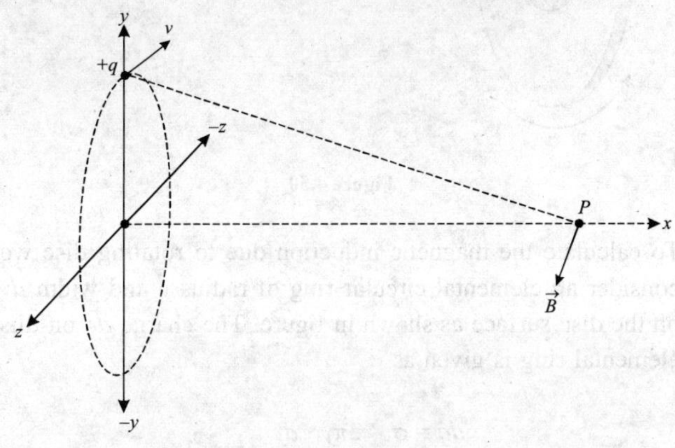

Figure 4.48

If we consider revolving charge as a continuous circulating current of magnitude given by equation-(4.46) then for an axial point at a distance x from the center of circle the magnetic induction direction will be given by right hand thumb rule as shown in figure-4.49 and its magnitude can be calculated by using equation-(4.28) given as

$$B = \frac{\mu_0 R^2}{2(R^2+x^2)^{3/2}}\left(\frac{q\omega}{2\pi}\right)$$

$$\Rightarrow \quad B = \frac{\mu_0 q\omega R^2}{4\pi(R^2+x^2)^{3/2}} \quad \ldots (4.49)$$

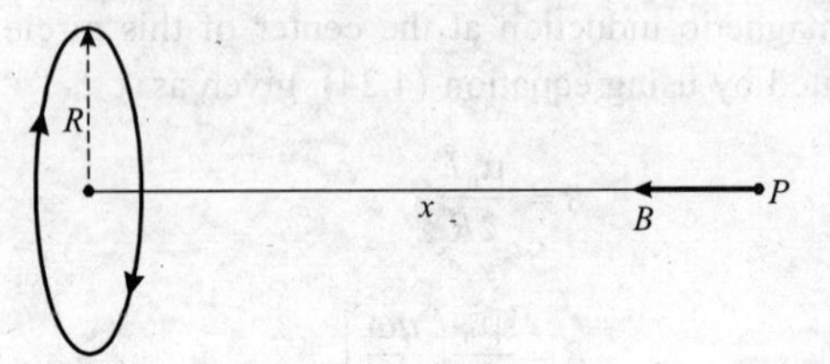

Figure 4.49

4.3.8 Magnetic Induction due to a Surface Charged Rotating Disc

Figure-4.50 shows a circular disc of radius R and charged with a surface charge density σ C/m². The disc is rotating at a constant angular velocity ω and due to the rotating charges we will determine the magnetic induction at the center of the disc.

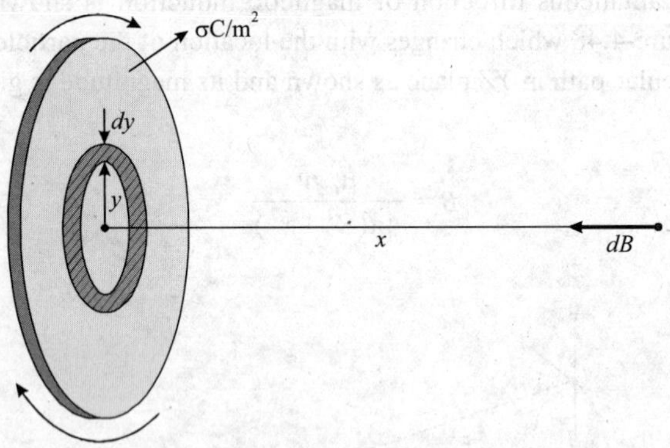

Figure 4.50

To calculate the magnetic induction due to rotating disc we consider an elemental circular ring of radius y and width dy on the disc surface as shown in figure. The charge dq on this elemental ring is given as

$$dq = \sigma \times 2\pi y \cdot dy$$

The current in elemental ring due to its rotation is given as

$$dI = \frac{dq\omega}{2\pi} = \sigma\omega y \cdot dy$$

The magnetic induction dB at the center of disc due to this elemental ring can be calculated by using the result of magnetic induction of a coil which is given as

$$dB = \frac{\mu_0 dI}{2y} = \frac{1}{2}\mu_0\sigma\omega dy$$

Net magnetic induction due to the whole disc at its center is given by integrating above expression within limits from 0 to R for the complete surface of disc which is given as

$$B = \int dB = \int_0^R \frac{1}{2}\mu_0\sigma\omega dy$$

$$\Rightarrow \quad B = \frac{1}{2}\mu_0\sigma\omega R \quad \ldots (4.50)$$

Magnetic induction at the axis point of above rotating disc can be calculated by integrating the magnetic induction at axial point due to the above chosen elemental ring. Students can try on their own to get the result and verify it with the result given below.

$$B_{\text{axis}} = \frac{\mu_0\sigma\omega R^4}{8(R^2+x^2)^{3/2}} \quad \ldots (4.51)$$

 # Illustrative Example 4.10

A very long straight semi-infinite solenoid has a cross-section radius R and n turns per unit length. A direct current I flows through the solenoid. Suppose that x is the distance from the one end of the solenoid, measured along its axis. Calculate

(a) The magnetic induction B on the axis of solenoid as a function of distance x.

(b) Draw an approximate plot of B v/s ratio x/R.

(c) The distance x_0 to the point on the axis at which the value of B differs by η = 1% from that in the middle section of the solenoid. (Consider $x_0 >> R$)

Solution

(a) In terms of angle θ_1 and θ_2, the magnetic field at a point on the axis is given as

$$B = \frac{\mu_0 ni}{2}\,[\cos\theta_1 + \cos\theta_2]$$

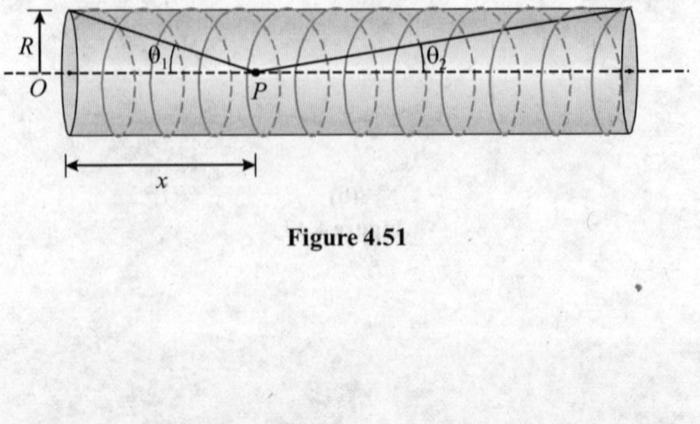

Figure 4.51

For a semi-infinite solenoid we use $\theta_1 = \theta$ and $\theta_2 = 0°$ and from figure we have

$$\cos\theta = \frac{x}{(x^2+R^2)^{1/2}}$$

Thus magnetic induction as a function of distance x is given as

$$B = \frac{\mu_0 ni}{2} \times \left[\frac{x}{(x^2+R^2)^{1/2}} + 1\right] \qquad \ldots (4.52)$$

(b) Equation-(4.52) is plotted as shown in figure-4.52.

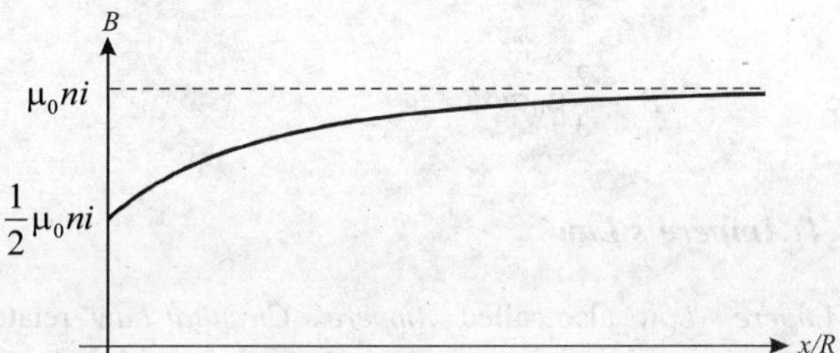

Figure 4.52

(c) At $x = x_0$ magnetic induction is taken as $0.99\ \mu_0 ni$ so from equation-(4.52) we use

$$\frac{\mu_0 ni}{2} \times \left[\frac{x_0}{(x_0^2+R^2)^{1/2}} + 1\right] = \frac{99}{100}\mu_0 ni$$

$$\Rightarrow \quad 50\left[\frac{x_0}{(x_0^2+R^2)^{1/2}} + 1\right] = 99$$

In above expression $x_0 >> R$ so we can use binomial approximation as

$$50\left[\left(1+\left(\frac{R}{x_0}\right)^2\right)^{-1/2} + 1\right] = 99$$

$$\Rightarrow \quad \left[\left(1-\frac{R^2}{2x_0^2}\right)+1\right] = \frac{99}{50}$$

$$\Rightarrow \quad 2 - 1.98 = \frac{R^2}{2x_0^2}$$

$$\Rightarrow \quad 0.04\, x_0^2 = R^2$$

$$\Rightarrow \quad x_0 = 5R$$

Illustrative Example 4.11

A straight long solenoid produces magnetic induction B at its centre. If it is cut into two equal parts and same number of turns wound on one part in double layer. Calculate magnetic field produced by new solenoid at its centre.

Solution

Magnetic induction produced by a long solenoid having n turns per unit length on its core and carrying a current I at its center is given as

$$B = \mu_0 nI$$

If same number of turns wound over half length in double layer on the solenoid core then number of turns per unit length on the new solenoid becomes $2n$ so for the same current in the solenoid the magnetic induction will become $2B$.

Illustrative Example 4.12

A very long straight solenoid carries a current I. The cross-sectional area of the solenoid is equal to S, the number of turns per unit length is equal to n. Find the magnetic flux of vector $\vec{B}$ through the end plane of the solenoid.

Solution

Magnetic induction at the end plane of a semi infinite solenoid is given as

$$B = \frac{1}{2}\mu_0 ni$$

Similar to the way we calculate electric flux using electric field strength as flux density, in the same manner magnetic flux can also be calculated using the magnetic induction at a plane. In this case as throughout the cross section magnetic induction is uniform and direction is perpendicular so to the cross sectional surface, here the magnetic flux can be given as

$$\phi = \int \overline{B}.\overline{dS}$$

$$\Rightarrow \quad \phi = \int BdS\cos(0°)$$

$$\Rightarrow \quad \phi = B\int dS = BS$$

$$\Rightarrow \quad \phi = \frac{1}{2}\mu_0 ni \times S = \frac{1}{2}\mu_0 niS$$

Illustrative Example 4.13

A non-conducting sphere of radius R charged uniformly with surface density σ rotates with an angular velocity ω about a diametrical axis passing through its centre. Find the magnetic induction due to the rotating charge at the centre of the sphere.

Solution

Figure-4.53 shows the charged sphere on which we consider an elemental ring at an angle θ from the axis of angular width $d\theta$. The surface area of the elemental ring is given as

$$dS = 2\pi R \sin\theta \times R d\theta$$

The charge on the elemental ring surface is given as

$$dq = \sigma dS$$

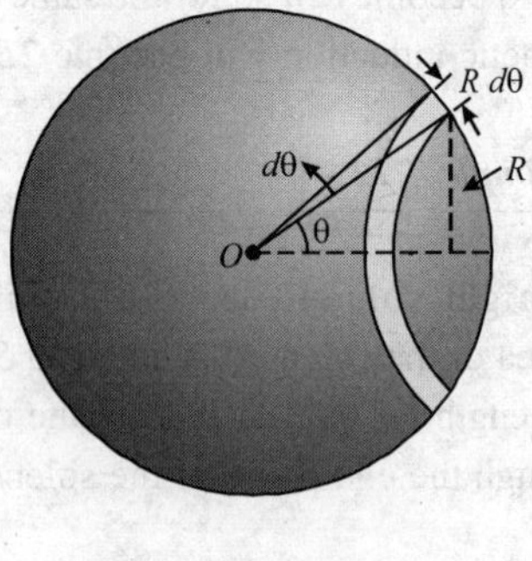

Figure 4.53

Current due to rotating charge on the elemental ring is given as

$$di = \frac{dq\omega}{2\pi}$$

$$\Rightarrow \quad di = \frac{(2\pi\sigma R^2 \sin\theta d\theta)\omega}{2\pi}$$

$$\Rightarrow \quad di = \sigma\omega R^2 \sin\theta d\theta$$

Magnetic induction at the centre O due to the current in elemental ring is given as

$$dB = \frac{\mu_0 di (R\sin\theta)^2}{2(R^2\cos^2\theta + R^2\sin^2\theta)^{3/2}}$$

$$\Rightarrow \quad dB = \frac{\mu_0 di \sin^2\theta}{2R}$$

Substituting the value of current di we get

$$dB = \frac{\mu_0}{2} \times \sigma\omega R^2 \sin\theta\, d\theta \times \frac{\sin^2\theta}{R}$$

$$\Rightarrow \quad dB = \frac{1}{2}\mu_0\sigma\omega R \sin^3\theta\, d\theta$$

Net magnetic induction at O is given by integrating above expression within limits of θ from 0 to π given as

$$B = \int dB = \frac{1}{2}\mu_0\sigma\omega R \int_0^{\pi} \sin^3\theta d\theta$$

$$\Rightarrow \quad B = \frac{1}{2}\mu_0\sigma\omega R\left[\frac{1}{3}\cos^3\theta - \cos\theta\right]_0^{\pi}$$

$$\Rightarrow \quad B = \frac{1}{2}\mu_0\sigma\omega R\left[\frac{1}{3}(-1) - (-1) - \frac{1}{3}(1) + (1)\right]_0$$

$$\Rightarrow \quad B = \frac{2}{3}\mu_0\sigma\omega R$$

4.4 Ampere's Law

'Ampere's Law' also called *'Ampere's Circuital Law'* relates the line integral of magnetic field along a given closed path and the currents which are enclosed by that closed path. The law is stated as

"Line integral of magnetic induction along a closed path is equal to μ_0 times the total current coming out and enclosed by that closed path."

In figure-4.54 M is a closed path in free space where some current carrying wires are present with direction of currents indicated in the figure. Such a path chosen for application of Ampere's law is called *'Ampere's Path'*. Along the path at a point we consider an element of length $\vec{dl}$ and at the location of this element if net magnetic induction due to all the wires in the region is $\vec{B}$ then line integral of magnetic induction along the given path M is written as

$$L_i = \oint_M \vec{B}.\vec{dl}$$

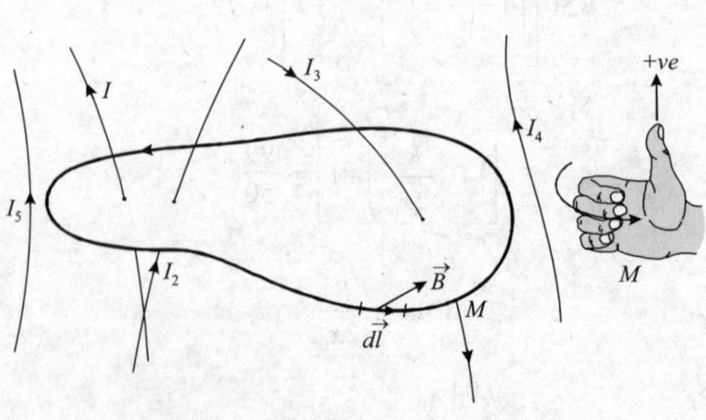

Figure 4.54

According to Ampere's law this line integral is equal to the product of μ_0 and the total current enclosed by the closed path. This gives

$$\oint_M \vec{B}.\vec{dl} = \mu_0 I_{enclosed} \quad \dots (4.53)$$

Expression in equation-(4.53) is the called '*Equation of Ampere's law*'. For the given situation as shown in figure there are three currents enclosed by the path M so we use

$$I_{enclosed} = I_1 + I_2 - I_3 \quad \dots (4.54)$$

Substituting the above value of $I_{enclosed}$ in equation-(4.53) gives

$$\oint_M \vec{B}.\vec{dl} = \mu_0(I_1 + I_2 - I_3) \quad \dots (4.55)$$

In equation-(4.54) direction of currents on right hand side of equality is decided by right hand thumb rule as shown in figure-4.54. Here right hand fingers are curled along the direction of line integral on the path M and thumb gives the positive direction or the currents in the direction of thumb are taken positive and opposite ones are taken negative.

It is important to note that in equation-(4.55) on LHS the magnetic induction $\vec{B}$ is due to all the currents in the region but on RHS only enclosed currents are included. This is because due to every individual currents magnetic field is closed loop in surrounding of that current thus line integral of magnetic field for a closed path in surrounding of any current is always zero if the path is not enclosing the current as shown in figure-4.55. If B_1 is the magnetic induction at the location of an element dl chosen on the path Z then we have

$$\oint_Z \vec{B_1}.\vec{dl} = 0$$

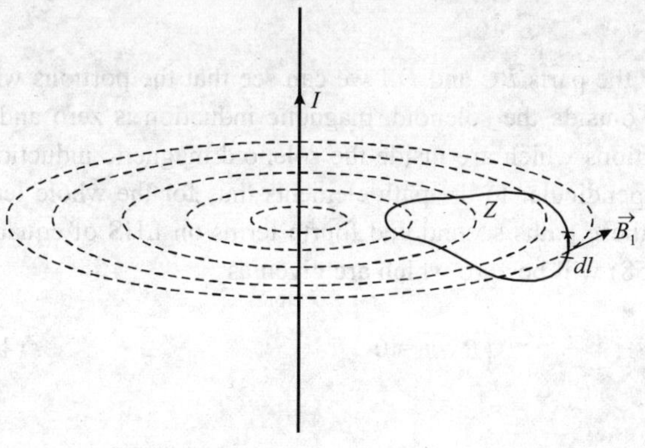

Figure 4.55

Qualitatively we can state that total inward magnetic lines on a path are equal to total outward magnetic lines from the path.

4.4.1 Applications of Ampere's Law

In application of Ampere's law under different situations we need to choose the path in such a way that the line integral of magnetic induction along the path can be carried out easily. If the path is randomly chosen then many times the integral can't be solved so students must be careful about the below mentioned general points for selection of Ampere's path for its application in different situations. These points are

(i) Path should be chosen in such a way that at every point of path magnetic induction should be either tangential to the path elements or normal to it so that '*dot*' product can be easily handled.

(ii) Path should be chosen in such a way that at every point of path magnetic induction should either be uniform or zero so that calculations become easy.

To have better understanding of applications of Ampere's law we consider some cases of determining magnetic field using Ampere's law which is one of the most common application.

Just like in electrostatics we've studied that in cases of symmetric and uniform charge distribution calculation of electric field becomes easier if we use Gauss's law similarly, in cases of uniform current configurations Ampere's law is easier than Biot Savart's law that is discussed in upcoming articles.

4.4.2 Magnetic Induction due to a Long Straight Wire

Figure-4.56 shows a straight wire carrying a current I and we will determine the magnetic induction due to this wire at a point P located a distance r from wire as shown in figure. This we've already done in article-4.2.1 but here we'll do this by using Ampere's law.

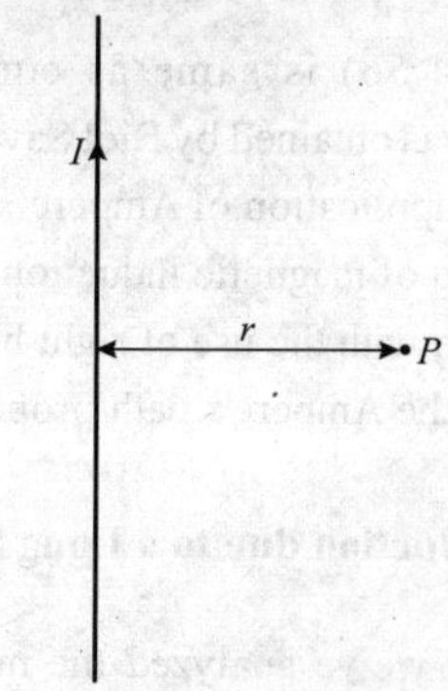

Figure 4.56

To apply Ampere's law we need to choose a path along which we will calculate the line integral of magnetic induction. As shown in figure-4.57 we consider a circular path M with point P located on this path. We've chosen this path because we know that direction of magnetic induction at every point of this path is tangential to the path or parallel to every element on this path and its magnitude remain constant because of symmetry.

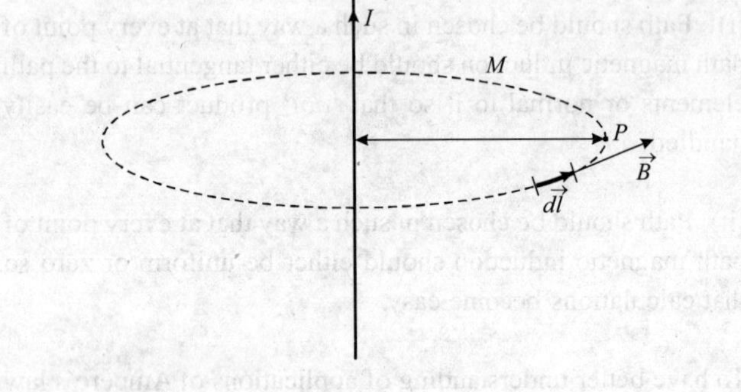

Figure 4.57

Total current enclosed by this path is I so on applying Ampere's law on this path, it gives

$$\oint_M \vec{B}.\vec{dl} = \mu_0 I_{\text{enclosed}}$$

$$\Rightarrow \quad \oint_M Bdl\cos(0°) = \mu_0 I$$

$$\Rightarrow \quad B\oint_M dl = \mu_0 I$$

$$\Rightarrow \quad B.\,2\pi R = \mu_0 I$$

$$\Rightarrow \quad B = \frac{\mu_0 I}{2\pi R} \qquad \dots (4.56)$$

Above equation-(4.56) is same as equation-(4.19) of article-4.2.1 which was obtained by Biot Savart's law. Students should note that for application of Ampere's law it is essential to know the direction of magnetic induction in surrounding of current configuration with the use of right hand thumb rule so that we can choose the Ampere's path properly.

4.4.3 Magnetic Induction due to a Long Solenoid

In article-4.3.1 also we've analyzed the magnetic induction due to a long solenoid which now we'll calculate again by using Ampere's law. Figure-4.58 shows a tightly wound long solenoid with core radius R, number of turns per unit length n and carrying a current I.

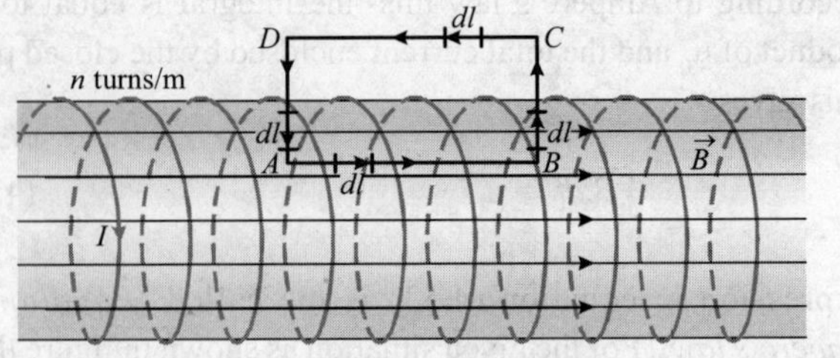

Figure 4.58

To apply Ampere's law we consider a rectangular path $ABCD$ as shown in figure such that the path lies in a radial plane passing through the axis of cylindrical core of solenoid and part CD of the path is lying outside and parallel to the axis of solenoid. The dimensions of the path are taken as $AB = x$ and $CD = y$ so the total number of turns passing through the path $ABCD$ are nx. Now applying Ampere's law on path $ABCD$ gives

$$\oint_{ABCD} \vec{B}.\vec{dl} = \mu_0 I_{\text{enclosed}}$$

$$\Rightarrow \quad \oint_{ABCD} \vec{B}.\vec{dl} = \mu_0(nxI) \qquad \dots (4.57)$$

In above equation to solve the line integral on LHS of equation-(4.57) we split the integral for the different parts of the closed path $ABCD$ as

$$\int_A^B \vec{B}\cdot\vec{dl} + \int_B^C \vec{B}\cdot\vec{dl} + \int_C^D \vec{B}\cdot\vec{dl} + \int_D^A \vec{B}\cdot\vec{dl} = \mu_0\,(nxI) \qquad \dots (4.58)$$

As the magnetic induction inside a tightly wound long solenoid is uniform, for path length AB magnetic induction vector is along the element length so first term in above equation-(4.58) can be given as

$$\int_A^B \vec{B}\cdot\vec{dl} = B\int_A^B dl = Bx \qquad \dots (4.59)$$

For the parts BC and DA we can see that the portions which are outside the solenoid, magnetic induction is zero and the portions which are inside the solenoid magnetic induction is perpendicular to the path elements thus for the whole length of these paths second and fourth terms on LHS of equation-(4.58) will be zero which are given as

$$\int_B^C \vec{B}\cdot\vec{dl} = 0 \qquad \dots (4.60)$$

and

$$\int_D^A \vec{B}\cdot\vec{dl} = 0 \qquad \dots (4.61)$$

For the remaining path CD as it is completely outside the solenoid where magnetic induction is zero so this term will also be zero as at every point of path CD, $B = 0$ given as

$$\int_C^D \vec{B}\cdot\vec{dl} = 0 \qquad \dots (4.62)$$

Substituting above values in equation-(4.58) gives

$$Bx = \mu_0\,(nxI)$$

$$\Rightarrow \qquad B = \mu_0 nI \qquad \dots (4.63)$$

Expression in above equation-(4.63) is same as equation-(4.38) of article-4.3.1 which was calculated by integrating the magnetic induction due to ring elements over the whole length of solenoid.

4.4.4 Magnetic Induction due to a Tightly Wound Toroid

In article-4.3.5 also we've analyzed the magnetic induction due to a large toroid which now we'll calculate it again by using Ampere's law. Figure-4.59 shows a tightly wound large toroid with average tore radius R, cross sectional radius r ($r << R$), number of turns per unit length n and carrying a current I.

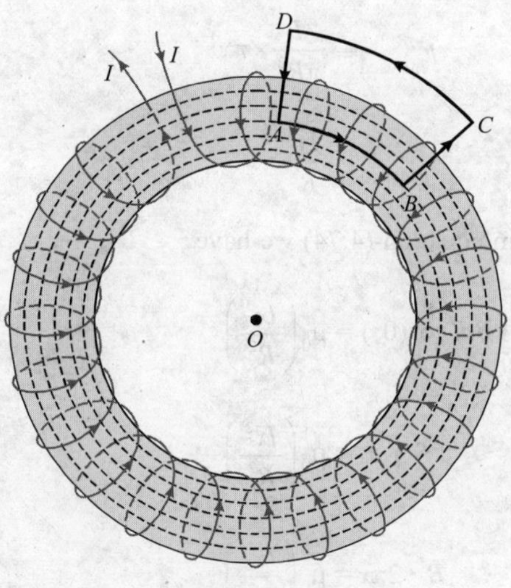

Figure 4.59

To apply Ampere's law we consider an approximately rectangular path $ABCD$ as shown in above figure similar to the case of solenoid such that the path lies in the plane perpendicular to the axis of toroid at point O and part CD of the path is lying outside the toroid. The dimensions of the paths are taken as $AB = x$ and $CD = y$ so the total number of turns passing through the path $ABCD$ are nx. Now applying Ampere's law on path $ABCD$ gives

$$\oint_{ABCD} \vec{B}.\vec{dl} = \mu_0 I_{enclosed}$$

$$\Rightarrow \qquad \oint_{ABCD} \vec{B}.\vec{dl} = \mu_0(nxI) \qquad \dots (4.64)$$

In above equation to solve the line integral on LHS of equation-(4.64) we split the integral for the different parts of the closed path $ABCD$ similar to the analysis we did for solenoid as

$$\int_A^B \vec{B}\cdot\vec{dl} + \int_B^C \vec{B}\cdot\vec{dl} + \int_C^D \vec{B}\cdot\vec{dl} + \int_D^A \vec{B}\cdot\vec{dl} = \mu_0\,(nxI) \qquad \dots (4.65)$$

As the magnetic induction inside a tightly wound long solenoid is uniform, for path length AB magnetic induction vector is along the element length so first term in above equation-(4.65) can be given as

$$\int_A^B \vec{B}\cdot\vec{dl} = B\int_A^B dl = Bx \qquad \dots (4.66)$$

For the parts BC and DA we can see that the portions which are outside the toroid magnetic induction is zero and the portions which are inside the toroid magnetic induction is perpendicular to the path elements thus for the whole length of these paths second and fourth terms on LHS of equation-(4.65) will be zero which are given as

$$\int_B^C \vec{B}\cdot\vec{dl} = 0 \qquad \dots (4.67)$$

and
$$\int_D^A \vec{B}\cdot\vec{dl} = 0 \qquad \dots (4.68)$$

For the remaining path CD as it is completely outside the solenoid where magnetic induction is zero so this term will also be zero as at every point of path CD, $B = 0$ given as

$$\int_C^D \vec{B}\cdot\vec{dl} = 0 \qquad \dots (4.69)$$

Substituting above values in equation-(4.65) gives

$$Bx = \mu_0\,(nxI)$$

$$\Rightarrow \qquad B = \mu_0 nI \qquad \dots (4.70)$$

If total number of turns in toroid are N then n is given as

$$n = \frac{N}{2\pi R}$$

Thus equation-(4.70) becomes

$$B = \mu_0\left(\frac{N}{2\pi R}\right)I$$

$$\Rightarrow \qquad B = \frac{\mu_0 NI}{2\pi R} \qquad \dots (4.71)$$

Expression in above equation-(4.71) is same as equation-(4.43) of article-4.3.5 which we've now calculated using Ampere's law.

4.4.5 Magnetic Induction due to a Cylindrical Wire

Figure-4.60 shows a long straight cylindrical wire of radius R carrying a current I. To determine the magnetic induction at outside point P located a distance x ($x > R$) from its axis we consider a circular Ampere′s path of radius x on which applying Ampere's law gives

$$\oint_M \vec{B}\cdot\vec{dl} = \mu_0 I_{enclosed}$$

$$\Rightarrow \quad \oint_M Bdl\cos(0°) = \mu_0 I$$

$$\Rightarrow \quad B\oint_M dl = \mu_0 I$$

$$\Rightarrow \quad B\cdot 2\pi x = \mu_0 I$$

$$\Rightarrow \quad B = \frac{\mu_0 I}{2\pi x} \quad \ldots (4.72)$$

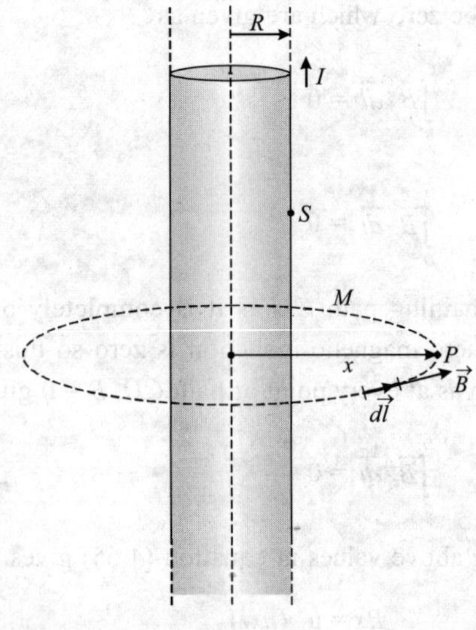

Figure 4.60

If point P is located on the surface of cylindrical wire we can use $x = R$ for which the magnetic induction is given by replacing x with R in equation-(4.72) as

$$B_S = \frac{\mu_0 I}{2\pi R} \quad \ldots (4.73)$$

To determine the magnetic induction at an interior point P at a distance x from the axis of wire again we consider a circular path as shown in figure-4.61 and apply Ampere's law on this path which gives

$$\oint_M \vec{B}.\vec{dl} = \mu_0 I_{enclosed} \quad \ldots (4.74)$$

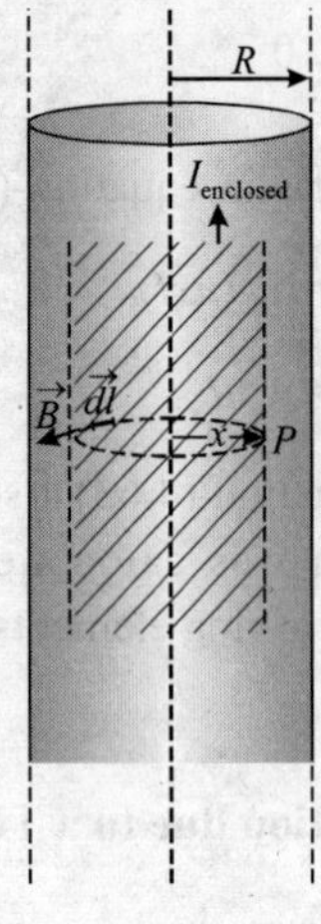

Figure 4.61

As the current I is considered to be uniformly distributed over the cross section of cylindrical wire, the current enclosed in the circular path M of radius x as shown in above figure is given as

$$I_{enclosed} = \frac{I}{\pi R^2}\times \pi x^2$$

$$\Rightarrow \quad I_{enclosed} = \frac{Ix^2}{R^2}$$

Thus from equation-(4.74) we have

$$\Rightarrow \quad \oint_M Bdl\cos(0°) = \mu_0\left(\frac{Ix^2}{R^2}\right)$$

$$\Rightarrow \quad B\oint_M dl = \mu_0\left(\frac{Ix^2}{R^2}\right)$$

$$\Rightarrow \quad B\cdot 2\pi x = \mu_0\left(\frac{Ix^2}{R^2}\right)$$

$$\Rightarrow \quad B = \frac{\mu_0 Ix}{2\pi R^2} \quad \ldots (4.75)$$

For outside and surface points of the cylindrical wire the expressions of magnetic induction as obtained in equations-(4.72) and (4.73) are same as obtained in equation-(4.56) thus for a uniform current carrying cylindrical wire on its outer and surface points we can determine magnetic induction by considering its current concentrated along the axis of wire.

If current density in the cylindrical wire is J then we can rewrite above expression in equation-(4.75) as

$$B = \frac{1}{2}\mu_0 Jx \quad \text{... (4.76)}$$

If position vector of point P is considered as $\vec{x}$ then direction of magnetic induction at point P is perpendicular to $\vec{x}$ thus equation-(4.76) can be vectorially written as

$$\vec{B} = \frac{1}{2}\mu_0 J\vec{x}_{\perp} \quad \text{... (4.77)}$$

Above equation-(4.77) can also be written as

$$\vec{B} = \frac{1}{2}\mu_0(\vec{J}\times\vec{x}) \quad \text{... (4.78)}$$

Using equation-(4.72), (4.73) and (4.75) we can plot the variation curve of magnetic induction magnitude in surrounding of the cylindrical current carrying wire which is shown in figure-4.62.

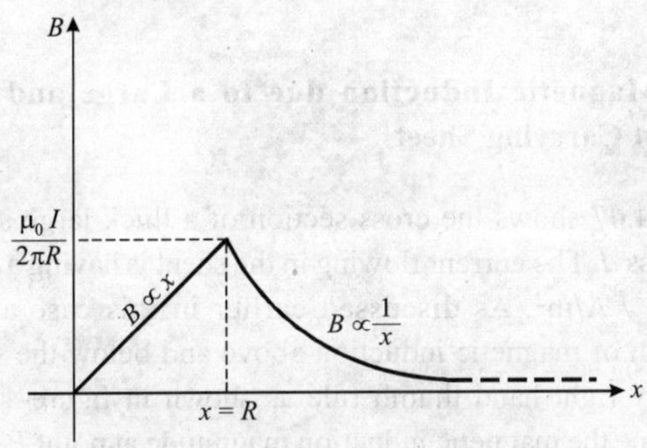

Figure 4.62

4.4.6 Magnetic Induction due to a Hollow Cylindrical Wire

Figure-4.63 shows a hollow thin walled long cylindrical wire carrying a current I. Similar to what we discussed in previous article here also we can say that due to uniform current distribution for outer and surface points we can consider that current is concentrated on the axis of cylinder thus magnetic induction at outer and surface points of the wire is given as

For $x > R$ $\qquad B_{out} = \frac{\mu_0 I}{2\pi x}$ $\qquad$ ... (4.79)

For $x = R$ $\qquad B_S = \frac{\mu_0 I}{2\pi R}$ $\qquad$ ... (4.80)

Above results can also be obtained by considering a circular Ampere's path and applying Ampere's law like the way we did for a solid cylindrical wire.

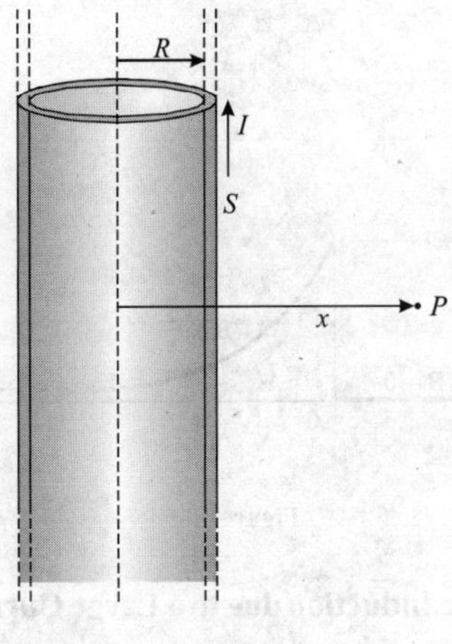

Figure 4.63

For interior points of the hollow cylindrical wire if we consider a point P as shown in figure-4.64 and apply Ampere's law on the circular path M shown then we have

$$\oint_M \vec{B}.\vec{dl} = \mu_0 I_{enclosed}$$

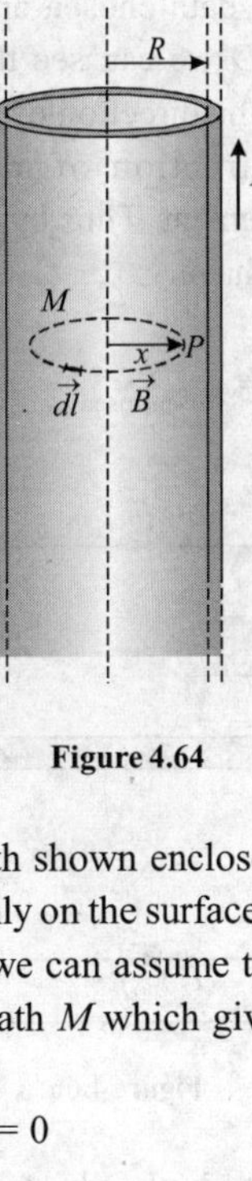

Figure 4.64

In this case for the path shown enclosed current will be zero as current is flowing only on the surface of the hollow cylinder. By symmetry of path we can assume that magnetic induction is uniform along the path M which gives

$$\oint_M \vec{B}.\vec{dl} = 0$$

$$\Rightarrow \quad B_{inside} = 0 \quad \text{... (81)}$$

Using equation-(4.79), (4.80) and (4.81) we can plot the variation curve of magnetic induction magnitude in surrounding of the cylindrical current carrying wire which is shown in figure-4.65.

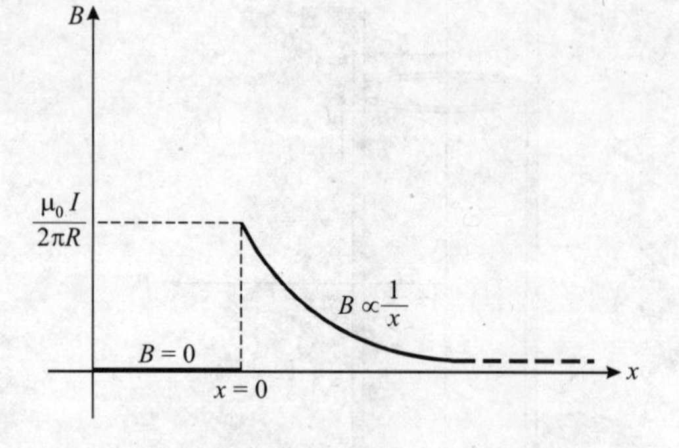

Figure 4.65

4.4.7 Magnetic Induction due to a Large Current Carrying Sheet

Figure-4.66 shows the cross section of a current carrying large sheet with linear current density i A/m flowing in it. In article-4.3.6 we have already discussed about the direction of magnetic induction above and below the sheet as shown in figure-4.45. To determine the magnetic induction at a point P located at a distance r above the sheet using Ampere's law, we consider a rectangular path $ABCD$ as shown in figure-4.66. The dimensions of the path chosen are $AB = x$ and $BC = y$. Along path AB and CD we can see that magnetic induction direction is parallel to the direction of element chosen and for paths BC and DA direction of magnetic induction is perpendicular to the element. Thus by applying Ampere's law on the path $ABCD$ we have

$$\oint_{ABCD} \vec{B}.\vec{dl} = \mu_0 I_{\text{enclosed}}$$

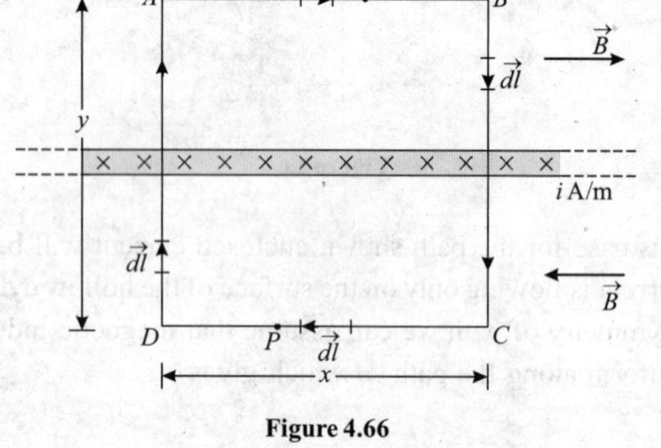

Figure 4.66

As linear current density in the sheet is i A/m, the current in length x of the sheet which is enclosed by the path $ABCD$ is given as ix ampere which gives

$$\oint_{ABCD} \vec{B}.\vec{dl} = \mu_0(ix) \qquad \dots (4.82)$$

In above equation to solve the line integral on LHS of equation-(4.82) we split the integral for the different parts of the closed path $ABCD$ similar to the analysis we did for solenoid as

$$\int_A^B \vec{B}\cdot\vec{dl} + \int_B^C \vec{B}\cdot\vec{dl} + \int_C^D \vec{B}\cdot\vec{dl} + \int_D^A \vec{B}\cdot\vec{dl} = \mu_0\,(ix) \qquad \dots (4.83)$$

Second and fourth term in LHS, the magnetic induction is perpendicular to the element along paths BC and DA thus dot product will result zero and for paths AB and CD magnetic field is uniform and parallel to the element this gives

$$B\int_A^B dl + B\int_C^D dl = \mu_0(ix)$$

$$\Rightarrow \qquad Bx + Bx = \mu_0(ix)$$

$$\Rightarrow \qquad 2Bx = \mu_0(ix)$$

$$\Rightarrow \qquad B = \frac{1}{2}\mu_0 i \qquad \dots (4.84)$$

Expression in above equation-(4.84) is same as obtained in equation-(4.44) which we solved by using long integration process.

4.4.8 Magnetic Induction due to a Large and Thick Current Carrying Sheet

Figure-4.67 shows the cross section of a thick large sheet of thickness d. The current flowing in the sheet is having a current density J A/m^2. As discussed earlier in this case also the direction of magnetic induction above and below the sheet is given by right hand thumb rule as shown in figure-4.45. To determine the magnetic induction magnitude at point P outside the sheet we consider the rectangular path $ABCD$ with point P located on the line AB of the path as shown in figure-4.67. The dimensions of the path are $AB = x$ and $BC = y$. By applying Ampere's law on this path we have

$$\oint_{ABCD} \vec{B}\cdot\vec{dl} = \mu_0 I_{\text{enclosed}}$$

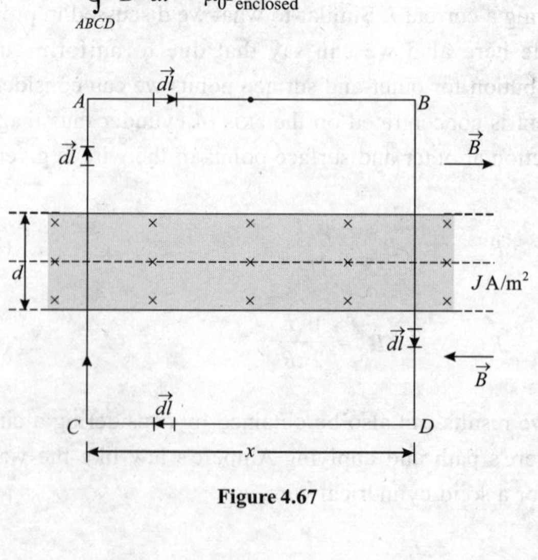

Figure 4.67

As current density in the cross section of sheet is J A/m^2, the current in length x of the sheet which is enclosed by the path $ABCD$ is given as Jxd ampere which gives

$$\oint_{ABCD} \vec{B}\cdot\vec{dl} = \mu_0(Jxd) \quad \ldots (4.85)$$

In above equation to solve the line integral on LHS of equation-(4.85) we split the integral for the different parts of the closed path $ABCD$ similar to the analysis we did earlier as

$$\int_A^B \vec{B}\cdot\vec{dl} + \int_B^C \vec{B}\cdot\vec{dl} + \int_C^D \vec{B}\cdot\vec{dl} + \int_D^A \vec{B}\cdot\vec{dl} = \mu_0\,(Jxd) \quad \ldots (4.86)$$

Second and fourth term in LHS, the magnetic induction is perpendicular to the element along paths BC and DA thus dot product will result zero and for paths AB and CD magnetic field is uniform and parallel to the element which gives

$$B\int_A^B dl + B\int_C^D dl = \mu_0(Jxd)$$

$$\Rightarrow \quad Bx + Bx = \mu_0(Jxd)$$

$$\Rightarrow \quad 2Bx = \mu_0(Jxd)$$

$$\Rightarrow \quad B = \frac{1}{2}\mu_0 Jd \quad \ldots (4.87)$$

To determine the magnetic induction at interior points of the thick sheet at a point P at a distance x from the central plane of the sheet as shown in figure-4.68, we consider a rectangular path $ABCD$ as shown with dimensions $AB = y$ and $BC = 2x$. On applying Ampere's law on this path, we have

$$\oint_{ABCD} \vec{B}\cdot\vec{dl} = \mu_0 I_{\text{enclosed}}$$

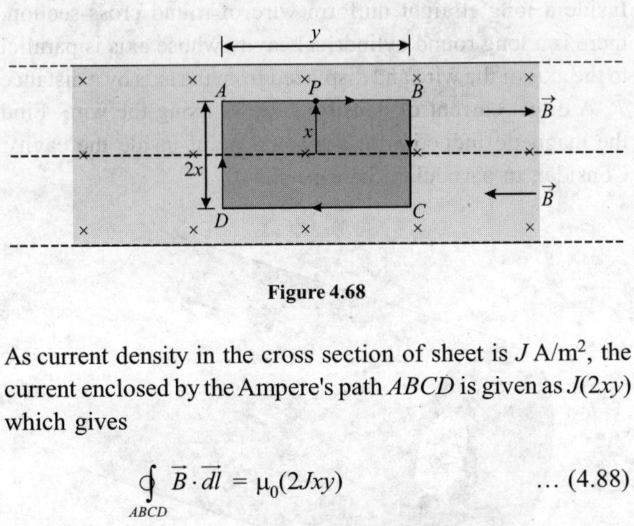

Figure 4.68

As current density in the cross section of sheet is J A/m^2, the current enclosed by the Ampere's path $ABCD$ is given as $J(2xy)$ which gives

$$\oint_{ABCD} \vec{B}\cdot\vec{dl} = \mu_0(2Jxy) \quad \ldots (4.88)$$

In above equation to solve the line integral on LHS of equation-(4.88) we split the integral for the different parts of the closed path $ABCD$ similar to the analysis we did earlier as

$$\int_A^B \vec{B}\cdot\vec{dl} + \int_B^C \vec{B}\cdot\vec{dl} + \int_C^D \vec{B}\cdot\vec{dl} + \int_D^A \vec{B}\cdot\vec{dl} = \mu_0\,(2Jxy) \quad \ldots (4.89)$$

Again like previous analysis second and fourth term in LHS of the expression above, the magnetic induction is perpendicular to the element along paths BC and DA thus dot product will result zero and for paths AB and CD magnetic field is uniform and parallel to the element this gives

$$B\int_A^B dl + B\int_C^D dl = \mu_0(2Jxy)$$

$$\Rightarrow \quad By + By = \mu_0(2Jxy)$$

$$\Rightarrow \quad 2By = \mu_0(2Jxy)$$

$$\Rightarrow \quad B = \mu_0 Jx \quad \ldots (4.90)$$

From equation-(4.87) and (4.90) we can plot the variation of magnetic induction with distance from the central plane of a thick sheet which is shown in figure-4.69.

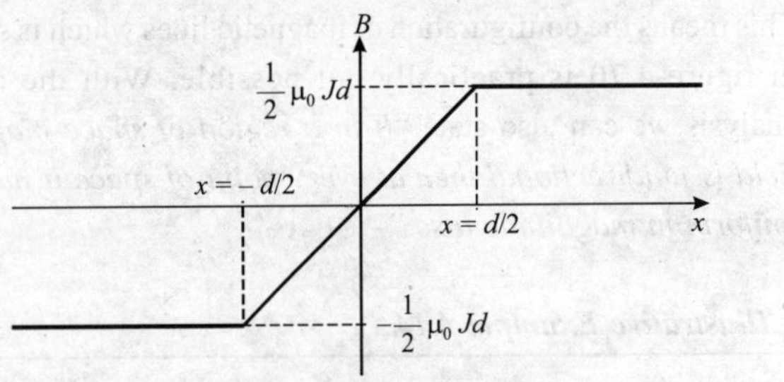

Figure 4.69

4.4.9 Unidirectional Magnetic Field in a Region

Consider the configuration of magnetic lines of forces as shown in figure-4.70 in a region. In this region at every point in space magnetic field is in same direction but the density of magnetic lines is different that means in this region magnetic induction is not uniform everywhere. If in this region we consider a rectangular path $PQRS$ as shown in figure and we apply Ampere's law on this path $PQRS$ then it gives

$$\oint_{PQRS} \vec{B}.\vec{dl} = 0 \quad \ldots (4.91)$$

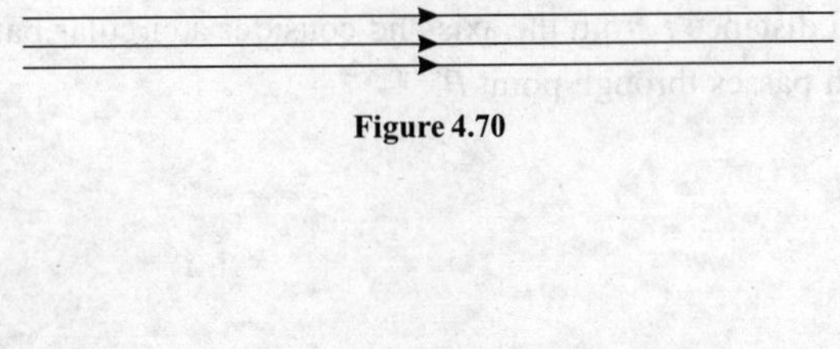

Figure 4.70

Right hand side of the above equation is zero as there is no current enclosed in the closed path. Equation-(4.91) can be expanded for the integrals on the four straight line paths as

$$\int_P^Q \vec{B}.\vec{dl} + \int_Q^R \vec{B}.\vec{dl} + \int_R^S \vec{B}.\vec{dl} + \int_S^P \vec{B}.\vec{dl} = 0 \qquad \dots (4.92)$$

For the path segments PQ and RS we can see that magnetic induction vector and $\vec{dl}$ are perpendicular to each other so first and third term of the above equation will vanish and if B_1 and B_2 are the magnetic inductions at path segments QR and SP which are of lengths x then we have

$$0 + B_1x + 0 - B_2x = 0$$

$$\Rightarrow \qquad B_1 = B_2 \qquad \dots (4.93)$$

Thus it is clear that above situation is possible if and only if magnetic induction at path segments QR and SP are equal. This means the configuration of magnetic lines which is shown in figure-4.70 is practically not possible. With the above analysis we can also state "*If in a region of space magnetic field is unidirectional then at every point of space it must be uniform in magnitude also.*"

Illustrative Example 4.14

Figure-4.71 shows a coaxial cable which consist of an inner solid cylindrical conductor of radius a and outer hollow cylindrical shell with inner radius b and outer radius c. A current I flows in both conductors in opposite directions as shown. Find the magnetic induction at a point located at a distance r from central axis with $b < r < c$.

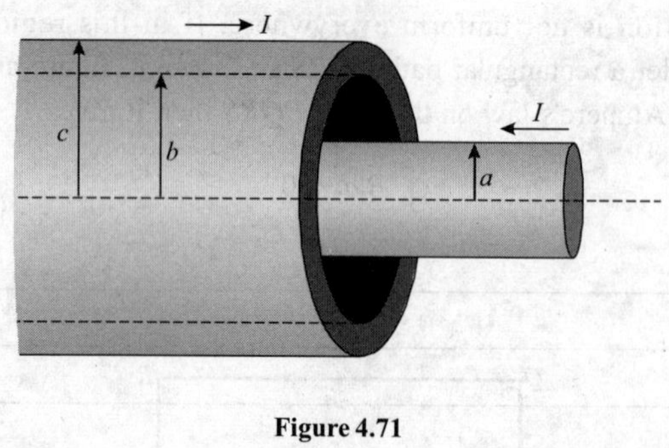

Figure 4.71

Solution

In the figure-4.72 shown below we consider a point P at a radial distance r from the axis and consider a circular path M which passes through point P.

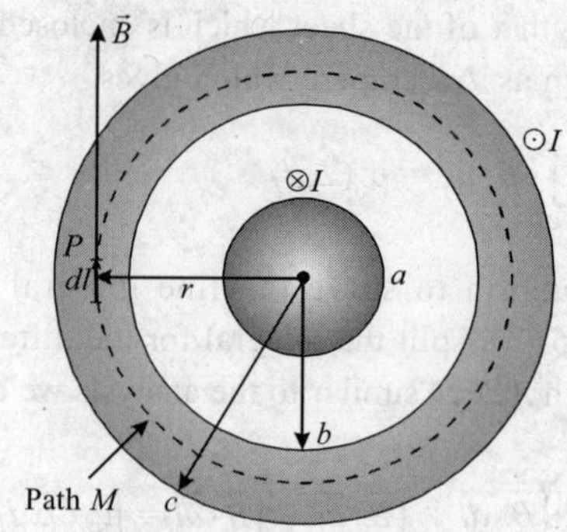

Figure 4.72

The current enclosed by the closed path M can be given as

$$I_{\text{enclosed}} = I - \frac{I}{\pi(c^2 - b^2)} \times \pi(r^2 - b^2)$$

Using Ampere's law on the path M gives

$$\oint_M \vec{B} \cdot \vec{dl} = \mu_0 \left[I - \frac{I}{\pi(c^2 - b^2)} \times \pi(r^2 - b^2) \right]$$

$$\Rightarrow \qquad B(2\pi r) = \mu_0 I \left[\frac{c^2 - r^2}{c^2 - b^2} \right]$$

$$\Rightarrow \qquad B = \frac{\mu_0 I}{2\pi r} \left(\frac{c^2 - r^2}{c^2 - b^2} \right)$$

Illustrative Example 4.15

Inside a long straight uniform wire of round cross-section, there is a long round cylindrical cavity whose axis is parallel to the axis of the wire and displaced from the axis by a distance $\vec{l}$. A direct current of density $\vec{J}$ flows along the wire. Find the magnetic induction at a general point inside the cavity. Consider, in particular, the case $\vec{l} = 0$.

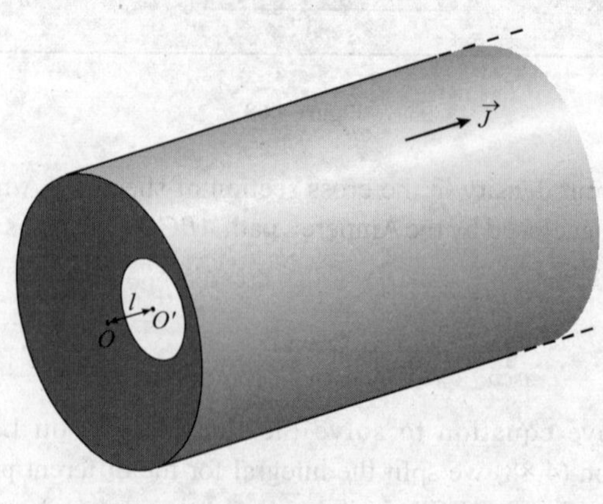

Figure 4.73

Solution

Consider a cross-section of the cylinder perpendicular to its axis as shown in figure-4.73. The cylindrical cavity is shown at a distance l from the axis O of the cylinder. We will calculate the magnetic induction at the point P inside the cavity. The cavity means an absence of current which we consider as an equivalent opposite current of same current density in the cavity. Magnetic induction at point P inside cavity is given by subtracting the magnetic induction due to opposite current considered in cavity region from the total magnetic induction at P due to complete solid cylindrical wire which is given as

$$\vec{B}_P = \vec{B}_{Wire} - \vec{B}_{Cavity}$$

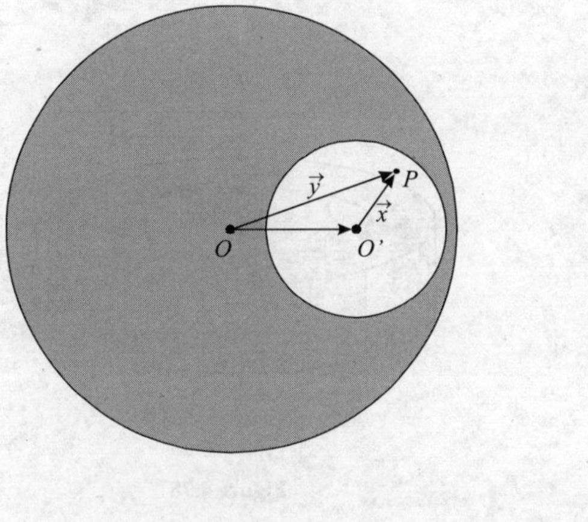

Figure 4.74

Expressions for the magnetic induction due to wire and that due to the opposite current in cavity is given by using equation-(4.77) as

$$\vec{B}_P = \frac{1}{2}\mu_0 J\,\vec{y}_\perp - \frac{1}{2}\mu_0 J\,\vec{x}_\perp$$

$$\Rightarrow \quad \vec{B}_P = \frac{1}{2}\mu_0 J(\vec{y}_\perp - \vec{x}_\perp)$$

$$\Rightarrow \quad \vec{B}_P = \frac{1}{2}\mu_0 J(\vec{l}_\perp) \qquad \ldots (4.94)$$

Above expression of magnetic induction as given in equation-(4.94) is a uniform magnetic induction in the direction normal to the line joining OO' as shown in figure-4.74.

If separation between O and O' becomes zero then the cavity will be coaxial with the axis of cylindrical wire and from above expression given in equation-(4.91) it gives there is no magnetic field in the cavity or inside of a hollow cylindrical current carrying wire.

 # Illustrative Example 4.16

In a long cylindrical wire of radius R, magnetic induction varies with the distance from axis as $B = cr^\alpha$. Find the function of current density in wire with the distance from axis of wire.

Solution

At a distance r from the axis of wire we consider a closed path M as shown in figure-4.75. We apply Ampere's law on this path gives

$$\oint_M \vec{B}\cdot\vec{dl} = \mu_0 I_{enclosed}$$

If $J(x)$ is the current density inside the wire as a function of distance x from the axis of wire, the enclosed current within the closed path M is given by integrating the current in the elemental ring of radius x and width dx considered in the cross section of wire as shown in figure-4.75 given as

$$I_{enclosed} = \int_0^r J(x).2\pi x.dx$$

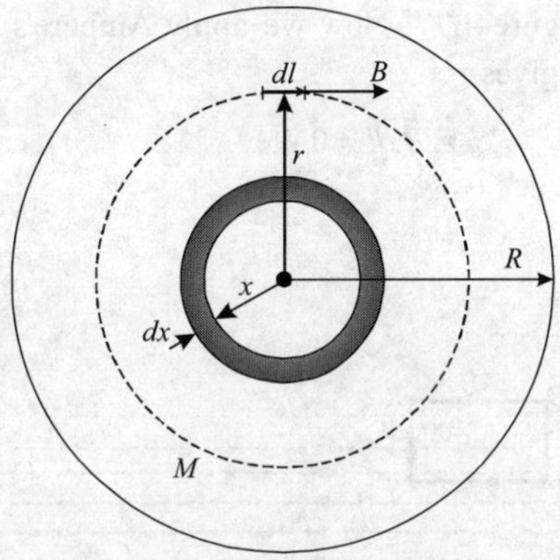

Figure 4.75

$$\Rightarrow \quad B\oint_M dl = \mu_0 \int_0^r J(x).2\pi x.dx$$

$$\Rightarrow \quad B(2\pi r) = \mu_0 \int_0^r J(x).2\pi x.dx$$

$$\Rightarrow \quad cr^{\alpha+1} = \mu_0 \int_0^r J(x).x.dx$$

Differentiating the above expression with respect to x gives

$$(\alpha + 1)cr^\alpha = \mu_0 J(r).\ r$$

$$\Rightarrow \quad J(r) = \left(\frac{(\alpha+1)c}{\mu_0}\right) r^{\alpha-1}$$

 # Illustrative Example 4.17

Figure-4.76 shows a region of space in which a uniform magnetic induction B_0 is present between the planes $z = 0$ and $z = a$. Using Ampere's law prove that such a field cannot exist between two planes as described here.

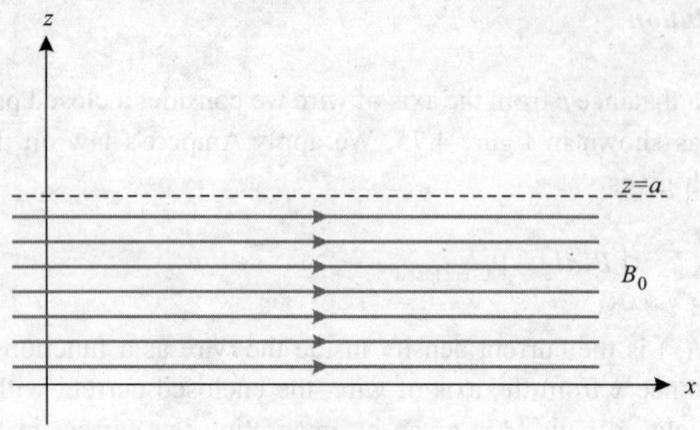

Figure 4.76

Solution

For the given magnetic field we consider a small rectangular path *PQRS* partly above and partly below the plane $z = a$ as shown in figure-4.77. Now we apply Ampere's law on this path which gives

$$\oint_{PQRS} \vec{B}.\vec{dl} = 0 \qquad \text{... (4.99)}$$

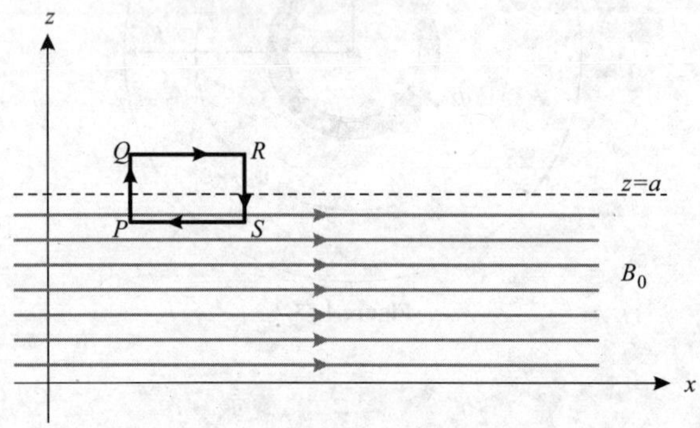

Figure 4.77

Right hand side of the above equation is zero as there is no current enclosed in the closed path. Equation-(4.95) can be expanded for the integrals on the four straight line paths as

$$\int_P^Q \vec{B}.\vec{dl} + \int_Q^R \vec{B}.\vec{dl} + \int_R^S \vec{B}.\vec{dl} + \int_S^P \vec{B}.\vec{dl} = 0 \qquad \text{... (4.96)}$$

For the path segments *PQ* and *RS* we can see that magnetic induction vector and $\vec{dl}$ are perpendicular to each other and for the path segment *QR* it is located outside the magnetic field where no magnetic induction exist so first, second and third term of the above equation will vanish and as B_0 is the magnetic inductions at path segments *SP* which is considered of lengths *x* then we have

$$0 + 0 + 0 - B_0 x = 0$$

$$\Rightarrow \qquad B_0 = 0$$

Thus with by applying Ampere's law on the path shown in above figure we get $B_0 = 0$ that means such a non-zero magnetic field cannot practically exist.

 # Illustrative Example 4.18

Figure-4.78 shows a toroidal solenoid whose cross-section is rectangular in shape. Find the magnetic flux through this cross-section if the current through the toroidal winding is *I*, total number of turns in winding is *N*, the inside and outside radii of the toroid are *a* and *b* respectively and the height of toroid is equal to *h*.

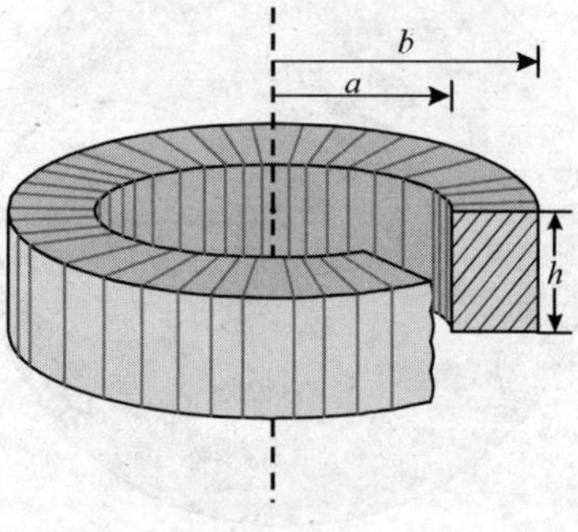

Figure 4.78

Solution

To find the magnetic flux through the cross section shown in figure, we consider an elemental strip of width *dx* at a distance *x* from the axis of toroid as shown in figure-4.79.

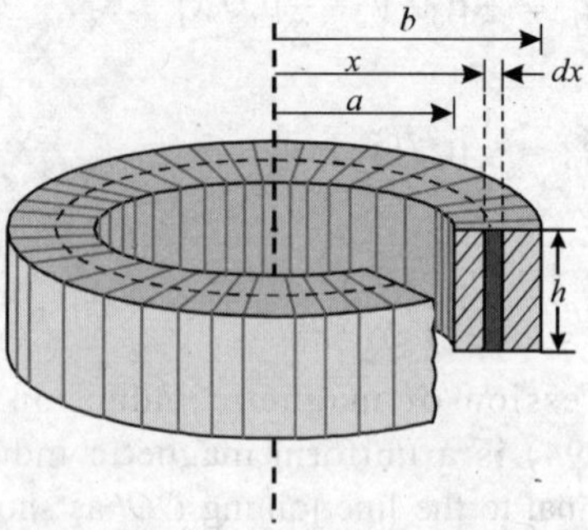

Figure 4.79

The magnetic field at a distance *x* from the axis of the toroid is given as

$$B = \mu_0 \left(\frac{N}{2\pi x}\right) I = \frac{\mu_0 NI}{2\pi x}$$

Magnetic flux through an elemental strip of radial thickness dx and height h as shown in figure is given as

$$d\phi = \vec{B}.\vec{dS} = BdS$$

$$\Rightarrow \quad d\phi = \frac{\mu_0 NI}{2\pi x}.hdx$$

Total magnetic flux through the cross section of the toroid is given by integrating the above elemental flux within limits from a to b which is given as

$$\phi = \int_a^b \frac{\mu_0 NIh}{2\pi x}dx$$

$$\Rightarrow \quad \phi = \frac{\mu_0 NIh}{2\pi}\int_a^b \frac{1}{x}dx$$

$$\Rightarrow \quad \phi = \frac{\mu_0 NIh}{2\pi}[\ln x]_a^b$$

$$\Rightarrow \quad \phi = \frac{\mu_0 NIh}{2\pi}[\ln b - \ln a]$$

$$\Rightarrow \quad \phi = \frac{\mu_0 NIh}{2\pi}\ln\left(\frac{b}{a}\right)$$

Web Reference at www.physicsgalaxy.com

Age Group - Grade 11 & 12 | Age 17-19 Years

Section - Magnetic Effects

Topic - Magnetic Effects of Current

Module Number - 21 to 35

Practice Exercise 4.2

(i) A tightly wound long solenoid having n turns per unit length is kept above a large metal sheet carrying a surface current of linear current density i A/m. The solenoid is oriented such that magnetic induction at its center is found to be zero when a current is passed through it.

(a) Find the current in the solenoid

(b) If the solenoid is rotated by 90° then find the magnetic induction at the center of solenoid.

[(a) $\frac{i}{2n}$; (b) $\frac{\mu_0 i}{\sqrt{2}}$]

(ii) A coaxial cable carries the a current i in the inside conductor of radius a as shown in figure-4.80 and the outer conductor of inner radius b and outer radius c carries a current i' in opposite direction. Find the magnetic induction due to the coaxial cable at distance r from the central axis of the cable for (a) $r < a$; (b) $a < r < b$ and (c) $b < r < c$

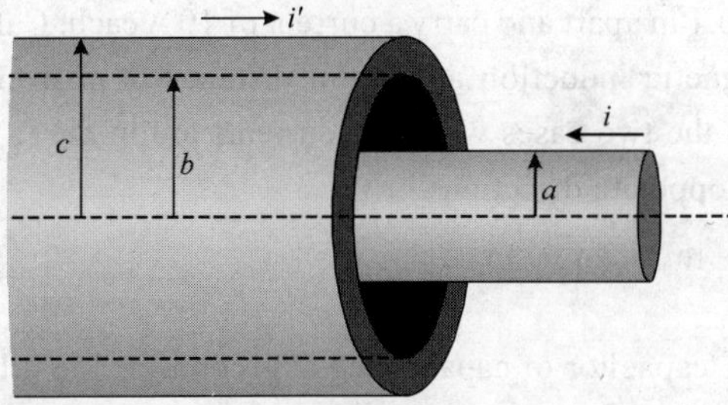

Figure 4.80

[(a) $\frac{\mu_0 ir}{2\pi a^2}$; (b) $\frac{\mu_0 i}{2\pi r}$; (c) $\frac{\mu_0}{2\pi r}\left[i - i'\left(\frac{r^2-b^2}{c^2-b^2}\right)\right]$]

(iii) A thin conducting strip of width h is tightly wound in the shape of a very long cylindrical coil with cross-sectional radius R to make a single layer straight solenoid as shown in figure-4.81. A direct current I flows through the strip. Find the magnetic induction inside and outside the solenoid as a function of the distance r from its axis.

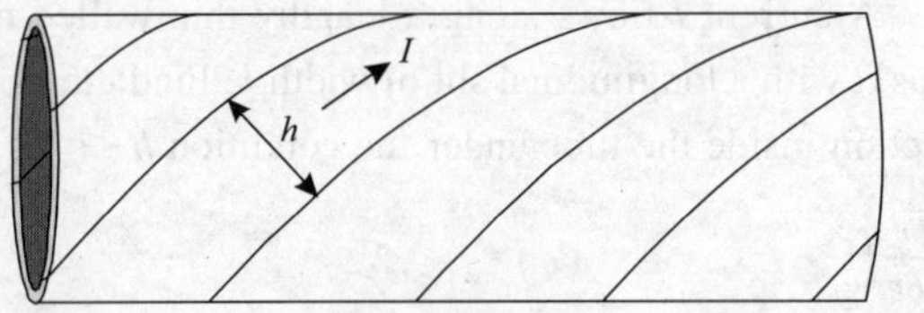

Figure 4.81

[$\frac{\mu_0 I}{h}\sqrt{1-\left(\frac{h}{2\pi R}\right)^2}$, $\frac{\mu_0 I}{2\pi r}$]

(iv) A long cylinder of uniform cross-section and radius R is carrying a current i along its length and the current density is uniform. There is a cylindrical cavity of uniform cross-section and radius r in the cylinder parallel to its length. The axis of the cylindrical cavity is separated by a distance d from the axis of the cylinder. Find the magnetic field at the axis of cylinder.

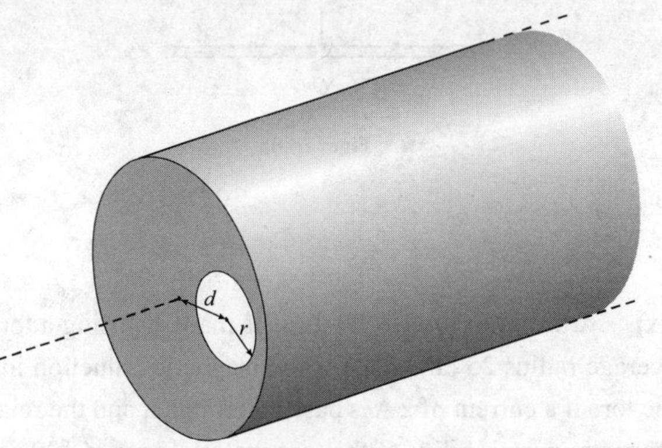

Figure 4.82

[$\frac{\mu_0 ir^2}{2\pi d(R^2-r^2)}$]

(v) Two straight infinitely long and thin parallel wires are spaced 0.1 m apart and carry a current of 10 A each. Calculate the magnetic induction at a point distant 0.1 m from both wires in the two cases when the currents are in the (a) same and (b) opposite directions.

[(a) 3.46×10^{-5} T; (b) 2×10^{-5} T]

(vi) A capacitor of capacitance C is connected to a battery of EMF E for a long time and then disconnected. The charged capacitor is then connected across a long solenoid having n turns per meter in its closely packed winding on its core. After connections it is found that the voltage across the capacitor drops to E/η in a time Δt. In this period estimate the average magnetic induction at the center of solenoid.

[$\frac{\mu_0 nCE}{\Delta t}\left(1-\frac{1}{\eta}\right)$]

(vii) A current I flows along a lengthy thin walled tube of radius R with a longitudinal slit of width h. Find the magnetic induction inside the tube under the condition $h << R$.

[$\frac{\mu_0 Ih}{4\pi^2 Rr}$]

(viii) A direct current I flows along a lengthy straight wire which terminates perpendicularly on an infinitely large conducting plane. From the point O, the current spreads all over the infinite conducting plane. Find the magnetic induction at all points of space above and below the conducting plane at a distance r from the axis of wire.

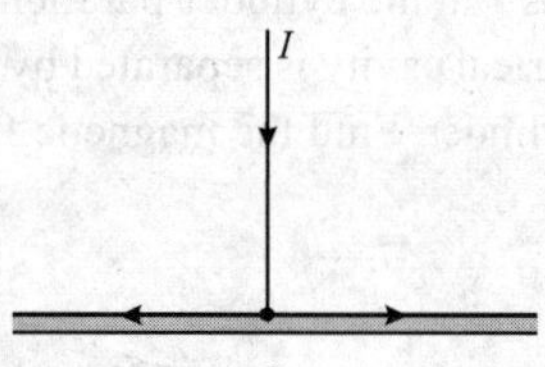

Figure 4.83

[$\frac{\mu_0 I}{2\pi r}$, 0]

(ix) A toroid of total 1000 turns is made by using a tore of average radius 25 cm. What is the magnetic induction inside the tore if a current of 2 A is passed through it and the relative magnetic permeability of the tore material is $\mu_r = 100$.

[16×10^{-2} T]

4.5 Electromagnetic Interactions

We've already discussed in beginning of this chapter about how electric and magnetic fields interact with static and moving charges. Electric field can exert force on both static and moving charges whereas magnetic field can only exert force on moving charges. As motion is always measured in a specific reference frame thus magnetic force is also dependent upon frame. Actually the electric and magnetic forces acting on a charge particle are two types of a single force called '*Electromagnetic Interaction*' which is the net force applied by these force fields on a charge. When the situation is observed from different frames of references then for all inertial reference frames the net electromagnetic force on charge particle remain same like what we discussed in topic of statics and dynamics but from different frames the electric and magnetic force vectors may be measured differently. Always the vector sum of electric and magnetic forces experienced by a charge particle remain constant in all inertial frames which gives the total electromagnetic force on the specific charge particle. In upcoming articles we will discuss upon these forces in more details.

4.5.1 Electromagnetic Force on a Moving Charge

When a charge q moving at velocity $\vec{v}$ enters in a region of magnetic field with magnetic induction $\vec{B}$, it experiences a force given as

$$\vec{F} = q(\vec{v} \times \vec{B}) \quad \text{... (4.97)}$$

If in space electric field $\vec{E}$ also exist then the net electromagnetic force on the charge particle is given as

$$\vec{F} = q\vec{E} + q(\vec{v} \times \vec{B}) \quad \text{... (4.98)}$$

The expression of force as given in equation-(4.98) is called '*Lorentz Force Equation*' which gives net electromagnetic force on a particle. First term in above equation is the electric force on charge and second term is the magnetic force on charge. The two forces may be different as observed from different frames of reference but for all inertial reference frames the total force given by this equation will be a constant. This is because in different frames due to their motion the effective electric and magnetic field changes as variation in one field induces the other and vice versa. This phenomenon of induction of one field due to variation in other will be studied in next chapter of electromagnetic induction.

For some upcoming articles we will restrict our discussion only upto magnetic forces as we've already discussed about electric forces at a decent level in previous chapters.

4.5.2 Direction of Magnetic Force on Moving Charges

As already discussed in previous article that the magnetic force on a moving charge in magnetic field is given by equation-(4.97).

The direction of magnetic force on charge particle can be given by the cross product using right hand thumb rule as shown in figure-4.84.

This figure shows a region with magnetic field in inward direction and a charge q enters the region with a velocity v toward right as shown.

Using cross product in equation-(4.97) we can rotate our right hand fingers from the direction of velocity vector (right) to the direction of magnetic induction vector (inward) and in this state direction of right hand thumb gives the direction of magnetic force shown in figure-4.84.

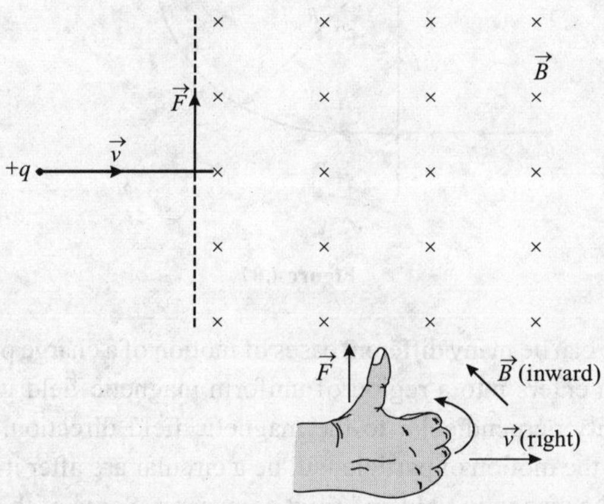

Figure 4.84

Right hand thumb rule is a common way of finding the direction of magnetic force on a moving charge but in many three dimensional cases another method '*Right Hand Palm Rule*' is also very helpful in determining the direction of magnetic force which is stated as

"*Stretch your right hand palm with fingers straight and thumb in same plane. If you point fingers along the direction of magnetic induction and thumb along the direction of velocity of positive charge motion then area vector of your right hand palm gives the direction of magnetic force.*"

For the above case shown in figure-4.84 we can also determine the direction of magnetic force using right hand palm rule as shown in figure-4.85.

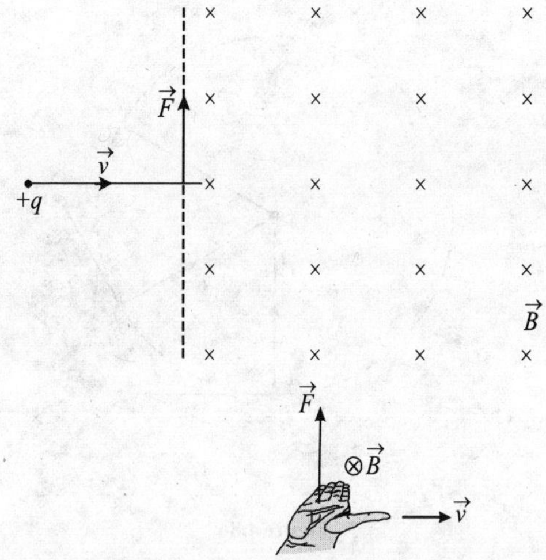

Figure 4.85

In many cases right hand palm rule is advantageous to apply so in upcoming cases we will prefer to use right hand palm rule however students are free to use any of the rule whichever they feel comfortable.

4.5.3 Work Done by Magnetic Force on Moving Charges

From equation-(4.97) it is clear that direction of magnetic force is always perpendicular to instantaneous velocity of the particle thus it can never do work on freely moving charge particles.

Thus in magnetic field we can state that speed of a freely moving charge particle can never be changed due to magnetic forces acting on it.

As magnetic force acts in direction perpendicular to the instantaneous velocity of particle, it can change the direction of motion of the moving charges. In upcoming articles we will discuss different cases of projection of charge particles in magnetic field.

4.5.4 Projection of a Charge Particle in Uniform Magnetic Field in Perpendicular Direction

When a charge particle with charge q is projected with an initial velocity v in magnetic field from point A as shown in figure-4.86 then as velocity is perpendicular to magnetic field, the magnetic force on charge at point A can be calculated by equation-(4.97) which is given as

$$F = qvB \qquad \dots (4.99)$$

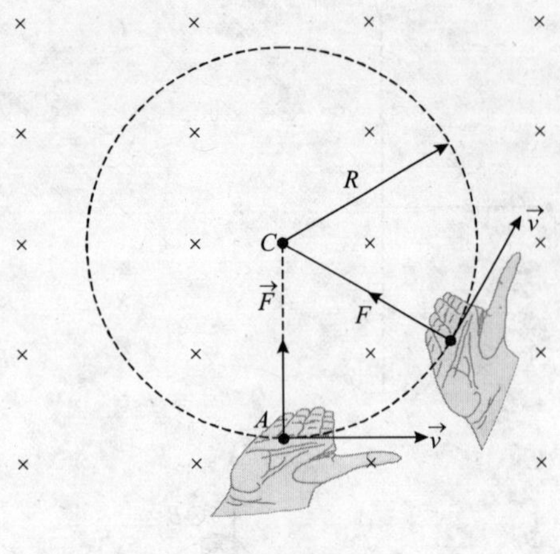

Figure 4.86

By right hand palm rule direction of force on q at point A is in vertically upward direction as shown. Due to this force the direction of motion of charge changes and with the change in direction of velocity of charge, the direction of magnetic force on it also changes with motion. As speed of particle is constant and force on it is always in normal direction so motion of particle will be circular and the magnetic force will provide the necessary centripetal force for this uniform circular motion. If particle is moving in a circle of radius R, we have

$$qvB = \frac{mv^2}{R}$$

$$\Rightarrow \qquad R = \frac{mv}{qB} \qquad \text{... (4.100)}$$

The angular speed of particle in circular motion is given as

$$\omega = \frac{v}{R} = \frac{qB}{m} \qquad \text{... (4.101)}$$

Time period of revolution of particle in circular motion is given as

$$T = \frac{2\pi}{\omega} = \frac{2\pi m}{qB} \qquad \text{... (4.102)}$$

From equation-(4.101) and (4.102) we can see that the revolution angular speed and time period does not depend upon the projection speed of particle, it only depends upon the specific charge and magnetic induction magnitude in the region.

4.5.5 Projection of a Charge Particle from Outside into a Uniform Magnetic Field in Perpendicular Direction

Figure-4.87 shows a situation in which a charge particle with charge q, mass m and moving at a velocity v is projected toward a region of magnetic field such that its velocity is perpendicular to the magnetic field as well as its boundary as shown.

As soon as the particle enters the region of magnetic field, it experiences a magnetic force $F = qvB$ of which the direction is given by right hand palm rule shown in figure. As discussed in previous article, the path of motion will be circular with center lying on the line of action of the force acting on it. The particle will follow a circular arc and come out of the field as shown. The radius of the circular arc is given by equation-(4.100).

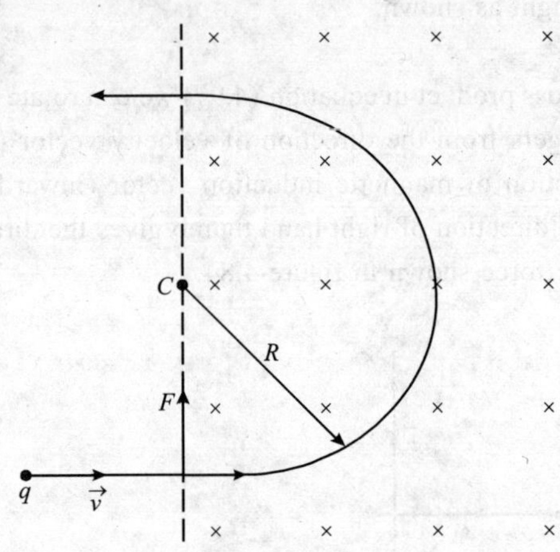

Figure 4.87

There can be many different cases of motion of a charge particle which enters into a region of uniform magnetic field with its velocity perpendicular to the magnetic field direction. In all cases the motion of particle will be a circular arc after it enters into the magnetic field and till it comes out. Some of the cases are shown in figure-4.88.

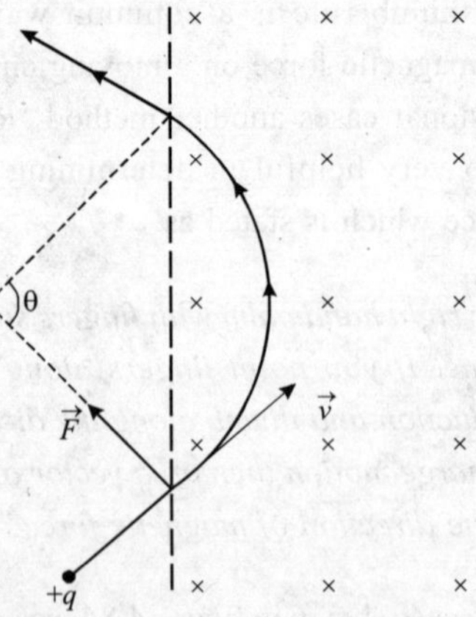

(a)

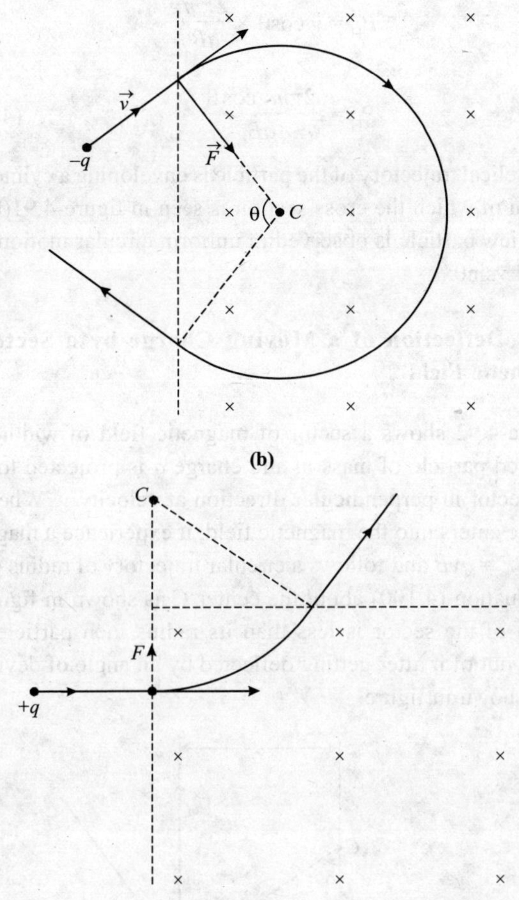

Figure 4.88

In each case when particle enters the magnetic field we can find the direction of magnetic force on particle and somewhere on the line of force we can locate the center of circular trajectory of particle and draw the arc until it comes out of the field.

Always remember that a charge particle which is projected into a magnetic field from outside space will never be able to complete the circle inside the field, it will certainly come out at some point. To complete the circle in magnetic field particle must be projected from a point inside the field as discussed in article-4.5.4 or this is possible if magnetic field vary with time in some cases, discussion of such cases is beyond the scope of this book.

4.5.6 Projection of a Charge Particle in Direction Parallel to the Magnetic Field

When a particle is projected such that its velocity vector is parallel to the direction of magnetic induction then from equation-(4.97) the magnetic force on the particle is zero and hence the trajectory of particle will be a straight line as shown in figure-4.89.

$$F = 0 \qquad \text{... (4.103)}$$

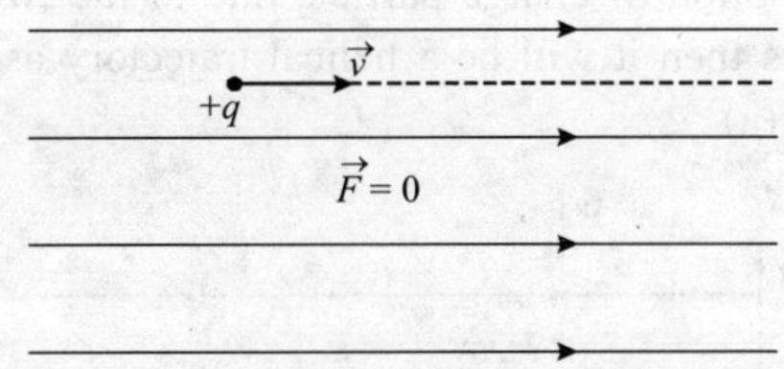

Figure 4.89

4.5.7 Projection of a Charge Particle at Some Angle to the Direction of Magnetic Field

Figure-4.90 shows a particle with charge q and mass m is projected with initial speed v at an angle θ with the direction of magnetic field vector of magnetic induction B. In this case the magnetic force on the charge particle can be calculated by equation-(4.97) which is given as

$$F = qvB \sin\theta \qquad \text{... (4.104)}$$

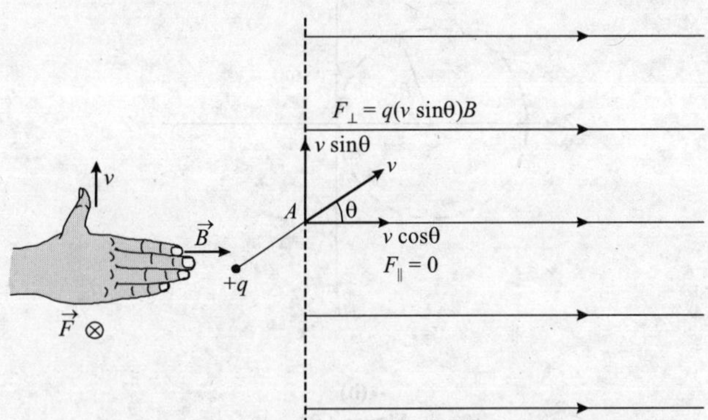

Figure 4.90

At the point A where the particle enters the magnetic field region, we resolve the particle's velocity in two rectangular components along and perpendicular to the magnetic field which are $v\cos\theta$ and $v\sin\theta$.

In this case the component $v\cos\theta$ is parallel to the magnetic field direction so it will not experience any magnetic force and due to this component we can consider the motion of charge particle will be straight line.

Other component $v\sin\theta$ is perpendicular to the magnetic field direction on which the magnetic force will be given by equation-(4.104) and the direction of this force is into the plane of paper (inward) which is given by right hand palm rule as shown in figure-4.90. As the component $v\sin\theta$ is perpendicular to the direction of magnetic induction, the motion due to this component will be circular and effectively if we see the resulting motion of charge particle due to the two velocity components then it will be a helical trajectory as shown in figure-4.91(a).

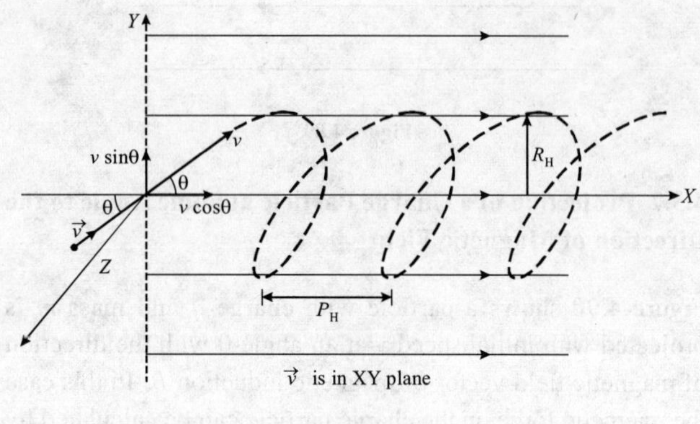

(a)

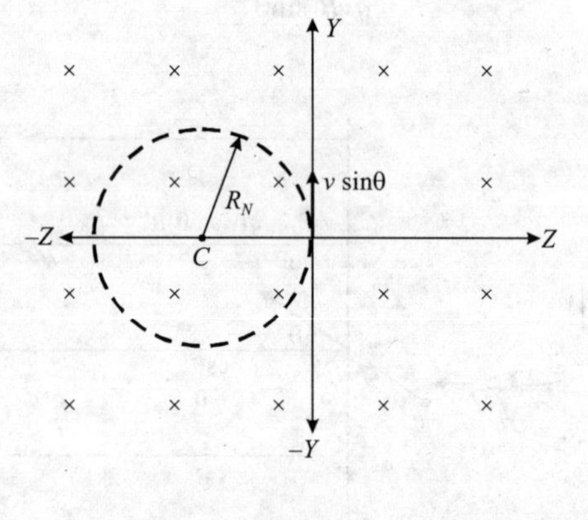

(b)

Figure 4.91

Figure-4.91(b) shows the side view of figure-4.91(a) if it is seen from left side. In this view only the component $v\sin\theta$ is seen as other component $v\cos\theta$ is into the plane of paper.

Thus whenever a charge is projected in a magnetic field at some angle, its trajectory is helical as shown above with radius of helical path is given as

$$R_H = \frac{mv\sin\theta}{qb} \quad \text{... (4.105)}$$

Another characteristic of the helical path is considered as its pitch P_H which is the distance travelled by the particle along the axis of helical path in one revolution as shown in figure-4.91(a) which is given as

$$P_H = v\cos\theta \times T$$

$$\Rightarrow \quad P_H = v\cos\theta \times \frac{2\pi m}{qB}$$

$$\Rightarrow \quad P_H = \frac{2\pi mv\cos\theta}{qB} \quad \text{... (4.106)}$$

The helical trajectory of the particle is enveloping a cylindrical region of which the cross section is seen in figure-4.91(b). In this view particle is observed in uniform circular motion with speed $v\sin\theta$.

4.5.8 Deflection of a Moving Charge by a Sector of Magnetic Field

Figure-4.92 shows a sector of magnetic field of width d. A charged particle of mass m and charge q is projected toward this sector in perpendicular direction at velocity v. When the charge enters into the magnetic field, it experience a magnetic force $F = qvB$ and follows a circular trajectory of radius given by equation-(4.100) about the center C as shown in figure. If width of the sector is less than its radius then particle will come out of it after getting deflected by an angle of deviation δ as shown in figure.

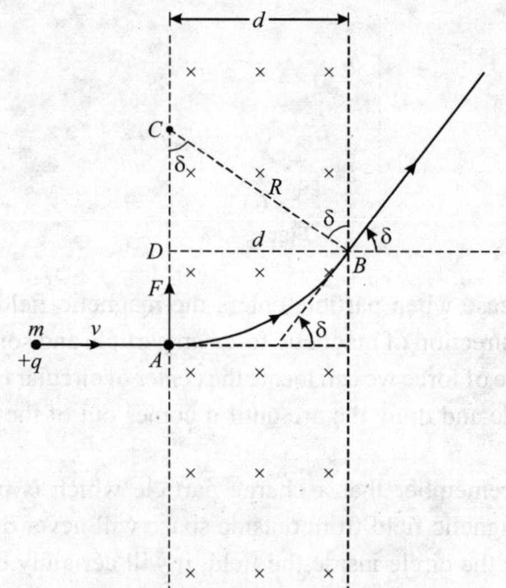

Figure 4.92

From the above figure we can calculate the angle of deviation in direction of motion of particle which is given from ΔBCD as

$$\sin\delta = \frac{d}{R}$$

$$\Rightarrow \quad \sin\delta = \frac{d}{(mv/qB)}$$

$$\Rightarrow \quad \delta = \sin^{-1}\left(\frac{qBd}{mv}\right) \quad \text{... (4.107)}$$

If in above situation the sector width is more than the radius of circular trajectory of the particle then as shown in figure-4.87 we can state that angle of deviation will be 180° and particle will return in the direction opposite to that at which it enters the magnetic field after following a semi-circle in the field.

Illustrative Example 4.19

A charge 4 μC enters in a region of uniform magnetic field with a velocity $(4\hat{i} - 7\hat{j})$ m/s experiences a force $(5\hat{i} - C\hat{j})$ N. Find the value of C.

Solution

As we know magnetic force is always ⊥ to velocity of charge particle, given as

$$\vec{F}_m = q(\vec{v} \times \vec{B})$$

As $\vec{F}$ is ⊥ to $\vec{v}$ we use

$$\vec{F} \cdot \vec{v} = 0$$

$$\Rightarrow \quad (5\hat{i} - C\hat{j}) \cdot (4\hat{i} + 7\hat{j}) = 0$$

$$\Rightarrow \quad 20 - 7C = 0$$

$$\Rightarrow \quad C = \frac{20}{7}$$

Illustrative Example 4.20

A charge particle of mass m and charge q is accelerated by a potential difference V volt. It enters in a region of uniform magnetic field B as shown in figure-4.93. Find the time after which it will come out from the magnetic field.

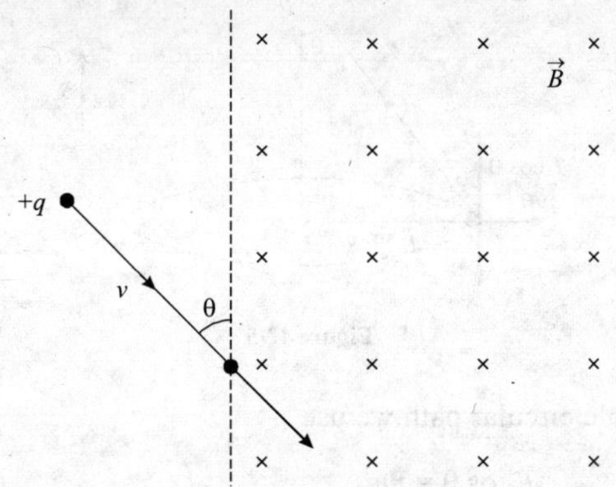

Figure 4.93

Solution

As charge is accelerated at a voltage V, the kinetic energy gained by the particle is written as

$$qV = \frac{1}{2}mv^2$$

As particle's velocity is perpendicular to the applied magnetic field, it follows a circular path with center lying on the line of force which acts on the particle when it enters the field as shown in figure-4.94. The angular speed of particle during its circular motion is given as

$$\omega = \frac{qB}{m}$$

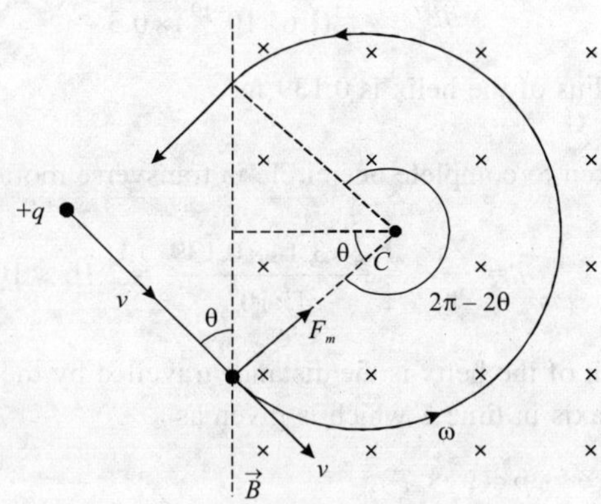

Figure 4.94

From above figure we can see that in the magnetic field the particle follows a circular arc subtending an angle 2π – 2θ at C so time spent any particle in magnetic field is given as

$$t = \frac{2\pi - 2\theta}{\omega}$$

$$\Rightarrow \quad t = \frac{2m}{qB}(\pi - \theta)$$

Illustrative Example 4.21

A proton of charge 1.6×10^{-19} C and mass $m = 1.67 \times 10^{-27}$ kg is shot with a speed 8×10^6 m/s at an angle of 30° with the X-axis. A uniform magnetic field $B = 0.30$ T exists along the X-axis. Show that path of the proton is a helix. Find the radius and pitch of the helical path followed by the proton.

Solution

The velocity components of the proton are given as

$$v_x = v\cos 30° = (8 \times 10^6)(0.866)$$

$$\Rightarrow \quad v_x = 6.93 \times 10^6 \text{ m/s}$$

$$v_y = v \sin 30° = (8 \times 10^6) \times (0.5)$$

$$\Rightarrow \quad v_y = 4.0 \times 10^6 \text{ m/s}$$

The magnetic force due to v_x is given as

$$F = qv_x B \sin 0° = 0$$

The magnetic force due to v_y has no x-component so the motion along x-axis is uniform at speed v_x and due to v_y proton moves in circular path and overall motion will be helical.

The radius of circular transverse motion is given as

$$r = \frac{mv_y}{qB} = \frac{(1.67\times10^{-27})(4\times10^6)}{(1.6\times10^{-19})\times0.3} = 0.139 \text{ m}$$

Thus radius of the helix is 0.139 m.

Time taken to complete one circle in transverse motion is

$$T = \frac{2\pi r}{v_y} = \frac{2\times3.14\times0.139}{4\times10^6} = 2.16 \times 10^{-7} \text{ s}$$

The pitch of the helix is the distance travelled by the proton along x-axis in time T which is given as

$$p = v_x \times T$$

$$\Rightarrow \quad p = (6.93 \times 10^6) \times (2.19 \times 10^{-7})$$

$$\Rightarrow \quad p = 1.515 \text{ m}$$

Illustrative Example 4.22

An α-particle is describing a circle of radius 0.45 m in a field of magnetic induction of 1.2 T. Find its speed, frequency of revolution and kinetic energy. What potential difference will be required which will accelerate the particle so as to give this much of the kinetic energy to it? The mass of α-particle is 6.8×10^{-27} kg and its charge is twice the charge of electron.

Solution

In case of circular motion in magnetic field we use

$$F = evB = \frac{mv^2}{r}$$

$$\Rightarrow \quad v = \frac{eBr}{m}$$

Substituting the given values, we get

$$v = \frac{3.2\times10^{-19}\times1.2\times0.45}{6.8\times10^{-27}} = 2.6 \times 10^7 \text{ m/s}$$

The frequency of revolution is given as

$$n = \frac{v}{2\pi r} = \frac{2.6\times10^7}{2\times3.14\times0.45} = 9.2 \times 10^6 \text{ s}^{-1}$$

The kinetic energy of α-particle is given by

$$K = \frac{1}{2}mv^2$$

$$\Rightarrow \quad K = \frac{1}{2} \times 6.8 \times 10^{-27} \times 2.6 \times 10^7 \text{ J}$$

$$\Rightarrow \quad K = 2.3 \times 10^{-12} \text{ J}$$

$$\Rightarrow \quad K = \frac{2.3\times10^{-12}}{1.6\times10^{-19}} \text{eV}$$

$$\Rightarrow \quad K = 14 \times 10^6 \text{ eV} = 14 \text{ MeV}$$

An electron will acquire this amount of energy (14 MeV) when it is accelerated through a potential difference of 14×10^6 V. Since α-particle carries a charge twice that of an electron it will gain this much amount of kinetic energy when accelerated through half of the potential difference of electron which is 7×10^6 V.

Illustrative Example 4.23

A small ball having mass m and with a charge q is suspended from a rigid support by means of an inextensible string of length l. It is made to revolve on a horizontal circular path in a uniform magnetic field of magnetic induction B which is in vertically upward direction. The time period of revolution of the ball is T. If the thread is always tight, calculate the radius of circular path on which the ball moves.

Solution

The situation described in question is shown in figure-4.95

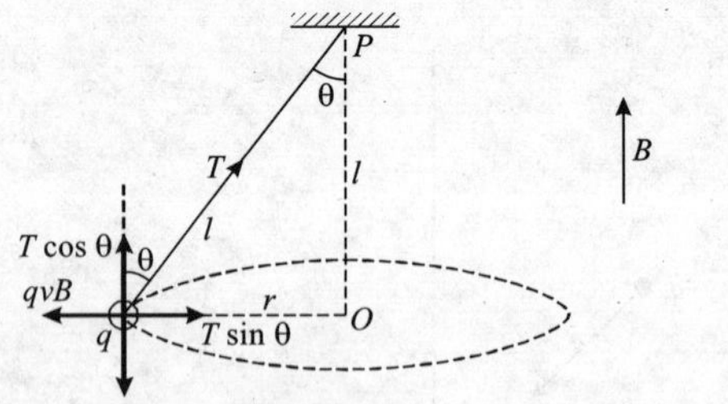

Figure 4.95

For stable circular path we use

$$T \cos \theta = mg \qquad \dots (4.108)$$

and

$$T \sin\theta - qvB = \frac{mv^2}{r} \qquad \dots (4.109)$$

From equation-(4.108) and (4.109) we have

$$\left(\frac{mg}{\cos\theta}\right)\sin\theta - qBr\omega = mr\omega^2$$

From figure, we have

$$\sin\theta = \frac{r}{l} \text{ and } \cos\theta = \frac{\sqrt{(l^2-r^2)}}{l}$$

$$\Rightarrow \quad \frac{mgr}{\sqrt{(l^2-r^2)}} - qBr\omega = mr\omega^2$$

$$\Rightarrow \quad \frac{1}{\sqrt{(l^2-r^2)}} = \frac{\omega^2}{g} + \frac{qB\omega}{mg}$$

$$\Rightarrow \quad (l^2-r^2) = \frac{(1/\omega)^2}{[(\omega/g)+(qB/mg)]^2}$$

$$\Rightarrow \quad (l^2-r^2) = \frac{(T/2\pi)^2}{[(2\pi/gT')+(qB/mg)]^2}$$

$$\Rightarrow \quad r = \left[l^2 - \frac{(T/2\pi)^2}{\{(2\pi/gT')+(qB/mg)\}^2}\right]$$

Illustrative Example 4.24

A particle of mass $m = 1.6 \times 10^{-27}$ kg and charge $q = 1.6 \times 10^{-19}$ C enters a region of uniform magnetic field of strength 1 T along the direction as shown in figure-4.96, the speed on the particle is 10^7 m/s. The magnetic field is directed along the inward normal to the plane of the paper. The particle leaves the region of the field at the point F.

(a) Find the distance EF and angle θ.

(b) If the direction of the magnetic field is reversed, find the time spent by the particle in the region of magnetic field after entering at E.

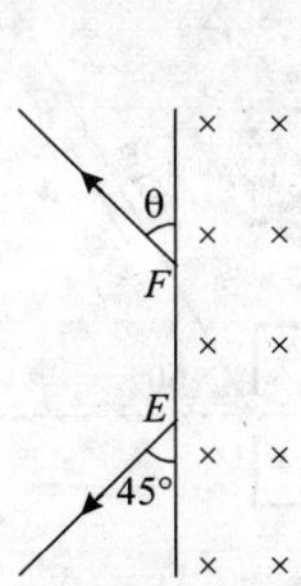

Figure 4.96

Solution

(a) If the direction of magnetic field is directed along the inward normal to the plane of the paper, the path of the particle will be an arc of a circle of radius OE as shown in figure-4.97.

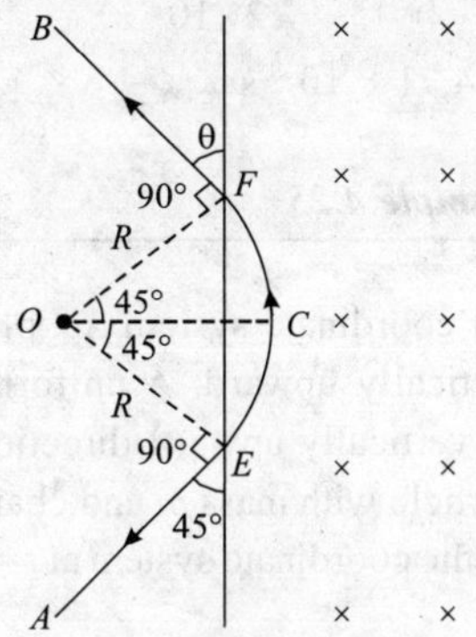

Figure 4.97

From the figure, we can see that $\theta = 45°$ and we have

$$EF = 2R\cos 45°$$

Radius of circular motion is given as

$$R = \frac{mv}{qB} = \frac{1.6\times10^{-27}\times10^7}{1\times1.6\times10^{-19}} = 0.1 \text{ m}$$

$$\Rightarrow \quad EF = 2 \times 0.1 \times (1/\sqrt{2}) = 0.141 \text{ m}$$

(b) If the direction of the magnetic field is directed along the outward normal to the paper, the path ECH of the particle in the region of magnetic field will be a circular arc in the clockwise direction with radius R as shown in figure-4.98 and from figure we can see that

$$\angle EO'H = 90°$$

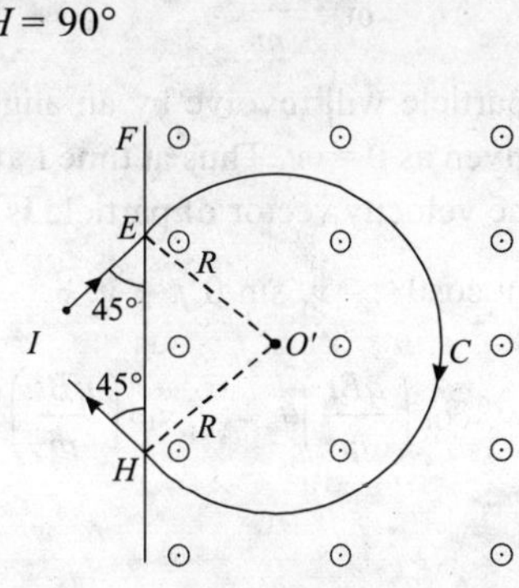

Figure 4.98

Radii $O'E$ and $O'H$ are perpendicular at points E and H so the length of arc is given as

$$ECH = 2\pi R - \frac{\pi R}{2} = \frac{3\pi R}{2}$$

Time spent by particle along arc ECH in the magnetic field is given as

$$t = \frac{3\pi R}{2v} = \frac{3\times3.14\times0.1}{2\times10^7}\ \text{s}$$

$$\Rightarrow \quad t = 4.71 \times 10^{-8}\ \text{s}$$

Illustrative Example 4.25

In a right handed coordinate system XY plane is horizontal and Z-axis is vertically upward. A uniform magnetic field exist in space in vertically upward direction with magnetic induction B. A particle with mass m and charge q is projected from the origin of the coordinate system at $t = 0$ with a velocity vector given as

$$\vec{v} = v_1\hat{i} + v_2\hat{k}$$

Find the velocity vector of the particle after time t.

Solution

The velocity component v_2 of the particle is along Z-axis and parallel to the magnetic field direction thus it will not experience any force and will remain constant. Due to the other velocity component v_1 which is in positive x-direction, particle will experience a force in negative y-direction and it will follow a circular path with center lying at a point C with position coordinates $(0, -R, 0)$ initially. Due to both velocity components the resulting motion of the particle will be a helical trajectory with axis parallel to Z-axis passing through the point $(0, -R, 0)$. The angular speed of the particle in its helical path is given as

$$\omega = \frac{qB}{m}$$

In a time t the particle will revolve by an angle θ along XY plane which is given as $\theta = \omega t$. Thus at time t after projection of the particle the velocity vector of particle is given as

$$\vec{v} = v_1\cos\theta\,\hat{i} - v_1\sin\theta\,\hat{j} + v_2\hat{k}$$

$$\Rightarrow \quad \vec{v} = v_1\cos\left(\frac{qBt}{m}\right)\hat{i} - v_1\sin\left(\frac{qBt}{m}\right)\hat{j} + v_2\hat{k}$$

Web Reference at www.physicsgalaxy.com

Age Group - Grade 11 & 12 | Age 17-19 Years
Section - Magnetic Effects
Topic - Electromagnetic Force
Module Number - 1 to 13

Practice Exercise 4.3

(i) A beam of singly ionized charged particles, having kinetic energy 1000 eV contain particles of masses 8×10^{-27} kg and 1.6×10^{-26} kg emerge from one end of an accelerator tube. There is a plate at a distance 0.01 m from end of tube placed perpendicular to it. Find minimum magnetic induction in the region so that beam will not strike to plate.

[$\sqrt{2}$T]

(ii) An electron moving with a velocity 10^8 m/s enters a magnetic field at an angle of 20° to the direction of the field. Calculate

(a) The value of magnetic induction so that the helical path radius will be 2 m.

(b) The time required to execute one revolution of the helical path.

(c) The pitch of helical path followed by the electron.

[(a) 9.6×10^{-5} T; (b) 3.69×10^{-7} s; (c) 34.68 m]

(iii) A stream of protons and deuterons in a vacuum chamber enters a uniform magnetic field. Both protons and deuterons have been subjected to same accelerating potential, hence the kinetic energies of the particles are the same. If the ion-stream is perpendicular to the magnetic field and the protons move in a circular path of radius 15 cm, find the radius of the path traversed by the deuterons. Given that mass of deuteron is twice that of a proton.

[0.212 m]

(iv) An electron gun G emits electron of energy 2 keV travelling in the positive X-direction. The electrons are required to hit the spot S where $GS = 0.1$ m, and the line GS makes an angle of 60° with the X-axis as shown in figure-4.99 a uniform magnetic field B parallel to GS exists in the region outside the electron gun. Find the minimum value of B needed to make the electrons hit point S.

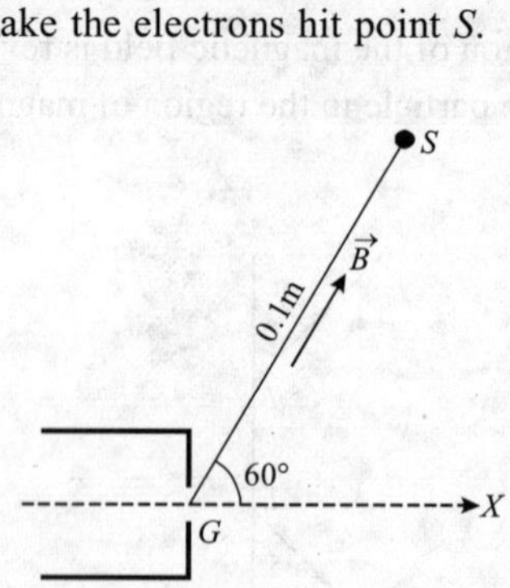

Figure 4.99

[4.73×10^{-3} T]

(v) A 15000 V electron is describing a circle in a uniform field of magnetic induction 250 G acting at right angle to it. Calculate the radius of the circle.

[1.66 cm]

(vi) A slightly divergent beam of charged particles is accelerated by a potential difference V propagates from a point A along the axis of a solenoid. The beam is focussed at a point P at a distance l from A by two successive values of magnetic inductions B_1 and B_2 one after another. Find specific charge of the particles.

[$\dfrac{8\pi^2 V}{l^2(B_2 - B_1)^2}$]

(vii) A direct current flowing through the winding of a long cylindrical solenoid of radius R produces a uniform magnetic induction B in it. An electron travelling at velocity v enters into the solenoid along the radial direction between its turn at right angles to the solenoid axis. After a certain time the electron deflected by magnetic field leaves the solenoid. Calculate the time which the electron spends inside the solenoid.

[$\dfrac{2m}{eB}\tan^{-1}\left(\dfrac{eBR}{mv}\right)$]

(viii) Two long parallel wires carrying currents 2.5A and I in the same direction directed into the plane of the paper are held at points P and Q as shown in figure-4.100 such that they are perpendicular to the plane of paper. The points P and Q are located at a distance of 5 m and 2 m respectively from a collinear point R as shown. An electron moving with a velocity of 4×10^5 m/s along the positive x-direction experiences a force of magnitude 3.2×10^{-20} N at the point R. Find the value of I.

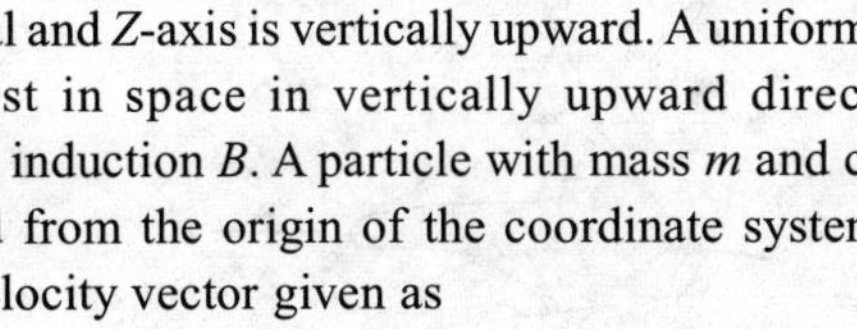

Figure 4.100

[4 A]

(ix) In a right handed coordinate system XY plane is horizontal and Z-axis is vertically upward. A uniform magnetic field exist in space in vertically upward direction with magnetic induction B. A particle with mass m and charge q is projected from the origin of the coordinate system at $t = 0$ with a velocity vector given as

$$\vec{v} = v_1\hat{i} + v_2\hat{k}$$

Find the position coordinates of the particle after time t.

[$\dfrac{mv_1}{qB}\sin\left(\dfrac{qBt}{m}\right), -\dfrac{mv_1}{qB}\left(1-\cos\left(\dfrac{qBt}{m}\right)\right), v_2 t$]

(x) Inside a cylindrical capacitor of inner radius a and outer radius b, an electron is projected from the surface of inner cylindrical shell perpendicular to it with an initial velocity. In the annular region between the two cylindrical shells a uniform magnetic induction B exist in direction parallel to the axis of capacitor. Find the maximum initial velocity with which the electron is to be projected so that it will not hit the outer shell.

[$\dfrac{eB(b^2 - a^2)}{2mb}$]

4.6 Magnetic Force on Current Carrying Conductors

In previous articles we've studied that a moving charge in magnetic field experiences a force given by equation-(4.97). A current carrying conductor contains free electrons continuously flowing at drift speed. So if a current carrying conductor is placed in a magnetic field then all its free electrons will experience same magnetic force and due to this, overall the conductor will experience a net magnetic force which is the sum of magnetic forces on all its moving free electrons.

There are many cases under which we'll study the force experienced by current carrying conductors. This force may cause translational or rotational motion of the conductors and will affect the overall motion as well. In upcoming articles and illustrations we will extend our knowledge of magnetic force for current carrying conductors.

4.6.1 Force on a Wire in Uniform Magnetic Field

Figure-4.46 shows a current carrying wire XY with current I placed in a region of uniform magnetic induction B. If the free electrons inside the conductor are moving at drift speed v_d then each free electron will experience a magnetic force $F_m = ev_dB$.

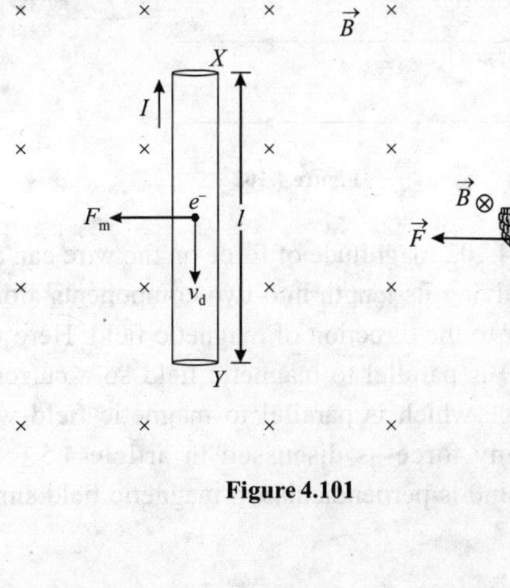

Figure 4.101

The direction of these forces on all free electron is given by right hand palm rule which is toward left as shown in figure. For applying the right hand palm rule in case of current carrying conductors we point thumb in the direction of current flow which is the flow of positive charges in the conductor as shown in figure-4.101.

If n be the free electron density of the conductor, S is the cross sectional area of this conductor then total number of free electrons in this wire XY are nlS. Thus total magnetic force on wire XY is given as

$$F = ev_dB \times nlS \qquad \dots (4.110)$$

In above equation-(4.110) nev_d is the current density and product with the cross sectional area S gives the current so it can be rewritten as

$$F = BIl \qquad \dots (4.111)$$

If the direction of force is expressed in form of cross product then we use the vectors for length of conductor $\vec{l}$ and that for magnetic field $\vec{B}$ and the magnetic force vector on current carrying conductor can be given as

$$\vec{F} = I(\vec{l} \times \vec{B}) \qquad \dots (4.112)$$

Thus if a wire is placed in a uniform magnetic field making an angle θ with the direction of magnetic field as shown in figure-4.102 then the magnetic force on this wire is given by equation-(4.112) as

$$F = BIl\sin\theta \qquad \dots (4.113)$$

The direction of this force can be given by cross product of equation-(4.112) which is into the plane of paper as shown.

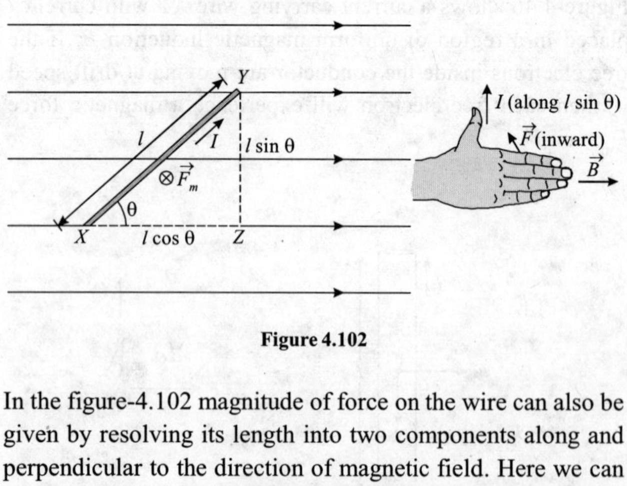

Figure 4.102

In the figure-4.102 magnitude of force on the wire can also be given by resolving its length into two components along and perpendicular to the direction of magnetic field. Here we can see that $l\cos\theta$ is parallel to magnetic field so a current or a moving charge which is parallel to magnetic field will not experience any force as discussed in article-4.5.6. Other component $l\sin\theta$ is perpendicular to magnetic field similar to the case shown in figure-4.101 thus the force on it is given by equation-(4.111) replacing l to $l\sin\theta$ which gives equation-(4.113).

4.6.2 Direction of Magnetic Force on Currents in Magnetic Field

As discussed in previous article about direction of magnetic force that it can be given by cross product in equation-(4.112). Same can be given by right hand palm rule as already discussed for force on moving charges in magnetic field. In case of current carrying conductor we need to point right hand thumb along the direction of current which denotes the flow of positive charges. Figure-4.103 again illustrates the application of right hand palm rule for force on a current carrying conductor XY placed in a magnetic field. In this case the direction of magnetic force on conductor XY is into the plane of paper (inward).

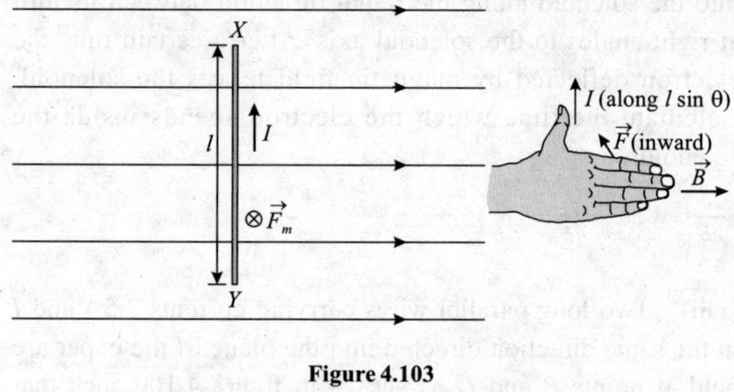

Figure 4.103

Another way of determining the direction of magnetic force on current carrying conductors in magnetic field is by '*Fleming's Left Hand Rule*' stated below

"To determine the direction of magnetic force stretch your index finger, thumb and middle finger of left hand in mutually perpendicular directions as shown in figure-4.104 and orient your hand such that your index finger points in the direction of magnetic field and middle finger along the current then your left hand thumb will give you the direction of magnetic force on the conductor."

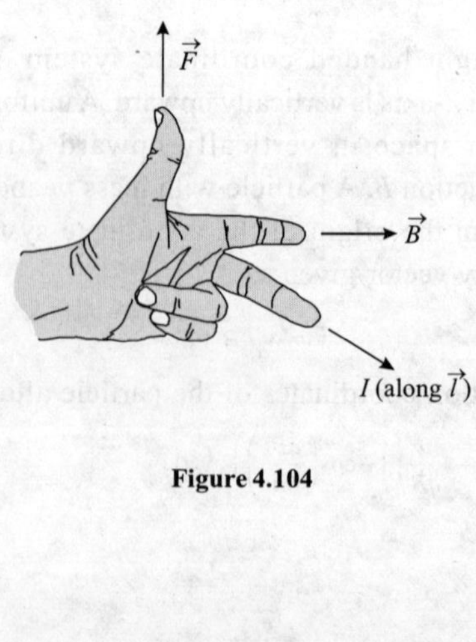

Figure 4.104

The situation shown in Figure-4.103 is redrawn again in figure-4.105 in which we can verify the direction of magnetic force on wire XY by using Fleming's left hand rule.

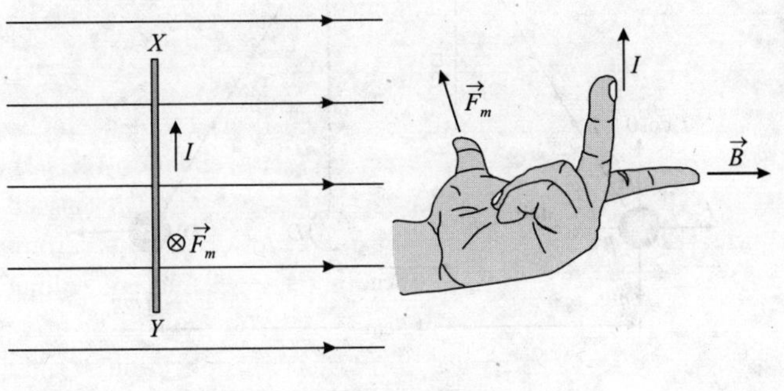

Figure 4.105

While applying Fleming's left hand rule if sometimes current is not flowing in conductor at right angle to the direction of magnetic field then resolve the components of the length of the conductor and point middle finger in the direction of the length component normal to magnetic field.

Students can also use Fleming's left hand rule to determine the direction of magnetic force on freely moving charges in magnetic field which is already discussed in previous articles.

4.6.3 Force Between Two Parallel Current Carrying Wires

Figure-4.106 shows two parallel wires at a separation r and carrying currents I_1 and I_2 in same direction. First wire is considered to be very long and second wire XY is of length l. The magnetic induction due to first wire at the location of second wire is in inward direction which is given as

$$B_1 = \frac{\mu_0 I_1}{2\pi r} \qquad \text{... (4.114)}$$

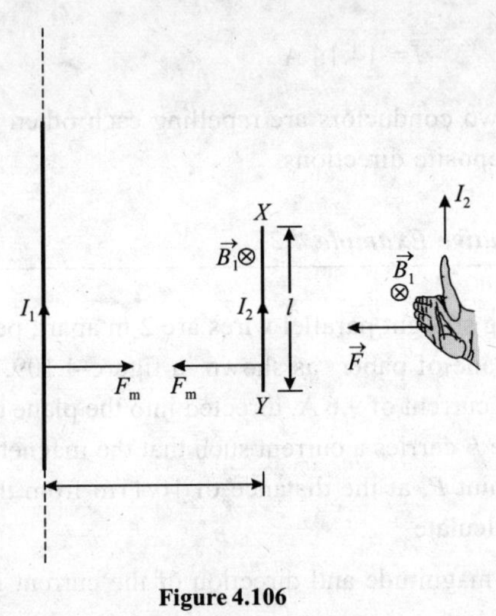

Figure 4.106

The force on second wire due to the magnetic field of first wire at its location is given by equation-(4.111) as

$$F = B_1 I_2 l$$

$$\Rightarrow \qquad F = \left(\frac{\mu_0 I_1}{2\pi r}\right) I_2 l$$

$$\Rightarrow \qquad F = \frac{\mu_0 I_1 I_2 l}{2\pi r} \qquad \text{... (4.115)}$$

Above equation-(4.115) gives the force of interaction between two parallel current carrying wires provided one wire is very long. The direction of magnetic force on wire XY can be given by right hand palm rule as shown in figure-4.106 which is toward left. According to Newton's third law the force by second wire on first will be opposite i.e. in rightward direction. Thus the two wires will attract each other when they carry currents in same direction. If the direction of currents in the two wires is opposite then they will repel each other which can be easily proven by using right hand palm rule, cross product or by using Fleming's left hand rule. Thus in general about force between two parallel current carrying wires we state that

"Two parallel wires carrying currents in same direction attract each other and those carrying currents in opposite direction repel each other because of magnetic force between them."

4.6.4 Magnetic Force on a Random Shaped Current Carrying Wire in Uniform Magnetic Field

Figure-4.107 shows a random shaped wire AB carrying a current I placed in magnetic induction B. The distance between end points of wire AB is l. To analyze the magnetic force on wire we consider coordinate axes as shown in figure with x-axis along AB and y-axis perpendicular to AB.

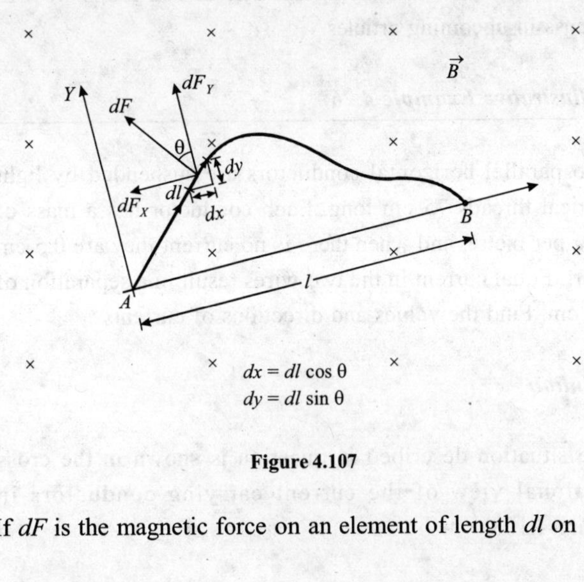

Figure 4.107

If dF is the magnetic force on an element of length dl on the wire then it is given as $dF = BIdl$ and direction of the force on dl is shown in the figure-4.107 which is given by right hand palm rule. Now we resolve this force in two components along x and y axis as dF_x and dF_y which are given as

$$dF_x = BIdl\sin\theta = BIdy \quad \text{... (4.116)}$$

and

$$dF_y = BIdl\cos\theta = BIdx \quad \text{... (4.117)}$$

If we calculate the total force on wire AB by integrating above components, we have

$$F_x = \int dF_x = \int BIdy = BI\int_0^0 dy = 0 \quad \text{... (4.118)}$$

and

$$F_y = \int dF_y = \int BIdx = BI\int_0^l dx = BIl \quad \text{... (4.119)}$$

Thus total force on wire is along y-axis i.e. in direction perpendicular to the line joining the ends of wire AB and it is given as

$$F_{wire} = BIl \quad \text{... (4.120)}$$

Above expression in equation-(4.120) shows that the net magnetic force on a random shaped current carrying wire which is equal to the force acting on a straight wire carrying same current and which has length equal to the line joining the end points of the random shaped wire.

If in this case we join terminals A and B of the wire and make a closed loop then $l = 0$ so $F = 0$. Thus we can also state that if there is a current carrying closed loop or coil then net magnetic force on the coil when placed in uniform magnetic field is zero. About current carrying coils or closed loops we will discuss in upcoming articles.

 # Illustrative Example 4.26

Two parallel horizontal conductors are suspended by light vertical threads 75 cm long. Each conductor has a mass of 40 g per metre, and when there is no current they are 0.5 cm apart. Equal current in the two wires result in a separation of 1.5 cm. Find the values and directions of currents.

Solution

The situation described in question is shown in the cross sectional view of the current carrying conductors in figure-4.108.

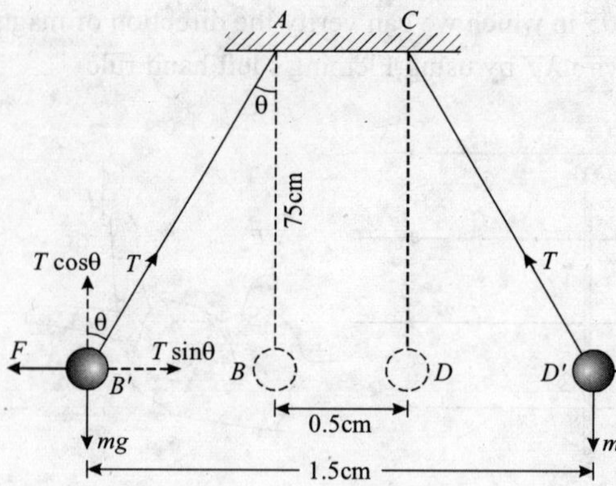

Figure 4.108

For equilibrium of conductors, we have

$$T\cos\theta = mg \quad \text{... (4.121)}$$

$$T\sin\theta = F = \frac{\mu_0 I^2 l}{2\pi d} \quad \text{... (4.122)}$$

From equations-(4.121) and (4.122) we have

$$\tan\theta = \frac{\mu_0 I^2 l}{2\pi dmg} \quad \text{... (4.123)}$$

When θ is small we use $\tan\theta \approx \sin\theta$ thus from figure we have

$$\sin\theta = \frac{0.5\times10^{-2}}{75\times10^{-2}} = \frac{1}{150}$$

Mass of each conductor of length l is given as

$$m = 40.0 \times 10^{-3}\, l \text{ kg}$$

Substituting the values in equation-(4.123), we get

$$\frac{1}{150} = \frac{2\times10^{-7}\times I^2}{1.5\times10^{-2}\times40\times10^{-3}\times10}$$

$$\Rightarrow \qquad I = 14.14 \text{ A}$$

As the two conductors are repelling each other, the currents are in opposite directions.

 # Illustrative Example 4.27

Two long straight parallel wires are 2 m apart, perpendicular to the plane of paper as shown in figure-4.109. The wire A carries a current of 9.6 A, directed into the plane of the paper. The wire B carries a current such that the magnetic induction at the point P, at the distance of 10/11m from the wire B is zero. Calculate

(a) The magnitude and direction of the current in B.

(b) The magnitude of the magnetic induction at the point S.

(c) The force per unit length on the wire B.

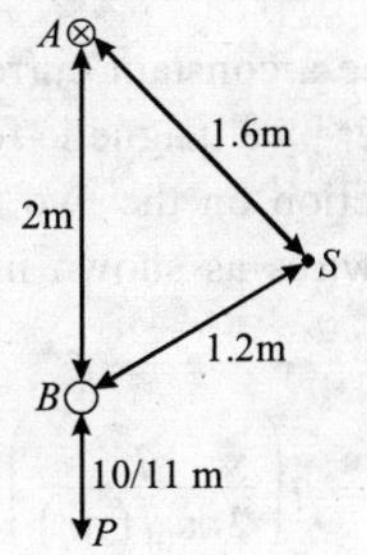

Figure 4.109

Solution

(a) As the magnetic field of induction at point P is zero, for this the magnetic induction at P produced by current carrying wires should be equal and opposite so the direction of current in B must be opposite to that of A directed upward and perpendicular to the plane of the paper.

Magnetic induction at P due to wire A is given as

$$B_1 = \frac{\mu_0 i_1}{2\pi r_1}$$

If current in wire B is taken as i_2 then magnetic induction at P due to wire B is given as

$$B_2 = \frac{\mu_0 i_2}{2\pi r_2}$$

As net magnetic induction at point P is zero, we have

$$B_1 = B_2$$

$$\Rightarrow \quad \frac{\mu_0 i_1}{2\pi r_1} = \frac{\mu_0 i_2}{2\pi r_2}$$

$$\Rightarrow \quad i_2 = \frac{r_2}{r_1} \times i_1$$

We have $\quad r_1 = AP = 2 + \frac{10}{11} = \frac{32}{11}\text{ m}$

and $\quad r_2 = BP = \frac{10}{11}\text{ m}$

$$\Rightarrow \quad i_2 = \frac{(10/11)}{(32/11)} \times 9.6 = 3\text{ A}$$

Thus the wire B carries a current 3 A directed upward and perpendicular to the plane of paper.

(b) The magnetic field produced by wire A at S

$$B_3 = \frac{\mu_0 i_1}{2\pi r_1'} = \frac{2\times10^{-7}\times9.6}{1.6}$$

$$\Rightarrow \quad B_3 = 12 \times 10^{-17}\text{ T}$$

The magnetic field produced by wire B at S

$$B_4 = \frac{\mu_0}{2\pi} \cdot \frac{i_2}{r_2'} = \frac{2\times10^{-7}\times3}{1.2}$$

$$\Rightarrow \quad B_4 = 5 \times 10^{-7}\text{ T}$$

According to figure, $\angle ASB = 90°$ the distances AB, AS and BS are related as

$$(AB)^2 = (AS)^2 + (BS)^2$$

Thus net magnetic induction at point S is given as

$$\Rightarrow \quad B_S = \sqrt{(B_3^2 + B_4^2)}$$

$$\Rightarrow \quad B_S = \sqrt{[(12\times10^{-4})^2 + (5\times10^{-7})^2]}$$

$$\Rightarrow \quad B_S = 1.3 \times 10^{-6}\text{ T}$$

(c) Force per unit length on wire B is given as

$$F = \frac{\mu_0 i_1 i_2}{2\pi r_{AB}} = \frac{2\times10^{-7}\times9.6\times3}{2}$$

$$\Rightarrow \quad F = 2.88 \times 10^{-6}\text{ N/m}$$

Illustrative Example 4.28

A rod AB of mass m and length l is placed on two smooth rails P and Q in a uniform magnetic induction B as shown in figure-4.110. The rails are connected to a current source supplying a constant current I. Find the speed attained by rod AB when it leaves off the other end of rails of length L.

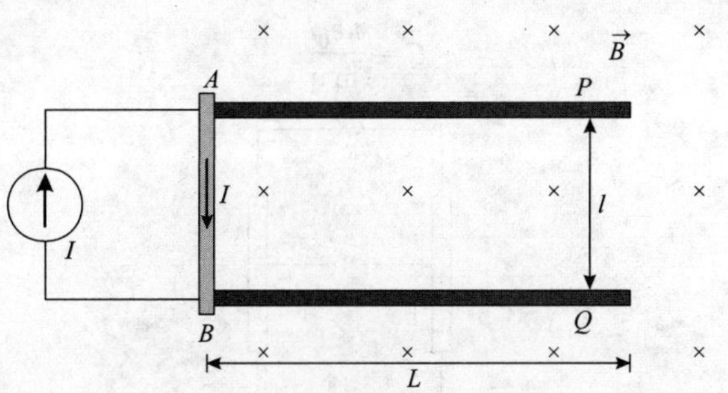

Figure 4.110

Solution

Due to magnetic force acceleration of rod *AB* when it slides on the rails is given as

$$a = \frac{BIl}{m}$$

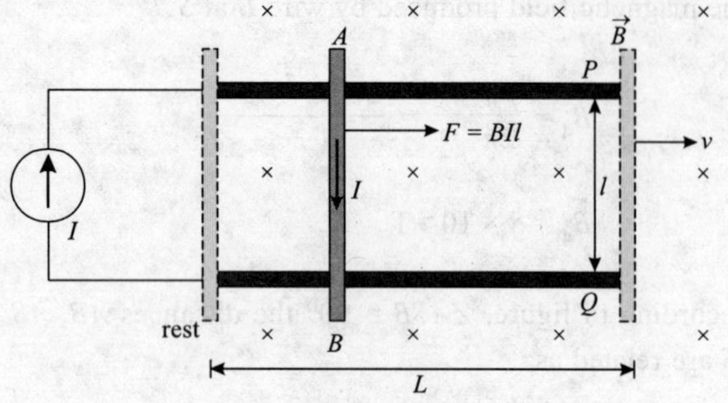

Figure 4.111

As shown in figure-4.111 after travelling a distance *L* on rails speed attained by rod *v* is given as

$$v^2 = d + 2aL$$

$$\Rightarrow \quad v = \sqrt{2aL}$$

$$\Rightarrow \quad v = \sqrt{\frac{2BIlL}{m}}$$

 # Illustrative Example 4.29

Two long parallel wires of negligible resistance are connected at one end to a resistance *R* and at the other end to a constant voltage source of voltage *V*. The distance between the axes of the wires is η times greater than the cross-sectional radius of each wire. At what value of resistance *R*, does the resultant force of interaction between the wires will become zero?

Solution

Figure-4.112 shows the situation described in the question. The two wires form a wire capacitor of which capacitance is given as

$$C = \frac{\pi\varepsilon_0 l}{\ln \eta}$$

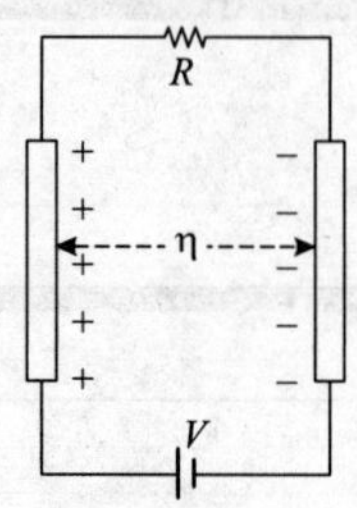

Figure 4.112

Charge on the capacitor in steady state is given as

$$q = CV = \frac{\pi\varepsilon_0 lV}{\ln \eta} \quad \text{... (4.124)}$$

Due to voltage source a constant current flows in the wires which repel each other by a magnetic force which is nullified by the force of attraction on the two wires due to opposite charges on the two wires as shown in figure. The force of attraction is given as

$$F_1 = qE = q\left(\frac{q}{2\pi\varepsilon_0 l(\eta r)}\right) \quad \text{... (4.125)}$$

Substituting the value of *q* from equation-(4.124) into (4.125),

$$F_1 = \frac{\left(\frac{\pi\varepsilon_0 lV}{\ln \eta}\right)^2}{2\pi\varepsilon_0 l(\eta r)} \quad \text{... (4.126)}$$

The current flow is in the opposite direction in the two wires so the net force of repulsion between these wires is given as

$$F_2 = \frac{\mu_0 I^2 l}{2\pi(\eta r)} = \frac{\mu_0 (V/R)^2 l}{2\pi\eta r} \quad \text{... (4.127)}$$

As the net force between the two wires is zero we use

$$\frac{\mu_0 (V/R)^2 l}{2\pi\eta r} = \frac{\left(\frac{\pi\varepsilon_0 lV}{\ln \eta}\right)^2}{2\pi\varepsilon_0 l(\eta r)}$$

$$\Rightarrow \quad R = \sqrt{\frac{\mu_0}{\varepsilon_0}}\frac{\ln \eta}{\pi}$$

 # Illustrative Example 4.30

A rectangular loop of wire *ABCD* is oriented with the left corner at the origin, one edge along *X*-axis and the other edge along *Y*-axis as shown in the figure-4.113. A magnetic field exist in space in direction perpendicular to the *XY* plane as shown and has a magnitude that is given as $B = \alpha y$ where α is a constant. Find the total magnetic force on the loop if it carries current *i*.

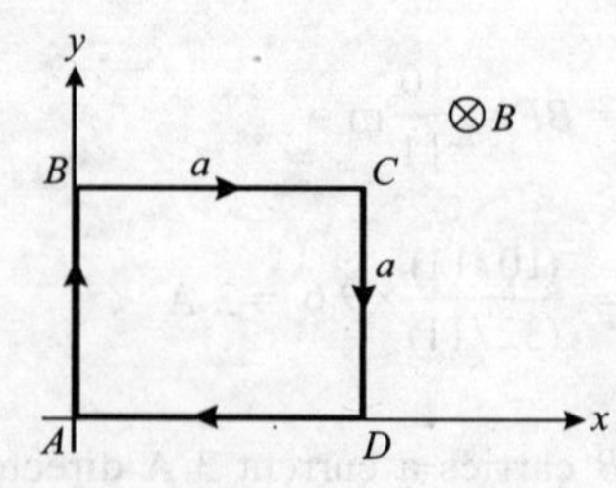

Figure 4.113

Solution

Due to the magnetic induction the four segments of the wire loop experience the forces as shown in figure-4.114. On the segment DA as $y = 0$ the magnetic induction is also zero so no force will act so we have

$$F_{AD} = 0$$

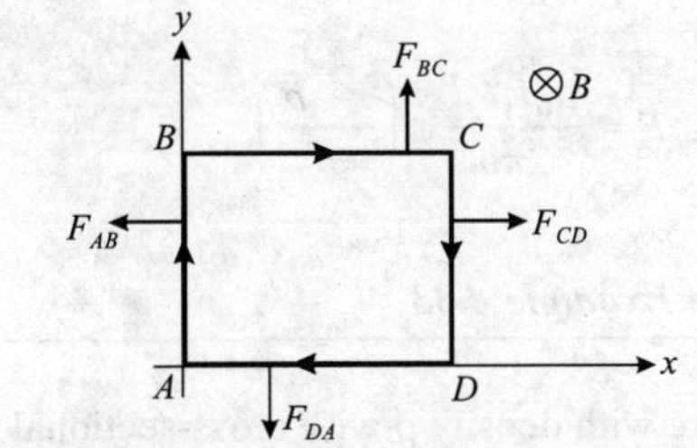

Figure 4.114

At the location of wire BC we have $y = a$ at which we have $B = \alpha a$ so the force on this segment is given as

$$F_{BC} = BIl = (\alpha a)ia = \alpha ia^2$$

For the remaining two segments AB and CD the forces are opposite and equal as for every element on segment AB at a position y there is a corresponding element on CD at same y for which the force is equal and opposite so the two forces on these segments will cancel each other so total force on the wire loop is along y direction and it is given as

$$\vec{F} = \alpha ia^2 \hat{j}$$

 # Illustrative Example 4.31

An infinite wire, placed along z-axis, has current I_1 in positive z-direction. A conducting rod PQ placed in xy plane parallel to y-axis has current I_2 in positive y-direction. The ends of the rod subtend angles 30º and 60º at the origin with positive x-direction as shown in figure-4.115. The rod is at a distance a from the origin. Find net force on the rod.

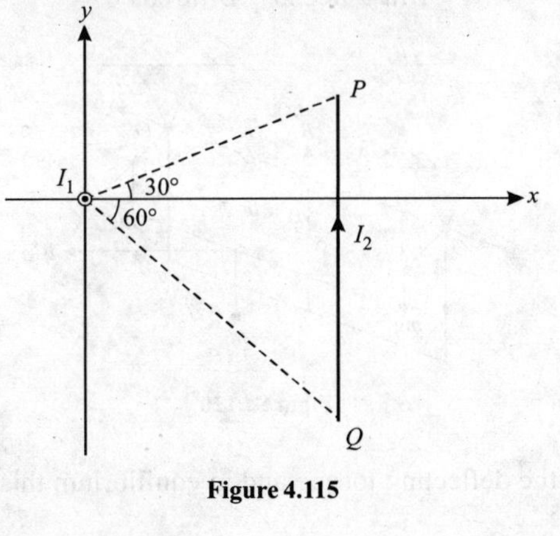

Figure 4.115

Solution

To calculate the force on rod PQ we consider an element of width dy at a distance y from the x-axis as shown in figure-4.116. The magnetic induction at the location of this element due to the wire at origin is given as

$$B = \frac{\mu_0 I_1}{2\pi\sqrt{y^2 + a^2}}$$

The force on element due to the magnetic induction of wire at origin is given as

$$dF = BI_2 dy \sin\theta$$

Net force on the rod PQ is given as

$$F = \int dF = \int BI_2 dy \sin\theta$$

$$\Rightarrow \quad F = \int_{-a\tan 60^\circ}^{+a\tan 30^\circ} \left(\frac{\mu_0 I_1}{2\pi\sqrt{a^2 + y^2}}\right) I_2 dy \left(\frac{y}{\sqrt{a^2 + y^2}}\right)$$

$$\Rightarrow \quad F = \frac{\mu_0 I_1 I_2}{2\pi} \int_{-\sqrt{3}a}^{+a/\sqrt{3}} \frac{y\,dy}{a^2 + y^2}$$

$$\Rightarrow \quad F = \frac{\mu_0 I_1 I_2}{2\pi} \left[\frac{1}{2}\ln(a^2 + y^2)\right]_{-\sqrt{3}a}^{+a/\sqrt{3}}$$

$$\Rightarrow \quad F = \frac{\mu_0 I_1 I_2}{4\pi} \left[\ln\left(\frac{4}{3}a^2\right) - \ln(4a^2)\right]$$

$$\Rightarrow \quad F = \frac{\mu_0 I_1 I_2}{4\pi} \ln 3$$

In above integration we ignore a negative sign as we are calculating the magnitude of force only and the direction is given by right hand palm rule.

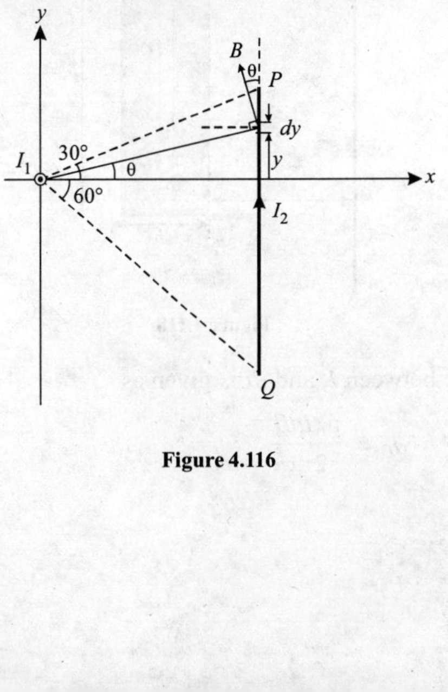

Figure 4.116

 # Illustrative Example 4.32

Figure-4.117 shows a long straight current carrying wire with a current I_1 and a thin strip of width b and length l placed parallel to it with a current I_2 as shown in figure. Find the magnetic force of interaction between current I_1 and I_2.

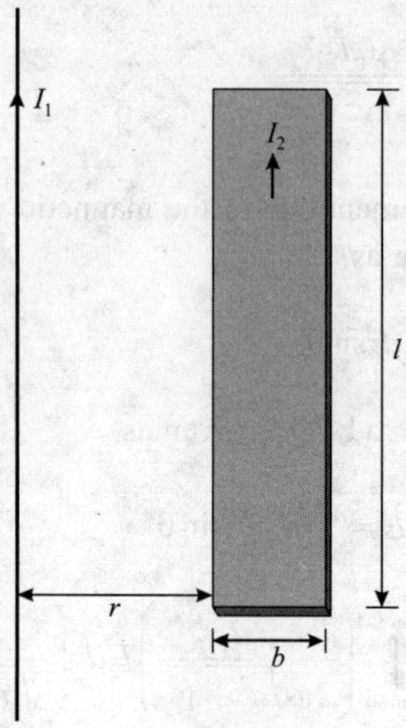

Figure 4.117

Solution

We consider an elemental strip of width dx in the strip at a distance x from the wire as shown in figure-4.118. The current in the elemental strip is given as

$$dI = \frac{I_2}{b}dx$$

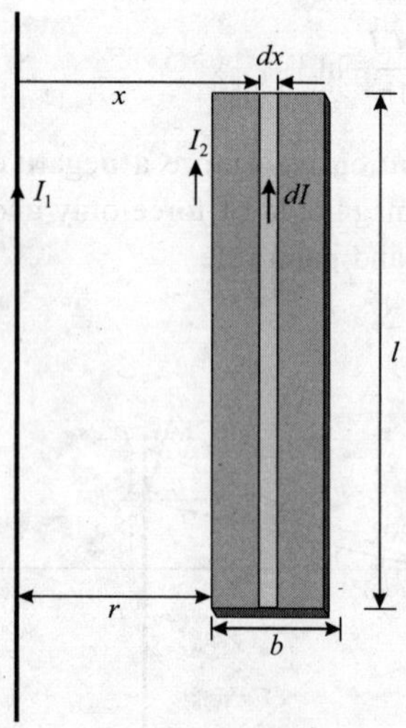

Figure 4.118

The force between I, and dI is given as

$$dF = \frac{\mu_0 I dI l}{2\pi x}$$

Total force on the strip can be calculated by integrating the above force within limits from $x = l$ to $x = l + b$ which is given as

$$F = \int dF = \frac{\mu_0 I_1 I_2 l}{2 \times b}\int_r^{r+b}\frac{dx}{x}$$

$$\Rightarrow \qquad F = \frac{\mu_0 I_1 I_2 l}{2\pi b}[\ln x]_r^{r+b}$$

$$\Rightarrow \qquad F = \frac{\mu_0 I_1 I_2 l}{2\pi b}\ln\left(\frac{r+b}{b}\right)$$

 # Illustrative Example 4.33

A copper wire with density ρ with cross-sectional area S bent to make three sides of a square frame which can turn about a horizontal axis OO' as shown in figure-4.119. The wire is located in uniform vertical magnetic field. Find the magnetic induction if on passing a current I through the wire the frame deflects by an angle θ in its equilibrium position.

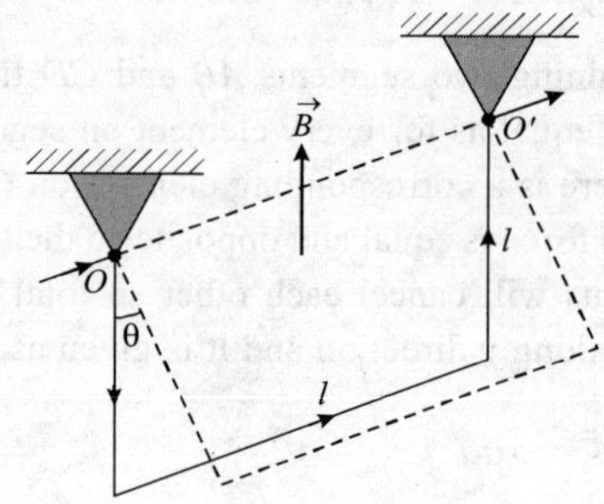

Figure 4.119

Solution

We consider the side of square wire frame is a. The horizontal wire of the frame will experience a rightward force BIl and due to this force it experiences a torque about the axis OO' and the frame will tilt. Torque on frame about OO' is given as

$$\tau = BIa \times a\cos\theta = BIa^2 \cos\theta$$

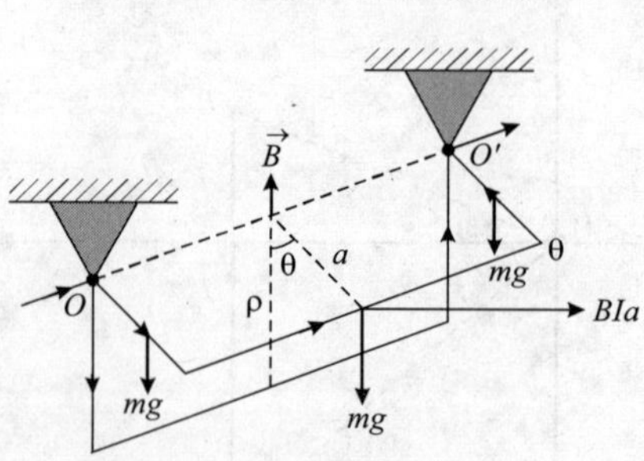

Figure 4.120

This is the deflecting torque and at equilibrium this torque is balanced by the torque on the frame due the weight mg of the three sides of the square acting at centre of the wires as shown in figure-4.120 so at equilibrium balancing of torques gives

$$BIa^2\cos\theta = \frac{Mg}{3} \times a\sin\theta + 2\left(\frac{Mg}{3}\right)\times\left(\frac{a}{2}\right)\sin\theta$$

$$\Rightarrow \quad BIa^2\cos\theta = \frac{2}{3}Mga\sin\theta$$

$$\Rightarrow \quad B = \frac{2Mg}{3Ia}\tan\theta$$

Mass of square wire frame can be written in terms of its density, length and cross sectional area as

$$M = 3aS\rho$$

$$\Rightarrow \quad B = \frac{2(3aS\rho)g}{3Ia}\tan\theta$$

$$\Rightarrow \quad B = \frac{2aS\rho g}{Ia}\tan\theta$$

4.7 Motion of a Charged Particle in Electromagnetic Field

In previous articles we've studied the magnetic force on a moving charge and a current carrying conductor in magnetic field. There are many cases in which both electric and magnetic forces simultaneously act on a moving charge particle. We've discussed that the total electromagnetic force acting on a moving charge remain constant when observed from different frames of reference whereas electric and magnetic forces may be observed differently from different frames as these two forces are different ways to analyze a single force called electromagnetic interaction. Right now we will restrict our mathematical analysis of the two forces in ground frame only.

4.7.1 Undeflected motion of a charge particle in Electric and Magnetic Fields

When a charge particle is moving in a straight line in a gravity free region where both electric and magnetic fields are present then it is possible under two conditions. First condition is if electric and magnetic forces on the charge particle balance each other and act in opposite direction with equal magnitudes and second condition is when both electric and magnetic fields are in same direction and charge is also moving in that direction. In first condition the charge is in uniform motion whereas in second condition due to electric force charge would be accelerating.

Figure-4.121 shows such a situation in which a charge q is moving in a region where mutually perpendicular electric and magnetic fields are present and charge is moving in direction perpendicular to both the fields.

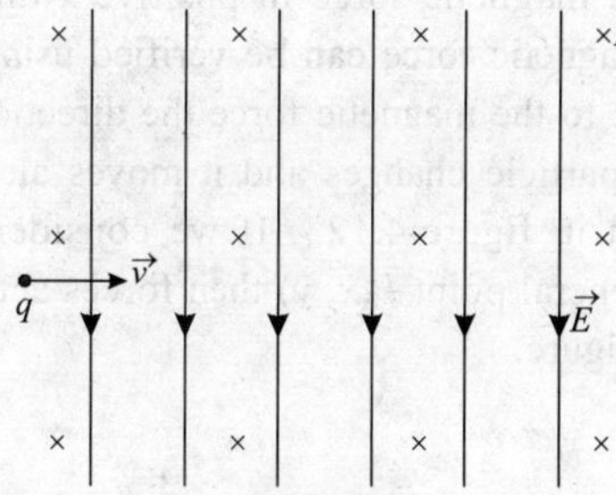

Figure 4.121

In the situation shown in figure-4.121 electric force on the charge will act in downward direction along the direction of electric field and the electric force on it is given as

$$F_e = qE$$

The magnetic force on the charge will act in upward direction which can be given by right hand palm rule. The magnitude of the magnetic force on the charge particle is given as

$$F_m = qvB$$

If charge is moving undeflected in a straight line then the two forces must balance each other and condition for undeflected motion of particle is given as

$$F_e = F_m$$

$$\Rightarrow \quad qE = qvB$$

$$\Rightarrow \quad v = \frac{E}{B} \qquad \text{... (4.128)}$$

4.7.2 Cycloidal Motion of a Charge Particle in Electromagnetic Field

Figure-4.122 shows a coordinate system in which an electric field E exist along positive y-direction and a magnetic field of magnetic induction B exist along positive z-direction. At the origin of coordinate system a point charge of mass m and charge q is placed and it is released from rest. We will analyze the motion of this charge under electromagnetic forces acting on it.

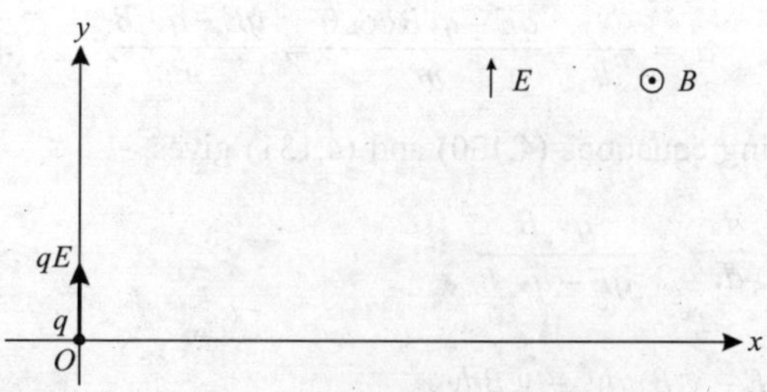

Figure 4.122

Just after release of charge particle it experiences only an electric force qE in positive y-direction. Due to this force as charge starts moving and as it gains some velocity it starts experiencing a magnetic force in positive x-direction. The direction of magnetic force can be verified using right hand palm rule. Due to the magnetic force the direction of motion of the charge particle changes and it moves along a curved path as shown in figure-4.123. If we consider the charge particle at a general point $P(x, y)$ then forces acting on it are shown in the figure.

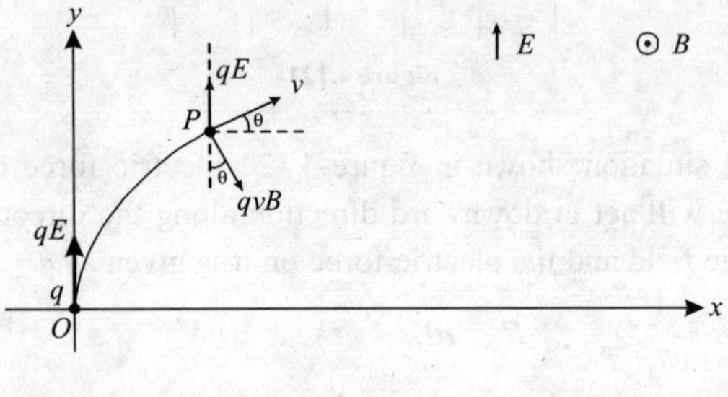

Figure 4.123

The velocity components of the particle at point P are given as

$$v_x = v\cos\theta$$

and $$v_y = v\sin\theta$$

During motion of particle at any point the particle gains velocity only due to the work done by electric force as magnetic force does not do any work and will not cause any gain in speed of particle so at any point $P(x, y)$ the kinetic energy of particle is given as

$$qEy = \frac{1}{2}mv^2 \quad \text{... (4.129)}$$

If a_x and a_y are the accelerations of the particle along x and y-directions then net forces acting on the particle along x and y-directions are given as

$$F_x = ma_x = qvB\sin\theta$$

and $$F_y = ma_y = qE - qvB\cos\theta$$

$$\Rightarrow \quad a_x = \frac{dv_x}{dt} = \frac{qvB\sin\theta}{m} = \frac{qv_yB}{m} \quad \text{... (4.130)}$$

$$\Rightarrow \quad a_y = \frac{dv_y}{dt} = \frac{qE - qvB\cos\theta}{m} = \frac{qE - qv_xB}{m} \quad \text{... (4.131)}$$

Dividing equations-(4.130) and (4.131) gives

$$\frac{dv_x}{dv_y} = \frac{qv_yB}{qE - qv_xB}$$

$$\Rightarrow \quad (E - v_xB)\, dv_x = v_yB dv_y$$

Integrating the above expression within limits from origin of coordinate system to point P gives

$$\int_0^{v_x}(E - v_xB)dv_x = B\int_0^{v_y} v_y dv_y$$

$$\Rightarrow \quad Ev_x - \frac{1}{2}Bv_x^2 = \frac{1}{2}Bv_y^2$$

$$\Rightarrow \quad Ev_x = \frac{1}{2}Bv^2 \quad (\text{As } v^2 = v_x^2 + v_y^2) \text{... (4.132)}$$

Above equation-(4.131) relates the net velocity of particle with its x-component. If we substitute the value of v_x from equation-(4.130) to equation-(4.129) we get

$$\frac{d}{dt}\left(\frac{E}{B} - \frac{m}{qB}\frac{dv_y}{dt}\right) = \frac{qv_yB}{m}$$

$$\Rightarrow \quad \frac{d^2v_y}{dt^2} + \left(\frac{qB}{m}\right)^2 v_y = 0 \quad \text{... (4.133)}$$

The expression in equation-(4.133) is the basic differential equation of SHM in v_y which indicates that the velocity component of particle in y-direction is executing SHM hence its y-coordinate will also execute SHM so the motion of particle will be oscillating in y-direction and progressive in x-direction as shown in figure-4.124. Even the x-direction motion of particle is also oscillating with moving mean position which can be verified by combining equations-(4.130) and (4.131) by eliminating v_y. This trajectory of particle in xy plane comes out to be cycloidal path which is similar to the path traced by a particle on rim of body in pure rolling on a surface. In-depth analysis of cycloidal motion is not in our scope so we will restrict our analysis upto the motion of charge particle under electromagnetic fields. Using equation-(4.132) and previous relations in the given parameters the time of periodic motion, oscillation amplitude (maximum height along y-direction), range in x-direction and other parameters can be calculated.

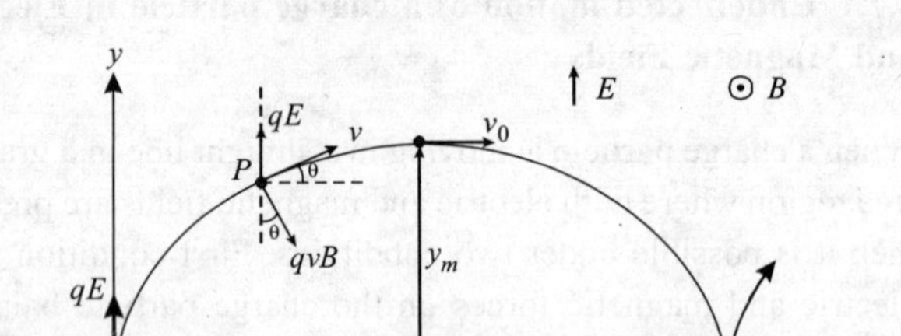

Figure 4.124

In y-direction motion of the particle, mean position is at a height where the net force on particle in y-direction becomes zero which happens at $y = y_m/2$ which would be the amplitude of oscillations of particle in y-direction. At the topmost point of the trajectory if v_0 is the velocity of the particle then it is given by equation-(4.129) as

$$qEy_m = \frac{1}{2}mv_0^2 \quad \text{... (4.134)}$$

At the topmost point as $v_x = 0$, at this point net downward force on particle must be equal to the net upward force when the particle was at origin so we have

$$qE = qv_0B - qE$$

$$\Rightarrow \quad v_0 = \frac{2E}{B} \quad \text{... (4.135)}$$

From equation-(4.134) and (4.135) we get

$$qEy_m = \frac{1}{2}\text{m}\left(\frac{2E}{B}\right)^2$$

$$\Rightarrow \quad y_m = \frac{2mE}{qB} \quad \text{... (4.136)}$$

Illustrative Example 4.34

A proton beam is fired in space where it passes without deviation through the region where there are uniform transverse mutually perpendicular electric and magnetic fields exist with electric field strength E and magnetic induction B. The beam strikes a fixed solid nonmetallic target. Find the force exerted by the beam on the target if the beam current is i. Take mass of proton m_p.

Solution

As the proton beam passes without deviation, so we use

$$evB = eE$$

$$\Rightarrow \quad v = \frac{E}{B}$$

Number of protons striking the target per second is given by using beam current as

$$n = \frac{i}{e}$$

Total mass of protons striking the target per second are

$$m = m_p \times \frac{i}{e}$$

Net force on the target is the total momentum imparted to the target per second which is given as

$$F = mv$$

$$\Rightarrow \quad F = \frac{m_p iE}{eB}$$

Illustrative Example 4.35

A particle of mass 1×10^{-26} kg and charge $+1.6 \times 10^{-19}$ C travelling with a velocity 1.28×10^6 m/s along positive x-direction in a region where uniform electric field E and a uniform magnetic field of induction B are present such that $E_x = E_y = 0$ and $E_z = 102.4$ kV/m and $B_x = B_z = 0$ and $B_y = 8 \times 10^{-2}$ T. The particle enters in this region at the origin of coordinate system at time $t = 0$. Determine the location x, y and z coordinates of the particle at $t = 5 \times 10^{-6}$ s. If only the electric field is switched off at this instant, what will be the position of the particle at $t = 7.45 \times 10^{-6}$ s?

Solution

The Electric force on the charge particle is given as

$$F_e = qE_z = (1.6 \times 10^{-19})\,(102.4 \times 10^3)\text{ N}$$

$$\Rightarrow \quad F_e = 163.84 \times 10^{-16}\text{ N}$$

Above electric force acts on the particle along negative z-direction.

The Magnetic force on the charge particle is given as

$$F_m = q\,v\,B$$

$$\Rightarrow \quad F_m = (1.6 \times 10^{-19})\,(1.28 \times 10^6)\,(8 \times 10^{-12})\text{ N}$$

$$\Rightarrow \quad F_m = 163.84 \times 10^{-16}\text{ N}$$

Above magnetic force acts on the particle along positive z-direction. Above two forces are exactly equal and opposite so the charge particle will go undeflected in the space along x-direction.

(a) At time $t = 5 \times 10^{-6}$ second, the distance x travelled by the particle is given as

$$x = v\,t = (1.28 \times 10^6)\,(5 \times 10^{-6}) = 6.4\text{ m}$$

Thus coordinates of the particle are given as (6.4, 0, 0).

(b) When the electric field is switched off, there will be a force 163.84×10^{-16} along $+z$-axis acting on the particle. The particle moves in uniform magnetic field and describes a circular path in xz plane as shown in figure-4.125. The radius of the circular trajectory of particle is given as

$$r = \frac{mv}{Bq}$$

$$\Rightarrow \quad r = \frac{(1\times10^{-26})(1.28\times10^6)}{(8\times10^{-2})(1.6\times10^{-19})} = 1\text{ m}$$

The time period t of revolution of particle due to magnetic field is given as

$$t = \frac{2\pi r}{v} = \frac{2\times3.14\times1}{1.28\times10^6} = 4.9 \times 10^{-6}\text{ s}$$

The time during which the magnetic field acts

$$t_1 = 7.45 \times 10^{-6} - 5 \times 10^{-6} = 2.45 \times 10^{-6}\text{ s}$$

As the time period is 4.9×10^{-6} s and the magnetic field acts only for a time 2.45×10^{-6} s which is half the time period so the particle covers a semicircle as shown in figure and displaces by 2 m along z-direction. Thus final coordinates of particle are (6.4 m, 0, 2 m).

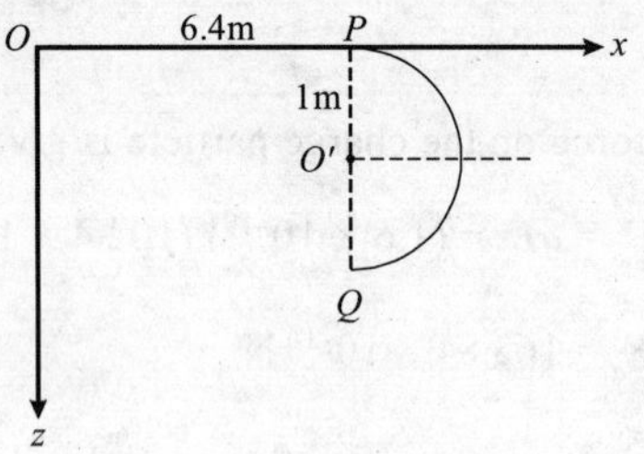

Figure 4.125

Illustrative Example 4.36

Uniform electric and magnetic fields with strength E and induction B respectively are directed along y-axis as shown in figure-126. A particle with specific charge q/m leaves the origin O in the direction of x-axis with an initial non-relativistic velocity v_0. Find

(a) The coordinate y_n of the particle when it crosses the y-axis for the nth time

(b) The angle α between the particles velocity vector and y-axis at that moment.

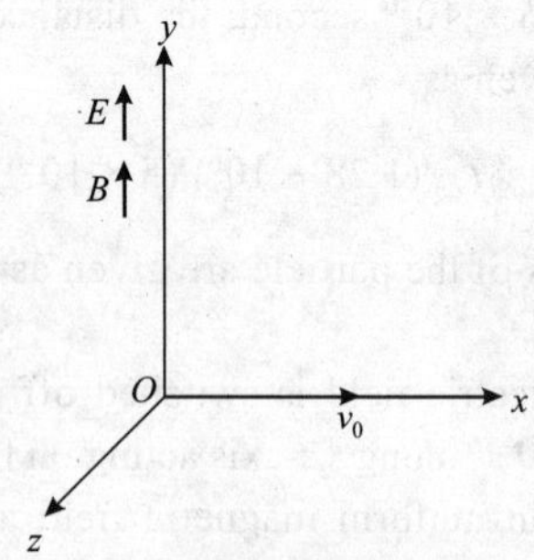

Figure 4.126

Solution

The resulting motion of the particle is helical with increasing pitch due to the electric field along y-direction and after every revolution the helical trajectory will be touching the y-axis when the particle crosses it.

(a) There will be an acceleration a_y on the particle due to electric force which acts along positive y-direction which is given as

$$a_y = \frac{qE}{m}$$

If the particle crosses y-axis n^{th} time after t second then we use

$$y_n = \frac{qE}{2m}t^2 \qquad \dots (4.137)$$

If n be the number of revolutions, then we have

$$t = n \times T = \frac{2\pi mn}{qB} \qquad \dots (4.138)$$

From equation-(4.137) and (4.138), we have

$$y_n = \frac{qE}{2m}\times\left(\frac{2\pi mn}{qB}\right)^2 = \frac{2\pi^2 mn^2 E}{qB^2}$$

(b) In y-direction the velocity of the particle is only due to electric field which is given as

$$v_y = a_y \times t$$

$$\Rightarrow \quad v_y = \left(\frac{qE}{m}\right)\times\left(\frac{2\pi mn}{qB}\right) = \frac{2\pi nE}{B}$$

As along xz plane the particle velocity component will remain constant at v_0, the angle which the velocity vector makes with y-axis is given as

$$\tan\alpha = \frac{v_0}{v_y} = \frac{v_0 B}{2\pi nE}$$

$$\Rightarrow \quad \alpha = \tan^{-1}\left(\frac{v_0 B}{2\pi nE}\right)$$

Illustrative Example 4.37

an electron beam passes through a magnetic field of magnetic induction 2×10^{-3} T and an electric field of strength 3.4×10^4 V/m both acting simultaneously in mutually perpendicular directions. If the path of electrons remains undeviated, calculate the speed of the electrons. If the electric field is removed, what will be the radius of curvature of the trajectory of the electron path after 2 s?

Solution

If motion of electron is undeviated then the magnetic and electric force must be balancing each other on electron so we have

$$qE = qvB$$

$$\Rightarrow \quad v = \frac{E}{B} = \frac{3.4\times10^4}{2\times10^{-3}} = 1.7 \times 10^7 \text{ m/s}$$

When the electric field is removed, then only under magnetic field acting in perpendicular direction motion of electron will be along a circular path of which the radius is given as

$$r = \frac{mv}{Be}$$

$$\Rightarrow \quad r = \frac{9\times10^{-31}\times(1.7\times10^7)}{(2\times10^{-3})\times(1.6\times10^{-19})}$$

$$\Rightarrow \quad r = 4.78 \times 10^{-2} \text{ m}$$

Illustrative Example 4.38

There is a constant homogeneous electric field of 100 V/m within the region $x = 0$ and $x = 0.167$ m pointing along positive x-direction. There is a constant homogeneous magnetic field B within the region $x = 0.167$ m and $x = 0.334$ m along the positive z-direction. A proton at rest at the origin ($x = 0$, $y = 0$) is released. Find the minimum strength of the magnetic field B, so that the proton is detected again at point $x = 0$, $y = 0.167$ m. Take mass of the proton 1.67×10^{-27} kg.

Solution

Figure-4.127 shows the resulting motion of the particle in the region where electric and magnetic fields are present as described in the question.

First the proton is accelerated in the electric field. Then it enters in magnetic field and describes a circular path of which radius is given as

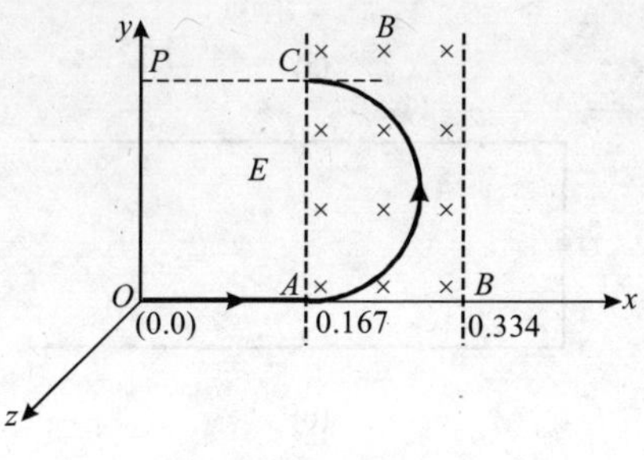

Figure 4.127

$$r = \frac{mv}{qB} \quad \text{... (4.139)}$$

After following a semicircular path it leaves the magnetic field in negative direction. Its motion is retarded in electric field. Finally it strikes y-axis at the same distance 0.167 m. Thus the radius of the circular path must be half of 0.167 m. Using work energy theorem the velocity of the particle when it enters the magnetic field is given as

$$\frac{1}{2}mv^2 = qE\,(0.167) \quad \text{... (4.140)}$$

From equations-(4.139) and (4.140) we have

$$B = \frac{m}{e(0.167/2)} \times \sqrt{\frac{2eE}{m}(0.167)}$$

$$\Rightarrow \quad B = 2\sqrt{\left(\frac{2m}{e} \times \frac{E}{0.167}\right)}$$

$$\Rightarrow \quad B = 2\sqrt{\left[\frac{2(1.67\times10^{-27})(100)}{(1.6\times10^{-19})(0.167)}\right]}$$

$$\Rightarrow \quad B = \frac{10^{-2}}{\sqrt{2}} = 7.07 \times 10^{-3} \text{ T}$$

Web Reference at www.physicsgalaxy.com

Age Group - Grade 11 & 12 | Age 17-19 Years
Section - Magnetic Effects
Topic - Electromagnetic Force
Module Number - 14 to 23

Practice Exercise 4.4

(i) Figure-4.128 shows a wire AB of mass m placed on a rough inclined plane of inclination α and static friction coefficient μ. The wire carries a current I. Find the minimum magnitude of magnetic induction required to slide the wire up the inclined plane if direction of magnetic induction is normal to plane as shown in figure.

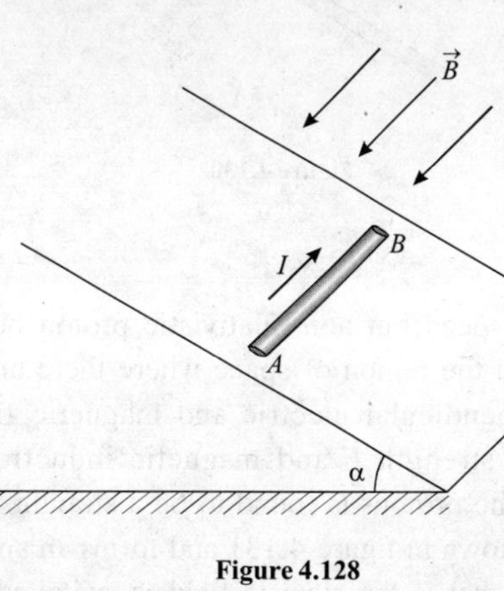

Figure 4.128

$$\left[\frac{mg(\sin\alpha + \mu\cos\alpha)}{Il}\right]$$

(ii) A wire of length 60 cm and mass 16 g is suspended by a pair of flexible supporting springs in a magnetic field of induction 0.60 T. What are the magnitude and direction of the current in the wire so that the supporting springs remain unstretched ?

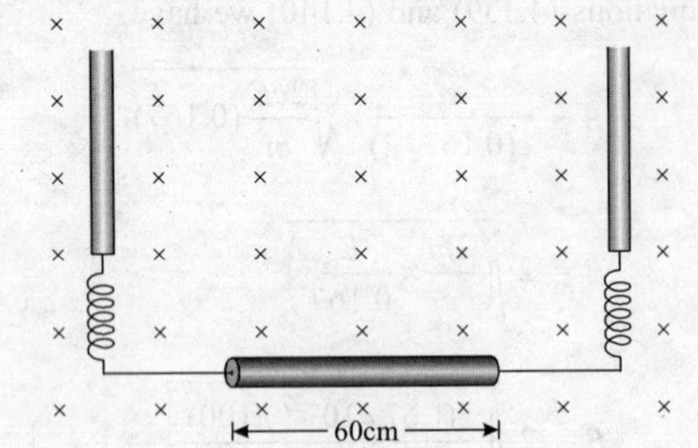

Figure 4.129

[0.41 A, left to right]

(iii) Two long parallel wires carry currents of equal magnitude but in opposite direction, these wires are suspended from ceiling by four strings of same length L as shown in figure-4.130. The mass per unit length of the wires is λ. Determine the value of the diverging angle θ assuming it to be small.

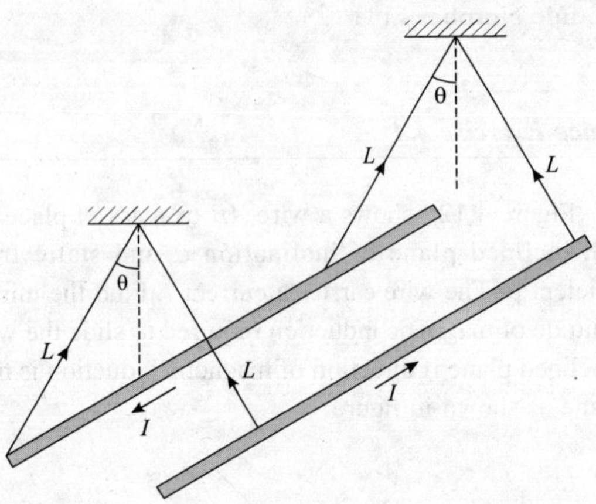

Figure 4.130

[$\sqrt{\mu_0 I^2 / 4\pi\lambda g l}$]

(iv) A high speed but non-relativistic proton beam move rectilinearly in the region of space where there are uniform mutually perpendicular electric and magnetic fields with electric field strength E and magnetic induction B. The trajectory of the protons is found to be a straight line in the XY plane as shown in figure-4.131 and forms an angle ϕ with X-axis. Show that if the electric field is switched off at an instant the protons will follow helical trajectory and find the pitch of the helical trajectory.

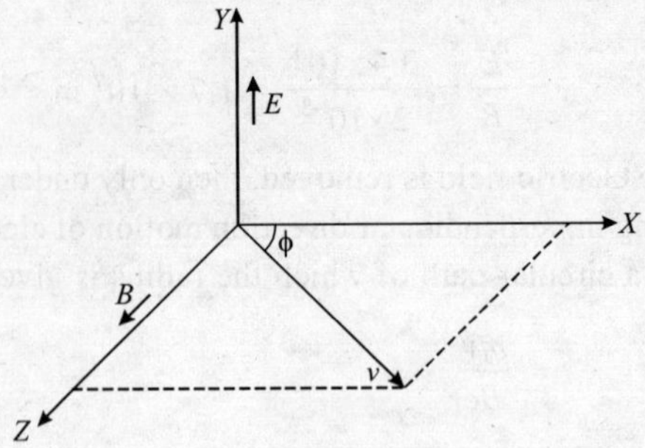

Figure 4.131

[$\frac{2\pi mE}{qB^2}\tan\phi$]

(v) A loop of flexible conducting wire of length 0.5 m lies in a magnetic field of 1.0 T perpendicular to the plane of the loop. Show that when a current is passed through the loop, it opens into a circle. Also calculate the tension developed in the wire if the current is of 1.57 A.

[0.125 N]

(vi) Find the magnitude and direction of a force acting per unit length of a wire, carrying a current i = 8.0 A, at a point O, if the wire is bent as shown in figures-4.132(a) and (b) as shown in figure-4.132. In figure-(a) wire is bent as semicircular loop of radius R = 10 cm and in figure-4.132(b) wire is bent as U-shaped with the straight segments very long with their separation equal to l = 20 cm.

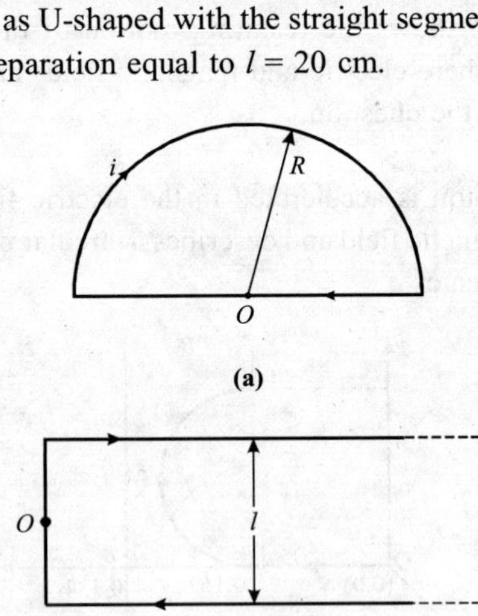

Figure 4.132

[(a) 2×10^{-4} N/m (b) 1280×10^{-7} N/m]

(vii) A square cardboard of side l and mass m is suspended from a horizontal axis XY as shown in figure-4.133. A single wire is wound along the periphery of board and carrying a clockwise current I. At t = 0, a vertical downward magnetic field of induction B is switched on. Find the minimum magnitude of B so that the board will be able to rotate up to horizontal level.

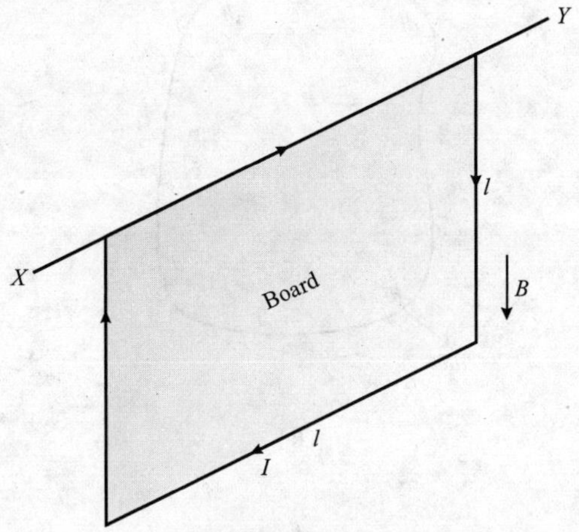

Figure 4.133

$[\frac{mg}{2Il}]$

(viii) Figure-4.134 shows a horizontal wire MN of length l and mass m is placed in a magnetic field B. The ends of wire are bent and dipped in two bowls containing Hg which are connected to an external circuit as shown. If key is pressed for a short time δt due to which a charge q suddenly flows in the circuit. Find the maximum height above initial level the wire MN, it will jump.

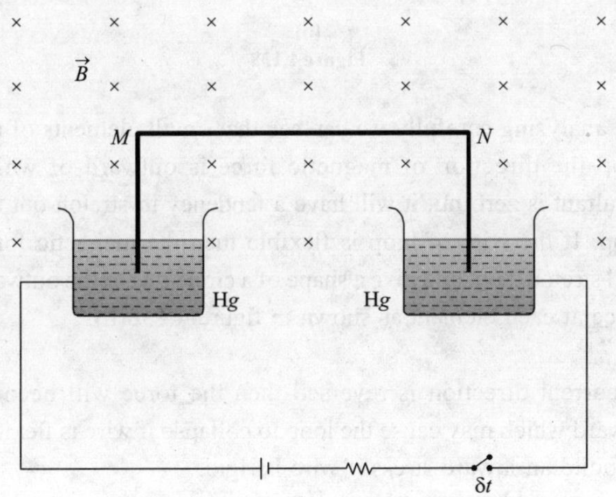

Figure 4.134

$[\frac{B^2q^2l^2}{2m^2g}]$

(ix) A straight segment OC of length L of a circuit carrying a current I is placed along the X-axis as shown in figure-4.135. Two infinitely long straight wires A and B, each extending from $Z = -\infty$ to $+\infty$, are fixed at $y = -a$ and $y = +a$ respectively as shown in figure-4.135. If the wires A and B each carry same current I into the plane of the paper, obtain the expression for the force acting on the segment OC. What will be the force on OC if the current in the wire B is reversed.

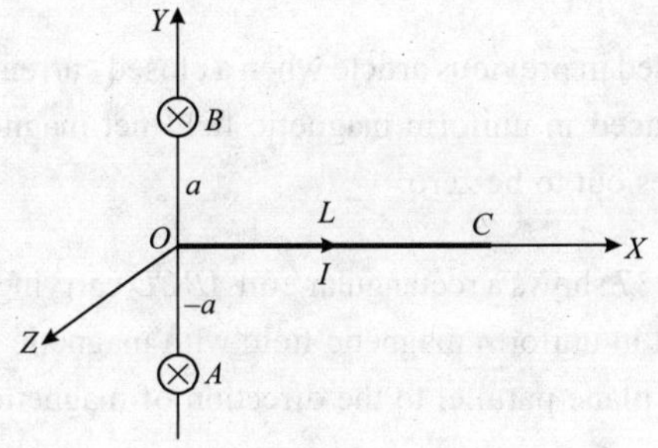

Figure 4.135

$[\frac{\mu_0 I^2}{2\pi}\ln\left(\frac{L^2+a^2}{a^2}\right), 0]$

(x) A positively charged particle having charge $q_1 = 1$ C and mass $m_1 = 40$ g, is revolving along a circle of radius $R = 40$ cm with velocity $v_1 = 5$ m/s in a uniform magnetic field with centre of circle at origin O of a three dimensional system. At $t = 0$, the particle was at (0, 0.4 m 0) and velocity was directed along positive X-direction. Another particle having charge $q_2 = 1$ C and mass $m_2 = 10$ g moving uniformly parallel to Z-direction with velocity $v_2 = (40/\pi)$ m/s collides with revolving particle at $t = 0$ and gets stuck to it. Neglecting gravitational force and coulomb force, calculate x, y and z coordinates of the combined particle at $t = \pi/40$ s.

[(0.2 m, 0.2 m, 0.2 m)]

(xi) From the surface of a round wire of radius a carrying a direct current i an electron is projected with a velocity v_0 perpendicular to the surface along radial direction. Find what will be the maximum distance of the electron from the axis of the wire before it turns back due to the magnetic force on the charge particle by the current flowing in the wire.

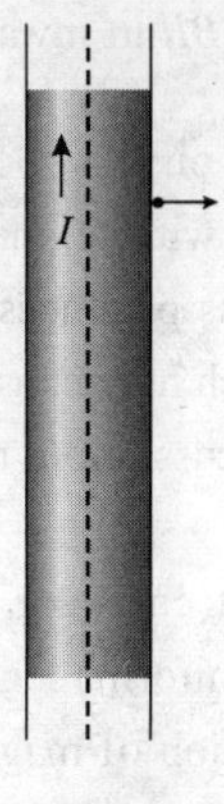

Figure 4.136

$[ae^{\frac{2\pi m v_0}{\mu_0 i q}}]$

4.8 A Closed Current Carrying Coil placed in Magnetic Field

As discussed in previous article when a closed current carrying loop is placed in uniform magnetic field net magnetic force on it comes out to be zero.

Figure-4.137 shows a rectangular coil *ABCD* carrying a current *I* is placed in uniform magnetic field with magnetic induction *B* with its plane parallel to the direction of magnetic field.

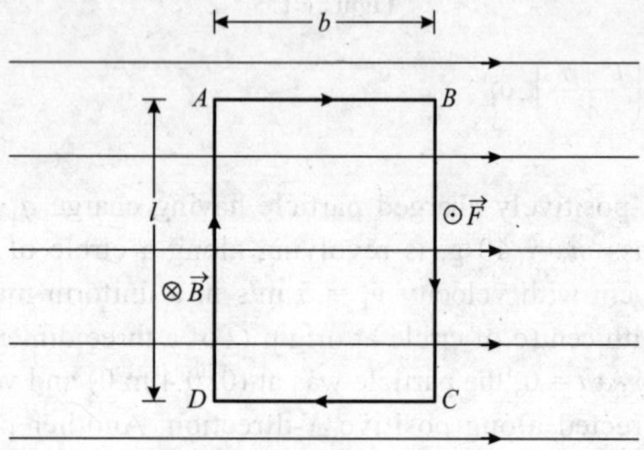

Area of coil $A = lb$

Figure 4.137

In this case if we analyze the directions of magnetic forces on different segments of the coil by using right hand palm rule then we find that

The force on *AB* is $F_{AB} = 0$

The force on *BC* is $F_{BC} = BIl$ in outward direction

The force on *CD* is $F_{CD} = 0$

The force on *DA* is $F_{DA} = BIl$ in inward direction

Thus total magnetic force on this loop is zero but the equal and opposite forces on the wire segments *BC* and *DA* on loop at different lines of actions produces a couple and coil will experience the torque which may cause it to rotate if it is free. In next article we will discuss about this torque in detail.

Consider another current carrying closed loop shown in figure-4.138(a) placed in uniform magnetic field with its plane perpendicular to the direction of magnetic field.

In this situation if we consider a small element on the loop as shown then by right hand palm rule the direction of magnetic force on this element is as shown in figure.

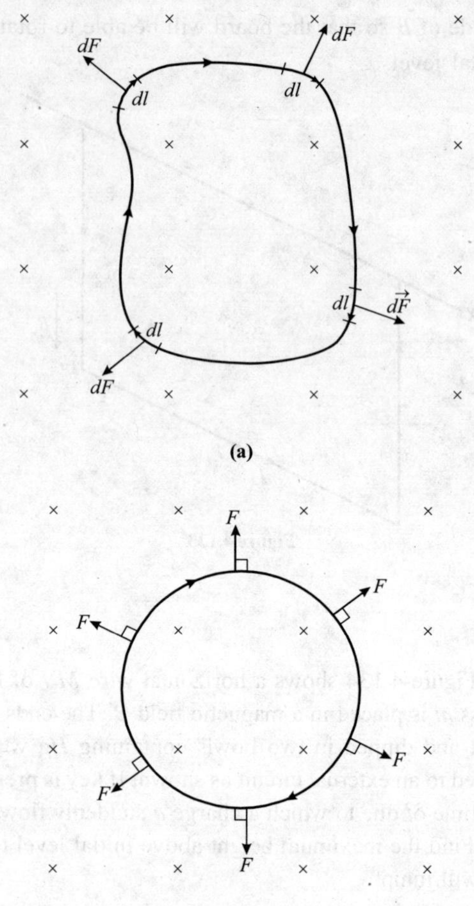

Figure 4.138

On analyzing carefully we can see that on all elements of the loop the direction of magnetic force is outward of which resultant is zero but it will have a tendency to stretch out the loop. If the wire of loop is flexible then the magnetic force will stretch it out and give a shape of a circle due to the outward force at each element as shown in figure-4.138(b).

If current direction is reversed then the force will become inward which may cause the loop to collapse if wire is flexible or build an inward stress if wire is rigid.

Above cases we analyzed for uniform magnetic field but if the closed current carrying loop is placed in a non uniform magnetic field then magnetic force on it may be non zero as at different locations of coil elements the magnetic induction magnitude can be different in non uniform magnetic field which will exert different forces on different elements of the coil which may not cancel each other.

We will see illustrations based on such situations.

4.8.1 Torque due to Magnetic Forces on a Current Carrying Loop in Magnetic Field

Consider the situation shown in figure-4.137 where we can see that the magnetic forces on wire segments *AB* and *CD* is zero as wires are parallel to magnetic induction direction and the forces on segments *BC* and *DA* are equal and in opposite direction which produce a couple. We've already studied in mechanics that torque due to couple forces is given by the product of force magnitude with the separation between lines of action of forces and this torque is independent of the location of axis of rotation. Here it is given as

$$\tau = BIl \times b = BIlb = BIA \quad \dots (4.141)$$

If number of turns in coil are *N* then due to *N* wire segments the total torque on the coil will be given as

$$\tau = BIA \times N = BINA \quad \dots (4.142)$$

Equation-(4.142) gives the net torque acting on the coil if coil is placed with its plane perpendicular to the magnetic induction direction. Consider the situation shown in figure-5.139 in which the coil is placed in such a way that its area vector is oriented at an angle θ to the direction of magnetic field or the plane of coil makes an angle (90° – θ) to the magnetic field.

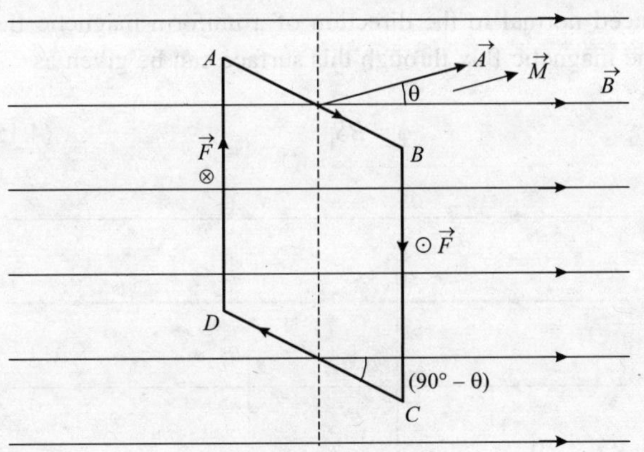

Figure 4.139

In above figure the force on wire segments *AB* and *CD* are opposite to each other along the same lines of actions so will cancel each other and the forces on wire segments *BC* and *DA* are same as before but the separation between their lines of action is now *b* sinθ as shown so the torque on coil is now given as

$$\tau = Bil \times b \sin\theta \times N$$

$$\Rightarrow \quad \tau = BINA \sin\theta \quad \dots (4.143)$$

In above expression the term *INA* is referred as magnetic moment of the coil which is defined as the product of current and area enclosed by all the turns of the coil. Magnetic moment of a current carrying coil is a vector quantity having direction along the area vector of the coil, given as

$$\vec{M} = NI\vec{A} \quad \dots (4.144)$$

The direction of area vector of the coil is given by right hand thumb rule for the direction of current in the coil as shown in figure-4.140

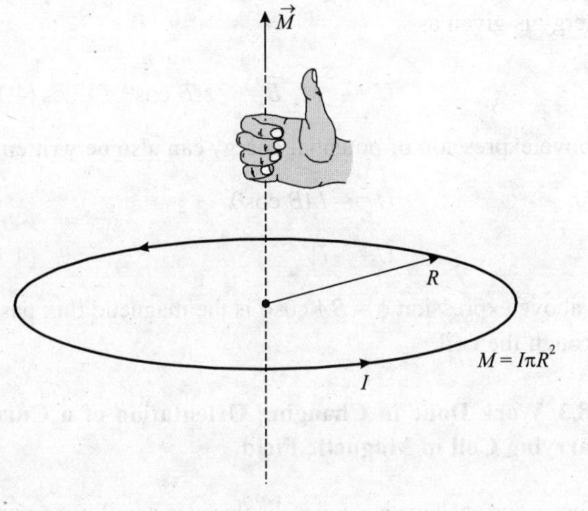

Figure 4.140

Magnetic moment of a current carrying coil is synonymous to the magnetic dipole moment of a small magnetic dipole about which we will discuss in the section of classical magnetism later in this chapter.

Using magnetic moment of the coil, equation-(4.143) can be rewritten as

$$\tau = MB \sin\theta \quad \dots (4.145)$$

Using the direction of torque, vectorially expression of torque can be given as

$$\vec{\tau} = \vec{M} \times \vec{B} \quad \dots (4.146)$$

4.8.2 Interaction Energy of a Current Carrying Loop in Magnetic Field

In classical magnetism we will discuss in detail about how a current carrying coil in magnetic field can be considered like a magnetic dipole but as of now we will use this fact for other analysis.

We will also study that a magnetic dipole placed in magnetic field acts similar to an electric dipole placed in electric field and we've already discussed in the chapter of electrostatics that the interaction potential energy of an electric dipole with dipole moment p placed in an external electric field E is given as

$$U = -\vec{p} \cdot \vec{E} = -pE\cos\theta \quad \text{... (4.147)}$$

Similar to this situation for a magnetic dipole with dipole moment M placed in a magnetic field with magnetic induction B with the angle between magnetic moment and magnetic induction θ as shown in figure-5.139, its interaction potential energy is given as

$$U = -\vec{M} \cdot \vec{B} = -MB\cos\theta \quad \text{... (4.148)}$$

Above expression of potential energy can also be written as

$$U = -IAB\cos\theta$$

$$\Rightarrow \quad U = -I\phi \quad \text{... (4.149)}$$

In above expression $\phi = BA\cos\theta$ is the magnetic flux passing through the coil.

4.8.3 Work Done in Changing Orientation of a Current Carrying Coil in Magnetic Field

When a current carrying coil is displaced in a uniform magnetic field in such a way that its orientation changes with angle between magnetic induction and magnetic moment of coil from q_1 to q_2 then the potential energy of the coil in magnetic field in initial and final state are given as

$$U_i = -MB\cos\theta_1 \quad \text{... (4.150)}$$

and $$U_f = -MB\cos\theta_2 \quad \text{... (4.151)}$$

Work done in changing the orientation of the coil during its displacement is given as

$$W = U_f - U_i$$

$$\Rightarrow \quad W = (-MB\cos\theta_2) - (-MB\cos\theta_1)$$

$$\Rightarrow \quad W = MB(\cos\theta_1 - \cos\theta_2) \quad \text{... (4.152)}$$

To change the orientation of coil externally we need to apply a torque against the magnetic torque of equal magnitude thus work done in changing the orientation in above situation can also be given as

$$W = \int dW = \int \tau d\theta$$

$$\Rightarrow \quad W = \int_{\theta_1}^{\theta_2} MB\sin\theta . d\theta$$

$$\Rightarrow \quad W = MB\,[-\cos\theta]_{\theta_1}^{\theta_2}$$

$$\Rightarrow \quad W = MB(\cos\theta_1 - \cos\theta_2) \quad \text{... (4.153)}$$

Above equation-(4.153) is same as equation-(4.152) we obtained by using difference of interaction energies of coil in final and initial states.

Above expression of work can be rewritten as

$$W = IAB(\cos\theta_1 - \cos\theta_2)$$

$$\Rightarrow \quad W = I(\phi_{initial} - \phi_{final})$$

$$\Rightarrow \quad W = -I(\phi_{final} - \phi_{initial})$$

$$\Rightarrow \quad W = -I\Delta\phi \quad \text{... (4.154)}$$

4.8.4 Magnetic Flux through a surface in Magnetic Field

In the region of magnetic field we can calculate the magnetic flux in the same way we did in electric field as magnetic induction is measured as magnetic flux density in a region similar to electric field.

Figure-4.141 shows a rectangular surface $ABCD$ of area S placed normal to the direction of a uniform magnetic field. The magnetic flux through this surface can be given as

$$\phi = BS \quad \text{... (4.155)}$$

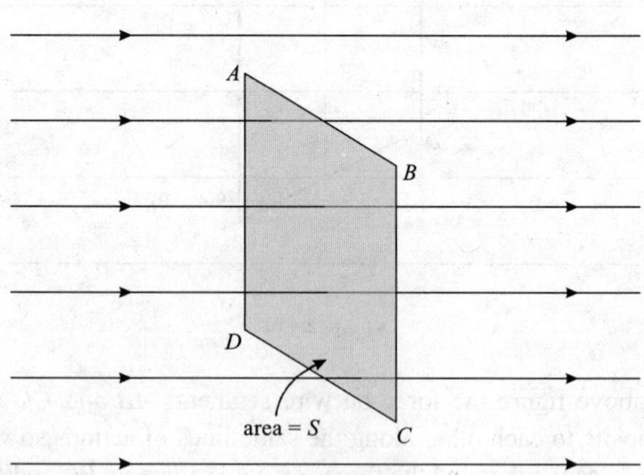

Figure 4.141

If the area is inclined to magnetic induction such that its area vector makes an angle θ with the direction of magnetic field or its plane makes an angle $(90° - \theta)$ with the magnetic field as shown in figure-4.142 then magnetic flux thorough this area will be same which passes through its normal component $S\cos\theta$ as other component of area $S\sin\theta$ is parallel to the magnetic field and no flux will pass through it as shown.

Thus magnetic flux through this surface is given as

$$\phi = BS\cos\theta \quad \dots (4.156)$$

$$\Rightarrow \quad \phi = \vec{B}\cdot\vec{S} \quad \dots (4.157)$$

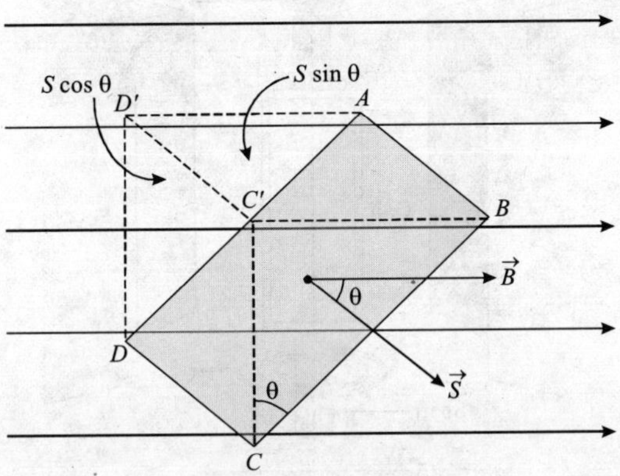

Figure 4.142

Figure-4.143 shows a region with non uniform magnetic induction in which there is a surface M placed in it.

To evaluate the magnetic flux passing through this surface, we consider an elemental area dS in this surface as shown with its area vector normal to the surface area dS at this point.

If $\vec{B}$ is the magnetic induction at the location of this area dS then magnetic flux $d\phi$ through the elemental area dS is given as

$$d\phi = BdS\cos\theta$$

$$\Rightarrow \quad d\phi = \vec{B}\cdot\vec{dS} \quad \dots (4.158)$$

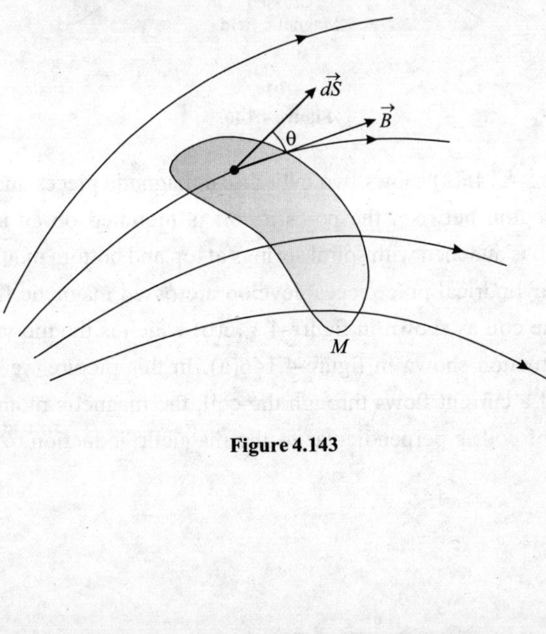

Figure 4.143

Thus total magnetic flux through the surface M is given by integrating the above elemental flux over the complete surface area given as

$$\phi = \int d\phi = \int_M \vec{B}\cdot\vec{dS} \quad \dots (4.159)$$

4.8.5 Stable and Unstable Equilibrium of a Current Carrying Loop in Magnetic Field

Figure-4.144 shows a current carrying rectangular loop placed in a plane perpendicular to the direction of magnetic field. The loop carries a current in clockwise direction due to which the direction vector of its magnetic moment is along the direction of magnetic induction due to which the angle between these two vectors is $\theta = 0$ and thus torque on loop is also $\vec{M}\times\vec{B} = 0$ and with the direction of magnetic forces on the segments of the loop we can see that all forces are acting in the plane of coil so net torque on it is zero and loop is in equilibrium.

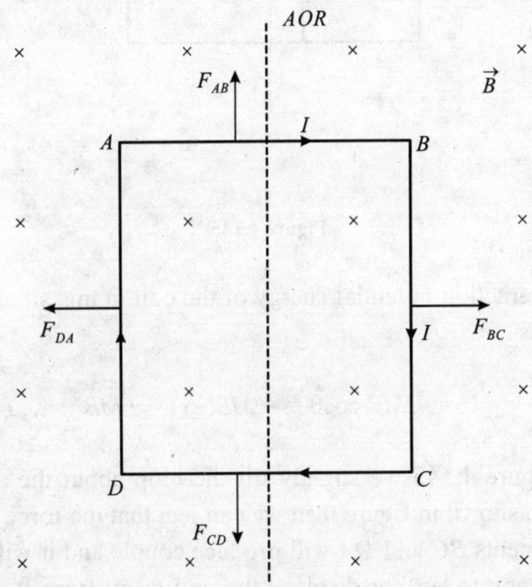

Figure 4.144

. The interaction potential energy of the coil is given as

$$U = -MB\cos\theta = -MB \quad \dots (4.160)$$

If in figure-4.144 we slightly tilt the loop about the axis of rotation shown in figure then we can feel that the force acting on segments BC and DA will produce couple and it will have a tendency to bring back the coil in its initial position thus in this case these forces will develope a restoring torque hence the equilibrium of coil is stable equilibrium.

We can also see from equation-(4.160) that the potential energy of loop in this state is at its minimum value which corresponds to the case of stable equilibrium.

Figure-4.145 shows a similar situation with the current direction in the loop is in anticlockwise direction. In this case the angle between magnetic moment and magnetic induction is $\theta = 180°$ and thus torque on loop is again $\vec{M} \times \vec{B} = 0$ and with the direction of magnetic forces on the segments of the loop we can see that all forces are acting in the plane of coil so net torque on it is zero and loop is in equilibrium.

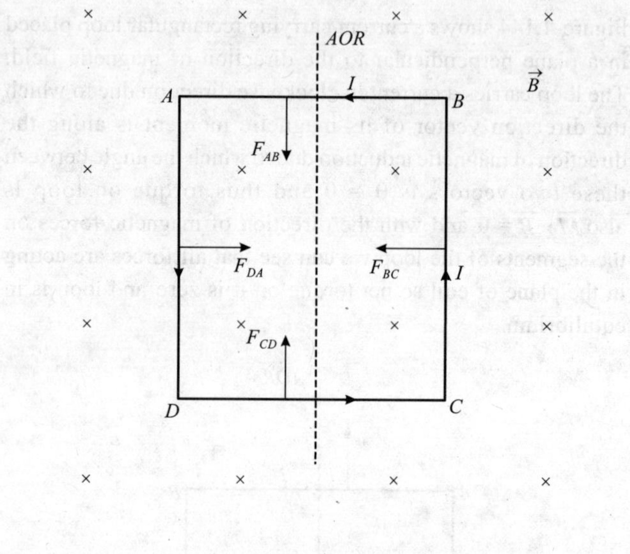

Figure 4.145

The interaction potential energy of the coil in this situation is given as

$$U = -MB\cos\theta = -MB(-1) = +MB \quad \dots (4.161)$$

If in figure-4.145 we slightly tilt the loop about the axis of rotation shown in figure then we can feel that the force acting on segments BC and DA will produce couple and it will have a tendency to further displace the coil away from its initial position thus in this case these forces will develope a torque away from initial position hence the equilibrium of coil is unstable equilibrium.

We can also see from equation-(4.161) that the potential energy of loop in this state is at its maximum value which corresponds to the case of unstable equilibrium.

4.8.6 Moving Coil Galvanometer

We've studied in previous chapter that a galvanometer is used to measure current in electrical circuits. A moving coil galvanometer is a normal deflection type meter we discussed in different experimental setups in previous chapter in which the deflection of needle is directly proportional to the current supplied through it.

In this section we will be discussing the working mechanism of galvanometer.

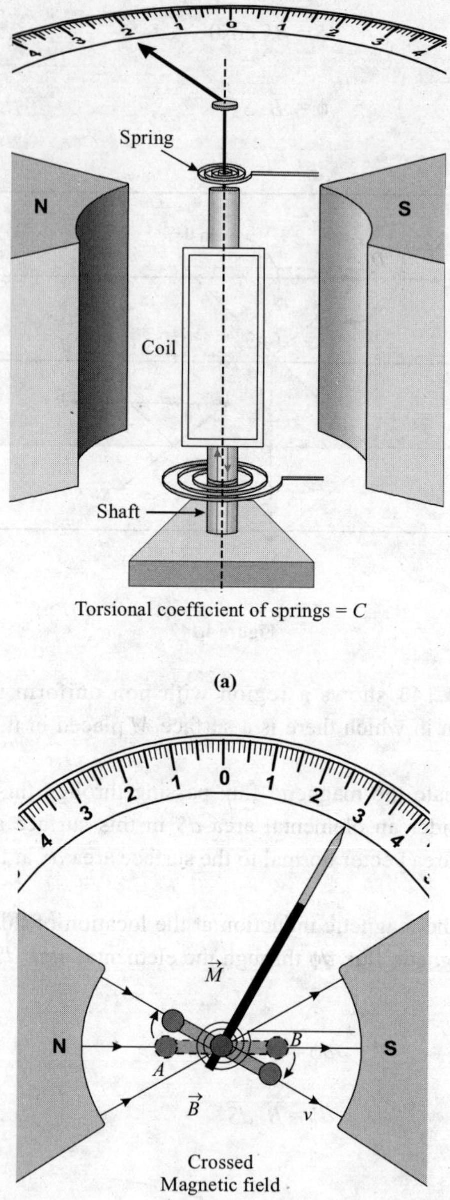

(b)

Figure 4.146

Figure-4.146(a) shows two cylindrical magnetic pieces and in the region between the poles a coil is mounted on an axle which is attached with spiral springs at top and bottom mounts. The cylindrical pole pieces develop a crossed magnetic field on the coil as shown in figure-4.146(b) which is the top view of situation shown in figure-4.146(a). In this picture we can see if a current flows through the coil, the magnetic moment $\vec{M}$ of coil is perpendicular to the magnetic induction $\vec{B}$ at initial position of coil. Due to magnetic torque in clockwise direction the coil rotates and because of crossed magnetic field at all orientations of coil its magnetic moment is always perpendicular to the magnetic induction at that orientation of the coil so the magnetic torque on coil is independent of the orientation angle of the coil and it is given as

$$\vec{\tau} = \vec{M} \times \vec{B}$$

$$\Rightarrow \quad \tau = MB \qquad [\text{As } \theta = 90°]$$

$$\Rightarrow \quad \tau = BINA \qquad \ldots (4.162)$$

Due to magnetic torque when coil rotates, spiral springs also twist which are attached at the top and bottom of the axle on which coil is mounted. These spiral springs exert a restoring torque on the shaft and have a tendency to bring the coil back to initial mean position. When a current flows through the coil, it experiences a magnetic torque given by equation-(4.162) due to which coil rotates and held at some angle where the restoring torque of spiral springs balances the magnetic torque. If overall stiffness coefficient of the spiral springs is C then at the equilibrium position if coil is deflected by an angle θ from initial position then we have

$$BINA = C\theta$$

$$\Rightarrow \quad \theta = \left(\frac{BNA}{C}\right) I \qquad \ldots (4.163)$$

Here we can see that the angle of deflection of coil is directly proportional to the current supplied through the coil. In figure-4.147 we can see if a light weight needle is attached to the axle of the coil then with proper calibration the needle can be used to show the reading of current on a round scale as shown in figure. After proper calibration the whole assembly of magnets, mounts with coil is placed inside a cabinet and from outside only the scale and needle is visible. This is the system we call moving coil galvanometer which is used in our labs for current measurements.

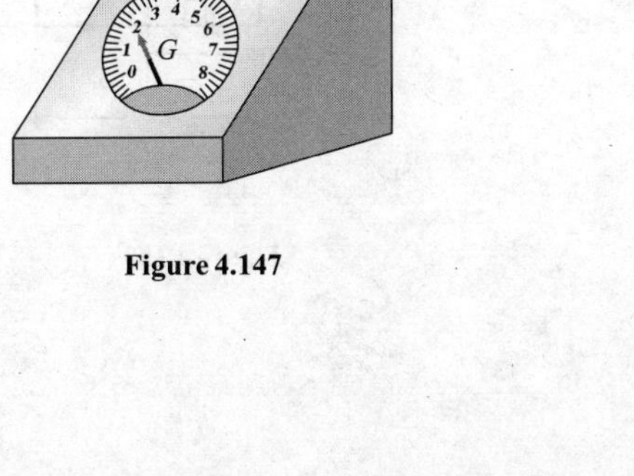

Figure 4.147

In above equation-(4.163) the proportionality constant is replaced by another constant S called '*Sensitivity of Galvanometer*' given as

$$S = \frac{BNA}{C} \qquad \ldots (4.164)$$

$$\Rightarrow \quad \theta = SI \qquad \ldots (4.165)$$

Here sensitivity of galvanometer indicates how sensitive the device is. If S is large then even for small currents flowing in the galvanometer coils deflection will be good enough to measure it and such a galvanometer is able to sense very small amounts of currents significantly and are called highly sensitive.

 # Illustrative Example 4.39

Figure-4.148 shows a coil of area A and N turns with a current I is placed in a uniform magnetic induction B. Find the work required to pull this coil out from magnetic field.

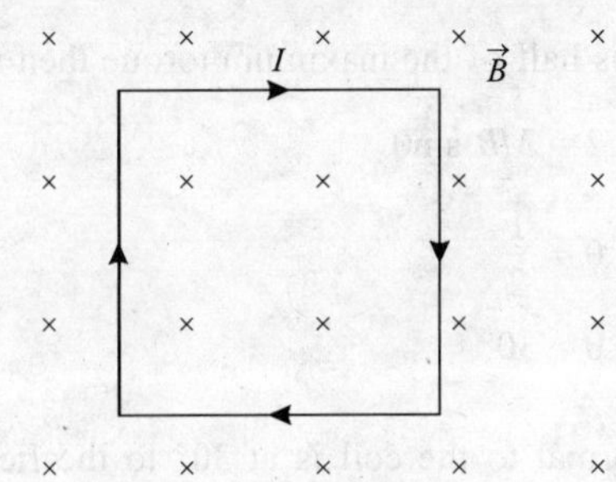

Figure 4.148

Solution

Work done in the process of pulling the coil out of field is given as

$$W = -I\Delta\phi = I(\phi_1 - \phi_2)$$

Initial flux through coil is given as

$$\phi_1 = BAN$$

Final flux through coil is given as

$$\phi_2 = 0$$

Work done $\quad W = I(BAN - 0) = BIAN$

 # Illustrative Example 4.40

A circular coil of wire 8 cm in diameter has 12 turns and carries a current of 5 A. The coil is placed in a field where magnetic induction is 0.6 T.

(a) What is the maximum torque on the coil?

(b) In what position would the torque be one half as great as in (a)?

Solution

(a) The magnetic moment of the coil is given as

$$M = NiA$$

Area of coil is given as

$$A = \pi r^2 = \pi(4 \times 10^{-2})^2$$

$$\Rightarrow \quad M = 12 \times 5 \times \pi \times (4 \times 10^{-2})^2$$

$$\Rightarrow \quad M = 0.302 \text{ Am}^2$$

Maximum torque on coil acts when it is placed in the plane of the magnetic field or when the angle between magnetic moment and magnetic induction is 90°.

$$\tau_{max} = MB = 0.302 \times 0.60 = 0.181 \text{ Nm}$$

(b) If θ is the angle between the area of the coil and the magnetic field direction then torque on coil is given as

$$\tau = MB \sin\theta$$

If this torqu is half of the maximum torque then we have

$$MB/2 = MB \sin\theta$$

$$\Rightarrow \quad \sin\theta = \frac{1}{2}$$

$$\Rightarrow \quad \theta = 30°$$

When the normal to the coil is at 30° to the field then the torque is half of the maximum torque on coil.

Illustrative Example 4.41

A square frame carrying a current I is located in the same plane as a long straight wire carrying a current I_0. The frame side has a length a. The axis of the frame passing through the midpoints of the opposite sides is parallel to the wire and is separated from it by the distance which is η times greater than the side of the frame. Find

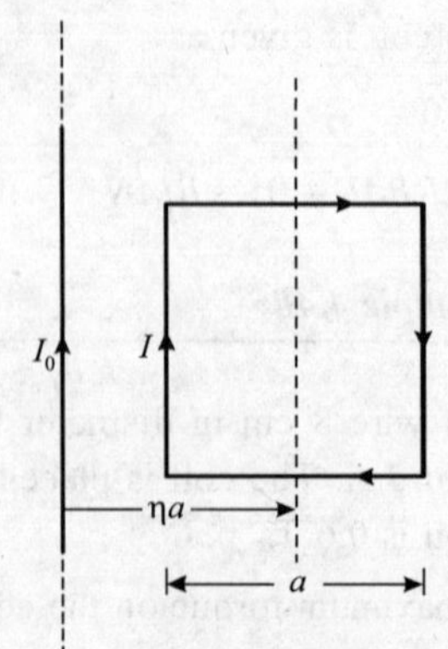

Figure 4.149

(a) Force acting on the frame

(b) The mechanical work to be performed in order to turn the frame through 180° about its axis, with the currents maintained constant.

Solution

(a) Force of attraction between parallel currents is given as

$$F_1 = \frac{\mu_0 I I_0}{2\pi\left(\eta a - \frac{a}{2}\right)} = \frac{\mu_0 I I_0}{\pi(2\eta - 1)a}$$

Similar force of repulsion between antiparallel currents is given as

$$F_2 = \frac{\mu_0 I I_0}{2\pi\left(\eta a + \frac{a}{2}\right)} = \frac{\mu_0 I I_0}{\pi(2\eta + 1)a}$$

Net force of attraction between the square frame and the long straight wire is

$$F = F_1 - F_2$$

$$\Rightarrow \quad F = \frac{\mu_0 I I_0}{\pi(2\eta - 1)a} - \frac{\mu_0 I I_0}{\pi(2\eta + 1)a}$$

$$\Rightarrow \quad F = \frac{2\mu_0 I I_0}{\pi(4\eta^2 - 1)}$$

(b) Work performed in turning the frame through 180° is given as

$$W = -I\Delta\phi = -I(-\phi - \phi) = 2I\phi$$

Where ϕ is the magnetic flux passing through the coil due to the current in the straight wire which is calculated by considering an elemental strip in the coil as shown in figure-4.150.

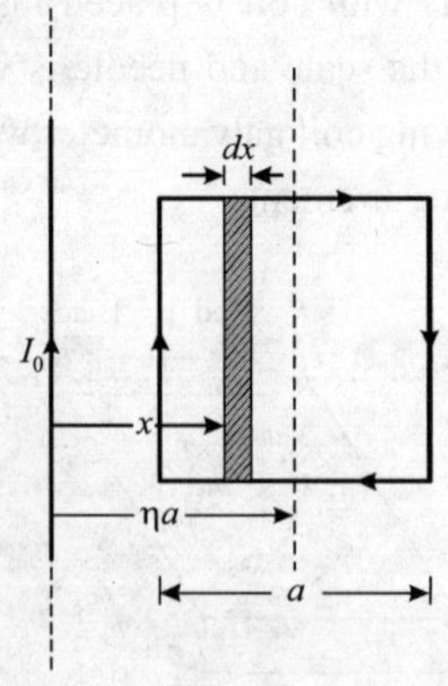

Figure 4.150

The magnetic flux through the elemental strip is given as

$$d\phi = B.dS$$

$$\Rightarrow \quad d\phi = \frac{\mu_0 I_0}{2\pi x}.adx$$

Total magnetic flux through the coil is given as

$$\phi = \int d\phi = \int_{\eta a-\frac{a}{2}}^{\eta a+\frac{a}{2}} \frac{\mu_0 I_0}{2\pi x}.adx$$

$$\Rightarrow \quad \phi = \frac{\mu_0 I_0 a}{2\pi}\int_{\eta a-\frac{a}{2}}^{\eta a+\frac{a}{2}} \frac{dx}{x}$$

$$\Rightarrow \quad \phi = \frac{\mu_0 I_0 a}{2\pi}[\ln x]_{\eta a-\frac{a}{2}}^{\eta a+\frac{a}{2}}$$

$$\Rightarrow \quad \phi = \frac{\mu_0 I_0 a}{2\pi}\left[\ln\left(\eta a+\frac{a}{2}\right)-\ln\left(\eta a-\frac{a}{2}\right)\right]$$

$$\Rightarrow \quad \phi = \frac{\mu_0 I_0 a}{2\pi}\ln\left(\frac{2\eta+1}{2\eta-1}\right)$$

Work done in rotation of coil is given as

$$W = 2I\phi$$

$$\Rightarrow \quad W = \frac{\mu_0 I I_0 a}{\pi}\ln\left(\frac{2\eta+1}{2\eta-1}\right)$$

Illustrative Example 4.42

Figure-4.151 shows a larger horizontal coil of radius R carrying a current I. Another small coil of radius r ($r << R$) carrying a current i & N turns is placed at the centre with its plane at an angle θ from the axis. Find the torque experienced by the smaller coil in this situation.

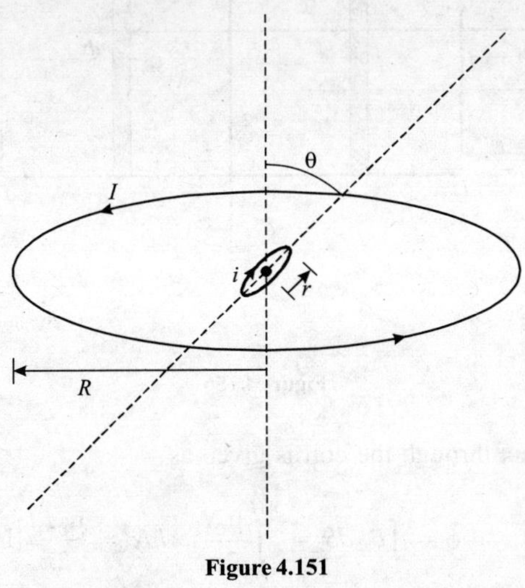

Figure 4.151

Solution

Magnetic moment of smaller coil is given as

$$M = i \times \pi r^2 N = Ni\pi r^2$$

Magnetic induction due to large coil at its centre is given as

$$B = \frac{\mu_0 I}{2R}$$

Angle between magnetic induction at center of large coil and magnetic moment of smaller coil is $\frac{\pi}{2}+\theta$ as shown in figure-4.152

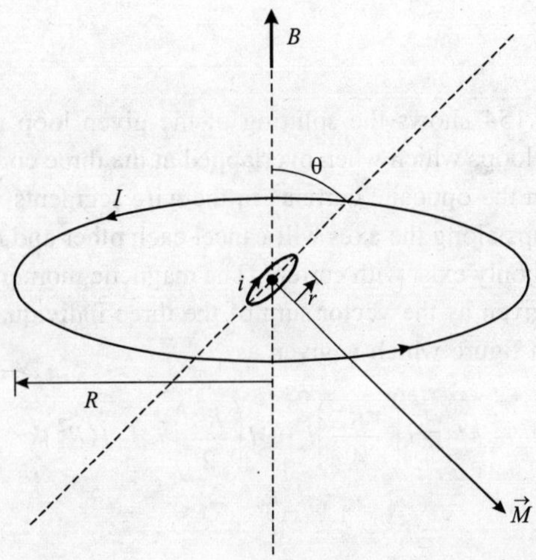

Figure 4.152

Torque on smaller coil due to the magnetic induction of larger coil at its center is given as

$$\vec{\tau} = \vec{M}\times\vec{B} = MB\sin\left(\frac{\pi}{2}+\theta\right)$$

$$\Rightarrow \quad \tau = Ni\pi r^2\left(\frac{\mu_0 I}{2R}\right)\cos\theta$$

$$\Rightarrow \quad \tau = \frac{\mu_0 iIN\pi r^2}{2R}\cos\theta$$

Illustrative Example 4.43

Find the magnetic moment of the current carrying loop shown in figure-4.153.

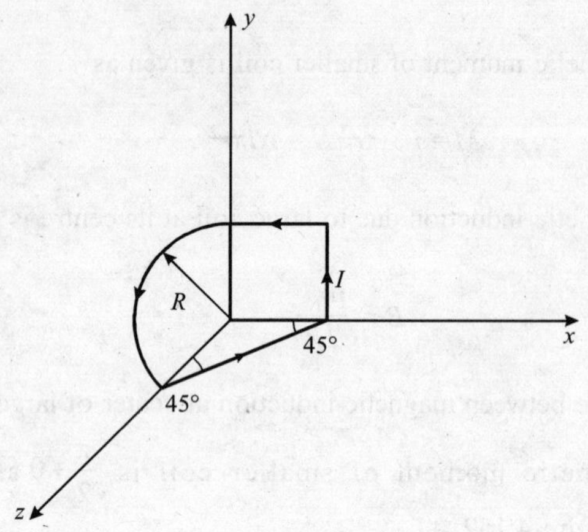

Figure 4.153

Solution

Figure-4.154 shows the splitting of the given loop in three separate loops which when overlapped at the three coordinate axes then the opposite currents in the wire segments in these three loops along the axes will cancel each other and original loop will only exist with current. The magnetic moment of the loop is given as the vector sum of the three individual loops shown in figure which is given as

$$\vec{M} = I\left(\frac{\pi R^2}{4}\right)\hat{i} + I\left(\frac{R^2}{2}\right)\hat{j} + I(R^2)\hat{k}$$

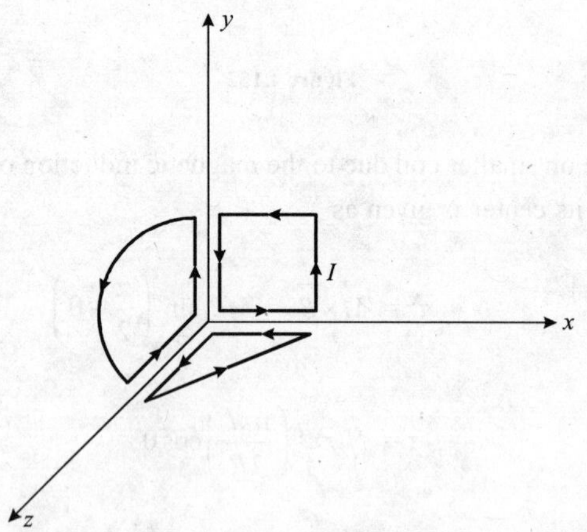

Figure 4.154

Illustrative Example 4.44

A square coil of edge l carrying a current I_2 is placed near to a long straight wire carrying current I_1 as shown in figure-4.155. Find work required to rotate the coil $ABCD$ about the axis along edge BC by 180° to the dotted position $A'BCD'$ as shown.

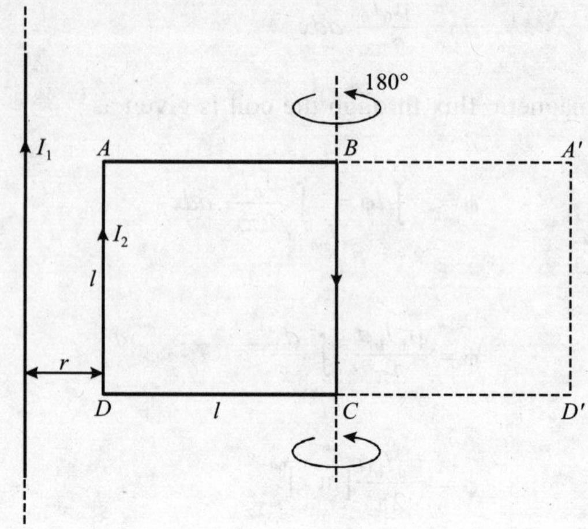

Figure 4.155

Solution

Work done in a process of changing the orientation of a coil in a magnetic field is given as

$$W = I_2(\phi_i - \phi_f)$$

We calculate the flux passing through the square coil at initial and final state by considering an elemental strip of width dx at a distance x from the long wire as shown in figure-4.156.

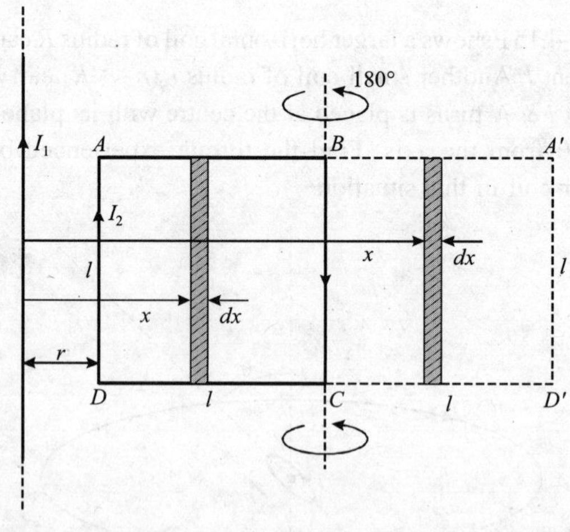

Figure 4.156

Initial flux through the coil is given as

$$\phi_i = \int B \cdot dS = \int_r^{r+l} \frac{\mu_0 I_1}{2\pi x} \times l dx = \frac{\mu_0 I_1 l}{2\pi}[\ln x]_r^{r+l}$$

$$\Rightarrow \quad \phi_i = \frac{\mu_0 I_1 l}{2\pi}\left(\frac{r+l}{r}\right)$$

Final flux through the coil is given as

$$\phi_f = \int_{r+l}^{r+2l} \frac{\mu_0 I_1}{2\pi x}\cdot l dx = \frac{\mu_0 I_1}{2\pi x}[\ln x]_{r+l}^{r+2l}$$

$$\Rightarrow \quad \phi_f = \frac{\mu_0 I_1}{2\pi}\ln\left(\frac{r+2l}{r+l}\right)$$

Work done this process is given as

$$W = I_2\left(\frac{\mu_0 I_1 l}{2\pi}\right)\left[\ln\frac{r+l}{r} - \ln\frac{r+2l}{r+l}\right]$$

$$\Rightarrow \quad W = \frac{\mu_0 I_1 I_2 l}{2\pi}\ln\left(\frac{r+2l}{r}\right)$$

Illustrative Example 4.45

A rectangular coil of area $5.0 \times 10^{-4}\,m^2$ and 60 turns is pivoted about one of its vertical sides. The coil is in a radial horizontal magnetic field of 9×10^{-3} T. What is the torsional constant of the spring connected to the coil if a current of 0.20 mA produces an angular deflection of 18º ?

Solution

From the equation of moving coil galvanometer we have

$$i = \left(\frac{C}{NAB}\right)\theta$$

The torsional constant of the spring is given as

$$C = \frac{NABi}{\theta}$$

Substituting the values in *SI* units we have

$$C = \frac{(60)(5.0\times10^{-4})(9\times10^{-3})(0.2\times10^{-3})}{18}$$

$$\Rightarrow \quad C = 3 \times 10^{-9} \text{ N-m/degree}$$

Illustrative Example 4.46

Figure-4.157 shows a coil bent with all edges of length 2 m and carrying a current of 2 A. There exists in space a uniform magnetic field of 2 T in positive *y*-direction. Find the torque on the loop.

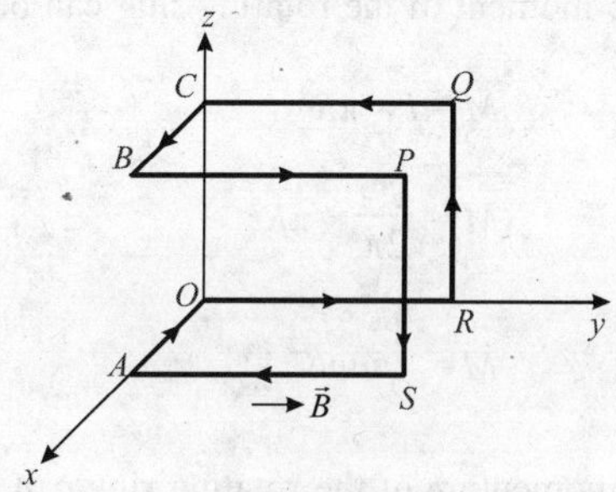

Figure 4.157

Solution

We assume equal and opposite currents in wires *PQ* and *RS*, then we split the given loop in three independent square loops and find magnetic moment vector of the loop which is only due to the square coil *PQRS* as top and bottom square coils magnetic moments are equal and opposite so will cancel each other. Thus magnetic moment of the given loop is given as

$$\vec{M} = Ia^2\hat{j} = 2\times(2)^2\hat{j} = 8\hat{j}$$

The magnetic induction vector in space is given as

$$\vec{B} = 2\hat{j}$$

The torque on the given loop is given as

$$\vec{\tau} = \vec{M}\times\vec{B} = 0$$

4.9 Relation in Magnetic Moment and Angular Momentum of uniformly charged and uniform dense rotating bodies

Figure-4.158 shows a thin ring of radius *R* with uniformly distributed charge *q* and mass *m* rotating at constant angular speed ω. The equivalent circulating current due to rotation of charge is given as

$$I = \frac{q\omega}{2\pi}$$

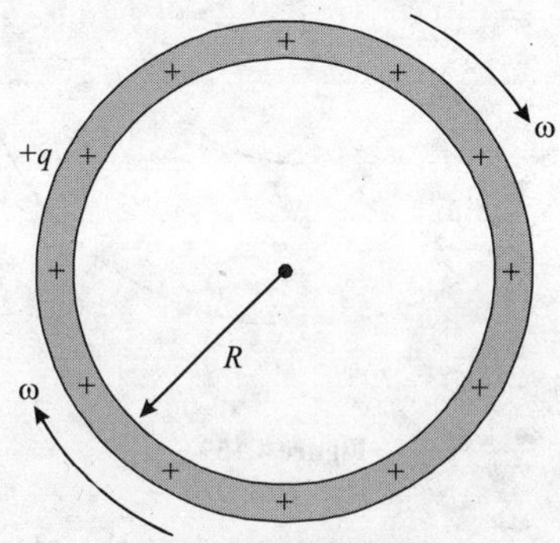

Figure 4.158

The magnetic moment of the rotating ring can be given as

$$M = I \times \pi R^2$$

$$\Rightarrow \quad M = \frac{q\omega}{2\pi} \times \pi R^2$$

$$\Rightarrow \quad M = \frac{1}{2} q\omega R^2 \quad \text{... (4.166)}$$

The angular momentum of the rotating ring can be given as

$$L = I\omega$$

$$\Rightarrow \quad L = MR^2\omega \quad \text{... (4.167)}$$

Dividing equation-(4.166) and (4.167) gives

$$\frac{M}{L} = \frac{\left(\frac{1}{2} q\omega R^2\right)}{(MR^2\omega)}$$

$$\Rightarrow \quad \frac{M}{L} = \frac{q}{2m} \quad \text{... (4.168)}$$

The ratio of magnetic moment to angular momentum as given in above equation-(4.117) is a standard relation which can be used for all uniformly charged and uniformly dense rotating bodies. In many cases above relation can be directly used for analysis of different situations mentioned in a question. Now we will consider one more illustration to verify the above result and its application. Figure-4.159 shows a uniform rod AB of length l, mass m, uniformly charged with a charge q is rotating at angular speed ω about one of its ends A.

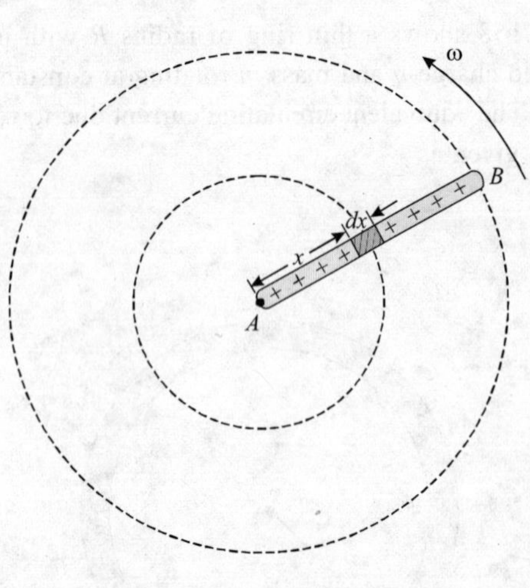

Figure 4.159

To calculate the magnetic moment of the rotating rod, we consider an element on rod of length dx at a distance x from the fixed end as shown in figure-4.159. The charge on this element is given as

$$dq = \frac{q}{l} dx$$

During rotation of the rod, this elemental charge will revolve in circle of radius x for which the corresponding equivalent current in this circle is given as

$$dI = \frac{dq\omega}{2\pi}$$

Due to the current in element, its magnetic moment is given as

$$dM = dI \times \pi x^2$$

$$\Rightarrow \quad dM = \left(\frac{dq\omega}{2\pi}\right)\pi x^2$$

$$\Rightarrow \quad dM = \frac{1}{2} dq\omega x^2$$

$$\Rightarrow \quad dM = \frac{1}{2}\left(\frac{q}{l} dx\right)\omega x^2$$

$$\Rightarrow \quad dM = \frac{q}{2l} \omega x^2 dx$$

Total magnetic moment of the rotating rod is given by integrating above expression for the whole length of the rod within limits from 0 to l which is given as

$$M = \int dM = \int_0^l \frac{q}{2l} \omega x^2 dx$$

$$\Rightarrow \quad M = \frac{q\omega}{2l} \int_0^l x^2 dx$$

$$\Rightarrow \quad M = \frac{q\omega}{2l}\left[\frac{x^3}{3}\right]_0^l$$

$$\Rightarrow \quad M = \frac{q\omega}{2l}\left(\frac{l^3}{3}\right)$$

$$\Rightarrow \quad M = \frac{1}{6} q\omega l^2 \quad \text{... (4.169)}$$

The angular momentum of the rotating rod is given as

$$L = I\omega$$

$$\Rightarrow \quad L = \left(\frac{1}{3} Ml^2\right)\omega$$

$$\Rightarrow \quad L = \frac{1}{3} Ml^2\omega \quad \text{... (4.170)}$$

By taking the ratio of equaiton-(4.169) and (4.170) we can verify equation-(4.168) for this case of rotating rod as well. If we use equation-(4.168) then the magnetic moment of the rotating rod as expressed in equation-(4.169) can be obtained directly by substituting the value of angular momentum from equation-(4.170) to equation-(4.168) and this saves the time of integration process we used in obtaining equation-(4.169) but here before applying equation-(4.168) for any situation of a rotating charge students must carefully analyze the given situation that the body must be uniformly charged and uniformly dense.

4.10 Magnetic Pressure and Field Energy of Magnetic Field

Similar to the case we've studied in electrostatic that a charged metal surface always experiences an electric pressure on it in outward direction due to its surface charge density, in case of a current carrying hollow conductor also if current is flowing on its surface and parallel currents always attract each other so the surface experiences an inward magnetic pressure on its surface. To determine the magnetic pressure on the surface we consider a long straight hollow cylindrical shell carrying a current *I*. We know at every interior point of this hollow wire magnetic induction is zero whereas just outside the surface the magnetic induction is given as

$$B = \frac{\mu_0 I}{2\pi R} \qquad \ldots (4.171)$$

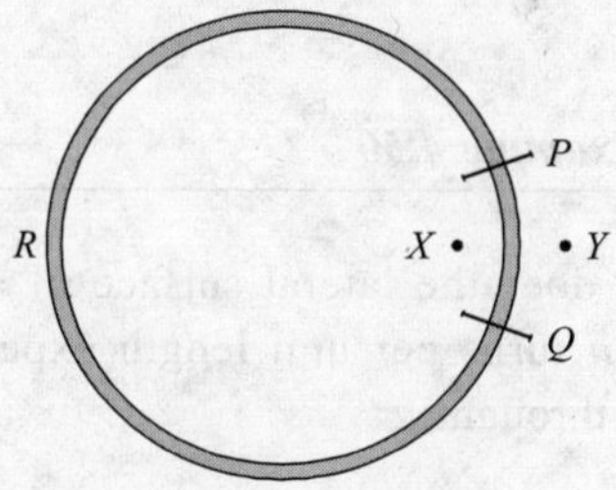

Figure 4.160

Figure-4.160 shows the cross sectional view of the hollow cylindrical wire in which we consider an elemental wire *PQ* of width *dw* and the remaining shell *PRQ* and consider two points *X* and *Y* just inside and outside of elemental wire *PQ*. At point *X* magnetic induction is zero and that at point *Y* is given by equation-(4.171). If B_1 and B_2 are the magnetic inductions at points *X* and *Y* due to the segments *PQ* and *PRQ* of the shells as shown in figure-4.160 then we have

$$B_X = B_1 - B_2 = 0 \qquad \ldots (4.172)$$

$$B_Y = B_1 + B_2 = B = \frac{\mu_0 I}{2\pi R} \qquad \ldots (4.173)$$

From equation-(4.172) and (4.173) we have

$$B_1 = B_2 = \frac{B}{2} \qquad \ldots (4.174)$$

Thus similar to the case of electrostatics the elemental part *PQ* of the shell contributes in half of the magnetic induction just outside the shell due to the whole current in it. If we consider a length *l* of the elemental wire *PQ* then force experienced by it due to the remaining section *PRQ* is given as

$$dF = B_2(dI)l$$

$$dF = B_2\left(\frac{I}{2\pi R} \times dw\right)l$$

$$dF = \left(\frac{\mu_0 I}{4\pi R}\right)\left(\frac{I}{2\pi R}\right)dwl$$

The area of the elemental wire strip is $dS = dwl$ so we can calculate the inward magnetic pressure on the elemental strip which is given as

$$p_m = \frac{dF}{dS} = \frac{\mu_0 I^2}{8\pi^2 R^2}$$

$$p_m = \frac{B^2}{2\mu_0} \qquad \ldots (4.175)$$

Above expression given in equation-(4.175) is the expression of magnetic pressure due to a surface current. Same expression can be used for magnetic energy density in the same way it is explained in article-1.19.1 in case of electrostatic energy density.

 # Illustrative Example 4.47

A flat disc of radius *R* charged uniformly on its surface at a surface charge density σ. About its central axis of rotation it rotates at an angular speed ω. Find the magnetic moment of disc due to rotation of charges.

Solution

We consider an elemental ring of radius *x* and width *dx* in the disc as shown in figure-4.161. Equivalent current in this elemental ring is given as

$$dI = \frac{dq\omega}{2\pi}$$

Magnetic moment of the rotating elemental ring is given as

$$dM = dI \times \pi x^2 = \frac{\sigma 2\pi x dx\omega}{2\pi} \times \pi x^2$$

$$\Rightarrow \qquad dM = \sigma\omega\pi x^3 dx$$

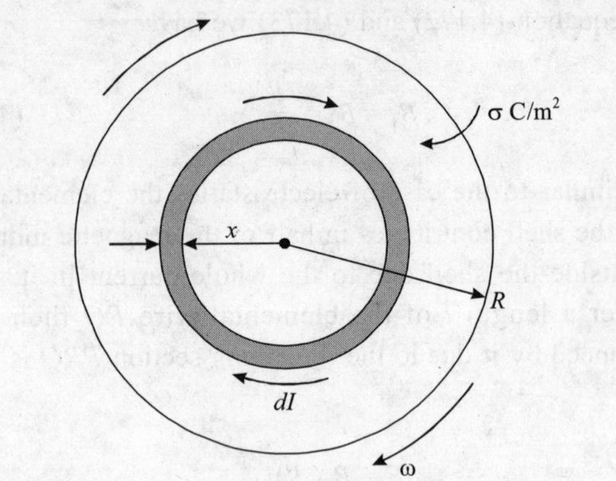

Figure 4.161

Total magnetic moment of the rotating disc is given as

$$M = \int dM = \sigma\pi\omega \int_0^R x^3 dx$$

$$\Rightarrow \quad M = \frac{1}{4}\sigma\pi\omega R^4$$

Above result can be directly calculated by using equation-(4.168). Students are advised to verify the above result by substituting the value of angular momentum of the disc in equation-(4.178).

Illustrative Example 4.48

A flat non-conducting disc of radius R carries an excess charge on its surface. The surface charge density is σ. The disc rotates about an axis perpendicular to its plane passing through the centre with angular velocity ω. Find the torque on the disc if it is placed in a uniform magnetic field B directed perpendicular to the rotation axis.

Solution

The situation described in question is shown in figure-4.162. As explained in previous illustration the magnetic moment of the rotating disc is given as

$$M = \frac{1}{4}\sigma\pi\omega R^4$$

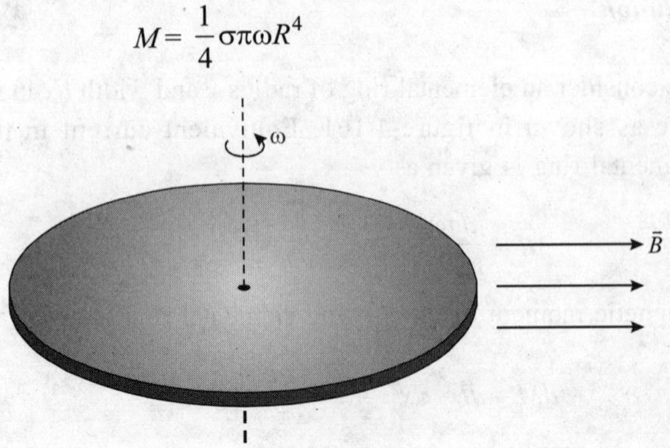

Figure 4.162

The torque on the disc due to magnetic field is given as

$$\tau = MB \sin 90°$$

$$\Rightarrow \quad \tau = \frac{\sigma\omega\pi BR^4}{4}$$

Illustrative Example 4.49

A solid sphere of radius R, uniformly charged with a charge Q is rotating about its central axis at angular speed ω. Find the magnetic moment of this rotating sphere.

Solution

The relation in magnetic moment and angular momentum of a uniformly charged and uniform body is given by equation-(4.168) as

$$\frac{M}{L} = \frac{Q}{2m}$$

The angular momentum of the rotating sphere is given as

$$L = I\omega = \frac{2}{5}mR^2\omega$$

Thus magnetic moment of the sphere is given as

$$M = \frac{Q}{2m} \times \frac{2}{5}mR^2\omega$$

$$\Rightarrow \quad M = \frac{1}{5}QR^2\omega$$

Illustrative Example 4.50

What pressure does the lateral surface of a long straight solenoid with n turns per unit length experience when a current I flows through it.

Solution

In case of a long solenoid outside magnetic induction is zero and inside it is given as $B = \mu_0 nI$. Thus the magnetic pressure on the surface of solenoid currents is given as

$$p_m = \frac{B^2}{2\mu_0} = \frac{1}{2}\mu_0 n^2 I^2$$

Above result we've directly written by using the expression of magnetic pressure but students can note that in article-4.10 while deriving this expression we consider a surface current along the length of a hollow shell whereas in case of solenoid current flows along the curved part of its core but still the result is valid. This can be verified by following the similar derivation process as well.

Illustrative Example 4.51

A conducting current-carrying plane is placed in an external uniform magnetic field. As a result, the magnetic induction becomes equal to B_1 on one side of the plane and equal to B_2 on the other side. Find the magnetic force acting per unit area of the plane in the cases illustrated in the figure-4.163(a, b, c).

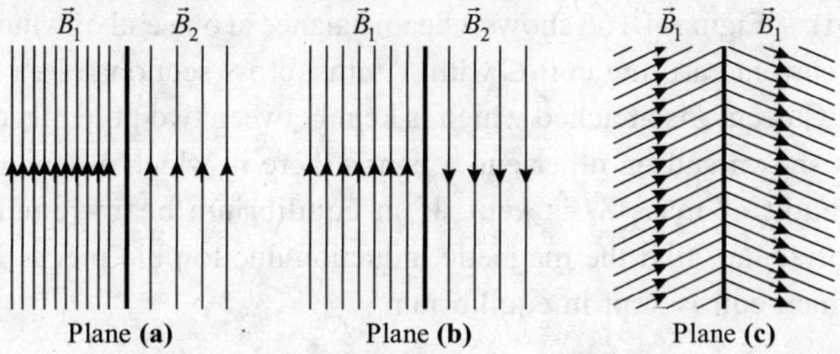

Figure 4.163

Determine the direction of the current in the plane in each case.

Solution

(a) As on the two sides of the plane fields are in same direction the external magnetic field induction B must be the average of B_1 and B_2 because on one side of the plane the external field will be added to the field of plane and on its other side it is subtracted.

So the magnetic induction due to the plane is $\frac{B_1 - B_2}{2}$ or $\frac{B_2 - B_1}{2}$ on opposite of the plane. If plane carries a liner current density I, we use

$$\frac{B_1 - B_2}{2} = \frac{1}{2}\mu_0 I$$

$$\Rightarrow \qquad I = \frac{B_1 - B_2}{\mu_0}$$

Force on the plane per unit area on the plane can be given as

$$p_m = \frac{B_1^2 - B_2^2}{2\mu_0} \qquad \ldots (4.176)$$

Students can derive and verify the result of magnetic pressure in equation-(4.176) in the same way it is done in article-4.10 for a long hollow current carrying cylindrical shell.

(b) As on the two sides of the plane fields are in opposite direction the external magnetic field in this case is given as

$$B_{ext} = \frac{B_1 - B_2}{2}$$

and the field due to the plane is given as

$$\frac{B_1 + B_2}{2} = \frac{1}{2}\mu_0 I$$

$$\Rightarrow \qquad I = \frac{B_1 + B_2}{2\mu_0}$$

Force on the plane per unit area on the plane can be given as

$$p_m = \frac{B_1^2 - B_2^2}{2\mu_0}$$

Students can derive and verify the result of magnetic pressure in equation-(4.176) in the same way it is done in article-4.10 for a long hollow current carrying cylindrical shell.

(c) In this case, external field is continuous across the plane and due to plane is directed parallel to the plane upward on the left and downward on the right side.

Similar to the analysis we did again the force on the plane per unit area on the plane can be given as

$$p_m = \frac{B_1^2 - B_2^2}{2\mu_0}$$

In each case, the current is in the direction directed into the plane of paper.

Web Reference at www.physicsgalaxy.com
Age Group - Grade 11 & 12 | Age 17-19 Years
Section - Magnetic Effects
Topic - Electromagnetic Force
Module Number - 24 to 38

Practice Exercise 4.5

(i) In Bohr model of hydrogen atom, the electron circulates round the nucleus in a path of radius 5.1×10^{-11} m at a frequency 6.8×10^{15} rev/s.

(a) What is the magnitude of magnetic induction at the centre of the orbit in Bohr model?

(b) What is the equivalent dipole moment of the rotating electron in Bohr model?

[13.6 T, 90×10^{-24} Am^2]

(ii) Figure-4.164 shows rectangular twenty-turn loop of wire with sides 10 cm and 5cm. It carries a current of 0.10 A and it is hinged at one side along *y*-axis as shown. Calculate the magnitude and direction of the torque acting on the loop if it is mounted with its plane at an angle of 30° to the direction of a uniform field of magnetic induction 0.50 T which exist along positive *x*-direction.

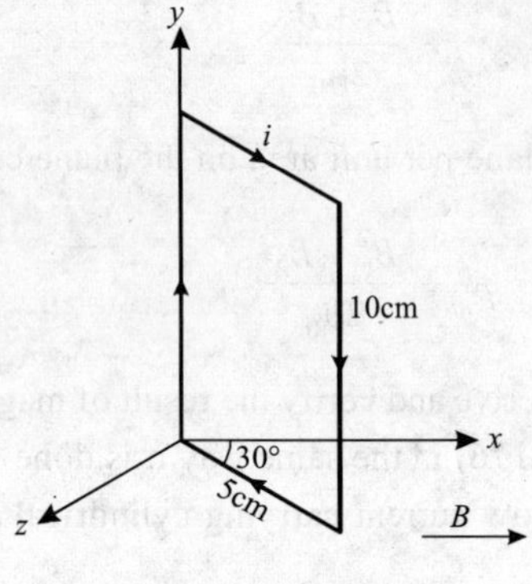

Figure 4.164

[4.3×10^{-3} Nm]

(iii) A coil in the shape of an equilateral triangle of side 0.02 m is suspended from a vertex such that it is hanging in a vertical plane between the pole pieces of a permanent magnet producing a horizontal magnetic induction 5×10^{-2} T. Find the couple acting on the coil when a current of 0.1 A is passed through it and the magnetic field is parallel to its plane.

[8.66×10^{-7} Nm]

(iv) A wire loop carrying a current *I* is placed in the *x*-*y* plane as shown in figure-4.165.

(a) If a particle with charge $+Q$ and mass *m* is placed at the centre *P* and given a velocity *v* along *NP* (see the figure), find its instantaneous acceleration of the particle at point *P*.

(b) If an external uniform magnetic induction field $\vec{B} = B\hat{i}$ is applied, find the force and the torque acting on the loop due to this field.

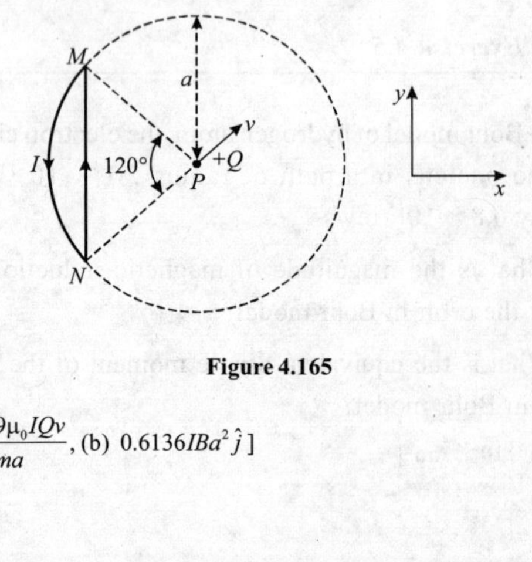

Figure 4.165

[(a) $\dfrac{0.109\mu_0 IQv}{ma}$, (b) $0.6136IBa^2\,\hat{j}$]

(v) A coil of radius *R* carries current i_1. Another concentric coil of radius $r(r << R)$ carries current i_2. Planes of two coils are mutually perpendicular and both the coils are free to rotate about common diameter. Find maximum kinetic energy of smaller coil when both the coils are released, masses of coils are *M* and *m* respectively.

[$\dfrac{\mu_0 \pi r^2 i_1 i_2 MR}{2(MR^2 + mr^2)}$]

(vi) Figure-4.166 shows a beam balance at one end of which a current carrying coil *C* with *N* turns, cross sectional area *A* & Current *I* is attached which is kept between two pole pieces as shown and on other end a pan is there in which a counter weight of mass *M* is kept. If in equilibrium beam remain horizontal, find the magnetic induction due to pole pieces in which coil is kept in equilibrium.

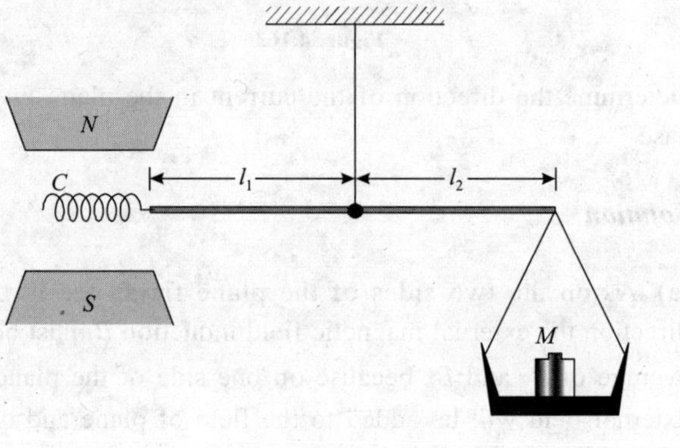

Figure 4.166

[$\dfrac{Mgl_2}{INA}$]

(vii) A uniform magnetic field of magnetic induction *B* is directed at an angle of 45° to the *x*-axis in *xy* plane in a coordinate system. *PQRS* is a rigid square wire frame carrying a steady current I_0, with its centre at the origin *O*. At time $t = 0$, the frame is at rest in the position shown in the figure-4.167, with its side parallel to *x* and *y* axes. Each side of the frame is of mass *M* and length *L*.

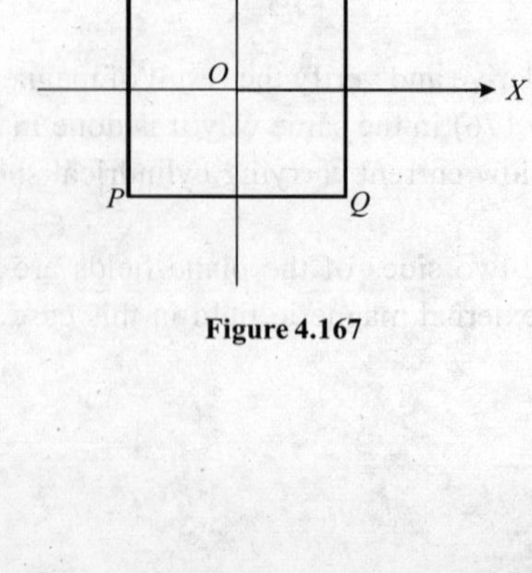

Figure 4.167

(a) Calculate the torque about O acting on the frame due to magnetic field?

(b) Find the angle by which the frame rotates under the action of this torque in a short interval of time Δt, and the axis about which this rotation occurs. Consider that Δt is so short that any variation in the torque during this interval may be neglected.

[(a) $\frac{I_0 L^2 B}{\sqrt{2}}(-\hat{i}+\hat{j})$; (b) $\frac{3I_0 B}{4M}(\Delta t)^2$]

(viii) Calculate the magnetic moment of a thin wire with a current I wound tightly on a half a tore of a toroid as shown in figure-4.168. The diameter of the cross-section of the tore is d and total number of turns are N.

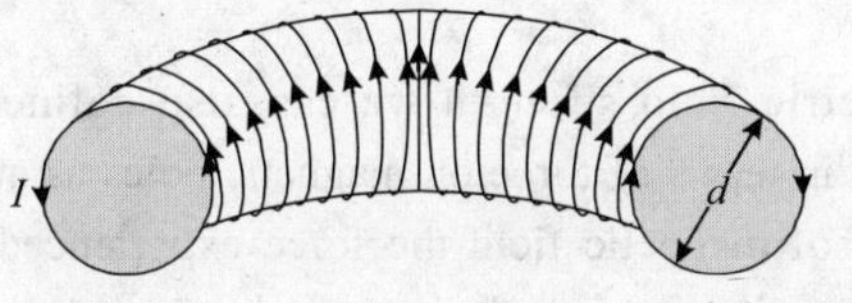

Figure 4.168

[$\frac{1}{2}Id^2N$]

(ix) A flat circular coil with 10 turns of wire on it has a diameter 20 mm and carries a current 0.5 A. It is mounted inside a long solenoid that has 200 turns and the length of the solenoid is 0.25 m. The current passing through the solenoid is 2.4 A. Calculate the torque needed to hold the coil with its axis perpendicular to that of solenoid.

[3.78×10^{-6} Nm]

(x) The coil of a moving coil galvanometer twists through 90° when a current of one microampere is passed through it. If the area of the coil is 10^{-4} m^2 and it has 100 turns, calculate the magnetic field of the magnetic poles in the galvanometer. Torsional constant of the spring system used in galvanometer is given as $C = 10^{-8}$ N-m/degree.

[90 T]

4.11 Classical Magnetism

About 4000 years ago in a Greek town Magnesia a shepherd named Magnes was herding his sheep and suddenly he found that after he took a step some iron nails in his shoes stuck fast to a black rock on which he was standing. In state of surprize he digged the rock further and found that this rock has character to attract some of the metal objects. On the name of the town this rock was named '*Magnetite*'. It was later analyzed and found containing a compound Fe_3O_4 because of which such properties are there in this material. Over a period of time these properties found in many other materials also are called '*Magnetic Properties*' and the force field because of which these material expert force on some specific metal objects is named '*Magnetic Field*'. Over long period of time many more discoveries and experiments evolved the knowledge of physicists in this domain and its applications helped making many industrial processes more effective and productive.

4.11.1 Pole Strength of a Magnetic Pole

Pole strength is a measurement of magnetic field produced by a magnetic pole. This is a physical quantity similar to electric charge in electrostatics like the magnitude of a charge is a measure of how strong electric field the charge can produce in its surrounding. Similarly if pole strength of a magnetic pole is high then it means this pole produces high magnetic field in its surrounding. Unit used for measurement of magnetic pole strength is '*ampere-meter*' or '*A–m*'.

Like positive and negative charges in magnetism there are two different poles exist which are called '*North and South Poles*' like positive charge from a north pole magnetic flux comes out and like a negative charge magnetic lines goes into a south pole. Similar to charges in magnetism also like poles repel each other and unlike poles attract each other.

If we consider two independent point magnetic poles, a north and a south pole as shown in figure-4.169 then magnetic field lines in their surrounding are considered radially outward and radially inward respectively as shown.

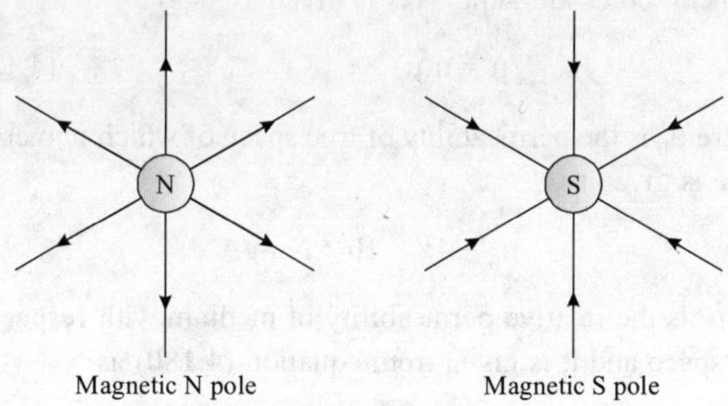

Figure 4.169

Above figure shows a theoretical configuration of magnetic field in surrounding of these point magnetic poles because practically independent poles (called '*monopoles*') never exist in nature which we will study later in upcoming articles.

4.11.2 Coulomb's Law for Magnetic Forces

This law gives the force of interaction between two magnetic poles and it is analogous to Coulomb's law for electric charges. First we will analyze this law at theoretical level. Figure-4.170 shows two magnetic monopoles with pole strengths m_1 and m_2 kept at a separation r between them. The interaction force between the two poles is

(i) Directly proportional to the product of magnetic pole strengths of the two poles

$$F \propto m_1 m_2 \quad \text{... (4.177)}$$

(ii) Inversely proportional to the square of the distance between the poles

$$F \propto \frac{1}{r^2} \quad \text{... (4.178)}$$

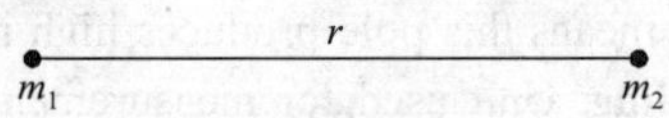

Figure 4.170

From above equations-(4.177) and (4.178) we have

$$F \propto \frac{m_1 m_2}{r^2}$$

$$\Rightarrow \quad F = K\frac{m_1 m_2}{r^2} \quad \text{... (4.179)}$$

In above expression shown in euqation-(4.179), K is a proportionality constant which depends upon the medium in which magnetic poles are placed. Value of K is given as

$$K = \frac{\mu}{4\pi}$$

Where μ is the magnetic permeability of the medium in which magnetic poles are kept. This is given as

$$\mu = \mu_0 \mu_r \quad \text{... (4.180)}$$

Where μ_0 is the permeability of free space of which numerical value is given as

$$\mu_0 = 4\pi \times 10^{-7} \text{ N-m/A}$$

and μ_r is the relative permeability of medium with respect to free space and it is given from equation-(4.180) as

$$\mu_r = \frac{\mu}{\mu_0}$$

Unlike to the value of relative permittivity of medium $\in_r$ which always has numerical value greater than unity for different material medium, in magnetism depending upon the type of material medium value of μ_r can be greater or less than unity which we will discuss more in upcoming articles.

Thus using the value of proportionality constant expression given in equation-(4.179) can be rewritten as

$$F = \frac{\mu_0}{4\pi}\frac{m_1 m_2}{r^2} \quad \text{... (4.181)}$$

In above expression we considered medium to be free space or air for which we take $\mu_r = 1$.

4.11.3 Magnetic Induction in terms of Force on Poles

Every magnetic pole produces magnetic induction in its surrounding space which can exert a force on any other pole placed in surrounding. As already discussed that behaviour of magnetic poles in study of magnetism is more or less similar to that of charges in electrostatics.

Like electric field strength we can also define magnetic induction in terms of force on magnetic poles as at any point in region of magnetic field the force experienced by a unit magnetic north pole gives the magnitude of magnetic induction at that point in space. Figure-4.171 shows a region of magnetic field in which a magnetic north pole of pole strength m_0 is placed. If it experiences a force $\vec{F}$ due to magnetic induction than at the location of the pole magnetic induction is given as

$$\vec{B} = \frac{\vec{F}}{m_0} \quad \text{... (4.182)}$$

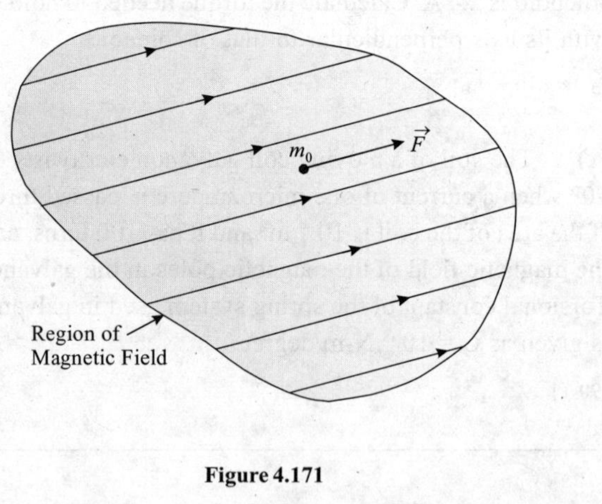

Figure 4.171

Always remember that similar to electrostatics, in magnetic field a north pole experiences force in the direction of magnetic field and a south pole experiences force opposite to the direction of magnetic field as shown in figure-4.172. The magnitude of force on a magnetic pole of strength m placed in magnetic induction B is given as

$$F = mB \quad \text{... (4.183)}$$

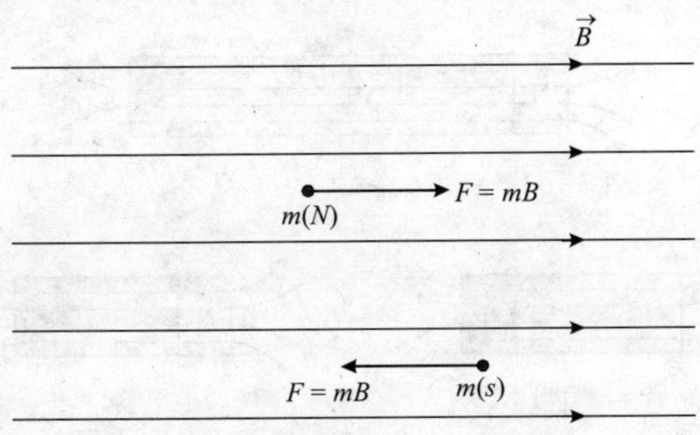

Figure 4.172

4.11.4 Magnetic Induction due to a Magnetic Pole

We've discussed in previous article that at any point magnetic induction is given as force experienced by a unit magnetic north pole placed at that point.

Thus to determine the magnetic induction in surrounding of a magnetic north pole of pole strength m, we place a test pole m_0 at a distance r from the pole at point P as shown in figure-4.173. The magnetic force on test pole placed at point P is given as

$$F = K\frac{mm_0}{r^2}$$

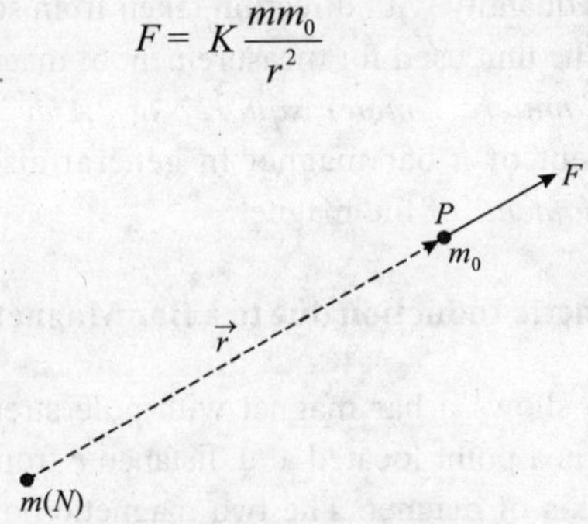

Figure 4.173

The magnetic induction at point P is given by equation-(4.182) as

$$B_P = \frac{F}{m_0}$$

$$\Rightarrow \quad B_P = \frac{Km}{r^2} \quad \ldots (4.184)$$

$$\Rightarrow \quad B_P = \frac{\mu_0}{4\pi}\frac{m}{r^2} \quad \ldots (4.185)$$

The expression given in equation-(4.184) is similar to the electric field produced by a point charge in its surrounding. About direction we've already discussed that due to a north pole magnetic induction is radially outward and in surrounding of a south pole magnetic induction is radially inward.

Vectorially equation-(4.185) can be written as

$$\vec{B}_P = \frac{\mu_0}{4\pi}\frac{m}{r^3}\vec{r} \quad \ldots (4.186)$$

4.11.5 Bar Magnet

A bar magnet is a rod shaped metal object which produces magnetic field in its surrounding and at the two ends of it there are two magnetic poles - North Pole and South Pole. Magnetic lines originate from north pole of a magnet and terminate on south pole as shown in figure-4.174. At the magnetic poles of magnet, the strength of magnetic field is maximum.

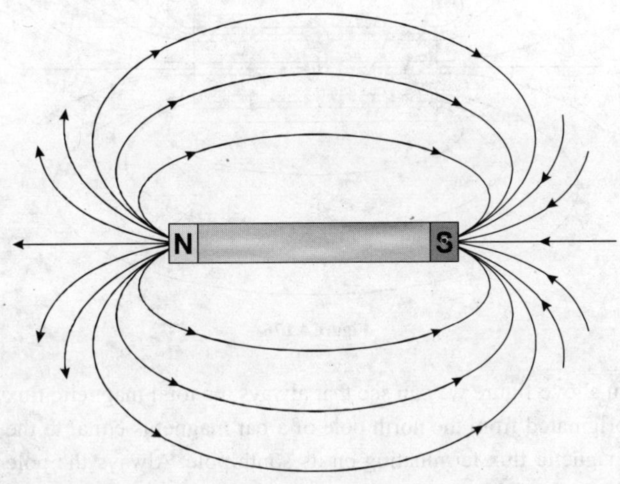

Figure 4.174

To understand how a bar magnet produces magnetic field, we first discuss about the magnetic field produced by an atom. If in an atom there are some unpaired electrons which are revolving around the nucleus then these revolving electrons can be considered as a current carrying coil which produces magnetic induction as shown in figure-4.175. Thus every atom which have unpaired electrons can be assumed like a very small coil producing its own non-zero magnetic induction.

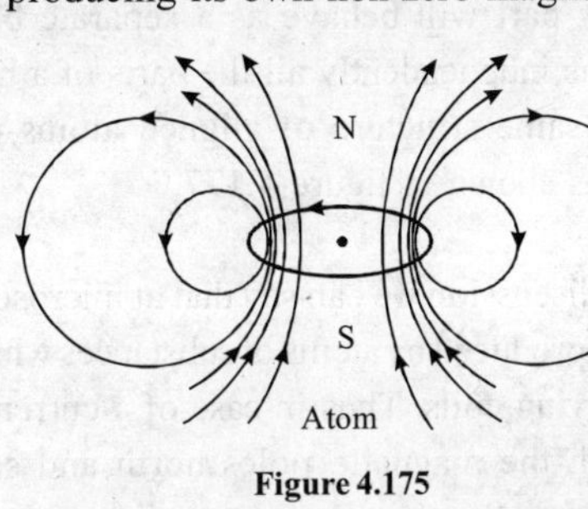

Figure 4.175

In fact every current carrying coil can be considered similar to a bar magnet. The face of coil from which the magnetic lines are emerging out can be regarded as its magnetic north pole and the other face of coil into which the magnetic lines are getting into can be regarded as its magnetic south pole. In a bar magnet all the atoms producing magnetic induction are aligned in such a way that these all atoms produce their magnetic induction in same direction so the resulting overall magnetic field will be high in magnitude as shown in figure-4.174 above. The microscopic view of atoms inside a bar magnet is shown in figure-4.176 which explains how a bar magnet produces magnetic field.

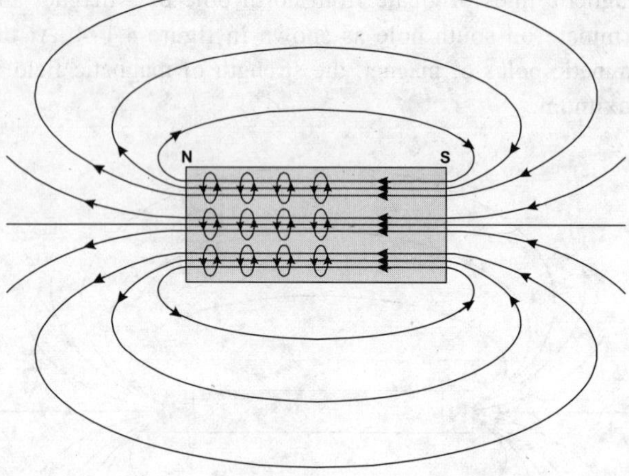

Figure 4.176

In above figure we can see that always the total magnetic flux originated from the north pole of a bar magnet is equal to the magnetic flux terminating on its south pole. Always the pole strengths of both the magnetic poles of a bar magnet are equal in magnitude.

With above explanation we can see that the magnetic lines due to a coil are closed loops thus for a bar magnet also magnetic lines are closed loops as inside the magnet the lines are in opposite direction travelling from south to north pole forming a closed loop.

Every bar magnet has a property that if it is cut or broken in parts then every part will behave as a separate bar magnet with two poles as independently all the parts of a bar magnet have internally same structure of aligned atoms producing magnetic field as shown in figure-4.177.

With the above discussion we can say that at microscopic level magnetic field is produced by atoms of substances which behave like current carrying coils. Thus in case of a current carrying coil always both the magnetic poles north and south exist together as magnetic lines are closed loop lines so we can also state that in nature magnetic unipole can never exist as the two poles can never be isolated in any situation of a device producing magnetic field.

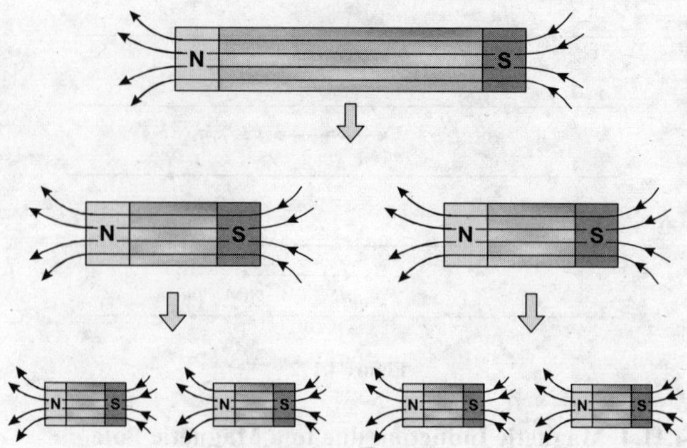

Figure 4.177

The strength of a bar magnet is characterized by its magnetic dipole moment. If the pole strength of either pole of a bar magnet is m and the separation between its poles is d then the magnetic dipole moment of a bar magnet is given as

$$\mu = md \quad \text{... (4.187)}$$

The symbol used for magnetic dipole moment is either μ or M. Like electric dipole moment, magnetic dipole moment is also a vector quantity with direction taken from south pole to north pole. The unit used for measurement of magnetic dipole moment is '*ampere - meter square*' or '*A-m²*'. Magnetic dipole moment of a bar magnet in general also called as '*Magnetic Moment*' of the magnet.

4.11.6 Magnetic Induction due to a Bar Magnet on its Axis

Figure-4.178 shows a bar magnet with pole strength m and length $2d$. P is a point located at a distance r from the center and on the axis of magnet. The two magnetic poles produce magnetic induction at point P in opposite directions as shown in figure.

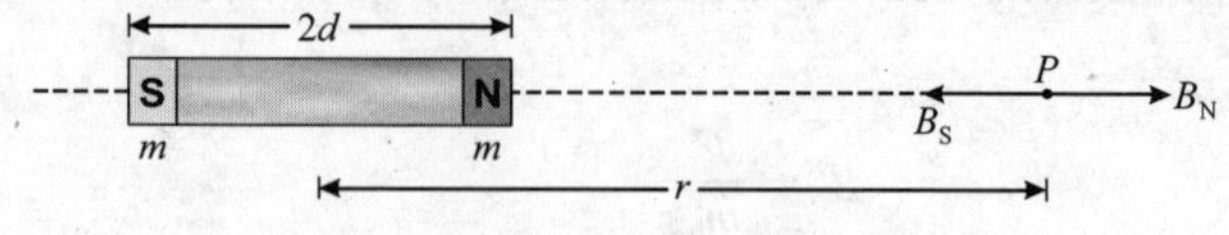

Figure 4.178

The net magnetic induction at point P is given as

$$B_P = B_N - B_S$$

$$\Rightarrow \quad B_P = \frac{\mu_0}{4\pi}\frac{m}{(r-d)^2} - \frac{\mu_0}{4\pi}\frac{m}{(r+d)^2}$$

$$\Rightarrow \quad B_P = \frac{\mu_0 m}{4\pi}\left[\frac{1}{(r-d)^2} - \frac{1}{(r+d)^2}\right]$$

$$\Rightarrow \quad B_P = \frac{\mu_0}{4\pi}\frac{4rd}{(r^2-d^2)^2}$$

$$\Rightarrow \quad B_P = \frac{\mu_0}{4\pi}\frac{2Mr}{(r^2-d^2)^2} \quad \ldots (4.188)$$

The expression in equation-(4.188) gives the magnetic induction due to a bar magnet on its axial point in which we used magnetic moment of the magnet as $M = 2md$. If the bar magnet is replaced with a magnetic dipole in which $d << r$ as shown in figure-4.179 then the above result will be modified as given below

$$B_P = \frac{\mu_0}{4\pi}\frac{2Mr}{(r^2-d^2)^2} \approx \frac{\mu_0}{4\pi}\frac{2M}{r^3}$$

$$\Rightarrow \quad B_P = \frac{2KM}{r^3} \quad \ldots (4.189)$$

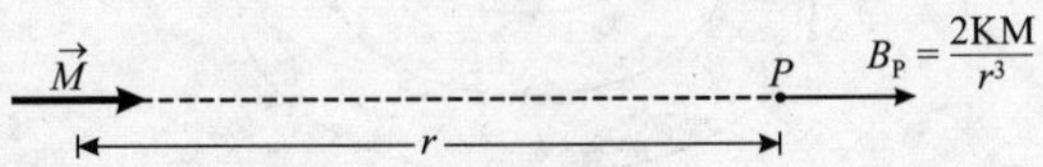

Figure 4.179

The result given in Equation-(4.189) is similar to the electric field due to an electric dipole at a point on its axis so this is easy to remember also.

4.11.7 Magnetic Induction due to a Bar Magnet on its Equatorial Line

Figure-4.180 shows a bar magnet with pole strength m and length $2d$. P is a point located at a distance r from the center and on the perpendicular bisector of magnet called its equatorial line. The two magnetic poles produce magnetic induction of equal magnitude at point P due to symmetry along the directions as shown in figure.

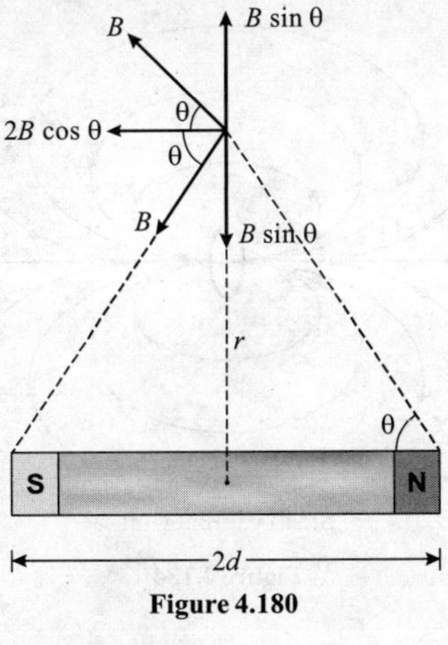

Figure 4.180

Thus the net magnetic induction at point P is given as

$$B_P = 2B\cos\theta$$

$$\Rightarrow \quad B_P = 2\left(\frac{\mu_0}{4\pi}\frac{m}{(r^2+d^2)}\right)\cdot\frac{d}{\sqrt{r^2+d^2}}$$

$$\Rightarrow \quad B_P = \frac{\mu_0}{4\pi}\frac{M}{(r^2+d^2)^{3/2}} \quad \ldots (4.190)$$

Similar to previous article if we calculate the magnetic induction at equatorial line of a magnetic dipole as shown in figure-4.181 then it is given by modifying expression in equation-(4.190) using $d << r$ as

$$B_P = \frac{\mu_0}{4\pi}\frac{M}{(r^2+d^2)^{3/2}} \approx \frac{\mu_0}{4\pi}\frac{M}{r^3}$$

$$\Rightarrow \quad B_P = \frac{KM}{r^3} \quad \ldots (4.191)$$

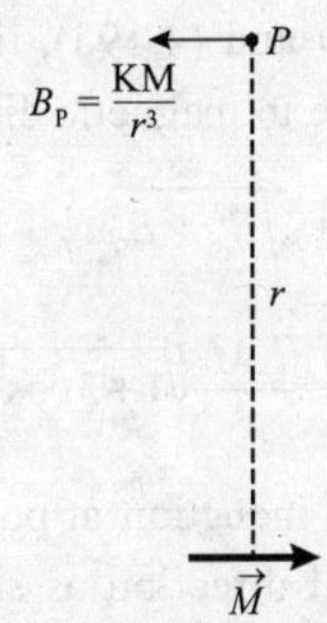

Figure 4.181

The result in equation-(4.191) is also similar to the electric field due to an electric dipole at a point on its equator.

4.11.8 Analogy between Electric and Magnetic Dipoles

In previous articles we've discussed that the expressions of magnetic induction due to a magnetic dipole at its axial and equatorial line are similar to those we've already studied for electric field produced by an electric dipole and with the analogy of these results we can analyze the magnetic induction due to a magnetic dipole in its surrounding along radial and transverse directions. Figure-4.182 shows a point P at a distance r from a magnetic dipole of dipole moment M. The line joining point P to the center of dipole is making an angle θ with the axis of dipole. With the analogy from electric dipole the radial and transverse components of magnetic induction at point P due to this magnetic dipole are given below.

Radial component of magnetic induction is given as

$$B_r = \frac{2KM\cos\theta}{r^3} \quad \text{... (4.192)}$$

Transverse component of magnetic induction is given as

$$B_\theta = \frac{KM\sin\theta}{r^3} \quad \text{... (4.193)}$$

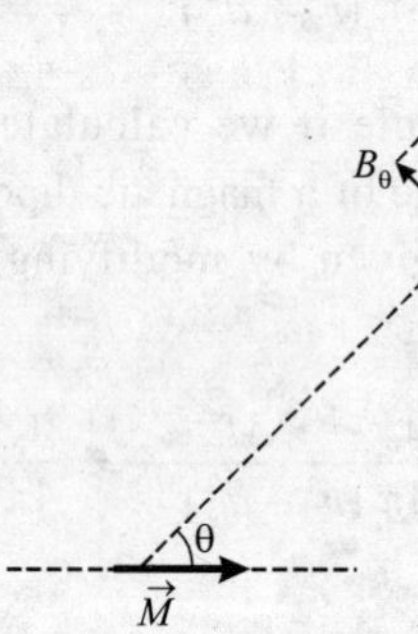

Figure 4.182

Using equation-(4.192) and (4.193), the resultant magnetic induction at point P due to magnetic dipole is given as

$$B_P = \sqrt{B_r^2 + B_\theta^2}$$

$$\Rightarrow \quad B_P = \frac{KM}{r^3}\sqrt{1+3\cos^2\theta} \quad \text{... (4.194)}$$

The resulting magnetic induction at point P is aligned at an angle ϕ from the radial direction as shown in figure-4.182 which is given as

$$\phi = \tan^{-1}\left(\frac{B_\theta}{B_r}\right)$$

$$\Rightarrow \quad \phi = \tan^{-1}\left(\frac{1}{2}\tan\theta\right) \quad \text{... (4.195)}$$

4.11.9 A Small Current Carrying Coil as a Magnetic Dipole

Figure-4.183 shows the magnetic field produced by a bar magnet and that of a current carrying coil which looks similar except the length of bar magnet but if we look at the figure-4.184 which shows the magnetic field in surrounding of a small magnetic dipole and that of a small current carrying coil. Both the configurations of magnetic field lines looks almost identical thus a very small current carrying coil can be regarded as a magnetic dipole and all the results we've obtained for a magnetic dipole can be used for such small current carrying loops with magnetic dipole moment of dipole replaced with the magnetic moment of the coil.

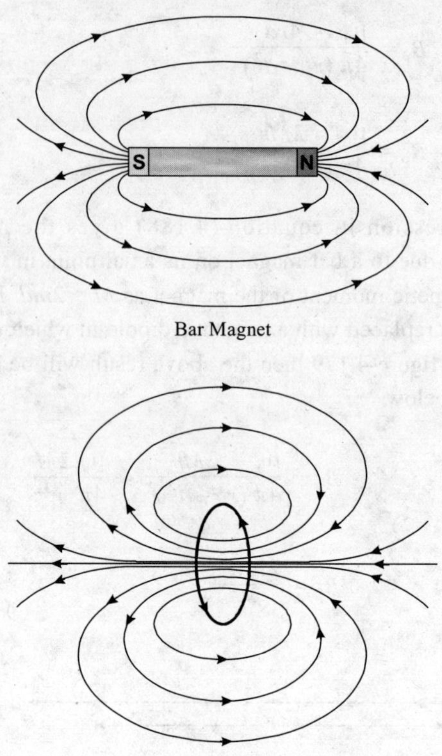

Figure 4.183

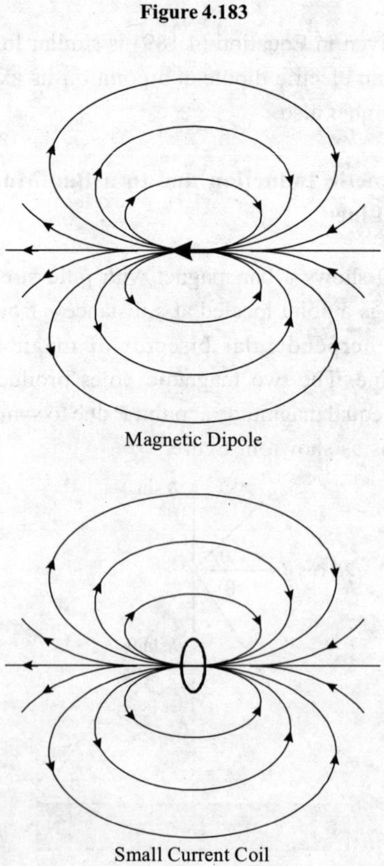

Figure 4.184

Figure-4.185 shows a tightly wound long solenoid and the magnetic induction produced by it by the magnetic field lines configuration. This magnetic field lines configuration is almost same as that produced by a bar magnet thus a current carrying solenoid can be considered to be behaving like a bar magnet with magnetic moment given as

$$M = NiA \quad \dots (4.196)$$

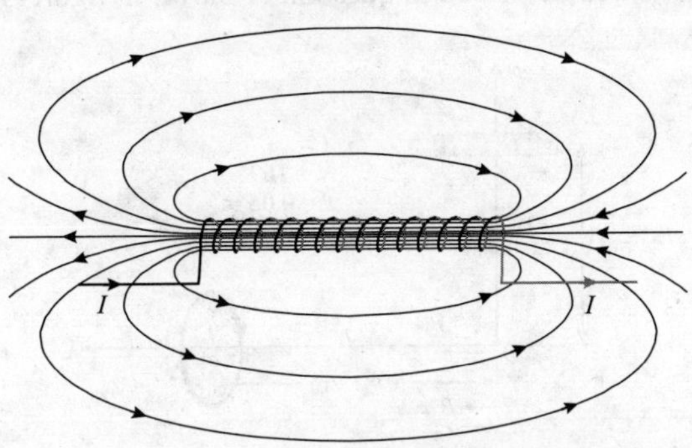

Figure 4.185

4.11.10 Force on a Magnetic Dipole in Magnetic Field

Figure-4.186 shows a magnetic dipole of dipole moment M placed in a uniform magnetic induction B. As both of its poles will experience equal and opposite forces as shown in figure, the net magnetic force on the dipole will be zero similar to an electric dipole placed in uniform electric field. Due to equal and opposite forces acting at different lines of action a couple will be produced and the torque on magnetic dipole due to these couple forces can be given by its analogy with the case of electric dipole already studied in the chapter of electrostatics as

$$\vec{\tau} = \vec{M} \times \vec{B} \quad \dots (4.197)$$

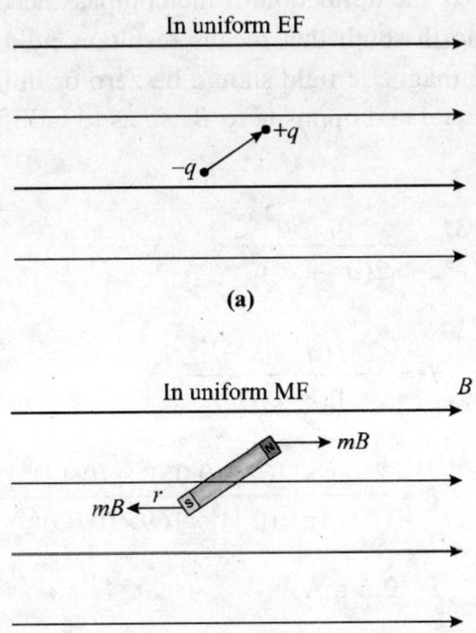

Figure 4.186

If the dipole is placed in a non uniform magnetic field then the force on it will also be non-zero which can also be given by the analogy with the case of electric dipole, given as

$$\vec{F} = \vec{M} \cdot \frac{d\vec{B}}{dx} \hat{n} \quad \dots (4.198)$$

In above case $\hat{n}$ is the unit vector along the direction of magnetic induction. Similar to the case of an electric dipole placed in non uniform electric field above equation-(4.198) gives the force on dipole along the direction of magnetic induction.

Above results obtained for a magnetic dipole can be directly applied to a small current carrying coil in different situations.

Illustrative Example 4.52

A bar magnet is 0.1 m long and its pole strength is 12 Am. Find the magnetic induction at a point on its axis at a distance of 0.2 m from its centre.

Solution

Net magnetic induction due to bar magnet at point P is given by the vector sum of the magnetic inductions at P due to the two poles given as

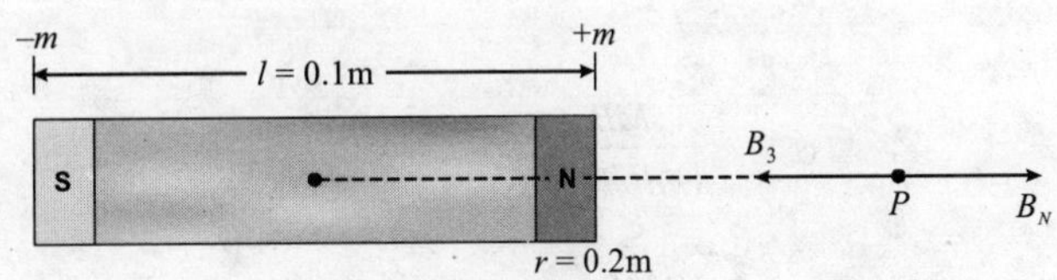

Figure 4.187

$$B_P = B_N - B_S$$

$$\Rightarrow \quad B_P = \frac{\mu_0}{4\pi} \cdot \frac{m}{(r - l/2)^2} - \frac{\mu_0}{4\pi} \cdot \frac{m}{(r + l/2)^2}$$

$$\Rightarrow \quad B_P = \frac{\mu_0}{4\pi} \left[\frac{2rl}{(r^2 - l^2/4)^2} \right] = \frac{32\mu_0 mrl}{4\pi(4r^2 - l^2)^2}$$

$$\Rightarrow \quad B_P = \frac{32 \times 10^{-7} \times 12 \times 0.2}{(4(0.2)^2 - (0.1)^2)^2}$$

$$\Rightarrow \quad B_P = 3.4 \times 10^{-4}\,\text{T}$$

Illustrative Example 4.53

A magnetic dipole of magnetic moment M is suspended by a string in a uniform horizontal magnetic field as shown in figure-4.188. If in horizontal plane this dipole is slightly tilted and released, show that it will execute simple harmonic motion and find its oscillation period. Consider the dipole as a uniform rod of mass m and length l.

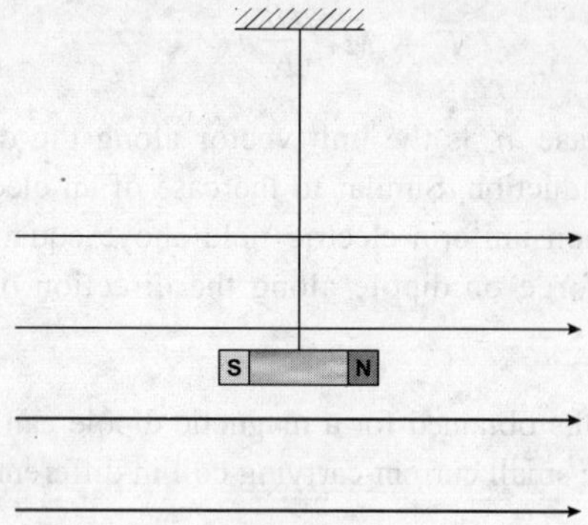

Figure 4.188

Solution

If dipole is tilted from its equilibrium position by a small angle θ, in horizontal plane, restoring torque on magnetic dipoles is given as

$$\tau_R = MB \sin\theta \simeq MB\theta$$

The angular acceleration of dipole is given as

$$\alpha = -\frac{\tau_A}{I}$$

$$\Rightarrow \quad \alpha = -\frac{MB}{(ml^2/12)}\theta$$

$$\Rightarrow \quad \alpha = -\frac{12MB}{ml^2}\theta \quad \text{... (4.199)}$$

Equation-(4.199) shows that restoring angular acceleration of the dipole is directly proportional to the angular displacement hence it will execute SHM. Comparing this with angular acceleration of standard angular SHM equation given as $\alpha = -\omega^2\theta$ we get

$$\omega = \sqrt{\frac{12MB}{ml^2}}$$

$$\Rightarrow \quad T = 2\pi\sqrt{\frac{ml^2}{12MB}}$$

 # *Illustrative Example 4.54*

A small magnetic dipole of magnetic moment $\pi \times 10^{-3}$ A-m^2 is placed on the Y-axis at a distance of 0.1 m from the origin with its axis parallel to X-axis. A coil having 169 turns and radius 0.05 m is placed on the X-axis at a distance of 0.12 m from the origin with the axis of the coil coinciding with X-axis. Find the magnitude and direction of the current in the coil for a compass needle placed at the origin, to point in the north-south direction.

Solution

The situation described in question is shown in figure-4.189.

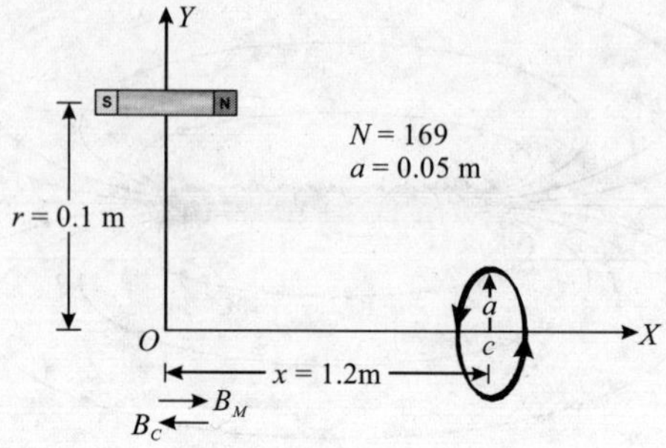

Figure 4.189

The magnetic induction at O due to magnetic dipole moment M is given as

$$B_M = \frac{\mu_0}{4\pi}\frac{M}{r^3} \text{ N/A-m} \quad \text{... (4.200)}$$

The direction of above magnetic induction is along positive X-direction. The magnetic induction at O due to the current carrying coil of radius a and having N turns is given as

$$B_C = \frac{\mu_0 Nia^2}{2(a^2+x^2)^{3/2}} \quad \text{... (4.201)}$$

The direction of above magnetic induction is along negative or positive X-direction depending upon the direction of current in the coil. As the deflection of the compass needle at O has to remain north-south that means resultant field at O other than Earth's magnetic field should be zero or in this case B_M should be equal and opposite to B_C so as to nullify it thus we have

$$\frac{\mu_0}{4\pi}\cdot\frac{M}{r^3} = \frac{\mu_0 Nia^2}{2(a^2+x^2)^{3/2}}$$

$$\Rightarrow \quad i = \frac{2M(a^2+x^2)^{3/2}}{4\pi r^3 \times Na^2} \quad \text{... (4.202)}$$

$$\Rightarrow \quad i = \frac{2\times(\pi\times10^{-3})[(0.05)^2+(0.12)^2]^{3/2}}{4\pi\times(0.1)^3\times169\times(0.05)^2}$$

$$\Rightarrow \quad i = 2.6 \text{ mA}$$

For the field B_C to be along negative X-direction, the current in the coil should be in anticlockwise direction.

Illustrative Example 4.55

Centres of two similar coils P and Q having same number of turns are located at the coordinates (0.4, 0) and (0, 0.3) such that the plane of coils are perpendicular to X and Y axes respectively. The areas of cross sections of coils P and Q are in the ratio 4 : 3. Coil P has 16 A current in clockwise direction and coil Q has $9\sqrt{3}$ A current in anti-clockwise direction as seen from the origin. A small compass needle is placed at the origin. Find the deflection of the needle, assuming the Earth's magnetic field negligible and the radii of the coils very small compared to their distance from the origin.

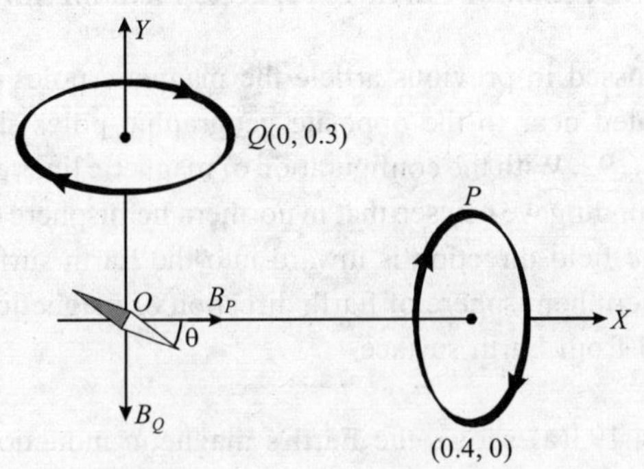

Figure 4.190

Solution

As the radius of coils is considered to be very small we can consider these coils as magnetic dipoles so the magnetic induction due to coil at a distance x along its axis is given as

$$B = \frac{2KM}{x^3} = \frac{\mu_0 NiA}{2\pi x^3}$$

Magnetic induction at O due to coil P is given as

$$B_P = \frac{\mu_0 Ni_P A_P}{2\pi x^3} \quad \text{(along } OX\text{)}$$

Similarly the magnetic induction due to coil Q at O is given as

$$B_Q = \frac{\mu_0 Ni_Q A_Q}{2\pi y^3} \quad \text{(along } YO\text{)}$$

If the compass needle makes an angle θ with X-axis, then it is along the direction of net magnetic induction at point O which is given as

$$\tan\theta = \frac{B_Q}{B_P} = \left(\frac{i_Q}{i_P}\right)\left(\frac{A_Q}{A_P}\right)\left(\frac{x^3}{y^3}\right)$$

$$\Rightarrow \quad \tan\theta = \left(\frac{9\sqrt{3}}{16}\right)\left(\frac{3}{4}\right)\left(\frac{0.4}{0.3}\right)^3 = \sqrt{3}$$

$$\Rightarrow \quad \theta = \tan^{-1}\sqrt{3} = 60°$$

Illustrative Example 4.56

A magnetic dipole with a dipole moment of magnitude 0.020 Am^2 is released from rest in a uniform magnetic field of magnetic induction 52 mT. When the dipole rotates due to magnetic couple on it through the orientations where its dipole moment is aligned with the magnetic field, its kinetic energy is 0.80 mJ.

(a) What is the initial angle between the dipole moment and the magnetic field?

(b) What is the angle when the dipole be at rest again next time?

Solution

(a) By energy conservation, we have

$$U_\theta + K_\theta = U_{0°} + K_{0°}$$

$$\Rightarrow \quad (-MB\cos\theta) + 0 = (-MB\cos 0°) + K_{0°}$$

$$\Rightarrow \quad MB(1-\cos\theta) = K_0$$

$$\Rightarrow \quad \cos\theta = 1 - \frac{K_0}{MB}$$

$$\Rightarrow \quad \cos\theta = 1 - \frac{0.8\times10^{-3}}{0.02\times52\times10^{-3}} = 0.23$$

$$\Rightarrow \quad \theta = \cos^{-1}(0.23) = 76.67°$$

(b) As already discussed that dipole will execute oscillatory motion so on the other side of equilibrium position it will come to rest at the same angle 76.67°.

Illustrative Example 4.57

Figure-4.191 shows two small bar magnets having dipole moments M_1 and M_2 placed at separation r. Find the magnetic interaction energy of this system of dipoles for $d << r$.

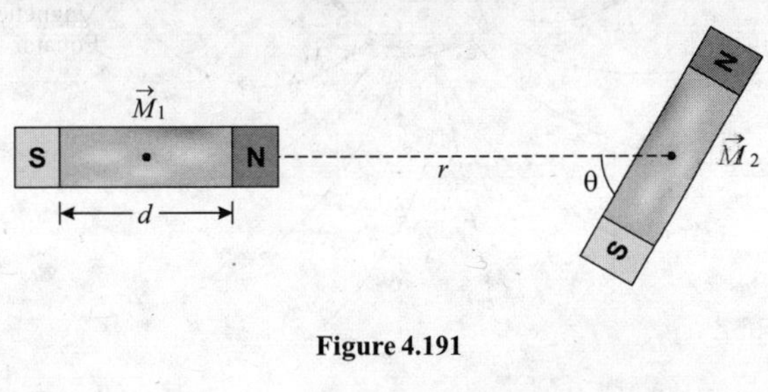

Figure 4.191

Solution

Magnetic induction at the location of M_2 due to M_1 is given as

$$B_1 = \frac{2KM_1}{r^3} = \frac{\mu_0 M_1}{2\pi r^3}$$

Interaction energy of M_2 in the field of M_1 is given as

$$U = -\vec{M_2} \cdot \vec{B_1}$$

$$\Rightarrow \quad U = -M_2 B_1 \cos\theta = -\frac{\mu_0 M_1 M_2}{2\pi r^3}\cos\theta$$

4.12 Terrestrial Magnetism

It has been known from centuries that on suspending a magnet freely it aligns with its axis along north-south direction. This leads physicists to study more about the magnetic field produced by Earth and magnetic properties associated with it. The study of Earth's magnetism and its magnetic properties is called '*Terrestrial Magnetism*'. Earth's magnetic field is also called '*Geomagnetic Field*'. Cause of Earth's magnetic field is the rotation of ionized particles in molten core of earth which constitutes the convection currents at the Earth's core and behave like a coil which produces magnetic field in surrounding and it extends from inner core to outer space. The configuration of Earth's magnetic field is shown in figure-4.192.

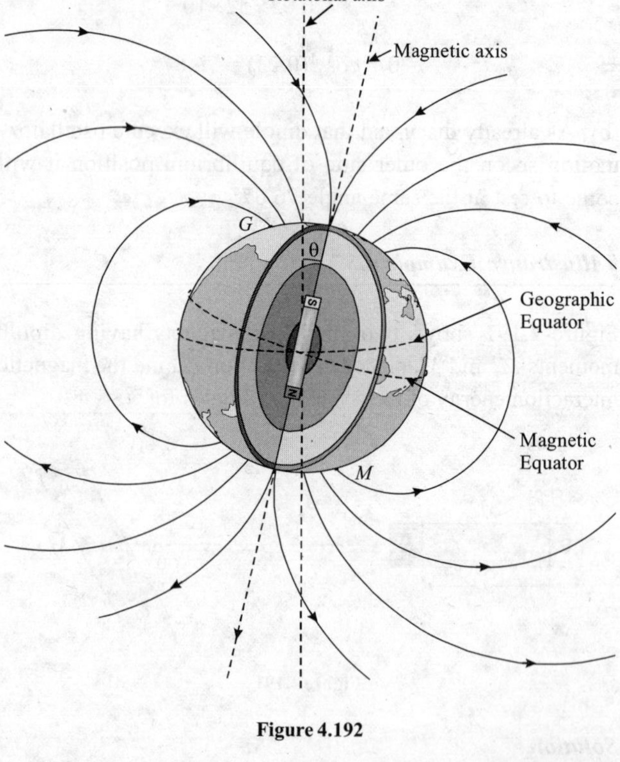

Figure 4.192

As shown in above figure, we can see that the axis of Earth's magnetic field is slightly tilted from its axis of rotation (Geographic Axis) at about 11°. This angle changes with time very slowly due to some geophysical factors not in scope of this book. This axis along which Earth's magnetic coil is considered is called '*Magnetic Axis*' of Earth.

The points on Earth surface where this magnetic axis meet are called magnetic poles. Due to the direction of convection current inside the core of Earth its magnetic induction comes out from the geographic south pole and it gets into the Earth at geographic north pole. Thus the magnetic poles of Earth are located near to the opposite geographic poles as shown in figure-4.192.

4.12.1 Direction of Earth's Magnetic Field on Surface

As discussed in previous article the magnetic poles of earth are located near to the opposite geographic poles shown in figure-4.192. With the configuration of magnetic lines of forces in surrounding we can see that in northern hemisphere of Earth magnetic field direction is inward into the Earth surface and in southern hemisphere of Earth direction of magnetic field is outward from Earth surface.

Figure-4.193(a) shows the Earth's magnetic induction B_E at surface of Earth in northern hemisphere at point G in figure-4.192. The angle θ which the magnetic induction makes with the horizontal at this point is called '*Dip Angle*'. Similarly in southern hemisphere of Earth at point H shown in figure-4.192 the magnetic induction is shown in figure-4.193(a). The horizontal and vertical components of Earth's magnetic induction at point G are given as

$$B_H = B_E \cos\theta \quad \text{... (4.203)}$$

and

$$B_V = B_E \sin\theta \quad \text{... (4.204)}$$

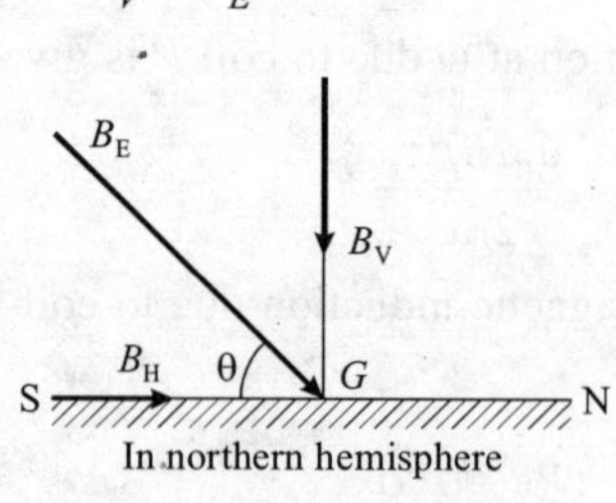

(a)

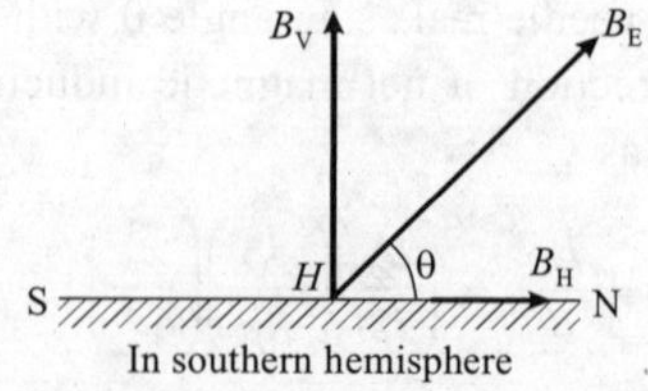

(b)

Figure 4.193

Dividing equations-(4.203) and (4.204), we have

$$\tan\theta = \left(\frac{B_V}{B_H}\right)$$

$$\Rightarrow \qquad \theta = \tan^{-1}\left(\frac{B_V}{B_H}\right) \qquad \dots (4.205)$$

At a point in southern or northern hemisphere we can see that always the horizontal component of Earth's magnetic induction points from approximately south to north at that point thats why when we suspend a magnet freely at any point due to the magnetic torque on it due to horizontal component of Earth's magnetic induction the magnet aligns along north-south direction.

A magnetic compass also works because of the torque on the magnetic needle due to horizontal component of Earth's magnetic induction. As we've discussed that magnetic poles of Earth do not exactly coincide with the geographic poles but still the direction of B_H approximately points from south to north direction at that point which fairly works well for the purpose of navigation as shown in figure-4.194.

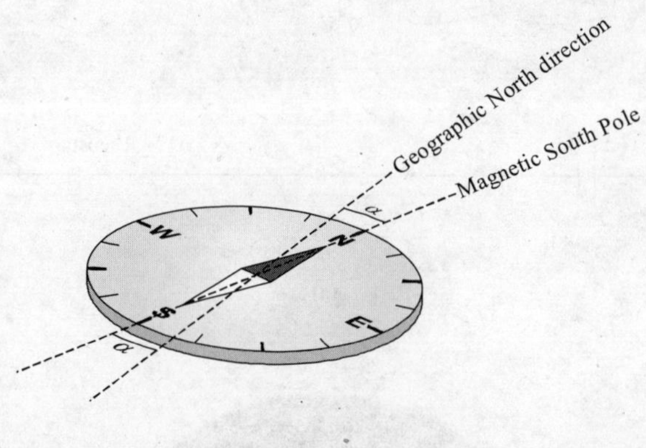

Figure 4.194

4.12.2 Some Definitions and Understanding Earth's Magnetic Field

While analyzing Earth's magnetism there are some terms we need to understand clearly which helps in various applications related to Earth's magnetism. We will discuss and understand all these terms one by one.

Geographic Meridian : At any point on Earth surface this is a vertical plane containing north-south direction at that point. Figure-4.195 shows the geographic meridian at a point A on Earth Surface. This can also be defined as a vertical plane at any point on earth surface such that every horizontal line along east-west direction passing through this plane will cross the plane normally.

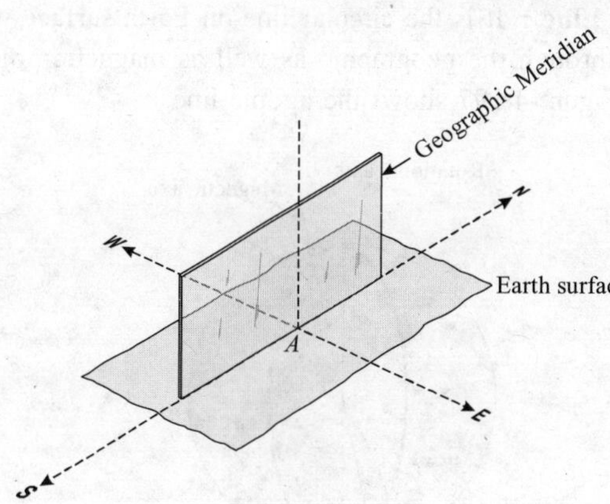

Figure 4.195

Magnetic Meridian : At any point on Earth surface this is a vertical plane containing the direction of net magnetic induction of Earth's field. If a surface is placed in this vertical plane then the magnetic flux of Earth's magnetic field through this surface is always zero. Figure-4.196 shows both Geographic and Magnetic Meridian at a point A on Earth surface.

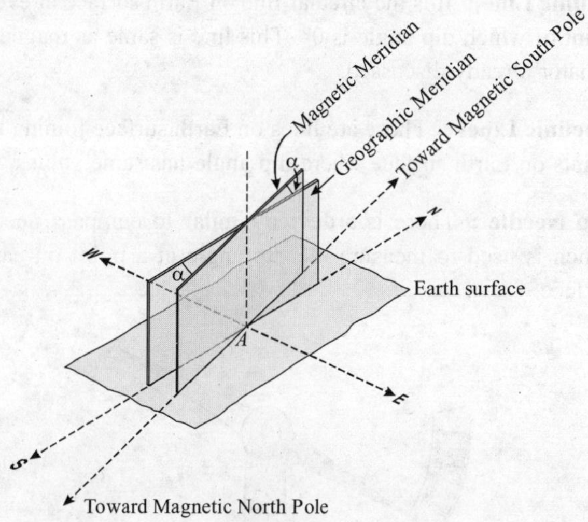

Figure 4.196

Geographic and Magnetic Equator : Geographic equator is the circular line on earth which divides the Earth in two equal hemispheres at a plane normal to the axis of rotation of Earth whereas magnetic equator is also a circular line on Earth surface at which Earth's magnetic field is horizontal or dip angle is 0°. Both geographic and magnetic equators are shown in figure-4.192.

Magnetic Declination : At any point on Earth surface it is the angle between the magnetic north-south direction and true north-south direction at that point. This is also defined as the angle between geographic and magnetic meridian at a point on Earth surface.

Agonic Line : It is the circular line on Earth surface which passes through the geographic as well as magnetic poles of Earth. Figure-4.197 shows the agonic line.

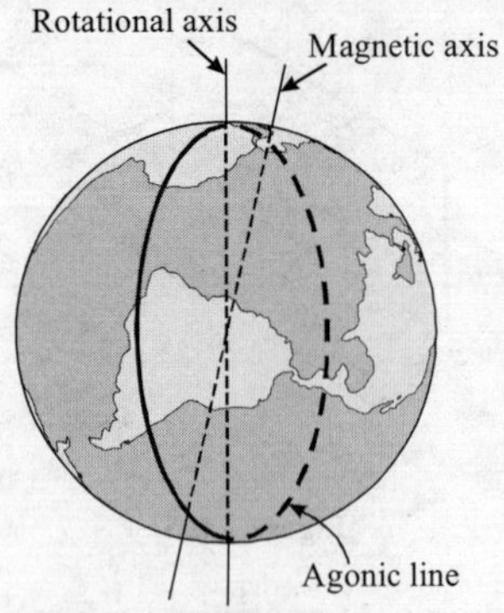

Figure 4.197

Isogonic Lines : These are lines on Earth surface joining the points on Earth surface where magnetic declination is same. Further details about these lines are not in our scope of discussion.

Aclinic Line : It is the circular line on Earth surface at every point of which dip angle is 0°. This line is same as magnetic equator already discussed.

Isoclinic Lines : These are lines on Earth surface joining the points on Earth surface where dip angle has same values.

Dip Needle : There is a device similar to compass needle which is used to measure the dip angle at a point on earth surface.

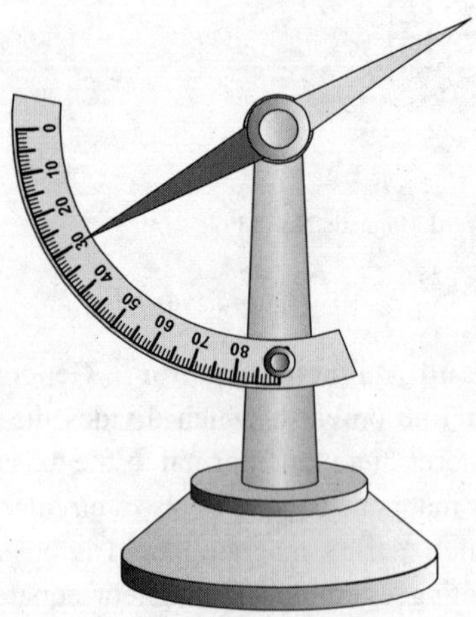

Figure 4.198

This is called '*Dip Needle*' shown in figure-4.198. This needle is mounted to rotate freely in a vertical plane. First the needle plane is placed in magnetic meridian so that the needle gets aligned along the direction of net magnetic induction of Earth as shown in figure then on the pre-calibrated scale dip angle can be measured.

4.12.3 Tangent Galvanometer

Tangent galvanometer is a device used to calculate horizontal component of Earth's magnetic induction. Figure-4.199(a) shows a tangent galvanometer in which there is a circular coil *C* mounted on a stand in vertical plane which can be rotated on the mount. A horizontal compass needle is fixed at the center of coil as shown. On the mount of the device the ends of the coil wire are connected to terminals at which external lead wires can be joined and current is passed in the coil *C*. Figure-4.199(b) shows the picture of an actual tangent galvanometer used in labs.

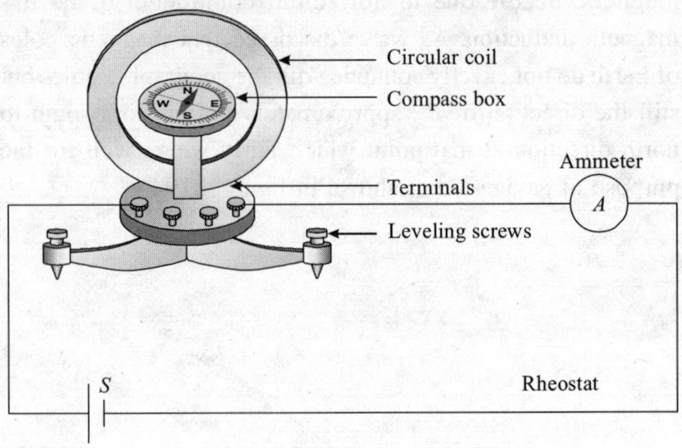

(a)

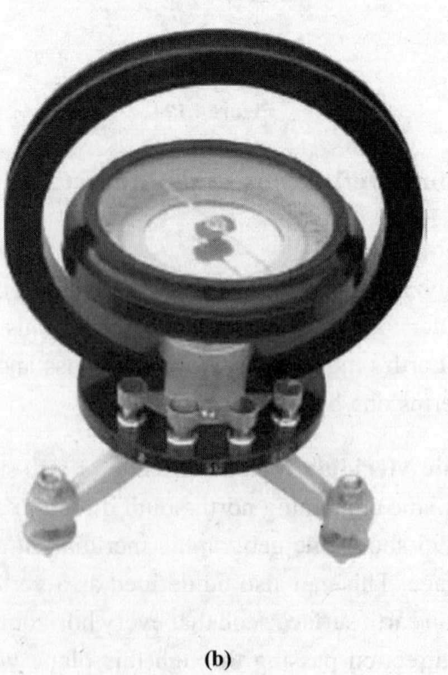

(b)

Figure 4.199

To setup the tangent galvanometer for experiment first the coil C is rotated and aligned along the magnetic meridian. For this coil C is to be rotated till the compass needle comes in the vertical plane of coil as the vertical plane in which compass needle naturally floats is the magnetic meridian at a point on earth surface.

Now a current is passed through the coil C and it is gradually increased by sliding the rheostat. Due to current in coil it produces a magnetic induction at its center due to which the magnetic needle deflects. If B_C is the magnetic induction at center of coil due to coil current and B_H is the horizontal component of earth's magnetic induction at this point then deflection of compass needle from its initial direction is given as

$$\theta = \tan^{-1}\left(\frac{B_C}{B_H}\right) \qquad \dots (4.206)$$

Figure-4.200 shows the deflection of compass needle at the center of coil C due to magnetic induction of the coil current.

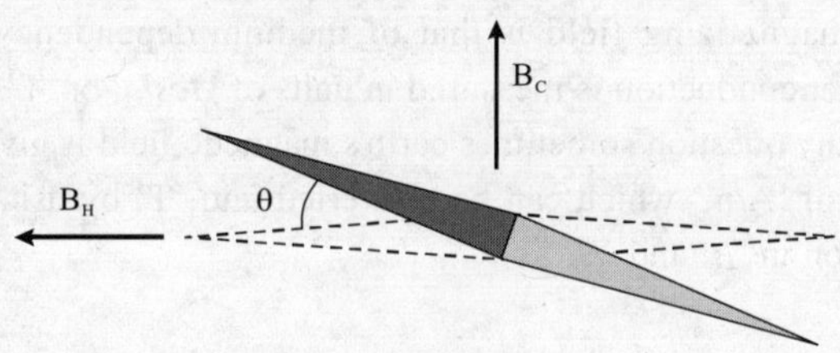

Figure 4.200

While executing the experiment we change the current in coil till the deflection angle of needle becomes 45° and at this state we measure the reading of ammeter, say this is I. Thus at $\theta = 45°$ we use

$$B_H = B_C$$

$$\Rightarrow \qquad B_H = \frac{\mu_0 IN}{2R} \qquad \dots (4.207)$$

By substituting the values on RHS of equation-(4.207) we can calculate the value of B_H. The experiment can be repeated for different values of N by selecting different terminals on the mount of tangent galvanometer and calculate several values of B_H of which average can be obtained along with error analysis and standard deviation of the experimental value of B_H.

4.12.4 Deflection Magnetometer

Deflection magnetometer is an experimental setup used to measure the magnetic moment and pole strength of a bar magnet. It is also used to compare the pole strengths of two bar magnets. A deflection magnetometer consists of a small magnetic compass needle pivoted at the center of a scale as shown in figure-4.201. The compass is fixed at the scale in such a way that its circular scale can be rotated which is marked with 0°– 90°– 0°– 90° in perpendicular direction as shown which are kept exactly perpendicular to the scale as shown in figure-4.201.

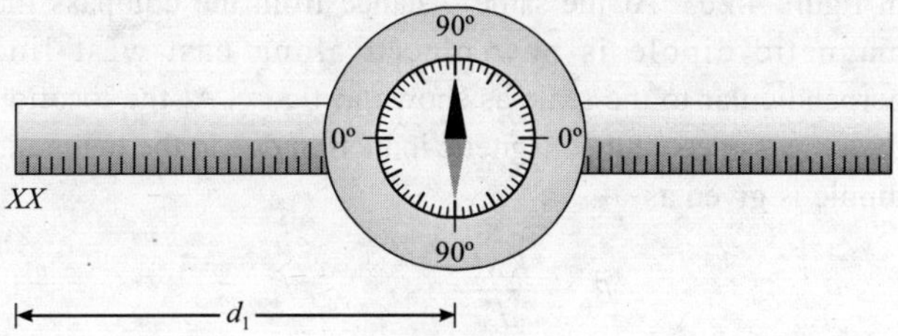

Figure 4.201

There are two positions of the magnetometer for measuring the magnetic moment of a bar magnet or a magnetic dipole. These are called 'tan$A$' and 'tan$B$' positions. In tan$A$ position of magnetometer, the scale of magnetometer is placed at a point along east-west line as shown in figure-4.202 and it is adjusted so that the compass needle points exactly along N-S direction of compass which is perpendicular to the scale. The magnetic dipole of which magnetic moment is to be measured is also placed along the scale line as shown at some distance d_1 from the compass needle. The magnetic induction due to the magnetic dipole at the location of compass is given as

$$B_r = \frac{2KM}{d_1^3}$$

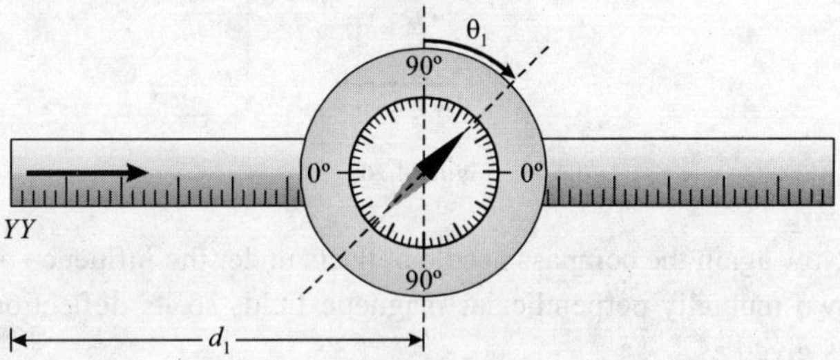

Figure 4.202

If horizontal component of earth's magnetic field is B_H then in tan$A$ position deflection of compass needle is given as

$$\tan\theta_1 = \frac{B_r}{B_H} \qquad \dots (4.208)$$

$$\Rightarrow \qquad B_r = B_H \tan\theta_1$$

$$\Rightarrow \qquad \frac{2KM}{d_1^3} = B_H \tan\theta_1$$

$$\Rightarrow \qquad M = \frac{2\pi B_H d_1^3 \tan\theta_1}{\mu_0} \qquad \dots (4.209)$$

Now the magnetometer scale is rotated by 90° and it is placed along north-south direction and its circular scale is also rotated with 90° – 90° line along N-S direction and it is adjusted so that magnetic needle exactly points parallel to the scale. This is called tan B position of the magnetometer which is shown in figure-4.203. At the same distance from the compass the magnetic dipole is now placed along east-west line perpendicular to the scale as shown in figure. At the location of compass needle the magnetic induction due to the magnetic dipole is given as

$$B_\theta = \frac{KM}{d_1^3}$$

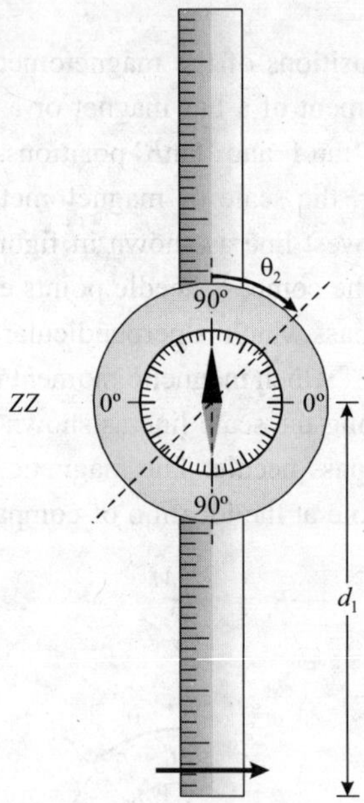

Figure 4.203

Now again the compass needle deflects under the influence of two mutually perpendicular magnetic fields so its deflection is given as

$$\tan\theta_2 = \frac{B_\theta}{B_H} \quad \text{... (4.210)}$$

$$\Rightarrow \quad B_r = B_H \tan\theta_2$$

$$\Rightarrow \quad \frac{KM}{d_1^3} = B_H \tan\theta_2$$

$$\Rightarrow \quad M = \frac{4\pi B_H d_1^3 \tan\theta_2}{\mu_0} \quad \text{... (4.211)}$$

Using equation-(4.209) and (4.211) magnetic moment of magnetic dipole can be calculated. If we use a bar magnet then instead of results of magnetic dipole we need to use the result of magnetic induction due to a bar magnet along its axial point in tan$A$ position and result of magnetic induction due to a bar magnet at its equatorial point in tan$B$ position.

4.12.5 Earth's Magnetic Field in Other Units

Earth's magnetic field is produced by the convection currents at the core of earth and the field which is observed outside the earth's surface magnetizes different materials found on earth surface and inside as well. Over a long period of time such materials transform into magnets as these are magnetised by earth's magnetic field. So it was considered that earth's magnetic field is independent of the type of material which is being magnetized and it was used to be referred as '*Earth's Magnetizing Field*' and it was denoted by the symbol $\vec{H}$ which is measured in units of '*Ampere per meter*' or 'A/m'. After the detailed study of magnetic induction over a period of time it was understood that magnetic induction changes when the field enters inside a material medium due to polarization of medium similar to the case of electric field when it enters in a dielectric medium. The only difference in magnetic induction and magnetizing field is that of medium dependency and magnetic induction is measured in units of '*Tesla*' or 'T'. Still in many question sometimes earth's magnetic field is given in units of 'A/m' which can be converted into 'T' by using the relation in $\vec{B}$ and $\vec{H}$ as

$$\vec{B} = \mu\vec{H}$$

$$\Rightarrow \quad \vec{B} = \mu_0\mu_r\vec{H} \quad \text{... (4.212)}$$

About the above relation given in equation-(4.212) and magnetizing field we will study in detail under the topic of magnetic properties of material in next chapter.

4.12.6 Apparent angle of dip at a point on Earth's Surface

When at a point on earth's surface dip needle is placed in magnetic meridian then it aligns along the direction of earth's magnetic field and on the vertical circular scale we can measure the dip angle at that location.

When the dip needle is placed in a plane which is at an angle θ to the magnetic meridian then in this plane the horizontal component of earth's magnetic field is given as

$$B'_H = B_H \cos\theta$$

If θ_D' is the dip angle measured by the dip needle which is called apparent dip angle at this location then it is given as

$$\tan\theta'_D = \frac{B_V}{B_H\cos\theta} \quad \text{... (4.213)}$$

True dip angle θ_D at this location is given as

$$\tan\theta_D = \frac{B_V}{B_H} \quad \text{... (4.214)}$$

From above equations-(4.213) and (4.214) we have

$$\tan\theta_D = \tan\theta'_D \cos\theta \quad \text{... (4.215)}$$

Above equation-(4.215) relates the true dip angle, apparent dip angle and the angle between the vertical plane and the magnetic meridian in which the dip angle is apparently measured.

Illustrative Example 4.58

At a point on earth surface horizontal component of earth's magnetic field is 40 μT and dip angle is 30°. Find the total magnetic field of earth at this point.

Solution

In this case we use

$$B_H = B_E \cos\theta$$

$$\Rightarrow \quad B_E = \frac{B_H}{\cos\theta} = \frac{40\times10^{-6}}{\sqrt{3}/2}$$

$$\Rightarrow \quad B_E = 46\ \mu T$$

Illustrative Example 4.59

The radius of tangent galvanometer coil is 16 cm. Find the number of turn in its coil if a current of 40 mA is required to produce a deflection of 30° in it from magnetic meridian. Horizontal component of earth's magnetic field is 36×10^{-6} T.

Solution

In a tangent galvanometer if needle deflection is θ from magnetic meridian as shown in figure-4.204 we use

$$B_C = B_H \tan\theta$$

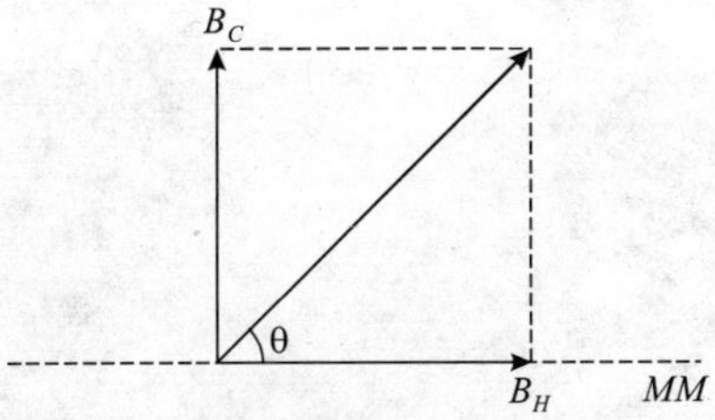

Figure 4.204

$$\Rightarrow \quad \frac{\mu_0 NI}{2R} = B_H \tan\theta$$

$$\Rightarrow \quad N = \frac{2RB_H \tan\theta}{\mu_0 I}$$

$$\Rightarrow \quad N = \frac{2\times0.16\times36\times10^{-6}\times1/\sqrt{3}}{4\pi\times10^{-7}\times40\times10^{-3}}$$

$$\Rightarrow \quad N = 0.0132 \times 10^4 = 132 \text{ turns}$$

Illustrative Example 4.60

In the magnetic meridian of a certain place at the center of the coil of a tangent galvanometer, the horizontal component of earth's magnetic field is 0.26 G and the dip angle is 60°. Find :

(a) Vertical component of earth's magnetic field

(b) The net magnetic field at this place.

(c) If a current is passed in tangent galvanometer, its coil produces a magnetic induction 3.47×10^{-3} T. Calculate the deflection in compass needle of tangent galvanometer.

Solution

(a) Vertical component of earth's field is given as

$$B_V = B_H \tan\theta$$

$$\Rightarrow \quad B_V = (0.26) \tan 60° = 0.45 \text{ G}$$

(b) Horizontal component and total field of earth are related as

$$B_H = B_E \cos\theta$$

$$\Rightarrow \quad B_E = \frac{B_H}{\cos\theta} = \frac{0.26}{\cos 60°} = 0.52 \text{ G}$$

(c) At the center of coil the horizontal component of earth's magnetic induction in tesla is given as

$$B_H = 0.26 \times 10^{-4} \text{ T}$$

The deflection in compass needle of a tangent galvanometer is given as

$$\theta = \tan^{-1}\left(\frac{B_C}{B_H}\right)$$

$$\Rightarrow \quad \theta = \tan^{-1}\left(\frac{3.47\times10^{-3}}{2.6\times10^{-3}}\right)$$

$$\Rightarrow \quad \theta = \tan^{-1}(1.33) = 63°$$

Web Reference at www.physicsgalaxy.com

Age Group - Grade 11 & 12 | Age 17-19 Years
Section - Magnetic Effects
Topic - Classical & Terrestrial Magnetism
Module Number - 1 to 26

Practice Exercise 4.6

(i) A short bar magnet is placed in magnetic meridian with its north pole pointing toward south. Its magnetic moment is 2 Am^2. Neutral point is obtained 10 cm from centre of magnet toward north. Calculate horizontal component of earth's magnetic field.

[40 μT]

(ii) A magnetic dipole of magnetic moment 6 Am^2 is lying in a horizontal plane with its north pole pointing toward 60° East of North. Find the net horizontal magnetic field at a point on the axis of the magnet 0.2 m away from it. Horizontal Component of earth field at this place is 30 μT.

[$30\sqrt{31}$μT]

(iii) A coil of 50 turns and 10 cm diameter is made out of a wire of resistivity 2×10^{-6} Ωcm and cross sectional radius 0.1 mm. The coil is connected to a source of EMF 10 V and of negligible internal resistance.

(a) Find the current through the coil

(b) What must be potential difference across the coil so as to nullify the horizontal component of earth's magnetic field, 0.314×10^{-4} T at the centre of the coil. How should the coil be placed to achieve this result?

[(a) 1 A; (b) 0.5 V, coil is placed in a plane normal to magnetic meridian]

(iv) Two circular coils, each of 100 turns are held such that one lies in the vertical plane and the other in the horizontal plane with their centres coinciding. The radii of the vertical and the horizontal coils are respectively 20 cm and 30 cm. If the directions of the currents in them are such that the earth's magnetic field at the centre of the coils is exactly neutralised, calculate the currents in each coil. Horizontal component of earth's field at common center of coils is 27.8 A/m and angle of dip at this point is 30°.

[111.2 mA, 96.3 mA]

(v) A magnetic needle suspended in a vertical plane at 30° from the magnetic meridian makes an angle of 45° with the horizontal. Find the true angle of dip.

[41°]

(vi) Two small magnets of magnetic moments 0.108 Am^2 and 0.192 Am^2 are placed at some separation that their axes are mutually perpendicular. If the distance of the point of intersection of axes of magnets be respectively 30 cm and 40 cm from these magnets, then find the resultant magnetic induction at the point of intersection. The magnetic moments of both the magnets are pointing toward the point of intersection of their axes.

[10^{-6}]

(vii) A short magnet produces a deflection of 30° in needle of a magnetometer when placed at certain distance in tan*A* position of magnetometer. If another short magnet of double the length and thrice the pole strength is placed at the same distance in tan*B* position of the magnetometer, what is the deflection produced ?

[60°]

(viii) A magnetic needle performs 20 oscillations per minute in a horizontal plane. If the angle of dip be 30°, then how many oscillations per minute will this needle perform in vertical north-south plane and in vertical east-west plane?

[21.5 min^{-1}, 15.2 min^{-1}]

Advance Illustrations Videos at www.physicsgalaxy.com

Age Group - Advance Illustrations for JEE(Adv)/IPhO
Section - Magnetic Effects
Topic - Magnetic Effects & Electromagnetic Induction
Illustrations - 66 In-depth Illustrations Videos

* * * * *

Discussion Questions

Q4-1 A bar magnet is stationary in magnetic meridian. Another similar magnet is kept parallel to it such that the centres lie on their perpendicular bisectors. If the second magnet is free to move, then what type of motion it will have : translatory, rotatory or both?

Q4-2 Does Ampere's law on a closed loop in a region is valid if no current is enclosed by the loop and there are some currents which exist outside the loop.

Q4-3 The electric current in a straight wire is constant and wire is kept along east-west line at a point in a horizontal plane. A point P is located to the north side of wire at some distance. What is the direction of magnetic induction at point P. If the wire is rotated in horizontal plane by an angle 30° then what will be the direction at point P.

Q4-4 Is it possible that a body's speed can be increased by magnetic forces? Explain.

Q4-5 Torques τ_1 and τ_2 are required for a magnetic needle to remain perpendicular to the magnetic fields at two different places. What is the ratio of magnetic fields at those places ?

Q4-6 If a wire carries a time varying current then in its surrounding will Ampere's law be valid for a closed loop.

Q4-7 If a compass-needle be placed on the magnetic north pole of the earth then how it behave? If a dip needle be placed at the same place, then what will be its behaviour?

Q4-8 A current carrying wire is placed along the axis of a uniformly charged circular ring. If the ring starts rotating about its central axis what will be force on the current carrying wire due to the moving charges of ring.

Q4-9 An isolated metal wire not carrying any current is placed in magnetic field. Does free electrons of this metal wire experience magnetic force due to thermal motion. If yes what is the effect of it.

Q4-10 If the horizontal and vertical components of earth's magnetic field are equal at a certain place, what is the angle of dip there?

Q4-11 In different electrical circuit generally connecting lead wires are twisted together in electrical appliances. Why this is done ?

Q4-12 For a three dimensional current carrying loop is it possible that in a magnetic field net torque on it is zero for some orientation? Explain the situation.

Q4-13 What is the maximum value of the angle of dip? At what places does it occur?

Q4-14 Why an iron pin is attracted to the ends of a bar magnet but not to the middle region of it. Is the material of a magnet at the end is differently or strongly polarized or it is something else? Explain.

Q4-15 Two wires carrying equal currents are placed at right angle to each other without contact at middle point. If one wire is kept fixed and other is released from rest. Describe the motion of this wire.

Q4-16 Cosmic rays are charged particles that strike out atmosphere from some external source. We find that more low-energy cosmic rays reach the earth at the north and south magnetic poles than at the (magnetic) equator. Why it is so?

Q4-17 Can you calculate magnetic induction due to a semi-infinite current carrying straight wire. If not then explain why?

Q4-18 When two magnets are placed in such a way along the same line that their opposite poles facing each other. Now if the magnets are released from rest they gain kinetic energy due to attractive forces. Is work done by magnetic forces in this case non-zero or it is something else.

Q4-19 Is there any point on earth surface where dip angle is 90°? If yes how many such points are there.

Q4-20 Two high energy proton beams if parallel to each other repel each other whereas two parallel wires carrying currents in same direction attract each other. Why ?

Q4-21 A charged particle moves with a velocity v near a current carrying wire experiences a magnetic force on it. If this charge is observed from a reference frame also moving at same velocity v as that of charge then this charge will appear at rest to the observer in moving frame. Will magnetic force and magnetic field in that reference frame become zero? Explain.

Q4-22 The neutron, which has no charge, has a magnetic dipole moment. Is this possible ?

Q4-23 Is it possible that a closed current carrying loop placed in a magnetic field experiences a non-zero magnetic force? Explain.

* * * * *

Conceptual MCQs Single Option Correct

4-1 A uniform magnetic field is at right angles to the direction of motion of protons. As a result, the protons describes a circular path of radius 2.5 cm. If the speed of the protons is doubled, then the radius of the circular path will be :

(A) 0.5 cm (B) 2.5 cm
(C) 5.0 cm (D) 7.5 cm

4-2 A current is passed through a straight wire bent at a point. The magnetic field established around it has its lines of forces :

(A) Circular and endless
(B) Oval in shape and endless
(C) Straight
(D) All are true

4-3 A charged particle moves in a circular path in a uniform magnetic field. If its speed is reduced then its time period will :

(A) Increase (B) Decrease
(C) Remain same (D) None of these

4-4 An electron of mass m_e, initially at rest, moves through a certain distance in a uniform electric field in time t_1. A proton of mass m_p, also, initially at rest, takes time t_2 to move through an equal distance in this uniform electric field. Neglecting the effect of gravity, the ratio of t_2/t_1 is nearly equal to :

(A) 1 (B) $(m_p/m_e)^{1/2}$
(C) $(m_e/m_p)^{1/2}$ (D) 1836

4-5 A proton, a deuteron and an α-particle having the same kinetic energy are moving in circular trajectories in a constant magnetic field. If r_p, r_d and r_α denote respectively the radii of the trajectories of these particles, then :

(A) $r_\alpha = r_p < r_d$ (B) $r_\alpha > r_d > r_p$
(C) $r_\alpha = r_d > r_p$ (D) $r_p = r_d = r_\alpha$

4-6 Identify the correct statement related to the direction of magnetic moment of a planar loop :

(A) It is always perpendicular to the plane of the loop
(B) It depends on the direction of current
(C) It can be obtained by right hand screw rule
(D) All of the above

4-7 Two free parallel wires carrying currents in the opposite directions :

(A) Attract each other
(B) Repel each other
(C) Do not affect each other
(D) Get rotated to be perpendicular to each other

4-8 A non-planer closed loop of arbitrary shape carrying a current I is placed in uniform magnetic field. The force acting on the loop :

(A) Is zero only for one orientation of loop in magnetic field
(B) Is zero for two symmetrically located positions of loop in magnetic field
(C) Is zero for all orientations
(D) Is never zero

4-9 A vertical straight conductor carries a current vertically upwards. A point P lies to the east of it a small distance and another point Q lies to the west at the same distance. The magnetic induction magnitude at P is :

(A) Greater than at Q
(B) Same as at Q
(C) Less than at Q
(D) Greater or less than at Q depending upon the strength of the current

4-10 A wire is placed parallel to the lines of force in a magnetic field and a current flows in the wire. Then :

(A) The wire will experience a force in the direction of the magnetic field
(B) The wire will not experience any force at all
(C) The wire will experience a force in a direction opposite to the field
(D) It experiences a force in a direction perpendicular to lines of force

4-11 The straight wire AB carries a current I. The ends of the wire subtend angles θ_1 and θ_2 at the point P as shown in figure-4.205. The magnetic field at the point P is :

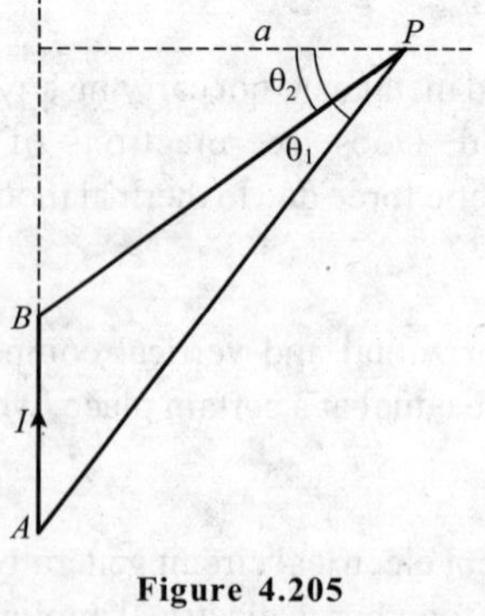

Figure 4.205

(A) $\frac{\mu_0 I}{4\pi a}(\sin\theta_1 - \sin\theta_2)$ (B) $\frac{\mu_0 I}{4\pi a}(\sin\theta_1 + \sin\theta_2)$

(C) $\frac{\mu_0 I}{4\pi a}(\cos\theta_1 - \cos\theta_2)$ (D) $\frac{\mu_0 I}{4\pi a}(\cos\theta_1 + \cos\theta_2)$

4-12 The coil of a tangent galvanometer is put in the magnetic meridian :
(A) To avoid the magnetic effect of the earth field
(B) To produce intense magnetic field at the centre of the coil
(C) To produce a field at right angle to the earth's field
(D) To avoid error due to parallax

4-13 Two circular coils X and Y having equal number of turns and carry equal currents in the same sense and subtend same solid angle at point O. If the smaller coil X is midway between O and Y, then if we represent the magnetic induction due to the bigger coil Y at O as B_y and that due to smaller coil x at O as B_x, then :

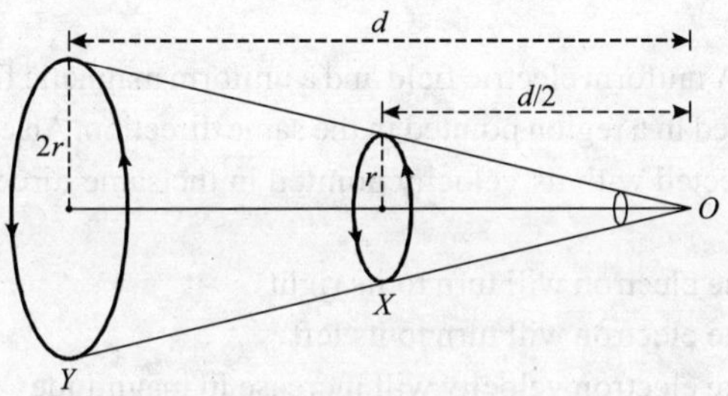

Figure 4.206

(A) $\frac{B_y}{B_x} = 0.25$ (B) $\frac{B_y}{B_x} = 0.5$
(C) $\frac{B_y}{B_x} = 1$ (D) $\frac{B_y}{B_x} = 2$

4-14 Two parallel wires carrying currents in the same direction attract each other because of :
(A) Potential difference between them
(B) Mutual inductance between them
(C) Electric forces between them
(D) Magnetic forces between them

4-15 Two straight long wires are set parallel to each other. Each carries a current i in the same direction and the separation between them is $2r$. The magnetic induction at a distance r between the two wires is :
(A) i/r (B) $2\,i/r$
(C) $4\,i/r$ (D) Zero

4-16 The magnetic field of a U-magnet is parallel to the surface of this paper with the N-pole on the left side. A conductor is placed in the field so that it is perpendicular to this page. When a current flows through the conductor out of the paper, it will tend to move :
(A) Downward
(B) Upward
(C) To the right
(D) First downward and then upward

4-17 The figure shows the cross-section of two long coaxial tubes carrying equal currents I in opposite directions. If B_1 and B_2 are magnetic fields at points 1 and 2, as shown in figure-4.207 then :

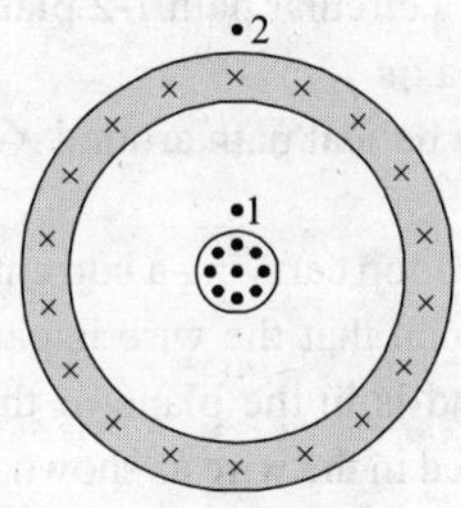

Figure 4.207

(A) $B_1 \neq 0; B_2 = 0$ (B) $B_1 = 0; B_2 = 0$
(C) $B_1 \neq 0; B_2 \neq 0$ (D) $B_1 = 0; B_2 \neq 0$

4-18 An insulating rod of length l carries a charge q uniformly distributed on it. The rod is pivoted at one of its ends and is rotated at a frequency f about a fixed perpendicular axis. The magnetic moment of the rod is :

(A) $\frac{\pi q f l^2}{12}$ (B) $\frac{\pi q f l^2}{2}$
(C) $\frac{\pi q f l^2}{6}$ (D) $\frac{\pi q f l^2}{3}$

4-19 The strength of the magnetic field around a long straight current carrying conductor :
(A) Is same everywhere around the conductor
(B) Obeys inverse square law
(C) Is directly proportional to the square of the distance from the conductor
(D) None of the above

4-20 The plane of a dip circle is set in the geographical meridian and the apparent dip angle is θ_1. It is then set in a vertical plane perpendicular to the geographical meridian, the apparent dip becomes θ_2. The angle of declination α at that place is given as :

(A) $\tan\alpha = \sqrt{(\tan\theta_1 \tan\theta_2)}$ (B) $\tan\alpha = \tan\theta_1/\tan\theta_2$
(C) $\tan\alpha = (\tan^2\theta_1 + \tan^2\theta_2)$ (D) $\tan\alpha = \tan\theta_2/\tan\theta_1$

4-21 A moving coil type of galvanometer is based upon the principle that :
(A) Wire carrying a current experiences a force in magnetic field
(B) Wire carrying current produces a force in magnetic field
(C) A current carrying loop in magnetic field experiences a torque
(D) All are true

4-22 A charge moving with velocity v in X-direction is subjected to a field of magnetic induction in negative X-direction. As a result, the charge will :

(A) Remain unaffected
(B) Start moving in a circular path Y-Z plane
(C) Retard along X-axis
(D) Moving along a helical path around X-axis

4-23 A rectangular loop carrying a current i is situated near a long straight wire such that the wire is parallel to one of the sides of the loop and is in the plane of the loop. If a steady current I is established in the wire as shown in figure-4.208, the loop will :

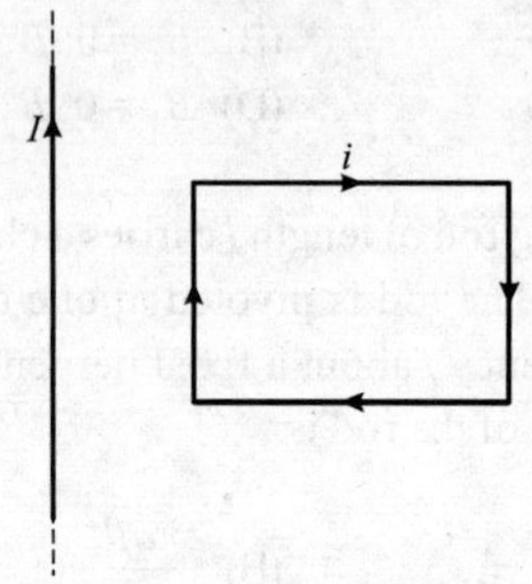

Figure 4.208

(A) Rotate about an axis parallel to the wire
(B) Move away from the wire
(C) Move towards the wire
(D) Remain stationary

4-24 An electron enters a region where magnetic induction B and electric field strength E are mutually perpendicular, then :

(A) It will always move in the direction of B
(B) It will always move in the direction of E
(C) It always possess circular motion
(D) It can go undeflected

4-25 A length of wire carries a steady current. It is bent first to form a circular plane coil of one turn. The same length is now bent more sharply to give a double loop of smaller radius. The magnetic field at the centre caused by the same current is :

(A) Quarter of its first value
(B) Unaltered
(C) Four times of its first value
(D) A half of its first value

4-26 A proton and an α-particle enter in a uniform magnetic field with the same velocity. The period of rotation of the α-particle will be :

(A) Four times that of the proton
(B) Two times that of the proton
(C) Three times that of the proton
(D) Same as that of the proton

4-27 Two particles X and Y having equal charges, after being accelerated through the same potential difference, enter a region of uniform magnetic field and describe circular paths of radii R_1 and R_2 respectively. The ratio of the masses of X to that of Y :

(A) $(R_1/R_2)^{1/2}$ (B) R_2/R_1
(C) $(R_1/R_2)^2$ (D) R_1/R_2

4-28 If a charged particle moves through a magnetic field perpendicular to it :

(A) Both momentum and energy of the particle change
(B) The momentum changes but the energy is constant
(C) Both momentum and energy are constant
(D) The momentum remains constant and energy is changed

4-29 A uniform electric field and a uniform magnetic field are produced in a region pointed in the same direction. An electron is projected with its velocity pointed in the same direction of fields :

(A) The electron will turn to its right
(B) The electron will turn to its left
(C) The electron velocity will increase in magnitude
(D) The electron velocity will decrease in magnitude

4-30 Two single turn circular coils P and Q are made from similar wires but radius of Q is twice that of P. What should be the value of potential difference across them so that the magnetic induction at their centre may be the same ?

(A) $V_q = 2V_p$ (B) $V_q = 3V_P$
(C) $V_q = 4V_p$ (D) $V_q = 1/4V_p$

4-31 A proton (mass m and charge $+e$) and an alpha particle (mass $4\,m$ and charge $+2\,e$) are projected with the same kinetic energy at right angles to a uniform magnetic field. Which one of the following statements will be true ?

(A) The alpha-particle will be bent in a circular path with a smaller radius that of the proton
(B) The radius of the path of the alpha-particle will be greater than that of the proton
(C) The alpha-particle and the proton will be bent in a circular path with the same radius
(D) The alpha-particle and the proton will go through the field in a straight line

4-32 A circular coil has one turn and carries a current i. The same wire is wound into a smaller coil of 4 turns and the same current is passed through it. The field at the centre :

(A) Decreases to 1/4 of the value
(B) Is the same
(C) Increases to 14 times the value
(D) Decreases to 16 times the value

4-33 Two electrons move parallel to each other with equal speed v. The ratio of magnetic and electrical forces between them is :

(A) v/c
(B) c/v
(C) v^2/c^2
(D) c^2/v^2

4-34 An electron having a charge $-e$ moves with a velocity v in positive X-direction. An electric field exist in region along positive Y-direction and a magnetic field exist in the region along negative X-direction. The force on the electron acts in :

(A) Positive direction of Y-axis
(B) Negative direction of Y-axis
(C) Positive direction of Z-axis
(D) Negative direction of Z-axis

4-35 A charged particle moving in a uniform magnetic field penetrates a layer of lead and loses one half of its kinetic energy. The radius of curvature changes to :

(A) Twice the original radius
(B) $\sqrt{2}$ times the original radius
(C) Half the original radius
(D) $(1/\sqrt{2})$ times the original radius

4-36 Protons are shot in a region perpendicular to a uniform magnetic field in a region :

(A) Magnetic field will have no influence on the motion of protons
(B) Protons will continue to move in the same direction but will gain momentum
(C) Protons will continue to move in the opposite directions but will gain momentum
(D) They will bend in an arc of circle

4-37 In the given diagram, two long parallel wires carry equal currents in opposite directions. Point O is situated midway between the wires and the X-Y plane contains the two wires and the positive Z-axis comes normally out of the plane of paper. The magnetic field B at O is non-zero along :

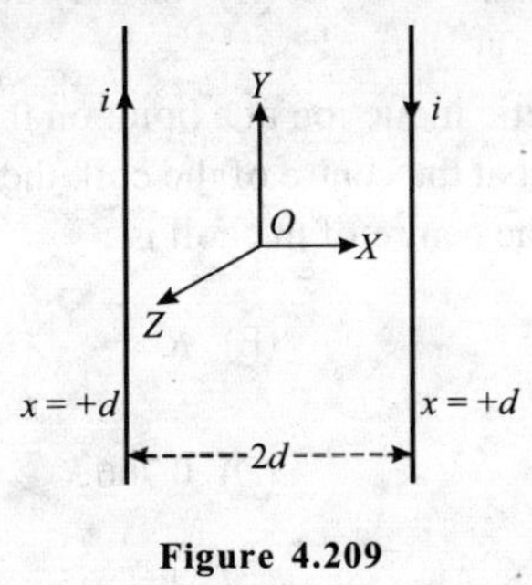

Figure 4.209

(A) X, Y and Z axes
(B) X-axis
(C) Y-axis
(D) Z-axis

4-38 Three very long current carrying wires are placed parallel to each other and perpendicular to the plane of paper as shown in the figure-4.210. All the wires are equally spaced. The magnetic field will be zero at :

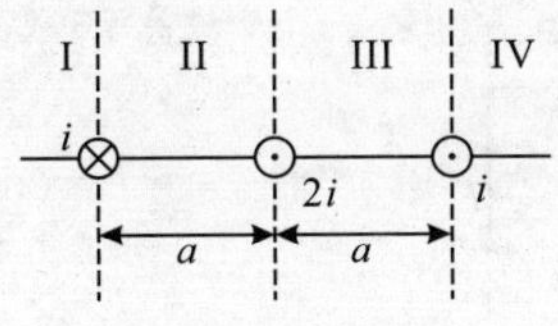

Figure 4.210

(A) Two points in region I
(B) One point in region I and one point in region II
(C) Two points in region III
(D) One point in region I and one point in region III

4-39 A circular loop is kept in that vertical plane which contains the north south direction. If carries a current that is towards north at the topmost point. Let P be a point on the axis of the circle to the east of it and Q a point on this axis to the west of it. The magnetic field due to the loop :

(A) Is toward east at P and towards west at Q
(B) Is towards west at P and towards east at Q
(C) Is towards east at both P and Q
(D) Is towards west at both P and Q

4-40 Two particles Y and Z emitted by a radioactive source at P made tracks in a chamber as illustrated in the figure-4.211. A magnetic field acts into the paper. Careful measurement showed that both tracks were circular, the radius of Y track being half that of the Z track. Which one of the following statements is certainly true ?

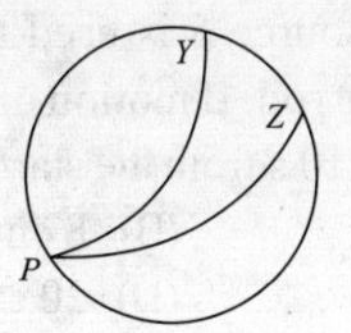

Figure 4.211

(A) Both particles Y and Z carried a positive charge
(B) The mass of particle Z was one-half that of particle Y
(C) The mass of particle Z was twice that of particle Y
(D) The charge of particle Z was twice that of particle Y

* * * * *

Numerical MCQs Single Option Correct

4-1 An infinitely long wire carrying current I is placed along Y axis with current away from origin such that its one end is at point A $(0, b)$ while the wire extends upto $+\infty$ as shown in figure-4.212. The magnitude of magnetic induction at point $(a, 0)$ is :

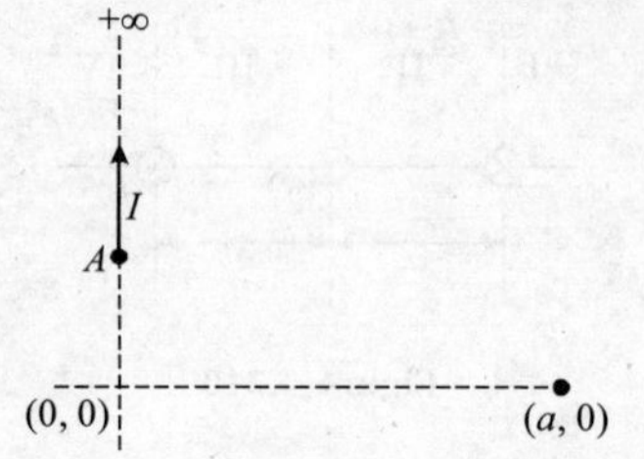

Figure 4.212

(A) $\frac{\mu_0 I}{4\pi a}\left(1+\frac{b}{\sqrt{a^2+b^2}}\right)$ (B) $\frac{\mu_0 I}{4\pi a}\left(1-\frac{b}{\sqrt{a^2+b^2}}\right)$

(C) $\frac{\mu_0 I}{4\pi a}\left(\frac{b}{\sqrt{a^2+b^2}}\right)$ (D) None of these

4-2 A conducting rod of mass 50 g and length 10 cm slide without friction on two long, horizontal rails as shown in figure-4.213.

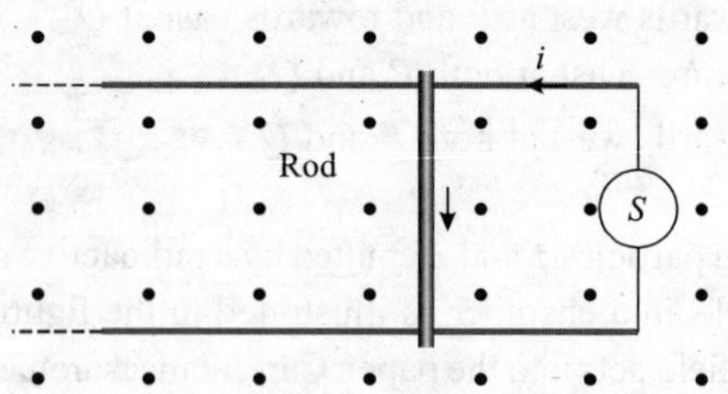

Figure 4.213

A uniform magnetic induction of magnitude 5 mT exists in the region, as shown. A source S is used to maintain a constant current 2 A through the rod. If motion of the rod starts from the rest, its speed after the 10 s from the start of the motion, will be :

(A) 2 cm/s (B) 8 cm/s

(C) 12 cm/s (D) 20 cm/s

4-3 Figure-4.214 shows a long straight wire carrying current I, is bent at its midpoint to form an angle of 45°. Magnetic induction at point P, distance R from point of bending is equal to :

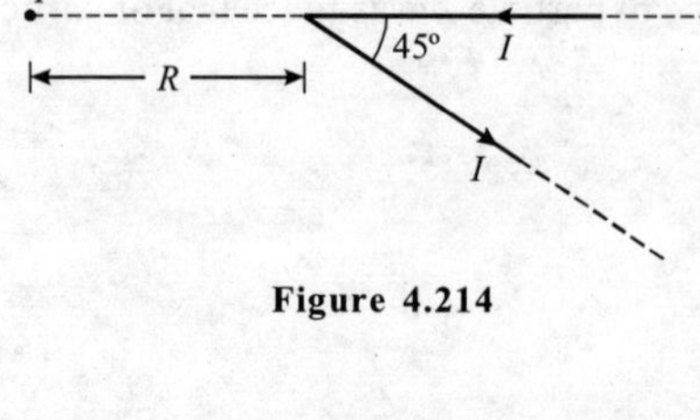

Figure 4.214

(A) $\frac{(\sqrt{2}-1)\mu_0 I}{4\pi R}$ (B) $\frac{(\sqrt{2}+1)\mu_0 I}{4\pi R}$

(C) $\frac{(\sqrt{2}+1)\mu_0 I}{4\sqrt{2}\pi R}$ (D) $\frac{(\sqrt{2}-1)\mu_0 I}{2\sqrt{2}\pi R}$

4-4 Two infinitely long stright wires are arranged perpendicular to each other and are in mutually perpendicular planes as shown in figure-4.215. If $I_1 = 2A$ along the y-axis and $I_2 = 3A$ along negative z-axis and $AP = AB = 1$ cm. The magnetic induction $\vec{B}$ at point P is :

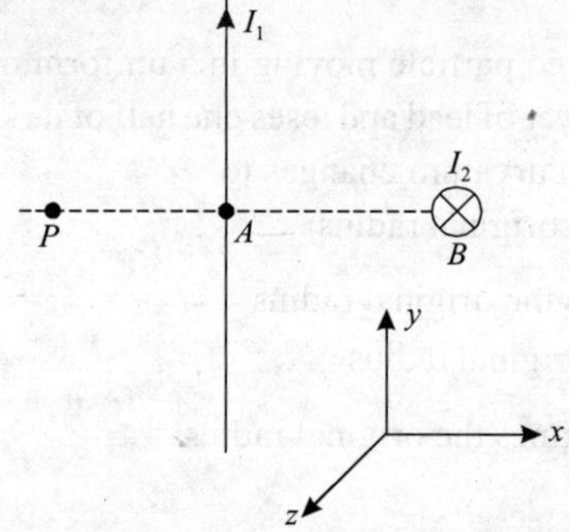

Figure 4.215

(A) $(3\times10^{-5}\text{ T})\,\hat{j}+(-4\times10^{-5}\text{ T})\,\hat{k}$

(B) $(3\times10^{-5}\text{ T})\,\hat{j}+(4\times10^{-5}\text{ T})\,\hat{k}$

(C) $(4\times10^{-5}\text{ T})\,\hat{j}+(3\times10^{-5}\text{ T})\,\hat{k}$

(D) $(-3\times10^{-5}\text{ T})\,\hat{j}+(4\times10^{-5}\text{ T})\,\hat{k}$

4-5 A particle of mass m and charge q is thrown from origin at $t = 0$ with velocity $2\hat{i}+3\hat{j}+4\hat{k}$ units in a region with uniform magnetic field $\vec{B} = 2\hat{i}$ units. After time $t = \pi m/qB$, an electric field $\vec{E}$ is switched on such that particle moves on a straight line with constant speed. $\vec{E}$ may be :

(A) $5\hat{k}-10\hat{j}$ units (B) $-6\hat{k}-9\hat{j}$ units

(C) $-6\hat{k}+8\hat{j}$ units (D) $6\hat{k}+8\hat{j}$ units

4-6 If the magnetic induction at a point on the axis of current coil is half of that at the centre of the coil, then the distance of that point from the centre of the coil is :

(A) $\frac{R}{2}$ (B) R

(C) $\frac{3R}{2}$ (D) $0.766R$

4-7 A current carrying circular coil of single turn of mass m is hanged by two ideal strings as shown in the figure-4.216. A constant magnetic field $\vec{B}$ is set up in the horizontal direction in the region. The ratio of tension (T_1/T_2) in the string will be : [Take $\pi BIR = \frac{mg}{4}$ and $\theta = 45°$ in the figure shown]

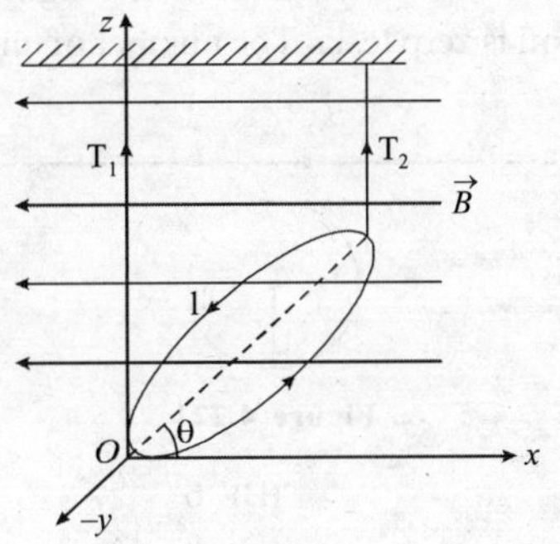

Figure 4.216

(A) 2 : 1 (B) 5 : 3
(C) 4 : 1 (D) 1 : 2

4-8 A helium nucleus is moving in a circular path of radius 0.8 m. If it takes 2 s to complete one revolution. Find out magnetic field produced at the centre of the circle :

(A) $\mu_0 \times 10^{-19}$ T (B) $\frac{10^{-19}}{\mu_0}$ T

(C) 2×10^{-19} T (D) $\frac{2 \times 10^{-19}}{\mu_0}$ T

4-9 A conductor of length l and mass m is placed along the east-west line on a table. Suddenly a certain amount of charge is passed through it and it is found to jump to a height h. The earth's horizontal magnetic induction is B. The charge passed through the conductor is :

(A) $\frac{1}{Bmgh}$ (B) $\frac{\sqrt{2gh}}{Blm}$

(C) $\frac{gh}{Blm}$ (D) $\frac{m\sqrt{2gh}}{Bl}$

4-10 An α particle is moving along a circle of radius R with a constant angular velocity ω. Point A lies in the same plane at a distance 2 R from the centre. The point A records magnetic field produced by α particle. If the minimum time interval between two successive times at which A records zero magnetic field is 't', the angular speed ω, in terms of t is :

(A) $\frac{2\pi}{t}$ (B) $\frac{2\pi}{3t}$

(C) $\frac{\pi}{3t}$ (D) $\frac{\pi}{t}$

4-11 Consider six wires coming into or out of the page as shown in figure-4.217, all with the same current. Rank the line integral of the magnetic field from most positive to most negative taken counterclockwise around each loop shown in figure :

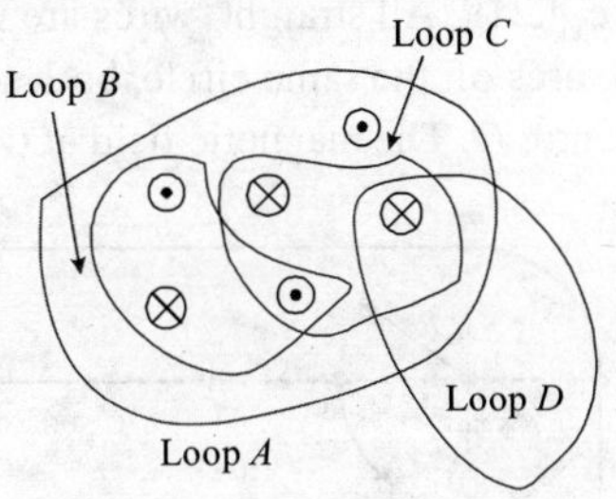

Figure 4.217

(A) $B > C > D > A$ (B) $B > C = D > A$
(C) $B > A > C = D$ (D) $C > B = D > A$

4-12 A current I flows in a closed path in a plane arcs as shown in the figure-4.218. The path consists of eight cars with alternating radii r and $2r$. Each segment of arc subtends equal angle at the common centre P. The magnetic field produced by current path at point P is :

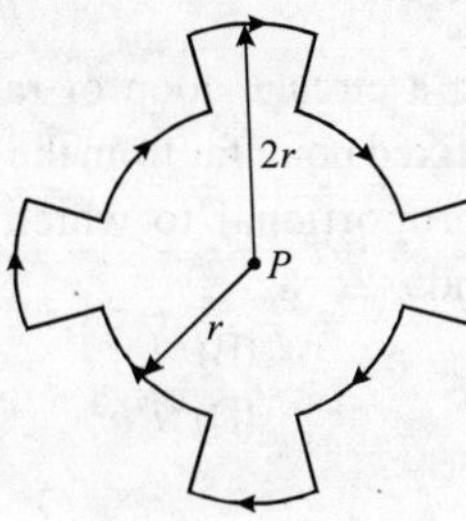

Figure 4.218

(A) $\frac{3}{8}\frac{\mu_0 I}{r}$; perpendicular to the plane of the paper and directed inward

(B) $\frac{1}{8}\frac{\mu_0 I}{r}$; perpendicular to the plane of the paper and directed outward

(C) $\frac{1}{8}\frac{\mu_0 I}{r}$; perpendicular to the plane of the paper and directed inward

(D) $\frac{3}{8}\frac{\mu_0 I}{r}$ perpendicular to the plane of the paper and directed outward

4-13 A charged particle of specific charge (charge/mass) α is released from origin at time $t = 0$ with a velocity given as

$$\vec{v} = v_0(\hat{i} + \hat{j})$$

The magnetic field in region is uniform with magnetic induction $\vec{B} = B_0\hat{i}$. Coordinates of the particle at time $t = \frac{\pi}{B_0\alpha}$ are :

(A) $\left(\frac{v_0}{2B_0\alpha}, \frac{\sqrt{2}v_0}{\alpha B_0}, \frac{-v_0}{B_0\alpha}\right)$ (B) $\left(\frac{-v_0}{2B_0\alpha}, 0, 0\right)$

(C) $\left(0, \frac{2v_0}{B_0\alpha}, \frac{v_0\pi}{2B_0\alpha}\right)$ (D) $\left(\frac{v_0\pi}{B_0\alpha}, 0, \frac{-2v_0}{B_0\alpha}\right)$

4-14 The configuration of some current carrying wires is shown in figure-4.219. All straight wires are very long. Both AB and CD are arcs of the same circle, both subtending right angles at the centre O. The magnetic field at O is :

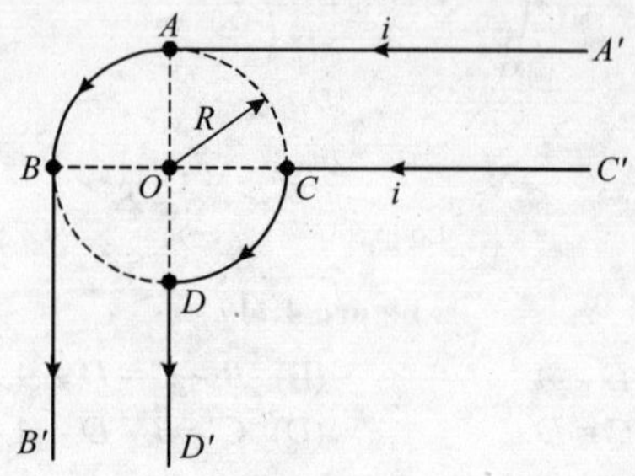

Figure 4.219

(A) $\frac{\mu_0 i}{4\pi R}$ (B) $\frac{\mu_0 i}{4\pi R}\sqrt{2}$

(C) $\frac{\mu_0 i}{2\pi R}$ (D) $\frac{\mu_0 i}{2\pi R}(\pi+1)$

4-15 A current i in a circular loop of radius b produces a magnetic field. At a fixed point far from the loop on its axis the magnetic field is proportional to which of the following combinations of i and b ?

(A) ib (B) ib^2

(C) i^2b (D) i/b^2

4-16 Two long conductors are arranged as shown above to form overlapping cylinders, each of radius r, whose centers are separated by a distance d. Current of density J flows into the plane of the page along the shaded part of one conductor and an equal current flows out of the plane of the page along the shaded portion of the other, as shown in figure-4.220. What are the magnitude and direction of the magnetic induction at point A?

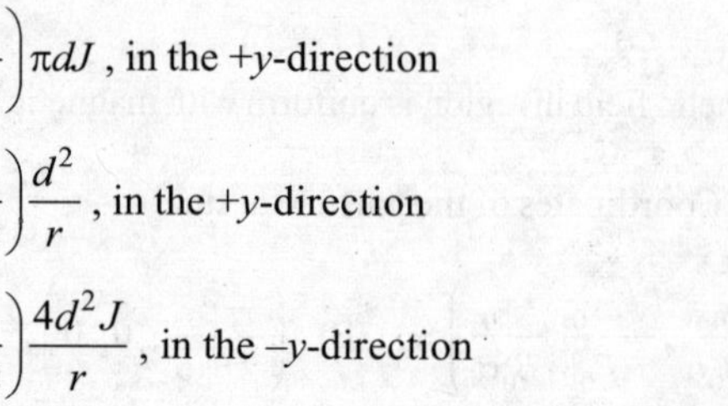

Figure 4.220

(A) $\left(\frac{\mu_0}{2\pi}\right)\pi dJ$, in the $+y$-direction

(B) $\left(\frac{\mu_0}{2\pi}\right)\frac{d^2}{r}$, in the $+y$-direction

(C) $\left(\frac{\mu_0}{2\pi}\right)\frac{4d^2J}{r}$, in the $-y$-direction

(D) $\left(\frac{\mu_0}{2\pi}\right)\frac{Jr^2}{d}$, in the $-y$-direction

4-17 The radius of a coil of wire with N turns is 0.22 m, and 3.5 A current flows clockwise in the coil as shown. A long straight wire carrying a current 54 A toward the left is located 0.05 m from the edge of the coil. The magnetic field at the centre of the coil is zero tesla. The number of turns N in the coil are :

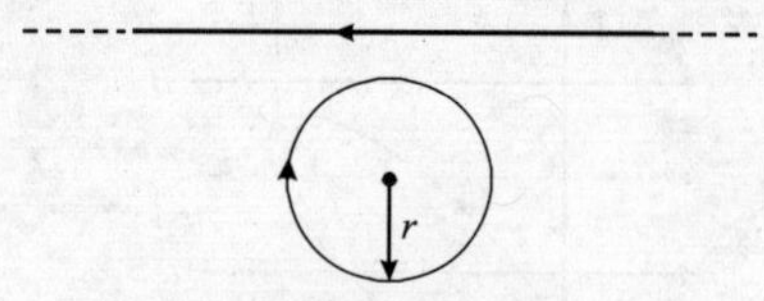

Figure 4.221

(A) 4 (B) 6

(C) 7 (D) 8

4-18 Two proton beams are moving with equal speed v in same direction. The ratio of electric force and magnetic force between them is : (Where c_0 is speed of light in vacuum)

(A) $\frac{c_0^2}{v^2}$ (B) $\frac{v^2}{c_0^2}$

(C) $\frac{c_0}{v}$ (D) $\frac{v}{c_0}$

4-19 A neutral atom of atomic mass number 100 which is stationary at the origin in gravity free space emits an α-particle (A) in z-direction. The product ion is P. A uniform magnetic field exists in the x-direction. Disregard the electromagnetic interaction between A and P. If the angle of rotation of A after which A and P will meet for the first time is $\frac{n\pi}{25}$ radians, what is the value of n ?

(A) 12 (B) 24

(C) 36 (D) 48

4-20 If the ratio of time periods of circular motion of two charged particles in magnetic field is 1/2, then the ratio of their kinetic energies must be :

(A) $1:\sqrt{2}$ (B) $\sqrt{2}:1$

(C) 2:1 (D) It can have any value

4-21 Figure-4.222 shows a charged particle of mass 2 g and charge –5 μC enters a circular region of radius 10 cm, in which there is a uniform magnetic field of strength 4 T and directed perpendicular to the plane of circular region in the figure. If the particle velocity vector rotates through 90° angle in passing through this region, then its speed is :

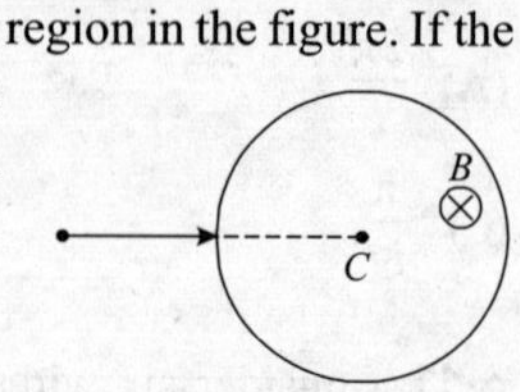

Figure 4.222

(A) 0.25 mm/s

(B) 4 mm/s

(C) 1 cm/s

(D) 1 mm/s

4-22 The magnetic field shown in the figure-4.221 consists of two uniform regions. The width of the first part is 5cm and the magnetic induction here is 0.001 T. The width of the other part is also 5 cm, with the direction of the induction being opposite in direction and 0.002 T in magnitude. What should be the minimum speed of the electron arriving from the direction indicated in the figure so that it can come out through the magnetic field II in region III ? Take mass of electron is 9×10^{-31} kg :

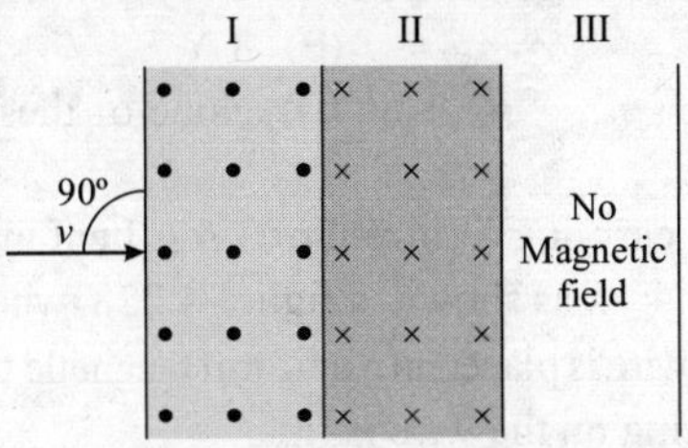

Figure 4.223

(A) $\frac{8}{9}\times10^{7}$ m/s (B) $\frac{4}{9}\times10^{7}$ m/s

(C) $\frac{16}{9}\times10^{7}$ m/s (D) $\frac{4}{7}\times10^{7}$ m/s

4-23 In the figure-4.222 the force on the wire ABC in the given uniform magnetic field of magnetic induction 2 T is :

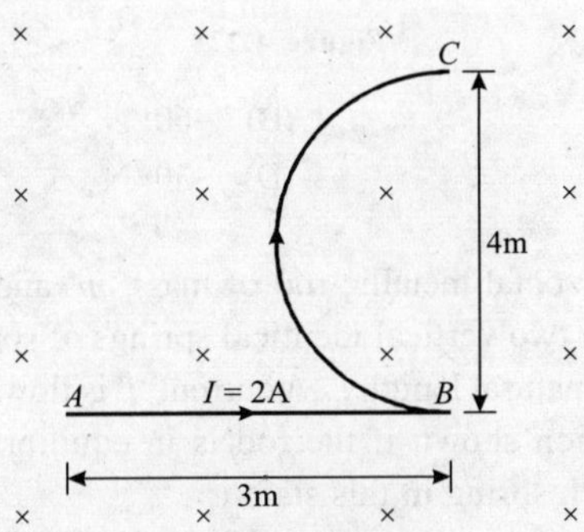

Figure 4.224

(A) $4(3+2\pi)$ N (B) 20N

(C) 30N (D) 40N

4-24 A uniform magnetic field exists in region which forms an equilateral triangle of side a. The magnetic field is perpendicular to the plane of the triangle. A charge q enters into this magnetic field perpendicularly with speed v along perpendicular bisector of one side and comes out along perpendicular bisector of other side. The magnetic induction in the triangle is :

(A) $\frac{mv}{qa}$ (B) $\frac{2mv}{qa}$

(C) $\frac{mv}{2qa}$ (D) $\frac{mv}{4qa}$

4-25 A charge particle of charge q, mass m is projected with a velocity $\vec{v}=v\hat{i}$ in a region of space where electric field strength $\vec{E}=E\hat{k}$ and magnetic induction $\vec{B}=B\hat{j}$ are present. The acceleration of the particle is :

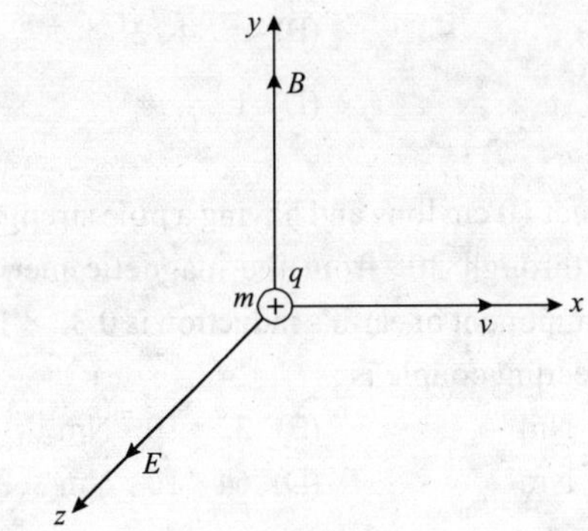

Figure 4.225

(A) $\frac{qvB}{m}\hat{k}$ (B) $\frac{qE}{m}\hat{k}$

(C) $\frac{q(E+vB)\hat{k}}{m}$ (D) $\frac{q(E-vB)\hat{k}}{m}$

4-26 A ring of radius 5 m is lying in the x-y plane is carrying current of 1 A in anti-clockwise sense. If a uniform magnetic field of magnetic induction $\vec{B}=3\hat{i}+4\hat{j}$ is switched on in space, then the co-ordinates of point about which the loop will have a tendency to lift up is :

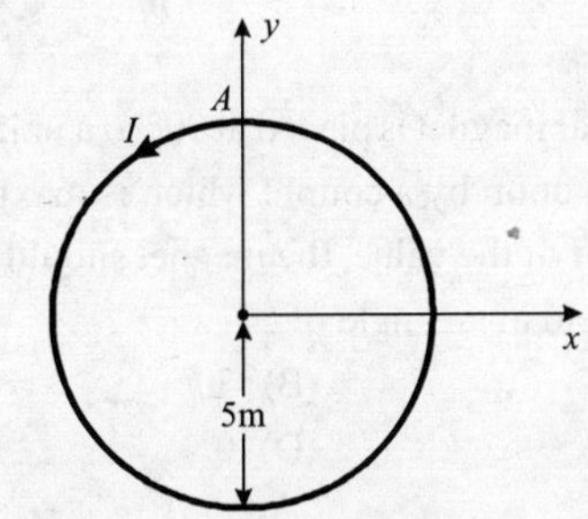

Figure 4.226

(A) (3,4) (2) (4,3)

(3) (3,0) (4) (0,3)

4-27 An electron is shot into one end of a solenoid. As it enters the uniform magnetic field within the solenoid, its speed is 800 m/s and its velocity vector makes an angle of 30° with the central axis of the solenoid. The solenoid carries 4.0 A current and has 8000 turn along its length. Find number of revolutions made by the electron within the solenoid by the time it emerges from the solenoid's opposite end. Charge to mass ratio e/m for electron is $\sqrt{3}\times10^{11}$ C/kg. Fill your answer in multiple of 10^3 :

(A) 1600 (B) 1200

(C) 800 (D) 600

4-28 Two identical wires each of length L are bent to form a circular loop and a square loop. If the same current i flows in the two wires, then the ratio of the magnetic inductions at the centre of the circular and square loops is :

(A) $\pi^2/ 2\sqrt{2}$ (B) $\pi^2/ 4\sqrt{2}$
(C) $\pi^2/ 8\sqrt{2}$ (D) 1

4-29 A magnet 10 cm long and having a pole strength of 2 Am is deflected through 30° from the magnetic meridian. The horizontal component of earth's induction is 0.32×10^{-4} T. The value of deflecting couple is :

(A) 16×10^{-7} Nm (B) 32×10^{-7} Nm
(C) 48×10^{-7} Nm (D) 64×10^{-7} Nm

4-30 In a gravity free space, a smooth insulating ring of radius R, with a bead having charge q is placed horizontally in a uniform magnetic field of induction B_0 and perpendicular to the plane of ring. Starting from $t = 0$, the magnetic field is varying with time as $B(t) = B_0 + \alpha t$, where α is a positive constant. The contact force between the ring and bead as a function of time is :

(A) $\frac{\alpha q^2 Rt}{m}(2B_0 + \alpha t)$ (B) $\frac{\alpha q^2 Rt}{4m}(2B_0 + \alpha t)$
(C) $\frac{\alpha q^2 Rt}{4m}(B_0 + \alpha t)$ (D) $\frac{4\alpha q^2 Rt}{m}(2B_0 + \alpha t)$

4-31 When a bar magnet is placed at 90° to a uniform magnetic field, it is acted upon by a couple which is maximum. For the couple to be half of the value, the magnet should be inclined to the magnetic field at an angle of :

(A) 45° (B) 30°
(C) 15° (D) 0°

4-32 Let B_P and B_Q be the magnetic field produced by the wire P and Q which are placed symmetrically in a rectangular loop $ABCD$ as shown in figure-4.225. Current in wire P is I directed inward and in Q is $2I$ directed outwards. Values of line integral of magnetic induction for different segments of the loop $ABCD$ are given as

$$\int_A^B \vec{B}_Q \cdot \vec{dl} = 2\mu_0$$

$$\int_D^A \vec{B}_P \cdot \vec{dl} = -2\mu_0$$

and $$\int_A^B \vec{B}_P \cdot \vec{dl} = -\mu_0$$

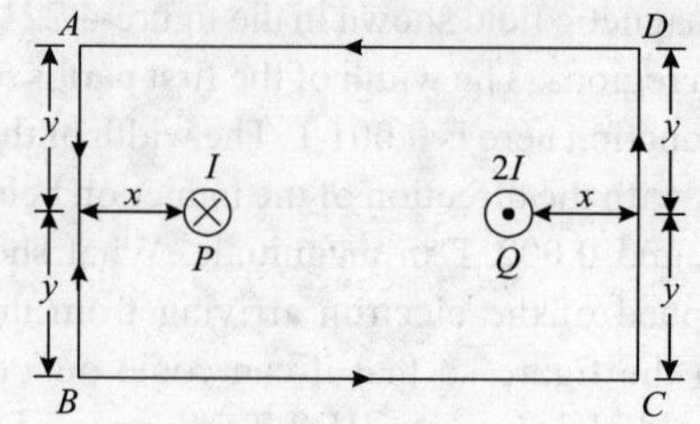

Figure 4.227

The value of I will be :

(A) 6 A (B) 8 A
(C) 10 A (D) None of these

4-33 A wire carrying a current of 3 A is bent in the form of a parabola $y^2 = 4 - x$ as shown in figure-4.228, where x and y are in metre. The wire is placed in a uniform magnetic field $\vec{B} = 5\hat{k}$ T. The force acting on the wire is :

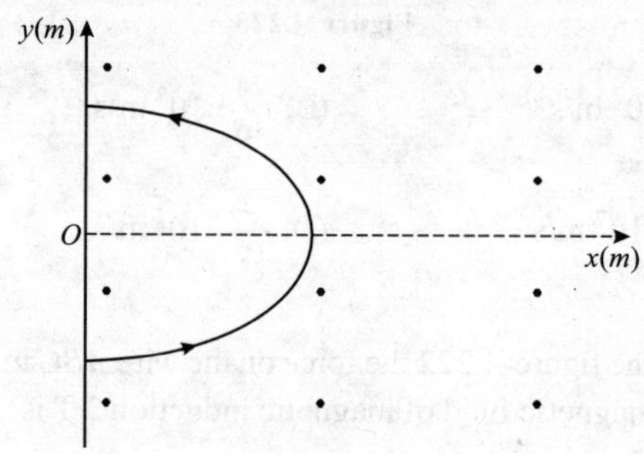

Figure 4.228

(A) $60\hat{i}$ N (B) $-60\hat{i}$ N
(C) $30\hat{i}$ N (D) $-30\hat{i}$ N

4-34 A horizontal metallic rod of mass 'm' and length 'l' is supported by two vertical identical springs of spring constant 'K' each and natural length l_0. A current 'i' is flowing in the rod in the direction shown if the rod is in equilibrium then the length of each spring in this state is :

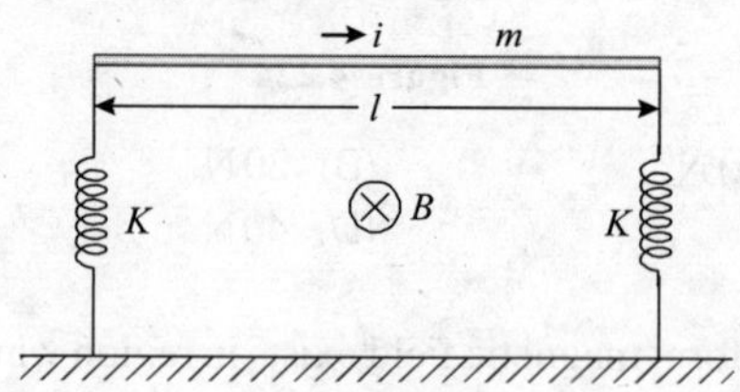

Figure 4.229

(A) $l_0 + \frac{ilB - mg}{K}$ (B) $l_0 + \frac{ilB - mg}{2K}$
(C) $l_0 + \frac{mg - ilB}{2K}$ (D) $l_0 + \frac{mg - ilB}{K}$

4-35 A dip circle is adjusted to set that it moves freely in the magnetic meridian. In this position, the angle of dip is 40°. Now the dip circle is rotated so that the plane in which the needle moves makes an angle of 30° with the magnetic meridian. In this position, the needle will dip by the angle :

(A) 40° (B) 30°

(C) More than 40° (D) Less than 40°

4-36 An infinite current carrying conductor is bent into three segments as shown in the figure-4.230. If it carries current i, the magnetic field at the origin is found to be $\frac{\mu_0 i}{4\pi a}((\sqrt{x}-1)\hat{j}+\hat{k})$. The value of x is :

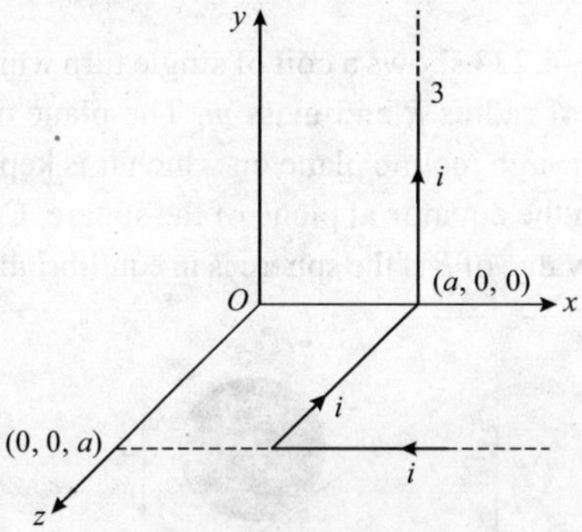

Figure 4.230

(A) 4 (B) 3

(C) 2 (D) 1

4-37 A charge particle moving along positive x-direction with a velocity v enters a region where there is a uniform magnetic field $\vec{B}=-B\hat{k}$, from $x=0$ to $x=d$. The particle gets deflected at an angle θ from its initial path. the specific charge of the particle is :

(A) $\frac{Bd}{v\cos\theta}$ (B) $\frac{v\tan\theta}{Bd}$

(C) $\frac{B\sin\theta}{vd}$ (D) $\frac{v\sin\theta}{Bd}$

4-38 Figure-4.231 shows a wire configuration carrying a constant current i. If the magnetic induction at point 'P' in the current configuration shown in figure-4.231 can be written as $K\tan\left(\frac{\alpha}{2}\right)$ then K is :

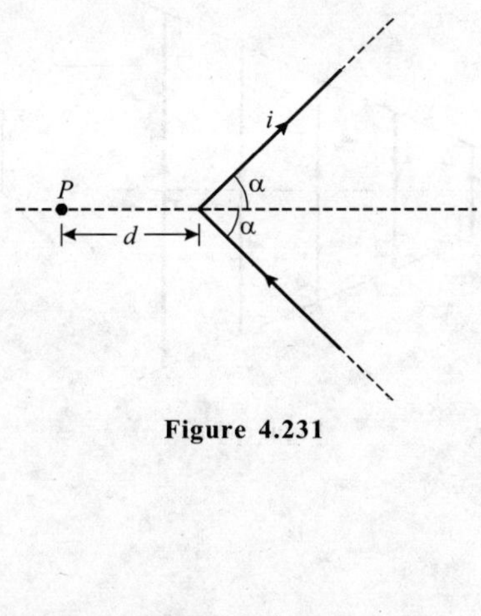

Figure 4.231

(A) $\frac{\mu_0 I}{4\pi d}$ (B) $\frac{\mu_0 I}{2\pi d}$

(C) $\frac{\mu_0 I}{\pi d}$ (D) $\frac{2\mu_0 I}{\pi d}$

4-39 The value of horizontal component of earth's magnetic field at a place is 0.35×10^{-4} T. If the angle of dip is 60°, the value of vertical component of earth's magnetic field is about :

(A) 0.10×10^{-4} T (B) 0.2×10^{-4} T

(C) 0.40×10^{-4} T (D) 0.6×10^{-4} T

4-40 A wire of mass 100 g is carrying a current of 2 A towards increasing x in the form of $y = x^2$ $(-2\text{m} \le x \le +2\text{m})$. This wire is placed in a magnetic field $\vec{B} = -0.02\,\hat{k}$ T. The acceleration of the wire is :

(A) $-1.6\hat{j}$ m/s² (B) $-3.2\hat{j}$ m/s²

(C) $1.6\hat{j}$ m/s² (D) Zero

4-41 A long straight wire along the z-axis carries a current I in the negative z direction. The magnetic vector field $\vec{B}$ at a point having coordinates (x, y) in the $z = 0$ plane is :

(A) $\frac{\mu_0 I(y\hat{i}-x\hat{j})}{2\pi(x^2+y^2)}$ (B) $\frac{\mu_0 I(x\hat{i}+y\hat{j})}{2\pi(x^2+y^2)}$

(C) $\frac{\mu_0 I(x\hat{j}-y\hat{i})}{2\pi(x^2+y^2)}$ (D) $\frac{\mu_0 I(x\hat{i}-y\hat{j})}{2\pi(x^2+y^2)}$

4-42 A magnetic needle vibrates in the vertical plane perpendicular to the magnetic meridian. Its time period is 2 seconds. if the same needle vibrates in the horizontal plane and the time period is again 2 seconds, what is the angle of dip at that place :

(A) 30° (B) 45°

(C) 60° (D) None of the above

4-43 A charged particle of mass m and charge q is accelerated through a potential difference of V volts. It enters a region of uniform magnetic field B which is directed perpendicular to the direction of motion of the particle. The particle will move on a circular path of radius :

(A) $\sqrt{\frac{Vm}{2qB^2}}$ (B) $\frac{2Vm}{qB^2}$

(C) $\sqrt{\frac{2Vm}{q}}\left(\frac{1}{B}\right)$ (D) $\sqrt{\frac{Vm}{q}}\left(\frac{1}{B}\right)$

4-44 Two magnets of equal mass are joined at right angles to each other as shown in figure-4.232. Magnet 1 has a magnetic moment three times that of magnet 2. This arrangement is pivoted at center so that it is free to rotate in the horizontal plane. In equilibrium what angle will the magnet 1 subtend with the magnetic meridian :

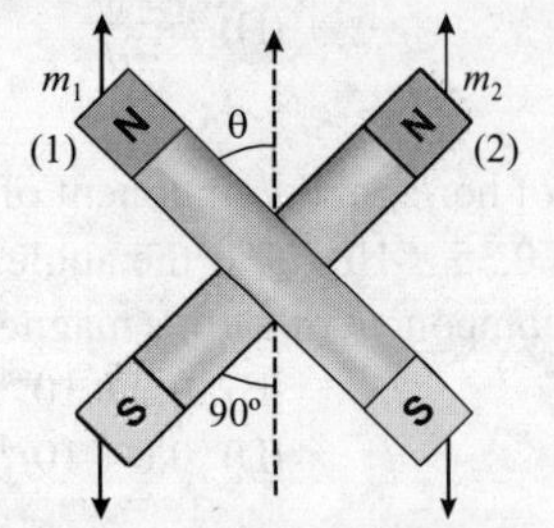

Figure 4.232

(A) $\tan^{-1}\left(\frac{1}{2}\right)$ (B) $\tan^{-1}\left(\frac{1}{3}\right)$

(C) $\tan^{-1}$(A) (D) 0°

4-45 A circular loop of radius 15.7 cm carries a current of 15 A. Another loop of radius 1.57 cm having 30 turns is placed at the center of the larger loop and a current of 1 A is passed through it. What torque acts on the small loop if the planes of two loops are at right angles and the induction due to large loop is considered uniform throughout the area of smaller loop ?

(A) 0.57×10^{-6} Nm (B) 1.13×10^{6} N/m

(C) 1.14×10^{-6} Nm (D) 2.26×10^{6} N/m

4-46 The magnetic moment of a short magnet is 8 Am^2. What is the magnetic induction at a point 20 cm away on its equatorial line from its mid point :

(A) 10^{-4} Web/m^2 (B) 2×10^{-4} Web/m^2

(C) 3×10^{4} Web/m^2 (D) 4×10^{-4} Web/m^2

4-47 A particle of charge -16×10^{-18} C moving with velocity 10 ms^{-1} along the x-axis enters region where a magnetic field of induction B is along the y-axis and an electric field of magnitude 10^4 V/m is along the negative z-axis If the charged particle continues moving along the x-axis, the magnitude of B is :

(A) 10^3 Wb/m^2 (B) 10^5 Wb/m^2

(C) 10^{16} Wb/m^2 (D) 10^{-3} Wb/m^2

4-48 The moment of a short magnet is 4 Am^2. The magnetic induction at a point on the axial line at a point 40 cm away from its mid point is :

(A) 0.125×10^{-4} Wb/m^2 (B) 0.150×10^{-4} Wb/m^2

(C) 0.175×10^{-4} Wb/m^2 (D) 2.0×10^{-4} Wb/m^2

4-49 An electron is projected with velocity v_0 in a uniform electric field E perpendicular to the field. Again it is projected with velocity v_0 perpendicular to a uniform magnetic field B. If r_1 is initial radius of curvature just after entering in the electric field and r_2 is initial radius of curvature just after entering in magnetic field then the ratio r_1/r_2 is equal to :

(A) $\frac{Bv_0^2}{E}$ (B) $\frac{B}{E}$

(C) $\frac{Ev_0}{B}$ (D) $\frac{Bv_0}{E}$

4-50 Magnetic field strength due to a short bar magnet on its axial line at a distance x is B. What is its value at the same distance on the equatorial line ?

(A) $B/2$ (B) B

(C) $2B$ (D) $4B$

4-51 Figure-4.233 shows a coil of single turn which is wound on a sphere of radius R and mass m. The plane of the coil is parallel to a rough incline plane on which it is kept. The plane of coil lies in the equatorial plane of the sphere. Current in the coil is i. The value of B if the sphere is in equilibrium on inclined plane is :

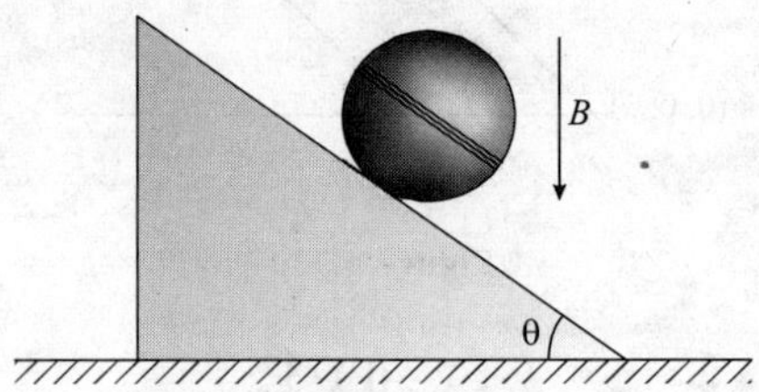

Figure 4.233

(A) $\frac{mg\cos\theta}{\pi iR}$ (B) $\frac{mg}{\pi iR}$

(C) $\frac{mg\tan\theta}{\pi iR}$ (D) $\frac{mg\sin\theta}{\pi iR}$

4-52 If a magnet is suspended at an angle 30° to the magnetic meridian and in this plane the dip needle makes an angle of 60° with the horizontal. The true value of dip is :

(A) $\tan^{-1}\left(\frac{2}{3}\right)$ (B) $\tan^{-1}\left(\frac{3}{2}\right)$

(C) $\tan^{-1}(3)$ (D) $\tan^{-1}(2)$

4-53 Infinite number of straight wires each carrying current I are equally spaced as shown in the figure-4.234. Adjacent wires have current in opposite direction. Net magnetic induction at point P is :

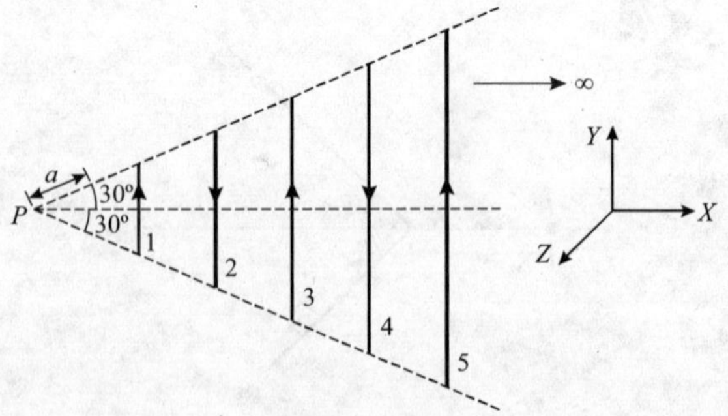

Figure 4.234

(A) $\frac{\mu_0 I}{4\pi}\frac{\ln 2}{\sqrt{3}a}\hat{k}$ (B) $\frac{\mu_0 I}{4\pi}\frac{\ln 4}{\sqrt{3}a}\hat{k}$

(C) $\frac{\mu_0 I}{4\pi}\frac{\ln 4}{\sqrt{3}a}(-\hat{k})$ (D) Zero

4-54 The magnetic induction due to a current carrying circular loop of radius 3 m at a point on the axis at a distance of 4 m from the centre is 54 μT. What will be its value at the centre of the loop?

(A) 250 μT (B) 150 μT

(C) 125 μT (D) 75 μT

4-55 An electron experiences no deflection if subjected to an electric field of 3.2×10^5 V/m and a magnetic induction of 2.0×10^{-3}T. Both the fields are applied perpendicular to the path of electron and also to each other. If the electric field is removed, then the electron will revolve in an orbit of radius :

(A) 45 m (B) 4.5 m

(C) 0.45 m (D) 0.045 m

4-56 An electron is accelerated through a potential difference V enters into a uniform transverse magnetic field and experiences a force F. if the accelerating potential increased to $2V$, the electron in the same magnetic field will experience a force :

(A) F (B) $F/2$

(C) $\sqrt{2}F$ (D) $2F$

4-57 A mass spectrometer is a device which select particle of equal mass. An ion with an electric charge $q > 0$ starts at rest from a source S and is accelerated through a potential difference V. It passes through a hole into a region of constant magnetic field $\vec{B}$ perpendicular to the plane of the paper as shown in the figure-4.235. The particle is deflected by the magnetic field and emerges through the bottom hole at a distance d from the top hole. The mass of the particle is :

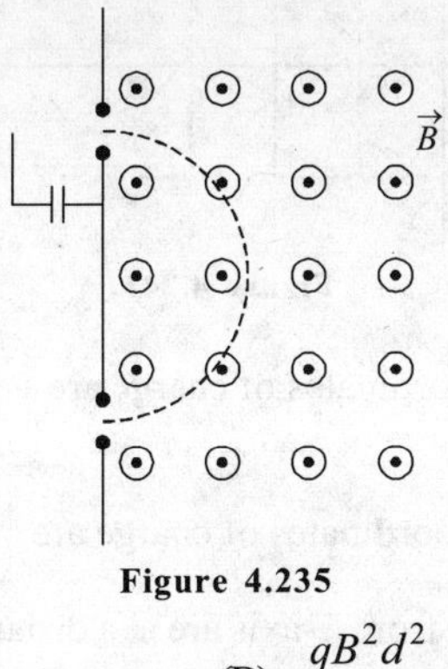

Figure 4.235

(A) $\frac{qBd}{V}$ (B) $\frac{qB^2d^2}{4V}$

(C) $\frac{qB^2d^2}{8V}$ (D) $\frac{qBd}{2V}$

4-58 The magnetic induction normal to the plane of circular coil of n turns and radius r which carries a current i is measured on the axis at a small distance h from the centre of the coil. This is smaller than the mangetic induction at the centre by the fraction :

(A) $\frac{2}{3}\frac{h^2}{r^2}$ (B) $\frac{3}{2}\frac{r^2}{h^2}$

(C) $\frac{3}{2}\frac{h^2}{r^2}$ (D) $\frac{2}{3}\frac{h^2}{r^2}$

4-59 A straight wire of diameter 0.5 mm carrying a current 2 A is replaced by another wire of diameter 1 mm carrying the same current. The magnetic induction at a distance 2 m away from the centre is :

(A) Half of the previous value

(B) Twice of the previous value

(C) Unchanged

(D) Quarter of its previous value

4-60 A block of mass m & charge q is released on a long smooth inclined plane with magnetic induction B is constant, uniform, horizontal and parallel to the surface as shown in figure-4.236. Find the time from start when block loses contact with the surface

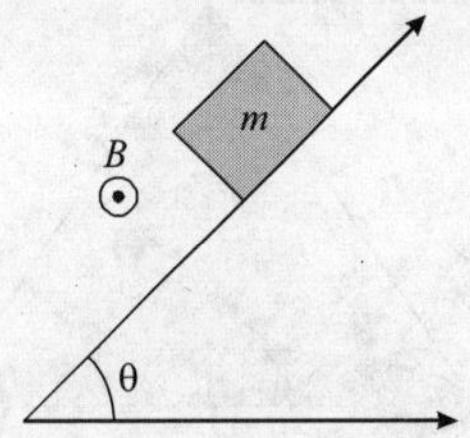

Figure 4.236

(A) $\frac{m\cos\theta}{qB}$ (B) $\frac{m\,\mathrm{cosec}\,\theta}{qB}$

(C) $\frac{m\cot\theta}{qB}$ (D) None

4-61 A circular current carrying coil has a radius R. The distance from the centre of the coil on the axis where the magnetic induction will be $(1/8)^{th}$ of its value at the centre of the coil is :

(A) $R\sqrt{3}$ (B) $2R\sqrt{3}$

(C) $R/\sqrt{3}$ (D) $2R/\sqrt{3}$

4-62 Two infinite length wires carries currents 8 A and 6 A respectively and placed along X and Y-axis. Magnetic field at a point $P(0, 0, d)$ m will be :

(A) $\frac{7\mu_0}{\pi d}$ (B) $\frac{10\mu_0}{\pi d}$

(C) $\frac{14\mu_0}{\pi d}$ (D) $\frac{5\mu_0}{\pi d}$

4-63 At $t = 0$, a positively charged particle of mass m is projected from the origin with velocity u_0 at an angle 37° from the x-axis as shown in the figure-4.237. A constant $\vec{B}_0 = B_0\hat{j}$ is present in space. After a time interval t_0 velocity of particle may be :

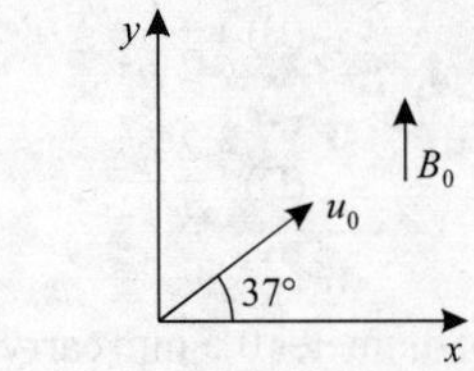

Figure 4.237

(A) $u_0\left[\frac{\sqrt{39}}{2}\hat{i}+\frac{3}{5}\hat{j}-\frac{\hat{k}}{\sqrt{3}}\right]$ (B) $u_0\left[\frac{\hat{i}}{\sqrt{3}}+\frac{\hat{j}}{\sqrt{2}}+\frac{\hat{k}}{\sqrt{6}}\right]$

(C) $u_0\left[\frac{\sqrt{39}}{10}\hat{i}+\frac{3}{5}\hat{j}+\frac{1}{4}\hat{k}\right]$ (D) $u_0\left[\frac{\sqrt{39}}{10}\hat{i}+\frac{3}{5}\hat{j}+\frac{1}{2}\hat{k}\right]$

4-64 A charge Q is uniformly distributed through out the volume of a right circular cone of semi-vertical angle θ and height h. The cone is rotated about its axis at a uniform angular velocity ω. Magnetic dipole moment of cone is :

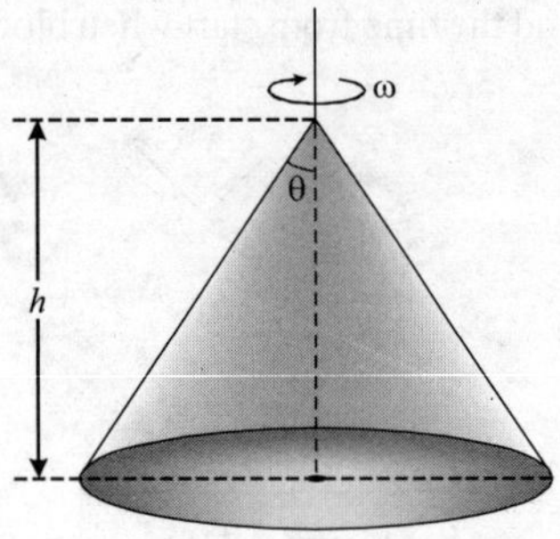

Figure 4.238

(A) $\frac{3Qh^2\omega\cot^2\theta}{20}$ (B) $\frac{Qh^2\omega\cot^2\theta}{20}$

(C) $\frac{Qh^2\omega\tan^2\theta}{20}$ (D) $\frac{3Qh^2\omega\tan^2\theta}{20}$

4-65 A steady current is flowing in a circular coil of radius R, made up of a thin conducting wire. The magnetic field at the centre of the loop is B_C. Now, a circular loop of radius R/n is made from the same wire without changing its length, by unfolding and refolding the loop, and the same current is passed through it. If new magnetic field at the centre of the coil is B_O, then the ratio B_C/B_O is :

(A) $1 : n^2$ (B) $n^{1/2}$

(C) $n : 1$ (D) None of these

4-66 A Wire carrying current i has configuration shown in figure below. Two semi infinite straight sections, both tangent to a circle, are connected by a circular arc of central angle θ, along the circumference of circle, with all sections lying in same plane. The value of θ in order for magnetic field B to be zero at the centre of circle is (in radian) :

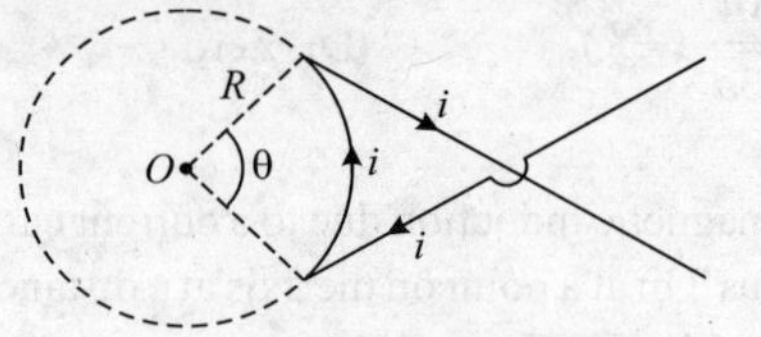

Figure 4.239

(A) $\frac{\pi}{8}$ (B) 8

(C) π (D) 2

4-67 A conducting wire carrying a current I is bent into the shape as shown in figure below. The net magnetic field at the centre O of the circular arc of radius R is given as :

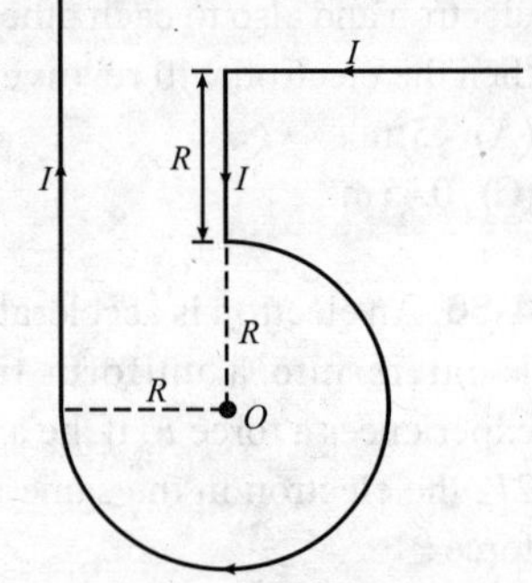

Figure 4.240

(A) $\frac{\mu_0 I}{2R}\left(\frac{1+3\pi}{\pi}\right)$

(B) $\frac{\mu_0 I}{4R}\left(\frac{1+3\pi}{\pi}\right)$

(C) $\frac{\mu_0 I}{8R}\left(\frac{1+3\pi}{\pi}\right)$

(D) $\frac{\mu_0 I}{8R}\left(\frac{2+3\pi}{\pi}\right)$

4-68 In a region, magnetic field along X-axis changes with time according to the given graph. If time period, pitch and radius of helical path of a positively charged particle are T_0, P_0 and R_0 respectively, then which of the following is incorrect, if the particle is projected at an angle θ_0 with the positive X-axis in X-Y plane ?

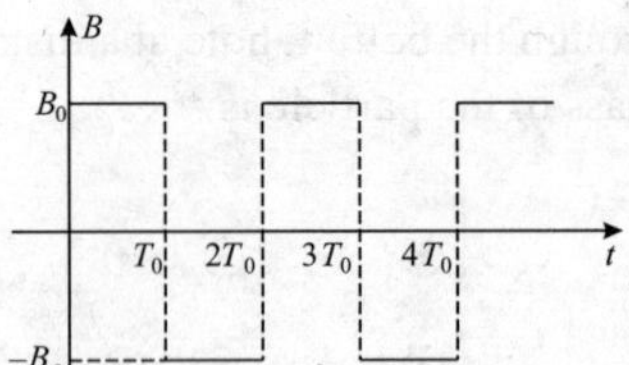

Figure 4.241

(A) At $t = \frac{T_0}{2}$, coordinates of charge are $\left(\frac{P_0}{2}, 0, -2R_0\right)$

(B) At $t = \frac{3T_0}{2}$, coordinates of charge are $\left(\frac{3P_0}{2}, 0, 2R_0\right)$

(C) Two extremes from X-axis are at a distance $2R_0$ from each other along Z-axis

(D) Two extremes from X-axis are at a distance $4R_0$ from each other along Z-axis

* * * * *

Advance MCQs with One or More Options Correct

4-1 Consider two rings of copper wire. One ring is scaled up version of the other, twice large in all regards (radius, cross sectional radius). If current around the rings are driven by equal voltage source then choose the **CORRECT** alternative(s). Assume that cross-sectional radius is very small as compared to radius of rings :

(A) Resistance of larger ring is half of the smaller ring

(B) Current in the larger ring is two times that in the smaller ring

(C) Magnetic field at their centres are same

(D) Magnetic field at centre of larger ring is twice as that at the centre of smaller ring

4-2 Two circular coils of radii 5 cm and 10 cm carry currents of 2 A. The coils have 50 and 100 turns respectively and are placed in such a way that their planes as well as their centres coincide. Magnitude of magnetic field at the common centre of coils is :

(A) $8\pi \times 10^{-4}$ T if currents in the coils are in same sense

(B) $4\pi \times 10^{-4}$ T if currents in the coils are in opposite sense

(C) Zero if currents in the coils are in opposite sense

(D) $8\pi \times 10^{-4}$ T if currents in the coils are in opposite sense

4-3 A tangent galvanometer is connected to an ideal battery. In which of the following options the deflection of magnetic needle of the tangent galvanometer will remain same :

(A) If battery voltage is doubled and number of turns in coil are also doubled

(B) If battery voltage is kept constant and number of turns in coil are doubled

(C) If number of turns and coil radius both are doubled

(D) If number of turns are halved and coil radius is doubled

4-4 The figure-4.242 contains an infinite slab having current per unit area of $\vec{J}_1 = J\hat{k}$ between the infinite planes at $x = -b$ and $x = b$. Slightly to the right of $x = b$, an infinite thin sheet is kept. It carries a current per unit length $\vec{k}_2 = 2bJ(-\hat{k})$. Choose the correct option(s) :

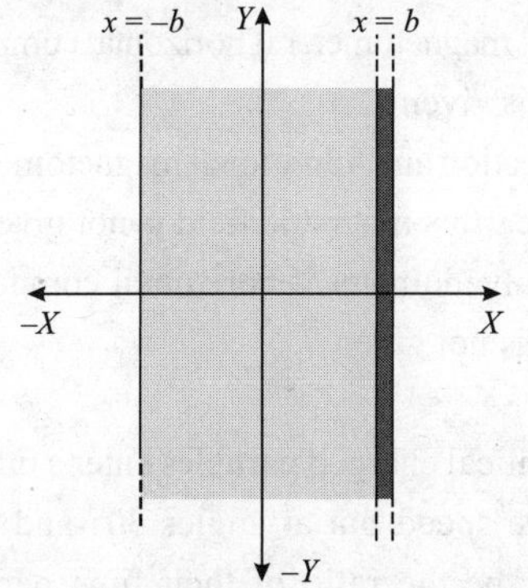

Figure 4.242

(A) The field due to sheet at any point is $\mu_0 Jb$

(B) The field due to sheet at any point is $\frac{\mu_0 Jb}{2}$

(C) The magnetic field due to slab at a point inside the slab must be independent of y co-ordinate and y component of field must be a function of x

(D) Magnetic field at a point (x, y) inside slab, due to slab is $\mu_0 Jx$

4-5 An infinitely long straight wire is carrying a current I_1. Adjacent to it there is another equilateral triangular wire having current I_2. Choose the wrong options :

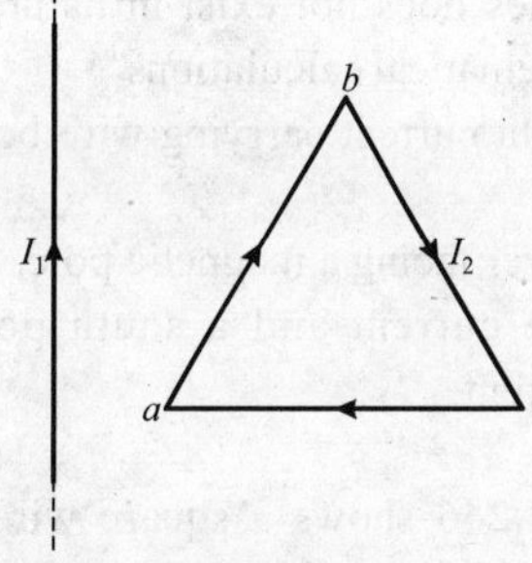

Figure 4.243

(A) Net force on loop is leftwards

(B) Net force on loop is rightwards

(C) Net force on loop is upwards

(D) Net force on loop is downwards

4-6 A charged particle having its charge to mass ratio as β goes in a conical pendulum of length L making an angle θ with vertical and angular velocity ω. If a magnetic field B is directed vertically downwards (see figure-4.244) :

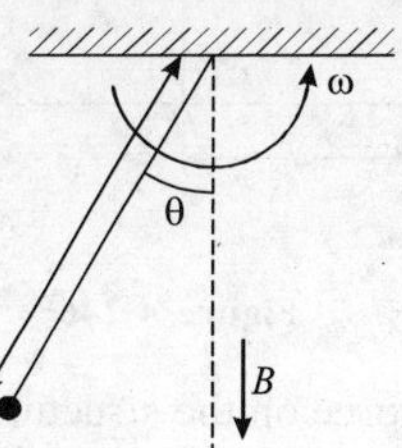

Figure 4.244

(A) $B = \frac{1}{\beta}\left[\omega - \frac{g}{\omega L\cos\theta}\right]$

(B) Angular momentum of the particle about the point of suspension remains constant

(C) If the direction of B were reversed maintaining same ω and L, then θ will remain unchanged

(D) Rate of change of angular momentum of the particle about the point of suspension is not a constant vector

4-7 Two long and parallel wires at P and Q carry currents 0.1 A and 0.2 A respectively in opposite directions as shown in figure-4.245. In which region(s) a neutral point may not exist, that is where the magnetic field is not zero?

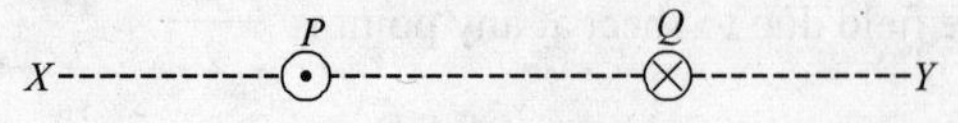

Figure 4.245

(A) Between X and P
(B) Between P and Q
(C) Between Q and Y
(D) In all the regions there exists no neutral point

4-8 Which of the following statements given below is/are correct
(A) Only electric charges can produce magnetic fields
(B) Magnetic poles does not exist in nature these are only assumed for mathematical calculations
(C) A long straight current carrying wire behaves like a bar magnet
(D) For an observer facing a magnetic pole, a north pole acts like a clockwise current and a south pole acts like an anticlockwise current

4-9 The figure-4.246 shows a square wire mesh made of conducting wires. Here, each small square has side a. The structure is kept in uniform magnetic field B perpendicular to the plane of paper:

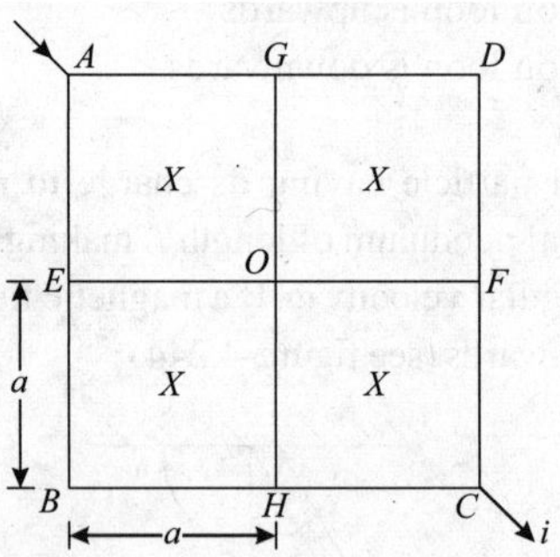

Figure 4.246

(A) The magnetic force on the structure is $2\sqrt{2}\ iBa$
(B) The potential of point B = potential of point D
(C) Potential of point O = potential of point B
(D) The magnetic force on the structure is $\sqrt{2}\ iBa$

4-10 A charged particle of unit mass and unit charge at some instant has velocity $\vec{v} = (8\hat{i} + 6\hat{j})\ \text{ms}^{-1}$ in magnetic field $\vec{B} = (2\hat{k})$ Tesla. (Neglect all other forces). Choose the CORRECT option(s):
(A) The path of particle may be $x^2 + y^2 - 4x - 21 = 0$
(B) The path of particle may be $x^2 + y^2 = 25$
(C) The path of particle may be $y^2 + z^2 = 25$
(D) Time period of particle will be 3.14 s

4-11 Consider the following statements regarding a charged particle in a magnetic field. Which of the statements are true?
(A) Starting with zero velocity, it accelerates in a direction perpendicular to the magnetic field
(B) While deflection in magnetic field its energy gradually increases
(C) Only the component of magnetic field perpendicular to the direction of motion of the charged particle is effective in deflecting it
(D) Direction of deflecting force on the moving charged particle is perpendicular to its velocity

4-12 A particle of specific charge 'α' is projected from origin at $t = 0$ with a velocity $\vec{V} = V_0(\hat{i} + \hat{k})$ in a magnetic field $\vec{B} = -B_0\hat{k}$. Then : (Mass of particle = 1 unit)

(A) At $t = \dfrac{\pi}{\alpha B_0}$, velocity of the particle is $-V_0(\hat{i} - \hat{k})$

(B) At $t = \dfrac{\pi}{4\alpha B_0}$, speed of the particle is V_0

(C) At $t = \dfrac{2\pi}{\alpha B_0}$, magnitude of displacement of the particle is more than $\dfrac{2V_0}{\alpha B_0}$

(D) At $t = \dfrac{2\pi}{\alpha B_0}$, distance travelled by the particle is less than $\dfrac{2\sqrt{2}\pi V_0}{\alpha B_0}$.

4-13 For experimental measurement of the magnetic moment of a bar magnet which of the following devices can be used
(A) Deflection magnetometer if horizontal component of earth's magnetic field is given
(B) Vibrational magnetometer if horizontal component of earth's magnetic field is given
(C) Both Deflection and vibrational magnetometer if horizontal component of earth's magnetic field is not given
(D) Tangent galvanometer if horizontal component of earth's magnetic field is not given

4-14 Two identical charged particles enter a uniform magnetic field with same speed but at angles 30° and 60° with field. Let a, b and c be the ratio of their time periods, radii and pitches of the helical paths than :

(A) $abc = 1$ (B) $abc > 1$

(C) $abc < 1$ (D) $a = bc$

4-15 A current carrying conductor is in the form of a sine curve as shown in figure-4.247, which carries current I. If the equation of this curve is $Y = 2\sin\left(\frac{\pi x}{L}\right)$ and a uniform magnetic field B exists in space :

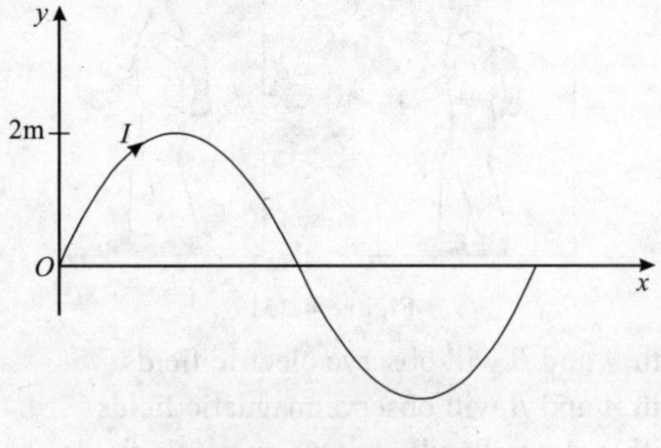

Figure 4.247

(A) Force on wire is BIL if field is along Z-axis

(B) Force on wire is $2BIL$ if field is along Y-axis

(C) Force on wire is zero if field is along X-axis

(D) Force on wire is BIL if field is in the XY plane making an angle 30° with X-axis

4-16 A straight conductor carries a current. Assume that all free electrons in the conductor move with the same drift velocity v. A and B are two observers on a straight line XY parallel to the conductor. A is stationary. B moves along XY with a velocity v in the direction of the free electrons :

(A) A and B observe the same magnetic field

(B) A observes a magnetic field, B does not

(C) A and B observe magnetic fields of the same magnitude but opposite directions

(D) A and B do not observe any electric field

4-17 A dip needle is taken at a point on geomagnetic equator line on earth surface. The dip needle is placed such that it can rotate in a vertical plane perpendicular to magnetic meridian at that point. At different points of the geomagnetic equator the dip needle in equilibrium can point in a direction which is :

(A) Horizontal

(B) Vertical

(C) At some angle to vertical

(D) At any direction except vertical

4-18 A square wire frame is hinged about one of it's sides AB. It carries a current of 0.5 A. Which of the following magnetic fields can hold it in equilibrium in horizontal position shown. It has a mass of 500 gm :

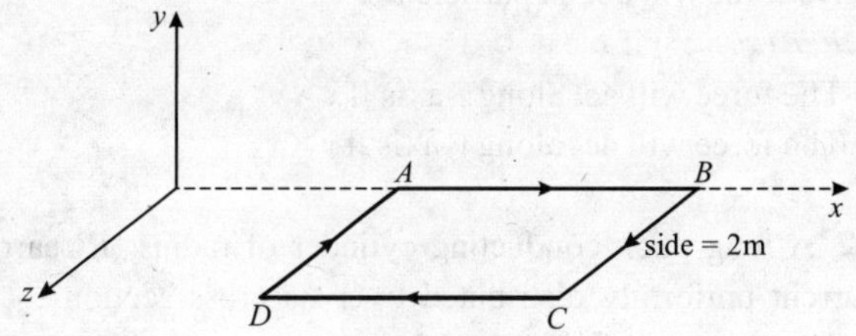

Figure 4.248

(A) $3\hat{i} + \frac{5}{2}\hat{k}$ (B) $\frac{5}{2}\hat{i} - 3\hat{j} + 2\hat{k}$

(C) $2\hat{j} - \frac{5}{2}\hat{k}$ (D) $\hat{i} + \frac{5}{2}\hat{j} + \frac{5}{2}\hat{k}$

4-19 A compass needle is taken to a geomagnetic pole and kept in a horizontal plane. The needle :

(A) May stay in north-south direction

(B) May stay in east-west direction

(C) May stay at 11° east of north

(D) May oscillate

4-20 A particle of charge $-q$ and mass m enters a uniform magnetic field $\vec{B}$ (perpendicular to paper inwards) at P with a velocity v_0 at an angle α and leaves the field at Q with velocity v at angle β as shown in figure-4.249, then :

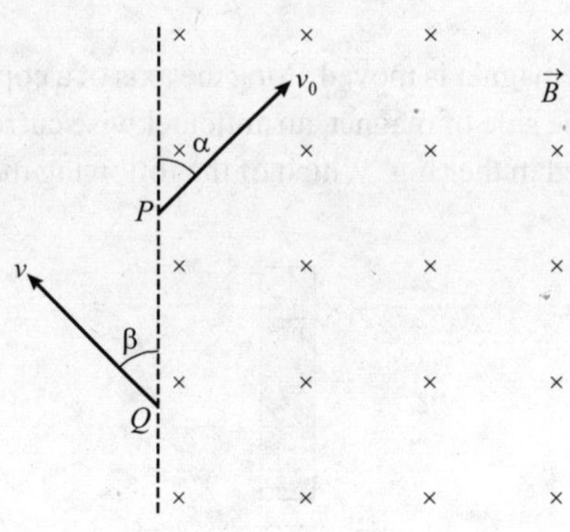

Figure 4.249

(A) $\alpha = \beta$

(B) $v = v_0$

(C) $PQ = \frac{2mv_0 \sin\alpha}{Bq}$

(D) Particle remains in the field for time $t = \frac{2m(\pi - \alpha)}{Bq}$

4-21 A charged particle with velocity $\vec{v} = x\hat{i} + y\hat{j}$ moves in a magnetic field $\vec{B} = y\hat{i} + x\hat{j}$. The magnitude of magnetic force acting on the particle is F. Which one of the following statement(s) is/are correct ?

(A) No force will act on particle if $x = y$

(B) $F \propto (x^2 - y^2)$ if $x > y$

(C) The force will act along z-axis if $x > y$

(D) The force will act along y-axis if $y > x$

4-22 A long thick conducting cylinder of radius 'R' carries a current uniformly distributed over its cross section :

(A) The magnetic field strength is maximum on the surface

(B) The magnetic field strength is zero on the surface

(C) The strength of the magnetic field inside the cylinder will vary as inversely proportional to r, where r is the distance from the axis

(D) The energy density of the magnetic field outside the conductor varies as inversely proportional to $1/r^2$, where 'r' is the distance from the axis.

4-23 Two parallel conductors carrying current in the same direction attract each other, while two parallel beams of electrons moving in the same direction repel each other. Which of the following statements provide part or all the reason for this ?

(A) The conductors are electrically neutral

(B) The conductors produce magnetic fields on each other

(C) The electron beams do not produce magnetic field on each other

(D) The magnetic forces caused by the electron beams on each other are weaker than the electrostatic force between them

4-24 A bar magnet is moved along the axis of a copper ring, as seen from the side of magnet, an anticlockwise current is found to be induced in the ring. Which of the following may be true ?

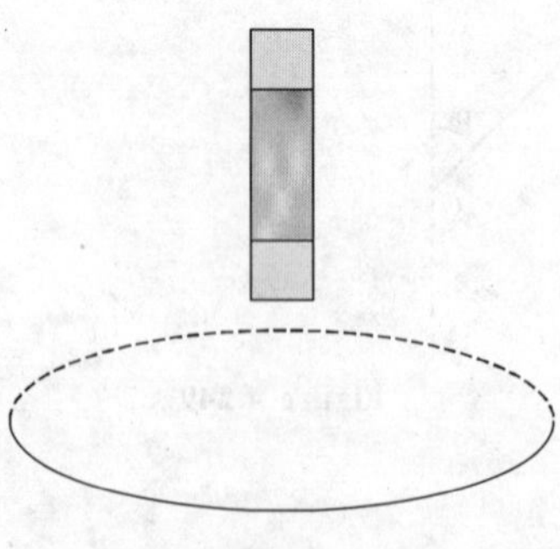

Figure 4.250

(A) The south pole faces the ring and the magnet moves toward it

(B) The north pole faces the ring and the magnet moves toward it

(C) The south pole faces the ring and the magnet moves away from it

(D) The north pole faces the ring and the magnet moves away from it

4-25 An observer A and a charge Q are fixed in a stationary frame F_1. An observer B is fixed in a frame F_2, which is moving with respect to F_1 :

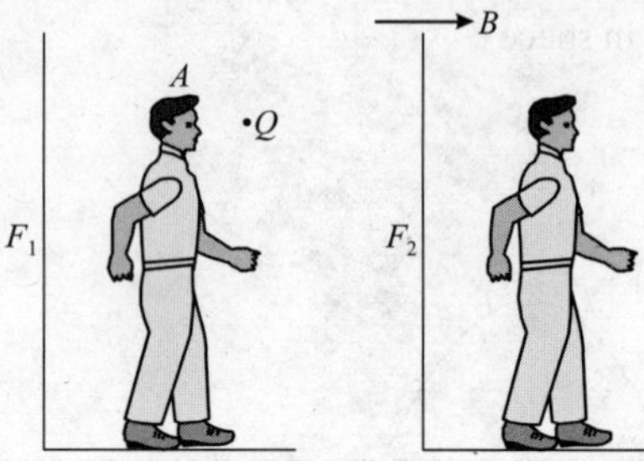

Figure 4.251

(A) Both A and B will observe electric fields

(B) Both A and B will observe magnetic fields

(C) Neither A nor B will observe magnetic fields

(D) B will observe a magnetic field, but A will not

4-26 There are two wires ab and cd in a vertical plane as shown in figure-4.252. Direction of current in wire ab is rightwards. Choose the correct options :

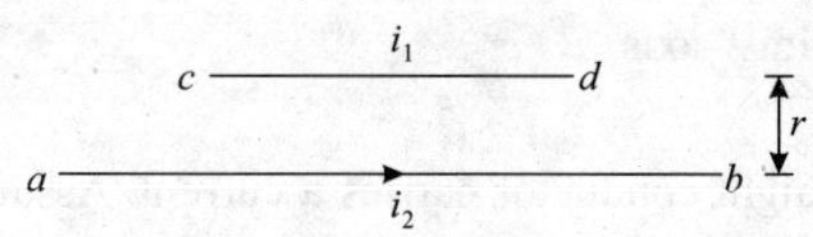

Figure 4.252

(A) If wire ab is fixed then wire cd can be kept in equilibrium by the current in cd in leftward direction

(B) Equilibrium of wire cd will be stable equilibrium

(C) If wire cd is fixed, then wire ab can be kept in equilibrium by flowing current in cd in rightward direction

(D) Equilibrium of wire ab will be stable equilibrium

4-27 An infinitely long, straight wire carrying current I_1 passes through the center of circular loop of wire carrying current I_2. The infinite wire is perpendicular to the plane of the loop. Which of the following statements is/are INCORRECT regarding the magnetic force on the loop due to the infinite wire :

(A) Force on the loop due to infinite wire is upward, along the axis of the loop

(B) Force on the loop due to infinite wire is downward, along the axis of the loop

(C) Although net force on the loop due to infinite wire is zero, but due to magnetic interaction between infinite wire and loop, a tensile stress is developed in the loop

(D) There is no magnetic force on the loop due to infinite wire.

4-28 Which of the following statement is correct ?

(A) A charge particle enters a region of uniform magnetic field at an angle 85° to magnetic lines of force. The path of the particle is a circle

(B) An electron and a proton are moving with the same kinetic energy along the same direction. When they pass through uniform magnetic field perpendicular to their direction of motion, they describe circular path

(C) There is no change in the energy of a charged particle moving in a magnetic field although magnetic force acts on it

(D) Two electrons enter with the same speed but in opposite direction in a uniform transverse magnetic field. Then the two describe circle of the same radius and these move in the same direction

4-29 A rectangular loop of dimensions $(a \times b)$ carries a current i. A uniform magnetic field $\vec{B} = B_0\hat{i}$ exists in space. Then :

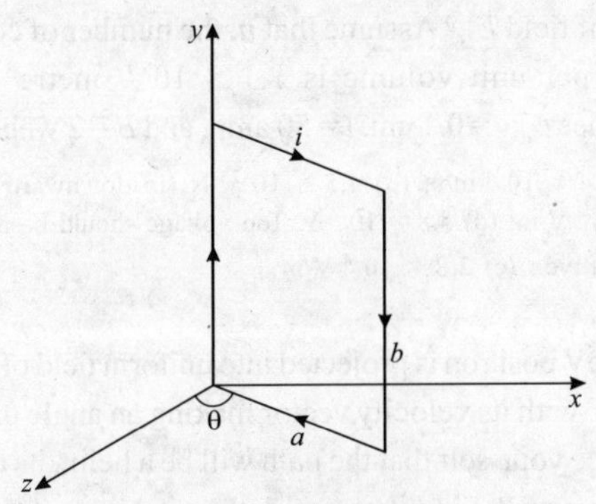

Figure 4.253

(A) Torque on the loop is $iabB_0 \sin\theta$

(B) Torque on the loop is in negative y-direction

(C) If allowed to move the loop turn so as to increase θ

(D) In allowed to move the loop turn so as to decrease θ

4-30 A particle of charge $+q$ and mass m moving under the influence of a uniform electric field $E\vec{i}$ and a uniform magnetic field $B\vec{j}$ follows a trajectory from P to Q as shown in figure-4.254. The velocities at P and Q are $v\vec{i}$ and $-2v\vec{j}$. Which of the following statement(s) is/are correct ?

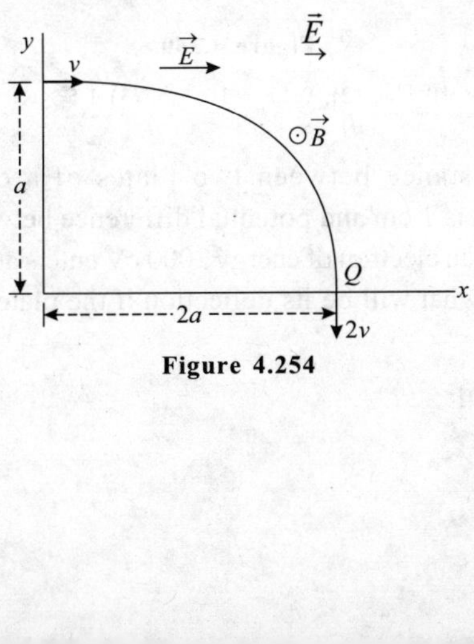

Figure 4.254

(A) $E = \frac{3}{4}\left(\frac{mv^2}{qa}\right)$

(B) Rate of work done by the electric field at P is $\frac{3}{4}\left(\frac{mv^3}{a}\right)$

(C) Rate of work done by the electric field at P is zero

(D) Rate of work done by both the fields at Q is zero

4-31 In the diagram shown, an irregular loop of the wire carrying a current lies in the plane of the paper here. Now, the loop is distorted into some other shape while remaining in the same plane. Point P is still within the loop in same plane. Which of the following is/are true?

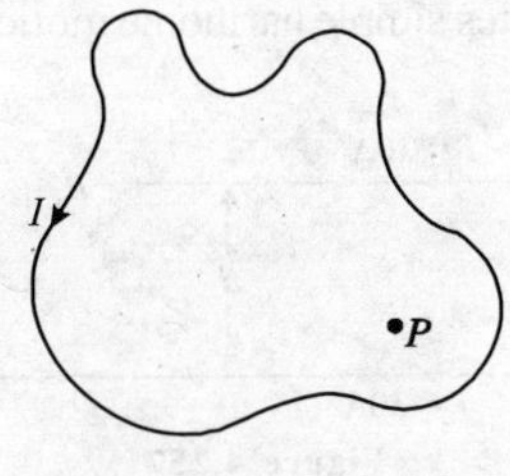

Figure 4.255

(A) The magnetic field at point P may be zero

(B) The magnetic field at point P will not change in magnitude when the loop is distorted.

(C) The magnetic field at P will not change in direction when the loop is distorted

(D) None of the above is true.

4-32 A long thin wooden cylindrical shell of radius R carries uniform surface charge density σ. It is rotating about its axis with angular velocity ω. The angular speed slowly increases with time t as $\omega = kt$ where k is constant. Which of the following statement is/are correct about magnetic and electric field inside the shell :

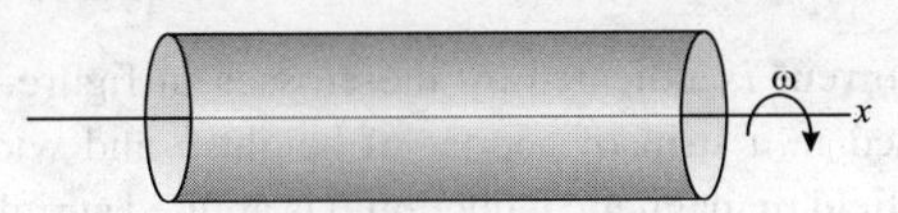

Figure 4.256

(A) Both the magnetic and the electric field due to shell are uniform and constant

(B) The magnetic field is uniform but not constant and the electric field is constant but not uniform

(C) The magnetic field is constant but not uniform electric field is uniform but not constant

(D) total energy U stored in both types of field varies with time as $U = a + bt^2$ where a and b are positive constant

* * * * *

Unsolved Numerical Problems for Preparation of NSEP, INPhO & IPhO

For detailed preparation of INPhO and IPhO students can refer advance study material on www.physicsgalaxy.com

4-1 An α-particle is accelerated by a potential difference of 10^4 V. Find the change in its direction of motion, if it enters normally in a region of thickness 0.1 m having transverse magnetic induction of 0.1 Tesla. (Given : mass of α-particle 6.4×10^{-7} kg)

Ans. [$\theta = 30°$]

4-2 A long horizontal wire *AB* which is free to move in a vertical plane and carries a steady current of 20 A, is in equilibrium at a height of 0.01 m over another parallel long wire *CD*, which is fixed in a horizontal plane and carries a steady current of 30 A, as shown in figure-4.257. Show that when *AB* is slightly depressed, it executes simple harmonic motion. Find the period of oscillations.

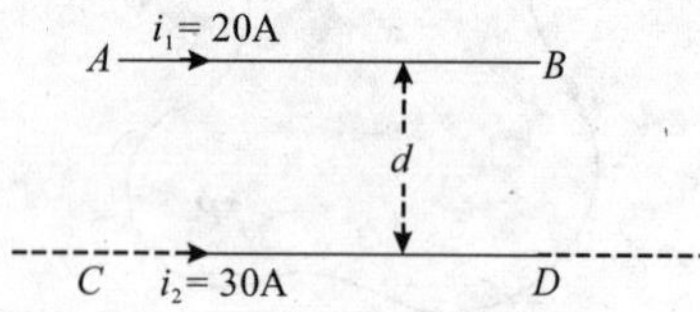

Figure 4.257

Ans. [0.2 s]

4-3 A beam of charged particles, having kinetic energy 10^3 eV, contains masses 8×10^{-27} kg and 1.6×10^{-26} kg emerge from the end of an accelerator tube. There is a plate at a distance 10^{-2} m from the end of the tube and placed perpendicular to the beam. Calculate the magnitude of the smallest magnetic field which can prevent the beam from striking the plate.

Ans. [$\sqrt{2}$ T]

4-4 A long straight cylindrical hollow pipe has inner and outer radii 1 cm and 2 cm respectively. It carries a current 100 A. Calculate the magnetic field at distance (a) 0.5 cm, (b) 1.5 cm and (c) 4 cm from the axis of pipe.

Ans. [(a) 0 (b) 5.56×10^{-4} T (c) 5×10^{-4} T]

4-5 A current *i*, indicated by the crosses in figure-4.258 is established in a strip of copper of height *h* and width *w*. A uniform field of magnetic induction *B* is applied at right angles to the strip.

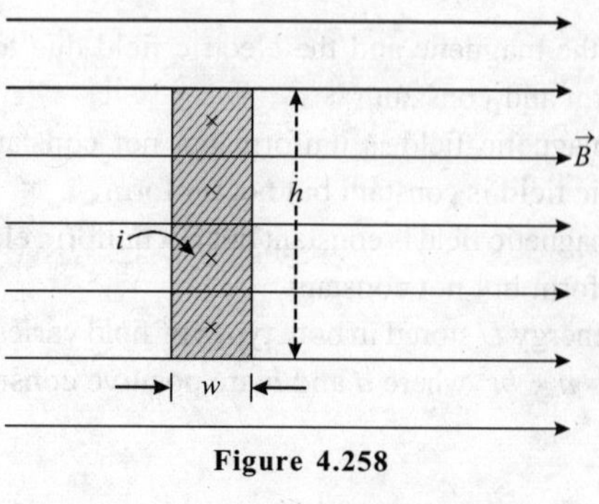

Figure 4.258

(a) Calculate the drift velocity v_d for the electrons.

(b) What are the magnitude and direction of the magnetic force *F* acting on the electrons.

(c) What would be the magnitude and direction of a homogeneous electric field *E* have to be in order to counterbalance the effect of magnetic field ?

(d) What is the voltage *V* necessary between two sides of the conductor in order to create this field *E*? Between which sides of the conductor would this voltage have to be applied ?

(e) If no electric field is applied from the outside, the electrons will be pushed somewhat to one side and therefore will give rise to a uniform electric field E_H across the conductor until the forces of this electrostatic field E_H balance the magnetic force encountered in part-(b). What will be the magnitude and direction of field E_H? Assume that *n*, the number of conduction electrons per unit volume is 1.1×10^{29}/ metre^3 and that $h = 0.02$ metre, $w = 0.1$ cm, $i = 50$ amp, and $B = 2$ weber/metre^2.

Ans. [(a) 1.4×10^{-4} m/s; (b) 4.5×10^{-23} N (in downward direction); (c) 2.8×10^{-4} V/m; (d) 5.8×10^{-6} V, Top voltage should be positive and bottom negative.; (e) 2.8×10^{-4} V/m]

4-6 A 2 keV positron is projected into uniform field of induction *B* of 0.10 T with its velocity vector making an angle of 89° with *B*. Convince your-self that the path will be a helix, its axis being the direction of *B*. Find the period, the pitch *p*, and the radius *r* of the helix, see figure-4.259.

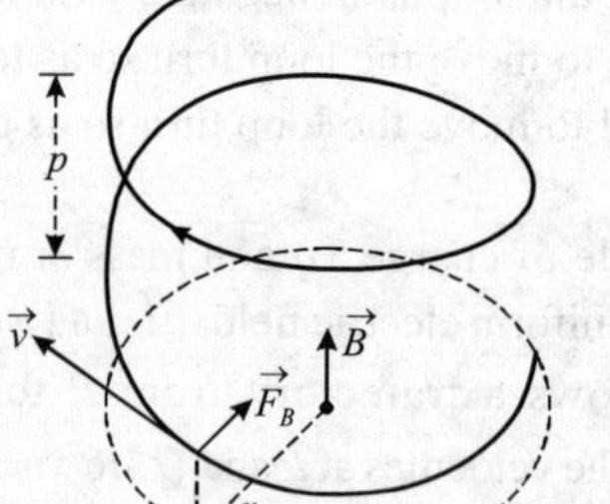

Figure 4.259

Ans. [(1) 3.6×10^{-10} s, (2), 0.17×10^{-3} m, (3) 1.5×10^{-3} m]

4-7 The distance between two plates of a cathode ray oscillograph is 1 cm and potential difference between them is 1200 volt. If an electron of energy 2000 eV enters at right angles to the field what will be its deflection if the plates be 1.5 cm long ?

Ans. [0.34 cm]

4-8 A solenoid of length 0.4 m and diameter 0.6 m consists of a single layer of 1000 turns of fine wire carrying a current of 5.0×10^{-3} ampere. Calculate the magnetic field intensity on the axis at the middle and at the ends of the solenoid.

Ans. [$2.775\ \pi \times 10^{-6}$ T, $2\ \pi \times 10^{-6}$ T]

4-9 A charge of 1 coul. is placed at one end of a non-conducting rod of length 0.6 m. The rod is rotated in a vertical plane about a horizontal axis passing through the other end of the rod with angular frequency $10^4\ \pi$ radian/sec. Find the magnetic field at a point on the axis of rotation at a distance of 0.8 from the centre of the path. Now half of the charge is removed from one end and placed on the other end. The rod is rotated in a vertical plane about horizontal axis passing through the mid-point of the rod with the same angular frequency. Calculate the magnetic field at a point on the axis at a distance of 0.4 m form the centre of the rod.

Ans. [1.13×10^{-3} T; 2.26×10^{-3} T]

4-10 A long horizontal wire P carries a current of 50 A. It is rigidly fixed. Another find wire Q is placed directly above and parallel to P. The weight of the wire Q is 0.075 N/m and it carries a current of 25 A. Find the position of the wire Q from the wire P so that Q remains suspended due to the magnetic repulsion. Also indicate the direction of current in Q with respect to P.

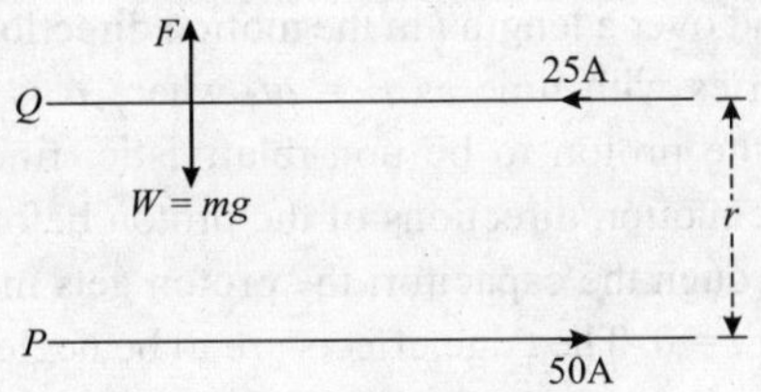

Figure 4.260

Ans. [3.33 mm]

4-11 A pair of parallel horizontal conducting rails of negligible resistance shorted at one end is fixed on a table. The distance between the rails is L. A conducting massless rod of resistance R can slide on the rails frictionlessly. The rod is tied to a massless string which passes over a pulley fixed to the edge of the table. A mass m, tied to the other end of the string, hangs vertically. A constant magnetic field B exists perpendicular to the table. If the system is released from rest, calculate.

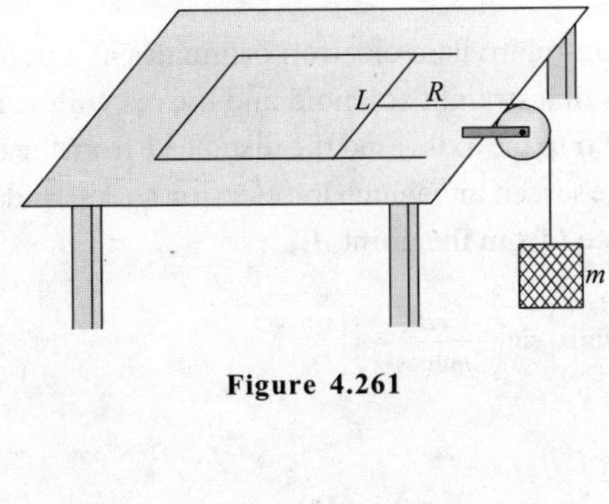

Figure 4.261

(a) The terminal velocity achieved by the rod, and

(b) The acceleration of the mass at the instant when the velocity of rod is half the terminal velocity.

Ans. [(a) $v_T = \frac{mgR}{B^2L^2}$, (b) $\frac{g}{2}$]

4-12 A uniformly conducting wire is bent to form a ring of mass m and radius r, and the ring in placed on a rough horizontal surface with its plane horizontal. There exists a uniform and constant horizontal magnetic field of induction B. Now a charge q is quickly passed through the ring in a very small time interval Δt. As a result the ring ultimately just becomes vertical. Find the value of q for this to happen. Assume that friction is sufficient to prevent slipping and ignore any loss in energy.

Ans. [$\frac{m}{\pi B}\sqrt{\frac{3g}{r}}$]

4-13 The region between $x = 0$ and $x = L$ is filled with uniform, steady magnetic field $B_0\hat{k}$. A particle of mass m positive charge q and velocity $v_0\hat{i}$ travels along X-axis and enters the region of magnetic field. Neglect the gravity throughout the question.

(a) Find the value If L if the particle emerges from the region of magnetic field with its final velocity at spent by it is the magnetic field.

(b) If the magnetic field now extends upto 2.1 L, find the time spent by the particle inside the field now.

Ans. [(a) $\frac{mv_0}{2qB}$; (b) $\frac{\pi m}{2qB}$]

4-14 Two straight parallel conductors are spaced 50 cm apart and carry oppositely directed currents, the first 20 A, the second 24 A. A point P is separated from the first conductor by a distance of 40 cm and from the second by 30 cm. Calculate the magnetic field of induction at P.

Ans. [188.68×10^{-7} T and $\alpha = 32°$]

4-15 The electron circulates round the nucleus in a path of radius 5.1×10^{-11} m at a frequency of 6.8×10^{15} revolutions/sec. Calculate B at the centre and magnetic dipole moment.

Ans. [14 T, 9×10^{-24} Am^2]

4-16 A coil carrying a current $I = 10$ mA is placed in a uniform magnetic field so that its axis coincides with the field direction. The single-layer winding of the coil is made of copper wire with diameter $d = 0.1$ mm, radius of turns is equal to $R = 30$ mm. At what value of the induction of the external magnetic field can be coil winding be ruptured ?

Ans. [8 kT]

4-17 A current $i = 5.0$ amp. flows along a thin wire shaped as shown in figure-4.262. The radius of a curved part of the wire is equal to $R = 120$ mm, the angle $2\phi = 90°$. Find the magnetic induction of the field at the point O.

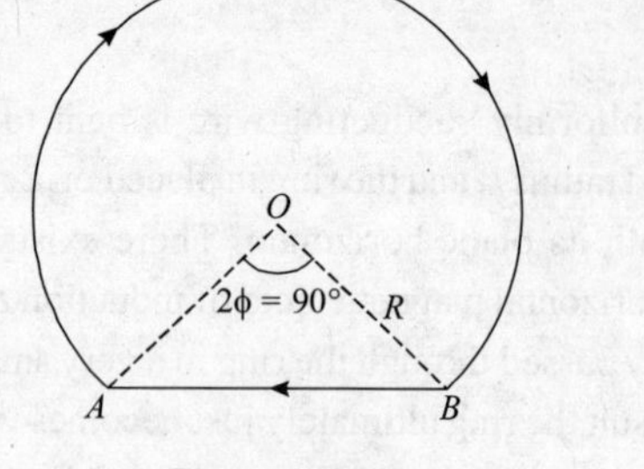

Figure 4.262

Ans. [28 μT]

4-18 In an electromagnetic pump designed for transferring molten metals in a pipe section with metal is located in a uniform magnetic induction B. A current I is made to flow across this pipe section in the direction perpendicular both to the vector $\vec{B}$ and to the axis of the pipe. Find the Gauge pressure produced by the pump if $B = 0.10$ T, $I = 100$ A and $a = 2.0$ cm.

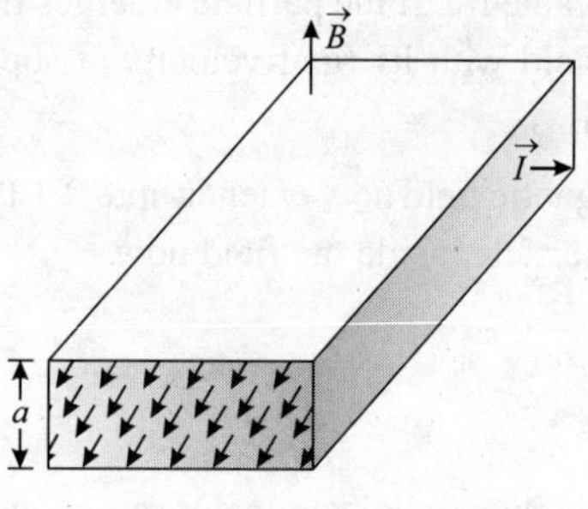

Figure 4.263

Ans. [0.5 kPa]

4-19 A current I flows in a long thin walled cylinder of radius R. What pressure do the wall of the cylinder experience ?

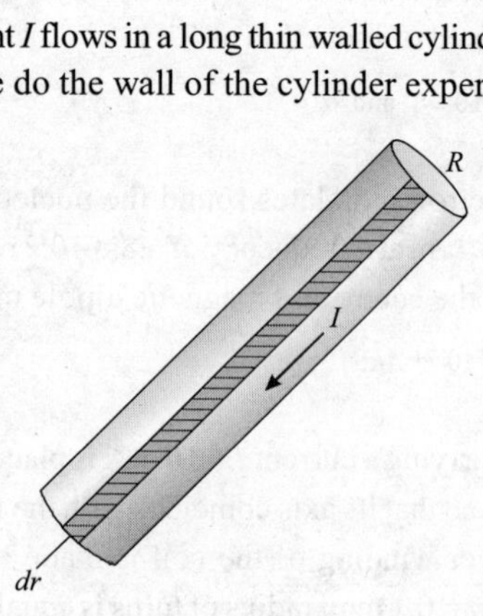

Figure 4.264

Ans. [$\frac{\mu_0 I^2}{8\pi^2 R^2}$]

4-20 At the moment $t = 0$ an electron leaves one plate of a parallel plate capacitor with a negligible velocity. An accelerating voltage, varying as $V = at$, where $a = 100$ V/s, is applied between the plates. The separation between the plates is $l = 5.0$ cm. What is the velocity of the electron at the moment it reaches the opposite plate?

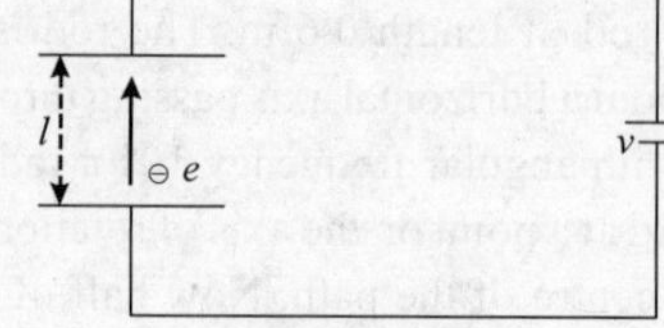

Figure 4.265

Ans. [16 km/s]

4-21 A proton beam passes without deviation through a region of space where there are uniform transverse mutually perpendicular electric and magnetic fields with $E = 120$ kV/m and $B = 50$ mT. Then the beam strikes a grounded target. Find the force which the beam acts on the target if the beam current is equal to 0.80 mA.

Ans. [2×10^{-5} N]

4-22 A proton accelerated by a potential difference V gets into the uniform electric field of a parallel plate capacitor whose plates extend over a length l in the motion direction. The field strength varies with time as $E = at$, where a is a constant. Assuming the proton to be non-relativistic, find the angle between the motion directions of the proton before and after its flight through the capacitor; the proton gets in the field at the moment $t = 0$. The edge effects are to be neglected.

Ans. [$\tan^{-1}\left(\frac{al^2}{4}\sqrt{\frac{m}{2eV^3}}\right)$]

4-23 A charged particle moves along a circle of radius $r = 100$ mm in a uniform magnetic field with induction $B = 10.0$ mT. Find its velocity and period of revolution if that particle is :

(a) A non-relativistic proton

(b) A relativistic electron

Ans. [(a) 6.5 μs; (b) 4.1 ns]

4-24 A non-relativistic electron originates at a point A lying on the axis of a straight solenoid and moves with velocity v at an angle of α to the axis. Find the distance r from the axis to the point on the screen into which the electron strikes and is located at a distance l from the point A.

Ans. [$\frac{2mv}{eB}\sin\alpha\left|\sin\left(\frac{eBl}{2mv\cos\alpha}\right)\right|$]

4-25 A non-relativistic charged particle flies through the electric field of a cylindrical capacitor and gets into a uniform transverse magnetic field with induction B. In the capacitor, the particle moves along the *arc* of a circle, in the magnetic field, along a semi-circle of radius r. The potential difference applied to the capacitor is equal to V, the radii of electrodes are equal to a and b, with $a < b$. Find the velocity of the particle and its specific charge q/m.

Ans. $\left[\dfrac{V}{rB\ln\dfrac{b}{a}}, \dfrac{V}{r^2B^2\ln\left(\dfrac{b}{a}\right)}\right]$

4-26 Uniform electric and magnetic fields with strengths E and induction B respectively are directed along y-axis. A particle with specific charge q/m leaves the origin O in the direction of the x-axis with an initial non-relativistic velocity v_0. Find :

(a) The co-ordinate y_n of the particle when it crosses the y-axis for the nth time;

(b) The angle α between the particle's velocity vector and y-axis at that moment.

Ans. [(a) $2\pi^2n^2mE/qB^2$; (b) $\tan^{-1}\left(\dfrac{Bv_0}{2\pi En}\right)$]

4-27 A narrow beam of identical ions with specific charge q/m, possessing different velocities, enters the region of space, where there are uniform parallel electric and magnetic fields with strengths E and B, at the point O. The beam direction coincides with the x-axis at the point O. A plane screen oriented at right angles to the x-axis is located at a distance l from O. Find the equation of trace that the ion leaves on the screen. Demonstrate that at $z << l$, it is the equation of a parabola.

Ans. $\left[z^2 = \left(\dfrac{B^2l^2q}{2mE}\right)y\right]$

4-28 A beam of non-relativistic charged particles moves without deviation through the region of space A where there are transverse mutually perpendicular electric and magnetic fields with strength E and induction B. When the magnetic field is switched off, the trace of the beam on the screen S shifts by Δx. Knowing the distance a and b, find the specific charge q/m of the particles.

Ans. $\left[\dfrac{2mE\Delta x}{a(a+2b)B^2}\right]$

4-29 An electron is accelerated through a PD of 100 V and then enters a region where it is moving perpendicular to a magnetic field $B = 0.2$ T. Find the radius of the circular path, Repeat this problem for a proton.

Ans. [0.0167 cm, 0.7 cm]

4-30 A proton, a deutron and an α-particle have equal kinetic energies. Compare the radii of their paths when a normal magnetic field is applied.

Ans. $[r_d = \sqrt{2}, r_p = \sqrt{2}r_\alpha]$

4-31 Determine the magnetic field at point P located a distance x from the corner of an infinitely long wire bent at right angle as shown in figure-4.266. The wire carries a steady current i.

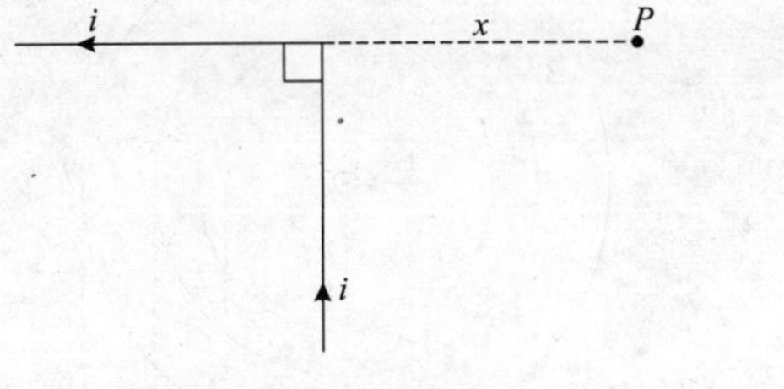

Figure 4.266

Ans. $\left[\dfrac{\mu_0 i}{4\pi x}\text{ into the page}\right]$

4-32 Consider the current carrying loop shown in figure-4.267 formed of radial lines and segments of circles whose centres are at point P. Find the magnitude and direction of $\vec{B}$ at point P.

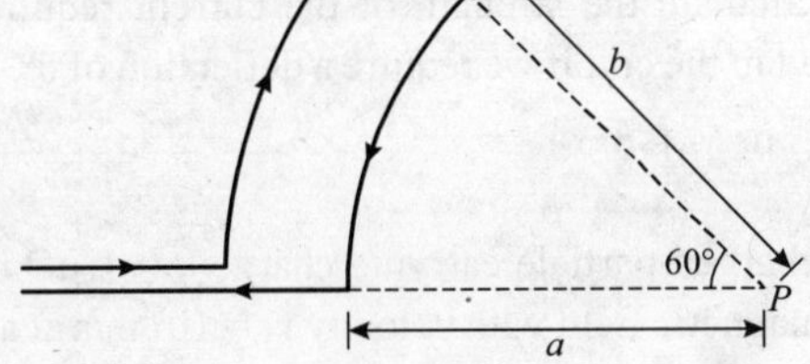

Figure 4.267

Ans. $\left[\dfrac{\mu_0 i}{12}\left(\dfrac{1}{a}-\dfrac{1}{b}\right)\text{ out of the page}\right]$

4-33 Four long, parallel conductors carry equal currents of 5.0 A. The direction of the currents is into the page at points A and B and out of the page at C and D. Calculate the magnitude and direction of the magnetic field at point P, located at the centre of the square.

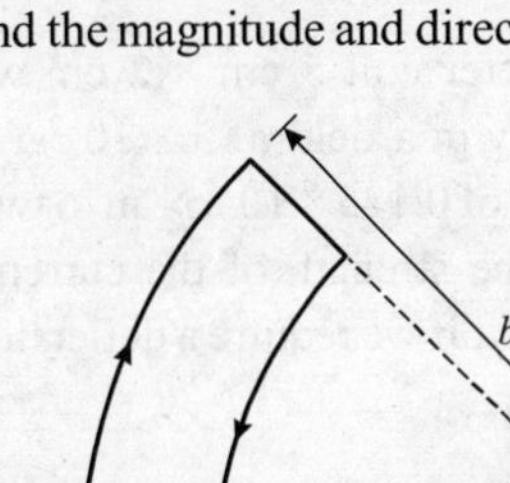

Figure 4.268

Ans. [20.0 μT toward the bottom of the square]

4-34 Figure given in the question is a cross-sectional view of a coaxial cable. The centre conductor is surrounded by a rubber layer, which is surrounded by an outer conductor, which is surrounded by another rubber layer. The current in the inner conductor is 1.0 A out of the page, and the current in the outer conductor is 3.0 A into the page. Determine the magnitude and direction of the magnetic field at points *a* and *b*.

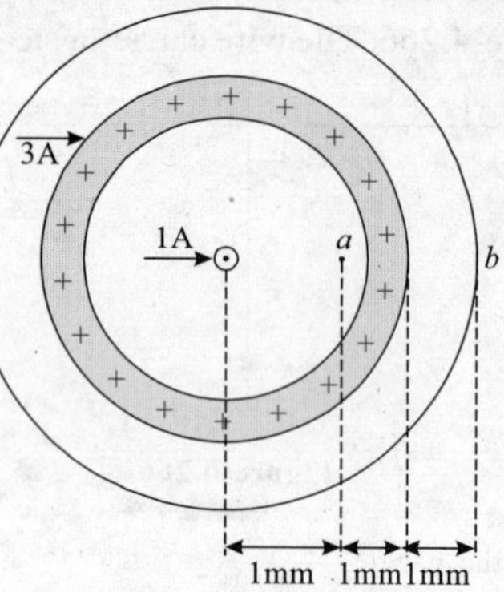

Figure 4.269

Ans. [200 μT toward the top of the page, 133 μT toward the bottom of the page]

4-35 A galvanometer coil 5 cm × 2 cm with 200 turns is suspended vertically in a field of 5×10^{-2} T. The suspension fiber needs a torque of 0.125×10^{-7} N-m to twist it through one radian. Calculate the strength of the current required to be maintained in the coil if we require a deflection of 6°.

Ans. [1.3×10^{-7} A]

4-36 A charged particle carrying charge $q = 1$ μC moves in uniform magnetic field with velocity $v_1 = 10^6$ m/s at angle 45° with *x*-axis in the *x*-*y* plane and experiences a force $F_1 = 5\sqrt{2}$ mN along the negative *z*-axis. When the same particle moves with velocity $v_2 = 10^6$ m/s along the *z*-axis it experiences a force F_2 in *y*-direction. Find :

(a) Magnitude and direction of the magnetic field,

(b) The magnitude of the force F_2.

Ans. [(a) $(10^{-2}\,\hat{i})$T; (b) 10^{-2} N]

4-37 A wire shaped to a regular hexagon of side 2 cm carries a current of 2 A. Find the magnetic field at the centre of the hexagon.

Ans. [1.38×10^{-4} T]

4-38 Three infinitely long thin wires, each carrying current *i* in the same direction, are in the *X-Y* plane of a gravity free space. The central wire is along the *y*-axis while the other two are along $x = \pm d$:

(a) Find the locus of the points for which the magnetic field *B* is zero

(b) If the central wire is displaced along the *z*-direction by a small amount and released, show that it will execute simple harmonic motion. If the linear density of the wires is λ, find the frequency of oscillation

Ans. [(a) $x = \frac{d}{\sqrt{3}}$ and $x = -\frac{d}{\sqrt{3}}$ (b) $\frac{i}{2\pi d}\sqrt{\frac{\mu_0}{\pi\lambda}}$]

4-39 Uniform electric and magnetic fields with strength *E* and *B* are directed along the *y*-axis. A particle with specific charge *q*/*m* leaves the origin in the direction of *x*-axis with an initial velocity v_0. Find :

(a) The *y*-coordinate of the particle when it crosses the *y*-axis for n^{th} time.

(b) The angle α between the particle's velocity vector and the *y*-axis at that moment.

Ans. [(a) $\frac{2n^2 mE\pi^2}{qB^2}$ (b) $\tan^{-1}\left(\frac{Bv_0}{2\pi nE}\right)$]

4-40 A particle of charge *q* and mass *m* is projected from the origin with velocity $\vec{v} = v_0\hat{i}$ in a nonuniform magnetic field $\vec{B} = -B_0 x\hat{k}$. Here v_0 and B_0 are positive constants of proper dimensions. Find the maximum positive *x*-coordinate of the particle during its motion.

Ans. [$\sqrt{\frac{2mv_0}{B_0 q}}$]

4-41 An electron moves through a uniform magnetic field given by $\vec{B} = B_x\hat{i} + (3B_x)\hat{j}$. At a particular instant, the electron has the velocity $\vec{v} = (2.0\hat{i} + 4.0\hat{j})$ m/s and magnetic force acting on it is $(6.4 \times 10^{-19}\text{ N})\hat{k}$. Find B_x.

Ans. [$B_x = -2.0$ T]

4-42 A neutral particle is at rest in a uniform magnetic field $\vec{B}$. At time $t = 0$ it decays into two charged particles. Each of mass *m* :

(a) If the charge of one of the particles is +*q*, what is the charge of the other ?

(b) The two particles moves off in separate paths, both of them lie in the plane perpendicular to $\vec{B}$. At a later time the particles collide. Express the time from decay until collision in terms of *m*, *B* and *q*.

Ans. [(a) $-q$ (b) $\frac{\pi m}{Bq}$]

4-43 Each of the points at the corners of the cube in figure represents a positive charge *q* moving with a velocity of magnitude *v* in the direction indicated. The region in the figure is in a uniform magnetic field $\vec{B}$, parallel to the x-axis and directed toward the right. Find the magnitude and direction of the force on each charge.

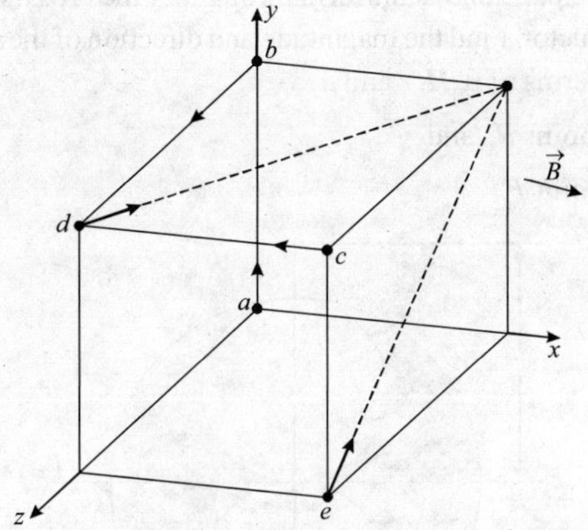

Figure 4.270

Ans. [(a) $-qvB\hat{k}$; (b) $+qvB\hat{j}$; (c) Zero; (d) $\frac{-qvB}{\sqrt{2}}\hat{j}$; (e) $\left(-\frac{qvB}{\sqrt{2}}\right)(\hat{j}+\hat{k})$]

4-44 A proton of charge e and mass m enters a uniform magnetic field $\vec{B}=B\hat{i}$ with an initial velocity $\vec{v}=v_x\hat{i}+v_y\hat{j}$. Find an expression in unit-vector notation for its velocity at time t.

Ans. [$\vec{v}=v_x\hat{i}+v_y\cos\omega t\hat{j}-v_y\sin\omega t\hat{k}$, Here $\omega=\frac{Be}{m}$]

4-45 A thin, 50.0 cm long metal bar with mass 750 g rests on, but is not attached to, two metallic supports in a 0.450 T magnetic field, as shown in figure-4.271. A battery and a resistance $R = 25.0\ \Omega$ in series are connected to the supports :

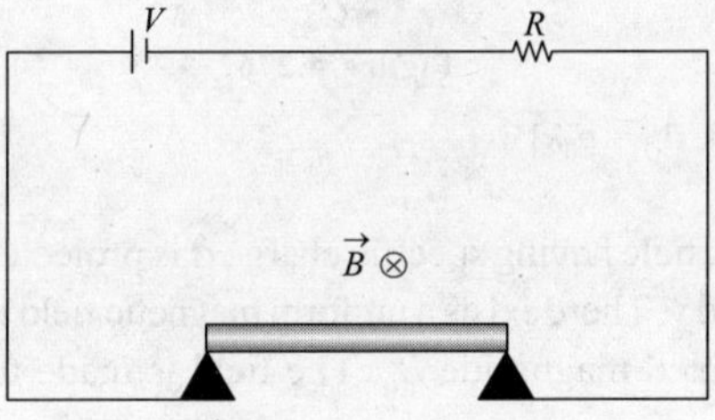

Figure 4.271

(a) What is the largest voltage the battery can have without breaking the circuit at the supports?

(b) The battery voltage has this maximum value calculated. Decreasing the resistance to 2.0 Ω, find the initial acceleration of the bar.

Ans. [(a) 817.5 V (b) 112.8 m/s^2]

4-46 In figure-4.272, the cube is 40.0 cm on each edge. Four straight segments of wire ab, bc, cd and da form a closed loop that carries a current $I = 5.00$ A, in the direction shown. A uniform magnetic field of magnitude $B = 0.020$ T is in the positive y-direction. Determine the magnitude and direction of the magnetic force on each segment.

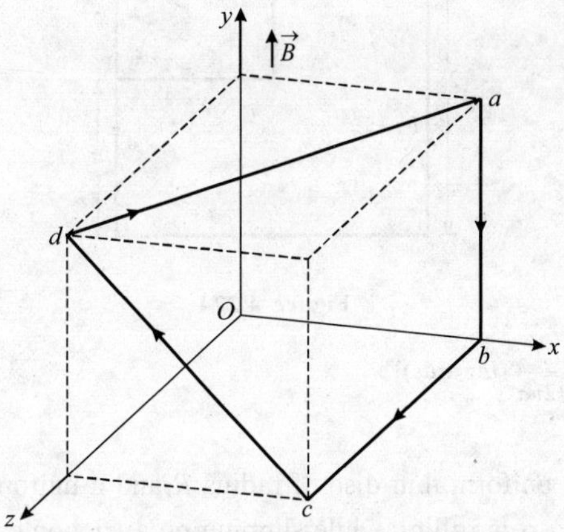

Figure 4.272

Ans. [$\vec{F}_{ab}=0$, $\vec{F}_{bc}=(-0.04\text{N})\hat{i}$, $\vec{F}_{cd}=(-0.04\text{N})\hat{k}$, $\vec{F}_{da}=(0.04\hat{i}+0.04\hat{k})\text{N}$]

4-47 A length L of wire carries a current i. Show that if the wire is formed into a circular coil, then the maximum torque in a given magnetic field is developed when the coil has one turn only, and that maximum torque has the magnitude $\tau = L^2 iB/4\pi$.

4-48 A coil with magnetic moment 1.45 A-m^2 is oriented initially with its magnetic moment antiparallel to a uniform 0.835 T magnetic field. What is the change in potential energy of the coil when it is rotated 180° so that its magnetic moment is parallel to the field ?

Ans. [– 2.42 J]

4-49 A current $I = \sqrt{2}$A flows in a circuit having the shape of isosceles trapezium. The ratio of the bases of the trapezium is 2. Find the magnetic induction B at symmetric point O in the plane of the trapexium. The length of the smaller base of the trapexium is 100 mm and the distance $r = 50$ mm.

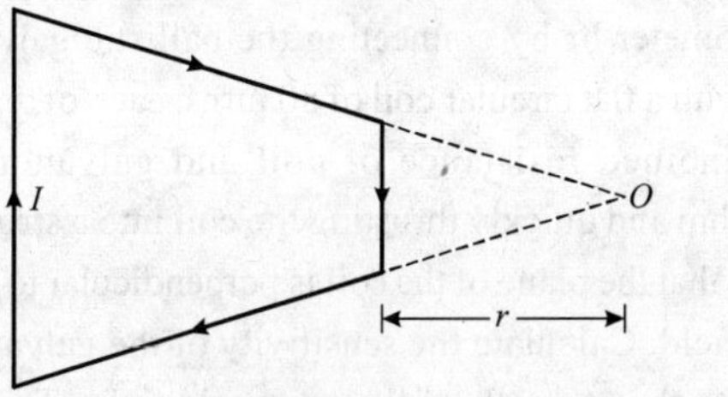

Figure 4.273

Ans. [2 × 10^{-6} T]

4-50 Find the magnetic field $\vec{B}$ at the point P in figure-4.274.

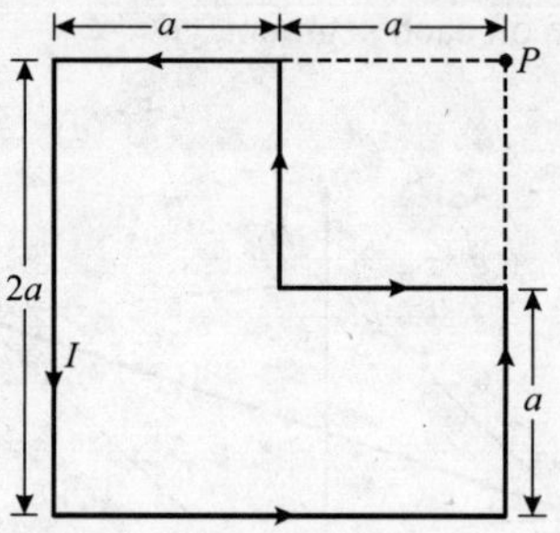

Figure 4.274

Ans. $[\frac{\mu_0 i}{4\sqrt{2}\pi a}$ (inwards)]

4-51 A uniform thin disc of radius R and a uniform charge density $+\sigma$ is rolling while slipping on a frictionless surface such that $v_{cm} = 3\omega R$ where v_{cm} is the velocity of the centre of the disc. Calculate the magnetic field at the centre of the disc.

Ans. $[\frac{\mu_0 \sigma v_{cm}}{6}]$

4-52 A closely wound coil has a radius of 6.00 cm and carries a current of 2.50 A. How many turns must it have if, at a point on the coil axis 6.00 cm from the centre of the coil, the magnetic field is 6.39×10^{-4} T ?

Ans. [69]

4-53 A closed curve encircles several conductors. The line integral $\oint \vec{B} \cdot d\vec{l}$ around this curve is 3.83×10^{-7} T-m.

(a) What is the net current in the conductors ?

(b) If you were to integrate around the curve in the opposite direction, what would be the value of the line integral?

Ans. [(a) 0.3 A; (b) 0.0184 m]

4-54 A deflection of 24 divisions of a ballistic galvanometer is obtained either by charging a capacitor of 3 μF capacitance to a potential difference of 2 V and discharging through the galvanometer or by connecting the ballistic galvanometer in series with a flat circular coil of 80 turns, each of diameter 1 cm, the combined resistance of coil and galvanometer being 4000 ohm and quickly thrusting the coil into a strong magnetic field so that the plane of the coil is perpendicular to the direction of the field. Calculate the sensitivity of the galvanometer and calculate the strength of the magnetic field. The strength of the earth's magnetic field may be neglected.

Ans. [4 div per μC, 3.82 T]

4-55 A long cylindrical conductor of radius a has two cylindrical cavities of diameter a through its entire length as shown in cross-section in figure-4.275. A current I is directed out of the page and is uniform throughout the cross-section of the conductor. Find the magnitude and direction of the magnetic field in terms of μ_0, I, r and a :

(a) At point P_1 and

(b) at point P_2

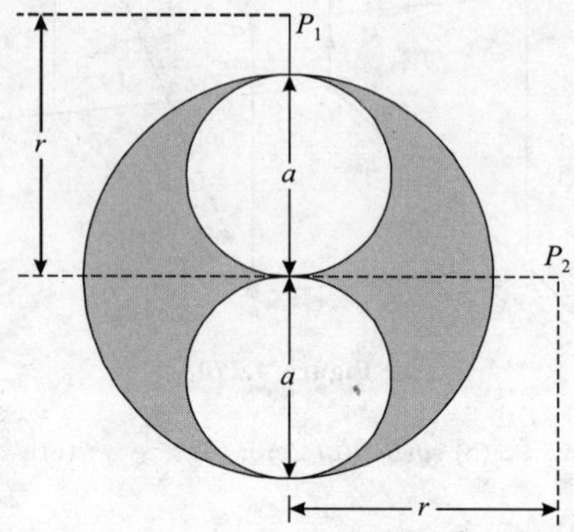

Figure 4.275

Ans. [(a) $\frac{\mu_0 I}{\pi r}\left(\frac{2r^2 - a^2}{4r^2 - a^2}\right)$ to the left; (b) $\frac{\mu_0 I}{\pi r}\left(\frac{2r^2 + a^2}{4r^2 + a^2}\right)$ towards the top of the page]

4-56 The two infinite plates shown in cross-section in figure-4.276 carry λ amperes of current out of the page per unit width of plate. Find the magnetic field at points P and Q.

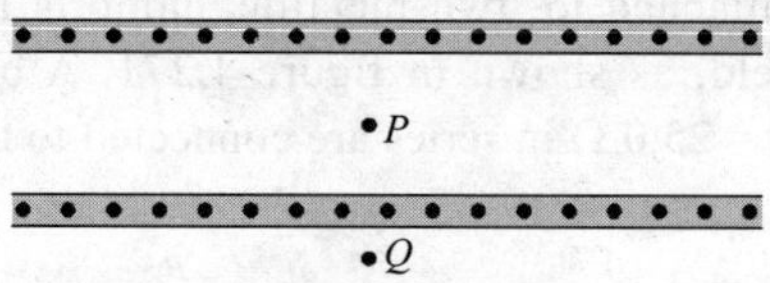

Figure 4.276

Ans. $[B_P = 0,\ B_Q = \mu_0 \lambda]$

4-57 A particle having specific charge σ is projected in xy plane with a speed v. There exists a uniform magnetic field in z-direction having a fixed magnitude B_0. The field is made to reverse its direction after every interval of $\frac{2\pi}{\sigma B_0}$. Calculate the maximum separation between two positions of the particle during its course of motion. Neglect any other force including gravity throughout the motion of charge.

Ans. $[\frac{4v}{\sigma B_0}]$

4-58 A magnet of length 0.1 m and pole strength 10^{-4} web kept in a magnetic field of intensity 30 N/Wb at an angle 30°. Find the couple acting on it.

Ans. [1.5×10^{-4} Nm]

4-59 Find the force experienced by a pole of strength 100 Am at a distance of 20 cm from a short bar magnet of length 5 cm and pole strength of 200 Am on its axial line.

Ans. [2.5×10^{-2} N]

4-60 A magnetic needle is suspended at a distance of 1 m from a short magnet on the eastern side on its axial line. The deflection produced is 30°. Calculate the horizontal component of earth's magnetic field if the magnetic moment of the magnet is 100 Am^2.

Ans. [3.46×10^{-5} T]

4-61 A copper wire having resistance 0.01 ohm in each metre is used to wind a 400 turn solenoid of radius 1.0 cm and length 20 cm. Find the emf of a battery which when connected across the solenoid will cause a magnetic field of 1.0×10^{-2} T near the centre of the solenoid.

Ans. [1 V]

4-62 A vibration magnetometer consists of two identical bar magnets placed one over the other such that they are mutually perpendicular and bisect each other. The time period of oscillation in a horizontal magnetic field is 4 s. If one of the magnets is taken away, find the period of oscillation of the other in the same field.

Ans. [3.36 s]

4-63 A small magnet of magnetic moment $\pi \times 10^{-10}$ amp-m^2 is placed on the Y-axis at a distance of 0.1 m from the origin with its axis parallel to the X-axis. A coil having 169 turns and radius 0.05 m is placed on the X-axis at a distance of 0.12 m from the origin with the axis of the coil coinciding with X-axis. Find the magnitude and direction of the current in the coil for a compass needle placed at the origin, to point in the north-south direction.

Ans. [2.6×10^{-10} A, clockwise direction when viewed from O]

4-64 A circular coil of radius 0.157 m has 50 turns. It is placed such that its axis is in magnetic meridian. A dip needle is supported at the centre of the coil with its axis of rotation horizontal and in the plane of the coil. The angle of dip is 30° when a current flows through the coil. The angle of dip becomes 60° on reversing the current. Find the current in the coil assuming that the magnetic field due to the coil is smaller than the horizontal component of earth's magnetic field, $B_H = 3 \times 10^{-5}$ T.

Ans. [0.75 A]

4-65 A small magnet of magnetic moment M is placed at broad-side on position of a magnet of magnetic moment M', length $2l'$ in such a way that the axis of former coincides with the perpendicular bisector of the latter. The separation between their centres is d. Calculate the nature of interaction (force or couple) among them. What is its limiting value when d becomes very large ?

Ans. [$\frac{\mu_0}{4\pi} \times \frac{M' \times m}{(d^2 + l'^2)^{3/2}}$, $\frac{\mu_0 M'M}{4\pi(d^2 + l'^2)^{3/2}}$, $\frac{\mu_0 M'M}{4\pi d^3}$]

4-66 A small coil of radius 0.002 m is placed on the axis of a magnet of magnetic moment 10^5 J/t and length 0.1 m at a distance of 0.15 m from the centre of the magnet. The plane of the coil is perpendicular to the axis of the magnet. Find the force on the coil when the current of 2.0 amp. is passed through it.

Ans. [4.396×10^{-3} N]

4-67 A magnet is suspended in the magnetic meridian with a untwisted wire. The upper end of the wire is rotated through 180° to deflect the magnet by 30° from magnetic meridian. Now this magnet is replaced by another magnet. Now the upper end of the wire is rotated through 270° to deflect the magnet 30° from magnetic meridian. Compare the magnetic moments of magnets.

Ans. [$M_1 : M_2 = 5 : 8$]

4-68 A coil is made with a wire having radius 0.1 mm and resistivity 2×10^{-6} Ωcm. The radius of the coil is 5 cm and it consists of 50 turns. The coil is connected to a cell of emf 10 V and negligible internal resistance :

(a) Find the current flowing through it

(b) What must be the potential difference across the coil so as to nullify the earth's horizontal magnetic induction of 3.14×10^{-5} T as the centre of the coil. How should the coil be placed to achieve the above result ?

Ans. [(a) 1 A (b) 0.5 V]

4-69 A magnet is suspended at an angle 60° to an external magnetic field 5×10^{-4} T. What is the workdone by the magnetic field in bringing it in its direction. The magnetic moment is 20 Am^2.

Ans. [-5×10^{-3} J]

4-70 The time period of a bar magnet oscillating in a uniform magnetic field is 3 seconds. If the magnet is cut into two equal parts along the equatorial line of the magnet and one part is made to vibrate in the same field, what is the time period ?

Ans. [$T' = 2\pi\sqrt{[I'/M'H]}$]

4-71 A small coil of radius 0.002 m is placed on the axis of a magnet of magnetic moment 10^5 m from the centre of the magnet. The plane of the coil is perpendicular to the axis of the magnet. Find the force on the coil when the current of 2.0 amp. is passed through it.

Ans. [43.96×10^{-4} N]

4-72 Find the interaction energy of two loops carrying currents I_1 and I_2 if both loops are shaped as circles of radii a and b, with $a << b$. The loop's centres are located at the same point and their planes form an angle θ between them.

Ans. [$\frac{\mu_0}{2b} \cdot \pi a^2 I_1 I_2 \cos\theta$]

4-73 An electron accelerated by a potential difference $V = 1.0$ kV moves in a uniform magnetic field at an angle $\alpha = 30°$ to the vector B whose modulus is $B = 29$ mT. Find the pitch of the helical trajectory of the electron.

Ans. [2 cm]

4-74 A particle accelerated by a potential difference V flies through a uniform transverse magnetic field with induction B. The field occupies a region of space d in thickness. Prove that the angle α through which the particle deviates from the initial direction of its motion is given by.

$$\alpha = \sin^{-1}\left(dB\sqrt{\frac{q}{2Vm}}\right)$$

where m is the mass of the particle.

4-75 A beam of proton with a velocity 4×10^{-5} m/s enters a uniform magnetic field of 0.3 T at an angle of 60° to the magnetic field. Find the radius of the helical path taken by the proton beam. Also find the pitch of the helix (which is the distance travelled by a proton in the beam parallel to the magnetic field during one period of revolution).

Ans. [12 mm, 43.7 mm]

4-76 A particle of mass m and charge q is moving in a region where uniform, constant electric and magnetic field E and B are present. E and B are parallel to each other. At time $t = 0$, the velocity v_0 of the particle is perpendicular to E. Find the velocity v of the particle at time t. You must express your answer in terms of t, q, m, the vectors v_0, E, B and their magnitudes v_0, E and B

Ans. [$\frac{qt}{m}\vec{E} + \vec{v}_0\cos\left(\frac{qBt}{m}\right) + \frac{v_0(\vec{v}_0\times\vec{B})}{|\vec{v}_0\times\vec{B}|}\sin\left(\frac{qBt}{m}\right)$]

4-77 A uniform magnetic field with a slit system as shown in figure-4.277. is to be used as a momentum filter for high-energy charged particles. With a field B Tesla, it is found that the filter transmits α-particles each of energy 5.3 MeV. The magnetic field is increased to 2.3 B Tesla and deuterons are passed into the filter. Find the energy of each deuteron transmitted by the filter.

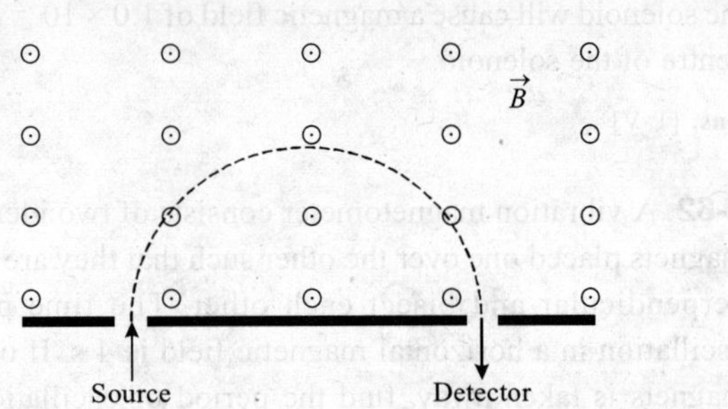

Figure 4.277

Ans. [14 MeV]

4-78 Find the ratio of magnetic dipole moment and magnetic field at the centre of a disc. Radius of disc is R and it is rotating at constant angular speed ω about its axis. The disc is non-conducting and uniformly charged.

Ans. [$\frac{\pi R^3}{2\mu_0}$]

* * * * *

5

Electromagnetic Induction and Alternating Current

FEW WORDS FOR STUDENTS

After the discovery of Faraday's law of Electromagnetic Induction only generation of electricity became easier and cheaper. In magnetism we studied that variation of electric field induces magnetic field and its converse is the phenomenon of electromagnetic induction. In this chapter we will study that according to the law of conservation of energy the work which is done in changing magnetic field associated with a conductor transforms into generation of electricity by induction and whenever work is done always there is some opposition due to which negative work is done and energy is extracted from some body. This negative work is also accounted in determining the direction of induced current and emf which is studied under Lenz's law. Overall this chapter is going to cover the most useful applications of electromagnetism in real life.

CHAPTER CONTENTS

COVER APPLICATION

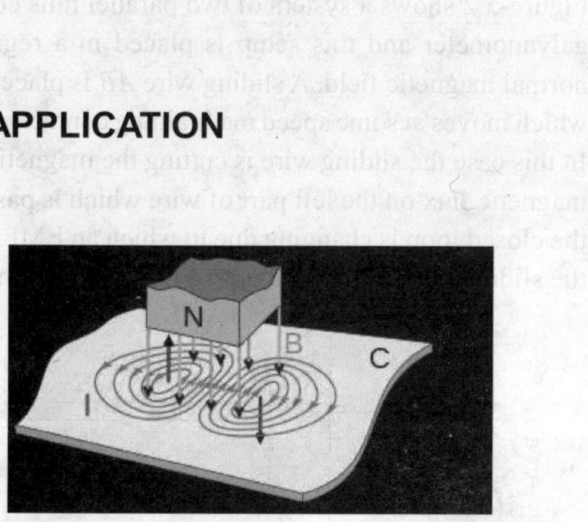

Figure-(a)

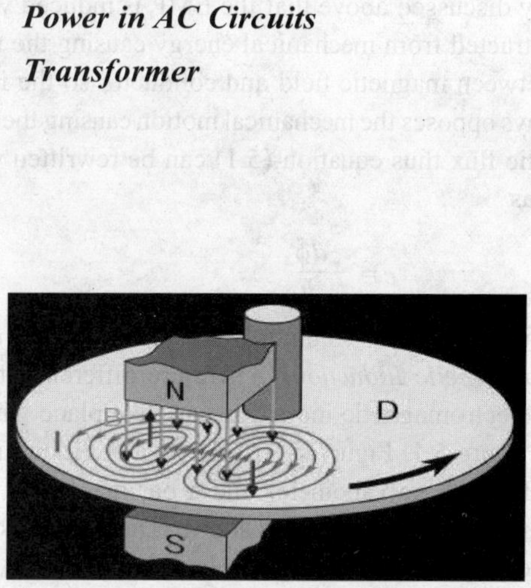

Figure-(b)

Figure-(a) shows a moving metal strip in the magentic field of a magnetic pole and due to motion of free electrons in the strip these electrons experience a magnetic force and starts flowing in closed loops within strip as shown. Such currents are called eddy currents and the magnetic field exerts an opposing magnetic force on these currents and the motion of metal body is opposed. Figure-(b) shows a rotating metal disc and a magnetic field due to magnetic poles passes through the disc as shown and it develops eddy currents and an opposing force on these currents which causes and opposite torque on the rotating disc. This phenomenon is used in design eddy current braking system for atuomobiles.

We've studied in previous chapter that magnetic field never does any work on charges as magnetic force acts in direction normal to their motion. We can modify this statement as net work done by magnetic force on moving charges is always zero but it is possible that there are work done involved by magnetic forces in a system but equal positive and negative work causes no net work done. In the phenomenon of electromagnetic induction magnetic force does negative work on mechanical agents who are displacing a body which contains charges and extract energy from mechanical work and does positive work on charges in inducing EMF in the conducting bodies which may cause induced current to flow if circuit is closed. Always total work by magnetic forces is zero in system but it acts as a mediator in transformation of mechanical energy to electrical energy.

5.1 Faraday's Law of Electromagnetic Induction

Based on several experiments Michael Faraday observed that due to relative motion between a magnetic field and a conductor if magnetic lines are cut by the conductor or total magnetic flux through a coil changes then an EMF is induced in the conductor or coil. This phenomenon is called Electromagnetic Induction.

It is analyzed that the magnitude of induced EMF is equal to the rate at which the magnetic flux associated with the conductor or coil changes or being cut. If in time dt the magnetic flux cut or change by $d\phi$ then the magnitude of induced EMF in the conductor or coil is given as

$$e = \left|\frac{d\phi}{dt}\right| \qquad \dots(5.1)$$

As already discussed above that the EMF is induced with the energy extracted from mechanical energy causing the relative motion between magnetic field and conductor so the induced EMF always opposes the mechanical motion causing the change of magnetic flux thus equation-(5.1) can be rewritten without modulus as

$$e = -\frac{d\phi}{dt} \qquad \dots(5.2)$$

Above equation-(5.2) is commonly known as '*Faraday's Law of Electromagnetic Induction*'. There are different situations in which electromagnetic induction can take place which are shown in figure-5.1. Figure-5.1(a) shows a fixed circular coil connected with a galvanometer and a bar magnet is coming close to the coil along its axis as shown. Due to the motion of magnet the magnetic flux through the coil changes and it induces an EMF in the coil. As wire of coil is forming a closed loop, an induced current also flows and galvanometer shows some deflection. Figure-5.1(b) shows a similar situation but in this case magnet is fixed and coil setup is moving. Again due to continuous change in magnetic flux through the coil an EMF is induced in the coil causing an induced current to flow through galvanometer. In both of these cases if the speed of motion between coil and magnet increases the rate of flux change increases causing higher EMF to be induced more induced current will flow.

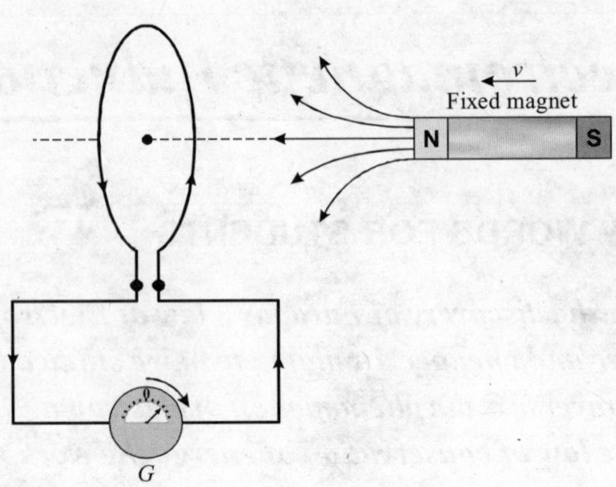

(a)

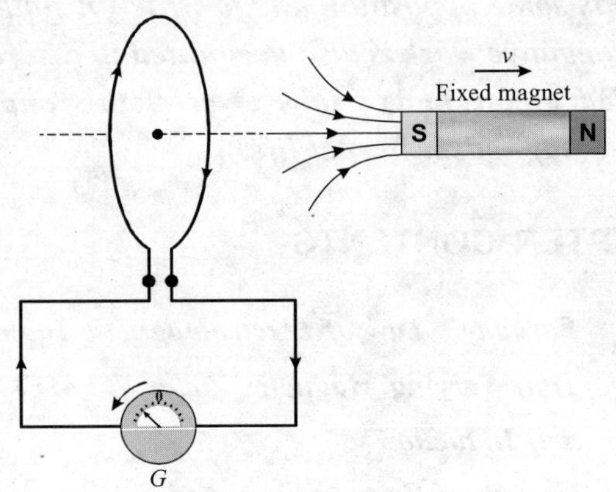

(b)

Figure 5.1

Figure-5.2 shows a system of two parallel rails connected to a galvanometer and this setup is placed in a region having a normal magnetic field. A sliding wire AB is placed on the rails which moves at some speed maintaining contacts with the rails. In this case the sliding wire is cutting the magnetic lines or the magnetic flux on the left part of wire which is passing through the closed loop is changing due to which an EMF is induced in the sliding wire causing a current flow through the circuit.

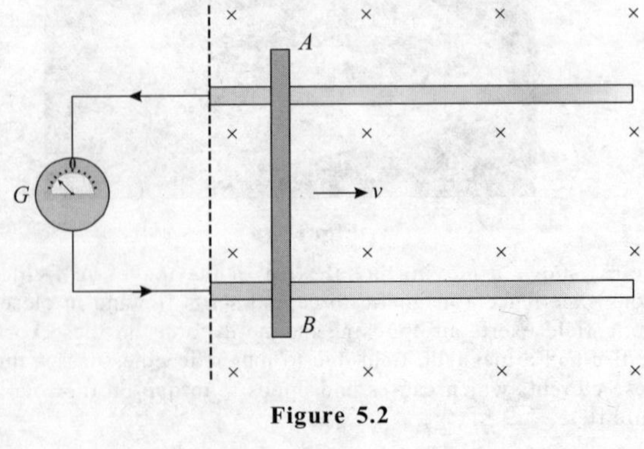

Figure 5.2

There can be many such practical situations in which the magnetic flux associated with a closed loop or a coil changes or flux is cut by a conductor then an EMF is induced.

5.1.1 Lenz´s Law

We've already discussed in previous article that the direction of induced EMF in electromagnetic induction is such that it opposes the causes of change of magnetic flux so that negative work done in processes causing change of flux will be used in generation of electrical EMF thats why in equation-(5.2) there is a negative sign which denotes that sign of induced EMF is opposite to the flux change.

Lenz´s Law is a way to understand the application of Newton´s third law and conservation of energy in circuits when electromagnetic induction takes place. According to Newton´s third law equal and opposite forces cause both positive and negative work to be done simultaneously and by conservation of energy the amount of energy extracted from the processes causing flux variation is equal to the electrical energy generated in form of EMF. In upcoming articles we will mathematically verify this fact also.

In different cases of electromagnetic induction Lenz´s law can be directly used to determine the direction of induced EMF or induced current in conductors or coils through which magnetic flux is changing. The Lenz´s law can be stated as

"The direction of induced EMF or induced current in a conductor or coil due to electromagnetic induction is such that the effects produced by the induced EMF or current opposes the cause of change in magnetic flux or the cause due to which electromagnetic induction is taking place."

Figure-5.3 shows a circular coil placed in plane perpendicular to a magnetic field. If magnetic field starts increasing with time then magnetic flux through the coil area starts increasing. This induces an EMF in the coil and an induced current also. The direction of induced current is such that it opposes the cause of induction.

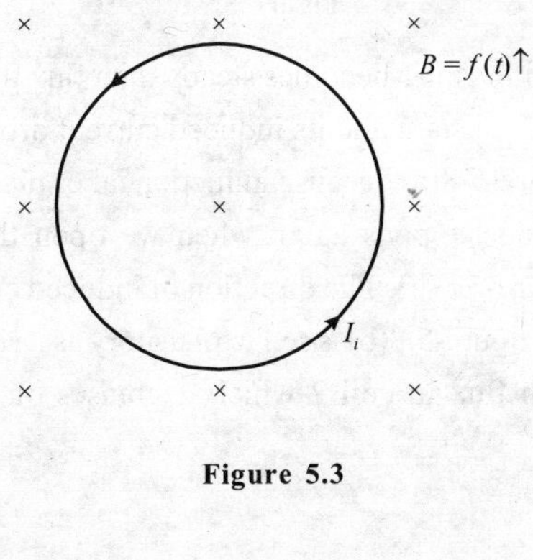

Figure 5.3

In this case the cause of induction is increase in magnetic flux so direction of induced current is such that it produces its own magnetic field in outward direction to oppose the increase in external magnetic field thus the direction of induced current must be anticlockwise in this case as shown.

Figure-5.4(a) and (b) shows a fixed coil toward which a bar magnet is moving along its axis with its north and south pole facing the coil. In these two cases we can see that current induced in coil by electromagnetic induction is such that it produces its own magnetic field in opposition to the fields of the bar magnet which was increasing due to motion of magnet toward the coil.

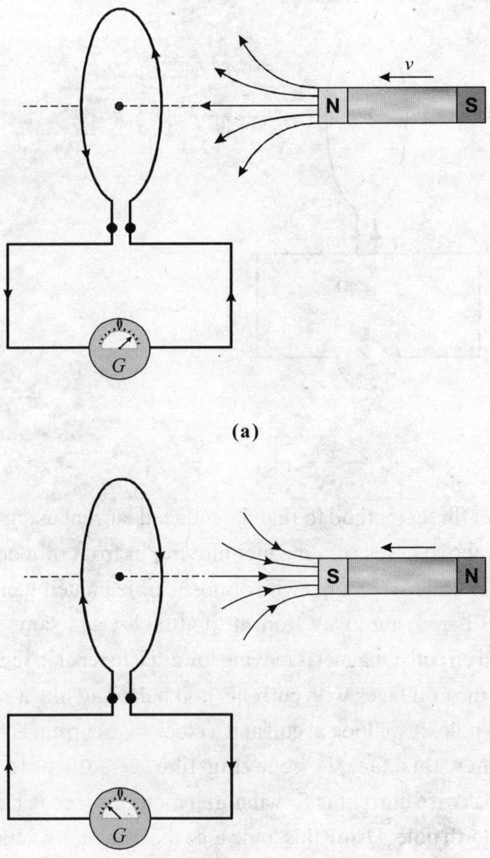

Figure 5.4

Figure-5.5(a) and (b) shows a situation similar to that shown in figure-5.4 but in this case bar magnet is moving away from the coil due to which the magnetic flux through the coil is decreasing. The current induced in coil in this case should be such that the magnetic induction due to induced current in coil is in the same direction as that of magnet because with the motion of magnet away from the coil magnetic flux through the coil decreases and the induced current should oppose the decrease of magnetic flux.

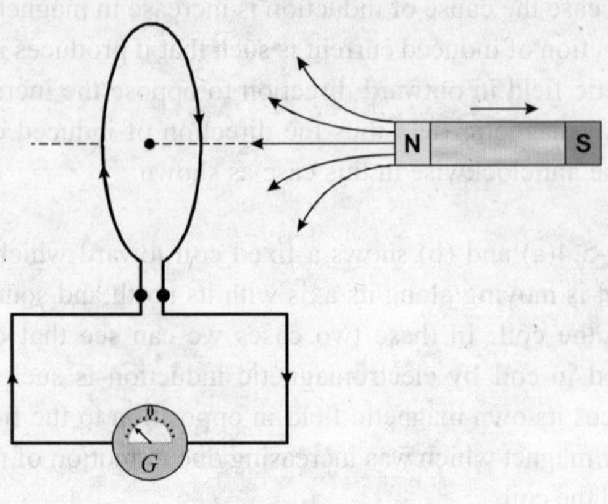

(a)

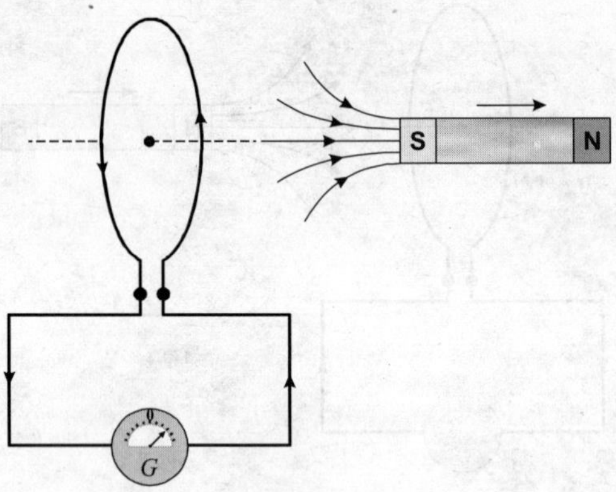

(b)

Figure 5.5

Another direct method to find the induced current using Lenz′s law in above cases of a magnet moving in front of a coil is to consider coil as a magnet with opposite pole inducing on coil if magnet is moving away from it to attract it and same pole is induced on coil if magnet is moving toward it to repel it. Figure-5.6 shows the coil faces with currents in it behaving like a south or a north pole. If we look at coil and a clockwise current is flowing in it then this face is behaving like a south pole and if anticlockwise current is flowing in it then this face is behaving like a north pole. Using this logic also the direction of current in coils shown in figure-5.4 and 5.5 can be determined quickly.

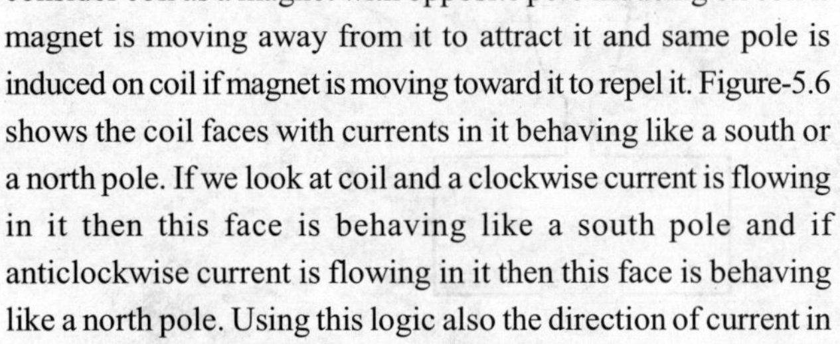

Figure 5.6

Figure-5.7(a) shows a setup of two coaxial coils. One connected with a battery and a switch and other with a galvanometer. When the switch is closed as shown in figure-5.7(b) just after closing the switch a current flows in coil 1 due to which it generates a magnetic induction and a part of its magnetic flux passes through coil 2 due to which a current is induced in coil 2 which opposes the flux of coil 1 because initially no flux was there in coil 2 and it grows because of closing the switch.

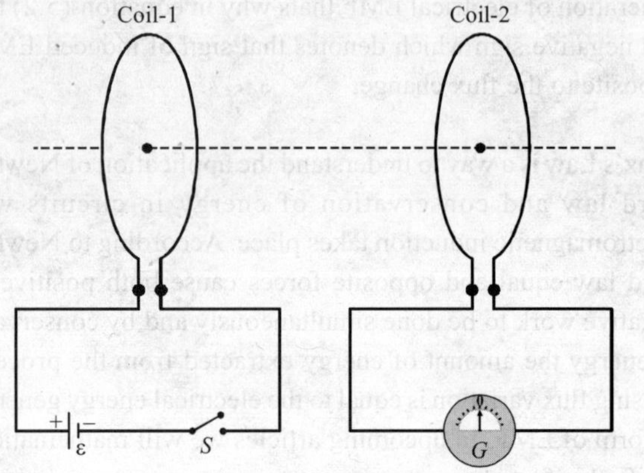

(a)

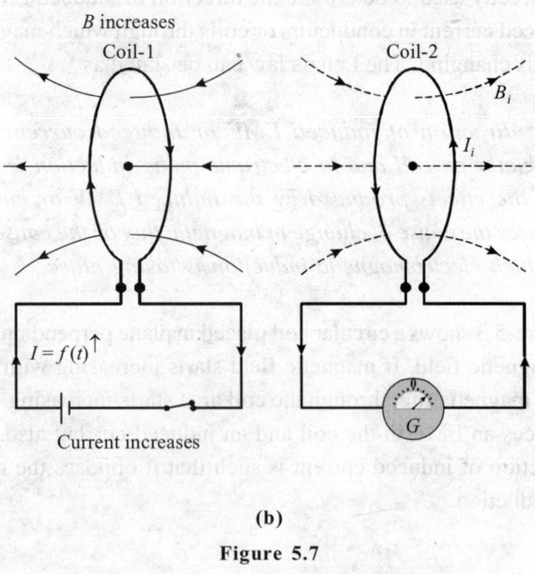

(b)

Figure 5.7

When current in coil 1 becomes steady then flux through coil 2 also becomes constant and its induced current drops to zero as shown in figure-5.8(a) because induction takes place when flux changes which happens again when we open the switch as shown in figure-5.8(b). The direction of induced current in coil 2 as shown in figure-5.8(b) is self explanatory as it should oppose the change in flux in coil 2 which decreases on opening the switch.

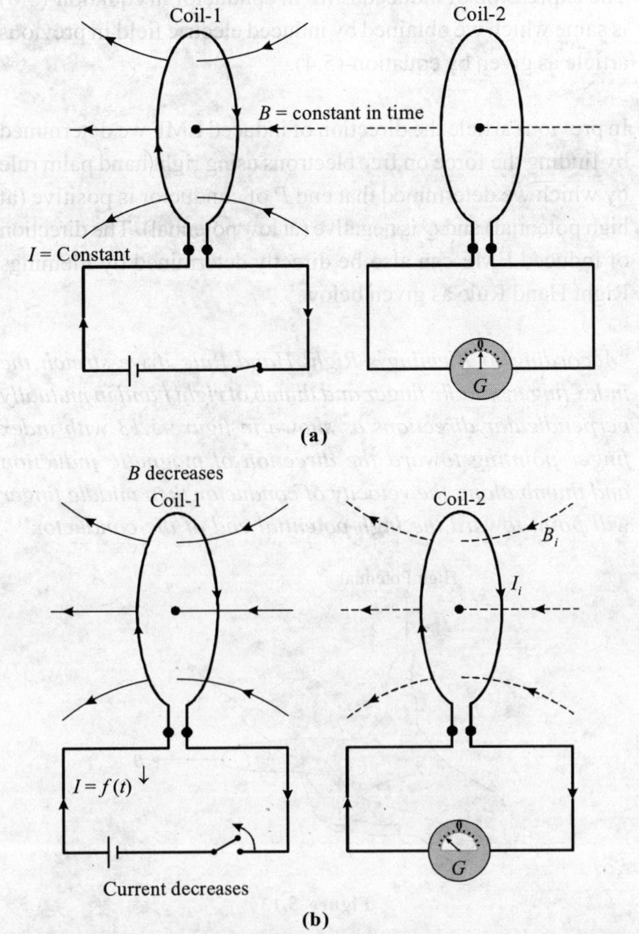

Figure 5.8

We will consider one more illustration to understand application of Lenz's law. Figure-5.9 shows a circular coil placed near to a long wire connected with a battery and a rheostat. Due to the current in long wire magnetic field is passing through the circular coil. If current in wire is steady, flux through the coil remain constant and thus no current is induced in coil.

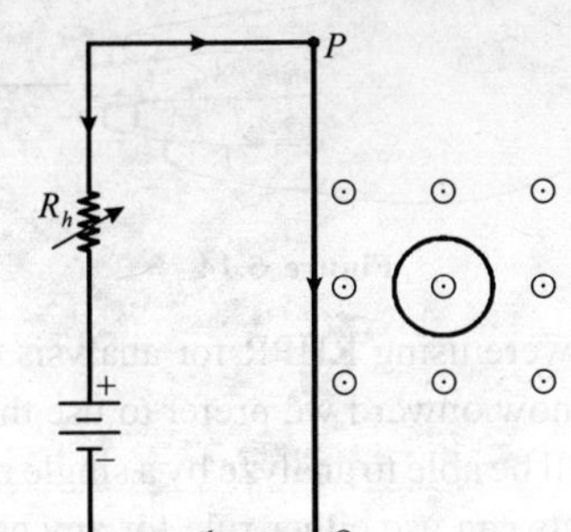

Figure 5.9

If in above case resistance of rheostat is gradually decreased then current in wire increases which also increases the magnetic flux through the coil and due to this a clockwise current is induced in coil as shown in figure-5.10(a) to oppose the outward increasing magnetic flux. If resistance of rheostat is increased gradually then current in wire decreases which also decreases the magnetic flux through coil and due to this an anticlockwise current is induced in coil as shown in figure-5.10(b) to oppose the outward decreasing magnetic flux.

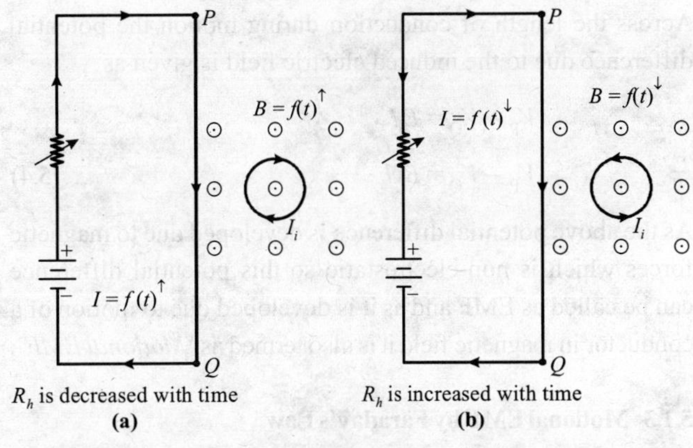

Figure 5.10

5.1.2 Motion EMF in a Straight Conductor Moving in Uniform Magnetic Field

Figure-5.11 shows a conductor PQ of length l moving in a uniform magnetic induction B at constant speed v. Along with conductor its free electrons inside are also moving so these free electrons experience a magnetic force $F = evB$ of which direction is given by right hand palm rule which comes in downward direction as shown in figure.

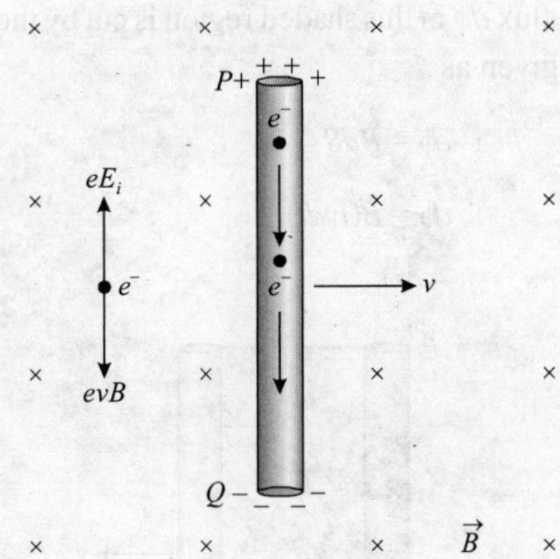

Figure 5.11

Due to this magnetic force electrons will drift to the end Q of the conductor and other end P will become slightly positive due to deficiency of electrons. This establishes an induced electric field from P to Q inside the conductor due to this separation of charges along the length of conductor because of magnetic force. Due to this induced electric field free electrons will experience an upward force eE_i as shown. These electrons will drift until the upward electric force balances the magnetic force on these electrons and then across the length of conductor electric field becomes steady and balances magnetic forces on free electrons. This electric field which is induced due to motion of a conductor in magnetic field is given as

$$eE_i = evB$$

$$\Rightarrow \quad E_i = vB \quad \dots(5.3)$$

Across the length of conduction during motion the potential difference due to the induced electric field is given as

$$V_P - V_Q = E_i l$$

$$\Rightarrow \quad V_P - V_Q = Bvl \quad \dots(5.4)$$

As the above potential difference is developed due to magnetic forces which is non-electrostatic so this potential difference can be called as EMF and as it is developed due to motion of a conductor in magnetic field it is also termed as '*Motional EMF*'.

5.1.3 Motional EMF by Faraday's Law

In previous article we discussed about EMF induced in a conductor moving in uniform magnetic field given by equation-(5.4). As due to motion of conductor magnetic lines were being cut according to Faraday's law the EMF induced in the conductor can be given as

$$e = \left|\frac{d\phi}{dt}\right| \quad \dots(5.5)$$

In figure-5.12 when the conductor moves by a distance vdt in time dt, it swaps an area $lvdt$ which is shown by shaded part, the magnetic flux $d\phi$ in this shaded region is cut by the conductor in time dt is given as

$$d\phi = BdS$$

$$\Rightarrow \quad d\phi = B(lvdt)$$

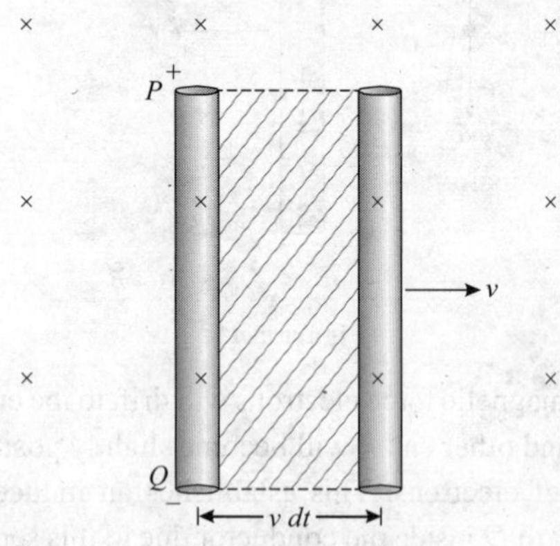

Figure 5.12

Thus from equation-(5.5) the induced EMF in the conductor is given as

$$e = \left|\frac{d\phi}{dt}\right| = Bvl \quad \dots(5.6)$$

The expression of induced EMF in conductor in equation-(5.6) is same which we obtained by induced electric field in previous article as given by equation-(5.4).

In previous article the direction of induced EMF we determined by finding the force on free electrons using right hand palm rule by which we determined that end P of conductor is positive (at high potential) and Q is negative (at low potential). The direction of induced EMF can also be directly determined by Flemings Right Hand Rule as given below.

"*According to Fleming's Right Hand Rule if we stretch the index finger, middle finger and thumb of right hand in mutually perpendicular directions as shown in figure-5.13 with index finger pointing toward the direction of magnetic induction and thumb along the velocity of conductor then middle finger will point toward the high potential end of the conductor.*"

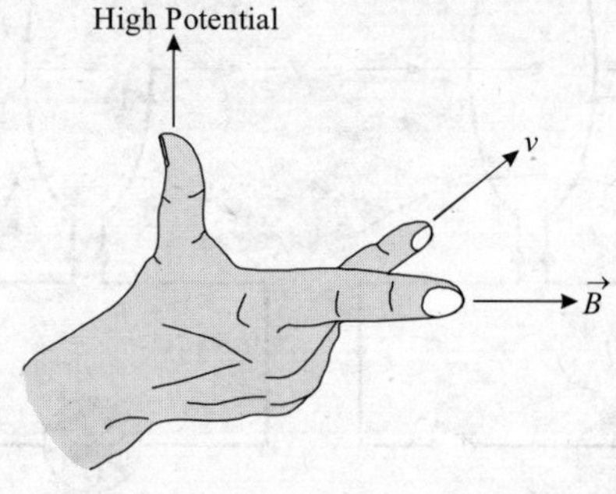

Figure 5.13

Above direction can also be given by Right Hand Palm Rule as shown in figure-5.14.

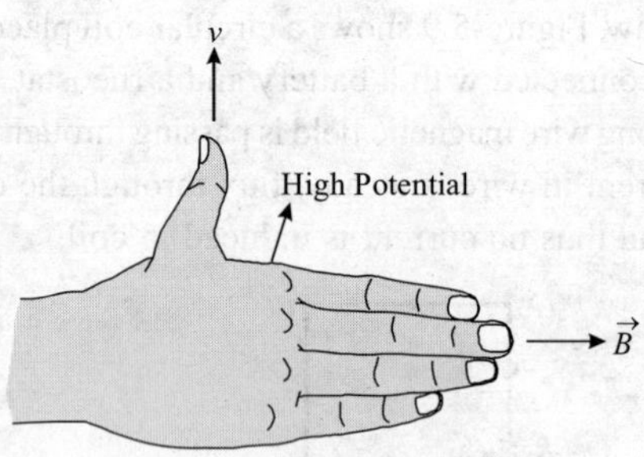

Figure 5.14

As till now we were using RHPR for analysis of direction of magnetic field, now onward we prefer to use the same rule so that all cases we'll be able to analyze by a single right hand only. However students can use either rule for any case.

5.1.4 Motional EMF as an Equivalent Battery

In different situations when a conductor moves in magnetic field, it can be considered like an equivalent battery or a source of potential difference with internal resistance equal to the resistance of the conductor which can supply current as shown in figure-5.15 in which a conductor of length l, resistance r moving at a velocity v in a uniform magnetic field B with l, v and B are perpendicular to each other can be replaced by an equivalent battery of EMF Bvl and internal resistance r as shown in figure.

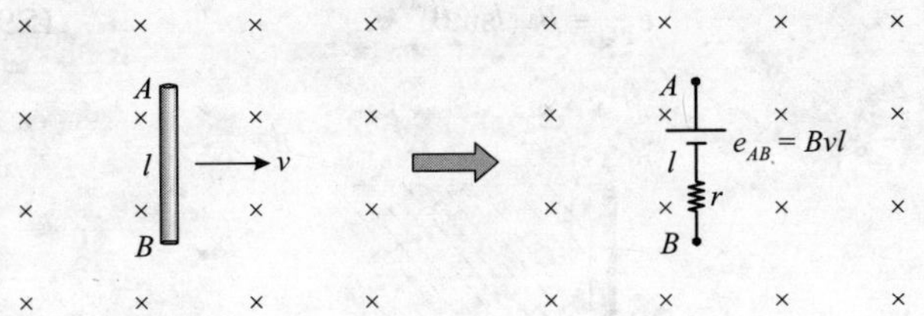

Figure 5.15

To understand the above situation better we consider an illustration shown in figure-5.16(a) in which two sliding wires PQ and RS are sliding on three conducting rails which are connected to some resistances at their ends as shown. In this case we can determine the currents through resistances and different sections of the setup by making an equivalent circuit of this setup as shown in figure-5.16(b).

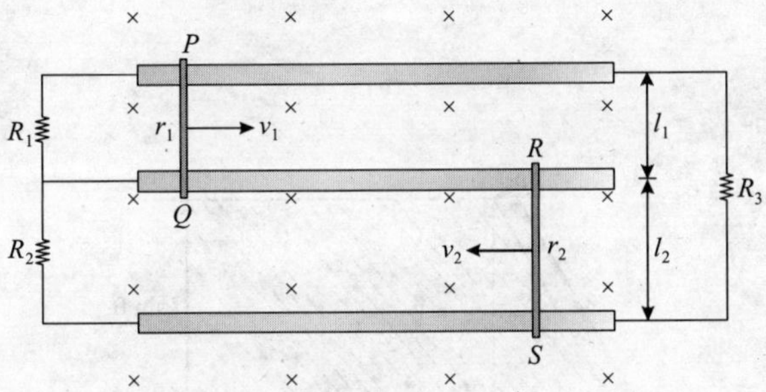

(a)

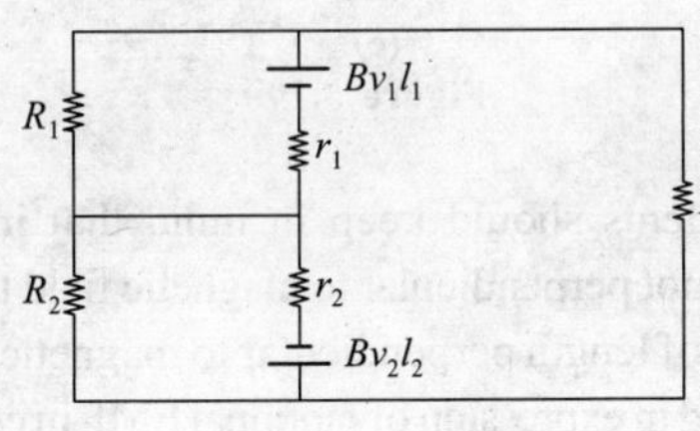

(b)

Figure 5.16

5.1.5 EMF Induced in a Rotating Conductor in Uniform Magnetic Field

Figure-5.17 shows a uniform conducting rod PQ of length l which is rotating in a plane perpendicular to the direction of a uniform magnetic field as shown about an axis of rotation passing through point P at an angular speed ω. As the conductor's motion is cutting the magnetic lines an EMF is induced in it and by right hand palm rule we can see that point P is at higher potential.

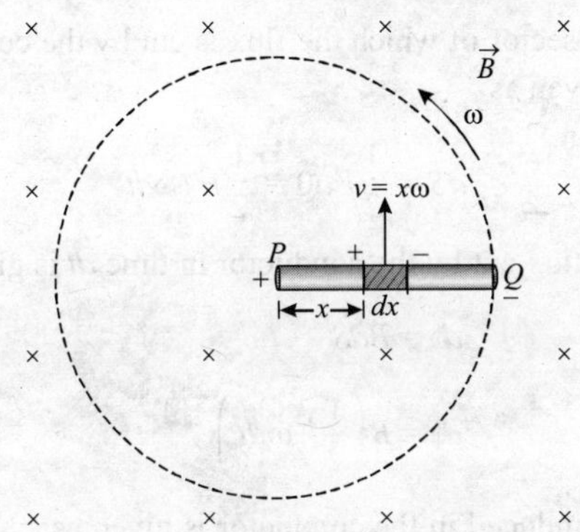

Figure 5.17

To calculate the induced EMF in the conductor we consider an elemental segment of width dx at a distance x from the end P of the rod as shown in figure-5.17. The speed of motion of this element is $v = x\omega$. The EMF induced in this element can be calculated by the expression of motional EMF given in equation-(5.4) as

$$de = Bvdx$$

$$\Rightarrow \quad de = B(x\omega)dx$$

Thus total EMF induced across the length of the conductor PQ is given by integrating above expression for the total length of the conductor from 0 to l as

$$e_{PQ} = \int de = \int_0^l B\omega x.dx$$

$$\Rightarrow \quad e_{PQ} = B\omega\left[\frac{x^2}{2}\right]_0^l$$

$$\Rightarrow \quad e_{PQ} = \frac{1}{2}B\omega l^2 \qquad \ldots (5.7)$$

Alternative Analysis by Faraday's law :

Figure-5.18 shows the area swapped by the rotating conductor in time dt. The angle by which the rod rotates in this time is given as

$$d\theta = \omega dt$$

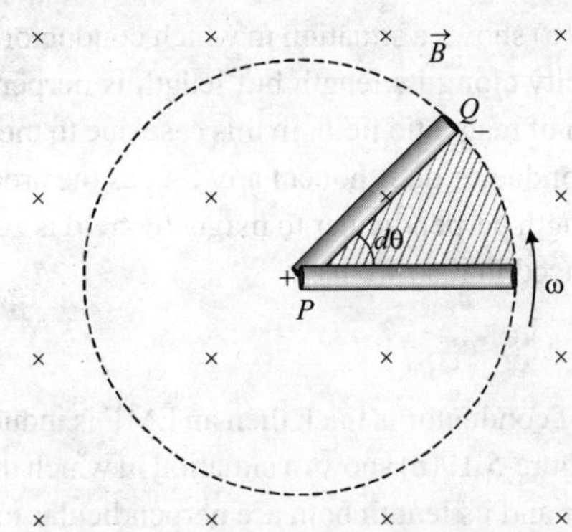

Figure 5.18

Area of the sector of which the flux is cut by the conductor in time at is given as

$$dS = \frac{1}{2} l^2 d\theta = \frac{1}{2} l^2 (\omega dt)$$

Amount of flux cut by the conductor in time dt is given as

$$d\phi = BdS$$

$$\Rightarrow \qquad d\phi = B\left(\frac{1}{2} l^2 \omega dt\right)$$

Thus EMF induced in the conductor is given as

$$e = \left|\frac{d\phi}{dt}\right| = \frac{1}{2} B\omega l^2 \qquad \text{...(5.8)}$$

Equation-(5.8) is same as that of equation-(5.7) but that was obtained by integrating motional EMF in small elements in the conductor whereas equation-(5.8) is obtained directly by Faraday´s law.

5.1.6 EMF induced in a Conductor in Magnetic Field which is Moving in Different Directions

In previous articles we´ve discussed when a conductor moves in a magnetic field such that it cuts magnetic lines then an EMF is induced in it which we call motional EMF. When the conductor´s length is oriented normal to the magnetic field direction and its velocity is also normal to the direction of its length as well as magnetic field as explained in figure-5.11 and 5.12 the motional EMF induced in the conductor is given by equation-(5.4) or (5.6) but if the conductor is moving in such a way that its length and/or velocity are not normal to the direction of magnetic field then we need to take the components of length as well as velocity normal to the magnetic field.

Figure-5.19(a) shows the situation, we´ve already discussed in which the conductor is moving normal to the field with its length also perpendicular to the field thus EMF induced in this case is given as

$$e_{PQ} = Bvl$$

Figure-5.19(b) shows a situation in which conductor is moving with a velocity along its length but length is perpendicular to the direction of magnetic field. In this case due to motion along the length conductor does not cut any flux as the area swapped out by its length perpendicular to magnetic field is zero thus no EMF is induced in it so we have

$$e_{PQ} = 0$$

In this case if conductor is thick then an EMF is induced across its width. Figure-5.19(c) shows a situation in which the velocity of conductor and its length both are perpendicular to magnetic field but velocity is not perpendicular to its length so the area swapped out by the conductor in magnetic field will be less and to calculate the induced EMF in conductor we consider the component of the length normal to its velocity which is $l\sin\theta$ here. Thus the motional EMF induced in the conductor in this case is given as

$$e_{PQ} = Bv(l\sin\theta) \qquad \text{...(5.9)}$$

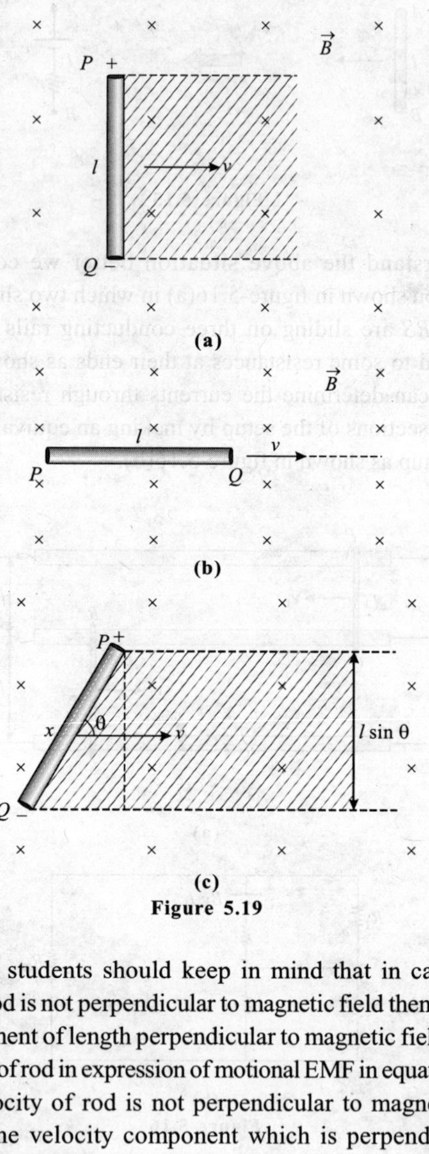

Figure 5.19

In general students should keep in mind that in case when length of rod is not perpendicular to magnetic field then consider the component of length perpendicular to magnetic field as well as velocity of rod in expression of motional EMF in equation-(5.4) and if velocity of rod is not perpendicular to magnetic field consider the velocity component which is perpendicular to magnetic field in the same expression.

5.1.7 Motional EMF in a Random Shaped Wire Moving in Magnetic Field

Figure-5.20 shows a random shaped wire AB in which the length between its ends A and B is l is moving with a velocity v perpendicular to line AB in a uniform magnetic field as shown. In this case we can consider a small element dl in the wire as shown in figure which will have its two components, one along the line AB and other perpendicular to the line AB. Due to motion of wire EMF will only be induced in the component of dl along line AB due to the reason discussed in previous article thus total motional EMF between ends AB of the wire can be directly given as

$$e_{AB} = Bvl$$

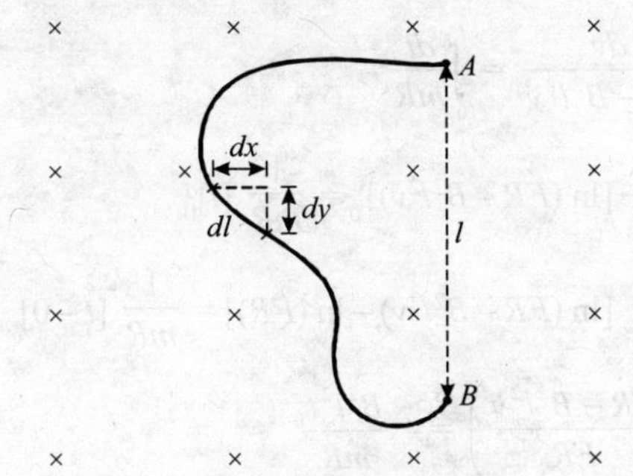

Figure 5.20

Similar to the previous article figures-5.21(a) and (b) shows the situations in which the random shaped wires are moving in different directions for which the EMF induced can be calculated by using the component of velocity perpendicular to the line AB which are given as $Bvl\sin\theta$ for figure-5.21(a) and zero for figure-5.21(b).

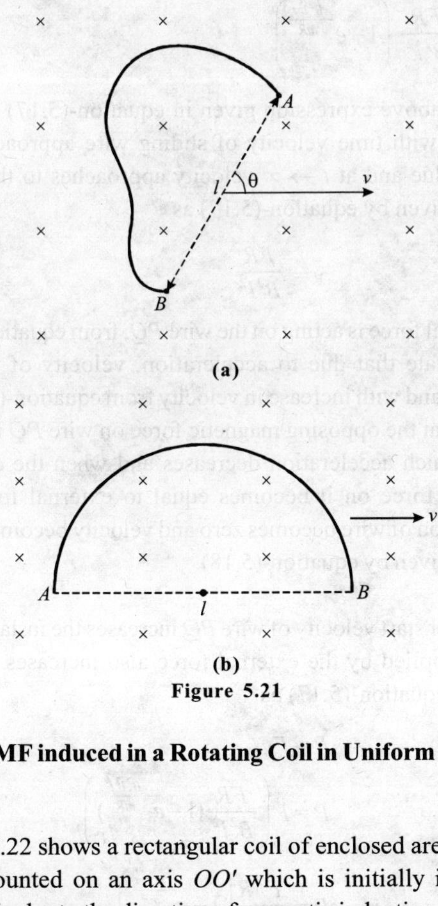

Figure 5.21

5.1.8 EMF induced in a Rotating Coil in Uniform Magnetic Field

Figure-5.22 shows a rectangular coil of enclosed area A and N turns mounted on an axis OO' which is initially in a plane perpendicular to the direction of magnetic induction B. It starts rotating at an angular velocity ω as shown. The initial magnetic flux linked with the coil at $t = 0$ is given as

$$\phi = BAN$$

After time $t = t$ the coil will rotate by an angle $\theta = \omega t$ so flux linked with all the turns of the coil is given as

$$\phi = (\vec{B}\cdot\vec{A})N$$

$$\Rightarrow \quad \phi = BAN\cos\theta$$

$$\Rightarrow \quad \phi = BAN\cos\omega t \quad \dots(5.10)$$

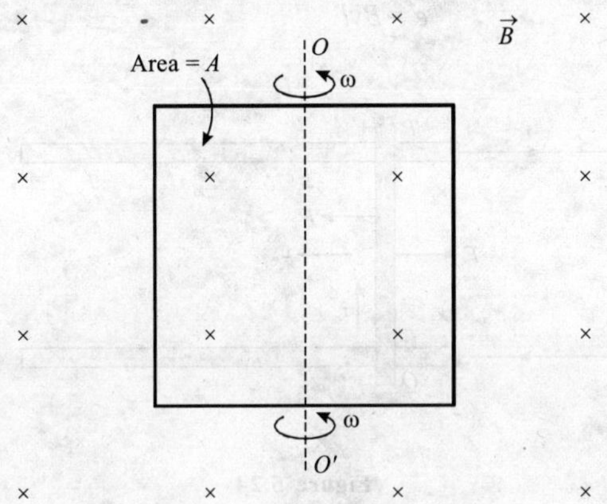

Figure 5.22

As the flux linked with the coil is changing with time, EMF induced in coil at time $t = t$ is given as

$$e = \left|\frac{d\phi}{dt}\right|$$

$$\Rightarrow \quad e = BAN\sin\omega t\ .\ \omega$$

$$\Rightarrow \quad e = BAN\omega\sin\omega t \quad \dots(5.11)$$

$$\Rightarrow \quad e = e_0\sin\omega t \quad \dots(5.12)$$

Where $e_0 = BAN\omega$ which is considered as the amplitude of the sinusoidal induced EMF given by equation-(5.11). Such a sinusoidal function of EMF is also called '*Alternating EMF*' which is a source of alternating current in electrical circuits and this EMF which is produced by rotating a coil in magnetic field is the basis of working for an AC (Alternating Current) Generator. The time function of alternating EMF induced in coil is shown in figure-5.23.

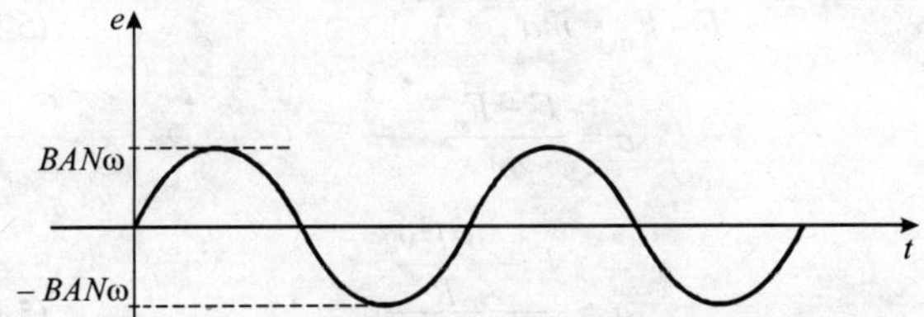

Figure 5.23

5.1.9 Motional EMF under External Force and Power Transfer

Figure-5.24 shows a setup with two long conducting rails with separation l in a plane perpendicular to a uniform magnetic field of magnetic induction B. A sliding wire PQ of mass m is placed on rails as shown. The rails are connected with a resistance R and the sliding wire is pulled with a constant external force F. If initially the sliding wire is at rest at $t = 0$ then at a general instant of time t it is considered to be moving at instantaneous velocity v then at this instant motional EMF induced in this wire is given as

$$e = Bvl$$

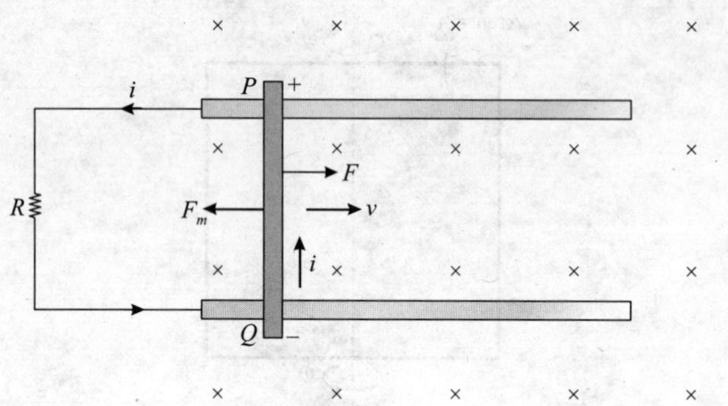

Figure 5.24

The current through the resistance due to induced EMF is given as

$$i = \frac{e}{R} = \frac{Bvl}{R} \quad \ldots(5.13)$$

Due to the direction of induced EMF current flows from Q to P in the sliding wire because of which magnetic field exerts a magnetic force on the sliding wire which is given as

$$F_m = Bil = \frac{B^2l^2v}{R} \quad \ldots(5.14)$$

By right hand palm rule we can analyze that the direction of this magnetic force on sliding wire PQ is toward left which is in opposition to the external force. This is also validating Lenz's law that the effects produced by induction oppose the causes of induction.

If at a general instant of time t acceleration of wire PQ is a then we have

$$F - F_m = ma \quad \ldots(5.15)$$

$$\Rightarrow \quad a = \frac{F - F_m}{m}$$

$$\Rightarrow \quad a = \frac{F - \frac{B^2l^2v}{R}}{m} \quad \ldots(5.16)$$

$$\Rightarrow \quad \frac{dv}{dt} = a = \frac{FR - B^2l^2v}{mR}$$

$$\Rightarrow \quad \frac{dv}{FR - B^2l^2v} = \frac{dt}{mR}$$

To find the velocity of wire PQ as a function of time we integrate the above expression from initial instant $t = 0$ to a general time instant $t = t$ given as

$$\int_0^v \frac{dv}{FR - B^2l^2v} = \int_0^t \frac{dt}{mR}$$

$$\Rightarrow \quad -\frac{1}{B^2l^2}[\ln(FR - B^2l^2v)]_0^v = \frac{1}{mR}[t]_0^t$$

$$\Rightarrow \quad -\frac{1}{B^2l^2}[\ln(FR - B^2l^2v) - \ln(FR)] = \frac{1}{mR}[t - 0]$$

$$\Rightarrow \quad \ln\left(\frac{FR - B^2l^2v}{FR}\right) = -\frac{B^2l^2t}{mR}$$

$$\Rightarrow \quad \frac{FR - B^2l^2v}{FR} = e^{-\frac{B^2l^2t}{mR}}$$

$$\Rightarrow \quad FR - B^2l^2v = FRe^{-\frac{B^2l^2t}{mR}}$$

$$\Rightarrow \quad B^2l^2v = FR\left(1 - e^{-\frac{B^2l^2t}{mR}}\right)$$

$$\Rightarrow \quad v = \frac{FR}{B^2l^2}\left(1 - e^{-\frac{B^2l^2t}{mR}}\right) \quad \ldots(5.17)$$

With the above expression given in equation-(5.17) it can be seen that with time velocity of sliding wire approaches to a steady value and at $t \to \infty$ velocity approaches to the steady velocity given by equation-(5.17) as

$$v = \frac{FR}{B^2l^2} \quad \ldots(5.18)$$

As external force is acting on the wire PQ, from equation-(5.15) we can state that due to acceleration, velocity of wire PQ increases and with increase in velocity from equation-(5.14) we can see that the opposing magnetic force on wire PQ increases due to which acceleration decreases and when the opposing magnetic force on it becomes equal to external force then acceleration of wire becomes zero and velocity becomes steady which is given by equation-(5.18).

When after start velocity of wire PQ increases the instantaneous power supplied by the external force also increases which is given by equation-(5.17) as

$$P = Fv$$

$$\Rightarrow \quad P = F\left(\frac{FR}{B^2l^2}(1 - e^{-\frac{B^2l^2t}{mR}})\right)$$

$$\Rightarrow \quad P = \frac{F^2R}{B^2l^2}\left(1 - e^{-\frac{B^2l^2t}{mR}}\right) \quad \ldots(5.19)$$

From equation-(5.19) we can analyze that the power supplied by external force increases with time and after a long time this power becomes steady which is given as

$$P_S = \frac{F^2R}{B^2l^2} \quad \ldots(5.20)$$

Initially when wire is accelerating, the supplied power by the external force is being used in two parts. One part of supplied power is increasing the kinetic energy of the wire and other part is being dissipated as heat in the resistance R which is given as

$$H = i^2R$$

In above expression, we substitute the value of current from equation-(5.13) as

$$H = \left(\frac{Blv}{R}\right)^2 R = \frac{B^2l^2v^2}{R}$$

Substituting the value of velocity from equation-(5.17) in above expression gives

$$H = \frac{B^2l^2}{R}\left(\frac{FR}{B^2l^2}(1-e^{-\frac{B^2l^2t}{mR}})\right)^2$$

$$\Rightarrow \quad H = \frac{F^2R}{B^2l^2}\left(1-e^{-\frac{B^2l^2t}{mR}}\right)^2 \quad \ldots(5.21)$$

After a long time above expression approaches to a steady value given as

$$H_S = \frac{F^2R}{B^2l^2} \quad \ldots(5.22)$$

Above expression in equation-(5.22) is same as equation-(5.20) so we can state that after wire PQ attains steady velocity then power supplied by the external agent is fully dissipated as heat in the resistor connected across the rails upto the time wire PQ attains steady velocity the a part of power supplied increases the kinetic energy of wire and remaining is dissipated as heat.

In different cases of electromagnetic induction in mechanical setups when external forces are present, due to induction some opposition is developed which causes the effect of external force to reduce and at some point of time the system attains a steady state when external force is balanced by the opposing effects. Under this state the power supplied by external force to the system is transformed into some other form. This happens due to magnetic field as magnetic forces does equal and opposite work to transform energy from one form to another. This phenomenon can be used in design of many electromechanical system for efficient transformation of energy from one form to another.

 # Illustrative Example 5.1

A copper rod of length L is moving at a uniform speed v parallel to a long straight wire carrying a current of I as shown in figure-5.25. The rod is perpendicular to the wire with its ends at distance a and b from it. Calculate the motional EMF induced in the rod.

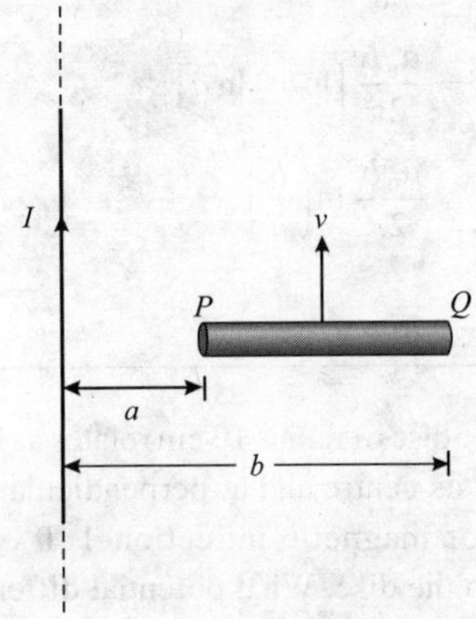

Figure 5.25

Solution

The magnetic field at a distance x from straight wire is given as

$$B = \frac{\mu_0 I}{2\pi x}$$

We consider an element of length dx in rod at a distance x from the straight wire as shown in figure-5.26. Due to the motion of the element dx in the rod in magnetic field B of straight wire, the motional induced EMF in the element is given as

$$de = Bvdx$$

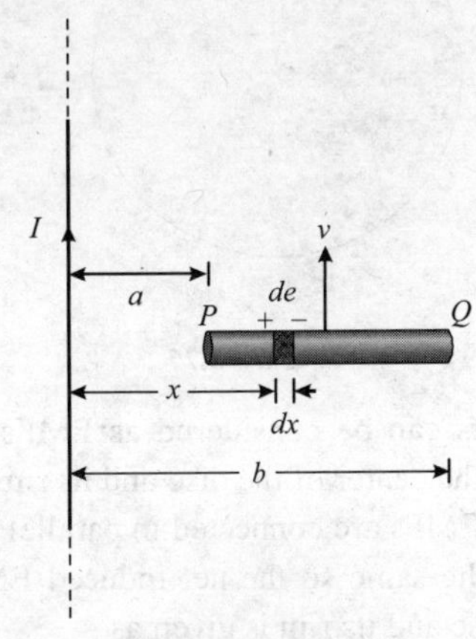

Figure 5.26

The direction of de is shown in figure by right hand palm rule. As all such de in all the elements in the rod are in series so induced EMF in whole rod PQ is given by integrating above expression within limits from a to b given as

$$e = \int de = \int_a^b Bvdx$$

$$\Rightarrow \quad e = \int_a^b \frac{\mu_0 Ivdx}{2\pi x}$$

$$\Rightarrow \quad e = \frac{\mu_0 Iv}{2\pi}[\ln x]_a^b$$

$$\Rightarrow \quad e = \frac{\mu_0 Iv}{2\pi}[\ln b - \ln a]$$

$$\Rightarrow \quad e = \frac{\mu_0 Iv}{2\pi}\ln\left(\frac{b}{a}\right)$$

Illustrative Example 5.2

A circular copper disc of radius 10 cm rotates at 1800 rpm about an axis through its centre and at perpendicular to the disc. A uniform field of magnetic induction 1 T exist in region perpendicular to the disc. What potential difference develops between the axis of the disc and its rim?

Solution

The disc can be considered to be made of several elemental sectors as shown in figure-5.27. Each such thin sectors can be considered like rotating rods across which the EMF induced is given as

$$e = \frac{1}{2}B\omega R^2$$

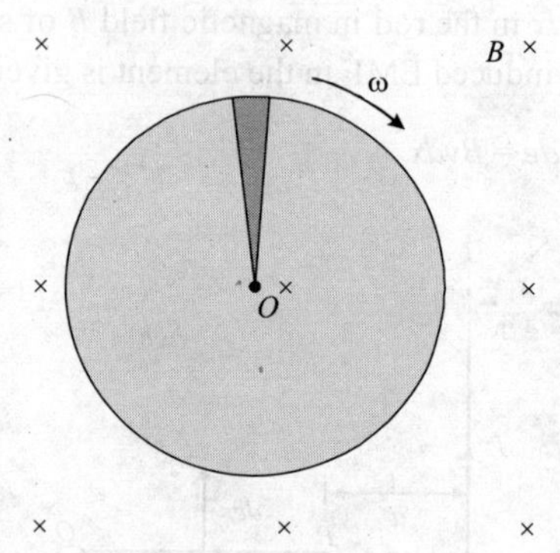

Figure 5.27

All such sectors can be considered as EMFs connected in parallel across the center of the disc and its rim and we know when identical EMFs are connected in parallel the equivalent EMF remains the same so the net induced EMF across the center of the disc and its rim is given as

$$e = \frac{1}{2}\times 1\times 2\times 3.14\times\frac{1800}{60}\times(0.1)^2$$

$$e = 0.942 \text{ V}$$

Illustrative Example 5.3

A copper rod PQ of mass m slides down two smooth copper bars which are set at an angle α to the horizontal as shown in figure-5.28. At the top of the bars these are interconnected through a resistance R. The separation between the bars is equal to l. The system is located in a uniform magnetic field of induction B in vertically upward direction as shown in figure. The resistances of the bars, the rod and the sliding contacts are considered to be negligible. If the rod is released from rest, find the velocity of rod as a function of time and its steady velocity attained.

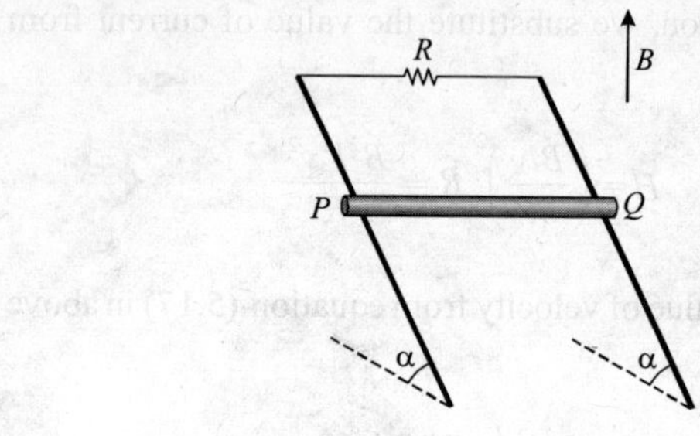

Figure 5.28

Solution

When the rod is released from rest and as it starts moving, it cuts the magnetic flux and an EMF is induced in it with polarity given by right hand palm rule as shown in figure-5.29. If at any instant conductor velocity is v and as it is moving perpendicular to the magnetic field component B cosα, the induced EMF in the rod is given as

$$e = (B\cos\alpha)vL = BvL\cos\alpha$$

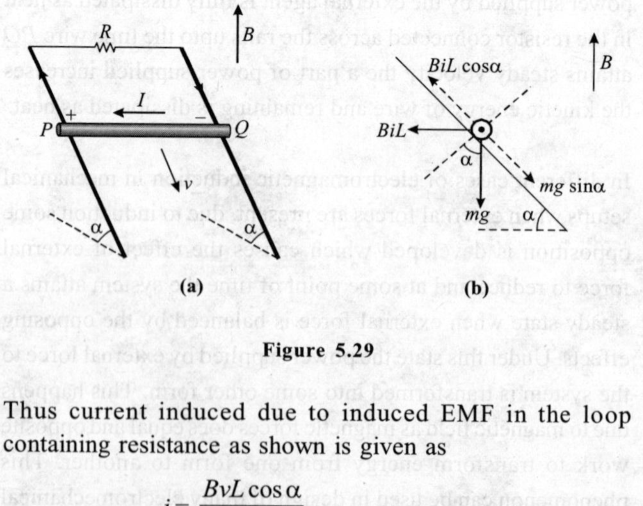

Figure 5.29

Thus current induced due to induced EMF in the loop containing resistance as shown is given as

$$i = \frac{BvL\cos\alpha}{R}$$

Figure-5.29(b) shows the side view of the sliding rod on which by right hand palm rule, we can see that magnetic force will act along leftward direction and if rod slides with an acceleration a then equation of motion of the rod is given as

$$mg\sin\alpha - BiL\cos\alpha = ma$$

$$\Rightarrow \quad m\left(\frac{dv}{dt}\right) = mg\sin\alpha - \frac{B^2L^2v\cos^2\alpha}{R}$$

$$\Rightarrow \quad dv = \left(g\sin\alpha - \frac{B^2L^2v\cos^2\alpha}{mR}\right)dt$$

$$\Rightarrow \quad \int_0^v \frac{dv}{mgR\sin\alpha - B^2L^2v\cos^2\alpha} = \int_0^t \frac{dt}{mR}$$

$$\Rightarrow \quad -\frac{1}{B^2L^2\cos^2\alpha}\left[\ln\left(mgR\sin\alpha - B^2L^2v\cos^2\alpha\right)\right]_0^v = \frac{t}{mR}$$

$$\Rightarrow \quad \ln\left(\frac{mgR\sin\alpha - B^2L^2v\cos^2\alpha}{mgR\sin\alpha}\right) = -\frac{B^2L^2t\cos^2\alpha}{mR}$$

$$\Rightarrow \quad v = \frac{mgR\sin\alpha}{B^2L^2\cos^2\alpha}\left(1 - e^{-\frac{B^2L^2t\cos^2\alpha}{mR}}\right)$$

Steady state is theoretically attained after a long time when velocity becomes

$$v_S = \frac{mgR\sin\alpha}{B^2L^2\cos^2\alpha}$$

In steady state the component of gravitational force is balanced by magnetic force on rod which gives

$$mg\sin\alpha = BiL\cos\alpha$$

$$\Rightarrow \quad mg\sin\alpha = \frac{B^2L^2v\cos^2\alpha}{R}$$

$$\Rightarrow \quad v_S = \frac{mgR\sin\alpha}{B^2L^2\cos^2\alpha}$$

 # Illustrative Example 5.4

A straight horizontal conductor PQ of length l, and mass m slides down on two smooth conducting fixed parallel rails, set inclined at an angle θ to the horizontal as shown in figure-5.30.

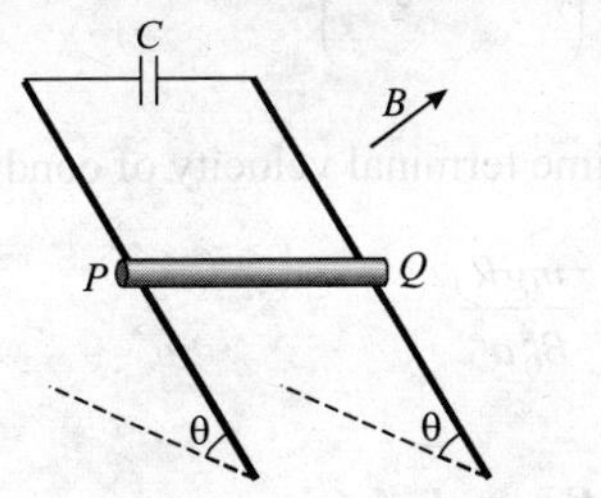

Figure 5.30

The top end of the bar are connected with a capacitor of capacitance C. The system is placed in a uniform magnetic field, in the direction perpendicular to the inclined plane formed by the rails as shown in figure. If the resistance of the bars and the sliding conductor are negligible calculate the acceleration of sliding conductor as a function of time if it is released from rest at $t = 0$.

Solution

When the conductor is released from rest and if at time $t = t$ its speed is v then induced EMF in the conductor is given as

$$e_{PQ} = Blv$$

This potential difference is across the capacitor so instantaneous charge on capacitor is given as

$$q = CV = CBlv$$

Current through the capacitor is given as

$$i = \frac{dq}{dt} = CBl\frac{dv}{dt} = CBla$$

In magnetic field the current carrying conductor experiences a magnetic force in upward direction by right hand palm rule as shown in figure-5.31(b) which shows the side view of sliding conductor and its free body diagram. This gives

$$F_{mag} = Bil = B^2l^2Ca$$

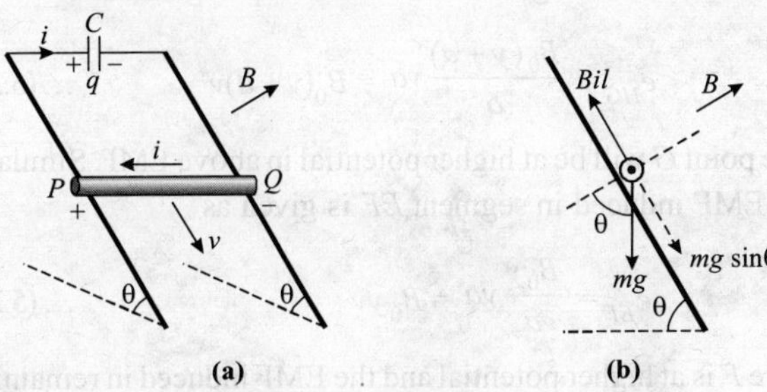

Figure 5.31

If a is the acceleration of conductor then its equation of motion is given as

$$ma = mg\sin\theta - B^2l^2Ca$$

$$\Rightarrow \quad a[m + B^2l^2C] = mg\sin\theta$$

$$\Rightarrow \quad a = \frac{mg\sin\theta}{m + B^2l^2C}$$

Here we can see that a is constant in time.

 # Illustrative Example 5.5

In a region of space a horizontal magnetic induction exist along $+Z$-direction which is into the plane of paper and magnitude of magnetic induction varies along Y-direction (vertically downward), is given as

$$\vec{B} = \frac{B_0 y}{a}\hat{k}$$

Where B_0 and a are positive constants. A square loop $EFGH$ of side a, mass m and resistance R is placed in X-Y plane and start falling under gravity from rest as shown in figure-5.32. Find

(a) The induced current in the loop as a function of instantaneous speed of the loop and indicate its direction

(b) The total Lorentz force acting on the loop as a function of instantaneous speed of the loop and indicate its direction

(c) An expression for the speed of the loop, $v(t)$ and its terminal velocity.

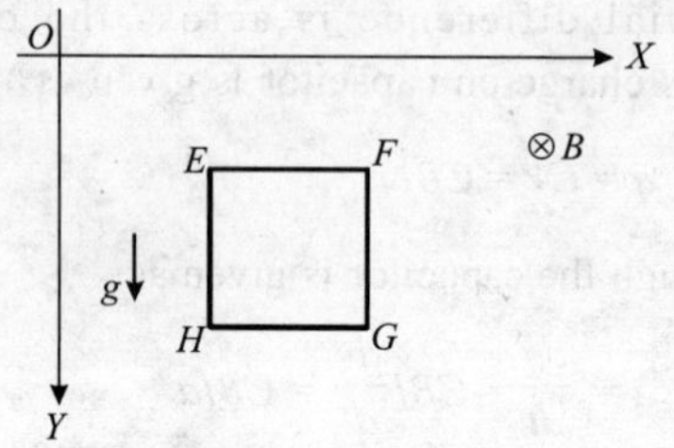

Figure 5.32

Solution

(a) If v be the instantaneous velocity of the loop at any time t. Induced EMF in segment HG of the loop is given as

$$e_{HG} = \frac{B_0(y+a)}{a} va = B_0(y+a)v \qquad \ldots (5.23)$$

The point G will be at higher potential in above EMF. Similarly the EMF induced in segment EF is given as

$$e_{EF} = \frac{B_0 y}{a} va = B_0 yv \qquad \ldots (5.24)$$

Here F is at higher potential and the EMF induced in remaining two segments are zero as these are not cutting any magnetic flux.

$$e_{EH} \text{ and } e_{FG} = 0$$

So, the current in the loop is given as

$$i = \frac{B_0(y+a)v - B_0 yv}{R} = \frac{B_0 av}{R}$$

The current will be in anticlockwise direction due to higher EMF in segment HG.

(b) The magnetic forces on EF and HG are given as

$$F_{EF} = \frac{B_0 y}{a} \times i \times a$$

$$F_{HG} = \frac{B_0(y+a)}{a} \times i \times a$$

Different elements along the vertical segments will experience different forces but in opposite direction as shown in figure-5.33 so will get cancelled out.

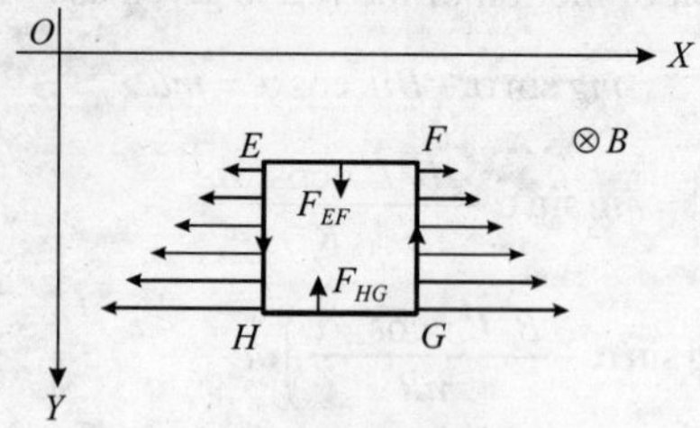

Figure 5.33

Net Lorentz force on loop is given as

$$F = B_0(y+a)i - B_0 yi = B_0 ai$$

$$\Rightarrow \quad \vec{F} = \frac{B_0^2 a^2 v}{R}(-\hat{j})$$

(c) Net force acting on loop in downward direction is

$$F = mg - \frac{B_0^2 a^2 v}{R}$$

$$\Rightarrow \quad m\frac{dv}{dt} = mg - \frac{B_0^2 a^2 v}{R}$$

$$\Rightarrow \quad \int_0^v \frac{dv}{mg - \frac{B_0^2 a^2 v}{R}} = \int_0^t \frac{dt}{m}$$

$$\Rightarrow \quad -\frac{R}{B_0^2 a^2}\left[\ln\left(mg - \frac{B_0^2 a^2 v}{R}\right)\right]_0^v = \frac{1}{m}[t]_0^t$$

$$\Rightarrow \quad \left[\ln\left(mg - \frac{B_0^2 a^2 v}{R}\right) - \ln(mg)\right] = -\frac{B_0^2 a^2 t}{mR}$$

$$\Rightarrow \quad \frac{mgR - B_0^2 a^2 v}{mgR} = e^{-\frac{B_0^2 a^2 t}{mR}}$$

$$\Rightarrow \quad v = \frac{mgR}{B_0^2 a^2}\left(1 - e^{-\frac{B_0^2 a^2 t}{mR}}\right)$$

After a long time terminal velocity of conductor is given as

$$v_{terminal} = \frac{mgR}{B_0^2 a^2}$$

Illustrative Example 5.6

Two parallel vertical metallic rails AB and CD are separated by 1 m. They are connected at the two ends by resistances R_1 and R_2 as shown in figure-5.34. A horizontal metallic bar PQ of mass

0.2 kg slides without friction with maintaining contacts with the rails, vertically downward under the action of gravity. There is a uniform horizontal magnetic field of 0.6 T perpendicular to the plane of the rails in the region. It is observed when the terminal velocity is attained, the powers dissipated in R_1 and R_2 are 0.75 W and 1.2 W respectively. Find the terminal velocity of the bar and the values of R_1 and R_2.

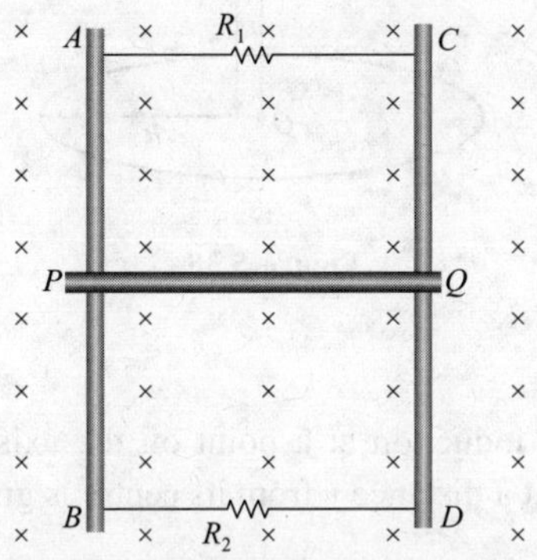

Figure 5.34

Solution

Due to sliding bar an EMF is induced in it which causes currents to flow in the resistances as shown in figure-5.35 the forces acting on the bar are the weight of rod in vertically downward direction and the magnetic force *Bil* in vertically upwards direction by right hand palm rule as shown.

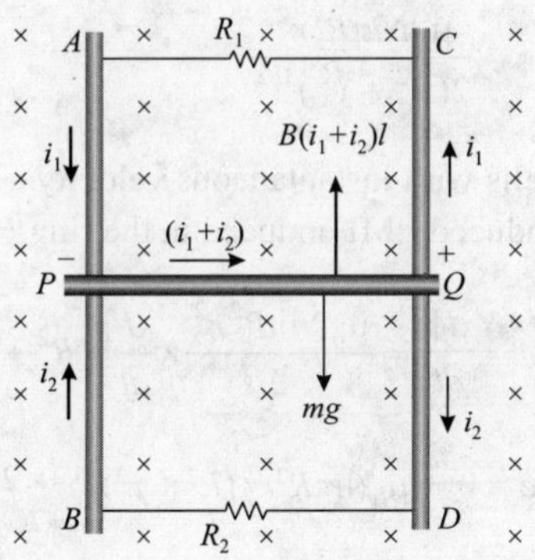

Figure 5.35

When the two forces are equal then the bar acquires terminal velocity v_T which happens when

$$mg = Bil$$

$$\Rightarrow \quad i = \frac{mg}{Bl}$$

$$\Rightarrow \quad i = \frac{0.2 \times 9.8}{0.6 \times 1} = \frac{49}{15} \text{ A}$$

If i_1 and i_2 be the currents in R_1 and R_2 respectively. Then above current is distributed in inverse ratio of resistances so we use

$$i = i_1 + i_2$$

$$\Rightarrow \quad \frac{49}{15} = i_1 + i_2 \qquad \ldots(5.25)$$

$$\text{and} \quad e = i_1 R_1 = i_2 R_2 \qquad \ldots(5.26)$$

We have

$$P_1 = ei_1$$

$$\Rightarrow \quad 0.76 = ei_1 \qquad \ldots(5.27)$$

$$\text{and} \quad P_2 = ei_2$$

$$\Rightarrow \quad 1.2 = ei_2 \qquad \ldots(5.28)$$

From equations-(5.27) and (5.28) we have

$$\frac{i_1}{i_2} = \frac{0.76}{1.2}$$

$$\Rightarrow \quad i_1 = \frac{19}{30} i_2 \qquad \ldots(5.29)$$

Solving equations-(5.25) and (5.29), we get

$$i_2 = 2 \text{ A}$$

$$\text{and} \quad i_1 = \frac{19}{15} \text{ A}$$

From equation-(5.28) we have

$$1.2 = e \times 2$$

$$\Rightarrow \quad e = 0.6 \text{ V} \qquad \ldots(5.30)$$

At terminal speed EMF is given as

$$e = Bv_T l$$

$$\Rightarrow \quad v_T = (e/Bl)$$

$$\Rightarrow \quad v_T = \frac{0.6}{0.6 \times 1} = 1 \text{ m/s}$$

Resistances are given as

$$R_1 = \frac{e}{i_1} = \frac{0.6 \times 15}{19} = 0.47\ \Omega$$

$$\text{and} \quad R_2 = \frac{e}{i_2} = \frac{0.6}{2} = 0.3\ \Omega$$

Illustrative Example 5.7

Figure-5.36 shows a conductor *OA* of length *l* placed along *y*-axis with one end at origin. In this region a non-uniform magnetic field exist along +*Z*-direction of which magnitude depends only on its *Y* coordinate which is given as

$$B = B_0\left(1 + \frac{y^2}{l^2}\right) \text{T}$$

If the conductor OA starts translating with velocity $\vec{v} = v_0\hat{i}$, find the EMF induced in conductor.

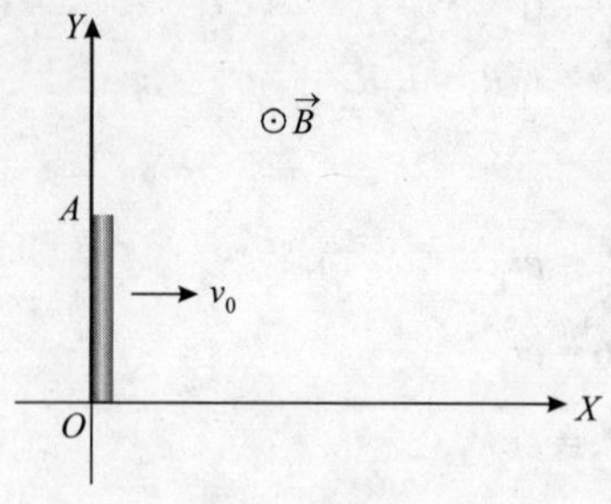

Figure 5.36

Solution

We consider an element of width dy at a distance y from origin in the conductor as shown in figure-5.37. Motional EMF induced in element dy is given as

$$de = Bv_0 dy = B_0 v_0\left(1+\frac{y^2}{l^2}\right)dy$$

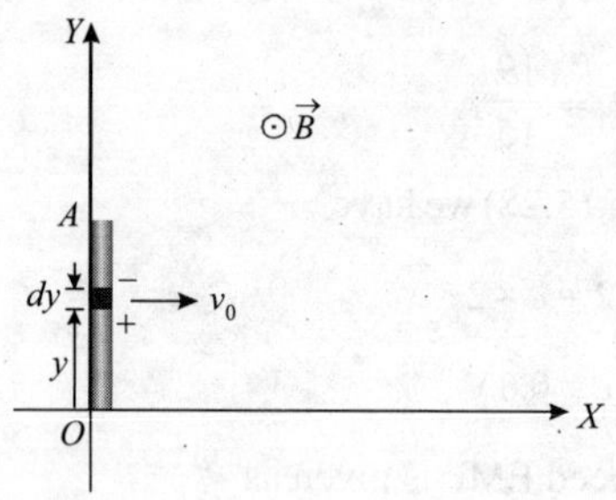

Figure 5.37

Total EMF induced in OA is given by integrating the above induced EMF in the element which is given as

$$e_{OA} = \int de = \int_0^l B_0 v_0\left(1+\frac{y^2}{l^2}\right)dy$$

$$\Rightarrow \quad e_{OA} = B_0 v_0\left[y+\frac{y^3}{3l^2}\right]_0^l$$

$$\Rightarrow \quad e_{OA} = \frac{4}{3}B_0 v_0 l$$

 # Illustrative Example 5.8

A coil A of radius R and number of turns n carries a current i and it is placed in a horizontal plane. A small conducting ring P of radius r ($r << R$) is placed at a height y_0 above the centre of the coil A as shown in figure-5.38. Calculate the induced EMF in the ring when the ring in allowed to fall freely. Express the induced EMF as a function of instantaneous speed of the falling ring and its height above the center of the coil A.

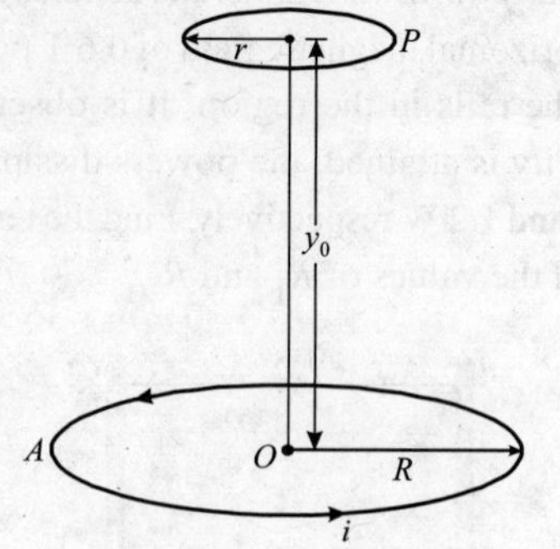

Figure 5.38

Solution

The magnetic induction at a point on the axis of a current carrying coil at a distance y from its centre is given by

$$B = \frac{\mu_0 NiR^2}{2(R^2+y^2)^{3/2}} \qquad \ldots(5.31)$$

Due to the coil A the magnetic flux linked with ring P is given as

$$\phi = BA$$

$$\Rightarrow \quad \phi = \frac{\mu_0 NiR^2}{2(R^2+y^2)^{3/2}} \times \pi r^2$$

$$\Rightarrow \quad \phi = \frac{\mu_0 Ni\pi R^2 r^2}{2(R^2+y^2)^{3/2}} \qquad \ldots(5.32)$$

If the ring P falls with instantaneous velocity v at any instant of time. The induced EMF induced in the ring P is given as

$$e = \frac{d\phi}{dt} = \frac{\mu_0 Ni\pi R^2 r^2}{2} \times \frac{d}{dt}\left[(R^2+y^2)^{-3/2}\right]$$

$$\Rightarrow \quad e = -\frac{3}{4}\mu_0 Ni\pi R^2 r^2 (R^2+y^2)^{-5/2} \times 2y\frac{dy}{dt}$$

$$\Rightarrow \quad e = -\frac{3}{2}\frac{\mu_0 \pi niR^2 r^2}{(R^2+y^2)^{5/2}}y(-v)$$

$$\Rightarrow \quad e = \frac{3}{2}\frac{\mu_0 \pi niR^2 r^2 yv}{(R^2+y^2)^{5/2}}$$

 # Illustrative Example 5.9

Figure-5.39 shows two vertical smooth rails AB and CD separated by a distance l. Ends A and C are connected with capacitor of capacitance C. A rod PQ of mass m is horizontally kept in touch with both rails as shown. If it is released at $t = 0$ and it remains in contact with rails during its fall, find the charge on capacitor as a function of time. Neglect resistance of connecting wires and rails.

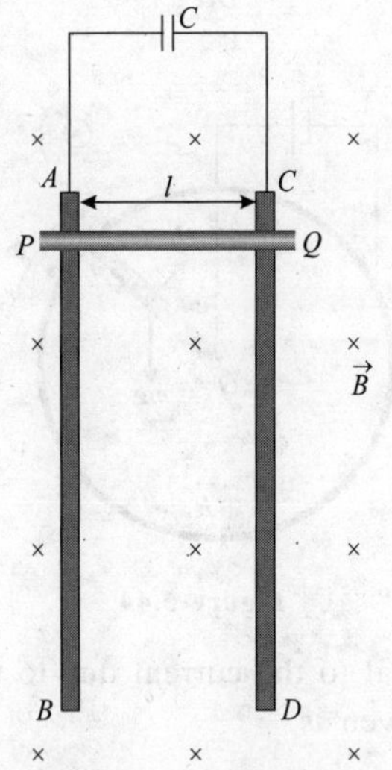

Figure 5.39

Solution

When the rod falls then at any instant when its speed is v, the motional emf across PQ is given as

$$e = Blv$$

As we can neglect the resistance of all connecting wires and rails the charge on capacitor is given as

$$q = Ce = CBlv \qquad \ldots(5.33)$$

Current through the capacitor is given as

$$i = \frac{dq}{dt} = CBla$$

The rod experiences an upward magnetic force and downward its weight as shown in figure-5.40.

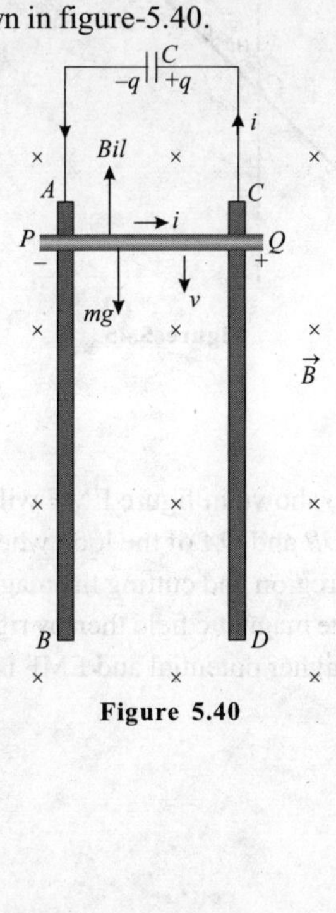

Figure 5.40

If rod has an acceleration a, it can be given as

$$a = \frac{mg - Bil}{m} = \frac{mg - B^2l^2Ca}{m}$$

$$\Rightarrow \qquad a = \frac{mg}{m + B^2l^2C}$$

As acceleration is constant, after time t its velocity is given as

$$v = at = \frac{mgt}{m + B^2l^2C}$$

Thus charge on capacitor after time t is given by equation-(5.33) as

$$q = CBl\left(\frac{mgt}{m + B^2l^2C}\right) = \frac{CBlmgt}{m + B^2l^2C}$$

Illustrative Example 5.10

Figure-5.41 shows a rectangular wire loop $ABCD$ with length l and breadth b. The wire is having a resistance λl per unit length. If the loop is pulled out from the magnetic field at a uniform speed v as shown in figure-5.00, find the potential difference across points of the loop $V_B - V_C$ and $V_A - V_D$.

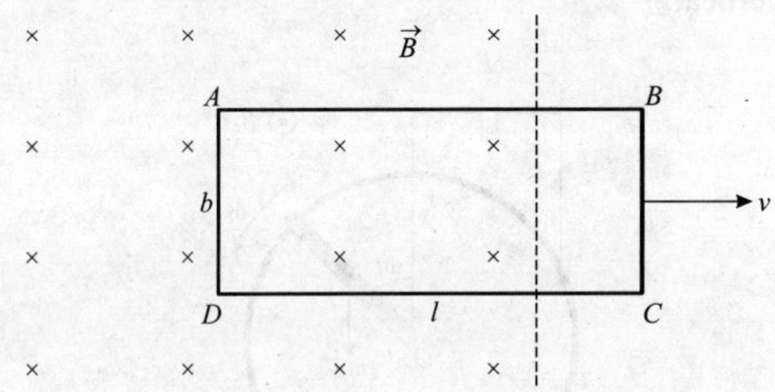

Figure 5.41

Solution

Due to motion of loop motional EMF is only induced across segment AD which is given as

$$e_{AD} = Bvb$$

The equivalent circuit of the loop with motional EMF is shown in figure-5.42

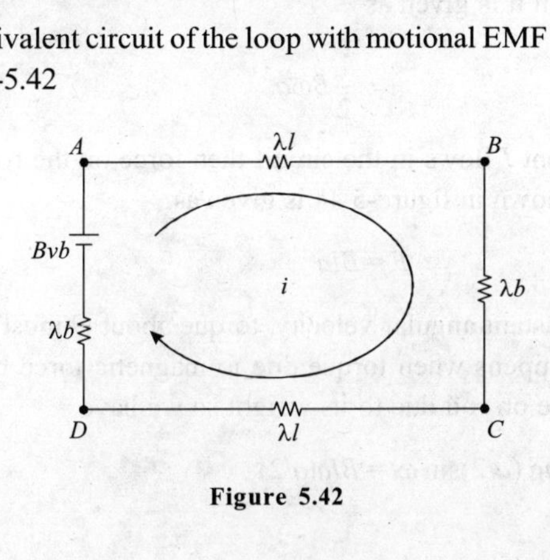

Figure 5.42

Induced current in above loop is given as

$$i = \frac{Bvb}{2\lambda(b+l)}$$

Now we can calculate the required potential differences as

$$V_B - V_C = i \times \lambda b = \frac{Bv \times b^2}{2 \times (b+l)} = \frac{Bvb^2}{2(b+l)}$$

$$V_A - V_D = i \times \lambda(b+2l) = \frac{Bvb(b+2l)}{2(b+l)}$$

Illustrative Example 5.11

A metal rod of mass m can rotate about a horizontal axis O, sliding along a circular wire ring mounted in a vertical plane of radius a as shown in figure-5.43. The arrangement is located in a uniform horizontal magnetic field of induction B directed perpendicular to the plane of ring. The axis and the ring are connected to an EMF to form a circuit of resistance R. Neglecting the friction and ring resistance, find the time function according to which the source EMF must vary to make the rod rotate at a constant angular velocity ω. Given that at $t = 0$ rod was vertical.

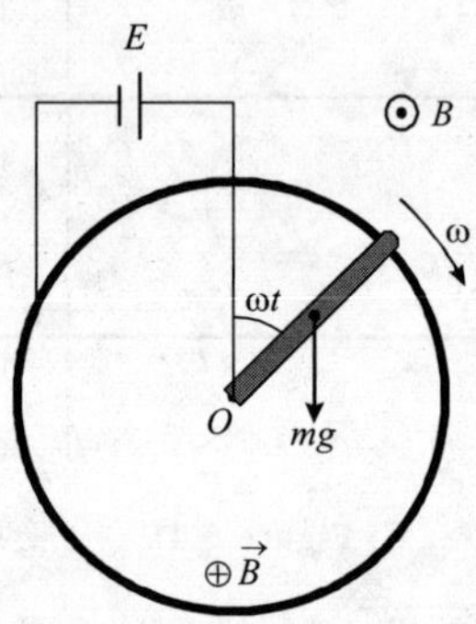

Figure 5.43

Solution

If rod is rotating at constant angular speed then motional EMF induced in it is given as

$$e = \frac{1}{2}B\omega a^2$$

If a current I flows in the circuit then force on the rod at the instant shown in figure-5.44 is given as

$$F = BIa$$

For a constant angular velocity, torque about O must be zero which happens when torque due to magnetic force balances the torque on rod due to its weight so we have

$$mg\,(a/2)\sin\omega t = BIa(a/2)$$

$$\Rightarrow \quad I = \frac{mg\sin\omega t}{Ba}$$

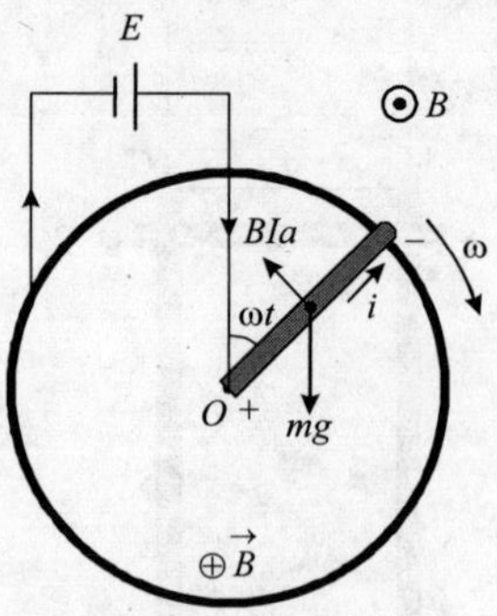

Figure 5.44

This must be equal to the current due to total EMF in the circuit which is given as

$$I = \frac{E - \frac{1}{2}B\omega a^2}{R} = \frac{mg\sin\omega t}{aB}$$

$$\Rightarrow \quad E = \frac{1}{2Ba}(2mgR\sin\omega t + B^2\omega a^3)$$

Illustrative Example 5.12

Figure-5.45 shows a semicircular wire loop of resistance R and radius a hinged at point O and rotating at an angular speed ω. Point O is located on the boundary of a uniform magnetic induction B. Plot the current as a function of time in the loop taking clockwise direction as positive. Take $\theta = 0$ at $t = 0$.

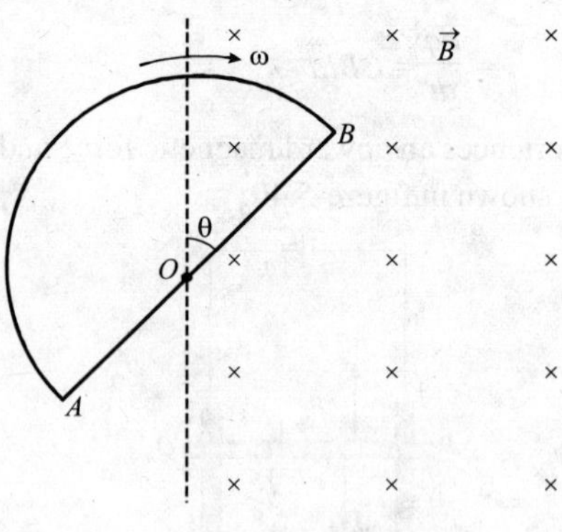

Figure 5.45

Solution

In the rotating loop shown in figure EMF will only be induced in the segment of OB and OA of the loop when these are inside the magnetic field region and cutting the magnetic lines. When segment OB is in the magnetic field then by right hand palm rule point B will be at higher potential and EMF induced across OB is given as

$$e=\frac{1}{2}B\omega a^2$$

This causes an anticlockwise current in the loop which is given as

$$i=\frac{e}{R}=\frac{B\omega a^2}{2R} \qquad \ldots(5.34)$$

After half revolution when segment OB comes out of the region of magnetic field, segment OA enters into the region and same EMF is induced in it and a clockwise current of same magnitude flows in the loop. Thus the plot of time function of current is shown in figure-5.46.

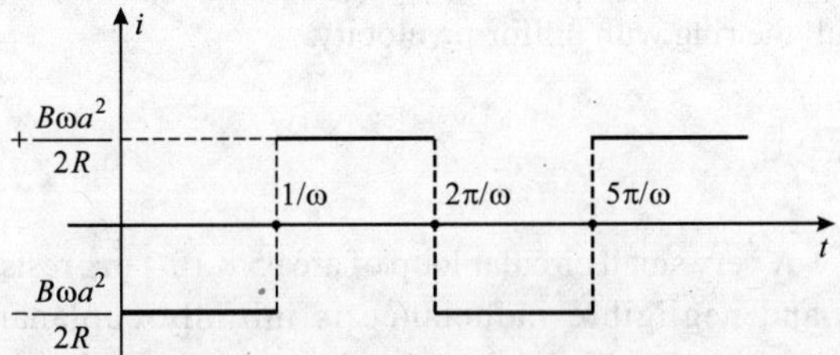

Figure 5.46

Illustrative Example 5.13

P and Q are two vertical infinite conducting plates kept parallel to each other and separated by a distance $2r$. A conducting ring of radius r falls vertically between the planes such that planes are always tangential to the ring. Both the planes are connected by a resistance R. There exists a uniform horizontal magnetic field of strength B perpendicular to the plane of ring. The arrangement is shown in figure-5.47. Plane Q is smooth and friction between the plane P and the ring is enough to prevent slipping between ring and plane P. At $t = 0$, the ring was at rest and neglect the resistance of the planes and the ring. Find

(a) The current through resistance R as a function of time

(b) Terminal velocity of the ring

(c) State the difference in analysis of situation if ring is also made up of a wire of resistance R.

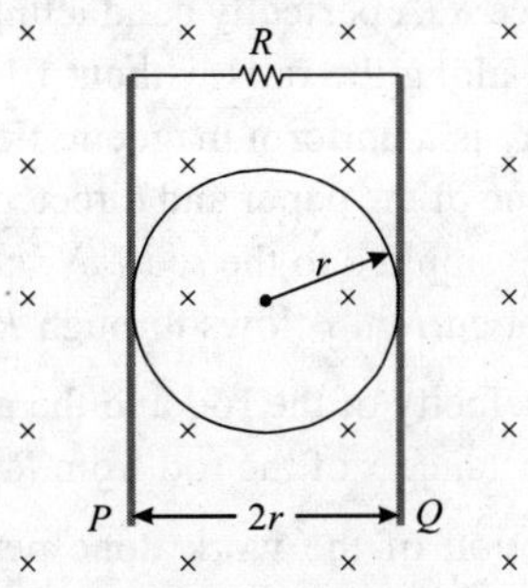

Figure 5.47

Solution

If v be the velocity of center of mass of the ring at any time t, the EMF across the diameter of ring is given as

$$e=2Bvr$$

Current through resistance is given as

$$i=\frac{2Bvr}{R} \qquad \ldots(5.35)$$

The forces acting on the ring are shown in figure-5.48. For rolling motion of ring its equation of motion for rotational motion is

$$fr=I\alpha$$

$$f=\frac{I\alpha}{r}=\frac{Ia}{r^2} \qquad \ldots(5.36)$$

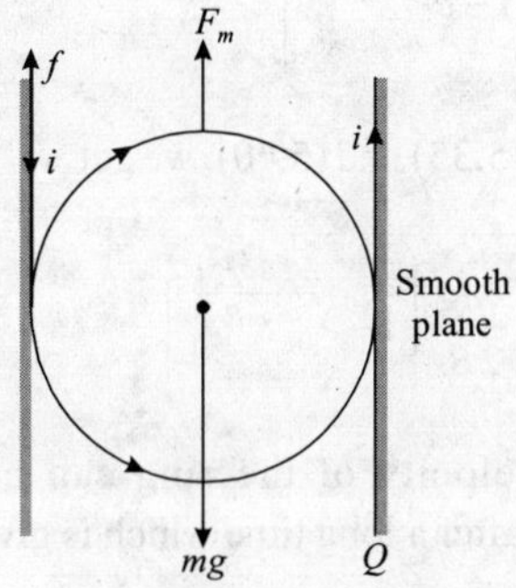

Figure 5.48

The upward magnetic force on ring is given as

$$F_m=Bi(2r)$$

$$\Rightarrow \quad F_m=\frac{4B^2r^2v}{R} \qquad \ldots(5.37)$$

Equation of motion for translational motion of the ring is

$$mg-f-F_m=ma \qquad \ldots(5.38)$$

$$\Rightarrow \quad mg-\frac{Ia}{r^2}-\frac{4B^2r^2}{R}v=ma$$

$$\Rightarrow \quad mg-\frac{4B^2r^2}{R}v=ma+\frac{Ia}{r^2}$$

$$\Rightarrow \quad mg-\frac{4B^2r^2}{R}v=a\left[m+\frac{I}{r^2}\right]$$

$$\Rightarrow \quad \left(mg-\frac{4B^2r^2}{B}v\right)=\frac{dv}{dt}\left[m+\frac{I}{r^2}\right]$$

$$\Rightarrow \quad \frac{dv}{\left(mg-\frac{4B^2r^2}{R}v\right)}\times\left(m+\frac{I}{r^2}\right)=dt$$

For a ring we use its moment of inertia is given as $I = mr^2$ which gives

$$\Rightarrow \qquad \frac{2mdv}{\left(mg - \frac{4B^2r^2}{R}v\right)} = dt \qquad \ldots(5.39)$$

Integrating equation-(5.39) within proper limits, we get

$$-\frac{mR}{2B^2r^2}\left[\ln\left(mg - \frac{4B^2r^2}{R}v\right)\right]_0^v = t$$

$$\Rightarrow \qquad -\frac{mR}{2B^2r^2}\left[\ln\left(mg - \frac{4B^2r^2}{R}v\right) - \ln(mg)\right] = t$$

$$\Rightarrow \qquad -\frac{mR}{2B^2r^2}\ln\left(\frac{mgR - 4B^2r^2v}{mgR}\right) = t$$

$$\Rightarrow \quad v = \frac{mgR}{4B^2r^2}\left(1 - e^{-\frac{2B^2r^2t}{mR}}\right) \qquad \ldots(5.40)$$

From equations-(5.35) and (5.40), we get

$$i = \frac{2Bvr}{R} = \frac{mg}{2Br}\left(1 - e^{-\frac{2B^2r^2t}{mR}}\right)$$

(b) Terminal velocity of the ring can be calculated by equation-(5.40) after a long time which is given as

$$v = \frac{mgR}{4B^2r^2}$$

(c) If ring is made up of a wire of resistance R then EMF induced in the two half rings will remain same but as both the half rings will have resistance $R/2$ and the two EMFs in these half rings are considered in parallel so the total resistance of the circuit will become $R + R/4 = 5R/4$. Thus the analysis done in part (a) and (b) remain same with the resistance value replaced with $5R/4$ instead of R.

Web Reference at www.physicsgalaxy.com

Age Group - Grade 11 & 12 | Age 17-19 Years

Section - Magnetic Effects

Topic - Electromagnetic Induction

Module Number - 1 to 19

Practice Exercise 5.1

(i) A coil of mean area 500 cm^2 and having 1000 turns is held perpendicular to a uniform field of 0.4 G. The coil is turned through 180° in 1/10 s. Calculate the average induced EMF.

[0.04 V]

(ii) Two long parallel conducting horizontal rails are connected by a conducting wire at one end. A uniform magnetic field B directed vertically downwards exists in the region of space. A light uniform ring of diameter d which is practically equal to separation between the rails, is placed over the rails as shown in figure-5.49.

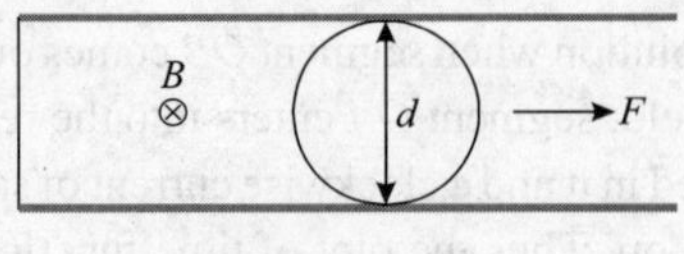

Figure 5.49

If resistance of ring be λ per unit length, calculate force required to pull the ring with uniform velocity.

$[\frac{4B^2vd}{\pi\lambda}]$

(iii) A very small circular loop of area 5×10^{-4} m^2, resistance 2 Ω and negligible inductance is initially coplanar and concentric with a much larger fixed circular loop of radius 0.1 m. A constant current of 1 A is passed in the bigger loop and the smaller loop is rotated with angular velocity ω rad/s about a diameter. Calculate

(a) Maximum flux linked with the smaller loop

(b) Average induced EMF in one rotation of the loop

(c) Induced current in the smaller loop, as a function of time.

[(a) $10\pi \times 10^{-10}$ Wb; (b) 10^{-9} ω; (c) 2.5×10^{-10} ω sinωt]

(iv) A plane spiral with a great number N of turns wound tightly to one another is located in a uniform magnetic field perpendicular to the spiral's plane. The outside radius of the spiral's turns is equal to a. The magnetic induction varies with time as $B = B_0 \sin \omega t$, where B_0 and ω are constants. Find the amplitude of induced EMF in the spiral.

$[\frac{1}{3}\pi N a^2 B_0 \omega]$

(v) Two long parallel horizontal rails, a distance d apart and each having a resistance λ per unit length, are joined at one end by a resistance R. A perfectly conducting rod MN of mass m is free to slide along the rails without friction as shown in figure-5.50. There is a uniform magnetic field of induction B normal to the plane of the paper and directed into the paper. A variable force F is applied to the rod MN such that, as the rod moves, a constant current i flows through R.

(a) Find the velocity of the rod and the applied force F as function of the distance x of the rod from R.

(b) What fraction of the work done per second by F is converted into heat?

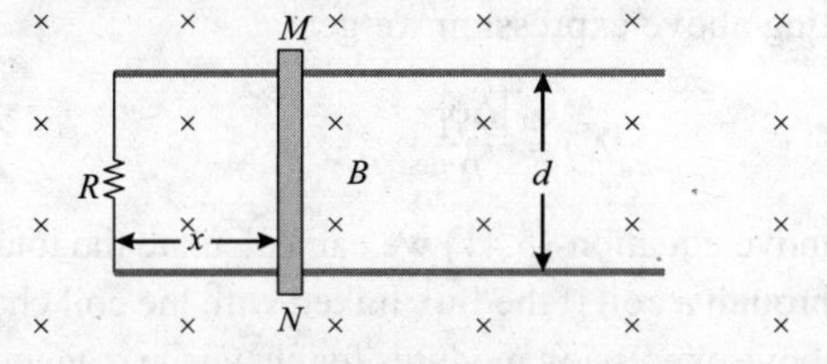

Figure 5.50

[(a) $\dfrac{i(r+2\lambda x)}{Bd}$, $m\left(\dfrac{2i^2\lambda(R+2\lambda x)}{B^2d^2}\right)$ (b) $\dfrac{B^3d^3}{2mi\lambda(R+2\lambda x)}$]

(vi) A wire frame of area 3.92×10^{-4} m^2 and resistance 20 Ω is suspended freely from a 0.392 m long thread. There is a uniform magnetic field of 0.784 T and the plane of wire-frame is perpendicular to the magnetic field. The frame is made to oscillate under gravity by displacing it through 2×10^{-2} m from its initial position along the direction of magnetic field. The plane of the frame is always along the direction of thread and does not rotate about it. What is the induced EMF in wire-frame as a function of time? Also find the maximum current in the frame.

[2×10^{-6} V, 10^{-7} A]

(vii) A square frame with side a and a long straight wire carrying a current i are located in the same plane as shown in figure-5.51. The frame translates to the right with a constant velocity v. Find the EMF induced in the frame as a function of distance x.

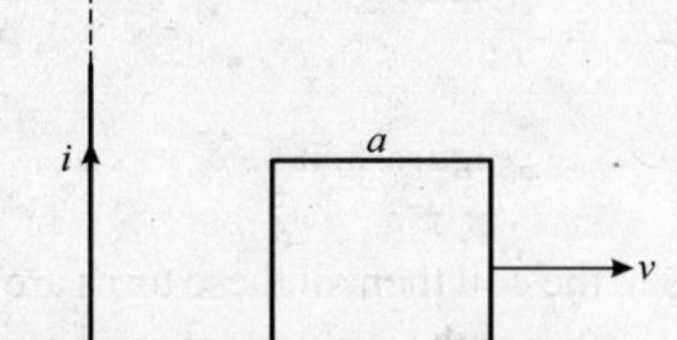

Figure 5.51

[$\dfrac{\mu_0 i a^2 xv}{2\pi x(x+a)}$]

(viii) A rod of length $2a$ is free to rotate in a vertical plane, about a horizontal axis O passing through its mid-point. A long straight, horizontal wire is in the same plane and is carrying a constant current i as shown in figure-5.52.

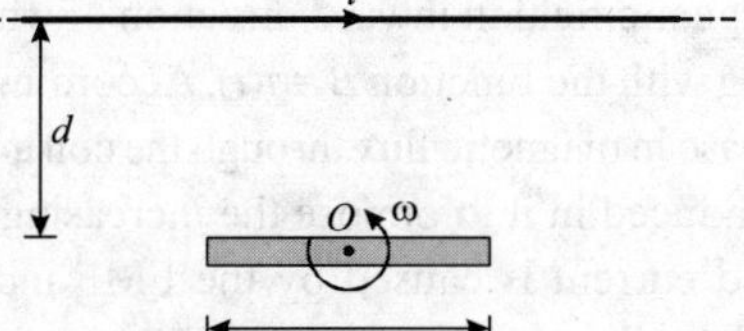

Figure 5.52

At initial moment of time. The rod is horizontal and starts to rotate with constant angular velocity ω, calculate EMF induced in rod as a function of time.

[$\dfrac{\mu_0 i\omega}{2\pi\sin^2\omega t}\left[d\ln\left(\dfrac{d-a\sin\omega t}{d+a\sin\omega t}\right)-2a\sin\omega t\right]$]

(ix) Two long wires are placed on a pair of parallel rails perpendicular to the wires. The spacing between the rails d is large compared with x, the distance between the wires. Both wires and rails are made of a material of resistivity ρ per unit length. A magnetic flux density B is applied perpendicular to the rectangle by the wires and rails. One wire is moved along the rails with a uniform speed v while the other is held stationary. Determine how the force on the stationary wire varies with x and show that it vanishes for a value of x approximately equal to $(\mu_0 v/4\pi\rho)$.

(x) A uniform rod AB of mass m and length l is placed over two smooth conducting rails P and Q. If the switch shown as closed at $t = 0$, find the velocity of rod AB as a function of time.

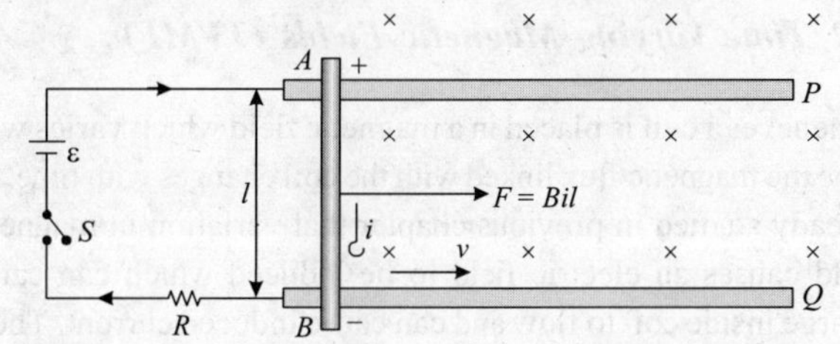

Figure 5.53

[$\dfrac{e}{Bl}(1-e^{-B^2l^2t/mR})$]

(xi) In figure-5.54 a wire ring of radius R is in pure rolling on a surface. Find the EMF induced across the top and bottom points of the ring at any instant.

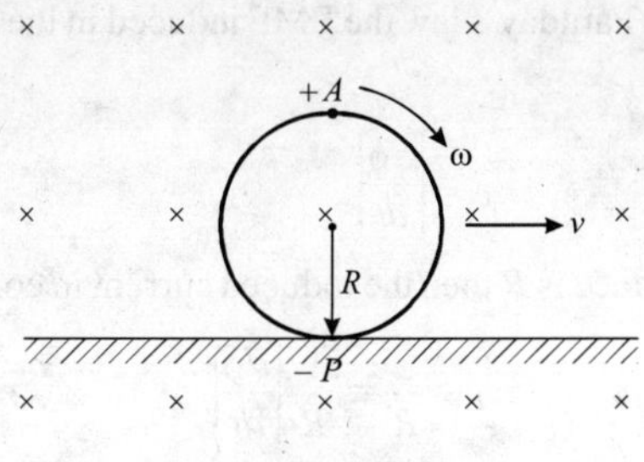

Figure 5.54

[$2B\omega R^2$]

(xii) Figure-5.55 shows a small circular coil of area A suspended from a point O by a string of length l in a uniform magnetic induction B in a uniform magnetic induction B in horizontal direction. If the coil is set into oscillations like a simple pendulum by displacing it a small angle θ_0 as shown, find EMF induced in coil as a function of time. Assume the plane of coil is always in plane of string.

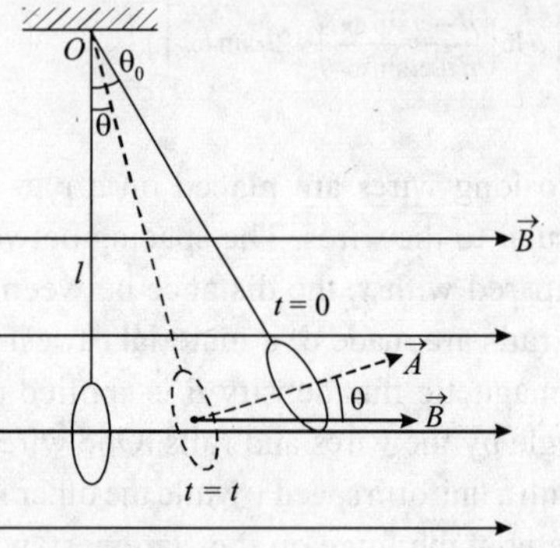

Figure 5.55

$[\frac{1}{2}BA\theta_0^2\omega\sin\left(2\sqrt{\frac{g}{l}}t\right)]$

5.2 Time Varying Magnetic Fields (TVMF)

Whenever a coil is placed in a magnetic field which varies with time the magnetic flux linked with the coil changes with time. As already studied in previous chapter that variation in magnetic field causes an electric field to be induced which can cause charge inside coil to flow and can cause induced current. There are several electrical parameters which can be calculated in any electrical circuit when magnetic flux associated with the circuit changes with time. In this section we'll discuss some of specific cases related to time varying magnetic fields.

5.2.1 Charge Flown through a Coil due to Change in Magnetic Flux

If magnetic flux associated with a coil changes with time then according to Faraday's law the EMF induced in the coil is given as

$$e = \left|\frac{d\phi}{dt}\right|$$

If coil resistance is R then the induced current in coil is given as

$$i = \frac{e}{R} = \frac{1}{R}\left|\frac{d\phi}{dt}\right|$$

If in time dt a charge dq flows through the coil when flux change is $d\phi$ in this time then we have

$$\frac{dq}{dt} = \frac{1}{R}\left|\frac{d\phi}{dt}\right|$$

$$\Rightarrow \quad dq = \frac{|d\phi|}{R}$$

Integrating above expression we get

$$\Delta q = \frac{|\Delta\phi|}{R} \quad \ldots(5.41)$$

Using above equation-(5.41) we can calculate the total charge flown through a coil if the flux linked with the coil changes by $\Delta\phi$. In above expression modulus for change in magnetic flux is used to avoid the sign for the charge flown as direction in which charge flows can be calculated by Lenz's law which we've already discussed.

5.2.2 Induced EMF in a Coil in Time Varying Magnetic Field

When a coil is placed in time varying magnetic field, as discussed in previous article the changing magnetic flux causes an EMF to be induced in the coil. If the coil area is A through which the magnetic flux is passing as shown in figure-5.56 then at any instant magnetic flux passing through the coil is given as

$$\phi_1 = BA$$

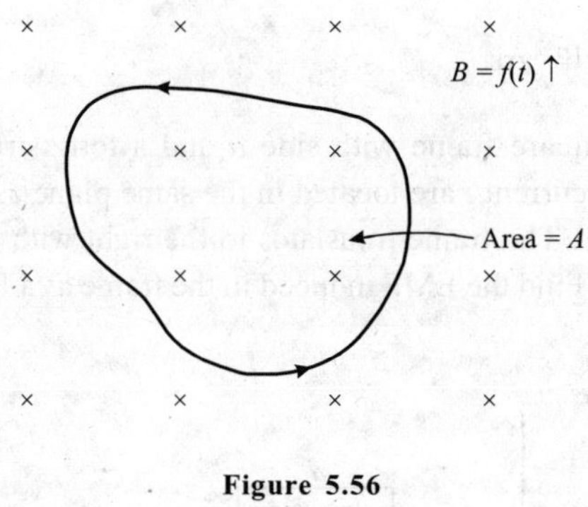

Figure 5.56

If there are N turns in the coil then all these turns are considered in series one after another at the same place so in such condition the magnetic flux '*linked*' with the coil is given as

$$\phi = BA \times N \quad \ldots(5.42)$$

The EMF induced in coil (in all turns) is given as

$$e = \left|\frac{d\phi}{dt}\right| = AN\frac{dB}{dt} \quad \ldots(5.43)$$

Above EMF is called '*Loop EMF*' induced in the coil which is distributed in every element of the coil.

Figure-5.57(a) shows a single turn circular coil placed in time varying magnetic field in inward direction of which magnitude is increasing with the function $B = f(t)$. According to Lenz's law due to increase in magnetic flux through the coil an anticlockwise current is induced in it to oppose the increasing flux. Actually this induced current is caused by the EMF induced in every element of the coil as shown in figure-5.57(b). Every small element of the coil behaves like an elemental EMF de and all such elemental EMFs are in series. Sum of all these EMFs in the coil is called loop EMF given by equation-(5.43).

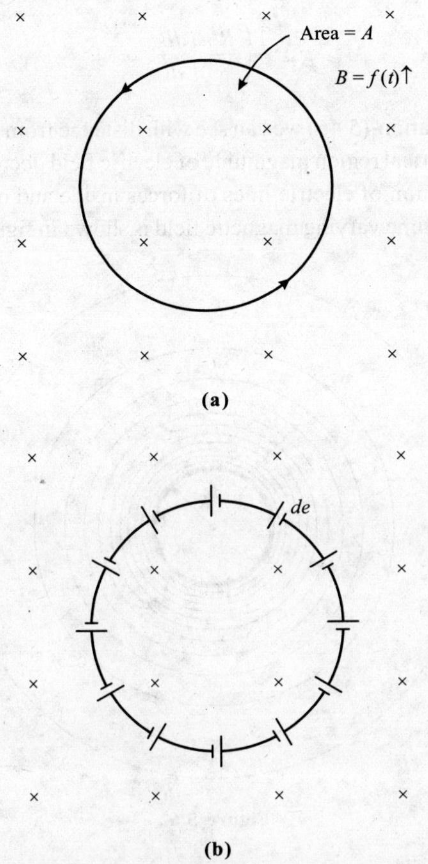

Figure 5.57

5.2.3 Induced Electric Field in Cylindrical Region Time Varying Magnetic Field

Figure-5.58 shows magnetic field along the axis of a cylindrical region of radius R. A coil of radius r is placed coaxially in the region as shown. If magnetic induction starts increasing with time an EMF is induced in the coil wire which causes an electric field to be induced in the wire due to which induced current flows.

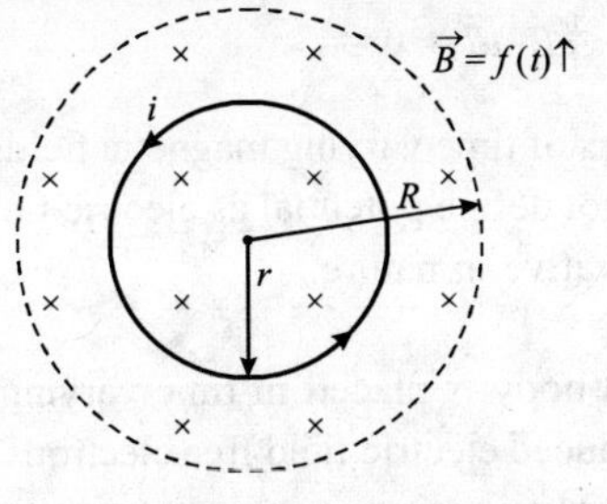

Figure 5.58

By symmetry of the region in which magnetic field exist, the direction of induced electric field in the coil wire must be same as that of the induced current so at every point of the coil we can consider electric field to be along the tangent as shown in figure-5.59(a). Even if coil is not placed here, induced electric field lines will be closed circles as shown in figure-5.59(b).

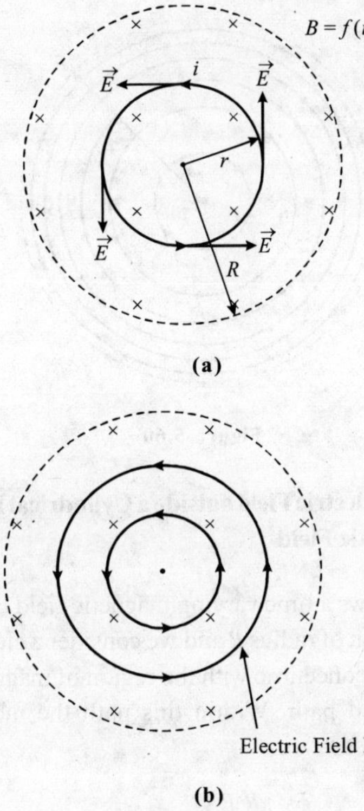

Figure 5.59

The induced EMF in the coil shown in figure-5.58 can be given as

$$e_{loop} = \pi R^2 \frac{dB}{dt} \quad \ldots (5.44)$$

If we consider an electric field line of radius x as shown in figure-5.59(a) then along this circular line total loop EMF induced is given as

$$e_{loop} = \pi x^2 \frac{dB}{dt}$$

If $\vec{E}$ be the strength of induced electric field along the above line of force in consideration then we can write

$$e_{loop} = \int_0^{2\pi x} \vec{E}.\vec{dl} = \pi x^2 \frac{dB}{dt}$$

By symmetry we can state that magnitude of electric field along the coaxial line of force should remain same and it is tangential to the line of force so we can write

$$E(2\pi x) = \pi x^2 \frac{dB}{dt}$$

$$\Rightarrow \qquad E = \frac{1}{2} x \frac{dB}{dt} \quad \ldots (5.45)$$

Equation-(5.45) shows that electric field increases with distance from axis of region thus the density of electric lines of forces increases as we move away from the central axis. The configuration of electric lines is shown in figure-5.60.

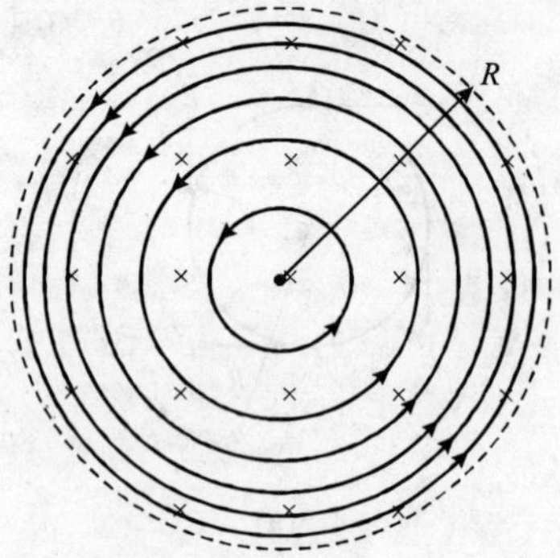

Figure 5.60

5.2.4 Induced Electric Field outside a Cylindrical Region Time Varying Magnetic Field

Figure-5.61 shows a time varying magnetic field confined in a cylindrical region of radius R and we consider a closed circular path of radius x concentric with the region of magnetic field as shown by dotted path. Within this path the magnetic flux passing is given as

$$\phi = \pi R^2 B$$

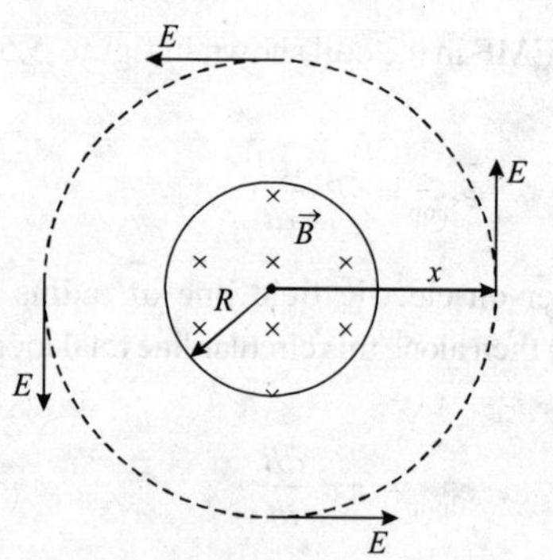

Figure 5.61

If we place a coil along this path then EMF induced in the coil is given as

$$e_{loop} = \pi R^2 \frac{dB}{dt}$$

By symmetry the direction of induced electric field will be tangential to the path as discussed in previous article and using induced electric field loop EMF can be given as

$$e_{loop} = \int_0^{2\pi x} \vec{E}.\vec{dl} = \pi R^2 \frac{dB}{dt}$$

$$\Rightarrow \qquad E(2\pi x) = \pi R^2 \frac{dB}{dt}$$

$$\Rightarrow \qquad E = \frac{1}{2}\left(\frac{R^2}{x}\right)\frac{dB}{dt} \qquad \ldots(5.46)$$

From equation-(5.46) we can see with distance from the axis of the cylindrical region magnitude of electric field decreases. The configuration of electric lines of forces inside and outside the region of time varying magnetic field is shown in figure-5.62.

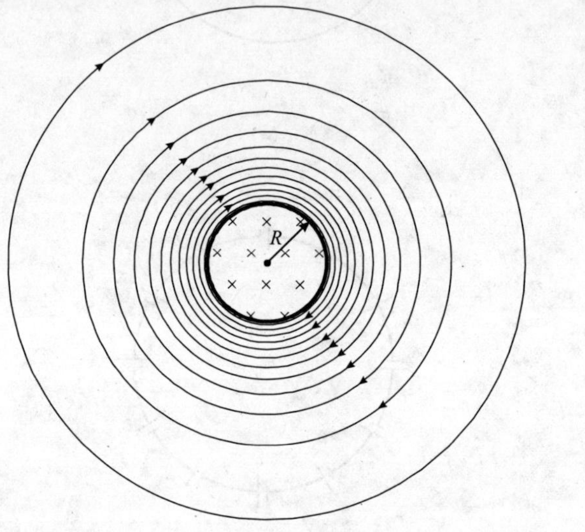

Figure 5.62

5.2.5 Electric Potential in Region of Time Varying Magnetic Field

We've discussed in previous article that induced electric field in time varying magnetic field have closed loop electric lines of forces as there are no static charges or source of electric field is present in this situation for which the field is non conservative in nature as for a charge going round the loop electric force acts in same direction and hence work done is non zero. Thus for the induced electric field in time varying magnetic field we have for a general closed path

$$\oint \vec{E} \cdot \vec{dl} \neq 0 \qquad \ldots(5.47)$$

Thus in regions of time varying magnetic fields at any point in space we cannot define potential as electric field in this region is non conservative in nature.

When a metal body is placed in time varying magnetic field then due to induced electric field free electrons of the metal are displaced which causes an opposing static electric field to be developed inside the metal due to static charges and at every point inside the metal its magnitude is equal to that of non conservative induced electric field of the region. To understand this we will discuss on an illustration shown in figure-5.63.

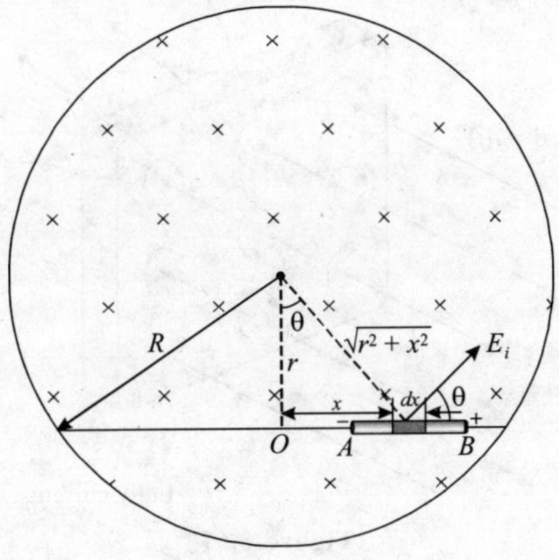

Figure 5.63

Inside a time varying magnetic field, a rod AB of length L is placed such that the axis of rod is at a distance r form the rod. We consider an element of length dx on rod at a distance x from point O as shown in figure above. The induced electric field at the location of element dx can be obtained by equation-(5.45), given as

$$E_i = \frac{1}{2}\sqrt{r^2+x^2}\,\frac{dB}{dt} \quad \ldots(5.48)$$

Due to the component of this electric field along the length of the rod its free electrons will drift toward left and left end A of rod becomes negative and due to deficiency of electrons end B becomes positive. These charges establishes another electric field inside the rod from B to A. In steady condition this electric field balances the component of E_i along the rod so that no further drift of free electrons take place. Thus the electric field inside the rod due to static charges which is conservative in nature is given as

$$E = E_i\cos\theta \quad \ldots(5.49)$$

$$\Rightarrow \quad E = \frac{1}{2}\sqrt{r^2+x^2}\,\frac{dB}{dt} \times \frac{r}{\sqrt{r^2+x^2}}$$

$$\Rightarrow \quad E = \frac{1}{2}r\frac{dB}{dt} \quad \ldots(5.50)$$

The expression in above equation-(5.50) shows that the static electric field inside the rod is uniform and depends only upon the distance of axis of rod from the center of the cylindrical region in which magnetic field is confined.

If this electric field is uniform, the potential difference across the rod is given as

$$V_B - V_A = EL$$

$$\Rightarrow \quad V_B - V_A = \left(\frac{1}{2}r\frac{dB}{dt}\right)L$$

$$\Rightarrow \quad V_B - V_A = \frac{1}{2}rL\frac{dB}{dt} \quad \ldots(5.51)$$

5.2.6 Eddy Currents

When a conductor moves in a magnetic field or there exist some relative motion between a conductor and magnetic field then localized currents are induced within the body of conductor in plane perpendicular to magnetic field if magnetic flux passing through the conductor changes. These currents are called '*Eddy Currents*' or '*Foucaults Currents*'.

Figure-5.64 shows a closed loop which is being pulled out from a magnetic field due to which the magnetic flux through the loop is decreasing and according to Faraday's law a motional EMF Bvl is induced in the segment DA of the conductor and a clockwise induced current flows in it. Due to this current segment DA experiences an opposing force Bil which opposes the loop to be pulled out from the magnetic field which is in accordance of Lenz's law.

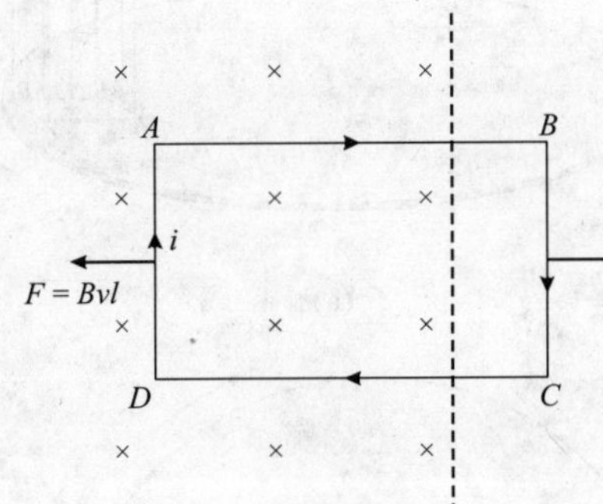

Figure 5.64

See figure-5.65 in which a sheet of metal is being pulled through a magnetic field. In this case there is no wire loop like figure-5.64 but the dotted segments of the sheets as shown in below figure will develop an induced EMF and tend to supply clockwise induced currents as shown in whichever path is available in the body of conductor. Due to these induced current these all segments within the magnetic fields experience a backward force by magnetic field and opposes the motion of sheet or develop a braking action for the moving conductor. These induced currents are '*Eddy Currents*'.

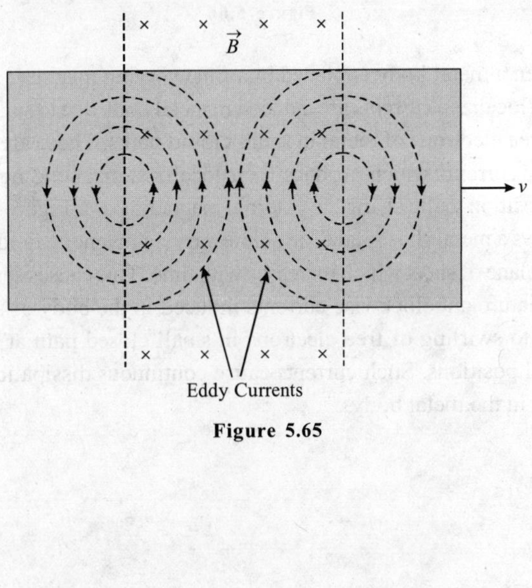

Figure 5.65

Figure-5.66 shows another illustration of braking of a rotating conducting disc by eddy currents. On the surface of a rotating metal disc we apply magnetic field on a part of its surface area as shown. Those segments of the metal disc which are moving through this region of magnetic field develop an induced EMF and eddy currents flow as shown in figure-5.66(b) which is the top view of the rotating disc. These currents are concentrated mainly in the part of disc where magnetic field is applied and outside these are scattered to form close loops. In this part of disc these currents will experience an opposing magnetic force to rotation of disc and hence it provides a braking action on rotating disc by the torque due to this magnetic force.

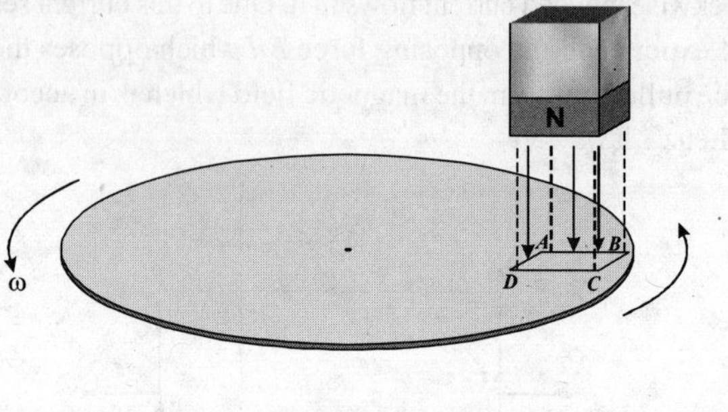

(a)

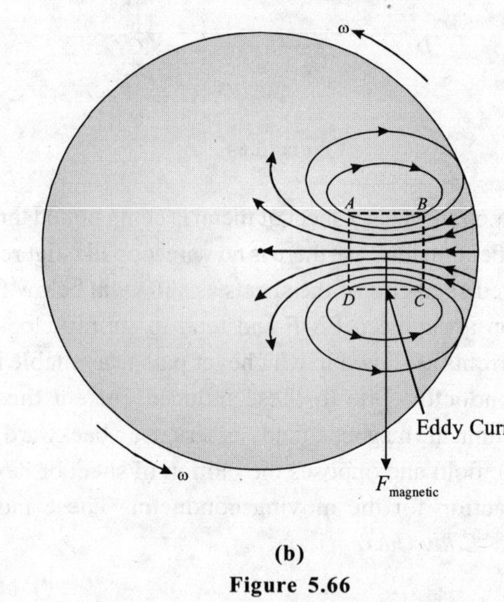

(b)

Figure 5.66

When a metal body is placed in a time varying magnetic field then localized currents are induced in metal body due to swirling of free electrons of metal in small closed paths. These are also eddy currents which produce their localized magnetic field in opposition to the change in external magnetic field. Figure-5.67 shows a metal sheet placed in a time varying magnetic field into the plane of sheet which increases with time. This causes several miniature anticlockwise currents induced in the body of sheet due to swirling of free electrons in small closed path at their local positions. Such currents cause continuous dissipation of heat in the metal body.

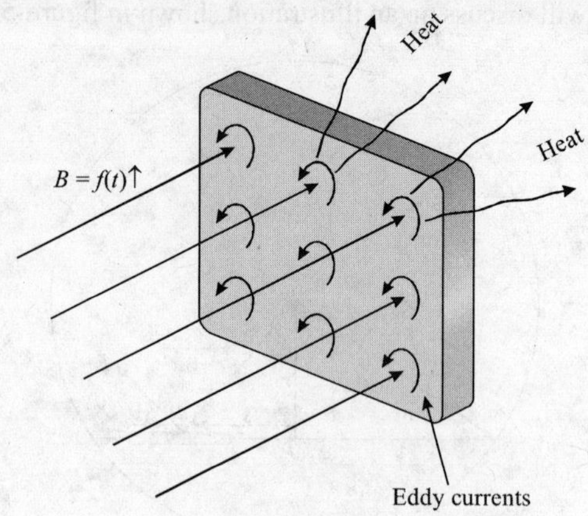

Figure 5.67

As discussed above whenever eddy currents are produced in a metal body these have two main effects on the specific situation under which these eddy currents are produced. One is the braking action on the relative motion of conductor and magnetic field and other is the heat dissipation in the body of conductor. Due to these actions there are many useful applications of eddy currents are developed at industrial and laboratory level.

Illustrative Example 5.14

Two concentric coplanar circular loops made of wire with resistance per unit length $10^{-4}\ \Omega$/m, have diameters 0.2 m and 2 m. A time varying potential difference $(4 + 2.5t)$ volt is applied to the larger loop. Calculate the current in the smaller loop.

Solution

The situation described in question is shown in figure-5.68

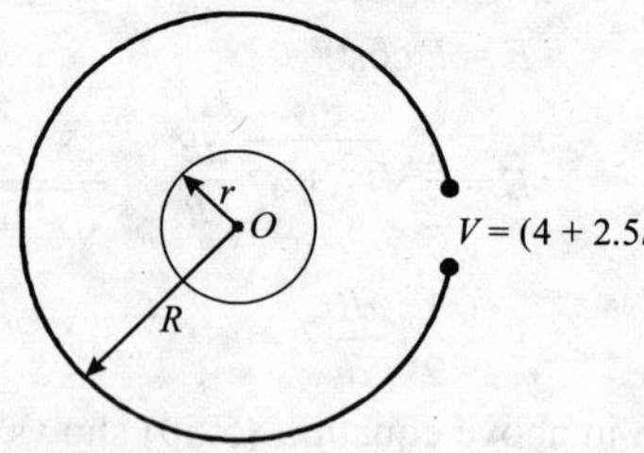

Figure 5.68

The magnetic induction at O, due to the current in large loop is given as

$$B_0 = \frac{\mu_0 i}{2R}$$

where $$i = \frac{V}{R} = \frac{(4+2.5t)}{(2\pi R)\rho}$$

$$\Rightarrow \qquad B_0 = \frac{\mu_0}{2R}\left[\frac{(4+2.5t)}{(2\pi R)\rho}\right]$$

Here we consider that the central loop is very small i.e., $r << R$, so the field may be considered as constant within the loop. Thus within the loop the field is B_0 so the flux through smaller loop is given as

$$\phi = B_0 \times (\pi r^2) = \frac{\mu_0}{2R}\left[\frac{(4+2.5t)}{(2\pi R)\rho}\right]\cdot \pi r^2$$

Induced EMF in the smaller loop is given as

$$e = \left|\frac{d\phi}{dt}\right| = \frac{\mu_0 r^2}{4R^2\rho}\times(2.5)$$

Thus current i in the smaller loop is given as

$$i = \frac{e}{R} = \frac{\mu_0 r^2}{4R^2\rho}\times 2.5\times\left(\frac{1}{2\pi r\rho}\right)$$

$$\Rightarrow \quad i = \frac{2.5\mu_0 r}{8\pi R^2\rho^2}$$

$$\Rightarrow \quad i = \frac{2.5\times(4\pi\times10^{-7})(0.1)}{8\pi\times1\times10^{-8}} = 1.25\text{ A}$$

Illustrative Example 5.15

A current $i = 3.36(1+2t)\times10^{-2}$ A increases at a steady rate in a long straight wire. A small circular loop of radius 10^{-3} m has its plane parallel to the wire and is placed at a distance of 1 m from the wire. The resistance of the loop is $8.4\times10^{-4}\ \Omega$. Find the magnitude and direction of induced current in the loop.

Solution

Situation described in question is shown in figure-5.69

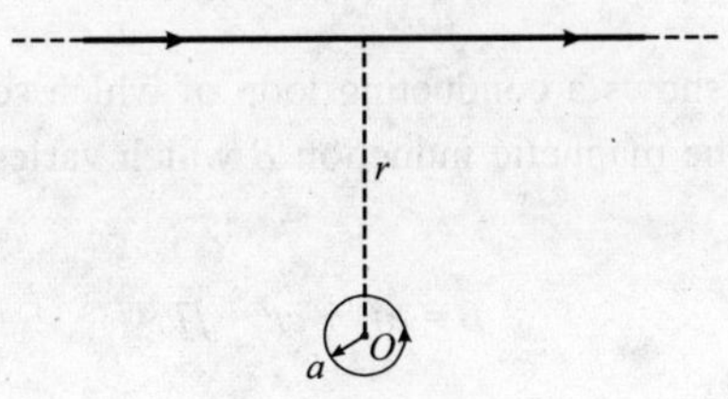

Figure 5.69

The magnetic flux passing through the loop is given as

$$\phi = B.A = \left(\frac{\mu_0 i}{2\pi r}\right)\pi a^2 = \frac{\mu_0 a^2 i}{2r}$$

$$\Rightarrow \quad \phi = \frac{\mu_0 a^2}{2\times1}[3.36\,(1+2t)\times10^{-2}]$$

The induced e.m.f. is given by

$$e = \frac{d\Phi}{dt} = \frac{\mu_0 a^2}{2}\times[3.36\times2\times10^{-2}]$$

$$\Rightarrow \quad e = 3.36\times10^{-2}\times\mu_0 a^2$$

So, the induced current i is given by

$$i = \frac{e}{R} = \frac{1}{R}\times3.36\times10^{-2}\times\mu_0 a^2$$

$$\Rightarrow \quad i = \frac{(3.36\times10^{-2})\times(4\pi\times10^{-7})(10^{-3})^2}{(8.4\times10^{-4})}$$

$$\Rightarrow \quad i = \frac{4.22\times10^{-14}}{8.4\times10^{-4}} = 5\times10^{-11}\text{ A}$$

Illustrative Example 5.16

A long straight solenoid of cross-sectional diameter d and with n turns per unit of its length has a round turn of copper wire of cross-sectional area A and density ρ is tightly put on its winding. Find the current flowing in the turn if the current in the solenoid winding is increased with a constant rate I ampere per second.

Solution

The magnetic field inside the solenoid is given as

$$B = \mu_0 ni$$

The flux through its cross section of copper winding is given as

$$\phi = BA = (\mu_0 ni)\frac{\pi d^2}{4}$$

EMF induced in the copper wire is given as

$$e = \left|\frac{d\phi}{dt}\right| = \mu_0 n\pi\frac{d^2}{4}\frac{di}{dt}$$

Current in the copper wire is given as

$$I_C = \frac{e}{R} = \frac{\mu_0 n\pi d^2 I}{4\cdot\rho\left(\frac{\pi d}{A}\right)} = \frac{\mu_0 ndAI}{4\rho}$$

Illustrative Example 5.17

For the situation described in figure-5.70 the magnetic field changes with time according to,

$$B = (2.00t^3 - 4.00t^2 + 0.8)\ T \text{ and } r_2 = 2R = 5.0\text{ cm}$$

(a) Calculate the force on an electron located at point P_2 at time instant $t = 2$ s

(b) What are the magnitude and direction of the electric field at P_1 when $t = 3$ s and $r_1 = 0.02$ m.

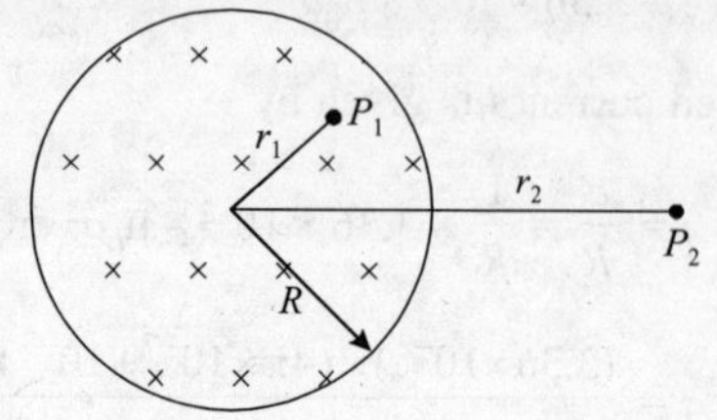

Figure 5.70

Solution

(a) At point P_2 the induced electric field strength is given as

$$E = \frac{R^2}{2r_2}\left(\frac{dB}{dt}\right)$$

$$F = qE = \frac{eR^2}{2r_2}(6t^2 - 8t)$$

Substituting the values we get

$$F = \frac{(1.6\times10^{-19})(2.5\times10^{-2})}{2\times5\times10^{-2}}[6(2)^2 - 8(2)]$$

$$\Rightarrow \quad F = 8.0\times10^{-21}\ \text{N}$$

(b) At P_1 being a point inside of the magnetic field, the induced electric field at this point is given as

$$E = \frac{r_1}{2}\left(\frac{dB}{dt}\right)$$

$$\Rightarrow \quad E = \frac{r_1}{2}[6t^2 - 8t]$$

$$\Rightarrow \quad E = \frac{0.02}{2}[6(3)^3 - 8(3)]$$

$$\Rightarrow \quad E = 0.3\ \text{V/m}$$

As discussed in the above part, direction of electric field is in the direction of induced current (anticlockwise) in an imaginary circular conducting loop passing through P_1.

Illustrative Example 5.18

A plane loop shown in figure-5.71 is shaped in the from of two squares with sides a and b and it is introduced into a uniform magnetic field at right angles, to the loop's plane. The magnetic induction varies with time as $B = B_0 \sin \omega t$. Find the amplitude of the current induced in the loop if its resistance per unit length is equal to r. The induction of the loop is negligible.

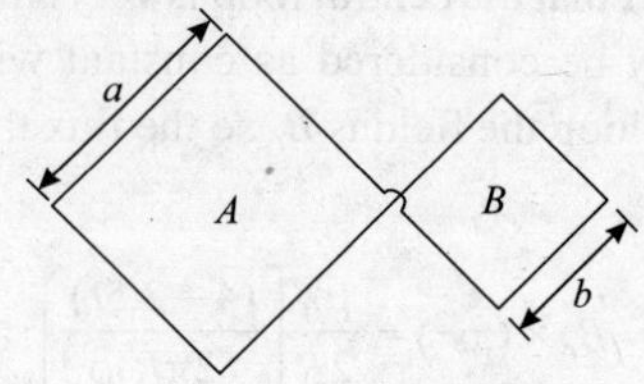

Figure 5.71

Solution

The loops are connected in such a way that EMFs in loops will oppose each other. The EMF induced in first loop is given as

$$e_A = \frac{d}{dt}(a^2 B) = a^2\frac{d}{dt}(B_0 \sin \omega t)$$

$$\Rightarrow \quad e_A = a^2 B_0\, \omega \cos \omega t$$

EMF induced in the second loop is given as

$$e_B = -b^2 B_0\, \omega \cos \omega t$$

Resistance of the circuit is given as

$$R = 4(a+b)r$$

Amplitude of current is given as

$$i_0 = \frac{(a^2 - b^2)B_0\omega}{4(a+B)r}$$

$$\Rightarrow \quad i_0 = \frac{1}{4}\frac{(a-b)B_0\omega}{r}$$

Illustrative Example 5.19

Figure-5.72 shows a conducting loop of which semi-circular part lies in the magnetic induction B which varies with time, given as

$$B = at^3 + ct^2 + fT$$

The wire is having a resistance $R\Omega$/m. Find current in loop at time $t = 2$ s.

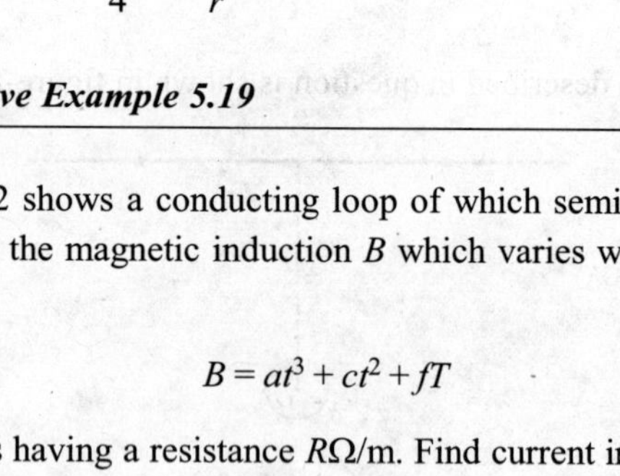

Figure 5.72

Solution

Induced emf in the loop is given as

$$e = A\frac{dB}{dt} = \frac{\pi r^2}{2}(3at^2 + 2ct)$$

Total resistance of the loop is given as

$$R_T = R\left[\frac{r}{2} + \frac{r}{2} + 2r + \pi r\right] = rR(3 + \pi)$$

Current in loop is given as

$$i = \frac{\varepsilon - e}{R_T}$$

$$\Rightarrow \quad i = \frac{\varepsilon - \frac{\pi r^2}{2}(3at^2 + 2ct)}{rR(3 + \pi)}$$

Illustrative Example 5.20

A thin non-conducting ring of mass m carrying a charge q can freely rotate about its axis. At the initial moment, the ring was at rest and no magnetic field was present. Then a practically uniform magnetic field was switched on, which was perpendicular to the plane of the ring and increased with time according to a certain law $B(t)$. Find the angular velocity attained by the ring as a function of the magnetic induction $B(t)$.

Solution

A changing magnetic field sets up an induced electric field due to which the torque on ring causes it to accelerate, we use

$$\tau = mR^2\frac{d\omega}{dt} \qquad \ldots(5.52)$$

But

$$\tau = q_0 ER = q\cdot\frac{1}{2}R^2\frac{dB}{dt} \qquad \ldots(5.53)$$

From equation-(5.52) and (5.53) we have

$$\frac{1}{2}R^2 q\frac{dB}{dt} = mR^2\frac{d\omega}{dt}$$

$$\Rightarrow \quad \frac{1}{2}qdB = m\,d\omega$$

Integrating above expression upto a time t we get

$$\frac{1}{2}qB(t) = m\omega$$

$$\Rightarrow \quad \omega = \frac{q}{2m}B(t)$$

The direction of ω will be opposite to the direction of magnetic induction.

Illustrative Example 5.21

An infinitesimally small bar magnet of dipole moment M is pointing and moving with the speed v is in the X-direction. A small closed circular conducting loop of radius a is placed in the Y-Z plane with its centre at $x = 0$, and its axis coinciding with the X-axis. Find the force opposing the motion of the magnet, if the resistance of the loop is R. Assume that the distance x of the magnet from the centre of the loop is much greater than a.

Solution

The varying magnetic field due to magnetic dipole will produce induced current in the coil. Due to induced current in circular conducting loop, it will also behave like a small bar magnet. This bar magnet will produce a force opposing the motion of the magnet. The situation is shown in figure-5.73.

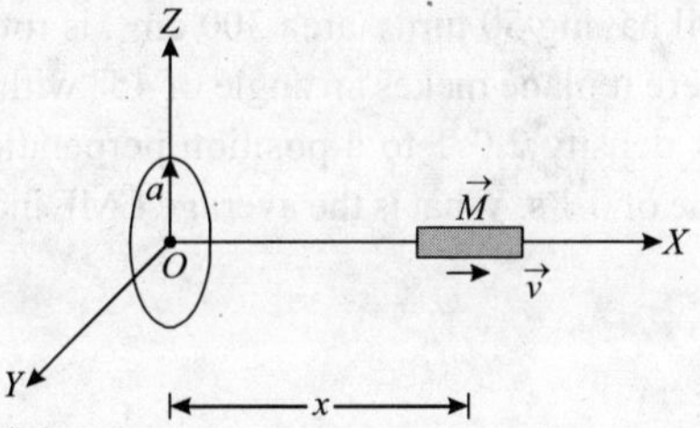

Figure 5.73

The magnetic field at the centre O of the coil due to bar magnet is given as

$$B = \frac{\mu_0}{4\pi}\times\frac{2M}{x^3}$$

The magnetic flux through the loop due to bar magnet is given as

$$\phi = \frac{\mu_0}{4\pi}\times\frac{2M}{x^3}\times(\pi a^2)$$

Induced EMF induced in circular loop is given as

$$e = -\frac{d\phi}{dt} = -\frac{d}{dt}\left[\frac{\mu_0}{4\pi}\times\frac{2M}{x^3}\times(\pi a^2)\right]$$

$$\Rightarrow \quad e = -\frac{\mu_0 Ma^2}{2}\left(\frac{-3}{x^4}\times\frac{dx}{dt}\right)$$

$$\Rightarrow \quad e = \frac{3\mu_0 Ma^2 v}{2x^4} \text{ where } v = \frac{dx}{dt}$$

Induced current in the circular loop is given as

$$i = \frac{e}{R} = \frac{3\mu_0 Ma^2 v}{2x^4 R}$$

If M_{coil} be the magnetic moment of the coil. Then we have

$$M_{coil} = i \times A = \frac{3\mu_0 M a^2 v}{2x^4 R} \times \pi a^2$$

$$\Rightarrow \quad M_{coil} = \frac{3\pi\mu_0 M a^4 v}{2x^4 R}$$

Now, opposing force on bar magnet is given as

$$F = M.\frac{dB}{dx} = \frac{\mu_0}{4\pi} \times \frac{6MM_{coil}}{x^4}$$

$$\Rightarrow \quad F = \frac{\mu_0}{4\pi}\frac{6M}{x^4}\left[\frac{3\pi\mu_0 M a^4 v}{2x^4 R}\right]$$

$$\Rightarrow \quad F = \frac{9\mu_0^2 M^2 a^4 v}{4Rx^8}$$

Illustrative Example 5.22

A closed coil having 50 turns, area 300 cm^2, is rotated from a position where it plane makes an angle of 45° with a magnetic field of flux density 2.0 T to a position perpendicular to the field in a time of 0.1 s. What is the average EMF induced in the coil?

Solution

Initially the flux linked with each turn of the coil is given as

$$\phi = \vec{B} \cdot \vec{A} = BA \cos\theta = BA \cos 45°$$

Substituting the values, we get

$$\phi = 2.0 \times 300 \times 10^4 \times 0.7071$$

$$\Rightarrow \quad \phi = 4.24 \times 10^{-2} \text{ Wb}$$

Finally flux linked with each turn of the coil is given as

$$\phi' = BA \cos 0° = BA$$

$$\Rightarrow \quad \phi' = 2.0 \times 300 \times 10^{-4} = 6.0 \times 10^{-2} \text{ Wb}$$

Change in flux in this process is given as

$$\Delta\phi = \phi' - \phi$$

$$\Rightarrow \quad \Delta\phi = (6.0 \times 10^{-2}) - 4.24 \times 10^{-2}$$

$$\Rightarrow \quad \Delta\phi = 1.76 \times 10^{-2} \text{ Wb}$$

This change is carried out in 0.1 s. The magnitude of the average EMF induced in the coil is given as

$$e = N\frac{d(\phi' - \phi)}{dt} = 50 \times \frac{1.76 \times 10^{-5}}{0.1}$$

$$\Rightarrow \quad e = 8.8 \text{ V}$$

Illustrative Example 5.23

A long solenoid has n turns per unit length, radius R and carries a current I is kept in gravity free region. From its axis at a distance twice that of its radius a charge $+q$ and mass m is placed. If the current in solenoid is suddenly switched off, find the velocity attained by the charge.

Solution

Magnetic induction inside the solenoid is given as

$$B_i = \mu_0 n I$$

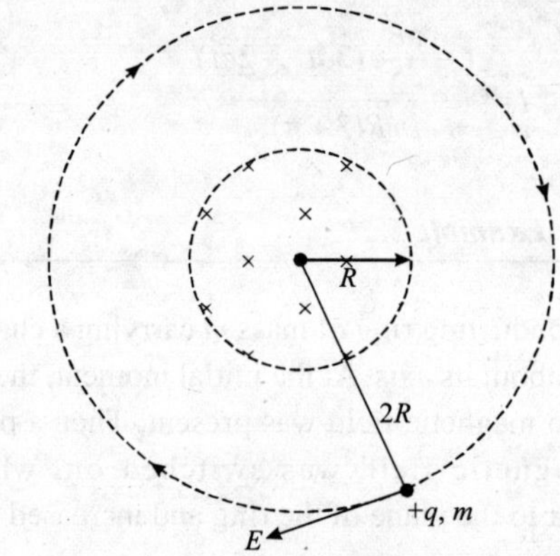

Figure 5.74

If the duration in which field drops to zero after switching off then electric field induced at a distance x outside in this duration δt is given as

$$E = \frac{1}{2}\frac{R^2}{x} \cdot \frac{dB}{dt} = \frac{R}{4} \cdot \frac{(\mu_0 NI - 0)}{\delta t}$$

Due to the induced electric field, impulse on the charge $+q$ in this duration is given as

$$J = qE\delta t = mv$$

$$\Rightarrow \quad v = \frac{qE\delta t}{m}$$

$$\Rightarrow \quad v = \frac{q}{m}\left(\frac{\mu_0 nIR}{4}\right) = \frac{\mu_0 nIRq}{4m}$$

Web Reference at www.physicsgalaxy.com

Age Group - Grade 11 & 12 | Age 17-19 Years

Section - Magnetic Effects

Topic - Electromagnetic Induction

Module Number - 20 to 34

Practice Exercise 5.2

(i) A magnetic flux through a stationary loop with a resistance R varies during the time interval τ as $\phi = a\,t(\tau - t)$. Find the amount of heat generated in the loop during that time. The inductance of the loop is to be neglected.

[$\dfrac{a^2\tau^3}{3R}$]

(ii) A long solenoid having 1000 turns per cm carries an alternating current of peak value 1 A. A search coil having a cross-sectional area of 1×10^{-4} m^2 and 20 turns is kept in the solenoid so that its plane is perpendicular to the axis of the solenoid. The search coil registers a peak voltage of 2.5×10^{-2} V. Find the frequency of the current in the solenoid.

[15.8 s^{-1}]

(iii) Two infinite long straight parallel wires A and B are separated by 0.1 m distance and carry equal currents in opposite directions. A square loop of wire C of side 0.1 m lies in the plane of A and B. The loop of wire C is kept parallel to both A and B at a distance of 0.1 m from the nearest wire. Calculate the EMF induced in the loop C while the currents in A and B are increasing at the rate of 10^3 A/s. Also indicate the direction of current in the loop C.

[$2 \times 10^{-5} \ln\left(\dfrac{4}{3}\right)$ volt, clockwise]

(iv) A flat circular coil of 200 turns of diameter 25 cm is laid on a horizontal table and connected to a ballistic galvanometer. The complete circuit is having resistance of 800 Ω. When the coil is quickly turned over, the spot of light swings to a maximum reading of 30 divisions. When a 0.1 μF capacitor charged to 6 V is discharged through the same ballistic galvanometer, a maximum reading of 20 divisions is obtained. Calculate the vertical component of the earth's magnetic induction.

[0.37×10^{-4} T]

(v) A rectangular frame $ABCD$ made of a uniform metal wire has a straight connection between E and F made of the same wire as shown in figure-5.75. $AEFD$ is a square of side 1 m and $EB = FC = 0.5$ m. The entire circuit is placed in a steadily increasing uniform magnetic field directed into the plane of the paper and normal to it. The rate of change of magnetic field is 1 T/s. The resistance per unit length of the wire is 1 Ω/m. Find the magnitudes and directions of the currents in the segment AE, BE and EF.

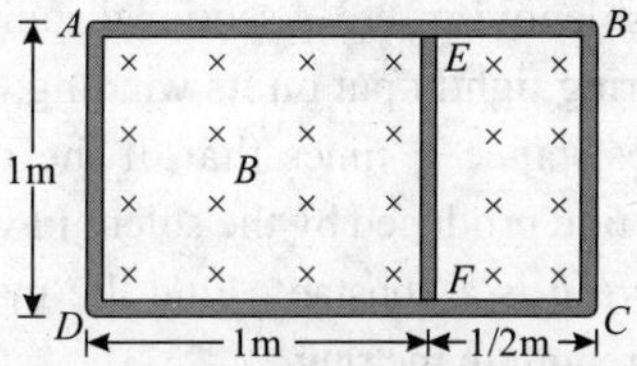

Figure 5.75

[$\dfrac{3}{11}$ A, $\dfrac{3}{11}$ A, $\dfrac{1}{22}$ A]

(vi) In a long straight solenoid with cross-sectional radius a and number of turns per unit length n a current varies with a constant velocity I ampere per second. Find the magnitude of the induced electric field strength as a function of the distance r from the solenoid axis. Draw the approximate plot of this function.

[For $r < a$, $\dfrac{1}{2} r\mu_0 nI$ and for $r > a$, $\dfrac{1}{2}\dfrac{a^2\mu_0 nI}{r}$]

(vii) A thin non-conducting ring of mass m radius a carrying a charge q rotates freely about its own axis which is vertical. At the initial moment, the ring was at rest and no magnetic field was present. At instant $t = 0$, a uniform magnetic field is switched on which is vertically downwards and increases with time according to the law $B = B_0 t$. Neglecting magnetism induced due to rotational motion of the ring, calculate

(a) The angular acceleration of the ring and its direction of rotation as seen from above.

(b) Power developed by the forces acting on the ring as function of time.

[(a) $\dfrac{B_0 q}{2m}$ (b) $\dfrac{q^2 B_0^2 a^2 t}{4m}$]

(viii) In the middle of a long solenoid, there is a coaxial ring of square cross-section, made of conducting material with resistivity ρ. The thickness of the ring is equal to h, its inside and outside radii are equal to a and b respectively. Find the current induced in the ring if the magnetic induction produced by the solenoid varies with time as $B = \beta t$, where β is a constant.

[$\dfrac{h\beta}{4\rho}(b^2 - a^2)$]

(ix) A long solenoid of diameter 0.1 m has 2×10^4 turns per meter. At the centre of the solenoid a 100 turn coil of radius 0.01 m is placed with its axis coinciding with the solenoid axis. The current in the solenoid is decreased at a constant rate from + 2A to – 2A in 0.05 s. Find the EMF induced in the coil. Also find the total charge flowing through the coil during this time if the resistance of the coil is 10 π^2 Ω.

[$6.4\ \pi^2 \times 10^{-3}$ V, 32 μC]

(x) A long solenoid of cross-sectional radius a has a thin insulated wire ring tightly put on its winding; one-half of the ring has the resistance η times that of the other half. The magnetic induction produced by the solenoid varies with time as $B = bt$, where b is a constant. Find the magnitude of the electric field strength in the ring.

[$\frac{ab}{2}\left(\frac{\eta-1}{\eta+1}\right)$]

(xi) A magnetic field induction is changing in magnitude at a constant rate dB/dt. A given mass m of copper is drawn into a wire of radius a and formed into a loop of radius r is placed perpendicular to the field. Show that the induced current in the loop is given by

$$i = \frac{m}{4\pi\rho\delta}\frac{dB}{dt}$$

where ρ is the specific resistance and δ, the density of copper.

(xii) A long solenoid of cross-sectional area 5.0 cm^2 is wound with 25 turns of wire per centimeter. It is placed in the middle of a closely wrapped coil of 10 turns and radius 25 cm as shown in figure-5.76.

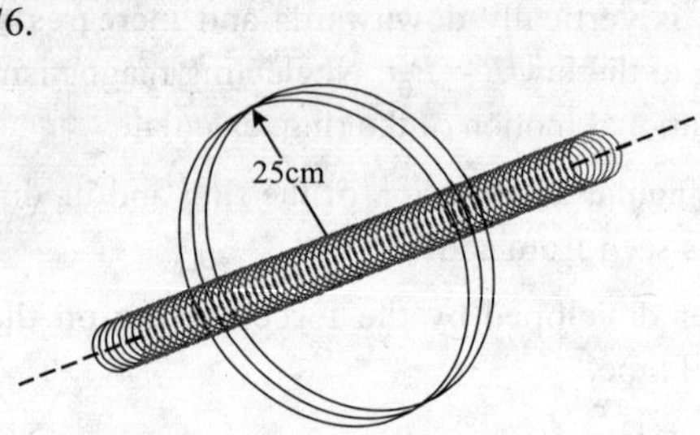

Figure 5.76

(a) What is the EMF induced in the coil when the current through the solenoid is decreasing at a rate – 0.20 A/s?
(b) What is the electric field induced in the coil?

[(a) 3.14×10^{-6} V; (b) 2.0×10^{-6} V/m]

(xiii) In a coil of resistance R, magnetic flux due to an external magnetic field varies with time as $\phi = k(C - t^2)$. Where k and C are positive constants. Find the total heat produced in coil in time $t = 0$ to $t = C$.

[$\frac{4k^2C^2}{3R}$]

(xiv) Figure-5.77 shows a fixed coil of N turns and radius a carrying a current I. At a distance x from its centre another small coaxial coil of radius $b (b << a)$ and resistance R is moving toward the first coil at a uniform speed v. Find the induced current in smaller coil.

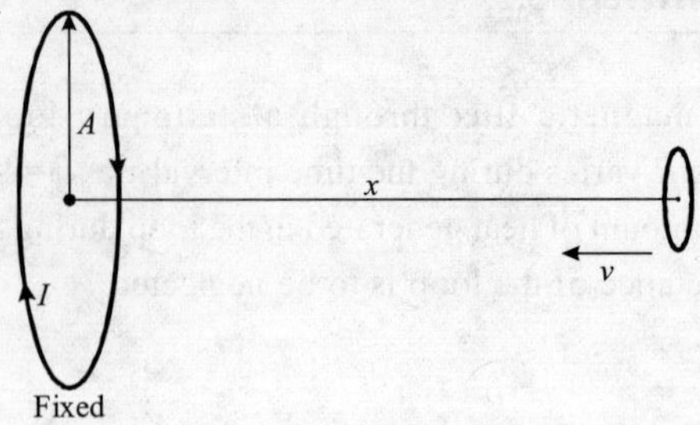

Figure 5.77

[$\frac{3\mu_0\pi NIa^2b^2vx}{2R(x^2+a^2)^{5/2}}$]

5.3 Self Induction

We've studied that current flows in a closed circuit only and a circuit may consist of one or more loops. Whenever current flowing through a conductor (part of a closed circuit) or a coil changes then magnetic field produced by that current also changes and it changes the magnetic flux through the loop or loops in that circuit of which the conductor or coil is a part.

Due to change in magnetic flux linked with the circuit of conductor or coil an EMF is induced in the coil which opposes the causes of induction i.e. the effects of induced EMF opposes the change in current. Thus every conductor or a coil when current flowing in it is changed due to the flux linked with the circuit of its own current, electromagnetic induction takes place which opposes the change in current in itself. This property of a conductor or coil by which it opposes change in current in itself is called '*Self Induction*'.

If in a coil or a conductor a current I is flowing then magnetic flux ϕ which is linked with the same coil or conductor is directly proportional to the current in it so we have

$$\phi \propto I$$

$$\Rightarrow \quad \phi = LI \qquad \ldots(5.54)$$

In above equation-(5.54), L is a proportionality constant which is called '*Coefficient of Self Induction*' for the coil or conductor and its associated circuit in which current I is flowing.

If current changes at a rate of dI/dt then EMF induced in the circuit of coil or conductor is given as

$$e = \left|\frac{d\phi}{dt}\right| = L\left|\frac{dI}{dt}\right| \qquad \ldots(5.55)$$

According to Lenz's law the direction of induced EMF is such that it opposes the causes of induction which is change in current thus signs of e and dI/dt are opposite in above equation which can be written without modulus as

$$e = -L\frac{dI}{dt} \quad \ldots(5.56)$$

Unit used for measurement of coefficient of Self Induction is '*Henery*' or '*H*' which is given as

$$1\text{H} = 1\ \text{V-s/A}$$

5.3.1 Understanding Self Induction

Consider two situations of a wire segment AB in a circuits as shown in figure-5.78. In first case shown in figure-5.78(a) its just a straight wire AB in which a current I flows when switch is closed. Here we consider that remaining part of circuit is far away from the wire and not affected by the magnetic induction produced by this wire AB. In second case shown in figure-5.78(b) in the middle of wire AB a loop is made by twisting the wire through which magnetic flux passes when current flows through wire AB.

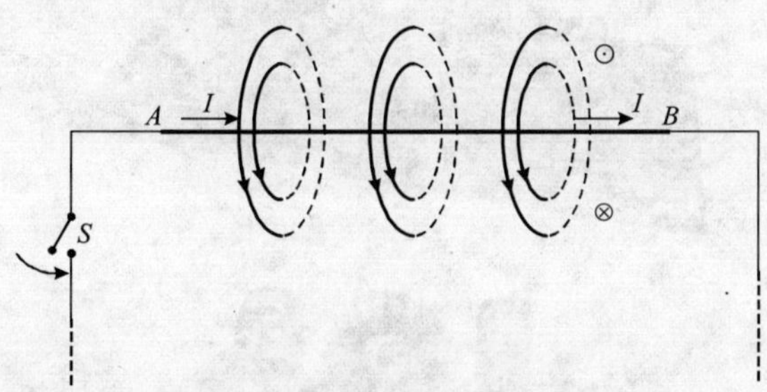

(a)

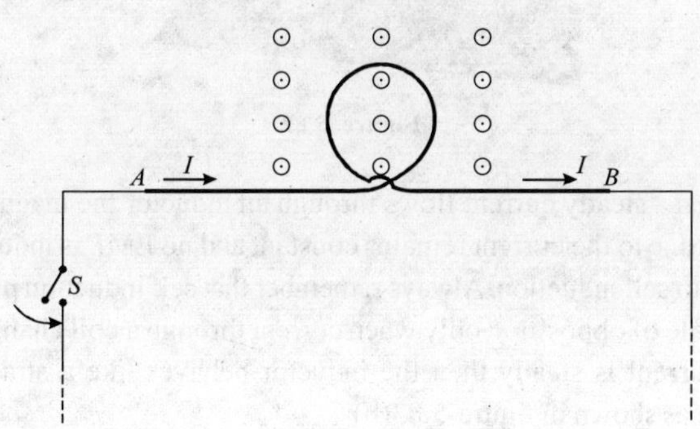

(b)
Figure 5.78

When the switch is closed in first case the current in wire quickly grows to a value I but in second case when switch is closed current grows but with this magnetic flux through the loop also increases which causes an EMF to be induced in the loop of which the direction is such that it opposes the change in flux. We've discussed that in time varying magnetic fields every element of the conductor or coil acts as an EMF thus the direction of such elemental EMFs in the loop are as shown in figure-5.79. Due to the induced EMF in the loop the growth of current in wire AB after closing the switch is opposed and it grows slowly as compared to the first case.

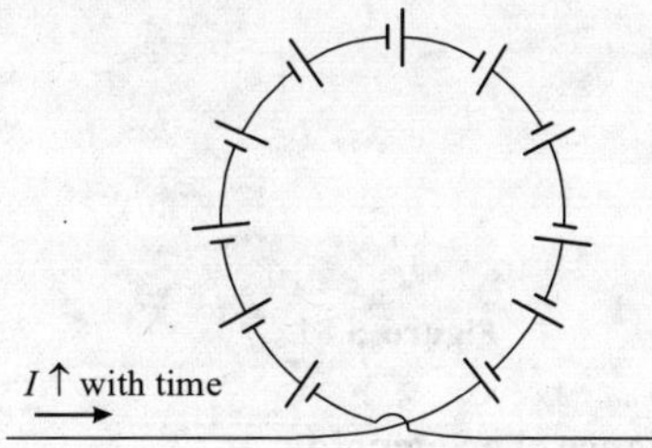

Figure 5.79

Figure-5.80(a) and (b) shows the time variation of current in wire AB in the above two cases. In second case the growth of current is slow due to the induced EMF in the loop while current increases.

(a)

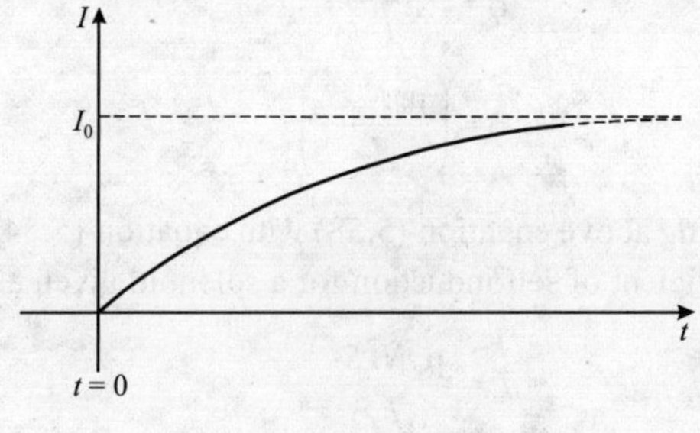

(b)
Figure 5.80

We can imagine a situation if instead of one we make three loops in wire AB as shown in figure-5.81. In this case EMF will be induced in all three loops which opposes the growth of current in wire AB hence opposition is more and growth of current will be even slower compared to the case with one loop in wire AB. Here we can say that with three loops self induction of wire AB is higher compared to the situation with one loop and that is more than the situation without a loop. With the above illustrations we've taken it is evident that self induction of a conductor or a coil depends upon the shape and size of the conductor.

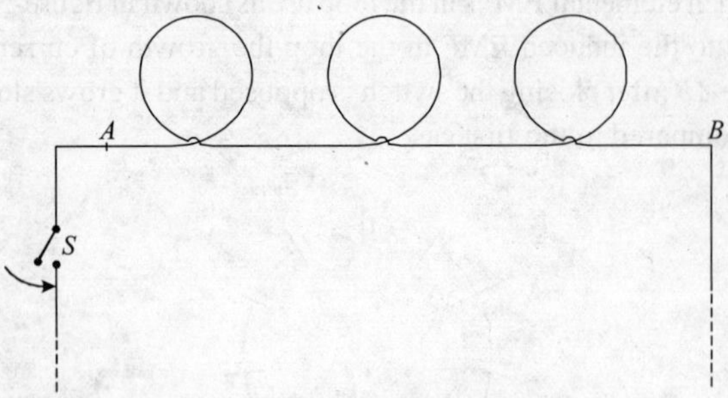

Figure 5.81

5.3.2 Self Inductance of a Solenoid

A solenoid is a coil with multiple turns wound on a cylindrical core. When a steady current I is flowing through a long solenoid of length l, total turns N with cross sectional area S, the magnetic induction inside is given as

$$B = \mu_0 nI = \mu_0\left(\frac{N}{l}\right)I$$

The magnetic flux through any cross section of the solenoid is given as

$$\phi_S = BS = \left(\frac{\mu_0 NI}{l}\right)S \qquad \ldots(5.57)$$

Magnetic flux linked with all the turns of the solenoid is given as

$$\phi = \phi_S \times N$$

$$\Rightarrow \qquad \phi = \frac{\mu_0 N^2 SI}{l}$$

$$\Rightarrow \qquad \phi = \left(\frac{\mu_0 N^2 S}{l}\right)I \qquad \ldots(5.58)$$

Comparing above equation-(5.58) with equation-(5.54) we get the coefficient of self induction for a solenoid given as

$$L = \frac{\mu_0 N^2 S}{l} \qquad \ldots(5.59)$$

Due to multiple turns connected in series in a solenoid when current flowing through it changes the EMF induced in it due to self induction is significant high compared to normal conductors and this property makes a solenoid very useful in different types of electrical circuits. When a solenoid is used in circuits it is called an '*Inductor*'.

Whenever current flowing through an inductor changes with time then the inductor behaves like a battery of EMF given as

$$e = L\frac{di}{dt}$$

In next article we'll discuss about the behaviour of an inductor when used in electrical circuits.

5.3.3 Behaviour of an Inductor in Electrical Circuits

For use of a solenoid in electrical circuits it is made in miniature form with close packed turns and cross sectional radius is kept very small compared to its length. Figure-5.82(a) shows a common commercial inductor which is used in electrical circuits. To save the space instead of keeping it as a straight solenoid the wire is wound in form of a toroid as shown. Figure-5.82(b) and (c) shows different types of inductors used in a circuit on a printed circuit board (PCB).

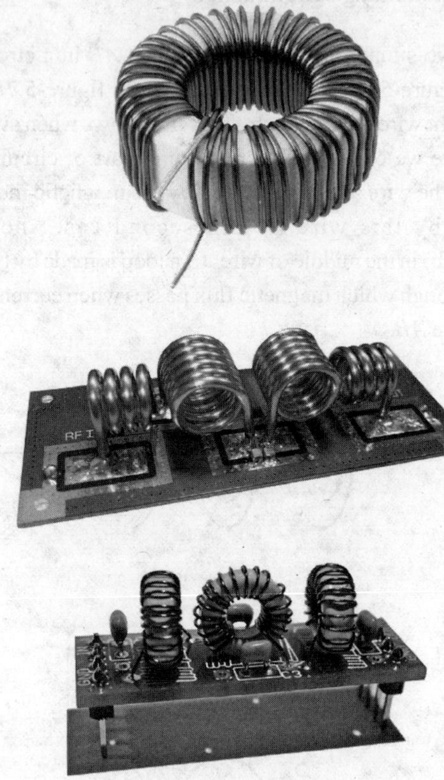

Figure 5.82

When a steady current flows through an inductor the magnetic flux due to the current remains constant and no EMF is induced due to self induction. Always remember that self induction plays its role of opposition only when current through a coil changes. If current is steady then the inductor behaves like a straight wire as shown in figure-5.83(b)

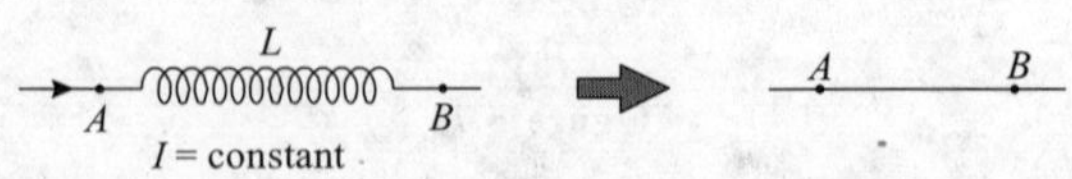

Figure 5.83

Consider the case shown in figure-5.84 when current flowing through the inductor increases with time. In this case due to self induction an EMF is induced in the inductor so as to oppose the change in current. In this case as current is increasing and flowing to the right then left end of inductor will have high potential and right end of inductor will be at low potential so that the EMF induced in the inductor tend to supply its current in direction opposite to the flowing current so that increase in current is opposed. In this situation the inductor behaves like an equivalent EMF across its terminals A and B as shown in figure-5.84(b).

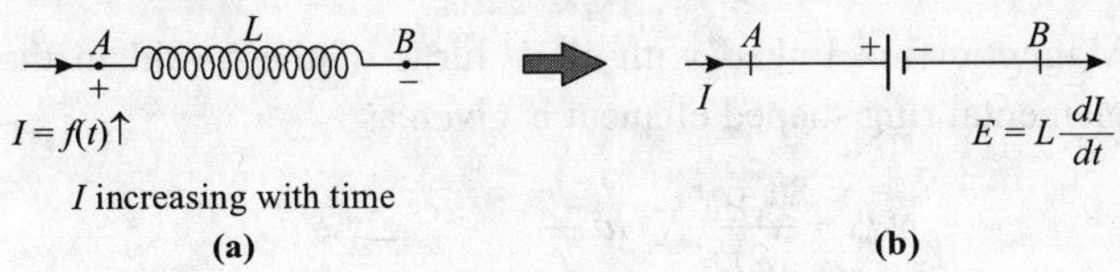

Figure 5.84

Figure-5.85 shows a case when current flowing through an inductor decreases with time. In this case due to self induction an EMF is induced so as to oppose the change in current. As current is decreasing, right end of inductor will be at higher potential and left end at lower potential so that the self induced EMF will tend to supply its current in the same direction as that of the existing current to oppose the decrement in current. In this situation the inductor behaves like an equivalent EMF across its terminals A and B as shown in figure-5.85(a) and (b).

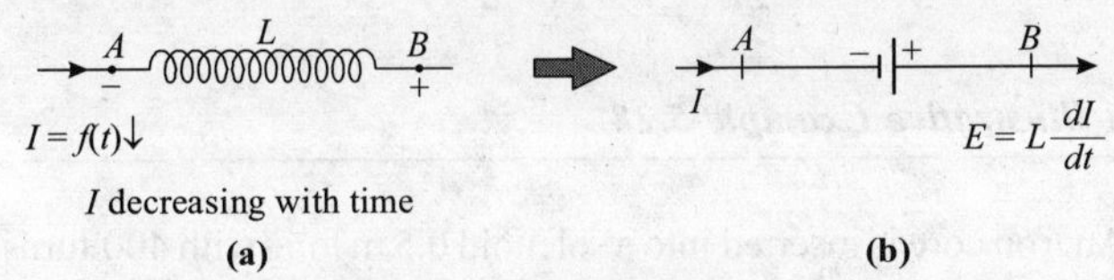

Figure 5.85

Illustrative Example 5.24

How many meters of a thin wire are required to manufacture a solenoid of length $l_0 = 100$ cm and inductance $L = 1.0$ mH, if the solenoid's cross-sectional diameter is considerably less than its length?

Solution

Self induction coefficient of a solenoid is given as

$$L = \frac{\mu_0 N^2 \pi r^2}{l_0}$$

Total length of wire is given as

$$l = N \times 2\pi r$$

$$\Rightarrow \quad L = \frac{\mu_0 l^2}{4\pi l_0}$$

$$\Rightarrow \quad l = \sqrt{\frac{4\pi l_0 L}{\mu_0}} = 0.1 \text{ km}$$

Illustrative Example 5.25

The inductor shown in figure-5.86 has inductance 0.54 H and carries a current in the direction shown that is decreasing at a uniform rate, $di/dt = -0.030$ A/s.

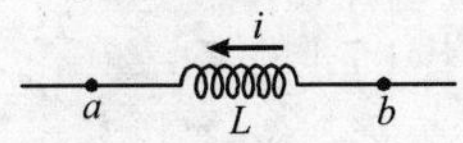

Figure 5.86

(a) Find the self-induced emf.

(b) Which end of the inductor, a or b, is at a higher potential?

Solution

(a) Self induced EMF is given as

$$e = L\left|\frac{di}{dt}\right| = 0.54 \times 0.03 \text{ V}$$

$$\Rightarrow \quad e = 1.62 \times 10^{-2} \text{ V}$$

(b) Current in the shown direction is decreasing. Hence induced EMF should produce current in the same direction. Hence induced battery polarity will be as shown in figure-5.87 below.

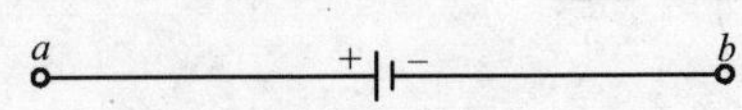

Figure 5.87

So we have

$$V_a > V_b$$

Illustrative Example 5.26

Calculate the inductance of a unit length of a double tape line if the tapes are separated by a distance h which is considerably less than their width b. Current flows in the two sheets of the tape line in opposite direction as shown in figure-5.88. Such a tapeline is used as connecting wires to industrial appliances where additional inductance is required for supply of current.

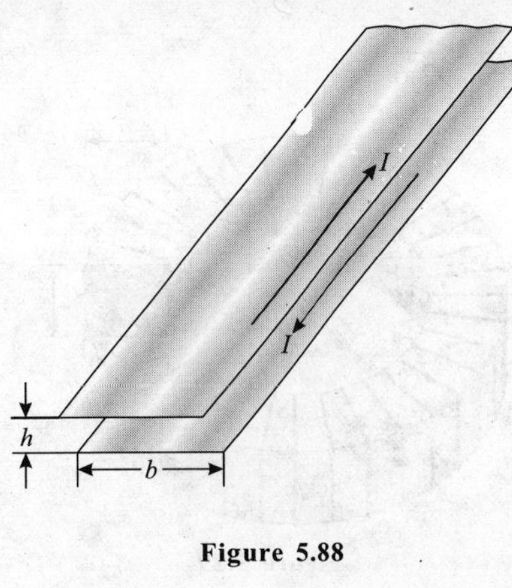

Figure 5.88

Solution

The current per unit length in the width of the sheets of tape line is I/b due to which each sheet of the line produces a magnetic induction between the sheets which is given as

$$B=\frac{1}{2}\mu_0\left(\frac{I}{b}\right)$$

In between the sheets of line the total magnetic induction due to both the sheets is given as

$$B=\frac{\mu_0 I}{b}$$

The magnetic flux passing through the region between the two sheets of tape line of length l is given as

$$\phi=\frac{\mu_0 I}{b}lh$$

$$\Rightarrow \qquad \frac{\phi}{I}=\frac{\mu_0}{b}lh$$

If self inductance of the tape line is L then we have

$$\Rightarrow \qquad L=\frac{\phi}{I}=\frac{\mu_0}{b}lh$$

Self inductance per unit length of the line is given as

$$\frac{L}{l}=\frac{\mu_0 h}{b}$$

Illustrative Example 5.27

Calculate the inductance of a toroid whose inside radius is equal to b and cross-section has the form of a small square of side a. The solenoid winding consists of N turns. The space inside the solenoid is filled with uniform paramagnetic material having relative permeability μ_r.

Solution

If we consider an elemental ring of radius r and width dr as shown in the figure-5.89. The number of turns per unit length in this ring shaped element is given as

$$n=\frac{N}{2\pi r}$$

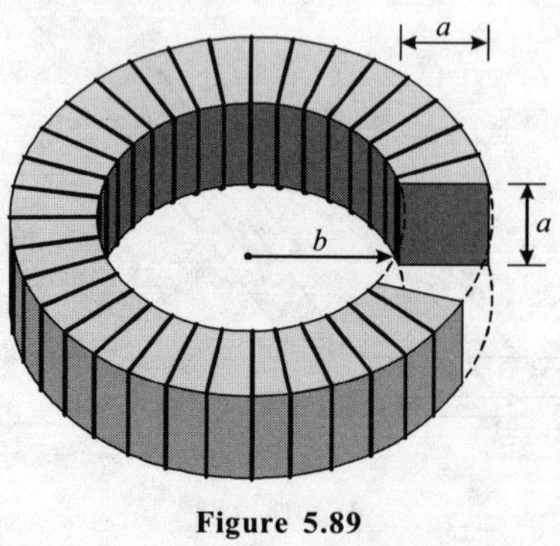

Figure 5.89

The magnetic induction inside the elemental toroid is given as

$$B=\mu_r\mu_0 nI=\frac{\mu_r\mu_0 NI}{2\pi r}$$

The magnetic flux through a cross section of the elemental ring shaped toroid is given as

$$d\phi=\frac{\mu_r\mu_0 NI}{2\pi r}\times adr$$

Magnetic flux linked with all N turns of the toroid in the elemental ring shaped element is given as

$$Nd\phi=\frac{\mu_r\mu_0}{2\pi}N^2 Ia\frac{dr}{r}$$

Total magnetic flux linked with the given toroid is given as

$$\phi=\int d\phi=\frac{\mu_r\mu_0}{2\pi}N^2 Ia\int_b^{b+a}\frac{dr}{r}$$

$$\Rightarrow \qquad \phi=\frac{\mu_r\mu_0}{2\pi}N^2 Ia\ln\left(\frac{b+a}{a}\right)$$

Self inductance of the toroid is given as

$$L=\frac{\phi}{I}$$

$$\Rightarrow \qquad L=\frac{\mu_r\mu_0}{2\pi}N^2 a\ln\left(\frac{b+a}{a}\right)$$

Illustrative Example 5.28

An iron core is inserted into a solenoid 0.5 m long with 400 turns per unit length. The area of cross-section of the solenoid is 0.001 m^2. (a) Find the relative permeability of the core when a current of 5 A flows through the solenoid winding. Under these conditions, the magnetic flux through the cross-section of the solenoid is 1.6×10^{-3} Wb. (b) Find the inductance of the solenoid under these conditions.

Solution

We know that the magnetic induction on the axis of a solenoid is given by

$$B=\mu\left(\frac{\mu_0}{4\pi}\right)4\pi ni \qquad \ldots(5.60)$$

where μ is the permeability of the medium.

(a) As magnetic flux $\phi=BA$ we use $B=\phi/A$ which gives

$$B=\frac{1.6\times10^{-3}}{10^{-3}}=1.6\,\text{T}$$

Substituting the values in equation-(5.60), we get

$$1.6=\mu(10^{-7})\times4\pi\times400\times5$$

$$\Rightarrow \qquad \mu\cong637$$

(b) Total number of turns in the solenoid are given as

$$N = n \times l = 400 \times 0.5 = 200$$

Total magnetic flux linked to the solenoid is given as

$$\phi_T = N \times \phi = 200 \times 1.6 \times 10^{-3} = 0.32 \text{ Wb}$$

$$\Rightarrow \quad L = \frac{N\phi}{i} = \frac{0.35}{5} = 0.064 \text{ H} = 64 \text{ mH}$$

5.4 *Growth of Current in an Inductor*

In previous articles we've discussed that an inductor behaves like an equivalent battery when current through it changes. Due to the self induction of an inductor it opposes the change in current in itself and depending upon the value of coefficient of self induction of the inductor the opposition to change in external current is different. In next article we will discuss and analyze the growth of current in an inductor when it is connected across a battery.

5.4.1 Growth of Current in an Inductor Connected Across a Battery

Figure-5.90(a) shows an inductor of self induction coefficient L is connected across an ideal battery of emf E. When the switch is closed a current starts growing in circuit which is opposed by the induced EMF in inductor as shown in figure-5.90(b).

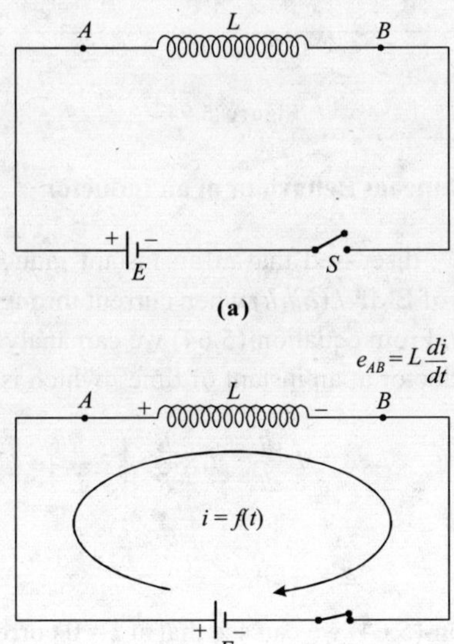

Figure 5.90

In figure-5.90(b) we can see that the inductor is connected across the battery so potential difference of battery is always equal to the induced EMF across the inductor. If at time $t = 0$ switch is closed and current in circuit at time $t = t$ is i then we have

$$E = L\frac{di}{dt}$$

$$\Rightarrow \quad Ldi = Edt$$

$$\Rightarrow \quad \int_0^i Ldi = \int_0^t Edt$$

$$\Rightarrow \quad L[i]_0^i = E[t]_0^t$$

$$\Rightarrow \quad Li = Et$$

$$\Rightarrow \quad i = \frac{Et}{L} \qquad \ldots(5.61)$$

Above expression in equation-(5.61) shows that current in circuit linearly grows with time and variation curve is shown in figure-5.91.

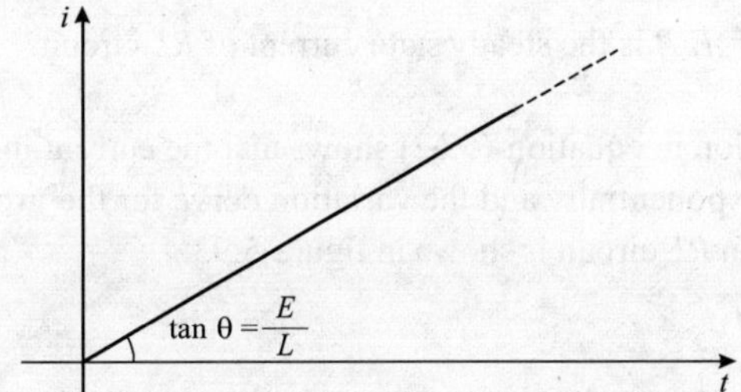

Figure 5.91

5.4.2 Growth of Current in RL Circuit across a battery

Figure-5.92 shows a circuit with an inductor of inductance L connected in series with a resistor of resistance R across a battery of EMF E. In this circuit when the switch is closed at $t = 0$, a current starts flowing and if at $t = t$ current flowing in circuit is considered to be i.

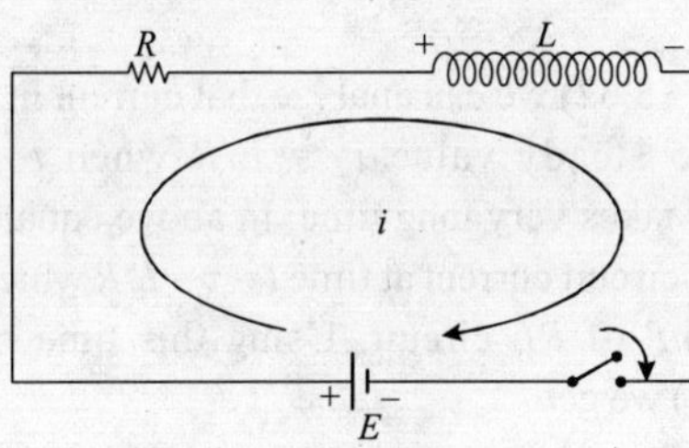

Figure 5.92

We write KVL equation for the above loop as

$$+E - iR - L\frac{di}{dt} = 0$$

$$\Rightarrow \quad \frac{di}{dt} = \frac{E - iR}{L}$$

$$\Rightarrow \quad \int_0^i \frac{di}{E - iR} = \int_0^t \frac{dt}{L}$$

$$\Rightarrow \quad -\frac{1}{R}[\ln(E - iR)]_0^i = \frac{1}{L}[t]_0^t$$

$$\Rightarrow \qquad [\ln(E-iR)-\ln(E)] = -\frac{R}{L}[t-0]$$

$$\Rightarrow \qquad \ln\left(\frac{E-iR}{E}\right) = -\frac{Rt}{L}$$

$$\Rightarrow \qquad \frac{E-iR}{E} = e^{-\frac{Rt}{L}}$$

$$\Rightarrow \qquad i = \frac{E}{R}\left(1-e^{-\frac{Rt}{L}}\right) \qquad \dots(5.62)$$

$$\Rightarrow \qquad i = i_S\left(1-e^{-\frac{Rt}{L}}\right) \qquad \dots(5.63)$$

Here $i_S = E/R$ is the steady state current of RL circuit.

Expression in equation-(5.62) shows that the current in circuit grows exponentially and the variation curve for the growth of current in RL circuit is shown in figure-5.93.

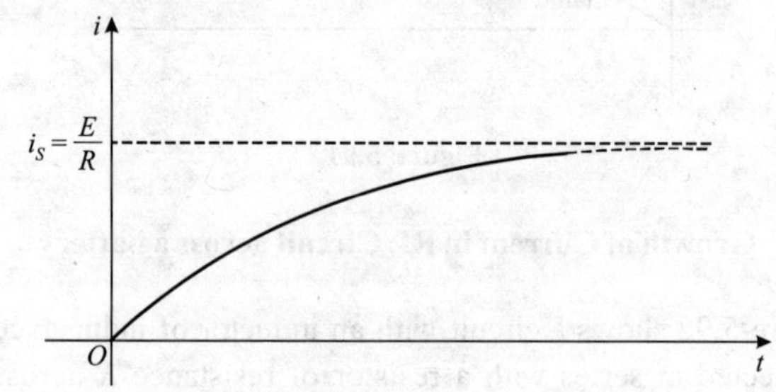

Figure 5.93

5.4.3 Time Constant of RL Circuit

From equation-(5.62) we can analyze that current in RL circuit approaches to steady value $i_S = E/R$ when $t \to \infty$ and theoretically it takes very long time. In above equation-(5.62) we analyze the circuit current at time $t = \tau = L/R$ which is called '*Time Constant*' of RL circuit. Using this time $t = L/R$ in equation-(5.62) we get

$$i = \frac{E}{R}(1-e^{-1})$$

$$\Rightarrow \qquad i = \frac{E}{R}\left(1-\frac{1}{e}\right)$$

$$\Rightarrow \qquad i = \frac{E}{R}\left(1-\frac{1}{2.718}\right)$$

$$\Rightarrow \qquad i = \frac{E}{R}(1-0.37)$$

$$\Rightarrow \qquad i = 0.63\frac{E}{R} \qquad \dots(5.64)$$

From equation-(5.64) we can state that time constant of a RL circuit is that time duration in which current in RL circuit grows to 63% of the steady state value. If in equation-(5.62) we analyze the current after five times the time constant then we have

$$i = \frac{E}{R}(1-e^{-5})$$

$$\Rightarrow \qquad i = 0.993\frac{E}{R} \qquad \dots(5.65)$$

From equation-(5.65) it can be seen that in duration equal to five times of time constant current attains 99.3% of steady state value and remaining 0.7% will be achieved theoretically in infinite time which can be ignored practically. Thus for analysis of RL circuits we consider that in approximately five times the time constant duration steady state arrives practically so transient period of growth of current in a RL circuit is approximately equal to $5L/R$. The growth of current is shown in the plot of current vs time in figure-5.94. In the below graph transient period and steady state are also mentioned.

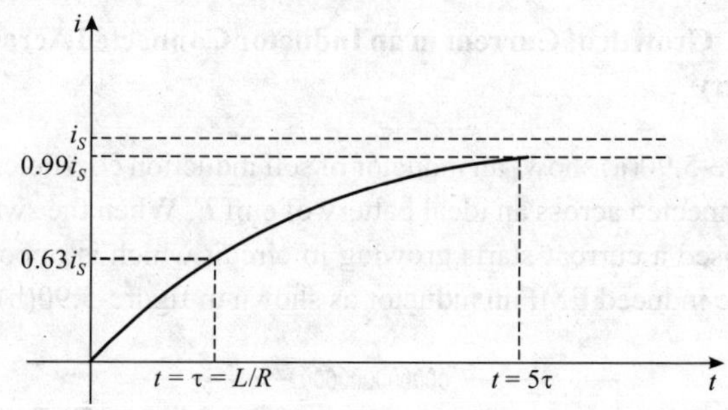

Figure 5.94

5.4.4 Instantaneous Behaviour of an Inductor

We've already discussed that at an instant inductor behaves like a battery of EMF $L(di/dt)$ when current through it changes at a rate di/dt. From equation-(5.64) we can analysis the EMF across the inductor at an instant of time t which is given as

$$e = L\frac{di}{dt} = L\times\frac{E}{R}\times\left(-\frac{R}{L}\right)e^{-\frac{Rt}{L}}$$

$$\Rightarrow \qquad e = -Ee^{-\frac{Rt}{L}} \qquad \dots(5.66)$$

From equation-(5.64) we can see that at $t = 0$ current $i = 0$ and from equation-(5.62) at $t = 0$ the EMF induced in inductor is $e = -E$ that means the EMF in inductor is in opposition to battery EMF and it is equal so current in circuit is zero at $t = 0$.

In other words we can state that just after closing the switch at $t = 0$ inductor in circuit behaves like open circuit through which no current can pass as shown in figure-5.95(a). After a long time when steady state is arrived we know that current becomes E/R and becomes steady due to which EMF induced in the inductor becomes zero so we can state that in steady state an inductor behaves like a straight wire or short circuit as shown in figure-5.95(b).

At $t = 0+$

At $t \to \infty$

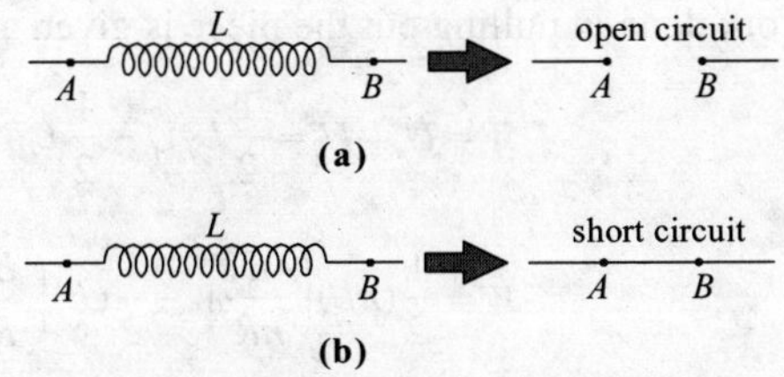

Figure 5.95

5.4.5 Transient Analysis of Advance RL Circuits

We've already discussed in the topic of capacitance that in case of a circuit if multiple resistors and batteries are present in a circuit then across the capacitor we can replace the remaining circuit by Thevenin's equivalent circuit and then we can use the results derived for simple *RC* circuit. In the same way for *RL* circuits also if multiple resistances and batteries are present then we can replace the circuit across inductor by a single equivalent battery and its internal resistance and use the results of simple *RL* circuit. Will analyze such cases in upcoming illustrations.

Illustrative Example 5.29

A solenoid has an inductance of 10 H and a resistance of 2 Ω. It is connected to a 10 V battery. How long will it take for the magnetic energy to reach one fourth of its maximum value?

Solution

(a) The *L-R* circuit is shown in figure-5.96 Let at a time instant *t*, after shorting of switch, current through the circuit is *i*.

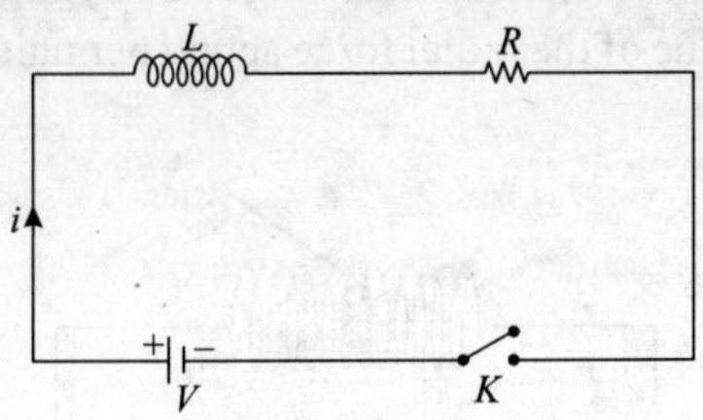

Figure 5.96

For the given loop of circuit current as a function of time is given as

$$i = \frac{V}{R}(1 - e^{-Rt/L}) = i_0(1 - e^{-Rt/L}) \qquad \ldots(5.67)$$

Where $i_0 = V/R$ is the maximum current in circuit. The magnetic energy stored in inductor is given as

$$U = \frac{1}{2}Li^2$$

Given that at an instant the magnetic energy attains one fourth of the maximum gives

$$\frac{1}{2}Li^2 = \frac{1}{4}\left(\frac{1}{2}Li_0^2\right)$$

$$\Rightarrow \qquad i = \frac{i_0}{2} = \frac{V}{2R}$$

Substituting the values in equation-(5.67), we get

$$\frac{V}{2R} = \frac{V}{R}(1 - e^{-2t/10}) \text{ or } 0.5 = 1 - e^{-0.2t}$$

or $\quad e^{-0.2t} = 0.5$ which gives $t = 3.478$ s

Illustrative Example 5.30

Calculate the time constant τ of a straight solenoid of length *l* having a single layer winding of copper wire whose total mass is equal to *m*. The cross-sectional diameter of the solenoid is assumed to be considerably less than its length. Take resistivity of copper to be ρ and density is equal to δ.

Solution

Time constant of *LR* circuit is given as

$$\tau = \frac{L}{R}$$

Inductance of a solenoid is given as

$$L = \frac{\mu_0 N^2 A}{l} = \frac{\mu_0 N^2}{l} \times \pi r^2$$

If l_0 is the total length of wire making the solenoid then we can rewrite above expression as

$$L = \frac{\mu_0}{4\pi}\frac{(2\pi N r)^2}{l} = \frac{\mu_0}{4\pi}\frac{l_0^2}{l}$$

The resistance of the wire is given as

$$R = \frac{\rho l_0}{A} = \frac{\rho l_0^2}{A l_0} = \frac{\rho l_0^2}{V} = \frac{\rho l_0^2}{(m/\delta)}$$

$$\Rightarrow \qquad R = \frac{\delta \rho l_0^2}{m}$$

$$\Rightarrow \qquad l_0^2 = \frac{mR}{\sigma\rho}$$

$$\Rightarrow \qquad L = \frac{\mu_0}{4\pi}\frac{mR}{\sigma\rho l}$$

$$\Rightarrow \qquad \tau = \frac{L}{R} = \frac{\mu_0 m}{4\pi\delta\rho l}$$

Illustrative Example 5.31

A battery of EMF E and of negligible internal resistance is connected in an LR circuit as shown in figure-97. The inductor has a piece of soft iron inside it. When steady state is reached the piece of soft iron is abruptly pulled out suddenly so that the inductance of the inductor decreases to nL with $n < 1$ with battery remaining connected. Find :

(a) Current as a function of time if at $t = 0$ is the instant when the soft iron piece is pulled out.

(b) The work done in pulling out the piece.

(c) Thermal power generated in the circuit as a function of time.

(d) Power supplied by the battery as a function of time.

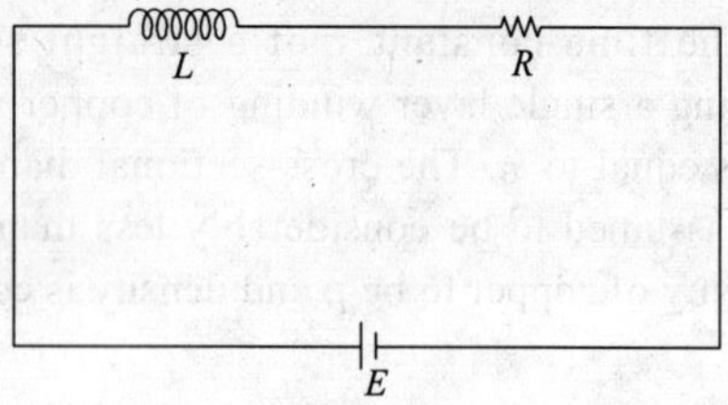

Figure 5.97

Solution

(a) At $t = 0$, steady state current in the circuit is $i_0 = E/R$. Suddenly L reduces to nL $(n < 1)$, so to keep the flux constant, the current in the circuit at time $t = 0$ will increase to $\frac{i_0}{n} = \frac{E}{nR}$.
If i be the current at time t in circuit as shown in figure-5.98 then by using Kirchhoff's law in the loop we have,

$$E - nL\left(\frac{di}{dt}\right) - iR = 0$$

$$\Rightarrow \qquad \frac{di}{E - iR} = \frac{1}{nL}dt$$

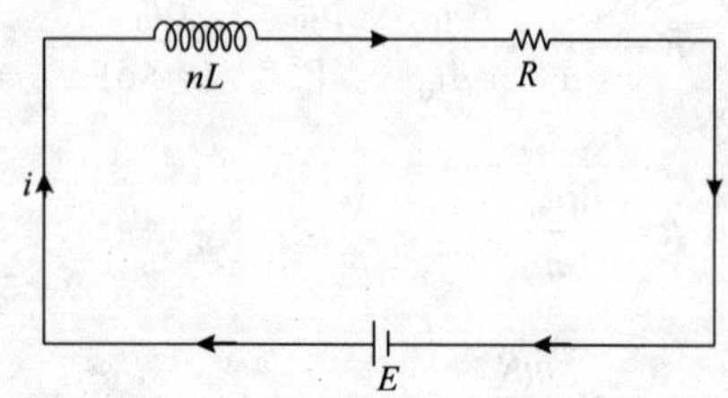

Figure 5.98

Integrating the above expression, gives

$$\int_{i_0/n}^{i} \frac{di}{E - iR} = \frac{1}{nL}\int_0^t dt$$

$$i = \frac{E}{R} - \frac{E}{R}\left(1 - \frac{1}{n}\right)e^{-Rt/nL}$$

(b) Work done in pulling out the piece is given as

$$W = U_f - U_i = \frac{1}{2}L_f i_f^2 - \frac{1}{2}L_i i_i^2$$

$$\Rightarrow \qquad W = \frac{1}{2}(nL)\left(\frac{E}{nR}\right)^2 - \frac{1}{2}(L)\left(\frac{E}{R}\right)^2$$

$$\Rightarrow \qquad W = \frac{1}{2}L\left(\frac{E}{R}\right)^2\left(\frac{1}{n} - 1\right)$$

$$\Rightarrow \qquad W = \frac{1}{2}L\left(\frac{E}{R}\right)^2\left(\frac{1-n}{n}\right)$$

(c) Thermal power generated in the circuit as a function of time is given as

$$P_1 = i^2R$$

Here, i the time function of current obtained in part (a).

(d) Power supplied by the battery as a function of time is,

$$P_2 = Ei$$

Here, i the time function of current obtained in part (a).

Illustrative Example 5.32

A thin wire ring of radius a and resistance r is located inside a long solenoid so that their axes coincide. The length of the solenoid is equal to l its cross-section radius to b. At a certain moment, the solenoid was connected to a source of constant voltage V. The total resistance of the circuit is equal to R. Assuming the inductance of the ring to be negligible, find the maximum value of the radial force acting per unit length of the ring.

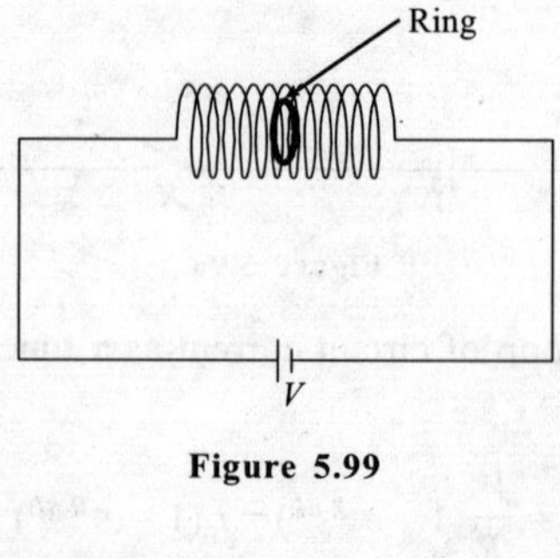

Figure 5.99

Solution

The inductance L of the solenoid is given as

$$L = \frac{\mu_0 N^2 A}{l} = \frac{\mu_0 (nl)^2(\pi b^2)}{l} = \mu_0 n^2 \pi b^2 l \quad \ldots(5.68)$$

The current through the solenoid varies with time as

$$i = \frac{V}{R}(1 - e^{-Rt/L})$$

Magnetic induction inside the solenoid varies with time as

$$B = \mu_0 ni$$

Magnetic flux passing through the ring is given as

$$\Rightarrow \quad \phi = B\pi a^2$$

$$\Rightarrow \quad \phi = \mu_0 ni\pi a^2$$

$$\Rightarrow \quad \phi = \frac{\mu_0 nV\pi a^2}{R}(1 - e^{-Rt/L})$$

EMF induced in the ring is given as

$$e = \frac{d\phi}{dt}$$

$$\Rightarrow \quad e = \frac{\mu_0 nV\pi a^2}{L} e^{-Rt/L}$$

Current induced in the ring is given as

$$i_R = \frac{e}{r} = \frac{\mu_0 nV\pi a^2}{rL} e^{-Rt/L}$$

Radial force per unit length on the ring circumference is given as

$$F_r = \frac{dF}{dl} = Bi_R$$

$$\Rightarrow \quad F_r = \mu_0 nI\left(\frac{\mu_0 nV\pi a^2}{rL} e^{-Rt/L}\right)$$

$$\Rightarrow \quad F_r = \left(\frac{\mu_0^2 n^2 \pi a^2 V}{rL} e^{-Rt/L}\right)\left(\frac{V}{R}(1 - e^{-Rt/L})\right)$$

$$\Rightarrow \quad F_r = \frac{\mu_0^2 n^2 \pi a^2 V^2}{rRL} e^{-Rt/L}(1 - e^{-Rt/L}) \quad \ldots(5.69)$$

Substituting the value of L from equation-(5.68) to equation-(5.69), we get

$$F_r = \frac{\mu_0 a^2 V^2}{rRb^2 l} e^{-Rt/L}(1 - e^{-Rt/L}) \quad \ldots(5.70)$$

In above equation we can see that at $t = 0$, $F_r = 0$ and also $F_r = 0$ at $t = \infty$. Thus at some intermediate time value of radial force per unit length is maximum for this we differentiate F_r with respect to time t and equate it to zero which gives the time at which this occurs and it is obtained as

$$e^{-Rt/L} = 1/2$$

Thus maximum value of F_r is given as

$$F_{max} = \frac{\mu_0 a^2 V^2}{4rRlb^2}$$

Illustrative Example 5.33

A section of an electrical circuit XY is shown in figure-5.100 which carries a current of 5 A which is decreasing at the rate of 10 A/s. Find the potential difference $V_y - V_x$.

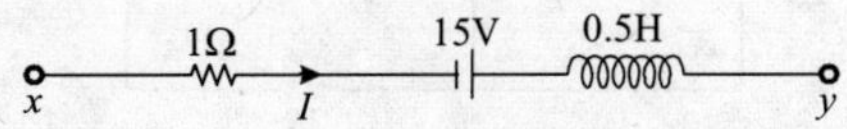

Figure 5.100

$$e = L\frac{di}{dt}$$

Solution

In the above circuit section as current is decreasing with time, the polarity of self induced EMF is shown in figure-5.101. In this branch of circuit we write equation of potential drop from point x to y which is given as

$$V_x - iR + E + L\frac{di}{dt} = V_y$$

$$\Rightarrow \quad V_x - 5 \times 1 + 15 + 0.5 \times 10 = V_y$$

$$\Rightarrow \quad V_y - V_x = 15\text{ V}$$

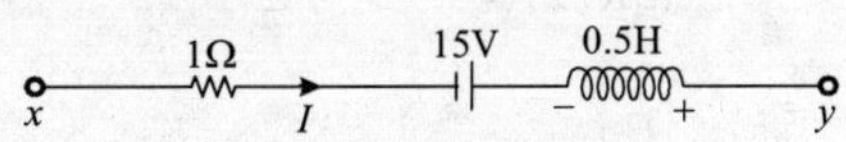

Figure 5.101

Illustrative Example 5.34

Figure-5.102 shows a RL circuit. If at $t = 0$ switch is closed, find the current in the inductor as a function of time.

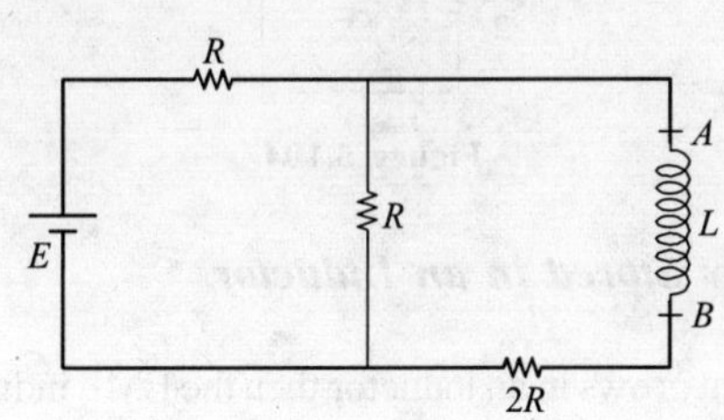

Figure 5.102

Solution

In the above circuit, we can remove inductor and calculate the Thevenin's equivalent battery across the terminals A and B as shown in figure-5.103. The internal resistance across terminals A and B can be calculated by shorting the battery which gives

$$r = 2R + \frac{R}{2} = \frac{5R}{2}$$

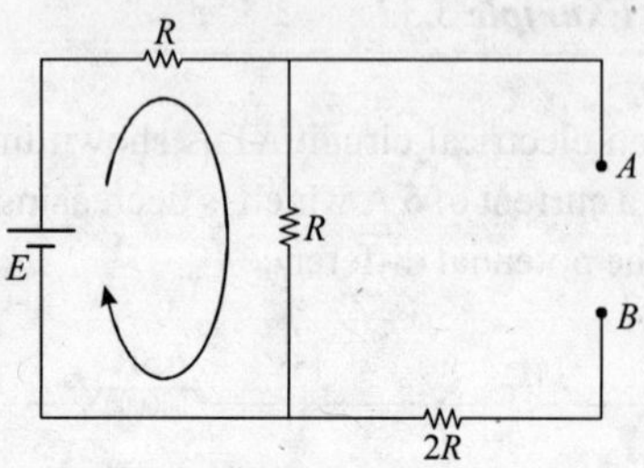

Figure 5.103

Due to removal of inductor right loop of circuit is now open and a current flows in the left loop which is given as

$$i=\frac{E}{2R}$$

The open circuit potential difference across terminals A and B is given as

$$V_{AB}=iR=\frac{E}{2}$$

Thus the reduced circuit for the given circuit is shown in figure-5.104. This circuit is now reduced to simple RL circuit and in this case the current as a function of time can be given as

$$i=\frac{(E/2)}{(5R/2)}\left(1-e^{-\frac{5Rt}{2L}}\right)$$

$$i=\frac{E}{5R}\left(1-e^{-\frac{5Rt}{2L}}\right)$$

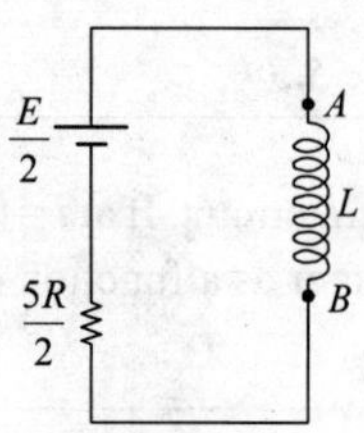

Figure 5.104

5.5 Energy Stored in an Inductor

When current grows in an inductor then the EMF induced across its terminals opposes the current flowing into it and the high potential of induced EMF is at that end of inductor from which the current is entering into it as shown in figure-5.105 and the inductor behaves like a battery as shown.

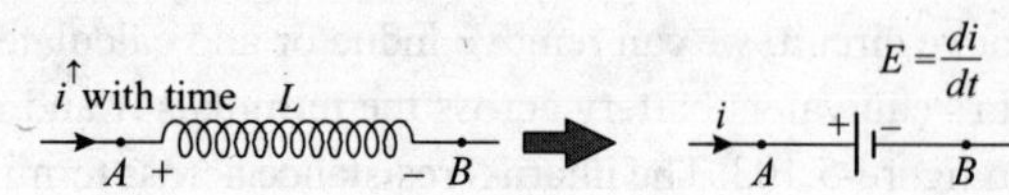

Figure 5.105

In the chapter of current electricity we've studied if current enters into a battery from its high potential end then power is absorbed by the battery and chemical energy of battery increases. Similarly in above case the EMF absorbs the power from the current flowing into it. As with current magnetic field increases in the inductor, the energy of magnetic field also increases. At any instant of time t the power absorbed by the inductor is given as

$$P=ei=\left(L\frac{di}{dt}\right)i \quad \text{...(5.71)}$$

In time dt, energy absorbed by the inductor is

$$dU=Pdt$$

$$\Rightarrow \quad dU=Lidi$$

When current in inductor increases from 0 to I, total energy absorbed upto this instant by the inductor is given as

$$U=\int dU=\int_0^I Lidi$$

$$\Rightarrow \quad U=L\left[\frac{i^2}{2}\right]_0^I$$

$$\Rightarrow \quad U=\frac{1}{2}LI^2 \quad \text{...(5.72)}$$

Above expression of energy stored in an inductor carrying a current I as given in equation-(5.72) is a standard result which can be used in different cases. Whenever in a given physical situation an inductor carrying a current I is given that means when this current was grown to I in the inductor that time this energy was stored by the inductor and it is maintained along with the current in it. This energy is actually stored in inductor in form of field energy of magnetic field within the volume of inductor which is an energy similar to the field energy of electric field we studied in the chapter of electrostatics. In next section same will be discussed in detail.

5.5.1 Magnetic Field Energy Density

In the chapter of electrostatics we discussed that in whole region wherever electric field is present there exist electric field energy of which the volume density is given as

$$u_e=\frac{1}{2}\epsilon_0E^2\ \text{J/m}^3$$

Similarly in region of magnetic field also there exist magnetic field energy which we've already discussed in article-4.10. The volume density of magnetic field energy in space is given as

$$u_m=\frac{B^2}{2\mu_0}\ \text{J/m}^3 \quad \text{...(5.73)}$$

5.5.2 Field Energy Stored in a Current Carrying Inductor

In an inductor of length l, cross sectional area S with N turns carrying a current I, the magnetic induction inside is given as

$$B = \mu_0\left(\frac{N}{l}\right)I$$

Total magnetic energy stored in the volume of inductor is given as

$$U = u_m \times Sl$$

$$\Rightarrow \quad U = \frac{B^2}{2\mu_0} \times Sl$$

$$\Rightarrow \quad U = \frac{Sl}{2\mu_0}\left(\frac{\mu_0 NI}{l}\right)^2$$

$$\Rightarrow \quad U = \frac{1}{2}\left(\frac{\mu_0 N^2 S}{l}\right)I^2$$

$$\Rightarrow \quad U = \frac{1}{2}LI^2 \quad \ldots(5.74)$$

Above equation-(5.74) is same as equation-(5.72) which verifies that the energy absorbed by the inductor during the time its current grows is stored in form of magnetic field energy in the volume of inductor.

When an inductor in which a current I_0 is flowing and it is suddenly cut from the circuit then the energy stored in it does not dissipate immediately as under ideal conditions it is considered to remain intact by magnetic polarization of molecules in the volume of inductor. This phenomenon of retention of magnetic field is called hysteresis about which we will discuss in magnetic properties of material later in this chapter. Such an isolated inductor which contains magnetic energy is called '*Active Inductor*' which is indicated by the direction of last current flowing in it as shown in figure-5.106. In this figure '*dot*' at one end of the inductor indicates the end which behaves like its north pole. This dot convention is used because on paper in two dimensional picture of inductor it is difficult to show the actual direction of current by which the magnetic field direction can be determined. Like in the below figure magnetic field inside solenoid exist from left to right.

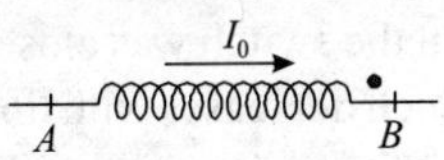

Figure 5.106

 # *Illustrative Example 5.35*

A solenoid of resistance 50 Ω and inductance 80 H are connected to a 200 V battery. How long will it take for the current to reach 50% of its final equilibrium value? Calculate the maximum energy stored in inductor.

Solution

The current i in RL circuit is given as

$$i = \frac{E}{R}(1 - e^{-Rt/L})$$

When $t \to \infty$ the final steady state or equilibrium value of current is given as

$$i_0 = \frac{E}{R}$$

If the current has half of this value at time t_0 then we have

$$\frac{1}{2}\frac{E}{R} = \frac{E}{R}(1 - e^{-Rt_0/L})$$

$$\Rightarrow \quad \frac{1}{2} = (1 - e^{-Rt_0/L})$$

$$\Rightarrow \quad e^{-Rt_0/L} = 1 - \frac{1}{2} = \frac{1}{2}$$

$$\Rightarrow \quad e^{Rt_0/L} = 2$$

$$\Rightarrow \quad t_0 = \frac{L}{R}\ln(2)$$

$$\Rightarrow \quad t_0 = \frac{80}{50} \times 0.693 = 1.104 \text{ s}$$

The maximum energy stored in inductor is given as

$$E_{max} = \frac{1}{2}Li_0^2 = \frac{1}{2} \times 80 \times \left(\frac{200}{50}\right)^2 = 640 \text{ J}$$

 # *Illustrative Example 5.36*

The current in a coil of self inductance 2.0 H is increasing according to $I = 2\sin(t^2)$ ampere. Find the amount of energy spend during the period when the current changes from zero to 2 A.

Solution

The energy stored in a coil of self inductance L when the current changes by 2 A is given as

$$E = \frac{1}{2}LI^2 = \frac{1}{2} \times (2.0) \times (2)^2 = 4 \text{ J}$$

This is equal to the amount of energy spent by the source which is supplying the current.

Illustrative Example 5.37

Find the magnetic field energy in a cubical region of edge 'a' above a large current carrying sheet carrying a uniform linear current density I A/m.

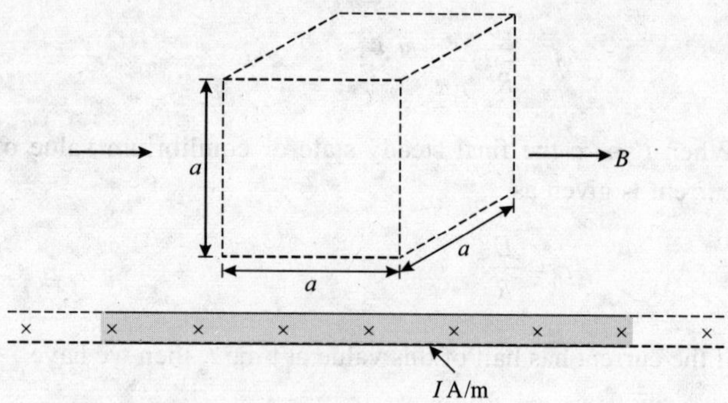

Figure 5.107

Solution

Magnetic induction due to a large current sheet in its surrounding is given as

$$B = \frac{1}{2}\mu_0 I$$

Magnetic field energy density is in space is given as

$$u = \frac{B^2}{2\mu_0} = \frac{\left(\frac{1}{2}\mu_0 I\right)^2}{2\mu_0} = \frac{1}{8}\mu_0 I^2 \text{ J/m}^3$$

Field energy in cubical region is given as

$$U = 4 \times a^3 = \frac{1}{8}\mu_0 a^3 I^2$$

Illustrative Example 5.38

What inductance would be needed to store 1.0 kWh of energy in a coil carrying a 200 A current.

Solution

Magnetic energy stored in an inductor of inductance L and carrying a current i is given as

$$U = \frac{1}{2}LI^2$$

$$\Rightarrow \quad L = \frac{2U}{i^2}$$

$$\Rightarrow \quad L = \frac{2(3.6\times10^6)}{(200)^2} = 180 \text{ H}$$

5.6 Decay of Current in RL Circuit

Figure-5.108 shows an active inductor carrying a current I_0 is connected to a resistor of resistance R via a switch S. As already discussed in previous article that I_0 was the last current flowing through the inductor when it was disconnected from a circuit. The magnetic flux through the inductor that time was $\phi = LI_0$. Because of hysteresis (also called magnetic inertia which we will study in article-5.9.17), the magnetic flux through a coil or inductor cannot change suddenly so if this active inductor is again connected in a circuit, the total flux linked in the circuit remain same. In figure below when switch is closed then immediately after closing the switch current through this inductor will be I_0 to keep the magnetic flux same.

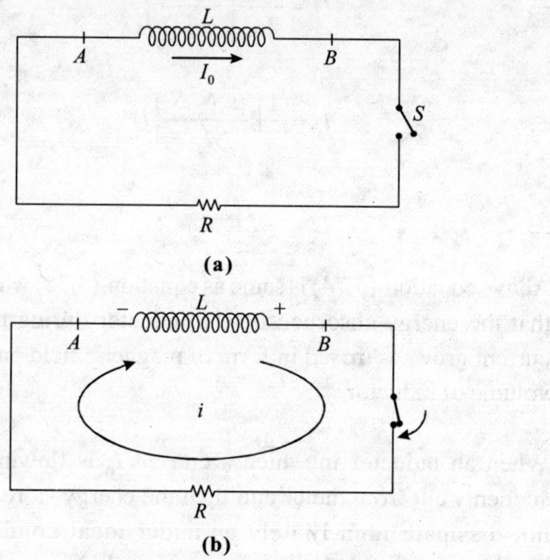

Figure 5.108

Due to current heat started dissipating in the resistor and the energy for this comes from the magnetic energy in inductor so current through the inductor gradually decreases and an EMF is induced across inductor with high and low potential terminals as shown in above figure. As current is decreasing for the inductor and resistor in parallel we can write

$$-L\frac{di}{dt} = iR$$

$$\Rightarrow \quad \frac{di}{i} = -\frac{R}{L}dt$$

In this situation when the switch was closed at $t = 0$ the current in inductor was I_0 which decreases with time. If after some time at $t = t$ current in circuit is i then integrating above expression from $t = 0$ to t, we have

$$\int_{I_0}^{i}\frac{di}{i} = -\frac{R}{L}\int_0^t dt$$

$$\Rightarrow \quad [\ln(i)]_{I_0}^{i} = \frac{-R}{L}[t]_0^t$$

$$\Rightarrow \quad [\ln(i) - \ln(I_0)] = -\frac{R}{L}[t-0]$$

$$\Rightarrow \quad \ln\left(\frac{i}{I_0}\right) = -\frac{Rt}{L}$$

$$\Rightarrow \quad i = I_0 e^{-\frac{Rt}{L}} \quad \ldots(5.75)$$

Expression in equation-(5.75) gives the current in *RL* circuit during its decay. Figure-5.109 shows the variation of decay current in inductor with time. We can also see that in one time constant current drops to 37% of the initial value. Substituting $t = L/R$ in above equation-(5.75), we have

$$i = I_0 e^{-1}$$

$$\Rightarrow \quad i = \frac{I_0}{e}$$

$$\Rightarrow \quad i = \frac{I_0}{2.718} = 0.37\, I_0 \quad \ldots(5.76)$$

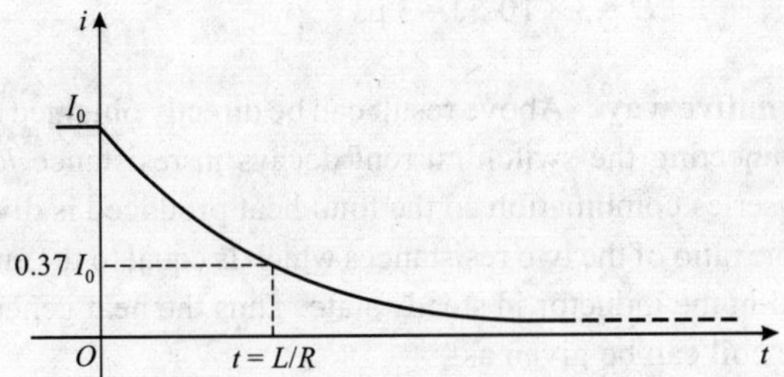

Figure 5.109

As current decays exponentially, after a long time in steady state current becomes zero and in this period whole of the magnetic energy stored in inductor is dissipated as heat which can also be verified by calculating the heat dissipation in resistor. Using expression of current in equation-(5.75), we can write the thermal power produced in resistor *R* is given as

$$P_{th} = i^2 R$$

$$\Rightarrow \quad P_{th} = I_0^2 R e^{-\frac{2Rt}{L}} \quad \ldots(5.77)$$

Heat dissipated in resistor during an elemental time *dt* is given as

$$dH = P_{th} dt$$

$$\Rightarrow \quad dH = I_0^2 R e^{-\frac{2Rt}{L}} dt$$

To calculate the total heat dissipated in resistance we integrate the above expression from $t = 0$ to $t \to \infty$ as theoretically it takes infinite time after which current will drop to zero.

$$\Rightarrow \quad H = \int dH = \int_0^\infty I_0^2 R e^{-\frac{2Rt}{L}} dt$$

$$\Rightarrow \quad H = I_0^2 R\left(-\frac{L}{2R}\right)\left[e^{-\frac{2Rt}{L}}\right]_0^\infty$$

$$\Rightarrow \quad H = -\frac{1}{2} L I_0^2 [0-1]$$

$$\Rightarrow \quad H = \frac{1}{2} L I_0^2 \quad \ldots(5.78)$$

Equation-(5.78) is the total magnetic energy initially stored in the inductor before closing the switch. This verifies that all the magnetic energy of inductor is dissipated as heat in resistor during the time current decays.

Illustrative Example 5.39

A thin charged ring of radius $a = 10$ cm rotates about its axis with an angular velocity $\omega = 100$ rad/s. Find the ratio of volume energy densities of magnet and electric field on the axis of the ring a point removed from its centre by a distance $l = a$.

Solution

We know the magnetic field at *P* a distance *l* from the centre *O* of the coil on the axis

$$B = \frac{\mu_0 I a^2}{2\pi(l^2 + a^2)^{3/2}}$$

Current due to revolving charge is given as

$$I = \frac{q\omega}{2\pi}$$

$$\Rightarrow \quad B = \frac{\mu_0}{4\pi} \frac{q\omega a^2}{(l^2 + a^2)^{3/2}}$$

Energy density of magnetic field is given as

$$u_M = \frac{B^2}{2\mu_0}$$

The electric field strength at an axial point is given as

$$E = \frac{1}{4\pi\varepsilon_0} \frac{ql}{(l^2 + a^2)^{3/2}}$$

The energy density of the electric field is given as

$$u_E = \frac{1}{2}\varepsilon E^2$$

Ratio of energy densities of magnetic and electric field are given as

$$\frac{u_M}{u_E} = \frac{(B/E)^2}{\mu_0 \varepsilon_0} = \left(\frac{\omega a^2}{l}\right)^2 \mu_0 \varepsilon_0$$

$$\frac{u_M}{u_E} = \frac{\left(\frac{\omega a^2}{l}\right)^2}{c^2} = 1.1 \times 10^{-15}$$

Illustrative Example 5.40

A 10 H inductor carries a current of 20 A. How much ice at 0°C could be melted by the energy stored in the magnetic field of the inductor? Latent heat of ice is 22.6×10^3 J/kg.

Solution

Energy stored in inductor is given as

$$U = \frac{1}{2}Li^2$$

This energy is completely used in melting the ice. If L_f is the latent heat of fusion, we use

$$\frac{1}{2}Li^2 = mL_f$$

$$\Rightarrow \quad m = \frac{Li^2}{2L_f}$$

Substituting the values we get

$$m = \frac{(10)(20)^2}{2(2.26 \times 10^3)} = 0.88 \text{ kg}$$

Illustrative Example 5.41

A coil of inductance $L = 2.0$ μH and resistance $R = 1.0\ \Omega$ is connected to a source of constant e.m.f. $E = 3.0$ V. A resistance $R_0 = 2.0\ \Omega$ is connected in parallel with the coil. Find the amount of heat generated in the coil after the switch *Sw* is disconnected. The internal resistance of the source is negligible.

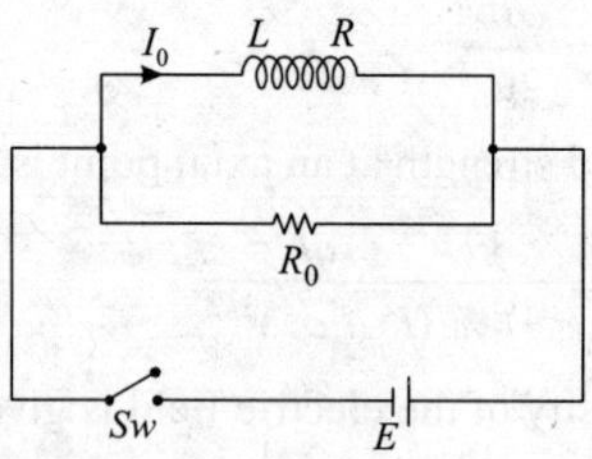

Figure 5.110

Solution

When the switch is disconnected the decay of current I_0 starts where I_0 is the steady state current in the inductor. KVL equation for the loop in which current decays at an instant when a current I exist in loop is given as

$$IR_0 + IR = -L\frac{dI}{dt}$$

$$\Rightarrow \quad \frac{dI}{I} = -\left(\frac{R_0 + R}{L}\right)dt$$

$$\Rightarrow \quad \int_{I_0}^{I}\frac{dI}{I} = \int_0^t \frac{R_0 + R}{L}dt$$

Solving the above integration gives

$$I = I_0 e^{-(R+R_0)t/L}$$

Heat generated in time dt is given as

$$dQ = I^2 R\, dt$$

$$\Rightarrow \quad Q = \int dQ = \int_0^{\infty} I^2 R dt$$

$$\Rightarrow \quad Q = I_0^2 R\frac{L}{2(R_0 + R)} = \frac{LE^2}{2R(R + R_0)} \quad [\text{As } I_0 R = E]$$

Substituting the values we get

$$Q = 3 \times 10^{-6} \text{ J} = 3\ \mu\text{J}$$

Alternative way : Above result can be directly obtained as on disconnecting the switch current decays in resistance R and R_0 in series combination so the total heat produced is divided in same ratio of the two resistances which is equal to the energy stored in the inductor in steady state. Thus the heat generated in the coil can be given as

$$H = \frac{1}{2}LI_0^2 \times \frac{R}{R + R_0}$$

Illustrative Example 5.42

In circuit shown in figure-5.111, find the current through battery just after closing the switch and after a long time in steady state.

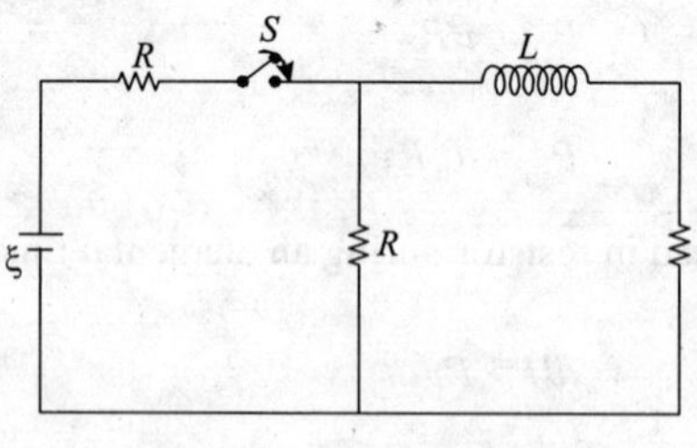

Figure 5.111

Solution

Just after closing the switch inductor behaves like open circuit so the circuit just after closing the switch is shown in figure-5.112 below.

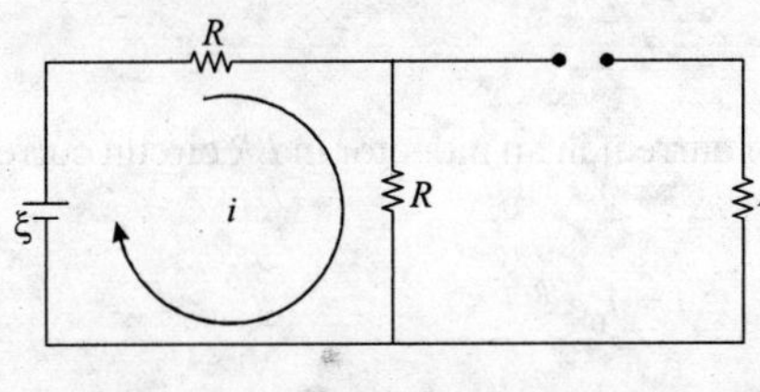

Figure 5.112

The current only flows in the left loop as shown which is given as

$$i_B = \frac{\xi}{2R}$$

In steady state after a long time the inductor behaves like a straight wire thus equivalent circuit in steady state is shown in figure-5.113 below. The two resistances on the right side can be considered in parallel and thus across the battery equivalent resistance will be $R + R/2 = 3R/2$.

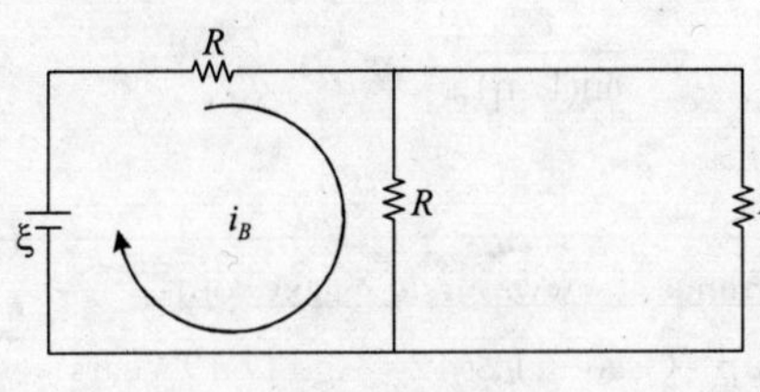

Figure 5.113

The current flowing through battery in steady state is given as

$$i_B = \frac{\xi}{3R/2} = \frac{2\xi}{3R}$$

Illustrative Example 5.43

For the circuit shown in figure-5.114. E = 50 V, R_1 = 10 Ω, R_2 = 20 Ω, R_3 = 30 Ω and L = 2.0 mH. Find the current through R_1 and R_2.

(a) Immediately after switch S is closed

(b) A long time after S is closed

(c) Immediately after S is reopened

(d) A long time after S is reopened

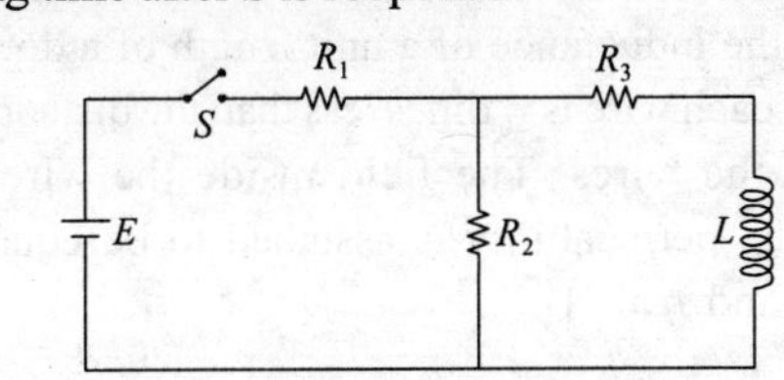

Figure 5.114

Solution

(a) Resistance offered by inductor immediately after switch is closed will be infinite as it behaves like open circuit. Therefore, current through R_3 will be zero and current through R_1 is given as

$$I_1 = \frac{E}{R_1 + R_2}$$

$$\Rightarrow \qquad I_1 = \frac{50}{10+20} = \frac{5}{3}\text{ A}$$

(b) After a long time of closing the switch, resistance offered by inductor will be zero as in steady state it behaves like short circuit. In that case R_2 and R_3 are in parallel, and the resultant of these two is then in series with R_1 thus equivalent resistance across the battery in steady state is given as

$$R_{net} = R_1 + \frac{R_2 R_3}{R_2 + R_3} = 10 + \frac{(20)(30)}{20+30} = 22\ \Omega$$

Current through the battery is given as

$$I_2 = \frac{E}{R_{net}} = \frac{50}{22}\text{ A}$$

This current will distribute in R_2 and R_3 in inverse ratio of resistance so current through R_2 is given as

$$R_2 = \left(\frac{50}{22}\right)\left(\frac{R_3}{R_2 + R_3}\right)$$

$$\Rightarrow \qquad R_2 = \left(\frac{50}{22}\right)\left(\frac{30}{30+20}\right) = \frac{15}{11}\text{A}$$

(c) Immediately after switch is reopened, the current through R_1 will become zero.

But current through R_2 will be equal to the steady state current through R_3, which is given as

$$I_3 = \left(\frac{50}{22} - \frac{15}{11}\right) = 0.91\text{ A}$$

(d) A long after S is reopened, current through all resistors will become zero.

Illustrative Example 5.44

In the circuit shown in figure-115, find the current in inductor as a function of time if switch is closed at $t = 0$.

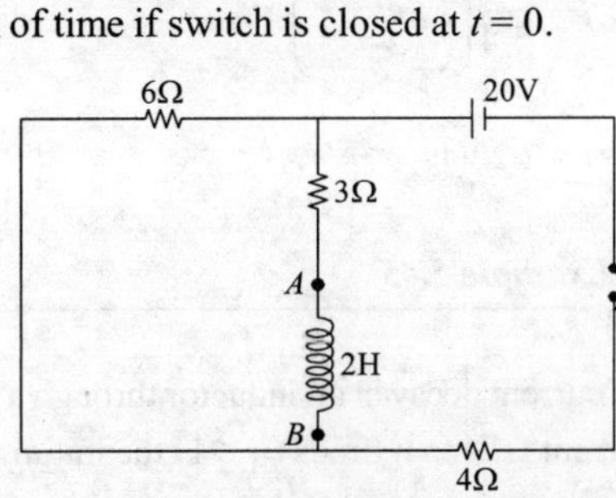

Figure 5.115

Solution

In above given circuit we remove the inductor and across terminals A and B we reduce the circuit by its Thevenin's equivalent battery as explained in figures-5.116 below.

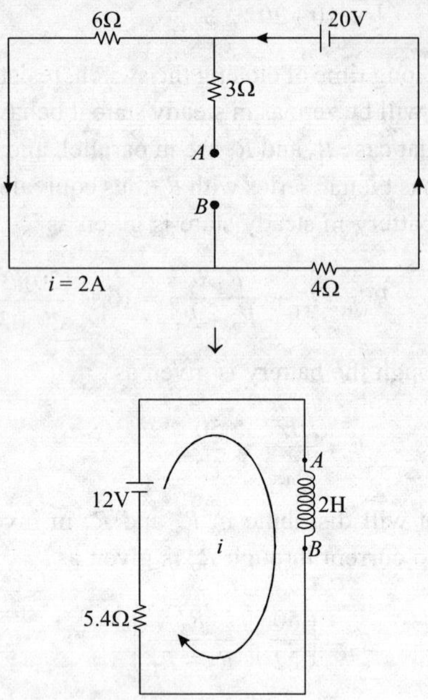

Figure 5.116

Internal resistance of circuit across A & B is given as

$$r = 3 + \frac{6\times 4}{6+4} = 5.4\,\Omega$$

Open circuit potential difference across A & B is given as

$$V_A - V_B = 12\,\text{V}$$

Growth of current in LR circuit can be directly given by the relation of simple LR circuit as

$$i = \frac{\varepsilon}{R}(1 - e^{-Rt/L})$$

$$\Rightarrow \quad i = \frac{12}{5.4}\left(1 - e^{-\frac{5.4t}{2}}\right)$$

$$\Rightarrow \quad i = 2.22(1 - e^{-2.7t})\,\text{A}$$

 # Illustrative Example 5.45

In a process of current decay in an inductor through a resistance, if in time t, current falls to η times ($\eta < 1$) the initial value, find the time constant of circuit.

Solution

For decay of current in an inductor in LR circuit current is given as

$$i = I_0 e^{-Rt/L}$$

In above situation time constant of circuit is given as

$$\tau = L/R$$

$$\Rightarrow \quad i = I_0 e^{-t/\tau}$$

Given that at $t = t$, $i = \eta I_0$ which gives

$$\eta I_0 = I_0 e^{-t/\tau}$$

$$\Rightarrow \quad \ln\left(\frac{1}{\eta}\right) = \frac{t}{\tau}$$

$$\Rightarrow \quad \tau = \frac{t}{\ln(1/\eta)}$$

<u>Web Reference at www.physicsgalaxy.com</u>

Age Group - Grade 11 & 12 | Age 17-19 Years
Section - Magnetic Effects
Topic - Self & Mutual Inductance
Module Number - 1 to 21

Practice Exercise 5.3

(i) Find the self inductance of a unit length of a cable consisting of two thin walled coaxial metallic cylinders if the radius of the outside cylinder is η ($\eta > 1$) times that of the inside one. The permeability of the medium between the cylinders is assumed to be equal to unity.

[$\frac{\mu_0}{2\pi}\ln(\eta)$]

(ii) Find the inductance of a unit length of a double line if the radius of each wire is η times less than the distance between the axes of the wires. The field inside the wires is to be neglected, the permeability is assumed to be equal to unity throughout, and $\eta >> 1$.

[$\frac{\mu_0}{\pi}\ln(\eta)$]

(iii) In the circuit shown in figure-5.117, find potential of point C at the instant shown. The rate of increase of current in resistance is 2.5 A/s.

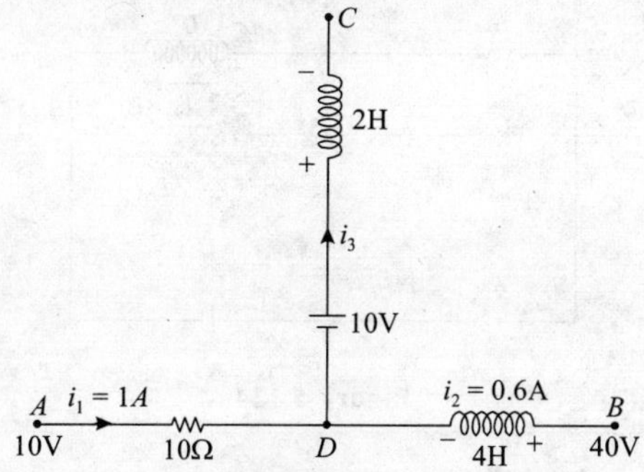

Figure 5.117

[– 15 V]

(iv) A long cylinder of radius a carrying a uniform surface charge rotates about its axis with an angular velocity ω. Find the magnetic field energy per unit length of the cylinder inside of it if the linear charge density equals λ and consider permeability of the medium is equal to unity.

[$\frac{\mu_0\lambda^2\omega^2a^2}{8\pi}$]

(v) A long coaxial cable consists of two concentric cylinders of radii a and b. The central conductor of the cable carries a steady current i and the outer conductor provides the return path of the current. Calculate the energy stored in the magnetic field of length l of such a cable

[$\frac{\mu_0 i^2 l}{4\pi}\ln\left(\frac{b}{a}\right)$]

(vi) In a branch of an electrical circuit shown in figure-5.118, $R = 10\ \Omega$, $L = 5$ H, $E = 20$ V, $i = 2$ A. This current is decreasing at a rate of 1.0 A/s. Find V_{ab} at this instant.

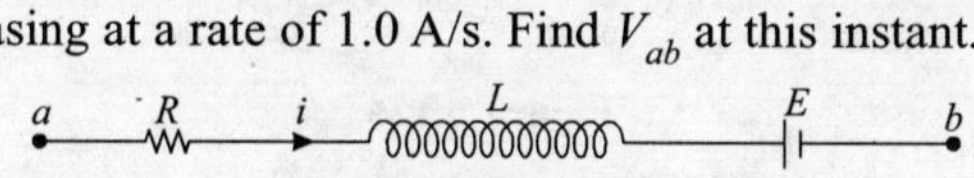

Figure 5.118

[35 V]

(vii) The potential difference across a 150 mH inductor as a function of time is shown in figure-5.119. Assume that the initial value of the current in the inductor is zero. What is the current when (a) $t = 2.0$ ms (b) $t = 4.0$ ms ?

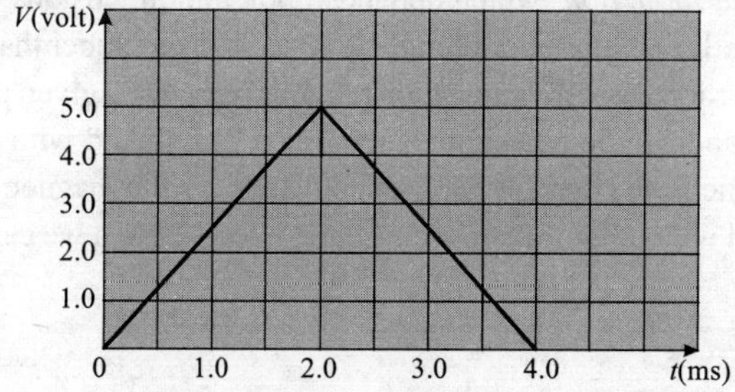

Figure 5.119

[(a) 3.33×10^{-2} A (b) 6.67×10^{-2} A]

(viii) A metal rod OA of mass m and length l is kept rotating with a constant angular speed ω in a vertical plane about a horizontal axis at the end O as shown in figure-5.120. The free end A is arranged to slide without friction along a fixed conducting circular ring in the same plane as that of rotation. A uniform and constant magnetic induction B is applied perpendicular and into the plane of rotation as shown in figure. An inductor and an external resistance R are connected through a switch S between the point O and a point C on the ring to form an electrical circuit. Neglect the resistance of the ring and the rod. Initially, the switch is open.

(a) What is the induced EMF across the terminals of the switch?

(b) The switch S is closed at time $t = 0$. Obtain an expression for the current as a function of time. In the steady state, obtain the time dependence of the torque required to maintain the constant angular speed, given that the rod OA was along the positive X-axis at $t = 0$.

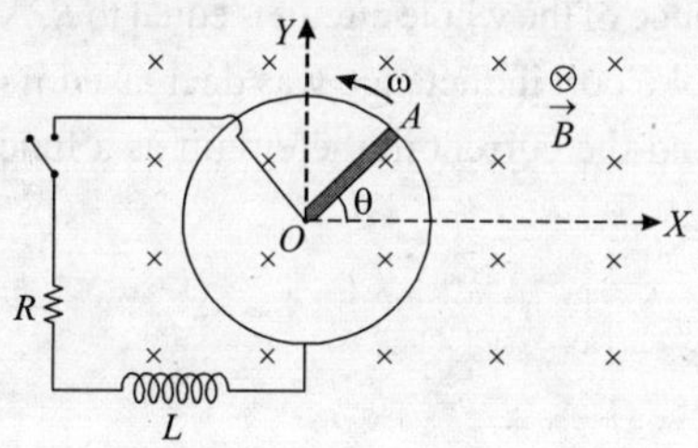

Figure 5.120

[(a) $\frac{1}{2}Br^2\omega$ (b) $\frac{Br^2\omega}{2R}(1 - e^{-Rt/L})$; $\frac{B^2r^2\omega}{4R}(1 - e^{-Rt/L})$]

(ix) A solenoid of inductance L with resistance r is connected in parallel to a resistance R. A battery of EMF E and of negligible internal resistance is connected across the parallel combination as shown in the figure-5.121.

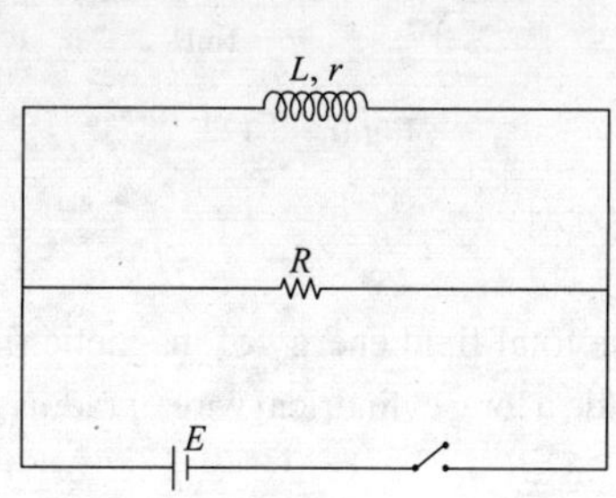

Figure 5.121

(a) Current through the solenoid after the switch is opened at $t = 0$.

(b) Amount of heat generated in the solenoid

[(a) $\frac{E}{r}e^{-\left(\frac{R+r}{L}\right)t}$; (b) $\frac{E^2L}{2r(R+r)}$]

(x) In the circuit diagram shown, initially there is no energy in the inductor and the capacitor. The switch is closed at $t = 0$. Find the current I as a function of time if $R = \sqrt{L/C}$

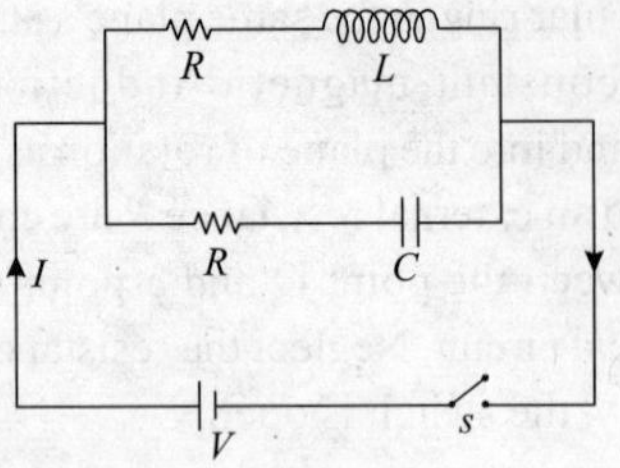

Figure 5.122

$[\frac{V}{R}]$

(xi) A closed circuit consists of a source of constant EMF ξ and a choke coil of inductance L connected in series. The active resistance of the whole circuit is equal to R. At the moment $t = 0$, the choke coil inductance was decreased η ($\eta < 1$) times suddenly. Find the current in the circuit as a function of t.

$[\frac{\xi}{R}\left[1-(\eta-1)e^{-\frac{\eta R t}{L}}\right]]$

(xii) In the circuit shown in figure-5.123, switch S is closed at time $t = 0$. Find the current through the inductor as a function of time t.

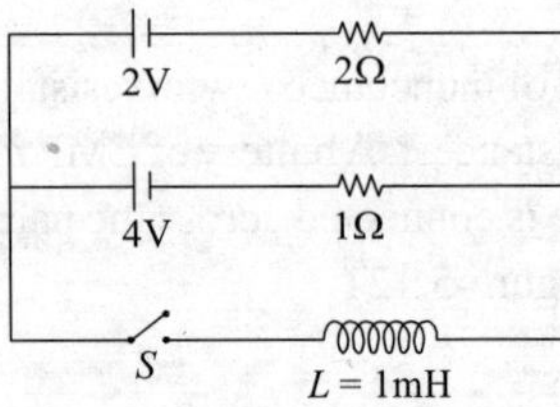

Figure 5.123

$[i = 5(1 - e^{-2000t/3})\ \text{A}]$

(xiii) Find the total field energy of magnetic field stored per unit length inside a long cylindrical wire of radius R and carrying a current I.

$[\frac{\mu_0 I^2}{16\pi}]$

(xiv) Figure-5.124 shows an active inductor with current I_0 connected in series with a resistance and a battery. If at $t = 0$ the switch is closed, find the current in inductor as a function of time.

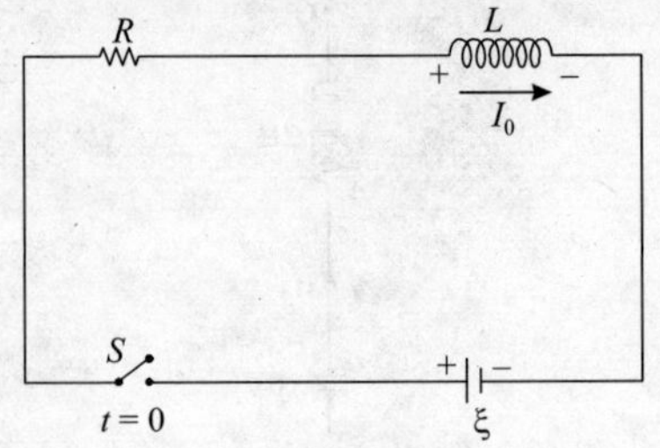

Figure 5.124

$[\frac{1}{R}[\xi - (\xi_0 - I_0 R)e^{-Rt/L}]]$

5.7 Mutual Induction

It is a property of a pair of coils due to which change in current in one coil is opposed by the EMF induced in other coil because of magnetic flux linkage in the two coils. Figure-5.125 shows two coils kept close to each other along same axis. When a current i_1 flows in coil-1 it develops a flux ϕ_1 of which some fraction passes through coil-2 as shown which is linked with it. When current in coil-1 is changed, the flux due to its current which is linked with coil-2 changes and induces an EMF in coil-2. This is called '*Mutually Induced EMF*' as its due to flux change in coil-1.

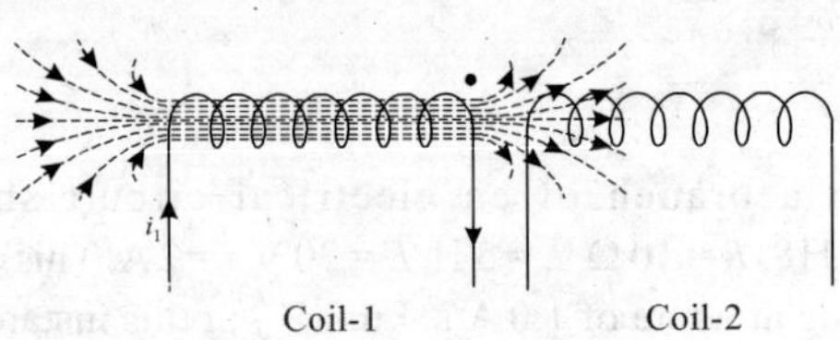

Figure 5.125

If ϕ_2 is the magnetic flux linked with coil-2 due to the current i_1 in coil-1 then we have

$$\phi_2 \propto i_1$$

$$\Rightarrow \quad \phi_2 = M i_1 \quad \dots(5.79)$$

Where M is the proportionality constant called '*Coefficient of Mutual Induction*' which depends upon the dimensions of the coil and separation between the two coils. Remember that M is bidirectional coefficient which remains same for a given pair of coils and can be used in calculation of flux linked with either coil due to the current in other coil. If ϕ_{12} is the magnetic flux linked with coil-1 due to a current i_2 in coil-2 then we can also write

$$\phi_{12} = M i_2 \quad \dots(5.80)$$

Thus mutually induced EMF in coils will depend upon the rate at which the current changes in other coils which are given as

$$e_2 = M\frac{di_1}{dt}$$

and $$e_1 = M\frac{di_2}{dt}$$

The direction of mutually induced EMF in either coil will be such that it opposes the change in current in the other coil.

5.7.1 Total Flux linked to a Coil with Mutual Induction

When there is a pair of coils kept fixed at some separation having their self induction coefficients L_1 and L_2 and mutual induction coefficient for the pair M then total magnetic flux linked with either coil will be the sum of magnetic flux linked with the coil due to both self induction and mutual induction if both the coils are connected to closed circuits and carry currents.

Figure-5.126 shows two coils which carry currents i_1 and i_2 and the direction of their magnetic flux is denoted by the dot at one end of the coil according to the dot convention we already discussed in previous article-5.5.2.

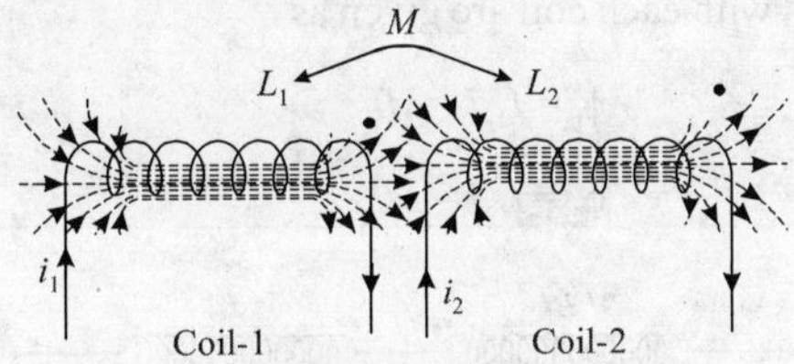

Figure 5.126

In figure-5.126 we can see that magnetic flux due to both coils are from left to right so the part of flux due to one coil which is linked with other coil is in same direction as that of their own flux so net flux linked with coil-1 and coil-2 are given as

$$\phi_1 = L_1 i_1 + M i_2 \quad \dots(5.81)$$

$$\phi_2 = L_2 i_2 + M i_1 \quad \dots(5.82)$$

If current in above coils starts changing then EMF induced in the two coils are given as

$$e_1 = \frac{d\phi_1}{dt} = L_1\frac{di_1}{dt} + M\frac{di_2}{dt}$$

and $$e_2 = \frac{d\phi_2}{dt} = L_2\frac{di_2}{dt} + M\frac{di_1}{dt}$$

Now consider a pair of coils shown in figure-5.127 in which the direction of magnetic flux due to the two coils are in opposite direction so the net magnetic flux linked with the two coils are given as

$$\phi_1 = L_1 i_1 - M i_2 \quad \dots(5.83)$$

$$\phi_2 = L_2 i_2 - M i_1 \quad \dots(5.84)$$

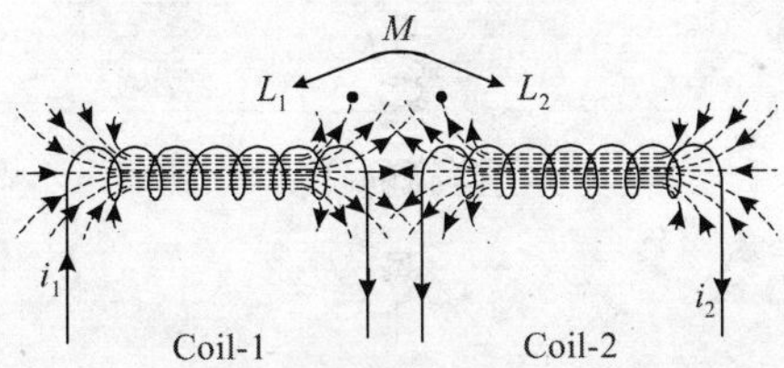

Figure 5.127

If current in above coils starts changing then EMF induced in the two coils are given as

$$e_1 = \frac{d\phi_1}{dt} = L_1\frac{di_1}{dt} - M\frac{di_2}{dt}$$

and $$e_2 = \frac{d\phi_2}{dt} = L_2\frac{di_2}{dt} - M\frac{di_1}{dt}$$

For a given pair of coils the coefficient of mutual induction is used for calculation of magnetic flux through one coil due to the current in either coil. This property of mutual induction for a pair of coils is called '*Reciprocity Property*' of mutual induction.

5.7.2 Relation between Coefficients of Self and Mutual Induction for a given Pair of Coils

Figure-5.128 shows a pair of coils with their coefficient of self induction L_1 and L_2 and coefficient of mutual induction M. The relationship between these coefficients is given as

$$M = k\sqrt{L_1 L_2} \quad \dots(5.85)$$

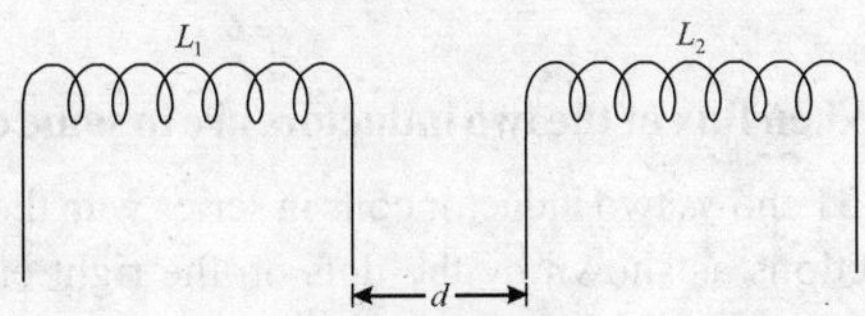

Figure 5.128

Where k is called '*Coupling factor*' which depends upon the orientation of coils and the separation between the two coils. If the fraction of magnetic flux produced by one coil which is linked with other is high then coupling factor between the two coils will be higher. In general $0 \le k \le 1$ for any set of coils. If there is no flux linkage between the two coils then $k = 0$ and for full flux linkage between the coils $k = 1$. No flux linkage means no part of flux of one coil passes through the other coil. This happens when the coils are separated by a very large distance as shown in figure-5.129(a) or when the coils are mounted at right angle to each other as shown in figure-5.129(b) in which flux of one coil does not link with turns of other coil.

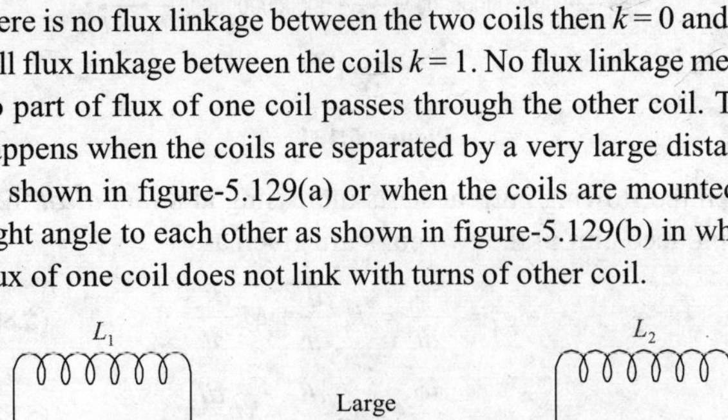

(a)

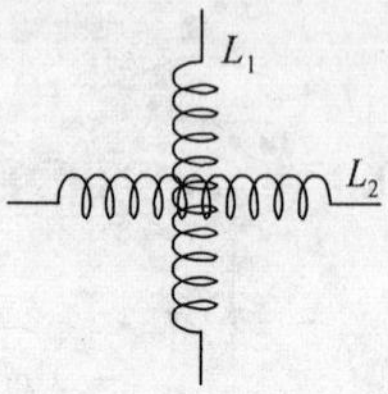

(b)
Figure 5.129

When coils are wound over each other as shown in figure-5.130 then complete flux of one coil is linked with the other coil so in this case we can consider the value of k to be equal to unity.

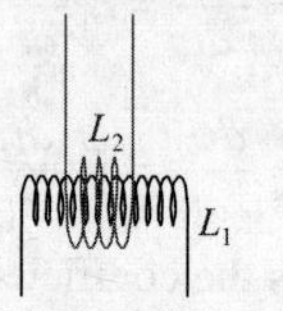

Figure 5.130

For partial linkage of flux between the two coils the coefficient of mutual induction is given by equation-(5.85) with value of k between 0 and 1. Students need not think about derivation of equation-(5.85) which is considered as a standard empirical relation here.

5.7.3 Inductors in Series Combination

There are two ways in which inductors can be connected in series combination with their flux in same direction or in opposite direction. We will discuss the two ways as different cases one by one.

Case I : When flux of the two inductors are in same direction

Figure-5.131 shows two inductor coils in series with their flux in same directions as shown by the dots on the right end of the two coils. If a current I flows through the coils the magnetic flux linked with each coil are given as

$$\phi_1 = L_1 I + MI$$

and
$$\phi_2 = L_2 I + MI$$

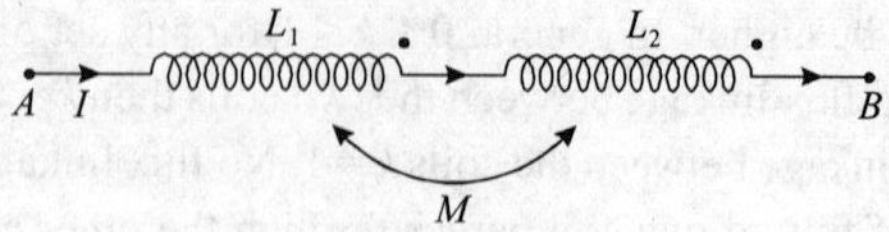

Figure 5.131

When the flowing current starts increasing at a rate dI/dt then the induced emf in the two coils are given as

$$e_1 = \frac{d\phi_1}{dt} = L_1\frac{dI}{dt} + M\frac{dI}{dt} \quad \ldots(5.86)$$

and
$$e_2 = \frac{d\phi_2}{dt} = L_2\frac{dI}{dt} + M\frac{dI}{dt} \quad \ldots(5.87)$$

As current is increasing with time the EMF induced in the two coils will oppose the increment in current and have their high and low potential ends across the two coils as shown in figure-5.131. Writing KVL equation from A to B in figure-5.131 we have

$$V_A - \left(L_1\frac{dI}{dt} + M\frac{dI}{dt}\right) - \left(L_2\frac{dI}{dt} + M\frac{dI}{dt}\right) = V_B$$

$$\Rightarrow \quad V_A - V_B = (L_1 + L_2)\frac{dI}{dt} + 2M\frac{dI}{dt}$$

$$\Rightarrow \quad V_A - V_B = (L_1 + L_2 + 2M)\frac{dI}{dt}$$

$$\Rightarrow \quad V_A - V_B = L_{eq}\frac{dI}{dt} \quad \ldots(5.88)$$

In above equation-(5.88) the equivalent self inductance of the two inductors in series is given as

$$L_{eq} = L_1 + L_2 + 2M \quad \ldots(5.89)$$

Case II : When the flux of the two inductors are in opposite direction

Figure-5.132 shows two inductor coils in series with their flux in opposite directions as shown by the dots on the different ends of the two coils. If a current I flows through the coils the magnetic flux linked with each coil are given as

$$\phi_1 = L_1 I - MI$$

and
$$\phi_2 = L_2 I - MI$$

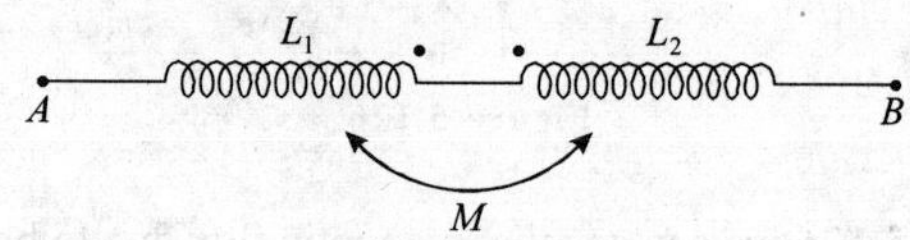

Figure 5.132

When the flowing current starts increasing at a rate dI/dt then the induced emf in the two coils are given as

$$e_1 = \frac{d\phi_1}{dt} = L_1\frac{dI}{dt} - M\frac{dI}{dt} \quad \ldots(5.90)$$

and
$$e_2 = \frac{d\phi_2}{dt} = L_2\frac{dI}{dt} - M\frac{dI}{dt} \quad \ldots(5.91)$$

As current is increasing with time the EMF induced in the two coils will oppose the increment in current and have their high and low potential ends across the two coils as shown in figure-5.131. Writing KVL equation from A to B in figure-5.131 we have

$$V_A - \left(L_1\frac{dI}{dt} - M\frac{dI}{dt}\right) - \left(L_2\frac{dI}{dt} - M\frac{dI}{dt}\right) = V_B$$

$$\Rightarrow \quad V_A - V_B = (L_1 + L_2)\frac{dI}{dt} - 2M\frac{dI}{dt}$$

$$\Rightarrow \quad V_A - V_B = (L_1 + L_2 - 2M)\frac{dI}{dt}$$

$$\Rightarrow \quad V_A - V_B = L_{eq}\frac{dI}{dt} \quad \ldots(5.92)$$

In above equation-(5.88) the equivalent self inductance of the two inductors in series is given as

$$L_{eq} = L_1 + L_2 - 2M \quad \text{...(5.93)}$$

5.7.4 Inductors in Parallel Combination

There are several ways in which inductors can be connected in parallel combination depending upon the orientation of inductors but here we will discuss simple combination without considering mutual induction between them.

Figure-5.133 shows the two inductors having self inductances L_1 and L_2 connected in parallel combination. If a current i flows through the combination and it divides as i_1 and i_2 in the two inductors which are changing with time then for parallel combination of inductors we use

$$L_1 \frac{di_1}{dt} = L_2 \frac{di_2}{dt}$$

$$\Rightarrow \quad L_1 di_1 = L_2 di_2$$

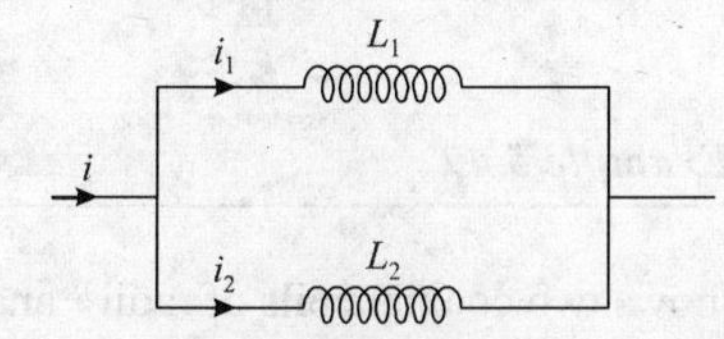

Figure 5.133

Integrating the above expression for any time limits when currents are i_1 and i_2 in the two inductors, we have

$$L_1 i_1 = L_2 i_2 \quad \text{...(5.94)}$$

and
$$i_1 + i_2 = i \quad \text{...(5.95)}$$

From equation-(5.94) and (5.95) we can calculate the current distribution in two parallel inductors at any time which gives

$$i_1 = \frac{L_2 i}{L_1 + L_2} \quad \text{...(5.96)}$$

and
$$i_2 = \frac{L_1 i}{L_1 + L_2} \quad \text{...(5.97)}$$

From equation-(5.95) we have

$$\frac{di}{dt} = \frac{di_1}{dt} + \frac{di_2}{dt} \quad \text{...(5.98)}$$

If L_{eq} is the equivalent self induction for the combination then for the terminals A and B across the inductors we have

$$V_{AB} = L_{eq} \frac{di}{dt} = L_1 \frac{di_1}{dt} = L_2 \frac{di_2}{dt} \quad \text{...(5.99)}$$

From equation-(5.98) and (5.99) we have

$$\frac{V_{AB}}{L_{eq}} = \frac{V_{AB}}{L_1} + \frac{V_{AB}}{L_2}$$

$$\Rightarrow \quad \frac{1}{L_{eq}} = \frac{1}{L_1} + \frac{1}{L_2} \quad \text{...(5.100)}$$

Equation-(5.100) gives the formula for calculation of equivalent self inductance for the inductors connected in parallel which can be generalized to multiple inductors if mutual induction is neglected between these inductors.

Illustrative Example 5.46

A coil of 100 turns and 1 cm radius is kept coaxially within a long solenoid of 8 turns per cm and 5 cm radius. Find the mutual inductance.

Solution

The magnetic field B inside the solenoid is given as

$$B = \mu_0 n_s i_s$$

The magnetic flux linked with the coaxial coil placed inside the solenoid is given as

$$\phi_c = N_c B A_c = N_c(\mu_0 n_s i_s) A_c$$

Where A_c is the cross sectional area of coil.

The mutual inductance between solenoid and coil can be given as

$$M = \frac{\phi_c}{i_s} = \mu_0 n_s N_c A_c$$

Substituting the given values, we get

$$M = 4\pi \times 10^{-7} \times 800 \times 100 \times \pi \times 10^{-4}\,\text{H}$$

$$\Rightarrow \quad M = 3.15 \times 10^{-5}\,\text{H}$$

Illustrative Example 5.47

Calculate the mutual inductance of a long straight wire and a rectangular frame with side a and b as shown in figure-5.134. The wire and the frame lie in the same plane, with side b being closest to the wire, separated by a distance l from it and oriented parallel to it.

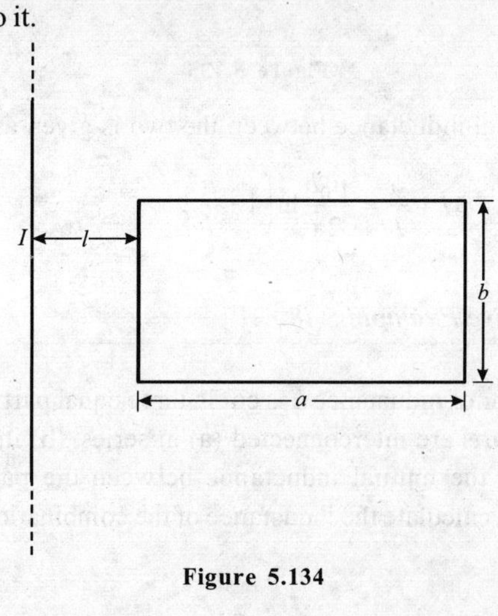

Figure 5.134

Solution

To calculate the mutual inductance between the wire and the frame we supply a current I through the wire and calculate the magnetic flux through the frame. For this we consider an elemental strip in the frame of width dr at a distance r from wire as shown in figure-5.135. The magnetic flux through the elemental strip is given as

$$d\phi = \left(\frac{\mu_0 I}{2\pi r}\right) bdr$$

$$\Rightarrow \quad \phi = \int_{l}^{a+l} \left(\frac{\mu_0 I}{2\pi r}\right) bdr$$

$$\Rightarrow \quad \phi = \frac{\mu_0 Ib}{2\pi} \int_{l}^{a+l} \frac{dr}{r}$$

$$\Rightarrow \quad \phi = \frac{\mu_0 Ib}{2\pi} [\ln r]_a^{a+l}$$

$$\Rightarrow \quad \phi = \frac{\mu_0 Ib}{2\pi} \ln\left(1+\frac{a}{l}\right)$$

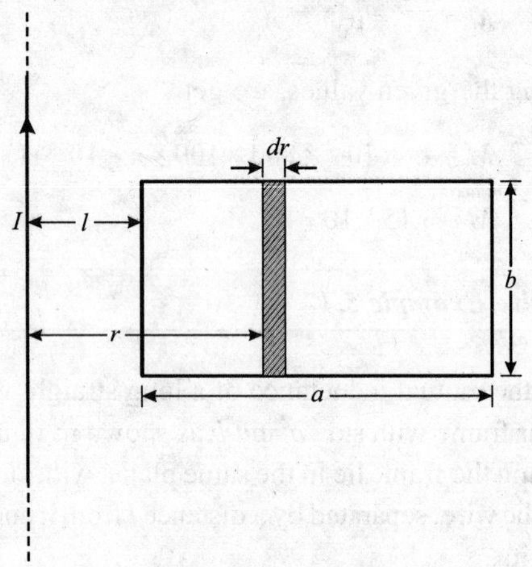

Figure 5.135

Thus mutual inductance between the two is given as

$$M = \frac{\phi}{I} = \frac{\mu_0 b}{2\pi} \ln\left(1+\frac{a}{l}\right)$$

 # Illustrative Example 5.48

An inductor of inductance L is cut in three equal parts and two of these parts are interconnected (a) in series, (b) in parallel. Assuming the mutual inductance between the parts to be negligible, calculate the inductance of the combination in both the cases.

Solution

(a) When the given inductor is cut in identical parts then each will have an inductance $L/3$. When two such coils are connected in series then equivalent self inductance of the combination is given as

$$L_s = L_1 + L_2$$

$$\Rightarrow \quad L_s = \frac{L}{3} + \frac{L}{3} = \frac{2L}{3}$$

(b) In parallel combination we use

$$\frac{1}{L_p} = \frac{1}{L_1} + \frac{1}{L_2}$$

$$\Rightarrow \quad \frac{1}{L_p} = \frac{1}{L/3} + \frac{1}{L/3}$$

$$\Rightarrow \quad L_p = \frac{L}{6}$$

 # Illustrative Example 5.49

Figure-5.136 shows two coaxial coils of radii r and R ($R >> r$) kept at large separation x ($x >> R$). Calculate the magnetic flux passing through coil A due to a current I in coil B.

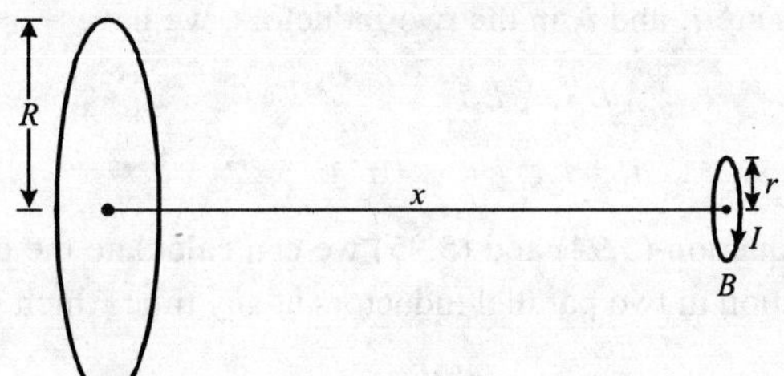

Figure 5.136

Solution

If M is the coefficient of mutual induction between the two coils then magnetic flux through coil A due to current in coil B is given as

$$\phi_A = MI_B \qquad \ldots(5.101)$$

First we will calculate the mutual induction coefficient between the two coils and for this we find the flux through coil B if a current I flows in coil A as shown in figure-5.136.

The magnetic induction at the location of coil B due to current in coil A is given as

$$B = \frac{\mu_0 I R^2}{2(x^2+R^2)^{3/2}}$$

The magnetic flux through coil B due to above magnetic induction is given as

$$\phi_B = B.\pi r^2$$

$$\Rightarrow \qquad \phi_B = \frac{\mu_0 \pi r^2 R^2}{2(x^2+R^2)^{3/2}} \cdot I$$

As coefficient of mutual inductance is a bidirectional coefficient, we can calculate it as

$$M = \frac{\phi_B}{I} = \frac{\mu_0 \pi r^2 R^2}{2(x^2+R^2)^{3/2}}$$

Above is the mutual inductance coefficient for the pair of these coil which can be used in calculation of flux from either coil due to current in other coil so from reciprocity property, we have

$$\phi_A = MI_B = \frac{\mu_0 \pi r^2 R^2 I}{2(x^2+R^2)^{3/2}}$$

Illustrative Example 5.50

In the electric circuit shown in figure-5.137 an EMF E, a resistance R and coils of inductances L_1 and L_2 are used. The internal resistance of the source and the coil resistances are negligible. Find the steady state currents in the coils long time after the switch Sw was shorted.

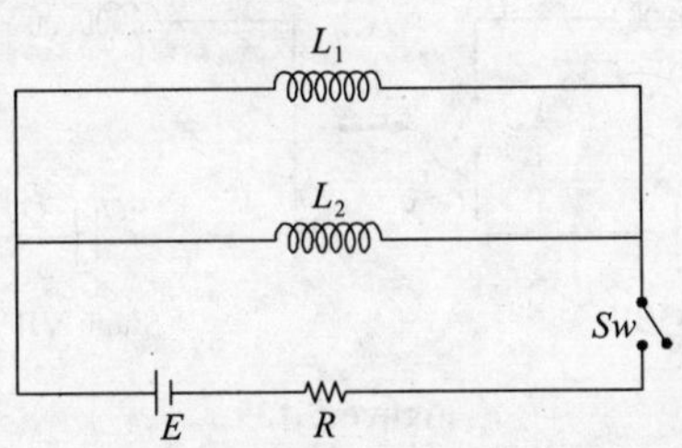

Figure 5.137

Solution

In steady state inductors behave like short circuits so the current through battery is given as

$$I = I_1 + I_2 = \frac{E}{R}$$

As already discussed in article-5.7.4 that current in inductors connected in parallel combination is divided in inverse ratio of their inductances so we have currents through inductors given as

$$I_1 = \frac{EL_2}{R(L_1+L_2)}$$

and
$$I_2 = \frac{EL_1}{R(L_1+L_2)}$$

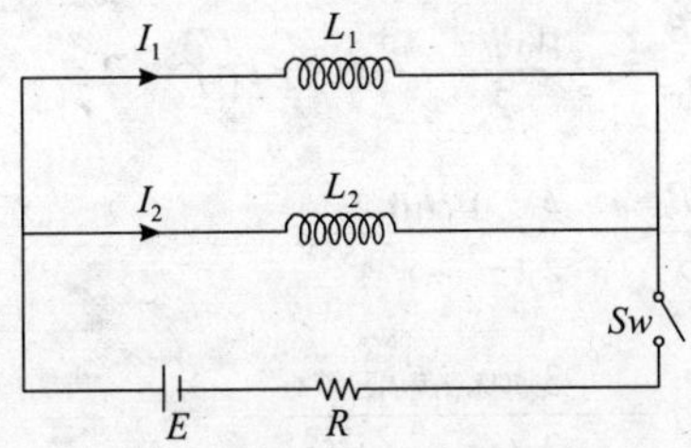

Figure 5.138

Illustrative Example 5.51

Two coaxial circular loops of radii 0.5 m and 0.05 m are separated by a distance 0.5 m and carry currents 2 A and 1 A respectively. Calculate the mutual inductance for this pair of coils and the force between the two coils.

Solution

Magnetic field at the location of smaller loop due to larger loop is given as

$$B = \frac{\mu_0 i_1 r_1^2}{2(x^2+r_1^2)^{3/2}}$$

Flux through the smaller loop is given as

$$\phi_2 = B \times (\pi r_2^2)$$

$$\Rightarrow \qquad \phi_2 = \frac{\mu_0 i_1 r_1^2}{2(x^2+r_1^2)^{3/2}} \times \pi r_2^2$$

If M is the coefficient of mutual induction between the pair of coils, we use

$$\phi_2 = Mi_1$$

$$\Rightarrow \qquad M = \frac{\phi_2}{i_1} = \frac{\mu_0 \pi r_1^2 r_2^2}{2(x^2+r_1^2)^{3/2}}$$

$$\Rightarrow \qquad M = \frac{(4\pi\times10^{-7})\pi\times0.25\times(25\times10^{-4})}{2(0.25+0.25)^{3/2}}$$

$$\Rightarrow \qquad M = 3.5\times10^{-9}\,\text{H}$$

If m is the magnetic moment of the coil then force on this coil is given as

$$F = m\left(\frac{dB}{dx}\right)$$

$$\Rightarrow \qquad F = (\pi r^2 i_2)\frac{dB}{dx}$$

As
$$B = \frac{\mu_0 i_1 r_1^2}{2(x^2+r_1^2)^{3/2}}$$

$$\Rightarrow \quad \frac{dB}{dx} = -\frac{\mu_0 i_1 r_1^2}{2} \times \frac{3}{2}(x^2 + r_1^2)^{-5/2}.2x$$

$$\Rightarrow \quad \frac{dB}{dx} = -\frac{3}{2}\frac{\mu_0 i_1 r_1^2 x}{(x^2 + r_1^2)^{5/2}}$$

$$\Rightarrow \quad F = -\frac{3}{2}\frac{\pi\mu_0 i_1 i_2 r_1^2 r_2^2 x}{(x^2 + r_1^2)^{5/2}}$$

$$\Rightarrow \quad F = \frac{-3 i_1 i_2 x}{(x^2 + r_1^2)} \times M_{12}$$

$$\Rightarrow \quad F = \frac{-3\times 2\times 1\times 0.5}{(0.25+0.25)} \times 3.5\times 10^{-9}$$

$$\Rightarrow \quad F = 2.1\times 10^{-8}\,\text{N}$$

Illustrative Example 5.52

There are two stationary loops with mutual inductance M. The current in one of the loops starts varying as $I_1 = \alpha t$, where α is a constant and t is any time instant starting from $t = 0$. Find the time dependence $I_2(t)$ of the current in the other loop which has self inductance L and resistance R.

Solution

The induced EMF in the second loop when the current changes in the first loop is given as

$$e_2 = M\frac{dI_1}{dt}$$

$$\Rightarrow \quad e_2 = M\alpha$$

For the second loop we use KVL equation which gives

$$I_2 R + L\frac{dI_2}{dt} = M\alpha$$

$$\Rightarrow \quad \int_0^{I_2} \frac{dI_2}{\left(I_2 - \frac{M\alpha}{R}\right)} = -\frac{R}{L}\int_0^t dt$$

$$\Rightarrow \quad I_2 = \frac{\alpha M}{R}(1 - e^{-Rt/L})$$

5.8 LC Oscillations

In article-5.6 we studied that on connecting an active inductor across a resistor current in inductor decays and its magnetic energy decays in resistor as heat. Figure-5.139 shows an active inductor connected across a capacitor via a switch. In this situation when switch is closed (Stage-I) then current flows in the loop with initial current I_0 and the current charges the capacitor due to which electrical energy of capacitor increases which comes from the magnetic energy of inductor thus current in loop decreases with time as capacitor energy increases and inductor energy decreases as shown in stage-II.

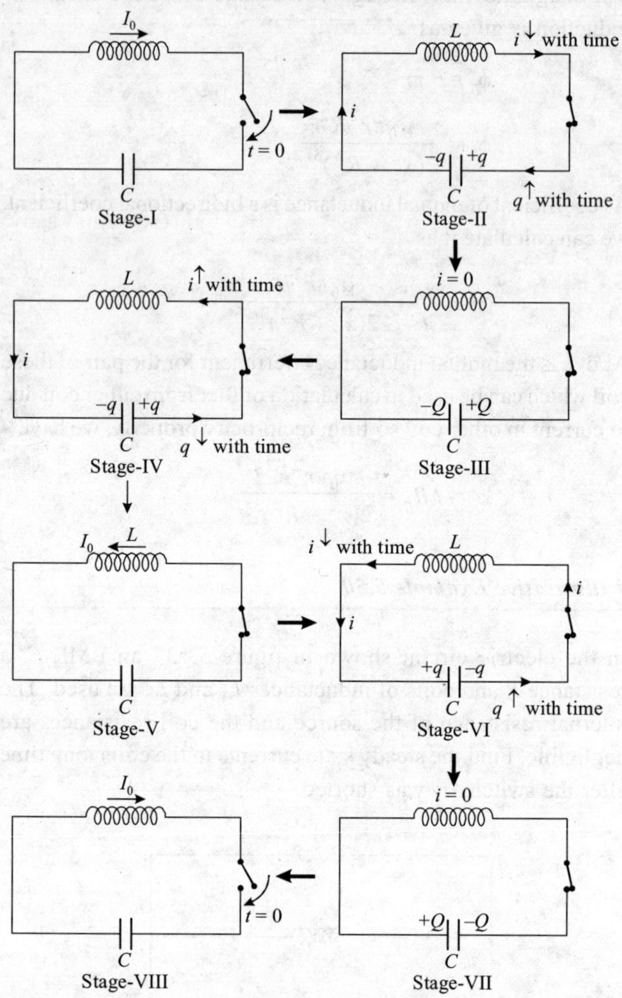

Figure 5.139

After sometime capacitor charge increases to maximum when current in loop becomes zero and at this instant magnetic energy in inductor becomes zero as shown in stage-III. We can state that whole initial magnetic energy of inductor is transformed into electrical energy of capacitor thats why its charge is maximum. After this instant capacitor starts discharging through the inductor for which a current flows in loop in anticlockwise direction and current increases and charge on capacitor starts decreasing and again electrical energy of capacitor starts transforming into magnetic energy of inductor as shown in stage-IV. After sometime stage-V comes when whole energy is transformed as magnetic and current in inductor becomes I_0 again and charge on capacitor becomes zero. After this further stages-VI, VII and VIII are self explanatory and finally in stage-VIII loop attains the initial state as shown in stage-I. With this cycle of oscillation of charge in the loop in above explained stages is called '*LC Oscillations*'. Under ideal conditions resistance of the circuit is considered zero with inductor and capacitor are considered ideal, no energy dissipation is considered so charge in an inductor and capacitor connected in parallel oscillates indefinitely.

5.8.1 Oscillation Period of LC Oscillations

As discussed in previous article when an inductor and a capacitor with some energy in either of these connected in parallel, charge and energy starts oscillating in the loop. At any instant if q is the charge on capacitor and i is the current in circuit then total energy of circuit can be given as

$$E=\frac{q^2}{2C}+\frac{1}{2}Li^2 \quad \ldots(5.102)$$

During oscillations energy periodically transforms from electrical to magnetic and then back to electric and vice versa and under ideal conditions of zero resistance no energy loss take place so the above energy of circuit E will remain constant in time. Differentiating the above equation-(5.102) gives

$$\frac{dE}{dt}=\frac{1}{2C}(2q)\frac{dq}{dt}+\frac{1}{2}L(2i)\frac{di}{dt}=0$$

$$\Rightarrow \quad \frac{q}{C}\frac{dq}{dt}+Li\frac{d^2q}{dt^2}=0$$

$$\Rightarrow \quad \frac{d^2q}{dt^2}+\left(\frac{1}{LC}\right)q=0 \quad \ldots(5.103)$$

Above equation-(5.103) is similar to the basic differential equation of SHM which is for displacement and it is written as

$$\frac{d^2x}{dt^2}+\omega^2x=0 \quad \ldots(5.104)$$

This shows that in LC oscillations charge executes SHM of which angular frequency can be given by comparing equations-(5.103) and (5.104) which gives

$$\omega=\frac{1}{\sqrt{LC}} \quad \ldots(5.105)$$

Thus time period of oscillating charge in LC circuit is given as

$$T=\frac{2\pi}{\omega}$$

$$\Rightarrow \quad T=2\pi\sqrt{LC} \quad \ldots(5.106)$$

From equation-(5.103) we've seen that charge on capacitor is executing SHM so by the general solution of SHM from equation-(5.103) the charge on capacitor plates as a function of time can be given as

$$q=q_0\sin(\omega t+\alpha) \quad \ldots(5.107)$$

In above equation q_0 is the charge amplitude which is the maximum charge on capacitor plates during oscillations, ω is the angular frequency of oscillations which is given by equation-(5.105) for the case when one capacitor and one inductor are connected in parallel. In other cases it can be obtained by differentiating energy equation for the given circuit and α is the initial phase of oscillating charge which depends upon the initial condition of the circuit when switch is closed. Initial phase can also be calculated by the uniform circular motion analysis like the way we did it in different illustrations while analyzing SHM. This will be further explained with the help of illustrations on LC oscillations.

During oscillations the current in circuit can be given as

$$i=\frac{dq}{dt}=q_0\,\omega\cos(\omega t+\alpha) \quad \ldots(5.108)$$

Above equation is similar to the velocity of a particle executing SHM thus current in circuit in terms of instantaneous charge on capacitor can be given as

$$i=\omega\sqrt{q_0^2-q^2} \quad \ldots(5.109)$$

As already discussed that circuit current becomes maximum when capacitor charge is zero thus maximum current in circuit is related to the maximum charge on capacitor as

$$i_{max}=\omega q_0 \quad \ldots(5.110)$$

$$\Rightarrow \quad i_{max}=\frac{q_0}{\sqrt{LC}} \quad \ldots(5.111)$$

Above expression of maximum current can also be obtained by conservation of energy. If maximum charge on capacitor is known then at the instant charge on capacitor is maximum current in circuit is zero as whole energy of circuit is electrical energy in capacitor and at the instant of maximum current whole energy is transformed into magnetic energy thus by energy conservation we have

$$\frac{q_0^2}{2C}=\frac{1}{2}Li_{max}^2$$

$$\Rightarrow \quad i_{max}=\frac{q_0}{\sqrt{LC}}$$

 # *Illustrative Example 5.53*

A capacitor of capacitance 25 μF is charged to 300 V. It is then connected across a 10 mH inductor. The resistance in the circuit is negligible.

(a) Find the frequency of oscillation of the circuit

(b) Find the potential difference across capacitor and magnitude of circuit current 1.2 ms after the inductor and capacitor are connected

(c) Find the magnetic energy and electric energy at $t = 0$ and $t = 1.2$ ms

Solution

(a) The frequency of oscillation of the LC circuit is given as

$$f = \frac{1}{2\pi\sqrt{LC}}$$

Substituting the given values we have

$$f = \frac{1}{2\pi\sqrt{(10\times10^{-3})(25\times10^{-6})}}$$

$$\Rightarrow \quad f = 318.3 \text{ Hz}$$

(b) Charge across the capacitor at time t will be given as

$$q = q_0 \cos \omega t$$

and $$i = -q_0\omega \sin \omega t$$

Given that initial maximum charge on capacitor is

$$q_0 = CV_0 = (25 \times 10^{-6})(300)$$

$$\Rightarrow \quad q_0 = 7.5 \times 10^{-3} \text{ C}$$

The charge in the capacitor after time $t = 1.2 \times 10^{-3}$ s is given as

$$q = (7.5 \times 10^{-3}) \cos (2\pi \times 318.3)(1.2 \times 10^{-3}) \text{ C}$$

$$\Rightarrow \quad q = -5.53 \times 10^{-3} \text{ C}$$

Potential difference across capacitor is given as

$$V = \frac{|q|}{C} = \frac{5.53\times10^{-3}}{25\times10^{-6}} = 221.2 \text{ V}$$

The magnitude of current in the circuit at $t = 1.2 \times 10^{-3}$ s is given as

$$|i| = q_0\omega \sin \omega t$$

$$\Rightarrow |i| = (7.5 \times 10^{-3})(2\pi)(318.3) \sin[(2\pi)(318.3)(1.2 \times 10^{-3})] \text{ A}$$

$$\Rightarrow |i| = 10.13 \text{ A}$$

(c) At $t = 0$ current in the circuit is zero so magnetic energy in inductor is also zero and charge in the capacitor is maximum so total energy is magnetic energy which is given as

$$U_C = \frac{1}{2}\frac{q_0^2}{C}$$

$$\Rightarrow \quad U_C = \frac{1}{2} \times \frac{(7.5\times10^{-3})^2}{(25\times10^{-6})} = 1.125 \text{ J}$$

Total energy in circuit at any instant which is stored in inductor and capacitor is also given as

$$E = U_L + U_C = 1.125 \text{ J}$$

At $t = 1.2$ ms, we use

$$U_L = \frac{1}{2}Li^2 = \frac{1}{2}(10 \times 10^{-3})(10.13)^2$$

$$\Rightarrow \quad U_L = 0.513 \text{ J}$$

and $$U_C = E - U_L = 1.125 - 0.513$$

$$\Rightarrow U_C = 0.612 \text{ J}$$

Otherwise U_C can be calculated as

$$U_C = \frac{1}{2}\frac{q^2}{C} = \frac{1}{2} \times \frac{(5.53\times10^{-3})^2}{(25\times10^{-6})}$$

$$\Rightarrow \quad U_C = 0.612 \text{ J}$$

 # Illustrative Example 5.54

In circuit shown in figure-5.140 charge on capacitor is $Q = 100$ μC. If switch is closed at $t = 0$ find current in circuit when charge on capacitor reduces to 50 μC. Also find the maximum current in circuit.

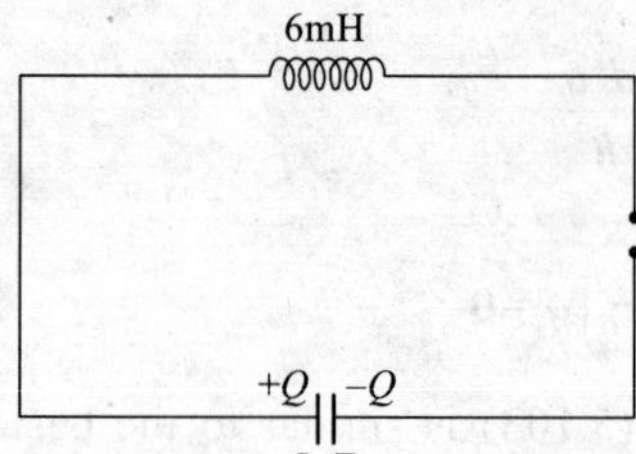

Figure 5.140

Solution

At $t = 0$ when switch is closed capacitor starts discharging through the inductor and current in circuit increases. When charge on capacitor is q and current in circuit is i by conservation of energy we have

$$\frac{q^2}{2C} + \frac{1}{2}Li^2 = \frac{Q^2}{2C}$$

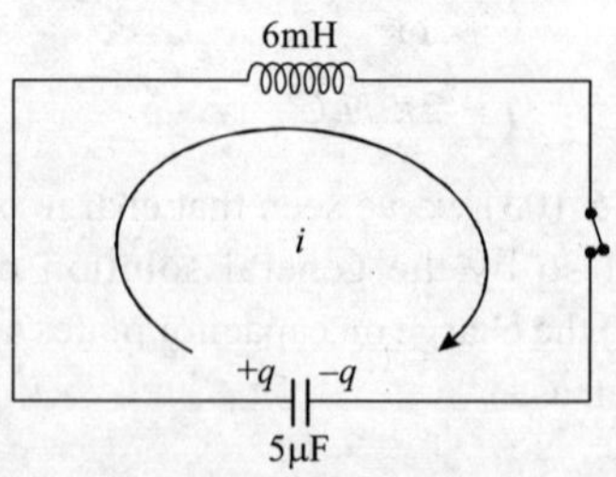

Figure 5.141

Current in circuit in terms of charge on capacitor is given as

$$i=\frac{1}{\sqrt{LC}}\sqrt{Q^2-q^2}=\frac{\sqrt{(100\mu)^2-(50\mu)^2}}{\sqrt{3\times10^{-8}}}$$

$$\Rightarrow\ i=\frac{10^{-6}}{\sqrt{3\times10^{-4}}}\sqrt{7500}$$

$$\Rightarrow\ i=0.5\text{ A}$$

Maximum energy stored in inductor is given as

$$\frac{1}{2}LI_{max}^2=\frac{Q^2}{2L}$$

$$\Rightarrow\quad I_{max}=\frac{Q}{\sqrt{LC}}=\frac{100\times10^{-6}}{\sqrt{3\times10^{-8}}}=\frac{1}{\sqrt{3}}\text{ A}$$

Illustrative Example 5.55

In an *L-C* circuit $L = 3.3$ H and $C = 840$ pF. At $t = 0$ charge on the capacitor is 105 μC and maximum. Compute the following quantities at $t = 2.0$ ms

(a) The energy stored in the capacitor

(b) The total energy in the circuit

(c) The energy stored in the inductor

Solution

The angular frequency of *L-C* oscillations is,

$$\omega=\frac{1}{\sqrt{LC}}$$

$$\Rightarrow\quad \omega=\frac{1}{\sqrt{3.3\times840\times10^{-12}}}$$

$$\Rightarrow\quad \omega=1.9\times10^4\text{ rad/s}$$

Charge stored in the capacitor at time *t*, is given as

$$q=q_0\cos\omega t$$

(a) At $t=2\times10^{-3}$ s

$$q=(105\times10^{-6})\cos[1.9\times10^4][2\times10^{-3}]$$

$$\Rightarrow\quad q=100.3\times10^{-6}\text{ C}$$

Energy stored in the capacitor at this instant is given as

$$U_C=\frac{1}{2}\frac{q^2}{C}$$

$$\Rightarrow\quad U_C=\frac{(100.3\times10^{-6})^2}{2\times840\times10^{-12}}$$

$$\Rightarrow\quad U_C=6.0\text{ J}$$

(b) Total energy in the circuit is the energy in capacitor at maximum charge which is given as

$$U=\frac{1}{2}\frac{q_0^2}{C}$$

$$\Rightarrow\quad U=\frac{(105\times10^{-6})^2}{2\times840\times10^{-12}}$$

$$\Rightarrow\quad U=6.56\text{ J}$$

(c) Energy stored in inductor in the given time is given by conservation of energy as

$$U_L=(6.56-6.0)\text{ J}$$

$$\Rightarrow\quad U_L=0.56\text{ J}$$

Illustrative Example 5.56

In an oscillating *LC* circuit in which $C = 4.00$ μF, the maximum potential difference across the capacitor during the oscillations is 1.50 V and the maximum current through the inductor is 50.0 mA.

(a) What is the inductance *L*?

(b) What is the frequency of the oscillations ?

(c) How much time does the charge on the capacitor take to rise from zero to its maximum value ?

Solution

(a) By conservation of energy we have

$$\frac{1}{2}Li_0^2=\frac{1}{2}CV_0^2$$

$$\Rightarrow\quad L=\frac{CV_0^2}{i_0^2}$$

$$\Rightarrow\quad L=\frac{(4\times10^{-6})(1.5)}{(50\times10^{-3})^2}$$

$$\Rightarrow\quad L=3.6\times10^{-3}\text{ H}$$

(b) Oscillation frequency of the LC circuit is given as

$$f=\frac{1}{2\pi\sqrt{LC}}$$

$$\Rightarrow\quad f=\frac{1}{2\pi\sqrt{(3.6\times10^{-3})(4\times10^{-6})}}$$

$$\Rightarrow\quad f=0.133\times10^4\text{ Hz}$$

$$\Rightarrow\quad f=1.33\text{ kHz}$$

(c) During oscillations the time taken for charge to rise from zero to maximum is one fourth of the oscillation period which is given as

$$t=\frac{T}{4}=\frac{1}{4f}$$

$$\Rightarrow \quad t=\frac{1}{4\times1.33\times10^{3}}\,s$$

$$\Rightarrow \quad t=0.188\times10^{-3}\,\text{s}$$

$$\Rightarrow \quad t=0.188\,\text{ms}$$

Illustrative Example 5.57

In the circuit shown in the figure-5.142, $E=50.0$ V, $R=250\,\Omega$ and $C=0.500\,\mu$F. The switch S is closed for a long time, and no voltage is measured across the capacitor. After the switch is opened, the voltage across the capacitor reaches a maximum value of 150 V. What is the inductance L?

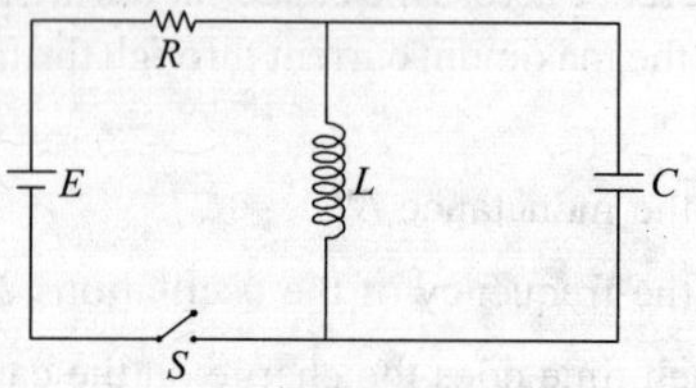

Figure 5.142

Solution

In steady state when switch was closed,

$$i_0=\frac{E}{R}=0.2\,\text{A}$$

After switch is opened, it becomes LC circuit in which peak current is 0.2 A. By energy conservation we have

$$\frac{1}{2}Li_0^2=\frac{1}{2}CV_0^2$$

$$\Rightarrow \quad L=\frac{V_0^2}{i_0^2}\cdot C$$

$$\Rightarrow \quad L=\frac{(150)^2}{(0.2)^2}\times0.5\times10^{-6}$$

$$\Rightarrow \quad L=0.28\,\text{H}$$

Illustrative Example 5.58

An inductor of inductance 2.0 mH is connected across a charged capacitor of capacitance 5.0 μF, and resulting L-C circuit is set oscillating at its natural frequency. Let Q denote the instantaneous charge on the capacitor, and I the current in the circuit. It is found that the maximum value of Q is 200 μC.

(a) When $Q=100\,\mu$C, what is the value of $\left|\frac{dI}{dt}\right|$

(b) When $Q=200\,\mu$C, what is the value of I?

(c) Find the maximum value of I.

(d) When I is equal to one half its maximum value, what is the value of $|Q|$?

Solution

Charge stored in the capacitor oscillates simple harmonically and charge as a function of time is given as

$$q=q_0\sin(\omega t\pm\phi)$$

Here we use $q_0=200\,\mu\text{C}=2\times10^{-4}\,\text{C}$

and $\quad \omega=\frac{1}{\sqrt{LC}}$

$$\Rightarrow \quad \omega=\frac{1}{\sqrt{(2\times10^{-3})(5.0\times10^{-6})}}=10^4\,\text{s}^{-1}$$

If at $t=0$, $q=q_0$

$$q=q_0\cos\omega t \qquad \ldots(5.112)$$

$$\Rightarrow \quad I=\frac{dq}{dt}=-q_0\omega\sin\omega t \qquad \ldots(5.113)$$

and $$\frac{dI}{dt}=-q_0\omega^2\cos\omega t \qquad \ldots(5.114)$$

(a) At $q=100\,\mu$C we have

$$\cos\omega t=\frac{1}{2}$$

$$\Rightarrow \quad \omega t=\frac{\pi}{3}$$

At $\cos(\omega t)=\frac{1}{2}$ and from equation-(5.114) we have

$$\left|\frac{dI}{dt}\right|=(2.0\times10^{-4}\,\text{C})(10^4\,\text{s}^{-1})^2\left(\frac{1}{2}\right)$$

$$\Rightarrow \quad \left|\frac{dI}{dt}\right|=10^4\,\text{A/s}$$

(b) At $q=200\,\mu$C we have

$$\cos\omega t=1$$

$$\Rightarrow \quad \omega t=0, 2\pi\ldots$$

At this time instant we have

$$I = -q_0\omega \sin \omega t$$

$$\Rightarrow \quad I = -0$$

(c) Current is given by equation-(5.113) as

$$I = -Q_0\omega \sin \omega t$$

Maximum value of current is $Q_0\omega$

$$\Rightarrow \quad I_{max} = Q_0\omega$$

$$\Rightarrow \quad I_{max} = (2.0 \times 10^{-4})(10^4)$$

$$\Rightarrow \quad I_{max} = 2.0\,\text{A}$$

(d) From energy conservation we have

$$\frac{1}{2}LI_{max}^2 = \frac{1}{2}LI^2 + \frac{1}{2}\frac{Q^2}{C}$$

$$\Rightarrow \quad Q = \sqrt{LC(I_{max}^2 - I^2)}$$

Using $I = \frac{I_{max}}{2} = 1.0\,\text{A}$

$$\Rightarrow \quad Q = \sqrt{(2.0\times10^{-3})(5.0\times10^{-6})(2^2-1^2)}$$

$$\Rightarrow \quad Q = \sqrt{3} \times 10^{-4}\,\text{C}$$

$$\Rightarrow \quad Q = 1.732 \times 10^{-4}\,\text{C}$$

Illustrative Example 5.59

In figure-5.143 if S is closed at $t = 0$, find charge on capacitor as a function of time. The inductor is active with initial current I_0 in it.

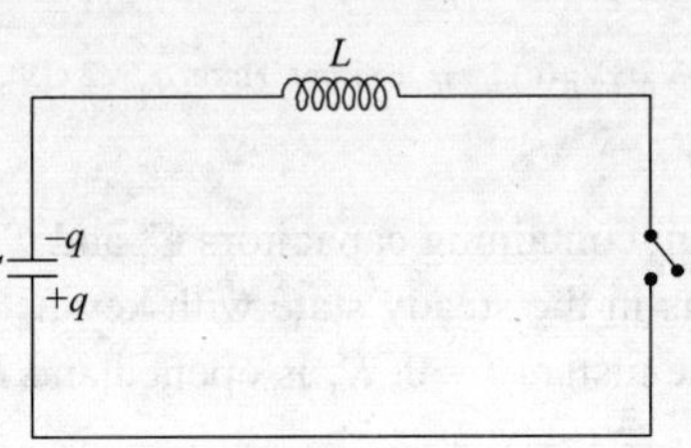

Figure 5.143

Solution

If q_0 is the maximum charge on capacitor then by energy conservation we have

$$\frac{1}{2}LI_0^2 = \frac{q_0^2}{2C}$$

$$\Rightarrow \quad q_0 = \sqrt{LC} \cdot I_0$$

Charge on capacitor as a function of time is given as

$$q = q_0 \sin(\omega t + \alpha)$$

Where $\omega = \frac{1}{\sqrt{LC}}$ and at $t = 0$, $q = 0$ we get $\alpha = 0$.

Thus charge on capacitor is given as

$$q = \sqrt{LC}\, I_0 \sin\left(\frac{t}{\sqrt{LC}}\right)$$

Web Reference at www.physicsgalaxy.com

Age Group - Grade 11 & 12 | Age 17-19 Years
Section - Magnetic Effects
Topic - Self & Mutual Inductance
Module Number - 22 to 36

Practice Exercise 5.4

(i) Two thin concentric wires shaped as circle with radii a and b lie in the same plane. Allowing for $a << b$, find

(a) Their mutual inductance

(b) The magnetic flux through the surface enclosed by the outside wire, when the inside wire carries a current I.

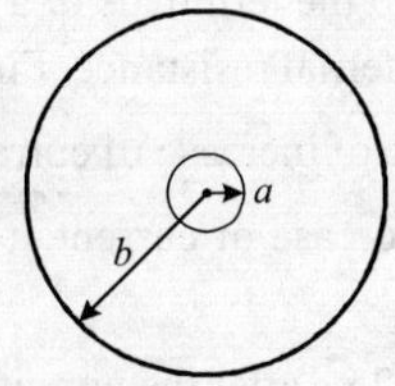

Figure 5.144

[(a) $\frac{\mu_0 \pi a^2}{2b}$; (b) $\frac{\mu_0 \pi a^2 I}{2b}$]

(ii) (a) Calculate the mutual inductance between two coils when a current of 4 A in first coil changes to 12 A in 0.5s and induces an EMF of 50 mV in the other coil.

(b) Also calculate the induced EMF in the second coil if current in the first changes from 3 A to 9 A in 0.02 s.

[(a) 3.125×10^{-3} H; (b) 0.9375 V]

(iii) Find the mutual inductance of two thin coaxial loops of the same radius a if their centres are separated by a distance l, with $l >> a$.

[$\frac{\mu_0 \pi a^4}{2l^3}$]

(iv) The equivalent inductance of two inductors is 2.4 H when connected in parallel and 10 H when connected in series. What is the value of inductance of the individual inductors. Neglect mutual inductance between the two inductors.

[4 H, 6 H]

(v) A circular coil P of 100 turns and radius 2 cm is placed coaxially at the centre of another circular coil Q of 1000 turns and radius 20 cm. Calculate

(a) The mutual inductance of the coils,

(b) The induced EMF in coil P when the current in the coil Q decreases from 5 A to 3 A in 0.04 s

(c) The rate of change of flux through the coil P at this instant

(d) The charge passing through coil P if its resistance is 8Ω.

[(a) 3.94×10^{-4} H (b) 19.72×10^{-3} V (c) 19.72×10^{-3} Wb/s (d) 9.86×10^{-5} C]

(vi) A long solenoid of length 1 m, cross-sectional area 10 cm², having 1000 turns has wound about its centre a small coil of 20 turns. Compute the mutual inductance of the pair of solenoid and the coil. What is the induced EMF in the coil when the current in the solenoid changes at the rate of 10 A/s ?

[251 μV]

(vii) An inductor with an inductance of 2.5 H and a resistance of 8 Ω is connected to the terminals of a battery with an EMF 6 V and negligible internal resistance. Find

(a) The initial rate of increase of current in the circuit

(b) The rate of increase of current at the instant when the current is 0.50 A

(c) The current 0.25 s after the circuit is closed

(d) The final steady state current

[(a) 2.40 A/s (b) 0.80 A/s (c) 0.413 A (d) 0.750 A]

(viii) In the given circuit shown in figure-5.145, find the current through the 5 mH inductor in steady state.

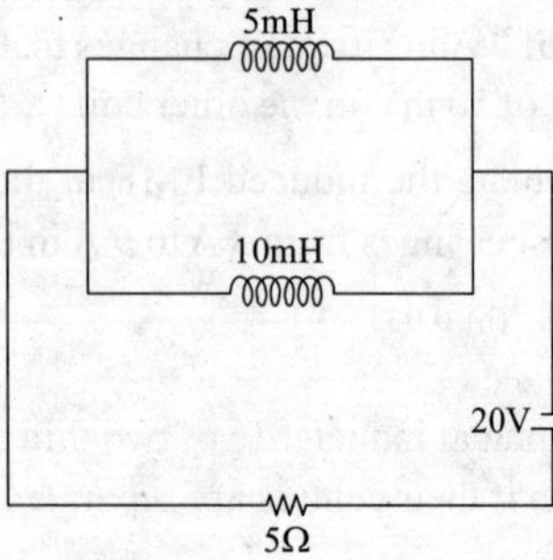

Figure 5.145

[$\frac{8}{3}$A]

(ix) In the LC circuit shown in figure-5.146, $C = 1$ μF. With capacitor charged to 100 V, switch S is suddenly closed at time $t = 0$. The circuit then oscillates at a frequency of 10^3 Hz.

(a) Calculate ω and T

(b) Express q as a function of time

(c) Calculate L

(d) Calculate the average current during the first quarter-cycle.

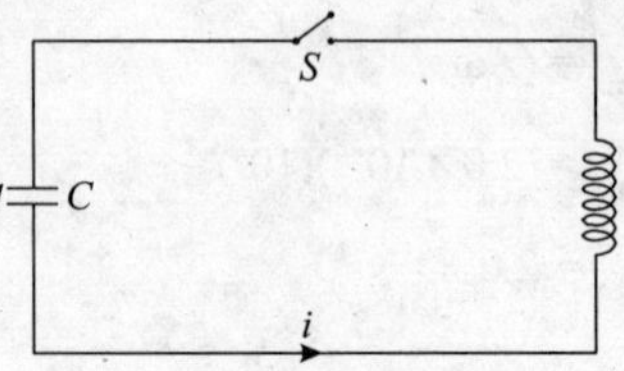

Figure 5.146

[(a) 6.28×10^3 rad/s, 10^{-3}s (b) $10^{-4} \cos (6.28 \times 10^3 t)$ (c) 0.0253 H (d) 0.4 A]

(x) Two capacitors of capacitances 2 C and C are connected in series with an inductor of inductance L. Initially capacitors have charge such that $V_B - V_A = 4V_0$ and $V_C - V_D = V_0$. Initial current in the circuit is zero. Find

(a) Maximum current that will flow in the circuit

(b) Potential difference across each capacitor at that instant

(c) Equation of current flowing towards left in the inductor

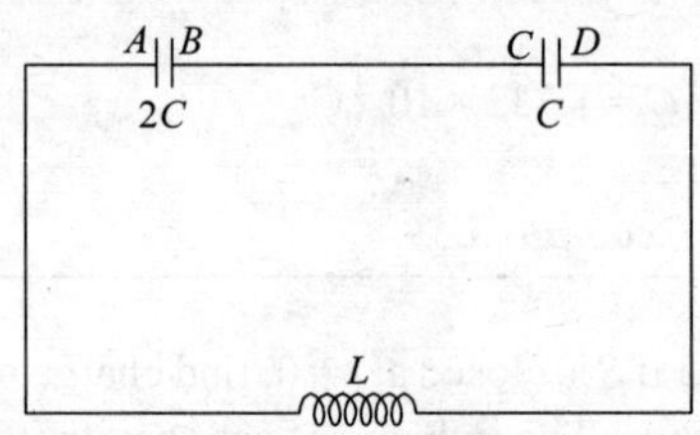

Figure 5.147

[(a) $2 CV_0\omega$ (b) $3V_0:3V_0$ (c) $i = q_0\omega \sin\omega t$. Here, $q_0 = 2 CV_0$ and $\omega = \sqrt{\frac{3}{2LC}}$]

(xi) A circuit containing capacitors C_1 and C_2, shown in the figure-5.148 is in the steady state with key K_1 closed and K_2 opened. At the instant $t = 0$, K_1 is opened and K_2 is closed.

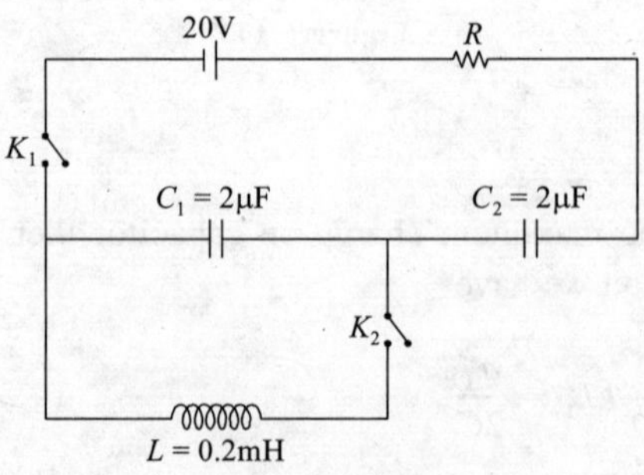

Figure 5.148

(a) Find the angular frequency of oscillations of LC circuit.

(b) Determine the first instant t, when energy in the inductor becomes one third of that in the capacitor.

(c) Calculate the charge on the plates of the capacitor at that instant.

[(a) 5×10^4 rad/s (b) 1.05×10^{-5}s (c) $10\sqrt{3}\mu C$]

(xii) In circuit shown in figure-5.149 if switches S_1 and S_2 are closed at $t = 0$, find the oscillation frequency of charge in this circuit. Neglect mutual induction between inductors.

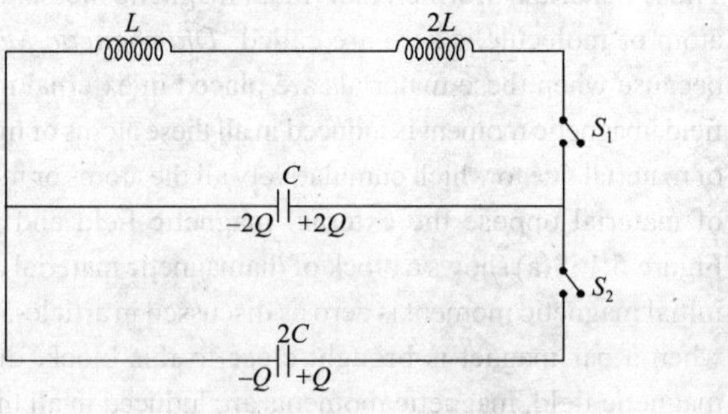

Figure 5.149

$[\frac{1}{6\pi\sqrt{LC}}]$

(xiii) Figure-5.150 shows LC circuit with initial charge on capacitor 200 μC. If at $t = 0$ switch is closed, find the first instant when energy stored in inductor becomes one third that of capacitor.

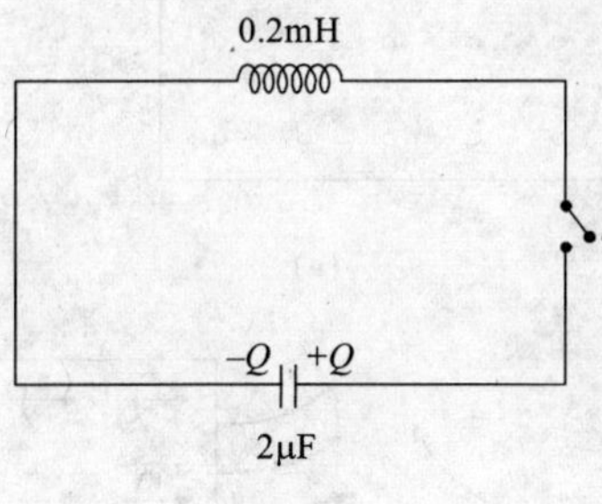

Figure 5.150

[10.5μs]

5.9 *Magnetic Properties of Matter*

In previous chapter and articles we've discussed about the origin of magnetic field by currents whether in a coil or by motion of charge particles or orbital motion of electrons in atoms. It is observed when a material is placed in an external magnetic field then the magnetic field of atomic electrons in the atoms of material interact with the external field. The magnetic properties of different materials depend upon how the atomic electrons interact with external magnetic field. The best way to discuss about the magnetic properties of materials is to analyze the behaviour and responses of different materials when placed in an external magnetic field. Based on the responses of materials in magnetic field, all materials are classified in three broad categories :

(i) Diamagnetic Materials

(ii) Paramagnetic Materials

(iii) Ferromagnetic Materials

To understand the behaviour and classification of materials as discussed above first we need to understand the magnetic moment of atoms in different materials due to the orbital motion of electrons.

5.9.1 Magnetic Moment of Hydrogen Atom

In a hydrogen atom a single electron revolves around a proton and by Bohr's postulate of quantisation of angular momentum the angular momentum of electron in its ground state is given as

$$L = \frac{h}{2\pi} \quad \ldots(5.114)$$

The magnetic moment μ of the atom due to electron motion can be directly given by equation-(4.168) as

$$\mu = \frac{e}{2m} \times L$$

$$\Rightarrow \quad \mu = \frac{e}{2m} \times \frac{h}{2\pi}$$

$$\Rightarrow \quad \mu = \frac{eh}{4\pi m} \quad \ldots(5.115)$$

The value given in equation-(5.115) is termed as *'Bohr Magneton'* and it is used as a basic unit for measurement of magnetic dipole moment due to electron spin or orbital motion in an atom.

5.9.2 Natural Magnetic Moment in Different Materials

In atoms of different materials there are many electrons in different orbits in their atoms. These electrons have orbital magnetic moment due to their orbital motion and in addition to that these electrons also have magnetic moment due to their spin angular momentum which may get added or subtracted in their resulting magnetic moment depending upon their direction.

Overall there can be two possibilities in a material. First is that magnetic moment due to an individual atom in a material is zero thus overall magnetic moment of the piece of material is also zero. Figure-5.151(a) shows magnified view of a small block of material in which each dot represent an atom which has zero dipole moment. Another possibility is that magnetic moment due to individual atoms in the material is non zero but all such dipole moments are randomly scattered in the volume of material so overall magnetic moment of the piece of material is zero. Figure-5.151(b) shows magnified view of a small block of material in which each of its atom has non zero magnetic dipole moment which is represented by a small arrow but all these magnetic moments are distributed in random directions thus overall sum of all the dipole moments can be taken zero.

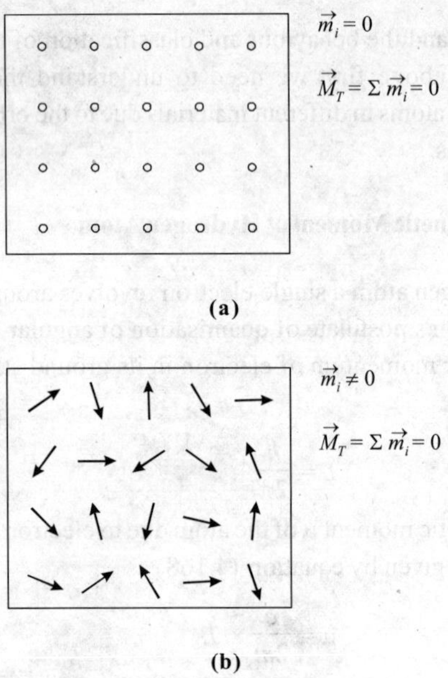

Figure 5.151

5.9.3 Diamagnetism

The property in a material because of which it has a tendency to repel external magnetic field is called '*Diamagnetism*'. To understand this see the figure-5.152 which shows a coil mounted on a rigid support and a bar magnet is moving toward the coil along its axis. We know that due to motion of magnet the magnetic flux through the coil changes and a current is induced in the coil in such a direction to oppose the motion of magnet. We can also say that a magnetic moment is induced in coil in opposition to the magnet.

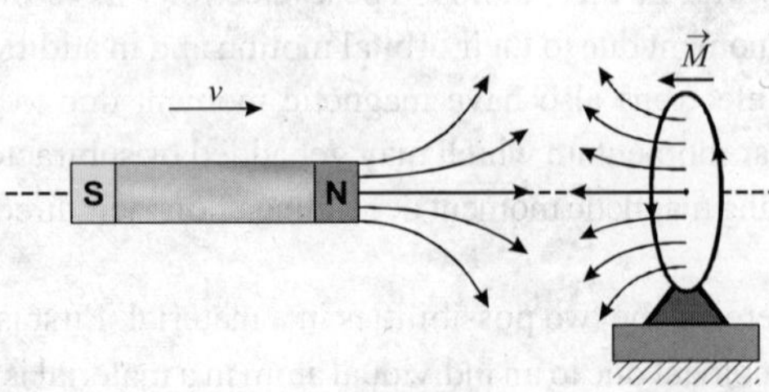

Figure 5.152

In every material there are atoms in which orbitting electrons behave like equivalent currents. Whenever an external magnetic field is applied on a material, all the orbits in atoms of the material have more or less tendency to oppose the external magnetic field and an opposite magnetic moment is induced in the coil which opposes the external field. Thus every material has some diamagnetic character in it.

5.9.4 Response of Diamagnetic Materials to External Magnetic Fields

Those materials in which individual magnetic moment of each atom or molecule is zero are called '*Diamagnetic Materials*' because when these materials are placed in external magnetic field, magnetic moment is induced in all these atoms or molecules of material due to which cumulatively all the atoms or molecules of material oppose the external magnetic field and repel it. Figure-5.153(a) shows a block of diamagnetic material of which initial magnetic moment is zero as discussed in article-5.9.2 and when a bar magnet is brought close to this block, due to its magnetic field, magnetic moments are induced in all the atoms in the block in opposite direction and because of all these dipoles block produces an induced magnetic field B_i in direction opposite to that of bar magnet as shown in figure-5.153(b) and this repels the bar magnet.

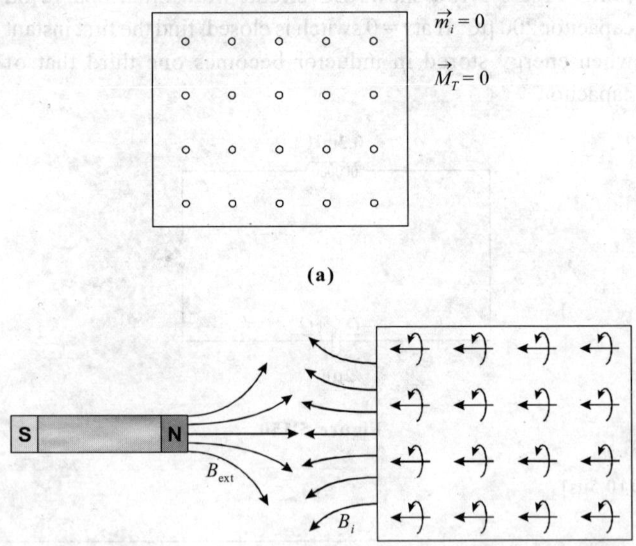

Figure 5.153

Always remember that diamagnetism is a weak phenomenon but in diamagnetic materials it can be seen in different ways like figure-5.154 shows a diamagnetic block placed between two opposite pole pieces repel the magnetic field and due to this magnetic lines bulge out as shown and almost every material has diamagnetic character upto some extent.

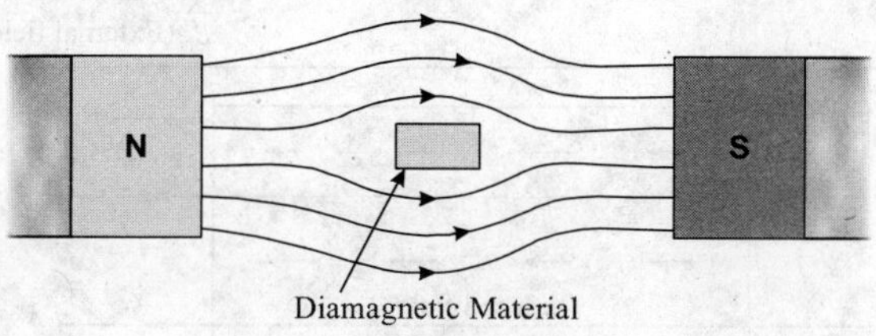

Figure 5.154

5.9.5 Magnetic Levitation in Diamagnetic Materials

As discussed in diamagnetic materials when subjected to external magnetic field then due to magnetization an opposite direction magnetic field is induced in the material and external magnetic field repels the magnetized block. This repulsive force can be used in suspension or propelling materials. This phenomenon is called '*Magnetic Levitation*'. Figure-5.155(a) shows a diamagnetic block placed at the top of an electromagnet on an insulating stand and as soon as the circuit switch is closed a magnetic field by electromagnet passes through the diamagnetic block and it is repelled. If the repulsive force is more than the weight of block it gets suspended in space above the electromagnet as shown in figure-5.155(b).

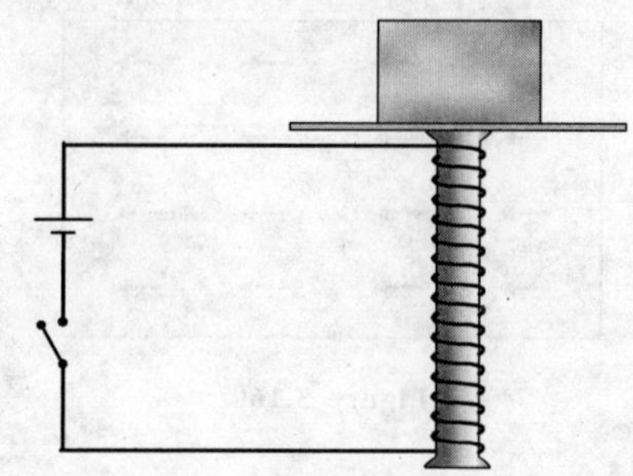

(a)

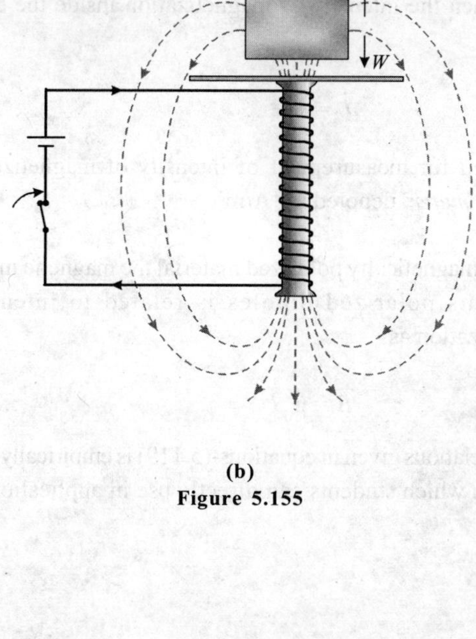

(b)

Figure 5.155

5.9.6 Paramagnetism

Whenever a magnetic dipole is placed in an external magnetic field, it exerts a torque on the dipole to align it along the direction of magnetic field. Figure-5.156 shows a free magnetic dipole placed in external magnetic field due to which it experiences a torque $\vec{M} \times \vec{B}$ in clockwise sense and as the dipole is free to rotate it will align along the direction of magnetic field as shown.

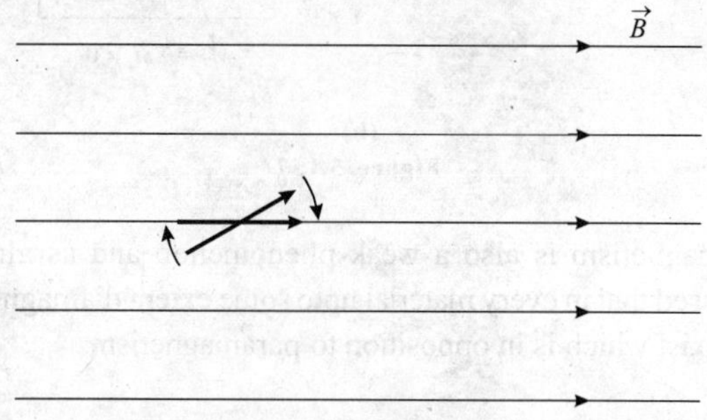

Figure 5.156

The materials in which their atoms or molecules have non zero magnetic moment randomly distributed in volume when placed in external magnetic field, these dipoles align along the direction of external field and then the total magnetic moment of the material will be non zero and along the direction of magnetic field. This phenomenon by which all the dipoles in a material align along the direction of external magnetic field and induces a magnetic field in the direction of external field is called '*Paramagnetism*' and such materials are called '*Paramagnetic Materials*'.

5.9.7 Response of Paramagnetic Materials to External Magnetic Fields

Figure-5.157(a) shows a block of paramagnetic material in which all its dipoles are randomly distributed with total dipole moment of the block zero as already discussed in article-5.9.2. When the block is subjected to an external magnetic field then all its dipoles align along the direction of external magnetic field as shown in figure-5.157(b). As all dipoles are in the direction of external magnetic field, thus the side of magnetically polarized block facing the magnet acts like a south pole which attracts the magnet or source of external magnetic field as shown in figure-5.157(b).

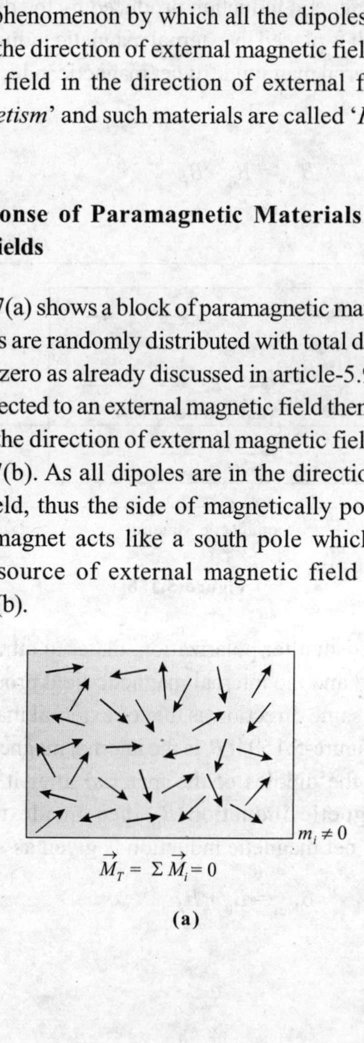

(a)

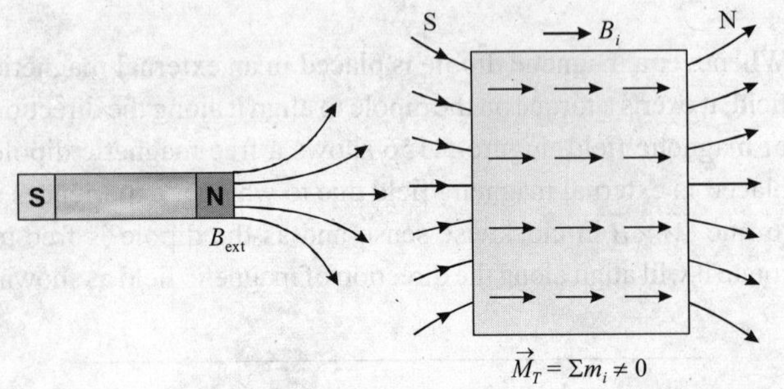

(b)

Figure 5.157

Paramagnetism is also a weak phenomenon and as already discussed that in every material upto some extent diamagnetism also exist which is in opposition to paramagnetism.

5.9.8 Magnetic Induction inside a Paramagnetic and Diamagnetic Materials

As already discussed in previous articles that in diamagnetism after polarization, material repel external magnetic field and the internal magnetic field produced by the material is in opposition to the external magnetic field. As shown in figure-5.158 if B_i is the internal magnetic induction produced by the dipoles of the material after it is placed in external magnetic induction B_0 then inside the material magnitude of net magnetic induction is given as

$$B_{\text{net}} = B_0 - B_i \qquad \ldots(5.116)$$

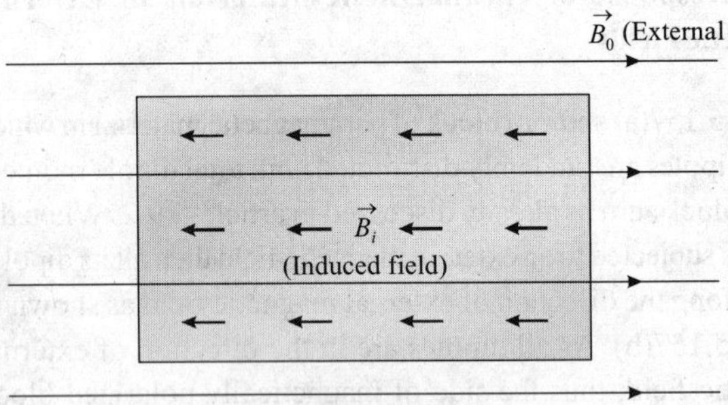

Figure 5.158

In paramagnetism after polarization, material attracts external magnetic field and the internal magnetic field produced by the material is in same direction as that of external magnetic field. As shown in figure-5.159 if B_i is the internal magnetic induction produced by the dipoles of the material after it is placed in external magnetic induction B_0 then inside the material magnitude of net magnetic induction is given as

$$B_{\text{Net}} = B_0 + B_i \qquad \ldots(5.117)$$

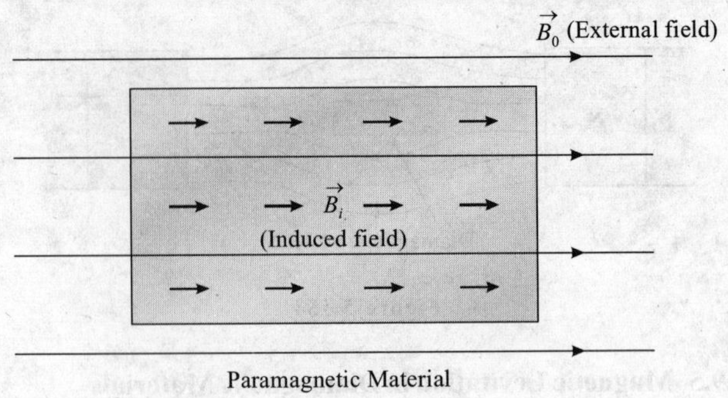

Figure 5.159

5.9.9 Intensity of Magnetization

As already discussed in article-5.9.2 due to random distribution of dipoles inside a material (if dipoles exist in the material) the total dipole moment of the whole block of material is zero but when it is subjected to an external magnetic field it gets magnetically polarized and net dipole moment exist. This net dipole moment direction is opposite to external magnetic field in diamagnetic materials and it is in same direction as that of external magnetic field in paramagnetic materials.

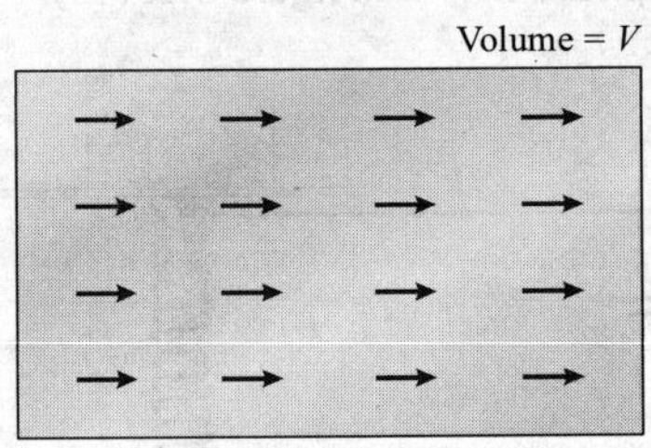

Figure 5.160

After magnetic polarization of a material the total dipole moment of the material per unit of its volume is called '*Intensity of Magnetization*'. Figure-5.160 shows a block of volume V which is magnetically polarized. If the total dipole moment of the block is $\overline{M}$ then the intensity of magnetization inside the block is given as

$$\vec{I} = \frac{\overline{M}}{V} \qquad \ldots(5.118)$$

Unit used for measurement of intensity of magnetization is '*ampere/meter*' denoted as 'A/m'.

Inside a magnetically polarized material the magnetic induction due to its polarized dipoles is related to intensity of magnetization as

$$\vec{B} = \mu_0 \vec{I} \qquad \ldots(5.119)$$

Above relations given in equations-(5.119) is empirically defined relations which students can directly use in applications.

5.9.10 Magnetic Field Vectors $\vec{B}$ and $\vec{H}$

In previous chapter we've discussed that in a region of magnetic field the magnetic induction is measured in units of '*Tesla*' and denoted by vector $\vec{B}$. In previous articles we've also discussed when external magnetic field passes through different materials then due to magnetization of materials net magnetic induction inside the magnetized (magnetically polarized) material changes so we need to define a physical quantity $\vec{H}$ for external magnetic field which does not change with medium. This $\vec{H}$ is called '*Magnetic Field Strength*' or '*Magnetizing Field*' of magnetic field. Magnetizing field in a given region is measured in units of 'ampere/meter' and denoted as 'A/m'.

In general both the vectors $\vec{B}$ and $\vec{H}$ are called commonly as magnetic field in practical situations. It is the unit of measurement which clarifies about which vector we are talking about. If unit used is 'tesla' then its $\vec{B}$ and if unit used is 'A/m' then its $\vec{H}$. In a given region of space both the vectors of magnetic field are related as

$$\vec{B} = \mu_0 \vec{H} \qquad \ldots(5.120)$$

Inside a material having magnetic permeability μ_r the relation is modified as

$$\vec{B} = \mu_0\mu_r \vec{H} \qquad \ldots(5.121)$$

5.9.11 Relation in $\vec{B}$, $\vec{H}$ and $\vec{I}$ in Magnetization of Materials

When a material is placed in external magnetic field of magnetic induction $\vec{B_0}$ then as discussed in article-5.9.8 due to magnetization of material an induced magnetic induction inside the material $\vec{B_i}$ is developed and net magnetic induction inside the material vectorially is given as

$$\vec{B} = \vec{B_0} + \vec{B_i} \qquad \ldots(5.122)$$

If magnetizing field of external magnetic induction is $\vec{H}$ and intensity of magnetization inside the material is $\vec{I}$ then from above equation-(5.122), we have

$$\vec{B} = \mu_0 \vec{H} + \mu_0 \vec{I}$$

$$\Rightarrow \qquad \vec{B} = \mu_0 (\vec{H} + \vec{I}) \qquad \ldots(5.123)$$

5.9.12 Magnetic Susceptibility

This is a constant parameter for each material which gives an idea about the ease with which the material can be magnetized when subjected to external magnetic field. For any material magnetic susceptibility is defined as the ratio of intensity of magnetization inside the material to the magnetizing field applied for magnetization of the material so it is given as

$$\chi = \frac{I}{H} \qquad \ldots(5.124)$$

$$\Rightarrow \qquad H = \chi I \qquad \ldots(5.125)$$

Vectorially above relation in equation-(5.125) can be given as

$$\vec{H} = \chi \vec{I} \qquad \ldots(5.126)$$

For any material having magnetic permeability μ_r net magnetic induction inside is given by equation-(5.121) and (5.123) which is given as

$$\mu_0\mu_r \vec{H} = \mu_0 (\vec{H} + \chi \vec{H})$$

$$\Rightarrow \qquad \mu_r = 1 + \chi \qquad \ldots(5.127)$$

As we know for diamagnetic materials $\vec{I}$ is in opposition to external field $\vec{H}$ thus χ is negative so magnetic permeability of diamagnetic materials is less than unity and for paramagnetic materials $\vec{I}$ is in same direction as that of external magnetic field $\vec{H}$ thus χ is positive so magnetic permeability of paramagnetic materials is more than unity.

5.9.13 Curie's Law

In previous article we've discussed that in paramagnetic materials intensity of magnetization is due to the alignment of all the dipoles of the material along external magnetic field after it gets magnetized. There are two main factors on which the intensity of magnetization depends. Intensity of magnetization is directly proportional to the external magnetizing field H. As H increases the dipoles of material will experience more torque and overall alignment of dipoles in the direction of external magnetic field increases. Thus we have

$$I \propto H \qquad \ldots(5.128)$$

Another factor on which intensity of magnetization depends is the temperature. As temperature increases then due to thermal agitation the alignment of dipoles gets disturbed and overall dipole moment of the material decreases. Intensity of magnetization is observed to be inversely proportional to the temperature of the material, thus we have

$$I \propto \frac{1}{T} \qquad \ldots(5.129)$$

From equations-(5.128) and (5.129) we have

$$I = C\left(\frac{H}{T}\right) \qquad \ldots(5.130)$$

In above equation C is called Curie's constant and at a specific temperature we can compare equation-(5.130) with equation-(5.131) which gives

$$\chi = \frac{C}{T} \qquad \ldots(5.131)$$

Thus the magnetic susceptibility of paramagnetic material is inversely proportional to its absolute temperature. This is called '*Curie's Law in Magnetism*'. In general diamagnetic materials do not obey Curie's law as in diamagnetic materials intensity of magnetization is weak and their susceptibility does not very significantly with temperature whereas paramagnetic materials obey Curie law and on heating their susceptibility decreases to lower values and a paramagnetic material lose its magnetic character on heating.

5.9.14 Ferromagnetic Materials

There are some specific materials like Fe, Co, Ni and some more elements in which atoms have non zero magnetic moments and in their solid lattice due to a quantum phenomenon called '*Exchange Coupling*' atomic groups are formed in different pockets of material which have their magnetic moment aligned in same direction in that pocket. This phenomenon exchange coupling is due to the alignment of all dipoles by the magnetic field of neighbouring dipole in a short neighbourhood. Different pockets in the material may have atomic groups aligned with their magnetic moment in different directions as shown in figure-5.161. Each of these atomic groups aligned in same direction are called '*Domains*' and such materials are called '*Ferromagnetic Materials*'. As all the domains in a ferromagnetic material are having direction of their dipole moment randomly distributed the net magnetic moment of such materials is zero.

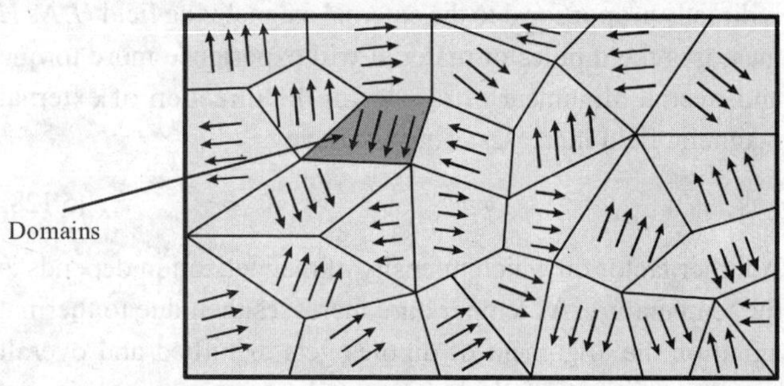

Figure 5.161

5.9.15 Magnetization of Ferromagnetic Materials

Due to exchange coupling all atoms in a domain have their individual dipole moment μ_i aligned in same direction. In this state even a very small magnitude external magnetic field can align all the domains along the direction of external magnetic field as shown in figure-5.162. This is because the internal magnetic field of already aligned atoms in a domain produce a torque on neighbouring domain atoms which supports the external field in this alignment process.

In ferromagnetic materials induced field B_i due to magnetization of material is much higher than the external field because of exchange coupling. Thus we have

$$B_i >> B_0$$

$$\Rightarrow \quad I >> H \qquad \ldots(5.132)$$

Thus for ferromagnetic materials we use $\chi >> 1$.

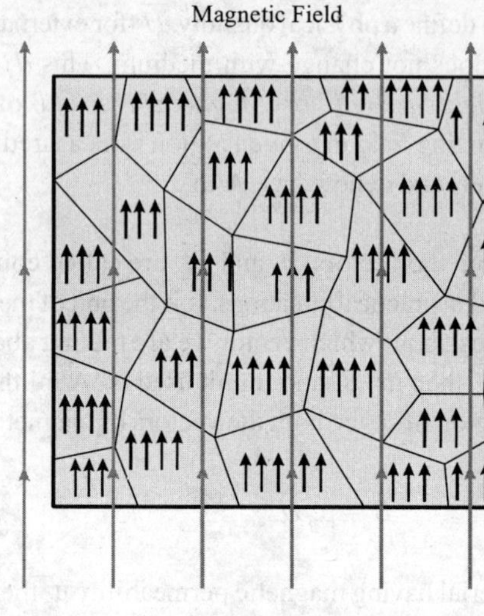

Figure 5.162

The susceptibility of ferromagnetic materials decrease with the rise in temperature in a different way. At a specific temperature called '*Curie Point*' or '*Curie Temperature*' a ferromagnetic material starts behaving like a paramagnetic material thus after Curie point, the susceptibility of a ferromagnetic material varies inversely with its absolute temperature or we can say that only above Curie point a ferromagnetic substance obeys Curie's law.

5.9.16 Superconductor as a Perfectly Diamagnetic Material

Superconducting materials are regarded as perfectly diamagnetic as on subjecting to external magnetic field, the free electrons in superconductors starts developing an eddy current which grows until it balances the external magnetic field inside the material.

When inside a magnetic field a conductor is cooled to the superconducting state and at a specific temperature material looses all its electrical resistance and at the same instant the material expels all the magnetic field inside it. This is called '*Meissner's Effect*'. Even when the material is not acting as a superconductor, it had some eddy currents due to application of external magnetic field which grows as its temperature decreases and at the superconducting state the eddy currents will increase so as to balance the external magnetic field and resulting zero magnetic field inside the material.

Figure-5.163 shows a theoretical situation of coil madeup of superconducting wire. When an external magnetic field is applied onto it then an induced current is developed in the coil which opposes the external magnetic field and due to zero resistance in the coil the current in it does not decay and grows to the limit till the net magnetic field at the plane of coil by its current balances the external magnetic field so theoretically we consider no magnetic flux passes through a superconducting coil when placed in an external magnetic field.

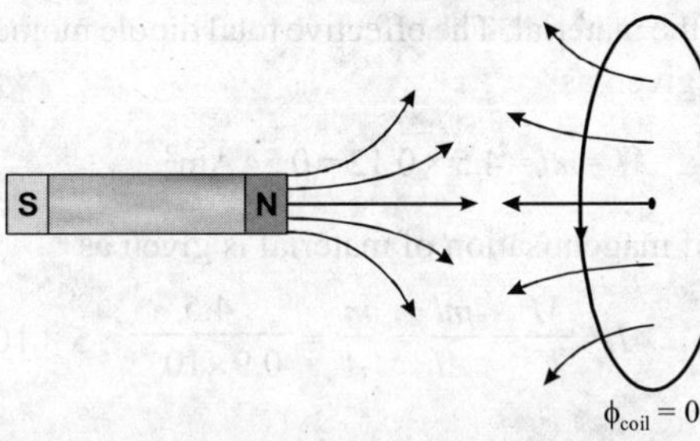

Figure 5.163

Another situation is shown in figure-5.164 in which a superconducting block is placed in an external magnetic field and in this situation inside the block eddy currents are induced to nullify the net magnetic field at all its interior points.

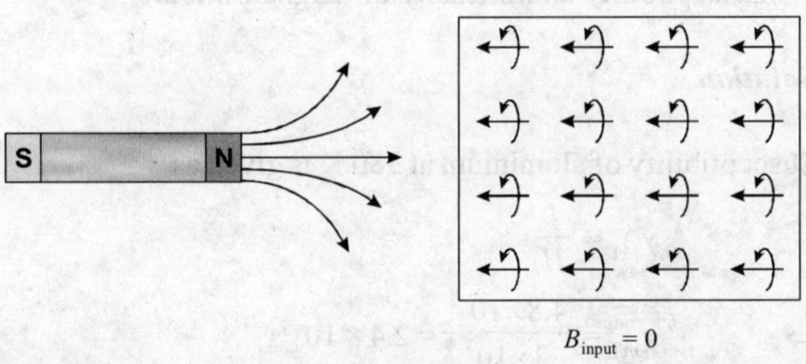

Figure 5.164

5.9.17 Magnetic Hysteresis

The phenomenon in which the value of a physical property lags behind the causes by which it is changing is called '*Hysteresis*'. When a ferromagnetic material is magnetized by an external magnetizing field the intensity of magnetization in the material increases with the external field and when magnetizing field decreases then intensity of magnetization also decreases but it lags behind the change in magnetizing field. This is called '*Magnetic Hysteresis*'. We will discuss magnetic hysteresis with the help of an illustration.

Consider a ferromagnetic material which is subjected to an external magnetic field which can be changed in magnitude as well as in direction. Figure-5.165 shows the variation of intensity of magnetization in the material with change in magnetizing field. The curve starts from origin when initial value of magnetizing field was zero and at that instant polarization of material was also zero and hence no initial magnetization was there. When H increases, I also increases and curve follows path O to point A after which it no further increase in I is observed with increase in H. This state is called magnetic saturation material at which I approaches maximum value.

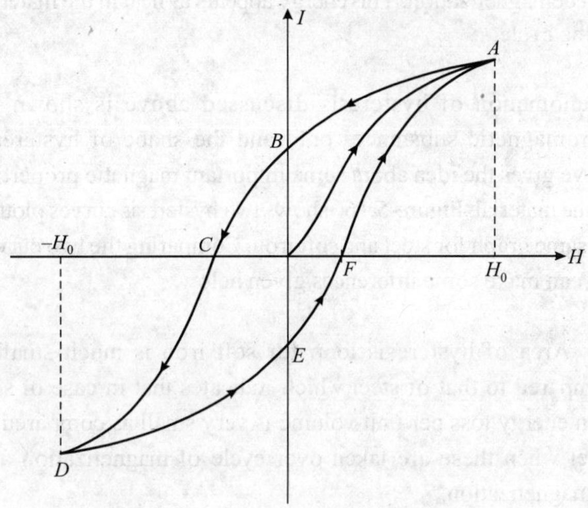

Figure 5.165

Now from the point of magnetic saturation H is decreases with which I also decreases along the path AB. When H becomes zero then at point B some magnetization is left in the material. This magnetization OB which is left in the material at the point when H is zero is called '*Retentivity*' of the material. This intensity of magnetization left in the material when magnetizing field is reduced to zero from saturation is also called '*Remanence*' or sometimes called '*Residual Magnetism*'. This residual magnetism is also termed as '*Magnetic Inertia*' due to which in absence of demagnetization the retention of magnetic flux in the material is there for a long term depending upon the retentivity of the material.

To reduce the intensity of magnetization to zero, the magnetising field is increased in reversed direction from B to C then at point C the intensity of magnetization becomes zero for which we had to apply a magnetizing field in reverse direction equal to OC. This magnetizing field OC is called '*Coercivity*' of the material. Thus the value of reverse magnetizing field required to reduce the retentivity in material to zero is called coercivity of the material.

Further when the magnetizing field is increased in reverse direction, intensity of magnetization increases along the curve CD and at point D again it is the state of magnetic saturation in reverse direction. Now magnetizing field is increased in original direction upto point A by passing through the point E and F which are corresponding to retentivity and coercivity in opposite directions as shown in figure-5.165. In this figure the closed curve *ABCDEFA* is traced between values of H and I is called '*Hysteresis Loop*'. Based on several experiments and analysis it is found that the area of the hysteresis loop which is also called '*I-H Curve*' is proportional to the net energy absorbed per unit volume by the material during one cycle of magnetization and demagnetization. This energy appears as heat in the material in the cycle.

Phenomenon of hysteresis discussed above is shown by ferromagnetic substances only and the shape of hysteresis curve gives the idea about some important magnetic properties of the material. Figure-5.166 shows two hysteresis curves plotted on same graph for steel and soft iron. Comparing the two curves we can make some inferences given below.

(i) Area of hysteresis loop for soft iron is much smaller compared to that of steel which indicates that in case of soft iron energy loss per unit volume is very small as compared to steel when these are taken over cycle of magnetization and demagnetization.

(ii) Soft iron gets magnetized to saturation value at less value of external magnetizing field compared to steel and on removing magnetizing field magnetic retention in case of soft iron is more than that of steel. That indicates that soft iron is strongly magnetized compared to steel by same magnetizing field.

(iii) Coercivity of steel is much greater than soft iron that means the residual magnetism in steel sustains for a longer time and for soft iron residual magnetism can be destroyed by a smaller value of reverse magnetizing field easily.

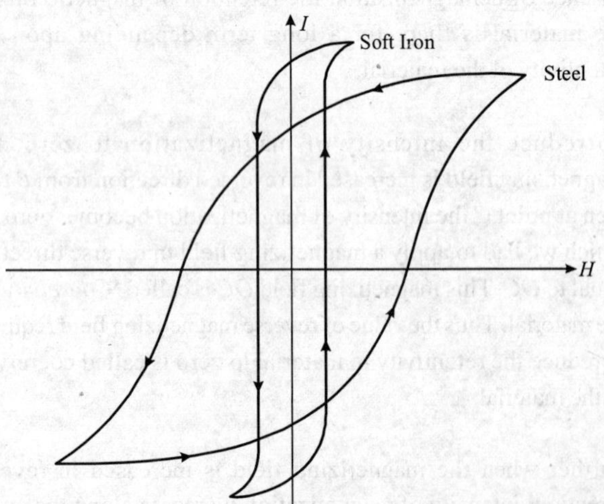

Figure 5.166

Illustrative Example 5.60

A bar magnet has its pole strength 4.5 Am and length 12 cm. The cross sectional area of the magnet is 0.9 cm^2. Find the total dipole moment of the magnet and intensity of magnetisation of the magnetic material.

Solution

The intensity of magentisation is the dipole moment per unit volume in the material. The effective total dipole moment of the magnet is given as

$$M = ml = 4.5 \times 0.12 = 0.54\ \text{Am}^2$$

Intensity of magentisation of material is given as

$$I = \frac{M}{V} = \frac{ml}{Al} = \frac{m}{A} = \frac{4.5}{0.9 \times 10^{-4}} = 5 \times 10^4\ \text{A/m}$$

Illustrative Example 5.61

In a region at 280 K temperature, on an aluminium sample a magnetising field of intensity 2×10^3 A/m is applied due to which the sample acquires an intensity of magnetisation 4.8×10^{-2} A/m. Calculate the susceptibility of aluminium at 280 K and if temperature of the sample is raised to 320 K, what will be the susceptibility and intensity of magnetisation.

Solution

Susceptibility of aluminium at 280 K is given as

$$\chi_{m1} = \frac{I}{H}$$

$$\Rightarrow \quad \chi_{m1} = \frac{4.8 \times 10^{-2}}{2 \times 10^3} = 2.4 \times 10^{-5}$$

As aluminium is a paramagnetic material, it obeys Curie's law so if χ_{m2} is the susceptibility of aluminium at 320 K temperature we use

$$\frac{\chi_{m1}}{\chi_{m2}} = \frac{T_2}{T_1}$$

$$\Rightarrow \quad \chi_{m2} = \chi_{m1} \times \frac{T_1}{T_2}$$

$$\Rightarrow \quad \chi_{m2} = 2.4 \times 10^{-5} \times \frac{280}{320} = 2.1 \times 10^{-5}$$

If I' is the intensity of magnetisation of aluminium at 320 K temperature then we have

$$I' = \chi_{m2} H$$

$$\Rightarrow \quad I' = 2.1 \times 10^{-5} \times 2 \times 10^3\ \text{A/m}$$

$$\Rightarrow \quad I' = 4.2 \times 10^{-2}\ \text{A/m}$$

Illustrative Example 5.62

A piece of iron of mass 8.4 kg is repeatedly magnetised and demagnetised by an external periodic time varying magnetic field of frequency 50 Hz. In the iron piece it is measured that rate of heat dissipation is 6.4×10^4 J/hr. If iron density is 7200 kg/m^3 find the energy dissipated in iron piece per cycle per unit volume of it.

Solution

The heat dissipation in the iron piece per unit volume per hour is given as

$$Q = \frac{Heat}{Volume} = \frac{6.4 \times 10^4}{8.4/7200} \text{ J/hr-m}^3$$

Period of one cycle of magnetisation is given as

$$T = \frac{1}{f} = \frac{1}{50 \times 3600} \text{ hr}$$

Thus heat dissipated per cycle per unit volume is given as

$$Q_v = \frac{6.4 \times 10^4}{8.4/7200} \times \frac{1}{50 \times 3600} = 305 \text{ J/m}^3$$

Web Reference at www.physicsgalaxy.com
Age Group - Grade 11 & 12 | Age 17-19 Years
Section - Magnetic Effects
Topic - Magnetic Properties of Materials
Module Number - 1 to 16

5.10 Alternating Current

A current which periodically changes direction is called an Alternating Current (AC). In an AC along with periodic change in direction of current its magnitude can also vary with time. Based on the ways in which magnitude and direction of an AC changes, several different types of ACs are analyzed.

Figure-5.167 shows some specific types of ACs in which current variation with time is shown. The most common type of AC which is widely used in AC applications is shown in figure-5.167(d) which varies with time according to sine function and it is called '*Sinusoidal AC*'.

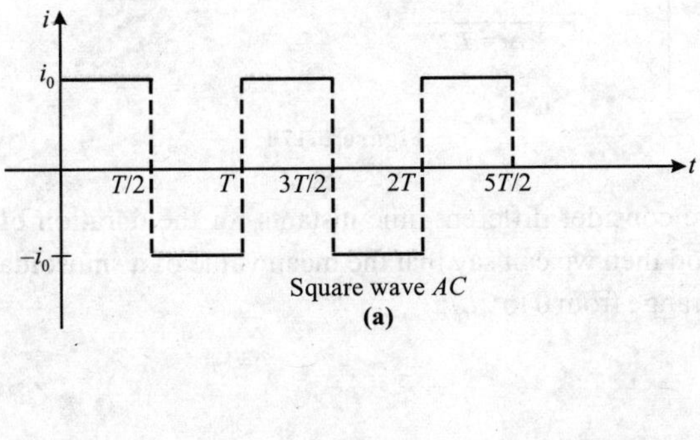

Square wave *AC*
(a)

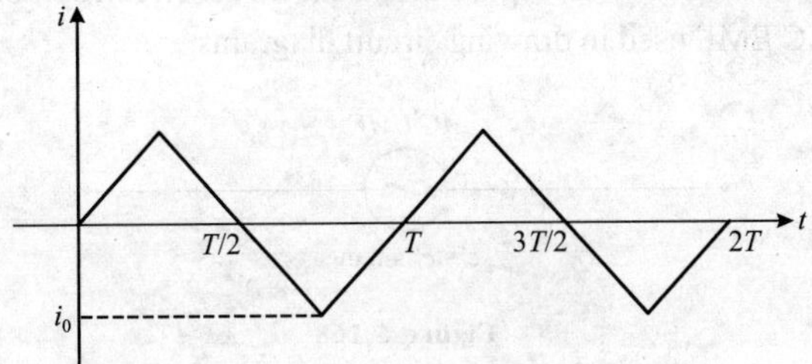

Triangular wave *AC*
(b)

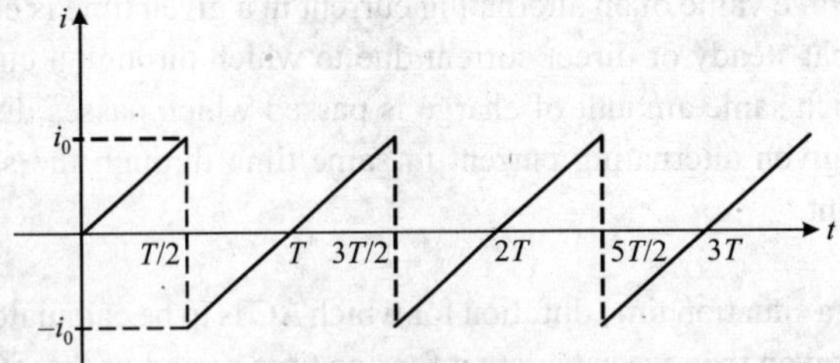

Saw tooth wave *AC*
(c)

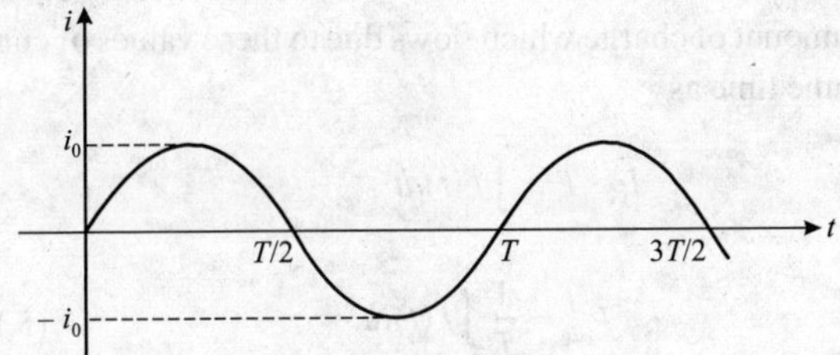

Sinusoidal wave AC
(d)

Figure 5.167

The alternating current which is used for domestic and industrial purposes is commonly the sinusoidal AC for which the time function is given as

$$i = i_0 \sin(\omega t) \qquad \ldots(5.133)$$

Here i_0 is called current amplitude or peak value of alternating current. ω is the angular frequency. The function given in equation-(5.133) gives the instantaneous value of alternating current.

Alternating current is produced due to an alternating EMF. An AC EMF also changes its direction periodically and its magnitude changes with time sinusoidally or in different ways. A sinusoidal EMF in general is expressed as

$$e = e_0 \sin \omega t \qquad \ldots(5.134)$$

The AC EMF shown in the above equation-(5.134) is considered as a reference for phase analysis of current and other circuit parameters in different types of AC circuits which we will discuss in upcoming articles. Figure-5.168 shows the circuit symbol of an AC EMF used in drawing circuit diagrams.

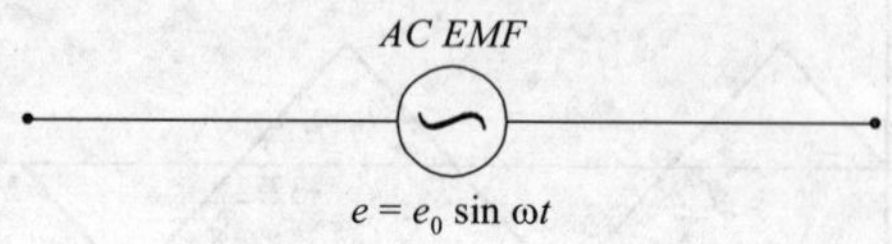

Figure 5.168

5.10.1 Mean or Average Value of an Alternating Current

Average value of an alternating current in a given time is equal to that steady or direct current due to which through a circuit branch same amount of charge is passed which passes due to the given alternating current in same time through the same circuit.

If in a situation time duration for which AC is to be calculated is not given then we calculate it for one time period of the AC.

If an alternating current is expressed as $i = f(t)$ then its average value I_{avg} for a time $t = 0$ to $t = T$ can be calculated by equating the amount of charge which flows due to these values of current in same time as

$$I_{avg}.T = \int_0^T f(t)dt$$

$$\Rightarrow \quad I_{avg} = \frac{1}{T}\int_0^T f(t)dt \quad \ldots(5.135)$$

Expression in above equation-(5.135) is the average function formula used to evaluate the time average of any given function and here we will use this function for calculation of average or mean value of current for any AC of which the instantaneous variation of current with time is given.

If we carefully see the integral part of the equation-(5.135) it is the area of the curve $f(t)$ vs t between time $t = 0$ to $t = T$. For current this area is the total charge flown in the specified duration thus in case charge quantity is known which flows in a given time like if a charge Δq flows in time Δt then mean value of current can be directly given as

$$I_{avg} = \frac{\Delta q}{\Delta t} \quad \ldots(5.136)$$

$$\Rightarrow \quad I_{avg} = \frac{Area\,under\,i-t\,curve}{\Delta t} \quad \ldots(5.137)$$

5.10.2 Mean Value of a Sinusoildal Alternating Current

A general sinusoidal alternating current is given by the time function expressed in equation-(5.133). The curve of variation of current with time is shown in figure-5.169. For one complete cycle we can see in this figure the positive and negative area are equal thus mean value of this sinusoidal current for one complete time period comes out to be zero.

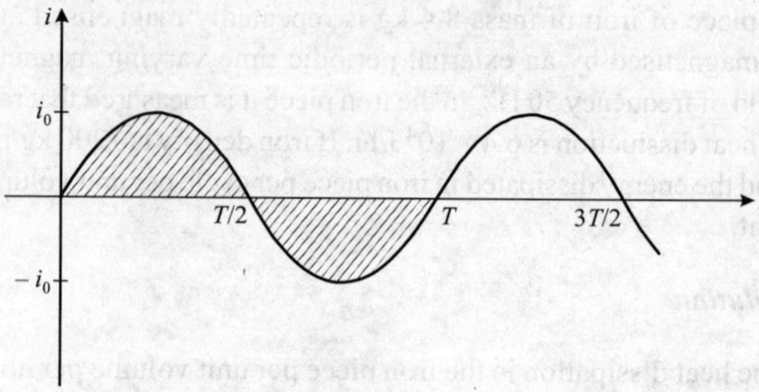

Figure 5.169

If we calculate the mean value of the sinusoidal current for half cycle then it can be calculated by using equation-(5.135) as

$$I_{avg} = \frac{1}{T/2}\int_0^{\pi/\omega} i_0 \sin(\omega t)dt$$

$$\Rightarrow \quad I_{avg} = \frac{1}{T/2}\left(-\frac{i_0}{\omega}[\cos(\omega t)]_0^{\pi/\omega}\right)$$

$$\Rightarrow \quad I_{avg} = \frac{1}{T/2}\left(\frac{i_0}{(2\pi/T)}[\cos(0°)-\cos(\pi)]\right)$$

$$\Rightarrow \quad I_{avg} = \frac{i_0}{\pi}[1-(-1)]$$

$$\Rightarrow \quad I_{avg} = \frac{2i_0}{\pi} = 0.636 i_0 \quad \ldots(5.138)$$

Above equation-(5.138) shows that average or mean value of a sinusoidal AC during half cycle is 63.6% of its peak value but the above equation is valid only if half cycle is considered from the duration $t = 0$ to $t = T/2$. For different half time periods the mean value may be different. Figure-5.170 shows the graph of same sinusoidal AC in which if we consider the time period from $t = T/4$ to $t = 3T/4$ then we can see that the total area of the graph is zero hence the mean current for this period which is also half of the total period comes out to be zero.

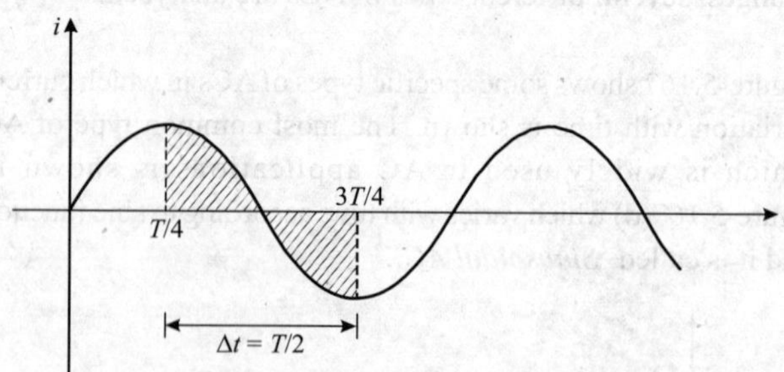

Figure 5.170

If we consider different time instants for the duration of half period then we can say that the mean value of a sinusoidal AC can range from 0 to $2i_0/\pi$.

5.10.3 Root Mean Square (RMS) value of an Alternating Current

RMS value of an alternating current for a given time duration is calculated by taking the square root of the average of square of the time function $i = f(t)$ of current as the name RMS implies. This can be mathematically calculated by using the average function formula for square of the time function of current which is given as

$$I_{RMS} = \sqrt{\frac{1}{T}\int_0^T [f(t)]^2 dt} \quad \ldots(5.139)$$

Theoretically this RMS value is defined as a steady constant current when passes through a given resistor produces same amount of heat in a given duration which is produced by the given alternating current when passed through the same resistor in same time duration.

If the alternating current $i = f(t)$ is passed through a resistor of resistance R then for a given time 0 to T total heat produced in this resistor can be given as

$$H = \int_0^T i^2 R dt$$

$$\Rightarrow \quad H = \int_0^T [f(t)]^2 dt \quad \ldots(5.140)$$

If I_{RMS} is the RMS value of the given alternating current then the total heat produced by this constant value in a resistance R in time 0 to T is given as

$$H = I_{RMS}^2 RT \quad \ldots(5.141)$$

From equations-(5.140) and (5.141) we have

$$I_{RMS}^2 RT = \int_0^T [f(t)]^2 dt$$

$$\Rightarrow \quad I_{RMS}^2 = \frac{1}{T}\int_0^T [f(t)]^2 dt$$

$$\Rightarrow \quad I_{RMS} = \sqrt{\frac{1}{T}\int_0^T [f(t)]^2 dt} \quad \ldots(5.142)$$

We can see that equation-(5.142) is same as equation-(5.139).

5.10.4 RMS value of a Sinusoidal Alternating Current

A general sinusoidal alternating current is given by the time function expressed in equation-(5.133). For calculation of its RMS value as we will find the average of squares half cycle or full cycle does not make any difference as square of positive or negative both cycles will be positive. To determine the RMS value of a sinusoidal alternating current first we will calculate the '*Mean Square*' value of this current which is given as

$$I_{RMS}^2 = \frac{1}{T}\int_0^T [f(t)]^2 dt$$

$$\Rightarrow \quad I_{RMS}^2 = \frac{1}{T/2}\int_0^{T/2} i_0^2 \sin^2 \omega t dt$$

$$\Rightarrow \quad I_{RMS}^2 = \frac{\omega i_0^2}{\pi}\int_0^{\pi/\omega} \sin^2 \omega t dt$$

$$\Rightarrow \quad I_{RMS}^2 = \frac{\omega i_0^2}{2\pi}\int_0^{\pi/\omega} [1-\cos(2\omega t)] dt$$

$$\Rightarrow \quad I_{RMS}^2 = \frac{\omega i_0^2}{2\pi}\left[t - \frac{1}{2\omega}\sin(2\omega t)\right]_0^{\pi/\omega}$$

$$\Rightarrow \quad I_{RMS}^2 = \frac{\omega i_0^2}{2\pi}\left[\left(\frac{\pi}{\omega} - 0\right) - (0-0)\right]$$

$$\Rightarrow \quad I_{RMS}^2 = \frac{i_0^2}{2}$$

$$\Rightarrow \quad I_{RMS} = \frac{i_0}{\sqrt{2}} = 0.707\, i_0 \quad \ldots(5.143)$$

The RMS value of sinusoidal alternating current as obtained in equation-(5.143) is a standard result for full or half cycle of it but for different periods the RMS value may come differently for this sinusoidal alternating current.

Illustrative Example 5.63

An electric bulb is designed to operate at 12 V *DC*. If this bulb is connected to an *AC* source and it gives same brightness, what would be the peak voltage of *AC*.

Solution

As brightness is same, this indicates that heat produced in the two cases is same so the effective (RMS) current supplied by *AC* source is same as that of *DC* current through the bulb. Thus effective (RMS) voltage of *AC* must be 12 V which is given in terms of peak value of voltage as

$$e_{rms} = \frac{e_0}{\sqrt{2}}$$

$$\Rightarrow \quad e_0 = \sqrt{2}\, e_{rms} = 12\sqrt{2}\text{ V}$$

Illustrative Example 5.64

The current decaying in *LR* circuit has a function $i = I_0 e^{-t/\tau}$ where τ is the time constant of the circuit. Find RMS value of this current for the period $t = 0$ to $t = \tau$.

Solution

We know that root mean square value of current is given as

$$I_{RMS}^2 = \frac{1}{T}\int_0^T [f(t)]^2\,dt$$

$$\Rightarrow \quad I_{RMS}^2 = \frac{1}{\tau}\int_0^{\tau} I_0^2 e^{-2t/\tau}\,dt$$

$$\Rightarrow \quad I_{RMS}^2 = \frac{I_2^2}{\tau}\left[\frac{e^{-2t/\tau}}{-t/\tau}\right]_0^{\tau}$$

$$\Rightarrow \quad I_{RMS}^2 = -\frac{I_0^2}{2}[e^{-2}-1]$$

$$\Rightarrow \quad I_{RMS}^2 = \frac{I_0^2}{2}\left(1-\frac{1}{e^2}\right)$$

$$\Rightarrow \quad I_{RMS} = \frac{I_0}{\sqrt{2}}\sqrt{1-\frac{1}{e^2}}$$

 # Illustrative Example 5.65

A direct current of 2 A and an AC of peak value 2 A flows through resistances 2 Ω and 1 Ω respectively. Find the ratio of heat produced in the two resistances in same interval.

Solution

In time t heat produced by a DC current I_1 is given as

$$H_1 = I^2 Rt$$

$$\Rightarrow \quad H_1 = (2)^2 (2)\, t = 8t$$

RMS value of AC is given as

$$i_{rms} = \frac{i_0}{\sqrt{2}} = \frac{2}{\sqrt{2}} = \sqrt{2}\text{ A}$$

Heat produced by the rms current in time t is given as

$$H_2 = i_{rms}^2 Rt$$

$$\Rightarrow \quad H_2 = (\sqrt{2})^2 (1)t = 2t$$

$$\Rightarrow \quad \frac{H_1}{H_2} = \frac{8t}{2t} = 4$$

 # Illustrative Example 5.66

Find the RMS value of the sawtooth voltage of peak value V_0 per cycle for which the time function is shown in figure-5.171.

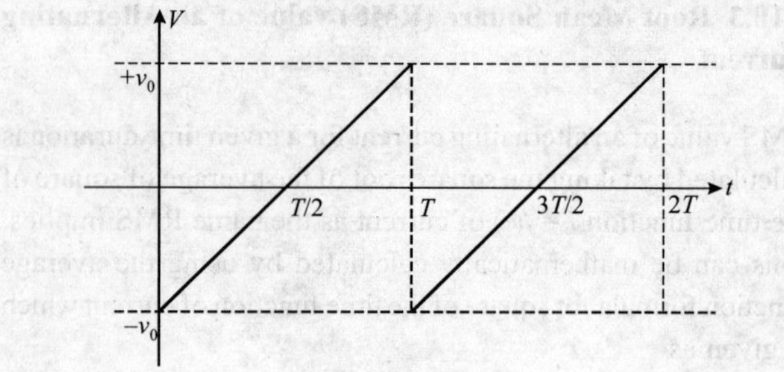

Figure 5.171

Solution

Time function of voltage for the above graph is given as

$$V = \frac{2V_0}{T}t - V_0$$

Mean square value of the voltage is given as

$$V_{ms} = \frac{1}{T}\int_0^T V^2\,dt$$

$$\Rightarrow \quad V_{ms} = \frac{1}{T}\int_0^T \left(\frac{2V_0}{T}t - V_0\right)^2 dt$$

$$\Rightarrow \quad V_{ms} = \frac{1}{T}\int_0^T \left(\frac{4V_0^2t^2}{T} - \frac{4V_0^2 t}{T} + V_0^2\right) dt$$

$$\Rightarrow \quad V_{ms} = \frac{1}{T}\left(\frac{4}{3}V_0^2 T - \frac{4V_0^2}{2}T + V_0^2 T\right)$$

$$\Rightarrow \quad V_{ms} = \left(\frac{V_0^2}{3}\right)$$

$$\Rightarrow \quad V_{rms} = \sqrt{V_{ms}} = \frac{V_0}{\sqrt{3}}$$

Practice Exercise 5.5

(i) An *AC* voltage is given as $e = e_1 \sin \omega t + e_2 \cos \omega t$. Find the *RMS* value of this voltage.

[$\sqrt{\frac{e_1^2 + e_2^2}{2}}$]

(ii) In a wire direct current i_1 and an AC current $i_2 = i_{20}\sin\omega t$ is superposed. Find the RMS value of current in wire.

[$\sqrt{i_1^2 + \frac{i_{20}^2}{2}}$]

(iii) Calculate the RMS value of the EMF for a cycle of which time variation is shown in figure-5.172

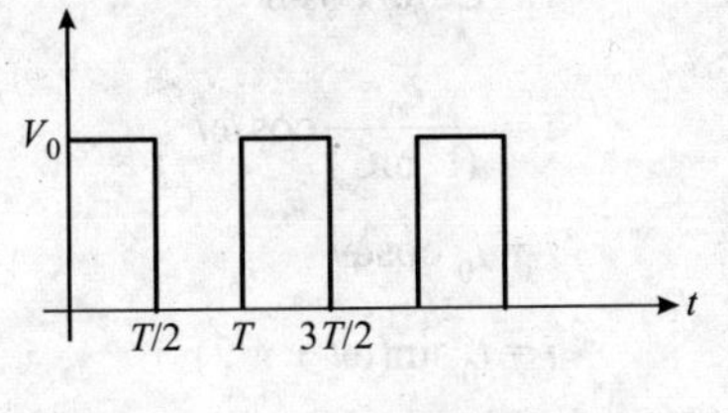

Figure 5.172

[$\frac{V_0}{\sqrt{2}}$]

(iv) In a given AC circuit through a specific branch the current varies as a function of time given as

$i = i_0\sin^2\omega t \quad 0 \le \omega t < \pi$

and $i = i_0\sin\omega t \quad \pi \le \omega t < 2\pi$

Calculate the average current per cycle of this AC.

[$i_0\left(\frac{1}{4} - \frac{1}{\pi}\right)$]

(v) Calculate the root mean square value of the voltage of the given variation of an alternating EMF with time in graph as shown in figure-5.173.

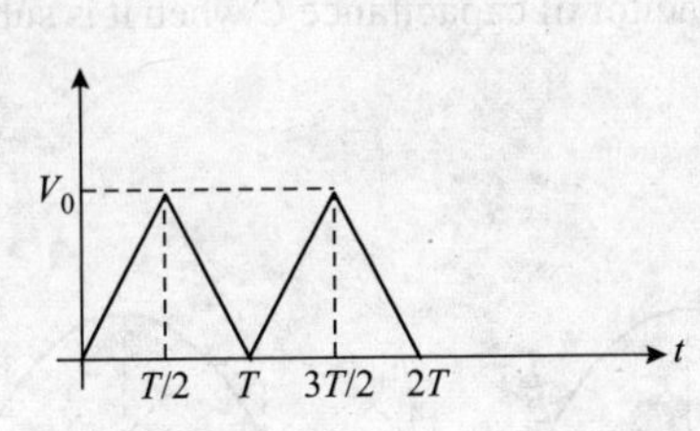

Figure 5.173

[$\frac{V_0}{\sqrt{3}}$]

(vi) In previous question calculate the average voltage per cycle of the alternating EMF.

[$\frac{V_0}{\sqrt{2}}$]

(vii) Calculate the average value of the AC per cycle for which time function of the current is shown in figure-5.174.

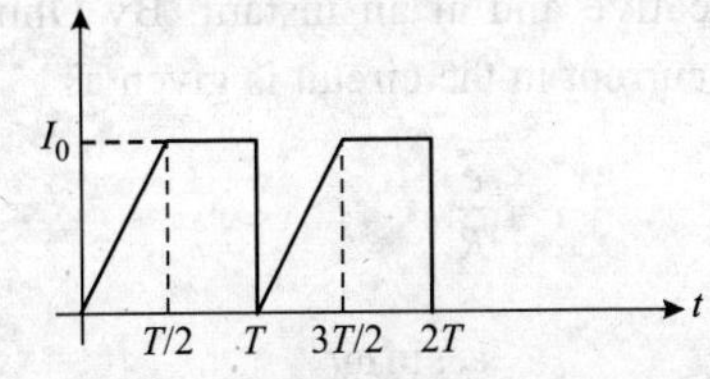

Figure 5.174

[$\frac{3}{4}I_0$]

5.11 AC Circuit Components

In different types of AC circuits mainly three passive circuit components are used which are resistors, capacitors and inductors. These may be connected in different combinations across and AC EMF. In analysis of AC circuits, currents and potential difference across different circuit components are to be analyzed when circuit is closed. While analyzing AC circuits an important factor has be taken care of along with magnitude of current and potential differences in different branches and for different circuit components which is the phase of current and potential difference being analyzed. Being a sinusoidal function when EMF is applied across a circuit, due to the behaviour of circuit components, currents in branches of circuit may lag or lead the applied EMF in phase so it is an essential parameter to be accounted in all calculations while solving an alternating current circuit. Later in upcoming articles we will see that power in AC circuit is also dependent upon the phase of current and potential difference for any circuit component. So we will build our understanding of solving AC circuits step by step.

5.11.1 A Resistor Across an AC EMF

Figure-5.175 shows a pure resistor of resistance R is connected across an AC EMF of which the time function is given as

$$e = e_0 \sin\omega t \qquad \ldots(5.144)$$

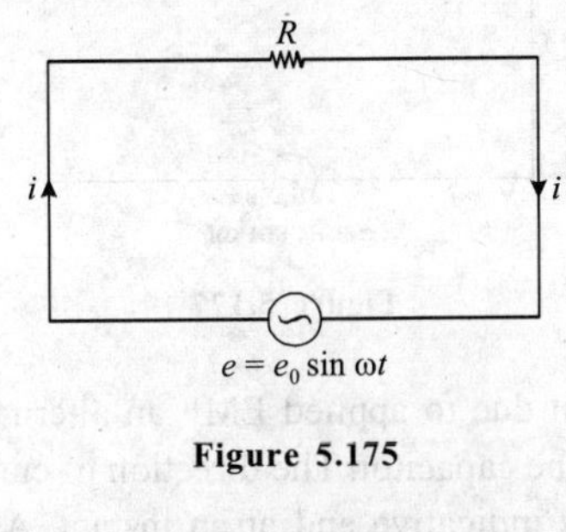

Figure 5.175

In above circuit due to applied EMF an alternating current i flows through the resistance. The direction of current shown in figure is indicative and at an instant. By Ohm's Law the instantaneous current in the circuit is given as

$$i = \frac{e}{R}$$

$$\Rightarrow \quad i = \frac{e_0 \sin \omega t}{R}$$

$$\Rightarrow \quad i = i_0 \sin\omega t \quad \ldots(5.145)$$

Where $$i_0 = \frac{e_0}{R} \quad \ldots(5.146)$$

From equation-(5.144) and (5.145) we can see that alternating EMF and alternating current produced due to this EMF in a resistance are in same phase. Equation-(5.146) gives the current amplitude of the alternating current produced in the resistance.

Figure-5.176 shows the time variation of AC EMF and current through the resistor of resistance R when it is subjected to the AC EMF.

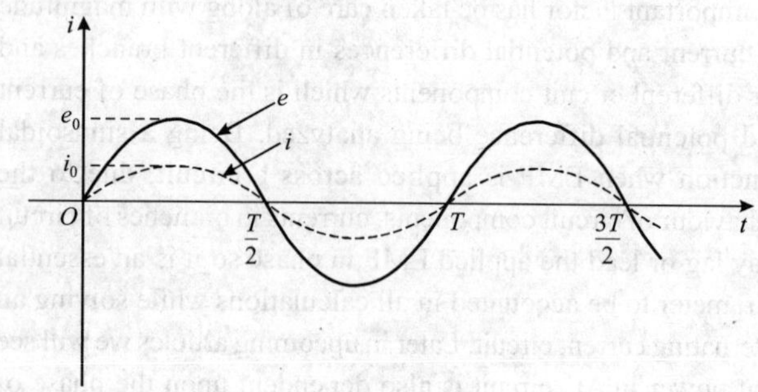

Figure 5.176

5.11.2 A Capacitor Across an AC EMF

Figure-5.177 shows a capacitor of capacitance C is connected across an AC EMF of which the time function is given as

$$e = e_0 \sin \omega t \quad \ldots(5.147)$$

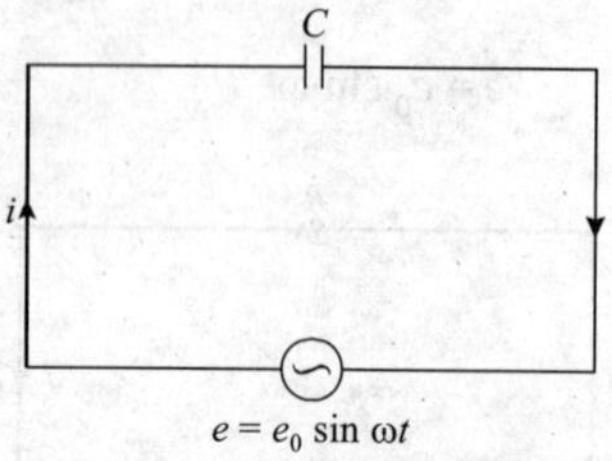

Figure 5.177

In above circuit due to applied EMF an alternating current i flows through the capacitor. The direction of current shown in above figure is indicative and at an instant. As capacitor is connected in parallel across the AC EMF, neglecting the resistance of connecting wires the instantaneous charge on capacitor is given as

$$q = Ce$$

$$\Rightarrow \quad q = Ce_0 \sin\omega t \quad \ldots(5.148)$$

The instantaneous current in the circuit can be given as

$$i = \frac{dq}{dt}$$

$$\Rightarrow \quad i = Ce_0\omega \cos\omega t$$

$$\Rightarrow \quad i = \frac{e_0}{(1/\omega C)} \cos \omega t$$

$$\Rightarrow \quad i = i_0 \cos\omega t$$

$$\Rightarrow \quad i = i_0 \sin(\omega t + \pi/2) \quad \ldots(5.149)$$

Where $$i_0 = \frac{e_0}{(1/\omega C)} \quad \ldots(5.150)$$

From equation-(5.147) and (5.149) we can see that alternating current produced due to the applied alternating EMF in a capacitor leads in phase over applied EMF by an angle $\pi/2$. Equation-(5.150) gives the current amplitude of the alternating current produced in the capacitor connected across AC EMF.

In equation-(5.150) the term $1/\omega C$ must have unit of '*ohm*' for the equation-(5.150) to be dimensionally correct. This value $1/\omega C$ is the ohmic opposition offered by capacitor in path of alternating current. This is called '*Capacitive Reactance*' of the capacitor which is denoted by X_C and given as

$$X_C = \frac{1}{\omega C} \quad \ldots(5.151)$$

Figure-5.178 shows the time variation of AC EMF and current through a capacitor of capacitance C when it is subjected to the AC EMF.

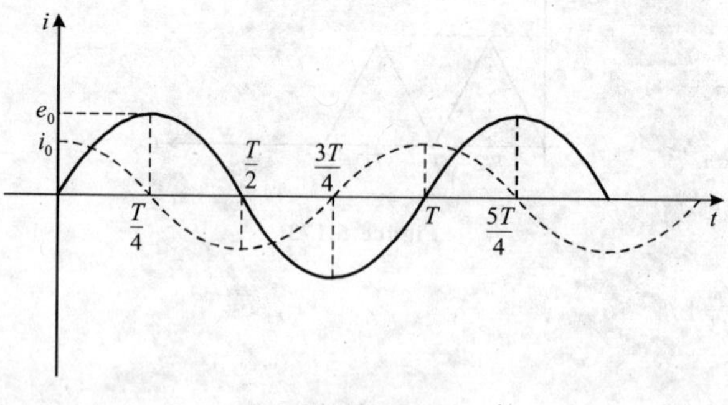

Figure 5.178

5.11.3 An Inductor Across an AC EMF

Figure-5.179 shows an inductor of self inductance L is connected across an AC EMF of which the time function is given as

$$e = e_0 \sin \omega t \quad \ldots(5.152)$$

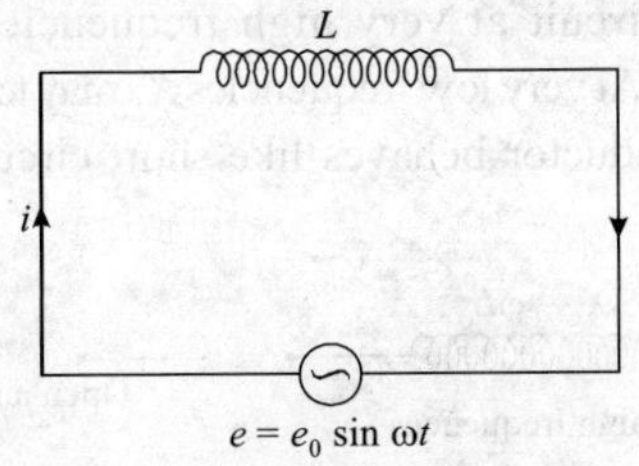

Figure 5.179

In above circuit due to applied EMF an alternating current i flows through the inductor. The direction of current shown in above figure is indicative and at an instant. As the inductor is connected in parallel across the AC EMF, neglecting the resistance of connecting wires we use

$$e = L\frac{di}{dt}$$

$$\Rightarrow \quad e_0 \sin \omega t = L\frac{di}{dt}$$

$$\Rightarrow \quad Ldl = e_0 \sin \omega t \, dt$$

Integrating the above expression we get

$$\int L di = \int e_0 \sin \omega t dt$$

$$Li = -\frac{1}{\omega}(e_0 \cos \omega t) + C$$

$$\Rightarrow \quad i = -\frac{1}{L\omega}(e_0 \cos \omega t) + \frac{C}{L} \quad \ldots(5.153)$$

In above equation first term on right hand side is the periodic current whereas second term is the direct current which does not change with time so alternating current produced in inductor due to AC EMF is given as

$$i = -\frac{1}{L\omega}(e_0 \cos \omega t)$$

$$\Rightarrow \quad i = \frac{e_0}{L\omega}\sin\left(\omega t - \frac{\pi}{2}\right)$$

$$\Rightarrow \quad i = i_0 \sin\left(\omega t - \frac{\pi}{2}\right) \quad \ldots(5.154)$$

Where $\quad i_0 = \dfrac{e_0}{\omega L} \quad \ldots(5.155)$

From equation-(5.154) and (5.155) we can see that alternating current produced due to the applied alternating EMF in an inductor lags behind in phase with the applied EMF by an angle $\pi/2$. Equation-(5.155) gives the current amplitude of the alternating current produced in the inductor connected across AC EMF.

In equation-(5.155) the term ωL must have unit of '*ohm*' for the equation-(5.155) to be dimensionally correct. This value ωL is the ohmic opposition offered by an inductor in path of alternating current. This is called '*Inductive Reactance*' of the inductor which is denoted by X_L and given as

$$X_L = \omega L \quad \ldots(5.156)$$

Figure-5.180 shows the time variation of AC EMF and current through an inductor of inductance L when it is subjected to the AC EMF.

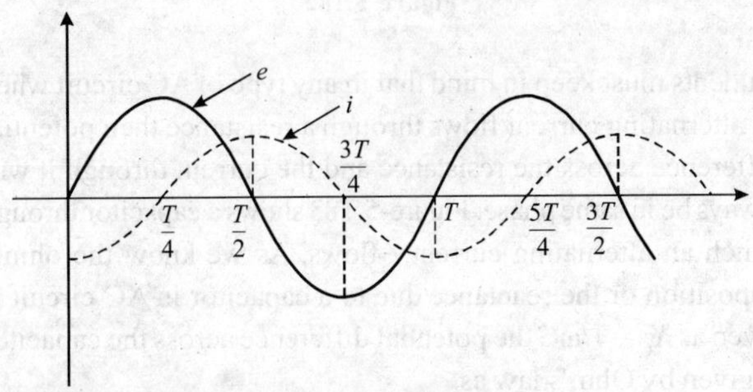

Figure 5.180

5.11.4 Comparison of AC Circuit Elements

In previous articles we've seen how a resistor, capacitor and an inductor behaves when connected across an AC EMF. In case of AC circuit a capacitor and an inductor also offers ohmic opposition which is called '*Reactance*' of the circuit measured in unit of ohm and denoted by 'Ω'. Unlike to the normal resistance of a resistor the reactance in AC circuit depends upon frequency as we've seen that both capacitive and inductive reactance are dependent upon frequency. Equation-(5.151) shows that capacitive reactance varies inversely with frequency of AC EMF whereas from equation-(5.156) shows that inductive reactance varies as directly proportional to the frequency.

Figure-5.181 shows the variation curve of the resistance and reactance with frequency of AC source.

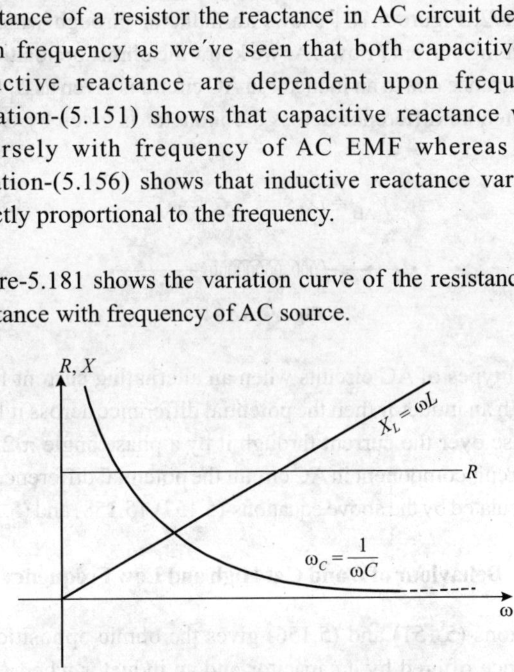

Figure 5.181

As discussed in previous articles we've also discussed the phase relationship between EMF and supplied current for different circuit components. Same phase relationships can be used in different AC circuits between potential difference and current across AC components. Figure-5.182 shows a resistance through which an alternating current i flows. In this situation the potential difference across the resistance can be given as

$$V_{AB} = iR \qquad \ldots(5.157)$$

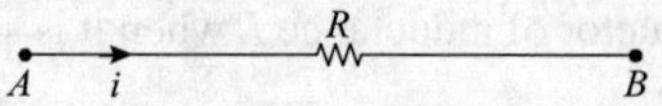

Figure 5.182

Students must keep in mind that in any type of AC circuit when an alternating current flows through a resistance then potential difference across the resistance and the current through it will always be in same phase. Figure-5.183 shows a capacitor through which an alternating current i flows. As we know the ohmic opposition or the reactance due to a capacitor in AC circuit is given as $X_C = 1/\omega C$ the potential difference across the capacitor is given by Ohm's law as

$$V_{AB} = iX_C \qquad \ldots(5.158)$$

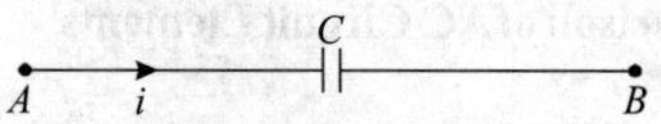

Figure 5.183

For all types of AC circuits when an alternating current flows through a capacitor then the potential difference across it lags behind in phase with the current flowing through it by a phase angle $\pi/2$. Figure-5.184 shows an inductor through which an alternating current i flows. As we know the ohmic opposition or the reactance due to an inductor in AC circuit is given as $X_L = \omega L$ the potential difference across the inductor is given by Ohm's law as

$$V_{AB} = iX_L \qquad \ldots(5.159)$$

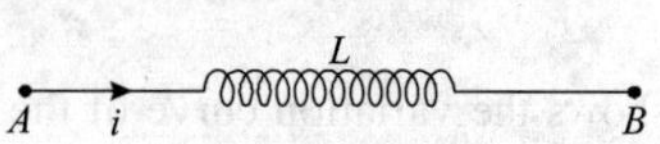

Figure 5.184

For all types of AC circuits when an alternating current flows through an inductor then the potential difference across it leads in phase over the current through it by a phase angle $\pi/2$. For any circuit component in AC circuit the potential difference can be calculated by the above equations-(5.157), (5.158) and (5.159).

5.11.5 Behaviour of L and C at High and Low Frequency AC

Equations-(5.151) and (5.156) gives the ohmic opposition or reactance offered by a capacitor and an inductor when AC is passes through these. For an inductor its reactance is given as $X_L = \omega L$ which is directly proportional to the frequency of applied AC thus as frequency of AC passing through an inductor increases its reactance also increases and at very high frequencies its X_L is also very high and an inductor behaves like an open circuit at very high frequencies as shown in figure-5.185(a). At very low frequencies X_L may tend to negligible value and an inductor behaves like short circuit as shown in figure-5.185(b).

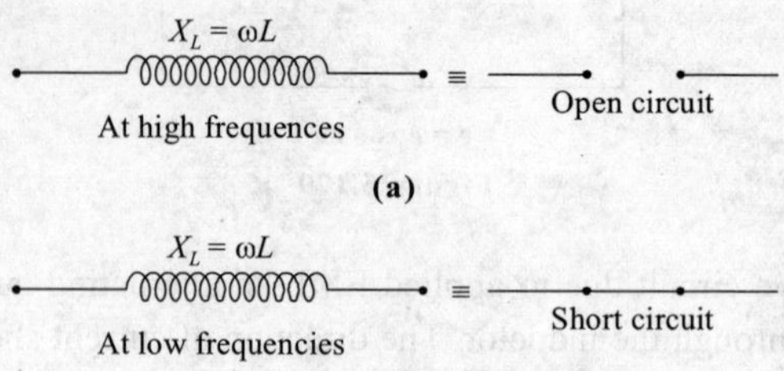

Figure 5.185

For a capacitor its reactance is given as $X_C = 1/\omega C$ which is inversely proportional to frequency of applied AC so as frequency of AC passing through the capacitor increases its reactance decreases and at very high frequencies X_C may tend to negligible value and a capacitor behaves like short circuit as shown in figure-5.186(a). At very low frequencies X_C will be very high and a capacitor behaves like open circuit as shown in figure-5.186(b).

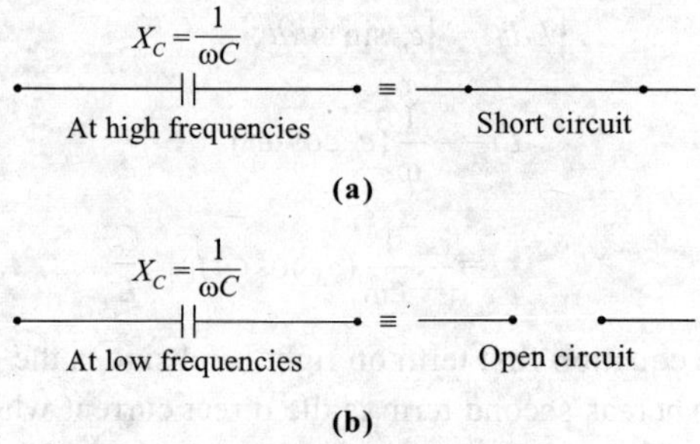

Figure 5.186

5.11.6 LR Series Circuit Across an AC EMF

Figure-5.187 shows a resistor of resistance R in series with an inductor of inductance L connected across an AC EMF. If at any instant current in circuit is i then KVL equation for the loop at that instant is written as

$$-iR - L\frac{di}{dt} + e_0 \sin \omega t = 0$$

$$\Rightarrow \qquad \frac{di}{dt} + \left(\frac{R}{L}\right) i = \frac{e_0}{L} \sin \omega t \qquad \ldots(5.160)$$

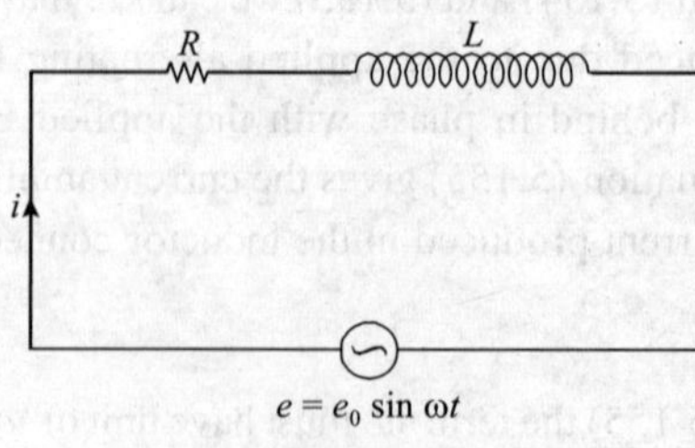

Figure 5.187

Equation-(5.160) is a first order differential equation of which the solution is given as

$$ie^{\int \frac{R}{L}dt} = \int\left(\frac{e_0 \sin \omega t}{L}\right)e^{\int \frac{R}{L}dt}\,dt + C$$

$$\Rightarrow \quad ie^{\frac{Rt}{L}} = \int\left(\frac{e_0 \sin \omega t}{L}\right)e^{\frac{Rt}{L}}\,dt + C$$

$$\Rightarrow \quad ie^{\frac{Rt}{L}} = \frac{e_0}{L}\int \sin \omega t \cdot e^{\frac{Rt}{L}}\,dt + C$$

In above expression we can drop the last term C as it is not a periodic term and it will not contribute in alternating current so considering only alternating current we have

$$ie^{\frac{Rt}{L}} = \frac{e_0}{L}\int \sin \omega t \cdot e^{\frac{Rt}{L}}\,dt = \frac{e_0}{L}(I_1) \quad \ldots(5.161)$$

Where $\qquad I_1 = \int \sin \omega t \cdot e^{\frac{Rt}{L}}\,dt \qquad \ldots(5.162)$

Above integration I_1 can be solved by-parts as

$$I_1 = \frac{L}{R}\sin \omega t \cdot e^{\frac{Rt}{L}} - \int \omega \cos \omega t \cdot \left(\frac{L}{R}e^{\frac{Rt}{L}}\right)dt$$

$$\Rightarrow I_1 = \frac{L}{R}\sin \omega t \cdot e^{\frac{Rt}{L}} - \frac{\omega L}{R}\int \cos \omega t \cdot e^{\frac{Rt}{L}}\,dt$$

$$\Rightarrow I_1 = \frac{L}{R}\sin \omega t \cdot e^{\frac{Rt}{L}} - \frac{\omega L}{R}\left[\frac{L}{R}\cos \omega t \cdot e^{\frac{Rt}{L}} + \frac{\omega L}{R}\int \sin \omega t \cdot e^{\frac{Rt}{L}}\,dt\right]$$

$$\Rightarrow I_1 = \frac{L}{R}\sin \omega t \cdot e^{\frac{Rt}{L}} - \frac{\omega L^2}{R^2}\cos \omega t \cdot e^{\frac{Rt}{L}} - \frac{\omega^2 L^2}{R^2}I_1$$

$$\Rightarrow \left(\frac{R^2 + \omega^2 L^2}{R^2}\right)I_1 = \frac{L}{R}\sin \omega t \cdot e^{\frac{Rt}{L}} - \frac{\omega L^2}{R^2}\cos \omega t \cdot e^{\frac{Rt}{L}}$$

$$\Rightarrow I_1 = \frac{Le^{\frac{Rt}{L}}}{R^2 + \omega^2 L^2}[R \sin \omega t - \omega L \cos \omega t] \quad \ldots(5.163)$$

Substituting the value of I_1 from above equation-(5.163) in equation-(5.161) gives

$$ie^{\frac{Rt}{L}} = \left(\frac{Le^{\frac{Rt}{L}}}{R^2 + \omega^2 L^2}[R \sin \omega t - \omega L \cos \omega t]\right)$$

$$\Rightarrow \quad i = \frac{e_0}{R^2 + \omega^2 L^2}[R \sin \omega t - \omega L \cos \omega t] \quad \ldots(5.164)$$

In above equation substituting

$$R = A\cos\phi$$

and $\qquad \omega L = A\sin\phi$

$$\Rightarrow \quad A = \sqrt{R^2 + \omega^2 L^2} \quad \ldots(5.165)$$

and $\qquad \phi = \tan^{-1}\left(\frac{\omega L}{R}\right) \qquad \ldots(5.166)$

Thus above equation-(5.164) can be reduced as

$$i = \frac{e_0}{R^2 + \omega^2 L^2}\left[\sqrt{R^2 + \omega^2 L^2}\sin\left(\omega t - \tan^{-1}\left(\frac{\omega L}{R}\right)\right)\right]$$

$$\Rightarrow \quad i = \frac{e_0}{\sqrt{R^2 + \omega^2 L^2}}\sin\left(\omega t - \tan^{-1}\left(\frac{\omega L}{R}\right)\right) \quad \ldots(5.167)$$

$$\Rightarrow \quad i = i_0 \sin(\omega t - \phi) \quad \ldots(5.168)$$

Where the peak current i_0 in circuit is given as

$$i_0 = \frac{e_0}{\sqrt{R^2 + \omega^2 L^2}} \quad \ldots(5.169)$$

In above equation the denominator is the total ohmic opposition offered by *LR* circuit connected across the AC EMF which is called '*Impedance*' of the AC circuit which is the resulting ohmic effect of the combination of resistance of resistor and inductive reactance of the inductor. So for a series *RL* circuit its impedance is given as

$$Z_{RL} = \sqrt{R^2 + \omega^2 L^2}$$

From equation-(5.168) we can see that the alternating current produced in a series *LR* circuit legs behind AC EMF by a phase angle ϕ which is given by equation-(5.166). As we know due to a pure resistance AC EMF and current remain in same phase whereas due to a pure inductor current legs behind EMF by a phase angle $\pi/2$. So when a pure resistance and an inductor are in series then due to the effect of both the current legs behind AC EMF but by an angle which is less than $\pi/2$.

Soon we will discuss a specific method of solving AC Circuits that is called '*Phasor Analysis*' with which in a much simpler way we can determine the alternating current given in equation-(5.167) but students must understand the whole analysis we did in solving a series *LR* circuit to determine the alternating current in flowing in it.

Figure-5.188 shows the variation of AC EMF and alternating current flowing through a series *LR* circuit.

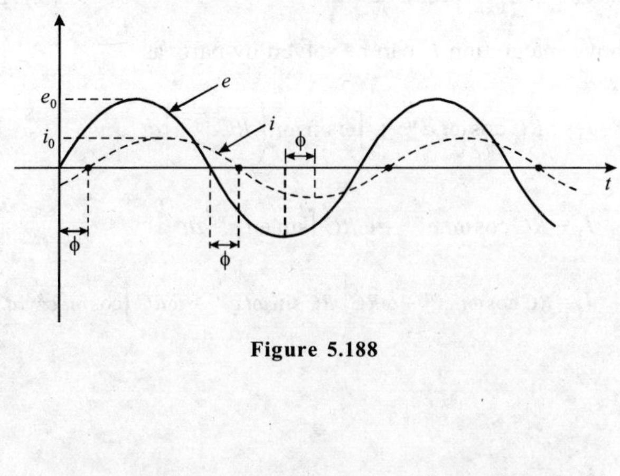

Figure 5.188

5.11.7 *RC* Series Circuit Across an AC EMF

Figure-5.189 shows a resistor of resistance R in series with a capacitor of capacitance C connected across an AC EMF. If at any instant current in circuit is i then KVL equation for the loop at that instant is written as

$$-iR - \frac{q}{C} + e_0 \sin \omega t = 0$$

Differentiating above equation, we get

$$\Rightarrow \quad \frac{di}{dt}R + \left(\frac{1}{C}\right)i = e_0\omega \cos \omega t$$

$$\Rightarrow \quad \frac{di}{dt} + \left(\frac{1}{RC}\right)i = \frac{e_0\omega}{R}\cos \omega t \qquad \ldots(5.170)$$

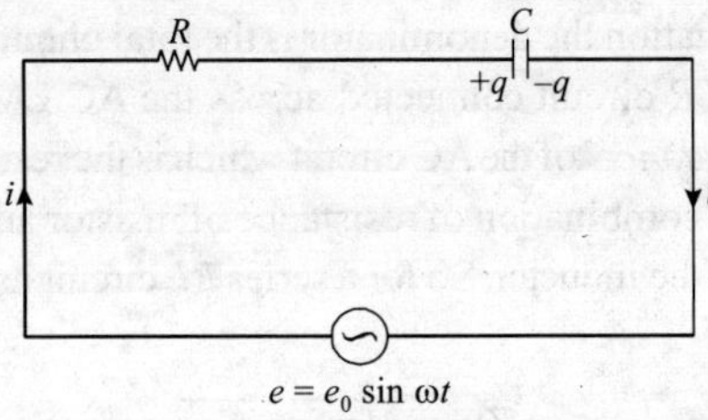

Figure 5.189

Equation-(5.170) is a first order differential equation of which the solution is given as

$$ie^{\int \frac{1}{RC}dt} = \int\left(\frac{e_0\omega \cos \omega t}{R}\right)e^{\int \frac{1}{RC}dt}\,dt + C_1$$

$$\Rightarrow \quad ie^{\frac{t}{RC}} = \int\left(\frac{e_0\omega \cos \omega t}{R}\right)e^{\frac{t}{RC}}\,dt + C_1$$

$$\Rightarrow \quad ie^{\frac{t}{RC}} = \frac{e_0\omega}{R}\int \cos \omega t . e^{\frac{t}{RC}}\,dt + C_1$$

In above expression we can drop the last term C_1 as it is not a periodic term and it will not contribute in alternating current so considering only alternating current we have

$$ie^{\frac{t}{RC}} = \frac{e_0\omega}{R}\int \cos \omega t . e^{\frac{t}{RC}}\,dt = \frac{e_0\omega}{R}(I_1) \qquad \ldots(5.171)$$

Where $\quad I_1 = \int \cos \omega t . e^{\frac{t}{RC}}\,dt \qquad \ldots(5.172)$

Above integration I_1 can be solved by-parts as

$$I_1 = RC \cos \omega t . e^{\frac{t}{RC}} + \int \omega \sin \omega t .\left(RCe^{\frac{t}{RC}}\right)dt$$

$$\Rightarrow \quad I_1 = RC \cos \omega t . e^{\frac{t}{RC}} + \omega RC\int \sin \omega t . e^{\frac{t}{RC}}\,dt$$

$$\Rightarrow \quad I_1 = RC \cos \omega t . e^{\frac{t}{RC}} + \omega RC\left[RC \sin \omega t . e^{\frac{t}{RC}} - \omega RC\int \cos \omega t . e^{\frac{t}{RC}}\,dt\right]$$

$$\Rightarrow \quad I_1 = RC \cos \omega t . e^{\frac{t}{RC}} + \omega R^2C^2 \sin \omega t . e^{\frac{t}{RC}} - \omega^2 R^2C^2 I_1$$

$$\Rightarrow \quad (1+\omega^2R^2C^2)\,I_1 = RC \cos \omega t \cdot e^{\frac{t}{RC}} + \omega R^2C^2 \sin \omega t \cdot e^{\frac{t}{RC}}$$

$$\Rightarrow \quad I_1 = \frac{RCe^{\frac{t}{RC}}}{1+\omega^2R^2C^2}[\cos \omega t + \omega RC \sin \omega t] \qquad \ldots(5.173)$$

Substituting the value of I_1 from above equation-(5.173) in equation-(5.171) gives

$$ie^{\frac{t}{RC}} = \frac{e_0\omega}{R}\left(\frac{RCe^{\frac{t}{RC}}}{1+\omega^2R^2C^2}[\cos \omega t + \omega RC \sin \omega t]\right)$$

$$\Rightarrow \quad i = \frac{e_0\omega C}{1+\omega^2R^2C^2}[\cos \omega t + \omega RC \sin \omega t] \qquad \ldots(5.174)$$

In above equation substituting

$$1 = A\cos\phi$$

and $\quad \omega RC = A\sin\phi$

$$\Rightarrow \quad A = \sqrt{1+\omega^2R^2C^2} \qquad \ldots(5.175)$$

and $\quad \phi = \tan^{-1}\left(\frac{1}{\omega RC}\right) \qquad \ldots(5.176)$

Thus above equation-(5.174) can be reduced as

$$\Rightarrow \quad i = \frac{e_0\omega C}{1+\omega^2R^2C^2}\left[\sqrt{1+\omega^2R^2C^2}\,\sin\left(\omega t + \tan^{-1}\left(\frac{1}{\omega RC}\right)\right)\right]$$

$$\Rightarrow \quad i = \frac{e_0}{\sqrt{R^2+1/\omega^2C^2}}\sin\left(\omega t + \tan^{-1}\left(\frac{1}{\omega RC}\right)\right) \qquad \ldots(5.177)$$

$$\Rightarrow \quad i = i_0 \sin(\omega t - \phi) \qquad \ldots(5.178)$$

Where the peak current i_0 in circuit is given as

$$i_0 = \frac{e_0}{\sqrt{R^2+1/\omega^2C^2}} \qquad \ldots(5.179)$$

In above equation the denominator is the total ohmic opposition offered by *RC* circuit connected across the AC EMF which is the resulting ohmic opposition of the combination of resistance of resistor and inductive reactance of the capacitor. So for a series *RC* circuit its impedance is given as

$$Z_{RL} = \sqrt{R^2+1/\omega^2C^2}$$

From equation-(5.178) we can see that the alternating current produced in a series *RC* circuit leads AC EMF by a phase angle ϕ which is given by equation-(5.176). As we know due to a pure resistance AC EMF and current remain in same phase whereas due to a pure capacitor current leads EMF by a phase angle $\pi/2$. So when a pure resistance and a capacitor are in series then due to the effect of both the current leads AC EMF but by an angle which is less than $\pi/2$.

By using phasor analysis we can simplify the above calculations which we did for calculation of current obtained in equation-(5.177). Figure-5.190 shows the variation of AC EMF and current through a series RC circuit.

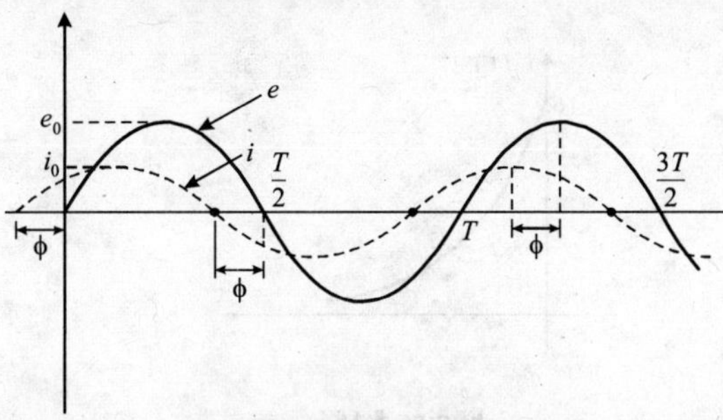

Figure 5.190

Illustrative Example 5.67

A 100 μF capacitor in series with a 40 Ω resistor is connected to a 110 V-60 Hz supply. What is the maximum current in the circuit? What is the time lag between current maxima and voltage maxima?

Solution

The peak current in a RC circuit is given as

$$i_0 = \frac{e_0}{\sqrt{[R^2 + (1/\omega C)^2]}}$$

Peak voltage is given as

$$e_0 = \sqrt{2} e_{rms} = 1.414 \times 110 = 155.5 \text{ V}$$

$$\Rightarrow \quad i_0 = \frac{155.5}{\sqrt{\left[(40)^2 + \left(\frac{1}{376.8 \times 10^{-4}}\right)^2\right]}}$$

$$\Rightarrow \quad i_0 = 3.24 \text{ A}$$

In RC circuit, the voltage lags behind the current by phase angle ϕ, where

$$\tan\phi = \frac{(1/\omega C)}{R} = \frac{1}{(376.8 \times 10^{-4})(40)}$$

$$\Rightarrow \quad \tan\phi = 0.6635$$

$$\Rightarrow \quad \phi = \tan^{-1}(0.6635) = 33.56°$$

The time lag is given as

$$t = \frac{\phi}{360} \times T = \frac{\phi}{360}\left(\frac{1}{f}\right)$$

$$\Rightarrow \quad t = \frac{33.56°}{360}\left(\frac{1}{60}\right) = 1.55 \times 10^{-3} \text{ s}$$

Illustrative Example 5.68

An electric lamp which runs at 40 V and consumes 10 A current is connected to AC mains at 100 V, 50 Hz supply. Calculate the inductance of the required choke for lamp to glow at full brightness.

Solution

Resistance of the lamp is given as

$$R = \frac{V}{I} = \frac{40}{10} = 4\,\Omega$$

Circuit current is given as

$$I = \frac{E}{\sqrt{[R^2 + (\omega L)^2]}}$$

$$\Rightarrow \quad 10 = \frac{100}{\sqrt{[(4)^2 + (2 \times 3.14 \times 50 \times L)^2]}}$$

$$\Rightarrow \quad L = 0.02916 \text{ H}$$

Illustrative Example 5.69

In the figure-5.191 shown the current in circuit is $i = 10e^{-4t}$ A. Find V_L and V_{ab}.

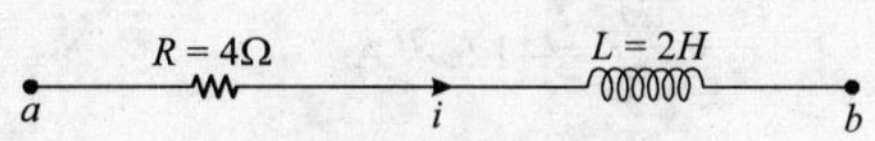

Figure 5.191

Solution

The voltage across the inductor is given as

$$V_L = L\frac{di}{dt}$$

$$\Rightarrow \quad V_L = (2)\frac{d}{dt}(10e^{-4t})$$

$$\Rightarrow \quad V_L = -80\, e^{-4t}$$

Writing equation of potential drop from point a to b gives

$$V_a - iR - L\frac{di}{dt} = V_b$$

$$\Rightarrow \quad V_a - V_b = iR + L\frac{di}{dt}$$

$$\Rightarrow \quad V_{ab} = (10e^{-4t})(4) - 80e^{-4t} = -40e^{-4t}$$

Illustrative Example 5.70

In the figure-5.192 shown, $i_1 = 10e^{-2t}$ A, $i_2 = 4$ A and $V_C = 3e^{-2t}$ V. Find

(a) i_L and V_L, also plot the time functions of i_L and V_L

(b) V_{ac}, V_{ab} and V_{cd}, also plot their time dependence curves

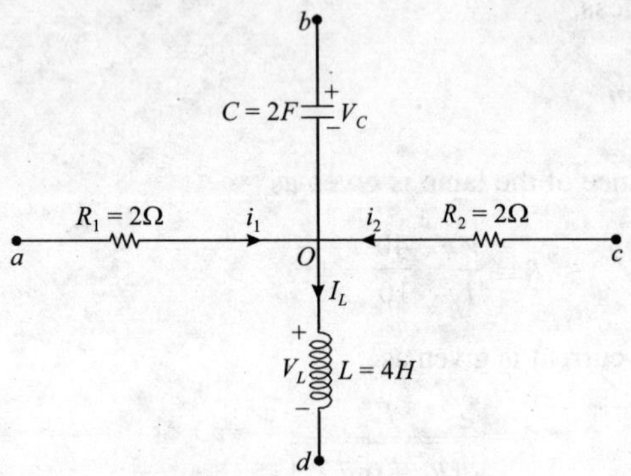

Figure 5.192

Solution

(a) Charge stored in the capacitor at time t is given as

$$q = CV_C$$

$$q = (2)(3e^{-2t})$$

$$q = 6e^{-2t}\ C$$

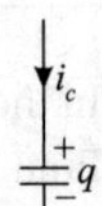

$$\Rightarrow \quad i_c = \frac{dq}{dt} = -12e^{-2t}\ A$$

Direction of current is from b to O, Applying KCL at O gives

$$i_L = i_1 + i_2 + i_c = 10e^{-2t} + 4 - 12e^{-2t}\ A$$

$$\Rightarrow \quad i_L = (4 - 2e^{-2t})\ A$$

$$\Rightarrow \quad i_L = [2 + 2(1 - e^{-2t})]\ A$$

i_L versus time graph is as shown in figure-5.193.

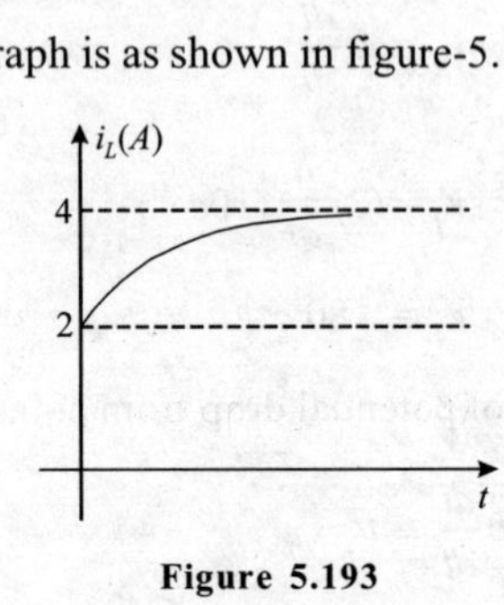

Figure 5.193

$$V_L = V_{od} = L\frac{di_L}{dt}$$

$$\Rightarrow \quad V_L = (4)\frac{d}{dt}(4 - 2e^{-2t})\ V$$

$$\Rightarrow \quad V_L = 16e^{-2t}\ V$$

V_L versus time graph is as shown in figure-5.194.

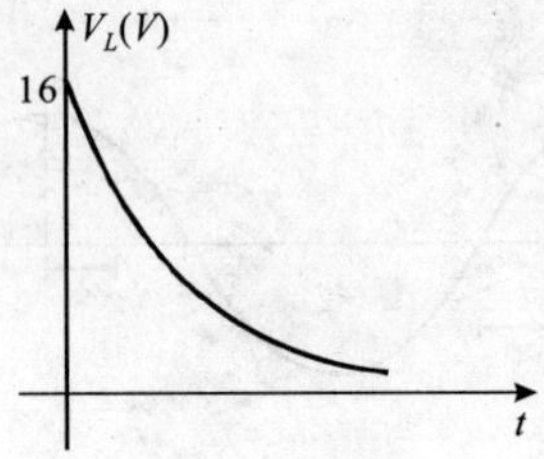

Figure 5.194

(b) Writing equation of potential drop from point a to c gives

$$V_a - i_1R_1 + i_2R_2 = V_c$$

$$\Rightarrow \quad V_a - V_c = V_{ac} = i_1R_1 - i_2R_2$$

Substituting the values we get

$$V_{ac} = (10e^{-2t})(2) - (4)(3)$$

$$V_{ac} = (20e^{-2t} - 12)\text{V}$$

Time dependence curve of V_{ac} is shown in figure-5.195.

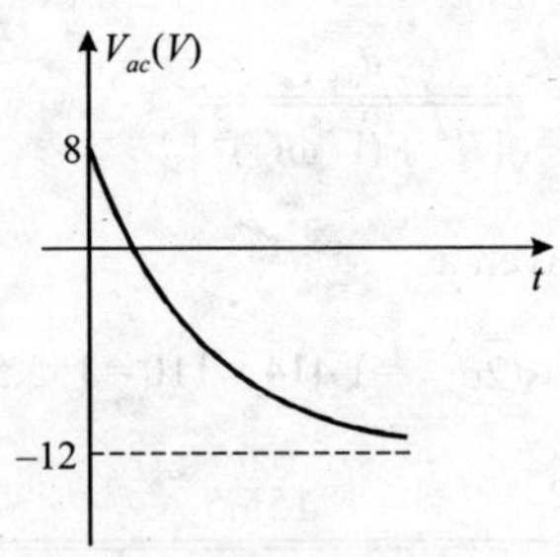

Figure 5.195

Writing equation of potential drop from point a to b gives

$$V_a - i_1R_1 + V_C = V_b$$

$$\Rightarrow \quad V_a - V_b = i_1R_1 - V_C$$

Substituting the values we get

$$V_{ab} = (10e^{-2t})(2) - 3e^{-2t}\ \text{V}$$

$$\Rightarrow \quad V_{ab} = 17e^{-2t}\ \text{V}$$

Time function curve of V_{ab} is shown in figure-5.196

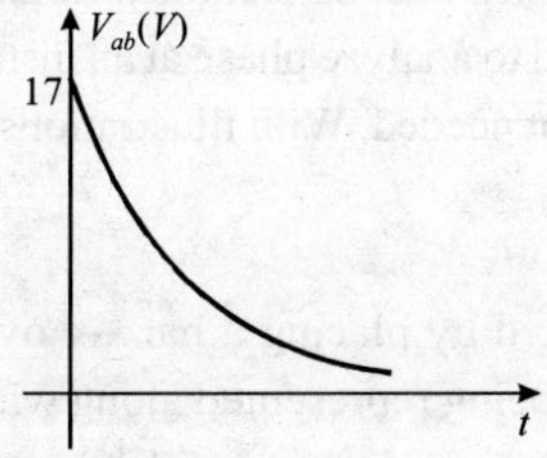

Figure 5.196

Writing equation of potential drop from point c to d gives

$$V_c - i_2R_2 - V_L = V_d$$

$$\Rightarrow \quad V_c - V_d = i_2R_2 + V_L$$

Substituting the values we get

$$V_{cd} = (4)(3) + 16e^{-2t}\text{V}$$

$$\Rightarrow \quad V_{cd} = (12 + 16e^{-2t})\text{V}$$

Time function curve of V_{cd} is shown in figure-5.197.

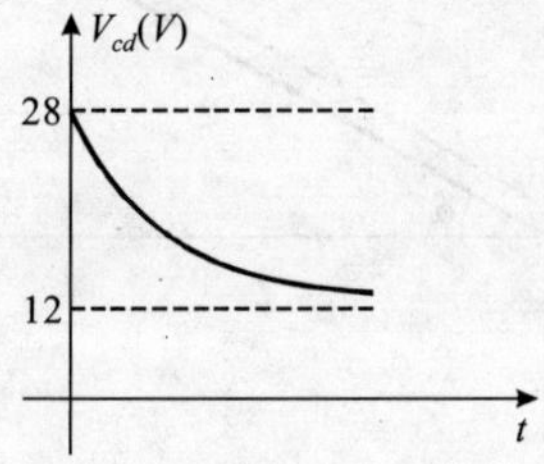

Figure 5.197

Illustrative Example 5.71

When 100 V DC is applied across a solenoid, a steady current of 1 A flows in it. When 100 V AC is applied across the same solenoid, current drops to 0.5 A. If the frequency of AC source is $\frac{150\sqrt{3}}{\pi}$ Hz, find the resistance and inductance of the solenoid.

Solution

Steady current through solenoid with DC source is given as

$$I = \frac{\varepsilon}{R} = \frac{100}{R} = 1$$

$$\Rightarrow \quad R = 100\,\Omega$$

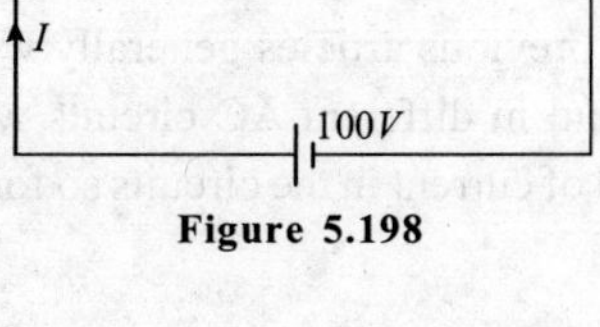

Figure 5.198

When AC is applied the current through the solenoid is given as

$$i = \frac{e}{z} = \frac{e}{\sqrt{R^2 + x_L^2}} = \frac{100}{\sqrt{R^2 + x_L^2}} = 0.5$$

$$\Rightarrow \quad \sqrt{R^2 + X_L^2} = 200$$

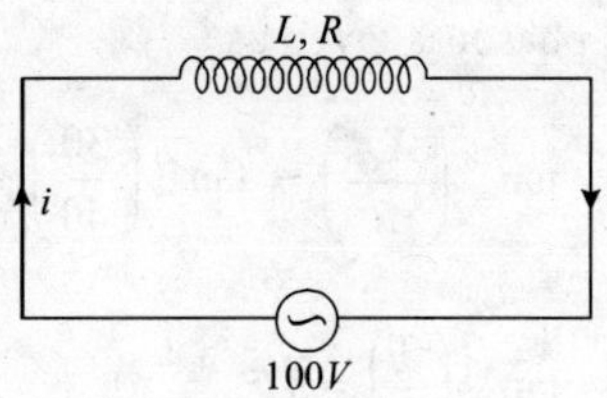

Figure 5.199

$$\Rightarrow \quad x_L^2 = 40000 - 10000 = 30000$$

$$\Rightarrow \quad x_L = 100\sqrt{3}\Omega$$

Inductive reactance is given as

$$x_L = \omega L$$

$$\Rightarrow \quad L = \frac{x_L}{\omega} = \frac{100\sqrt{3}}{2\pi}\frac{\pi}{150\sqrt{3}} = \frac{1}{3}\text{H}$$

Illustrative Example 5.72

In a circuit a resistance of 40 Ω and capacitor of capacitance $\frac{1250}{9\pi}$ μF are connected in series across a 500 V, 120 Hz AC source. Find the effective current in circuit and phase difference between current and source EMF.

Solution

Circuit impedance of a *RC* Circuit is given as

$$\bar{Z} = \bar{R} + \bar{X}_C$$

$$\Rightarrow \quad Z = \sqrt{R^2 + X_C^2}$$

Capacitive reactance is given as

$$X_C = \frac{1}{\omega C} = \frac{1}{2\pi f C}$$

$$\Rightarrow \quad X_C = \frac{9\pi \times 10^6}{2\pi(120)(1250)}\Omega$$

$$\Rightarrow \quad X_C = \frac{3 \times 10^6}{10^5} = 30\,\Omega$$

Circuit impedance is given as

$$Z = \sqrt{(40)^2 + (30)^2} = 50\,\Omega$$

Thus circuit current is given as

$$i_{rms} = \frac{e_{rms}}{Z} = \frac{500}{50} = 10\,\text{A}$$

Phase angle of Z phasor is given as

$$\phi = \tan^{-1}\left(\frac{X_C}{R}\right) = \tan^{-1}\left(\frac{30}{40}\right)$$

$$\Rightarrow \qquad \phi = \tan^{-1}\left(\frac{3}{4}\right) = 37°$$

As in RC circuit current leads EMF so here current will lead EMF in phase by 37°.

5.12 Phasor Analysis

In the chapter of Simple Harmonic Motion (SHM) we've studied that instantaneous displacement of a particle in SHM can be represented by projection of tip of a rotating vector at uniform angular speed on the diameter of circle in which the tip is moving. The uniform circular motion of the tip can be used to analyze instantaneous displacement and phase of the particle as shown in figure-5.200. Here the displacement of P' which is in SHM can be given as

$$y = A\sin(\omega t + \alpha) \qquad \dots(5.180)$$

Where α is the initial phase of the particle.

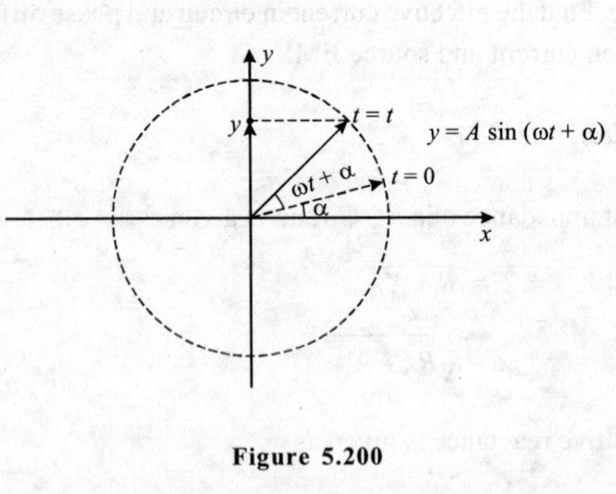

Figure 5.200

Above equation-(5.180) is similar function with which we represent AC EMF and current so this method can also be used to represent such alternating circuit parameters for sinusoidal functions. Such rotating vectors which are used to represent AC circuit parameters are called '*Phasors*' and for time function and analysis AC circuits we used these phasors to represent the magnitude and phase of the circuit parameter. In general phasors are drawn in static manner only. Rotation is considered only when we need to analyze phase at an instant, in general for AC circuits it is not needed. With illustrations taken here it will be more clear.

A phasor is denoted by placing a bar '–' over the symbol of physical quantity being represented along with its initial phase angle. If we consider y in equation-(5.180) represents a physical quantity of an AC circuit then its phasor is written as

$$\bar{y} = L\angle\alpha \qquad \dots(5.181)$$

The diagrammatic representation of the static phasor as given by equation-(5.181) is shown in below figure-5.201. For diagrammatic representation the peak value of a phasor is drawn as length of phasor and its phase angle (also called as its '*argument*') is the angle from the reference axis in anticlockwise sense at which it is drawn as shown in below figure.

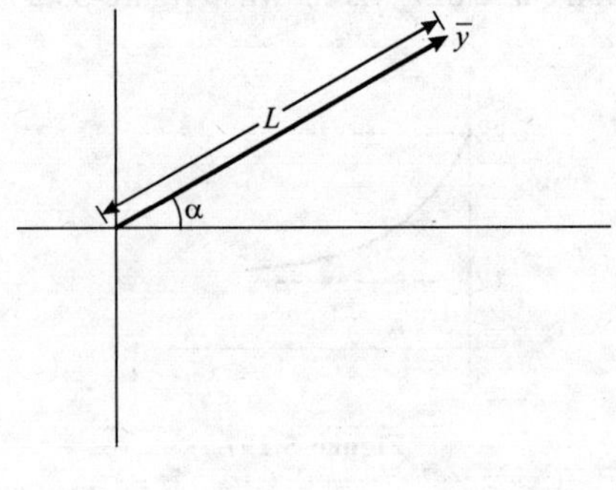

Figure 5.201

If in an AC circuit an AC EMF is used for which time function is given as $e = e_0 \sin\omega t$ then the phasor form of this AC EMF is written as

$$\bar{e} = e_0\angle 0° \qquad \dots(5.182)$$

The diagrammatic representation of the EMF phasor as given by equation-(5.182) is shown in below figure-5.202.

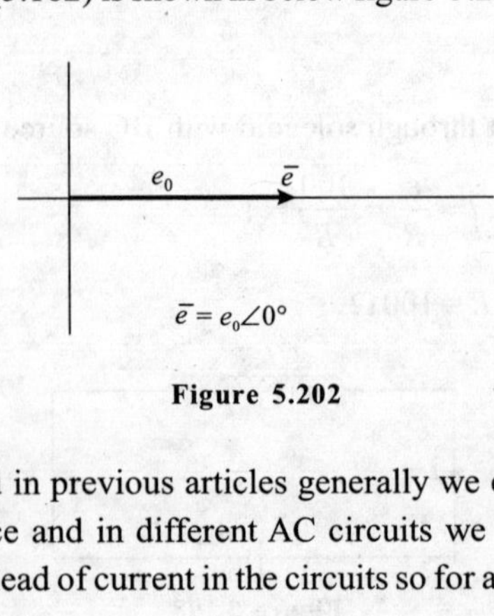

Figure 5.202

As discussed in previous articles generally we consider EMF as a reference and in different AC circuits we determine the phase lag or lead of current in the circuits so for a an alternating current $i = i_0 \sin(\omega t + \phi)$ its phasor form is written as

$$\bar{i} = i_0 \angle \phi \qquad \ldots(5.183)$$

The diagrammatic representation of the current phasor as given by equation-(5.183) is shown in below figure-5.203.

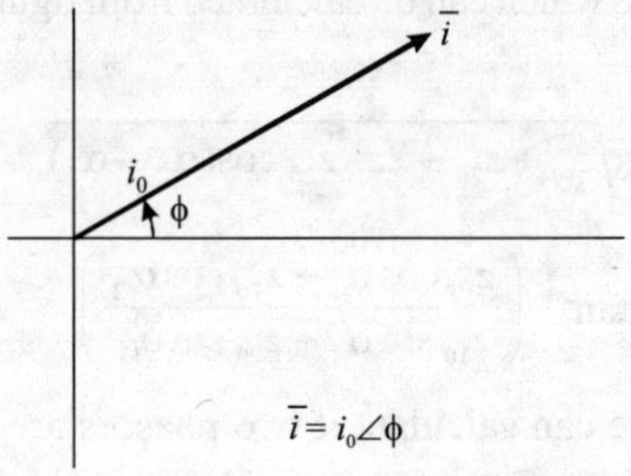

Figure 5.203

5.12.1 Standard Phasors for Resistances and Reactances in AC Circuits

In any AC circuit EMF and current are time varying functions for which phasors can be considered as rotating vectors like SHM if the time phase analysis of these is required. For mathematical analysis of AC circuits we also define standard phasors for resistances, capacitors and inductors with standard values for their magnitude and phasor angles. As resistances and reactances in a given AC circuit are not time varying so their vectors are never considered as rotating vectors. Standard phasors corresponding to these are given below.

(i) Standard Phasor for a Resistance : For a pure resistor of resistance R its phasor is written as

$$\bar{R} = R \angle 0^\circ \qquad \ldots(5.184)$$

Diagrammatically it is represented as shown in figure-5.204.

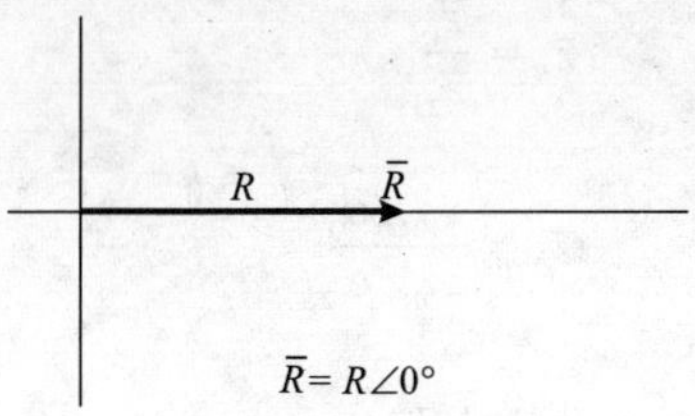

Figure 5.204

(ii) Standard Phasor for Capacitive Reactance : For a pure capacitor of capacitance C its phasor for capacitive reactance is written as

$$\overline{X_C} = \frac{1}{\omega C} \angle(-\pi/2) \qquad \ldots(5.185)$$

Diagrammatically it is represented as shown in figure-5.205.

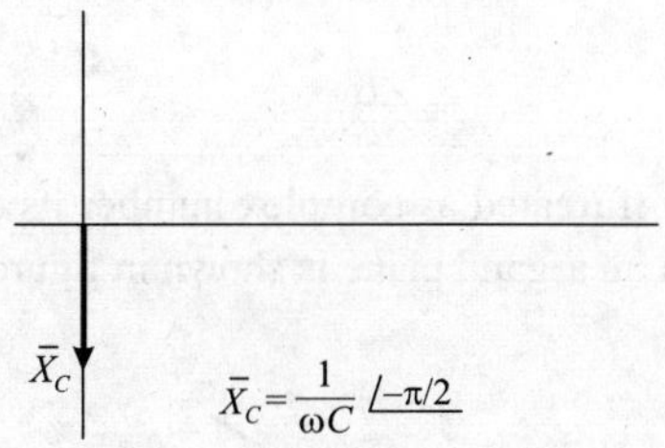

Figure 5.205

(iii) Standard Phasor for Inductive Reactance : For a pure inductor of inductance L its phasor for inductive reactance is written as

$$\overline{X_C} = \omega L \angle(+\pi/2) \qquad \ldots(5.186)$$

Diagrammatically it is represented as shown in figure-5.206.

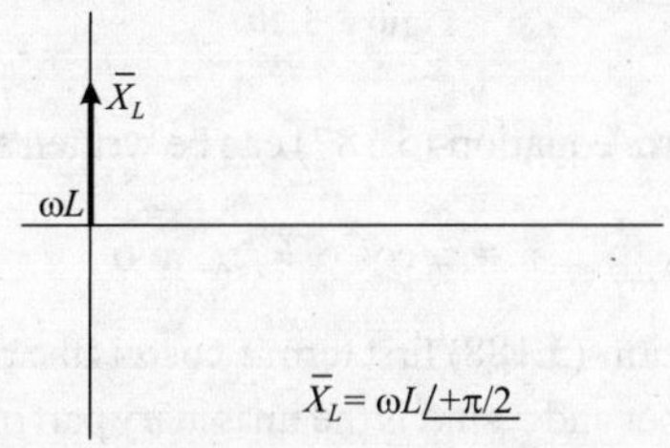

Figure 5.206

In above equations-(5.184), (5.185) and (5.186) many times students get confuse about the phasor angles taken. Here the above values defined for phasor angles are standard values which are defined to analyze and solve AC circuits so one should not think about the derivation or approach of these values. With different illustrations of these standard phasor values applications can be understood at good level.

5.12.2 Phasor Algebra

For calculations in different AC circuits some rules are defined according to which different circuit parameters are used in mathematical operations, set of such rules for solving and analysis of AC circuit studied under '*Phasor Algebra*'. We will discuss some basic rules and applications in solving simple AC circuits here. For basic mathematical operations these rules are listed below in pointwise manner.

(i) Phasors as Complex Numbers : For mathematical calculations phasors are treated like complex numbers with magnitude and argument and the diagrammatic representation of a phasor can be considered the representation of a complex number on argand plane with horizontal and vertical axes as real and imaginary axis of the argand plane. A specific phasor

$\overline{z}$ with its magnitude z_0 and argument α can be written as

$$\overline{z} = z_0 \angle\alpha \quad \text{...(5.187)}$$

Above phasor if treated as complex number its diagrammatic representation on argand plane is shown in figure-5.207

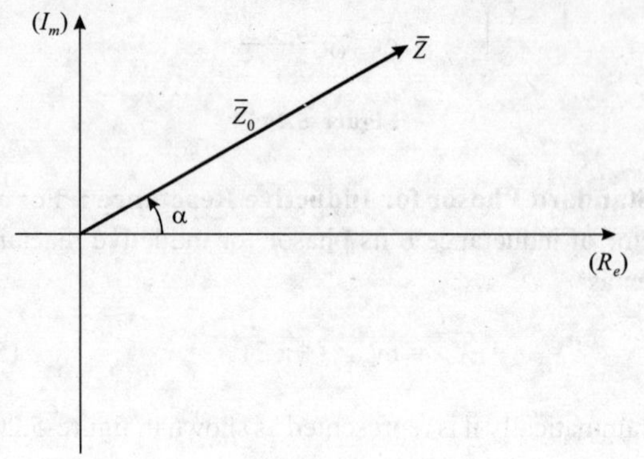

Figure 5.207

In complex form equation-(5.187) can be written as

$$\overline{z} = z_0 \cos\alpha + jz_0 \sin\alpha \quad \text{...(5.188)}$$

In above equation-(5.188) first term $z_0\cos\alpha$ is the real part of the complex number and $z_0\sin\alpha$ is the imaginary part of the complex number and $j = \sqrt{-1}$.

(ii) Addition of Two Phasors : When two phasors $\overline{z}_1$ and $\overline{z}_2$ are given as

$$\overline{z} = z_{10} \angle\alpha_1 \quad \text{...(5.189)}$$

and $$\overline{z}_2 = z_{20} \angle\alpha_2 \quad \text{...(5.190)}$$

Sum of the above two phasors can be done diagrammatically as shown in figure-5.208.

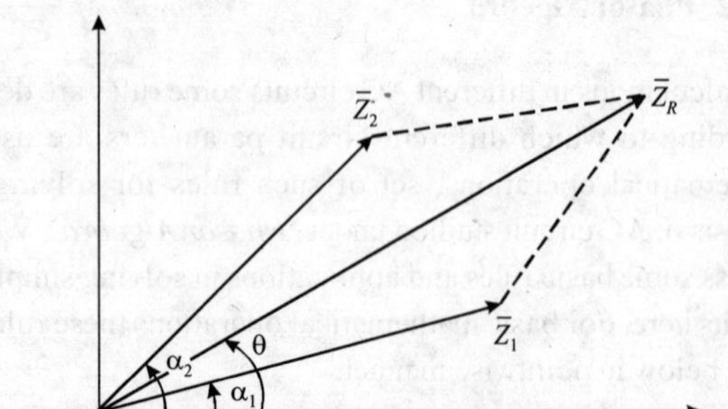

Figure 5.208

Thus the resultant phasor which is the sum of the two phasors is given as

$$\overline{z}_R = \overline{z}_1 + \overline{z}_2$$

$$\Rightarrow \quad \overline{z}_R = z_{10} \angle\alpha_1 + z_{20} \angle\alpha_2$$

$$\Rightarrow \quad \overline{z}_R = |\overline{z}_R| \angle\theta$$

Where $|\overline{z}_R|$ is the magnitude of resultant phasor and θ is its argument angle which can be calculated from figure-5.208 given as

$$|\overline{z}_R| = \sqrt{z_{10}^2 + z_{20}^2 + 2z_{10}z_{20}\cos(\alpha_2 - \alpha_1)} \quad \text{...(5.191)}$$

and $$\theta = \tan^{-1}\left(\frac{z_{10}\cos\alpha_1 + z_{20}\cos\alpha_2}{z_{10}\sin\alpha_1 + z_{20}\sin\alpha_2}\right) \quad \text{...(5.192)}$$

In the same we can calculate if two phasors are subtracted by changing the direction of second phases and adding it to the first. It is done in the same way we add or subtract vectors or complex numbers diagrammatically.

(iii) Product of Two Phasors : When two phasors $\overline{z}_1$ and $\overline{z}_2$ as given by equations-(5.189) and (5.190) are multiplied then in the product phasor will have magnitude given by the product of their individual magnitudes and its argument angle will be given by the sum of the argument angles of the individual phasors as it is done in product of complex numbers.

$$\overline{z}_P = \overline{z}_1 . \overline{z}_2$$

$$\Rightarrow \quad \overline{z}_P = z_{10} \angle\alpha_1 \times z_{20} \angle\alpha_2$$

$$\Rightarrow \quad \overline{z}_P = (z_{10} \times z_{20}) \angle(\alpha_1 + \alpha_2) \quad \text{...(5.193)}$$

(iv) Division of Two Phasors : When two phasors $\overline{z}_1$ and $\overline{z}_2$ as given by equations-(5.189) and (5.190) are divided then in the resultant phasor it will have magnitude given by the division of their individual magnitudes and its argument angle will be given by the difference of the argument angles of the individual phasors as it is done in case of division of complex numbers.

$$\overline{z}_P = \frac{\overline{z}_1}{\overline{z}_2}$$

$$\Rightarrow \quad \overline{z}_P = \frac{z_{10}\angle\alpha_1}{z_{20}\angle\alpha_2}$$

$$\Rightarrow \quad \overline{z}_P = \left(\frac{z_{10}}{z_{20}}\right) \angle(\alpha_1 - \alpha_2) \quad \text{...(5.194)}$$

With the above basic rules we can analyze all types of simple AC Circuits however the above calculations can also be done by considering phasors in complex notation form as given in equation-(5.188) and for calculations real and imaginary parts can be separated and finally given again in form of magnitude argument form which can be transformed as time function whenever needed.

In next upcoming articles we will re-analyze the cases of AC Circuits in which different circuit components are connected across an AC EMF by using phasor analysis.

5.12.3 Phasor Analysis of a Resistance Across an AC EMF

Figure-5.209 shows a resistor resistance R is connected across an AC EMF. Using Ohm's law the phasor current through the circuit is given as

$$\bar{i} = \frac{\bar{e}}{\bar{R}}$$

$$\Rightarrow \quad \bar{i} = \frac{e_0\angle 0°}{R\angle 0°}$$

$$\Rightarrow \quad \bar{i} = \frac{e_0}{R}\angle 0° = i_0\angle 0° \qquad \ldots(5.195)$$

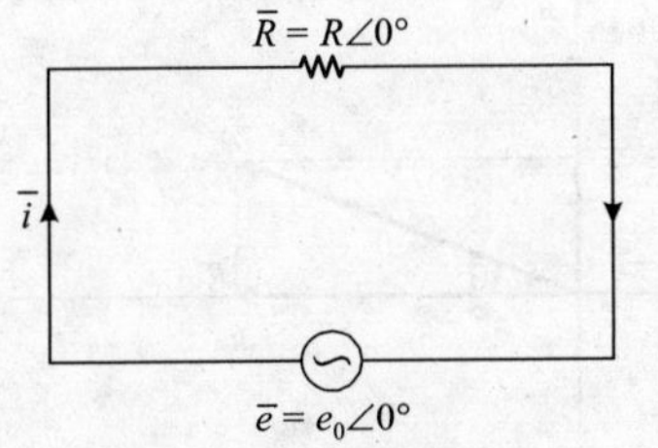

Figure 5.209

Using equation-(5.195) we can write the time function of the phasor current which is given as

$$i = i_0 \sin(\omega t + 0°) \qquad \ldots(5.196)$$

Where $\quad i_0 = \dfrac{e_0}{R} \qquad \ldots(5.197)$

Above equations are same as equations-(5.145) and (5.146) as discussed in article-5.11.1 but here these are obtained by using phasor analysis. Figure-5.210 shows the phasor diagram of AC EMF and current through a pure resistance.

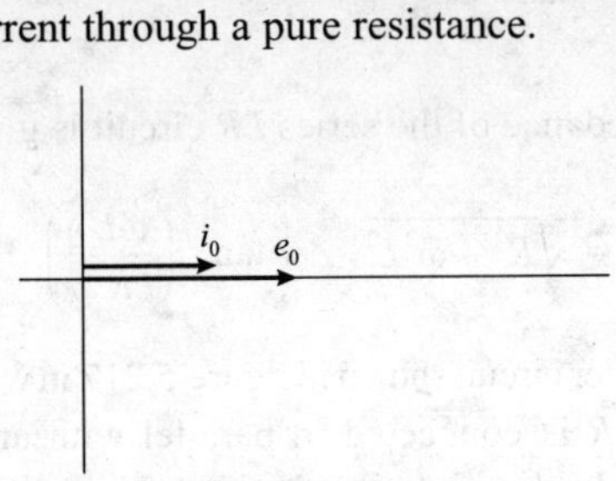

Figure 5.210

5.12.4 Phasor Analysis of a Capacitor Across an AC EMF

Figure-5.211 shows a capacitor of capacitance C connected across an AC EMF. Using Ohm's law in phasor form, phasor current in circuit is given as

$$\bar{i} = \frac{\bar{e}}{\bar{X}_C}$$

$$\Rightarrow \quad \bar{i} = \frac{e_0\angle 0°}{(1/\omega C)\angle(-\pi/2)}$$

$$\Rightarrow \quad \bar{i} = \frac{e_0}{1/\omega C}\angle(+\pi/2) = i_0\angle(+\pi/2) \quad \ldots(5.198)$$

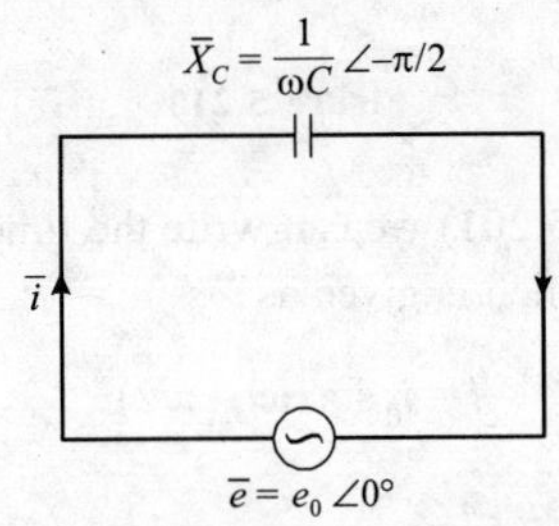

Figure 5.211

Using equation-(5.198) we can write the time function of the phasor current which is given as

$$i = i_0 \sin(\omega t + \pi/2) \qquad \ldots(5.199)$$

Where $\quad i_0 = \dfrac{e_0}{1/\omega C} = \dfrac{e_0}{X_C} \qquad \ldots(5.200)$

Above equations are same as equations-(5.149) and (5.150) as discussed in article-5.11.2 but here these are obtained by using phasor analysis. Figure-5.212 shows the phasor diagram of AC EMF and current through a pure capacitance.

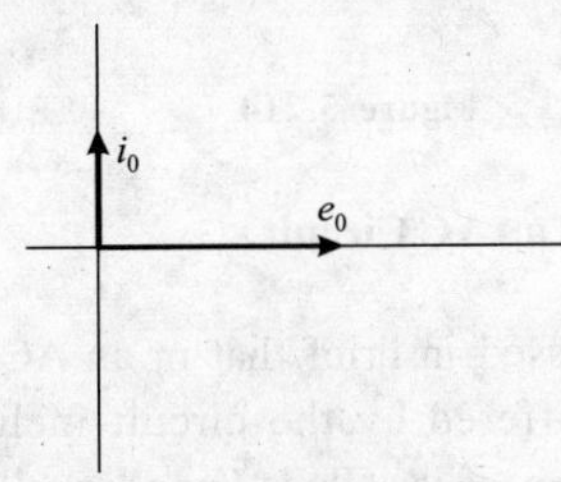

Figure 5.212

5.12.5 Phasor Analysis of an Inductor Across an AC EMF

Figure-5.213 shows an inductor of inductance L which is connected across an AC EMF. Using Ohm's law the phasor current through the circuit is given as

$$\bar{i} = \frac{\bar{e}}{\bar{X}_L}$$

$$\Rightarrow \quad \bar{i} = \frac{e_0\angle 0°}{\omega L\angle(+\pi/2)}$$

$$\Rightarrow \quad \bar{i} = \frac{e_0}{\omega L}\angle(-\pi/2) = i_0\angle(-\pi/2) \quad \ldots(5.201)$$

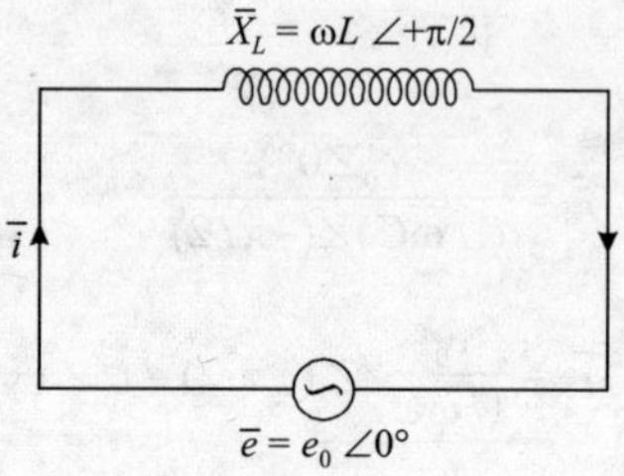

Figure 5.213

Using equation-(5.201) we can write the time function of the phasor current which is given as

$$i = i_0 \sin(\omega t - \pi/2) \quad \dots (5.202)$$

Where
$$i_0 = \frac{e_0}{\omega L} \quad \dots (5.203)$$

Above equations are same as equations-(5.154) and (5.155) as discussed in article-5.11.3 but here these are obtained by using phasor analysis. Figure-5.214 shows the phasor diagram of AC EMF and current through a pure inductor.

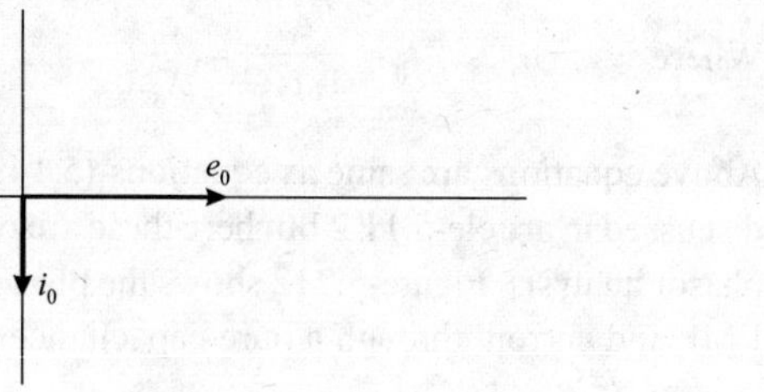

Figure 5.214

5.12.6 Impedance of an AC Circuit

We've already discussed in brief that in an AC circuit total ohmic opposition offered by the circuit including its all resistances and reactances is called '*Impedance*' of the circuit and it is denoted by '*Z*' and its phasor is denoted by $\bar{Z}$ and measured in unit of '*ohm*'. In a circuit impedance is caused by either of its resistances or reactances. For purely resistive, capacitive and inductive circuits impedances are given as

Purely Resistive Impedance $\bar{Z} = \bar{R}$

Purely Capacitive Impedance $\bar{Z} = \bar{X}_C$

Purely Inductive Impedance $\bar{Z} = \bar{X}_L$

When different types of circuit components are connected in series or parallel then we calculate impedance of the circuit by using series and parallel combination of these components in the same way we used to calculate equivalent resistance for DC circuits. The only difference in case of AC circuits is that instead of simple calculations we use rules of phasor algebra for calculations which will be clearly understood with the help of some illustrations. Figure-5.215 shows series combination of a resistor of resistance *R* with an inductor of inductance *L*. Here the impedance of the circuit across terminals *A* and *B* is given as

$$\bar{Z}_{AB} = \bar{R} + \bar{X}_L$$

$$\Rightarrow \quad \bar{Z}_{AB} = R\angle 0° + \omega L \angle(+\pi/2) \quad \dots (5.204)$$

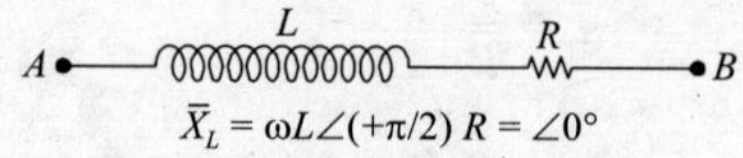

Figure 5.215

Above equation can be solve diagrammatically as shown in figure-5.216 where we add resistance phasor and inductive reactance phasor like vectors or complex numbers.

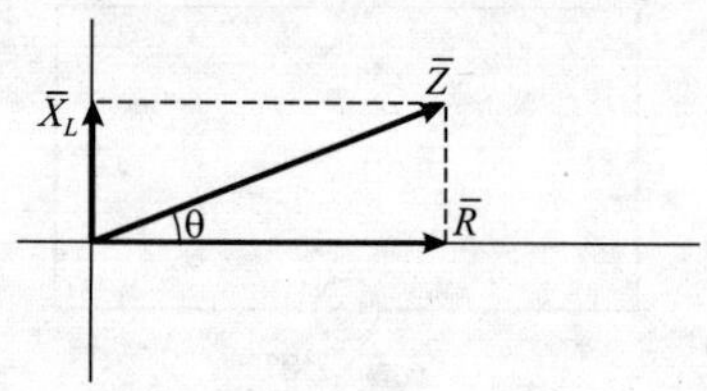

Figure 5.216

From above figure-5.216, the magnitude of impedance phasor is given as

$$Z = \sqrt{R^2 + X_L^2}$$

$$\Rightarrow \quad Z = \sqrt{R^2 + \omega^2 L^2} \quad \dots (5.205)$$

The argument of the impedance phasor is given as

$$\theta = \tan^{-1}\left(\frac{\omega L}{R}\right) \quad \dots (5.206)$$

Thus the impedance of the series *LR* circuit is given as

$$\bar{Z}_{AB} = \sqrt{R^2 + \omega^2 L^2} \angle \left(\tan^{-1}\left(\frac{\omega L}{R}\right)\right) \quad \dots (5.207)$$

Consider another circuit shown in figure-5.217 in which a resistor or resistance *R* is connected in parallel with an inductor of inductance *L*. In this situation the impedance of the circuit is given as

$$\frac{1}{\bar{Z}_{AB}} = \frac{1}{\bar{R}} + \frac{1}{\bar{X}_L}$$

$$\Rightarrow \quad \frac{1}{\bar{Z}_{AB}} = \frac{1}{R\angle 0°} + \frac{1}{\omega L\angle(+\pi/2)}$$

$$\Rightarrow \quad \frac{1}{\bar{Z}_{AB}} = \frac{1}{R}\angle 0^\circ + \frac{1}{\omega L}\angle(-\pi/2) \qquad \ldots(5.208)$$

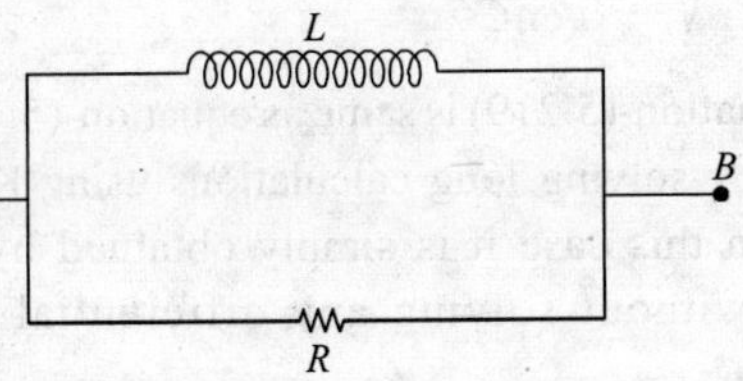

Figure 5.217

Above equation can be diagrammatically solved for adding the two terms on the RHS of the equation as shown in figure-5.218.

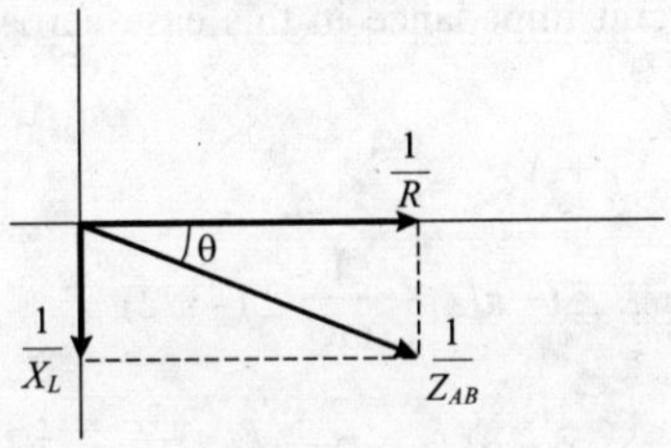

Figure 5.218

From the above figure the magnitude of the reciprocal of impedance phasor is given as

$$\left|\frac{1}{\bar{Z}_{AB}}\right| = \sqrt{\left(\frac{1}{R}\right)^2 + \left(\frac{1}{\omega L}\right)^2}$$

$$\Rightarrow \quad \left|\frac{1}{\bar{Z}_{AB}}\right| = \frac{\sqrt{R^2+\omega^2 L^2}}{R\omega L} \qquad \ldots(5.209)$$

The argument of the reciprocal of impedance phasor is given as

$$\theta = -\tan^{-1}\left(\frac{1/\omega L}{1/R}\right) = -\tan^{-1}\left(\frac{R}{\omega L}\right) \qquad \ldots(5.210)$$

Thus reciprocal of impedance phasor is given as

$$\frac{1}{\bar{Z}_{AB}} = \frac{\sqrt{R^2+\omega^2 L^2}}{R\omega L}\angle\left(-\tan^{-1}\left(\frac{R}{\omega L}\right)\right)$$

$$\Rightarrow \quad \bar{Z}_{AB} = \frac{R\omega L}{\sqrt{R^2+\omega^2 L^2}}\angle\left(\tan^{-1}\left(\frac{R}{\omega L}\right)\right) \qquad \ldots(5.211)$$

Above equation-(5.211) gives the impedance of the parallel LR circuit shown in figure-5.217.

For any given AC circuit in which different circuit components are connected in some combination if it is connected across an AC EMF then alternating current supplied by the EMF can be given as

$$\bar{i} = \frac{\bar{e}}{\bar{Z}} \qquad \ldots(5.212)$$

5.12.7 Phasor Analysis of Series RL Circuit Across AC EMF

Figure-5.219 shows a series RL circuit connected across an AC EMF. As already discussed in previous article, circuit impedance in this case across AC EMF is given as

$$\bar{Z}_{AB} = \bar{R} + \bar{X}_L$$

$$\Rightarrow \quad \bar{Z}_{AB} = R\angle 0^\circ + \omega L\angle(+\pi/2)$$

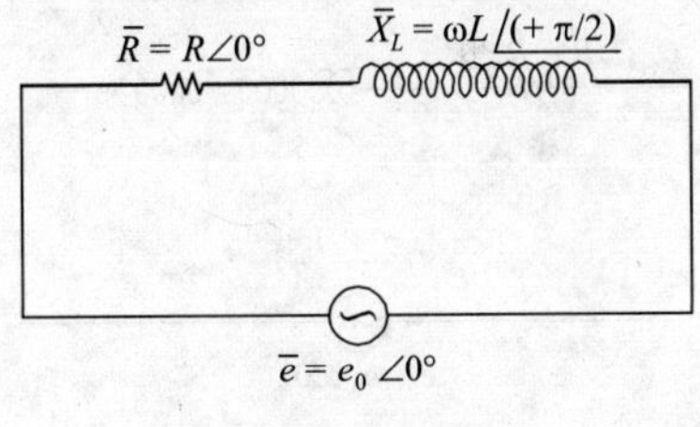

Figure 5.219

Above equation is solved graphically as shown in figure-5.216 which gives

$$\bar{Z}_{AB} = \sqrt{R^2+\omega^2 L^2}\angle\left(\tan^{-1}\left(\frac{\omega L}{R}\right)\right) \qquad \ldots(5.213)$$

The current supplied by the AC EMF is given as

$$\bar{i} = \frac{\bar{e}}{\bar{Z}}$$

$$\Rightarrow \quad \bar{i} = \frac{e_0\angle 0^\circ}{\sqrt{R^2+\omega^2 L^2}\angle\left(\tan^{-1}\left(\frac{\omega L}{R}\right)\right)}$$

$$\Rightarrow \quad \bar{i} = \frac{e_0}{\sqrt{R^2+\omega^2 L^2}}\angle\left(-\tan^{-1}\left(\frac{\omega L}{R}\right)\right) \qquad \ldots(5.214)$$

Current phasor as given in equation-(5.214) can be written in time function as

$$\bar{i} = \frac{e_0}{\sqrt{R^2+\omega^2 L^2}}\sin\left(\omega t - \tan^{-1}\left(\frac{\omega L}{R}\right)\right) \qquad \ldots(5.215)$$

$$\Rightarrow \quad i = i_0 \sin(\omega t - \phi) \qquad \ldots(5.216)$$

Where $i_0 = \frac{e_0}{\sqrt{R^2+\omega^2 L^2}}$ and $\phi = \tan^{-1}\left(\frac{\omega L}{R}\right)$

Above equation-(5.215) is same as equation-(5.167) which was obtained by solving long calculations using Kirchhoff's law whereas in this case it is simply obtained by using phasor analysis without solving any differential equation and integration.

5.12.8 Phasor Analysis of Series RC Circuit Across AC EMF

Figure-5.220 shows a series LR circuit connected across an AC EMF. The circuit impedance in this case across AC EMF is given as

$$\bar{Z}_{AB} = \bar{R} + \bar{X}_C$$

$$\Rightarrow \quad \bar{Z}_{AB} = R\angle 0° + \frac{1}{\omega C}\angle(-\pi/2)$$

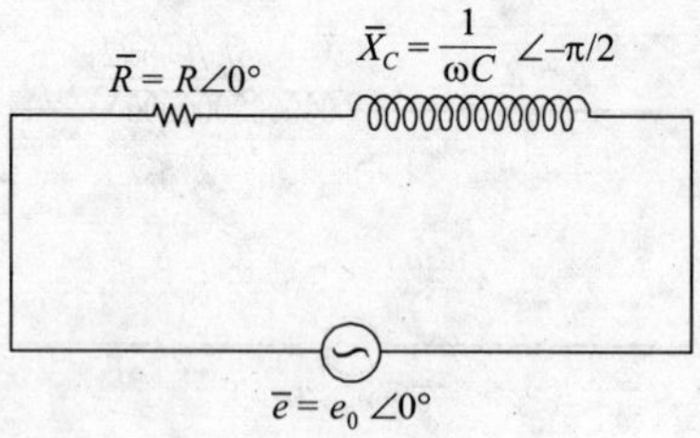

Figure 5.220

Above equation is solved graphically as shown in figure-5.221 which gives

$$\bar{Z}_{AB} = \sqrt{R^2 + \frac{1}{\omega^2 C^2}}\angle\left(-\tan^{-1}\left(\frac{1}{R\omega C}\right)\right) \quad \text{...(5.217)}$$

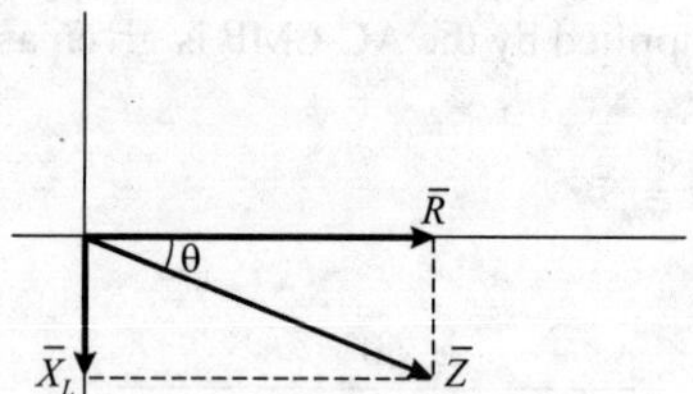

Figure 5.221

The current supplied by the AC EMF is given as

$$\bar{i} = \frac{\bar{e}}{\bar{Z}}$$

$$\Rightarrow \quad \bar{i} = \frac{e_0\angle 0°}{\sqrt{R^2 + \frac{1}{\omega^2 C^2}}\angle\left(-\tan^{-1}\left(\frac{1}{R\omega C}\right)\right)}$$

$$\Rightarrow \quad \bar{i} = \frac{e_0}{\sqrt{R^2 + \frac{1}{\omega^2 C^2}}}\angle\left(\tan^{-1}\left(\frac{1}{R\omega C}\right)\right) \quad \text{...(5.218)}$$

Current phasor as given in equation-(5.218) can be written in time function as

$$i = \frac{e_0}{\sqrt{R^2 + \frac{1}{\omega^2 C^2}}}\sin\left(\omega t + \tan^{-1}\left(\frac{1}{R\omega C}\right)\right) \quad \text{...(5.219)}$$

$$\Rightarrow \quad i = i_0 \sin(\omega t + \phi) \quad \text{...(5.220)}$$

Where $i_0 = \frac{e_0}{\sqrt{R^2 + \frac{1}{\omega^2 C^2}}}$ and $\phi = \tan^{-1}\left(\frac{1}{R\omega C}\right)$

Above equation-(5.219) is same as equation-(5.177) which was obtained by solving long calculations using Kirchhoff's law whereas in this case it is simply obtained by using phasor analysis without solving any differential equation and integration.

5.12.9 Phasor Analysis of Series LC Circuit Across AC EMF

Figure-5.222 shows a series LC circuit connected across an AC EMF. The circuit impedance in this case across AC EMF is given as

$$\bar{Z}_{AB} = \bar{X}_L + \bar{X}_C$$

$$\Rightarrow \quad \bar{Z}_{AB} = \omega L\angle(+\pi/2) + \frac{1}{\omega C}\angle(-\pi/2)$$

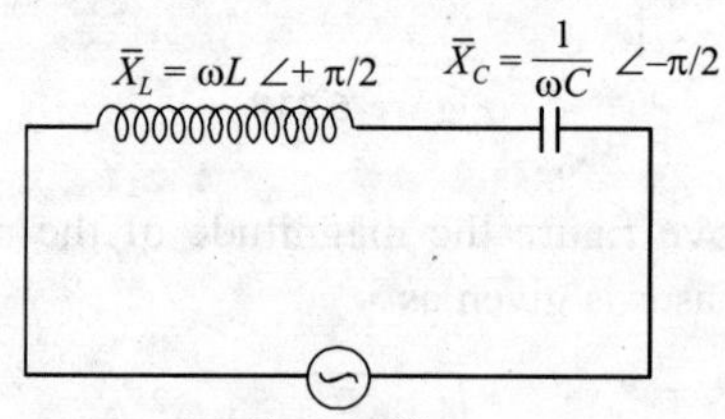

Figure 5.222

Above equation is solved graphically as shown in figure-5.223. Considering $\omega L > 1/\omega C$ gives

$$\bar{Z}_{AB} = \left(\omega L - \frac{1}{\omega C}\right)\angle(+\pi/2) \quad \text{...(5.221)}$$

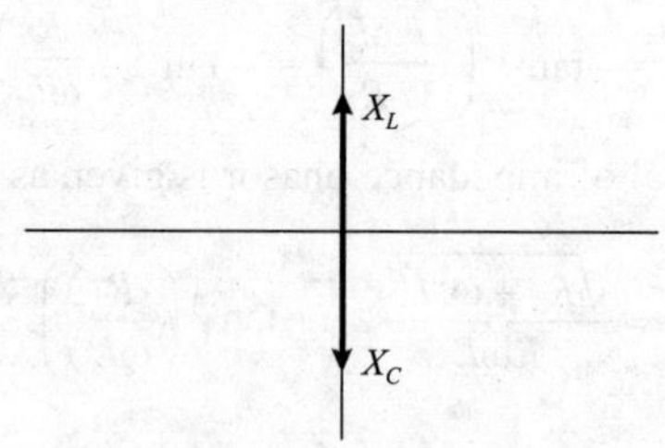

Figure 5.223

The current supplied by the AC EMF is given as

$$\bar{i} = \frac{\bar{e}}{\bar{Z}}$$

$$\Rightarrow \quad \bar{i} = \frac{e_0\angle 0°}{\left(\omega L - \frac{1}{\omega C}\right)\angle(+\pi/2)}$$

$$\Rightarrow \quad \bar{i} = \frac{e_0}{\left(\omega L - \frac{1}{\omega C}\right)}\angle(-\pi/2) \quad \text{...(5.222)}$$

Current phasor as given in equation-(5.222) can be written in time function as

$$i = \frac{e_0}{\left(\omega L - \frac{1}{\omega C}\right)} \sin\left(\omega t - \frac{\pi}{2}\right) \quad \ldots(5.223)$$

$$\Rightarrow \quad i = i_0 \sin(\omega t - \pi/2) \quad \ldots(5.224)$$

Where $i_0 = \frac{e_0}{\left(\omega L - \frac{1}{\omega C}\right)}$

In case of an inductor in series with a capacitor across AC EMF always current is either lagging or leading in phase by an angle $\pi/2$ with EMF as phasors of capacitive or inductive reactance are in opposite directions. If capacitive reactance is more then current will lead EMF and if inductive reactance is more then current will lag behind EMF.

5.12.10 Series RLC Circuit Across AC EMF

Figure-5.224 shows a circuit in which *R*, *L* and *C* are connected in series across an AC EMF. In this case the circuit impedance is given as

$$\bar{Z}_{AB} = \bar{R} + \bar{X}_L + \bar{X}_C$$

$$\Rightarrow \quad \bar{Z}_{AB} = R\angle 0^\circ + \omega L \angle(+\pi/2) + \frac{1}{\omega C}\angle(-\pi/2)$$

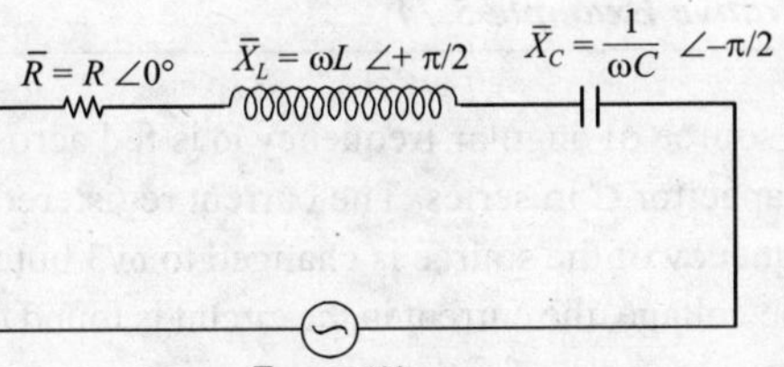

Figure 5.224

Above equation is solved graphically as shown in figure-5.225 in which we consider $\omega L > 1/\omega C$ which gives

$$\bar{Z}_{AB} = \sqrt{R^2 + \left(\omega L + \frac{1}{\omega C}\right)^2} \angle \tan^{-1}\left(\frac{\omega L - \frac{1}{\omega C}}{R}\right) \quad \ldots(5.225)$$

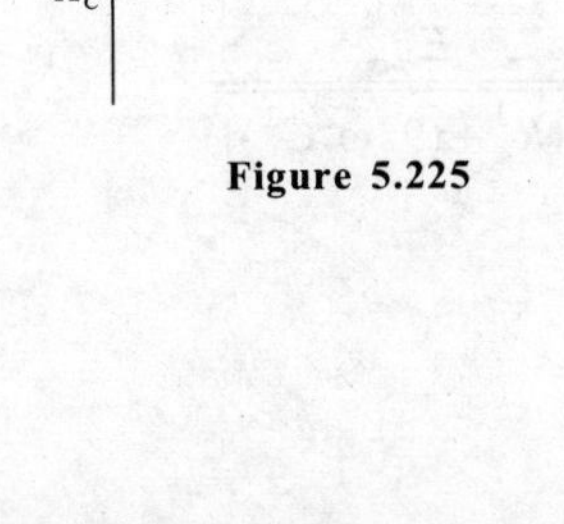

Figure 5.225

The current supplied by the AC EMF in above case is given as

$$\bar{i} = \frac{\bar{e}}{\bar{Z}}$$

$$\Rightarrow \quad \bar{i} = \frac{e_0\angle 0^\circ}{\sqrt{R^2 + \left(\omega L - \frac{1}{\omega C}\right)^2} \angle \tan^{-1}\left(\frac{\omega L - \frac{1}{\omega C}}{R}\right)}$$

$$\Rightarrow \quad \bar{i} = \frac{e_0}{\sqrt{R^2 + \left(\omega L - \frac{1}{\omega C}\right)^2}} \angle -\tan^{-1}\left(\frac{\omega L - \frac{1}{\omega C}}{R}\right) \quad \ldots(5.226)$$

Using above equation-(5.226) which gives the phasor current in series RLC circuit, we can write the time function of the current which is given as

$$i = \frac{e_0}{\sqrt{R^2 + \left(\omega L + \frac{1}{\omega C}\right)^2}} \sin\left(\omega t - \tan^{-1}\left(\frac{\omega L - \frac{1}{\omega C}}{R}\right)\right) \quad \ldots(5.227)$$

5.12.11 Phase Relations in Series RLC Circuit

Figure-5.226 shows a series RLC components in a branch of an AC circuit in which a current *i* flows. The impedance of the branch across terminals *A* and *B* is given as

$$\bar{Z}_{AB} = \sqrt{R^2 + \left(\omega L - \frac{1}{\omega C}\right)^2} \angle \tan^{-1}\left(\frac{\omega L - \frac{1}{\omega C}}{R}\right) \quad \ldots(5.228)$$

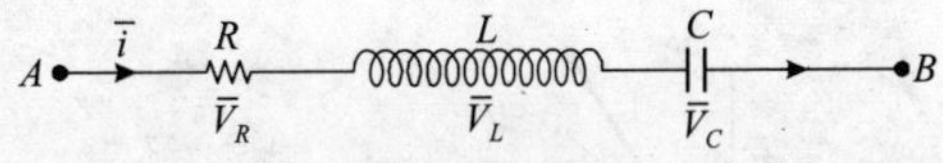

Figure 5.226

The potential difference across terminals *A* and *B* is given by Ohm's law as

$$\bar{V}_{AB} = \bar{i} \cdot \bar{Z}$$

As in above equation-(5.228) we considered $\omega L > 1/\omega C$ so in the circuit current will be lagging behind the potential difference. Actually the phase relation between the current and potential difference depends upon the frequency of AC EMF in above circuit. There are three cases in different situations.

Case-I : When $\omega L = \frac{1}{\omega C} \Rightarrow \omega = \frac{1}{\sqrt{LC}}$

In this case $\theta = 0$ where θ is the phase with which current will lag behind the potential difference across terminals *A* and *B* or at the above frequency current and potential difference will be in same phase.

Case-II : When $\omega L > \dfrac{1}{\omega C} \Rightarrow \omega > \dfrac{1}{\sqrt{LC}}$

In this case θ is positive and current will lag behind the potential difference across terminals A and B.

Case-III : When $\omega L < \dfrac{1}{\omega C} \Rightarrow \omega < \dfrac{1}{\sqrt{LC}}$

In this case θ is negative thus current will lead the potential difference across terminals A and B.

If we analyze the potential differences across each of R, L and C and these are given as $\bar{V}_R$, $\bar{V}_L$ and $\bar{V}_C$ then we use

$$\bar{V}_{AB} = \bar{V}_R + \bar{V}_L + \bar{V}_C \quad \ldots(5.229)$$

As current $\bar{i}$ through all the three components is same the potential difference across resistance $\bar{V}_R$ is in same phase with this current, potential difference across inductor $\bar{V}_L$ will lead this current by an angle π/2 and the potential difference across the resistance $\bar{V}_C$ will lag behind this current by an angle π/2.

Figure-5.227 shows the phasors of current and potential differences in this circuit branch and by this we can write the relation in magnitudes of all the potential difference mentioned in equation-(5.229) which is in phasor form.

$$V_{AB} = \sqrt{V_R^2 + (V_L - V_C)^2} \quad \ldots(5.230)$$

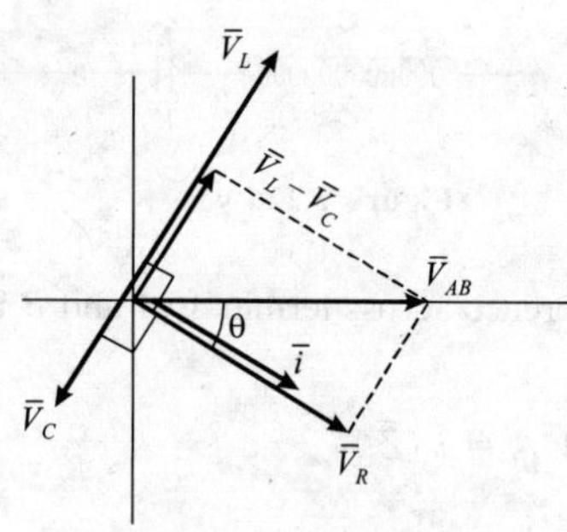

Figure 5.227

Illustrative Example 5.73

A 12 Ω resistance and an inductance of 0.05/π H with negligible resistance are connected in series. Across the end of this circuit is connected a 130 V alternating voltage of frequency 50 Hz. Calculate the alternating current in the circuit and potential difference across the resistance and that across the inductance.

Solution

The impedance of the circuit is given as

$$Z = \sqrt{(R^2 + \omega^2 L^2)}$$

$$\Rightarrow \quad Z = \sqrt{[R^2 + (2\pi fL)^2]}$$

$$\Rightarrow \quad Z = \sqrt{[(12)^2 + \{2\times 3.14\times 50\times (0.05/3.14)\}^2]}$$

$$\Rightarrow \quad Z = \sqrt{(144+25)} = 13\ \Omega$$

Current in the circuit is given as

$$i = \frac{E}{Z} = \frac{130}{13} = 10\text{ A}$$

Potential difference across resistance is given as

$$V_R = iR = 10\times 12 = 120\text{ V}$$

Inductive reactance of coil is given as

$$X_L = \omega L = 2\pi fL$$

$$\Rightarrow \quad X_L = 2\pi\times 50\times\left(\frac{0.05}{\pi}\right) = 5\ \Omega$$

Potential difference across inductance is given as

$$V_L = i\times X_L = 10\times 5 = 50\text{ V}$$

Illustrative Example 5.74

An AC source of angular frequency ω is fed across resistor R and a capacitor C in series. The current registered is i. If now the frequency of the source is changed to ω/3 but maintaining the same voltage, the current in the circuit is found to be halved. Calculate the ratio of reactance to resistance at the original frequency.

Solution

At angular frequency ω, the current in RC circuit is given as

$$i_{rms} = \frac{E_{rms}}{\sqrt{\{R^2 + (1/\omega^2 C^2)\}}} \quad \ldots(5.231)$$

When frequency is changed to ω/3, the current is halved so we have

$$\frac{i_{rms}}{2} = \frac{E_{rms}}{\sqrt{\{R^2 + 1/(\omega/3)^2 C^2\}}}$$

$$\Rightarrow \quad \frac{i_{rms}}{2} = \frac{E_{rms}}{\sqrt{\{R^2 + (9/\omega^2 C^2)\}}} \quad \ldots(5.232)$$

From equation-(5.231) and (5.232), we have

$$\frac{1}{\sqrt{\{R^2+(1/\omega^2C^2)\}}} = \frac{2}{\sqrt{\{R^2+(9/\omega^2C^2)\}}}$$

$$\Rightarrow \quad 3R^2 = \frac{5}{\omega^2C^2}$$

Thus the ratio of reactance to resistance is given as

$$\frac{X_C}{R} = \frac{(1/\omega C)}{R} = \sqrt{\left(\frac{3}{5}\right)}$$

 # *Illustrative Example 5.75*

In a series *RL* circuit with $L = \frac{175}{11}$ mH and $R = 12\ \Omega$ an AC source of emf $e = 130\sqrt{2}$V, 50 Hz is applied. Find the circuit impedance and phase difference of EMF and current in circuit.

Solution

For a series *RL* circuit, impedance is given as

$$\bar{Z} = \bar{R} + \bar{X}_L$$

$$\Rightarrow \quad Z = \sqrt{R^2 + x_L^2}$$

Inductive reactance is given as

$$X_L = \omega L = 2\pi FL$$

$$\Rightarrow \quad X_L = 2\cdot\left(\frac{2L}{7}\right)\cdot 50\frac{175}{11}m$$

$$\Rightarrow \quad X_L = 5000\times10^{-5} = 5\,\Omega$$

Circuit impedance is calculated as

$$Z = \sqrt{(12)^2+(5)^2}$$

$$\Rightarrow \quad Z = \sqrt{144+25} = \sqrt{169} = 13\,\Omega$$

With phase angle of impedance calculated from phasor diagram, given as

$$\phi = \tan^{-1}\left(\frac{X_L}{R}\right)$$

$$\Rightarrow \quad \phi = \tan^{-1}\left(\frac{5}{12}\right)$$

 # *Illustrative Example 5.76*

A coil has inductance 2.2/π H and is joined in series with a resistance of 220 Ω. An AC EMF 220 V, 50 Hz is applied to it, find the wattless current in circuit.

Solution

In series *RL* circuit, impedance is given as

$$Z = \sqrt{R^2 + X_L^2}$$

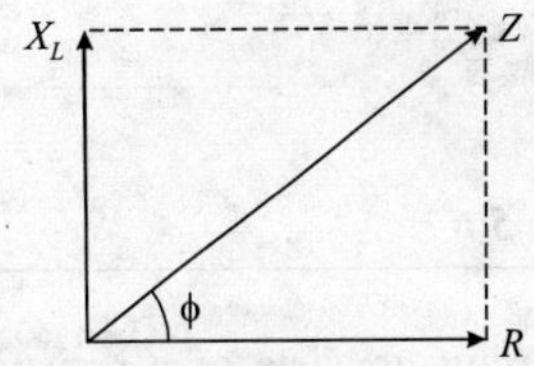

Figure 5.228

Inductive reactance is given as

$$X_L = \omega L$$

$$\Rightarrow \quad X_L = 2\pi(50)\times\frac{2.2}{\pi}$$

$$\Rightarrow \quad X_L = 220\,\Omega$$

As $X_L = R$ we have $\phi = 45°$

Circuit current is given as

$$i = \frac{e}{Z} = \frac{220}{220\sqrt{2}} = \frac{1}{\sqrt{2}}\text{ A}$$

Wattless current in AC circuit is given as

$$i_{\text{WL}} = i\sin\phi$$

$$\Rightarrow \quad i_{\text{WL}} = \frac{1}{\sqrt{2}}\times\frac{1}{\sqrt{2}} = \frac{1}{2} = 0.5\text{ A}$$

 # *Illustrative Example 5.77*

A 200 km long telegraph wire has a capacitance of 0.014 μF/km. If it carries an alternating current of 50 kHz, what should be the value of an inductance required to be connected in series so that impedance is minimum.

Solution

The total capacitance of telegraph line is given as

$$C = 0.014\times200 = 2.8\ \mu\text{F} = 2.8\times10^{-6}\text{F}$$

For minimum impedance, we have

$$\omega L = \frac{1}{\omega C}$$

$$\Rightarrow \quad L = \frac{1}{\omega^2C} = \frac{1}{(2\pi f)^2C} = \frac{1}{4\pi^2f^2C}$$

$$\Rightarrow \quad L = \frac{1}{4\times(3.14)^2\times(50\times10^3)^2\times(2.8\times10^{-6})}\text{H}$$

$$\Rightarrow \quad L = 0.36\times10^{-3} = 0.36\text{ mH}$$

Web Reference at www.physicsgalaxy.com

Age Group - Grade 11 & 12 | Age 17-19 Years
Section - Magnetic Effects
Topic - Alternating Current
Module Number - 14 to 33

Practice Exercise 5.6

(i) A series circuit consists of a resistance of 15 Ω, an inductance of 0.08 H and a capacitor of capacitance 30 μF. The applied voltage has a frequency of 500 rad/s. Does the current lead or lag the applied voltage and by what angle.

[60.65° lead]

(ii) An 220 V AC voltage at a frequency of 40 cycles/s is applied to a circuit containing a pure inductance of 0.01 H and a pure resistance of 6 Ω in series. Calculate

(a) The current supplied by source

(b) The potential difference across the resistance

(c) The potential difference across the inductance

(d) The time lag between maxima of current and EMF in circuit

[(a) 33.83 mA (b) 202.98 V (c) 96.83 V (d) 0.01579 s]

(iii) A box P and a coil Q are connected in series with an AC source of variable frequency. The EMF of source is constant at 10 V. Box P contains a capacitance of 1 μF in series with a resistance of 32 Ω. Coil Q has a self inductance 4.9 mH and a resistance of 68 Ω. The frequency is adjusted so that the maximum current flows in P and Q. Find the impedance of P and Q at this frequency. Also find the voltage across P and Q respectively.

[76 Ω, 98 Ω, 7.6 V, 9.8 V]

(iv) An AC source is connected to two circuits as shown in figure-5.229. Obtain the current through resistance R at resonance in both the circuits.

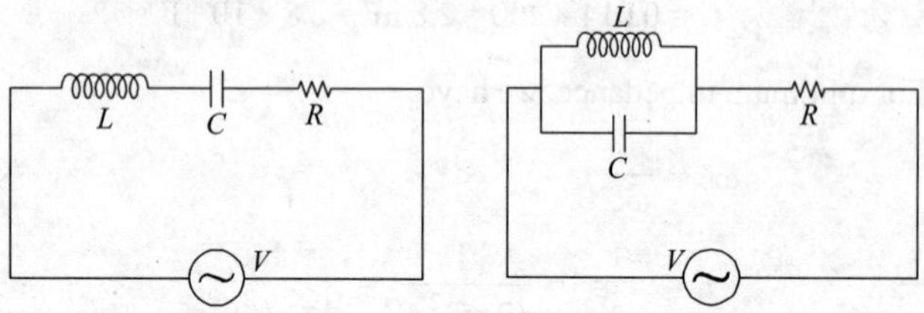

Figure 5.229

[$\frac{V}{R}$, 0]

(v) A resistance R, and inductance L and a capacitor C are all connected in series with an AC supply. The resistance is of 16 Ω and for a given frequency, the inductive reactance of L is 24 Ω and capacitive reactance of C is 12 Ω. If the current in the circuit is 5 A, find

(a) The potential difference across R, L and C

(b) The impedance of the circuit

(c) The voltage of AC supply

(d) The phase angle between current and voltage

[(a) 80 V, 120 V, 60 V (b) 20 Ω (c) 100 V (d) 37°]

(vi) A series circuit consists of a resistance, inductance and capacitance. The applied voltage and the current at any instant are given as

$$e = 141.4 \cos (300t - 10°)$$

and $$i = 5 \cos (3000t - 55°)$$

The inductance is 0.01 H. Calculate the values of the resistance and capacitance.

[33.33 μF]

(vii) A circuit with R = 70 Ω in series with a parallel combination of L = 1.5 H and C = 30 μF is driven by a 230 V supply of angular frequency 300 rad/s.

(a) Find the impedance of the circuit.

(b) What is the RMS value of total current?

(c) What are the current amplitudes in the L and C arms of the circuit?

(d) How will the circuit behave at $\omega = 1/\sqrt{LC}$?

[(a) 163.3 Ω (b) 1.414 A (c) 0.653 A, 2.64 A (d) Circuit current becomes zero]

(viii) A resistance of 10 Ω is joined in series with an inductance of 0.5 H. What capacitance should be put in series with the combination to obtain the maximum current? What will be this maximum current? What will be the potential difference across the resistance, inductance and capacitance? The current is being supplied by 200 V, 50 Hz AC mains.

[20.24 μF, 20 A, 200 V, 3142 V, 3142 V]

(ix) In the circuit shown in figure-5.230 AC EMF is $e = 10 \cos 100\pi t$. Find circuit impedance and the potential difference across points A and B when it is half of the voltage of source at that instant.

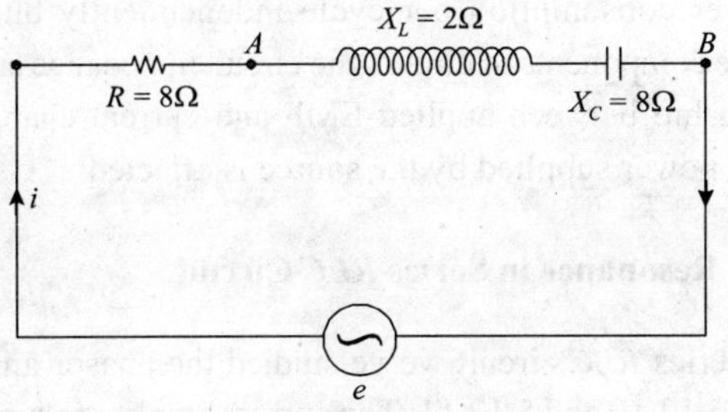

Figure 5.230

5.13 Power in AC Circuits

In the chapter of current electricity we've studied that the power supplied by a source to the circuit is given by the product of the EMF and the current supplied by the source. In DC circuits current and EMF remain constant in steady state but in AC circuits with time EMF and current continuously vary and depending upon the phase difference between EMF and the current their instantaneous values will be different for different circuits as phase relationship between EMF and current depend upon the type of circuit used so instantaneous power supplied by an AC source continuously vary with time thats why in AC circuits we analyze average power supplied by the AC source.

5.13.1 Average Power in AC Circuits

Figure-5.231 shows an AC Circuit in which an AC EMF is connected across an impedance $\overline{Z}$ which may be a combination of two or more components or a single component. The current in this circuit is given by Ohm's law as

$$\overline{i} = \frac{\overline{e}}{\overline{Z}}$$

$$\Rightarrow \quad \overline{i} = \frac{e_0\angle 0^\circ}{Z_0\angle\phi} = \frac{e_0}{Z_0}\angle -\phi = i_0\angle -\phi$$

$$\Rightarrow \quad i = i_0 \sin(\omega t - \phi) \qquad \ldots(5.233)$$

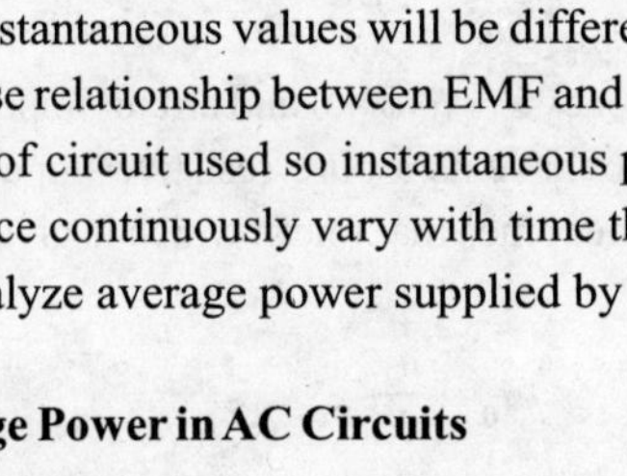

Figure 5.231

In this circuit instantaneous power supplied by the AC source can be given as

$$P = ei$$

$$\Rightarrow \quad P = e_0 \sin \omega t \times i_0 \sin(\omega t - \phi)$$

$$\Rightarrow \quad P = e_0 i_0 \sin \omega t \times (\sin \omega t \cos\phi - \cos \omega t \sin\phi)$$

$$\Rightarrow \quad P = e_0 i_0 \sin^2 \omega t \cos\phi - e_0 i_0 \sin \omega t \cos \omega t \sin\phi \qquad \ldots(5.234)$$

Above equation-(5.234) gives the instantaneous power supplied by the AC source of which average value can be given by replacing the sinusoidal time functions on RHS of this equation by their average values which gives

$$P_{avg} = e_0 i_0 \langle \sin^2 \omega t\rangle \cos\phi - e_0 i_0 \langle \sin \omega t \cos \omega t\rangle \sin\phi$$

$$\Rightarrow \quad P_{avg} = e_0 i_0 \left(\frac{1}{2}\right)\cos\phi - e_0 i_0 (0) \sin\phi$$

$$\Rightarrow \quad P_{avg} = \frac{1}{2} e_0 i_0 \cos\phi$$

$$\Rightarrow \quad P_{avg} = \frac{e_0}{\sqrt{2}}\frac{i_0}{\sqrt{2}}\cos\phi$$

$$\Rightarrow \quad P_{avg} = e_{rms}\, i_{rms} \cos\phi \qquad \ldots(5.235)$$

Above equation-(5.235) gives the average power supplied by an AC source to the connected circuit. In general average is defined for one cycle or for large number of cycles or over a significant duration. The term of '$\cos\phi$' on RHS of equation-(5.235) is called '*Power Factor*' of the AC circuit. Thus average power supplied to an AC circuit depends upon the phase difference between the AC EMF and the current supplied by the source.

5.13.2 Wattless Current in AC Circuits

If in a given AC circuit ϕ is the phase difference between the applied EMF and the current then phasor diagram for EMF and current drawn is shown in figure-5.232.

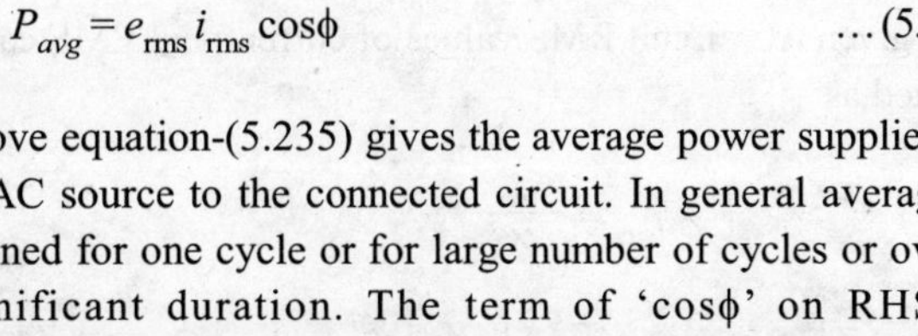

Figure 5.232

In above figure we've resolved the current phasor in two components, one along the EMF and other normal to it. For this circuit the average power delivered by the AC source can be given as

$$P_{avg} = e_{rms}\, i_{rms} \cos\phi$$

We can see in above expression of average power that it is due to the current component $i_{RMS}\cos\phi$ and there is no contribution of the current component $i_{RMS}\sin\phi$ in average power supplied by the AC source so this current component '$i_{RMS}\sin\phi$' is called '*Wattless Current*' of the AC circuit.

This wattless current does not have significance for calculation of average power in an AC circuit but for current calculations it is useful if mentioned specifically in some situation.

5.13.3 Maximum Power in an AC Circuit

As discussed in article-5.13.1 that average power supplied by an AC source to the circuit is given as

$$P_{avg} = e_{rms}\, i_{rms} \cos\phi$$

In a given AC circuit RMS values of current and EMF can be related as

$$i_{rms} = \frac{e_{rms}}{Z}$$

Where Z is the circuit impedance across the AC source. Using this average power can be written as

$$P_{avg} = \frac{e_{rms}^2}{Z} \cos\phi$$

With the change in phase difference between AC EMF and current in the circuit average power supplied changes. If in a circuit $\phi = 0$ then in that circuit, impedance will be purely resistive ($Z = R$) and power supplied will be maximum which is given as

$$P_{avg} = i_{rms}\, e_{rms} = i_{rms}^2 R = \frac{e_{rms}^2}{R} \quad \ldots(5.236)$$

Thus when $\phi = 0$ then in the circuit capacitive reactance and inductive reactance nullify the effect of each other and circuit behave as a purely resistive circuit across AC EMF.

If in a circuit $\phi = \pm\pi/2$ then the circuit impedance will be either purely capacitive or purely inductive and in this case average power supplied by the AC source will be zero. It is to be noted that in AC circuits inductors and capacitors never consume any average power. This is because in one half cycle for reactive components of AC circuits power is positive and for other half cycle power is negative so these components do not contribute in power consumption per cycle independently but due to reactive components of circuit, the circuit impedance and phase relationship between applied EMF and current changes thus overall power supplied by the source is affected.

5.13.4 Resonance in Series *RLC* Circuit

For a series *RLC* circuit we've studied the phasor analysis in article-5.12.10 and 5.12.11. The current amplitude supplied by the AC source in series *RLC* circuit is given as

$$i_0 = \frac{e_0}{Z} = \frac{e_0}{\sqrt{R^2 + \left(\omega L - \frac{1}{\omega C}\right)^2}}$$

In above equation we can see that i_0 will be maximum when in denominator $X_L = X_C$ which occurs at a specific frequency for a specific circuit which is given as

$$\omega = \frac{1}{\sqrt{LC}} \quad \ldots(5.237)$$

At above frequency $Z = R$, $\phi = 0$ and circuit impedance becomes minimum and behave as a pure resistive impedance at which circuit current becomes maximum which is given as

$$i_0 = \frac{e_0}{R} \quad \ldots(5.238)$$

At above frequency given by equation-(5.237) the current as well as power supplied by the AC source to the circuit becomes maximum and circuit impedance is purely resistive. This state is called '*Resonance*' or '*Resonating State*' of AC circuit and the frequency given by equation-(5.237) at which it occurs is called '*Resonating Frequency*'.

5.13.5 Variation of Current with Frequency in Series *RLC* Circuit

In series RLC circuit the RMS current is given as

$$i_{rms} = \frac{e_{rms}}{Z} = \frac{e_{RMS}}{\sqrt{R^2 + \left(\omega L - \frac{1}{\omega C}\right)^2}}$$

In previous article we've discussed that at resonating frequency the current and power supplied in circuit becomes maximum thus at frequencies below and above the resonating frequency current will be less than maximum of which the variation is shown in figure-5.233.

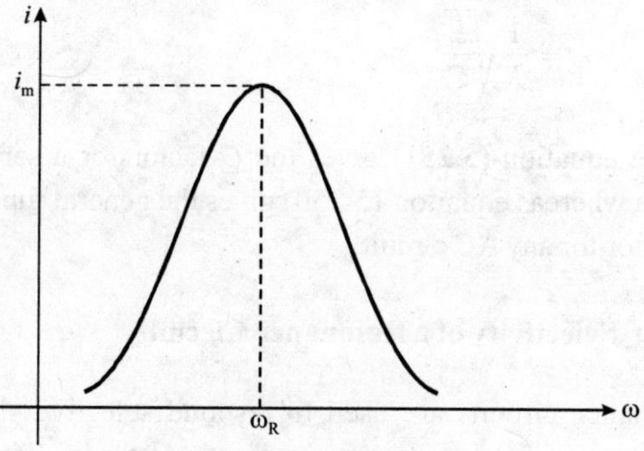

Figure 5.233

The resonating frequency at which current and power in circuit becomes maximum as shown above is given as

$$\omega_R = \frac{1}{\sqrt{LC}}$$

$$\Rightarrow \quad f_R = \frac{1}{2\pi\sqrt{LC}}$$

It is already discussed when frequency of AC source is $f = f_R$ then $\phi = 0$ and circuit impedance is purely resistive with current approaches to maximum value. When $f < f_R$ circuit impedance behave as combination of resistance and capacitance and ϕ is positive in this case and current leads EMF and when $f > f_R$ circuit impedance behave as combination of resistance and inductance and ϕ is negative so in this case current lags behind EMF.

5.13.6 Half Power Frequencies in Series RLC Circuit

As discussed in previous article that current and power in series *RLC* circuit are maximum at resonant frequency given by equation-(5.237). In the graph shown in figure-5.233 on the two sides of resonant frequency there are two side frequencies ω_1 and ω_2 at which power supplied is half of the maximum power. These frequencies are shown in figure-5.234.

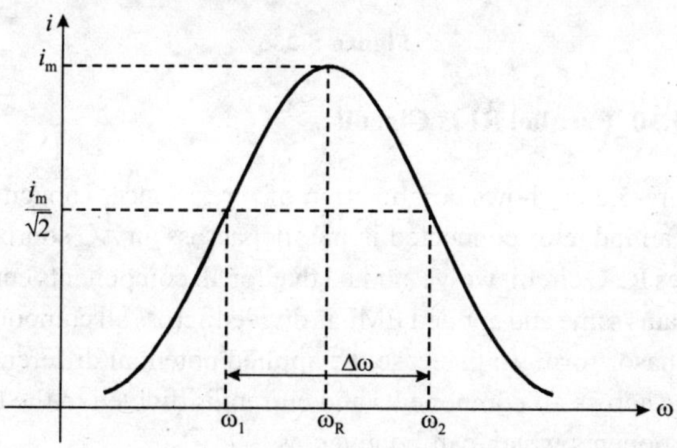

Figure 5.234

In AC circuits power consumed is only by the resistance of circuit as average power consumed by inductor and capacitor is always zero. Thus power of an AC Circuit is given as

$$P_{avg} = i_{rms}\, e_{rms} \cos\phi$$

$$\Rightarrow \quad P_{avg} = i_{rms}^2 Z \cos\phi$$

$$\Rightarrow \quad P_{avg} = i_{rms}^2 R \qquad \ldots(5.239)$$

Power is maximum when current is maximum at resonant frequency which is given as

$$P_m = i_m^2 R$$

When frequency is deviated from the resonant frequency power in circuit decreases and when power is reduced to half then current in circuit is called half power current which is given as

$$i_{hp} = \sqrt{\frac{(P_m/2)}{R}} = \frac{i_m}{\sqrt{2}}$$

The range of frequencies ω_1 to ω_2 at which the power in circuit is more than half of maximum is called '*Circuit Bandwidth*' which is given as

$$\Delta\omega = \omega_2 - \omega_1$$

5.13.7 Bandwidth for a Series RLC Circuit

The effective current in a series RLC circuit is given as

$$i_{rms} = \frac{e_{rms}}{Z} \qquad \ldots(5.240)$$

At maximum power in circuit we've discussed that $Z = R$ thus we use

$$i_m = \frac{e_{rms}}{R} \qquad \ldots(5.241)$$

Half power current is given as

$$i_{hp} = \frac{i_m}{\sqrt{2}}$$

From equations-(197) and (198) we can see that at half power frequency we have

$$Z = \sqrt{2}R \qquad \ldots(5.242)$$

For Series RLC circuit impedance is given as

$$Z = \sqrt{R^2 + X^2} = \sqrt{2}R$$

$$\Rightarrow \quad X = \pm R \qquad \ldots(5.243)$$

$$\Rightarrow \quad \left(\omega L - \frac{1}{\omega C}\right) = \pm R \qquad \ldots(5.244)$$

There are two quadratic equations in equation-(5.244) for the '+' and '–' signs on the RHS of the equation. Positive sign will correspond to positive reactance of series RLC circuit in which current will lag behind the EMF so for the right side half power frequency ω_2 we use positive sign and similarly negative sign correspond to negative reactance of series RLC circuit in which current will lead the EMF so for the left side half power frequency ω_1 we use negative sign.

For ω_1 we use

$$\omega L-\frac{1}{\omega C}=-R \qquad \ldots(5.245)$$

Solving the above equation gives

$$\omega_1=-\frac{R}{2L}+\sqrt{\frac{R^2}{4L^2}+\frac{1}{LC}} \qquad \ldots(5.246)$$

For ω_2 we use

$$\omega L-\frac{1}{\omega C}=+R \qquad \ldots(5.247)$$

Solving the above equation gives

$$\omega_2=\frac{R}{2L}+\sqrt{\frac{R^2}{4L^2}+\frac{1}{LC}} \qquad \ldots(5.248)$$

From equations-(5.246) and (5.248) bandwidth of series RLC circuit is given as

$$\Delta\omega=\omega_2-\omega_1=\frac{R}{L} \qquad \ldots(5.249)$$

5.13.8 Quality Factor of Series RLC Circuit

The ratio of energy stored in circuit to the energy loss per cycle at resonance in an AC circuit is defined as '*Quality Factor*' or '*Q-Factor*' of the circuit. This is given as

$$Q=\frac{\textit{Maximum Energy Stored per Cycle}}{\textit{Energy Loss per Cycle}}$$

It is numerically calculated as the ratio of resonating frequency to the circuit bandwidth which is given as

$$Q=\frac{\omega_R}{\Delta\omega} \qquad \ldots(5.250)$$

For series RLC circuit we substitute the values of resonating frequency and bandwidth which gives

$$Q=\frac{\omega_R L}{R}$$

$$\Rightarrow \quad Q=\frac{1}{R}\sqrt{\frac{L}{C}} \qquad \ldots(5.251)$$

Above equation-(5.251) gives the Q-factor for a series RLC circuit whereas equation-(5.250) gives the general function for Q-factor for any AC circuit.

5.13.9 Selectivity of a Resonance Circuit

Resonance circuits are used to respond selective signals of some specific frequency in communication systems. If in a circuit resonance is having a narrow peak at the chosen frequency then the circuit is called '*Highly Selective*'. Figure-5.235 shows the current variation with frequency for three different circuits named 1, 2 and 3. For circuit-1 at the same resonant frequency bandwidth is less and the curve is narrow compared to circuit-2 and 3 so in very short neighbourhood of the circuit, the power drops to a level below half power level and because of this, its Q-factor is high and this circuit is said to have 'Selectivity' more than circuit-2 and 3. Circuit-3 has higher bandwidth at same resonance frequency in which to a far variation of frequency away from the resonance frequency, circuit power is not going below the half power level so the frequency band upto its half power frequencies is blocked by this channel only so this is said to be a '*Poorly Selective*' circuit. Indirectly we can say that selectivity is a qualitative term and Q-factor is a quantitative term used to analyze the suitability of circuit to be used for a communication system.

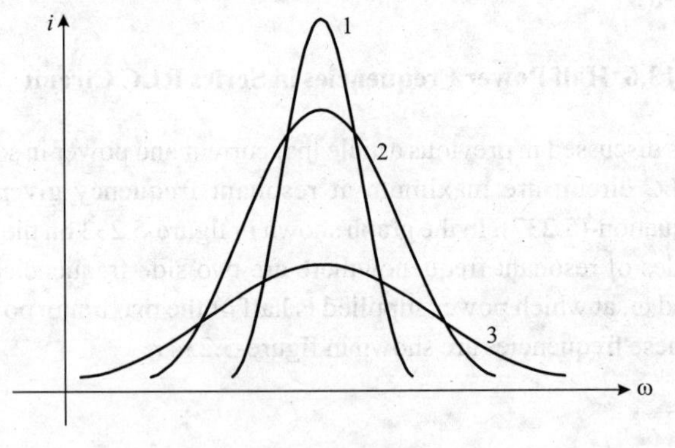

Figure 5.235

5.13.10 Parallel RLC Circuit

Figure-5.236 shows combination of a resistance, capacitance and an inductor connected in parallel across an AC source. In series RLC circuit we've studied that for all components current remains same and applied EMF is divided across all components in phasor form. In this case the applied potential difference is same across all components and current is divided in the three components which can be given as

$$\bar{i}=\bar{i_R}+\bar{i_C}+\bar{i_L} \qquad \ldots(5.252)$$

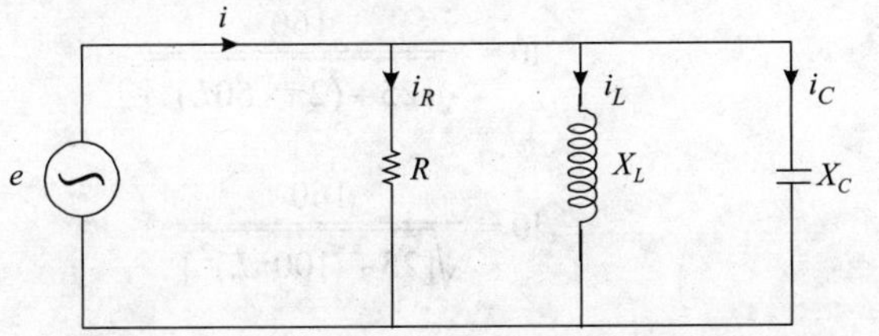

Figure 5.236

In above case the total current supplied by the AC source will not be the mathematical sum of the three currents through the three components as the phase of the three currents will differ. As the applied voltage is same to all, the current through resistance will be in same phase as that of the applied voltage, the current in inductor will lag behind the applied voltage by 90° and current in capacitor will lead the applied voltage by 90°. If the reference phase is taken from EMF then equation-(5.252) can be rewritten in phasor forms using the phasor diagram as shown in figure-5.237 of currents as

$$\bar{i} = i_R\angle 0° + i_C\angle 90° + i_L\angle -90° \quad \ldots(5.253)$$

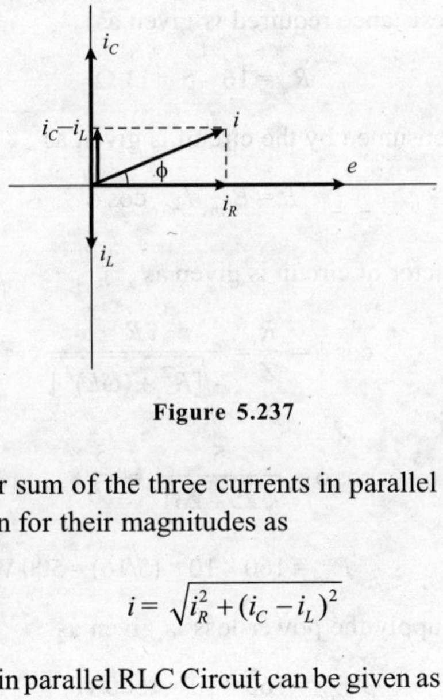

Figure 5.237

Thus phasor sum of the three currents in parallel RLC circuit can be given for their magnitudes as

$$i = \sqrt{i_R^2 + (i_C - i_L)^2} \quad \ldots(5.254)$$

Impedance in parallel RLC Circuit can be given as

$$\frac{1}{Z} = \frac{1}{R} + \frac{1}{X_L} + \frac{1}{X_C}$$

$$\Rightarrow \frac{1}{Z} = \frac{1}{R\angle 0°} + \frac{1}{\omega L\angle 90°} + \frac{1}{1/\omega C\angle -90°}$$

$$\Rightarrow \frac{1}{Z} = \frac{1}{R}\angle 0° + \frac{1}{\omega L}\angle -90° + \frac{1}{1/\omega C}\angle 90°$$

$$\Rightarrow \frac{1}{Z} = \sqrt{\left(\frac{1}{R}\right)^2 + \left(\omega C - \frac{1}{\omega L}\right)^2}$$

$$\Rightarrow Z = \frac{1}{\sqrt{\left(\frac{1}{R}\right)^2 + \left(\omega C - \frac{1}{\omega L}\right)^2}}$$

Thus current in parallel *RLC* Circuit can be given as

$$i = \frac{e}{Z} = e\sqrt{\left(\frac{1}{R}\right)^2 + \left(\omega C - \frac{1}{\omega L}\right)^2}$$

For the above current the frequency response curve is shown in figure-5.238. Here we can see that the frequency at which capacitive and inductive reactance are equal and impedance is purely resistive, the current in circuit is minimum. Such a circuit is called '*Rejector Circuit*' in which at a specific frequency the power supplied or current from the source is minimum. This state is called resonance of parallel RLC circuit and the resonant frequency ω_R is given as

$$\omega_R C - \frac{1}{\omega_R L} = 0$$

$$\Rightarrow \omega_R = \frac{1}{\sqrt{LC}}$$

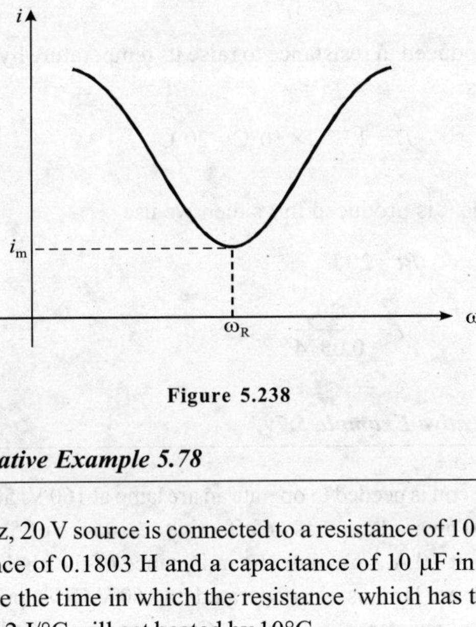

Figure 5.238

Illustrative Example 5.78

A 750 Hz, 20 V source is connected to a resistance of 100 Ω, an inductance of 0.1803 H and a capacitance of 10 μF in series. Calculate the time in which the resistance which has thermal capacity 2 J/°C will get heated by 10°C.

Solution

The inductive and capacitive reactance are given as

$$X_L = \omega L = (2\times 3.14\times 750)\times 0.1803 = 850\ \Omega$$

$$X_C = \frac{1}{\omega C} = \frac{1}{(2\times 3.14\times 750)\times(10^{-5})} = 21.2\ \Omega$$

Impedance of series RLC circuit is given as

$$Z = \sqrt{\left[R^2 + \left(\omega L - \frac{1}{\omega L}\right)^2\right]}$$

$$\Rightarrow \quad Z = \sqrt{[(100)^2 + (850 - 21.2)^2]} = 835\ \Omega$$

Power dissipated in circuit is given as

$$P = E_{rms} \times I_{rms} \times \cos\phi$$

Where power factor is given as

$$\cos\phi = \frac{R}{Z}$$

$$\Rightarrow \quad P = E_{rms} \times I_{rms} \times \frac{R}{Z}$$

$$\Rightarrow \quad P = E_{rms} \times \left(\frac{E_{rms}}{Z}\right) \times \frac{R}{Z}$$

$$\Rightarrow \quad P = \frac{E_{rms}^2 \times R}{Z^2}$$

$$\Rightarrow \quad P = \frac{(20)^2 \times 100}{(835)^2} = 0.0574\ \text{W}$$

Heat produced in resistance to raise its temperature by 10°C is given as

$$H = 2\ \text{J/°C} \times 10\text{°C} = 20\ \text{J}$$

If this heat is produced in t s then we use

$$Pt = 20\ \text{J}$$

$$\Rightarrow \quad t = \frac{20}{0.0574} = 384\ \text{s}$$

 # Illustrative Example 5.79

A choke coil is needed to operate an arc lamp at 160 V, 50 Hz AC supply. The arc lamp has an effective resistance of 5 Ω when running at 10 A. Calculate the inductance of the choke coil if the same arc lamp is to be operated on 160 V DC supply, what additional resistance is required. Compare the power losses in both cases.

Solution

The effective current through the circuit with lamp and choke coil in series is given as

$$I_{rms} = \frac{E_{rms}}{\sqrt{(R^2 + \omega^2 L^2)}}$$

$$\Rightarrow \quad 10 = \frac{160}{\sqrt{[25 + (2\pi \times 50L)^2]}}$$

$$\Rightarrow \quad 10 = \frac{160}{\sqrt{[25 + (100\pi L)^2]}}$$

$$\Rightarrow \quad \sqrt{[25 + (100\pi L)^2]} = 16$$

$$\Rightarrow \quad 25 + (100\pi)^2 L^2 = 256$$

$$\Rightarrow \quad 25 + 10^5 L^2 = 256$$

$$\Rightarrow \quad L^2 = \frac{231}{10^5} = 231 \times 10^{-5}$$

$$\Rightarrow \quad L = 0.048\ \text{H}$$

For 160 V DC if R_A be the additional resistance, then we have

$$10 = \frac{160}{(R_A + 5)}$$

$$\Rightarrow \quad R_A + 5 = 16$$

Additional resistance required is given as

$$R_A = 16 - 5 = 11\ \Omega$$

AC power consumed by the circuit is given as

$$P = E_{rms} I_{rms} \cos\phi$$

The power factor of circuit is given as

$$\cos\phi = \frac{R}{Z} = \frac{R}{\sqrt{[R^2 + (\omega L)^2]}}$$

$$\Rightarrow \quad \cos\phi = \frac{5}{\sqrt{25 + 231}} = \frac{5}{16}$$

$$\Rightarrow \quad P_{ac} = 160 \times 10 \times (5/16) = 500\ \text{W}$$

Across DC supply the power loss is given as

$$P_{dc} = 160 \times 10 = 1600\ \text{W}$$

 # Illustrative Example 5.80

An inductor of 2 H, capacitance 18 μF and a resistance of 10 kΩ are connected in series to an AC source of 20 V with adjustable frequency. At what frequency the current in circuit will be maximum and what will be this maximum current.

Solution

If i is maximum current at Resonance in series RLC circuit, the resonant frequency is given as

$$f_R = \frac{1}{2\pi\sqrt{LC}} = \frac{1}{2\pi\sqrt{2\times 18\times 10^{-6}}}$$

$$\Rightarrow \quad f_R = \frac{1}{12\pi}\times 10^3\,\text{Hz} = \frac{250}{3\pi}\,\text{Hz}$$

Maximum current in circuit is given as

$$i_{max} = \frac{e}{R} = \frac{20}{10\times 10^3} = 2\text{ mA}$$

Illustrative Example 5.81

A series *RLC* circuit with 100 Ω resistance is connected to an AC source of 200 V and angular frequency 300 rad/s. When only the capacitance is removed, the current lags behind the voltage by 60°. When only the inductance is removed, the current leads the voltage by 60°. Calculate the current and power dissipated in *RLC* circuit.

Solution

As per given condition in RLC circuit we have

$$\tan 60 = \frac{\omega L}{R}$$

and $$\tan 60 = \frac{1/\omega C}{R}$$

$$\Rightarrow \quad \omega L = \frac{1}{\omega C}$$

Impedance of circuit is given as

$$Z = \sqrt{\left[R^2 + \left(\omega L - \frac{1}{\omega C}\right)^2\right]} = R$$

Current in the circuit is given as

$$I_0 = \frac{V_0}{Z} = \frac{V_0}{R} = \frac{200}{100} = 2\text{A}$$

Average power dissipated in circuit is given as

$$\bar{P} = \frac{1}{2}V_0 I_0 \cos\phi$$

$$\Rightarrow \quad \bar{P} = \frac{1}{2}\times 200\times 2\times 1 = 200\text{ W}$$

Illustrative Example 5.82

A *RLC* series circuit has L = 10 mH, R = 3 Ω and C = 1 μF connected in series to a source of 15 cosωt volt. Calculate the current amplitude and the average power dissipated per cycle at a frequency that is 10% lower than the resonant frequency.

Solution

Resonant frequency of circuit is given as

$$\omega_R = \frac{1}{\sqrt{LC}}$$

$$\Rightarrow \quad \omega_R = \sqrt{\left(\frac{1}{(10\times 10^{-3})(1\times 10^{-6})}\right)} = 10^4\text{ rad/s}$$

10% less frequency of above resonant frequency is given as

$$\omega = 10^4 - 10^4\times\frac{10}{100} = 9\times 10^3\text{ rad/s}$$

At this frequency, the reactances are given as

$$X_L = \omega L = 9\times 10^3\times(10\times 10^{-3}) = 90\,\Omega$$

and $$X_C = \frac{1}{\omega C} = \frac{1}{(9\times 10^3)(1\times 10^{-6})} = 11.11\,\Omega$$

$$\Rightarrow \quad Z = \sqrt{[R^2 + (90 - 11.11)^2]} = 21.32\,\Omega$$

Current amplitude is given as

$$I_0 = \frac{E_0}{Z} = \frac{15}{21.32} = 0.704\text{ A}$$

Average power consumed by circuit is given as

$$P = \frac{1}{2}E_0 I_0\cos\phi$$

Power factor of the circuit is given as

$$\cos\phi = \frac{R}{Z} = \frac{3}{21.32} = 0.141$$

$$\Rightarrow \quad P = \frac{1}{2}\times 15\times 0.704\times 0.141 = 0.744\text{ W}$$

Illustrative Example 5.83

In an AC circuit EMF applied is e = 5 sinωt due to which a current i = 3 cosωt flows in circuit. Find the average power dissipated in the circuit.

Solution

From the given information we can see that the phase difference between EMF and the current supplied is $\pi/2$ so the circuit impedance is reactive for which the average power dissipated in circuit will be zero.

Illustrative Example 5.84

A current of 4 A flows in a coil when connected to a 12 V DC source. If the same coil is connected to a 132 V, 50 rad/s, AC source, a current of 2.4 A flows in the circuit. Determine the inductance of the coil. Also find the power developed in the circuit if a 2500 μF capacitor is connected in series with the coil.

Solution

When the coil is connected to a DC source, its resistance R is given as

$$R = \frac{V}{I} = \frac{12}{4} = 3\,\Omega$$

When it is connected to AC source, the impedance Z of the coil is given as

$$Z = \frac{V_{rms}}{I_{rms}} = \frac{12}{2.4} = 5\,\Omega$$

For a coil its impedance is given as

$$Z = \sqrt{[R^2 + (\omega L)^2]}$$

$$\Rightarrow \quad 5 = \sqrt{[(3)^2 + (50L)^2]}$$

$$\Rightarrow \quad 25 = [(3)^2 + (50L)^2]$$

$$\Rightarrow \quad L = 0.08\,\text{H}$$

When the coil is connected with a condenser in series, its impedance Z' is given by

$$Z' = \sqrt{\left[R^2 + \left(\omega L - \frac{1}{\omega L}\right)^2\right]}$$

$$\Rightarrow \quad Z' = \left[(3)^2 + \left(50 + 0.8 - \frac{1}{50 \times 2500 \times 10^{-6}}\right)^2\right]^{1/2}$$

$$\Rightarrow \quad Z' = 5\,\Omega$$

Average power developed in circuit is given as

$$P = V_{rms} \times I_{rms} \times \cos\phi$$

Where power factor of circuit is given as

$$\cos\phi = \frac{R}{Z'} = \frac{3}{5} = 0.6$$

$$\Rightarrow \quad P = 12 \times 2.4 \times 0.6 = 17.28\,\text{W}$$

5.14 Transformer

A transformer is a device used to increase or decrease AC voltage by using the concept of mutual induction between two coils. Figure-5.239 shows a transformer in which on a soft iron core two coils are wound named '*Primary Coil*' and '*Secondary Coil*' of the transformer. These are also called '*P-Coil*' and '*S-Coil*' of transformer. Primary coil of transformer is considered as input coil at which an AC source is connected of which the voltage is to be increased or decreased and secondary coil is considered as output coil from which desired output voltage is taken out. Figure-5.239(b) shows a three dimensional view of transformer for understanding its structure.

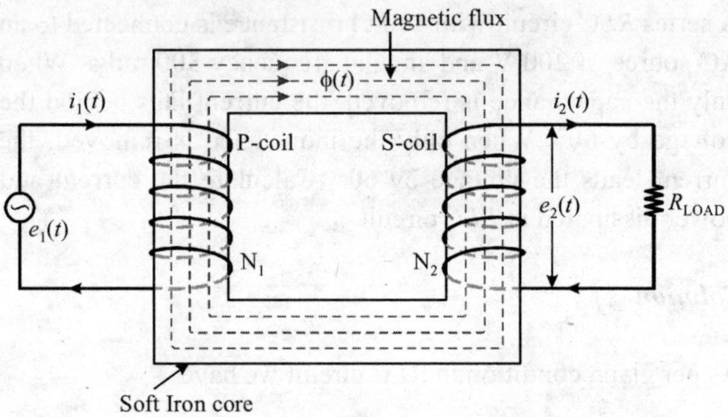

(a)

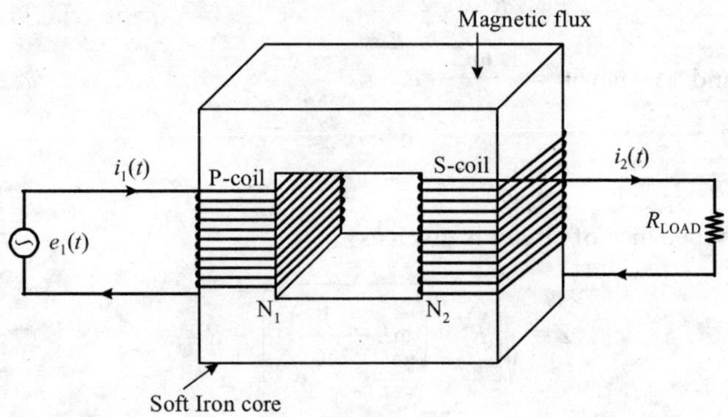

(b)

Figure 5.239

When an AC source of EMF $e(t)$ is connected across the primary coil of the transformer which is considered to be supplying a current $i_1(t)$ in primary coil as shown in figure. This current produces a total magnetic flux $\phi(t)$ in the core of transformer. If N_1 and N_2 are the total number of turns in primary and secondary coils then the magnetic flux linked with primary coil f_1 and f_2 are given as

$$\phi_1 = N_1\phi(t)$$

and

$$\phi_2 = N_2\phi(t)$$

Due to above time varying magnetic flux linked with the two coils of transformer the EMF induced in the two coils are given as

$$e_1 = \frac{d\phi_1}{dt} = N_1\frac{d\phi(t)}{dt} \quad \text{...(5.255)}$$

and
$$e_2 = \frac{d\phi_2}{dt} = N_2\frac{d\phi(t)}{dt} \quad \text{...(5.256)}$$

Dividing equations-(5.255) and (5.256) gives

$$\frac{e_1}{e_2} = \frac{N_1}{N_2} \quad \text{...(5.257)}$$

Above equation-(5.257) which relates the EMFs in primary and secondary coils with their number of turns is called '*Transformer Equation*'.

5.14.1 Power Relations in a Transformer

Figure-5.240 shows a transformer with AC source of EMF e_1 connected at primary coil and supplying a current i_1 into it. From secondary coil a load resistance R is connected across which the EMF induced is e_2 and current through it is i_2.

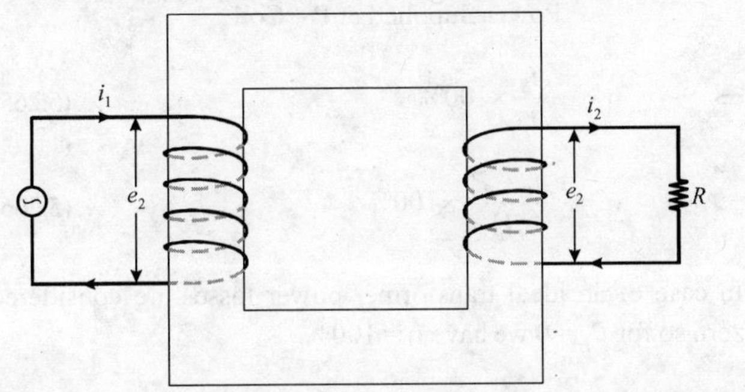

Figure 5.240

In above situation the power supplied at primary coil of transformer by AC source is given as

$$P_1 = e_1 i_1 \quad \text{...(5.258)}$$

At the secondary coil power delivered to the load resistance is given as

$$P_1 = e_2 i_2 \quad \text{...(5.259)}$$

For an ideal transformer energy losses are neglected so we have by conservation of energy

$$P_1 = P_2$$

$$\Rightarrow \quad e_1 i_1 = e_2 i_2 \quad \text{...(5.260)}$$

Using transformer equation, above equation-(5.260) can be rewritten as

$$\frac{e_1}{e_2} = \frac{i_2}{i_1} = \frac{N_1}{N_2} \quad \text{...(5.261)}$$

Above equation-(5.261) is called '*Ideal Power Equation*' of a transformer. In case of power losses in a transformer if total power losses is P_L then power equation is written as

$$e_1 i_1 - P_L = e_2 i_2 \quad \text{...(5.262)}$$

5.14.2 Types of Transformers

Depending upon the output voltage of a transformer it is classified in two categories - '*Step-up Transformers*' and '*Step-down Transformers*'.

Step-up Transformer : In step-up transformer the output voltage at secondary coil is more than voltage applied at primary coil. As $e_2 > e_1$ in a step-up transformer then from transformer equation we get $N_2 > N_1$ and from ideal power equation we get $i_2 < i_1$.

Step-down Transformer : In step-down transformer the output voltage at secondary coil is less than voltage applied at primary coil. As $e_2 < e_1$ in a step-down transformer then from transformer equation we get $N_2 < N_1$ and from ideal power equation we get $i_2 > i_1$.

5.14.3 Losses in Transformers

There are two types of power losses occur in transformer when its operating. These are - '*Copper Losses*' and '*Iron Losses*'. We will discuss both of these in some details.

Copper Losses in Transformer : These are dissipation losses in primary and secondary coils of transformer due to the resistance of coil windings. If resistance of the primary and secondary coil of a transformer are R_P and R_S and current in the two coils are i_P and i_S then total copper losses in a transformer circuit are given as

$$P_{CL} = i_P^2 R_P + i_S^2 R_S \quad \text{...(5.263)}$$

Copper losses in a transformer can only be reduced by proper selection of low resistance windings.

Iron Losses in Transformer : These are the dissipation losses in the core of transformer due to eddy currents. As time varying magnetic field continuously exist in the core of transformer due to which in all the cross sectional planes of the core eddy currents develop and produces heat. There is no direct mathematical way to analyze iron losses in a transformer. If P_T is the total power losses in a transformer then iron losses can be calculated by subtracting copper losses from it which is given as

$$P_{IL} = P_T - P_{CL} \quad \text{...(5.264)}$$

To reduce iron losses we can break eddy currents by making the transformer core by joining laminated soft iron thin sheets instead of using a solid soft iron core. Figure-5.241(a) shows a solid transformer core and figure-5.241(b) shows a transformer core which is made up of joining thin laminated sheets. In solid core cross-section eddy currents flow in larger paths as shown in figure-5.242(a) which causes severe losses whereas figure-5.242(b) shows the cross section of a core made up of laminated sheet in which eddy currents are restricted within the cross sections of thin sheets as lamination does not allow conduction between the sheets due to which eddy current losses are reduced.

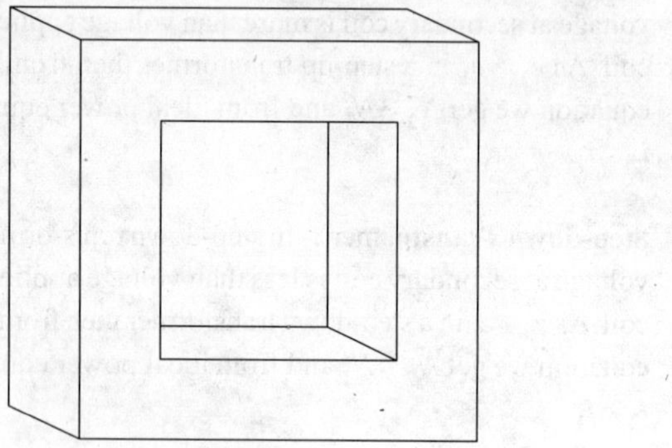
(a)

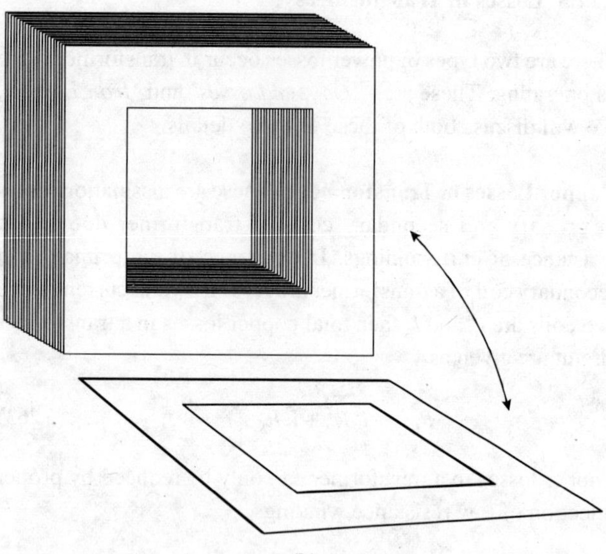
(b)

Figure 5.241

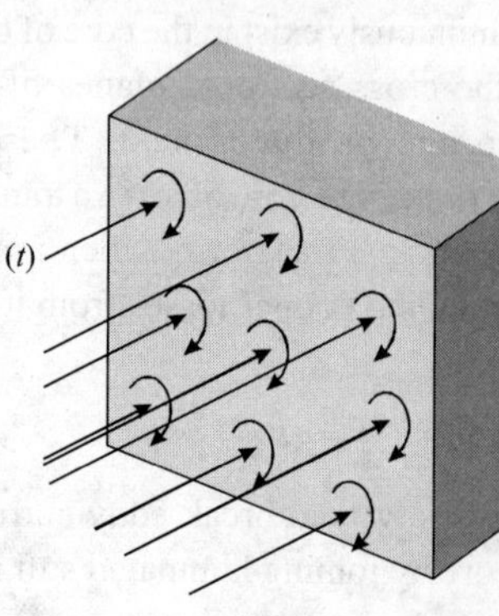

(a)

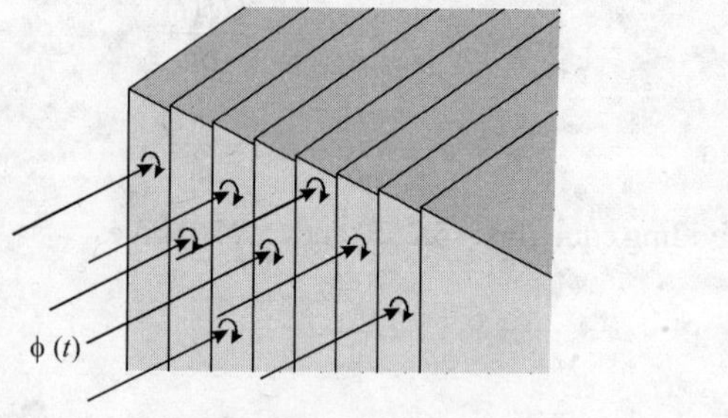

(b)

Figure 5.242

5.14.4 Efficiency of a Transformer

Due to power losses in a transformer its efficiency decreases and due to losses the power output taken from the secondary coil of the transformer is less than the power input at the primary coil. The efficiency of a transformer is given as

$$\eta = \frac{\text{Power Delivered at S – Coil}}{\text{Power Supplied at P – Coil}} \times 100\%$$

$$\Rightarrow \quad \eta = \frac{e_S i_S}{e_P i_P} \times 100\% \quad \ldots(5.265)$$

$$\Rightarrow \quad \eta = \frac{e_P i_P - P_L}{e_P i_P} \times 100\% \quad \ldots(5.266)$$

In case of an ideal transformer power losses are considered zero so for $P_L = 0$ we have $\eta = 100\%$.

 # Illustrative Example 5.85

An ideal transformer has 50 turns in its primary winding and 25 turns in its secondary winding. If the current in the secondary winding in 4 A what is the current in primary winding if a 200 V AC is applied across it?

Solution

With the ratio of turns in primary to secondary winding it is a 2 : 1 step down transformer for which by transformer equation we have

$$\frac{e_s}{e_p} = \frac{N_s}{N_p}$$

$$\Rightarrow \quad e_s = \frac{N_s}{N_p} \times e_p$$

$$\Rightarrow \quad e_s = \frac{25}{50} \times 200 = 100 \text{ V}$$

Power equation of ideal transformer gives

$$e_s i_s = e_p i_p$$

$$\Rightarrow \quad i_p = \frac{e_s i_s}{e_p} = \frac{100 \times 4}{200} = 2\text{ A}$$

Illustrative Example 5.86

An ideal power transformer is used to step up an alternating EMF of 220 V to 4.4 kV to transmit 0.6 kW of power. If the primary coil has 1000 turns, find

(a) The number of turns in the secondary coil

(b) The current rating of the secondary

Solution

(a) By transformer equation we have

$$N_s = \frac{e_s}{e_p} \times N_p$$

$$\Rightarrow \quad N_s = \left(\frac{4.4 \times 1000}{220}\right) \times 1000 = 20000 \text{ turns}$$

(b) Power supplied at primary coil is given as

$$i_p e_p = 6.6 \times 10^3 \text{ W}$$

$$\Rightarrow \quad i_p = \frac{6.6 \times 10^3}{220} = 30\text{ A}$$

For an ideal transformer we use

$$\frac{i_s}{i_p} = \frac{N_p}{N_s} = \left(\frac{1000}{20{,}000}\right) = \frac{1}{20}$$

$$\Rightarrow \quad i_s = \left(\frac{1}{20} \times i_p\right) = 1.5\text{ A}$$

Illustrative Example 5.87

A transformer has turns ratio $N_s/N_p = 4$. If a 200 V AC voltage is applied across its primary and it carries 1 A current, find current in circuit connected to secondary coil if transformer is 80% efficient.

Solution

Power supplied at primary coil is

$$P_1 = e_1 i_1 = 200 \times 1 = 200\text{ W}$$

Voltage across secondary coil is

$$e_2 = e_1 \times \frac{N_2}{N_1} = 200 \times 4 = 800\text{ V}$$

In the given conditions power losses are 20%

$$\Rightarrow \quad P_L = 200 \times \frac{20}{100} = 40\text{ W}$$

Power available at secondary coil is

$$P_2 = 200 - 40 = 160\text{ W}$$

$$\Rightarrow \quad P_2 = e_2 i_2 = 160\text{ W}$$

$$\Rightarrow \quad i_2 = \frac{160}{800} = 0.2\text{ A}$$

Illustrative Example 5.88

In a transformer there are 10000 turns in primary coil and 25000 turns in secondary coil. An AC EMF $e = 50 \sin \pi t$ is applied across primary coil, find the peak EMF across secondary coil in ideal conditions.

Solution

As per given turns ratio, this is a 1 : 2.5 step up transformer. Using transformer equation we have

$$\frac{e_1}{e_2} = \frac{N_1}{N_2}$$

$$\Rightarrow \quad e_2 = \frac{N_2}{N_1} \times e_1 = \frac{25000}{10000} \times 50\text{ V}$$

$$\Rightarrow \quad e_2 = 125\text{ V}$$

Web Reference at www.physicsgalaxy.com

Age Group - Grade 11 & 12 | Age 17-19 Years
Section - Magnetic Effects
Topic - Alternating Current
Module Number - 34 to 60

Practice Exercise 5.7

(i) A series LCR circuit containing a resistance of 120 Ω has resonant frequency 4×10^5 rad/s. At resonance the voltage across resistance and inductance area 60 V and 40 V respectively. Find the values of L and C and at what frequency the current in the circuit lags the voltage by 45°?

[2×10^{-4}H, $\frac{1}{32}$ μF, 8×10^5 rad/s]

(ii) 2000 V – 200 V, 20 kVA transformer has 66 turns in the secondary. Calculate the primary and secondary full-load current, neglect power losses in transformer.

[10 A, 100 A]

(iii) A circuit draws a power of 550 W from a source of 220 V, 50 Hz. The power factor of the circuit is 0.8 and the current lags in phase behind the potential difference. To make the power factor of the circuit as 1.0, what capacitance is needed to be connected in series with it.

[75 μF]

(iv) A series *RLC* circuit with inductance 0.12 H, capacitance 480 nF and resistance 23 Ω is connected to a 230 V variable frequency supply.

(a) What is the source frequency for which current amplitude is maximum? Find the maximum value.

(b) What is the source frequency for which average power absorbed by the circuit is maximum? Obtain the value of maximum power.

(c) For which angular frequencies of the source, the power transferred to the circuit is half of the power at resonant frequency?

(d) What is the *Q* factor of the circuit?

[(a) 663.5 Hz, 14.14 A (b) 663.5 Hz, 2300 W (c) 4263 rad/s, 4071 rad/s, (d) 21.74]

(v) A 20 V, 5 W lamp is used on AC mains of 220 V, 50 Hz. Calculate the (a) capacitance (b) inductance to be put in series to run the lamp at its peak brightness. (c) How much pure resistance should be included in place of the above devices so that the lamp can run on its peak brightness. (d) Which of the above arrangements will be more economical and why?

[(a) 4.0 μF (b) 2.53 H (c) 720 Ω; (d) Using *L* or *C* will be more economical]

(vi) An inductor coil, a capacitor and an AC source of 24 V are connected in series. When the frequency of the source is varied, a maximum current of 6 A is observed. If the inductor coil is connected to a battery of emf 12 V and internal resistance 4 Ω, what will be steady state current through battery.

[1.5 A]

(vii) In a step down transformer having primary to secondary turn ratio 20 : 1, the input voltage applied is 250 V and output current is 8 A. Assuming 100% efficiency, calculate

(a) Voltage across secondary coil

(b) Current in primary coil

(c) Power output

[(a) 12.5 V (b) 0.4 A (c) 100 W]

(viii) A box contains *L*, *C* and *R*. When 250 V DC voltage is applied to the terminals of the box, a current of 1 A flows in the circuit. When an AC source of 250 V, 2250 rad/s is applied across the box, a current of 1.25 A flows through it. It is observed that the current rises with frequency and becomes maximum at 4500 rad/s. Find the values of *L*, *C* and *R* in the box. Also draw the circuit diagram.

[250 Ω, 1 μF, $\frac{4}{81}$ H]

(ix) In a series *LCR* circuit $R = 120\ \Omega$ and it has resonant frequency 4000 rad/sec. At resonance, the voltage across resistance and inductance is 60 V and 40 V respectively. Find the value of *L* and *C* in circuit.

[20 mH, $\frac{25}{8}$ μF]

(x) A transformer has 200 turns in primary coil and 600 turns in secondary coil. If a 220 V DC is applied across primary coil what will be the voltage across secondary coil.

[0]

(xi) A transformer is used to light a 140 W, 24 V lamp from 240 V AC mains. The current in mains cable is 0.7 A, find the efficiency of transformer.

[83.33%]

* * * * *

Discussion Questions

Q5-1 How will be inductive reactance and capacitive reactance change on decreasing the frequency of alternating current to zero from an initial value ?

Q5-2 A cylindrical bar magnet is kept along the axis of a circular coil. Will there be a current induced in the coil, if the magnet is rotated about its axis?

Q5-3 An electric heater is heated turn by turn with direct and alternating currents. For both currents the effective potential difference across the ends of the heater is same. Will the rate of production of heat in both cases be the same?

Q5-4 Is the inductance per unit length for a solenoid near its centre the same as the inductance per unit length near its end?

Q5-5 A capacitor only is connected to an AC source. What will be the phase difference between the current flowing in the circuit and the potential difference between the plates of the capacitor?

Q5-6 What is the maximum value of power factor in an AC circuit? When does it occur ?

Q5-7 A copper ring is suspended in a vertical plane By a thread. A steel bar is passed through the ring in a horizontal direction and then a magnet is passed through it moving along the axis of ring. Will the motion of the bar and the magnet affect the position of the ring?

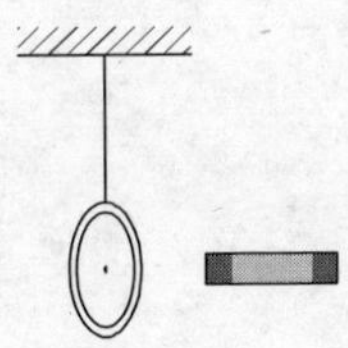

Figure 5.243

Q5-8 For tuning radio for various stations, we change the capacitance of an air-capacitor. In order to tune the radio with a high frequency station, whether the moving plates of the variable capacitor will have to be taken inside the stationary plates or outside them ?

Q5-9 Why coils in the resistance boxes are made from doubled up insulated wire?

Q5-10 A current flows in a straight from A to B as shown in figure-5.244 which is increasing in magnitude. What is the direction of induced current, if any, in the loop?

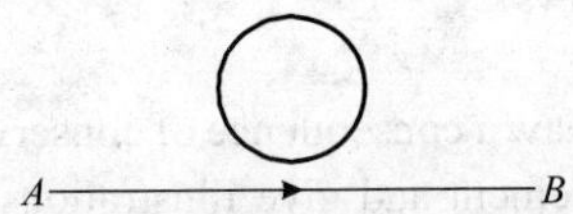

Figure 5.244

Q5-11 Can a transformer be used to alter DC voltage?

Q5-12 A pure inductance is connected to an AC source. What will be the phase difference between the current and the EMF in the circuit?

Q5-13 Why is the core of transformer laminated ?

Q5-22 A copper ring and a wooden ring of same dimension are placed so that there is same magnetic flux through each. Is induced current or induced EMF same in each case when flux starts varying at the same rate in both.

Q5-14 Three identical coils A, B and C shown in figure 2.245 are placed with their planes parallel to one another. Coil A and C carry current as shown. Coils B and C are fixed in position and coil A is moved towards B with uniform motion. Is there any induced current in B? If no, give reason. If yes, make the direction of induced current in the diagram.

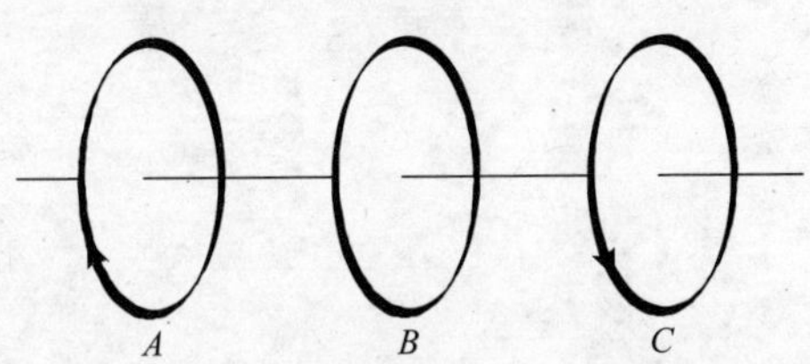

Figure 5.245

Q5-15 The resistance of a coil for direct current is R. An alternating current is sent through it. Will its resistance remain the same for AC as well?

Q5-16 A copper ring is held horizontally and a bar magnet is dropped through the ring with its length along the axis of the ring. Will the acceleration of the falling magnet be equal to, greater than or less than that due to gravity?

Q5-17 A bulb and a capacitor are connected in series to an AC source. What will happen with the brightness of bulb on increasing the frequency of the current source ?

Q5-18 A current is sent through a vertical spring from whose lower end a weight is hanging. What will happen to the weight when current flows?

Q5-19 "Lenz's law a consequence of conservation of energy" Explain this statement and give illustrations to support your explanation?

Q5-20 An artificial satellite with a metal surface has an orbit over the equator. Will the earth's magnetism induce a current in it in its orbital motion?

* * * * *

Conceptual MCQs Single Option Correct

5-1 For a *RLC* series circuit with an *AC* source of angular frequency ω.

(A) Circuit will be capacitive if $\omega > \frac{1}{\sqrt{LC}}$

(B) Circuit will be inductive if $\omega = \frac{1}{\sqrt{LC}}$

(C) Power factor of circuit will by unity if capacitive reactance equals inductive reactance

(D) Current will be leading voltage if $\omega > \frac{1}{\sqrt{LC}}$

5-2 Two identical metallic square loops L_1 and L_2 are placed next to each other with their sides parallel on a smooth horizontal table. Loop L_1 is fixed and a current which increases as a function of time is passed through it. Then loop L_2 :

(A) rotates about its center of mass
(B) moves towards L_1
(C) remains stationary
(D) moves away from L_1

5-3 The total charge flown through a conducting loop in a given time duration when it is moved in magnetic field depend on :

(A) The rate of change of magnetic flux
(B) Initial magnetic flux only
(C) The total change in magnetic flux
(D) Final magnetic flux only

5-4 When the current through a solenoid increases at a constant rate, the induced current in the solenoid

(A) Is a constant and is in the direction of the increasing current in it
(B) Is a constant and is opposite to the direction of the increasing current in it
(C) Increases with time and is in the direction of increasing current in it
(D) Increases with time and is opposite to the direction of the increasing current in it

5-5 The figure-5.246 shows four wire loops, with edge lengths of either *L* or 2 *L*. All four loops will move through a region of uniform magnetic field of induction *B* outward from the plane of paper. The loops will move at the same constant velocity. Rank the four loops according to the maximum magnitude of the EMF induced as they move through the field, greatest first :

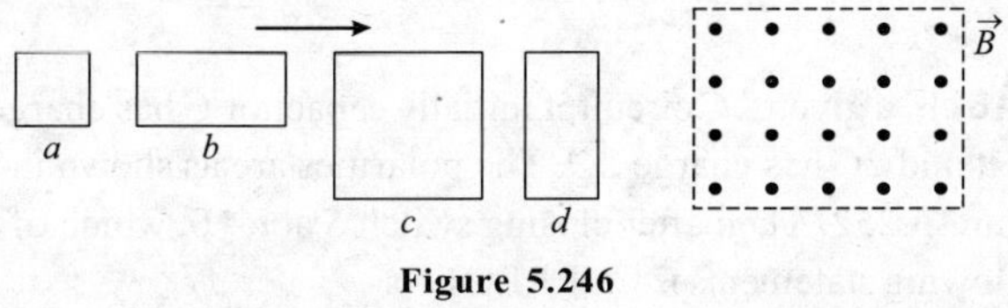

Figure 5.246

(A) $(e_c = e_d) < (e_a = e_b)$
(B) $(e_c = e_d) > (e_a = e_b)$
(C) $e_c > e_d > e_b > e_a$
(D) $e_c < e_d < e_b < e_a$

5-6 Two circular, similar, coaxial loops carry equal currents in the same direction. If the loops are brought nearer, what will happen?

(A) Current will increase in each loop
(B) Current will decrease in each loop
(C) Current will remain same in each loop
(D) Current will increase in one and decrease in the other

5-7 A coil is suspended in a uniform magnetic field, with the plane of the coil parallel to the magnetic lines of force. When a current is passed through the coil it starts oscillating, it is very difficult to stop. But if an aluminium plate is placed near to the coil, it stops. This is due to :

(A) Electromagnetic induction in the aluminium plate giving rise to electromagnetic damping by eddy currents
(B) Development of air current when the plate is placed
(C) Induction of electrical charge on the plate
(D) Shielding of magnetic lines of force as aluminium is a paramagnetic material

5-8 In a given solenoid if the number of turns and the length of the solenoid are doubled keeping the area of cross-section same, then its inductance :

(A) Remains the same
(B) Is halved
(C) Is doubled
(D) Becomes four times

5-9 Eddy currents are produced when :

(A) A metal body is kept in a time varying magnetic field
(B) A metal body is kept in the steady magnetic field
(C) A circular coil is placed in a magnetic field
(D) Through a circular coil current is passed

5-10 In figure-5.247, a lamp *P* is in series with an iron-core inductor *L*. When the switch *S* is closed, the brightness of the lamp rises relatively slowly to its full brightness than it would do without the inductor. This is due to :

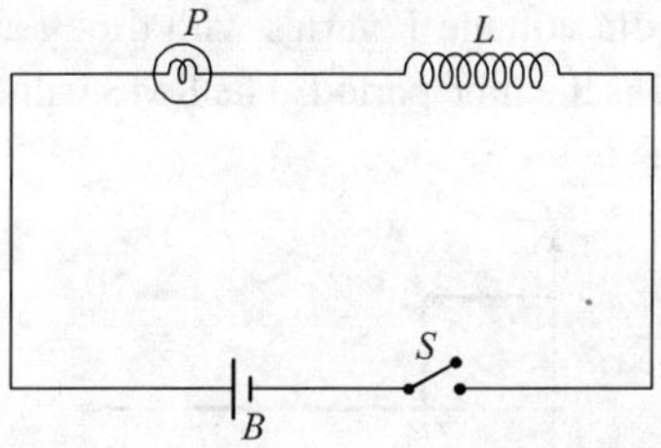

Figure 5.247

(A) the low resistance of *P*
(B) the induced EMF in *L*

(C) the low resistance of L

(D) the high voltage of the battery B

5-11 A current carrying ring is placed in a horizontal plane. A charged particle is dropped along the axis of the ring so that it falls under gravity, then :

(A) The current in the ring may increase

(B) The current in the ring may decrease

(C) The velocity of the particle will increase till it reaches the centre of the ring

(D) The acceleration of the particle will decrease continuously till it reaches the centre of the ring

5-12 A circuit element is placed in a closed box. At time $t = 0$, constant current generator supplying a current of 1 A, is connected across the box. Potential difference across the box varies according to graph shown in figure-5.248. The element in the box is :

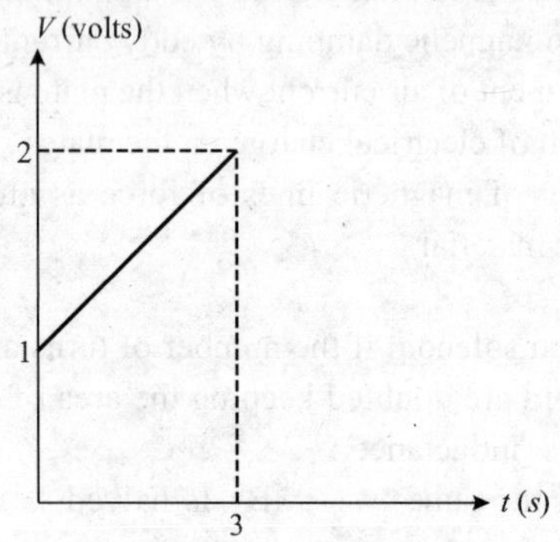

Figure 5.248

(A) Resistance of 2 Ω (B) Battery of emf 6 V

(C) Inductance of 2 H (D) Capacitance of 3 F

5-13 Identify the INCORRECT statement. Induced electric field in a region :

(A) is produced by varying magnetic field

(B) is non conservative in nature

(C) cannot exist in a region not occupied by magnetic field

(D) None of the above

5-14 A periodic voltage V varies with time t as shown in the figure 5.249. T is the time period. The RMS value of the voltage for one cycle is :

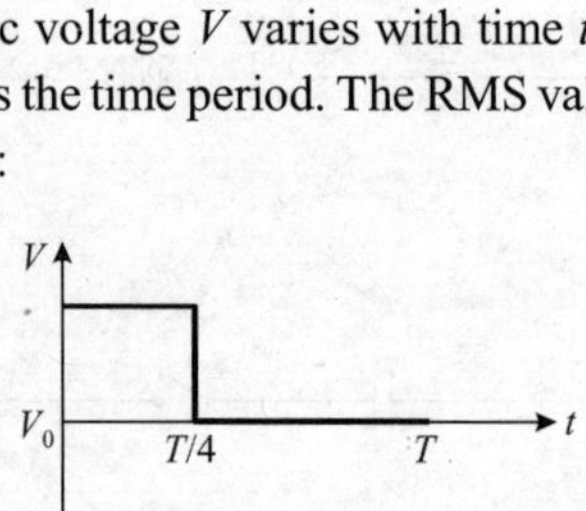

Figure 5.249

(A) $\frac{V_0}{8}$ (B) $\frac{V_0}{2}$

(C) V_0 (D) $\frac{V_0}{4}$

5-15 The current i in an induction coil varies with time t according to the graph shown in the figure-5.250. Which of the following graphs shows the induced EMF in the coil with time ?

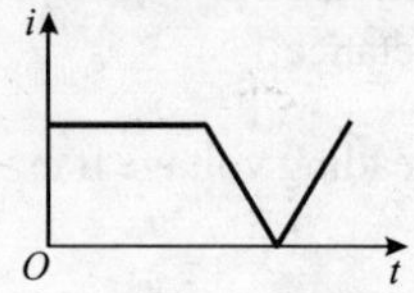

Figure 5.250

(A)

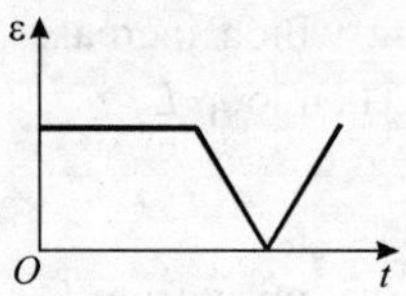

(B)

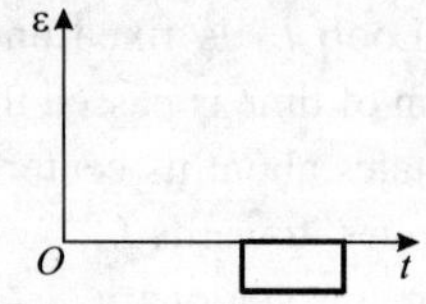

(C)

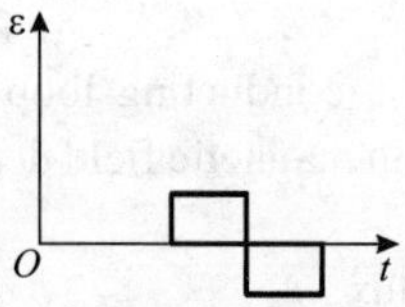

(D)

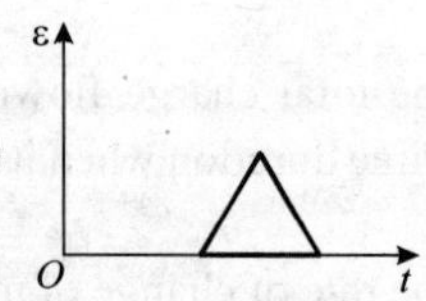

5-16 In an RLC circuit, capacitance is changed from C to $2C$. For the resonant frequency to remain unchanged, the inductance should be changed from L to :

(A) $4L$ (B) $2L$

(C) $L/2$ (D) $L/4$

5-17 In the shown AC circuit phase different between currents I_1 and I_2 is :

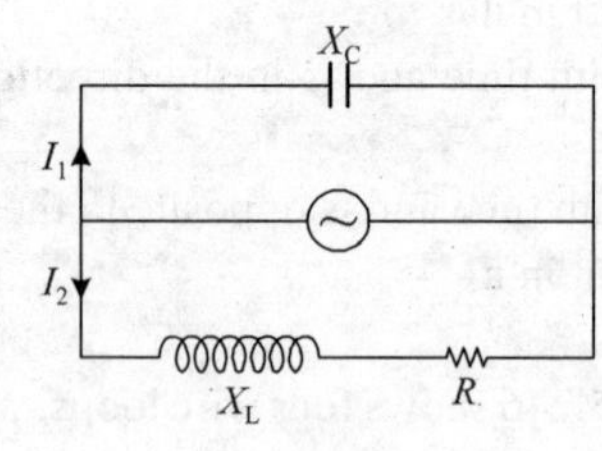

Figure 5.251

(A) $\frac{\pi}{2} - \tan^{-1}\frac{X_L}{R}$ (B) $\tan^{-1}\frac{X_L - X_C}{R}$

(C) $\frac{\pi}{2} + \tan^{-1}\frac{X_L}{R}$ (D) $\tan^{-1}\frac{X_L - X_C}{R} + \frac{\pi}{2}$

5-18 In a given LC circuit if initially capacitor C has charge Q on it and $2C$ has charge $2Q$. The polarities are as shown in the figure-5.252. Then after closing switch S at $t = 0$, which of the following statements is CORRECT :

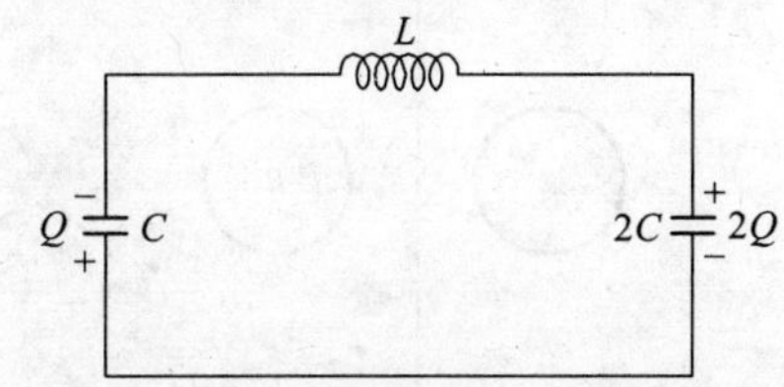

Figure 5.252

(A) Energy will get equally distributed in both the capacitor just after closing the switch.
(B) Initial rate of growth of current in inductor is $2Q/3CL$
(C) Maximum energy in the inductor will be $4Q^2/3C$
(D) None of these

5-19 In a series *RLC* circuit, the frequency of the source is half of the resonance frequency. The nature of the circuit will be :

(A) Capacitive (B) Inductive
(C) Purely resistive (D) Selective

5-20 A magnet is made to oscillate with a particular frequency, passing through a coil as shown in figure-5.253. The time variation of the magnitude of EMF generated across the coil during one cycle is :

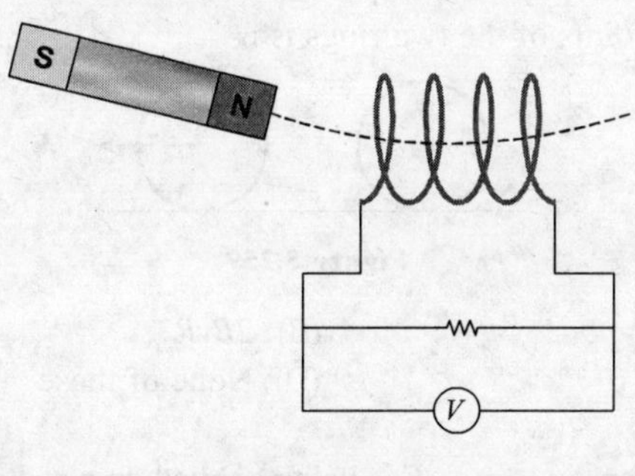

Figure 5.253

(A) 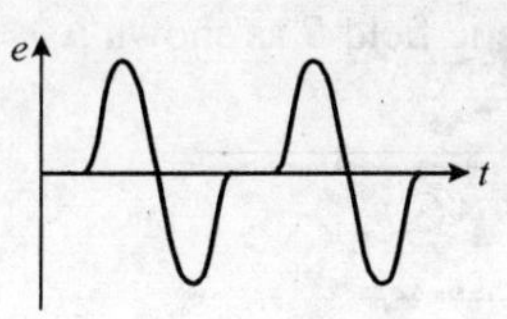 (B) 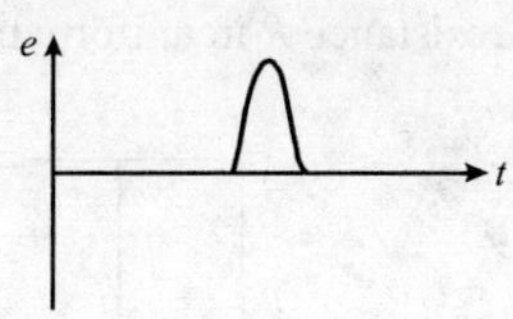

(C) 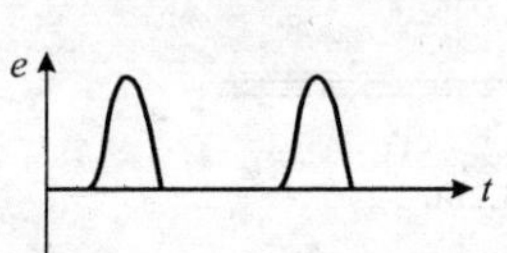 (D) 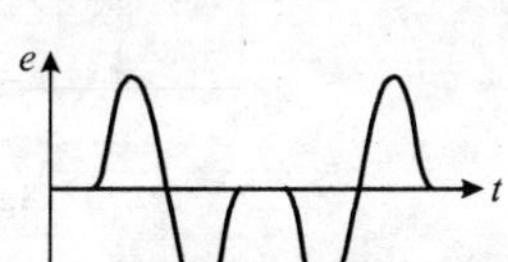

5-21 The magnetic materials having negative magnetic susceptibility are :

(A) Non magnetic (B) Para magnetic
(C) Diamagnetic (D) Ferromagnetic

5-22 The average and RMS value of voltage for square wave shown in figure-5.254 having peak value V_0 are :

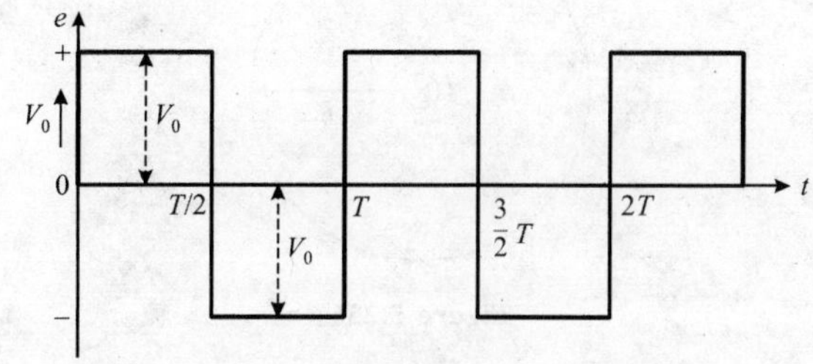

Figure 5.254

(A) $\frac{V_0}{\sqrt{2}}, \sqrt{2}V_0$ (B) $\sqrt{2}V_0, \frac{V_0}{\sqrt{2}}$

(C) V_0, V_0 (D) Zero, V_0

5-23 When a loop moves towards a stationary magnet with speed *v*, the induced EMF in the loop is *E*. If the magnet also moves away from the loop with the same speed, then the EMF induced in the loop is :

(A) E (B) $2E$
(C) $\frac{E}{2}$ (D) Zero

5-24 In AC circuit when AC ammeter is connected it reads a current *i*. If a student uses DC ammeter in place of AC ammeter the reading in the DC ammeter will be :

(A) $\frac{i}{\sqrt{2}}$ (B) $\sqrt{2}i$
(C) $0.637\,i$ (D) Zero

5-25 If value of *R* is changed in the series *RLC* circuit shown in figure-5.255, then :

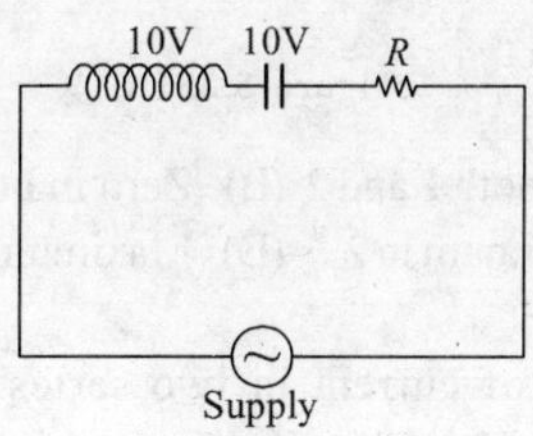

Figure 5.255

(A) voltage across *L* remains same
(B) voltage across *C* remains same
(C) voltage across *LC* combination remains same
(D) voltage across *LC* combination changes

5-26 A circuit consists of a circular loop of radius *R* kept in the plane of paper and an infinitely long current carrying wire kept perpendicular to the plane of paper and passing through the centre of loop. The mutual inductance of wire and loop will be :

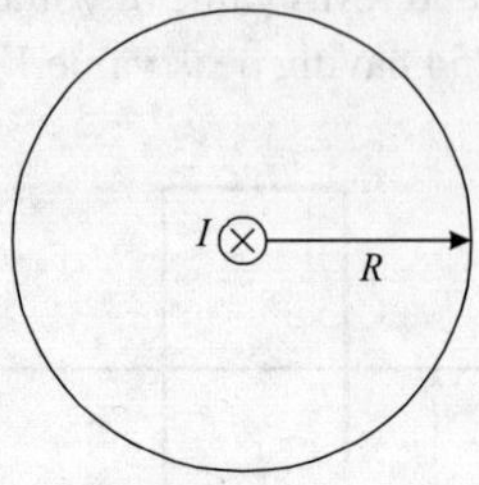

Figure 5.256

(A) $\frac{\mu_0 \pi R}{2}$ (B) 0

(C) $\mu_0 \pi R^2$ (D) $\frac{\mu_0 R^2}{2}$

5-27 Which of the following material is ferromagnetic
(A) Bismuth (B) Nickel
(C) Quartz (D) Aluminium

5-28 In a series *RLC* AC circuit, at resonance, the current is:
(A) Always in phase with the generator voltage.
(B) Always lags the generator voltage
(C) Always leads the generator voltage
(D) May lead or lag behind the generator voltage.

5-29 In the circuit given below (1) and (2) are ammeters. Just after key *K* is pressed to complete the circuit, the reading is :

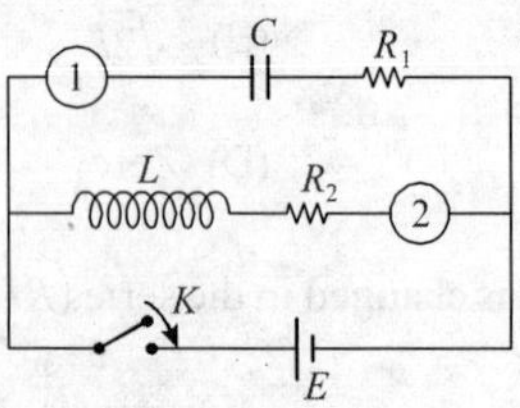

Figure 5.257

(A) Maximum in both 1 and 2 (B) Zero in both 1 and 2
(C) Zero in 1, minimum in 2 (D) Maximum in 1, zero in 2

5-30 The value of current in two series *RLC* circuits at resonance is same when connected across a sinusoidal voltage source. Then :
(A) Both circuits must be having same value of capacitance and inductor
(B) In both circuits ratio of *L* and *C* will be same
(C) For both the circuits X_L/X_C must be same at that frequency
(D) Both circuits must have same impedance at all frequencies.

5-31 *A* and *B* are two metallic rings placed at opposite sides of an infinitely long straight conducting wire as shown. If current in the wire is slowly decreased, the direction of induced current will be :

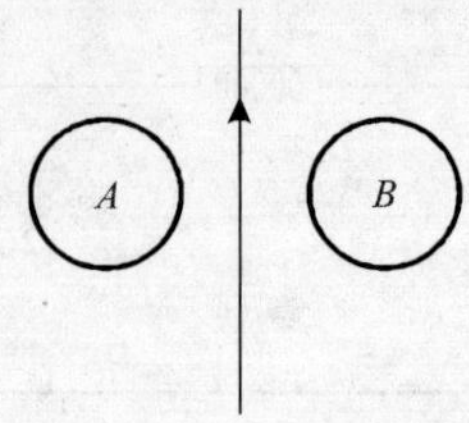

Figure 5.258

(A) Clockwise in *A* and anticlockwise in *B*
(B) Anticlockwise in *A* and clockwise in *B*
(C) Clockwise in both *A* and *B*
(D) Anticlockwise in both *A* & *B*

5-32 The area of *B-H* hysteresis curve is an indication of :
(A) The permeability of the substance
(B) The susceptibility of the substance
(C) The retentivity of the substance
(D) The energy dissipated per cycle per unit volume of the substance

5-33 Two identical conducting rings *A* & *B* of radius *R* are in pure rolling over a horizontal conducting plane with same speed of center of mass *v* but in opposite direction. A constant horizontal magnetic field *B* is exist in the space pointing inside the plane of paper. The potential difference between the topmost points of the two rings is :

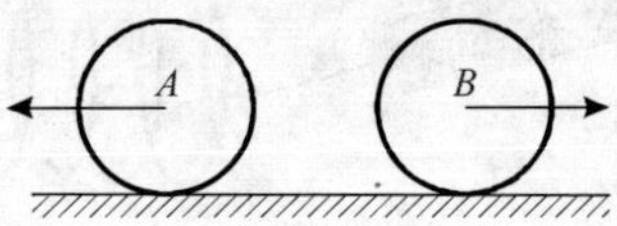

Figure 5.259

(A) Zero (B) $2BvR$
(C) $4BvR$ (D) None of these

5-34 A constant force *F* is being applied on a rod of length *l* kept at rest on two parallel conducting rails connected at ends by resistance *R* in uniform magnetic field *B* as shown :

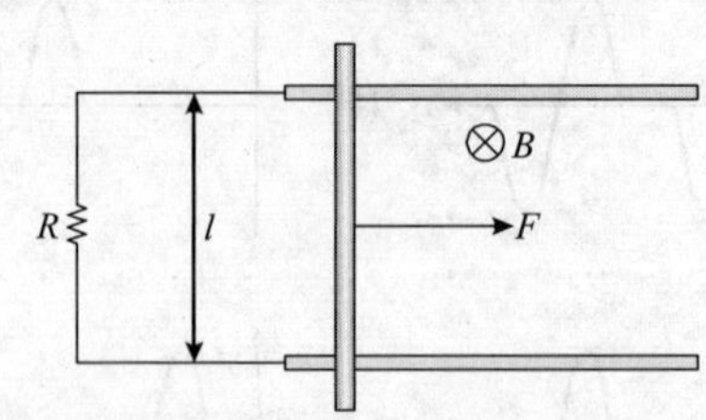

Figure 5.260

(A) The power delivered by force will be constant with time
(B) The power delivered by force will be increasing first and then will decrease
(C) The rate of power delivered by the external force will be increasing continuously
(D) The rate of power delivered by external force will be decreasing continuously.

5-35 AB and CD are fixed conducting smooth rails placed in a vertical plane and joined by a constant current source at its upper end. PQ is a horizontal conducting rod which is free to slide on the rails. A horizontal uniform magnetic field exists in space as shown. If the rod PQ in released from rest then :

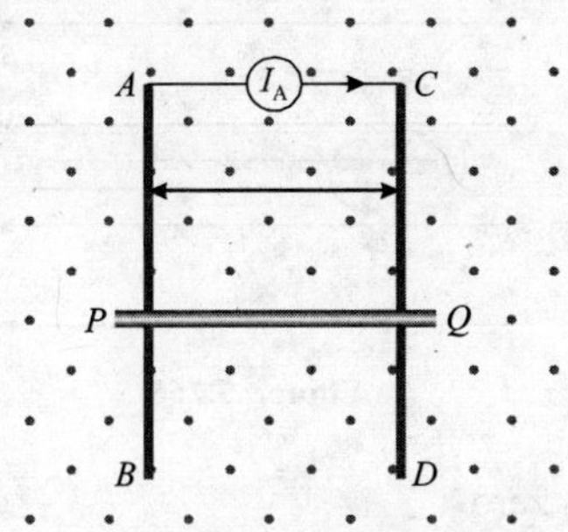

Figure 5.261

(A) The rod PQ will move downward with constant acceleration
(B) The rod PQ will move upward with constant acceleration
(C) The rod will move downward with decreasing acceleration and finally acquire a constant velocity
(D) Either A or B.

5-36 An alternating current I in an inductance coil varies with time t according to the graph as shown :

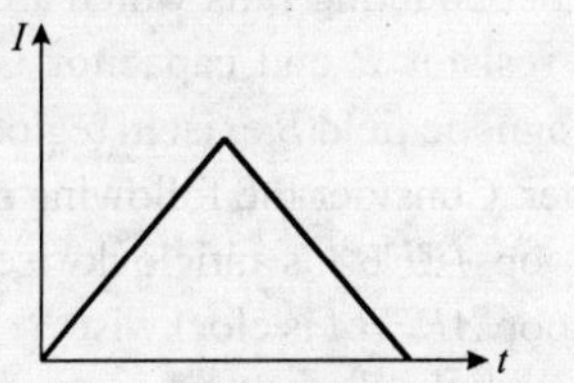

Figure 5.262

Which one of the following graphs gives the variation of voltage with time ?

(A) 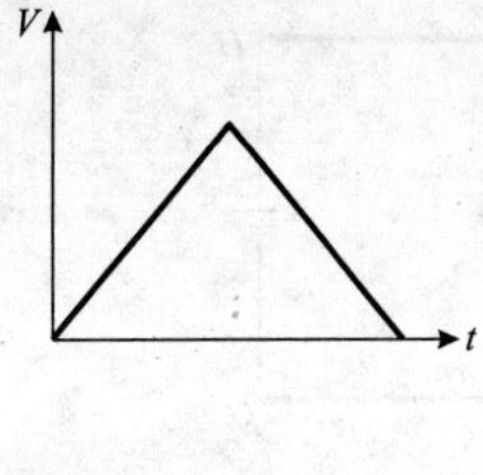

(B) 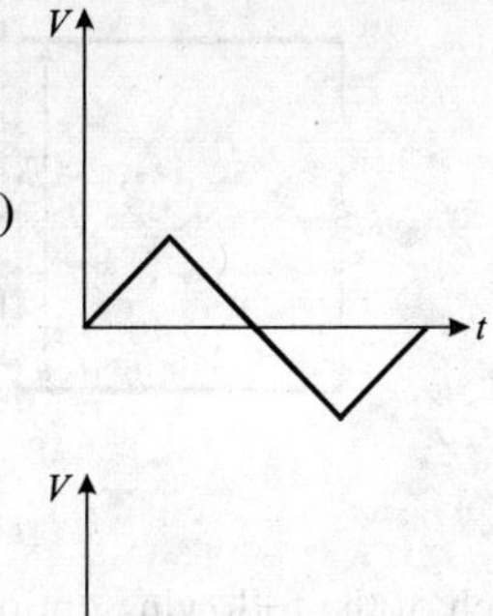

(C) 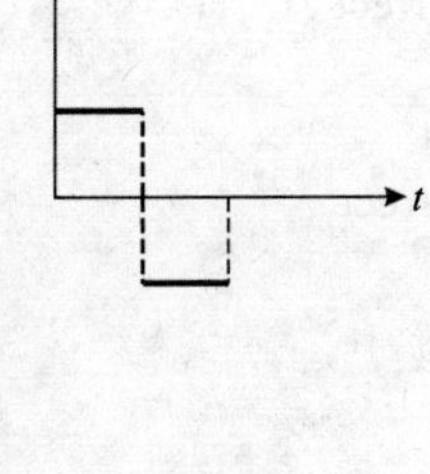

(D) 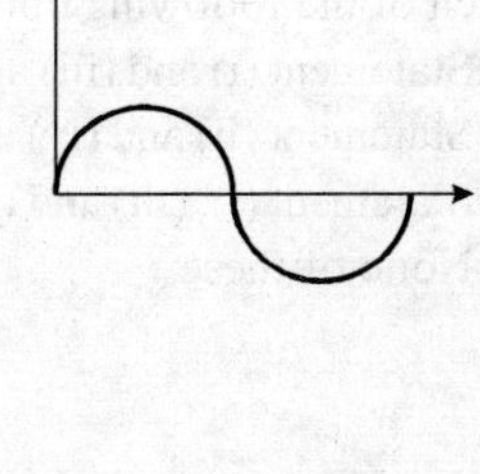

5-37 A small circular loop is suspended from an insulating thread. Another coaxial circular loop carrying a current I and having radius much larger than the first loop starts moving towards the smaller loop. The smaller loop will :

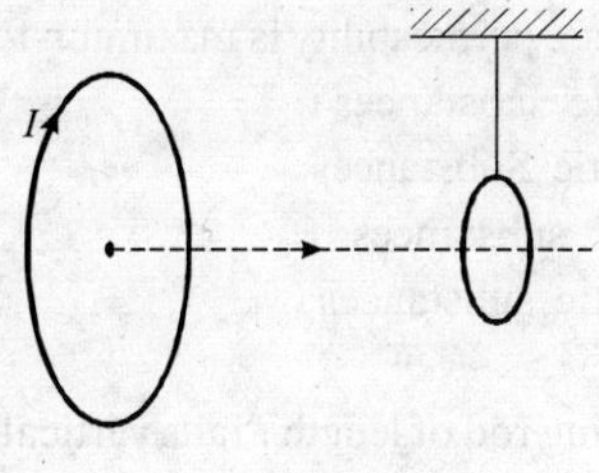

Figure 5.263

(A) Be attracted towards the bigger loop
(B) Be repelled by the bigger loop
(C) Experience no force
(D) All of the above

5-38 As shown in figure-5.264, a T-shaped conductor moves with constant angular velocity ω in a plane perpendicular to uniform magnetic field $\vec{B}$. The potential difference $V_A - V_B$ is :

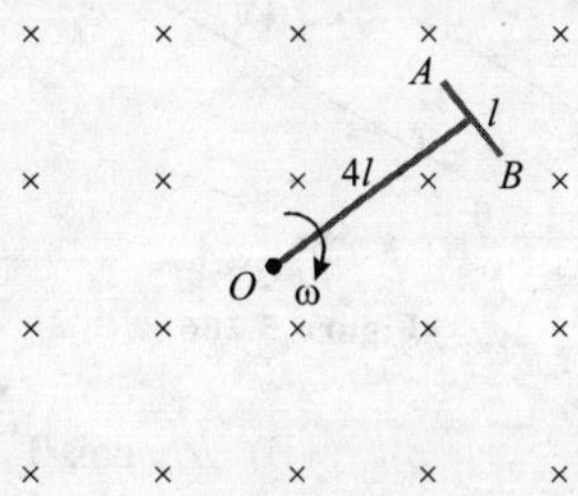

Figure 5.264

(A) Zero (B) $\frac{1}{2}B\omega l^2$
(C) $2B\omega l^2$ (D) $B\omega l^2$

5-39 If the permanent magnetic moment of the atoms of a substance is zero, then it is called :
(A) Diamagnetic (B) Paramagnetic
(C) Ferromagnetic (D) Antiferromagnetic

5-40 A ring B is placed coaxially with a solenoid A as shown in figure-5.265. As the switch S is closed at $t = 0$, the ring B :

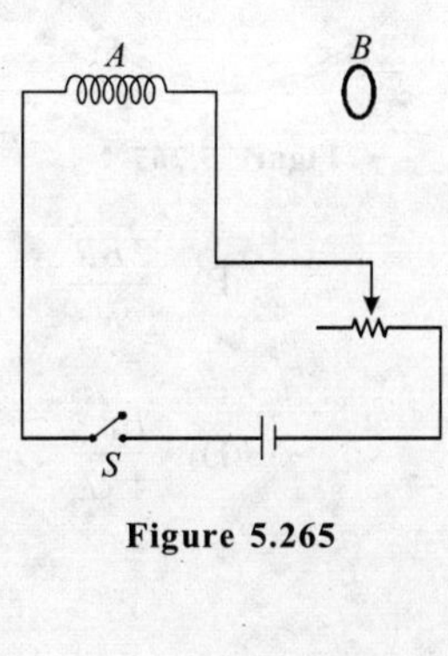

Figure 5.265

(A) Is attracted towards A
(B) Is repelled by A
(C) Is initially repelled and then attracted
(D) Is initially attracted and then repelled

5-41 The magnetic permeability is maximum for :
(A) Paramagnetic substances
(B) Ferromagnetic Substances
(C) Diamagnetic substances
(D) Non-magnetic substances

5-42 A conducting rod of length l falls vertically under gravity in a region of uniform magnetic induction $\vec{B}$. The field vectors are inclined at an angle θ with the horizontal as shown in figure-5.266. If the instantaneous velocity of the rod is v, the induced EMF in the rod ab is :

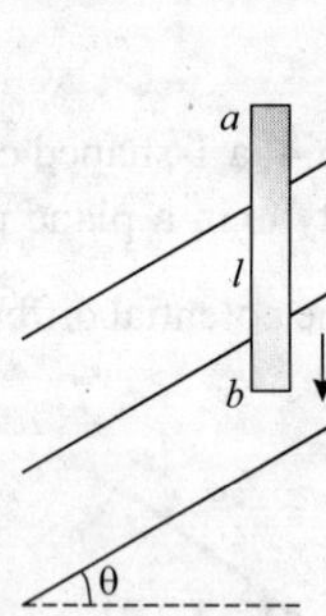

Figure 5.266

(A) Blv
(B) $Blv \cos\theta$
(C) $Blv \sin\theta$
(D) Zero

5-43 Figure-5.267 shows a conducting ring of radius R. A uniform steady magnetic field B lies perpendicular to the plane of the ring in a circular region of radius r ($< R$). If the resistance per unit length of the ring is λ, then the current induced in the ring when its radius gets doubled is :

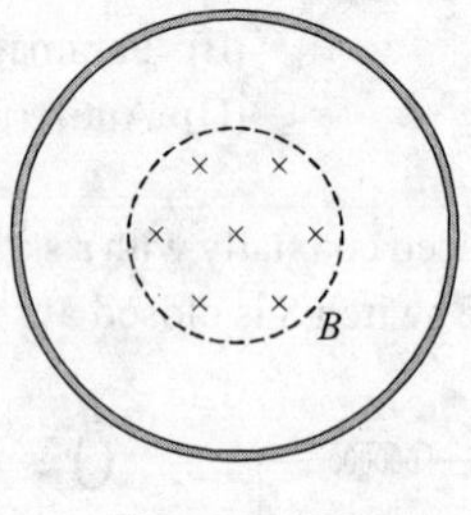

Figure 5.267

(A) $\frac{BR}{\lambda}$
(B) $\frac{2BR}{\lambda}$
(C) Zero
(D) $\frac{Br^2}{4R\lambda}$

5-44 A metallic rod of length l is hinged at the point M and it is rotating about an axis perpendicular to the plane of paper with a constant angular velocity ω. A uniform magnetic field of intensity B exist in the region as shown in figure-5.268 parallel to the plane of paper. The potential difference between the points M and N :

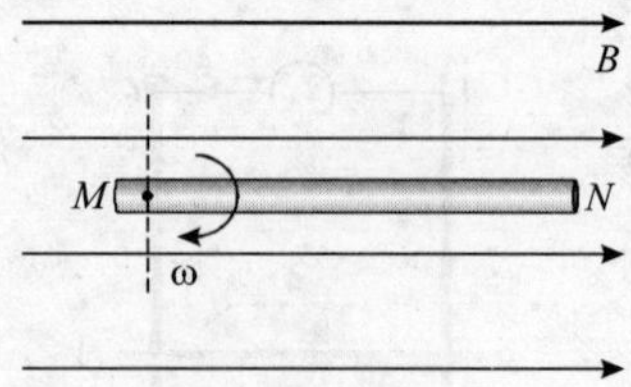

Figure 5.268

(A) Is always zero
(B) Varies between $\frac{1}{2}B\omega l^2$ to 0
(C) Is always $\frac{1}{2}B\omega l^2$
(D) Is always $B\omega l^2$

4-45 At Curie point, a ferromagnetic material transforms into :
(A) Diamagnetic
(B) Paramagnetic
(C) Ferromagnetic
(D) Antiferromagnetic

5-46 A conducting rod is moving with a constant velocity v over the parallel conducting rails which are connected at the ends through a resistor R and capacitor C as shown in the figure-5.269. Magnetic field B exist in region perpendicular to the plane of paper. Consider the following statements :
(i) Current in loop $AEFBA$ is anticlockwise
(ii) Current in loop $AEFBA$ is clockwise
(iii) Current through the capacitor is zero
(iv) Energy stored in the capacitor is $\frac{1}{2}CB^2L^2v^2$

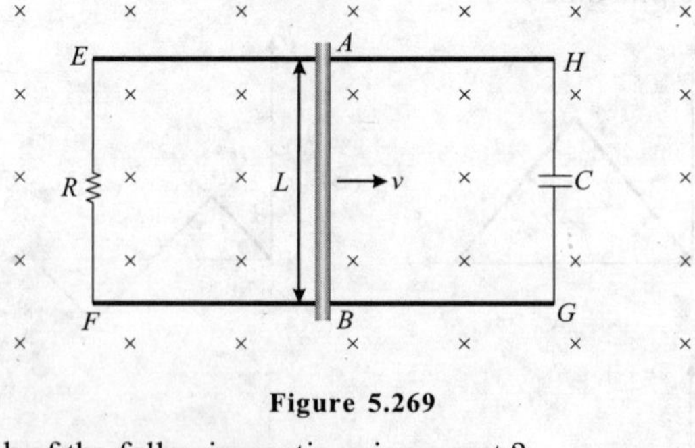

Figure 5.269

Which of the following options is correct ?
(A) Statement (i) and (iii) are correct
(B) Statement (ii) and (iv) are correct
(C) Statement (i), (iii) and (iv) are correct
(D) None of these

5-47 A rod is rotating with a constant angular velocity ω about point O at its center in a uniform magnetic field of induction B as shown in figure-5.270. Which of the following figure correctly shows the distribution of charge inside the rod ?

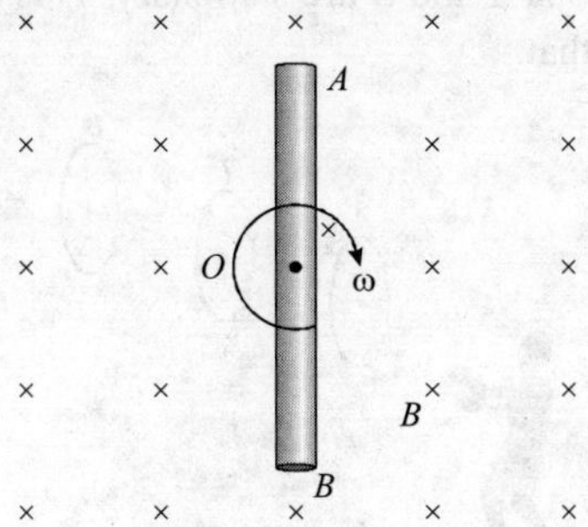

Figure 5.270

(A) 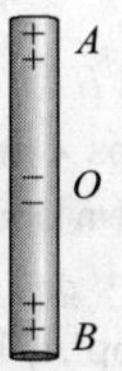

(B) 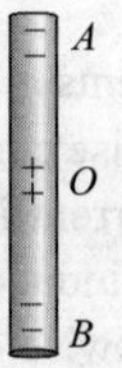

(C) 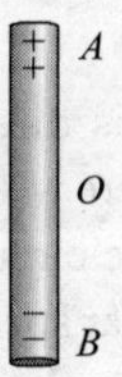

(D) 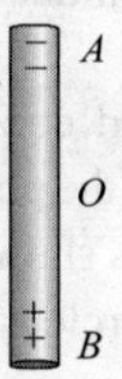

5-48 A straight conducting rod PQ is executing SHM in xy plane from $x = -d$ to $x = +d$. Its mean position is $x = 0$ and its length is along y-axis. There exists a uniform magnetic field B from $x = -d$ to $x = 0$ pointing inward normal to the paper and from $x = 0$ to $= +d$ there exists another uniform magnetic field of same magnitude B but pointing outward normal to the plane of the paper. At the instant $t = 0$, the rod is at $x = 0$ and moving to the right. The variation of induced EMF across the rod PQ with time is best represented as :

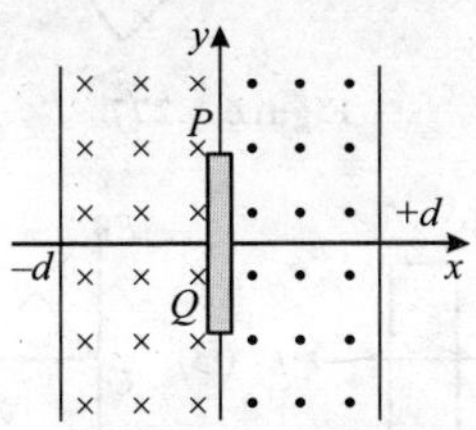

Figure 5.271

(A) 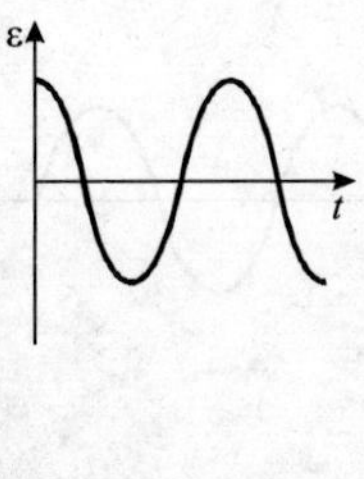

(B) 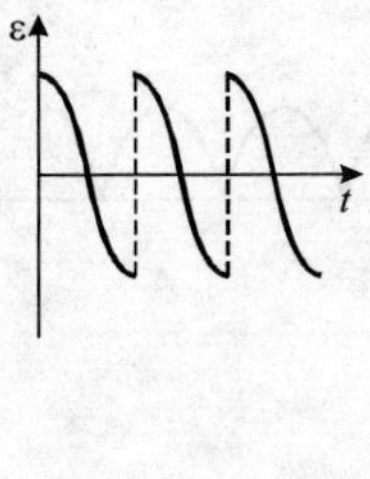

(C) 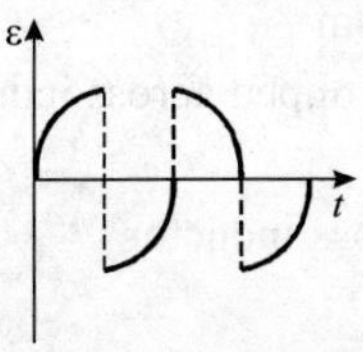

(D) 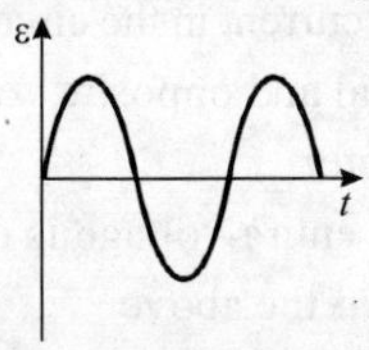

5-49 A wire is bent in the form of a V-shape and placed in a horizontal plane in a uniform magnetic field of induction B perpendicular to the plane of the wire as shown in figure-5.272. A uniform conducting rod starts sliding over the V-shaped wire with a constant speed v. If the wire has no resistance, the current in rod will :

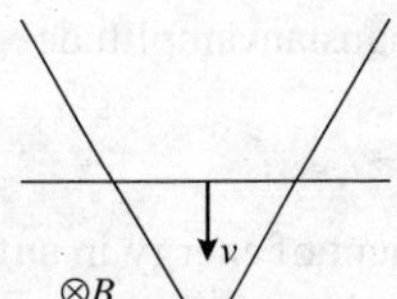

Figure 5.272

(A) Increase with time (B) Decrease with time
(C) Remain constant (D) Always be zero

5-50 In the circuit shown in figure-5.273 initially the switch is in position 1 for a long time, then suddenly at $t = 0$, the switch is shifted to position 2. It is required that a constant current should flow in the circuit, the value of resistance R in the circuit.

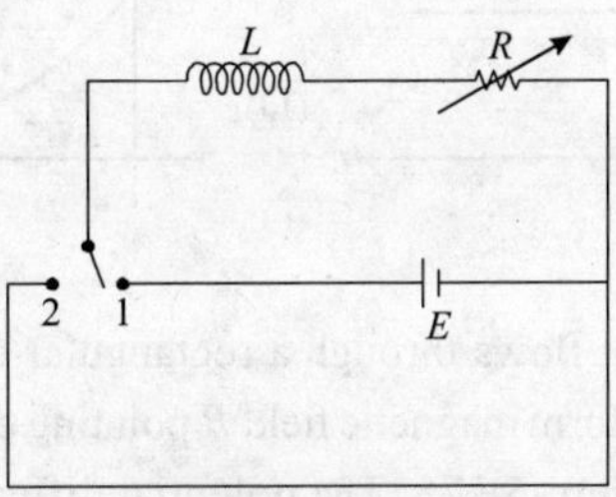

Figure 5.273

(A) Should be decreased at a constant rate
(B) Should be increased at a constant rate
(C) Should be maintained constant
(D) Not possible

5-51 When the switch S is closed at $t = 0$, identify the correct statement just after closing the switch as shown in figure-5.274 :

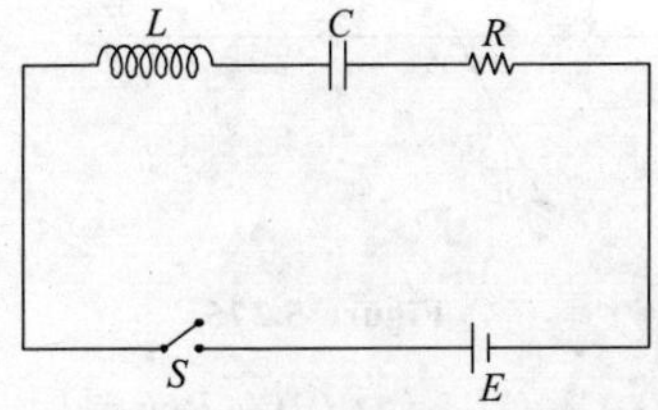

Figure 5.274

(A) The current in the circuit is maximum

(B) Equal and opposite voltages are dropped across inductor and resistor

(C) The entire voltage is dropped across inductor

(D) All of the above

5-52 A diamagnetic liquid solution is poured into a U-tube and one arm of this U-tube is placed between the poles of a strong magnet with the meniscus of liquid in that arm in line with the magnetic field. The level of solution in this arm will :

(A) will rise

(B) will fall

(C) will oscillate at constant amplitude

(D) remain as it is

5-53 Rate of increment of energy in an inductor with time in series *RL* circuit getting charged with battery of EMF *E* is best represented by :

(A) 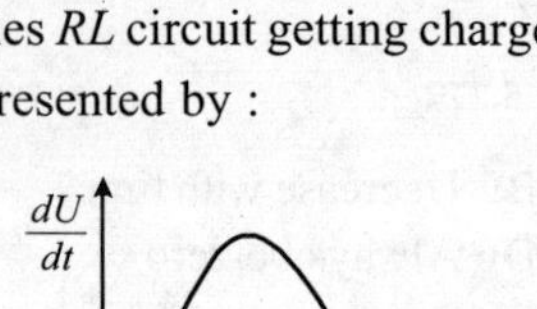

(B) 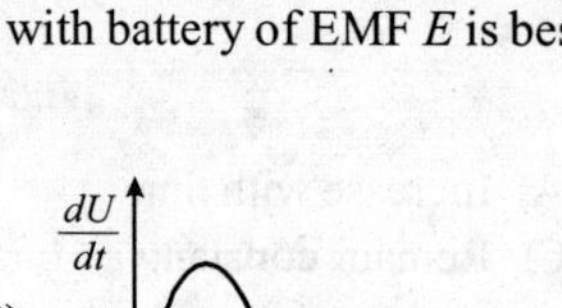

(C) 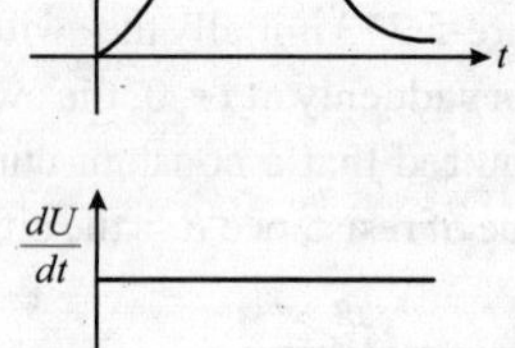

(D) 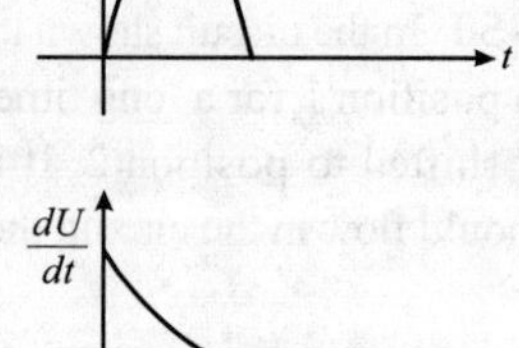

5-54 A current flows through a rectangular conductor in the presence of uniform magnetic field *B* pointing out in Z-direction as shown in figure-5.275. The potential difference $V_P - V_Q$ is equal to :

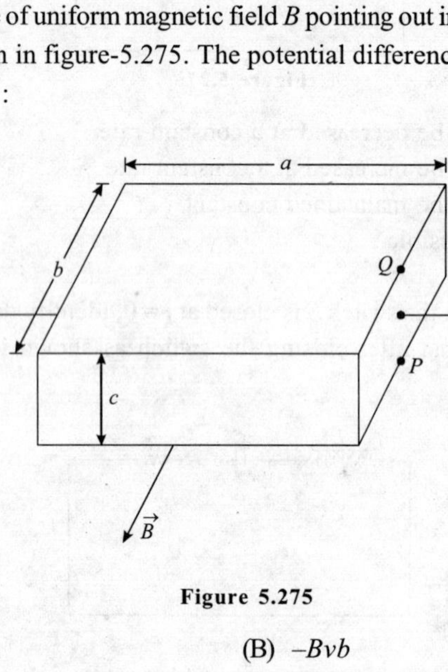

Figure 5.275

(A) *Bvb* (B) –*Bvb*

(C) *Bvc* (D) –*Bvc*

5-55 Three coaxial circular wire loops and an stationary observer are positioned as shown in figure-5.276. From the observers point of view, a current *I* flows counter clockwise in the middle loop, which is moving towards the observer with a velocity *v*. Loops *A* and *B* are stationary. This same observer would notice that.

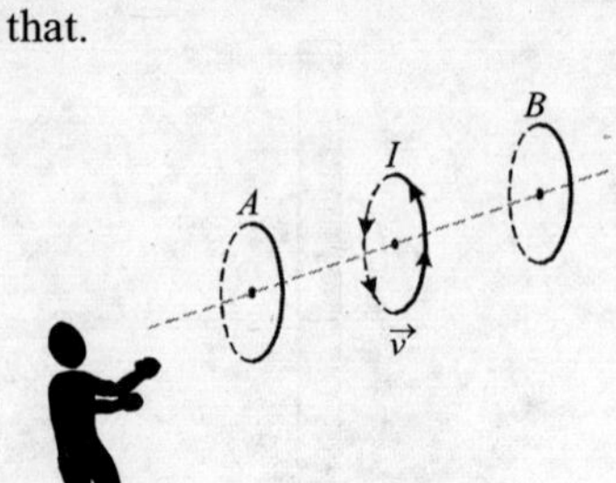

Figure 5.276

(A) Clockwise currents are induced in loops *A* and *B*.

(B) Counter clockwise currents are induced in loops *A* and *B*.

(C) A clockwise current is induced in loop *A*, but a counter clockwise current is induced in loop *B*.

(D) A counter clockwise current is induced in loop *A*, but a clockwise current is induced in loop *B*.

5-56 A uniform and constant magnetic field *B* is directed perpendicularly into the plane of the page everywhere within a rectangular region as shown in figure-5.277. A wire circuit in the shape of a semicircle is rotated at uniform angular speed in counter clockwise direction in the plane of the page about an axis passing through point *A*. The axis *A* is perpendicular to the page at the edge of the field and directed through the centre of the straight line portion of the circuit. Which of the following graphs best approximates the EMF *E* induced in the circuit as a function of time *t* ?

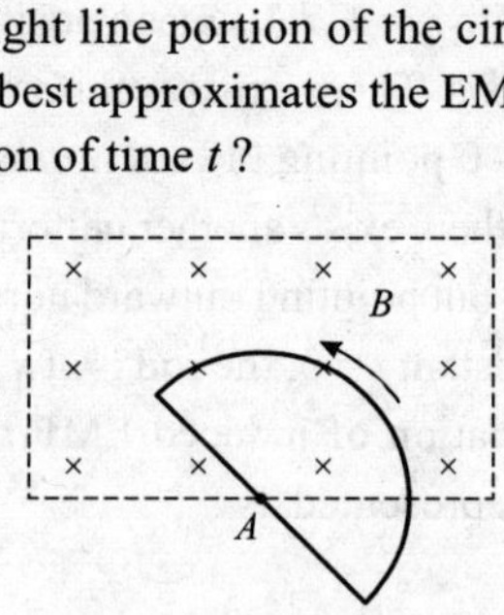

Figure 5.277

(A) 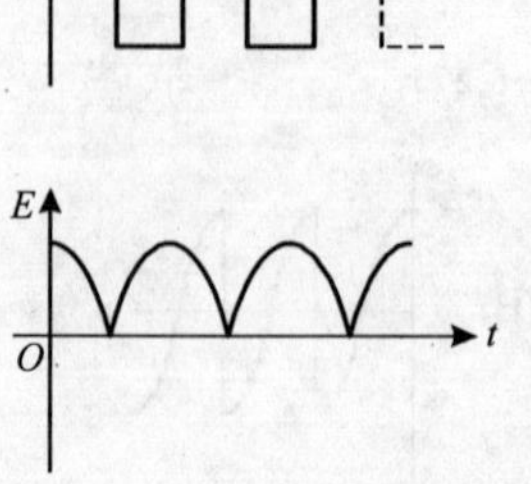

(B) 

(C)

(D) 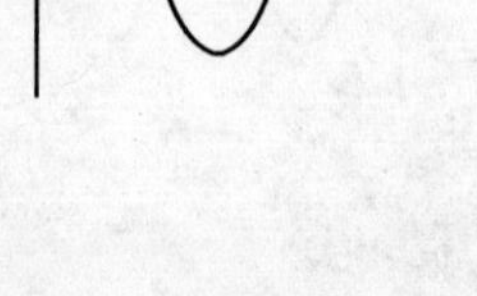

5-57 A short-circuited coil is placed in a time-varying magnetic field. Electrical power is dissipated due to the current induced in the coil. If the number of turns were to be quadrupled and the wire radius halved, the electrical power dissipated would be :

(A) Halved (B) Remain same
(C) Doubled (D) Quadrupled

5-58 A conducting ring is placed around the core of an electromagnet as shown in figure-5.278. When key K is pressed, the ring :

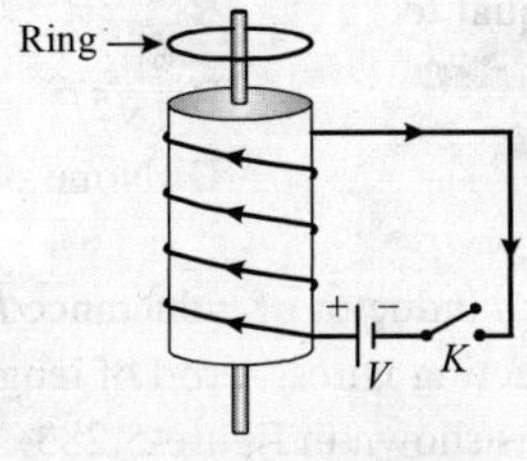

Figure 5.278

(A) Remain stationary
(B) Is attracted towards the electromagnet
(C) Jumps out of the core
(D) None of the above

5-59 The north and south poles of two identical magnets approach a coil, containing a capacitor with equal speeds from opposite sides. Then :

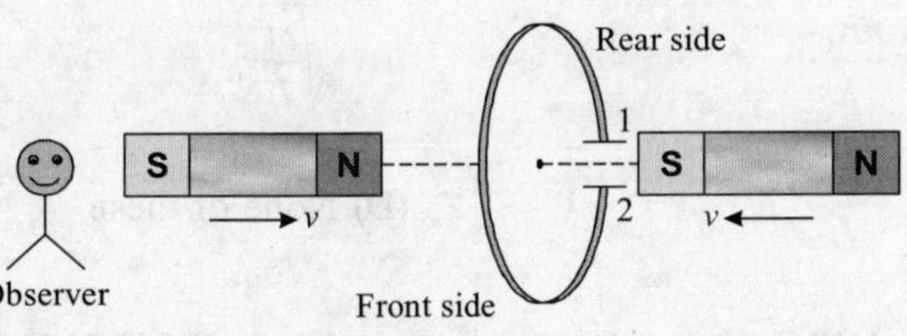

Figure 5.279

(A) Plate 1 will be negative and plate 2 positive
(B) Plate 1 will be positive and plate 2 negative
(C) Both the plates will be positive
(D) Both the plates will be negative

5-60 A metallic ring connected to a rod oscillates freely like a pendulum. If a magnetic field is applied in horizontal direction in a region as shown in figure-5.280 so that the pendulum now swings through the field, the pendulum will :

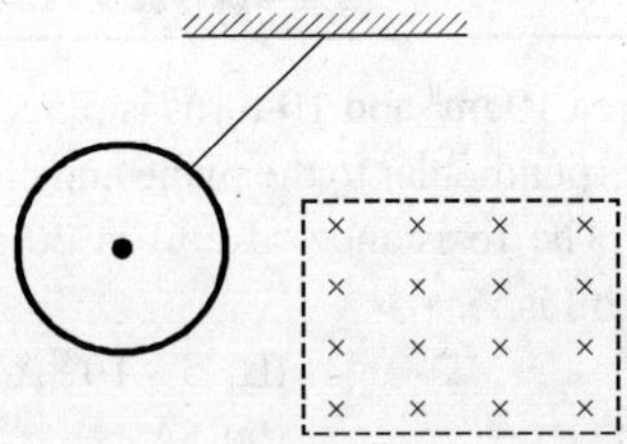

Figure 5.280

(A) Keep oscillating with the old time period
(B) Keep oscillating with a smaller time period
(C) Keep oscillating with a larger time period
(D) Come to rest very soon

5-61 The frequency of AC mains domestic and commercial supply in India is :

(A) 30 Hz (B) 50 Hz
(C) 60 Hz (D) 120 Hz

5-62 A bulb and a capacitor are connected in series to a source of alternating current. If its frequency is increased, while keeping the voltage of the source constant, then :

(A) Bulb will give more intense light
(B) Bulb will give less intense light
(C) Bulb will give light of same intensity as before
(D) Bulb will stop radiating light

5-63 Which of the following plots may represent the reactance of a series LC combination :

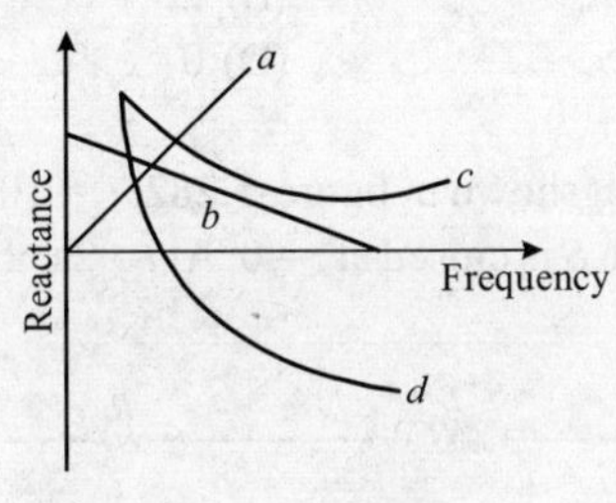

Figure 5.281

(A) a (B) b
(C) c (D) d

* * * * *

Numerical MCQs Single Option Correct

5-1 A coil of area $10 cm^2$ and 10 turns is placed in a magnetic field directed perpendicular to the plane and changing at a rate of 10^8 gauss/s. The resistance of coil is 20 Ω. The current induced in the coil is :

(A) 0.5A (B) 5×10^{-3}A
(C) 0.05A (D) 5A

5-2 The potential difference V and the current i flowing through an instrument in an AC circuit of frequency f are given as $V = \cos \omega t$ volts and $i = 2 \sin \omega t$ amperes. The power dissipated in the instrument is :

(A) Zero (B) 10 W
(C) 5 W (D) 2.5 W

5-3 In a step up transformer, the turn ratio is 3 : 2. A battery of EMF 4.5 V is connected across the primary windings of transformer. The voltage developed in the secondary would be :

(A) 4.5 V (B) 30 V
(C) 1.5 V (D) Zero

5-4 A flat circular coil of n turns, area A and resistance R is placed in a uniform magnetic field B. The plane of coil is initially perpendicular to B. When the coil is rotated through an angle of 180° about one of its diameter, a charge Q_1 flows through the coil. When the same coil after being brought to its initial position, is rotated through an angle of 360° about the same axis a charge Q_2 flows through it. Then Q_2/Q_1 is :

(A) 1 (B) 2
(C) 1/2 (D) 0

5-5 In the circuit shown in figure-5.282, $L = 10$ H, $R = 5 \Omega$, $E = 15$ V. The switch S is closed at $t = 0$. At $t = 2$s, the current in the circuit is :

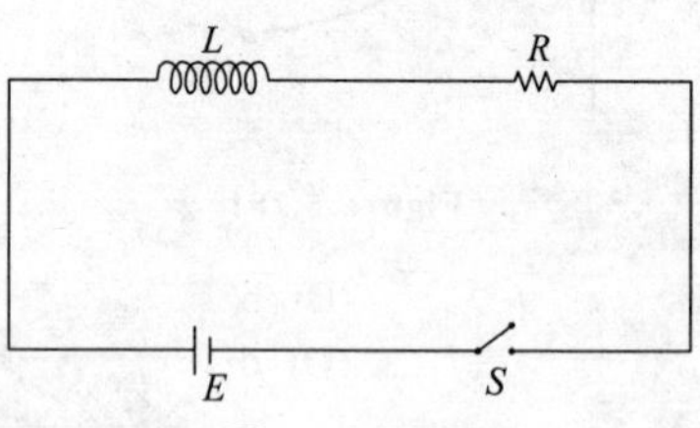

Figure 5.282

(A) $3\left(1-\frac{1}{e}\right)A$ (B) $3\left(1-\frac{1}{e^2}\right)A$
(C) $3\left(\frac{1}{e}\right)A$ (D) $3\left(\frac{1}{e^2}\right)A$

5-6 In an AC circuit, V and I are given as

$V = 100 \sin(100t)$ volt

and $I = 100 \sin\left(100t + \frac{\pi}{3}\right)$

The power dissipated in circuit is :

(A) 104 W (B) 10 W
(C) 2.5 W (D) 5 W

5-7 The ratio of secondary to the primary turns in a transformer is 5. If the power output be P, the input power neglecting all losses, must be equal to :

(A) $5P$ (B) $\sqrt{5}P$
(C) $P/5$ (D) None of these

5-8 Two ends of an inductor of inductance L are connected to two parallel conducting wires. A rod of length l and mass m is given velocity v_0 as shown in figure-5.283. The whole system is placed in perpendicular magnetic field B. Find the maximum current in the inductor. Neglect gravity and friction anywhere :

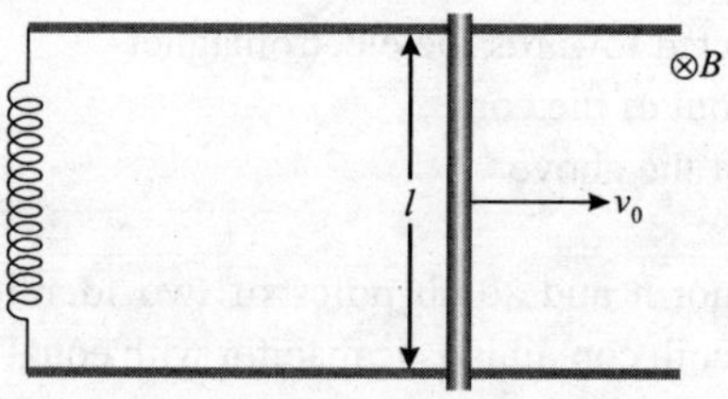

Figure 5.283

(A) $\frac{mv_0}{L}$ (B) $\sqrt{\frac{m}{L}}v_0$
(C) $\frac{mv_0^2}{L}$ (D) None of these

5-9 A 40 Ω electric heater is connected to a 200 V, 50 Hz mains supply. The peak value of electric current flowing in the circuit is approximately :

(A) 2.5 A (B) 5.0 A
(C) 7 A (D) 10 A

5-10 A transformer is used to light a 100 W, 110 V lamp from 220V mains supply. If the supply current is 0.5 A the efficiency of transformer is :

(A) 11% (B) 50%
(C) 80% (D) 90%

5-11 Two parallel long straight conductors having λ resistance per unit length lie on a smooth plane surface. Two identical other parallel conductors rest on them at right angles so as to form a square of side a. A uniform magnetic field B exists at right angles to the plane containing the conductors. Now conductors start moving outward with a constant velocity v_0 at $t = 0$. Then induced current in the loop at any time t is :

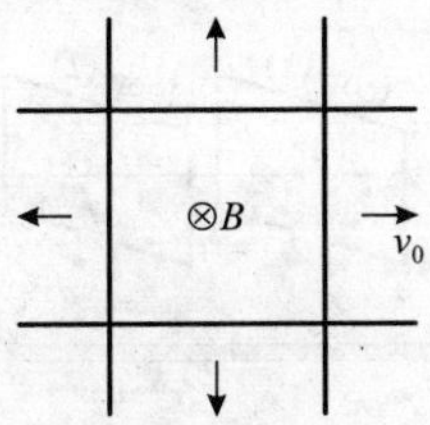

Figure 5.284

(A) $\frac{aBv_0}{\lambda(a+v_0t)}$ (B) $\frac{aBv_0}{2\lambda}$

(C) $\frac{Bv_0}{\lambda}$ (D) $\frac{Bv_0}{2\lambda}$

5-12 An alternating voltage is connected in series with a resistance R and an inductance L. If the potential drop across the resistance is 200 V and across the inductance is 150 V, then the applied voltage is :

(A) 350 V (B) 250 V

(C) 500 V (D) 300 V

5-13 A magnet is taken towards a conducting ring in such a way that a constant current of 10 mA is induced in it. The total resistance of the ring is 0.5 Ω. In 5 s, the magnetic flux through the ring changes by :

(A) 0.25 m Wb (B) 25 m Wb

(C) 50 m Wb (D) 15 m Wb

5-14 A straight conducting wire PQ of length l is fixed along a diameter of a non-conducting ring as shown in the figure-5.285. The ring is given a pure rolling motion on a horizontal surface such that its centre of mass has a velocity v. There exists a uniform horizontal magnetic field B in horizontal direction perpendicular to the plane of ring. The magnitude of induced EMF in the wire PQ at the position shown in the figure will be :

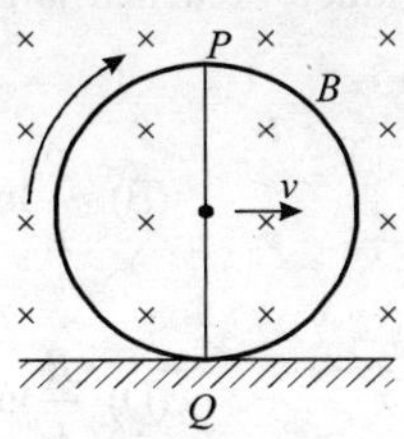

Figure 5.285

(A) Bvl (B) $2Bvl$

(C) $3Bvl/2$ (D) Zero

5-15 An inductive circuit contains a resistance of 10 Ω and an inductance of 20 H. If an AC voltage of 120 V and frequency 60 Hz is applied to this circuit, the current would be nearly :

(A) 0.32 A (B) 0.016 A

(C) 0.48 A (D) 0.80 A

5-16 A rectangular loop with a sliding connector of length 10cm is situated in a uniform magnetic field perpendicular to plane of loop. The magnetic induction is 0.1T and resistance of connector is 1Ω. The sides AB and CD have resistances 2Ω and 3Ω respectively. Find the current in the connector during its motion with constant velocity 1m/s :

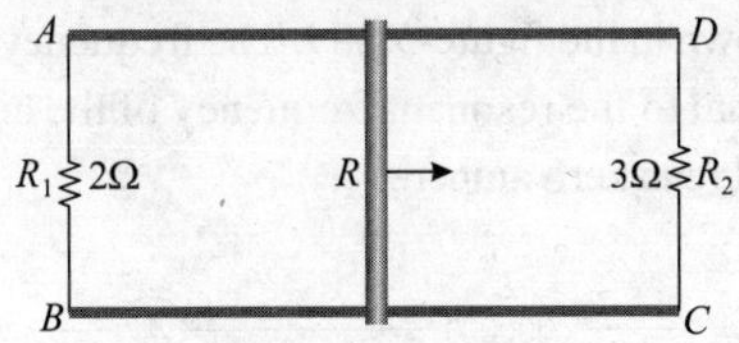

Figure 5.286

(A) $\frac{1}{220}$A (B) $\frac{1}{110}$A

(C) $\frac{1}{440}$A (D) $\frac{1}{55}$A

5-17 A 20V AC is applied to a circuit consisting of a resistance and a coil with negligible resistance. If the voltage across the resistance is 12V, the voltage across the coil is :

(A) 16V (B) 10V

(C) 8V (D) 6V

5-18 A square loop of side b is rotated in a constant magnetic field B at angular frequency ω as shown in the figure-5.287. What is the EMF induced in it ?

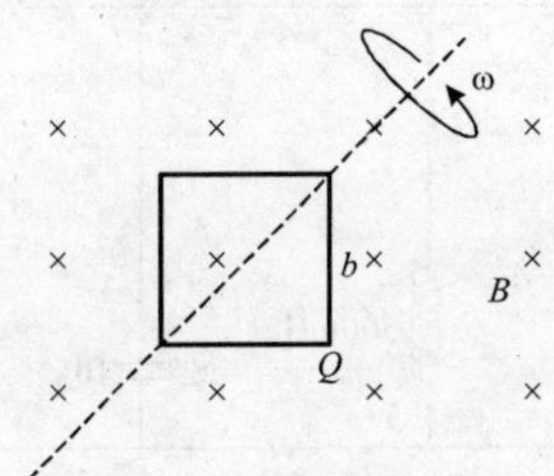

Figure 5.287

(A) $b^2 B\omega \sin \omega t$ (B) $bB\omega \sin^2 \omega t$

(C) $bB^2\omega \cos \omega t$ (D) $b^2 B\omega$

5-19 In the given branch AB of a circuit a current $I = (10t + 5)$ A is flowing, where t is time in second. At $t = 0$, the potential difference between points A and B $(V_A - V_B)$ is :

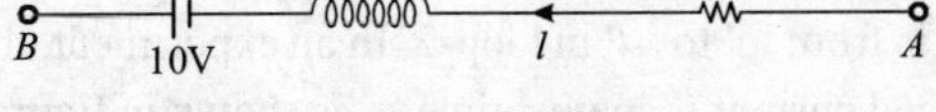

Figure 5.288

(A) 15 V (B) –5 V

(C) –15 V (D) 5 V

5-20 A resistance of 300 Ω and an inductance of $(1/\pi)$H are connected in series to an AC of 20 V, 200 Hz supply. The phase angle between the voltage and current is :

(A) $\tan^{-1}\frac{4}{3}$ (B) $\tan^{-1}\frac{3}{4}$

(C) $\tan^{-1}\frac{3}{2}$ (D) $\tan^{-1}\frac{2}{5}$

5-21 An inductor L and a capacitor C are connected in the circuit as shown in the figure-5.289. The frequency of the power supply is equal to the resonant frequency of the circuit. Which ammeter will read zero ampere :

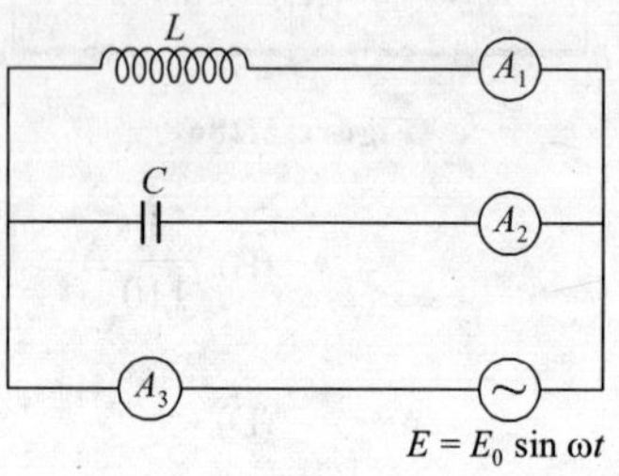

Figure 5.289

(A) A_1 (B) A_2

(C) A_3 (D) None of these

5-22 Switch S is closed at t = 0, in the circuit shown in figure-5.290. The change in flux in the inductor (L = 500mH) from t = 0 to an instant when it reaches steady state is :

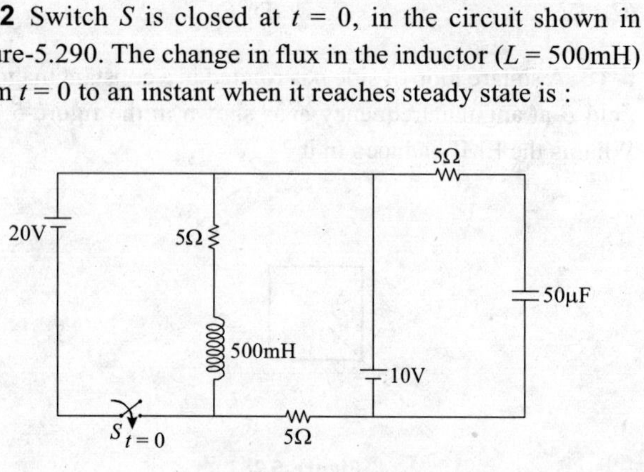

Figure 5.290

(A) 2Wb (B) 1.5Wb

(C) 0Wb (D) None of the above

5-23 An electric current i_1 can flow in either direction through loop-1 and induced current i_2 in loop-2. Positive i_1 is when current is from 'a' to 'b' in loop-1 and positive i_2 is when the current is from 'c' to 'd' in loop-2. In an experiment, the graph of induced current i_2 against time 't' is shown in figure-5.291. Which one of the following graphs options for current i_1 could have caused i_2 to behave as shown :

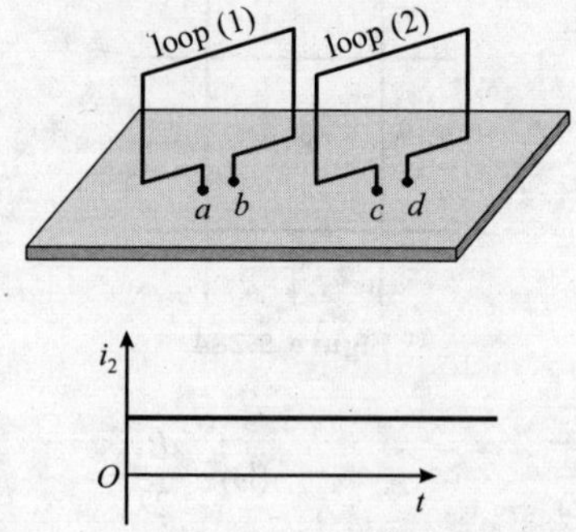

Figure 5.291

(A) 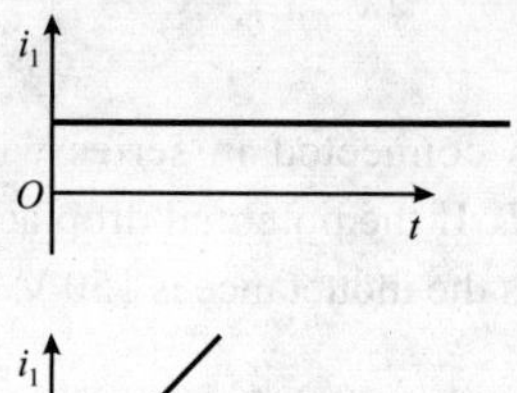

(B) 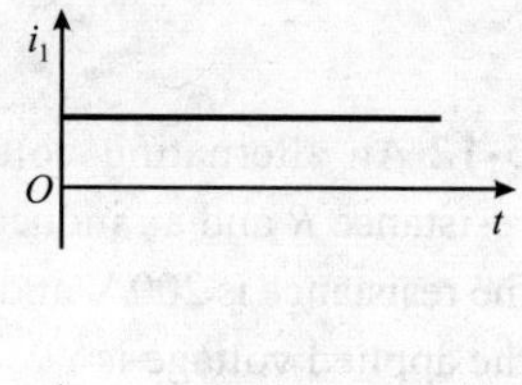

(C) 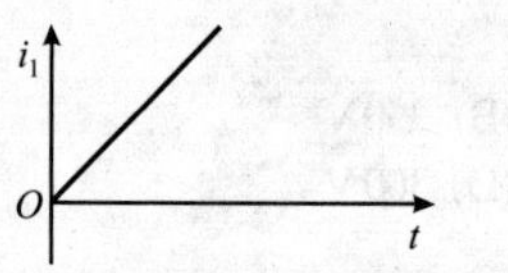

(D) 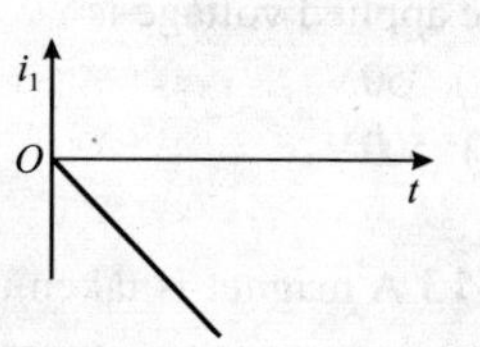

5-24 A branch of circuit is shown in the figure-5.292 which is part of a complete circuit. What is the potential difference $V_B - V_A$ when the current I is 5A and is decreasing at a rate of 10^3 A/s?

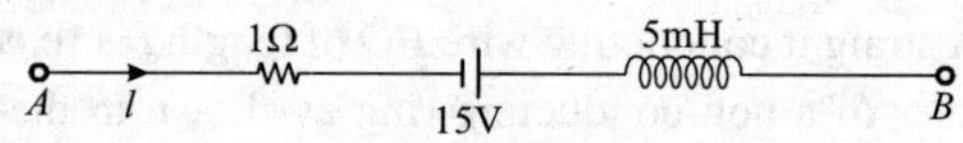

Figure 5.292

(A) 5V (B) 10V

(C) 15V (D) 20V

5-25 An LR circuit is connected to a battery at time t = 0. The energy stored in the inductor reaches half its maximum value at time :

(A) $\frac{R}{L}\ln\left[\frac{\sqrt{2}}{\sqrt{2}-1}\right]$ (B) $\frac{R}{L}\ln\left[\frac{\sqrt{2}-1}{\sqrt{2}}\right]$

(C) $\frac{R}{L}\ln\left(\frac{\sqrt{2}}{\sqrt{2}-1}\right)$ (D) $\frac{R}{L}\ln\left[\frac{\sqrt{2}-1}{\sqrt{2}}\right]$

5-26 A 120 V AC source is connected across a pure inductor of inductance 0.70 H. If the frequency of the source is 60 Hz, the current passing through the inductor is :

(A) 4.55 A (B) 0.355 A

(C) 0.455 A (D) 3.55 A

5-27 Two coils X and Y are placed in a circuit such that a current change of 3A in coil X causes the change in magnetic flux by 1.2Wb in coil Y. The value of mutual inductance of the coil is :

(A) 0.2H (B) 0.4H
(C) 0.6H (D) 3.6H

5-28 Charge q is distributed uniformly over a rod of length l. The rod is placed parallel to a long wire carrying a current i. The separation between the rod and the wire is a. The force needed to move the rod along its length with a uniform velocity v is :

(A) $\frac{\mu_0 iqv}{2\pi a}$ (B) $\frac{\mu_0 iqv}{4\pi a}$

(C) $\frac{\mu_0 iqvl}{2\pi a}$ (D) $\frac{\mu_0 iqvl}{4\pi a}$

5-29 A triangular wire frame having each side equal to 2m is placed in a region of time varying magnetic field having $dB/dt = \sqrt{3}$ T/s. The magnetic field is perpendicular to the plane of the triangle as shown in figure-5.293. The base of the triangle AB has a resistance 1Ω while the other two sides have resistance 2Ω each. The magnitude of potential difference between the points A and B will be :

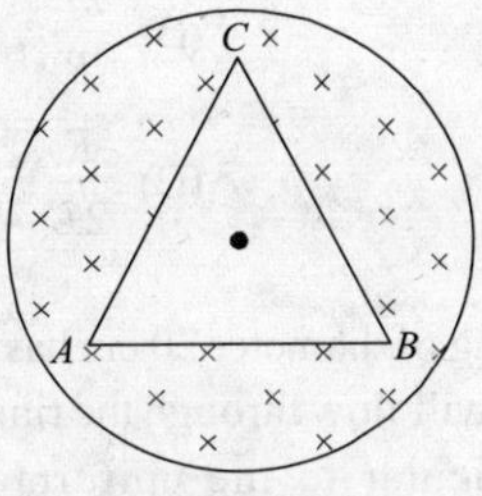

Figure 5.293

(A) 0.4 V (B) 0.6 V
(C) 1.2 V (D) None

5-30 In the circuit shown below, what will be the readings of the voltmeter V_3 and ammeter A :

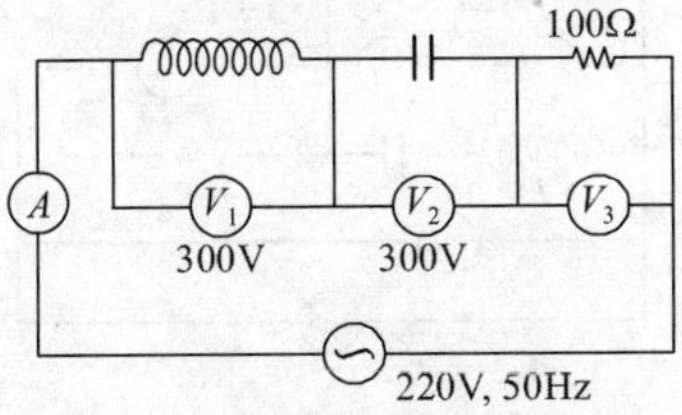

Figure 5.294

(A) 800 V, 2A (B) 300 V, 2A
(C) 220 V, 2.2 A (D) 100 V, 2A

5-31 A galvanometer is connected to the secondary coil. The galvanometer shows an instantaneous maximum deflection of 7 divisions when current is started in the primary coil of the solenoid. Now if the primary coil is rotated through 180°, then the new instantaneous maximum deflection will be :

(A) 7 units (B) 14 units
(C) 0 units (D) 21 units

5-32 A conducting ring of radius $2R$ rolls on a smooth horizontal conducting surface as shown in figure-5.295. A uniform horizontal magnetic field B is perpendicular to the plane of the ring. The potential of A with respect to O is :

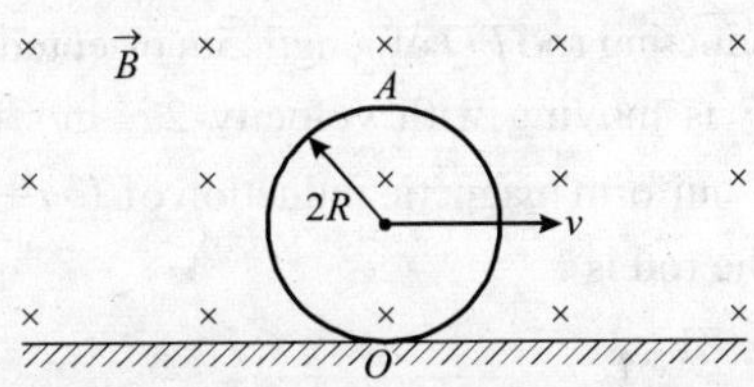

Figure 5.295

(A) $2\,BvR$ (B) $\frac{1}{2}BvR$
(C) $8\,BvR$ (D) $4\,BvR$

5-33 In the circuit shown in the figure-5.296, the AC source gives a voltage $V = 20\cos(2000t)$. Neglecting source resistance, the voltmeter and ammeter reading will be :

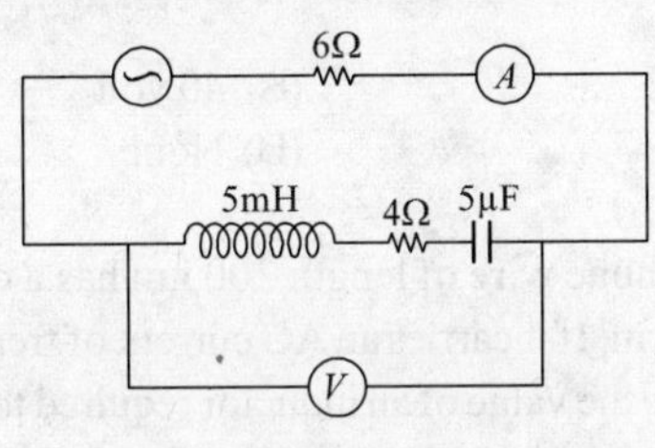

Figure 5.296

(A) 0V, 0.47A (B) 1.68V, 0.47A
(C) 0V, 1.4 A (D) 5.6V, 1.4 A

5-34 A coil of area 100cm² having 50 turns is perpendicular to a magnetic field of intensity 0.02T. The resistance of the coil is 2Ω. If it is removed from magnetic field in 1s the charge flown through the coil is :

(A) 5C (B) 0.5 C
(C) 0.05 C (D) 0.005 C

5-35 When a choke coil carrying a steady current is short circuited, the current in it decreases to β (< 1) times its initial value in a time T. The time constant of the choke coil is :

(A) $\frac{T}{\beta}$ (B) $\frac{T}{\ln\left(\frac{1}{\beta}\right)}$

(C) $\frac{T}{\ln \beta}$ (D) $T \ln \beta$

5-36 A force of 10N is required to move a conducting loop through a non-uniform magnetic field at 2m/s. The rate of production of internal energy in loop is :

(A) 25W (B) 5W
(C) 10W (D) 20W

5-37 A conducting rod PQ of length 5m oriented as shown in figure-5.297 is moving with velocity $2\hat{i}$ m/s without any rotation in a uniform magnetic induction of $(3\hat{j}+4\hat{k})$ T. EMF induced in the rod is :

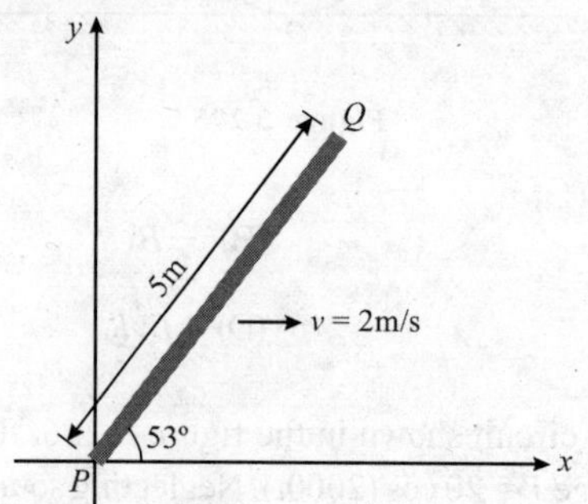

Figure 5.297

(A) 32 volt (B) 40 volt
(C) 50 volt (D) None

5-38 A telephone wire of length 200 km has a capacitance of 0.014 μF per km. If it carries an AC current of frequency 5 kHz, what should be the value of an inductor required to be connected in series so that the impedance of the circuit is minimum :

(A) 0.35 mH (B) 35 mH
(C) 3.5 mH (D) Zero

5-39 In the steady state condition, the rate of heat produced in a choke coil is P. The time constant of the choke coil it τ. If now the choke coil is short circuited, then the total heat dissipated in the coil is :

(A) $P\tau$ (B) $\frac{1}{2}P\tau$

(C) $\frac{P\tau}{\ln 2}$ (D) $P\tau \ln 2$

5-40 An aeroplane is flying horizontally with a velocity of 360 km/hr. The distance between the tips of wings is 50 m. If the vertical component of earth's magnetic field is 4×10^{-4} T, induced EMF across the wings is :

(A) Zero (B) 2 μV
(C) 2mV (D) 2 V

5-41 In a certain circuit current changes with time according to $i = 2\sqrt{t}$ RMS value of current between $t = 2$ s to $t = 4$ s will be :

(A) $3A$ (B) $3\sqrt{3}A$
(C) $2\sqrt{3}A$ (D) $(2-\sqrt{2})A$

5-42 The figure-5.298 shows a specific RL circuit, the time constant for this circuit is :

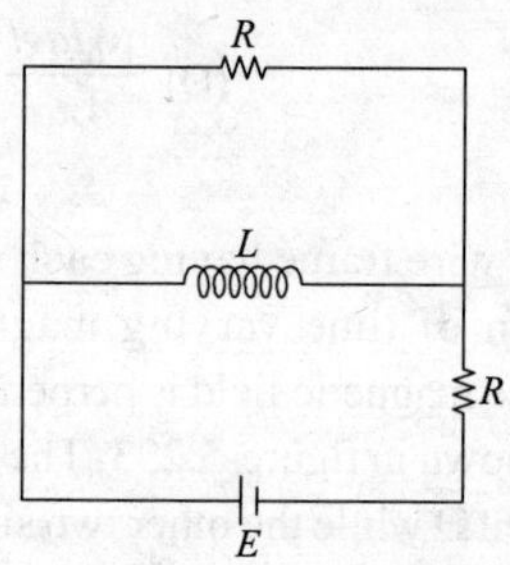

Figure 5.298

(A) $\frac{L}{2R}$ (B) $\frac{2L}{R}$

(C) $\frac{2R}{L}$ (D) $\frac{R}{2L}$

5-43 A circular ring of diameter 20 cm has a resistance 0.01 Ω. How much charge will flow through the ring if it is rotated from position perpendicular to the uniform magnetic field of $B = 2$ T to a position parallel to field ?

(A) 4C (B) 6.28C
(C) 3.14C (D) 25.12C

5-44 In the AC circuit shown in figure-5.299 the voltmeter whose reading will be zero at resonance is :

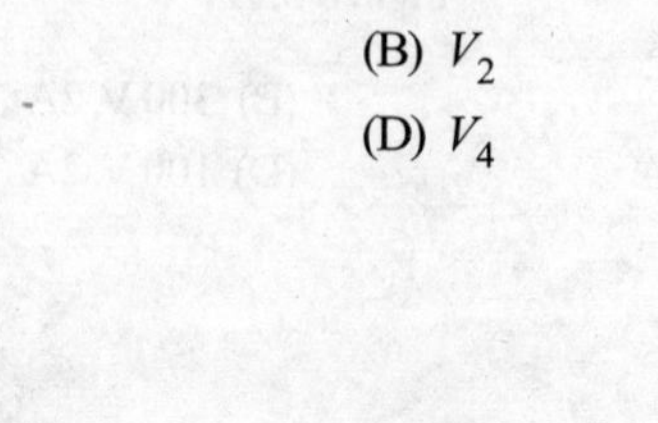

Figure 5.299

(A) V_1 (B) V_2
(C) V_3 (D) V_4

5-45 A square loop of side a and a straight long wire are placed in the same plane as shown in figure-5.300. The loop has a resistance R and inductance L. The frame is turned through 180° about the axis OO'. What is the charge that flows through the loop in this process ?

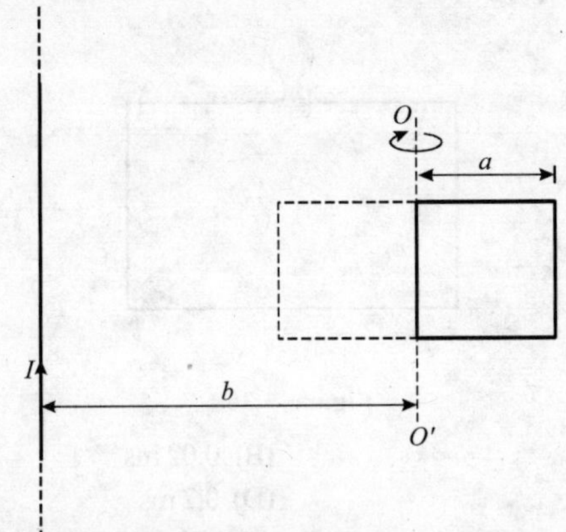

Figure 5.300

(A) $\frac{\mu_0 Ia}{2\pi R}\ln\left(\frac{2a+b}{b}\right)$ (B) $\frac{\mu_0 Ia}{2\pi R}\ln\left(\frac{b}{b^2-a^2}\right)$

(C) $\frac{\mu_0 Ia}{2\pi R}\ln\left(\frac{a+2b}{b}\right)$ (D) None of these

5-46 In the adjoining figure-5.301 the impedance of the circuit will be :

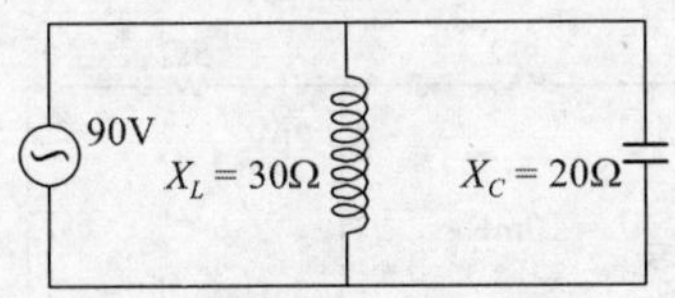

Figure 5.301

(A) 120 Ω (B) 50 Ω
(C) 60 Ω (D) 90 Ω

5-47 In figure-5.302, the switch is in the position 1 for a long time, then switch is shifted to position 2 at $t = 0$. At this instant the value of i_1 and i_2 are :

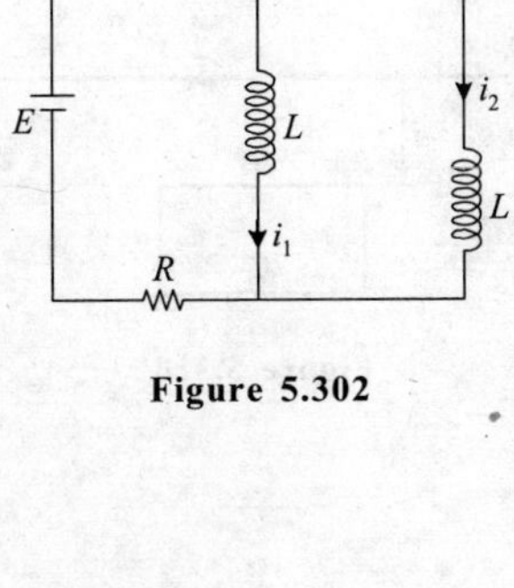

Figure 5.302

(A) $\frac{E}{R}, 0$ (B) $\frac{E}{R}, \frac{-E}{R}$

(C) $\frac{E}{2R}, \frac{-E}{2R}$ (D) None of these

5-48 When an AC source of EMF $e = E_0 \sin(100t)$ is connected across a circuit, the phase difference between the EMF e and the current i in the circuit is observed to be $\pi/4$, as shown in the figure-5.303. If the circuit consists possibly only of RC or LC in series, find the relationship between the two elements :

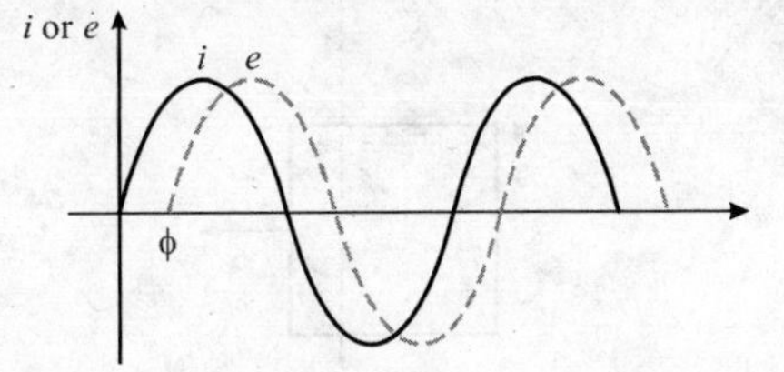

Figure 5.303

(A) $R = 1\ \text{k}\Omega, C = 10\ \mu\text{F}$ (B) $R = 1\ \text{k}\Omega, C = 1\ \mu\text{F}$
(C) $R = 1\ \text{k}\Omega, C = 10\ \text{H}$ (D) $R = 1\ \text{k}\Omega, L = 1\ \text{H}$

5-49 In the part of a circuit branch shown in figure-5.304 the potential difference V_{ab} at $t = 1$s is :

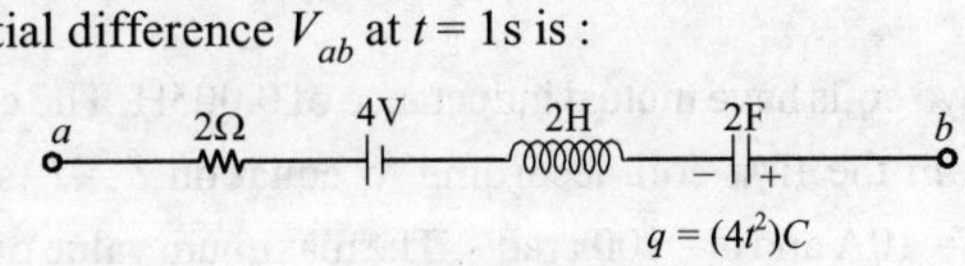

Figure 5.304

(A) 30 V (B) –30 V
(C) 20 V (D) –20 V

5-50 A circular coil of mean radius of 7 cm and having 4000 turns is rotated at the rate of 1800 revolutions per minute in the earth's magnetic field ($B = 0.5$ gauss), the maximum EMF induced in coil will be :
(A) 1.158 V (B) 0.58 V
(C) 0.29 V (D) 5.8 V

5-51 Initially in the circuit shown in figure-5.305, the switch is in position-1 for a long time and then shifted to position-2 at $t = 0$ as shown in figure-5.305. Just after closing the switch, the magnitude of current through the capacitor is :

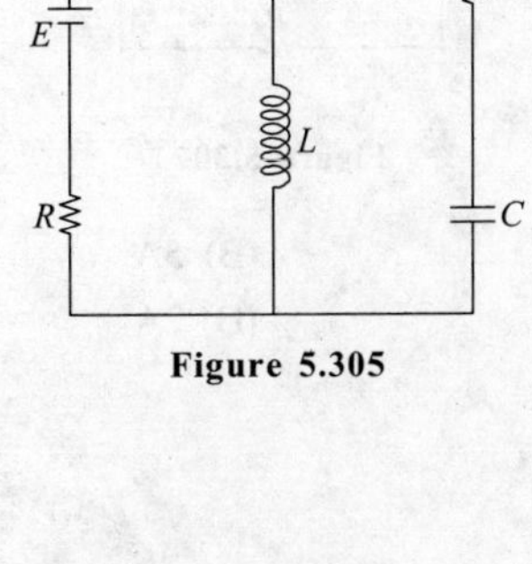

Figure 5.305

(A) Zero (B) $\frac{E}{2R}$

(C) $\frac{E}{R}$ (D) None of these

5-52 A square loop of area 2.5×10^{-3} m^2 and having 100 turns with a total resistance of 100 Ω is moved out of a uniform magnetic field of 0.40 T in 1 sec with a constant speed. Then work done, in pulling the loop is :

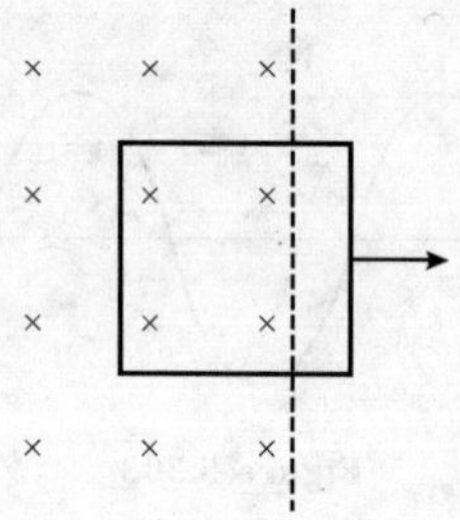

Figure 5.306

(A) zero (B) 1 mJ

(C) 1 μJ (D) 0.1 mJ

5-53 Two coils have mutual inductance of 0.005H. The current changes in the first coil according to equation $I = I_0 \sin \omega t$, where $I_0 = 10$A and $\omega = 100\pi$ rad/s. The maximum value of EMF induced in the second coil is :

(A) 2πV (B) 5πV

(C) πV (D) 4πV

5-54 Find the current passing through battery immediately after the key K is closed. It is given that initially all the capacitors are uncharged. Take $R = 6\Omega$ and $C = 4\mu$F.

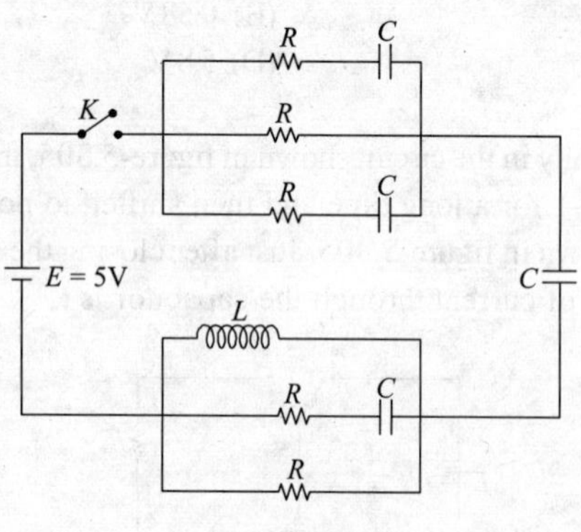

Figure 5.307

(A) 1A (B) 5A

(C) 3A (D) 2A

5-55 A square wire loop of 10.0cm side lies at right angles to a uniform magnetic field of 20T. A 10V light bulb is in a series with the loop as shown in the figure-308. The magnetic field is decreasing steadily to zero over a time interval Δt. The bulb will shine with full and sustained brightness if Δt is equal to :

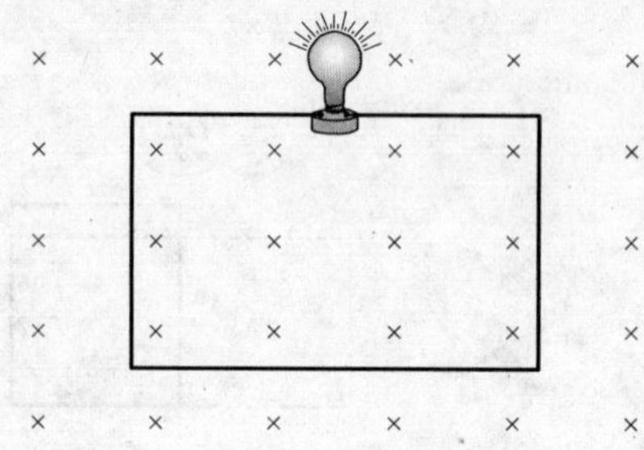

Figure 5.308

(A) 20 ms (B) 0.02 ms

(C) 2 ms (D) 0.2 ms

5-56 A rectangular loop of sides a and b is placed in x-y plane. A uniform but time varying magnetic field of strength $\vec{B} = 20t\hat{i} + 10t^2\hat{j} + 50\hat{k}$ is present in the region. The magnitude of induced EMF in the loop at time t is :

(A) $20 + 20t$ (B) 20

(C) $20t$ (D) Zero

5-57 In the circuit shown, the key K is closed at $t = 0$, the current through the key at the instant $t = 10^{-3} \ln 2$, is :

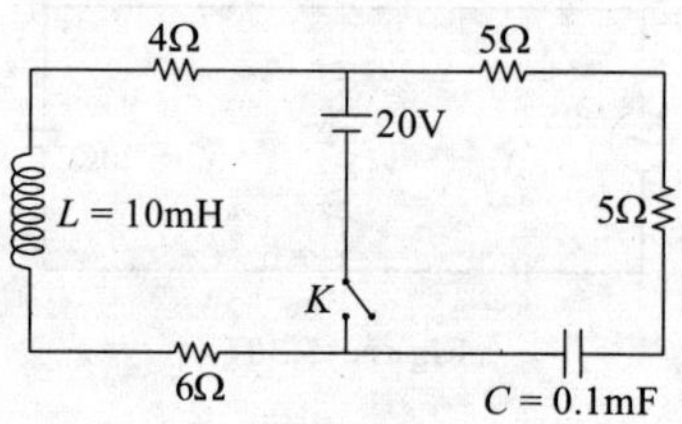

Figure 5.309

(A) 2A (B) 8A

(C) 4A (D) Zero

5-58 A long straight wire is parallel to one edge of a rectangular loop as shown in figure-5.310. If the current in the long wire varies with time as $I = I_0 e^{-t/\tau}$, what will be the induced emf in the loop at $t = \tau$?

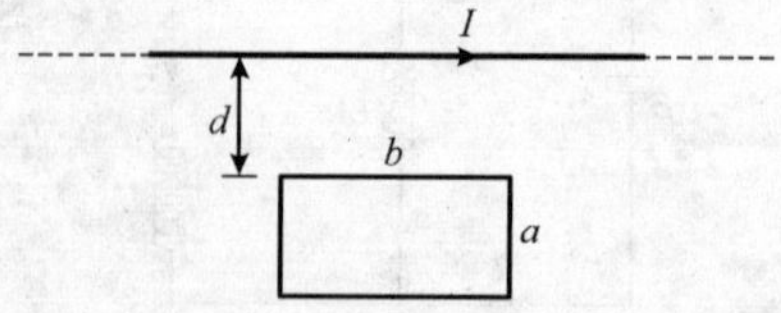

Figure 5.310

(A) $\frac{\mu_0 bI}{\pi\tau}\ln\left(\frac{d+a}{d}\right)$ (B) $\frac{\mu_0 bI}{2\pi\tau}\ln\left(\frac{d+a}{d}\right)$

(C) $\frac{2\mu_0 bI}{\pi\tau}\ln\left(\frac{d+a}{d}\right)$ (D) $\frac{\mu_0 bI}{\pi\tau}\ln\left(\frac{d}{d+a}\right)$

5-59 A constant voltage is applied to a series *RL* circuit by closing the switch. The voltage across inductor of inductance 2 H is 20 V at $t = 0$ and drops to 5 V at 20 ms. The value of *R* is :

(A) $100 \ln 2\Omega$ (B) $100(1 - \ln 2)\Omega$

(C) $100 \ln 4\Omega$ (D) $100(1 - \ln 4)$

5-60 A loop shown in the figure-5.311 is immersed in the varying magnetic field $B = B_0 t$, directed into the page. If the total resistance of the loop is *R*, then the direction and magnitude of induced current in the inner circle is :

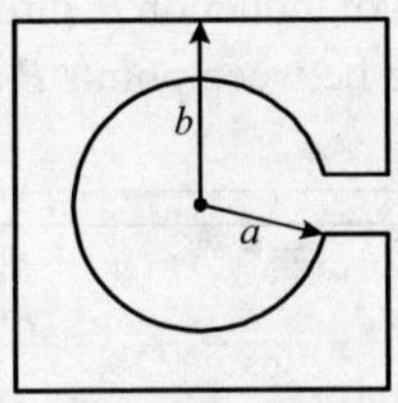

Figure 5.311

(A) Clockwise $\frac{B_0(\pi a^2 - b^2)}{R}$

(B) Anticlockwise $\frac{B_0\pi(a^2 + b^2)}{R}$

(C) Clockwise $\frac{B_0(\pi a^2 + 4b^2)}{R}$

(D) Clockwise $\frac{B_0(4b^2 - \pi a^2)}{R}$

* * * * *

5-61 Figure-5.312 shows an isosceles triangular wire frame with apex angle equal to $\pi/2$. The frame starts entering into the region of uniform magnetic field *B* with constant velocity *v* at $t = 0$. The longest side of the frame is perpendicular to the direction of velocity. If *i* is the instantaneous current through the frame then choose the alternative showing the correct variation of *i* with time :

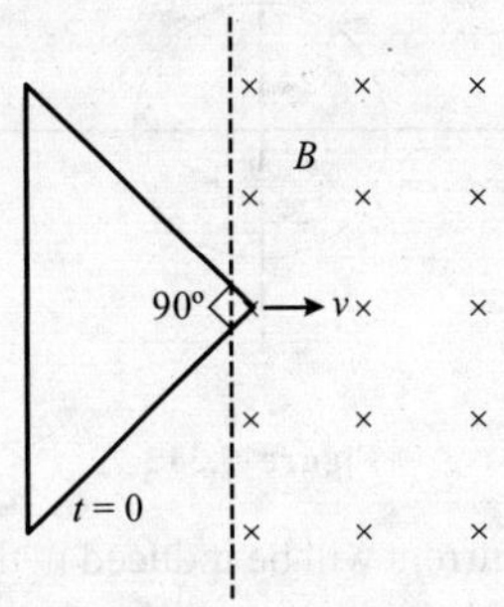

Figure 5.312

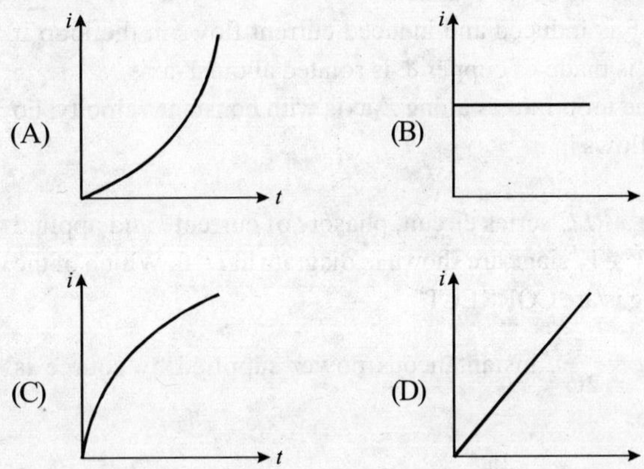

Advance MCQs with One or More Options Correct

5-1 A conducting loop is kept with its center lies at the origin of a coordinate system. A magnetic field has magnetic induction B pointing along Z-axis as shown in the figure-5.313

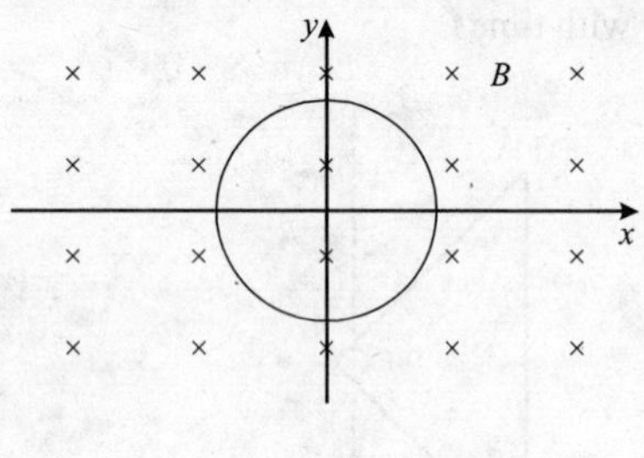

Figure 5.313

(A) No EMF and current will be induced in the loop if it rotates about Z-axis

(B) EMF is induced but no current flows if the loop is a fiber when it rotates about *Y*-axis.

(C) EMF is induced and induced current flows in the loop if the loop is made of copper & is rotated about *Y*-axis.

(D) If the loop moves along *Z*-axis with constant velocity, no current flows in it.

5-2 For a *RLC* series circuit, phasors of current *i* and applied voltage $V = V_0 \sin\omega t$ are shown in diagram at $t = 0$. Which of the following is/are CORRECT?

(A) At $t = \frac{\pi}{2\omega}$, instantaneous power supplied by source is negative.

(B) From $0 < t < \frac{2\pi}{3\omega}$, average power supplied by source is positive.

(C) At $t = \frac{5\pi}{6\omega}$, instantaneous power supplied by source is negative.

(D) If ω is increased slightly, angle between the two phasors decreases.

5-3 Two different coils have self inductances $L_1 = 8$ mH, $L_2 = 2$ mH. The current in one coil is increased at a constant rate. The current in the second coil is also increased at the same constant rate. At a certain instant of time, the power given to the two coils is the same. At that time the current, the induced voltage and the energy stored in the first coil are i_1, V_1 and W_1 respectively. Corresponding values for the second coil at the same instant are i_2, V_2 and W_2 respectively. Then :

(A) $i_1/i_2 = 1/4$
(B) $i_1/i_2 = 4$
(C) $W_2/W_1 = 4$
(D) $V_2/V_1 = 1/4$

5-4 Which of the following factor/factors is/are responsible for deciding the mutual inductance of two coils?

(A) The number of turns of each coil
(B) The shape of each coil
(C) Current through each coil
(D) Separation between the coils.

5-5 Which of the following statements is/are correct ?

(A) Self-induced emf may tend to decrease the current
(B) Self-induced emf may tend to increase the current
(C) Self-induced emf tries to keep the current constant
(D) None of these

5-6 The loop shown in figure-5.314 moves with a velocity *v* in a uniform magnetic field of induction *B*, directed into the paper. The potential difference between points *P* and *Q* is *e*. Then

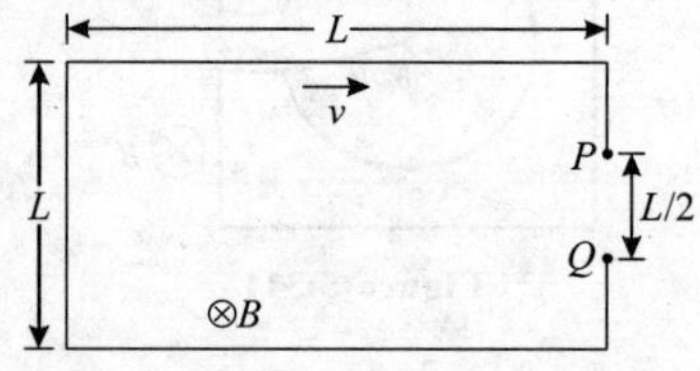

Figure 5.314

(A) $e = \frac{1}{2}BLv$
(B) $e = BLv$
(C) *P* is positive with respect to *Q*
(D) *Q* is positive with respect to *P*

5-7 Initially key was placed at position-1 till the capacitor got fully charged. Key is placed on position-2 at $t = 0$. The time when the energy in both capacitor and inductor will be same:

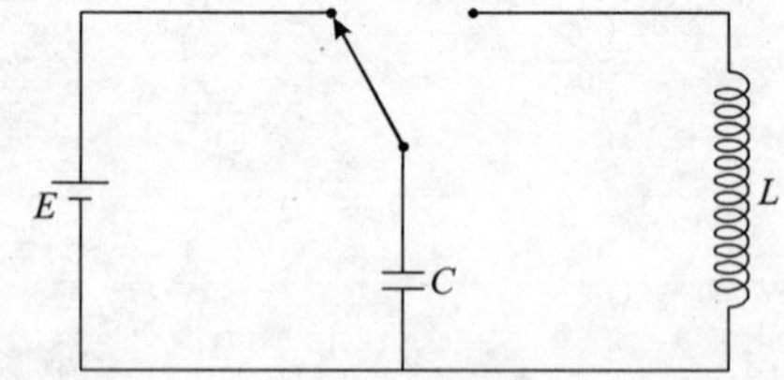

Figure 5.315

(A) $\frac{\pi\sqrt{LC}}{4}$
(B) $\frac{\pi\sqrt{LC}}{2}$
(C) $\frac{5\pi\sqrt{LC}}{4}$
(D) $\frac{5\pi\sqrt{LC}}{2}$

5-8 An infinitely long wire is placed near a square loop as shown in figure-5.316. Choose the correct options :

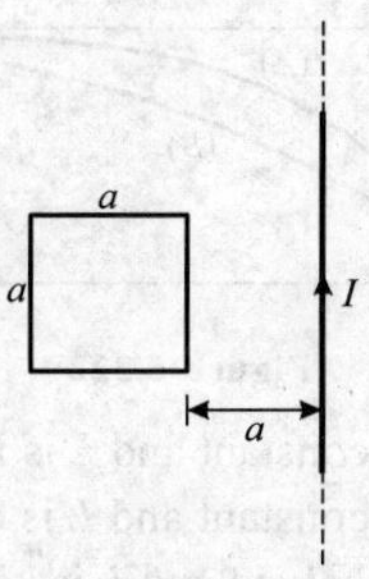

Figure 5.316

(A) The mutual inductance between the two is $\frac{\mu_0 a}{2\pi}\ln(2)$

(B) The mutual inductance between the two is $\frac{\mu_0 a^2}{2\pi}\ln(2)$

(C) If a constant current is passed in the straight wire in upward direction and loop is brought close to the wire then induced current in the loop is clockwise

(D) In the above condition, induced current in the loop is anticlockwise

5-9 A circuit is set up by connecting $L = 100$ mH, $C = 5\ \mu$F and $R = 100\ \Omega$ in series. An alternating emf of $150\sqrt{2}$ V, $\frac{500}{\pi}$ Hz is applied across this series combination. Which of the following is correct :

(A) the impedance of the circuit is 141.4 Ω

(B) the average power dissipated across resistance 225 W

(C) the average power dissipated across inductor is zero

(D) the average power dissipated across capacitor is zero

5-10 Choose the CORRECT statements :

(A) SI unit of magnetic flux is henry-ampere

(B) SI unit of coefficient of self-inductance is J/A

(C) SI unit of coefficient of self inductance is $\frac{\text{volt-second}}{\text{ampere}}$

(D) SI unit of magnetic induction is weber

5-11 In the figure shown a conducting wire PQ of length $l = 1$ m, is moved in a uniform magnetic field $B = 4T$ with constant velocity $v = 2$ m/s towards right. Given: $R = 2\ \Omega$, $C = 1$ F and $L = 4$ H

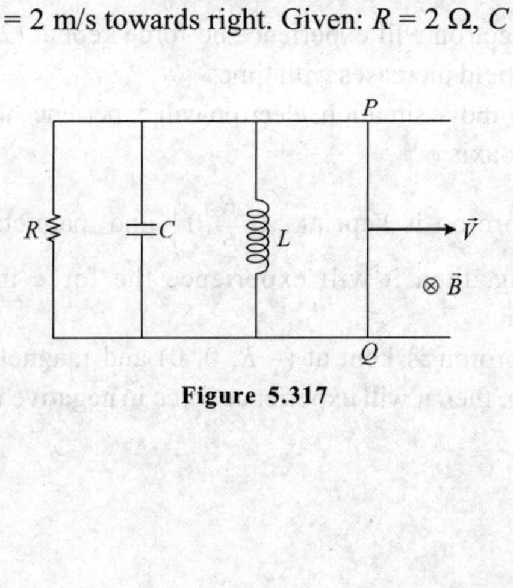

Figure 5.317

Currents through resistance, capacitor and inductor at any time t are I_1, I_2 and I_3 respectively, Current through wire PQ is I. Find the force required to move the wire with the given constant velocity of 2 m/s at $t = 2$ s:

(A) 8 N (B) 16 N

(C) 24 N (D) 32 N

5-12 In the circuit shown in figure-5.318, circuit is closed at time $t = 0$. At time $t = \ln(2)$ second :

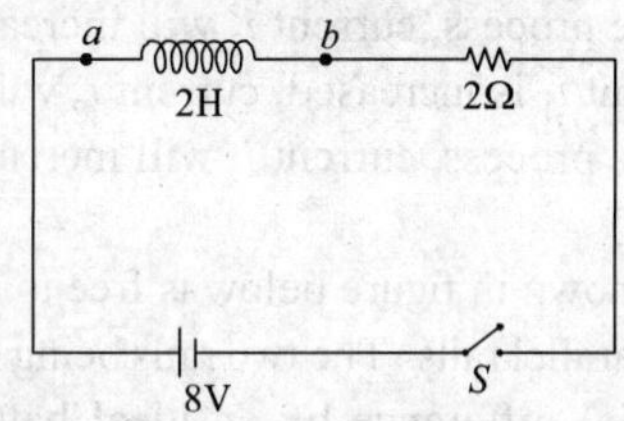

Figure 5.318

(A) Rate of energy supplied by the battery is 16 J/s

(B) Rate of heat dissipated across resistance is 8 J/s

(C) Rate of heat dissipated across resistance is 16 J/s

(D) $V_a - V_b = 4$ V

5-13 Choose the CORRECT statement(s) in the following :

(A) Diamagnetism exist in all materials

(B) Diamagnetism is the result of partial alignment of permanent magnetic moment in the material

(C) The magnetic field due to induced magnetic moment is opposite to the applied field

(D) The magnetising field intensity is always zero in free space

5-14 In the circuit shown in figure-5.319, if both the bulbs B_1 and B_2 are identical :

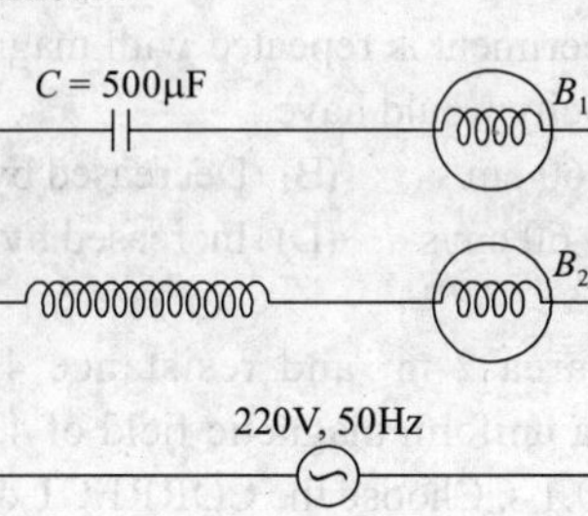

Figure 5.319

(A) their brightness will be the same

(B) B_2 will be brighter than B_1

(C) as frequency of supply voltage is increased the brightness of bulb B_1 will increase and that of B_2 will decrease

(D) only B_2 will glow because the capacitor has infinite impedance

5-15 Two circular coils are placed adjacent to each other. The coils are kept in same plane and currents through them i_1 and i_2 are in same directions. Choose the correct options :

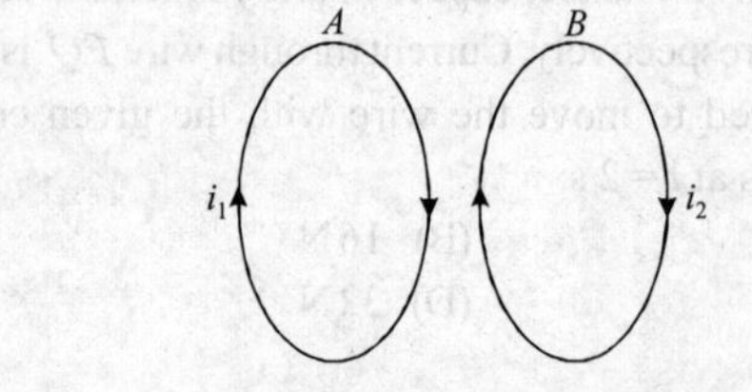

Figure 5.320

(A) When A is brought near B, current i_2 will increase
(B) In the above process, current i_2 will increase
(C) When current i_1 is increased, current i_2 will decrease
(D) In the above process, current i_2 will increase

5-16 The rod shown in figure below is free to slide along the two horizontal parallel rails. The two rails being maintained at a constant potential difference by an ideal battery. The only resistance is in the circuit is that of rod itself. A student performs an experiment by keeping this setup in a uniform magnetic field B. In first case when rod is kept initially at rest and released, the rod is found to move with a uniform velocity after a sufficiently long time. In second case when a force of F_0 is applied along with first case, so as to retard the rod, its terminal velocity changes and finally decreases by 20 cm/sec.

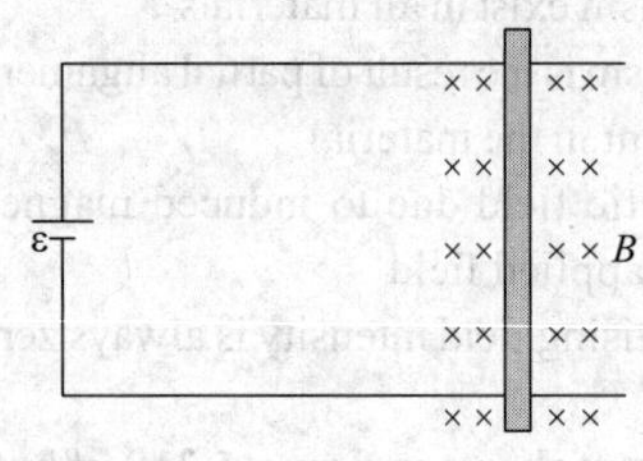

Figure 5.321

Now if above experiment is repeated with magnetic field $B/3$ then terminal velocity would have :

(A) Increased by 60 cm/s (B) Decreased by 180 cm/s
(C) Decreased by 60 cm/s (D) Increased by 20/9 cm/s

5-17 A coil of area 2 m^2 and resistance 4 Ω is placed perpendicular to a uniform magnetic field of 4T. The loop is rotated by 90° in 0.1 s. Choose the CORRECT options:

(A) Average induced emf in the coil is 8 V
(B) Average induced current in the circuit is 20 A
(C) 2 C charge will flow in the coil in above period
(D) Heat produced in the coil in the above period can't be determined from the given data

5-18 A circuit consisting of a constant EMF E, a self-inductance L and a resistance R in series is closed at time $t = 0$. The relation between the current i in the circuit and the time t is as shown by the curve A in the figure-5.321. When one or more of parameters E, R and L are changed, the curve B is obtained. Then it is possible that :

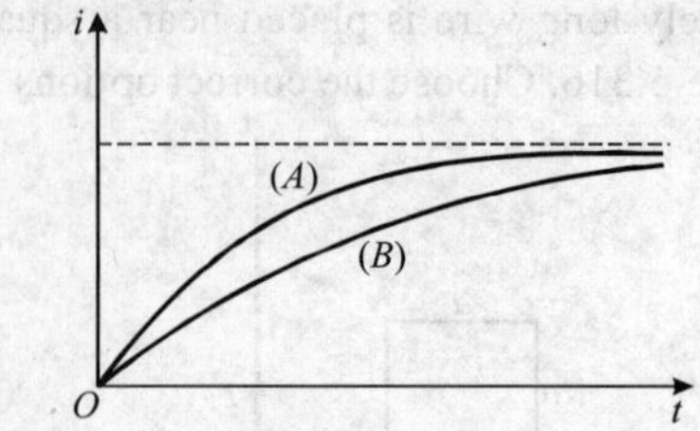

Figure 5.322

(A) E and R are kept constant and L is increased
(B) E and R are kept constant and L is decreased
(C) E and R are both halved and L is kept constant
(D) E and L are kept constant and R is decreased

5-19 In LC oscillations of a capacitor with an initial charge q_0 is connected in parallel :

(A) Time period of oscillations is $\dfrac{2\pi}{\sqrt{LC}}$
(B) Maximum current in circuit is $\dfrac{q_0}{\sqrt{LC}}$
(C) Maximum rate of change of current in circuit is $\dfrac{q_0}{2C}$
(D) Maximum potential difference across the inductor is $\dfrac{q_0}{2C}$

5-20 A solenoid is connected to a source of constant EMF for a long time. A soft iron piece is inserted into it. Then :

(A) Self-inductance of the solenoid gets increased
(B) Flux linked with the solenoid increases, hence steady state current gets decreased
(C) Energy stored in the solenoid gets increased
(D) Magnetic moment of the solenoid gets increased

5-21 Magnetic field in a cylindrical region of radius R in inward direction is as shown in figure-5.323 :

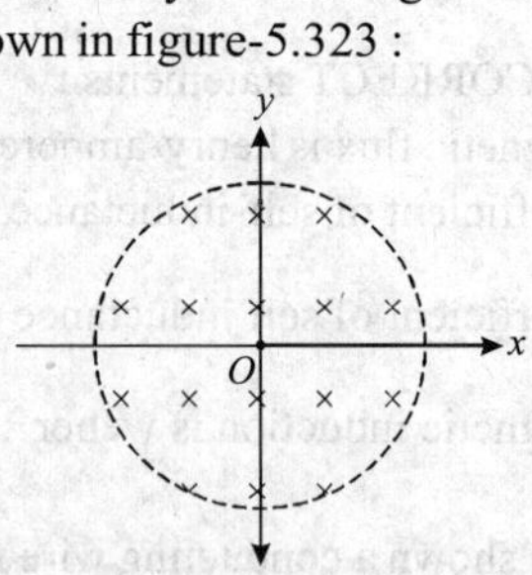

Figure 5.323

(A) An electron will experience no force kept at $(2P, 0, 0)$ if magnetic field increases with time
(B) In the above situation, electron will experience the force in negative y-axis
(C) If a proton is kept at $\left(0, \dfrac{R}{2}, 0\right)$ and magnetic field is decreasing, then it will experience the force in positive x-direction
(D) If a proton is kept at $(-R, 0, 0)$ and magnetic field is increasing, then it will experience force in negative y-axis

5-22 Two identical coaxial circular loops carry a current i in each flowing in the same direction. If the loops approach each other then :

(A) the current in each will tend to increase
(B) the current in each will tend to decrease
(C) both may repel each other
(D) both may attract each other

5-23 In the part of a circuit shown in Figure-5.323, q is in coulomb and t in second. At time $t = 1$s :

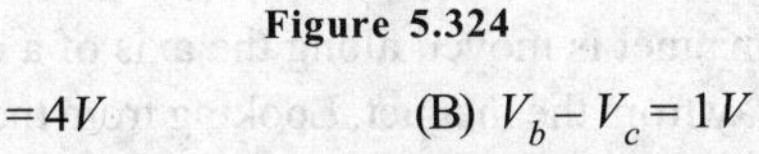

Figure 5.324

(A) $V_a - V_b = 4V$ (B) $V_b - V_c = 1V$
(C) $V_c - V_d = 16V$ (D) $V_a - V_d = 20V$

5-24 An equilateral triangular conducting frame is rotated with angular velocity ω in uniform magnetic field B as shown in figure-5.325. Side of triangle is l. Choose the correct options :

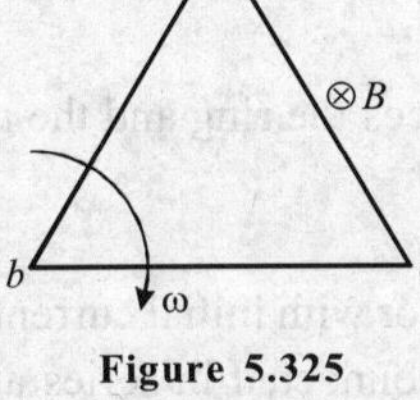

Figure 5.325

(A) $V_a - V_c = 0$ (B) $V_a - V_c = \frac{B\omega l^2}{2}$

(C) $V_a - V_b = \frac{B\omega l^2}{2}$ (D) $V_c - V_b = -\frac{B\omega l^2}{2}$

5-25 In the figure-5.326 shown 'R' is a fixed conducting ring of negligible resistance and radius 'a'. PQ is a uniform rod of resistance r. It is hinged at the centre of the ring and rotated about this point in clockwise direction with a uniform angular velocity ω. There is a uniform magnetic field of strength 'B' pointing inwards. 'r' is a fixed resistance connected between center of ring and its circumference which does not hinder the path of rotating rod :

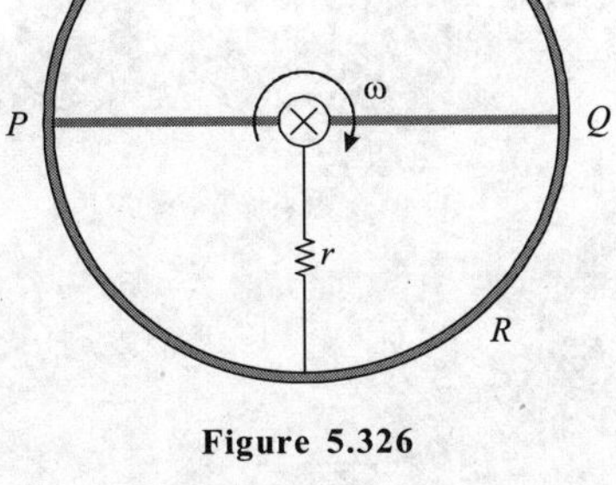

Figure 5.326

(A) Current through 'r' is zero

(B) Current through 'r' is $\frac{2B\omega a^2}{5r}$

(C) Direction of current in external 'r' is from centre to circumference

(D) Direction of current in external 'r' is from circumference to centre

5-26 A capacitor of capacity C is charged to a steady potential difference V and connected in series with an open key and a pure resistor R. At time $t = 0$, the key is closed. If I is the current at time t, a plot of ln I against t is shown as in the graph-1 of figure-5.327, one of the parameters i.e., V, R or C is changed, keeping the other two constant, and the graph-2 is recorded again. Then :

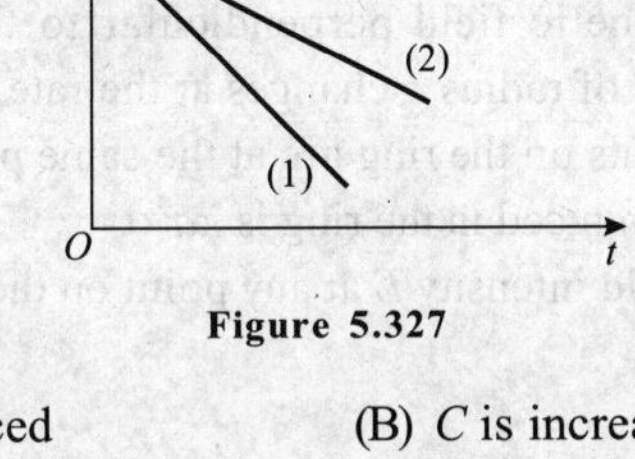

Figure 5.327

(A) C is reduced (B) C is increased
(C) R is reduced (D) R is increased

5-27 Plane rectangular loop is placed in a magnetic field. The EMF induced in the loop due to this field is e_i whose maximum value is e_{im}. The loop was pulled out of the magnetic field at a velocity which is not constant. Assume the magnetic induction in the region is $\vec{B}$ and it is uniform and constant. ε_i is plotted against time t as shown in the graph. Which of the following are/is correct statement(s) :

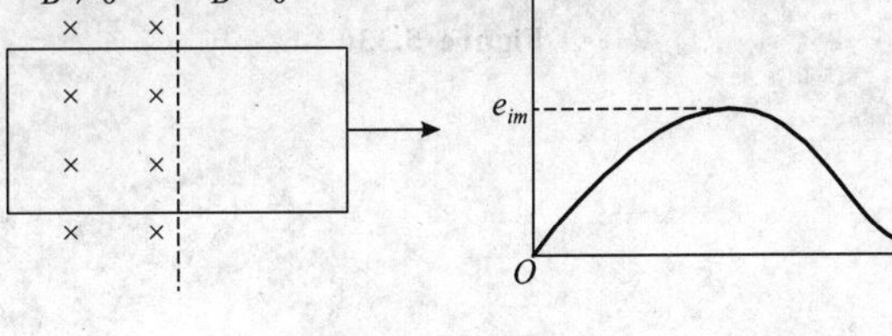

Figure 5.328

(A) e_{im} is independent of rate of removal of coil from the field.
(B) The total charge that passes through any point of the loop in the process of complete removal of the loop does not depend on velocity of removal.
(C) The total area under the curve (e_i vs t) is independent of rate of removal of coil from the field.
(D) The area under the curve is dependent on the rate of removal of the coil.

5-28 A conducting rod of length l is hinged at point O. It is free to rotate in a vertical plane. There exists a uniform magnetic field $\vec{B}$ in horizontal direction. The rod is released from the position shown. The potential difference between the two ends of the rod is proportional to :

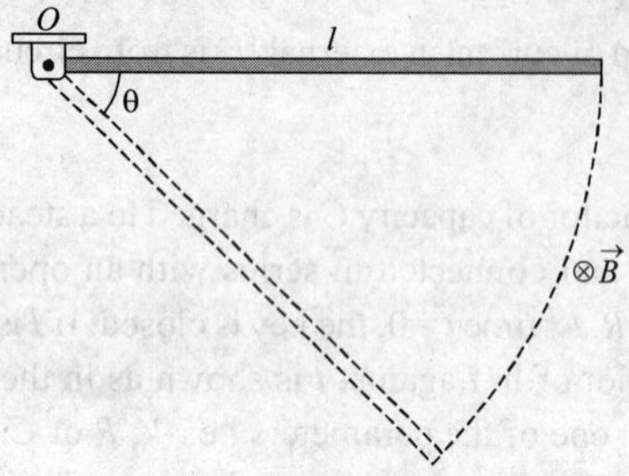

Figure 5.329

(A) $l^{3/2}$ (B) l^2
(C) $\sin\theta$ (D) $(\sin\theta)^{1/2}$

5-29 The magnetic field perpendicular to the plane of a conducting ring of radius a changes at the rate of α, then :
(A) All the points on the ring are at the same potential
(B) The EMF induced in the ring is $\pi a^2\alpha$
(C) Electric field intensity E at any point on the ring is zero
(D) $E = \frac{1}{2}a\alpha$

5-30 A bent rod PQR with $PQ = QR = l$ shown in figure-5.330 is rotating about its end P with a constant angular speed ω in a region of transverse magnetic field of induction B :

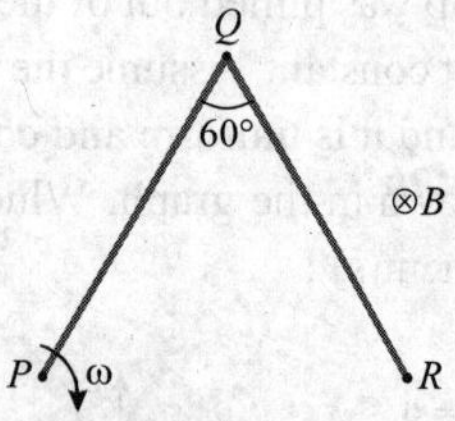

Figure 5.330

(A) EMF induced across the rod is $B\omega l^2$
(B) EMF induced across the rod is $B\omega l^2/2$
(C) Potential difference between points Q and R on the rod is $B\omega^2 l/2$
(D) Potential difference between points Q and R on the rod is zero

5-31 A semicircular conducting ring of radius R is placed in the xy-plane. A uniform magnetic field is set up along the x-axis. No EMF will be induced in the ring, if :
(A) It moves along the x-axis (B) It moves along the y-axis
(C) It moves along the z-axis (D) It remains stationary

5-32 A bar magnet is moved along the axis of a copper ring placed far away from the magnet. Looking from the side of the magnet, an anticlockwise current is found to be induced in the ring. Which of the following may be true ?
(A) the south pole faces the ring and the magnet moves towards it
(B) the north pole faces the ring and the magnet moves towards it
(C) the south pole faces the ring and the magnet moves away from it
(D) the north pole faces the ring and the magnet moves away from it

5-33 An ideal inductor with initial current zero, a resistor and an ideal battery are connected in series at time $t = 0$. At any time t, the battery supplies energy at the rate P_B, the resistor dissipates energy at the rate P_R and the inductor stores energy at the rate P_L then :
(A) $P_B = P_R + P_L$ for all times t
(B) $P_R < P_L$ for all times t
(C) $P_L < P_R$ in steady state
(D) $P_R > P_L$ only near the starting of the circuit

* * * * *

Unsolved Numerical Problems for Preparation of NSEP, INPhO & IPhO

For detailed preparation of INPhO and IPhO students can refer advance study material on www.physicsgalaxy.com

5-1 A coil of inductance L and resistance R is connected to a constant voltage source. How soon will the coil current attains η ($\eta < 1$) fraction of the steady state value ?

Ans. [$-\frac{L}{R}\ln(1-\eta)$]

5-2 A conducting circular loop of radius a and resistance per unit length R is moving with a constant velocity v_0, parallel to an infinite conducting wire carrying current i_0. a conducting rod of length $2a$ is approaching the centre of the loop with a constant velocity $v_0/2$ along the direction of the current. At the instant $t = 0$, the rod comes in contact with the loop at A and starts sliding on the loop with the constant velocity. Neglecting the resistance of the rod and any self inductance in the circuit, find the following when the rod slides on the loop.

(a) The current through the rod when it is at a distance of (a/2) from the point A of the loop.

(b) Force required to maintain the velocity of the rod at that instant.

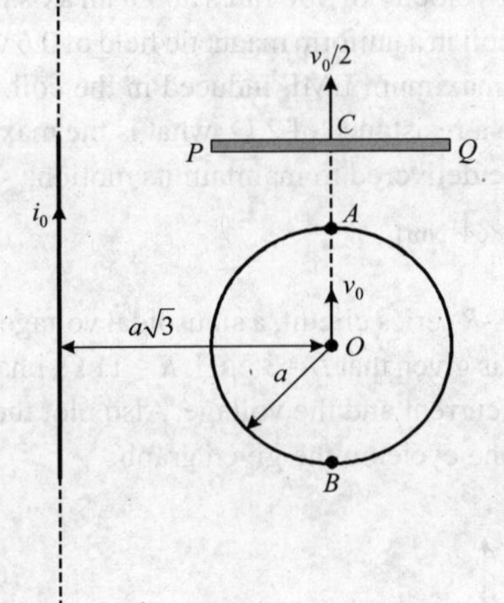

Figure 5.331

Ans. [(a) $i = \frac{9 v_0 \mu_0 i_0}{16 a R \pi^2}\ln(3)$; (b) $\frac{9\mu_0^2 i_0^2 v_0}{32 a R \pi^3}(\ln 3)^2$]

5-3 A metal disc of radius 25 cm rotates at a constant angular velocity 130 rad/s about its central axis. Find the potential difference between the centre and the rim of the disc if

(a) The external magnetic field is absent

(b) The external uniform magnetic field of induction 5 mT exist which is directed perpendicular to the disc.

Ans. [(a) 3 nV; (b) 20 mV]

5-4 Find out impedance of given circuit.

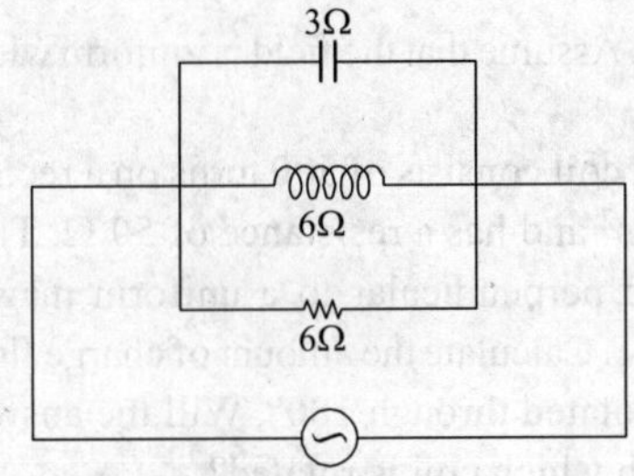

Figure 5.332

Ans. [$\frac{6}{\sqrt{2}}$ Ω]

5-5 U-frame $ABCD$ and a sliding rod PQ of resistance R, start moving with velocities v and $2v$ respectively, parallel to a long wire carrying current i_0. When the distance $AP = l$ at $t = 0$, determine the current through the inductor of inductance L just before connecting rod PQ loses contact with the U-frame.

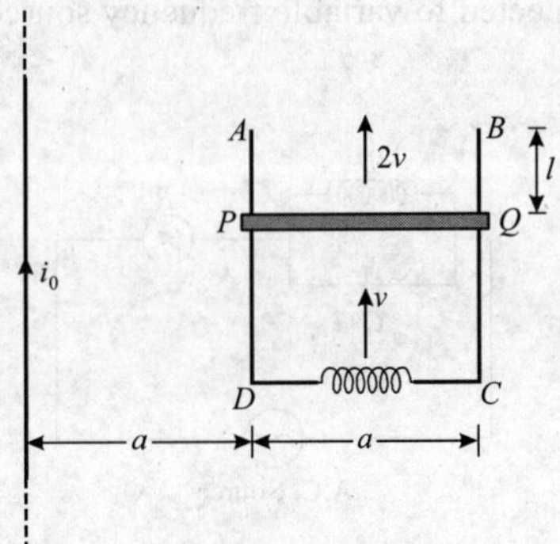

Figure 5.333

Ans. [$i = \left(\frac{e}{R}\right)[1 - e^{-Rl/Lv}]$, where $e = \frac{\mu_0 i_0 v}{2\pi}\ln(2)$]

5-6 Radio receiver receives a message at 300 m band, If the available inductance is 1 mH, then calculate required capacitance.

Ans. [25 pF]

5-7 An inductor-coil a capacitor and an AC source of rms voltage 24 V are connected in series. When the frequency of the source is varied a maximum rms current of 6.0 A is observed. If this inductor coil is connected to a battery of emf 12 V and internal resistance 4.0 Ω, what will be the steady current ?

Ans. [1.5 A]

5-8 A toroid is a long coil of wire, wound over a circular air core. Show that the coefficient of self induction L of the toroid of radius R containing N turns each of radius r on the air core is given as

$$L=\frac{\mu_0 N^2 r^2}{2R}$$

Where $R >> r$. Assume that the field is uniform within the toroid.

5-9 A closed coil consists of 500 turns on a rectangular frame of area 4.0 cm^2 and has a resistance of 50 Ω. The coil is kept with its plane perpendicular to a uniform magnetic field of induction 0.2 T. Calculate the amount of charge flowing through the coil if is rotated through 180°. Will the answer depend on the speed with which coil is rotated?

Ans. [16 × 10^{-4}C, No]

5-10 An electromagnetic wave of wavelength 300 metre can be transmitted by a transmission centre. A condenser of capacity 2.5 μF is available. Calculate the inductance of the required coil for a resonant circuit. Use $\pi^2 = 10$.

Ans. [1 × 10^{-8}H]

5-11 An LC circuit (inductance 0.01 henry and capacitance 1 μF) in connected to variable frequency source as shown in figure-5.334

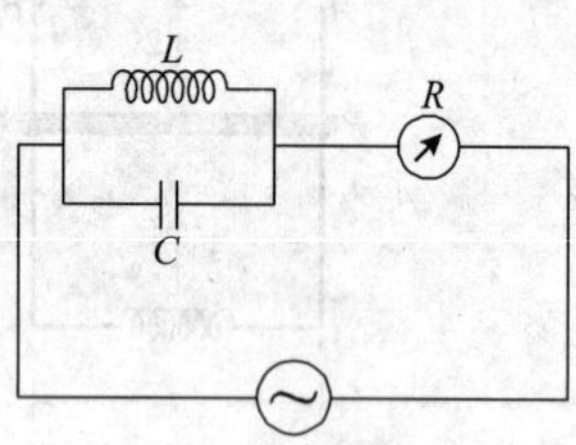

Figure 5.334

Draw a rough sketch of the current-variation as the frequency is changed from 1 kHz to 2 kHz.

Ans. [1.592 kHz]

5-12 A coil of 5 turns has dimension 9 cm × 7 cm. It rotates at the rate of 15 π rad/s in a uniform magnetic field whose flux density is 0.8 T. What maximum EMF is induced in the coil? What is the EMF 1/90 s after it reaches the value zero?

Ans. [0.594 V]

5-13 A circuit containing a 0.1 H inductor and a 500 μF capacitor in series is connected to a 230 V, 100/π Hz supply. The resistance of the circuit is negligible.

(a) Obtain the current amplitude and rms values.

(b) Obtain the rms value of potential drops across each element.

(c) What is the average power transferred to the inductor ?

(d) What is the average power transferred to the capacitor ?

(e) What is the total average power absorbed by the circuit ? ['*Average*' implies average over one cycle.]

Ans. [(a) 23 $\sqrt{2}$A, 23A (b) 460V, 230V (c) zero (d) zero (e) zero]

5-14 In a LC circuit parallel combination of inductance of 0.01 H and a capacitor of 1 μF is connected to a variable frequency alternating current source. Draw a rough sketch of the current variation as the frequency is changed from 1 kHz to 3 kHz.

Ans. [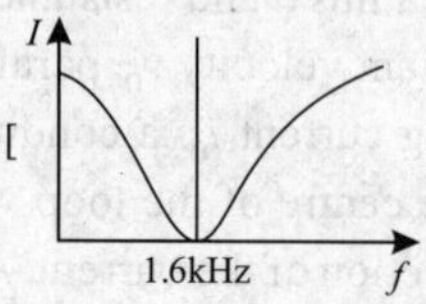]

5-15 Prove that in a series LCR circuit, the frequencies f_1 and f_2 at which the current amplitude falls to $1/\sqrt{2}$ of the current at resonance are separated by an interval equal to

$$\Delta f=\frac{R}{2\pi L}$$

5-16 A coil of 160 turns of cross-sectional area 250 cm^2 rotates at an angular velocity of 300 rad/s about an axis parallel to the plane of the coil in a uniform magnetic field of 0.6 weber/metre^2. What is the maximum EMF induced in the coil. If the coil is connected to a resistance of 2 Ω, what is the maximum torque that has to be delivered to maintain its motion.

Ans. [720 V, 864 Nm]

5-17 In an L-R series circuit, a sinusoidal voltage $V = V_0 \sin \omega t$ is applied. It is given that $L = 35$ μH, $R = 11$ Ω, phase difference between the current and the voltage. Also plot the variation of current for one cycle on the given graph.

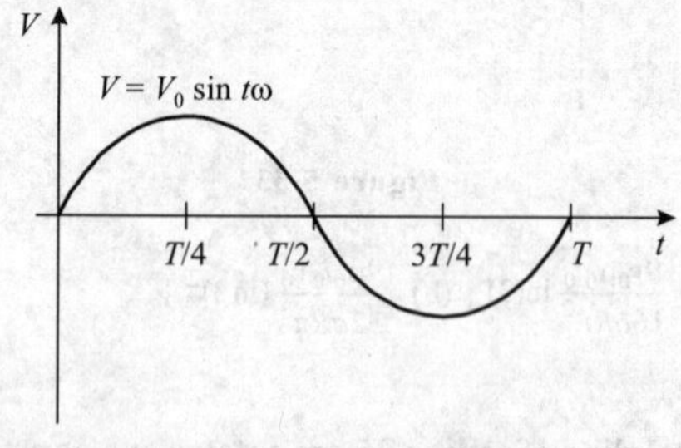

Figure 5.335

Ans. [20A, $\frac{\pi}{4}$]

5-18 A square metal wire loop of side 10 cm and resistance 1 Ω is moved with a constant velocity v_0 in a uniform magnetic field of induction 2 T as shown in figure-5.336 the magnetic field lines are perpendicular to the plane of the loop directed into the paper. The loop is connected to a network of resistors each of value 3 Ω. The resistance of the lead wires *OS* and *PQ* are negligible. What should be the speed of the loop so as to have a steady current of 1 mA in the loop? Give the direction of current in the loop.

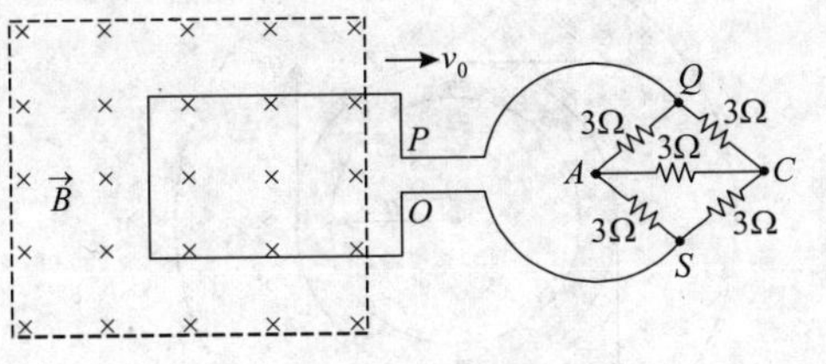

Figure 5.336

Ans. [2×10^{-2} m/s]

5-19 One end of a non-conducting spring of force constant *k* is connected to the mid-point of a conducting rod of mass *m* and length *l*, which can slide freely on a pair of parallel and smooth horizontal conducting rails. The other end of the spring is connected to a rigid wall. There exists a uniform magnetic field *B* normal to the plane of paper and into it. Electrical resistance of the rails and rod are negligible. The rails are connected to a capacitor of capacitance *C*. If the wire is pushed towards left and released, the time period of its oscillation will be. [Given $m = 2CB^2l^2$]

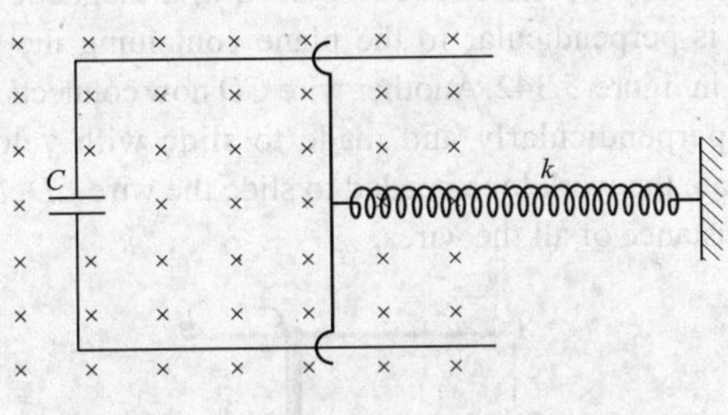

Figure 5.337

Ans. [$T = 2\pi\sqrt{\dfrac{3m}{2k}}$]

5-20 Two parallel conducting rails separated by a distance *l* are fixed on a plane surface inclined at an angle α to the horizontal as shown in figure-5.338. Rails are connected at the bottom by a resistance *R*. A copper rod of mass *m* slides without friction on the rails due to gravity. A uniform vertical field *B* exists throughout the region. Find the steady state velocity of the rod. Show that the rate at which thermal energy is produced in the circuit is equal to the rate at which rod is losing gravitational potential energy. What will happen if the direction of *B* is reversed ?

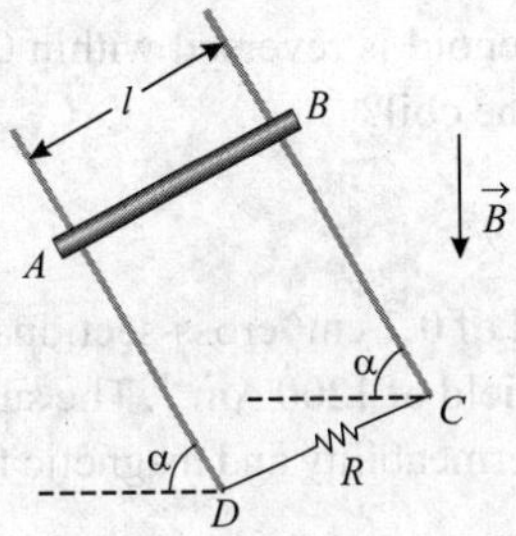

Figure 5.338

Ans. [$\dfrac{mgR\sin\alpha}{B^2l^2\cos^2\alpha}$, rod will continuously accelerate if *B* is reversed]

5-21 A small town with a demand of 800 kW of electric power at 220 V is situated 15 km away from an electric power plant generating power at 440 V. The resistance of the two wire line carrying power is 0.5 Wper km. The town gets from the line through a 4000 – 220 V step down transformer at a sub-station in the town.

(a) Estimate the line power loss in the form of heat.

(b) How much power must be plant supply, assuming there is a negligible power loss due to leakage?

(c) Voltage rating of the step up transformer at the plant.

Ans. [(a) 600 kW (b) 1400 kW (c) 440 – 7000 V]

4-22 A magnetising field of 1600 Am^{-1} produces a magnetic flux of 2.4×10^{-5} Wb in an iron bar of cross-sectional area 0.2 cm^2. Calculate permeability and susceptibility of the bar.

Ans. [7.5×10^{-4} N/A^2, 596]

5-23 A periodic voltage wave form has been shown in figure-5.339.

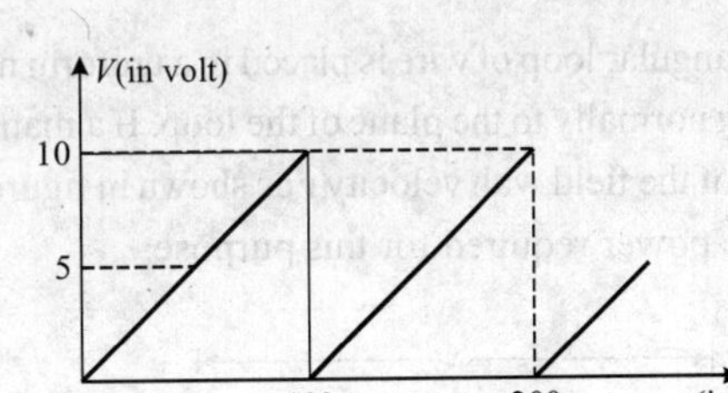

Figure 5.339

Determine. (a) Frequency of the wave form. (b) Average value of the voltage.

Ans. [(a) 10 Hz (b) 5 V]

5-24 A long solenoid having 200 turns per cm carries a current of 1.5 A. At the centre of it, a 100 turn coil is placed which is of cross-sectional area 3.14×10^{-4} m^2 having its axis parallel to the field produced by the solenoid. When the direction of current in the solenoid is reversed within 0.05 s., what is the EMF induced in the coil?

Ans. [0.048 V]

4-25 An iron rod of 0.2 cm^2 cross-sectional area is subjected to a magnetising field of 1200 Am^{-1}. The susceptibility of iron is 599. Find the permeability and magnetic flux produced.

Ans. [7.536×10^{-4} TmA^{-1}, 1.81×10^{-5} Wb]

5-26 When 10 V, DC is applied across a coil current through it is 2.5 A, if 10 V, 50 Hz A.C. is applied current reduces to 2 A. Calculate reactance of the coil.

Ans. [3Ω]

5-27 A long cylindrical coil of inductance L_1 is wound on a bobbin of diameter d_1. The magnetic induction in the coil connected to a current source is B_1. After rewinding the coil on a bobbin of diameter d_2 its inductance become L_2. Find the magnetic induction B_2 of the field in the new coil connected to the same current source assuming that the length of wire is much larger than that of coil.

Ans. [$B_1\left(\frac{L_2 d_1}{L_1 d_2}\right)$]

4-28 An airplane with a 20m wingspread is flying at 250 m/s straight south parallel to the earth's surface. The earths magnetic field has a horizontal component of 2×10^{-5} Wb/m^2 and the dip angle is 60°. Calculate the induced e.m.f. between the plane tips.

Ans. [0.1732 V]

5-29 A rectangular loop of wire is placed in a uniform magnetic field B acting normally to the plane of the loop. If a man attempt to pull it out of the field with velocity v as shown in figure-5.340, calculate the power required for this purpose.

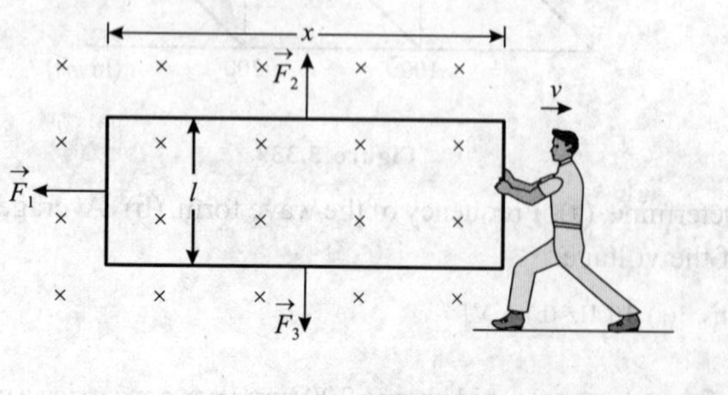

Figure 5.340

Ans. [$\frac{B^2 l^2 v^2}{R}$]

5-30 A thin non-conducting ring of mass m, radius a and uniformly distributed charge q is place inside a solenoid magnetic field with its plane normal to $\vec{B}$ and coaxially with solenoid as shown. If B is changing with time as $B = kt$, find the angular speed attained by ring after time t.

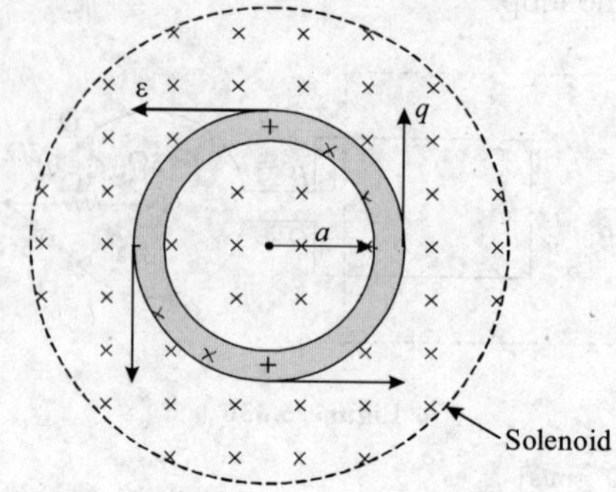

Figure 5.341

Ans. [$\frac{qkt}{2m}$]

5-31 Calculate (a) resistance or (b) inductance required in series to operate a lamp (60 V, 10 W) from a source of (100 V, 50 Hz)

Ans. [(a) 240 Ω (b) 1.5 H]

5-32 Two parallel wires AL and KM placed at a distance l are connected by a resistor R and placed in a magnetic field B which is perpendicular to the plane containing the wire as shown in figure-5.342. Another wire CD now connects the two wires perpendicularly and made to slide with velocity v. Calculate the workdone needed to slide the wire CD. Neglect the resistance of all the wires.

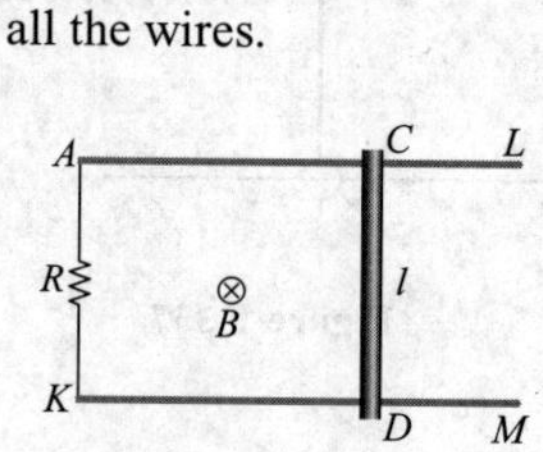

Figure 5.342

Ans. [$\frac{B^2 l^2 v^2}{R}$].

5-33 An inductor of inductance L = 400 mH and resistors R_1 = 2 Ω and R_2 = 2 Ω are connected to a battery of EMF E = 12 V as shown in the figure-5.343. The internal resistance of the battery is negligible. The switch S is closed at time t = 0. What is the potential drop across L as function of time ? After the steady state is reached, the switch is opened. What is the direction and the magnitude of current through R_1 as a function of time?

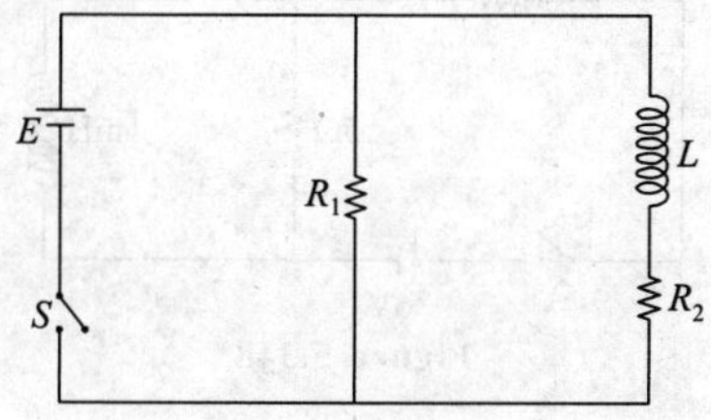

Figure 5.343

Ans. $[12e^{-5t}$ V, $6e^{-10t}$A, Clockwise]

5-34 A long straight wire carries a current i_0. At distance a and b from it there are two other wires, parallel to the former one, which are interconnected by a resistance R (figure-5.344) A connector slides without friction along the wires with a constant velocity v. Assuming the resistances of the wires, the connector, the sliding contacts and the self inductance of the frame to be negligible, find

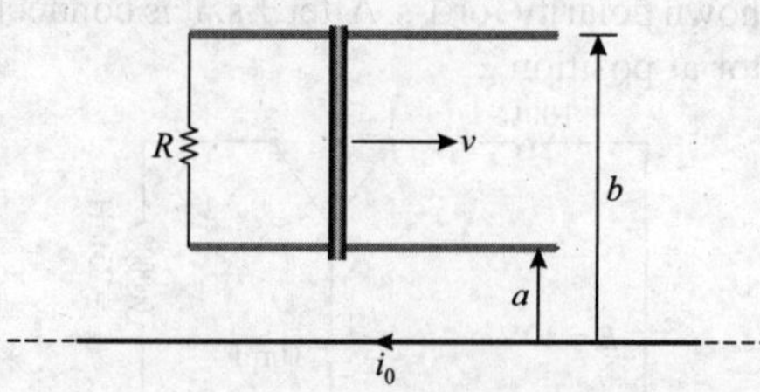

Figure 5.344

(a) The magnitude and the direction of current induced in the connectors,

(b) The force required to maintain the connector's velocity constant.

Ans. [(a) $\frac{\mu_0 i_0 v}{2\pi R}\ln\left(\frac{b}{a}\right)$, anticlockwise, (b) $\left[\frac{\mu_0 i_0 \ln(b/a)}{2\pi}\right]^2 \frac{v}{R}$]

5-35 An L-C circuit consists of an inductor with $L = 0.0900$ H and a capacitor of $C = 4 \times 10^{-4}$ F. The initial charge on the capacitor is 5.00 μC, and the initial current in the inductor is zero.

(a) What is the maximum voltage across the capacitor ?

(b) What is the maximum current in the inductor ?

(c) What is the maximum energy stored in the inductor ?

(d) When the current in the inductor has half its maximum value, what is the charge on the capacitor and what is the energy stored in the inductor ?

Ans. [(a) 1.25×10^{-2} V, (b) 8.33×10^{-4} A, (c) 3.125×10^{-8} J, (d) 4.33×10^{-6} C, 7.8×10^{-7} J]

5-36 A circuit has a coil of resistance 50 ohms and inductance $\frac{3}{\pi}$ henry. It is connected in series with a condenser of $\frac{40}{\pi}$ μF and AC supply voltage of 200 V and 50 cycles/sec. Calculate :

(i) the impedance of the circuit.

(ii) the p.d. across inductance coil and condenser.

Ans. [$Z = 50\sqrt{2}\ \Omega$, $V_C = 500\sqrt{2}$ V and $V_L = 600\sqrt{2}$ V]

5-37 A connecting rod AB of mass m slides without friction over two long conducting rails separated by a distance l (figure-5.345). At the left end, the rails are interconnected by a resistance R. The system is located in a uniform magnetic field perpendicular to the plane of the loop. At the moment $t = 0$ the rod AB starts moving to the right with an initial velocity v_0. Neglecting the resistances of the rails and the rod AB, as well as the self inductance, find :

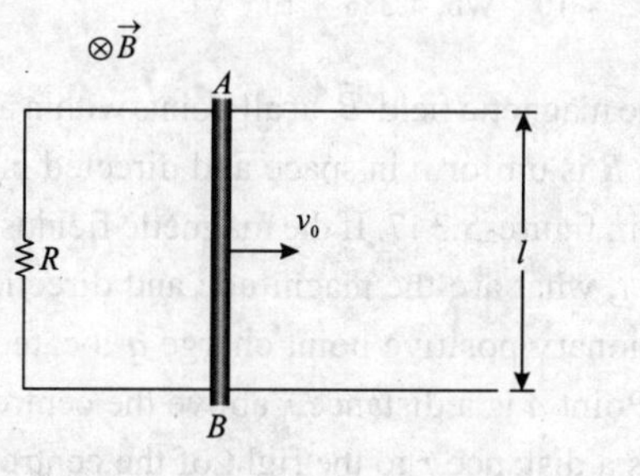

Figure 5.345

(a) The distance covered by the rod until it comes to a stand still,

(b) The amount of heat generated in the resistance R during the process.

Ans. [(a) $\frac{mv_0R}{B^2l^2}$ e(b) $\frac{1}{2}mv_0^2$]

5-38 An L-C circuit like that illustrated in figure-5.346 consists of a 3.30 H inductor and an 840 μF capacitor, initially carrying a 105 μC charge. At $t = 0$ the switch is thrown closed.

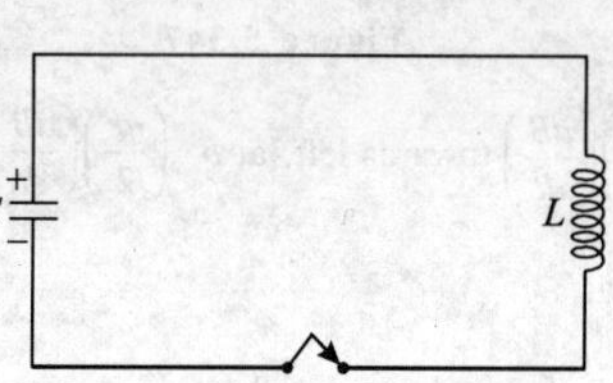

Figure 5.346

Compute the following quantities at $t = 2.00$ ms.

(a) The energy stored in the capacitor,

(b) The energy stored in the inductor,

(c) The total energy in the circuit.

Ans. [(a) 6.5531 μJ (b) 0.0094 μJ (c) 6.5625 μJ]

5-39 A vertical copper disc of diameter 20 cm makes 10 revolutions per second about a horizontal axis passing through it centre. A uniform magnetic field 10^{-2} weber/m^2 acts perpendicular to the plane of the disc. Calculate the potential difference between its centre and rim.

Ans. [3.14×10^{-3} V]

5-40 A current of 10 A is flowing in a long straight wire situated near a rectangular circuit whose two sides of length 0.2 m are parallel to the wire. One of them is at a distance of 0.05 m and the other at a distance of 0.10 m from the wire. The wire is in the plane of the rectangle. Find the magnetic flux through the rectangular circuit. If the current decays uniformly to zero in 0.02 s, find the EMF induced in the circuit and indicate the direction in which the induced current flows.

Ans. [2.772×10^{-7} Wb, 1.386×10^{-5} V]

5-41 The magnetic field $\vec{B}$ at all points within a circular region of radius R is uniform in space and directed into the plane of the page in figure-5.347. If the magnetic field is increasing at a rate dB/dt, what are the magnitude and direction of the force on a stationary positive point charge q located at points a, b and c? (Point a is a distance r above the centre of the region, point b is a distance r to the right of the centre, and point c is at the centre of the region.)

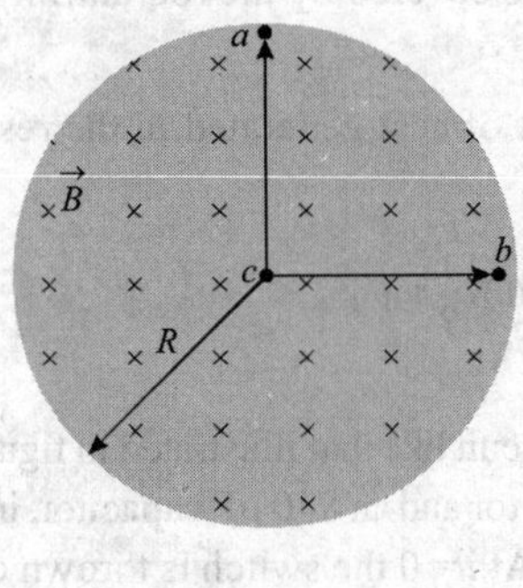

Figure 5.347

Ans. [At a : $\left(\frac{qr}{2}\right)\left(\frac{dB}{dt}\right)$ towards left, at b : $\left(\frac{qr}{2}\right)\left(\frac{dB}{dt}\right)$ towards top of the page, at c : zero]

5-42 The rails of a railway track are 1.5 m apart and assumed to be insulated from one another. Calculate the EMF that will exist between the rails if a train is passing at 100 km/hr. Assume the horizontal component of earth's magnetic field is 0.36×10^{-4} T and tan θ = 1.036 where θ is the angle of dip.

Ans. [1.554×10^{-3} V]

5-43 In the circuit arrangement shown in figure-5.348, the switch S is closed at $t = 0$. Find the current in the inductance as a function of time ? Does the current through 10 Ω resistor vary with time or remains constant.

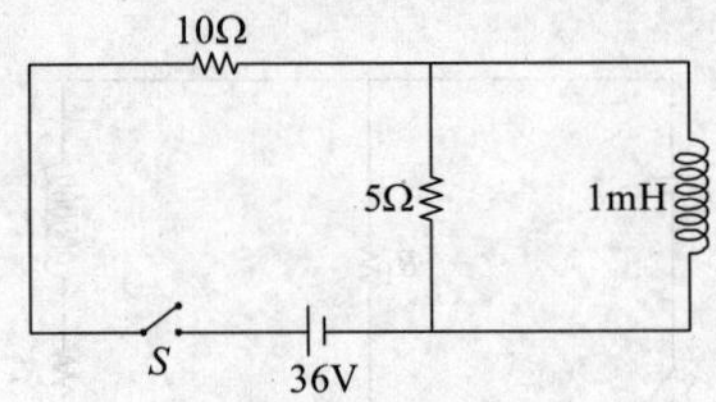

Figure 5.348

Ans. [3.6 $(1 - e^{-t/\tau})$ A where τ = 300 μs, Current through 10 Ω resistor varies with time]

5-44 A closed coil having 50 turns, area 300 cm^2 and resistance 40 Ω is held at right angles to uniform field of induction 0.02 T. If it is then turned through an angle of 30° about an axis at right angles to the field, find the charge flown through the coil.

Ans. [1.005×10^{-4} C]

5-45 Initially the capacitor in circuit shown in figure-5.349 is charged to a potential of 5 V and then connected to position 1 with the shown polarity for 1 s. After 1 s, it is connected across the inductor at position 2.

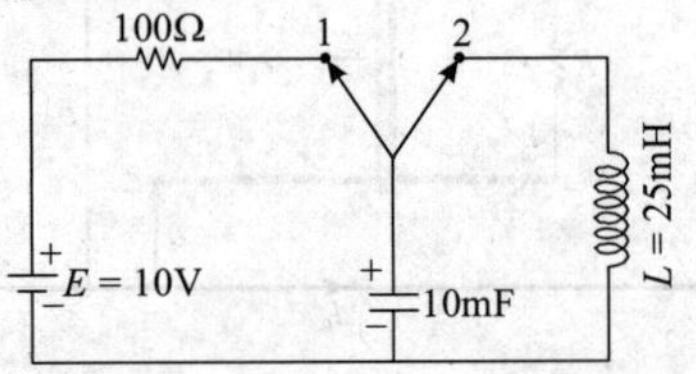

Figure 5.349

(a) Find the potential across the capacitor after 1 s of its connection to position 1.

(b) Find the maximum current flowing in the LC circuit when capacitor is connected across the inductor. Also find the frequency of LC oscillations.

Ans. [(a) 8.16 V, (b) 5.16 A, 10 Hz]

5-46 A space is divided by the line AD into two regions as shown in figure-5.348. Region I is free from magnetic field and region II has a uniform magnetic field B directed into the plane of paper. ACD is semicircular conducting loop of radius r with centre at O [Figure-5.350], the plane of the loop being in the plane of the paper. The loop is now made to rotate with a constant angular velocity ω about an axis passing through O and perpendicular to the plane of the paper. The effective resistance of the loop is R.

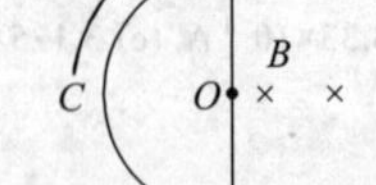

Figure 5.350

(a) Obtain an expression for the magnitude of the induced current in the loop.
(b) Show the direction of the current when the loop is entering into the region II.
(c) Plot a graph between the induced EMF and time of rotation for two periods of rotation.

Ans. [(a) $\frac{1}{2}\frac{Br^2\omega}{R}$; (b) anticlockwise; (c)

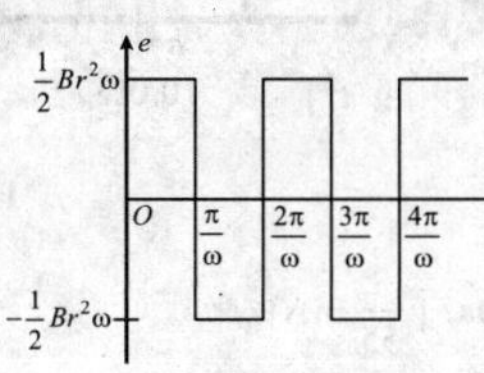

]

5-47 An inductance of 2.0 H, a capacitance of 18 μF and a resistance of 10 kΩ are connected to an AC source of 20 V with adjustable frequency. (a) What frequency should be chosen to maximise the current (RMS) in the circuit ? (b) What is the value of this maximum current (RMS) ?

Ans. [(a) $\frac{250}{3\pi}$ Hz; (b) 2 mA]

5-48 A conducting light string is wound on the rim of a metal ring of radius r and mass m. The free end of the string is fixed to the ceiling. A vertical infinite smooth conducting plane is always tangent to the ring as shown in the figure-5.351. A uniform magnetic field B is applied perpendicular to the plane of the ring. The ring is always inside the magnetic field. The plane and the string are connected by a resistance R. When the ring is released, find :

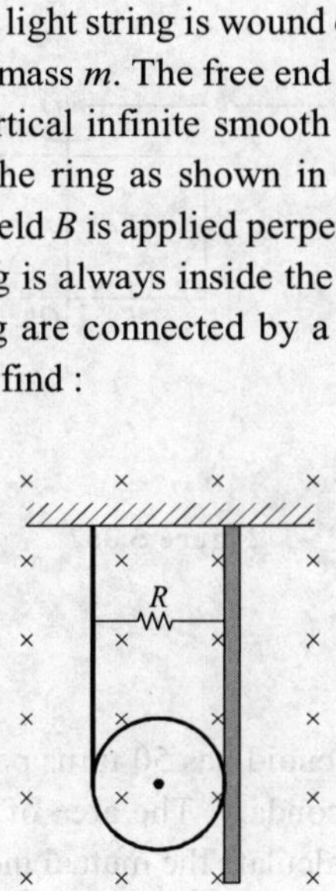

Figure 5.351

(a) The current in the resistance R as a function of time
(b) The terminal velocity of the ring

Ans. [(a) $i = \frac{mg}{2Br}\left(1-e^{-\frac{2B^2r^2}{mR}t}\right)$; (b) $v_T = \frac{mgR}{4B^2r^2}$]

5-49 A stiff wire bent into a semicircle of radius R is rotated at a frequency f in a uniform magnetic field B. Calculate the amplitude and frequency of the induced voltage. If this circuit has negligible resistance and the internal resistance of the ammeter is 1000 Ω, calculate the amplitude of induced current.

Ans. [$\frac{\pi^2R^2Bf}{1000}$]

5-50 A rectangular loop with a sliding conductor of length l is located in a uniform magnetic field perpendicular to the plane of loop. The magnetic induction perpendicular to the plane of loop is equal to B. The part ad and bc has electric resistance R_1 and R_2 respectively. The conductor starts moving with constant acceleration a_0 at time $t = 0$. Neglecting the self inductance of the loop and resistance of conductor. Find

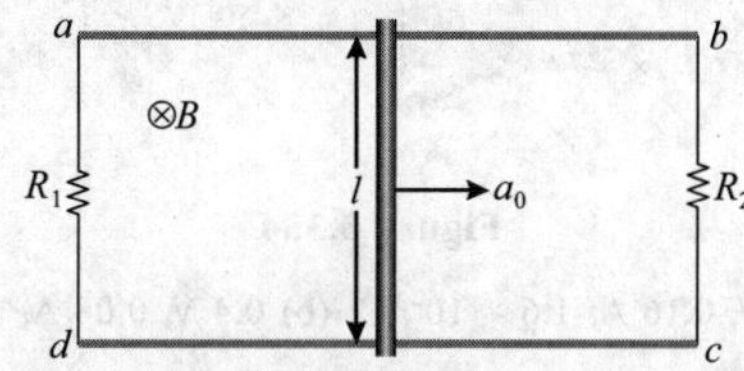

Figure 5.352

(a) The current through the conductor during its motion
(b) The polarity of $adcd$ terminal
(c) External force required to move the conductor with the given acceleration.

Ans. [(a) $i = \frac{Bla_0t}{R_1R_2}(R_1 + R_2)$ (b) Polarity of a, b is positive and polarity of c, d is negative, (c) $F_{ext} = a_0\left[m + \frac{B^2l^2t}{R_1R_2}(R_1 + R_2)\right]$]

5-51 A long straight wire carries a current $I = I_0 \sin(\omega t + \delta)$ and lies in the plane of a rectangular loop of N turns of wire as shown in figure-5.353. The quantities I_0, ω and δ are all constants. Determine the EMF induced in the loop by the magnetic field due to the current in the straight wire. Assume I_0 = 50 A, ω = 200 π/s, N = 100, a = b = 5 cm cm and l = 20 cm.

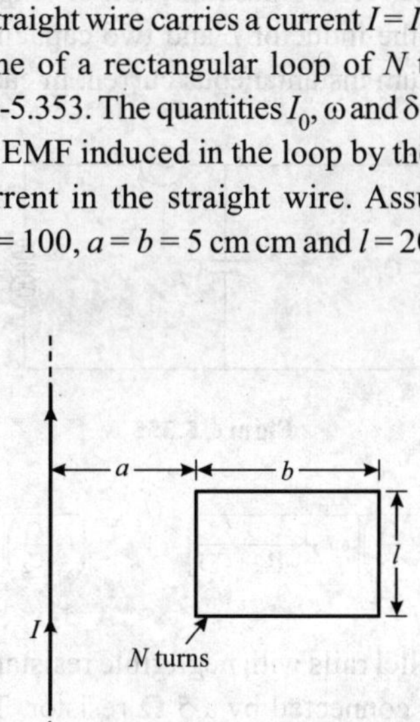

Figure 5.353

Ans. [$\frac{\mu_0 NI_0 l\omega}{2\pi}\ln\left(\frac{a+b}{a}\right)\cos(\omega t + \delta)$]

5-52 A square loop *ACDE* of area 20 cm^2 and resistance 5 Ω shown in figure-5.354 is rotated in a magnetic field of induction 2 T through 180° (a) in 0.01 s and (b) in 0.02 s. Find the magnitude of e, i and Δq in both the cases.

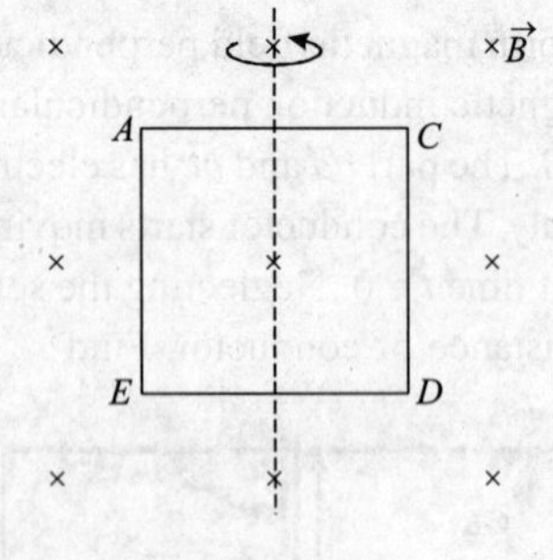

Figure 5.354

Ans. [(a) 0.8 V, 0.16 A, 1.6 × 10^{-3} C; (b) 0.4 V, 0.08 A, 1.6 × 10^{-3} C]

5-53 Two long parallel wire of zero resistance are connected to each other by a battery of 1.0 V. The separation between the wires is 0.5 m. A metallic bar, which is perpendicular to the wires and of resistance 10 Ω moves on these wires when magnetic field of 0.02 T is acting perpendicular to the plane containing the bar and the wires. Find the steady state velocity of the bar. If the mass of the bar is 0.002 kg, find its velocity as a function of time.

Ans. [100 m/s, $100(1 - e^{-t/200})$ m/s]

5-54 Consider the circuit shown in figure-5.355. The oscillating source of emf deliver a sinusoidal emf of amplitude e_{max} and frequency ω to the inductor L and two capacitors C_1 and C_2. Find the maximum instantaneous current in each capacitor.

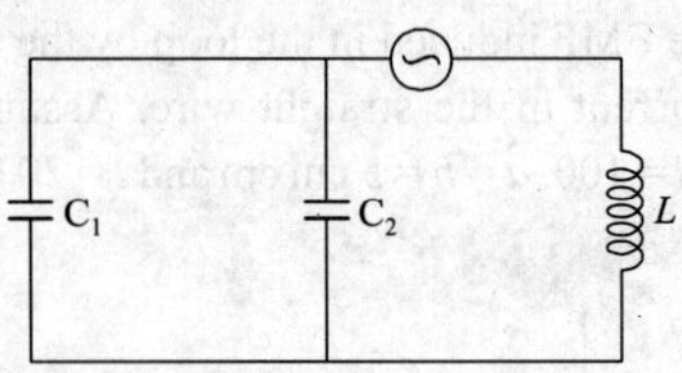

Figure 5.355

Ans. [$(I_1)_{max} = \dfrac{E_{max}}{\dfrac{C_2}{C_1}\left(1+\dfrac{C_1}{C_2}\right)\left[\omega L - \dfrac{1}{\omega(C_1+C_2)}\right]}$, $(I_2)_{max} = \dfrac{E_{max}}{\left(1+\dfrac{C_1}{C_2}\right)\left[\omega L - \dfrac{1}{\omega(C_1+C_2)}\right]}$]

5-55 Two parallel rails with negligible resistance are 10.0 cm apart. They are connected by a 5 Ω resistor. The circuit also contains two metal rods having resistances of 10 Ω and 15 Ω along the rails. The rods are pulled away from the resistor at constant speeds 4 m/s and 2 m/s respectively. A uniform magnetic field of magnitude 0.01 T is applied perpendicular to the plane of the rails. Determine the current in the 5 Ω resistor.

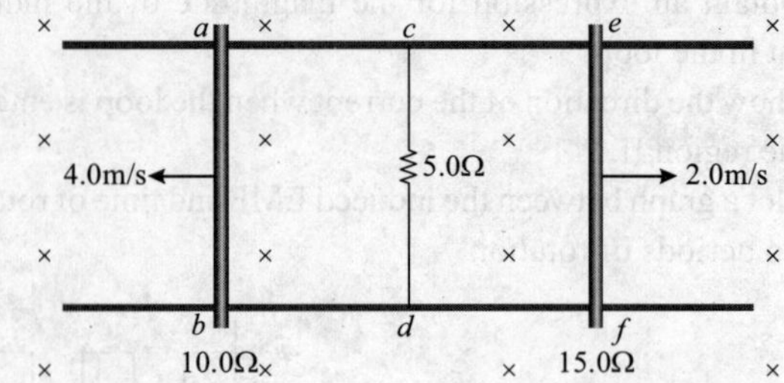

Figure 5.356

Ans. [$\frac{8}{55}$ mA]

5-56 A square frame with side a and a straight conductor carrying a constant current I are located in the same plane. The inductance and the resistance of the frame are equal to L and R respectively. The frame was turned through 180° about the axis OO' separated from the current carrying conductor by a distance b as shown in figure-5.357. Find the electric charge having flown through the frame.

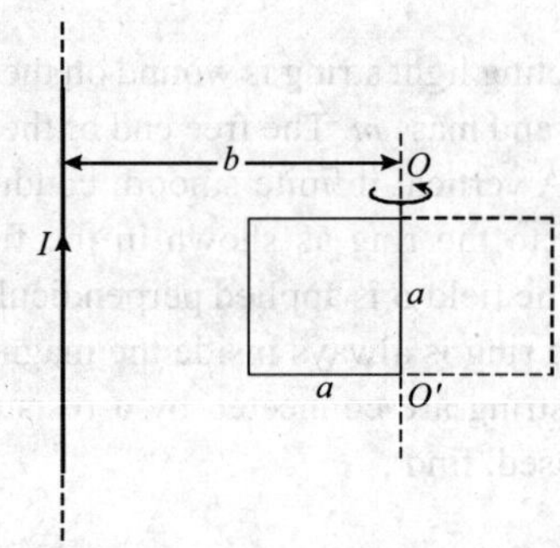

Figure 5.357

Ans. [$\frac{\mu_0 a I}{2\pi R}\ln\left(\frac{a+b}{b-a}\right)$]

5-57 A straight solenoid has 50 turns per cm in primary and 200 turns in the secondary. The area of cross section of the solenoid is 4cm^2. Calculate the mutual inductance.

Ans. [5.0 × 10^{-4} H]

5-58 A connector *AB* can slide without friction along U-shaped wire frame located in a horizontal plane. The connector has a length l, mass m and resistance R. The whole system is located in a uniform magnetic field of induction B directed vertically downward as shown in figure-5.358. At the moment $t = 0$ a constant horizontal force F starts acting on the connector shifting it translation wise to the right. Find how the velocity of the connector varies with time t. The inductance of the loop and the resistance of the U-shaped conductor are assumed to be negligible.

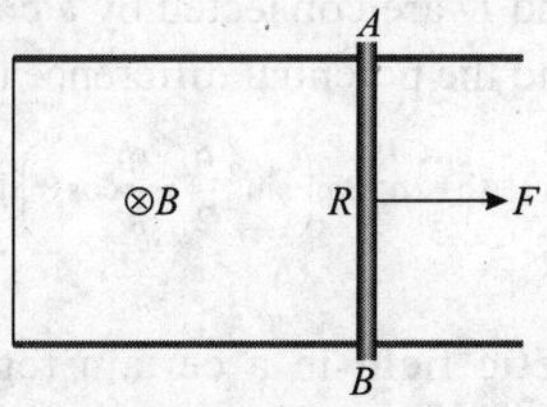

Figure 5.358

Ans. $\left[\frac{FR}{B^2l^2}\left(1-e^{-\frac{B^2l^2t}{mR}}\right)\right]$

5-59 A 5 H inductor is placed in series with a 10 Ω resistor. An EMF of 5 V being suddenly applied to the combination. Using these values prove the principle of conservation of energy, for time equal to the time constant.

5-60 When an alternating voltage of 220 V is applied across a device X, a current of 0.5 A flows through the circuit and is in phase with the applied voltage. When the same voltage is applied across another device Y, the same current again flows through the circuit but it leads the applied voltage by $p/2$ radians.

(a) Name the devices X and Y.

(b) Calculate the current flowing in the circuit when same voltage is applied across the series combination of X and Y.

Ans. [(a) X is resistor and Y is a capacitor (b) 0.35 A]

5-61 Two toroidal solenoids are wound around the same pipe so that the magnetic field of one passes through the turns of the other. Solenoid 1 has 700 turns and solenoid 2 has 400 turns. When the current in solenoid 1 is 6.52 A, the average flux through each turn of solenoid 2 is 0.0320 Wb.

(a) What is the mutual inductance of the pair of solenoids?

(b) When the current in solenoid 2 is 2.54 A, what is the average flux through each turn of solenoid 1?

Ans. [(a) 1.96 H (b) 7.12×10^{-3} Wb]

5-62 A square frame $PQRS$ of each side l, with a steady current i_1 is near a long straight conductor carrying a current i_2. The frame and the conductor are in one plane, with the length of the conductor parallel to the side PS and QR of the square frame as shown in figure-5.359. Calculate the workdone in moving the conductor from position P_1 to P_2.

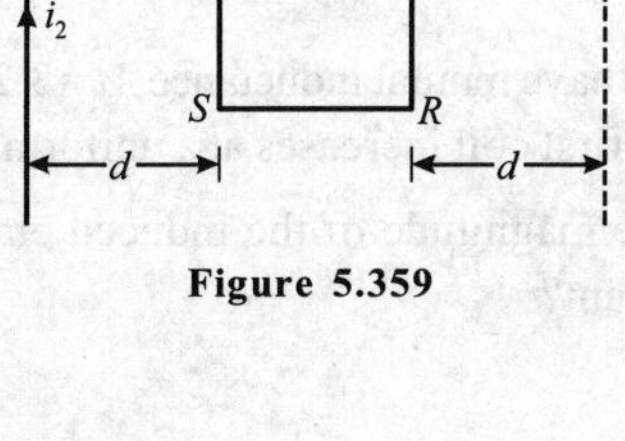

Figure 5.359

Ans. $\left[\frac{\mu_0 i_1 i_2 l}{2\pi}\ln\left(\frac{d+l}{d}\right)\right]$

5-63 A rectangular loop with a sliding connector of length l is located in a uniform magnetic field perpendicular to the loop plane as shown in figure-5.360. The magnetic induction is equal to B. The connector has an electric resistance R, the sides AB and CD have resistances R_1 and R_2 respectively. Neglecting the self inductance of the loop, find the current flowing in the connector during its motion with a constant velocity v.

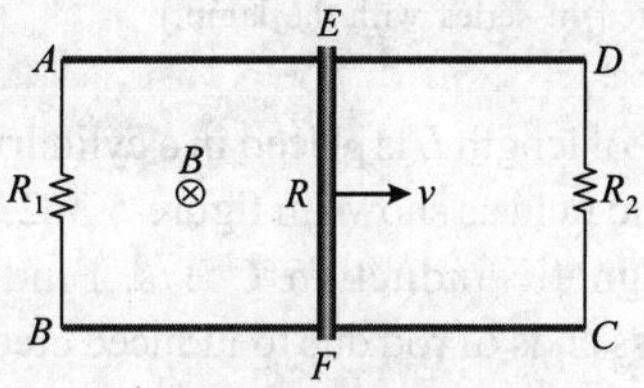

Figure 5.360

Ans. $\left[\frac{Blv}{R+\left(\frac{R_1R_2}{R_1+R_2}\right)}\right]$

5-64 (a) What is the magnetic flux through one turn of a solenoid of self inductance 8.0×10^{-5} H when a current of 3.0 A flown through it ? Assume that the solenoid has 1000 turns and is wound from wire of diameter 1.0 mm. (b) What is the cross-sectional area of the solenoid ?

Ans. [(a) 2.4×10^{-7} Wb (b) 6.37×10^{-5} m^2]

5-65 A long straight wire carrying a current i and a U-shaped conductor with sliding connector are located in the same plane as shown in figure-5.361. The connector of length l and resistance R slides to the right with a constant velocity v. Find the current induced in the loop as a function of separation r between the connector and the straight wire. The resistance of the U-shaped conductor and the self inductance of the loop are assumed to be negligible.

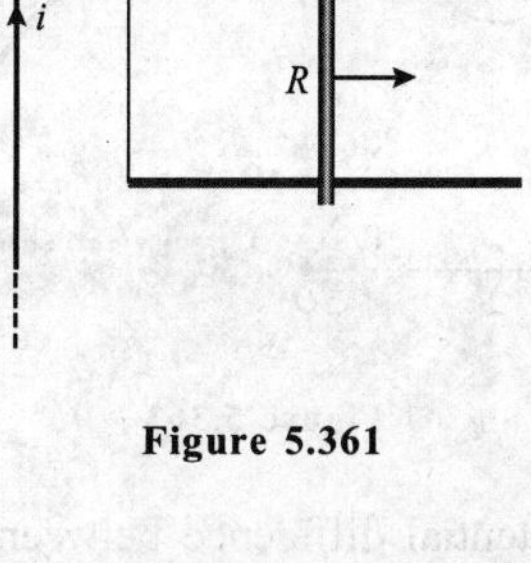

Figure 5.361

Ans. $\left[\frac{\mu_0 ivl}{2\pi rR}\right]$

5-66 A 20 volts 5 watt lamp is used on AC mains of 200 volts and $\frac{50}{\pi}\sqrt{11}$ c.p.s. Calculate the (i) capacitor, (ii) inductor, to be put in the series to run the lamp. (iii) How much pure resistance should be included in place of the above device so that the lamp can run on its rated voltage. (iv) Which is more economical, the capacitor, the inductor or the resistor.

Ans. [(i) $\frac{125}{33}$ μF, (ii) 2.4 H, (iii) 720 W, (iv) It will be more economical to use inductance or capacitance in series with the lamp to run it as it. It consumes no power while there would be dissipation of power when resistance is inserted in series with the lamp.]

5-67 A rod AB of length L is placed in a cylindrical region time varying magnetic field as shown in figure-5.362, with the rate of increasing magnetic induction C T/s. Find the potential difference across ends of rod due to induced electric field in the region.

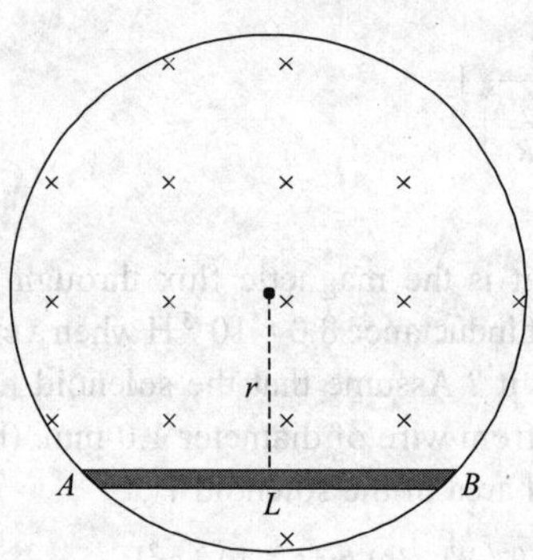

Figure 5.362

Ans. [$\frac{1}{2}CrL$]

5-68 A uniform wire of resistance per unit length λ is bent into a semicircle of radius a. The wire rotates with angular velocity ω in a vertical plane about a horizontal axis passing through C. A uniform magnetic field B exists in space in a direction perpendicular to paper inwards.

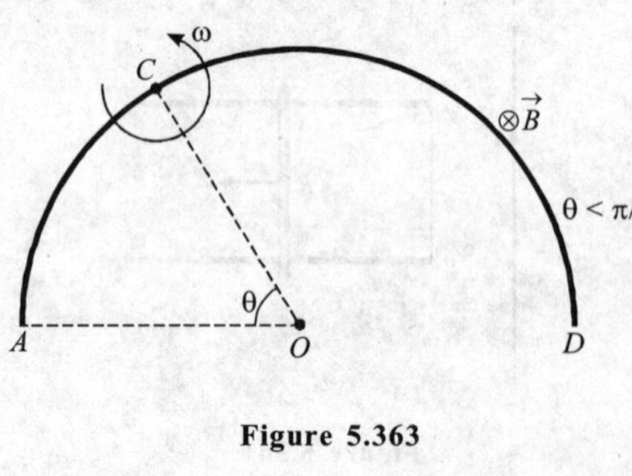

Figure 5.363

(a) Calculate potential difference between points A and D. Which point is at higher potential?

(b) If points A and D are connected by a conducting wire of zero resistance find the potential difference between A and C.

Ans. [(a) $2a^2B\omega\cos\theta$, (b) $2a^2B\omega\left(\sin^2\frac{\theta}{2}+\frac{\theta}{\pi}\cos\theta\right)$]

5-69 The magnetic field in a certain region is given by $\vec{B}=(4.0\hat{i}-1.8\hat{k})\times 10^{-3}$ T. How much flux passes through a loop of area 5.0 cm^2 in this region if the loop lies flat on the x-y plane ?

Ans. [9.0×10^{-7} Wb]

5-70 On a smooth horizontal table a disc is placed with non conducting ring with uniformly distributed charge q fixed on its circumference. Both disc and ring are of mass m and radius r. If a uniform magnetic field of induction B which is symmetric with centre of disc is switched on in vertically downward direction, find the angular speed attained by disc due to this.

Ans. [$\frac{qB}{3m}$]

5-71 A coil has 600 turns which produces 5×10^{-3} Wb/turn of flux when 3 A current flows in the wire. This produced 6×10^{-3} Wb/turn in 1000 turns of a secondary coil. When the switch is opened the current drops to zero in 0.2 s in primary coil. Find (a) mutual inductance, (b) the induced EMF in the secondary, (c) the self inductance of the primary coil.

Ans. [(a) 2 H, (b) 30 V, (c) 1 H]

5-72 Figure-5.364 shows a circuit in which an inductor of 5 H is connected to a 20 V battery and a fuse of rating 30 A. Neglect any resistance in the circuit, if switch is closed at $t=0$ find the time after which fuse will blow up.

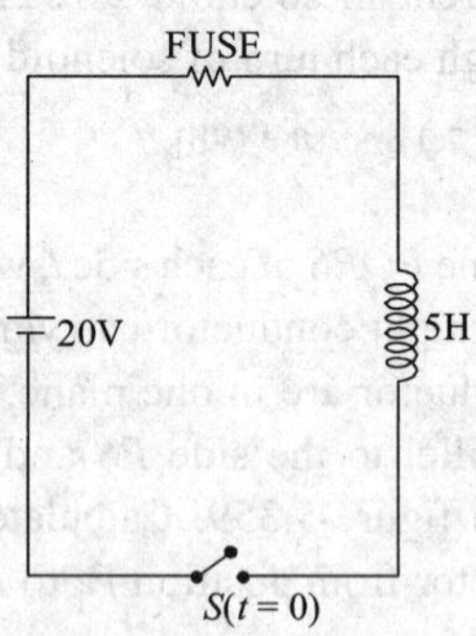

Figure 5.364

Ans. [7.5 s]

5-73 Two coils have mutual inductance $M=3.25\times 10^{-4}$ H. The current i_1 in the first coil increases at a uniform rate of 830 A/s.

(a) What is the magnitude of the induced emf in the second coil? Is it constant?

(b) Suppose that the current described is in the second coil rather than the first. What is the induced emf in the first coil?

Ans. [(a) 0.27 V, Yes (b) 0.27 V]

5-74 A small coil of radius r is placed at the centre of another coaxial coil of radius $R(R >> r)$. Find the coefficient of mutual induction for this pair of coils.

Ans. [$\frac{\mu_0 \pi r^2}{2R}$]

5-75 A Rowland ring of mean radius 15 cm has 4500 turns of wire wound on a ferromagnetic core of relative permeability 800. Find the magnitude of the magnetic field in the core for a magnetising current of 1.2 A.

Ans. [5.76 T]

* * * * *

ANSWERS & SOLUTIONS

CONCEPTUAL MCQS Single Option Correct

1	(C)	2	(B)	3	(C)
4	(B)	5	(A)	6	(D)
7	(B)	8	(C)	9	(B)
10	(B)	11	(A)	12	(C)
13	(B)	14	(D)	15	(D)
16	(B)	17	(A)	18	(D)
19	(D)	20	(B)	21	(C)
22	(A)	23	(C)	24	(D)
25	(C)	26	(B)	27	(C)
28	(B)	29	(D)	30	(C)
31	(C)	32	(D)	33	(C)
34	(B)	35	(D)	36	(D)
37	(D)	38	(D)	39	(D)
40	(A)				

NUMERICAL MCQS Single Option Correct

1	(B)	2	(D)	3	(A)
4	(B)	5	(C)	6	(D)
7	(B)	8	(A)	9	(D)
10	(B)	11	(C)	12	(A)
13	(D)	14	(C)	15	(B)
16	(A)	17	(A)	18	(A)
19	(D)	20	(D)	21	(D)
22	(A)	23	(B)	24	(B)
25	(C)	26	(A)	27	(A)
28	(C)	29	(B)	30	(B)
31	(B)	32	(A)	33	(A)
34	(B)	35	(C)	36	(C)
37	(D)	38	(B)	39	(D)
40	(C)	41	(A)	42	(B)
43	(C)	44	(B)	45	(A)
46	(A)	47	(A)	48	(A)
49	(D)	50	(A)	51	(B)
52	(B)	53	(B)	54	(A)
55	(C)	56	(C)	57	(C)
58	(C)	59	(C)	60	(C)
61	(A)	62	(D)	63	(D)
64	(D)	65	(A)	66	(D)
67	(C)	68	(C)		

ADVANCE MCQs One or More Options Correct

1	(A, B, C)	2	(A, C)	3	(A)
4	(A, C, D)	5	(All)	6	(A, D)
7	(B, C)	8	(A, B)	9	(A, B, C)
10	(A, B, D)	11	(C, D)	12	(A, C)
13	(A, B, C)	14	(A, D)	15	(B, C, D)
16	(A, D)	17	(A, B, C)	18	(A, D)
19	(A, B, C)	20	(All)	21	(A, B, C)
22	(A, D)	23	(A, B, D)	24	(B, C)
25	(A, D)	26	(A, B, C)	27	(A, B, C)
28	(B, C)	29	(A, B, D)	30	(A, B, D)
31	(C)	32	(B, D)		

Solutions of PRACTICE EXERCISE 4.1

(i) The rectangular wire frame as described in question is shown in figure. The magnetic induction due to a straight finite length current carrying wire with angles ϕ_1 and ϕ_2 as shown in figure at a perpendicular distance r is given as

$$B = \frac{\mu_0 i}{4\pi r}[\sin\phi_1 + \sin\phi_2]$$

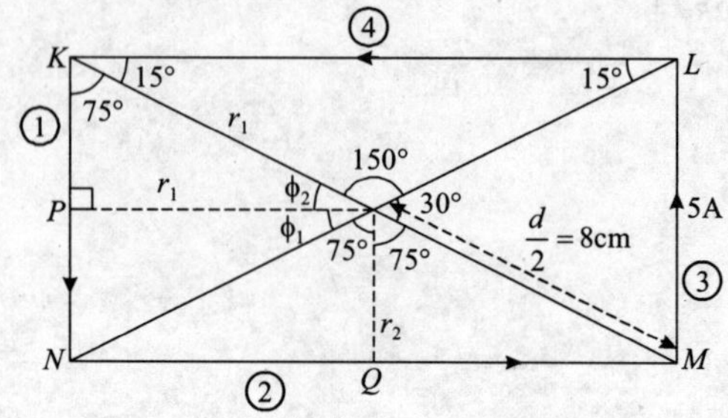

If B_1 and B_3 be the magnetic inductions at O due to wires KN and LM, then we have

$$B_1 = B_3 = \frac{\mu_0 i}{4\pi(d/2)\cos 15°}[\sin 15° + \sin 15°]$$

$$B_1 = B_3 = \frac{4\mu_0 i}{4\pi d}\tan 15°$$

If B_2 and B_4 be the magnetic inductions at O due to wires NM and LK, then we have

$$B_2 = B_4 = \frac{\mu_0 i}{4\pi(d/2)\cos 15°}[\sin 75° + \sin 75°]$$

$$B_2 = B_4 = \frac{4\mu_0 i}{4\pi d}\tan 75°$$

Net magnetic induction at center is given as

$$B = B_1 + B_2 + B_3 + B_4$$

$$\Rightarrow \quad B = 2\left[\frac{\mu_0}{4\pi}\times\frac{4i}{d}\tan 15°\right] + 2\left[\frac{\mu_0}{4\pi}\times\frac{4i}{d}\tan 75°\right]$$

$$\Rightarrow \quad B = \frac{\mu_0}{4\pi}\times\frac{8i}{d}[\tan 15° + \tan 75°]$$

$$\Rightarrow \quad B = 10^{-7}\times\frac{8\times 5}{16\times 10^{-2}}[0.2679\times 3.7321]\,\text{T}$$

$$\Rightarrow \quad B = 10^{-7}\times\frac{8\times 5}{16\times 10^{-2}}\times 4 = 1\times 10^{-4}\,\text{T}$$

$$\Rightarrow \quad B = 0.1\,\text{mT}$$

(ii) (a) Magnetic field at O due to straight wires at O is zero as the line of wire is passing through point O. The magnetic field at O due to semicircular part LM is given as half of the magnetic induction due to the complete circular coil given as

$$B = \frac{\mu_0 i}{4R}$$

(b) The magnetic induction at O due to wire MN is zero because O lies on the line MN. Magnetic induction at O due to circular portion ML of the wire which is a circular arc three fourth of the circle is given as

$$B_1 = \frac{\mu_0 i}{2R} \times \frac{3}{4} = \frac{3\mu_0 i}{8R}$$

The magnetic induction at O due to infinitely long straight wire LK is given by using the result of a semi-infinite wire given as

$$B_2 = \frac{\mu_0 i}{4\pi R}$$

Net magnetic induction at O is given as

$$B = B_1 + B_2 = \frac{3\mu_0 i}{8R} + \frac{\mu_0 i}{4\pi R}$$

$$\Rightarrow \quad B = \frac{\mu_0 i}{4\pi R}\left[1 + \frac{3\pi}{2}\right]$$

(c) In this case, the magnetic field will be due to a semi circular wire and two semi-infinite wires all in same directions so all will be added up given as

$$B = \frac{\mu_0 i}{4\pi R} + \frac{\mu_0 i}{4R} + \frac{\mu_0 i}{4\pi R}$$

$$\Rightarrow \quad B = \frac{\mu_0 i}{4\pi R}(2 + \pi)$$

(iii) (a) The magnetic induction due to the three wire segments at O is given vectorially as

$$\vec{B}_0 = \vec{B}_1 + \vec{B}_2 + \vec{B}_3 = \frac{\mu_0}{4\pi}\left[\frac{I}{R}(-\vec{k}) + \frac{I\pi}{R}(-1) + \frac{I}{R}(-\vec{k})\right]$$

$$\Rightarrow \quad \vec{B}_0 = -\frac{\mu_0 I}{4\pi R}[2\vec{k} + \pi\vec{i}\,]$$

$$\Rightarrow \quad |\vec{B}_0| = \frac{\mu_0 I}{4\pi R}\sqrt{\pi^2 + 4}$$

(b) The magnetic induction due to the three wire segments at O is given vectorially as

$$\vec{B}_0 = \vec{B}_1 + \vec{B}_2 + \vec{B}_3 = \frac{\mu_0 I}{4\pi R}[-\vec{k} + \pi(-\vec{i}\,) + (-\vec{i}\,)]$$

$$\vec{B}_0 = -\frac{\mu_0 I}{4\pi R}[\vec{k} + (\pi + 1)\vec{i}\,]$$

$$|\vec{B}_0| = \frac{\mu_0 I}{4\pi R}\sqrt{1 + (\pi + 1)^2}$$

(c) The magnetic induction due to the three wire segments at O is given vectorially as

$$\vec{B}_0 = \vec{B}_1 + \vec{B}_2 + \vec{B}_3 = \frac{\mu_0 I}{4\pi R}[(-\vec{k}) + \pi(-\vec{i}\,) + \pi/2(-\vec{i}\,) + (-\vec{j}\,)]$$

$$\Rightarrow \quad \vec{B}_0 = -\frac{\mu_0 I}{4\pi R}\left[\vec{k} + \vec{j} + \frac{3\pi}{2}\vec{i}\right]$$

$$\Rightarrow \quad |\vec{B}_0| = \frac{\mu_0 I}{4\pi R}\sqrt{\left(\frac{3\pi}{2}\right)^2 + 1 + 1}$$

$$\Rightarrow \quad |\vec{B}_0| = \frac{\mu_0 I}{8\pi R}\sqrt{9\pi^2 + 8}$$

(iv) The magnetic induction at center O due to the two circular arcs will be in same inward direction. If $\hat{n}$ is the unit vector in inward direction then it is given as

$$\vec{B}_0 = \vec{B}_a + \vec{B}_b$$

$$\Rightarrow \quad \vec{B}_0 = \left[\frac{\mu_0 I(3\pi/2)}{4\pi a} + \frac{\mu_0 I(\pi/2)}{4\pi b}\right]\hat{n}$$

$$\Rightarrow \quad \vec{B}_0 = \frac{\mu_0 I}{8}\left[\frac{3}{a} + \frac{1}{b}\right]\hat{n}$$

(v) We use the result of magnetic induction due to a finite wire segment which is given as

$$B_P = \frac{\mu_1 I}{4\pi l}[\cos\alpha + \cos\beta]$$

$$\Rightarrow \quad B_P = \frac{\mu_0 I}{4\pi l}[\cos 90° + \cos 30°]$$

$$\Rightarrow \quad B_P = \frac{\sqrt{3}\mu_0 I}{8\pi l}$$

(vi) The magnetic induction at point O will be due to straight segment and the circular arc will be in opposite direction which will be subtracted and it is given as

$$B_0 = B_1 - B_2$$

Where B_1 and B_2 are given as

$$B_1 = \frac{\mu_0 I}{4\pi(R/2)}[\cos 30° + \cos 30°]$$

and

$$B_2 = \frac{\mu_0 I(2\pi/3)}{4\pi R}$$

$$\Rightarrow \quad B_0 = \frac{\mu_0 I}{2\pi R}\sqrt{3} - \frac{\mu_0 I}{6R}$$

$$\Rightarrow \quad B_0 = \frac{\mu_0 I}{2R}\left[\frac{\sqrt{3}}{\pi} - \frac{1}{3}\right]$$

(vii) Due to the wire segments BC and DE no magnetic induction will be produced at O as it lies along the two lines and for the remaining wire segments we use the vector sum which is given as

$$\vec{B}_0 = \vec{B}_{AB} + \vec{B}_{CD} + \vec{B}_{EF} + \vec{B}_{FG}$$

$$\Rightarrow \quad \vec{B}_0 = \frac{\mu_0 I}{4\pi a}(-\hat{k}) + \frac{\mu_0 I}{4\pi(\sqrt{2}a)} \cdot \sqrt{2}(-\hat{k}) + \frac{\mu_0 I}{8a}(-\hat{j}) + \frac{\mu_0 I}{4\pi a}(\hat{i})$$

$$\Rightarrow \quad \vec{B}_0 = \frac{\mu_0 I}{4\pi a}\left[\hat{i} - \frac{\pi}{2}\hat{j} - 2\hat{k}\right]$$

(viii) In the given spiral along the radial direction number of turns per unit radial length is given as

$$n = \frac{N}{b-a}$$

We consider an elemental circular coil of radius x and width dx as shown in figure. The number of turns in this elemental coil are given as

$$dN = n dx = \frac{N}{b-a} \cdot dx$$

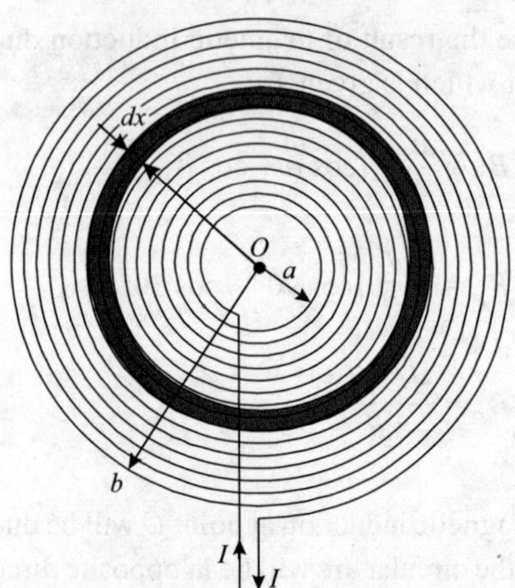

Magnetic induction due to the elemental coil at center O is given as

$$dB = \frac{\mu_0 I}{2x} \times \frac{N}{(b-a)} dx$$

Net magnetic induction at center O is given as

$$B_0 = \int dB = \frac{\mu_0 IN}{2(b-a)} \int_a^b \frac{dx}{x}$$

$$\Rightarrow \quad B_0 = \frac{\mu_0 IN}{2(b-a)} [\ln x]_a^b$$

$$\Rightarrow \quad B_0 = \frac{\mu_0 IN}{2(b-a)} \ln\left(\frac{b}{a}\right)$$

(ix) We consider an elemental wire of width dx at a distance x from the point P as shown in figure. The current in elemental wire is given as

$$dI = \frac{I}{b} \cdot dx$$

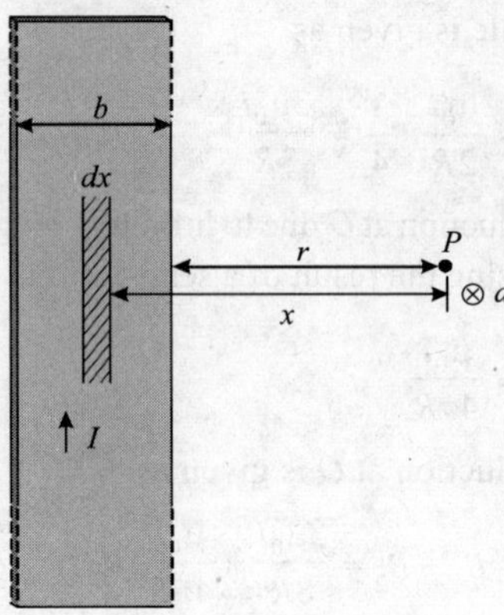

Magnetic induction at point P due to dI is given as

$$dB = \frac{\mu_0 dI}{2\pi x}$$

Total magnetic induction at point P is given as

$$B_P = \int dB = \frac{\mu_0 I}{2\pi b} \int_r^{r+b} \frac{dx}{x}$$

$$\Rightarrow \quad B_P = \frac{\mu_0 I}{2\pi b} [\ln x]_r^{r+b}$$

$$\Rightarrow \quad B_P = \frac{\mu_0 I}{2\pi b} \ln\left(\frac{r+b}{r}\right)$$

(x) The magnetic field induction at point R due to current in wires P and Q is given as

$$B = B_1 + B_2 = \left(\frac{\mu_0 I_1}{2\pi r_1} + \frac{\mu_0 I_2}{2\pi r_2}\right)$$

$$\Rightarrow \quad \vec{B} = -2 \times 10^{-7}\left[\frac{2.5}{5} + \frac{4}{2}\right]\hat{j}$$

$$\Rightarrow \quad \vec{B} = -5 \times 10^{-7}\,\hat{j}$$

If the third wire is placed at a distance x on the left of point R and if the wire carries a current outwards/inward perpendicular to the plane of paper Then for net magnetic induction at R to be zero we use

$$\frac{\mu_0 I}{2\pi x} = 5 \times 10^{-7}$$

$$\Rightarrow \quad x = 1\text{ m}$$

Thus third wire is to be placed at a distance of ± 1 m from point R along x-axis.

Solutions of PRACTICE EXERCISE 4.2

(i) (a) The magnetic induction above the large metal sheet carrying a surface current is given as

$$B = \frac{1}{2}\mu_0 i$$

If i_1 is the current flowing in the solenoid then the magnetic induction at the center of a long solenoid is given as $\mu_0 n i_1$ which nullifies the magnetic induction due to the metal sheet to make net magnetic induction at center of solenoid to be equal to zero thus we have

$$\mu_0 n i_1 = \frac{1}{2}\mu_0 i$$

$$\Rightarrow \quad i_1 = \frac{i}{2n}$$

(b) When solenoid is rotated by 90° then the two magnetic inductions due to solenoid and that due to the metal sheet will be at right angle to each other which are equal in magnitude, so net magnetic induction at the center of solenoid is given by the vector sum of the two vectors which is given as

$$B = \sqrt{B^2 + B^2} = \sqrt{2}B = \sqrt{2}\left(\frac{1}{2}\mu_0 i\right) = \frac{\mu_0 i}{\sqrt{2}}$$

(ii) As current is uniformly distributed over the cross-sections of outer and inner conductors. The current density in inner and outer conductor are given as

$$J_i = \frac{i}{\pi a^2}$$

$$J_o = \frac{i}{\pi(c^2 - b^2)}$$

(a) When $r < a$ we can consider a coaxial circular path of radius r as shown in figure. If B be the magnitude of magnetic field at this path then using Ampere's law we have

$$B(2\pi r) = \mu_0 I_{enclosed}$$

$$\Rightarrow \quad B(2\pi r) = \mu_0\left(\frac{i}{\pi a^2} \times \pi r^2\right)$$

$$\Rightarrow \quad B = \frac{\mu_0 i r}{2\pi a^2}$$

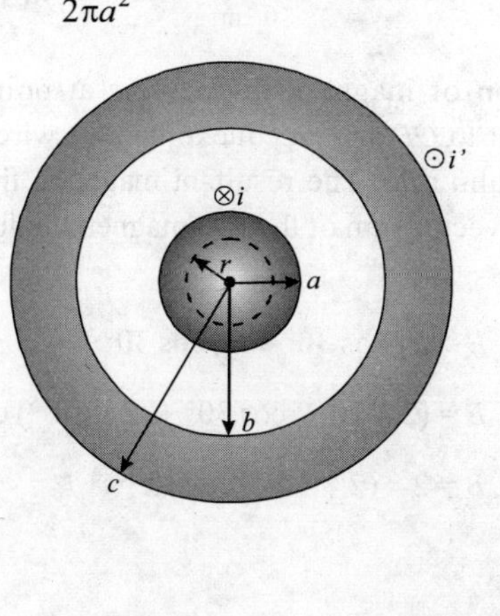

(b) When $a < r < b$ we can consider the circular path of radius r as shown in figure which encloses the current passing through inner conductor only so by using Ampere's law we have

$$B(2\pi r) = \mu_0 i$$

$$\Rightarrow \quad B = \frac{\mu_0 i}{2\pi r}$$

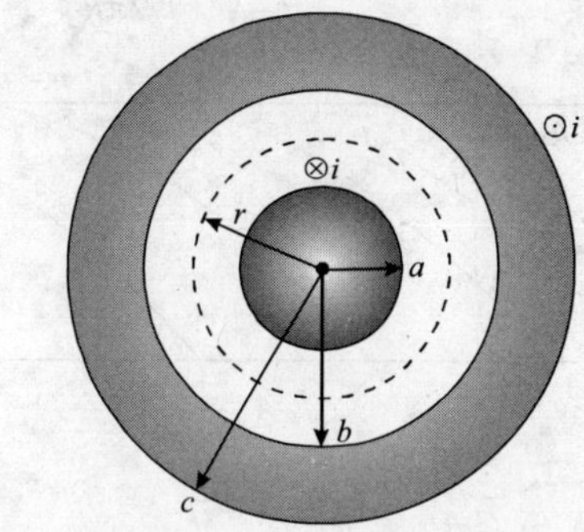

(c) When $b < r < c$ we consider the circular path of radius r as shown in figure. In this case the current enclosed by this coaxial circular path is given as

$$I_{enclosed} = i - \frac{i'}{\pi(c^2 - b^2)} \times \pi(r^2 - b^2)$$

Using Ampere's law we have

$$B(2\pi r) = \mu_0\left[i - \frac{i'}{\pi(c^2 - b^2)} \times \pi(r^2 - b^2)\right]$$

$$\Rightarrow \quad B = \frac{\mu_0}{2\pi r}\left[i - i'\left(\frac{r^2 - b^2}{c^2 - b^2}\right)\right]$$

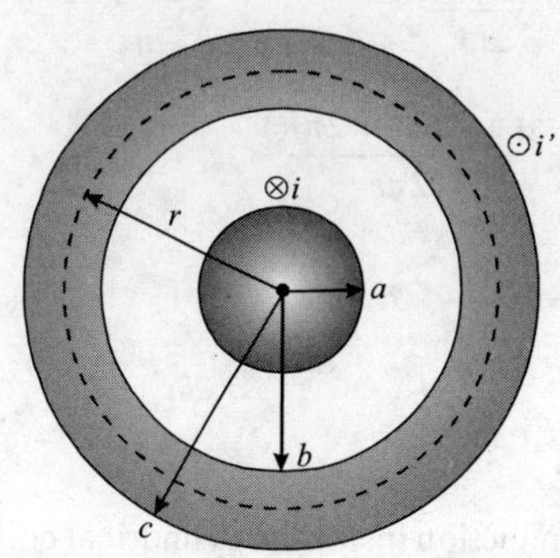

(iii) As current is flowing in a strip of width h, current density per unit length along the thickness of the strip is given as

$$J = \frac{I}{h}$$

Figure-(a) shows that the current density vector is at an angle θ from the cross sectional plane of the cylindrical coil and to calculate the angle θ we straightened one turn of the strip which is shown in figure-(b) from which we can calculate the sine and cosine components of the angle θ which are given as

$$\sin\theta = \frac{h}{2\pi R}$$

and $$\cos\theta = \sqrt{1-\sin^2\theta} = \sqrt{1-\left(\frac{h}{2\pi R}\right)^2}$$

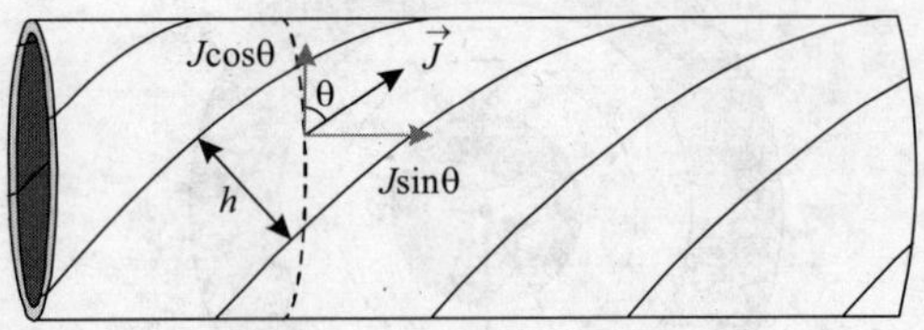

(a)

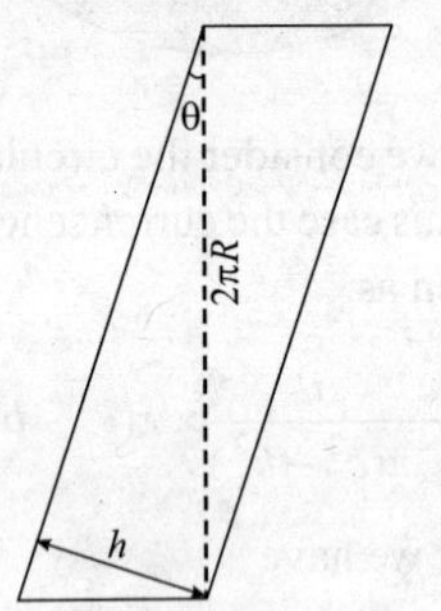

(a)

Magnetic induction outside the coil will be due to the current in the cylindrical coil along its axis which is due to the current along the axis of the cylindrical coil which is calculated by the current density component $J\sin\theta$ given as

$$B_{out} = \frac{\mu_0 I_{axial}}{2\pi r}$$

$$\Rightarrow \quad B_{out} = \frac{\mu_0 (J\sin\theta \times 2\pi R)}{2\pi r}$$

$$\Rightarrow \quad B_{out} = \frac{\mu_0 J h}{2\pi r}$$

$$\Rightarrow \quad B_{out} = \frac{\mu_0 I}{2\pi r}$$

The magnetic induction inside the cylindrical coil is due to the current circulating along the curved part on the surface of cylindrical coil which is given as

$$B_{in} = \mu_0 J\cos\theta$$

$$\Rightarrow \quad B_{in} = \mu_0\left(\frac{I}{h}\right)\sqrt{1-\left(\frac{h}{2\pi R}\right)^2}$$

(iv) Current density in the cylindrical wire is given as

$$J = \frac{i}{\pi(R^2 - r^2)}$$

Current through the smaller cross-section of cavity if it is not present is given as

$$i' = J\pi r^2$$

Magnetic induction due to this current at a point on the axis of cylinder is given as

$$B_1 = \frac{\mu_0 i'}{2\pi d} = \frac{\mu_0}{2\pi d} \times J\pi r^2 = \frac{\mu_0 i r^2}{2\pi d(R^2 - r^2)}$$

If B_2 be the magnetic induction due to remaining portion then in case of full solid cylinder net magnetic induction at axial point is zero so we have

$$B_1 + B_2 = 0$$

$$\Rightarrow \quad B_2 = -B_1$$

$$\Rightarrow \quad B_2 = \frac{\mu_0 i r^2}{2\pi d(R^2 - r^2)}$$

(v) (a) When the currents are in the same direction the situation is shown in figure. If the currents in both the wires are perpendicular to the plane of the paper and directed outward then the magnetic inductions B_1 and B_2 at point O due to the two current carrying wires are given as

$$B_1 = B_2 = \frac{\mu_0}{2\pi}\frac{i}{r}$$

$$\Rightarrow \quad B_1 = B_2 = 2\times 10^{-7}\left(\frac{10}{0.1}\right) = 2\times 10^{-5}\ \text{T}$$

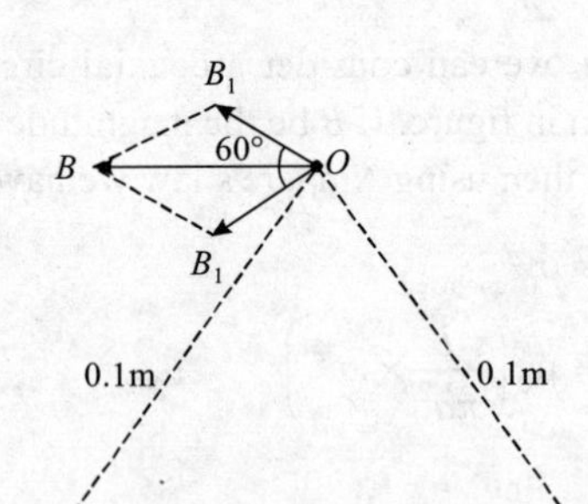

The direction of magnetic inductions at point O will be perpendicular to OP and OQ due to the two wires as given by right hand palm rule. The resultant magnetic field B at O is given by the vector sum of the two magnetic inductions which is given as

$$B = B_1\cos 30° + B_2\cos 30°$$

$$\Rightarrow \quad B = (2\times 10^{-5})\cos 30° + (2\times 10^{-5})\cos 30°$$

$$\Rightarrow \quad B = 2\times(2\times 10^{-5})\cos 30°$$

$\Rightarrow \quad B = 2 \times (2 \times 10^{-5}) \times (\sqrt{3}/2)$

$\Rightarrow \quad B = 3.46 \times 10^{-5}\,T$

(b) When the currents are in opposite directions. The situation is shown in figure. If the current in wire P is inward and that in wire Q be directed outward then from the previous part the magnetic inductions due to the two wires will be given as

$$B_1 = 2 \times 10^{-5}\,T$$

and $$B_2 = 2 \times 10^{-5}\,T$$

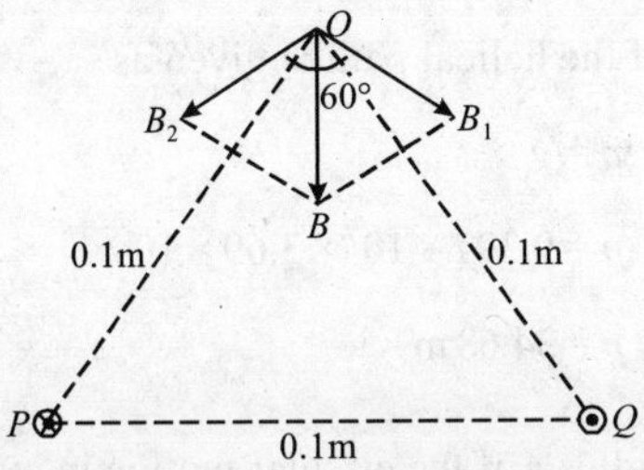

The direction of B_1 will be perpendicular to OP towards right and the direction of B_2 will be perpendicular to OQ towards left. The resultant magnetic induction at O is given by the vector sum of the two inductions which is given as

$$B = B_1 \cos 60° + B_2 \cos 60°$$

$$\Rightarrow \quad B = 2 \times (2 \times 10^{-5}) \times \frac{1}{2}$$

$$\Rightarrow \quad B = 2 \times 10^{-5}\,T$$

(vi) Charge on capacitor after time Δt is given as

$$q = \frac{CE}{\eta}$$

Charge flown through the solenoid in this duration is given as

$$\Delta q = CE - \frac{CE}{\eta} = CE\left(1 - \frac{1}{\eta}\right)$$

Average current in solenoid in this period is given as

$$i_{avg} = \frac{\Delta q}{\Delta t} = \frac{CE}{\Delta t}\left(1 - \frac{1}{\eta}\right)$$

Average magnetic induction at the center of solenoid is given as

$$B_{avg} = \mu_0 n i_{avg}$$

$$\Rightarrow \quad B_{avg} = \frac{\mu_0 nCE}{\Delta t}\left(1 - \frac{1}{\eta}\right)$$

(vii) The magnetic induction due to a current carrying thin walled tube at an internal point is always zero. However if a longitudinal cut of width h is made in the tube as shown in figure, then symmetry will no longer exist and inside magnetic induction will not be zero. A net magnetic induction will exists at an internal point. We consider a point P inside the tube at a distance r from the slit as shown. The net magnetic induction due to the tube at point P is equal to the magnetic induction produced at P due to the current in the portion of tube which is removed to make the slit. As slit width is very small the current in the slit width h is given as

$$I_S = \frac{I}{2\pi R} \times h$$

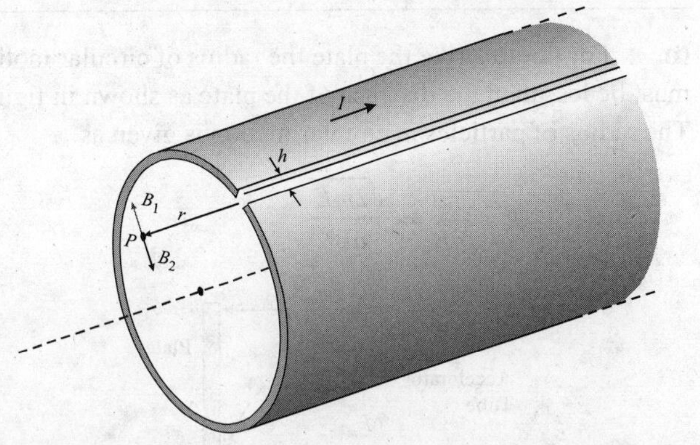

The magnetic induction at point P due to the current in the slit portion of tube is B_1 as shown in figure which is given as

$$B_1 = \frac{\mu_0 I_s}{2\pi r} = \frac{\mu_0}{2\pi}\frac{\left(\frac{I}{2\pi R}\right)h}{r} = \frac{\mu_0 Ih}{4\pi^2 Rr}$$

The magnetic induction due to the tube with the slit is given as B_2 which is equal and opposite to B_1 so that when tube is complete both the fields will nullify each other.

(viii) Above the plane at a general point P as shown in figure we apply Ampere's law on the circular path and because of symmetry about the axis of wire, the magnetic induction at every point of the circular path is along the path so we have

$$B(2\pi r) = \mu_0 I$$

$$\Rightarrow \quad B = \frac{\mu_0 I}{2\pi r}$$

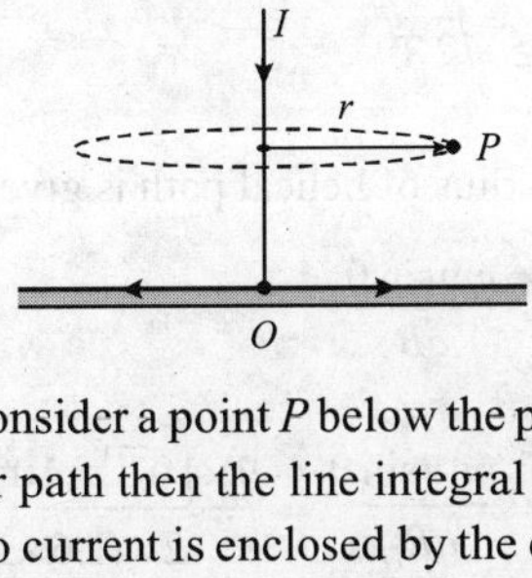

Similarly if we consider a point P below the plane and consider a similar circular path then the line integral of magnetic field will be zero as no current is enclosed by the closed path so the magnetic induction at all the points below the plane will be zero.

(ix) The magnetic induction inside the tore of the toroid is given as

$$B=\frac{\mu_r\mu_0 NI}{2\pi R}$$

$$\Rightarrow \quad B=\frac{100\times 4\pi\times 10^{-7}\times 1000\times 2}{2\pi\times 0.25}$$

$$\Rightarrow \quad B=16\times 10^{-2}\,\text{T}$$

Solutions of PRACTICE EXERCISE 4.3

(i) For not to strike the plate the radius of circular motion must be less than the distance of the plate as shown in figure. The radius of particles in circular motion is given as

$$R=\frac{mv}{qB}=\frac{\sqrt{2mE}}{qB}$$

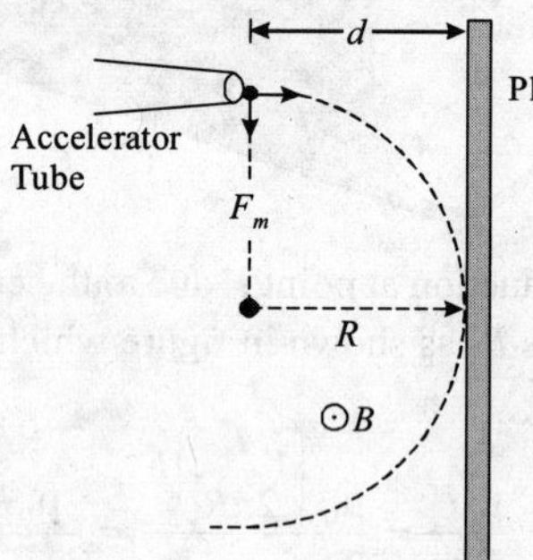

Larger radius will be for heavy particles and for not to strike the plate we use

$$R\le d$$

$$\Rightarrow \quad \frac{\sqrt{2mE}}{qB}\le d$$

$$\Rightarrow \quad B\ge\frac{\sqrt{2mE}}{qd}$$

$$\Rightarrow \quad B\ge\frac{\sqrt{2\times 1.6\times 10^{-26}\times 1000\times 1.6\times 10^{-19}}}{1.6\times 10^{-19}\times 0.01}$$

$$\Rightarrow \quad B\ge\sqrt{2}\,\text{T}$$

(ii) (a) The radius of helical path is given as

$$R_{\text{H}}=\frac{mv\sin\theta}{qB}$$

$$\Rightarrow \quad B=\frac{m_e v\sin\theta}{qR_H}=\frac{9\times 10^{-31}\times 10^{8}\times\sin 20^\circ}{2\times(1.6\times 10^{-19})}$$

$$\Rightarrow \quad B=9.6\times 10^{-5}\,\text{T}$$

(b) The time period of circular motion in magnetic field by a charge particle is given as

$$T=\frac{2\pi m_e}{Bq}=\frac{2\pi\times(9\times 10^{-31})}{(9.6\times 10^{-5})(1.6\times 10^{-19})}$$

$$\Rightarrow \quad T=3.69\times 10^{-7}\,\text{s}$$

(c) Velocity component parallel to magnetic field is given as

$$v_y=v\cos 20^\circ=10^8\times 0.9397$$

$$\Rightarrow \quad v_y=9.397\times 10^7\,\text{m/s}$$

Thus pitch of the helical path is given as

$$p=v_y\times t$$

$$\Rightarrow \quad p=9.397\times 10^7\times 3.69\times 10^{-7}$$

$$\Rightarrow \quad p=34.68\,\text{m}$$

(iii) The radius r of the circular motion in magnetic field is given as

$$r=\frac{mv}{qB}$$

For proton, we have

$$r_p=\frac{m_p v_p}{d_p B}$$

For deuteron, we have

$$r_d=\frac{m_d v_d}{d_d B}$$

$$\Rightarrow \quad \frac{r_d}{r_p}=\frac{m_d v_d}{m_p v_p}\times\frac{q_p}{q_d} \quad \ldots(1)$$

Given that kinetic energies of the two particles are same so we have

$$\frac{1}{2}m_p v_p^2=\frac{1}{2}m_d v_d^2$$

$$\Rightarrow \quad \frac{v_d}{v_p}=\left(\frac{m_p}{m_d}\right)^{1/2} \quad \ldots(2)$$

Substituting the value of v_d/v_p from equation-(2) in equation-(1), we get

$$\frac{r_d}{r_p}=\frac{m_d}{m_p}\times\left(\frac{m_p}{m_d}\right)^{1/2}=\left(\frac{m_d}{m_p}\right)^{1/2}=\sqrt{2}$$

$$\Rightarrow \quad r_d=\sqrt{2}\cdot r_p=1.414\times 0.15=0.212\,\text{m}$$

(iv) Given that the kinetic energy of electrons is 2 keV. So we can calculate the momentum of electrons as

$$\frac{1}{2}mv^2 = 2\text{ keV}$$

$$\Rightarrow \quad \frac{1}{2}mv^2 = 2\times10^3\times(1.6\times10^{-19})\text{ J}$$

$$\Rightarrow \quad m^2v^2 = 2\,m\times2\times10^3\times(1.6\times10^{-19})$$

$$\Rightarrow \quad mv = [2\,(9.1\times10^{-31})\times2\times10^3\times(1.6\times10^{-19})]^{1/2}$$

$$\Rightarrow \quad mv = 2.41\times10^{-23}\text{ N-s}$$

To hit the point S distance GS should be at least equal to one pitch of the helical path followed by electrons so we have

$$GS = \frac{2\pi mv\cos\theta}{qB}$$

$$\Rightarrow \quad B = \frac{2\pi mv\cos\theta}{q(GS)}$$

$$\Rightarrow \quad B = \frac{2\times3.14\times2.41\times10^{-23}\times0.5}{1.6\times10^{-19}\times0.1} = 4.73\times10^{-3}\text{ T}$$

(v) The kinetic energy of electron is 15000 eV. Thus we use

$$\frac{1}{2}mv^2 = 15000\text{ eV} = 15000\times(1.6\times10^{-19})\text{ J}$$

$$\Rightarrow \quad \frac{1}{2}mv^2 = 2.4\times10^{-15}\text{ J}$$

$$\Rightarrow \quad v = \sqrt{\left(\frac{2\times(2.4\times10^{-15})}{9.1\times10^{-31}}\right)} = 7.3\times10^7\text{ m/s}$$

Radius of circular motion is given as

$$r = \frac{mv}{qB}$$

$$\Rightarrow \quad r = \frac{(9.1\times10^{-31})(7.3\times10^7)}{(1.6\times10^{-19})\times(250\times10^4)} = 0.0166\text{ m}$$

(vi) Figure below shows the situation described in the question. When the beam will be focussed on point P then the distance AP must be an integral multiple of the pitch of helical path. For a slightly divergent beam for which we can consider $\cos\theta$ to be approximately equal to unity the pitch of helical path is given as

$$p_H = \frac{2\pi mv}{qB} = \frac{2\pi\sqrt{2mqV}}{qB}$$

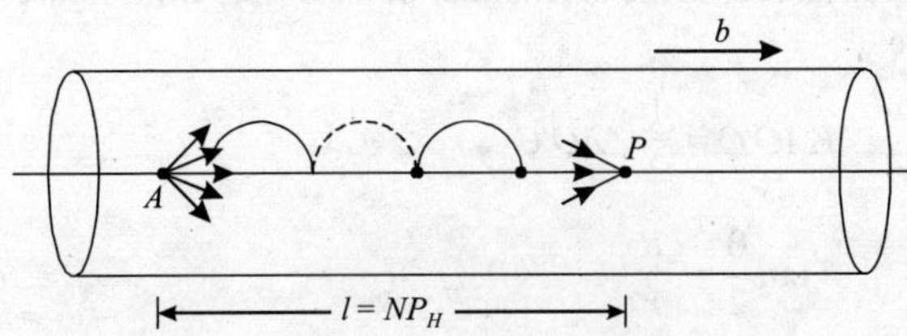

For the magnetic induction B_1 if the distance AP is N times that of the pitch then for the magnetic induction B_2 this distance will be $(N+1)$ times the pitch so we use

$$l = N\left(\frac{2\pi\sqrt{2mqV}}{qB_1}\right) \quad \ldots(1)$$

and $$l = (N+1)\left(\frac{2\pi\sqrt{2mqV}}{qB_2}\right) \quad \ldots(2)$$

$$\Rightarrow \quad (B_2 - B_1)l = \frac{2\pi\sqrt{2mqV}}{q}$$

$$\Rightarrow \quad (B_2 - B_1)^2l^2 = \frac{8\pi^2mqV}{q^2}$$

$$\Rightarrow \quad \frac{q}{m} = \frac{8\pi^2V}{l^2(B_2-B_1)^2}$$

(vii) The magnetic induction of the solenoid is directed along its axis. The magnetic force on the electron at any instant will be in a plane perpendicular to solenoid axis and the trajectory of the electron in the solenoid will be an arc of a circle. The radius r of the circular arch is given as

$$r = \frac{mv}{eB} \quad \ldots(1)$$

The trajectory of the electron is shown in figure below

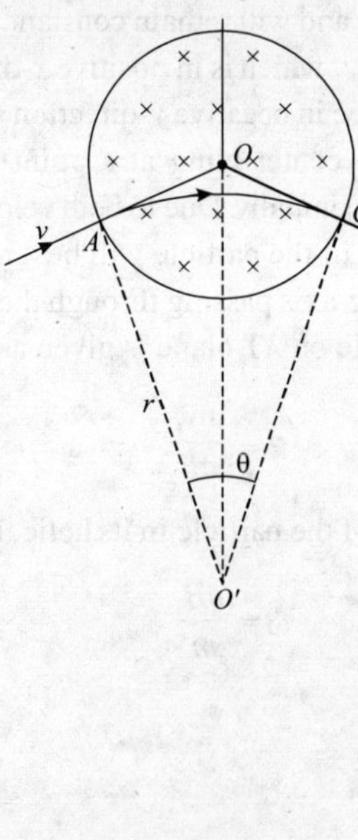

If electron leaves the solenoid at point C then from figure we have

$$\angle AO'O = \frac{1}{2}\angle AO'C$$

$$\Rightarrow \quad \tan\frac{\theta}{2} = \frac{R}{r} \quad \dots(2)$$

From equations-(1) and (2) we have

$$\theta = 2\tan^{-1}\left(\frac{eBR}{mv}\right) \quad \dots(3)$$

The magnitude of velocity remains constant over the entire trajectory so the transit time of electron inside the solenoid is given as

$$t = \frac{r\theta}{v} = \frac{m}{eB}\times\theta$$

$$t = \frac{2m}{eB}\tan^{-1}\left(\frac{eBR}{mv}\right)$$

(viii) The force on electron is given as

$$F = qvB$$

Magnetic induction at point R is given as

$$B = \frac{\mu_0(2.5)}{2\pi(5)} + \frac{\mu_0 I}{2\pi(2)} = \frac{\mu_0}{4\pi}(1+I)$$

Substituting the values, we get the force on electron as

$$F = 1.6\times10^{-19}\times4\times10^{5}\times10^{-7}(1+I)$$

$$\Rightarrow \quad F = 6.4\times10^{-21}(1+I)$$

$$\Rightarrow \quad F = 6.4\times10^{-21}(1+I) = 3.2\times10^{-20}\text{ N}$$

$$\Rightarrow \quad I = 4\text{ A}$$

(ix) The velocity component v_2 of the particle is along Z-axis and parallel to the magnetic field direction thus it will not experience any force and will remain constant. Due to the other velocity component v_1 which is in positive x-direction, particle will experience a force in negative y-direction and it will follow a circular path with center lying at a point C with position coordinates $(0, -R, 0)$ initially. Due to both velocity components the resulting motion of the particle will be a helical trajectory with axis parallel to z-axis passing through the point $(0, -R, 0)$ where radius of circle on XY plane is given as

$$R = \frac{mv_1}{qB}$$

The angular speed of the particle in its helical path is given as

$$\omega = \frac{qB}{m}$$

In a time t the particle will revolve by an angle θ along XY plane which is given as $\theta = \omega t$. X and Y coordinates of the particle can be calculated by considering the projection of the helical path on XY plane which is a circle. The position coordinates of particle at time t are given as

$$x = R\sin\theta = \frac{mv_1}{qB}\sin\left(\frac{qBt}{m}\right)$$

and $y = -R(1-\cos\theta) = -\dfrac{mv_1}{qB}\left(1-\cos\left(\dfrac{qBt}{m}\right)\right)$

and $z = v_2 t$

(x) Figure shows the situation described in the question. The electron follows a circular path with center C such that it just escapes the outer shell tangentially and does not collide with it. The radius of the circular path is given as

$$r = \frac{mv}{eB}$$

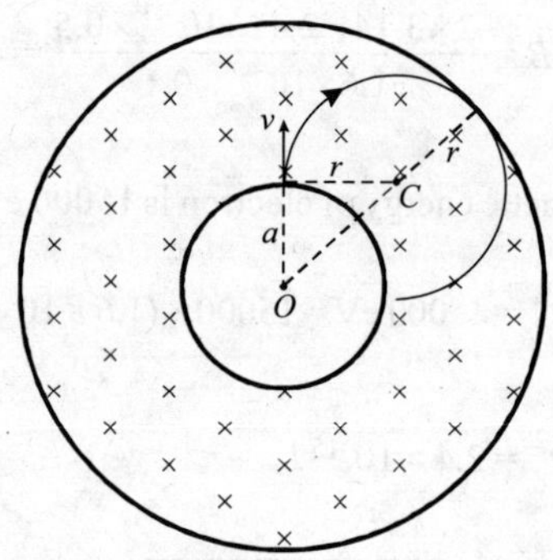

From the above figure we have the length OC given as

$$b - r = \sqrt{a^2 + r^2}$$

$$\Rightarrow \quad b^2 + r^2 - 2br = a^2 + r^2$$

$$\Rightarrow \quad r = \frac{b^2 - a^2}{2b}$$

$$\Rightarrow \quad \frac{mv}{eB} = \frac{b^2 - a^2}{2b}$$

$$\Rightarrow \quad v = \frac{eB(b^2 - a^2)}{2mb}$$

Solutions of PRACTICE EXERCISE 4.4

(i) For wire to slide up the incline we use

$$BIl \geq mg\sin\alpha + \mu\, mg\cos\alpha$$

$$B \geq \frac{mg(\sin\alpha + \mu\cos\alpha)}{Il}$$

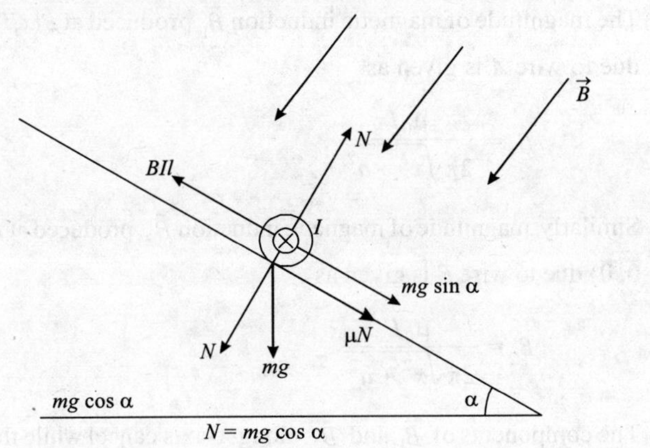

(ii) For the springs to remain unstretched the weight of the wire must be balanced by the magnetic force acting on the wire in upward direction. So for equilibrium of wire we have

$$Bil = mg$$

$$\Rightarrow \quad i = \frac{mg}{lB} = \frac{1.0\times10^{-2}\times9.8}{0.6\times0.4}\,\text{A}$$

$$\Rightarrow \quad i = 0.41\,\text{A}$$

For the magnetic force on wire to act in upward direction , the direction of current should be from left to right.

(iii) Repulsive magnitude force on wires per unit length is given as

$$F_m = \frac{\mu_0 I^2}{2\pi r}$$

Figure below shows the forces on the wires in equilibrium state.

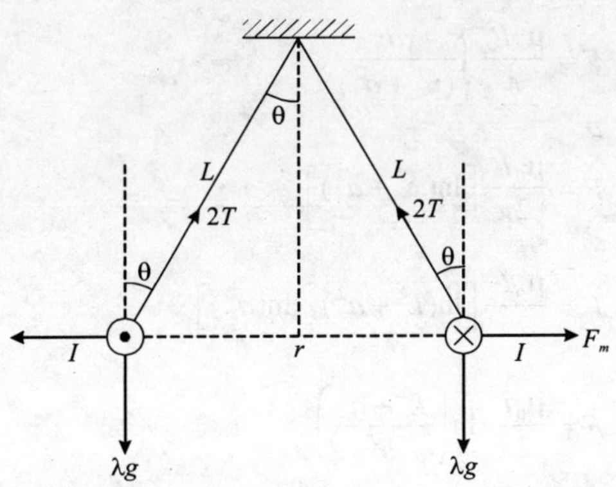

For equilibrium of wires we use

$$2T\sin\theta = \mu_0 I^2/2\pi r$$

$$2T\cos\theta = \lambda g$$

$$\Rightarrow \quad \tan\theta = \frac{\mu_0 I^2}{2\pi\lambda r g} = \frac{\mu_0 I^2}{2\pi\lambda(L\tan\theta)g}$$

$$\Rightarrow \quad \theta^2 = \frac{\mu_0 I^2}{4\pi\lambda g L} \quad \text{(for small angles we use } \tan\theta \approx \theta\text{)}$$

$$\Rightarrow \quad \theta = \sqrt{\mu_0 I^2/4\pi\lambda g l}$$

(iv) Initially the particle is moving undeflected that means electric and magnetic forces on the particle are balanced which is given as

$$qE = qvB\cos\phi$$

$$\Rightarrow \quad v = \frac{E}{B\cos\phi} \qquad \ldots(1)$$

When electric field is switched off, the protons are moving at an angle (90° – ϕ) to the direction of magnetic field thus path followed by the particle will be helical of which pitch is given as

$$p_H = v\sin\phi \times \frac{2\pi m}{qB} \qquad \ldots(2)$$

Substituting the value of v from equation-(1) in equation-(2), we get

$$p_H = \left(\frac{E}{B\cos\phi}\times\sin\phi\right)\times\frac{2\pi m}{qB}$$

$$\Rightarrow \quad p_H = \frac{2\pi m E}{qB^2}\tan\phi$$

(v) Force on every element of width dl on wire is $Bidl$. This is perpendicular to the element in outward direction on all elements so the loop opens into a circle. The tension in circular loop can be directly given as

$$T = \frac{\textit{Total scalar sum of radial force}}{2\pi}$$

$$\Rightarrow \quad T = \frac{Bil}{2\pi} = \frac{1.57\times1.0\times0.5}{2\times3.14}\,\text{N}$$

$$\Rightarrow T = 0.125\,\text{N}$$

(vi) (a) The magnetic field at O will be only due to the curved path which is given as

$$B = \frac{\mu_0 i}{4R}$$

The magnetic force per unit length of the wire at point O is given as

$$F = Bi$$

$$\Rightarrow \quad F = \frac{\mu_0 i^2}{4R}$$

$$\Rightarrow \quad F = \frac{4\times3.14\times10^{-7}\times(64)}{r\times(0.1)}\,\text{N/m}$$

$$\Rightarrow \quad F = 2\times10^{-4}\,\text{N/m}$$

(b) The magnetic induction at O will be only due to two semi-infinite segments of wire which is given as

$$B = 2\times\frac{\mu_0 i}{4\pi(l/2)}$$

The magnetic force per unit length of the wire at point O is given as

$$F = Bi$$

$$\Rightarrow \quad F = \frac{\mu_0 i^2}{\pi l}$$

$$\Rightarrow \quad F = 1280\times10^{-7}\,\text{N/m}$$

(vii) By work-energy theorem we can state that the work done by magnetic force in rotation of the square loop from initial position to horizontal position is equal to the work done against gravity in the process which is written as

$$W_{MF} - W_{gravity} = 0$$

$$\Rightarrow \quad BIl^2 = \frac{mgl}{2}$$

$$\Rightarrow \quad B = \frac{mg}{2Il}$$

(viii) By impulse of magnetic force, if the wire attains a velocity v in upward direction then we use

$$BIl\delta t = mv$$

$$\Rightarrow \quad v = \frac{Bql}{m}$$

Maximum height attained by wire MN is given as

$$h = \frac{v^2}{2q} = \frac{B^2q^2l^2}{2m^2g}$$

(ix) We consider a small element P of length dx at a distance x from the end O as shown in figure.

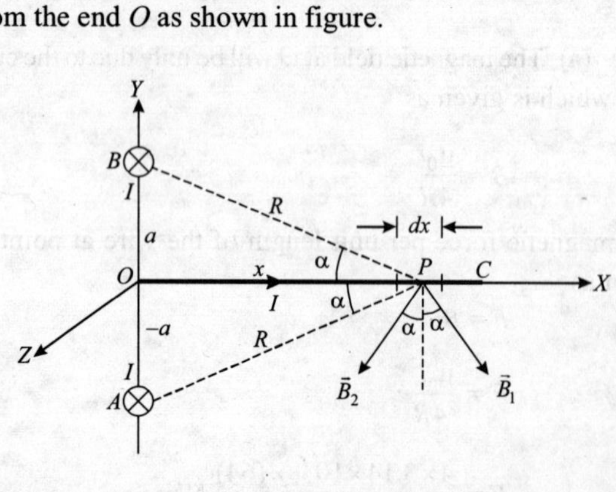

The magnetic inductions produced at point P due to A and B are perpendicular to AP and BP which are given as $\vec{B}_1$ and $\vec{B}_2$.

The magnitude of magnetic induction $\vec{B}_1$ produced at $P(x, 0, 0)$ due to wire A is given as

$$B_1 = \frac{\mu_0 I}{2\pi\sqrt{x^2+a^2}}$$

Similarly, magnitude of magnetic induction $\vec{B}_2$ produced at $P(x, 0, 0)$ due to wire B is given as

$$B_2 = \frac{\mu_0 I}{2\pi\sqrt{x^2+a^2}}$$

The components of $\vec{B}_1$ and $\vec{B}_2$ along X-axis cancel while those along Y-axis are added up. As $B_1 = B_2 = B$, we use the total field at point P is given as

$$B_P = 2B\cos\alpha$$

$$\Rightarrow \quad B_P = 2\times\frac{\mu_0 I}{2\pi\sqrt{x^2+a^2}}\times\frac{x}{\sqrt{x^2+a^2}}$$

$$\Rightarrow \quad B_P = \frac{\mu_0 Ix}{\pi(x^2+a^2)}$$

The force dF acting on the current element due to net magnetic induction at point P is given as

$$dF = BIdx$$

$$\Rightarrow \quad dF = \frac{\mu_0 I^2 xdx}{\pi(x^2+a^2)}$$

Net force on the whole conductor is given as

$$F = \int dF = \int_0^L \frac{\mu_0 I^2 x}{\pi(x^2+a^2)}dx$$

$$\Rightarrow \quad F = \frac{\mu_0 I^2}{\pi}\int_0^L \frac{xdx}{(x^2+a^2)}$$

$$\Rightarrow \quad F = \frac{\mu_0 I^2}{2\pi}\left[\ln(x^2+a^2)\right]_0^L$$

$$\Rightarrow \quad F = \frac{\mu_0 I^2}{2\pi}\left[\ln(L^2+a^2)-\ln(a^2)\right]$$

$$\Rightarrow \quad F = \frac{\mu_0 I^2}{2\pi}\ln\left(\frac{L^2+a^2}{a^2}\right)$$

If the current in wire B is reversed, the resultant magnetic field due the two wires will be along X-direction and the force on the conductor along X-direction will be zero.

(x) At $t = 0$, the particle is at (0, 0.4 m, 0) and velocity is directed along positive direction of X. Thus the particle is moving in clockwise direction. As the particle is positively charged, the current associated with its motion is also clockwise or along positive X-direction at (0, 0.4 m, 0). The magnetic force on particle is towards origin so by right hand palm rule we can see that the magnetic induction will be along positive Z-direction.

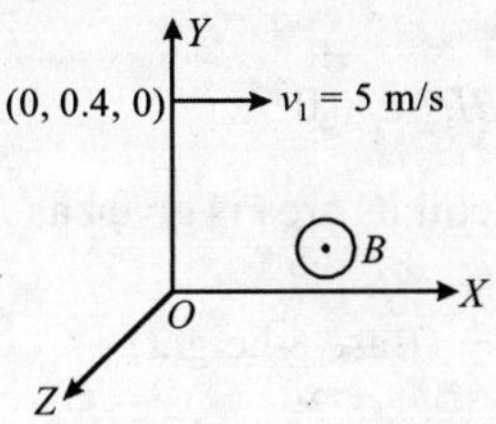

The radius of circular motion is given as

$$r_1 = \frac{m_1 v_1}{q_1 B}$$

$$\Rightarrow \quad B = \frac{m_1 v_1}{q_1 r_1}$$

$$\Rightarrow \quad B = \frac{0.04\times 5}{1\times 0.4} = 0.5\text{ T}$$

Now we consider the collision with second particle. Using the law of conservation of momentum, we have

$$(m_1+m_2)\vec{v} = m_1\vec{v}_1 + m_2\vec{v}_2$$

$$(0.04+0.010)\vec{v} = 0.04\times 5\vec{i} + 0.010\times(40/\pi)\vec{k}$$

$$\Rightarrow \quad 0.05\vec{v} = 0.20\vec{i} + (0.40/\pi)\vec{k}$$

$$\Rightarrow \quad v_x = 4\text{ m/s and } v_z = 8\text{ m/s}$$

Due to v_x combined particle tend to move clockwise along a circular path. But due to velocity v_z it tires to move uniformly along Z-axis. So its resulting path becomes helical.

The radius of helical path is given as

$$R = \frac{(m_1+m_2)v_x}{(q_1+q_2)B} = \frac{0.05\times 4}{2\times 0.5} = 0.2\text{ m}$$

Time period of revolution is given as

$$T = \frac{2\pi(m_1+m_2)}{(q_1+q_2)B} = \frac{2\pi\times 0.05}{2\times 0.5} = \frac{\pi}{10}\text{ s}$$

The axis of helix is located at

$$y_0 = (r_1 - R) = 0.4 - 0.2 = 0.2\text{ m}$$

Angular displacement of the particle due to circular motion along helical path in given time is given as

$$\theta = 2\pi\left(\frac{t}{T}\right) \text{ or } \theta = 2\pi\left[\frac{(\pi/40)}{(\pi/10)}\right] = \frac{\pi}{2}$$

Thus after the given time final coordinates of the particle are given as

$$x = R\sin\theta = R = 0.2\text{ m}$$

$$y = y_0 - R\cos\theta = 0.2\text{ m}$$

$$z = v_z t = 0.2\text{ m}$$

(xi) If we consider the wire is placed along Z-axis and the initial direction of the electron is along X-axis then the magnetic induction in surrounding of wire exist in the XZ plane and it is in the direction of Y-axis in the plane of paper acting on electron outside the wire. By right hand palm rule the magnetic force on electron will act in negative Z direction due to which its path is deflected as shown in figure. The magnetic induction at the location of electron when it is at a distance x from the axis of wire is given as

$$B = B_y = \frac{\mu_0 i}{2\pi x}$$

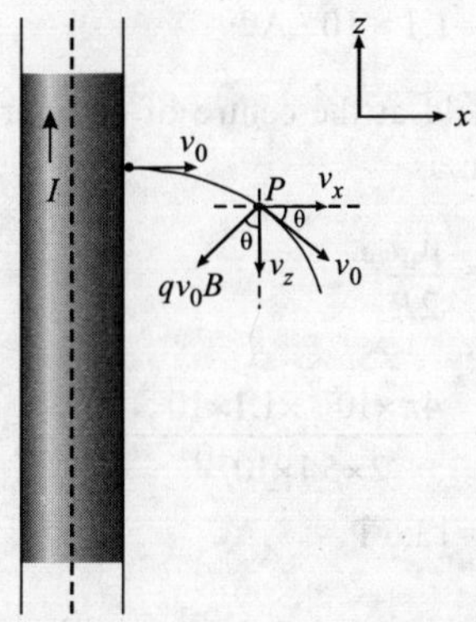

Along x and z direction the acceleration of the electron is given as

$$a_x = -\frac{qv_0 B\sin\theta}{m} = \frac{qv_z B}{m} \quad \ldots(1)$$

$$\text{and} \quad a_z = \frac{qv_0 B\cos\theta}{m} = \frac{qv_x B}{m} \quad \ldots(2)$$

As no work is done by magnetic force on electron, its speed remain constant so we use

$$v_x^2 + v_z^2 = v_0^2$$

$$\Rightarrow \quad v_z = \sqrt{(v_0^2 - v_x^2)}$$

From equation-(1) we have

$$v_x\frac{dv_x}{dx} = -\frac{q}{m}\sqrt{(v_0^2 - v_x^2)}\,\frac{\mu_0 i}{2\pi x} \quad \ldots(3)$$

$$\Rightarrow \quad -\frac{v_x dv_x}{\sqrt{(v_0^2 - v_x^2)}} = \frac{\mu_0 iq}{2\pi m}\frac{dx}{x}$$

Integrating the above expression we have

$$-\int_{v_o}^{v_x}\frac{v_x dv_x}{\sqrt{(v_0^2-v_x^2)}} = \int_a^x \frac{\mu_0 iq}{2\pi m}\frac{dx}{x}$$

$$\Rightarrow \quad \sqrt{(v_0^2-v_x^2)} = \frac{\mu_0 iq}{2\pi m}\ln\left(\frac{x}{a}\right)$$

When x is maximum $x = x_m$ we have $v_x = 0$ which gives

$$x_{\max} = ae^{\frac{2\pi m v_o}{\mu_0 iq}}$$

Solutions of PRACTICE EXERCISE 4.5

(i) (a) The equivalent current due to revolution of electron in orbit is given as

Current = Charge × Frequency

$$i = (1.6\times10^{-19})\times(6.8\times10^{15})$$

$$\Rightarrow \quad i = 1.1\times10^{-3}\text{ A}$$

The magnetic field at the centre of circular orbit carrying a current i is given as

$$B = \frac{\mu_0 i}{2R}$$

$$\Rightarrow \quad B = \frac{4\pi\times10^{-7}\times1.1\times10^{-3}}{2\times5.1\times10^{-11}}$$

$$\Rightarrow \quad B = 13.6\text{ T}$$

(b) Equivalent dipole moment of the rotating electron is given as

$$M = iA = i\times\pi r^2$$

$$\Rightarrow \quad M = (1.1\times10^{-3})\,\pi\,(5.1\times10^{-11})^2$$

$$\Rightarrow \quad M = 90\times10^{-24}\text{ Am}^2.$$

(ii) The torque on a coil in magnetic field is given as

$$\tau = BINA\sin\theta$$

Where θ is the angle which area vector or magnetic moment vector of the loop makes with the direction of magnetic induction.

As the angle between the plane of the loop and the magnetic field is 30° which gives that θ = 90° – 30° = 60°. Thus torque on coil is given as

$$\tau = 0.5\times0.1\times20\times0.05\times\sin60°$$

$$\Rightarrow \quad \tau = 4.3\times10^{-3}\text{ Nm}$$

The torque vector direction is given by right hand thumb rule for cross product of magnetic moment and magnetic induction which is parallel to the 10 cm side of the coil and points downward along negative y-direction.

(iii) The couple acting on a closed loop in magnetic field is given as

$$\tau = BINA\sin\theta$$

For the triangular coil its area is given as

$$A = \frac{1}{2}(\text{Base}\times\text{height})$$

$$\Rightarrow \quad A = \frac{1}{2}(0.02\times0.01732) = 1.732\times10^{-4}\text{m}^2$$

Thus torque on coil is given as

$$\tau = 5\times10^{-2}\times0.1\times1\times(1.732\times10^{-4})\times)\times\sin90°$$

$$\Rightarrow \quad \tau = 8.66\times10^{-7}\text{ Nm}$$

(iv) (a) The magnetic induction at P is due to the circular arc subtending an angle 120° and the straight wire MN. The magnetic induction B_1 at P due to the circular arc is given as

$$B_1 = \frac{\mu_0 nI}{2a} = \frac{\mu_0\left(\frac{1}{3}\right)I}{2a} = \frac{\mu_0 I}{6a}\text{ along }Z\text{-axis}$$

The magnetic induction B_2 due to straight wire at point P is calculated by using the result of magnetic induction due to a finite wire which is given as

$$B_2 = \frac{\mu_0 I}{4\pi d}(\sin60° + \sin60°)$$

The distance of the wire from P is given as

$$d = a\cos60° = a/2$$

$$\Rightarrow \quad B_2 = \frac{\mu_0 nI}{4\pi(a/2)}\left(\frac{\sqrt{3}}{2}+\frac{\sqrt{3}}{2}\right)$$

$$\Rightarrow \quad B_2 = \frac{\sqrt{3}\mu_0 I}{2\pi a}\text{ along }(-Z)\text{ axis}$$

Net magnetic field at point P is given as

$$B = B_1 - B_2 = \frac{\mu_0 I}{6a} - \frac{\sqrt{3}}{2}\frac{\mu_0 I}{\pi a}$$

$$\Rightarrow \quad B = \frac{\mu_0 I}{a}\left[\frac{1}{6}-\frac{\sqrt{3}}{2\pi}\right]\text{ along }Z\text{-axis}$$

Vectorially the magnetic induction at point P is given as

$$\vec{B} = \frac{\mu_0 I}{a}\left[\frac{1}{6}-\frac{\sqrt{3}}{2\pi}\right]\hat{k}$$

The velocity of particle v makes an angle of 60° with X-axis so its velocity vector is given as

$$\vec{v} = v\cos 60°\hat{i} + v\sin 60°\hat{j} = \frac{v}{2}\hat{i} + \frac{\sqrt{3}v}{2}\hat{j}$$

$$\Rightarrow \quad \vec{v} = \frac{v}{2}(\hat{i} + \sqrt{3}\hat{j})$$

The magnetic force on charge Q at point P is given by Lorentz force equation as

$$\vec{F}_m = Q(\vec{v} \times \vec{B})$$

The acceleration of particle at point P is given as

$$\vec{a}_m = \frac{\vec{F}_m}{m} = \frac{q}{m}(\vec{v} \times \vec{B})$$

$$\Rightarrow \quad \vec{a}_m = \frac{q}{m}\left[\frac{v}{2}(\hat{i} + \sqrt{3}\hat{j}) \times \frac{\mu_0 I}{a}\left(\frac{1}{6} - \frac{\sqrt{3}}{2\pi}\right)\hat{k}\right]$$

$$\Rightarrow \quad \vec{a}_m = \frac{0.109\mu_0 IQv}{ma}$$

(b) The torque on the current loop is given as

$$\vec{\tau} = \vec{M} \times \vec{B}$$

The magnetic moment of the loop is given as

$$\vec{M} = I \times (\text{Area of the loop})$$

Area of loop = Arc of the sector MNP– area of ΔPMN

$$A = \frac{1}{3}\pi a^2 - \frac{1}{2}\left(\frac{a}{2}\right)(\sqrt{3}a)$$

$$\Rightarrow \quad A = \frac{\pi a^2}{3} - \frac{\sqrt{3}a^2}{4} = 0.6136\, a^2$$

The area is in X-Y plane as shown in figure so vectorially it is written as

$$\vec{A} = 0.6136\, a^2\hat{k}$$

Thus torque on loop is given as

$$\vec{\tau} = (I \times 0.6136\, a^2)\hat{k} \times B\hat{i}$$

$$\Rightarrow \quad \vec{\tau} = 0.6136\, IBa^2\,\hat{j}$$

The direction of the torque will be along Y-axis.

(v) Figure shows the situation described in the question. When a magnetic dipole moment M is rotated through angle θ from equilibrium position, in a uniform magnetic field B, the workdone on it is given as

$$W = MB(1 - \cos\theta) \quad \ldots(1)$$

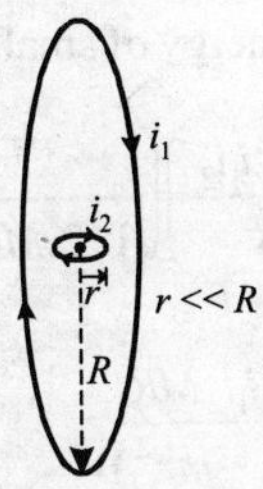

Magnetic induction at common centre due to current in larger coil is given as

$$B = \frac{\mu_0 i_1}{2R} \quad \ldots(2)$$

Magnetic moment of smaller coil is given as

$$M_2 = \pi r^2 i_2 \quad \ldots(3)$$

Initially, the planes of two coils are mutually perpendicular so $\theta = 90°$ thus work done is given as

$$W = (\pi r^2 i_2)(\mu_0 i_1/2R)(1 - \cos 90°)$$

The workdone is equal to the final energy of the system which is given as

$$U = \frac{\mu_0 \pi r^2 i_1 i_2}{2R} \quad \ldots(4)$$

When the system is released, dipole starts rotating to attain equilibrium position. The magnetic energy is converted into kinetic energy of both the coils. The kinetic energy is maximum when it reaches the equilibrium position or the kinetic energies are maximum when the coils become coplanar. The two coils rotate due to their mutual interaction only and if one coil rotates clockwise, then the other coil rotates anticlockwise.

If ω_1 and ω_2 be the angular velocities of larger and smaller coils when they become coplanar then by law of conservation of angular momentum we have

$$I_1\omega_1 = I_2\omega_2 \quad \ldots(5)$$

According to law of conservation of energy we have

$$\frac{1}{2}I_1\omega_1^2 + \frac{1}{2}I_2\omega_2^2 = U \quad \ldots(6)$$

From equations (5) and (6), we get

$$\frac{1}{2}I_1\left(\frac{I_2\omega_2}{I_1}\right)^2 + \frac{1}{2}I_2\omega_2^2 = U$$

$$\Rightarrow \quad \frac{1}{2}I_2\omega_2^2\left[\frac{I_2}{I_1} + 1\right] = U$$

$$\Rightarrow \quad \frac{1}{2}I_2\omega_2^2 = \frac{UI_1}{I_1+I_2} \quad \ldots(7)$$

Thus maximum kinetic energy of smaller coil is given as

$$\frac{1}{2}I_2\omega_2^2 = \left(\frac{\mu_0\pi r^2 i_1 i_2}{2R}\right)\left(\frac{1/2.MR^2}{1/2.MR^2+1/2.mr^2}\right)$$

$$\Rightarrow \quad \frac{1}{2}I_2\omega_2^2 = \frac{\mu_0\pi r^2 i_1 i_2 MR}{2(MR^2+mr^2)}$$

(vi) For equilibrium of beam balance as given in question magnetic torque on coil C is balanced by the torque of weight placed on pan so we use

$$\tau_{\text{magnetic on } C} = \tau_{\text{weight of } M}$$

$$\Rightarrow \quad BINA = Mg \times l_2$$

$$\Rightarrow \quad B = \frac{Mgl_2}{INA}$$

(vii) (a) Magnetic induction in space is given as

$$\vec{B} = B(\cos 45\,\hat{i} + \sin 45\,\hat{j})$$

The area vector of the coil is given as

$$\vec{A} = L^2\hat{k}$$

Torque on coil due to magnetic field is given as

$$\vec{\tau} = I_0(\vec{A}\times\vec{B})$$

$$\Rightarrow \quad \vec{\tau} = I_0[L^2\hat{k}\times B(\cos 45\hat{i} + \sin 45\hat{j})]$$

$$\Rightarrow \quad \vec{\tau} = I_0L^2B[\cos 45^\circ\hat{j} + \sin 45^\circ(-\hat{i})]$$

$$\Rightarrow \quad \vec{\tau} = \frac{I_0L^2B}{\sqrt{2}}(-\hat{i}+\hat{j})$$

(b) Axis of rotation of the coil is along the direction of torque so unit vector along the axis of rotation is given as $(-\hat{i}+\hat{j})/\sqrt{2}$. The frame will experience a torque about axis SQ in its plane and magnitude of torque is given as

$$\tau = I_0L^2B$$

Using the perpendicular axes theorem, the moment of inertia of frame about the axis of rotation SQ is given as

$$I = \frac{1}{2}\left[\frac{4}{3}ML^2\right] = \frac{2}{3}ML^2$$

The angular acceleration of the coil is given as

$$\alpha = \frac{\tau}{I}$$

$$\Rightarrow \quad \alpha = \frac{I_0L^2B}{2/3ML^2} = \frac{3I_0B}{2.M}$$

Angular rotation of coil in time Δt is given as

$$\theta = \frac{1}{2}\alpha(\Delta t)^2$$

$$\Rightarrow \quad \theta = \frac{1}{2}\times\frac{3I_0B}{2M}\times\Delta t^2$$

$$\Rightarrow \quad \theta = \frac{3I_0B}{4M}(\Delta t)^2$$

(viii) To calculate the magnetic moment of the given half toroid we consider an elemental coil of angular width $d\theta$ at an angle θ from the central line as shown in figure.

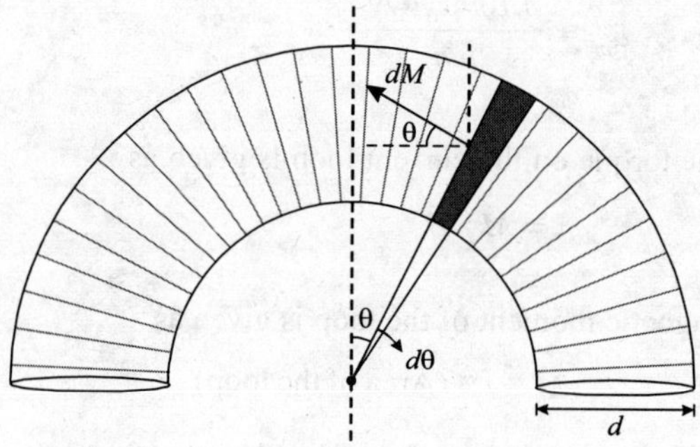

The number of turns in the elemental coil are given as

$$dN = \frac{N}{\pi}d\theta$$

The magnetic moment vector of the coil is in the direction normal to the area of this elemental coil as shown in figure which is given as

$$dM = I\times\frac{\pi d^2}{4}\times\frac{N}{\pi}d\theta$$

$$dM = \frac{1}{4}Id^2N\,d\theta$$

The component $dM\sin\theta$ will get cancelled out due to the symmetrical elemental coils on the other side of central line and the component $dM\cos\theta$ will be added up as all these components are directed toward left. Thus total magnetic moment of the half toroid is given as

$$M = \int dM\cos\theta$$

$$\Rightarrow \quad M = \int_{-\pi/2}^{+\pi/2}\frac{1}{4}Id^2N\cos\theta\,d\theta$$

$$\Rightarrow \quad M = \frac{1}{4} Id^2 N[\sin\theta]_{-\pi/2}^{+\pi/2}$$

$$\Rightarrow \quad M = \frac{1}{4} Id^2 N[(1)-(-1)]$$

$$\Rightarrow \quad M = \frac{1}{2} Id^2 N$$

(ix) The magnetic induction at the centre of solenoid is given by

$$B = \mu_0 ni$$

$$\Rightarrow \quad B = (4\pi \times 10^{-7}) \times \left(\frac{200}{0.25}\right) \times (2.4)\,\text{T}$$

$$\Rightarrow \quad B = 2.41 \times 10^{-3}\,\text{T}$$

The torque τ required to keep the coil at an angle of 90° with B is given as

$$\tau = BINA \sin 90°$$

$$\Rightarrow \quad \tau = [2.41 \times 10^{-3} \times 0.5 \times 10 \times [\pi \times (10 \times 10^{-3})^2]$$

$$\Rightarrow \quad \tau = 3.78 \times 10^{-6}\,\text{Nm}$$

(x) For a moving coil galvanometer we use

$$i = \left(\frac{C}{NBA}\right)\theta$$

$$\Rightarrow \quad B = \frac{C\theta}{NiA} = \frac{(10^{-8})(90)}{100 \times 10^{-6} \times 10^{-4}}$$

$$\Rightarrow \quad B = 90\,\text{T}$$

Solutions of PRACTICE EXERCISE 4.6

(i) At neutral point net magnetic induction is zero. Thus at point P in figure the magnetic induction of magnetic is toward south and that due to earth's horizontal component is toward north. The two fields cancel each other at neutral point so we use at point P

$$B_H = B_r$$

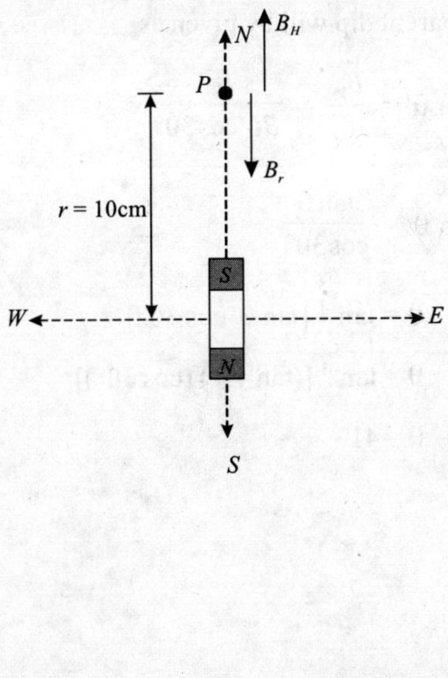

$$\Rightarrow \quad B_H = \frac{2KM}{r^3}$$

$$\Rightarrow \quad B_H = \frac{2 \times 10^{-7} \times 0.2}{(0.1)^3} = 4 \times 10^{-5}\,\text{T}$$

$$\Rightarrow \quad B_H = 40\,\mu\text{T}$$

(ii) Figure shows the situation described in the question. At Point P, radial magnetic induction due to dipole is given as

$$B_r = \frac{2KM}{r^3} = \frac{2 \times 10^{-7} \times 6}{(0.2)^3}\,\text{T}$$

$$\Rightarrow \quad B_r = 1.5 \times 10^{-4}\,\text{T} = 150\,\mu\text{T}$$

Magnetic induction along east direction at point P, due to dipole is given as

$$B_x = B_r \sin 60° = 150 \times \frac{\sqrt{3}}{2}$$

$$\Rightarrow \quad B_x = 75\sqrt{3}\,\mu\text{T}$$

Magnetic induction along north direction at point P, due to dipole and that due to earth is given as

$$B_y = B_H + B_r \cos 60°$$

$$\Rightarrow \quad B_y = 30 + 150(1/2) = 105\,\mu\text{T}$$

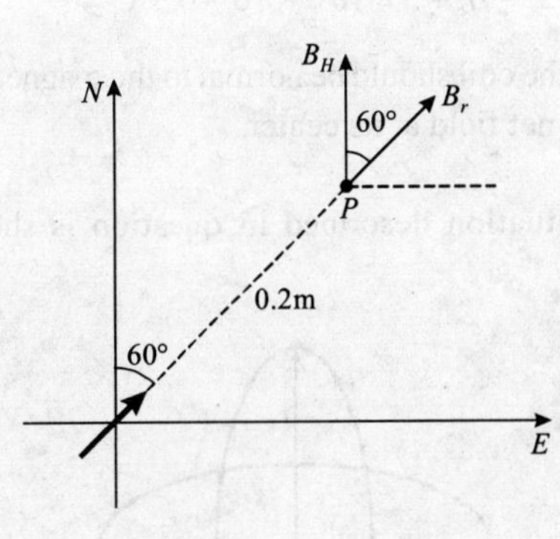

Net magnetic induction at point P in horizontal plane is given as

$$B_P = \sqrt{B_x^2 + B_y^2} = \sqrt{(105)^2 + (75\sqrt{3})^2}\,\mu\text{T}$$

$$\Rightarrow \quad B_P = 30\sqrt{31}\,\mu\text{T}$$

(iii) (a) The resistance of wire is given as

$$R = \frac{\rho l}{A}$$

Where length of coil wire is given as

$$l = (2\pi r) \times 50 = 2\pi \times 5 \times 50\,\text{cm} = 500\pi\,\text{cm}$$

Cross sectional area of coil wire is given as

$$A = \pi \times (0.01)^2 = \pi \times 10^{-4}\,\text{cm}^2$$

$$\Rightarrow \quad R = \frac{2\times10^{-6}\times500\pi}{\pi\times10^{-4}} = 10\,\Omega$$

Thus current in the coil is given as

$$i = \frac{E}{R} = \frac{10}{10} = 1\,\text{A}$$

(b) The magnetic induction B at the centre of a circular coil is given by

$$B = \frac{\mu_0 NI}{2R}$$

$$\Rightarrow \quad B = \frac{4\pi\times10^{-7}\times50\times I}{2\times5\times10^{-2}}$$

Above calculated magnetic induction is to be equal in magnitude to that of the earth's horizontal component of magnetic induction and in opposite direction so we have

$$\frac{4\pi\times10^{-7}\times50\times I}{2\times5\times10^{-2}} = 0.314\times10^{-4}$$

$$\Rightarrow \quad I = 5\times10^{-2}\,\text{A}$$

Potential difference across the coil

$$V = IR = 5\times10^{-2}\times10 = 0.5\,\text{V}$$

The plane of the coil should be normal to the magnetic meridian to nullify the net field at its center.

(iv) The situation described in question is shown in the figure

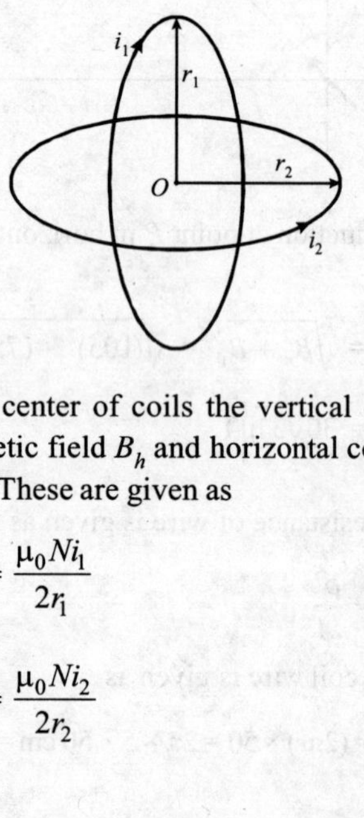

At the common center of coils the vertical coil produces a horizontal magnetic field B_h and horizontal coil produces the vertical field B_v. These are given as

$$B_h = \frac{\mu_0 N i_1}{2r_1}$$

$$B_v = \frac{\mu_0 N i_2}{2r_2}$$

If B_H and B_V are the horizontal and vertical components of earth's magnetic field at the common center respectively, then these are given as

$$B_H = \mu_0 H_H = 4\pi\times10^{-7}\times27.8\,\text{T}$$

and $$B_V = B_H\tan\theta = 4\pi\times10^{-7}\times27.8\times\tan30°\,\text{T}$$

To neutralize net magnetic field at center we use

$$B_h = \frac{\mu_0 N i_1}{2r_1} = B_H$$

$$\Rightarrow \quad i_1 = \frac{2r_1 B_H}{N} \quad \ldots(1)$$

and $$B_v = \frac{\mu_0 N i_2}{2r_2} = B_V$$

$$\Rightarrow \quad i_2 = \frac{2r_2 B_V}{N} \quad \ldots(2)$$

Substituting values in equations-(1) and (2), we get

$$i_1 = 111.2\,\text{mA}$$

and $$i_2 = 96.3\,\text{A}$$

(v) From figure we can see that in a vertical plane at 30° from the magnetic meridian, the horizontal component of earth's magnetic field is given as

$$B_H' = B_H\cos30°$$

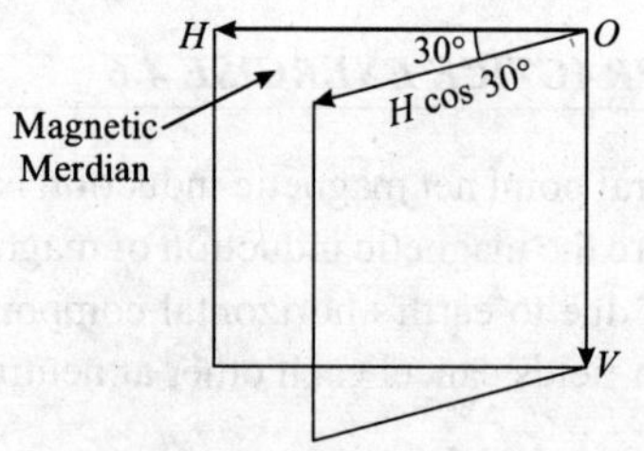

Vertical component of earth's field at the point will remain same as B_V. So apparent dip will by given as

$$\tan\theta' = \frac{B_V}{B_H'} = \frac{B_V}{B_H\cos30°}$$

$$\Rightarrow \quad \tan\theta' = \frac{\tan\theta}{\cos30°}$$

$$\Rightarrow \quad \theta = \tan^{-1}[\tan\theta'\cos30°]$$

$$\Rightarrow \quad \theta = \tan^{-1}[(\tan45°)(\cos30°)]$$

$$\Rightarrow \quad \theta = 41°$$

(vi) The situation described in question is shown in figure

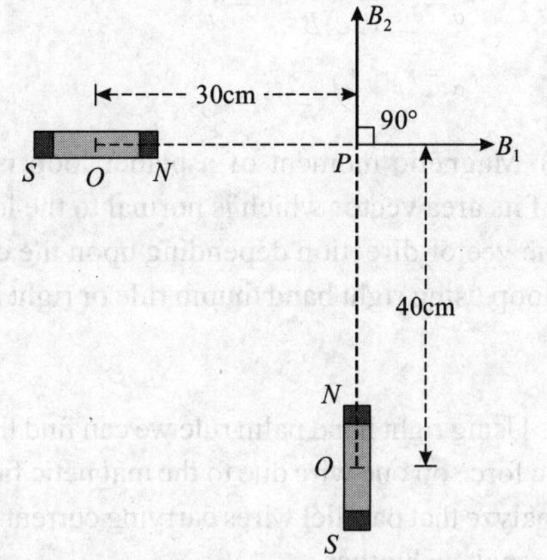

At point P the magnetic induction due to first magnet is given as

$$B_1 = \frac{2KM}{r_1^3}$$

$$\Rightarrow \quad B_1 = \frac{10^{-7} \times 2 \times 0.108}{(0.3)^2} \text{T}$$

$$\Rightarrow \quad B_1 = 8 \times 10^{-7} \text{T}$$

At point P the magnetic induction due to second magnet is given as

$$B_2 = \frac{\mu_0}{4\pi} \times \frac{2M_2}{d_2^3}$$

$$\Rightarrow \quad B_2 = \frac{10^{-7} \times 2 \times 0.192}{(0.4)^2} \text{T}$$

$$\Rightarrow \quad B_2 = 6 \times 10^{-7} \text{T}$$

B_1 and B_2 are mutually perpendicular to each other so the resultant field at P is given as

$$B = \sqrt{(B_1^2 + B_2^2)} = 10 \times 10^{-7} = 10^{-6} \text{T}$$

(vii) In tan A position of magnetometer we have

$$\frac{2KM}{d^3} = B_H \tan 30 = \frac{B_H}{\sqrt{3}} \quad \ldots(1)$$

The magnetic moment M' of second magnet is given as

$$M' = (3 \text{ m})(2 \times 2l) = 6M$$

In tan B position,

$$\frac{K(6M)}{d^3} = B_H \tan\theta \quad \ldots(2)$$

Dividing equation-(2) by equation-(1), we get

$$\frac{6}{2} = \frac{\tan\theta}{(1/\sqrt{3})}$$

$$\Rightarrow \quad \tan\theta = \frac{6}{2} \times \frac{1}{\sqrt{3}}$$

$$\Rightarrow \quad \tan\theta = 3 \times \frac{1}{\sqrt{3}} = \sqrt{3} \text{ or } \theta = 60°$$

(viii) In horizontal plane, the magnetic needle oscillates due to horizontal component of earth's magnetic field B_H for which the time period of oscillation is given as

$$T = 2\pi\sqrt{\frac{I}{MB_H}}$$

Above result of time period is already discussed earlier in an illustrative example. Students are advised to remember this result for oscillation of a magnet in magnetic field.

In the vertical north-south plane in magnetic meridian the needle oscillates in the total earth's magnetic field B_E, and in vertical east-west plane which is a plane perpendicular to the magnetic meridian it oscillates only in earth's vertical component B_V. If the time period be T_1 and T_2, then we have

$$T_1 = 2\pi\sqrt{\frac{I}{MB_E}} \text{ and } T_2 = 2\pi\sqrt{\frac{I}{MB_V}}$$

From above equations, we have

$$\frac{T_1^2}{T^2} = \frac{B_H}{B_E}$$

If n is the initial frequency of oscillation in horizontal plane then we have

$$\frac{n_1^2}{n^2} = \frac{B_E}{B_H}$$

and
$$\frac{n_2^2}{n^2} = \frac{B_V}{B_H}$$

We also have
$$\frac{B_E}{B_H} = \sec 30° = \frac{2}{\sqrt{3}}$$

and
$$\frac{B_V}{B_H} = \tan 30° = \frac{1}{\sqrt{3}}$$

$$\Rightarrow \quad n_1^2 = n^2\left(\frac{B_e}{H}\right) = (20)^2\left(\frac{2}{\sqrt{3}}\right)$$

$$\Rightarrow \quad n_1 = 21.5 \text{ oscillations/min}$$

and
$$n_2^2 = n^2\left(\frac{V}{H}\right) = (20)^2\left(\frac{1}{\sqrt{3}}\right)$$

$$\Rightarrow \quad n_2 = 15.2 \text{ oscillations/min}$$

Solutions of CONCEPTUAL MCQS Single Option Correct

Sol. 1 **(C)** The radius of circular trajectory of a particle in uniform magnetic field is given as

$$r=\frac{mv}{qB}$$

When v is doubled, r is also doubled and becomes 5.0 cm.

Sol. 2 **(B)** We know that magnetic lines around a straight long conductor are concentric circles. If the wire is bent at a point then due to non symmetric orientation of wire lines will no longer be circular so these become oval in shape.

Sol. 3 **(C)** Time period of circular motion in magnetic field is given as

$$T=\frac{2\pi m}{Bq}$$

Above relation is independent of speed so it will remain the same.

Sol. 4 **(B)** For electron the distance is given as

$$s_e=\frac{1}{2}\left(\frac{eE}{m_e}\right)t_1^2$$

and for proton the distance is given as

$$s_p=\frac{1}{2}\left(\frac{eE}{m_e}\right)t_1^2$$

$$\Rightarrow \quad \frac{t_2^2}{t_1^2}=\frac{m_p}{m_e} \quad \text{or} \quad \frac{t_2}{t_1}=\sqrt{\left(\frac{m_p}{m_e}\right)}$$

Sol. 5 **(A)** In the situation described in question we have kinetic energies of the particles

$$K_p=K_d=K_\alpha=K(\text{say})$$

We know that charges on particles are

$$q_p=e,\, q_d= \text{ and } q_\alpha=2e$$

and $\quad m_p=m,\, m_d=2\text{ m and } m_\alpha=4\text{ m}$

In uniform magnetic field radius of circular motion is given as

$$r=\frac{mv}{qB}=\frac{\sqrt{2mK}}{qB}$$

$$\Rightarrow \quad r_p=\frac{\sqrt{2mK}}{eB}$$

$$\Rightarrow \quad r_d=\frac{\sqrt{2(2m)K}}{eB}$$

$$\Rightarrow \quad r_\alpha=\frac{\sqrt{2(4m)K}}{(2e)B}=r_p$$

$$\Rightarrow \quad r_\alpha=r_p<r_d$$

Sol. 6 **(D)** Magnetic moment of a planer loop is along the direction of its area vector which is normal to the loop and we consider the vector direction depending upon the direction of current in loop using right hand thumb rule or right hand screw rule.

Sol. 7 **(B)** Using right hand palm rule we can find the direction of magnetic force on one wire due to the magnetic field of other wire and analyze that parallel wires carrying current in opposite directions repel each other.

Sol. 8 **(C)** In uniform magnetic field the force on any current carrying loop is always zero.

Sol. 9 **(B)** At the same distance from the wire magnetic induction is same in magnitude and direction is tangential to the circular line of force passing through that point.

Sol. 10 **(B)** By the expression of Lorentz force we can see that if the angle between motion of charge particle and magnetic field is 0° or 180° then net force comes out to be zero due to the cross product in expression of force.

Sol. 11 **(A)** For a finite wire carrying a current the magnetic induction is given by equation-(4.20) in which we can substitute the values of θ_1 and θ_2.

Sol. 12 **(C)** Initially the tangent galvanometer coil is kept in magnetic meridian so that its magnetic induction is at right angle to the horizontal component of earth's magnetic field so the calculation of deflection angle in terms of both the field induction is easier.

Sol. 13 **(B)** Here we use for the bigger coil, magnetic induction at axial point of a coil, it is given as

$$B_y=\frac{\mu_0}{2}\times\frac{i(2r)^2}{[(2r)^2+(d)^2]^{3/2}}$$

Here we use for the smaller coil, magnetic induction at axial point of a coil, it is given as

$$B_x=\frac{\mu_0}{2}\times\frac{ir^2}{[r^2+(d/2)^2]^{3/2}}$$

$$\Rightarrow \quad \frac{B_y}{B_x}=\frac{4}{(4r^2+d^2)^{3/2}}\times\left(\frac{4r^2+d^2}{4}\right)^{3/2}$$

$$\Rightarrow \quad \frac{B_y}{B_x}=\frac{4}{8}=\frac{1}{2}$$

Sol. 14 (D) Using right hand palm rule we can find the direction of magnetic force on one wire due to the magnetic field of other wire and analyze that parallel wires carrying current in same directions attract each other.

Sol. 15 (D) At the symmetrically located point between the two wires magnetic induction due to the two wires will be equal in magnitude and opposite in direction so net resultant will be zero.

Sol. 16 (B) Using right hand palm rule we can find the direction of magnetic force on one wire due to the magnetic field and analyze that it acts in upward direction.

Sol. 17 (A) At a distance r from centre we have the magnetic induction is given as

$$B = \frac{\mu_0}{2\pi}\frac{(i_{in})}{r}$$

For point 1 inner current is I but for path 2 enclosed current through the symmetric ampere's path is zero so option (A) is correct.

Sol. 18 (D) We use the relation

$$\frac{M}{L} = \frac{q}{2m}$$

$$\Rightarrow \quad M = \left(\frac{q}{2m}\right)(I\omega) = \left(\frac{q}{2m}\right)\left(\frac{ml^2}{3}\right)(2\pi f) = \frac{\pi q f l^2}{3}$$

Sol. 19 (D) Magnetic field around a straight current carrying conductor is in form of concentric circles and inversely proportional to the distance from the wire and same only in magnitude at the same distant points from the conductor.

Sol. 20 (B) For geographical meridian,

$$\tan\theta_1 = \frac{B_V}{B_H\cos\alpha}$$

In a plane perpendicular to magnetic meridian

$$\tan\theta_2 = \frac{B_V}{B_H\cos(90-\alpha)} = \frac{B_V}{B_H\sin\alpha}$$

$$\Rightarrow \quad \frac{\tan\theta_1}{\tan\theta_2} = \frac{\sin\phi}{\cos\alpha} = \tan\alpha$$

Sol. 21 (C) In magnetic field the torque on a current carrying loop is given as

$$\vec{\tau} = \vec{M}\times\vec{B}$$

Due to restoring torque on coil when a current flows in it, needle attached to the coil axis gives deflection on a calibrated scale to measure the current.

Sol. 22 (A) The force acting on a charged particle in magnetic field is given by

$$\vec{F} = q(\vec{v}\times\vec{B})$$

$$\Rightarrow \quad F = qvB\sin\theta$$

When angle between v and B is 180° the force becomes

$$F = 0$$

Sol. 23 (C) As the wire segment in loop which is parallel and close to the wire carry current in same direction the attractive force on this segment by the wire will be more than the parallel segment of loop which is farther away of wire so it will be overall attracted toward the wire.

Sol. 24 (D) When the electric and magnetic forces on electron are equal and opposite then it can go undeflected in the region.

Sol. 25 (C) The magnetic induction at the center of the current carrying circular coil is given as

$$B = \frac{\mu_0 NI}{2R}$$

Thus in the situation described in question it will become four times of the initial value.

Sol. 26 (B) Time period of revolution of a charge in magnetic field is given as

$$T = \frac{2\pi m}{Bq}$$

$$\Rightarrow \quad \frac{T_1}{T_2} = \frac{m_1}{q_1}\times\frac{q_2}{m_2}$$

$$\Rightarrow \quad T_2 = T_1\times\left(\frac{q_1\times m_2}{q_2\times m_1}\right)$$

$$\Rightarrow \quad T_2 = T_1\times\left(\frac{1}{2}\right)\times\left(\frac{1}{4}\right) = 2T_1$$

Sol. 27 (C) If R_1 and R_2 be the radius of the circular paths described by the particles X and Y respectively in uniform magnetic field B. Then we have

$$\frac{m_1 v_1}{R_1} = qB$$

and

$$\frac{m_2 v_2}{R_2} = qB$$

$$\Rightarrow \quad \frac{m_1 v_1}{R_1} = \frac{m_2 v_2}{R_2}$$

$$\Rightarrow \quad \frac{m_1}{m_2} = \left(\frac{R_1}{R_2}\right)\left(\frac{v_2}{v_1}\right) \quad \ldots(1)$$

As these are accelerated by the same potential, the kinetic energy acquired by these will be the same so we use

$$\frac{1}{2} m_1 v_1^2 = \frac{1}{2} m_2 v_2^2$$

$$\Rightarrow \quad m_1 v_1^2 = m_2 v_2^2$$

$$\Rightarrow \quad \left(\frac{m_1}{m_2}\right) = \left(\frac{v_2}{v_1}\right)^2$$

$$\Rightarrow \quad \frac{v_2}{v_1} = \sqrt{\left(\frac{m_1}{m_2}\right)} \quad \ldots(2)$$

Substituting the value of (v_2/v_1) from equation-(2) in equation-(1), we get

$$\frac{m_1}{m_2} = \left(\frac{R_1}{R_2}\right)\sqrt{\left(\frac{m_1}{m_2}\right)}$$

$$\Rightarrow \quad \sqrt{\frac{m_1}{m_2}} = \left(\frac{R_1}{R_2}\right)$$

$$\Rightarrow \quad \frac{m_1}{m_2} = \left(\frac{R_1}{R_2}\right)^2$$

Sol. 28 (B) We know that magnetic force is always perpendicular to the direction of motion of charged particle thus its energy remains constant. Momentum changes because velocity of particle changes due to change in direction.

Sol. 29 (D) As velocity of electron is parallel to electric and magnetic fields it will not experience any magnetic force and electric force in direction opposite to its motion so its speed decreases.

Sol. 30 (C) Magnetic induction due to the single turn circular coils at their centre is given as

$$B_1 = \frac{\mu_0 i_1}{2r_1}$$

and $$B_2 = \frac{\mu_0 i_2}{2r_2}$$

Given that $r_2 = 2r_1$, $B_1 = B_2$ and $i_2 = 2i_1$

$$\Rightarrow \quad \frac{V_q}{V_p} = \frac{i_2 \times r_2}{i_1 \times r_1} = \frac{2i_1}{i_1} \times \frac{2r_1}{r_1} = \frac{4}{1}$$

Sol. 31 (C) The radius of a charge particle in magnetic field is given as

$$r = \frac{mv}{qB}$$

$$\Rightarrow \quad r = \frac{\sqrt{2mK}}{qB}$$

Here charge of alpha particle is twice that of proton and its mass is four times that of proton thus radius of both will be same as their kinetic energies are same.

Sol. 32 (D) As we know that magnetic induction due to a circular coil has a proportional relationship given as

$$B \propto \frac{n}{r}$$

Here number of turns becomes 4 times while the radius becomes (1/4) times. Hence B becomes 16 times.

Sol. 33 (C) Electrostatic force between electrons is given as

$$F_e = \frac{1}{4\pi\varepsilon_0} \times \frac{e^2}{r^2}$$

Magnetic force between electrons is given as

$$F_m = \frac{\mu_0}{4\pi}\left(\frac{e^2 v^2}{r^2}\right)$$

$$\Rightarrow \quad \frac{F_m}{F_e} = \mu_0 \varepsilon_0 v^2 = \frac{v^2}{c^2} \quad \text{(As we use } \mu_0 \varepsilon_0 = 1/c^2\text{)}$$

Sol. 34 (B) As velocity of electron is along the same line of magnetic field, it will not experience any magnetic force and electric force on electron will act in direction opposite to electric field.

Sol. 35 (D) The radius of curvature of a charged particle moving in uniform magnetic field is given as

$$r = \frac{mv}{qB} = \frac{\sqrt{2mK}}{qB}$$

$$\Rightarrow \quad r' = \frac{\sqrt{2mK'}}{qB}$$

$$\Rightarrow \quad \frac{r'}{r} = \sqrt{\left(\frac{K'}{K}\right)} = \sqrt{\frac{K/2}{K}} = \frac{1}{\sqrt{2}}$$

$$\Rightarrow \quad r' = \frac{1}{\sqrt{2}} \cdot r$$

Sol. 36 (D) For the perpendicular motion a charge particle moves in a circular trajectory in magnetic field.

Sol. 37 (D) In the given situation the currents are in opposite direction. The magnetic fields will be added up at O. Thus the net magnetic field is along negative Z-axis.

Sol. 38 (D) If upward direction of B is considered positive the variation of magnetic field in the given region of wires can be plotted with position as shown in figure below.

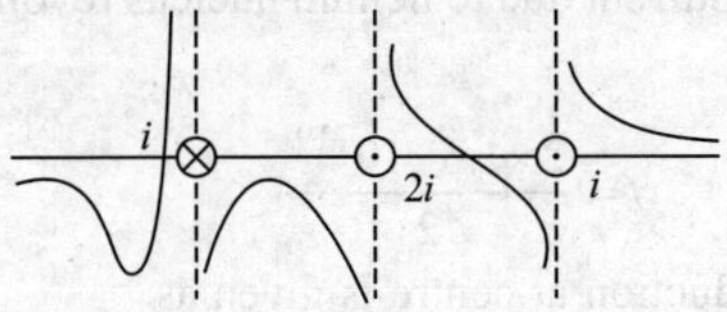

The curve cuts the x axis at one point in region I an done point in region III.

Sol. 39 (D) Figure below shows the loop in a vertical plane containing north-south direction with axis of loop along east-west direction and direction of current as explained in the question. By right hand thumb rule we can see that at both the points P and Q the direction of magnetic induction is along west.

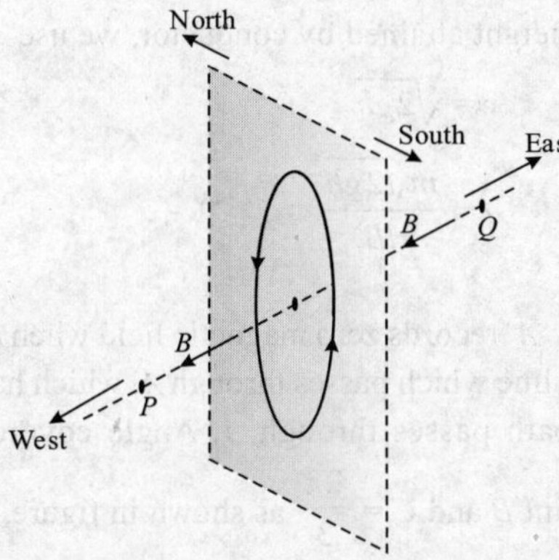

Sol. 40 (A) As magnetic field is acting into the plane of paper and the force on moving charges is acting toward the centre of curvature of the path shown, from Right Palm Rule it is clear that the particles are positively charged. The radius of curvature of path is given as

$$r = \frac{mv}{qB}$$

The radius of path is a function of m, v and q thus from options (B), (C) and (D) we cannot make clear statement specifically about mass or charge of particles, but statement (A) is certainly true.

Solutions of NUMERICAL MCQS Single Option Correct

Sol. 1 (B) Magnetic induction due to a straight current carrying wire is given as

$$B = \frac{\mu_0}{4\pi}\frac{i}{a}(\sin 90 + \sin(-\theta))$$

$$\Rightarrow \quad B = \frac{\mu_0}{4\pi}\frac{i}{a}(1 - \sin\theta)$$

$$\Rightarrow \quad B = \frac{\mu_0}{4\pi}\frac{i}{a}\left(1 - \frac{b}{\sqrt{a^2 + b^2}}\right)$$

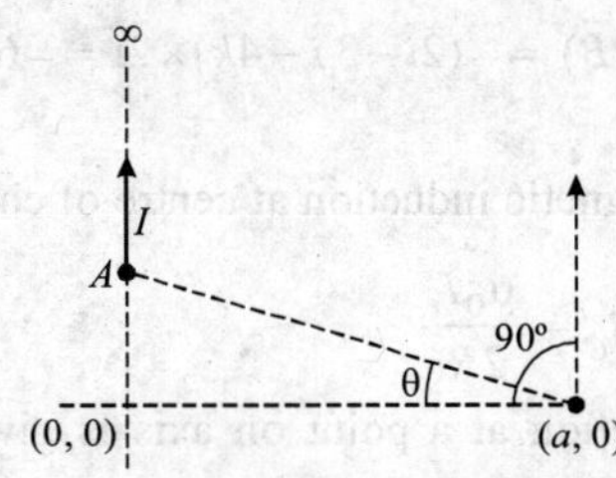

Sol. 2 (D) The acceleration of the rod is given as

$$a = \frac{ilB}{m}$$

Speed attained by the rod after time t is given as

$$V = \left(\frac{ilB}{m}\right)t$$

Substituting values we get

$$V = 20 \text{ cm/s}$$

Sol. 3 (A) Magnetic induction due to a straight current carrying wire is given as

$$B = \frac{\mu_0 I}{4\pi \cdot \frac{R}{\sqrt{2}}}(\sin 90° + \sin 135°)$$

$$\Rightarrow \quad B = \frac{\mu_0 I}{4\pi R}(\sqrt{2} - 1)$$

Sol. 4 (B) Magnetic induction at point P due current I_1 is given as

$$\vec{B}_1 = \frac{\mu_0 I_1}{2\pi(AP)}\hat{k} = \frac{4\pi \times 10^{-7} \times 2}{2\pi \times 1 \times 10^{-2}}\hat{k} = (4 \times 10^{-5}\text{T})\hat{k}$$

Magnetic induction at point P due current I_2 is given as

$$\vec{B}_2 = \frac{\mu_0 I_2}{2\pi(BP)}\hat{j} = \frac{4\pi \times 10^{-7} \times 3}{2\pi \times 2 \times 10^{-2}}\hat{j} = (3 \times 10^{-5}\text{T})\hat{j}$$

So net magnetic induction at point P is given as

$$\vec{B} = (3 \times 10^{-5}\text{ T})\hat{j} + (4 \times 10^{-5}\text{ T})\hat{k}$$

Sol. 5 (C) In time $\frac{T}{2} = \frac{\pi m}{qB}$ which is half of revolution time velocity will get reversed in *yz* plane which is given as

$$\vec{v} = 2\hat{i} - 3\hat{j} - 4\hat{k}$$

Net force on the particle is

$$q(\vec{E} + \vec{v} \times \vec{B}) = 0$$

$$\Rightarrow \quad \vec{E} = -(\vec{v} \times \vec{B}) = -(2\hat{i} - 3\hat{j} - 4\hat{k}) \times 2\hat{i} = -6\hat{k} + 8\hat{j}$$

Sol. 6 (D) Magnetic induction at centre of coil is given as

$$B_C = \frac{\mu_0 I}{2R}$$

Magnetic induction at a point on axis is given as

$$B_A = \frac{\mu_0 I 2\pi R^2}{4\pi (R^2 + x^2)^{3/2}}$$

According to given condition we have

$$\frac{\mu_0 I}{4R} = \frac{\mu_0 I \times 2\pi R^2}{4\pi (R^2 + x^2)^{3/2}}$$

$$\Rightarrow \quad \frac{1}{2R} = \frac{R^2}{(R^2 + x^2)^{3/2}}$$

$$\Rightarrow \quad \frac{1}{2} = \frac{R^3}{(R^2 + x^2)^{3/2}}$$

$$\Rightarrow \quad (R^2 + x^2)^{3/2} = 2R^3$$

$$\Rightarrow \quad ((R^2 + x^2)^{3/2})^{2/3} = (2R^3)^{2/3}$$

$$\Rightarrow \quad R^2 + x^2 = (2)^{2/3} R^2$$

$$\Rightarrow \quad x^2 = R^2 ((2)^{2/3} - 1)$$

$$\Rightarrow \quad x = 0.766R$$

Sol. 7 (B) From the diagram in question, for equilibrium, we can write

$$T_1 + T_2 = Mg \qquad \ldots(1)$$

Torque on ring is given as

$$t = M \times B = ipR^2 B \sin 45°$$

$$t = \frac{i\pi R^2 B}{\sqrt{2}}$$

Above torque is anticlockwise as viewed from top on *xz*-plane. Balancing torque about mid point, we have

$$\frac{T_1 R}{\sqrt{2}} = \frac{T_2 R}{\sqrt{2}} + \frac{i\pi R^2 B}{\sqrt{2}}$$

$$\Rightarrow \quad T_1 = T_2 + \pi i R B$$

$$\Rightarrow \quad T_1 - T_2 = \frac{mg}{4} \qquad \ldots(2)$$

Using equations-(1) & (2), we get

$$T_1 = \frac{5mg}{8}, \; T_2 = \frac{3mg}{8}$$

$$\Rightarrow \quad \frac{T_1}{T_2} = \frac{5}{3}$$

Sol. 8 (A) Current due to helium nucleus revolution is given as

$$I = \frac{2 \times 1.6 \times 10^{-19}}{2}$$

Magnetic induction at centre is given as

$$B = \frac{\mu_0 I}{2R}$$

$$\Rightarrow \quad \frac{4\pi \times 10^{-7} \times 1.6 \times 10^{-19}}{2 \times 0.8} = \mu_0 \times 10^{-19}\,\text{T}$$

Sol. 9 (D) Impulse on conductor when charge '*q*' passes through it is

$$F = Bql = mv$$

If '*h*' is the height attained by conductor, we use

$$v = \sqrt{2gh}$$

$$\Rightarrow \quad q = \frac{m\sqrt{2gh}}{lB}$$

Sol. 10 (B) '*A*' records zero magnetic field when α particle is moving on a line which passes through *A*, which happen when tangent to path passes through *A*. Angle covered between two such point *B* and $C = \frac{2\pi}{3}$ as shown in figure.

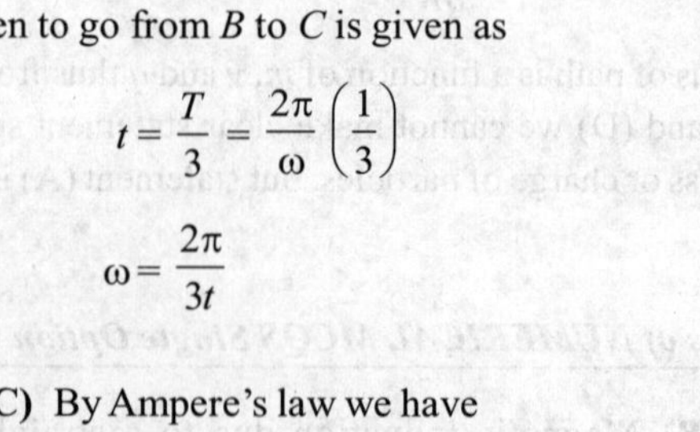

Time taken to go from *B* to *C* is given as

$$t = \frac{T}{3} = \frac{2\pi}{\omega}\left(\frac{1}{3}\right)$$

$$\Rightarrow \quad \omega = \frac{2\pi}{3t}$$

Sol. 11 (C) By Ampere's law we have

$$\oint \vec{B} \cdot \vec{dl} = \mu_0 I$$

For loop A, $\oint \vec{B}\cdot\vec{dl} = \mu_0(0) = 0$

For loop B, $\oint \vec{B}\cdot\vec{dl} = \mu_0(1+1-1)I = \mu_0 I$

For loop C, $\oint \vec{B}\cdot\vec{dl} = -\mu_0 I$

For loop D, $\oint \vec{B}\cdot\vec{dl} = -\mu_0 I$

$\Rightarrow \quad B > A > C = D$

Sol. 12 (A) The angle subtends by each wire segment are given as

$$\theta = \frac{360}{8} = 45°$$

Magnetic induction at P due to arc of radius r is given as

$$\Rightarrow \quad B = \frac{\mu_0 I}{4\pi r^2} \times l$$

Where l is the arc length which is given as

$$l = r\theta = \frac{\pi}{4} r$$

$$\Rightarrow \quad B = \frac{\mu_0 I}{4\pi r^2} \times \frac{\pi}{4} r$$

$$\Rightarrow \quad B = \frac{\mu_0 I}{16 r}$$

Total magnetic induction is given as

$$B_{T1} = \frac{\mu_0 I}{16r} \times 4 = \frac{\mu_0 I}{4r} \text{ inwards}$$

Magnetic induction due arc of radius $2r$ is given as

$$\Rightarrow \quad B = \frac{\mu_0 I}{4\pi(2r)^2} \times l$$

Where l is the arc length given as

$$l = \theta.(2r) = \frac{\pi}{4} \times 2r$$

$$\Rightarrow \quad B = \frac{\mu_0 I}{16\pi r^2} \times \frac{\pi}{4} \times 2r$$

Total magnetic induction due to all these arcs is given as

$$B_{T2} = \frac{\mu_0 I}{16\pi r^2} \times \frac{\pi}{4} \times 2r \times 4 \Rightarrow \frac{\mu_0 I}{8r} \text{ inwards}$$

Net magnetic induction at P is given as

$$B_P = \frac{\mu_0 I}{4r} + \frac{\mu_0 I}{8r} = \frac{3\mu_0 I}{8r} \text{ inwards}$$

Sol. 13 (D) Particle rotates in a circle in y-z plane, with radius of circle given as

$$r = \frac{mv_0}{qB} = \frac{v_0}{\alpha B}$$

Its time period of motion is given as

$$T = \frac{2\pi}{\alpha B}$$

After time $t = \frac{\pi}{B_0 \alpha}$, which is half the time period, particle would have completed half circle in y-z plane, and will be at $y = 0$ and $z = -2r = \frac{-2v_0}{\alpha B}$ as shown in figure.

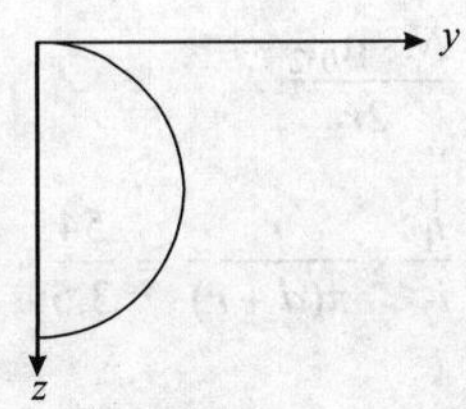

Particle continuous to move with constant velocity in x-direction and will be at a location given as

$$x = v_0\left(\frac{\pi}{B_0\alpha}\right)$$

$$\Rightarrow \quad \text{Position is } \left(\frac{v_0\pi}{B_0\alpha}, 0, -\frac{2v_0}{\alpha B}\right)$$

Sol. 14 (C) Magnetic induction due to AA' and BB' is given as

$$B_1 = \frac{\mu_0 i}{4\pi R}$$

Magnetic induction due to CC' and DD' is zero at O.

Magnetic induction due to BA is given as

$$B_2 = \frac{\mu_0 i}{8R}$$

Magnetic induction due to CD is given as

$$B_3 = \frac{-\mu_0 i}{8R}$$

Thus net magnetic induction at O is given as

$$B_O = \frac{\mu_0 i}{2\pi R}$$

Sol. 15 (B) The magnetic field at a far away fixed point on axis of current carrying ring is directly proportional to dipole moment of ring so we have

$$B \propto ib^2$$

Sol. 16 (A) At point A, the magnetic induction due to both the cylinders is along $+y$ direction. The magnitude of induction due to one cylinder is given as

$$B_1 = \frac{\mu_0 Jd}{4}$$

Net magnetic induction at point A is given as

$$B = B_1 + B_2$$

$$\Rightarrow \quad B = \frac{\mu_0 Jd}{2} \text{ in the } +y \text{ direction.}$$

Sol. 17 (A) As net magnetic induction at the center of coil is zero, we have

$$\frac{\mu_0 \cdot i_1}{2\pi(d+r)} = \frac{N \times \mu_0 i_2}{2r}$$

$$\Rightarrow \quad N = \frac{i_1}{i_2} \cdot \frac{r}{\pi(d+r)} = \frac{54}{3.5} \cdot \frac{0.22 \times 7}{22(0.27)} = 4$$

Sol. 18 (A) The magnetic induction due to one proton on the other is given as

$$B = \frac{\mu_0 qv}{4\pi r^2}$$

The magnetic force on protons due to other is given as

$$F_B = qvB = \frac{\mu_0 q^2 v^2}{4\pi r^2}$$

Electric force on the proton due to the beam is given as

$$F_E = qE = \frac{qkq}{r^2} = \frac{kq^2}{r^2}$$

$$\Rightarrow \quad \frac{F_E}{F_B} = \frac{1}{4\pi\varepsilon_0} \frac{q^2}{r^2} \div \frac{\mu_0 q^2 v^2}{4\pi r^2}$$

$$\Rightarrow \quad \frac{F_E}{F_B} = \frac{1}{\mu_0 \varepsilon_0 v^2} = \frac{c^2}{v^2}$$

Sol. 19 (D) A and P will have the same momentum in magnitude and they will move in opposite directions. They will move in the circle of same radius and the same centre but in opposite directions. If they meet after time t then we have

$$\omega_A t + \omega_P t = 2\pi$$

$$\Rightarrow \quad t = \frac{2\pi}{\omega_A + \omega_P} = \frac{2\pi}{\frac{2e.B}{4m} + \frac{2eB}{(A-4)m}}$$

$$\Rightarrow \quad t = \frac{4(A-4)m\pi}{eBA}$$

$$\theta_A = \omega_A t = \frac{2eB}{4m} \times \frac{4m(A-4)}{eBA}$$

$$\Rightarrow \quad \theta_A = \frac{2(A-4)\pi}{A} = \frac{48}{25}\pi$$

$$\Rightarrow \quad n = 48$$

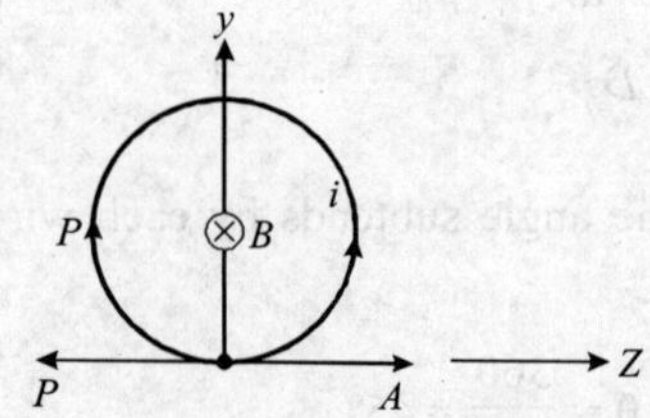

Sol. 20 (D) As time period of circular motion of a charge particle in magnetic field does not depend upon its speed so it does not depend upon its kinetic energy.

Sol. 21 (D) The particle will move along a circle of radius equal to the radius of circular region in which magnetic field is present as shown in figure.

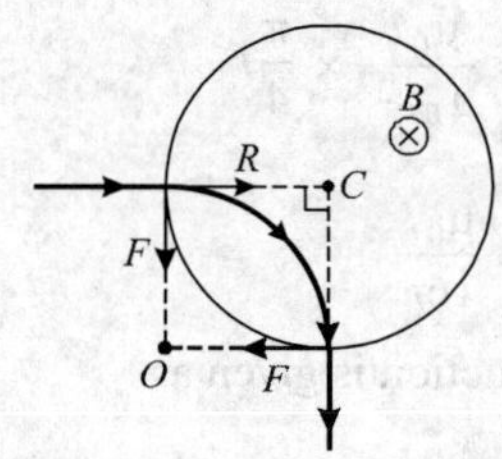

Radius of circular motion is given as

$$R = \frac{mv}{qB}$$

$$\Rightarrow \quad v = \frac{qBR}{m}$$

$$\Rightarrow \quad v = \frac{5 \times 10^{-6} \times 4 \times (0.1)}{2 \times 10^{-3}} = 10^{-3} \text{ m/s} = 1 \text{ mm/s}$$

Sol. 22 (A) To enter region 2, radius or particle in region 1 should be greater than d so we have

$$R = \frac{mV}{qB} > d$$

$$\Rightarrow \quad V > \frac{qBd}{m}$$

$$\Rightarrow \quad V > \frac{1.6 \times 10^{-19} \times 0.001 \times 5 \times 10^{-2}}{9 \times 10^{-31}}$$

$$\Rightarrow \quad V > \frac{8}{9} \times 10^7 \text{ m/s}$$

To come out of region 2 we use

$$2R > d$$

$$\Rightarrow \quad \frac{2mV}{qB} > d$$

$$\Rightarrow \quad V > \frac{qBd}{2m}$$

$$\Rightarrow \quad V > \frac{1.6\times10^{-19}\times0.002\times5\times10^{-12}}{2\times9\times10^{-31}}$$

$$\Rightarrow \quad V > \frac{8}{9}\times10^{7}\ \text{m/s}$$

Sol. 23 (B) Force on wire ABC is given as

$$|\vec{F}_{ABC}| = ilB$$

$$\Rightarrow \quad |\vec{F}_{ABC}| = (2)(5)(2) = 20\ \text{N}$$

Sol. 24 (B) The charged particle moves in a circle of radius $\frac{a}{2}$ so we have

$$qvB = \frac{mv^2}{a/2}$$

$$\Rightarrow \quad B = \frac{2mv}{qa}$$

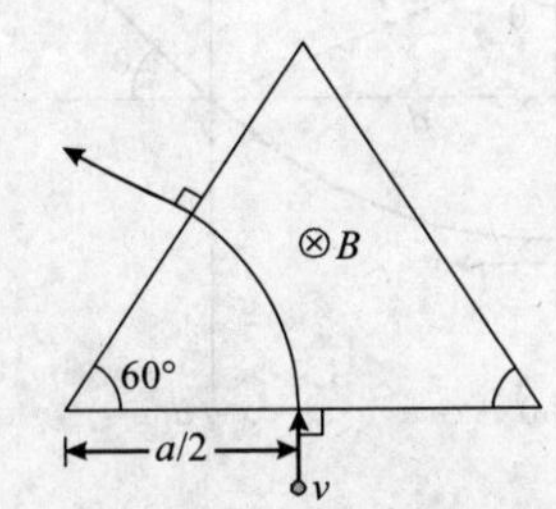

Sol. 25 (C) Acceleration of particle is given as

$$a = \frac{q(v\hat{i}\times B\hat{j}) + qE\hat{k}}{m} = \frac{q(vB+E)}{m}\hat{k}$$

Sol. 26 (A) Unit vector along z direction is given as

$$\hat{\mu} = \hat{k}$$

Magnetic induction in region is given as

$$\vec{B} = 3\hat{j} + 4\hat{i}$$

Torque vector on the ring acts along the direction

$$\hat{\mu}\times\vec{B} = 3\hat{j} - 4\hat{i}$$

Thus the ring will topple about a point located on the line perpendicular to the direction of torque vector which is $3\hat{i}+4\hat{j}$. Thus the point on ring located in this direction is (3, 4)

Sol. 27 (A) Magnetic induction inside the solenoid is given as

$$B = \mu_0\frac{N}{L}i$$

Where N are total number of turns & L is length of the solenoid. Time period of revolution of electron is given as

$$T = \frac{2\pi m}{qB}$$

Pitch of helical path is given as

$$p = V_{\|}T$$

Number of revolution in covering a distance L along the length of solenoid is given as

$$N = \frac{L}{\text{pitch}} = \frac{L\cdot qB}{V_{\|}\cdot 2\pi m}$$

$$\Rightarrow \quad N = \frac{\mu_0\cdot Ni}{V_{\|}\cdot 2\pi}\cdot\frac{q}{m}$$

Substituting values gives

$$N = \frac{4\pi\times10^{-7}\times8000\times4\times\sqrt{3}\times10^{11}}{400\cdot\sqrt{3}\times2\pi} = 1600\times10^{3}$$

Sol. 28 (C) Magnetic induction at the center of square and circular loop are given as

$$B_1 = 2\sqrt{2}\frac{\mu_0 I}{\pi L},\quad B_2 = \frac{\mu_0 I}{2R}$$

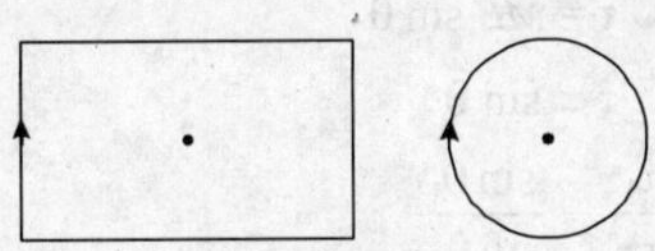

Ratio of magnetic inductions is given as

$$\frac{B_1}{B_2} = \frac{4\sqrt{2}}{\pi}\frac{R}{L}$$

As length of wires is equal, we use

$$4L = 2\pi R$$

$$\Rightarrow \quad \frac{B_1}{B_2} = \frac{8\sqrt{2}}{\pi^2},\quad \frac{B_2}{B_1} = \frac{\pi^2}{8\sqrt{2}}$$

Sol. 29 (B) The magnetic moment of the magnet is given as

$$M = 10\times10^{-2}\times2 = 20\times10^{-2}\ \text{Am}^2$$

$$\Rightarrow \quad M = 0.2\ \text{Am}^2$$

Torque on the magnet due to earth's magnetic induction is given as

$$\tau = MB\sin\theta$$

$\Rightarrow \quad \tau = 0.2 \times (0.32 \times 10^{-4}) \sin 30°$

$\Rightarrow \quad \tau = 0.2 \times (0.32 \times 10^{-4}) \times (1/2)$

$\Rightarrow \quad \tau = 32 \times 10^{-7}$ Nm

Sol. 30 (B) Induced electric field at a distance R from center is given as

$$E = \frac{R}{2}\frac{dB}{dt} = \frac{R}{2}\alpha$$

Speed attained by the bead is given as

$$v = \frac{qE}{m}t$$

For circular motion of bead, from below figure, we have

$$qvB - N = \frac{mv^2}{R}$$

$$\Rightarrow \quad N = \frac{\alpha q^2 Rt}{4m}(2B_0 + \alpha t)$$

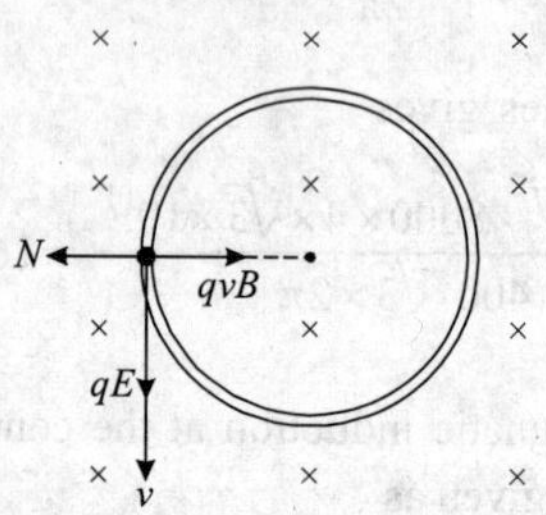

Sol. 31 (B) Torque on bar magnet is given as

$$\tau = MB \sin\theta$$

$$\Rightarrow \quad \tau \propto \sin\theta$$

$$\Rightarrow \quad \frac{\tau_1}{\tau_2} = \frac{\sin\theta_1}{\sin\theta_2}$$

$$\Rightarrow \quad \frac{\tau \times 2}{\tau_1} = \frac{1}{\sin\theta_2} \quad \text{or} \quad \sin\theta_2 = 1/2$$

$$\Rightarrow \quad \theta_2 = 30°$$

Sol. 32 (A) Using Ampere's law for the given loop, we have

$$\oint (\vec{B}_P + \vec{B}_Q)\vec{dl} = \mu_0 I$$

$$\Rightarrow \quad +12\mu_0 - 6\mu_0 = \mu_0 I$$

$$\Rightarrow \quad I = 6\text{ A}$$

Sol. 33 (A) At $x = 0$ and $y = \pm 2$m we use

$$\vec{F}_{MNP} = \vec{F}_{MP} = i[\overrightarrow{MP} \times \vec{B}]$$

$$\vec{F}_{MNP} = 60\hat{i}$$

Sol. 34 (B) If the springs are compressed by a distance x_0, we use for equilibrium of rod

$$2Kx_0 + mg = ilB$$

$$\Rightarrow \quad x_0 = \frac{ilB - mg}{2K}$$

Length of spring becomes

$$l = l_0 + x_0$$

Sol. 35 (C) Let new angle of dip be θ'. Then we have

$$\tan\theta' = \frac{\tan 40}{\cos 30} = \frac{\tan 40 \times 2}{\sqrt{3}}$$

This is more than 40°

Sol. 36 (C) Magnetic induction at O is given as

$$\vec{B} = \frac{\mu_0 I}{4\pi a}\left[\left(1 - \frac{1}{\sqrt{2}}\right)(-\hat{j}) + \left(\frac{1}{\sqrt{2}}\right)\hat{j} + \hat{k}\right]$$

$$\Rightarrow \quad x = 2$$

Sol. 37 (D) Figure below shows the path of motion of the particle.

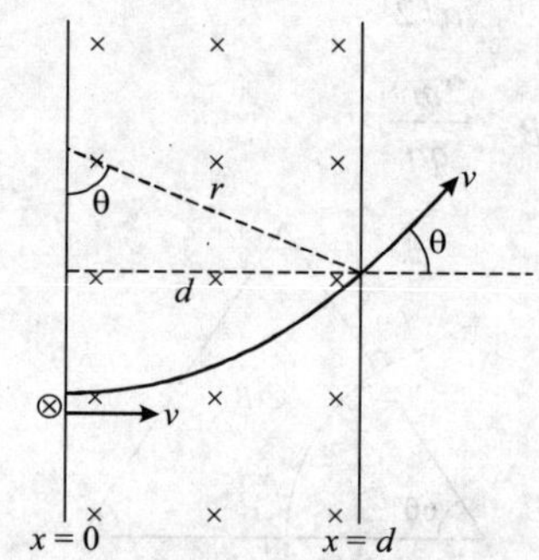

Deviation angle of particle is given as

$$\sin\theta = \frac{d}{r} = \frac{d}{(mv/Bq)}$$

$$\Rightarrow \quad \frac{q}{m} = \frac{v\sin\theta}{Bd}$$

Sol. 38 (B) The magnetic induction due to any one segment of wire is given as

$$B = \frac{\mu_0 i}{4\pi(d\sin\alpha)}(\cos 0° + \cos(180 - \alpha))$$

$$\Rightarrow \quad B = \frac{\mu_0 i}{4\pi(d\sin\alpha)}(1 - \cos\alpha)$$

$$\Rightarrow \quad B = \frac{\mu_0 i}{4\pi d}\tan\frac{\alpha}{2}$$

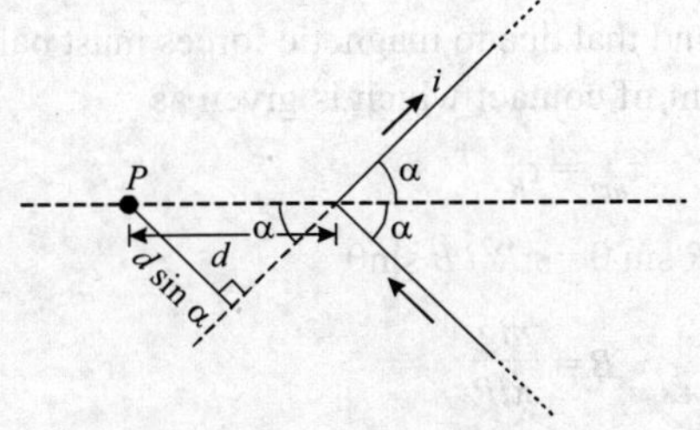

Resultant magnetic induction at P is given as

$$B_P = 2B = \frac{\mu_0 i}{2\pi d}\tan\frac{\alpha}{2}$$

$$\Rightarrow \quad K = \frac{\mu_0 i}{2\pi d}$$

Sol. 39 (D) Dip angle is given as

$$\tan\theta = B_V/B_H$$

$$\Rightarrow \quad B_V = B_H\tan\theta = (0.35\times10^{-4})\tan 60°$$

$$\Rightarrow \quad B_V = 0.60\times10^{-4}\,\text{T}$$

Sol. 40 (C) In uniform magnetic field, magnetic force on POQ is equal to the magnetic force on straight wire PQ having the same current as shown in figure below.

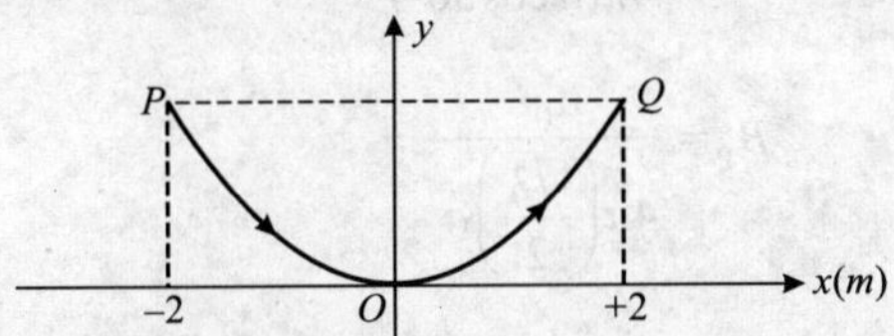

Thus force is given as

$$\vec{F} = i(\vec{l}\times\vec{B}) = i(\overrightarrow{PQ}\times\vec{B})$$

$$\Rightarrow \quad \vec{F} = 2[(4\hat{i})\times(-0.02\hat{k})] = (0.16\hat{j})$$

$$\Rightarrow \quad \vec{a} = \frac{\vec{F}}{m} = \frac{(0.16\hat{j})}{0.1} = (1.6\hat{j})\,\text{m/s}^2$$

Sol. 41 (A) Magnetic field at P is $\vec{B}$, perpendicular to OP in the direction shown in figure.

So we have

$$\vec{B} = B\sin\theta\,\hat{i} - B\cos\theta\,\hat{j}$$

Where $\quad B = \dfrac{\mu_0 I}{2\pi r}$

$$\sin\theta = \frac{y}{r} \text{ and } \cos\theta = \frac{x}{r}$$

$$\vec{B} = \frac{\mu_0 I}{2\pi}\times\frac{1}{r^2}(y\hat{i} - x\hat{j}) = \frac{\mu_0 I(y\hat{i} - x\hat{j})}{2\pi(x^2+y^2)}$$

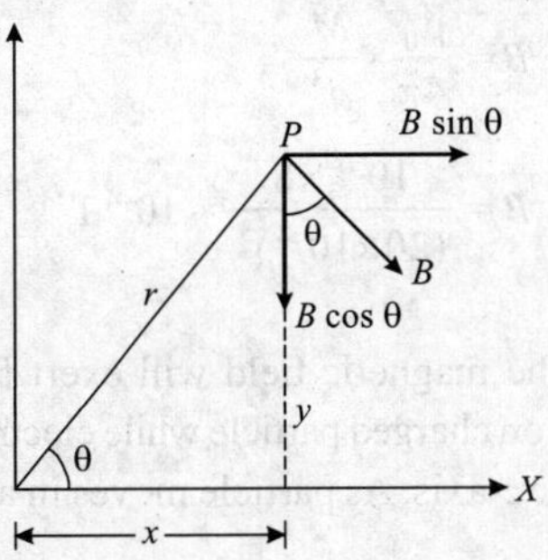

Sol. 42 (B) As time period is same in both horizontal and vertical plane we have

$$B_V = B_H$$

$$\Rightarrow \quad \tan\theta = \frac{B_V}{B_H} = 1$$

$$\Rightarrow \quad \theta = 45°$$

Sol. 43 (C) The radius of circular motion is given as

$$r = \frac{mv}{qB} = \sqrt{\frac{2qVm}{Bq}} = \sqrt{\frac{2Vm}{q}}\left(\frac{1}{B}\right)$$

Sol. 44 (B) For equilibrium of the system, torques on M_1 and M_2 due to B_H must counter balance each other so we have

$$M_1\times B_H = M_2\times B_H$$

If θ is the angle between M_1 and B_H then angle between M_2 and B_H will be $(90-\theta)$ so we have

$$M_1 B_H\sin\theta = M_2 B_H\sin(90-\theta)$$

$$\Rightarrow \quad \tan\theta = \frac{M_2}{M_1} = \frac{M}{3M} = \frac{1}{3}$$

$$\Rightarrow \quad \theta = \tan^{-1}\left(\frac{1}{3}\right)$$

Sol. 45 (A) Magnetic induction set up by large loop at the centre of smaller loop is given by

$$B = \frac{\mu_0 i}{2R} = \frac{4\pi\times10^{-7}\times15}{2\times0.157}$$

$$= 6\times10^{-5}\,\text{Wb/m}^2$$

$$\text{Torque} = \mu B\sin\theta = (NiA)B\sin 90$$

$$= \{30\times1\times\pi(0.01)^2\}(6\times10^{-5})(1)$$

$$= (9.42\times10^{-3})\times(6\times10^{-5})$$

$$= 0.57\times10^{-6}\,\text{Nm}$$

Sol. 46 (A) Magnetic induction at equatorial line due to a dipole is given as

$$B = \frac{\mu_0}{4\pi} \times \frac{M}{d^3}$$

$$\Rightarrow \quad B = \frac{10^{-7} \times 8}{(20 \times 10^{-2})^3} = 10^{-4}\,\text{T}$$

Sol. 47 (A) The magnetic field will exert force in negative z-axis direction on charged particle while electric field will exert force in positive z-axis. As particle moves in a straight line, we have

$$qE = qvB$$

$$\Rightarrow \quad B = \frac{E}{V}$$

$$\Rightarrow \quad B = 10^3\,\text{T}$$

Sol. 48 (A) Magnetic induction along the axial line is given as

$$B = \frac{\mu_0}{4\pi} \times \frac{M}{d^3}$$

$$\Rightarrow \quad B = \frac{10^{-7} \times 8}{(20 \times 10^{-2})^3}$$

$$\Rightarrow \quad B = 0.125 \times 10^{-4}\,\text{T}$$

Sol. 49 (D) When electron is projected in electric field, we have

$$\frac{mv_0^2}{r_1} = eE \qquad \ldots(1)$$

When electron is projected in magnetic field, we have

$$\frac{mv_0^2}{r_2} = ev_0B \qquad \ldots(2)$$

Dividing equation-(1) and (2)

$$\frac{r_2}{r_1} = \frac{eE}{ev_0B}$$

$$\Rightarrow \quad \frac{r_1}{r_2} = \frac{Bv_0}{E}$$

Sol. 50 (A) Magnetic induction at axial and equatorial line is given as

$$B_{axial} = \frac{\mu_0}{4\pi}\left(\frac{2M}{x^3}\right)$$

and $$B_{eq} = \frac{\mu_0}{4\pi}\left(\frac{M}{x^3}\right)$$

$$\Rightarrow \quad \frac{B_{eq}}{B_{axial}} = \frac{1}{2}$$

$$\Rightarrow \quad B_{eq} = \frac{B}{2}$$

Sol. 51 (B) For equilibrium of sphere net torque on it due to its weight and that due to magnetic forces must balance about bottom point of contact which is given as

$$\tau_{mg} = \tau_B$$

$$\Rightarrow \quad mg\,R \sin\theta = \pi R^2 i\,B \sin\theta$$

$$\Rightarrow \quad B = \frac{mg}{\pi i R}$$

Sol. 52 (B) The apparent dip angle is related to the angle between magnetic meridian and the vertical plane in which it is measured is given as

$$\tan 60 = \frac{V}{H\cos 30}$$

$$\Rightarrow \quad \sqrt{3} = \frac{V}{H\cos 30}$$

$$\Rightarrow \quad \tan\delta = \frac{V}{H} = \sqrt{3} \times \cos 30 = \sqrt{3} \times (\sqrt{3}/2)$$

$$\Rightarrow \quad \delta = \tan^{-1}(3/2)$$

Sol. 53 (B) Magnetic field due to wire 1 at P is given as

$$B_1 = \frac{\mu_0 i}{4\pi(a\cos 30°)}(\sin 30 + \sin 30)$$

$$\Rightarrow \quad B_1 = \frac{\mu_0 i}{4\pi\left(\frac{\sqrt{3}}{2}\right)a}$$

Due to wire 2 magnetic induction at point P is given as

$$B_2 = -\frac{\mu_0 i}{4\pi\left(\frac{\sqrt{3}}{2}\right)2a}$$

Summing infinite terms of such magnetic induction at point P is given as

$$B = \frac{\mu_0 i}{4\pi\left(\frac{\sqrt{3}}{2}\right)a}\left[1 - \frac{1}{2} + \frac{1}{3} - \frac{1}{4} \ldots\ldots\right]$$

$$\Rightarrow \quad B = \frac{\mu_0 i 2\ln 2}{4\pi\sqrt{3}a} = \frac{\mu_0 I}{4\pi}\frac{\ln 4}{\sqrt{3}a}[\hat{k}]$$

Sol. 54 (A) Magnetic induction at an axial point of the circular loop is given as

$$B_x = \frac{\mu_0 NiR^2}{2(R^2 + x^2)^{3/2}}$$

and $$B_c = \frac{\mu_0 Ni}{2R} \qquad [x = 0]$$

$$\Rightarrow \quad \frac{B_c}{B_x} = \frac{(R^2+x^2)^{3/2}}{R^3}$$

$$\Rightarrow \quad \frac{B_c}{B_x} = \frac{(25)^{3/2}}{(3)^3} = \frac{125}{27}$$

$$\Rightarrow \quad B_c = \frac{125}{27} \times 54 = 250\,\mu\text{T}$$

Sol. 55 **(C)** Initially we have

$$eE = eVB$$

$$V = \frac{E}{B} = \frac{3.2\times10^5}{2\times10^{-3}} = 1.6\times10^8\text{ m/s}$$

When electric field is removed, electron will only be moving in the influence of magnetic field and it follows a circular motion with radius given as

$$r = \frac{mV}{eB} = \frac{9.1\times10^{-31}\times1.6\times10^8}{1.6\times10^{-19}\times2\times10^{-3}}$$

$$\Rightarrow \quad r = \frac{9.1\times10^{-1}}{2} = 0.45\text{ m}$$

Sol. 56 **(C)** The kinetic energy of the electron is given as

$$\frac{1}{2}mv^2 = eV$$

$$\Rightarrow \quad v = (2\,eV/m)^{1/2}$$

Force on electron is given as

$$F = evB = eB\,(2eV/m)^{1/2}$$

When V is doubled, then we have

$$F' = \sqrt{2}F$$

Sol. 57 **(C)** As charge enters magnetic field in direction normal to it, it follows a circular path of radius given as

$$r = \frac{mv}{qB}$$

$$\Rightarrow \quad \frac{d}{2} = \frac{mv}{qB} \quad \ldots(1)$$

As the particle is accelerated by a potential difference V, we have

$$qV = \frac{1}{2}mv^2$$

$$\Rightarrow \quad \frac{2qV}{m} = v^2 \quad \ldots(2)$$

By solving equation-(1) and (2), we have

$$m = \frac{qB^2d^2}{8V}$$

Sol. 58 **(C)** The fields at axis and centre respectively are given as

$$B_{axis} = \frac{\mu_0}{4\pi}\times\frac{2\pi ir^2}{(r^2+h^2)^{3/2}}$$

and $$B_{centre} = \frac{\mu_0}{4\pi}\times\frac{2\pi i}{r}$$

$$\Rightarrow \quad \frac{B_{axis}}{B_{centre}} = \frac{r^3}{(r^2+h^2)^{3/2}} = \frac{r^3}{r^3\left[1+\frac{h^2}{r^2}\right]^{3/2}}$$

$$\Rightarrow \quad \frac{B_{axis}}{B_{centre}} = \left[1+\frac{h^2}{r^2}\right]^{-3/2} = \left(1-\frac{3h^2}{2r^2}\right)$$

$$\Rightarrow \quad \left(1-\frac{B_{axis}}{B_{centre}}\right) = \frac{3h^2}{2r^2}$$

$$\Rightarrow \quad \frac{B_{centre}-B_{axis}}{B_{centre}} = \frac{3h^2}{2r^2}$$

Sol. 59 **(C)** The magnetic induction due to a straight wire at some distance from it is given as

$$B = \frac{\mu_0}{2\pi}\frac{i}{r}$$

Above result is independent of diameter of wire so magnetic induction will remain same.

Sol. 60 **(C)** To break off from the surface the magnetic force on block is given as

$$f_B = mg\cos\theta$$

$$\Rightarrow \quad qvB = mg\cos\theta$$

$$\Rightarrow \quad q(g\sin\theta.t)B = mg\cos\theta$$

$$\Rightarrow \quad t = \frac{m\cot\theta}{qB}$$

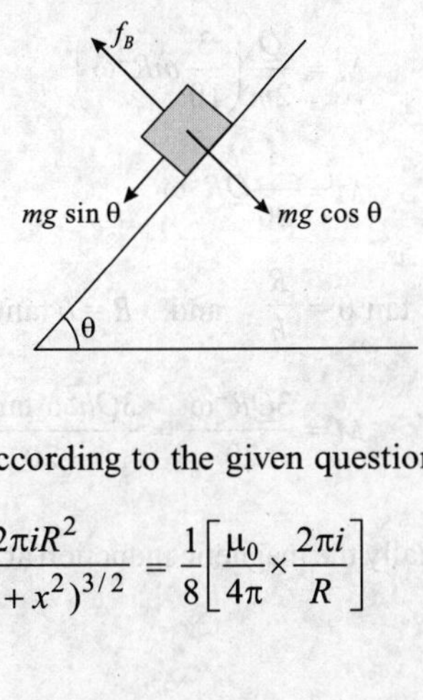

Sol. 61 **(A)** According to the given question, we use

$$\frac{\mu_0}{4\pi}\times\frac{2\pi iR^2}{(R^2+x^2)^{3/2}} = \frac{1}{8}\left[\frac{\mu_0}{4\pi}\times\frac{2\pi i}{R}\right]$$

$\Rightarrow \quad 8R^3 = (R^2+x^2)^{3/2}$ or $(2R)^3 = (R^2+x^2)^{3/2}$

$\Rightarrow \quad 2R = (R^2+x^2)^{1/2}$ or $4R^2 = R^2+x^2$

$\Rightarrow \quad x = \sqrt{3}R$

Sol. 62 (D) At any instant $|v| = v_0$ & component along y-axis must remain constant.

Sol. 63 (D) Magnetic field at P due to wire 1,

$$B_1 = \frac{\mu_0}{4\pi}\cdot\frac{2(8)}{d}$$

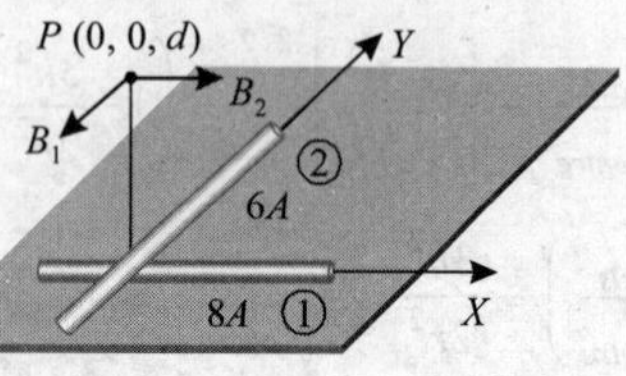

Due to wire 2, magnetic field at P is

$$B_2 = \frac{\mu_0}{4\pi}\cdot\frac{2(6)}{d}$$

$$\Rightarrow \quad B_{net} = \sqrt{B_1^2+B_2^2} = \sqrt{\left(\frac{\mu_0}{4\pi}\cdot\frac{16}{d}\right)^2+\left(\frac{\mu_0}{4\pi}\cdot\frac{12}{d}\right)^2}$$

$$= \frac{\mu_0}{4\pi}\times\frac{2}{d}\times 10 = \frac{5\mu_0}{\pi d}$$

Sol. 64 (D) The moment of inertia of cone is

$$I = \frac{3}{10}MR^2$$

Thus angular momentum of rotating cone is given as

$$L = I\omega = \frac{3}{10}mR^2\omega$$

Magnetic moment of a rotating cone is given as

$$M = \frac{Q}{2m}L$$

$$\Rightarrow \quad M = \frac{Q}{2m}\left(\frac{3}{10}mR^2\omega\right)$$

$$\Rightarrow \quad M = \frac{3}{20}QR^2\omega$$

As $\quad \tan\theta = \frac{R}{h}$ and $R = h\tan\theta$

$$\Rightarrow \quad M = \frac{3QR^2\omega}{20} = \frac{3Qh^2\omega\tan^2\theta}{20}$$

Sol. 65 (A) Initially the magnetic induction at centre of loop is given as

$$B_C = \frac{\mu_0 I}{2\pi R}$$

Now for same length of wire if the radius is made R/n then the number of turns will become n so new magnetic induction at centre is given as

$$B_O = \frac{n\mu_0 I}{2\pi(R/n)} = n^2\frac{\mu_0 I}{2\pi R}$$

$$\Rightarrow \quad \frac{B_C}{B_O} = \frac{1}{n^2}$$

Sol. 66 (D) Magnetic induction at O due to each of semi infinite straight wires is into the plane of paper and its magnitude is given as

$$B_1 = \frac{\mu_0 i}{4\pi R}$$

Magnetic induction due to circular arc at point O is outward from the plane of paper and its magnitude is given as

$$B_2 = \frac{\mu_0}{2R}\left(\frac{\theta}{2\pi}\right)i$$

For net magnetic induction at point O to be zero, we use

$$2B_1 = B_2$$

$$\Rightarrow \quad 2\frac{\mu_0 i}{4\pi R} = \frac{\mu_0\left(\frac{\theta}{2\pi}\right)i}{2R}$$

$$\Rightarrow \quad \theta = 2 \text{ radian}$$

Sol. 67 (C) To calculate the net magnetic field at the centre O, the magnetic field is calculated due to the three parts of the wire frames (1), (2) and (3) as shown in figure below.

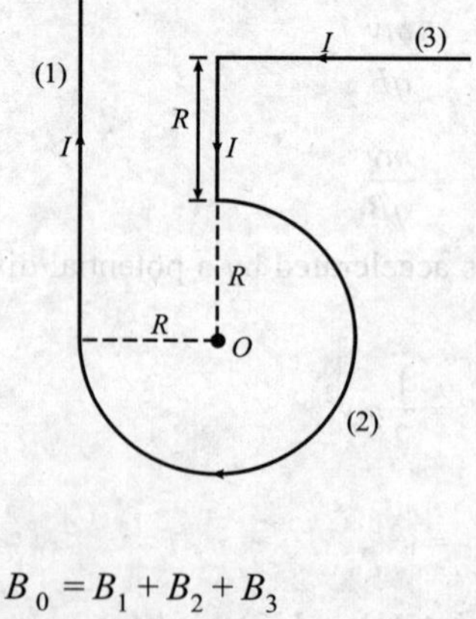

$$B_0 = B_1 + B_2 + B_3$$

$$\Rightarrow \quad B_0 = \frac{\mu_0 I}{4\pi R} + \frac{3\mu_0 I}{8R} - \frac{\mu_0 I}{8\pi R}$$

$$\Rightarrow \qquad B_0 = \frac{\mu_0 I}{8\pi R} + \frac{3\mu_0 I}{8R}$$

$$\Rightarrow \qquad B_0 = \frac{\mu_0 I}{8R}\left(\frac{1+3\pi}{\pi}\right)$$

Sol. 68 (C) At $t = \frac{T_0}{2}$ particle is at

$$x = \frac{P_0}{2},\ \theta = \pi,\ y = 0 \text{ and } z = -2R_0$$

and at $t = \frac{3T_0}{2}$ particle is at

$$x = \frac{3T_0}{2},\ \theta = \pi,\ y = 0 \text{ and } z = 2R_0$$

Thus along z axis maximum distance of the extreme positions from x axis is $2R_0 + 2R_0 = 4R_0$.

ADVANCE MCQs One or More Options Correct

Sol. 1 (A, B, C) Resistance of the rings is given as

$$R = \frac{\rho l}{A}$$

Current through the rings by equal voltage sources is given as

$$i = \frac{V}{R}$$

Magnetic field at the center of ring is given as

$$B = \frac{\mu_0 I}{2r}$$

If we double radius and cross-sectional radius, then length of wire will get doubled and cross sectional area becomes four times so resistance will be halved and current will get doubled. As current and radius of ring both get doubled magnetic induction at their center will remain same. Hence options (A), (B) and (C) are correct.

Sol. 2 (A, C) Magnetic induction at the center of first coil is given as

$$B_1 = \frac{\mu_0 N_1 i_1}{2R_1}$$

$$B_1 = \frac{(4\pi\times10^{-7})(50)(2)}{2(5\times10^{-2})} = 4\pi\times10^{-4}\,\text{T}$$

At the center of second coil it is given as

$$B_2 = \frac{\mu_0 N_2 i_2}{2R_2} = \frac{(4\pi\times10^{-7})(100)(2)}{(2)(10\times10^{-2})}$$

$$B_2 = 4\pi\times10^{-4}\,\text{T}$$

When currents are in the same direction, we use

$$B_{net} = B_1 + B_2$$

When currents are in the opposite direction, we use

$$B_{net} = B_1 - B_2$$

Sol. 3 (A) The deflection in magnetic needle of tangent galvanometer depends upon the magnetic induction at the center of its coil which is given as

$$B_C = \frac{\mu_0 IN}{2r} = \frac{\mu_0 (V/R)N}{2r} = \frac{\mu_0 VN}{2r[\rho(2\pi rN)/S]} = \frac{\mu_0 VS}{4\pi r^2\rho}$$

From the above expression we can see that only option (A) is correct.

Sol. 4 (A, C, D) Due to sheet the magnetic induction is given as

$$B = \frac{1}{2}\mu_0 i = \frac{\mu_0(2bJ)}{2} = \mu_0 JB$$

The magnetic induction inside the sheet is given as

$$B = \mu_0 Jx$$

Sol. 5 (All) Net upward and downward forces on the loop will get cancelled out and leftward component on wire segment ab is more than that on wire segment bc so net force on loop will act leftwards.

Sol. 6 (A, D) While revolving in conical pendulum force equations on the charge can be written as

$$T\sin\theta + F = m\omega^2(L\sin\theta)$$

$$T\sin\theta = mg$$

$$\Rightarrow \qquad \frac{mg}{\cos\theta}\sin\theta + \theta(\omega L\sin\theta)B = m\omega^2 L\sin\theta$$

$$\Rightarrow \qquad B = \frac{m\omega^2 L\sin\theta}{(\omega L\sin\theta)q} - \frac{\frac{mg\sin\theta}{\cos\theta}}{(\omega L\sin\theta)q}$$

$$\Rightarrow \qquad B = \frac{m\omega}{q} - \frac{mg}{q\omega L\cos\theta} = \frac{1}{\beta}\left[\omega - \frac{g}{\omega L\cos\theta}\right]$$

Sol. 7 (B, C) The magnetic induction directions at different locations in surrounding of wire on the line are shown in figure below.

Sol. 8 (A, B) We've discussed that magnetic field is produced by moving charges. Even in magnets the magnetic field is due to the revolving unpaired electrons in the material. Practically in a magnet magnetic field is produced throughout the volume of the material of magnet not just at its ends or poles. Magnetic poles is a theoretical concept for understanding the calculation of magnetic field mathematically. The magnetic lines in case of a current carrying straight wire are concentric circles whereas a bar magnet produces magnetic field which is similar to that of a solenoid. In case of a clockwise current magnetic induction is inward so it behaves like a south pole and vice versa. Thus options (A) and (B) are correct.

Sol. 9 (A, B, C) For a random shaped current carrying wire we've studied that the net magnetic force is equal to the force acting on a straight wire carrying same current and length equal to the line joining the end points of the wire. In above case the mesh can be replaced by a straight wire of length AC so force is given as

$$F = Bi(\sqrt{2}a) \times 2$$

By symmetry we have $V_B = V_D = V_O$

Hence options (A), (B) and (C) are correct.

Sol. 10 (A, B, D) As $\vec{v} \perp \vec{B}$ particle is performing circular motion in xy plane with radius of circle given as

$$r = \frac{mv}{Bq} = \frac{1\times10}{2} = 5\text{ m}$$

Radius of $x^2 + y^2 - 4x - 21 = 0$ is 5 m

Radius of $x^2 + y^2 = 25$ is 5 m

The time period of revolution of particle is given as

$$T = \frac{2\pi m}{Bq} = \frac{2\pi\times1}{1\times2} = 3.14\text{ s}$$

Sol. 11 (C, D) Magnetic field can not increase speed of a charged particle. Since magnetic field never changes speed thus no change in energy will happen. Since the component of magnetic field perpendicular to the motion can affect the direction of velocity it can make it in circular path centripetal force is always perpendicular to it's velocity direction.

Sol. 12 (A, C) Time period of motion is given as

$$T = \frac{2\pi m}{Bq} = \frac{2\pi}{\alpha B_0}$$

At $$t = \frac{\pi}{\alpha B_0} = \frac{T}{2}$$

Velocity of particle is $-v_0\hat{i} + v_0\hat{k}$

Speed of charge in magnetic field always remains constant so it will be

$$v = v_0\sqrt{2}$$

At $$t = \frac{2\pi}{\alpha B_0} = T$$

Displacement is equal to pitch which is given as

$$\Delta x = V_0 T = \frac{2\pi V_0}{\alpha B_0}$$

At $$t = \frac{2\pi}{\alpha B_0} = T$$

Distance is given as

$$\Delta x = v \times T = \frac{2\sqrt{2}V_0\pi}{\alpha B_0}$$

Sol. 13 (A, B, C) Already we've studied that both deflection and vibrational magnetometer are used to determine magnetic moment of a bar magnet in terms of the earth's horizontal component of magnetic field. If both are given then value of B_H can be eliminated and we can calculate the value of magnetic moment of bar magnet without using the value of B_H. A tangent galvanometer is used to determine B_H not magnetic moment of a bar magnet. Thus options (A), (B) and (C) are correct.

Sol. 14 (A, D) Radius of the helical path is given as

$$R_1 = b_1 = \frac{mv\sin\theta_1}{qB} = \frac{mv\sin 30°}{qB} = \frac{1}{2}\text{constant}$$

$$R_2 = b_2 = \frac{mv\sin\theta_2}{qB} = \frac{mv\sin 60°}{qB} = \frac{\sqrt{3}}{2}\times\text{constant}$$

Time period of motion in helical path is given as

$$T_1 = a_1 = \frac{2\pi R_1}{V_0\sin\theta_1} = \frac{2\pi\times mv\sin 30°}{qBv\sin 30°}$$

$$= \frac{2\pi m}{qB} = \text{constant}$$

and $$T_2 = a_2 = \frac{2\pi R_2}{V\sin\theta_2} = \frac{2\pi mv\sin 60°}{qBv\sin 60°} = \frac{2\pi m}{qB}$$

$$\Rightarrow \qquad b = \frac{R_1}{R_2} = \frac{1/2}{\sqrt{3}/2} = \frac{1}{\sqrt{3}}$$

$$\Rightarrow \qquad \frac{T_1}{T_2} = \frac{a_1}{a_2} = a = 1$$

Pitch of helical path is given as

$$P = v\cos\theta \times T$$

$\Rightarrow$ $P_1 = T_1 \times v \times \cos 30°$

$\Rightarrow$ $P_2 = T_2 \times v \times \cos 60°$

$\Rightarrow$ $$c = \frac{P_1}{P_2} = \frac{T_1 \cos 30°}{T_2 \cos 60°} = \frac{\sqrt{3}/2}{1/2} = \sqrt{3}$$

From above equations we have

$$a = 1;\ b = \frac{1}{\sqrt{3}};\ c = \sqrt{3}$$

$\Rightarrow$ $abc = 1;\ a = bc$

Sol. 15 (B, C, D) Let O and P be the end points of wire. Hence force on current carrying wire placed in uniform magnetic induction is given as

$$\vec{F} = I(\overrightarrow{OP} \times \vec{B})$$

Sol. 16 (A, D) Since the conductor is electrically neutral, both A and B do not observe electric field. Current in conductor is same for both A and B so both will observe same magnetic field. Hence options (A) and (D) are correct.

Sol. 17 (A, B, C) As the dip needle is placed in a plane which is normal to the magnetic field, it will not experience any torque which can rotate the dip needle so it can stay in equilibrium in any direction. Hence options (A), (B) and (C) are correct.

Sol. 18 (A, D) Torque on the wire frame due to its weight is given as

$$\tau_{mg} = 0.5\,g \times 1\,\hat{i} = 5\,\hat{i}$$

Magnetic torque on wire frame is given as

$$\tau_B = (-0.5 \times 4\,\hat{i}) \times \vec{B}$$

x and y component of magnetic induction does not exert a torque on the loop as it is hinges along side AB so only z direction magnetic field is required which can counterbalance the torque on the loop due to its weight so options (A) and (D) are correct.

Sol. 19 (A, B, C) At geomagnetic pole the direction of earth's magnetic field is only in vertical direction so it will not exert any net force or torque on the magnetic compass needle in horizontal plane thus it can stay in equilibrium along any line in horizontal plane. As there is no restoring force on needle for any position it cannot oscillate. Thus options (A), (B) and (C) are correct.

Sol. 20 (All) v is equal v_0 as speed of particle never changes in magnetic field as force is perpendicular to velocity always. And if speed is not changing then their components also not change

$$v_0 \cos\alpha = v\cos\beta$$

$\Rightarrow$ $v_0 = v$

$\Rightarrow$ $\alpha = \beta$

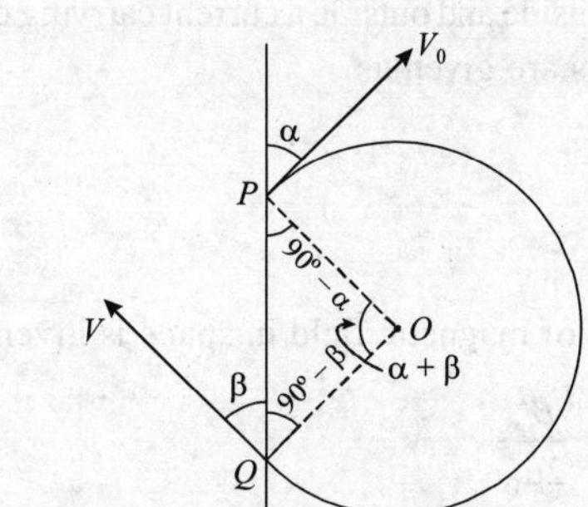

In triangle POQ, we have

$$\frac{PQ}{\sin(\alpha+\beta)} = \frac{OQ}{\sin(90-\alpha)} = \frac{OQ}{\cos\alpha}$$

$$OQ = \text{radius of that circle} = \frac{mv}{qB}$$

$$PQ = \frac{\sin(\alpha+\beta)\times R}{\cos\alpha}$$

$\Rightarrow$ $$PQ = \frac{(\sin 2\alpha)}{\cos\alpha} \times \frac{mv_0}{qB}$$

As $\alpha = \beta$, we have

$\Rightarrow$ $$PQ = \frac{2\sin\alpha\cos\alpha}{\cos\alpha}\frac{mv_0}{qB}$$

$\Rightarrow$ $$PQ = \frac{2mV_0 \sin\alpha}{qB}$$

We know that to cover complete circle particle will take time

$$T = \frac{2\pi m}{qB}$$

As shown in figure in this case particle has covered $360 - (\alpha+\beta)$ angle or we have

$$(360 - 2\alpha) = 2\,(180 - \alpha) = 2\,(\pi - \alpha) \text{ angle}$$

Time taken by particle in covering this angle is given as

$$t = \frac{2m(\pi - \alpha)}{Bq}$$

Sol. 21 (A, B, C) The magnetic force on charge is given as

$$F = q\vec{v} \times \vec{B}$$

$\Rightarrow \quad F = q[(x\hat{i} + y\hat{j}) \times (y\hat{i} + x\hat{j})]$

$\Rightarrow \quad F = q(x^2 - y^2)\hat{k}$

No force acts on particle if $x = y$

$F \propto (x^2 - y^2)$ if $x > y$

F is along z axis if $x > y$

Sol. 22 (A, D) As inside and outside a current carrying cylinder magnetic inductions are given as

$$B_{\text{in}} \propto r$$

and $$B_{\text{out}} \propto \frac{1}{r}$$

The energy density of magnetic field in space is given as

$$u_m = \frac{B^2}{2\mu_0}$$

Sol. 23 (A, B, D) Conductors are electrically neutral and produce magnetic fields on each other. Magnetic forces caused by the electrons on each other are weaker than the electrostatic force between them.

Sol. 24 (B, C) The current in coil is anticlockwise which produces a magnetic induction in upward direction so according to Lenz's law the magnetic field due to magnet is either increasing in downward direction or decreasing in upward direction. Hence options (B) and (C) are correct.

Sol. 25 (A, D) Observer A will observe that charge Q is stationary whereas B will feel that charge Q is moving in left direction. Since magnetic fields are produced whenever charge moves so magnetic fields are observed by B and electric field is observer by both A and B.

Sol. 26 (A, B, C) On wire ab in equilibrium magnetic repulsion will be balancing its weight and by slight displacement of wire ab in either direction vertically we can see that its equilibrium is stable.

Sol. 27 (A, B, C) Since $\vec{dl}$ and $\vec{B}$ are parallel for all elements on the loop so, $\vec{dF} = I_2(\vec{dl} \times \vec{B}) = 0$ for each small element.

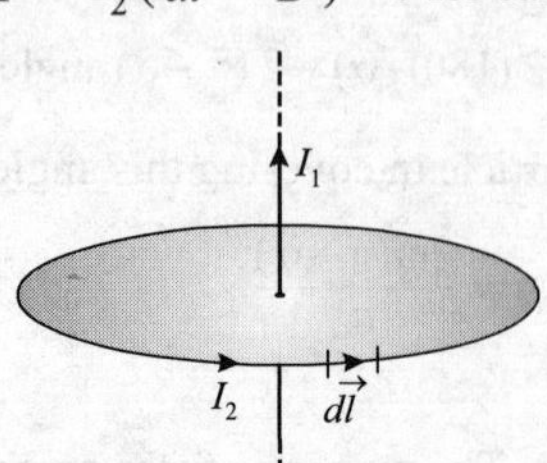

So, no magnetic force acts on loop.

Sol. 28 (B, C) Path will be helix in (A) and circular for $q = 90°$. For (B) since velocity is perpendicular to magnetic field so path will be circular. In (C) magnetic field never changes speed as work done by magnetic force on a freely moving charge is always zero. In (D) electrons will move in opposite direction since their velocity is opposite.

Sol. 29 (A, B, D) Torque acting on loop is given as

$$t = iabB_0 \sin\theta$$

The torque direction can be given by right hand thumb rule which is along $-y$ direction and it has a tendency to decrease θ.

Sol. 30 (A, B, D) By work energy theorem we have

$$qE \times 2a = \frac{1}{2}m(2v)^2 - \frac{1}{2}mv^2$$

$$2qEa = 2mv^2 - \frac{1}{2}mv^2 = \frac{3}{2}mv^2$$

$$\Rightarrow \quad E = \frac{3mv^2}{4qa}$$

Rate of workdone by electric field at P is given as

$$P_{\text{p}} = \vec{F}.\vec{v} = Fv\cos\theta$$

$$\Rightarrow \quad P_{\text{p}} = qEv$$

$$\Rightarrow \quad P_{\text{p}} = q \times \frac{3mv^2}{4qa} \cdot v = \frac{3}{4}\left(\frac{mv^3}{a}\right)$$

Rate of workdone by electric field Q

$$P_Q = \vec{F} \cdot \vec{v} = Fv\cos 90° = 0$$

As magnetic force is always normal to the velocity of particle so rate of workdone by magnetic field is always zero.

Sol. 31 (C) By right hand thumb rule we can analyze that for every small element of the loop the magnetic field direction at point P is in upward direction so for any shape of loop the direction of magnetic field at point P will remain same.

Sol. 32 (B, D) In the given situation due to rotation of shell a circulating surface current exist on the shell surface of which linear density is given as

$$i = \sigma(2\pi R)\frac{\omega}{2\pi} = \sigma Rkt$$

The magnetic induction inside the shell is given as

$$B = \mu_0 i = \mu_0 \sigma Rkt$$

The electric field inside the shell is due to time varying magnetic field and at a distance r from axis, its magnitude is given as

$$E_{in} = \frac{1}{2} r \frac{dB}{dt} = \frac{1}{2} r\mu_0 Rk \text{ (Constant in time)}$$

Thus inside the shell magnetic field is uniform but time varying and induced electric field is varying with distance from axis but not changing with time hence option (B) is correct and options (A) and (D) are NOT correct.

The total energy stored in field energy per unit volume inside the shell is calculated as

$$U = \frac{1}{2}\varepsilon_0 E^2 + \frac{B^2}{2\mu_0}$$

On substituting the values of E and B, it takes up the form as given in option (D) as $U = a + bt^2$ hence option (D) is correct.

* * * * *

ANSWERS & SOLUTIONS

CONCEPTUAL MCQS Single Option Correct

1	(C)	2	(D)	3	(C)
4	(B)	5	(B)	6	(B)
7	(A)	8	(C)	9	(A)
10	(B)	11	(C)	12	(D)
13	(C)	14	(B)	15	(C)
16	(C)	17	(C)	18	(C)
19	(A)	20	(A)	21	(C)
22	(D)	23	(D)	24	(D)
25	(C)	26	(B)	27	(B)
28	(D)	29	(D)	30	(C)
31	(B)	32	(D)	33	(C)
34	(D)	35	(D)	36	(C)
37	(B)	38	(A)	39	(A)
40	(B)	41	(B)	42	(D)
43	(C)	44	(A)	45	(B)
46	(C)	47	(A)	48	(B)
49	(C)	50	(D)	51	(C)
52	(B)	53	(A)	54	(C)
55	(C)	56	(A)	57	(B)
58	(C)	59	(B)	60	(D)
61	(B)	62	(A)	63	(D)

NUMERICAL MCQS Single Option Correct

1	(D)	2	(A)	3	(D)
4	(D)	5	(A)	6	(C)
7	(D)	8	(B)	9	(C)
10	(D)	11	(C)	12	(B)
13	(B)	14	(A)	15	(B)
16	(A)	17	(A)	18	(A)
19	(A)	20	(A)	21	(C)
22	(B)	23	(D)	24	(C)
25	(C)	26	(C)	27	(B)
28	(A)	29	(A)	30	(C)
31	(B)	32	(D)	33	(D)
34	(B)	35	(B)	36	(D)
37	(A)	38	(A)	39	(B)
40	(D)	41	(C)	42	(B)
43	(B)	44	(D)	45	(D)
46	(C)	47	(B)	48	(A)
49	(B)	50	(B)	51	(C)
52	(D)	53	(B)	54	(A)
55	(A)	56	(D)	57	(A)
58	(B)	59	(C)	60	(D)
61	(D)				

ADVANCE MCQs One or More Options Correct

1	(A, C, D)	2	(B, C, D)	3	(A, B, D)
4	(A, B)	5	(A, B, C)	6	(A, C)
7	(A, C)	8	(A, C)	9	(All)
10	(A, C)	11	(D)	12	(A, B, D)
13	(A, C)	14	(C)	15	(A, C)
16	(B)	17	(B, C, D)	18	(A, C)
19	(B, C)	20	(A, C, D)	21	(B, C, D)
22	(B, C, D)	23	(A, B, C)	24	(A, C)
25	(B, D)	26	(B)	27	(B, C)
28	(A, D)	29	(A, B, D)	30	(B, D)
31	(All)	32	(B, C)	33	(A, C)

Solutions of PRACTICE EXERCISE 5.1

(i) When the plane of coil is perpendicular to the field, magnetic flux linked with the coil is given as

$$\phi_1 = NBA$$

When the coil is turned through 180°, magnetic flux linked with it is given as

$$\phi_2 = -NBA$$

Change in flux linked with the coil is given as

$$\Delta\phi = -2NBA$$

Average induced EMF in the coil is given as

$$e = \left|\frac{\Delta\phi}{\Delta t}\right| = \frac{2NBA}{\Delta t}$$

$$\Rightarrow \qquad e = \frac{2\times1000\times0.4\times10^{-4}\times500\times10^{-4}}{0.1}$$

$$\Rightarrow \qquad e = 0.04\,\text{V}$$

(ii) When the ring moves towards right, then its due to its displacement the EMF induced in each of the two semicircles is given as

$$e = Bdv \qquad \text{... (1)}$$

By right hand palm rule the upper point of the ring is at high potential so current flows in the left loop in anticlockwise direction. The two semicircles behave like two identical sources in parallel with each of EMF given by equation-(1) with internal resistance given as

$$r = (\pi d/2)\lambda$$

Therefore equivalent resistance of parallel combination of the two semicircles is $r/2$ which is equal to

$$\frac{r}{2} = \frac{\pi d\lambda}{4}$$

As rails have negligible resistance and hence the equivalent resistance of the circuit is given by

$$R = \frac{r}{2} = \frac{\pi d\lambda}{4}$$

Induced current in circuit is given as

$$i = \frac{e}{R} = \frac{4Bv}{\pi\lambda}$$

Current through each semi-circle is given as

$$i_1 = \frac{i}{2} = \frac{e}{2R}$$

Force required to maintain velocity of ring is equal to the opposing magnetic force on the two semicircular parts which is given as

$$F = 2 \times B(i/2)d = Bid = \frac{4B^2vd}{\pi\lambda}$$

(iii) (a) Magnetic field produced by the bigger loop at the centre is given as

$$B = \frac{\mu_0 Ni}{2R}$$

$$\Rightarrow \quad B = \frac{(4\pi \times 10^{-7})(1)(1)}{2 \times 0.1} = 2\pi \times 10^{-6}\,\text{T}$$

The field is perpendicular to the plane of the loop.

The magnetic flux linked with the coil is maximum when its surface is perpendicular to the magnetic field and it is given as

$$\phi = BA$$

$$\Rightarrow \quad \phi = 2\pi \times 10^{-6} \times 5 \times 10^{-4} = 10\,\pi \times 10^{-10}\,\text{Wb}$$

(b) Average induced EMF in one rotation of loop is given as

$$e = \left|\frac{\Delta\phi}{\Delta t}\right| = \frac{2 \times 10\pi \times 10^{-10}}{2\pi/\omega}$$

$$\Rightarrow \quad e = 10^{-9}\,\omega$$

(c) Induced current in the smaller loop as a function of time is given as

$$i = \frac{e}{R} = \frac{1}{R}\left|\frac{d(BA\cos\omega t)}{dt}\right|$$

$$\Rightarrow \quad i = \frac{5 \times 10^{-10}\,\omega \sin\omega t}{2}$$

$$\Rightarrow \quad i = 2.5 \times 10^{-10}\,\omega \sin\omega t$$

(iv) We consider an elemental circular strip of radius r and width dr in the spiral as shown in figure. If the elemental strip/coil consist of dN turns then induced EMF across these dN number of turns at radius is given as

$$de = \left|\frac{d\phi}{dt}\right| = \frac{d}{dt}(\pi r^2 B N)$$

$$\Rightarrow \quad de = dN\,\pi r^2 \frac{d}{dt}(B_0 \sin\omega t)$$

$$\Rightarrow \quad de = dN\,\pi r^2 B_0 \omega \cos\omega t$$

$$\Rightarrow \quad de = \left(\frac{N}{a}dr\right)\pi r^2 B_0 \omega \cos\omega t$$

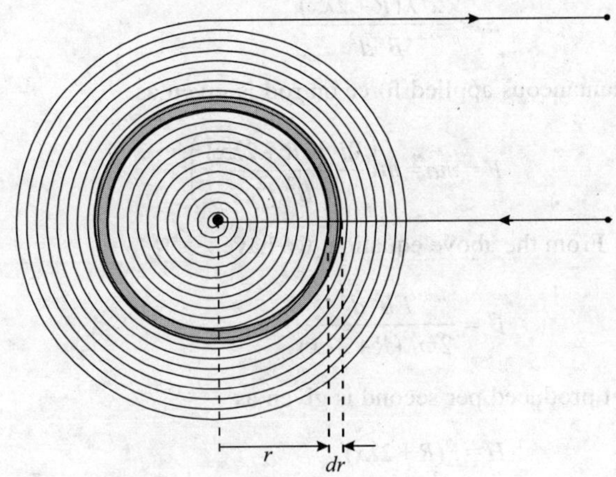

Total induced EMF in the spiral is given by integrating the above expression for the whole radius of the spiral which is given as

$$e = \int dt = \int_0^a \frac{N}{a} dr \,.\, \pi\,\omega\,B_0 \cos\omega t\, r^2$$

$$\Rightarrow \quad e = \frac{1}{3}\pi N B_0\, a^2\,\omega \cos\omega t = e_0 \cos\omega t$$

Amplitude of induced EMF in spiral is given as

$$e_0 = \frac{1}{3}\pi N a^2 B_0 \omega$$

(v) (a) If F is the instantaneous force acting on the rod MN at any instant t when the rod is at a distance x from the left end and moving at a velocity v as shown in figure. The induced EMF across the rod is given as

$$e = Bvd$$

The instantaneous total resistance of the circuit at this instant is given as

$$R_T = R + 2\lambda x$$

The current in the circuit is given as

$$i = \frac{e}{R_T} = \frac{Bvd}{(R + 2\lambda x)}$$

The velocity of the rod as a function of x is given as

$$\frac{dx}{dt} = \frac{i(r + 2\lambda x)}{Bd} \qquad \ldots (1)$$

The instantaneous acceleration a is given by

$$a = \frac{d^2x}{dt^2} = \frac{2i\lambda}{Bd}\left(\frac{dx}{dt}\right) = \frac{2i\lambda}{Bd}\left[\frac{i(r + 2\lambda x)}{Bd}\right]$$

$$\Rightarrow \quad a = \frac{2i^2\lambda(R+2\lambda x)}{B^2d^2}$$

Instantaneous applied force on rod is given as

$$F = ma = m\left(\frac{2i^2\lambda(R+2\lambda x)}{B^2d^2}\right)$$

(b) From the above equation, we have

$$i^2 = \frac{FB^2d^2}{2m\lambda(R+2\lambda x)}$$

Heat produced per second is given as

$$H = i^2(R+2\lambda x)$$

$$\Rightarrow \quad H = \frac{FB^2d^2}{2m\lambda}$$

Mechanical power supplied is given as

$$W = F\cdot\left(\frac{dx}{dt}\right)$$

$$\Rightarrow \quad W = F\times\frac{i(R+2\lambda x)}{Bd}$$

Calculating the fraction of mechanical power which is dissipated as heat gives

$$\frac{\text{Heat produced}}{\text{work done}} = \frac{H}{W} = \frac{FB^2d^2}{2m\lambda}\times\frac{Bd}{Fi(R+2\lambda x)}$$

$$\Rightarrow \quad \frac{H}{W} = \frac{B^3d^3}{2mi\lambda(R+2\lambda x)} \quad \ldots(2)$$

(vi) The situation is shown in figure.

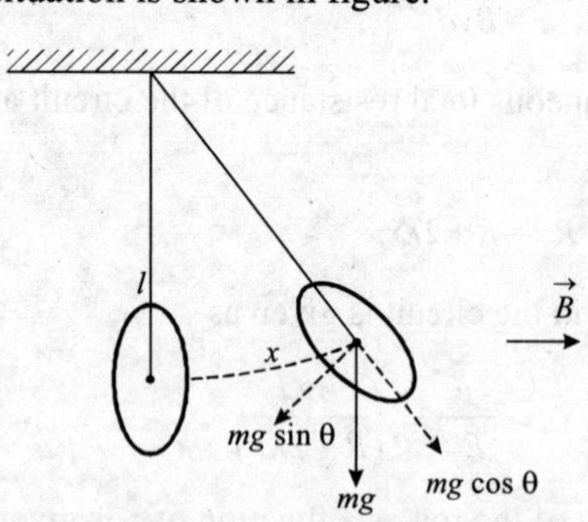

The instantaneous flux through the frame when displaced by an angle θ is given as

$$\phi = BA\cos\theta$$

Instantaneous induced EMF

$$e = -\frac{d\phi}{dt}\ BA\sin\theta\ \frac{d\theta}{dt}$$

$$\Rightarrow \quad e = BA\,\theta\frac{d\theta}{dt} \quad [\text{As } \sin\theta = \theta] \quad \ldots(1)$$

As the loop is very small in size compared to the length of string so we can consider it like a simple pendulum of which the motion equation is given as

$$\theta = \theta_0 \sin\omega t \quad \ldots(2)$$

Substituting the value of θ in equation-(1), we have

$$e = BA\,(\theta_0\sin\omega t)\frac{d}{dt}(\theta_0\sin\omega t)$$

$$\Rightarrow \quad e = BA\,\theta_0\sin\omega t\,\theta_0\,\omega\cos\omega t$$

$$\Rightarrow \quad e = \frac{1}{2}Ba\omega\theta_0^2\sin 2\omega t$$

Here we have

$$\omega = \sqrt{\left(\frac{g}{l}\right)} = \sqrt{\left(\frac{9.8}{0.392}\right)} = 5 \text{ rad/s}$$

and $\quad \theta_0 = \frac{x_0}{l} = \frac{2\times10^{-2}}{0.392}$ rad

Substituting the values, we get

$$e = \frac{1}{2}\times 0.784\times 3.92\times 10^{-4}\times 5\times\left(\frac{2\times10^{-2}}{0.392}\right)^2 \sin 10t$$

$$\Rightarrow \quad e = 2\times10^{-6}\sin 10t$$

$$\Rightarrow \quad e_{max} = 2\times10^{-6}\text{ V}$$

and $\quad i_{max} = \frac{e_{max}}{R} = \frac{2\times10^{-6}}{20} = 10^{-7}\text{ A}$

(vii) Consider a strip of the square as shown in figure.

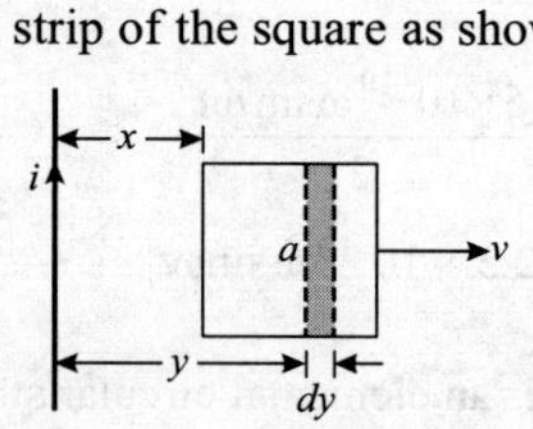

Area of the elemental strip is given as

$$dS = ady$$

Magnetic flux through this element due to the straight wire is given as

$$d\phi = B(ady) = \frac{\mu_0 i}{2\pi y}(ady) \quad \ldots(1)$$

The magnetic field at a distance y due to current i flowing in a wire is given as

$$B = \frac{\mu_0 i}{2\pi y}$$

Total flux through the square frame is given as

$$\phi = \int d\phi = \frac{\mu_0 ia}{2\pi}\int_x^{x+a}\frac{dy}{y}$$

$$\Rightarrow \quad \phi = \frac{\mu_0 ia}{2\pi}\ln\left(\frac{x+a}{x}\right)$$

Induced EMF in the square frame is given as

$$e = \left|\frac{d\phi}{dt}\right|$$

$$\Rightarrow \quad e = \frac{\mu_0 ia}{2\pi}\left(\frac{x}{x+a}\right)\left(\frac{a}{x^2}\right)\frac{dx}{dt}$$

$$\Rightarrow \quad e = \frac{\mu_0 ia^2 xv}{2\pi x(x+a)}$$

Above result can be directly obtained by calculating the motional EMF in left and right segments of the square frame which are parallel to the straight wire and subtracting the induced EMF in them.

(viii) The rotated position of the rod after a time t is shown in figure. Consider a small element of length dx of the rod at a distance x from the centre. The velocity of the element $v = x\omega$ and its distance from the wire is $r = (d - x\sin\omega t)$. Magnetic induction at this position is given as

$$B = \frac{\mu_0 i}{2\pi r} = \frac{\mu_0 i}{2\pi(d - x\sin\omega t)}$$

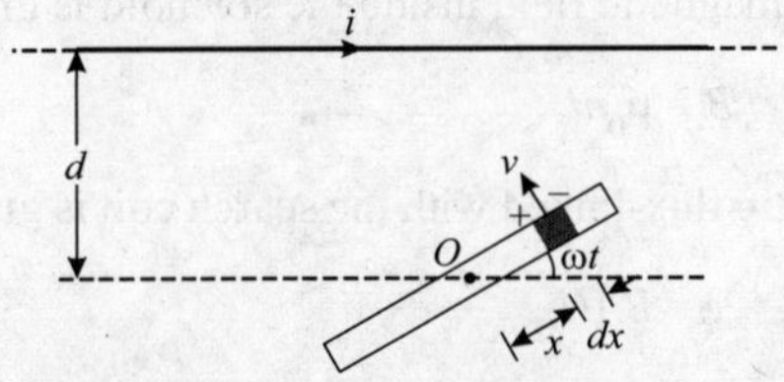

The induced EMF in this element is given as

$$de = Bvdx = \frac{\mu_0 i(x\omega)dx}{2\pi(d - x\sin\omega t)}$$

In order to obtain the resultant EMF, we integrate this expression from $-a$ to $+a$ which gives

$$e = \frac{\mu_0 i\omega}{2\pi}\int_{-a}^{a}\frac{xdx}{(d - x\sin\omega t)}$$

$$e = \frac{\mu_0 i\omega}{2\pi}\left(\frac{-1}{\sin^2\omega t}\right)\left[2a\sin\omega t - d\ln\left(\frac{d - a\sin\omega t}{d + a\sin\omega t}\right)\right]$$

$$\Rightarrow \quad e = \frac{\mu_0 i\omega}{2\pi\sin^2\omega t}\left[d\ln\left(\frac{d - a\sin\omega t}{d + a\sin\omega t}\right) - 2a\sin\omega t\right]$$

It should be noted that the lower end of the rod is at higher potential than upper end.

(ix) The situation described in question is shown in figure. If at any instant of time t, during the motion of second wire, the second wire is at a distance x. The area of the rectangle between the two wires is xd.

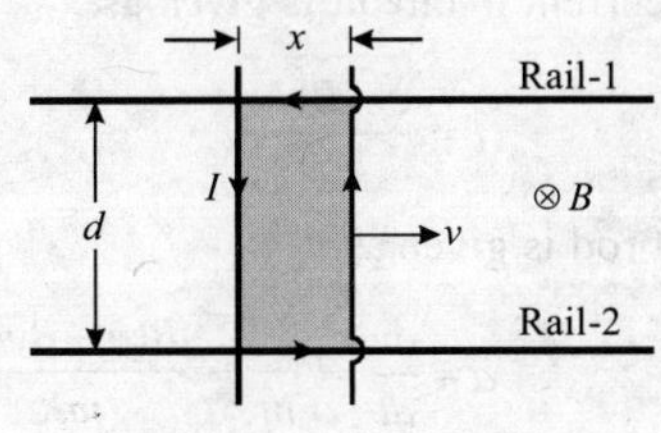

Rate of change of magnetic flux through the rectangle or motional EMF in the moving wire is given as

$$e = \frac{d\phi}{dt} = Bvd$$

So, the current induced in the rectangle is given as

$$i = \frac{e}{R} = \frac{Bdv}{2(d+x)\rho}$$

The force between the two wires due to current flow is given as

$$F = \frac{\mu_0 I^2 d}{2\pi x} = \frac{\mu_0 d}{2\pi x}\left[\frac{Bdv}{2(d+x)\rho}\right]^2$$

The force F', due to magnetic field on stationary wire is given as

$$F' = Bid = Bd\left[\frac{Bdv}{2(d+x)\rho}\right] = \frac{B^2d^2v}{2(d+x)\rho}$$

The force on stationary wire initially is directed towards left hand side because opposite currents repel each other while the force due to magnetic field will be directed towards right hand side according to right hand palm rule so the resultant force is given as

$$F_{net} = F' - F$$

$$\Rightarrow \quad F_{net} = \frac{B^2d^2v}{2(d+x)\rho} - \frac{\mu_0 d}{2\pi x}\left[\frac{Bdv}{2(d+x)\rho}\right]^2$$

$$\Rightarrow \quad F_{net} = \frac{B^2d^2v}{2(d+x)\rho}\left[1 - \frac{\mu_0 dv}{4\pi x(d+x)\rho}\right]$$

The force will be zero, when

$$\frac{\mu_0 dv}{4\pi x(d+x)\rho} = 1$$

For $d >> x$, we have

$$x = \frac{\mu_0 v}{4\pi\rho}$$

(x) When rod is moving at speed v, motional EMF induced in rod is given as

$$e = Bvl$$

At this instant current in circuit is given as

$$i = \frac{e - Bvl}{R}$$

Acceleration of rod is given as

$$a = \frac{dv}{dt} = \frac{F}{m} = \frac{B(e - Bvl)l}{mR}$$

$$\Rightarrow \quad \frac{dv}{e - Blv} = \frac{Bl}{mR}dt$$

$$\Rightarrow \quad \int_0^v \frac{dv}{\varepsilon - Blv} = \int_0^t \frac{Bl}{mR}dt$$

$$\Rightarrow \quad -\frac{1}{Bl}[\ln(e - Blv)]_0^v = \frac{Blt}{mR}$$

$$\Rightarrow \quad \ln\left(\frac{e - Blv}{e}\right) = -\frac{B^2l^2t}{mR}$$

$$\Rightarrow \quad \frac{e - Blv}{e} = e^{-B^2l^2t/mR}$$

$$\Rightarrow \quad v = \frac{e}{Bl}(1 - e^{-B^2l^2t/mR})$$

At $t \to \infty$ after a long time the terminal velocity is given as

$$v \to \frac{e}{Bl}$$

(xi) For pure rolling we use

$$v = R\omega$$

Motional EMF induced across points A and P is given as

$$e = Bvl = B(R\omega)(2R)$$

$$\Rightarrow \quad e = 2B\omega R^2$$

(xii) After the t, the angular position of coil from vertical is given as

$$\theta = \theta_0 \cos \omega t$$

$$\Rightarrow \quad \frac{d\theta}{dt} = -\theta_0 \omega \sin \omega t$$

At time t, magnetic flux through the coil is given as

$$\phi = BA \cos \theta = BA \cos\left[\theta_0 \cos\left(\sqrt{\frac{g}{l}}t\right)\right]$$

EMF induced in coil is given as

$$e = \left|\frac{d\phi}{dt}\right| = BA \sin \theta \frac{d\theta}{dt}$$

For small θ we use $\sin \theta \simeq \theta$, thus we have

$$e = BA\theta \frac{d\theta}{dt}$$

$$\Rightarrow \quad e = BA\left[\theta_0 \cos\sqrt{\frac{g}{l}}t\right]\left[\theta_0 \omega \sin\sqrt{\frac{g}{l}}t\right]$$

$$\Rightarrow \quad e = \frac{1}{2}BA\theta_0^2\omega \sin\left(2\sqrt{\frac{g}{l}}t\right)$$

Solutions of PRACTICE EXERCISE 5.2

(i) Induced EMF in the loop is given as

$$e = \frac{d\Phi}{dt} = 2at - a\tau$$

Induced current in the loop is given as

$$I = \frac{E}{R} = \frac{2at - a\tau}{R}$$

If in an elemental time dt, heat generated is dQ then we have

$$dQ = I^2 R\, dt$$

$$\Rightarrow \quad Q = \int dQ = \int_0^\tau I^2 R dt = \frac{a^2\tau^3}{3R}$$

(ii) The magnetic field inside the solenoid is given as

$$B = \mu_0 ni \quad \ldots(1)$$

The magnetic flux-linked with the search coil is given as

$$\phi = BAN_s \quad \ldots(2)$$

$$\Rightarrow \quad \phi = (\mu_0 iN) AN_s$$

EMF induced in search coil is given as

$$e = \frac{d\phi}{dt} = \mu_0 A NN_s \frac{di}{dt}$$

$$\Rightarrow \quad e = \mu_0 A NN_s (i_0 \omega \cos \omega t) \quad \ldots(3)$$

The peak value of EMF is given as

$$e_0 = \mu_0 A NN_s i_0 \omega \quad \ldots(4)$$

Substituting the given values, we have

$$2.5 \times 10^{-2} = (4\pi \times 10^{-7}) \times (1 \times 10^{-4}) \times (10^5) \times (20) \times 1 \times \omega$$

$$\Rightarrow \quad \omega = 99.47 \text{ rad/s}$$

$$\Rightarrow \quad f = \frac{\omega}{2\pi} = \frac{99.47}{2 \times 3.14} = 15.8 \text{ s}^{-1}$$

(iii) Figure shows the situation described in the question. Consider an element of width dx in the loop C at a distance x from the wire A as shown.

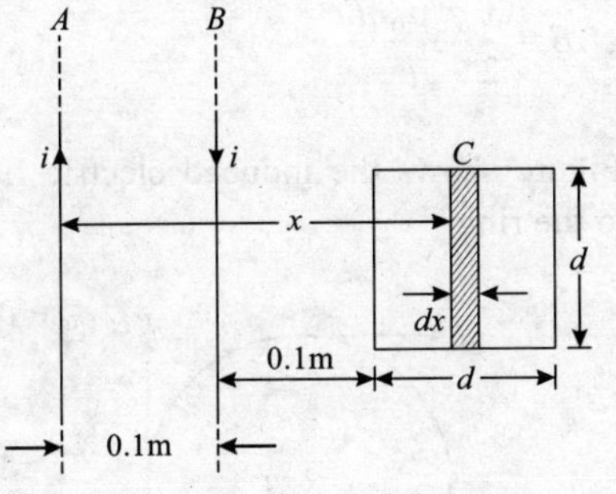

Magnetic field at the location of the element due to current i in A

$$B = \frac{\mu_0 i}{2\pi x}$$

Area of the element = $d \times dx$

Magnetic flux linked with the elemental area is given as

$$d\phi = \frac{\mu_0 i}{2\pi x} \times d \times dx$$

The magnetic flux linked with the entire loop C is given as

$$\phi_1 = \int d\phi = \int_{2d}^{3d}\left(\frac{\mu_0 i}{2\pi x}\right) d \times dx = \frac{\mu_0 i d}{2\pi}\int_{2d}^{3d}\frac{dx}{x}$$

$$\Rightarrow \quad \phi_1 = \frac{\mu_0 i d}{2\pi}[\ln x]_{2d}^{3d} = \frac{\mu_0 i d}{2\pi}\ln\left(\frac{3}{2}\right)$$

This flux is directed into the plane of paper. Similarly, the magnetic flux linked with the loop C due to the current i in wire B is given as

$$\phi_2 = \int_d^{2d}\left(\frac{\mu_0 i}{2\pi x}\right) d \times dx = \frac{\mu_0 i d}{2\pi}\ln(2)$$

This flux is directed outward perpendicular to the plane of paper. Net magnetic flux linked with the loop C is given as

$$\phi_C = \phi_2 - \phi_1$$

$$\phi_C = \frac{\mu_0 i d}{2\pi}\ln\left(\frac{4}{3}\right)$$

The induced EMF in the loop is given as

$$e = \left|\frac{d\phi}{dt}\right| = \frac{\mu_0 d}{2\pi}\log_e\left(\frac{3}{4}\right)\frac{di}{dt}$$

$$\Rightarrow \quad e = 2 \times 10^{-7} \times 0.1 \times \ln\left(\frac{4}{3}\right) \times 10^3$$

$$\Rightarrow \quad e = 2 \times 10^{-5}\ln\left(\frac{4}{3}\right) \text{ volt}$$

According to Lenz's law, the current in the arm of loop C nearest the wire B will be opposite to the current in B, so the current in the loop will be clockwise.

(iv) Let B_v be the vertical flux density of earth. The flux through the coil of area A and number of turns n is given by

$$\phi = n B_v A$$

On turning over of coil, the flux changes to

$$\phi' = -nB_v A$$

Change in flux is given as

$$\Delta\phi = \phi - \phi' = n B_v A - (-n B_v A) = 2 n B_v A$$

The charge passing through ballistic galvanometer is given as

$$q = \frac{\Delta\phi}{R}$$

$$\Rightarrow \quad q = \frac{2 \times 200 \times B_v \times (3.14 \times 0.125 \times 0.125 m^2)}{800} \text{ C}$$

$$\Rightarrow \quad q = 0.024 B_v \text{ C}$$

This charge gives a throw of 30 divisions. If k be the ballistic constant, then we use

$$q = 0.0245 B_v = 36 \text{ k} \quad \ldots(1)$$

The charge on the capacitor is given as

$$q' = CV = 0.1 \times 10^{-6} \times 6$$

$$\Rightarrow \quad q' = 6 \times 10^{-7} \text{ C}$$

The discharge of capacitor gives a throw of 20 divisions so we have

$$q' = 6 \times 10^{-7} = 20 \text{ k} \quad \ldots(2)$$

From equations-(1) and (2), we get

$$\frac{0.245 B_v}{6 \times 10^{-7}} = \frac{30}{20}$$

$$\Rightarrow \quad B_v = 0.37 \times 10^{-4} \text{ T}$$

(v) The induced EMF is given as

$$e = -\frac{d\phi}{dt} = -\frac{d}{dt}(BA) = -A\frac{dB}{dt}$$

So for loop $AEFDA$, we have

$$e_1 = (1 \times 1) \times 1 = 1 \text{ V}$$

For loop $EBCFE$, we have

$$e_2 = \left(\frac{1}{2} \times 1\right) \times 1 = 0.5 \text{ V}$$

Using Lenz's law, the directions of e_1, e_2, i_1 and i_2 in the two loops are shown in figure using Kirchoff's law at junction F, we have

$$i_1 = i + i_2 \qquad \ldots(1)$$

Applying Kirchoff's second law to loop 1, we have

$$1 \times i_1 + 1 \times i_1 + 1 \times i + 1 \times i_1 = 1$$

$$\Rightarrow 3i_1 + (i_1 - i_2) = 1$$

$$\Rightarrow 4i_1 - i_2 = 1 \qquad \ldots(2)$$

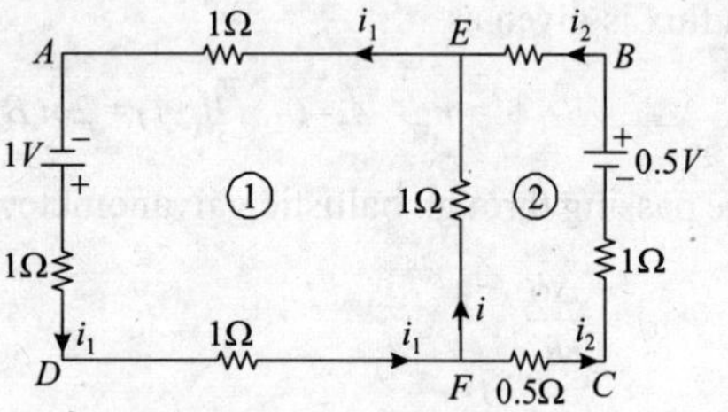

Applying Kirchoff's Second law to loop-2, we get

$$0.5i_2 - 1 \times i + 0.5 \times i_2 + 1 \times i_2 = 0.5$$

$$\Rightarrow 2i_2 - (i_1 - i_2) = 0.5$$

$$\Rightarrow 3i_2 - i_1 = 0.5 \qquad \ldots(3)$$

Solving equations-(2) and (3), we get

$$\Rightarrow i_2 = \frac{3}{11}\text{A}$$

and $i_1 = \dfrac{7}{22}\text{A}$

From equation-(1)

$$i = i_1 - i_2 = \frac{7}{22} - \frac{3}{11} = \frac{1}{22}\text{A}$$

(vi) The induced electric field is set up as a result of the changing current through the solenoid.

Inside the solenoid the induced electric field is given as

$$E = \frac{1}{2} r \frac{dB}{dt}$$

Inside the solenoid magnetic induction is given as

$$B = \mu_0 ni$$

$$\Rightarrow \quad E = \frac{1}{2} r \frac{d}{dt}(\mu_0 ni) = \frac{1}{2} r \mu_0 nI$$

This above field is for $r < a$, and for an outside point when $r > a$ it is given as

$$E = \frac{1}{2}\frac{a^2}{r}\frac{dB}{dt}$$

$$\Rightarrow \quad E = \frac{1}{2}\frac{a^2 \mu_0 nI}{r}$$

(vii) (a) Figure shows the induced electric field which is tangential to the ring

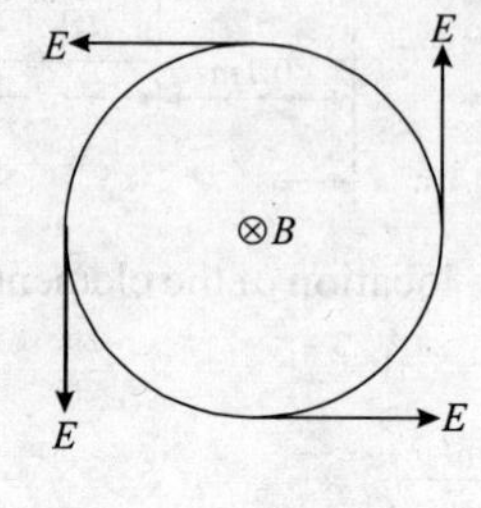

Magnitude of induced EMF is given as

$$e = \frac{d\phi}{dt} \pi a^2, \frac{dB}{dt} = \pi a^2 B_0$$

The induced EMF sets up the induced electric field and tend to setup a current which opposes the change of flux linked with the ring. As the flux linked along downward direction increases and hence the flux due to induced current must be upward. So, induced EMF tend to setup an anticlockwise current as seen from above.

The magnitude of the induced electric field established in the ring is given as

$$E = \frac{e}{2\pi a} = \frac{1}{2} a B_0$$

Torque on the ring due to the tangential electric field is given as

$$\tau = qEa$$

$$\Rightarrow \quad \tau = \frac{1}{2} a^2 B_0 q$$

The angular acceleration of ring is given as

$$\alpha = \frac{\tau}{I}$$

$$\Rightarrow \quad \alpha = \frac{1}{2}\frac{a^2 B_0 q}{ma^2} = \frac{B_0 q}{2m} \qquad \ldots(1)$$

(b) The angular velocity of the ring at time t is given as

$$\omega = \alpha t = \frac{qB_0 t}{2m}$$

Thus instantaneous power developed by the forces acting on the ring is given as

$$P = \tau\omega = \frac{1}{2}a^2 B_0 q \times \left(\frac{qB_0 t}{2m}\right)$$

$$\Rightarrow \quad P = \frac{q^2 B_0^2 a^2 t}{4m}$$

(viii) Consider an elemental ring of radius r and width dr within the cross section of the material. The EMF induced in this elemental ring is given as

$$de = \pi r^2 \frac{d}{dt}(\beta t) = \pi r^2 \beta$$

Current through this elemental ring is given as

$$dI = \frac{de}{R} = \frac{\pi r^2 \beta}{R} = \frac{\pi r^2 \beta}{\rho \cdot 2\pi r / hdr}$$

where $h\,dr$ is the area of the cross-section of the ring.

$$\Rightarrow \quad dI = \frac{h\beta r dr}{2\rho}$$

$$\Rightarrow \quad I = \int dI = \frac{h\beta}{2\rho}\int_a^b r dr = \frac{1h\beta}{4\rho}(b^2 - a^2)$$

(ix) Magnetic induction due to the solenoid at its centre is given by

$$B = \mu_0 ni \text{ T}$$

Flux linked with each turn of the coil is

$$\phi = BA = \mu_0 n i A$$

Induced EMF in N turns of coil is given as

$$e = N\frac{d\phi}{dt} = N\frac{d}{dt}(\mu_0 niA) = N\mu_0 n A\frac{di}{dt}$$

We have

$$\frac{di}{dt} = \frac{4}{0.05} = 80$$

$$\Rightarrow \quad e = 100 \times 4\pi \times 10^{-7} \times 2 \times 10^4 \times \pi \times 10^{-4} \times 80$$

$$\Rightarrow \quad e = 6.4\,\pi^2 \times 10^{-3} \text{ V}$$

Charge flown through the coil is given as

$$q = i \times t = \frac{e}{R} \times t$$

$$q = \frac{(6.4\pi^2 10^{-3})(0.05)}{10\pi^2}$$

$$= 3.2 \times 10^{-5} \text{ C}$$

$$q = 32\,\mu\text{C}$$

(x) Induced EMF in the coil is given as

$$e = \left|\frac{d\phi}{dt}\right| = \pi a^2 b$$

If E is the induced electric field in the ring then for one half of the ring which if we consider to be of resistance r and current in the ring is I then we have

$$rI = \frac{e}{2} - \pi a E$$

and for the other half of the ring the resistance is ηr for which we have

$$\eta r I = \frac{e}{2} + \pi a E$$

$$\Rightarrow \quad (\eta - 1)rI = 2\,\pi a E$$

$$\Rightarrow \quad (\eta + 1)rI = e = \pi a^2 b$$

$$\Rightarrow \quad E = \frac{ab}{2}\left(\frac{\eta - 1}{\eta + 1}\right)$$

(xi) The magnetic flux through the loop is given as

$$\phi = BA = B \times \pi r^2$$

EMF induced in the loop is given as

$$e = \frac{d\phi}{dt} = \pi r^2 \frac{dB}{dt}$$

The current induced in the loop is given as

$$i = \frac{e}{R} = \frac{\pi r^2}{R}\frac{dB}{dt} \quad \ldots(1)$$

Where R is the resistance of the loop which is given as

$$R = \rho \cdot \frac{l}{\pi a^2}$$

Where l is the length and πr^2 is the cross sectional area of the wire. Mass m of the wire is given as

$$m = \pi a^2 l \delta$$

Where δ is the density of copper.

$$\Rightarrow \quad R = \rho\frac{l}{m / l\delta} = \rho\frac{l^2 \delta}{m}$$

$$\Rightarrow \quad R = \rho\frac{(2\pi r)^2 \delta}{m}$$

$$\Rightarrow \quad R = \rho\frac{4\pi^2 r^2 \delta}{m} \quad \ldots(2)$$

Substituting the value of R from equation-(2) in equation-(1), we get

$$i = \frac{\pi r^2}{\rho(4\pi^2 r^2 \delta / m)}\frac{dB}{dt} = \frac{m}{4\pi\rho\delta}\frac{dB}{dt}$$

(xii) (a) We have already discussed that the mutual inductance between solenoid and coil can be given as

$$M=\frac{\mu_0 N_1 N_2(\pi R_1^2)}{l_1}$$

$$\Rightarrow \quad M=\frac{\mu_0 N_1 N_2 S_1}{l_1}$$

Induced EMF in coil is given as

$$e_2=\left|M\frac{di}{dt}\right|=\left|\frac{\mu_0 N_1 N_2 S_1}{l_1}\frac{di_1}{dt}\right|$$

$$\Rightarrow \quad e_2=\frac{(4\pi\times10^{-7})(25)(10)(5\times10^{-4})(0.2)}{10^{-2}}$$

$$\Rightarrow \quad e_2=3.14\times10^{-6}\,\text{V}$$

(b) Induced electric field is given as

$$E=\frac{e}{l}=\frac{e}{2\pi R_2}$$

$$\Rightarrow \quad E=\frac{3.14\times10^{-6}}{(2\pi)(0.25)}$$

$$\Rightarrow \quad E=2\times10^{-6}\,\text{V/m}$$

(xiii) EMF induced in coil is given as

$$e=\left|\frac{d\phi}{dt}\right|=2kt$$

Induced current in coil is given as

$$i=\frac{e}{R}=\frac{2kt}{R}$$

Heat produced in coil is given as

$$H=\int_0^C i^2 R\,dt=\int_0^C\frac{4k^2t^2}{R}dt$$

$$\Rightarrow \quad H=\frac{4k^2}{R}\left[\frac{t^3}{3}\right]_0^C$$

$$\Rightarrow \quad H=\frac{4k^2C^2}{3R}$$

(xiv) Magnetic induction the location of smaller coil due to larger coil is given as

$$B=\frac{\mu_0 N I a^2}{2(x^2+a^2)^{3/2}}$$

Magnetic flux through smaller coil is given as

$$\phi=B.\pi b^2$$

EMF induced in smaller coil is given as

$$e=\left|\frac{d\phi}{dt}\right|=\frac{\mu_0\pi N I a^2 b^2}{2}\left(\frac{3}{2}\cdot\frac{1\cdot 2x}{(x^2+a^2)^{5/2}}\cdot\frac{dx}{dt}\right)$$

$$\Rightarrow \quad e=\frac{3\mu_0\pi N I a^2 b^2 x v}{2(x^2+a^2)^{5/2}}$$

Current in smaller coil is given as

$$i=\frac{e}{R}=\frac{3\mu_0\pi N I a^2 b^2 v x}{2R(x^2+a^2)^{5/2}}$$

Solutions of PRACTICE EXERCISE 5.3

(i) A coaxial cable carries equal and opposite current in the two cylinders. If the current is I then the magnetic field in the region between the two cylinders is given as

$$B=\frac{\mu_0 I}{2\pi r} \qquad a\le r\le b$$

Where a and b are the radii of inner and outer cylindrical shells of the cable. The magnetic flux in an elemental section of width dr at a distance r from the axis of cable within its unit length is $d\phi$ then it is given as

$$d\phi=B.(1.dr)$$

Total magnetic flux through a cross section in the region between the shells is given as

$$\phi=\int d\phi=\int B\cdot dr$$

$$\Rightarrow \quad \phi=\frac{\mu_0 I}{2\pi}\int_a^b\frac{dr}{r}$$

$$\Rightarrow \quad \phi=\frac{\mu_0 I}{2\pi}\ln\left(\frac{b}{a}\right)$$

$$\Rightarrow \quad \phi=\frac{\mu_0 I}{2\pi}\ln(\eta)$$

Self inductance per unit length of the cable is given as

$$L=\frac{\phi}{I}$$

$$\Rightarrow \quad L=\frac{\mu_0}{2\pi}\ln(\eta)$$

(ii) If the separation between the wires of double lines is b and if the wires carry a current I in opposite directions then between the wires at a distance x from one wire the magnetic induction is given as

$$B=\frac{\mu_0}{2\pi}\left(\frac{I}{x}+\frac{I}{b-x}\right)$$

If we consider an elemental strip of width dx at a distance x from one wire which is of unit length then magnetic flux through this strip is given as

$$d\phi=BdA=B(1.dx)$$

$$\Rightarrow \quad \phi=\int d\phi=\frac{\mu_0 I}{2\pi}\left(\int_a^{b-a}\frac{dx}{x}+\int_a^{b-a}\frac{dx}{b-x}\right)$$

$$\Rightarrow \quad \phi=\frac{\mu_0 I}{\pi}\ln\left(\frac{b-a}{a}\right)$$

Self inductance per unit length of this double line is given as

$$L=\frac{\phi}{I}=\frac{\mu_0}{\pi}\ln\left(\frac{b-a}{a}\right)$$

$$\Rightarrow \quad L=\frac{\mu_0}{\pi}\ln\left(\frac{b}{a}\right)=\frac{\mu_0}{\pi}\ln(\eta)$$

(iii) From the circuit shown in figure the potential of point D is equal to zero. Thus for the 4 H inductor we can write

$$L\frac{di_2}{dt}=V_D-V_B=-40$$

$$\Rightarrow \quad \frac{di_2}{dt}=-10\text{ A/s}$$

At the junction D by KCL we have

$$i_1=i_2+i_3$$

$$\Rightarrow \quad \frac{di_1}{dt}=\frac{di_2}{dt}+\frac{di_3}{dt}$$

$$\Rightarrow \quad 2.5=-10+\frac{di_3}{dt}$$

$$\Rightarrow \quad \frac{di_3}{dt}=12.5\text{ A/s}$$

Writing equation of potential drop from point D to C gives

$$V_D+10-2\times 12.5=V_C$$

$$V_C=-15\text{ V}$$

(iv) Current due to rotation of the cylinder of length l is given as

$$I=\frac{q\omega}{2\pi}=\frac{\lambda l\omega}{2\pi}$$

By Ampere's law the magnetic induction inside the cylinder can be given as

$$B=\frac{\mu_0 I}{l}$$

The magnetic field energy density inside the cylinder is given as

$$u_m=\frac{B^2}{2\mu_0}$$

Energy per unit length of the cylinder is given as

$$U_m=\frac{u_m v}{l}=\frac{1}{l}\cdot\frac{B^2}{2\mu_0}\times\pi a^2 l$$

$$\Rightarrow \quad U_m=\frac{1}{2\mu_0 l}\times\left(\frac{\mu_0\lambda l\omega}{2\pi l}\right)^2\times\pi a^2 l$$

$$\Rightarrow \quad U_m=\frac{\mu_0\lambda^2\omega^2 a^2}{8\pi}$$

(v) Figure shows the cross sectional view of the coaxial cable described in the question. The magnetic field B in the space between the two conductors is given by

$$B=\frac{\mu_0 i}{2\pi r'}$$

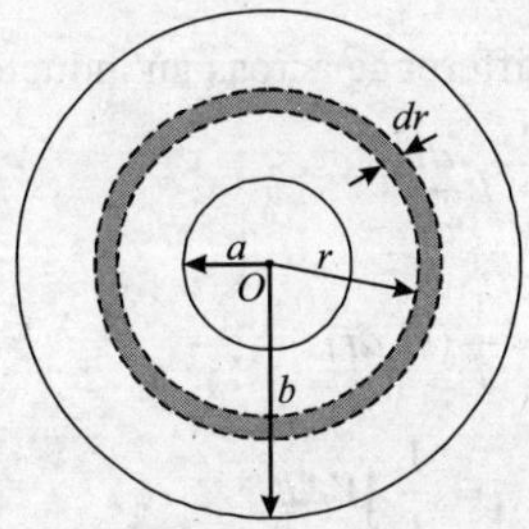

The energy density in the space between the conductors is given as

$$u_m=\frac{B^2}{2\mu_0}=\frac{1}{2\mu_0}\left[\frac{\mu_0 i}{2\pi r}\right]^2=\frac{\mu_0 i^2}{8\pi^2 r^2}$$

Consider a volume element dV in the form of a cylindrical shell of radii r and $(r+dr)$ as shown in the figure. Energy stored in this elemental volume is given as

$$dU=u_m dV=\frac{\mu_0 i^2}{8\pi^2 r^2}\times 2\pi r l dr$$

$$\Rightarrow \quad dU=\frac{\mu_0 i^2 l}{4\pi}\left(\frac{dr}{r}\right)$$

Total magnetic energy can be obtained by integrating this expression between the limits $r=a$ to $r=b$ which gives

$$U=\int dU=\frac{\mu_0 i^2 l}{4\pi}\int_a^b\left(\frac{dr}{r}\right)$$

$$\Rightarrow \quad U=\frac{\mu_0 i^2 l}{4\pi}\ln\left(\frac{b}{a}\right)$$

(vi) The potential difference across inductor is given as

$$V_L = L\frac{di}{dt} = 5 \times 1.0 = 5\ \text{V}$$

As the current is decreasing the inductor can be replaced by a source of emf $e = \left|L \cdot \frac{di}{dt}\right| = 5$ V in such a manner that this emf supports the decreasing current, or it sends the current in the circuit in the same direction as the existing current. So, positive terminal of this source is towards b. Thus, the given circuit can be drawn as

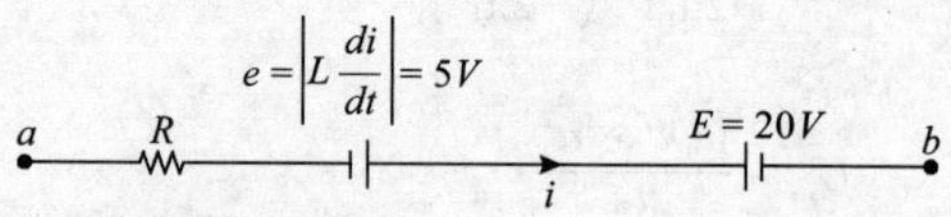

We write the equation of potential drop from a to b in above circuit branch which gives

$$V_a - iR + V_L - E = V_b$$

$$\Rightarrow \quad V_{ab} = V_a - V_b = E + iR - V_L$$

$$\Rightarrow \quad V_{ab} = 20 + (2)(10) - 5 = 35\ \text{V}$$

(vii) Potential difference across an inductor is given as

$$V_L = L\frac{di}{dt}$$

$$\Rightarrow \quad di = \frac{1}{L}(V_L dt)$$

$$\Rightarrow \quad \int di = i = \frac{1}{L}\int V_L dt$$

$$\Rightarrow \quad i = \frac{1}{L} \times (\text{area under } V_L \text{ versus } t \text{ graph})$$

(a) At $t = 2$ ms

$$i = (150 \times 10^{-3})^{-1}\left(\frac{1}{2} \times 2 \times 10^{-3} \times 5\right)$$

$$\Rightarrow \quad i = 3.33 \times 10^{-2}\ \text{A}$$

(b) At $t = 4$ ms

Area is just double. Hence current is also doubled.

(viii) (a) Due to rotation of rod motional EMF induced in it is given as

$$e = \frac{1}{2}Br^2\omega$$

In the figure by right hand palm rule we can see that the point O will be at high potential and point A will be at low potential.

(b) Here we can replace the rod by a battery of EMF obtained in part (a). Now switch, resistance and inductance are connected in series as shown in figure which shows the equivalent circuit of the given situation. At $t = 0$, the switch is closed.

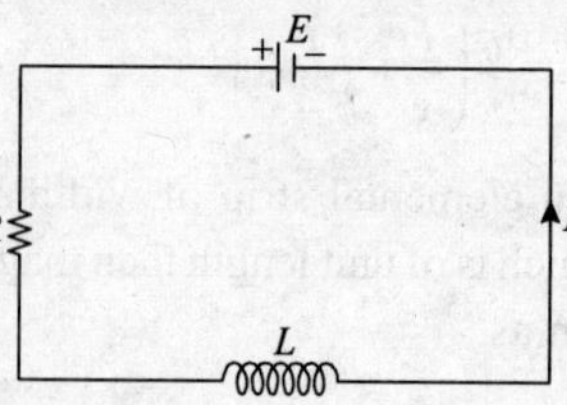

If a current I flows through the circuit then by KVL, we have

$$E - IR - L\frac{dI}{dt} = 0$$

$$\Rightarrow \quad L\frac{dI}{dt} = E - IR$$

$$\Rightarrow \quad \frac{dI}{E - IR} = \frac{dt}{L}$$

$$\Rightarrow \quad \int_0^I \frac{dI}{E - IR} = \int_0^t \frac{dt}{L}$$

$$\Rightarrow \quad -\frac{1}{R}[\ln(E - RI) - \ln E] = \frac{t}{L}$$

$$\Rightarrow \quad -\frac{1}{R}\ln\left(\frac{E - RI}{E}\right) = \frac{t}{L}$$

$$\Rightarrow \quad \frac{E - RI}{E} = e^{-Rt/L}$$

$$\Rightarrow \quad E - RI = Ee^{-Rt/L}$$

$$\Rightarrow \quad RI = E[1 - e^{-Rt/L}]$$

$$\Rightarrow \quad I = \frac{E}{R}[1 - e^{-Rt/L}]$$

$$\Rightarrow \quad I = \frac{Br^2\omega}{2R}(1 - e^{-Rt/L})$$

The force acting on rod due to induced current I is given as

$$F = BIr = \frac{B^2r^3\omega}{2R}(1 - e^{-Rt/L})$$

$$\Rightarrow \quad F = \frac{B^2r^3\omega}{2R}(1 - e^{-Rt/L})$$

This force may be regarded as acting on the middle point of rod OA. The torque produced is given as

$$\tau = F \times \frac{r}{2} = \frac{B^2r^2\omega}{4R}(1 - e^{-Rt/L})$$

The above magnetic torque acts in clockwise direction. To maintain a constant angular speed ω, an external torque τ is needed to be applied in anticlockwise direction with time dependence.

(ix) Steady state current in the inductor is given as

$$i_0 = \frac{E}{r}$$

(a) This current in inductor starts decaying down exponentially through resistances r and R in series thus the current as a function of time in inductor is given as

$$i = i_0 e^{-(R+r)t/L} = \frac{E}{r} e^{\frac{-(R+r)t}{L}}$$

(b) Energy stored in inductor at $t = 0$ is given as

$$U_0 = \frac{1}{2} L i_0^2$$

$$\Rightarrow \quad U_0 = \left(\frac{1}{2} L\right)\left(\frac{E}{r}\right)^2$$

During decay of current the above energy is dissipated in r and R in same ratio of resistances so the heat produced in the inductor is given as

$$H_r = \left(\frac{r}{R+r}\right) U_0$$

$$\Rightarrow \quad H_r = \frac{E^2 L}{2r(R+r)}$$

(x) When the switch is closed at $t = 0$ both RL and RC branches in above circuit will bet connected across the constant potential difference V of the battery. Due to this transient currents will start flowing in the two branches independently which are given as

$$i_C = \frac{V}{R} e^{-\frac{t}{RC}} = V\sqrt{\frac{C}{L}} e^{-\frac{t}{\sqrt{LC}}}$$

and $$i_L = \frac{V}{R}\left(1 - e^{-\frac{Rt}{L}}\right) = V\sqrt{\frac{C}{L}}\left(1 - e^{-\frac{t}{\sqrt{LC}}}\right)$$

Total current through battery is given as

$$I = I_1 + I_2 = V\sqrt{\frac{C}{L}} = \frac{V}{R}$$

(xi) If at any instant I is the current in the circuit, we use KVL for the loop of given LR circuit, we have

$$IR + \frac{L}{\eta}\frac{dI}{dt} = \xi \qquad \ldots(1)$$

We use at $t = 0, I = \eta \frac{E}{R} = \eta I_0$ where I_0 is the maximum current in circuit which is given as

$$I_0 = \frac{\xi}{R}$$

From the equation-(1), after integration we have

$$\int_{\eta I_0}^{I} \frac{dI}{(\xi/R - I)} = \int_0^t \frac{\eta R}{L} dt$$

$$\Rightarrow \quad \left[-\ln\left(\frac{\xi}{R} - 1\right)\right]_{\eta I_0}^{I} = \frac{\eta R}{L} t$$

$$\Rightarrow \quad I = \frac{\xi}{R}\left[1 - (\eta - 1) e^{-\frac{\eta R t}{L}}\right]$$

(xii) In the given circuit the upper two branches can be replaced by a single equivalent battery by considering these in parallel combination. Thus the equivalent EMF of the battery is given as

$$E = \frac{\frac{2}{2} + \frac{4}{1}}{\frac{1}{2} + \frac{1}{1}} = \frac{10}{3} \text{V}$$

Equivalent internal resistance of the equivalent battery is given as

$$r = \frac{2 \times 1}{2 + 1} = \frac{2}{3} \Omega$$

Now considering the above circuit as a simple LR circuit the current through the inductor can be given as

$$i = \frac{E}{r}\left(1 - e^{-\frac{rt}{L}}\right)$$

$$\Rightarrow \quad i = 5\left(1 - e^{-\frac{2000t}{3}}\right) \text{A}$$

(xiii) We consider an elemental shell of radius x and wall width dx inside the cylinder as shown in figure. The magnetic induction inside the wire at a distance x from axis is given as

$$B = \frac{1}{2}\mu_0 J x = \frac{\mu_0 I x}{2\pi R^2}$$

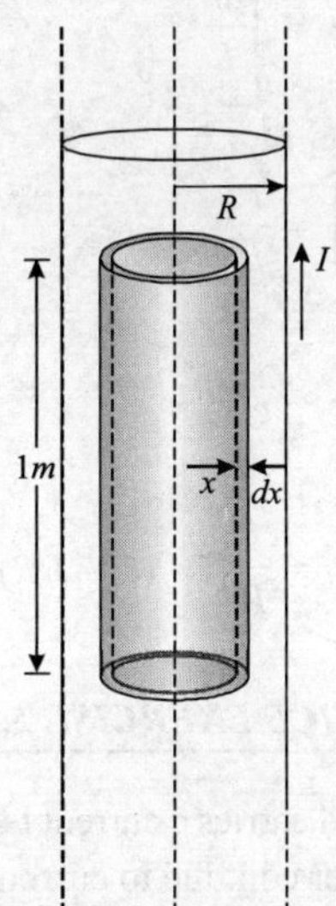

The volume of the elemental shell of length 1 m is given as

$$dV = 2\pi x \, dx \times 1$$

Field energy stored in elemental cylindrical shell is given as

$$dU = \frac{B^2}{2\mu_0} \times dV = \frac{1}{2\mu_0}\left(\frac{\mu_0 Ix}{2\pi R^2}\right) \times 2\pi x dx$$

$$dU = \frac{\mu_0 I^2 x^3 dx}{4\pi R^4}$$

Total field energy inside the cylinder per unit length is given by integrating above expression within limits from 0 to R which is given as

$$U = \int dU = \int_0^R \frac{\mu_0 I^2}{4\pi R^4} \cdot x^3 dx$$

$$\Rightarrow \quad U = \frac{\mu_0 I^2}{4\pi R^4} \cdot \frac{R^4}{4} = \frac{\mu_0 I^2}{16\pi}$$

(xiv) In the given circuit applying KVL equation for the loop gives

$$\xi - iR - L\frac{di}{dt} = 0$$

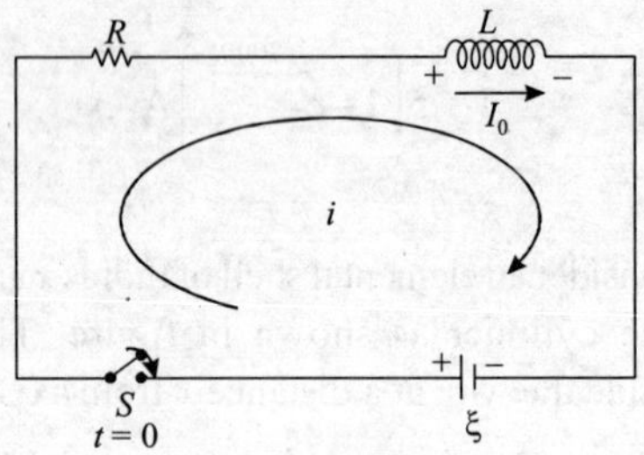

$$\Rightarrow \quad \int_{I_0}^{i} \frac{di}{\varepsilon - iR} = \int_0^t \frac{dt}{L}$$

$$\Rightarrow \quad -\frac{1}{R}\ln\left(\frac{\xi - iR}{\xi - I_0 R}\right) = \frac{t}{L}$$

$$\Rightarrow \quad \frac{\xi - iR}{\xi - I_0 R} = e^{-Rt/L}$$

$$\Rightarrow \quad i = \frac{1}{R}[\xi - (\xi_0 - I_0 R)e^{-Rt/L}]$$

Solutions of PRACTICE EXERCISE 5.4

(i) (a) If outer coil carries a current I then the magnetic flux at the location of inner coil due to current in coil 2.

$$\phi_i = \frac{\mu_0 I}{2b} \times \pi a^2$$

The mutual induction coefficient between the two coils can be given as

$$M = \frac{\phi}{I} = \frac{\mu_0 \pi a^2}{2b}$$

(b) By reciprocity theorem same coefficient of mutual induction can be used to calculate the magnetic flux linked with the outer coil if a current flows in inner coil. So the magnetic flux through the outer coil area due to a current I in inner coil is given as

$$\phi_o = MI = \frac{\mu_0 \pi a^2 I}{2b}$$

(ii) (a) We use

$$\frac{di}{dt} = \frac{4-12}{0.5} = -16 \text{ A/s}$$

EMF induced in second coil can be given as

$$e = -M\frac{di}{dt}$$

$$\Rightarrow \quad M = -\frac{e}{di/dt}$$

$$\Rightarrow \quad M = (50 \times 10^{-3})/16$$

$$\Rightarrow \quad M = 3.125 \times 10^{-3} \text{ H}$$

(b) We use

$$\frac{di}{dt} = \frac{3-9}{0.02} = -300 \text{ A/s}$$

EMF induced is given as

$$e = -M\frac{di}{dt}$$

$$\Rightarrow \quad e = -(3.125 \times 10^{-3})(-300)$$

$$\Rightarrow \quad e = 0.9375 \text{ V}$$

(iii) The magnetic field at the location of one loop due to the other loop carrying a current i in it, considering it as a magnetic dipole is given as

$$B_2 = \frac{2KM}{l^3} = \frac{\mu_0}{2\pi}\frac{i\pi a^2}{l^3}$$

Flux passing through the first loop is given as

$$\phi_{12} = B.\pi a^2$$

$$\Rightarrow \quad \phi_{12} = \frac{\mu_0}{2\pi}\frac{i\pi a^2}{l^3} \times \pi a^2$$

$$\Rightarrow \quad \phi_{12} = \frac{\mu_0 \pi a^4 i}{2l^3}$$

If M is the mutual inductance between the two loops then we have

$$M=\frac{\phi_{12}}{i}=\frac{\mu_0\pi a^4}{2l^3}$$

(iv) For parallel combination, we use

$$\frac{L_1L_2}{L_1+L_2}=2.4$$

$$\Rightarrow \quad L_1L_2=24 \quad [\text{As } L_1+L_2=10]$$

$$\Rightarrow \quad L_1=\frac{24}{L_2}$$

For series combination, we use

$$L_1+L_2=10$$

$$\Rightarrow \quad \frac{24}{L_2}+L_2=10$$

$$\Rightarrow \quad L_2^2-10L_2+24=0$$

$$\Rightarrow \quad L_2=\frac{10\pm\sqrt{100-96}}{2}=5\pm1=4\text{ H or }6\text{ H}$$

(v) (a) The magnetic induction B at the location of coil P due to coil Q is given by

$$B=\frac{\mu_0N_Qi}{2R}$$

Flux linked with the coil P is given by

$$\phi=BAN_P=B\times\pi r^2\times N_P$$

$$\phi=\frac{\mu_0N_QN_Pi\pi r^2}{2R}$$

Mutual inductance between the two coils is given as

$$M=\frac{\phi}{i}=\frac{\mu_0N_QN_P\pi r^2}{2R}$$

$$M=\frac{4\pi\times10^{-7}\times100\times1000\times\pi\times(2\times10^{-2})^2}{2\times0.2}$$

$$M=3.94\times10^{-4}\text{H}$$

(b) Induced EMF in coil P is given as

$$e=M\frac{di}{dt}$$

$$\Rightarrow \quad e=(3.944\times10^{-4})\left(\frac{5-3}{0.04}\right)$$

$$\Rightarrow \quad e=19.72\times10^{-3}\text{ V}$$

(c) Rate of change of flux through coil P is given by

$$\frac{d\phi}{dt}=e=19.72\times10^{-3}\text{ Wb/s}$$

(d) Charge passing through coil P is given by

$$q=\frac{\Delta\phi}{R}$$

$$\Rightarrow \quad q=\frac{19.72\times10^{-3}}{8}$$

$$\Rightarrow \quad q=9.86\times10^{-5}\text{C}$$

(vi) The mutual inductance between solenoid and coil is given by

$$M=\mu_0N_cN_sA$$

$$\Rightarrow \quad M=(4\pi\times10^{-7})(1000)(20)(10\times10^{-4})$$

$$\Rightarrow \quad M=25.1\times10^{-6}\text{H}$$

$$\Rightarrow \quad M=25.1\ \mu\text{H}$$

Induced EMF in the coil is given as

$$e=M\frac{di}{dt}=25.1\times10=251\ \mu\text{V}$$

(vii) (a) Initial potential difference across the inductor is given as

$$L\frac{di}{dt}=E$$

$$\Rightarrow \quad \frac{di}{dt}=\frac{E}{L}=\frac{6}{2.5}=2.4\text{ A/s}$$

(b) In the circuit when current is i, the potential difference across the inductor is given as

$$V_L=E-iR$$

$$\Rightarrow \quad L\frac{di}{dt}=E-iR$$

$$\Rightarrow \quad \frac{di}{dt}=\frac{E-iR}{L}$$

$$\Rightarrow \quad \frac{di}{dt}=\frac{6-0.5\times9}{2.5}=0.8\text{ A/s}$$

(c) The current in circuit as a function of time is given as

$$i=\frac{V}{R}(1-e^{-Rt/L})$$

Substituting values, we get

$$i=\frac{6}{8}(1-e^{-8\times0.25/2.5})$$

$$\Rightarrow \quad i=0.75\times(1-0.45)$$

$$\Rightarrow \quad i=0.413\text{ A}$$

(d) Steady state current in circuit is given as

$$i_0 = \frac{V}{R} = \frac{6}{8} = 0.75\,\text{A}$$

(viii) In steady state, current through the battery is given as

$$i_0 = \frac{E}{R} = \frac{20}{5}$$

$$\Rightarrow \quad i_0 = 4\,\text{A}$$

This current distributed in inverse ratio of inductances when connected in parallel. This gives the current through 5 H inductor as

$$i = \left(\frac{10}{10+5}\right) \times 4\,\text{A}$$

$$\Rightarrow \quad i = 2.67\,\text{A}$$

(ix) (a) Angular frequency of oscillations is given as

$$\omega = \frac{2\pi}{f} = 6.28 \times 10^3\ \text{rad/s}$$

Time period of oscillations is given as

$$T = \frac{1}{f} = 10^{-3}\,\text{s}$$

(b) Charge on capacitor as a function of time is given as

$$q = q_0 \sin(\omega t + \alpha)$$

At $t = 0$, $q = q_0 = CV_0 = 100\ \mu\text{C}$ which gives

$$q = q_0 \cos \omega t$$

(c) $$\omega = \frac{1}{\sqrt{LC}}$$

$$\Rightarrow \quad L = \frac{1}{\omega^2 C}$$

$$\Rightarrow \quad L = \frac{1}{(6.28 \times 10^3)^2 \times 10^{-6}} = 0.0253\,\text{H}$$

(d) Instantaneous current in circuit is given as

$$i = \left|\frac{dq}{dt}\right| = q_0 \omega \sin \omega t$$

Average value of current in first quarter cycle is given as

$$i_{avg} = \frac{\int_0^{T/4} i dt}{T/4} = 0.4\,\text{A}$$

(x) Initial charges on the capacitors are given as

$$q_1 = 8CV_0$$

$$q_2 = CV_0$$

$$q_1 + q_2 = 9CV_0$$

In the absence of inductor, this $9C_0V$ will distribute as $6CV_0$ in $2C$ and $3CV_0$ in C. Thus, mean position of q_1 is $6CV_0$ and mean position of q_2 is $3CV_0$ during oscillations of charge.

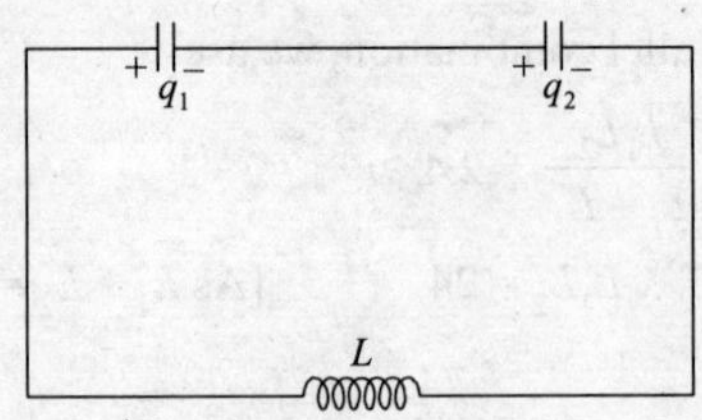

At $t = 0$, q_1 is $2CV_0$ more than its mean position and q_2 is $2CV_0$ less than its mean position. So charge amplitude will be given as

$$q_0 = 2CV_0$$

Net capacitance of the system is

$$C_{net} = \frac{2C}{3}$$

The angular frequency of oscillations is given as

$$\omega = \frac{1}{\sqrt{LC_{net}}} = \sqrt{\frac{3}{2LC}}$$

(a) Maximum current flowing in the circuit is given as

$$I_{max} = q_0\omega = 2CV_0\omega$$

(b) At the point of maximum current system is at mean position and at this instant potential difference across capacitors are given as

$$V_1 = \frac{6CV_0}{2C} = 3V_0$$

and $$V_2 = \frac{3CV_0}{C} = 3V_0$$

(c) Equation of current flow is given as

$$i = q_0\omega \sin \omega t$$

(xi) With key K_1 closed, C_1 and C_2 are in series with the battery in steady state, we have charges on the capacitors given as

$$q_0 = C_{eq}V = 1 \times 20 = 20\ \mu\text{C}$$

(a) With K_1 opened and K_2 closed, charge on C_2 will remain as it is, while charge on C_1 will oscillate in LC_1 circuit with frequency given as

$$\omega = \frac{1}{\sqrt{LC_1}}$$

$$\Rightarrow \quad \omega = \frac{1}{\sqrt{0.2\times10^{-3}\times2\times10^{-6}}}$$

$$\Rightarrow \quad \omega = 5\times10^{4}\text{ rad/s}$$

(b) Since at $t = 0$, charge is maximum which is equal to q_0. Therefore current will be zero. When energy in inductor is one third of the capacitor is given as

$$\frac{1}{2}Li^2 = \frac{1}{3}\left(\frac{1}{2}\frac{q^2}{C}\right)$$

$$\Rightarrow \quad i = \frac{q}{\sqrt{3LC}} = \frac{q\omega}{\sqrt{3}}$$

In LC oscillations current in circuit is given as

$$i = \omega\sqrt{q_0^2 - q^2}$$

$$\Rightarrow \quad q = \frac{\sqrt{3}}{2}q_0$$

Since at $t = 0$, charge is maximum or q_0, so we can write,

$$q = q_0\cos\omega t$$

$$\Rightarrow \quad \frac{\sqrt{3}q_0}{2} = q_0\cos\omega t$$

$$\Rightarrow \quad \omega t = \frac{\pi}{6}$$

$$\Rightarrow \quad t = \frac{\pi}{6\omega} = \frac{\pi}{6\times5\times10^4}$$

$$\Rightarrow \quad t = 1.05\times10^{-5}\text{ s}$$

(c) At the above instant charge on capacitor plates is given as

$$q = \frac{\sqrt{3}}{2}q_0 = \frac{\sqrt{3}}{2}\times20 = 10\sqrt{3}\ \mu\text{C}$$

(xii) For the given LC circuit the equivalent circuit is shown in figure. The oscillation frequency of charge in this circuit is given as

$$f = \frac{1}{2\pi\sqrt{(3L)(3C)}} = \frac{1}{6\pi\sqrt{LC}}$$

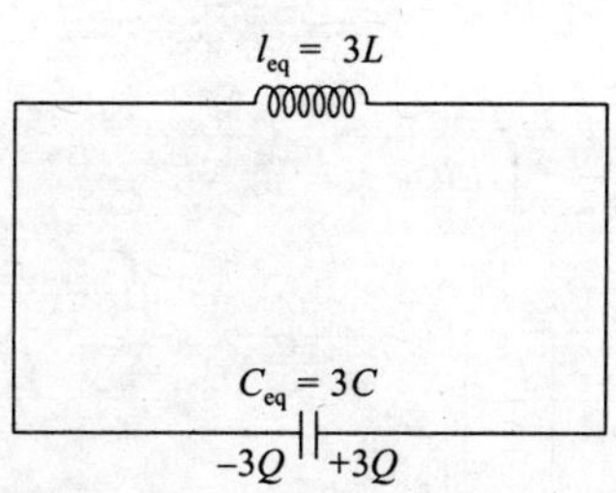

(xiii) When switch is closed a current flows in the circuit as shown in figure and as per given condition, we have

$$U_L = \frac{1}{3}U_C$$

Total energy of system is given as

$$U_L + U_C = \frac{Q^2}{2C}$$

When charge of capacitor is q during oscillations the energy stored in capacitor is given as

$$U_C = \frac{q^2}{2C}$$

$$\Rightarrow \quad \frac{1}{3}U_C + U_C = \frac{Q^2}{2C}$$

$$\Rightarrow \quad \frac{4}{3}\cdot\frac{q^2}{2C} = \frac{Q^2}{2C}$$

$$\Rightarrow \quad q = \frac{\sqrt{3}}{2}Q$$

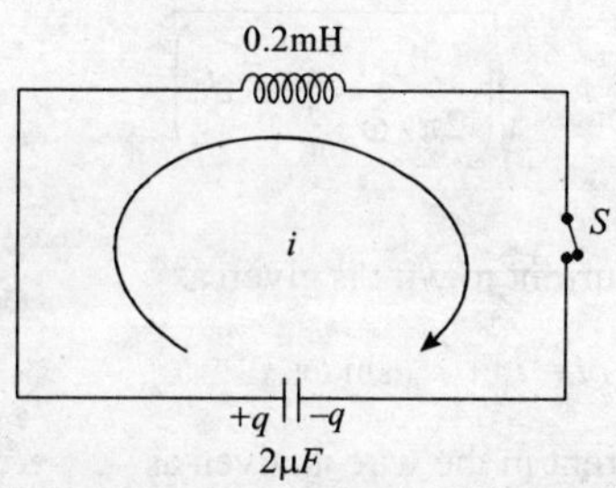

For LC oscillation the angular frequency is given as

$$\omega = \frac{1}{\sqrt{LC}}$$

Charge as a function of time on capacitor is given as

$$q = Q\cos\omega t$$

$$\Rightarrow \quad \frac{\sqrt{3}}{2}Q = Q\cos\left(\frac{t}{\sqrt{LC}}\right)$$

$$\Rightarrow \quad \frac{t}{\sqrt{LC}} = \frac{\pi}{6}$$

$$\Rightarrow \quad t = \frac{\pi}{6}\sqrt{LC} = \frac{\pi}{6}\sqrt{0.2\times10^{-3}\times2\times10^{-6}}$$

$$\Rightarrow \quad t = \frac{\pi}{6}\times2\times10^{-5} = 10.5\ \mu\text{s}$$

Solutions of PRACTICE EXERCISE 5.5

(i) The given AC voltage can be written as

$$e = e_1\sin\omega t + e_2\cos\omega t$$

We substitute the below values in the above function to reduce it

$$e_1 = e_0 \cos\theta \quad \ldots(1)$$

$$e_2 = e_0 \sin\theta \quad \ldots(2)$$

This gives

$$e = e_0 \sin(\omega t + \theta)$$

Squaring and adding equation-(1) and (2), we get

$$e_1^2 + e_2^2 = e_0^2$$

$$\Rightarrow \quad e_0 = \sqrt{e_1^2 + e_2^2}$$

$$\Rightarrow \quad e_{rms} = \frac{e_0}{\sqrt{2}} = \sqrt{\frac{e_1^2 + e_2^2}{2}}$$

Alternative method :

We can calculate the RMS value of the given time function of voltage by using the formula for RMS value given as

$$e_{rms} = \sqrt{\left(\frac{1}{2\pi/\omega}\int_0^{2\pi/\omega} e^2 dt\right)}$$

(ii) Total current in wire is given as

$$i = i_1 + i_{20}\sin\omega t$$

Square of current in the wire is given as

$$i^2 = (i_1 + i_{20}\sin\omega t)^2$$

$$\Rightarrow \quad i^2 = i_I^2 + i_{20}^2\sin^2\omega t + 2i_1 i_{20}\sin\omega t$$

Mean square of the current is given as

$$I_{ms} = i_1^2 + i_{20}^2\left(\frac{1}{2}\right) + (0)$$

$$\Rightarrow \quad I_{ms} = i_1^2 + \frac{i_{20}^2}{2}$$

$$\Rightarrow \quad I_{rms} = \sqrt{I_{rms}} = \sqrt{i_1^2 + \frac{i_{20}^2}{2}}$$

(iii) For the given time function as shown in graph the *RMS* value of the time function of EMF is given as

$$V_{rms} = \sqrt{\frac{1}{T}\int_0^{T/2} V_0 dt}$$

$$V_{rms} = \sqrt{\frac{1}{T}\left(V_0 \times \frac{T}{2}\right)}$$

$$V_{rms} = \frac{V_0}{\sqrt{2}}$$

(iv) Average value of the given *AC* current can be calculated as

$$\Rightarrow \quad I_{avg} = \frac{1}{T}\left[\int_0^{T/2}\left(i_0\sin^2\omega t\right)dt + \int_{T/2}^{T}\left(i_0\sin\omega t\right)dt\right]$$

$$\Rightarrow \quad I_{avg} = \frac{1}{T}\left(\frac{i_0}{2}\int_0^{T/2}(1-\cos 2\omega t)dt + i_0\left[-\frac{\cos\omega t}{\omega}\right]_{T/2}^{T}\right)$$

$$\Rightarrow \quad I_{avg} = \frac{1}{T}\left(\frac{i_0}{2}\left[t - \frac{1}{2\omega}\sin 2\omega t\right]_0^{T/2} - \frac{i_0}{\omega}[1-(-1)]\right)$$

$$\Rightarrow \quad I_{avg} = \frac{1}{T}\left[\frac{i_0}{2}\left(\frac{T}{2}\right) - \frac{2i_0}{\omega}\right]$$

$$\Rightarrow \quad I_{avg} = i_0\left(\frac{1}{4} - \frac{1}{\pi}\right)$$

(v)

$$V_{rms} = \sqrt{\frac{\int_0^{T/2}\left(\frac{2V_0}{T}t\right)^2 dt}{T/2}}$$

$$\Rightarrow \quad V_{rms} = \sqrt{\frac{\frac{4V_0^2}{T^2}\int_0^{T/2} t^2 dt}{T/2}}$$

$$\Rightarrow \quad V_{rms} = \frac{2\sqrt{2}V_0}{T^{3/2}}\sqrt{\left[\frac{t^3}{3}\right]_0^{T/2}}$$

$$\Rightarrow \quad V_{rms} = \frac{V_0}{\sqrt{3}}$$

(vi) For time $t = 0$ to $t = T/2$ the average voltage will be same as that of full cycle which is given as

$$V_{avg} = \frac{\int_0^{T/2}\frac{2V_0}{T}t\,dt}{T/2}$$

$$\Rightarrow \quad V_{avg} = \frac{4V_0}{T^2}\int_0^{T/2} t\,dt$$

$$\Rightarrow \quad V_{avg} = \frac{4V_0}{T^2}\left[\frac{t^2}{2}\right]_0^{T/2}$$

$$\Rightarrow \quad V_{avg} = \frac{V_0}{\sqrt{2}}$$

(vii) The charge flown in one cycle from $t = 0$ to $t = T$ is given as

$$q = \text{area under } i\text{-}t \text{ curve}$$

$$\Rightarrow \quad q = \frac{1}{2} I_0 \left(\frac{T}{2}\right) + I_0 \left(\frac{T}{2}\right)$$

$$\Rightarrow \quad q = \frac{3}{4} I_0 T$$

Average current per cycle is given as

$$I_{avg} = \frac{q}{T} = \frac{3}{4} I_0$$

Solutions of PRACTICE EXERCISE 5.6

(i) The inductive reactance of the circuit is given as

$$\omega L = 500 \times 0.08 = 40\ \Omega$$

The capacitive reactance of the circuit is given as

$$\frac{1}{\omega C} = \frac{1}{500 \times (30 \times 10^{-6})} = 66.7\ \Omega$$

As capacitive reactance is more so in circuit current will lead the applied voltage by an angle ϕ which is given as

$$\tan\phi = \left(\frac{(1/\omega C) - \omega L}{R}\right) = \frac{66.7 - 40}{15} = 1.78$$

$$\Rightarrow \quad \phi = 60.65°$$

Thus the current leads the applied voltage by 60.65°.

(ii) The impedance of *RL* series circuit is given as

$$Z = \sqrt{R^2 + \omega^2 L^2}$$

$$\Rightarrow \quad Z = \sqrt{R^2 + (2\pi f L)^2}$$

$$\Rightarrow \quad Z = \sqrt{(6)^2 + (2 \times 3.14 \times 40 \times 0.01)^2}$$

$$\Rightarrow \quad Z = 6.504\ \Omega$$

(a) Effective current supplied by source is

$$I_{rms} = \frac{E_{rms}}{Z} = \frac{220}{6.504} = 33.83 \text{ mA}$$

(b) The potential difference across the resistance is given as

$$V_R = I_{rms} \times R = 33.83 \times 6 = 202.98 \text{ V}$$

(c) Potential difference across inductance is given as

$$V_L = I_{rms} \times (\omega L) = 33.83 \times (2 \times 3.14 \times 40 \times 0.01)$$

$$\Rightarrow \quad V_L = 96.83 \text{ V}$$

(d) Phase angle between current and EMF is given as

$$\phi = \tan^{-1}\left(\frac{\omega L}{R}\right)$$

$$\Rightarrow \quad \phi = \tan^{-1}\left[\frac{2 \times 3.14 \times 40 \times 0.01}{6}\right]$$

$$\Rightarrow \quad \phi = \tan^{-1}(0.4189) = 22°46'$$

Time lag corresponding to the above phase angle is given as

$$\delta t = \frac{\phi}{360} \times T = \frac{\phi}{360} \times \frac{1}{f}$$

$$\Rightarrow \quad \delta t = \frac{22°46'}{360 \times 40} = 0.01579 \text{ s}$$

(iii) Figure shows the situation described in question.

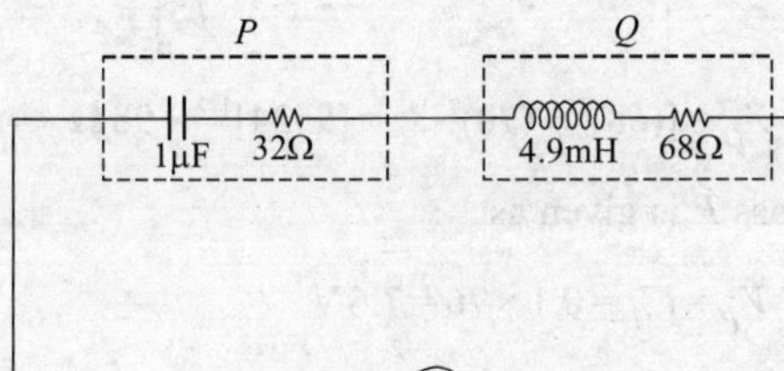

The current flowing is the *LCR* a.c. circuit is given as

$$i = \frac{e}{\sqrt{\left[R^2 + \left(\omega L - \frac{1}{\omega c}\right)^2\right]}}$$

The current in maximum at resonance, when

$$\left(\omega L - \frac{1}{\omega c}\right) = 0$$

$$\Rightarrow \quad \omega L = \frac{1}{\omega C}$$

$$\Rightarrow \quad \omega^2 = \frac{1}{LC}$$

$$\Rightarrow \quad \omega = \frac{1}{\sqrt{LC}}$$

$$\Rightarrow \quad \omega = \frac{1}{[(4.9 \times 10^{-3})(10^{-6})]^{1/2}} = \frac{10^5}{7} \text{ rad/s}$$

The current flowing in the circuit is given as

$$i_{max} = \frac{e}{R_1 + R_2} = \frac{10}{(32+68)} = \frac{1}{10} = 0.1\,\text{A}$$

The impedance of P is given as

$$Z_p = \sqrt{(R_1^2 + X_c^2)} = \sqrt{\left[R_1^2 + \left(\frac{1}{\omega c}\right)^2\right]}$$

$$\Rightarrow \quad Z_p = \left[(32)^2 + \left(\frac{7}{10^5} \times \frac{1}{10^{-6}}\right)^2\right]^{1/2}$$

$$\Rightarrow \quad Z_p = [(32)^2 + (70)^2]^{1/2}$$

$$\Rightarrow \quad Z_p = [1024 + 4900]^{1/2} = (5024)^{1/2} = 76\,\Omega$$

The impedance of Q is given as

$$Z_Q = \sqrt{[(R_2^2 + \omega^2 L^2)]}$$

$$\Rightarrow \quad Z_Q = \left[(68)^2 + \left(\frac{10^5}{7} \times 4.9 \times 10^{-3}\right)^2\right]^{1/2}$$

$$\Rightarrow \quad Z_Q = [(68)^2 + (70)^2]^{1/2} = [9524]^{1/2} = 98\,\Omega$$

Voltage across P is given as

$$V_P = iZ_P = 0.1 \times 76 = 7.6\,\text{V}$$

Voltage across Q is given as

$$V_Q = iZ_Q = 0.1 \times 98 = 9.8\,\text{V}$$

(iv) The first circuit is a series LCR circuit. The impedance in this circuit is given as

$$Z = \sqrt{[R^2 + \{\omega L - (1/\omega C)\}^2]}$$

In state of resonance we have

$$\omega L = \frac{1}{\omega C}$$

and $\quad Z = R$

The current in the circuit at resonance is given as

$$I = \frac{V}{Z} = \frac{V}{R}$$

In the second circuit, the inductance and capacitance are joined in parallel. The potential difference across each will be the same. At resonance $X_L = X_C (\omega L = 1/\omega C)$ and hence the current in both will be equal in magnitude. Further, a phase difference between currents through inductor L and capacitor C will be 180° or it is out of phase). So, two currents will be equal in magnitude but opposite in phase thus current through R will be zero in this circuit.

(v) (a) Potential difference across resistance is

$$V_R = IR = 5 \times 16 = 80\,\text{V}$$

Potential difference across inductance

$$V_L = I \times (\omega L) = 5 \times 24 = 120\,\text{V}$$

Potential difference across condenser

$$V_C = I \times (1/\omega C) = 5 \times 12 = 60\,\text{V}$$

(b) The impedance of circuit is given as

$$Z = \sqrt{\left[R^2 + \left(\omega L - \frac{1}{\omega C}\right)^2\right]}$$

$$Z = \sqrt{[(16)^2 + (24-12)^2]} = 20\,\Omega$$

(c) The voltage of AC supply is given as

$$E = IZ = 5 \times 20 = 100\,\text{V}$$

(d) Phase angle between current and voltage is given as

$$\phi = \tan^{-1}\left[\frac{\omega L - (1/\omega C)}{R}\right]$$

$$\Rightarrow \quad \phi = \tan^{-1}\left[\frac{24-12}{16}\right]$$

$$\Rightarrow \quad \phi = \tan^{-1}(0.75) = 37°$$

(vi) The phase difference between current and voltage is given as

$$\phi = 55 - 10 = 45°$$

From the given equations of current and voltage we can see that voltage is leading in phase over current.

For a series RLC circuit we use

$$\tan\phi = \tan 45° = 1$$

$$\Rightarrow \quad \tan\phi = \frac{\omega L - (1/\omega C)}{R} = 1$$

$$\Rightarrow \quad \omega L - \frac{1}{\omega C} = R \qquad \ldots(1)$$

$$\Rightarrow \quad Z = \sqrt{\left[R^2 + \left(\omega L - \frac{1}{\omega C}\right)^2\right]}$$

$$\Rightarrow \quad Z = \sqrt{(R^2 + R^2)} = 1.414\,R$$

$$\Rightarrow \quad Z = \frac{E_0}{I_0} = \frac{141.4}{5} = 28.28$$

$\Rightarrow \quad 1.414\,R = 28.28$

$\Rightarrow \quad R = 20\,\Omega \quad \ldots(2)$

From equation-(1) we have

$$\omega L - \frac{1}{\omega C} = 20$$

$$\Rightarrow (3000 \times 0.01) - \frac{1}{3000C} = 20$$

$$\Rightarrow \quad 30 - 20 = \frac{1}{3000C}$$

$$\Rightarrow \quad C = \frac{1}{3000 \times 10} = 33.33 \times 10^{-6}\,\text{F}$$

$$\Rightarrow \quad C = 33.33\,\mu\text{F}$$

(vii) Figure shows the situation described in the question.

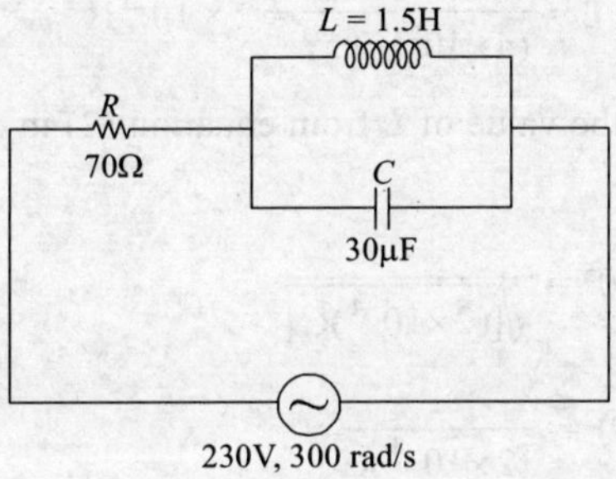

(a) In the given circuit, the inductor and capacitor are connected in parallel. Let Z' be their complex impedance. Then

$$\frac{1}{Z'} = \frac{1}{j\omega L} + \frac{1}{(1/j\omega C)} = \frac{1}{j\omega L} + j\omega C$$

$$\Rightarrow \quad \frac{1}{Z'} = \frac{1-\omega^2 LC}{j\omega L}$$

$$\Rightarrow \quad Z' = \frac{j\omega L}{1-\omega^2 LC}$$

The total complex impedance of the circuit is given by

$$Z = R + Z'$$

$$\Rightarrow \quad Z = R + \frac{j\omega L}{(1-\omega^2 LC)}$$

$$\Rightarrow \quad |Z| = \sqrt{\left[R^2 + \left(\frac{\omega L}{1-\omega^2 LC}\right)^2\right]}$$

Substituting these values and solving it, we get

$$|Z| = 163.3\,\Omega$$

(b) $$I_{rms} = \frac{E_{rms}}{Z} = \frac{230V}{163.3\Omega} = 1.41\,\text{A}$$

(c) Let I_L and I_C be the rms values of current in L and C respectively

$$I_L = \frac{Z_C}{(Z_L + Z_C)} I_{rms} \text{ and } I_C = \frac{Z_L}{(Z_L + Z_C)} I_{rms}$$

Here $\quad Z_L = j\omega L$ and $Z_C = 1j/\omega C$

Substituting these values, we get

$$I_L = \frac{I_{rms}}{1-\omega^2 LC} \text{ and } I_C = \frac{(\omega^2 LC) I_{rms}}{\omega^2 LC - 1}$$

Substituting the values and solving, we get

$$I_L = 0.462\,\text{A}$$

and $\quad I_C = 1.87\,\text{A}$

The corresponding current amplitudes are

$$I_{L0} = \sqrt{2} \times 0.462 = 1.414 \times 0.462 = 0.653\,\text{A}$$

and $\quad I_{C0} = \sqrt{2} \times 1.87 = 1.414 \times 1.87 = 2.64\,\text{A}$

(d) When $\omega = \dfrac{1}{\sqrt{(LC)}}$, then $\omega^2 LC = 1$

At this state circuit impedance becomes

$$Z = \frac{j\omega L}{1-\omega^2 LC} = \frac{j\omega L}{0} = \infty$$

Thus current in the circuit would be zero.

(viii) The current in the circuit would be maximum at resonance when

$$\omega L = \frac{1}{\omega C}$$

$$\Rightarrow \quad C = \frac{1}{\omega^2 L}$$

$$\Rightarrow \quad C = \frac{1}{(2\pi f)^2 L} = \frac{1}{(2 \times 3.14 \times 50)^2 \times 0.5}$$

$$\Rightarrow \quad C = 20.24 \times 10^{-6}\,\text{F}$$

At resonance circuit impedance is purely resistive so it is given as

$$Z = \sqrt{\left[R^2 + \left(\omega L - \frac{1}{\omega C}\right)^2\right]} = R = 10\,\Omega$$

$$\Rightarrow \quad I = \frac{E}{R} = \frac{200}{10} = 20\,\text{A}$$

Potential difference across resistance

$$V_R = IR = 20 \times 10 = 200\,\text{V}$$

Potential difference across inductor

$$V_L = I\omega L = (2\pi \times 50 \times 0.5) \times 20 = 3142\,\text{V}$$

Potential difference across capacitor

$$V_C = \frac{I}{\omega C} = I\omega L = 3142\text{ V}$$

(ix) Circuit impedance is given as

$$\bar{Z} = \bar{R} + \bar{X}_L + \bar{X}_C$$

$$\Rightarrow \quad Z = \sqrt{R^2 + (X_L - X_C)^2} = \sqrt{(8)^2 + (6)^2}$$

$$\Rightarrow \quad Z = 10\,\Omega$$

and $\quad \phi = -\tan^{-1}\frac{6}{8} = -37°$

Thus phasor impedance is given as

$$\bar{Z} = 10\,\Omega\angle -37°$$

Circuit current is given as

$$i = \frac{e}{Z} = \frac{10\cos(100\pi t)}{10\angle -37°} = \frac{10\angle 0°}{10\angle -37°} = 1\angle 37°$$

$$\Rightarrow \quad i = \cos(100\pi t + 37°)$$

Potential difference across points A and B is given as

$$\bar{V}_{AB} = \bar{i}(\bar{X}_C - \bar{X}_L)$$

$$\Rightarrow \quad \bar{V}_{AB} = 1\angle 37° \times 6\angle -90° = 6\angle -53°$$

$$\Rightarrow \quad V_{AB} = 6\cos(100\pi t - 53°)$$

$\bar{V}_{AB}$ will leg behind $\bar{i}$ by 90° because $X_C > X_L$. Given condition is that

$$V_{AB} = \frac{1}{2}e$$

$$\Rightarrow \quad 6\cos(100\pi t - 53°) = 5\cos 100\pi t$$

$$\Rightarrow \quad 6\cos(100\pi t) \times \frac{3}{5} + 6\sin(100\pi t) \times \frac{4}{5} = 5\cos(100\pi t)$$

$$\Rightarrow \quad \frac{24}{5}\sin(100\pi t) = \frac{7}{8}\cos(100\pi t)$$

$$\Rightarrow \quad \tan(100\,\pi t) = \frac{7}{24}$$

$$\Rightarrow \quad \cos(100\pi t) = \frac{24}{25}$$

$$\Rightarrow \quad V_{AB} = 5\cos(100\pi t) = 5 \times \frac{24}{25}\text{ V}$$

$$\Rightarrow \quad V_{AB} = \frac{24}{5}\text{ V}$$

Solutions of PRACTICE EXERCISE 5.7

(i) The resonant frequency ω_0 is given by

$$\omega_0 = \frac{1}{\sqrt{(LC)}}$$

$$\Rightarrow \quad 4 \times 10^5 = \frac{1}{\sqrt{(LC)}} \quad \ldots (1)$$

Current through the circuit at resonance is given

$$I = \frac{60}{120} = 0.5\text{ A}$$

The voltage across inductance is given as

$$V_L = (L\,\omega_0) \times I$$

$$\Rightarrow \quad 40 = L \times (4 \times 10^5) \times 0.5$$

$$\Rightarrow \quad L = \frac{40}{(4\times 10^5)(0.5)} = 2 \times 10^{-4}\text{ H} \quad \ldots (2)$$

Substituting the value of L from equation-(2) in equation-(1) gives

$$4 \times 10^5 = \frac{1}{\sqrt{[(2\times 10^{-4})C]}}$$

$$\Rightarrow \quad (4 \times 10^5)^2 = \frac{1}{(2\times 10^{-4})C}$$

$$\Rightarrow \quad C = \frac{1}{(4\times 10^5)^2 \times (2\times 10^{-4})}\text{ F}$$

$$\Rightarrow \quad C = \frac{1}{32} \times 10^{-6}\,\mu\text{F} = \frac{1}{32}\,\mu\text{F}$$

We are given with the phase angle $\phi = 45°$ so we use

$$\tan\phi = \frac{X_L - X_C}{R}$$

$$\Rightarrow \quad \tan 45° = \frac{X_L - X_C}{120}$$

$$\Rightarrow \quad X_L - X_C = 120$$

$$\Rightarrow \quad \omega L - \frac{1}{\omega C} = 120$$

$$\Rightarrow \quad \omega L - L\left(\frac{\omega_0^2}{\omega}\right) = 120$$

$$\Rightarrow \quad \omega^2(2 \times 10^{-4}) - \omega_0^2(2 \times 10^{-4}) = 120\,\omega$$

$$\Rightarrow \quad \omega^2 - 60 \times 10^4\,\omega - \omega_0^2 = 0$$

$$\Rightarrow \quad \omega = \left[\frac{(60\times 10^4 \pm \sqrt{[(60\times 10^4)^2 + 4\times(4\times 10^5)^2]})}{2}\right]$$

$$\Rightarrow \quad \omega = \frac{6\times10^5 \pm 10\times10^5}{2}$$

Here we consider the positive sign because the current lags voltage i.e., $X_L > X_C$

$$\Rightarrow \quad \omega = \frac{6\times10^5 + 10\times10^5}{2} = 8\times10^5 \text{ rad/s}$$

(ii) Primary and secondary coil voltage is given as

$$e_p = 2000\text{ V}$$

and $$e_s = 200\text{ V}$$

Power of transformer at primary coil is given as

$$e_p i_p = 20\times10^3$$

$$\Rightarrow \quad i_p = \frac{20\times10^3}{2000} = 10\text{ A}$$

Power of transformer at secondary coil is given as

$$e_s I_s = 20\times10^3$$

$$\Rightarrow \quad I_s = \frac{20\times10^3}{200} = 100\text{ A}$$

(iii) As the current lags behind the potential difference, the circuit contains resistance and inductance. The power consumed by the circuit is given as

$$P = E_{rms}\times I_{rms}\times\cos\phi$$

$$\Rightarrow \quad P = \frac{E_{rms}^2\times\cos\phi}{Z}$$

$$\Rightarrow \quad Z = \frac{E_{rms}^2\times\cos\phi}{P}$$

$$\Rightarrow \quad Z = \frac{(220)^2\times0.8}{550} = 70.4\,\Omega$$

Power factor of the circuit is given as

$$\cos\phi = \frac{R}{Z}$$

$$\Rightarrow \quad R = Z\cos\phi$$

$$\Rightarrow \quad R = 70.4\times0.8 = 56.32\,\Omega$$

Circuit impedance is given as

$$Z^2 = R^2 + (\omega L)^2$$

$$\Rightarrow \quad \omega L = \sqrt{(Z^2 - R^2)}$$

$$\Rightarrow \quad \omega L = \sqrt{(70.4)^2 - (56.32)^2} = 42.24\,\Omega$$

When capacitor is connected in the circuit, the circuit impedance becomes

$$Z = \sqrt{\left[R^2 + \left(\omega L - \frac{1}{\omega C}\right)^2\right]}$$

and $$\cos\phi = \frac{R}{\sqrt{\left[R^2 + \left(\omega L - \frac{1}{\omega C}\right)^2\right]}}$$

In the circuit $\cos\phi = 1$ when

$$\omega L = \frac{1}{\omega C}$$

$$\Rightarrow \quad C = \frac{1}{\omega(\omega L)} = \frac{1}{2\pi f(\omega L)}$$

$$\Rightarrow \quad C = \frac{1}{(2\times3.14\times50)(42.24)}$$

$$\Rightarrow \quad C = 75\times10^{-6}\text{ F} = 75\,\mu\text{F}$$

(iv) (a) The current amplitude i_0 in circuit is given as

$$i_0 = \frac{e_0}{\sqrt{\left[R^2 + \left(\omega L - \frac{1}{\omega C}\right)^2\right]}}$$

This is maximum at resonance when $\omega L = 1/\omega C$. If it happens at frequency ω_0. Then we have

$$\omega_0 = \frac{1}{\sqrt{(LC)}} = \frac{1}{\sqrt{[(0.12)(480\times10^{-9})]}}$$

$$\Rightarrow \quad \omega_0 = 4167\text{ rad/s}$$

The resonant frequency f_0 is given as

$$f_0 = \frac{\omega_0}{2\pi} = \frac{4167}{2\times3.14} = 663.5\text{ Hz}$$

At resonance maximum current amplitude is given as

$$i_{0\max} = \frac{e_0}{R} = \frac{\sqrt{2}\times230}{23} = 14.14\text{ A}$$

(b) The average power absorbed by the circuit is given as

$$P = e_{rms} i_{rms}\cos\phi$$

This is maximum when $\cos\phi = 1$

$$\Rightarrow \quad P_{max} = e_{rms}\times i_{rms}$$

$$\Rightarrow \quad P_{max} = \frac{(E_{rms})^2}{R} = \frac{(230)^2}{23} = 2300\text{ W}$$

This also happens at resonant frequency.

(c) The half power frequencies are the frequencies at which the power in the circuit is half the maximum power. These are given as

$$\omega_{hp} = \omega_0 \pm \frac{R}{2L} = 4167 \pm \left(\frac{23}{2\times 0.12}\right)$$

$$\Rightarrow \quad \omega_{hp} = 4263 \text{ rad/s and } 4071 \text{ rad/s}$$

(d) The quality factor of the circuit is given as

$$Q = \frac{\omega_0 L}{R} = \frac{4167\times 0.12}{23} = 21.74$$

(v) The current required by the lamp to run at its peak brightness is given as

$$I = \frac{P}{V} = \frac{5}{20} = 0.25 \text{ A}$$

The resistance of the lamp is given as

$$R = \frac{V}{I} = \frac{20}{0.25} = 80\,\Omega$$

(a) When a capacitor C is placed in series with lamp, then its impedance is given as

$$Z = \sqrt{\left[R^2 + \left(\frac{1}{\omega C}\right)^2\right]}$$

The current through the circuit becomes

$$I = \frac{200}{\sqrt{[R^2 + (1/\omega C)^2]}} = 0.25$$

$$\Rightarrow \quad \frac{200}{\sqrt{(80)^2 + \left(\frac{1}{4\pi^2 \times 50^2 \times C^2}\right)}} = 0.25$$

$$\Rightarrow \quad C = 4.0 \times 10^{-6}\,\text{F} = 4.0\,\mu\text{F}$$

(b) When an inductance L is placed in series with the lamp then the inductance is given as

$$Z = \sqrt{[R^2 + (\omega L)^2]}$$

The current through the circuit becomes

$$I = \frac{200}{\sqrt{[R^2 + (\omega L)^2]}} = 0.25$$

$$\Rightarrow \quad \frac{200}{\sqrt{[(80)^2 + (4\pi^2 \times 50^2 \times L^2)]}} = 0.25$$

$$\Rightarrow \quad L = 2.53\,\text{H}$$

(c) When a resistance r is placed in series with lamp of resistance then the current through the lamp is given as

$$\frac{200}{R + r} = 0.25$$

$$\Rightarrow \quad \frac{200}{80 + r} = 0.25$$

$$\Rightarrow \quad r = 720\,\Omega$$

(d) It will be more economical to use inductance or capacitance in series with the lamp to run it as the reactive components of circuit does not consume any power while there would be dissipation of power when resistance is inserted in series with the lamp.

(vi) At resonance the maximum current in circuit is

$$i_{\max} = \frac{e}{R} = \frac{24}{R} = 6$$

$$\Rightarrow \quad R = 4\,\Omega$$

Across DC source the steady current in circuit is given as

$$I = \frac{12}{4 + R} = \frac{12}{8} = 1.5 \text{ A}$$

(vii) (a) Using transformer equation, we have

$$\frac{n_s}{n_p} = \frac{1}{20}$$

Using $e_p = 250$ V and $i_s = 8$ A, we have

$$\Rightarrow \quad \frac{e_s}{e_p} = \frac{n_s}{n_p}$$

$$\Rightarrow \quad e_s = \frac{n_s}{n_p} \times e_p$$

$$\Rightarrow \quad e_s = \frac{1}{20} \times 250 = 12.5 \text{ V}$$

(b) Using ideal conditions and transformer equation, we have

$$\frac{i_p}{i_s} = \frac{n_s}{n_p}$$

$$\Rightarrow \quad i_p = \frac{n_s}{n_p} \times i_s$$

$$\Rightarrow \quad i_p = \frac{1}{20} \times 8 = 0.4 \text{ A}$$

(c) Power output of transformer is given as

$$P = e_s i_s$$

$$\Rightarrow \quad P = 12.5 \times 8 = 100 \text{ W}$$

(viii) For DC source we use

$$R=\frac{V_{d.c.}}{I_{d.c.}}=\frac{250}{1}=250\,\Omega$$

When a DC voltage is applied to the circuit containing L, C and R a current flows through it so we consider R is in parallel with L and C as shown in figure.

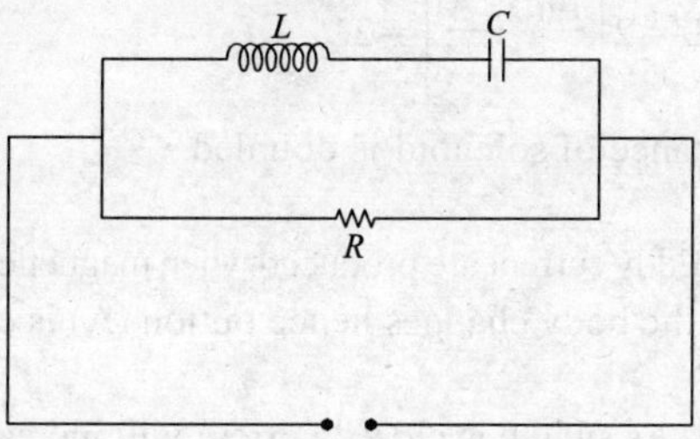

Impedance Z of the circuit at frequency 2250 rad/s is given as

$$\frac{1}{Z}=\sqrt{\left[\frac{1}{R^2}+\frac{1}{\left(\omega L-\frac{1}{\omega L}\right)^2}\right]}$$

Circuit impedance can also be directly given as

$$Z=\frac{V}{i}=\frac{250}{1.25}=200\,\Omega$$

$$\Rightarrow \quad \frac{1}{(200)^2}=\frac{1}{R^2}+\frac{1}{\left(\omega L-\frac{1}{\omega L}\right)^2}$$

$$\Rightarrow \quad \frac{1}{\left(\omega L-\frac{1}{\omega L}\right)^2}=\frac{1}{(200)^2}-\frac{1}{(250)^2}=\frac{9}{(10)^6}$$

$$\Rightarrow \quad \left(\omega L-\frac{1}{\omega L}\right)=\frac{1000}{3}$$

$$\Rightarrow \quad \left(2250L-\frac{1}{2250C}\right)=\frac{1000}{3} \qquad \ldots(1)$$

At resonance the frequency is given as

$$\omega_0{}^2=\frac{1}{LC}$$

$$\Rightarrow \quad 4500\times 4500=\frac{1}{LC}$$

$$\Rightarrow \quad 2250L=\frac{1}{9000C} \qquad \ldots(2)$$

From equation-(1), we have

$$\frac{1}{9000C}-\frac{1}{2250C}=\frac{1000}{3}$$

$$\Rightarrow \quad C=10^{-6}\,\text{F}=1\,\mu\text{F}$$

From equation-(2), we have

$$2250L=\frac{1}{9000\times 10^{-6}}$$

$$\Rightarrow \quad L=\frac{1}{2250\times 9000\times 10^{-6}}=\frac{4}{81}\,\text{H}$$

(ix) At resonance the circuit current is given as

$$i=\frac{e}{R}=\frac{V_R}{R}=\frac{60}{R}=0.5\,\text{A}$$

Voltage across inductance is given as

$$V_L=iX_L=(0.5)\omega L=40$$

$$L=\frac{40\times 2}{0.5\times 4000}$$

$$\Rightarrow \quad L=20\,\text{mH}$$

At resonance we have

$$\omega L=\frac{1}{\omega C}$$

$$\Rightarrow \quad C=\frac{1}{\omega^2 L}=\frac{1}{(4000)^2\times 20\times 10^{-3}}$$

$$\Rightarrow \quad C=\frac{1}{32}\times 10^{-4}=\frac{25}{8}\,\mu\text{F}$$

(x) By applying a DC voltage no flux variation takes place in core of transformer so no voltage is induced in secondary coil.

(xi) Voltage at primary and secondary coil of transformer are given as

$$e_1=240\,V \text{ and } e_2=24\,\text{V}$$

Resistance of lamp is given as

$$R=\frac{V^2}{P}=\frac{(24)^2}{140}=\frac{144}{35}\,\Omega$$

Current in secondary coil is given as

$$i_2=\frac{e_2}{R}=\frac{24}{144}\times 35=\frac{35}{6}\,\text{A}$$

Power at primary coil is given as

$$P_1=e_1i_1=240\times 0.7=168\,\text{W}$$

Power at secondary coil is given as

$$P_2=e_2i_2=24\times\frac{35}{6}=140\,\text{W}$$

Transformer efficiency is given as

$$\eta=\frac{e_2i_2}{e_1i_1}\times 100=\frac{148}{168}\times 100$$

$$\Rightarrow \quad \eta=83.33\%$$

Solutions of CONCEPTUAL MCQS Single Option Correct

Sol. 1 (C) The circuit will have inductive nature if $\omega > \frac{1}{\sqrt{LC}}$ and capacitive nature if $\omega < \frac{1}{\sqrt{LC}}$. If circuit has inductive nature the current will lag behind voltage. At resonance when capacitive and inductive reactance are equal power factor is equal to unity. Hence option (C) is correct.

Sol. 2 (D) Figure below shows the two loops placed on a table in same plane as described in question.

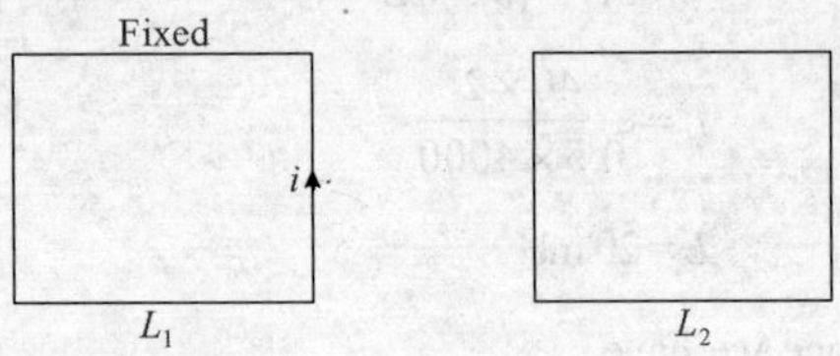

When current through L_1 increases then flux linked through L_2 will increase in direction into the plane of paper. Due to this according to lenz law, an anticlockwise current is induced in L_2 and in the two nearby parallel sides of the two loops currents will be in opposite directions so the loops will repel each other and L_2 will move away.

Sol. 3 (C) The total charge flown through a conducting loop in magnetic field is given as

$$\Delta q_f = \frac{\Delta\phi}{R}$$

Thus option (C) is correct.

Sol. 4 (B) According to Lenz's law the direction of induced current is such that it opposes the cause of induction. As current is increasing in the solenoid the induced current will be opposite to it. As (di/dt) is a constant thus induced current is constant.

Sol. 5 (B) EMF induces across the length of the wire which cuts the magnetic field. So in this case we have (Length of c = Length d) > (Length of a = b)
So we have $(e_c = e_d) > (e_a = e_b)$. Hence option (B) is correct.

Sol. 6 (B) When the loops are brought nearer, magnetic flux linked with each loop increases. Thus the current will be induced in each loop in a direction opposite to its own current according to Lenz's law. So, the current will decrease in each loop.

Sol. 7 (A) Due to conducting nature of aluminium, eddy currents are produced force on which causes damping in oscillations.

Sol. 8 (C) The inductance of solenoid is given as

$$L = \mu_0 \frac{N^2}{l} A$$

$$\Rightarrow \quad L' = \mu_0 \times \frac{(2N)^2}{2l} \times A$$

$$\Rightarrow \quad L' = 2\left[\frac{\mu_0 N^2 A}{l}\right] = 2L$$

Thus inductance of solenoid is doubled.

Sol. 9 (A) Eddy current are produced when magnetic flux linked with a metallic body changes hence option (A) is correct.

Sol. 10 (B) As switch is closed current will increase from its zero value to a finite value. In this process flux will change which induces an EMF to oppose the change. Thus brightness of bulb would increase slowly.

Sol. 11 (C) Magnetic field of ring is also along it axis, parallel to the direction of velocity of charged particle so no magnetic force will act on charged particle. But due to g velocity of charge particle will increase.

Sol. 12 (D) Voltage as function of time is given as

$$V(t) = \frac{t}{3} + 1$$

Current = 1 A

For capacitor, we have

$$I = \frac{Cdv}{dt}$$

$$\Rightarrow \quad 1 = C\left[\frac{1}{3} + 0\right]$$

$$\Rightarrow \quad C = 3\text{ F}$$

Sol. 13 (C) If magnetic field in a region is charging, then induced electric field exists even outside the region where magnetic field does not exist because if outside a closed loop is considered the magnetic flux through the loop changes with change in magnetic field.

Sol. 14 (B) Root mean square value is given as

$$V_{\text{RMS}} = \sqrt{\frac{\int_0^{T/4} V_0^2 dt}{\int_0^T dt}} = \sqrt{\frac{V_0^2\left(\frac{T}{4}\right)}{T}} = \sqrt{\frac{V_0^2\left(\frac{T}{4}\right)}{T}} = \sqrt{\frac{V_0^2}{4}} = \frac{V_0}{2}$$

Sol. 15 (C) The induced EMF in the coil is given as

$$e = L\left|\frac{di}{dt}\right| = L \times (\text{Slope of } i - t \text{ graph})$$

So initially EMF is zero as slope of $i - t$ curve is zero and then remaining two regions slopes are constants but of opposite signs. Hence induced EMF are constants but in opposite direction hence option (C) is correct.

Sol. 16 (C) The resonant frequency of a series RLC circuit is given as

$$\omega_r = \frac{1}{\sqrt{LC}}$$

For $\omega_1 = \omega_2$ we use

$$\frac{1}{\sqrt{L_1C}} = \frac{1}{\sqrt{L_2 2C}}$$

On squaring both sides, we get

$$\frac{1}{L_1C} = \frac{1}{L_2(2C)}$$

$$\Rightarrow \quad \frac{L_2}{L_1} = \frac{1}{2}$$

$$\Rightarrow \quad L_2 = \frac{L_1}{2}$$

Sol. 17 (C) In capacitor current leads reference voltage by $\frac{\pi}{2}$. In inductor in series with a resistor combination current legs reference voltage by an angle $\tan^{-1}\frac{X_L}{R}$. Thus phase difference between the two currents is given as $\frac{\pi}{2} + \tan^{-1}\frac{X_L}{R}$. Hence option (C) is correct.

Sol. 18 (C) When the circuit is switched on the charge starts oscillating between the capacitors and mean position of oscillations is when the two capacitors will be at same potential (minimum energy state). The energy stored in capacitors at same potential is given as

$$U_{\text{mean}} = \frac{Q^2}{6C}$$

Initial energy in capacitors is given as

$$U_{\text{initial}} = \frac{Q^2}{2C} + \frac{(2Q)^2}{4C} = \frac{3Q^2}{2C}$$

Thus maximum energy stored in inductor is when system is at mean position which is given as

$$U_{\text{magnetic}} = U_{\text{initial}} - U_{\text{mean}}$$

$$\Rightarrow U_{\text{magnetic}} = \frac{3Q^2}{2C} - \frac{Q^2}{6C} = \frac{4Q^2}{3C}$$

If initial rate of growth of current is di/dt then we have

$$L\frac{di}{dt} = 2\left(\frac{Q}{C}\right)$$

$$\Rightarrow \quad \frac{di}{dt} = \frac{2Q}{LC}$$

Hence option (C) is correct.

Sol. 19 (A) The capacitive and inductive reactance of the circuit are given as

$$X_C = \frac{1}{\omega C} \text{ and } X_L = \omega L$$

At $\omega < \omega_{\text{res}}$, $X_C > X_L$ so the circuit is capacitive.

Sol. 20 (A) When magnet enters in the coil then for a short duration flux through the coil remain constant so no EMF is induced and when it comes out and goes back into the coil EMF changes direction every time when magnet is outside and reverses the direction of motion. Hence option (A) is most suitable for this case.

Sol. 21 (C) In diamagnetic substances on placing these in external magnetic fields the dipoles are induced in direction opposite to external field thats why the susceptibility of such substances is negative.

Sol. 22 (D) Average value of the function shown in graph is given as

$$V_{\text{average}} = \frac{\int_0^{T/2} V_0 dt}{T/2} + \frac{\int_{T/2}^{T} (-V_0) dt}{T/2} = 0$$

RMS value of the function shown in graph is given as

$$V_{\text{rms}} = \sqrt{\frac{\int_0^T V_0^2 dt}{T}} = V_0$$

Sol. 23 (D) The magnetic flux passing through the loop is a function of distance between magnet and the loop. When magnet moves then rate of change of flux will be directly proportional to the speed of the magnet and if loop also moves away from the magnet then relative speed of the two is zero and no EMF will be induced in the loop.

Sol. 24 (D) A DC ammeter only measures DC current and when AC is passed through it then it measures average value of current which is zero.

Sol. 25 (C) In given circuit initially voltage across inductor and capacitor are same and in this case we have

$$X_L = X_C$$

Thus the potential difference across the combination of L and C will remain same at zero because the circuit is in resonance.

Sol. 26 (B) If currents is passed through the straight wire, magnetic lines are circular and tangential to the loop. So, no flux is linked with the loop so no mutual induction will exist between the two.

Sol. 27 (B) Out of given substances only in Nickel there are unpaired electrons present in its orbital configuration.

Sol. 28 (D) In a series RLC circuit, at resonance, the power factor is given as

$$\cos\phi = \frac{R}{Z} = \frac{R}{\sqrt{R^2 + \left(\varpi L - \frac{1}{\varpi C}\right)^2}}$$

Now depending on whether ωL is greater or less than $\frac{1}{\omega C}$ the lag or lead will occur.

Sol. 29 (D) At $t = 0$, for the purpose of current calculation in circuit inductor can be assumed as open circuit and capacitor as short circuited.

Sol. 30 (C) As $X_L = X_C$ at resonance

$$\Rightarrow \frac{X_L}{X_C} = 1 \text{ for both circuits.}$$

Sol. 31 (B) The field at A and B are out of the paper and inside the paper respectively. As the current in the straight wire decreases the field also decreases. The change in the magnetic field causes induced current in both A and B. According to lenz's law induced currents in coils A & B tend to oppose the variation of change in magnetic field so induced current in A is anticlockwise and in B is clockwise.

Sol. 32 (D) B-H curve area represents the energy dissipated per unit volume per cycle of the curve. More the area more energy is dissipated in depolarization of dipoles after polarization in half cycle.

Sol. 33 (C) EMF induced in the two rings between their topmost and bottommost points is given as

$$e = Bv(2R)$$

In Ring "A" and Ring "B" the direction of EMF is opposite so we have

$$V_{BT} - V_{AT} = 4BvR$$

Hence option (C) is correct.

Sol. 34 (D) The rate of power delivered by the external force is given as

$$\frac{dp}{dt} = \frac{d}{dt}(\vec{F}\cdot\vec{V}) = F\frac{dV}{dt} = Fa$$

As acceleration in this case is decreasing with time so rate of power also decreases.

Sol. 35 (D) There is a force BIl acting on the rod carrying a current I due to current source. By right hand palm rule we can see that this force is acting in vertically upward direction. The acceleration of rod is given as

$$a = \frac{F - W}{m}$$

The magnitude of acceleration will be constant, but the direction will depend on the mass of the rod.
Hence option (D) is correct.

Sol. 36 (C) The induced EMF in the coil is given as

$$e = L\left|\frac{di}{dt}\right| = L \times (\text{Slope of } i - t \text{ graph})$$

Thus option (C) is correct.

Sol. 37 (B) By Lenz's law, induced effects always oppose the cause of induction. So when the first loop is moved towards the smaller loop it will be repelled by the induced current in the loop.

Sol. 38 (A) In segment AB, both points A and B are equidistant from the center O of rotation so both points will be at same potential.

Sol. 39 (A) If dipoles does not exist in a material then always these are induced in opposition to the external magnetic field as already discussed and the substance is called diamagnetic.

Sol. 40 (B) After closing the switch current in solenoid increases with time so flux passing through B will increase with time. By Lenz's law, it should have a tendency to move away from the coil to decrease the flux.

Sol. 41 (B) In ferromagnetic substances due to exchange coupling the inside magnetic field increases the external magnetic field by a large extent so these have very high permeability.

Sol. 42 (D) As velocity of rod is parallel to its length, it will not cut any magnetic flux due to its motion so no EMF will be induced in it across its length.

Sol. 43 (C) As magnetic field is steady and not changing with time so no EMF is induced in the ring in any of the two states mentioned.

Sol. 44 (A) During motion the rod is not cutting any magnetic flux so no EMF will be induced in the rod.

Sol. 45 (B) Above Curie point temperature the alignment of dipoles in polarized ferromagnetic material gets disturbed and it looses the property of exchange coupling so it gets converted to a paramagnetic material.

Sol. 46 (C) EMF induced across the rod is given as

$$V_C = Bvl$$

Thus charge on capacitor is given as

$$q = CV_C = BvlC = \text{constant.}$$

$$\Rightarrow \quad I_C = \frac{dq}{dt} = 0$$

$$\Rightarrow \quad U_C = \frac{1}{2}CV^2 = \frac{1}{2}CB^2L^2v$$

Thus option (C) is correct.

Sol. 47 (A) From right hand palm rule, we can analyze that both A and B points are at higher potential than O.

Sol. 48 (B) At mean position, velocity is maximum. Hence motional EMF Bvl is also maximum. Velocity v oscillates simple harmonically so motional emf will also vary simple harmonically. Further, polarity of induced emf will keep on changing.

Sol. 49 (C) Instantaneous current in the wire is given as

$$i = \frac{Bvl}{R}$$

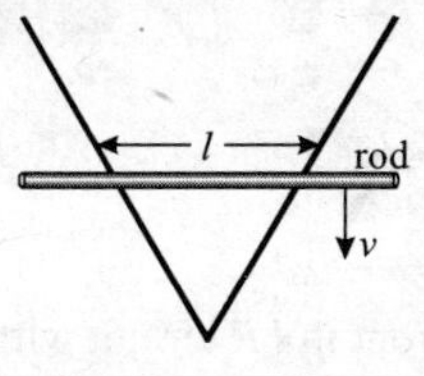

If λ is the resistance per unit length of conducing rod then we use

$$i = \frac{Bvl}{\lambda l} = \frac{Bv}{\lambda} = \text{constant}$$

Sol. 50 (D) In decay of current through RL circuit, current always decays and it cannot remains constant.

Sol. 51 (C) At $t = 0+$ an inductor behaves like open circuit and a capacitor behaves like short circuit so whole voltage of the battery will appear across the inductor just after closing the switch.

Sol. 52 (B) Due to diamagnetic nature the dipole polarization in the solution will be opposite to the applied field and field will repel the material away from it so the liquid solution level will fall in this tube.

Sol. 53 (A) Rate of increment of energy in inductor is given as

$$\frac{dU}{dt} = \frac{d}{dt}\left(\frac{1}{2}Li^2\right) = Li\frac{di}{dt}$$

Current in the inductor at time t is given as

$$i = i_0\left(1 - e^{-\frac{t}{\tau}}\right)$$

$$\Rightarrow \quad \frac{di}{dt} = \frac{i_0}{\tau}e^{-\frac{t}{\tau}}$$

$$\Rightarrow \quad \frac{dU}{dt} = \frac{Li_0}{\tau}e^{-\frac{t}{\tau}}\left(1 - e^{-\frac{t}{\tau}}\right)$$

$$\frac{dU}{dt} = 0 \text{ at } t = 0 \text{ as well as at } t = \infty$$

Hence option (A) is the best representation.

Sol. 54 (C) Magnetic force on charge carriers due to magnetic field is balanced by the electric force due to induced electric field, thus we have

$$avB = qE_i$$

$$\Rightarrow \quad E_i = vB$$

$$\Rightarrow \quad V_P - V_Q = E_i C$$

$$\Rightarrow \quad V_P - V_Q = BvC$$

Sol. 55 (C) The magnetic flux in loop A will increase while the magnetic flux in loop B will decrease. By Lenz's law, the induced current in loop A will tend to decrease the flux in loop A and induced current in loop B will tend to increase the flux in loop B. So clockwise current is induced in loop A and counterclockwise current is induced in loop B. Hence option (C) is correct.

Sol. 56 (A) The EMF is induced only in the straight radial wire rotating inside the magnetic field which is given as

$$e = \frac{1}{2} B r^2 \omega$$

Here ω = constant so emf remain constant in magnitude. Since magnetic flux increases for half cycle and decreases for the other half. Hence emf changes sign every half cycle. So the correct graph is drawn as

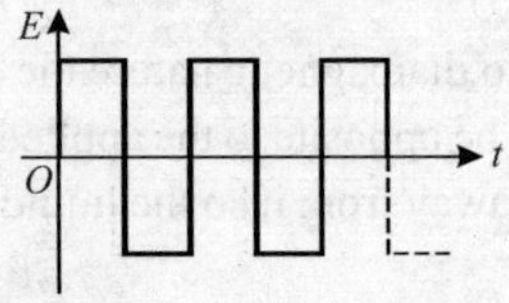

Hence option (A) is correct.

Sol. 57 (B) Power dissipated in the coil is given as

$$P = \frac{e^2}{R}$$

Where induced EMF e is given as

$$e = -\left(\frac{d\phi}{dt}\right)$$

Where linked flux with the coil is given as

$$\phi = NBA$$

$$\Rightarrow \quad e = -NA\left(\frac{dB}{dt}\right)$$

The coil resistance depends upon its wire length and cross section which is given as

$$R \propto \frac{l}{r^2}$$

$$\Rightarrow \quad P \propto \frac{N^2 r^2}{l}$$

$$\Rightarrow \quad \frac{P_1}{P_2} = 1$$

Sol. 58 (C) When key K is pressed, current through the electromagnet start increasing and flux linked with ring increases and according to Lenz's law it produces repulsion effect to oppose the increment in flux through the ring.

Sol. 59 (B) Due to the movement of both the magnets, current will be anticlockwise, as seen from left side so plate 1 will be positive and 2 will be negative.

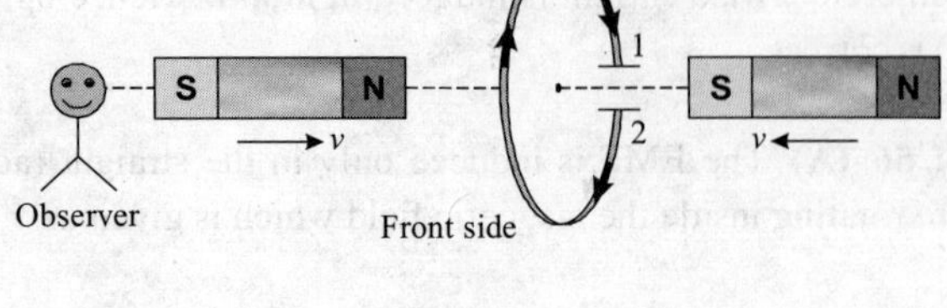

Sol. 60 (D) EMF induces in ring and it will opposes the motion. Hence due to the resistance of the ring its energy dissipates every time it passes through the region of magnetic field.

Sol. 61 (B) In India electricity generation in all power plants is done at 50 Hz as a national standard.

Sol. 62 (A) When a bulb and a capacitor are connected in series to an AC source, then on increasing the frequency the current in the circuit is increased, because the impedance of the circuit is decreased. So the bulb will give more intense light.

Sol. 63 (D) Reactance of circuit is given as

$$X = X_L - X_C = 2\pi f L - \frac{1}{2\pi f C}$$

Solutions of NUMERICAL MCQS Single Option Correct

Sol. 1 (D) Induced current in the coil is given as

$$i = \frac{e}{R}$$

$$\Rightarrow \quad i = \frac{N(\Delta\phi/\Delta t)}{R} = \frac{NS(\Delta B/\Delta t)}{R}$$

$$\Rightarrow \quad i = \frac{10(10 \times 10^{-4})(10^4)}{20}$$

$$\Rightarrow \quad i = 5\text{ A}$$

Sol. 2 (A) The given voltage and current can be written as

$$V = 5\cos\omega t = 5\sin\left(\omega t + \frac{\pi}{2}\right)$$

and $\quad i = 2\sin\omega t$

So the phase difference between voltage and current is $\phi = \pi/2$ and power dissipated in the instrument is given as

$$P = V_{rms} i_{rms} \cos\phi = 0$$

Sol. 3 (D) Transformer does not work with DC.

Sol. 4 (D) In second rotation of coil the initial and final flux passing through the coil are same so we have

$$\Delta\phi = 0$$

$$\Rightarrow \quad Q_2 = \frac{\Delta\phi}{R} = 0$$

Sol. 5 (A) The current in LR circuit with time is given as

$$i = \frac{E}{R}(1 - e^{-Rt/L})$$

$$\Rightarrow \quad i = \frac{15}{5}(1 - e^{-5 \times 2/10})$$

$\Rightarrow \quad i = 3\left(1 - \frac{1}{e}\right)$ A

Sol. 6 (C) Power dissipated in AC circuit is given as

$$P = V_{rms} i_{rms} \cos\phi$$

$$\Rightarrow \quad P = \frac{100}{\sqrt{2}} \times \frac{100 \times 10^{-3}}{\sqrt{2}} \times \cos\frac{\pi}{3}$$

$$\Rightarrow \quad P = \frac{10^4 \times 10^{-3}}{2} \times \frac{1}{2} = \frac{10}{4} = 2.5 \text{ W}$$

Sol. 7 (D) In case of a transformer if power losses are neglected then output power is same as input power

Sol. 8 (B) By energy conservation we use

$$\frac{1}{2} m v_0^2 = \frac{1}{2} L i_{max}^2$$

$$\Rightarrow \quad i_{max} = \sqrt{\frac{m}{L}} v_0$$

Sol. 9 (C) The circuit current is given as

$$i_{rms} = \frac{V_{rms}}{R} = \frac{200}{40} = 5 \text{ A}$$

$$\Rightarrow \quad i_0 = i_{rms} \sqrt{2} = 7.07 \text{ A}$$

Sol. 10 (D) Input power = 220 V × 0.5 A = 110 W

Output power is 100 W

$$\eta = \frac{100}{110} = 90.9\%, 90\%$$

Sol. 11 (C) At $t = t$ side of square is given as

$$l = (a + 2v_0 t)$$

Area of square is given as

$$S = l^2 = (a + 2v_0 t)^2$$

Magnetic flux through the square is given as

$$\phi = BS = B(a + 2v_0 t)^2$$

EMF induced in the square loop is given as

$$e = \frac{d\phi}{dt} = 4Bv_0 (a + 2v_0 t)$$

Resistance of the loop is given as

$$R = \lambda[4l] = 4\lambda (a + 2v_0 t)$$

Thus current in the loop is given as

$$i = \frac{e}{R} = \frac{Bv_0}{\lambda}$$

Sol. 12 (B) The applied voltage is given by $V = \sqrt{V_R^2 + V_L^2}$

$$V = \sqrt{(200)^2 + (150)^2} = 250 \text{ V}$$

Sol. 13 (B) The total charge flown through the ring is given as

$$\Delta q = \frac{\Delta\phi}{R}$$

$$\Rightarrow \quad i\Delta t = \frac{\Delta\phi}{R}$$

$$\Rightarrow \quad \Delta\phi = i(\Delta t)R$$

$$\Rightarrow \quad \Delta\phi = 10 \times 10^{-3} \times 5 \times 0.5 \text{ Wb}$$

$$\Rightarrow \quad \Delta\phi = 25 \times 10^{-3} \text{ Wb}$$

Sol. 14 (A) At the instant shown in figure, for pure rolling instantaneous axis of rotation is at the bottom point of contact and the conducting rod appears to be rotating about the bottom point Q. Thus the EMF induced in the rod is given as

$$e = \frac{B\omega l^2}{2}$$

$$\Rightarrow \quad e = \frac{B\left(\frac{2v}{l}\right) l^2}{2} = Bvl$$

Sol. 15 (B) The current in circuit is given as

$$i = \frac{V}{\sqrt{R^2 + \omega^2 L^2}} = \frac{120}{\sqrt{100 + 4\pi^2 \times 60^2 \times 20^2}}$$

$$\Rightarrow \quad i = 0.016 \text{ A}$$

Sol. 16 (A) Induced EMF in the sliding connector is given as

$$e = Blv$$

This acts as a cell of EMF Blv and internal resistance R. Effective resistance of the circuit is given as

$$R_{eq} = \frac{R_1 R_2}{R_1 + R_2}$$

Total resistance of the circuit is

$$R_T = R + \frac{R_1 R_2}{R_1 + R_2}$$

Current in circuit is given as

$$i = \frac{Blv}{[R + \{R_1R_2/(R_1 + R_2)\}]}$$

$$\Rightarrow \quad i = \frac{0.1 \times (1/10) \times 1}{[1 + \{(2 \times 3)/(2 + 3)\}]} = \frac{1}{220}\,\text{A}$$

Sol. 17 (A) The voltage across LR series combination is given as

$$V^2 = V_R^2 + V_L^2$$

$$\Rightarrow \quad V_L = \sqrt{V^2 - V_R^2} = \sqrt{400 - 144} = \sqrt{256} = 16\,\text{V}$$

Sol. 18 (A) At time t, angle rotated by loop is $\theta = \omega t$. This is also the angle between direction of magnetic induction and area vector of the loop. At this instant magnetic flux through the loop is given as

$$\phi = BS\cos\theta$$

$$\phi = Bb^2\cos\omega t$$

The EMF induced in the loop is given as

$$e = \left|\frac{d\phi}{dt}\right| = b^2 B\omega \sin\omega t$$

Sol. 19 (A) Given current varies at a rate given as

$$I = (10t + 5)\text{A}$$

$$\frac{dI}{dt} = 10\text{ A/s} = \text{constant}$$

At, $t = 0$, $I = 5$ A so writing equation of potential drop gives

$$V_A - 3 \times 5 - 1 \times 10 + 10 = V_B$$

$$\Rightarrow \quad V_A - V_B = 15\,\text{V}$$

Sol. 20 (A) Phase angle between voltage and current in series LR circuit is given as

$$\tan\phi = \frac{\omega L}{R} = \frac{2\pi \times 200}{300} \times \frac{1}{\pi} = \frac{4}{3}$$

$$\Rightarrow \quad \phi = \tan^{-1}\frac{4}{3}$$

Sol. 21 (C) At resonance $X_L = X_C$ so the currents in the inductance and capacitance branch will be equal and in opposite phase so their phasor sum will be zero and in that case ammeter A_3 will read zero.

Sol. 22 (B) Initial current in the inductor is given as

$$I_i = \frac{10}{10} = 1\text{A}$$

$$\Rightarrow \quad \phi_i = LI_i = 500\text{ m Wb} = 0.5\text{ Wb}$$

Final current through inductor in steady state after closing the switch is given as

$$I_f = \frac{20}{5} = 4\text{A}$$

$$\Rightarrow \quad \phi_f = LI_f = 0.5 \times 4 = 2\text{ Wb}$$

$$\Rightarrow \quad \Delta\phi = 1.5\text{ Wb}$$

Sol. 23 (D) Current will induced in loop-2 if flux changes through loop-2. So current should change with respect to time in loop-1. If current in loop-1 increases with negative value then induced current in loop-2 would be from c to d. As flux produced due to loop-1 is directly proportional to current i_1 then to produce constant current in loop-2 i_1 should linearly increase with time. Hence option (D) is correct.

Sol. 24 (C) Writing equation of potential drop from point A to B gives

$$V_A - 1 \times 5 + 15 + (5 \times 10^{-3})(10^3) = V_B$$

$$\Rightarrow \quad V_B - V_A = 15\,\text{V}$$

Sol. 25 (C) The current as a function of time in LR circuit after closing the switch is given as

$$i = \frac{E}{R}\left(1 - e^{-\frac{Rt}{L}}\right) = i_0\left(1 - e^{-\frac{Rt}{L}}\right)$$

When energy stored in inductor is half the maximum then we have

$$\frac{1}{2}Li^2 = \frac{1}{2}\left[\frac{1}{2}Li_0^2\right]$$

$$\Rightarrow \quad i = \frac{i_0}{\sqrt{2}} = i_0\left(1 - e^{-\frac{Rt}{L}}\right)$$

$$\Rightarrow \quad e^{-\frac{Rt}{L}} = 1 - \frac{1}{\sqrt{2}} = \frac{\sqrt{2} - 1}{\sqrt{2}}$$

$$\Rightarrow \quad \frac{Rt}{L} = \ln\left(\frac{\sqrt{2}}{\sqrt{2} - 1}\right)$$

$$\Rightarrow \quad t = \frac{L}{R}\ln\left(\frac{\sqrt{2}}{\sqrt{2} - 1}\right)$$

Sol. 26 (C) Inductive reactance of the inductor is given as

$$Z = X_L = 2\pi \times 60 \times 0.7$$

Thus circuit current is given as

$$\Rightarrow \quad i=\frac{120}{Z}=\frac{120}{2\pi\times 60\times 0.7}=0.455\text{ A}$$

Sol. 27 (B) Flux change in coil *Y* is related to current change in coil *X* as

$$\phi = Mi$$

$$\Rightarrow \quad d\phi = M\,di$$

$$\Rightarrow \quad M=\frac{d\phi}{di}$$

$$\Rightarrow \quad M=\frac{1.2}{3}=0.4\text{ H}$$

Sol. 28 (A) The magnetic induction due to wire at a distance a from wire is given as

$$B=\frac{\mu_0}{2\pi}\frac{i}{a}$$

Force on a charge q moving in magnetic induction is given as

$$F = Bqv\sin 90°$$

$$\Rightarrow \quad F=\frac{\mu_0 iqv}{2\pi a}$$

Sol. 29 (A) EMF induced in the triangular loop is given as

$$e=\frac{d\phi}{dt}$$

$$\Rightarrow \quad e = A\frac{dB}{dt}$$

Area of Triangle is given as

$$A=\frac{\sqrt{3}}{4}\times(\text{side})^2$$

$$\Rightarrow \quad A=\frac{\sqrt{3}}{4}\times 2\times 2=\sqrt{3}\text{ m}^2$$

$$\Rightarrow \quad e=\sqrt{3}\times\sqrt{3}=3\text{ V}$$

By symmetry in each rod emf will be 1 V. The current in the triangular loop is given as

$$i=\frac{e}{R}=\frac{3}{5}=0.6\text{ A}$$

Voltage drop between *A* and *B* = 0.6 × 1 = 0.6 V

So voltage across *AB* is given as

$$V_{AB}=e_{AB}-iR=1-0.6\times 1$$

$$V_{AB}=1-0.6=0.4\text{ V}$$

Sol. 30 (C) Voltages in the given circuit are related as

$$V^2=V_R^2+(V_L-V_C)^2$$

$$\Rightarrow \quad V_R=V=220\text{ V}$$

Circuit current is given as

$$i=\frac{220}{100}=2.2\text{ A}$$

Sol. 31 (B) When the coil is rotated through 180°, the flux changes from ϕ to $-\phi$. Hence change in flux is $\phi-(-\phi)=2\phi$ and we use $\phi = Mi$.

So change in current is $2i$. This causes a deflection of 14 units.

Sol. 32 (D) At the instant shown in figure, for pure rolling instantaneous axis of rotation is at the bottom point of contact and the conducting rod appears to be rotating about the bottom point *Q*. Thus the EMF induced in the rod is given as

$$e=\frac{B\omega l^2}{2}$$

$$\Rightarrow \quad e=\frac{(B)(v/2R)(4R)^2}{2}$$

$$\Rightarrow \quad e=2BvR$$

Sol. 33 (D) Circuit impedance for series *RLC* circuit is given as

$$Z=\sqrt{(R)^2+(X_L-X_C)^2}$$

$$R=10\,\Omega,\ X_L=\omega L=2000\times 5\times 10^{-3}=10\,\Omega$$

$$X_C=\frac{1}{\omega C}=\frac{1}{2000\times 50\times 10^{-6}}=10\,\Omega \text{ i.e. } Z=10\,\Omega$$

As $X_L=X_C$ so circuit is in resonance and current in circuit is given as

$$i_0=\frac{V_0}{Z}=\frac{20}{10}=2\text{ A}$$

$$\Rightarrow \quad i_{\text{rms}}=\frac{2}{\sqrt{2}}=1.41\text{ A}$$

Voltmeter reading is equal to the voltage across the resistance as at resonance phasor voltage of capacitor and inductor gets cancelled out

$$V_{\text{rms}}=i_{\text{rms}}R=4\times 1.41=5.64\text{ V}$$

Sol. 34 (B) Charge flown q is given as

$$q=\frac{\Delta\phi}{R}$$

$$\Rightarrow \quad q=\frac{NBA}{R}$$

$$\Rightarrow \quad q = \frac{50 \times 0.2 \times (100 \times 10^{-4})}{2}\,\text{C}$$

$$\Rightarrow \quad q = 0.5\,\text{C}$$

Sol. 35 (B) The decaying current in a short circuited choke coil is given as

$$i = i_0 e^{-Rt/L}$$

$$\Rightarrow \quad \beta i_0 = i_0 e^{-T/\tau}$$

$$\Rightarrow \quad \tau = \frac{T}{\ln(1/\beta)}$$

Sol. 36 (D) Power supplied by external agent in moving the loop will be used as internal energy in the loop which is given as

$$P = Fv = 10 \times 2 = 20\,\text{W}$$

Sol. 37 (A) Induced EMF in the rod is given as

$$e = (\vec{v} \times \vec{B}) \cdot \vec{l}$$

Velocity of the rod is given as

$$\vec{v} = 2\hat{i}$$

Magnetic induction in the region is given as

$$\vec{B} = 3\hat{i} + 4\hat{k}$$

Vector length of the rod is given as

$$\vec{l} = (5\cos 53^\circ)\,\hat{i} + (5\sin 53^\circ)\,\hat{i} = 3\hat{i} + 4\hat{k}$$

So EMF induced is given as

$$e = [(2\hat{i}) \times (3\hat{j} + 4\hat{k})] \cdot [3\hat{i} + 4\hat{j}]$$

$$\Rightarrow \quad e = (6\hat{k} - 8\hat{i}) \cdot (3\hat{i} + 4\hat{j})$$

$$\Rightarrow \quad e = -32\,\text{V}$$

Sol. 38 (A) Capacitance of wire is given as

$$C = 0.014 \times 10^{-6} \times 200 = 2.8 \times 10^{-6}\,\text{F} = 2.8\,\mu\text{F}$$

For impedance of the circuit to be minimum, we use

$$X_L = X_C$$

$$\Rightarrow \quad 2\pi\nu L = \frac{1}{2\pi\nu C}$$

$$\Rightarrow \quad L = \frac{1}{4\pi^2\nu^2 C} = \frac{1}{4(3.14)^2 \times (5 \times 10^3)^2 \times 2.8 \times 10^{-6}}\,\text{H}$$

$$\Rightarrow \quad L = 0.35 \times 10^{-3}\,\text{H} = 0.35\,\text{mH}$$

Sol. 39 (B) Heat dissipated in choke coil will be the amount of magnetic energy stored in it which appears as joule heat. In steady state condition it is given that

$$P = i_0^2 R$$

$$\Rightarrow \quad i_0^2 = \frac{P}{R}$$

and we have time constant of circuit as

$$\tau = \frac{L}{R}$$

$$\Rightarrow \quad L = \tau R$$

Heat dissipated in current decay is given as

$$H = \frac{1}{2} L i_0^2$$

$$\Rightarrow \quad H = \frac{1}{2}(\tau R)\left(\frac{P}{R}\right) = \frac{1}{2} P\tau$$

Sol. 40 (D) Motional EMF across the wings is given as

$$e = vBl$$

$$\Rightarrow \quad e = (360 \times 5/18) \times (4 \times 10^{-4}) \times 50$$

$$\Rightarrow \quad e = 2\,\text{V}$$

Sol. 41 (C) Mean square current is given as

$$\langle i^2 \rangle = \frac{\int_{t_1}^{t_2} i^2 dt}{\int_{t_1}^{t_2} dt}$$

$$\Rightarrow \quad \langle i^2 \rangle = \frac{\int_{t_1}^{t_2} (4t) dt}{\int_{t_1}^{t_2} dt}$$

$$\Rightarrow \quad \langle i^2 \rangle = \frac{4\left[\frac{t^2}{2}\right]_2^4}{(4-2)} = [16-4] = 12\,\text{s}$$

$$\Rightarrow \quad i_{\text{rms}} = \sqrt{\langle i^2 \rangle} = \sqrt{12} = 2\sqrt{3}\,\text{A}$$

Sol. 42 (B) By short circuiting the battery, Thevenin's resistance across inductor is given as

$$r_{th} = \frac{R}{2}$$

$$\Rightarrow \quad \tau = \frac{L}{r_{th}} = \frac{2L}{R}$$

Sol. 43 (B) Charge flown through the ring due to change in flux is given as

$$\Delta q = \frac{\Delta\phi}{R}$$

Where change in flux through the ring is given as

$$\Delta\phi = \frac{\pi d^2 B}{4} - 0$$

$$\Rightarrow \quad \Delta q = \frac{\pi d^2 B}{4R} = \frac{3.14\times(0.2)^2\times 2}{4\times 0.01}$$

$$\Rightarrow \quad \Delta q = 6.28\,\text{C}$$

Sol. 44 (D) At resonance net voltage across L and C in series is zero so reading of V_4 is zero.

Sol. 45 (D) Initial magnetic flux passing through the square loop can be calculated by integrating the flux through an elemental strip considered in the square loop as shown in figure below, which is given as

$$\phi_i = \int_b^{b+a} \frac{\mu_0}{2\pi}\frac{i}{x}(adx)$$

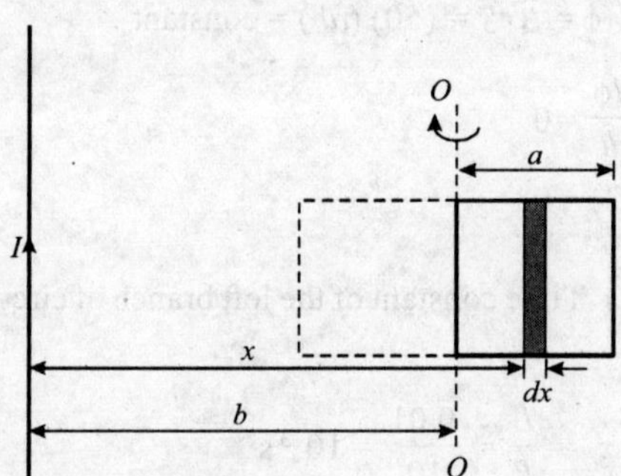

$$\phi_i = \frac{\mu_0 ia}{2\pi}\ln\left(\frac{b+a}{b}\right)$$

Similarly after 180° rotation, final flux is given as

$$\phi_f = \frac{\mu_0 ia}{2\pi}\ln\left(\frac{b-a}{b}\right)$$

$$\Rightarrow \quad \Delta\phi = |\phi_i - \phi_f| = \frac{\mu_0 ia}{2\pi}\ln\left(\frac{b+a}{b-a}\right)$$

Charge flown through the loop in process of rotation is given as

$$\Rightarrow \quad \Delta q = \frac{\Delta\phi}{R} = \frac{\mu_0 ia}{2\pi R}\ln\left(\frac{b+a}{b-a}\right)$$

Sol. 46 (C) $i_L = \frac{90}{30} = 3\,\text{A}, i_C = \frac{90}{20} = 4.5\,\text{A}$

Net current through the AC source is given by phasor sum of the two currents which are in opposite phase which is given as

$$i = i_C - i_L = 1.5\,\text{A}$$

Thus circuit impedance is given as

$$Z = \frac{V}{i} = \frac{90}{1.5} = 60\,\Omega$$

Sol. 47 (B) At $t = 0$, $i = E/R$ in steady state when switch is in position-1.

Now this current will decay in closed loop in anti-clockwise direction when switch is shifted to position-2. So $i_{20} = E/R$ is the initial current after witch is shifted to position-2.

Thus we have

$$i_1 = \frac{E}{R}$$

and

$$i_2 = -\frac{E}{R}$$

Sol. 48 (A) As the current i leads the voltage by $\frac{\pi}{4}$, it is an RC circuit, for which the phase difference between EMF and current is given as

$$\tan\phi = \frac{X_C}{R}$$

$$\Rightarrow \quad \tan\frac{\pi}{4} = \frac{1}{\omega CR}$$

$$\Rightarrow \quad \omega CR = 1$$

$$\Rightarrow \quad CR = \frac{1}{100}\,\text{s}^{-1}$$

From all the given options only option-(A) is correct.

Sol. 49 (B) Current in the circuit branch shown is given as

$$i = \frac{dq}{dt} = (8t)\text{A}$$

At $t = 1$ s, $q = 4$ C and $i = 8$ A

$$\Rightarrow \quad \frac{di}{dt} = 8\,\text{A/s}$$

Charge on capacitor is increasing, so charge on positive plate is also increasing. Hence direction of current is towards left as shown in figure.

We write the equation of potential drop from point a to b which gives

$$V_a + 2\times 8 - 4 + 2\times 8 + \frac{4}{2} = V_b$$

$$\Rightarrow \quad V_a - V_b = -30\text{ V}$$

Sol. 50 (B) EMF induced in a rotating coil in uniform magnetic induction is given as

$$e = NBA\omega \sin\omega t$$

Maximum EMF induced is given as

$$e_0 = \omega NBA$$

$$\Rightarrow \quad e_0 = (2\pi\nu)\,\text{NB}\,(\pi r^2)$$

$$\Rightarrow \quad e_0 = 2\pi^2 \nu\, NBr^2$$

$$\Rightarrow \quad e_0 = 2\times(3.14)^2 \times \frac{1800}{60}\times 4000\times 0.5\times 10^{-4}\times(7\times 10^{-2})^2$$

$$\Rightarrow \quad e_0 = 0.58\text{ V}$$

Sol. 51 (C) Steady state current through inductor in initial stage when switch is in position-1 is E/R. So at $t = 0$, current in closed loop when switch is shifted to position-2 will remain same as at initial instant capacitor behaves like short circuit.

Sol. 52 (D) Work done in pulling the loop out of magnetic field is given as

$$W = I\Delta\phi$$

$$\Rightarrow \quad W = \left(\frac{E}{R}\right)\Delta\phi$$

$$\Rightarrow \quad W = \left(\frac{\Delta\phi}{R\Delta t}\right)\Delta\phi$$

$$\Rightarrow \quad W = \frac{(BS)^2}{R\Delta t} = \frac{(0.4\times 2.5\times 10^{-3}\times 100)^2}{100\times 1} = 0.1\text{ mJ}$$

Sol. 53 (B) Rate of current variation is given as

$$\frac{dI}{dt} = I_0\omega\cos\omega t$$

EMF induced in the second coil is given as

$$e = M\frac{dI}{dt} = MI_0\omega\cos\omega t$$

$$\Rightarrow \quad e_{\text{max}} = MI_0\omega$$

$$e_{\text{max}} = 0.005\times 10\times 100\,\pi$$

$$e_{\text{max}} = (5\pi)\text{ V}$$

Sol. 54 (A) At time $t = 0$, resistance capacitor behaves like short circuit and inductor behaves like open circuit so at this instant circuit resistance across the battery will be

$$R_{\text{net}} = \frac{R}{2} + \frac{R}{3} = \frac{5R}{6} = 5\,\Omega$$

Current through the battery at $t = 0$ is given as

$$i = \frac{E}{R_{\text{net}}} = \frac{5}{5} = 1\text{ A}$$

Sol. 55 (A) EMF induced in the loop is given as

$$e = \frac{d\phi}{dt} = \frac{d}{at}(BA) = A\frac{dB}{dt} = A\frac{\Delta B}{\Delta t}$$

$$\Rightarrow \quad 10 = \frac{10}{100}\times\frac{10}{100}\times\frac{20}{\Delta t}$$

$$\Rightarrow \quad \Delta t = 20\text{ ms}$$

Sol. 56 (D) Area vector of the loop which is perpendicular to x-y plane, is given as

$$\vec{S} = (ab)\,\vec{k}$$

Magnetic flux through the area of loop is given as

$$\phi = \vec{B}\cdot\vec{S} = (50)\,(ab) = \text{constant}$$

$$\Rightarrow \quad \frac{d\phi}{dt} = 0$$

$$\Rightarrow \quad e = 0$$

Sol. 57 (A) Time constant of the left branch of circuit is given as

$$\tau_L = \frac{L}{R} = \frac{0.01}{10} = 10^{-3}\text{ s}$$

Time constant of the right branch of circuit is given as

$$\tau_C = CR = (0.1\times 10^{-3})(10) = 10^{-3}\text{s}$$

Steady state currents in left and right branch of circuit are given as

$$(i_0)_L = \frac{20}{10} = 2\text{ A}$$

$$(i_0)_C = \frac{20}{10} = 2\text{ A}$$

The given time is the half-life time of both left and right branches of the circuit so current in branches at this instant are given as

$$i_L = i_C = \frac{2}{2} = 1\text{ A}$$

Thus total current through the battery at this instant is 2 A.

Sol. 58 (B) To calculate the magnetic flux through the rectangular loop, we consider an elemental strip in the loop as shown in figure.

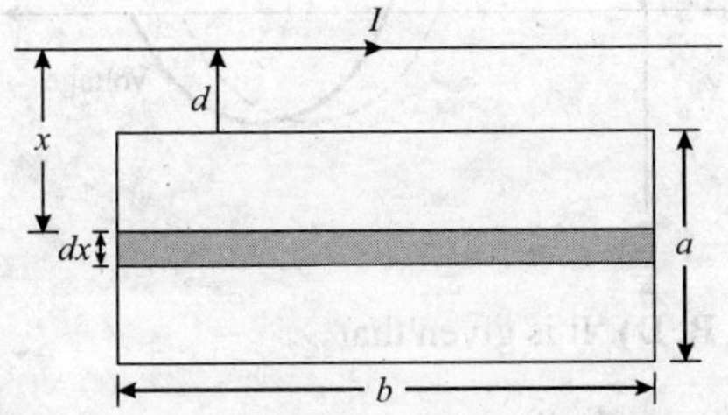

The strip is of width dx and at a distance x distance from wire carrying current I, the magnetic flux through the strip is given as

$$d\phi = \frac{\mu_0 I}{2\pi x} \cdot b dx$$

Total magnetic flux linked with the loop is given as

$$\phi = \int d\phi$$

$$\Rightarrow \quad \phi = \int_a^{a+b} \frac{\mu_0 I}{2\pi x} . b dx$$

$$\Rightarrow \quad \phi = \frac{\mu_0 I b}{2\pi} [\ln x]_a^{a+b}$$

$$\Rightarrow \quad \phi = \frac{\mu_0 I b}{2\pi} [\ln (a+b) - \ln a]$$

$$\Rightarrow \quad \phi = \frac{\mu_0 I b}{2\pi} \ln\left(\frac{a+b}{a}\right)$$

EMF induced in the loop is given as

$$e = \left|\frac{d\phi}{dt}\right|$$

$$\Rightarrow \quad e = \frac{\mu_0 b}{2\pi} \ln\left(\frac{a+b}{a}\right) \cdot \frac{dI}{dt}$$

$$\Rightarrow \quad e = \frac{\mu_0 b}{2\pi} \ln\left(\frac{a+b}{a}\right) \cdot \frac{d}{dt}(I_0 e^{-t/\tau})$$

$$\Rightarrow \quad e = \frac{\mu_0 b I_0}{2\pi\tau} \ln\left(\frac{a+b}{a}\right) e^{-t/\tau}$$

Sol. 59 (C) Value remains $\frac{1}{4}$ th in 20 ms times. Hence two half lives are equal to 20 ms. So, one half-life is 10 ms thus we use

$$t_{1/2} = (\ln 2)\,\tau_C = (\ln 2)\frac{L}{R}$$

$$\Rightarrow \quad R = \frac{(\ln 2)L}{t_{1/2}}$$

$$\Rightarrow \quad R = \frac{(\ln 2)(2)}{10\times 10^{-3}} = (100 \ln 4)\,\Omega$$

Sol. 60 (D) EMF induced in a loop in time varying magnetic field is given as

$$|e| = \frac{d\phi}{dt} = S\frac{dB}{dt}$$

$$\Rightarrow \quad |e| = (4b^2 - \pi a^2)B_0$$

Induced current in the loop is given as

$$i = \frac{|e|}{R} = \frac{(4b^2 - \pi a^2)B_0}{R}$$

The direction of induced current is given by Lenz's law to oppose the increasing magnetic induction as shown in figure below.

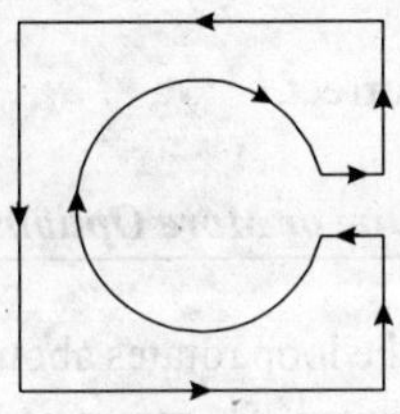

Sol. 61 (D) EMF induced in the wire frame is given as

$$e = \frac{-d}{dt}\phi$$

$$\Rightarrow \quad e = -B\frac{d}{dt}\text{A}$$

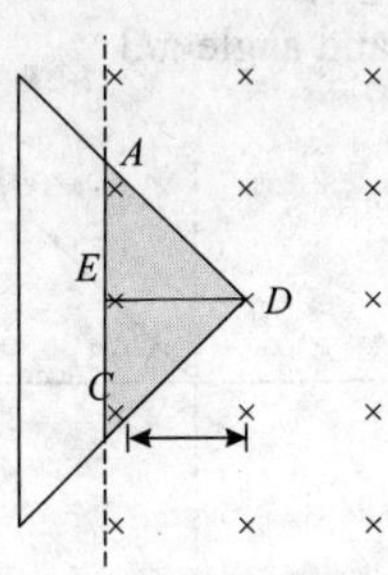

The shaded triangle area will change as loop will move towards magnetic field and the flux in this area through the loop increases with time. In the above figure shown, we have

$$\angle ADC = \frac{\pi}{2}$$

and $\angle AED = \dfrac{\pi}{4}$

If $ED = x$ then $AC = 2x$

So area of ΔACD is given as

$$S = \frac{1}{2} \times x \times 2x = x^2$$

Here we use $\dfrac{dx}{dt} = v$ and $\dfrac{dA}{dt} = \dfrac{2xdx}{dt} = 2xv$

Thus EMF induced is given as

$$e = 2Bxv$$

As $x = vt$, EMF induced is given as

$$e = 2Bv^2t$$

Induced current in the loop is given as

$$I = \frac{2Bv^2}{R}t$$

$$\Rightarrow \quad I \propto t$$

Thus option (D) is correct.

ADVANCE MCQs One or More Options Correct

Sol. 1 (A, C, D) If the loop rotates about Z axis, the variation of flux linkage will be zero. Therefore no EMF is induced in the ring consequently no current flows in the loop. When it rotates about y axis, its flux linkage changes. However, in insulators there can not be motional EMF. If the loop is made of copper, it is conductive therefore induced current is set up. If the loop moves along the Z axis variation of flux linkage is zero. Therefore the EMF and current will be equal to zero.

Sol. 2 (B, C, D) The graph below shows V & I phasors. Current leads the voltage by and angle $\pi/3$

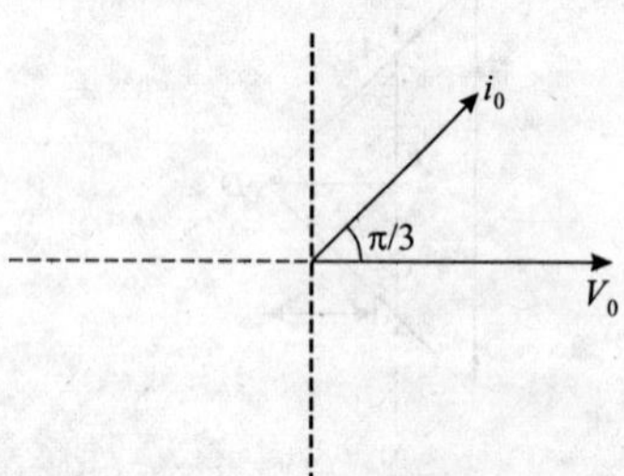

Power is positive if V & I are of same sign

Power is negative if V & I are of opposite sign

If $\omega\uparrow \Rightarrow \dfrac{1}{\omega C}\downarrow$ thus angle decreases

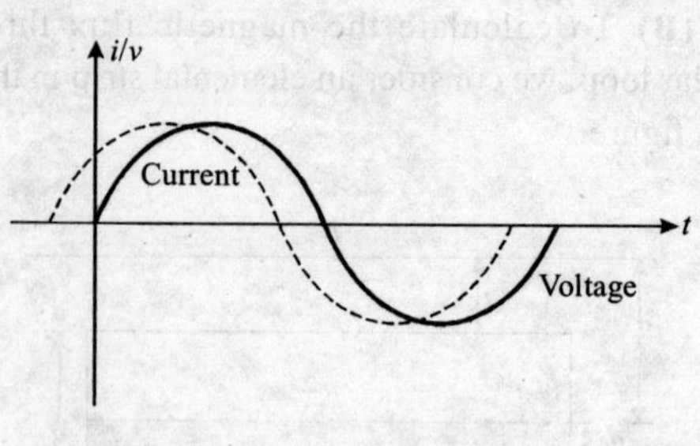

Sol. 3 (A, B, D) It is given that

$$(di/dt)_1 = (di/dt)_2$$

$$\Rightarrow \quad \frac{e_1}{e_2} = \frac{L_1}{L_2} = \frac{8\text{mH}}{2\text{mH}} = 4\text{ mH}$$

$$\Rightarrow \quad \frac{V_2}{V_1} = \frac{e_2}{e_1} = \frac{1}{4}$$

As power given to the two coils is same at an instant, we have

$$P_1 = P_2$$

$$\Rightarrow \quad V_1 i_1 = V_2 i_2$$

$$\Rightarrow \quad (i_1/i_2) = (V_2/V_1) = 1/4 \qquad \ldots(1)$$

$$\Rightarrow \quad \frac{W_1}{W_2} = \frac{\frac{1}{2}L_1 i_1^2}{\frac{1}{2}L_2 i_2^2} = \left(\frac{L_1}{L_2}\right)\left(\frac{i_1}{i_2}\right)^2$$

$$\Rightarrow \quad \frac{W_1}{W_2} = 4 \times \left(\frac{1}{4}\right)^2 = \frac{1}{4}$$

$$\Rightarrow \quad \frac{W_2}{W_1} = 4 \qquad \ldots(2)$$

Sol. 4 (A, B) The mutual inductance between two coils is given as

$$M = \frac{\mu_0 N_1 N_2 \pi r_2^2}{2r_1}$$

So, it depends upon the number of turns in each coil and area of cross-section of the coils.

Sol. 5 (A, B, C) Self induced EMF will have a direction such that it opposes the change in current in the conductor/coil. If current is decreasing, it tend to increase the current and if current is increasing, it tend to decrease the current. Self induced EMF have a tendency to keep the current same and opposes the change in current in the conductor/coil.

Sol. 6 (A, C) Motional EMF induced across the points P and Q is given as

$$e = Bvl$$

Where $l = \frac{L}{2}$

Polarity of this motional EMF is given by right palm rule.

Sol. 7 (A, C) For the given situation

$$\frac{q}{C} + L\frac{di}{dt} = 0$$

$$\Rightarrow \quad \frac{d^2q}{dt^2} + \frac{q}{LC} = 0$$

Comparing with standard differential equation of SHM for oscillation of q which is given as

$$\frac{d^2q}{dt^2} + \omega^2 q = 0$$

The solution to above equation is given as

$$q = q_0 \cos \omega t$$

and $\quad i = -q_0\omega \sin \omega t$

According to given conditions

$$\frac{q^2}{2C} = \frac{1}{2}Li^2$$

$$\Rightarrow \quad \frac{q_0 \cos^2 \omega t}{2C} = \frac{1}{2}Lq_0{}^2\omega^2 \sin^2\omega t$$

$$\Rightarrow \quad \cot^2\omega t = 1$$

$$\Rightarrow \quad \omega t = \frac{\pi}{4}, \frac{3\pi}{4}, \frac{5\pi}{4}, \frac{7\pi}{4} \ldots\ldots$$

$$\Rightarrow t = \frac{\pi\sqrt{LC}}{4}, \frac{3\pi\sqrt{LC}}{4}, \frac{5\pi\sqrt{LC}}{4}, \frac{7\pi\sqrt{LC}}{4} \ldots\ldots$$

Sol. 8 (A, C) The magnetic flux through the square loop due to the current in straight wire can be obtained by considering an elemental strip in the loop as shown in figure.

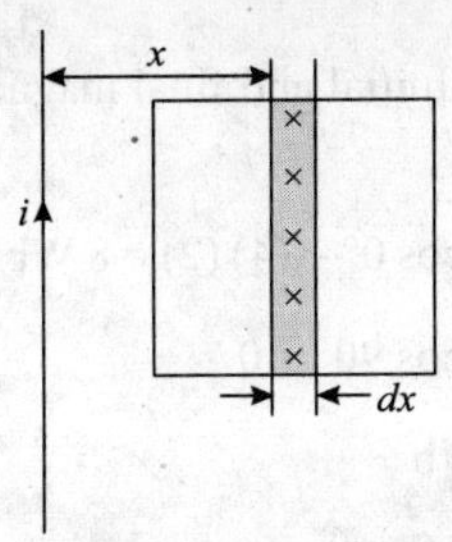

The magnetic flux through the elemental strip is given as

$$d\phi = (B_x)\, dS = \left(\frac{\mu_0\, i}{2\pi\, x}\right)(adx)$$

Total magnetic flux through the loop can be given as

$$\phi = \int_a^{2a} d\phi = \frac{\mu_0 ia}{2\pi}\ln 2$$

Thus mutual induction between the wire and the loop can be given as

$$M = \frac{\phi}{i} = \frac{\mu_0 a}{2\pi}\ln 2$$

Current in straight wire produces an outward magnetic field over the loop. If the loop is brought close to the wire outward magnetic field passing through the loop increases. According to Lenz's law induced current produces an inward magnetic field to oppose the increment in the magnetic flux through it. Thus induced current in loop is clockwise.

Hence options (A) and (C) are correct.

Sol. 9 (All) For a series RLC circuit, impedance is given as

$$Z = \sqrt{R^2 + \left(\omega L - \frac{1}{\omega C}\right)^2}$$

$$\Rightarrow Z = \sqrt{100^2 + \left(2\pi\left(\frac{500}{\pi}\right)(100\times10^{-3}) - \frac{1}{2\pi\left(\frac{500}{\pi}\right)(5\times10^{-6})}\right)^2}$$

$$\Rightarrow Z = 100\sqrt{2}\,\Omega = 141.4\,\Omega$$

Circuit Current is given as

$$i = \frac{e}{Z} = \frac{150\sqrt{2}}{100\sqrt{2}} = 1.5\text{ A}$$

Average power dissipated across resistance is given as

$$P = i^2R = (1.5)^2 \times 100 = 225\text{ W}$$

Across inductor and capacitor being reactive circuit components no average power is consumed.

Hence all options are correct.

Sol. 10 (A, C) Self inductance of a coil is given as

$$L = \frac{N\phi}{i}$$

$$\Rightarrow \quad \phi = \frac{Li}{N}$$

Thus SI unit of magnetic flux is henry-ampere. Self inductance can also be expressed as

$$L = \frac{-e}{\Delta i/\Delta t} = \frac{-e\Delta t}{\Delta i}$$

Thus SI unit of self inductance can also be given as V-s/ampere.

Sol. 11 (D) To move the conductor with uniform velocity net force on conductor must be equal to zero. Thus the force required toward right will balance the magnetic force on conductor in leftward direction, so we have

$$F_{\text{applied}} \text{ (rightwards)} = F_{magnetic} \text{ (leftwards)}$$

$$F_{\text{applied}} = IlB = (I_1 + I_2 + I_3)lB$$

Emf induced across the conductor is given as

$$e = Bvl = 4 \times 2 \times 1 = 8\text{ V}$$

Current through resistance is given as

$$I_1 = \frac{V_R}{R} = \frac{8}{2} = 4\text{A}$$

As potential difference across capacitor is constant, current through it will be zero as its charge will remain constant in steady state. Thus we have

$$I_2 = \frac{dq}{dt} = \frac{d}{dt}(CV_C) = \frac{d}{dt}(8) = 0$$

For inductor we, the potential difference across it will remain constant at 8 V so its current is given as

$$I_3 = \frac{Vt}{L} = \frac{8 \times 2}{4} = 4\text{ A}$$

Thus applied force on conductor toward right is given as

$$F_{\text{applied}} = (4+4)(1)(4) = 32\text{ N}$$

Sol. 12 (A, B, D) Time constant of the circuit is given as

$$\tau_L = \frac{L}{R} = \frac{2}{2} = 1\text{ s}$$

Half life time of the above circuit for the current growth is given as

$$t_{1/2} = (\ln 2)\,\tau_L = (\ln 2)\text{ s}$$

Thus the given time is half life time so in this period current reduces to half which is given as

$$i = \frac{i_0}{2} = \frac{8/2}{2} = 2\text{ A}$$

Rate of energy supplied by battery is given as

$$P = Ei = 8 \times 2 = 16\text{ J/s}$$

Power dissipated as heat across resistance is given as

$$P_R = i^2R = (2)^2(2) = 8\text{ J/s}$$

Potential difference across the inductor is given as

$$V_a - V_b = E - iR = 8 - 2 \times 2 = 4\text{ V}$$

Sol. 13 (A, C) In all materials due to phenomenon of induction always dipole induction take place in direction opposite to the external magnetic field so upto some level diamagnetic character always exist in all materials.

Sol. 14 (C) As inductance is not known we cannot compare the potential difference across the two bulbs so their brightness cannot be compared when glowing. As frequency of supply voltage increases the reactance of the upper branch decreases so and that of lower branch increases so current in upper branch increases and in lower branch decreases. Thus brightness of bulb B_1 increase and that of B_2 will decrease.

Sol. 15 (A, C) According to Lenz's law, induced effects always oppose the change i_1 and i_2 both are in same direction. Hence magnetic lines from B due to both currents are from right to left. By bringing A closer to B or increasing i_1 right to left magnetic field from B will increase. So i_2 should decrease.

Sol. 16 (B) In first case, terminal speed is attained when current in circuit becomes zero. It happens when

$$E = Bvl$$

$$v_0 = \frac{E}{Bl} \quad \text{...(i)}$$

In second case, when a force F_0 is applied, the terminal speed is attained when the external force balances the magnetic force on the rod, given as

$$F_0 - \left(\frac{E - Blv}{r}\right) \times Bl = 0$$

$$\Rightarrow \quad v = \frac{E}{Bl} - \frac{FR}{B^2l^2} \quad \text{...(ii)}$$

The difference in terminal speed in presence of external force is given as

$$\Delta v = \frac{FR}{B^2l^2}$$

Now if magnetic field is decreased to $B/3$, the new terminal speed will become

$$\Delta v' = \frac{FR}{\left(\frac{B}{3}\right)^2 l^2} = 9\,\Delta v$$

$$\Rightarrow \quad \Delta v' = 9 \times 20 = 180\text{ cm/s}$$

Sol. 17 (B, C, D) Initial and final magnetic flux through the coil are given as

$$\phi_i = BS\cos 0° = (4)(2) = 8\text{ Wb}$$

$$\phi_f = BS\cos 90° = 0$$

$$\Delta\phi = 8\text{ Wb}$$

EMF induced in the coil is given as

$$|e| = \frac{\Delta\phi}{\Delta t} = \frac{8}{0.1} = 80\text{ V}$$

Current through the coil is given as

$$i = \frac{|e|}{R} = 20\text{ A}$$

Charge flown through the coil is given as

$$\Delta q = \frac{\Delta\phi}{R} = 2\text{ C}$$

This current is not constant. So, we cannot find the heat generated unless current function with time is not known.

Sol. 18 (A, C) The current as a function of time in series RL circuit is given as

$$i = \frac{E}{R}\left(1 - e^{-\frac{Rt}{L}}\right)$$

Differentiating above equation we get the slope of above curve which is given as

$$\frac{di}{dt} = \frac{E}{L}e^{-\frac{Rt}{L}}$$

In curve B shown in figure slope is less but saturation current is same that means E/R is constant but E/L is decreased. Hence options (A) and (C) are correct.

Sol. 19 (B, C) The current in circuit is given as

$$i_{max} = \omega q_0 = \left(\frac{1}{\sqrt{LC}}\right)q_0$$

$$\Rightarrow \quad \left(\frac{di}{dt}\right)_{max} = \omega^2 q_0 = \left(\frac{1}{LC}\right)q_0$$

Sol. 20 (A, C, D) Soft iron is a ferromagnetic material so it has high permeability and self inductance of a solenoid is directly proportional to permeability of the inside medium. This increases the inside flux but no effect on the steady state current. Due to increase in L energy stored in it and magnetic moment increases.

Sol. 21 (B, C, D) If inward magnetic field increases than induced electric lines are anti-clockwise and if inward magnetic field decreases, then induced electric lines are clockwise both inside and outside the cylindrical region.

On positive charge, force is in the direction of $\vec{E}$. On negative charge, force is in the opposite direction of $\vec{E}$. Hence options (B), (C) and (D) are correct.

Sol. 22 (B, C, D) As loops are approaching each other, the magnetic flux due to each other increases so according to Lenz's law the induced current in the two will have a tendency to oppose this and induced current will be in opposite direction. The induced current may or may not be higher in magnitude than their initial current so the loops may attract or repel each other depending upon their final currents are in same direction or opposite directions.

Sol. 23 (A, B, C) The current in circuit branch is given as

$$q = 2t^2$$

$$\Rightarrow \quad i = \frac{dq}{dt} = 4t$$

$$\Rightarrow \quad \frac{di}{dt} = 4\text{ A/s}$$

At $t = 1$ s, $q = 2C$, $i = 4$ A and $\frac{di}{dt} = 4$ A/s, the potential difference across the inductor is given as

$$V_a - V_b = L\frac{di}{dt} = 1 \times 4 = 4\text{ V}$$

Potential difference across the capacitor is given as

$$V_b - V_c = \frac{q}{C} = \frac{2}{2} = 1\text{ V}$$

Potential difference across the resistor is given as

$$V_c - V_d = iR = 4 \times 4 = 16\text{ V}$$

Summing up all the above three equations gives

$$V_a - V_d = 21\text{ V}$$

Sol. 24 (A, C) As ba and bc are equal the potential difference of a and c will be same so we have

$$V_a - V_c = 0$$

$$\text{and} \quad V_a - V_b = V_c - V_b = \frac{B\omega l^2}{2}$$

Sol. 25 (B, D) The two halves of the rotating rod behave as motional EMFs so the equivalent circuit of the given system looks like shown in figure.

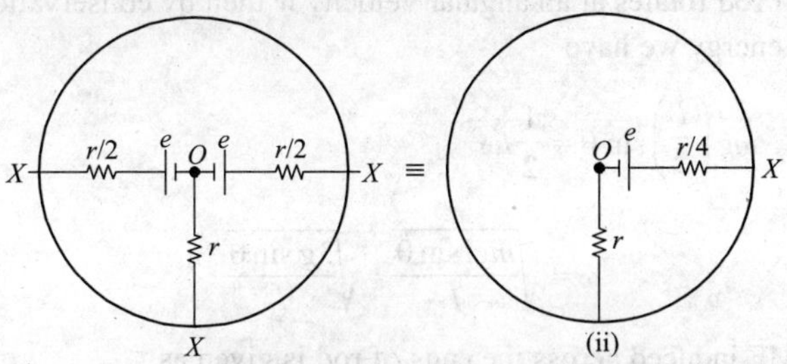

Induced emf in each half of rod is given as

$$e = \left(\frac{B\omega a^2}{2}\right)$$

If X is the potential of ring and taking potential at O to be zero, using *KCL* equation gives

$$4\left(\frac{X-e}{r}\right)+\left(\frac{X-0}{r}\right)=0$$

$$\Rightarrow \quad 5X=4e$$

$$\Rightarrow \quad X=\frac{4e}{5}=\frac{2B\omega a^2}{5}$$

and $\quad I=\frac{X}{r}=\frac{2B\omega a^2}{5r}$

The direction of current in '*r*' will be towards low potential terminal i.e. from rim to origin.

Sol. 26 (B) The current as a function of time in discharging of a capacitor is given as

$$i=\frac{V}{R}e^{-\frac{t}{RC}}$$

$$\Rightarrow \quad \ln i=-\left(\frac{1}{RC}\right)t+\ln\left(\frac{V}{R}\right)$$

In graph-2 the intercept on *y*-axis is same but slope is decreased so from above equation we can see that (*V*/*R*) remain same and (1/*RC*) is decreased. Hence only option (B) is correct.

Sol. 27 (B, C) EMF induced in the loop is given as

$$e=\left|\frac{d\phi}{dt}\right|$$

The area under the curve gives

$$\phi_i-\phi_i=\int d\phi=\int e\,dt$$

Which is change in flux that remain constant
Charge flow through the loop is given as

$$\Delta q=\frac{\text{flux change}}{R}=\text{constant}$$

Sol. 28 (A, D) When rod is released from rest then at an angle θ if rod rotates at an angular velocity *w* then by conservation of energy we have

$$mg\left(\frac{l}{2}\right)\sin\theta=\frac{1}{2}I\omega^2$$

$$\omega=\sqrt{\frac{mgl\sin\theta}{I}}=\sqrt{\frac{3g\sin\theta}{l}}$$

EMF induced across the ends of rod is given as

$$e=\frac{1}{2}B\omega l^2=\frac{1}{2}B\left(\sqrt{\frac{3g\sin\theta}{l}}\right)l^2$$

Sol. 29 (A, B, D) In a time varying magnetic field the EMF induced in the ring is given as

$$e=A\frac{dB}{dt}=\pi a^2\alpha$$

This EMF is distributed in all the elements of the ring and a steady current flows in the ring due to which across all elements the EMF induced and potential drop due to current remain same so all points of the ring will remain at same potentials. The electric field intensity at the points on ring is given as

$$E=\frac{1}{2}a\frac{dB}{dt}=\frac{1}{2}a\alpha$$

Sol. 30 (B, D) The rod is equivalent to a rod joining the ends *P* and *R* of the rod rotating in the same sense as shown in figure below.

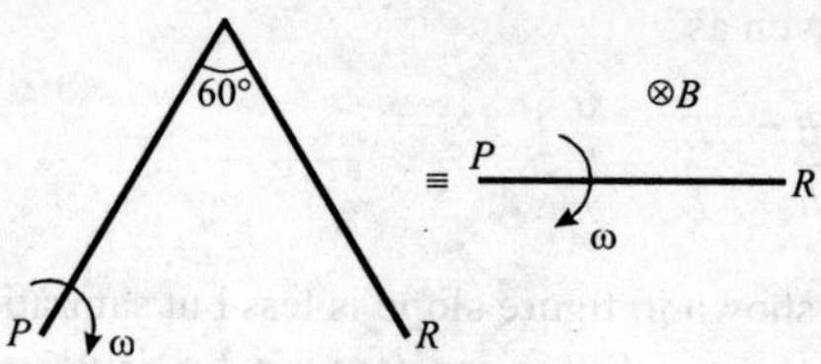

The EMF induced across points *P* and *R* is given as

$$V_R-V_P=\frac{B\omega l^2}{2}$$

EMF induced across points *Q* and *P* is given as

$$V_Q-V_P=\frac{B\omega l^2}{2}$$

$$\Rightarrow \quad V_R-V_P=\frac{B\omega l^2}{2}$$

$$\Rightarrow \quad V_Q-V_R=0$$

Sol. 31 (All) In the given situation if ring moves according to all the options given, it does not cut the magnetic flux so no EMF will be induced in the ring.

Sol. 32 (B, C) According to Lenz's law the induced current is such that it opposes the motion of magnet by applying a force on magnet opposite to its motion direction.

Sol. 33 (A, C) By principal of energy conservation we have

$$P_B=P_R+P_L$$

When the circuit was just closed, we have

$$P_R=i^2R \text{ and } P_L=L\,i\frac{di}{dt}$$

As $\frac{di}{dt}$ has greater value at the time the circuit is just closed so we have $P_L>P_R$ and in steady state $P_R>P_L$ as P_L becomes zero in steady state. Hence options (A) and (C) are correct.

* * * * *